Regulation of Lawyers:
Statutes and Standards

1998 Edition

Regulation of Lawyers: Statutes and Standards

1998 Edition

Stephen Gillers
Professor of Law
New York University

Roy D. Simon
Professor of Law
Hofstra University

Formerly published by
Little, Brown & Company

ASPEN LAW & BUSINESS
A Division of Aspen Publishers, Inc.

Permissions
Aspen Law & Business
1185 Avenue of the Americas
New York, NY 10036

Printed in the United States of America

ISBN 1-56706-575-9

Library of Congress Catalog Card No. 95-80254

About Aspen Law & Business, Law School Division

In 1996, Aspen Law & Business welcomed the Law School Division of Little, Brown and Company into its growing business — already established as a leading provider of practical information to legal practitioners.

Acquiring much more than a prestigious collection of educational publications by the country's foremost authors, Aspen Law & Business inherited the long-standing Little, Brown tradition of excellence — born over 150 years ago. As one of America's oldest and most venerable publishing houses, Little, Brown and Company commenced in a world of change and challenge, innovation and growth. Sharing that same spirit, Aspen Law & Business has dedicated itself to continuing and strengthening the integrity begun so many years ago.

ASPEN LAW & BUSINESS
A Division of Aspen Publishers, Inc.
A Wolters Kluwer Company

Summary of Contents

Summary of Contents

Acknowledgments

The authors appreciate the time and effort of the following people who helped the authors keep this book accurate and up-to-date: Joanne Pitulla, Assistant Ethics Counsel to the ABA Standing Committee on Ethics and Professional Responsibility; Carol Weiss, Staff Director of the ABA Section of Legal Education and Admissions to the Bar; Donna Spilis, Staff Director of the ABA Commission on Impaired Attorneys; Nancy Coleman, Director of the ABA Commission on Legal Problems of the Elderly; Barrie Althoff of the Washington State Bar Association; Alan Flink of Edwards & Angell, and John Tarantino and Pat Rocha of Adler, Pollock & Sheehan, in Providence, Rhode Island; Tom Smith, Staff Counsel to the ABA Section on Criminal Justice; Randall Difuntorum, Larry Doyle, Ann Wassam, and Mengesha Wondaferow of the California State Bar; David Brent, an Ethics Research Attorney at the ABA Center for Professional Responsibility; Michael Albano and Arthur Balbirer, past presidents of the American Academy of Matrimonial Lawyers, and Lorraine West, its Executive Director; David Isbell of Covington & Burling in Washington, D.C.; Professor Charles Wolfram of Cornell Law School, Reporter for the ALI's developing Restatement of the Law Governing Lawyers; Michael Greenwald, Elena Capella, and Todd Feldman of the American Law Institute; Rex Perschbacher and Richard Wydick, professors at University of California-Davis School of Law, and Richard Zitrin, a past Chair of the California State Bar's Committee on Professional Responsibility and Conduct, who kept us abreast of California developments; Dennis Rendleman, General Counsel to the Illinois State Bar Association; Gene Whetzel, General Counsel, and Albert Bell, former General Counsel, to the Ohio Bar Association; Greg Finnerty of the Ohio Bar Association's Government Affairs Office; Alice Moseley, Assistant Director of the North Carolina State Bar; Cynthia Kuhn of the District of Columbia Bar; John Howe, Sam Phillips, and Sara Rittman of Missouri's Office of Chief Disciplinary Counsel;

Acknowledgments

Tony Boggs of the Florida Bar; George Kuhlman, Ethics Counsel to the ABA Standing Committee on Ethics and Professional Responsibility; William Hornsby, Staff Counsel to the ABA Commission on Lawyer Advertising; Becky Stretch, Special Counsel in the ABA Center for Professional Responsibility; Alec Schwartz, Staff Director of the ABA Standing Committee on Specialization, and Jeremy Perlin, Staff Counsel to the Committee; Robert Bloom, who works at the Supreme Judicial Court of Massachusetts; John Rabiej, Chief of the Rules Committee Support Office of the Administrative Office of the United States Courts; Margaret Downie of the Arizona State Bar's Discipline Department; attorney Keefe Brooks, Chair of the Michigan State Bar's Committee on Professional and Judicial Ethics; Todd Sidor of the New Jersey State Bar; Kathleen Mulligan Baxter, Counsel to the New York State Bar Association's Committee on Professional Ethics; Michael Colodner, Counsel to New York's Chief Administrative Judge, the Hon. Jonathan Lippman; Jim McCauley, Ethics Counsel to the Virginia State Bar; Louise Lamoreaux, Ethics Coordinator for the Pennsylvania Bar Association; Frances Kahn Zemans and Cynthia Gray of the American Judicature Society; Jessica Reynolds of the office of Assemblyman Paul Horcher in California; Marge Dover, Executive Director of the National Association of Legal Assistants, Inc.; Peter Jarvis of Stoel Rives Boley Jones & Grey in Portland, Oregon; and many others who provided us with helpful information about changes in the standards and statutes governing lawyers.

The authors also thank the editors of the ABA/BNA Lawyer's Manual on Professional Conduct, whose bi-weekly Current Reports are indispensible to keeping up with state and national developments in the legal profession.

Stephen Gillers thanks his Secretary, Shirley Gray, and Roy Simon thanks his Secretary, Nancy Grasser, for their indispensable work in managing the manuscript for this book. Roy Simon is also grateful to his excellent Research Assistants, John Massaro and Darlene Rosch, Hofstra University School of Law Class of 1998.

Finally, the authors deeply appreciate the exceptional work done by Richard Audet, Julie Nahil, Lisa Wehrle, Emily White, and Bob Caceres, manuscript editors at Little, Brown and Company, and by Rosemary DeStefano, manuscript editor, and Beth Helferich, editorial assistant, at our new publisher Aspen Law and Business, who have helped to produce this and previous editions of this book.

The American Bar Association, for permission to reprint the ABA Model Rules of Professional Conduct, the Model Code of Professional Conduct, and numerous other items, all of which are separately acknowledged where the materials first appear.

The American Law Institute, for permission to reprint excerpts from Tentative Drafts Nos. 2-8 and Proposed Final Draft No. 1 of the Restatement (Third) of the Law Governing Lawyers, copyright © 1989-1997.

The American Trial Lawyer's Association, for permission to reprint its 1988 Code of Conduct and its 1986 Victim's Bill of Rights.

The Federal Bar Association, for permission to reprint excerpts from the Model Rules of Professional Conduct for Federal Lawyers © 1990.

The American Academy of Matrimonial Lawyers (AAML), for permission to reprint excerpts from the Bounds of Advocacy. AAML reserves all rights in the Bounds of Advocacy.

The Roscoe Pound Foundation (formerly the Roscoe Pound-American Trial Lawyers Foundation), for permission to reprint excerpts from the 1982 Revised Draft of the American Lawyer's Code of Conduct.

TRIAL magazine, for permission to reprint excerpts from the Preface to the American Lawyer's Code of Conduct. (The Preface originally appeared in TRIAL magazine.)

The National Association of Legal Assistants, Inc., 1601 South Main St., Suite 300, Tulsa, OK 74119, for permission to reprint excerpts from the NALA's Model Standards and Guidelines for Utilization of Legal Assistants.

Introduction to the
Regulation of Lawyers

This book contains rules regulating the behavior of lawyers and judges. These rules come from many sources: statutes, administrative regulations, rules of evidence and procedure, and, most prominently, ethical codes. These rules continue to grow and change.

What's Different About the 1998 Edition?

The 1998 edition contains hundreds of changes. Many of these changes reflect new items, especially in the Selected State Variations following each ABA Model Rule of Professional Conduct. Other changes reflect significant additions or deletions. For example:

- For the first time, we are including the full text of the New York Code of Professional Responsibility. The New York Code largely parallels the ABA Model Code, but at our press deadline in September of 1997 the courts were considering extensive revisions.
- For the first time, we are separately reprinting the District of Columbia Rules of Professional Conduct, which were significantly amended effective November 1, 1996. In the Related Materials following each ABA Model Rule, we note whether each D.C. rule differs significantly from the parallel ABA Model Rule.
- We have finally deleted the ABA Model Code of Professional Responsibility, which has not been amended since 1980. Those who still want to teach the Model Code, and those who feel more

comfortable with the Model Code numbering system (e.g., "DR 5-101"), can consult the New York Code of Professional Responsibility or the table near the end of the book that correlates the Model Code to the Model Rules. Of course, we continue to reprint the ABA's own Code Comparison after the Comment to every ABA Model Rule of Professional Conduct.

- We have deleted the Specialized Ethical Codes and Selected Professionalism Materials, Federal Sanctions and Discovery Provisions, New York's Rules Governing Attorneys in Domestic Relations Matters, various provisions of the ABA Standards for the Administration of Criminal Justice, and some of the less important statutes that we formerly reprinted from California and New York.

The net result is a leaner book that is more tightly focused on the rules and statutes at the core of most law school courses on professional responsibility.

Developments in the Regulation of Lawyers

Turning to specific news, here are brief summaries of major developments in the regulation of lawyers that have occurred since our last edition or were anticipated in the foreseeable future when we went to press in September of 1997:

NATIONAL DEVELOPMENTS

American Bar Association

Model Rules of Professional Conduct: During 1997, the only change in the Model Rules of Professional Conduct was an amendment to the Comment to Rule 1.14 ("Client Under a Disability"). The amended Comment clarifies a lawyer's duties in emergency situations where a person with a disability needs immediate legal services. The amendment was widely supported and passed by a voice vote. We detail the development of the amended Comment in the Legislative History following Rule 1.14.

Bigger changes to the Model Rules lie ahead, however. In the Spring of 1997, the ABA appointed a ten-member Special Committee on the Evaluation of the Rules of Professional Conduct chaired by Chief Justice E. Norman Veasey of the Delaware Supreme Court. The new committee, commonly called the "Ethics 2000 Committee," will consider whether the ABA Model Rules need updating in light of changes in the legal profession, such as the increased size and mobility of law firms, the proliferation of in-house counsel, the increase in specialization, and the impact of global communications and technology on the legal community. The committee will examine the emerging Restatement of the Law Governing Lawyers and state variations on the ABA Model Rules, conduct original research, take surveys, hold hearings, and make recommendations for action. It plans to issue a final report in the year 2000. In the meantime, the ABA's Standing Committee on Ethics and Professional Responsibility, the ABA entity that traditionally drafts new rules, will continue to draft new rules at the request of ABA entities.

Code of Judicial Conduct: At the 1997 Annual Meeting, the ABA amended the Commentary to (but not the text of) Canon 5C(2) of the ABA Model Code of Judicial Conduct to highlight the conflicts of interest that may arise when judges subject to election receive campaign contributions from lawyers who appear before them. We discuss the development of the amendment and reprint excerpts from an ABA Committee Report in an Editors' Note immediately preceding the amended Commentary to Canon 5C(2).

ABA Resolutions: At its 1997 Mid-Year Meeting, the ABA passed a resolution urging law firms to promote "alternative work schedules" such as: "(a) restructured full-time work schedules such as compressed work weeks, telecommuting, flexiplace, and flex-time; and (b) reduced work schedules such as part-time employment, job-sharing and phased retirement." At its 1997 Annual Meeting, the ABA passed three other resolutions bearing directly on the regulation of lawyers. One resolution condemns so-called "pay-to-play" practices under which only lawyers who contribute to the campaign chests of political officials are eligible to perform legal work for public entities, especially municipal finance work. The resolution also directs the ABA President to appoint a task force to review issues related to "pay-for-play" practices and to recommend effective solutions. Another resolution criticized courts that limit the attorney-client privilege for in-house lawyers. A third resolution urged state bars to develop procedures to protect clients when a lawyer dies or becomes disabled. A proposed resolution urging state bars to implement ABA Model Rule 6.1 ("Voluntary Pro Bono Publico Service") by "establishing a structure for annual fund campaigns in support of legal service programs" was withdrawn.

Legal Malpractice Study: The ABA Standing Committee on Lawyers' Professional Liability issued a study entitled Legal Malpractice Claims in the 1990s. It covers national data on legal malpractice claims from 1990 through 1995. Like a similar 1986 study, the new study shows that personal injury lawyers and real estate lawyers are most likely to be sued for legal malpractice. However, claims in both of these areas have dropped since the 1986 study, while claims against lawyers practicing business transaction and commercial law have increased. The study concludes that most malpractice insurers have seen only a small and gradual increase in the frequency and severity of legal malpractice claims since the mid-1980s. The study (report no. PC 45140028) is available from the ABA by calling (800) 285-2221.

Federal Court Ethics Rules

The Standing Committee on Rules of Practice and Procedure (a committee of the Judicial Conference of the United States) continues to study avenues to greater uniformity for ethics rules in federal courts. Because each district decides for itself what ethics rules to follow, the current situation is a confusing jumble of references to the ABA Model Rules, the ABA Model Code, state ethics rules, local rules, and special codes. At meetings in 1996, the Standing Committee was about equally divided over three options for bringing order to the situation:

1. The Judicial Conference could adopt a model local rule (binding only on courts that adopt it) providing that a federal court adopts the ethics rules of the state in which it sits, "except as otherwise provided by specific Rule of this Court after consideration of comments by representatives of bar associations within the state." This would amount to a modified *Erie* approach, generally deferring to state ethics codes but reserving federal power to depart from them; or

2. The Judicial Conference could recommend a mandatory (as opposed to model) federal *Erie* rule that would require a federal court to adopt the ethics rules of the state in which it sits; or

3. The Judicial Conference could recommend uniform federal rules of ethics in about half a dozen areas of particular concern to federal court litigators (such as conflicts of interest, confidentiality, and communications with represented persons by federal prosecutors).

To help choose from these three options, the Standing Committee asked the Federal Judicial Center and the Standing Committee's Reporter, Professor Daniel Coquillette of Boston College School of Law, to undertake four studies. At the Standing Committee's June 1997 meeting, Professor Coquillette presented all four studies to the Committee. The Committee then narrowed the field to two options: either a model local rule, or a set of federal ethics rules covering five or six areas of particular federal concern (leaving the rest to the states). The Committee instructed Professor Coquillette to draft language both for a model local rule and for proposed federal ethics rules, and to present the drafts at the Standing Committee's Winter meeting in January of 1998. At that time, the Standing Committee is expected to recommend one of the two options. For current information about the Standing Committee and the rulemaking process, readers may telephone John Rabiej, Chief of the Rules Committee Support Office, at (202)273-1820.

Restatement of the Law Governing Lawyers

In March of 1997, the ALI published Tentative Draft No. 8 of the American Law Institute's monumental Restatement of the Law Governing Lawyers, which contains a revised version of Chapter 4 (Lawyer Civil Liability). The new draft which had been sent back to the Reporters in 1994 for further work, and two new chapters: Chapter 6 (Representing Clients — In General) and Chapter 7 (Representing Clients in Litigation).

At the ALI's May 1997 Annual Meeting, the ALI membership approved all of revised Chapter 4, as well as §§151 through 159 of Chapter 6 (relating to the lawyer as counselor), but did not reach Chapter 7. The membership is scheduled to consider the remainder of Chapter 6 and all of Chapter 7 in 1998. In addition, in either 1998 or 1999, the membership will debate two chapters not yet written: Chapter 1, which will cover regulation of the legal profession, and Chapter 9, which will address the structure of the legal profession and the delivery of legal services. In addition, the membership must eventually revisit several sections that the membership has voted to amend (including §§209, 215, and 117A) but that have not yet been drafted in their amended form.

The ALI has now tentatively approved five of the nine chapters planned for the Restatement. Chief Reporter Charles Wolfram has predicted that the entire project will be completed in 1999. For updated information, check the ALI's web site at www.ali.org.

STATE-BY-STATE DEVELOPMENTS

Arizona

Arizona has not amended its Rules of Professional Conduct since our last edition, but in June of 1997 a committee that had been studying possible amendments to Rule 4.2 recommended that no changes be made. Thus, Arizona decided not to change the word "party" to "person" in the text of Rule 4.2, as the ABA did in 1995.

A different committee was appointed by the Arizona Judicial Council within the past year to study Rule 8.3 (Reporting Professional Misconduct). The particular focus is whether a lawyer must report another lawyer's misconduct if the reporting lawyer learned about misconduct from a client who is seeking damages from the other lawyer for malpractice or other wrongs.

California

California is always active. For detailed, up-to-date information, check out the California State Bar's web site at www.calbar.org. Click on "Bar Business" and "Public Comment Proposals" to learn news about proposed or possible amendments to the California Rules of Professional Conduct, or on "Publication 250" to view redlined versions of amended rules and statutes.

Rules of Professional Conduct: Since our last edition, the California Supreme Court approved only one new rule, Rule 1-400(D)(6). It became effective on June 1, 1997 and requires lawyers claiming specialty certification to disclose the full name of the certifying agency. We reprint the new rule in legislative style in our California materials.

Two proposals were pending before the California Supreme Court when we went to press. They would add a new Rule 1-700 ("Member as Candidate for Judicial Office") and a new Rule 1-710 ("Member as Temporary Judge, Referee, or Court-Appointed Arbitrator"). Both proposals incorporate California's mandatory Code of Judicial Ethics by reference, and would thus subject lawyers who are judicial candidates, temporary judges, referees, or court-appointed arbitrators to discipline by the Bar for violating the Code of Judicial Ethics. We reprint the pending proposals at the end of the California Rules of Professional Conduct.

A proposed Rule 4-110, was circulated for public comment during 1997. The rule would have required lawyers to deposit advance fees in a trust account unless the client waived this requirement in writing after being fully informed of information specified in the rule. Comments on the rule were overwhelmingly negative, so the Bar did not forward the proposal to the Supreme Court. Instead, the Bar will continue to study the problem.

In addition, a proposed confidentiality rule that circulated for public comment in 1996 was redrafted during 1997 in light of the 1996 comments. Proposed new Rule 3-100, which would address confidentiality for the first time in California's ethics rules, is similar to ABA Model Rule 1.6. (Confidentiality is addressed in §6068(e) of California's State Bar Act, which imposes a duty of confidentiality without exception.) In July of 1997, a bar committee headed by the President-elect of the California State Bar recommended that the proposal for Rule 3-100 be forwarded to the Supreme Court, but the Board of Governors had not yet acted on that recommendation as of our press deadline.

Proposed amendments to Rule 3-310, which also originally circulated in 1996, would prohibit a lawyer from opposing a current client in certain circumstances even if the lawyer had no confidential information material to the adverse representation would require written disclosure of a conflict in some additional situations. The proposed changes, which are quite complex, would bring Rule 3-310 into line with the California Supreme Court's decision in Flatt v. Superior Court, 9 Cal. 4th 275 (1994). The public comment period ended September 1, 1997, and the Bar hoped to forward a final proposal to the Board of the State Bar for action by end of the 1997.

Two other proposals can now be officially pronounced dead. In September of 1996, the State Bar circulated a proposed rule, patterned on the rule upheld in Florida Bar v. Went for It, Inc., 515 U.S. 618 (1995), to ban unsolicited communications by mail or equivalent means in accident or disaster cases for 30 days after the accident or disaster. (Simultaneously, the State Bar considered "the need for proposed legislation to address insurance companies who contact accident and disaster victims less than 30 days after an accident or disaster.") Public comments showed little concern about such solicitation. The Bar concluded that targeted mail to accident victims is not causing problems in California, and it decided not to pursue a rule in this area.

Also dead is a proposal to publish the name of a disciplined lawyer's law firm, or at least to divulge the size and type of law firm. The proposal would have countered the perception that the discipline system mainly attacks sole practitioners. Critics said the proposal imposed guilt by association, deprived law firms of due process, would be difficult to apply to lawyers associated with multiple firms (or who had been with various firms over the years), gave law firms an incentive to fire lawyers instead of helping them, and was irrelevant to conduct outside of law practice (e.g., DUI convictions). Following a review of public comments, the Bar decided not to take any further action.

Proposed new Rule 3-520 has been rejected by the California Supreme Court twice, but it is not totally dead. The State Bar is still exploring a rule or rule amendment to satisfy §6068(n) of the State Bar Act, which requires an attorney to "provide copies to the client of certain documents under time limits and as prescribed in a rule of professional conduct which the board shall adopt."

Mandatory Continuing Legal Education: California is also in the midst of a court battle over mandatory continuing legal education. In Warden v. California State Bar, 53 Cal. App. 4th 510, 62 Cal. Rptr. 2d 32 (1st Dist. Ct. of App.), review granted, 938 P.2d 371, 64 Cal. Rptr. 2d 577 (Cal. 1997), the appellate court declared California's mandatory CLE program unconstitutional under the Equal Protection Clause because it found no rational basis sufficient to support the CLE program and its exemptions. The California Supreme Court granted review on June 5, 1997, and the appeal was pending when we went to press.

Legislative Action: The California legislature did not enact any major new provisions of the State Bar Act during the past year. However, the legislature substantially expanded §6090.5, which prohibits agreements not to file a bar complaint as part of the settlement of a civil action. The legislature also amended several of the provisions governing fee arbitration (§§6200 through 6206), and slightly amended §§6147 and 6148. Other amendments were not noteworthy.

Civility Project: In January of 1997, the State Bar Board of Governors voted to try out a pilot program of peer-review counseling for "uncivil attorneys." When a bar complaint is filed accusing a lawyer of uncivil or obnoxious conduct that does not warrant discipline, the lawyer may be referred to a panel of respected lawyers for counseling. However, the case would remain on the bar counsel's docket and could be prosecuted if the counseling does not work.

Voter Initiatives: In November of 1997, voters rejected two propositions that would have significantly restricted attorney fees in contingent fee cases. The rejected propositions were essentially redrafts of propositions that had been rejected in March of 1996. Nevertheless, sponsors of the initiatives plan to try again in the future.

District of Columbia

Effective November 1, 1996, the District of Columbia significantly amended its Rules of Professional Conduct. The amendments reflect the work of a committee chaired by attorney F. Whitten Peters, which completed its proposals in December of 1993. The Bar forwarded the proposals with few changes to the District of Columbia Court of Appeals in 1994. The Court finally acted on the proposals on October 15, 1996, making the amended rules effective on November 1, 1996. Because the District of

Columbia rules now differ in so many ways from the ABA Model Rules, we are reprinting the D.C. rules in full in this volume.

Florida

In July of 1997, the Florida Supreme Court added a new paragraph to the Comment to Rule 4-5.6 of its Rules of Professional Conduct. The new comment provides in part as follows:

> This rule is not a per se prohibition against severance agreements between lawyers and law firms. Severance agreements containing reasonable and fair compensation provisions designed to avoid disputes required by time-consuming quantum meruit analysis are not prohibited by this rule. Severance agreements, on the other hand, that contain punitive clauses, the effect of which are to restrict competition or encroach upon a client's inherent right to select counsel, are prohibited. . . .

Of greater interest, the Florida Supreme Court rejected the State Bar's petition to change Florida's rule on pro bono reporting. The rule, adopted in 1993 by a divided court, requires Florida lawyers to report their pro bono hours each year. The Bar petitioned the Court to make reporting voluntary, but on May 22, 1997 a sharply divided Supreme Court, by a per curiam opinion, rejected the petition. One judge separately concurred, stating that the rule had been effective and nothing had changed since 1993 to warrant an amendment. Two other judges agreed that the rule should remain mandatory, but said no lawyer should be disciplined under the rule until an enforcement procedure is in place. One judge dissented, calling the mandatory reporting requirement "inappropriate if not counterproductive." See Amendments to Rule 4-6.1 of the Rules Regulating the Florida Bar — Pro Bono, Public Service, No. 88,646 (Fla. 1997).

Illinois

The Illinois State Bar Association is always active, and maintains a web site reachable at either of two addresses: www.isba.org or www.illinoisbar.org.

Rules of Professional Conduct: Illinois has not changed its Rules of Professional Conduct since our last edition, but on March 11, 1997, the Illinois Supreme Court denied the State Bar's proposal to permit the sale of a law practice. The Court has yet to act on a 1996 proposal to prohibit lawyers from initiating sexual relationships with their clients, but in In re Rinella, 175 Ill. 2d 504; 677 N.E.2d 909; 222 Ill. Dec. 375 (Ill. 1997), the Court suspended a lawyer for three years for having sexual relations with three different clients (and then lying about it during the Bar's investigation). The lawyer contended that he could not be sanctioned for engaging in sex with clients because no rule of ethics specifically prohibited such conduct, but the Court said that no lawyer could reasonably have considered such conduct acceptable under the rules governing the legal profession.

Specialty Certification: At its June 1997 Annual Meeting, the State Bar Assembly overwhelmingly ratified a task force recommendation that Illinois should recognize specialty certification. The Bar plans to appoint a joint committee of city, county, and specialized bar associations to develop a comprehensive certification proposal.

Unauthorized Practice of Law: The Illinois State Bar has been very active in the area of unauthorized practice. On March 7, 1997, the State Bar issued a study that examined the range of activities engaged in by non-lawyers in Illinois and attempted to educate the public about the risks of using a non-lawyer to handle real estate transactions, property tax disputes, insurance settlements, estate planning, and other matters.

Massachusetts

On June 9, 1997, the Massachusetts Supreme Court has adopted new Rules of Professional Conduct that will become effective on January 1, 1998. The rules were informed by an oral argument on April 2, 1997 featuring such well known law professors as Andrew Kaufman, Daniel Coquillette, Susan Koniak, and Monroe Freedman. The new rules convert the Massachusetts rules from the old Code format (Canons, ECs, and DRs) to a Model Rules format, but many of the new provisions differ sharply from the Model Rules. The Supreme Judicial Court has published a red-lined version comparing the new rules to both the ABA Model Rules and the old Massachusetts rules, and the new rules are available on the Boston Bar Association's website at www.bostonbar.org.

Despite the amendments, a few items remain open. For example:

- Rule 6.1 on pro bono service has, according to a press release issued by the Supreme Judicial Court, been left blank pending a report by the court's committee on pro bono legal services.
- The new advertising rules are little changed from the former rules, but the Court has appointed a new Committee on Lawyer Advertising issues.

- Rule 7.4, one of the most liberal specialization rules in the country, permits lawyers to hold themselves out publicly as specialists whether or not they are certified as specialists "if the holding out does not include a deceptive statement or claim."
- New Rule 8.3 provides that a lawyer having knowledge of another lawyer's serious violation of the rules "should" (not shall) inform the Bar Counsel's office. This contradicts an earlier announcement that the Court had voted in favor of mandatory reporting, but the "shall" version of the rule and related comments "will be published separately with an invitation for the bar to comment on the alternative versions of the rule."

The Court also announced plans to refer issues about government lawyers to a separate committee to be appointed sometime in 1997. In addition, the Court announced that it would establish a Standing Advisory Committee on the Rules of Professional Conduct to keep the rules current and to deal with problems arising under the new rules.

Michigan

Michigan has not changed its ethics rules since our last edition, and the Michigan State Bar has opposed various efforts to amend them. The Michigan Grievance Administrator, Phil Thomas, floated a proposal to require all fee agreements to be in writing, but the State Bar's Ethics Committee recommended against it, and the Bar's Board of Commissioners agreed. The Supreme Court could publish the proposal for comment anyway, but that seems unlikely. Mr. Thomas also recommended a rule prohibiting sex with clients, but the Ethics Committee also decided not to support that proposal.

A proposal to amend Rule 4.2 by changing "party" to "person" (consistent with the 1995 ABA amendment to Rule 4.2) made it all the way to the Michigan State Bar's Representative Assembly, but was then voted down. The main opposition came from the United States Attorney's office and various state prosecutors from around the state, who argued that the change would hamper law enforcement. However, Michigan ethics opinions and court decisions have consistently interpreted the term "party" to mean "person" anyway, so the rejection of the proposed amendment is not likely to have any practical impact.

Two other proposals have brighter prospects. One proposal, modeled on the ban that the Supreme Court approved in The Florida Bar v. Went for It, Inc. in 1995, would prohibit solicitation within 30 days of disaster or accident. This proposal is now in the formative stages and is likely to be proposed sometime during 1997 or early 1998. Another proposal would require banks that maintain client trust accounts to notify the disciplinary authorities about overdrafts from lawyer trust accounts.

Missouri

Missouri has not amended its Rules of Professional Conduct since our last edition, and the Missouri Bar is not working on any proposals to amend the rules. However, the Bar is thinking about publishing the Chief Disciplinary Counsel's ethics advisory opinions on the Bar's web site, www.mobar.org.

New Jersey

New Jersey has an extremely active State Bar. Here are some important recent developments:

Rules of Professional Conduct: Effective May 5, 1997, New Jersey adopted a new Rule 7.3(b)(4) to control solicitation after mass disasters. The new rule prohibits lawyers from engaging in unsolicited targeted mail or other contact with mass-disaster victims and their families within 30 days after a disaster. At the same time, New Jersey amended its rule governing targeted mail relating to events other than mass disasters. Under amended Rule 7.3(b)(5) (renumbered effective May 5, 1997), a targeted letter is generally permitted if it satisfies a series of conditions, including: (i) the word "ADVERTISEMENT" in capital letters at the top of page one; (ii) a notice that "[b]efore making your choice of attorney, you should give this matter careful thought. The selection of an attorney is an important decision."; and (iii) a notice that the recipient may report anything inaccurate or misleading to the Committee on Attorney Advertising.

Diversionary Program: In 1997, New Jersey adopted a statewide ethics diversionary program to deal with de minimis conduct by attorneys that does not rise to the level of professional misconduct yet, but might if it persists in the future. The program will have three components: a mediation component to handle lawyer-client or lawyer-lawyer disputes, a continuing legal education component, and a law office management program. The Director of the Office of Attorney Ethics will determine which lawyers to refer to the program and which components of the program they must complete.

Mandatory CLE: In Tolchin v. Supreme Court of New Jersey, 111 F.3d 1099 (3d Cir. 1997), the Third Circuit rejected a New York resident's Commerce Clause and Privileges and Immunities Clause challenge to New Jersey's tough rule requiring new attorneys to attend a 40-hour skills and methods course. The same case also upheld the validity of New Jersey's Rule 1:21-1(a), which prohibits anyone from practicing law in New Jersey who does not maintain a "bona fide office for the practice of law" in New Jersey regardless of where the attorney lives.

New York

New York is in the midst of major changes. The courts are considering the State Bar's extensive recommendations for amending the Code of Professional Responsibility, and the courts themselves have circulated proposals on various topics. For updates, readers should check the New York State Bar Association's home page at www.nysba.org. At press time, here is what we knew:

Code of Professional Responsibility: On March 4, 1997, the State Bar sent the Appellate Divisions extensive proposals to change the Code of Professional Responsibility. A few changes follow the ABA Model Rules, but most of the changes would create rules unique to New York. For example, one proposed rule prohibits solicitation if a lawyer "intends or expects, but does not disclose, that the legal services necessary to handle the matter competently will be performed primarily by another lawyer who is not affiliated with the soliciting lawyer as a partner, associate or of counsel." (The courts have since circulated a slightly different proposal on the same subject.) A proposed subdivision on communicating with represented parties allows a lawyer to "cause a client to communicate with a represented person . . . and counsel the client with respect to those communications, provided the lawyer gives reasonable advance notice to the represented person's counsel that such communications will be taking place." (New language in EC 7-18 would define "reasonable advance notice.")

Open Disciplinary Hearings: In mid-March of 1997, the Office of Court Administration, supported by Chief Judge Judith Kaye, proposed amendments to §90 of the New York State Judiciary Law that would open disciplinary proceedings to the public. Charges, responses, hearings, and the referee's report and recommendation would all be public. But the proposed changes would be accompanied by several new procedural protections for lawyers: (1) before charges are brought, lawyers could appear before the grievance committee — and, with leave of court, present witnesses — to rebut the proposed charges; (2) many complaints would be subject to a four-year statute of limitations; (3) New York's current "preponderance" standard for proving disciplinary charges would be raised to the "clear and convincing" standard used in most jurisdictions; (4) public disclosure of charges would be delayed for 40 days to allow either side time to ask the court to close the proceedings, and the courts could close proceedings for "good cause." Although these changes were proposed by the courts, they can be adopted only by the Legislature, which has rejected past efforts to open the disciplinary process.

Mandatory Continuing Legal Education: Effective October 1, 1997, the courts adopted new rules requiring all new attorneys to complete 32 hours of continuing legal education in their first two years after admission to the bar. Three of these hours each year would have to concern ethics and professionalism. Within a few years, the courts are likely to require mandatory CLE for all New York attorneys.

Standards of Civility: On September 17, 1997, effective immediately, the courts adopted voluntary guidelines called Standards of Civility. These Standards set forth "principles of behavior to which the bar, the bench and court employees should aspire." They are "not intended as rules to be enforced by sanction or disciplinary action," and they will not "supplement or modify" the Code of Professional Responsibility.

Statement of Client's Rights: Effective January 1, 1998, the courts have adopted a Statement of Client's Rights that will be promulgated as Part 1210 of the Joint Appellate Division Rules. The Statement, which is less detailed than the one already required in domestic relations matters (see 22 NYCRR §1400.2), will not have to be given to clients but will have to be posted conspicuously in every law office in New York.

New Local Rules in Federal Court: Effective April 15, 1997, the Eastern and Southern Districts of New York jointly adopted new local rules to replace the old local rules and a series of standing orders that had governed discovery and various other matters. Among other things, the new rules provide that the New York Code of Professional Responsibility governs lawyers in federal court. This settles a three-year debate over whether the Eastern District should adopt a special set of ethics rules to govern lawyers who practice before it.

Sanctions for Frivolous Litigation Conduct: Effective January 1, 1998, the courts have amended 22 NYCRR Part 130, the main sanctions provision in the New York court rules. The amendments have three main features. First, the amended rule requires that every paper served or filed in a civil action be signed by an attorney (or by an unrepresented party) to certify that, to the best of the attorney's knowledge and belief, the filing of the paper and the contentions made in the paper are not frivolous, and the substance of the factual arguments is not false. Second, the current limit of $10,000 per case for sanctions and costs is rescinded; instead, courts may impose sanctions of up to $10,000 per incident, and there is no limit at all on an award of costs. Third, Part 130-2 now permits an award of both costs and sanctions if an attorney unjustifiably fails to attend a scheduled court appearance.

North Carolina

On July 24, 1997, effective immediately, the North Carolina Supreme Court substantially amended the North Carolina Rules of Professional Conduct. The court adopted without any changes the proposals that the State Bar forwarded on April 4, 1997. Those proposals resulted from an exhaustive two-year study by the Committee to Review the Rules of Professional Conduct (commonly called the Rewrite Committee) comparing every rule in the North Carolina Rules of Professional Conduct to the ABA Model Rules of Professional Conduct. The revisions bring the numbering of North Carolina's rules into line with the ABA Model Rules. The new rules were announced too late for us to incorporate systematically in this edition, but we mention the following highlights of the amended rules:

- Rule 1.6(d) permits a lawyer to reveal confidential client information if necessary to rectify the consequences of a client's criminal or fraudulent act if the lawyer's services were used in the commission of the act.
- Rule 1.18 prohibits lawyers from initiating sexual relations with current clients.
- Rule 3.3, the only proposed rule that was revised by the State Bar Council during its debate, reflects the view that the duty of confidentiality should be paramount. The text is the same as ABA Model Rule 3.3, but the Comment makes clear that the duty to take "reasonable remedial measures" does not require disclosure of client perjury to the court. Instead, a lawyer may exercise discretion in choosing whether to disclose perjury to the court or not.

Ohio

Changes and proposed changes are in the works in Ohio on many different fronts. Eventually, readers will be able to get news from Ohio on the Bar's web site at www.ohiobar.org, but the most useful information at this site was available only to members of the Ohio Bar. Here are some current developments in Ohio:

Sale of a Law Practice: On June 4, 1997, the State Bar's Council of Delegates approved a proposed rule that would permit the sale of law practice and forwarded it to the Ohio Supreme Court. The Court referred the proposal to its Rules Advisory Committee, which will hold hearings on the proposal and then make a recommendation to the Supreme Court. The process typically takes a year or more.

Child Support and Student Loan Delinquencies: Since our last edition, the Ohio Supreme Court has amended Supreme Rule 3 to permit the Court to suspend the law license of any attorney who is in arrears in child support. Several lawyers have already lost their licenses under this new rule. Now, legislation is pending that would ask (but not command) the Supreme Court to suspend the licenses of lawyers who are delinquent in their student loans.

Disciplinary Process: In the Spring of 1997, Ohio's Committee to Review Ohio's Disciplinary Process completed a two-year study and issued a report covering topics such as bridging-the-gap courses, ethics schools, discipline by consent, and lawyers who threaten immediate harm to the public. In June of 1997, the Ohio Bar Council of Delegates revised the report and forwarded it to the Ohio Supreme Court for its review.

Pennsylvania

Pending Proposals: When we went to press, two proposals to amend the Rules of Professional Conduct were pending before the Pennsylvania Supreme Court. One proposal would amend Rule 4.2 by changing the word "party" to "person," as the ABA did in 1995. Another proposal, sponsored by the Bar's Solo and Small Practice Committee, would adopt a new Rule 1.17 to permit the sale of a law practice. The proposed rule is similar to ABA Model Rule 1.17. In August of 1997, the Disciplinary Board of the Supreme Court invited public comments on proposed Rule 1.17. The comment deadline was September 15, 1997.

Sex with Clients: The Pennsylvania State Bar's Ethics Committee has drafted a proposal to prohibit sex with clients, but the Ethics Committee does not plan to forward the proposal to the Bar's Board at this time because the Board is unlikely to approve it. Instead, the Ethics Committee plans to issue an advisory ethics opinion on the subject during the Fall of 1997. Eventually, the Ethics Committee may forward a proposed rule to the Board, but the Committee has not set any timetable for doing so.

Targeted Mail: The State Bar's Advertising Committee is drafting a rule to prohibit lawyers from soliciting accident victims by mail within thirty days after an accident. The rule, which has the support of the State Bar President, is modeled on the Florida rule upheld in Florida Bar v. Went for It.

Texas

Texas has not amended any of the Texas Disciplinary Rules of Professional Conduct since our last edition. Texas can amend its rules only by holding a referendum in which all members of the bar in good standing have the right to vote, and this does not happen often.

Virginia

Effective September 18, 1996, Virginia amended DR 1-103 to provide that information acquired as part of a "lawyers helping lawyers" program is to be treated as a confidence or secret under DR 4-101, and lawyers participating in the program need not (and must not) report the information.

Much larger changes are likely in the next year or two because the Virginia State Bar is in the midst of a major overhaul of its ethics rules. The aim is to convert Virginia's Code of Professional Responsibility to a Model Rules format by amending and renumbering the Code. So far, the Council of the Virginia State Bar has approved in substance Rules 1.1 through 1.5. The Council is scheduled to consider Rules 2.1 through 5.5 at its October meeting, and is scheduled to consider the balance of the rules in February of 1998. When the Council has completed its work, it will submit the entire package of proposed amendments to the Supreme Court of Virginia. The State Bar does not anticipate making any piecemeal amendments until the entire revised draft is forwarded to the Court.

For current information on Virginia ethics developments, readers may contact the Virginia State Bar at www.vsb.org. However, a more comprehensive source of on-line information is the home page maintained by the Virginia State Bar's Ethics Counsel, James McCauley. His home page address, which must be entered entirely in lower case letters, is: http:\\home.att.net\~j.mccauley. Mr. McCauley's page contains full text of proposed ethics rules, plus significant Virginia legal ethics opinions and links to other ethics resources.

A Brief History of Ethical Codes

The most important ethical codes for lawyers are those promulgated by the American Bar Association. The ABA's first effort at codifying ethical rules was the adoption of the Canons of Professional Ethics in 1908. These (as amended) remained in effect — though with diminishing influence — for 62 years.

Effective in 1970, the ABA replaced the Canons with the Model Code of Professional Responsibility. Within a few years, every state had adopted the new Code in some form. States varied somewhat in their adoptions, changing a word here or a sentence there, but most of the variations were modest. The only variation that was truly different appeared in California, which rejected or substantially revised many of the Model Code's Disciplinary Rules and deleted all of the Ethical Considerations.

In 1977, the President of the American Bar Association appointed a new commission to prepare a new set of rules. That commission soon became known as the Kutak Commission, after Robert J. Kutak, an energetic and visionary lawyer from Omaha, Nebraska, who chaired the commission until his death in early 1983. After much debate and several drafts, the ABA House of Delegates approved the Model Rules of Professional Conduct on August 2, 1983.

It is often instructive to compare the Model Rules as adopted with parallel provisions in the Kutak Commission's drafts. Many of these parallel provisions are contained in the Legislative History sections following each Model Rule. It is also often instructive to compare the Model Rules as adopted with state variations governing the same conduct. The states have been giving careful attention to the Model Rules. As of fall 1997, about 41 states and the District of Columbia have adopted all or significant portions of the Model Rules.

Several states, including California, New York, Oregon, and Vermont, have rejected the Model Rules. New York, however, amended its Code in 1990 to include provisions of the Model Rules. California also has amended its Rules of Professional Conduct to incorporate a few Model Rules provisions.

Many states that have adopted the Model Rules have deviated from the ABA's "model" text in significant ways. Sometimes a state will opt for language derived from a draft of the Model Rules. Sometimes a state will choose to retain language contained in the Model Code of Professional Responsibility. We have identified interesting state variations on particular Model Rules in a section called "Selected State Variations" following each Model Rule. While we have presented Model Rules variations from dozens of American jurisdictions, we have concentrated on these: Arizona, District of Columbia, Florida, Georgia, Illinois, Massachusetts, Michigan, Missouri, New Jersey, Pennsylvania, Texas, and Virginia.

Areas Deserving Special Attention

Several areas of variation deserve special attention. These areas include confidentiality, corporate representation, and lawyer advertising and solicitation. Model Rules 1.6, 1.9(c), 3.3, and 4.1 prominently address the issue of confidentiality. Rule 1.13 addresses the responsibilities of a lawyer whose client is an organization. Rules 7.1, 7.2, 7.3, and 7.4 are concerned with various methods for marketing legal services.

Other areas in which we see significant variation among jurisdictions or between drafts of the Model Rules and the final document include conflicts of interest (Rules 1.7, 1.8, 1.9, 1.10, and 1.11); fairness to opposing parties and counsel (Rule 3.4); relationships between lawyers and nonlawyers (Rule 5.4); and pro bono service (Rule 6.1).

Two dominant concerns underlie the provisions containing these variations. The first concern is the proper scope of the lawyer's loyalty to current and former clients, including the scope of the lawyer's duty to protect client confidences. Competing demands on this loyalty come from the justice system, third persons, other clients, and the lawyer's personal or financial interests.

The second concern is competition, from within and from outside the profession, in marketing and profiting from legal services. One question is whether non-lawyers should be permitted to invest in or share profits from organizations that sell legal services for a profit. This question brings up competition between lawyers and persons outside the legal profession. Another question is what limits should be placed on the ways in which lawyers compete with other lawyers. This question addresses issues of lawyer advertising and solicitation. Recently, a tangential issue has emerged: Should lawyers be permitted to own "ancillary" non-law businesses (such as title insurance companies, investment advisors, and real estate developers) that serve both clients and non-clients? By a slim vote, the ABA said "no" when it adopted Rule 5.7 in 1991. But only a year later, again by a slim margin, the ABA repealed Rule 5.7. In 1994, the ABA adopted a redrafted, permissive version of Rule 5.7.

Some Special Features of Our Book

The areas we have just identified are, we believe, those where controversy is most prominent and variation among jurisdictions is most frequent and pronounced. But other provisions of the Model Rules were also seriously debated and are also the subject of variation among the states. As we show in the Legislative History section for each Model Rule, the Kutak Commission's early drafts usually differed markedly from the Rules as finally adopted. And as we show in the Selected State Variations sections for each Model Rule, the states have often adopted divergent provisions. The legislative history and the selected state variations for each Rule, together with our extensive California, District of Columbia, and New York materials, should thus dispel any misconception that the ABA Model Rules are "the rules." The Model Rules are influential, but they continue to generate considerable disagreement.

To make it easier to roam within the Model Rules, we have prepared a comprehensive list of cross-references identifying every mention of a Rule in any other Rule or Comment. These cross-references, which follow each Rule, should help readers appreciate each Rule's implications throughout the Rules as a whole.

The Model Rules are only one source of authority and guidance within the legal profession. As our Related Materials show, lawyers may be subject to many obligations and restrictions beyond those imposed by the Model Rules. In addition, the Model Rules give little or no guidance in many areas of practice. We have therefore included other sources of authority, such as federal statutes, rules of evidence, and the tentative Restatement (Third) of the Law Governing Lawyers (still in progress). We have also reprinted significant parts of several specialized codes, such as the ABA Standards for Criminal Justice, the Bounds of Advocacy of the American Academy of Matrimonial Lawyers, and the Federal Bar Association's Model Rules of Professional Conduct for Federal Lawyers.

Finally, judges are subject to special regulations beyond those that govern practicing lawyers. Some of these are in statutory law, such as §455 of Title 28 of the United States Code. Others are in codes of judicial ethics. The most prominent ethics code is the ABA's Code of Judicial Conduct, first promulgated in 1972 and at one point adopted by 47 states and the District of Columbia. In 1990 the ABA revised the Code of Judicial Conduct. The revised document has been adopted in whole or in part in about 20 jurisdictions, including the United States Judicial Conference.

We always appreciate news about developments and proposals in the states and in bar organizations. Please contact us by e-mail at LAWRDS@hofstra.edu (Roy Simon) and SGILLERS@counsel.com (Stephen Gillers).

Stephen Gillers
Roy D. Simon

September 1997

Regulation of Lawyers: Statutes and Standards

1998 Edition

Model Codes and Standards

ABA Model Rules of Professional Conduct*
As amended through August 1997

Editors' Introduction. In 1977, only eight years after adopting the Model Code of Professional Responsibility, the ABA appointed a Commission on the Evaluation of Professional Standards to recommend revisions to the Code. The Commission was chaired by attorney Robert Kutak and is commonly referred to as the Kutak Commission.

It soon became clear to the Kutak Commission that the Code needed to be substantially rewritten and reorganized. Between 1979 and 1982, the Kutak Commission circulated four major drafts of its proposed Model Rules of Professional Conduct: the 1979 Unofficial Pre-Circulation Draft; the 1980 Discussion Draft; the 1981 Draft; and the 1982 Draft. After making some significant revisions, the ABA House of Delegates formally adopted the Model Rules on August 2, 1983.

Since 1983, about forty jurisdictions have adopted substantial portions of the Model Rules. However, there are significant variations among the states, especially regarding such key issues as conflicts, confidentiality, and advertising.

We have used a seven-part format to present each Rule:

(1) the black letter Model Rule itself;

(2) the official ABA Comment (with the paragraphs numbered, in brackets, for convenience);

(3) the Model Code Comparison, written by the ABA to compare each Rule to the Model Code of Professional Responsibility;

(4) Cross-references in the Rules, compiled especially for this book to show each place in the Rules and Comments where a particular Rule is mentioned;

(5) Legislative History, which we compiled to show interesting excerpts from earlier drafts, and amendments to the Rules since their adoption;

(6) Selected State Variations, which we compiled to show some of the ways in which states have diverged from the ABA Model Rule; and

(7) Related Materials, which we compiled to show such things as historical antecedents in the old ABA Canons of Professional Ethics, counterparts in the American Lawyer's Code of Conduct, the Restatement of the Law Governing Lawyers (in progress), the Bounds of Advocacy of the American Academy of Matrimonial Lawyers, and brief descriptions of or quotations from other items that shed light on a particular Rule.

Since our last edition, the ABA has not added any new rules or amended the text of any of the existing rules. However, at the ABA's 1997 Mid-Year Meeting, the House of Delegates amended the Comment to Rule 1.14 ("Client Under a Disability") to clarify a lawyer's duties in emergency situations. The language was jointly proposed by the Standing Committee on Ethics and Professional Responsibility (the traditional source of new rules), the ABA Commission on Legal Problems of the Elderly (which originally proposed amendments to Rule 1.14), the ABA Section of Real Property, Probate and Trust Law, and the Senior Lawyers Division of the ABA. The amendment passed by a voice vote.

The Commission on Legal Problems of the Elderly had originally sought changes to the text of Rule 1.14 in 1995. The changes that the Commission proposed at that time are reprinted in our Legislative History following Rule 1.14. However, the Commission withdrew its proposals right before the ABA's 1995 Annual Meeting to give the ABA Standing Committee on Ethics and Professional Responsibility time to study them. The Standing Committee responded with a two-pronged approach. First, the Standing Committee issued ABA Ethics Op. 96-404 (1996), which addressed ethical issues that arise when clients no longer seem mentally able to handle their own affairs. Second, the Standing Committee cosponsored the 1997 amendment to the Comment to Rule 1.14. We reprint the amended Comment to Rule 1.14 in legislative style, underscoring additions and striking through deletions. We also reprint the full text of the Committee Report submitted in support of the amendments.

Looking ahead, sweeping changes are in the offing — but not for a few years. In the spring of 1997 the ABA appointed a ten-member Special Committee on Evaluation of the Rules of Professional Conduct, commonly called the "Ethics 2000 Committee," which will comprehensively examine the Model Rules to determine whether amendments are needed. The Chair of the Committee is the Honorable E. Norman Veasey, Chief Justice of the Delaware Supreme Court. The Ethics 2000 Committee plans to issue a final report in the year 2000.

An overview of the Rules, including the legislative history of ABA codes of professional conduct, the major differences between the Rules and the Model Code, and the trends in state variations on the Rules, is contained in our introductory essay at the front of the book.

Contents

Preamble: A Lawyer's Responsibilities
Scope
Terminology

Article 1. Client-Lawyer Relationship

Article 2. Counselor

Article 3. Advocate

PREAMBLE: A LAWYER'S RESPONSIBILITIES

[1] A lawyer is a representative of clients, an officer of the legal system and a public citizen having special responsibility for the quality of justice.

[2] As a representative of clients, a lawyer performs various functions. As advisor, a lawyer provides a client with an informed understanding of the client's legal rights and obligations and explains their practical implications. As advocate, a lawyer zealously asserts the client's position under the rules of the adversary system. As negotiator, a lawyer seeks a result advantageous to the client but consistent with requirements of honest dealing with others. As intermediary between clients, a lawyer seeks to reconcile their divergent interests as an advisor and, to a limited extent, as a spokesman for each client. A lawyer acts as evaluator by examining a client's legal affairs and reporting about them to the client or to others.

[3] In all professional functions a lawyer should be competent, prompt and diligent. A lawyer should maintain communication with a client concerning the representation. A lawyer should keep in confidence information relating to representation of a client except so far as disclosure is required or permitted by the Rules of Professional Conduct or other law.

[4] A lawyer's conduct should conform to the requirements of the law, both in professional service to clients and in the lawyer's business and personal affairs. A lawyer should use the law's procedures only for legitimate purposes and not to harass or intimidate others. A lawyer should demonstrate respect for the legal system and for those who serve it, including judges, other lawyers and public officials. While it is a lawyer's duty, when necessary, to challenge the rectitude of official action, it is also a lawyer's duty to uphold legal process.

[5] As a public citizen, a lawyer should seek improvement of the law, the administration of justice and the quality of service rendered by the legal profession. As a member of a learned profession, a lawyer should cultivate knowledge of the law beyond its use for clients, employ that knowledge in reform of the law and work to strengthen legal education.

A lawyer should be mindful of deficiencies in the administration of justice and of the fact that the poor, and sometimes persons who are not poor, cannot afford adequate legal assistance, and should therefore devote professional time and civic influence in their behalf. A lawyer should aid the legal profession in pursuing these objectives and should help the bar regulate itself in the public interest.

[6] Many of a lawyer's professional responsibilities are prescribed in the Rules of Professional Conduct, as well as substantive and procedural law. However, a lawyer is also guided by personal conscience and the approbation of professional peers. A lawyer should strive to attain the highest level of skill, to improve the law and the legal profession and to exemplify the legal profession's ideals of public service.

[7] A lawyer's responsibilities as a representative of clients, an officer of the legal system and a public citizen are usually harmonious. Thus, when an opposing party is well represented, a lawyer can be a zealous advocate on behalf of a client and at the same time assume that justice is being done. So also, a lawyer can be sure that preserving client confidences ordinarily serves the public interest because people are more likely to seek legal advice, and thereby heed their legal obligations, when they know their communications will be private.

[8] In the nature of law practice, however, conflicting responsibilities are encountered. Virtually all difficult ethical problems arise from conflict between a lawyer's responsibilities to clients, to the legal system and to the lawyer's own interest in remaining an upright person while earning a satisfactory living. The Rules of Professional Conduct prescribe terms for resolving such conflicts. Within the framework of these Rules many difficult issues of professional discretion can arise. Such issues must be resolved through the exercise of sensitive professional and moral judgment guided by the basic principles underlying the Rules.

[9] The legal profession is largely self-governing. Although other professions also have been granted powers of self-government, the legal profession is unique in this respect because of the close relationship between the profession and the processes of government and law enforcement. This connection is manifested in the fact that ultimate authority over the legal profession is vested largely in the courts.

[10] To the extent that lawyers meet the obligations of their professional calling, the occasion for government regulation is obviated. Self-regulation also helps maintain the legal profession's independence from government domination. An independent legal profession is an important force in preserving government under law, for abuse of legal authority is more readily challenged by a profession whose members are not dependent on government for the right to practice.

[11] The legal profession's relative autonomy carries with it special responsibilities of self-government. The profession has a responsibility to assure that its regulations are conceived in the public interest and not in furtherance of parochial or self-interested concerns of the bar. Every lawyer is responsible for observance of the Rules of Professional Conduct. A lawyer should also aid in securing their observance by other lawyers. Neglect of these responsibilities compromises the independence of the profession and the public interest which it serves.

[12] Lawyers play a vital role in the preservation of society. The fulfillment of this role requires an understanding by lawyers of their relationship to our legal system. The Rules of Professional Conduct, when properly applied, serve to define that relationship.

SCOPE

[1] The Rules of Professional Conduct are rules of reason. They should be interpreted with reference to the purposes of legal representation and of the law itself. Some of the Rules are imperatives, cast in the terms "shall" or "shall not." These define proper conduct for purposes of professional discipline. Others, generally cast in the term "may," are permissive and define areas under the Rules in which the lawyer has professional discretion. No disciplinary action should be taken when the lawyer chooses not to act or acts within the bounds of such discretion. Other Rules define the nature of relationships between the lawyer and others. The Rules are thus partly obligatory and disciplinary and partly constitutive and descriptive in that they define a lawyer's professional role. Many of the Comments use the term "should." Comments do not add obligations to the Rules but provide guidance for practicing in compliance with the Rules.

[2] The Rules presuppose a larger legal context shaping the lawyer's role. That context includes court rules and statutes relating to matters of licensure, laws defining specific obligations of lawyers and substantive and procedural law in general. Compliance with the Rules, as with all law in an open society, depends primarily upon understanding and voluntary compliance, secondarily upon reinforcement by peer and public opinion and finally, when necessary, upon enforcement through disciplinary proceedings. The Rules do not, however, exhaust the moral and ethical considerations that should inform a lawyer, for no worthwhile human activity can be completely defined by legal rules. The Rules simply provide a framework for the ethical practice of law.

[3] Furthermore, for purposes of determining the lawyer's authority and responsibility, principles of substantive law external to these Rules determine whether a client-lawyer relationship exists. Most of the duties flowing from the client-lawyer relationship attach only after the client has requested the lawyer to render legal services and the lawyer has agreed to do so. But there are some duties, such as that of confidentiality under Rule 1.6, that may attach when the lawyer agrees to consider whether a client-lawyer relationship shall be established. Whether a client-lawyer relationship exists for any specific purpose can depend on the circumstances and may be a question of fact.

[4] Under various legal provisions, including constitutional, statutory and common law, the responsibilities of government lawyers may include authority concerning legal matters that ordinarily reposes in the client in private client-lawyer relationships. For example, a lawyer for a government agency may have authority on behalf of the government to decide upon settlement or whether to appeal from an adverse judgment. Such authority in various respects is generally vested in the attorney general and the state's attorney in state government, and their federal counterparts, and the same may be true of other government law officers. Also, lawyers under the supervision of these officers may be authorized to represent several government agencies in intragovernmental legal controversies in circumstances where a private lawyer could not represent multiple private clients. They also may have authority to represent the "public interest" in circumstances where a private lawyer would not be authorized to do so. These Rules do not abrogate any such authority.

[5] Failure to comply with an obligation or prohibition imposed by a Rule is a basis for invoking the disciplinary process. The Rules presuppose that disciplinary assessment of a lawyer's conduct will be made on the basis of the facts and circumstances as they existed at the time of the conduct in question and in recognition of the fact that a lawyer often has to act upon uncertain or incomplete evidence of the situation. Moreover, the Rules presuppose that whether or not discipline should be imposed for a violation, and the severity of a sanction, depend on all the circumstances, such as the willfulness and seriousness of the violation, extenuating factors and whether there have been previous violations.

[6] Violation of a Rule should not give rise to a cause of action nor should it create any presumption that a legal duty has been breached. The Rules are designed to provide guidance to lawyers and to provide a structure for regulating conduct through disciplinary agencies. They are not designed to be a basis for civil liability. Furthermore, the purpose of the Rules can be subverted when they are invoked by opposing parties as procedural weapons. The fact that a Rule is a just basis for a lawyer's self-

assessment, or for sanctioning a lawyer under the administration of a disciplinary authority, does not imply that an antagonist in a collateral proceeding or transaction has standing to seek enforcement of the Rule. Accordingly, nothing in the Rules should be deemed to augment any substantive legal duty of lawyers or the extra-disciplinary consequences of violating such a duty.

[7] Moreover, these Rules are not intended to govern or affect judicial application of either the attorney-client or work product privilege. Those privileges were developed to promote compliance with law and fairness in litigation. In reliance on the attorney-client privilege, clients are entitled to expect that communications within the scope of the privilege will be protected against compelled disclosure. The attorney-client privilege is that of the client and not of the lawyer. The fact that in exceptional situations the lawyer under the Rules has a limited discretion to disclose a client confidence does not vitiate the proposition that, as a general matter, the client has a reasonable expectation that information relating to the client will not be voluntarily disclosed and that disclosure of such information may be judicially compelled only in accordance with recognized exceptions to the attorney-client and work product privileges.

[8] The lawyer's exercise of discretion not to disclose information under Rule 1.6 should not be subject to reexamination. Permitting such reexamination would be incompatible with the general policy of promoting compliance with law through assurances that communications will be protected against disclosure.

[9] The Comment accompanying each Rule explains and illustrates the meaning and purpose of the Rule. The Preamble and this note on Scope provide general orientation. The Comments are intended as guides to interpretation, but the text of each Rule is authoritative. Research notes were prepared to compare counterparts in the ABA Model Code of Professional Responsibility (adopted 1969, as amended) and to provide selected references to other authorities. The notes have not been adopted, do not constitute part of the Model Rules, and are not intended to affect the application or interpretation of the Rules and Comments.

Cross-References in Rules

Rule 1.3, Comment 7: "[I]n a matter involving the conduct of government officials, a government lawyer may have authority to question such conduct more extensively than that of a lawyer for a private organization in similar circumstances. This Rule does not limit that authority. See note on **Scope**."

Rule 1.6, Comment 5: "A lawyer may not disclose such confidential information except as authorized or required by the Rules of Professional Conduct or other law. See also **Scope**."

Rule 1.7, Comment 2: "As to whether a client-lawyer relationship exists or, having once been established, is continuing, see Comment to Rule 1.3 and **Scope**."

Rule 1.7, Comment 15: "Where the conflict is such as clearly to call in question the fair or efficient administration of justice, opposing counsel may properly raise the question. Such an objection should be viewed with caution, however, for it can be misused as a technique of harassment. See **Scope**."

Legislative History

1980 Discussion Draft contained the following Preface:

The decade past has witnessed an extraordinary concern with professional responsibility. Barely ten years ago, the American Bar Association adopted its Model Code of Professional Responsibility, the product of a committee chaired by Edward L. Wright. . . . [I]n every sphere one finds searching inquiry into the meaning of professionally responsible conduct.

That inquiry has led to reconsideration of the Model Code, the creation of the Commission on Evaluation of Professional Standards, and, finally, the development of this document — the Discussion Draft of the Model Rules of Professional Conduct.

In reconsidering the concepts of professional standards, the Commission soon realized that more than a series of amendments or a general restatement of the Model Code of Professional Responsibility was in order. The Commission determined that a comprehensive reformulation was required. We have built on the Code's foundation, but we make no apology for having pushed beyond it. . . .

Selected State Variations

District of Columbia: D.C. "Scope" differs significantly from the ABA Model Rules Scope — see District of Columbia Rules of Professional Conduct below.

Massachusetts: Effective January 1, 1998, Scope, quoting case precedent, provides that "if a plaintiff can demonstrate that a disciplinary rule was intended to protect one in his position, a violation of that rule may be some evidence of the attorney's negligence."

Related Materials

ABA Canons: The Preamble to the Canons* provided as follows:

*This and all other excerpts from the ABA Canons of Professional Ethics have been reprinted with the permission of the American Bar Association. Copyright © by the American Bar Association. All rights reserved.

In America, where the stability of Courts and of all departments of government rests upon the approval of the people, it is peculiarly essential that the system for establishing and dispensing Justice be developed to a high point of efficiency and so maintained that the public shall have absolute confidence in the integrity and impartiality of its administration. The future of the Republic, to a great extent, depends upon our maintenance of Justice pure and unsullied. It cannot be so maintained unless the conduct and the motives of the members of our profession are such as to merit the approval of all just men.

No code or set of rules can be framed, which will particularize all the duties of the lawyer in the varying phases of litigation or in all the relations of professional life. The following canons of ethics are adopted by the American Bar Association as a general guide, yet the enumeration of particular duties should not be construed as a denial of the existence of others equally imperative, though not specifically mentioned.

American Academy of Matrimonial Lawyers: The American Academy of Matrimonial Lawyers (AAML) is an organization of approximately 1,200 members who have "devoted their professional lives to representing husbands, wives, and other family members in the throes or aftermath of marital dissolution." In 1991, the AAML published a set of ethical standards entitled Bounds of Advocacy directed specifically at matrimonial lawyers. The Reporter was Professor Robert Aronson. Excerpts from the Bounds of Advocacy are reprinted, with the kind permission of the AAML, in our Related Materials sections throughout the Model Rules. The following excerpts from the Preliminary Statement to the Bounds of Advocacy explain the project's purpose and scope.

Preliminary Statement to the Bounds of Advocacy
The primary purpose of the Standards of Conduct is to provide guidance to matrimonial lawyers confronting moral and ethical problems; that is, to establish bounds of advocacy. Existing codes often do not provide adequate guidance to the matrimonial lawyer. First, their emphasis on zealous representation of individual clients in criminal and some civil cases is not always appropriate in family law matters. Second, the existing codes delineate the minimum level necessary to avoid professional discipline, rather than describe optimum ethical behavior toward which attorneys should strive. Third, the rules are often vague and provide contradictory guidelines in some of the most difficult family law situations. The Standards of Conduct are an effort to provide clear, specific guidance in areas most important to matrimonial lawyers.

In many ways, matrimonial practice is unique. Family disputes occur in a volatile and emotional atmosphere. It is difficult for matrimonial lawyers to represent the interests of their clients without addressing the interests of other family members. Unlike most other concluded disputes in which the parties may harbor substantial animosity without practical effect, the parties to matrimonial disputes may be required to interact for years to come. In addition, many matrimonial lawyers believe themselves obligated to consider the best interests of children, regardless of which family member they represent. A survey of Academy Fellows indicated that the harm to children in an acrimonious family dispute was seen as the most significant problem for which there is insufficient guidance in existing ethical codes.

13

Canon 7 of the ABA Code of Professional Responsibility (CPR) provided: ''A Lawyer Should Represent a Client Zealously Within the Bounds of the Law.'' Ethical Consideration 7-1 indicates that ''bounds of the law'' include ''Disciplinary Rules and enforceable professional regulations.'' Many courts, bar disciplinary committees and individual lawyers interpreted the CPR to require an attorney to do everything, short of violating the law, to achieve the client's goals. Attorneys of this persuasion were therefore obligated to carry out even those client directives which the attorney found harsh, ethically distasteful or unnecessarily harmful to opposing parties, counsel or other persons, such as children.

Partly in response to the overzealous representation occasioned by the CPR and overly narrow interpretations of ''bounds of the law,'' the ABA Rules of Professional Conduct (RPC) eliminated the zealous representation language. However, the Rules neither clearly indicate the appropriate level of representation to replace zealousness nor do they ''exhaust the moral and ethical considerations that should inform a lawyer, for no worthwhile human activity can be completely defined by legal rules.''

In recent years, an increasing number of individual lawyers and associations have observed a widening gap between the minimum level of ethical conduct mandated by the RPC and the much greater level of professionalism to which attorneys should aspire. Some attorneys have ignored the caveat that the Rules do not ''exhaust the moral and ethical considerations'' which characterize the practice of law at the highest level. Local and state bar associations, along with a number of state and federal courts, have adopted codes of professionalism attempting to raise the level of ethical practice above the minimum necessary to avoid discipline.

The RPC are addressed to all lawyers, regardless of the nature of their practices. This generality means that, with rare exceptions, issues relevant only to a specific area of practice cannot be dealt with in detail or cannot be addressed at all.

The Preamble to the RPC states: ''Virtually all difficult ethical problems arise from conflict between a lawyer's responsibilities to clients, to the legal system and to the lawyer's own interest in remaining an upright person while earning a satisfactory living.''

The RPC's rules of general applicability may not, however, be the most appropriate framework to resolve these conflicting responsibilities for a particular area of practice. Many Fellows of the American Academy of Matrimonial Lawyers have encountered instances where the RPC provided insufficient, or even undesirable, guidance. Most attorneys — and presumably all Academy Fellows — are able to distinguish ''black'' (unethical or illegal conduct) from ''white'' (ethical and proper practice). This work, therefore, is directed primarily to the ''gray'' zone where even experienced, knowledgeable matrimonial lawyers might have doubts.

Conduct permitted by the RPC cannot be the basis for state bar or court discipline. Hence, the Standards here established for matrimonial lawyers use the terms ''should'' and ''should not,'' rather than ''must,'' ''shall,'' ''must not'' and ''shall not.'' Clearly, since these Standards promote a level of practice above the minimum established in the RPC, their use to establish a duty of care in a malpractice action is inappropriate.

However, the Standards have perhaps weighed certain principles more heavily in the balancing process than previous codes. While reaffirming the attorney's obligation of competent and zealous representation, the Standards promote greater professionalism, trust, fair dealing and concern for opposing parties and counsel,

14

third persons and the public. In addition, they encourage efforts to reduce costs, delay and emotional trauma and urge interaction between parties and attorneys on a more reasoned, cooperative level. . . .

American Lawyer's Code of Conduct: In 1982, the Roscoe Pound-American Trial Lawyer's Foundation circulated a revised draft of a proposed code of legal ethics entitled the American Lawyer's Code of Conduct (ALCC). The ALCC was intended as an alternative to the ABA's Model Rules of Professional Conduct, drafts of which were then being circulated for public comment by the Kutak Commission. The ALCC differs from the ABA Model Rules on many issues, especially confidentiality. The overall tone of the differences is reflected in the Preface and Preamble to the ALCC, which harshly criticized the Kutak Commission's 1982 Draft of the ABA Model Rules. The Preface and the Preamble state:

Preface to American Lawyer's Code of Conduct*

The Kutak Commission sees lawyers as ombudsmen, who serve the system as much as they serve clients. This is a collectivist, bureaucratic concept. It is the sort of thinking you get from a commission made up of lawyers who work for institutional clients, in institutional firms, and who have lost sight of the lawyer's basic function. Lawyers are not licensed to write prospectuses for giant corporations, or to haggle with federal agencies over regulations and operating rights. We are licensed to represent people in court, which often means people in trouble with the law, and with the government. We are the citizens' champions against official tyranny.

We cannot continue to have a democratic system, as we know it, without a legal profession whose members are free to perform that function. The Kutak Rules . . . embody a core conviction about the lawyer's role that is fundamentally at odds with the American constitutional system. . . .

Preamble to American Lawyer's Code of Conduct

The legal system that gives context and meaning to basic American rights is the adversary system. It is the adversary system which assures each of us a "champion against a hostile world," and which thereby helps to preserve and enhance our dignity as individuals.

Recognizing that the American attorney functions in an adversary system, and that such a system expresses fundamental American values, helps us to appreciate the emptiness of some cliches of lawyers' ethics. . . . In the context of the adversary system, it is clear that the lawyer for a private party is and should be an officer of a court only in the sense of serving a court as a zealous, partisan advocate of one side of the case before it, and in the sense of having been licensed by a court to play that very role.

TERMINOLOGY

[1] "Belief" or "Believes" denotes that the person involved actually supposed the fact in question to be true. A person's belief may be inferred from circumstances.

[2] "Consult" or "Consultation" denotes communication of information reasonably sufficient to permit the client to appreciate the significance of the matter in question.

[3] "Firm" or "Law Firm" denotes a lawyer or lawyers in a private firm, lawyers employed in the legal department of a corporation or other organization and lawyers employed in a legal services organization. See Comment, Rule 1.9.

[4] "Fraud" or "Fraudulent" denotes conduct having a purpose to deceive and not merely negligent misrepresentation or failure to apprise another of relevant information.

[5] "Knowingly," "Known," or "Knows" denotes actual knowledge of the fact in question. A person's knowledge may be inferred from circumstances.

[6] "Partner" denotes a member of a partnership and a shareholder in a law firm organized as a professional corporation.

[7] "Reasonable" or "Reasonably" when used in relation to conduct by a lawyer denotes the conduct of a reasonably prudent and competent lawyer.

[8] "Reasonable belief" or "Reasonably believes" when used in reference to a lawyer denotes that a lawyer of reasonable prudence and competence would ascertain the matter in question.

[9] "Reasonably should know" when used in reference to a lawyer denotes that a lawyer of reasonable prudence and competence would ascertain the matter in question.

[10] "Substantial" when used in reference to degree or extent denotes a material matter of clear and weighty importance.

Selected State Variations

District of Columbia: D.C. Terminology differs significantly from the ABA Model Rules Terminology. D.C. adds definitions for "Consent," "Law clerk,"

"Matter," and "Tribunal," which are not defined in the ABA Model Rules — see District of Columbia Rules of Professional Conduct below.

Illinois retains the Model Code definitions of "confidence" and "secret" and adds the following terminology:

> "Contingent fee agreement" denotes an agreement for the provision of legal services by a lawyer under which the amount of the lawyer's compensation is contingent in whole or in part upon the successful completion of the subject matter of the agreement, regardless of whether the fee is established by formula or is a fixed amount.
>
> "Disclose" or "disclosure" denotes communication of information reasonably sufficient to permit the client to appreciate the significance of the matter in question.
>
> "Person" denotes natural persons, partnerships, business corporations, not-for-profit corporations, public and quasi-public corporations, municipal corporations, State and Federal governmental bodies and agencies, or any other type of lawfully existing entity.

Louisiana adds Rule 1.1(b), which provides: "A lawyer is required to comply with the minimum requirements of continuing legal education as prescribed by Louisiana Supreme Court rule."

Missouri: Effective January 1, 1994, reflecting the surging popularity of limited liability companies across the country, Missouri expanded its definition of "partner" to include "a member of a law firm organized as a limited liability company."

New Jersey: Rule 1.6(d) states:

> Reasonable belief for purposes of RPC 1.6 is the belief or conclusion of a reasonable lawyer that is based upon information that has some foundation in fact and constitutes prima facie evidence of the matters referred to in subsection (b) or (c).

New York defines "fraud" as follows:

> "Fraud" does not include conduct, although characterized as fraudulent by statute or administrative rule, which lacks an element of scienter, deceit, intent to mislead, or knowing failure to correct misrepresentations which can be reasonably expected to induce detrimental reliance by another.

Pennsylvania defines "partner" to denote "an equity owner in a law firm, whether in the capacity of a partner in a partnership, a shareholder in a professional corporation, a member in a limited liability company, a beneficiary of a business trust, or otherwise."

Texas adds or modifies the following definitions:

> "Adjudicatory Official" denotes a person who serves on a Tribunal.
>
> "Adjudicatory Proceeding" denotes the consideration of a matter by a Tribunal.
>
> "Competent" or "Competence" denotes possession or the ability to timely acquire the legal knowledge, skill, and training reasonably necessary for the representation of the client.

"Consult" or "Consultation" denotes communication of information and advice reasonably sufficient to permit the client to appreciate the significance of the matter in question.

"Firm" or "Law firm" denotes a lawyer or lawyers in a private firm; or a lawyer or lawyers employed in the legal department of a corporation, legal services organization, or other organization, or in a unit of government.

"Fitness" denotes those qualities of physical, mental and psychological health that enable a person to discharge a lawyer's responsibilities to clients in conformity with the Texas Rules of Professional Conduct. Normally a lack of fitness is indicated most clearly by a persistent inability to discharge, or unreliability in carrying out, significant obligations.

"Should know" when used in reference to a lawyer denotes that a reasonable lawyer under the same or similar circumstances would know the matter in question.

"Substantial" when used in reference to degree or extent denotes a matter of meaningful significance or involvement.

"Tribunal" denotes any governmental body or official or any other person engaged in a process of resolving a particular dispute or controversy. "Tribunal" includes such institutions as courts and administrative agencies when engaging in adjudicatory or licensing activities as defined by applicable law or rules of practice or procedure, as well as judges, magistrates, special masters, referees, arbitrators, mediators, hearing officers and comparable persons empowered to resolve or to recommend a resolution of a particular matter; but it does not include jurors, prospective jurors, legislative bodies or their committees, members or staffs, nor does it include other governmental bodies when acting in a legislative or rule-making capacity.

Related Materials

American Lawyer's Code of Conduct uses the following terminology:

A lawyer *knows* certain facts, or acts *knowingly* or with *knowledge* of facts, when a person with that lawyer's professional training and experience would be reasonably certain of those facts in view of all the circumstances of which the lawyer is aware. A duty to investigate or inquire is not implied by the use of these words, but may be explicitly required under particular rules. Even in the absence of a duty to investigate, however, a studied rejection of reasonable inferences is inadequate to avoid ethical responsibility.

Reasonable belief, reasonably believes or *reasonable understanding* is the standard used to denote a lawyer's mental state when the lawyer may be required or permitted to act on the basis of incomplete knowledge of relevant facts, as when the lawyer is predicting future events, or is compelled to act on the basis of assumptions or inferences because all the relevant facts cannot be ascertained. The lawyer must understand or suppose the fact or circumstance to be so, and the circumstances must make that understanding or supposition a reasonable one.

Model Rules of Professional Conduct for Federal Lawyers* add the following definitions:

---

*This and all other excerpts from the Model Rules of Professional Conduct for Federal Lawyers, copyright © 1990 Federal Bar Association, 1815 H Street, NW, Washington,

"Federal Agency" means: (1) An Executive agency, including an Executive department, military department, Government corporation, Government controlled corporation, and an independent establishment; (2) The Congress, committees of Congress, members of Congress who employ lawyers, and Congressional agencies; (3) The courts of the United States and agencies of the Judiciary; (4) The Governments of the territories and possessions of the United States; or (5) The Government of the District of Columbia.

"Federal lawyer" means a Government lawyer or a Non-Government lawyer, as hereinafter defined.

"Government lawyer" means a Government employee who holds a position as an attorney with a Federal Agency or serves as a judge advocate in one of the Armed Forces, but only while performing official duties. The term includes a lawyer in private practice who has contracted with or been specially retained by a Federal Agency to represent the Agency or another person while engaged in the performance of the contractual obligation.

"Non-Government lawyer" means an individual who is a member of the bar of a Federal court or the highest court of a State or Territory, who represents persons before a Federal Agency. When a Government lawyer is engaged in the private practice of law or pro bono representation not related to the Government lawyer's official duties, the lawyer is considered a Non-Government lawyer.

"Supervisory lawyer" means a Federal lawyer within an office or organization with authority over or responsibility for the direction, coordination, evaluation, or assignment of responsibilities and work of subordinate lawyers, contract legal representation, nonlawyer assistants (e.g., paralegals), and clerical personnel.

ARTICLE 1. CLIENT-LAWYER RELATIONSHIP

Editors' Note. The 1980 Discussion Draft included the following introduction to Article 1:

A client usually seeks legal assistance to deal with unfamiliar circumstances and relationships. The client's position is ordinarily one of need and frequently one of adversity; the client's problem may involve significant personal and property interests, individual freedom and responsibility, or even life itself. To obtain effective advice and assistance in such matters, the client must place trust in the lawyer. To provide such advice and assistance the lawyer must be skillful, diligent, and trustworthy. At the same time, the lawyer must be faithful to the requirements of law and the Rules of Professional Conduct and respectful of the interests of third persons.

These responsibilities commence when a lawyer is asked to assist a client. They continue in all the functions that a lawyer may perform on behalf of a client. . . .

D.C. 20006-3697, have been directly quoted here with the permission of the Federal Bar Association.

Rule 1.1 Competence

A lawyer shall provide competent representation to a client. Competent representation requires the legal knowledge, skill, thoroughness and preparation reasonably necessary for the representation.

COMMENT

Legal Knowledge and Skill

[1] In determining whether a lawyer employs the requisite knowledge and skill in a particular matter, relevant factors include the relative complexity and specialized nature of the matter, the lawyer's general experience, the lawyer's training and experience in the field in question, the preparation and study the lawyer is able to give the matter and whether it is feasible to refer the matter to, or associate or consult with, a lawyer of established competence in the field in question. In many instances, the required proficiency is that of a general practitioner. Expertise in a particular field of law may be required in some circumstances.

[2] A lawyer need not necessarily have special training or prior experience to handle legal problems of a type with which the lawyer is unfamiliar. A newly admitted lawyer can be as competent as a practitioner with long experience. Some important legal skills, such as the analysis of precedent, the evaluation of evidence and legal drafting, are required in all legal problems. Perhaps the most fundamental legal skill consists of determining what kind of legal problems a situation may involve, a skill that necessarily transcends any particular specialized knowledge. A lawyer can provide adequate representation in a wholly novel field through necessary study. Competent representation can also be provided through the association of a lawyer of established competence in the field in question.

[3] In an emergency a lawyer may give advice or assistance in a matter in which the lawyer does not have the skill ordinarily required where referral to or consultation or association with another lawyer would be impractical. Even in an emergency, however, assistance should be limited to that reasonably necessary in the circumstances, for ill considered action under emergency conditions can jeopardize the client's interest.

[4] A lawyer may accept representation where the requisite level of competence can be achieved by reasonable preparation. This applies as well to a lawyer who is appointed as counsel for an unrepresented person. See also Rule 6.2.

Thoroughness and Preparation

[5] Competent handling of a particular matter includes inquiry into and analysis of the factual and legal elements of the problem, and use of methods and procedures meeting the standards of competent practitioners. It also includes adequate preparation. The required attention and preparation are determined in part by what is at stake; major litigation and complex transactions ordinarily require more elaborate treatment than matters of lesser consequence.

Maintaining Competence

[6] To maintain the requisite knowledge and skill, a lawyer should engage in continuing study and education. If a system of peer review has been established, the lawyer should consider making use of it in appropriate circumstances.

Model Code Comparison

DR 6-101(A)(1) provided that a lawyer shall not handle a matter "which he knows or should know that he is not competent to handle, without associating himself with a lawyer who is competent to handle it"; DR 6-101(A)(2) requires "preparation adequate in the circumstances." Rule 1.1 more fully particularizes the elements of competence. Whereas DR 6-101(A)(3) prohibited the "neglect of a legal matter," Rule 1.1 does not contain such a prohibition. Instead, Rule 1.1 affirmatively requires the lawyer to be competent.

Cross-References in Rules

Rule 1.2, Comment 5: "[T]he client may not be asked to agree to representation so limited in scope as to violate **Rule 1.1.**"

Rule 1.7, Comment 6: "[A] lawyer's need for income should not lead the lawyer to undertake matters that cannot be handled competently and at a reasonable fee" (citing **Rule 1.1**).

Rule 1.17, Comment 11 provides that a lawyer selling a law practice has an "obligation to exercise competence in identifying a purchaser qualified to assume the practice and the purchaser's obligation to undertake the representation competently (see **Rule 1.1**)."

Rule 6.2, Comment 2: A lawyer has good cause to decline appointment by a court to represent a person "if the lawyer could not handle the matter competently, see **Rule 1.1.** . . ."

Legislative History

1979 Unofficial Pre-Circulation Draft:

. . . (b) A lawyer acts incompetently in a particular matter, if:

(i) He or she fails to use the knowledge, skill, preparation, and judgment that a reasonably competent lawyer would use in the circumstances; and

(ii) The result of the lawyer's act or failure to act is substantial expense, delay, harm, or risk of harm to a client or other person for whose benefit the advice or assistance is provided.

1980 Discussion Draft: "A lawyer shall undertake representation only in matters in which the lawyer can act with adequate competence. . . ."

1981 Draft defined competence to include "efficiency."

1982 Draft was adopted.

Selected State Variations

Alaska: Rule 1.1 adds language from the ABA Comment to the Rule, allowing the lawyer, in emergency situations, to give advice or assistance in a matter in which the lawyer does not have the skill ordinarily required.

California: See Rule 3-110 (Failing to Act Competently).

District of Columbia: D.C. Rule 1.1(b) differs significantly from the ABA Model Rule — see District of Columbia Rules of Professional Conduct below.

Illinois adds the following subparagraphs to Rule 1.1:

(b) A lawyer shall not represent a client in a legal matter in which the lawyer knows or reasonably should know that the lawyer is not competent to provide representation, without the association of another lawyer who is competent to provide such representation.

(c) After accepting employment on behalf of a client, a lawyer shall not thereafter delegate to another lawyer not in the lawyer's firm the responsibility for performing or completing that employment, without the client's consent.

Louisiana adds Rule 1.1(b), which provides: "A lawyer is required to comply with the minimum requirements of continuing legal education as prescribed by Louisiana Supreme Court rule."

Michigan retains the language of the Code in its Rule 1.1.

New Hampshire substitutes for Rule 1.1:

(a) A lawyer shall provide competent representation to a client.

(b) Legal competence requires at a minimum:

(1) specific knowledge about the fields of law in which the lawyer practices;

(2) performance of the techniques of practice with skill;

(3) identification of areas beyond the lawyer's competence and bringing those areas to the client's attention;

(4) proper preparation; and

(5) attention to details and schedules necessary to assure that the matter undertaken is completed with no avoidable harm to the client's interest.

(c) In the performance of client service, a lawyer shall at a minimum:

(1) gather sufficient facts regarding the client's problem from the client, and from other relevant sources;

(2) formulate the material issues raised, determine applicable law and identify alternative legal responses;

(3) develop a strategy, in collaboration with the client, for solving the legal problems of the client; and

(4) undertake actions on the client's behalf in a timely and effective manner including, where appropriate, associating with another lawyer who possesses the skill and knowledge required to assure competent representation.

New Jersey: A lawyer shall not:

(a) Handle or neglect a matter entrusted to the lawyer in such manner that the lawyer's conduct constitutes gross negligence.

(b) Exhibit a pattern of negligence or neglect in the lawyer's handling of legal matters generally.

New York: Same or substantially the same as the ABA Model Code — see Model Code Comparison above.

Texas: Rule 1.01 provides:

(a) A lawyer shall not accept or continue employment in a legal matter which the lawyer knows or should know is beyond the lawyer's competence, unless:

(1) another lawyer who is competent to handle the matter is, with the prior informed consent of the client, associated in the matter; or

(2) the advice or assistance of the lawyer is reasonably required in an emergency and the lawyer limits the advice and assistance to that which is reasonably necessary in the circumstances.

(b) In representing a client, a lawyer shall not:

(1) neglect a legal matter entrusted to the lawyer; or

(2) frequently fail to carry out completely the obligations that the lawyer owes to a client or clients.

(c) As used in this Rule, "neglect" signifies inattentiveness involving a conscious disregard for the responsibilities owed to a client or clients.

Virginia: DR 6-101 (A) provides that a lawyer may undertake representation "only in matters in which: (1) The lawyer can act with competence and demonstrate the specific legal knowledge, skill, efficiency, and thoroughness in preparation employed in acceptable legal practice by lawyers undertaking similar matters; or (2) The lawyer has associated another lawyer who is competent in those matters."

Related Materials

ABA Model Rule for Minimum Continuing Legal Education (MCLE): In 1988, to give states guidance on implementing MCLE programs, the ABA adopted a Model Rule for MCLE. It is reprinted in the ABA/BNA Lawyers' Manual on Professional Conduct.

ABA Standards for Imposing Lawyer Sanctions:*

> 4.51. Disbarment is generally appropriate when a lawyer's course of conduct demonstrates that the lawyer does not understand the most fundamental legal doctrines or procedures, and the lawyer's conduct causes injury or potential injury to a client.
>
> 4.52. Suspension is generally appropriate when a lawyer engages in an area of practice in which the lawyer knows he or she is not competent, and causes injury or potential injury to a client.

American Academy of Matrimonial Lawyers: The "Bounds of Advocacy" drafted by the American Academy of Matrimonial Lawyers contains the following provisions and commentary:

> 1.3. An attorney should not advise a client about a matter concerning which the attorney is not sufficiently competent.

Comment to Rule 1.3

> No attorney has complete command of every field of the law or every issue that may be encountered in a family law matter. Clients, however, often ask matrimonial lawyers to provide psychological or investment counseling or to provide advice on issues of real estate and corporate law. A matrimonial lawyer should recommend that such a client consult more knowledgeable lawyers or other professionals when in the best interest of the client.

American Lawyer's Code of Conduct: Rule 4.2 provides:

> 4.2. A lawyer who has held himself or herself out to a client as having special skill and competence relative to a matter in which the client has retained the lawyer shall serve the client with that skill and care generally afforded to clients by lawyers of such skill and competence.

Mandatory Continuing Legal Education: About two-thirds of the states have adopted mandatory continuing legal education ("MCLE") programs, requiring lawyers to take a minimum number of hours of CLE each year. About half of these states require that a portion of the MCLE hours be devoted to "ethics" or "professionalism." (One state, Pennsylvania, mandates CLE *only* in the subjects of ethics and professionalism.) Many states adopted their MCLE programs after

---

*This and all subsequent ABA Standards for Imposing Lawyer Sanctions are copyright © 1986 by the American Bar Association. All rights reserved. Reprinted with permission of the American Bar Association.

the ABA passed a resolution in 1986 supporting the idea of continuing legal education for all active lawyers.

The latest state to adopt MCLE is New York, which will require CLE for newly admitted lawyers beginning in 1997 and for veteran lawyers beginning in 1998. In the District of Columbia, however, lawyers voted overwhelmingly against two MCLE proposals in a December 1995 advisory referendum. Only one state, Michigan, has repealed an MCLE program. In 1994, after trying MCLE for a few years, the Michigan Supreme Court dropped the program as "ineffective."

Restatement of the Law Governing Lawyers: The American Law Institute has tentatively approved the following provisions:

§28. *Lawyer's Duties to Client in General*

To the extent consistent with the lawyer's other legal duties and subject to the other provisions of this Restatement, a lawyer must, in matters within the scope of the representation:

(1) proceed in a manner reasonably calculated to advance a client's lawful objectives, as defined by the client after consultation;

(2) act with reasonable competence and diligence;

(3) comply with obligations concerning the client's confidences and property, avoid impermissible conflicting interests, deal honestly with the client, and not employ advantages arising from the client-lawyer relationship in a manner adverse to the client; and

(4) fulfill valid contractual obligations to the client.

§71. *Elements and Defenses Generally*

In addition to the other possible bases of civil liability described in §§76A and 77, a lawyer is civilly liable to a person to whom the lawyer owes a duty of care within the meaning of §72 or §73, if the lawyer fails to exercise care within the meaning of §74 and if that failure is a legal cause of injury within the meaning of §75, unless the lawyer has a defense within the meaning of §76.

§72. *Duty of Care to Client*

For purposes of liability under §71, a lawyer owes a client the duty to exercise care within the meaning of §74 in pursuing the client's lawful objectives in matters covered by the representation and in fulfilling the fiduciary duties to the client set forth in §28(3).

§73. *Duty of Care to Certain Non-Clients*

For purposes of liability under §71, a lawyer owes a duty to use care within the meaning of §74:

(1) to a prospective client, as stated in §27;

(2) to a non-client when and to the extent that:

(a) the lawyer or (with the lawyer's acquiescence) the lawyer's client invites the non-client to rely on the lawyer's opinion or provision of other legal services, and the non-client so relies, and

(b) the non-client is not, under applicable tort law, too remote from the lawyer to be entitled to protection;

(3) to a non-client when and to the extent that:

(a) the lawyer knows that a client intends as one of the primary objectives of the representation that the lawyer's services benefit the non-client; and

(b) such a duty would not significantly impair the lawyer's performance of obligations to the client, and the absence of such a duty would make enforcement of those obligations unlikely;

(4) to a non-client when and to the extent that:

(a) the lawyer's client is a trustee, guardian, executor, or fiduciary acting primarily to perform similar functions for the non-client; . . .

(The rest of Restatement §73 is reprinted after Model Rule 1.6.)

§74. Standard of Care

(1) For purposes of liability under §71, a lawyer who owes a duty of care must exercise the competence and diligence normally exercised by lawyers in similar circumstances, unless the lawyer represents that the lawyer will exercise greater competence or diligence.

(2) Proof of a violation of a rule or statute regulating the conduct of lawyers:

(a) does not give rise to an implied cause of action for lack of care;

(b) does not preclude other proof concerning the duty of care in Subsection (1); and

(c) may be considered by a trier of fact as an aid in understanding and applying the standard of Subsection (1) to the extent that (i) the rule or statute was designed for the protection of persons in the position of the claimant and (ii) proof of the content and construction of such a rule or statute is relevant to the claimant's claim.

§75. Causation and Damages

A lawyer is liable under §71 only for injury of which the lawyer's breach of a duty of care was a legal cause, as determined under generally applicable principles of causation and damages.

§76. Defenses; Prospective Liability Waiver; Settlement

(1) An agreement prospectively limiting a lawyer's liability to a client for malpractice is unenforceable.

(2) The client or former client may void an agreement settling a claim by the client or former client against the person's lawyer if:

(a) the client or former client was subjected to improper pressure by the lawyer in reaching the settlement; or

(b) (i) the client or former client was not independently represented in negotiating the settlement, and (ii) the settlement was not fair and reasonable to the client or former client.

(3) For purposes of professional discipline, a lawyer may not:

(a) make an agreement prospectively limiting the lawyer's liability to a client for malpractice; or

(b) settle a claim for such liability with an unrepresented client or former client without first advising that person in writing that independent representation is appropriate in connection therewith.

(4) Except as otherwise provided in this Section, liability under §71 is subject to the defenses available under generally applicable principles of law governing professional negligence actions. A lawyer is not liable under §71 for any action or inaction the lawyer reasonably believed to be required by law, including a professional rule.

§76A. *Civil Liability to Client Other Than for Malpractice*

(1) A lawyer is subject to liability to a client for injury caused by breach of contract in the circumstances and to the extent provided by contract law.

(2) A lawyer is subject to liability to a client for injury caused by intentional breach of the fiduciary duties set forth in §28(3) in the circumstances and to the extent provided by law governing intentional breach of fiduciary duties.

(3) A client is entitled to restitutionary, injunctive, or declaratory remedies against a lawyer in the circumstances and to the extent provided by generally applicable law governing such remedies.

§77. *Liability to Client or Non-Client Under General Law*

Except as provided in §78, and in addition to liability under §§71-76A, a lawyer is subject to liability to a client or non-client when a nonlawyer would be in similar circumstances.

§78. *Non-Client Claims — Certain Defenses and Exceptions to Liability*

(1) In addition to other absolute or conditional privileges provided by the law of defamation, a lawyer is absolutely privileged under the law of defamation to publish defamatory matter concerning a non-client in communications preliminary to a reasonably anticipated proceeding before a tribunal, or in the institution or during the course and as a part of such a proceeding, in which the lawyer participates as counsel, if the matter is published to a person who will be involved in the proceeding and has some relation to the proceeding.

(2) A lawyer representing a client in a civil proceeding, or procuring the institution of criminal proceedings by a client, is not liable to a non-client for wrongful use of civil proceedings or for malicious prosecution if the lawyer has probable cause for acting, or if the lawyer acts primarily to help the client obtain a proper adjudication of the client's claim.

(3) A lawyer who advises or assists a client to make or break a contract, to enter or dissolve a legal relationship, or to enter or not enter a contractual relation, is not liable to a non-client for interference with contract or with prospective con-

tractual relations or with a legal relationship, if the lawyer acts to advance the client's objectives without using wrongful means.

§79. *Vicarious Liability*

(1) A law firm is subject to civil liability for injury legally caused to a person by any wrongful act or omission of any principal or employee of the firm who was acting in the ordinary course of the firm's business or with actual authority.

(2) Each of the principals of a law firm organized as a general partnership is liable jointly and severally with the firm.

(3) A principal of a law firm organized other than as a general partnership as authorized by law is vicariously liable for the acts of another principal or employee of the firm to the extent provided by law.

Sixth Amendment: The Sixth Amendment to the United States Constitution guarantees criminal defendants "the assistance of counsel" for their defense. This phrase has consistently been interpreted to guarantee the *effective* assistance of counsel, which means that lawyers for criminal defendants must perform at a certain minimum level of competence to satisfy the Sixth Amendment guarantee of effective assistance. If a convicted defendant believes that his lawyer was ineffective, the defendant can challenge the conviction. In Strickland v. Washington, 466 U.S. 668 (1984), the Supreme Court said that whether a lawyer was "ineffective" depended on "whether, in light of all the circumstances, the identified acts or omissions were outside the wide range of professionally competent assistance." Model Rule 1.1, which requires a lawyer to be "competent," may help to determine the range of professionally "competent" assistance.

Rule 1.2 Scope of Representation

(a) A lawyer shall abide by a client's decisions concerning the objectives of representation, subject to paragraphs (c), (d) and (e), and shall consult with the client as to the means by which they are to be pursued. A lawyer shall abide by a client's decision whether to accept an offer of settlement of a matter. In a criminal case, the lawyer shall abide by the client's decision, after consultation with the lawyer, as to a plea to be entered, whether to waive jury trial and whether the client will testify.

(b) A lawyer's representation of a client, including representation by appointment, does not constitute an endorsement of the client's political, economic, social or moral views or activities.

(c) A lawyer may limit the objectives of the representation if the client consents after consultation.

(d) A lawyer shall not counsel a client to engage, or assist a client, in conduct that the lawyer knows is criminal or fraudulent, but a lawyer may discuss the legal consequences of any proposed course of conduct with a client and may counsel or assist a client to make a good faith effort to determine the validity, scope, meaning or application of the law.

(e) When a lawyer knows that a client expects assistance not permitted by the rules of professional conduct or other law, the lawyer shall consult with the client regarding the relevant limitations on the lawyer's conduct.

COMMENT

Scope of Representation

[1] Both lawyer and client have authority and responsibility in the objectives and means of representation. The client has ultimate authority to determine the purposes to be served by legal representation, within the limits imposed by law and the lawyer's professional obligations. Within those limits, a client also has a right to consult with the lawyer about the means to be used in pursuing those objectives. At the same time, a lawyer is not required to pursue objectives or employ means simply because a client may wish that the lawyer do so. A clear distinction between objectives and means sometimes cannot be drawn, and in many cases the client-lawyer relationship partakes of a joint undertaking. In questions of means, the lawyer should assume responsibility for technical and legal tactical issues, but should defer to the client regarding such questions as the expense to be incurred and concern for third persons who might be adversely affected. Law defining the lawyer's scope of authority in litigation varies among jurisdictions.

[2] In a case in which the client appears to be suffering mental disability, the lawyer's duty to abide by the client's decisions is to be guided by reference to Rule 1.14.

Independence from Client's Views or Activities

[3] Legal representation should not be denied to people who are unable to afford legal services, or whose cause is controversial or the subject of popular disapproval. By the same token, representing a client does not constitute approval of the client's views or activities.

Services Limited in Objectives or Means

[4] The objectives or scope of services provided by a lawyer may be limited by agreement with the client or by the terms under which the lawyer's services are made available to the client. For example, a retainer may be for a specifically defined purpose. Representation provided through a legal aid agency may be subject to limitations on the types of cases the agency handles. When a lawyer has been retained by an insurer to represent an insured, the representation may be limited to matters related to the insurance coverage. The terms upon which representation is undertaken may exclude specific objectives or means. Such limitations may exclude objectives or means that the lawyer regards as repugnant or imprudent.

[5] An agreement concerning the scope of representation must accord with the Rules of Professional Conduct and other law. Thus, the client may not be asked to agree to representation so limited in scope as to violate Rule 1.1, or to surrender the right to terminate the lawyer's services or the right to settle litigation that the lawyer might wish to continue.

Criminal, Fraudulent and Prohibited Transactions

[6] A lawyer is required to give an honest opinion about the actual consequences that appear likely to result from a client's conduct. The fact that a client uses advice in a course of action that is criminal or fraudulent does not, of itself, make a lawyer a party to the course of action. However, a lawyer may not knowingly assist a client in criminal or fraudulent conduct. There is a critical distinction between presenting an analysis of legal aspects of questionable conduct and recommending the means by which a crime or fraud might be committed with impunity.

[7] When the client's course of action has already begun and is continuing, the lawyer's responsibility is especially delicate. The lawyer is not permitted to reveal the client's wrongdoing, except where permitted by Rule 1.6. However, the lawyer is required to avoid furthering the purpose, for example, by suggesting how it might be concealed. A lawyer may not continue assisting a client in conduct that the lawyer originally supposes is legally proper but then discovers is criminal or fraudulent. Withdrawal from the representation, therefore, may be required.

[8] Where the client is a fiduciary, the lawyer may be charged with special obligations in dealings with a beneficiary.

[9] Paragraph (d) applies whether or not the defrauded party is a party to the transaction. Hence, a lawyer should not participate in a sham transaction; for example, a transaction to effectuate criminal or fraudulent escape of tax liability. Paragraph (d) does not preclude undertaking a criminal defense incident to a general retainer for legal services to a lawful enterprise. The last clause of paragraph (d) recognizes that determining the validity or interpretation of a statute or regulation may require a course of action involving disobedience of the statute or regulation or of the interpretation placed upon it by governmental authorities.

Model Code Comparison

Paragraph (a) has no counterpart in the Disciplinary Rules of the Model Code. EC 7-7 stated: "In certain areas of legal representation not affecting the merits of the cause or substantially prejudicing the rights of a client, a lawyer is entitled to make decisions on his own. But otherwise the authority to make decisions is exclusively that of the client. . . ." EC 7-8 stated that "[I]n the final analysis, however, the . . . decision whether to forego legally available objectives or methods because of nonlegal factors is ultimately for the client. . . . In the event that the client in a nonadjudicatory matter insists upon a course of conduct that is contrary to the judgment and advice of the lawyer but not prohibited by Disciplinary Rules, the lawyer may withdraw from the employment." DR 7-101(A)(1) provided that a lawyer "shall not intentionally . . . fail to seek the lawful objectives of his client through reasonably available means permitted by law. . . . A lawyer does not violate this Disciplinary Rule, however, by . . . avoiding offensive tactics. . . ."

Paragraph (b) has no counterpart in the Model Code.

With regard to paragraph (c), DR 7-101(B)(1) provided that a lawyer may, "where permissible, exercise his professional judgment to waive or fail to assert a right or position of his client."

With regard to paragraph (d), DR 7-102(A)(7) provided that a lawyer shall not "counsel or assist his client in conduct that the lawyer knows to be illegal or fraudulent." DR 7-102(A)(6) provided that a lawyer shall not "participate in the creation or preservation of evidence when he knows or it is obvious that the evidence is false." DR 7-106 provided that a lawyer shall not "advise his client to disregard a standing rule of a tribunal or a ruling of a tribunal . . . but he may take appropriate steps in good faith to test the validity of such rule or ruling." EC 7-5 stated that a lawyer "should never encourage or aid his client to commit criminal acts or counsel his client on how to violate the law and avoid punishment therefor."

With regard to Rule 1.2(e), DR 2-110(C)(1)(c) provided that a lawyer may withdraw from representation if a client "insists" that the lawyer engage in "conduct that is illegal or that is prohibited under the Disciplinary Rules." DR

9-101(C) provided that "a lawyer shall not state or imply that he is able to influence improperly . . . any tribunal, legislative body or public official."

Cross-References in Rules

Rule 1.3, Comment 1: "A lawyer has professional discretion in determining the means by which a matter should be pursued. See **Rule 1.2.**"

Rule 1.4, Comment 1: "A lawyer who receives from opposing counsel an offer of settlement in a civil controversy or a proffered plea bargain in a criminal case should promptly inform the client of its substance unless prior discussions with the client have left it clear that the proposal will be unacceptable. See **Rule 1.2(a).**"

Rule 1.6, Comment 10: "[T]he lawyer may not counsel or assist a client in conduct that is criminal or fraudulent. See **Rule 1.2(d).** Similarly, a lawyer has a duty under Rule 3.3(a)(4) not to use false evidence. This duty is essentially a special instance of the duty prescribed in **Rule 1.2(d)** to avoid assisting a client in criminal or fraudulent conduct."

Rule 1.6, Comment 11: "[T]he lawyer may have been innocently involved in past conduct by the client that was criminal or fraudulent. In such a situation the lawyer has not violated **Rule 1.2(d)**, because to 'counsel or assist' criminal or fraudulent conduct requires knowing that the conduct is of that character."

Rule 1.13, Comment 6: "If the lawyer's services are being used by an organization to further a crime or fraud by the organization, **Rule 1.2(d)** can be applicable."

Rule 1.14, Comment 4: "If the lawyer represents the guardian as distinct from the ward, and is aware that the guardian is acting adversely to the ward's interest, the lawyer may have an obligation to prevent or rectify the guardian's misconduct. See **Rule 1.2(d).**"

Rule 3.3, Comment 2: "The obligation prescribed in **Rule 1.2(d)** not to counsel a client to commit or assist the client in committing a fraud applies in litigation. Regarding compliance with **Rule 1.2(d)**, see the Comment to that Rule."

Rule 3.3, Comment 6: The alternative to disclosing a client's deception to the court or to the other party is that the lawyer "cooperate in deceiving the court, thereby subverting the truth-finding process which the adversary system is designed to implement. See **Rule 1.2(d).**"

Rule 3.3, Comment 10: "[A]n advocate has an obligation, not only in professional ethics but under the law as well, to avoid implication in the commission of perjury or other falsification of evidence. See **Rule 1.2(d).**"

Rule 6.4, Comment: "Lawyers involved in organizations seeking law reform generally do not have a client-lawyer relationship with the organization. . . . See also **Rule 1.2(b).**"

Rule 8.4, Comment 2: "The provisions of **Rule 1.2(d)** concerning a good faith challenge to the validity, scope, meaning or application of the law apply to challenges of legal regulation of the practice of law."

Legislative History

1980 Discussion Draft (then called Rule 1.3):

    (a) A lawyer shall accept a client's decisions concerning the objectives of the representation and the means by which they are to be pursued except as stated in paragraphs (b) and (c).

    (b) A lawyer shall not pursue a course of action on behalf of a client in violation of law or the rules of professional conduct.

    (c) The lawyer may decline to pursue a lawful course of action . . . and, if the client insists upon such course of action, the lawyer may withdraw from representation subject to the provisions of Rule 1.16.

The 1980 Draft also contained the following separate rules (then called Rules 2.3 and 2.4):

Advice Concerning Wrongful Conduct

    (a) A lawyer shall not give advice which the lawyer can reasonably foresee will:

    (1) Be used by the client to further an illegal course of conduct except as part of a good faith effort to determine the validity, scope, meaning, or application of the law; or

    (2) Aid the client in contriving false testimony or making a legally wrongful misrepresentation.

    (b) A lawyer may decline to give advice that might assist the client in any conduct that would violate the law or . . . that the lawyer considers repugnant.

Duty to Offer Advice

    A lawyer who knows that a client contemplates a course of action which has a substantial likelihood of serious legal consequences shall warn the client of the legal implications of the conduct, unless a client has expressly or by implication asked not to receive such advice.

The 1980 Draft also contained the following rule (then called Rule 4.1) similar to the adopted version of Rule 1.2(a):

Disclosures to a Client

    A lawyer conducting negotiations for a client shall:

    (a) inform the client of facts relevant to the matter and of communications from another party that may significantly affect resolution of the matter;

    (b) in connection with an offer, take reasonable steps to assure that the judgment of the client rather than that of the lawyer determines whether the offer will be accepted.

1981 Draft of Rule 1.2(d) prohibited a lawyer from counseling or assisting a client "in the preparation of a written instrument containing terms the lawyer knows or reasonably should know are legally prohibited. . . ."

1982 Draft of Rule 1.2 was the same as adopted, except that Rule 1.2(d) also prohibited a lawyer from counseling or assisting "in the preparation of a written instrument containing terms the lawyer knows are expressly prohibited by law. . . ."

Selected State Variations

Alaska: Rule 1.2 (a) adds: "[A] lawyer in a criminal case must also abide by the client's decision whether to take an appeal."

California: See Rule 3-210 (Advising the Violation of Law) and B & P Code §6068(c).

Colorado adds paragraph (f), which prohibits a lawyer from engaging in conduct that

> exhibits or is intended to appeal to or engender bias against a person on account of that person's race, gender, religion, national origin, disability, age, sexual orientation, or socioeconomic status, whether that conduct is directed to other counsel, court personnel, witnesses, parties, judges, judicial officers, or any persons involved in the legal process.

District of Columbia: D.C. Rule 1.2(d) differs significantly from the ABA Model Rule — see District of Columbia Rules of Professional Conduct below.

Florida adds the words "or reasonably should know" in Rule 1.2(d) and (e). In addition, Florida's Statement of Client's Rights, which must be provided to every contingent fee client (see Florida Rule 1.5(D)), provides that "[y]ou, the client, have the right to make the final decision regarding settlement of a case. . . ."

Georgia forbids a lawyer to "institute, cause to be instituted or settle a legal proceeding or claim without obtaining proper authorization from his client." DR 7-102(A)(9).

Illinois includes language from DR 7-102(A)-(B) as paragraphs (f)-(h), and adds the following new paragraph (based on DR 7-105) as Rule 1.2(e): "A lawyer shall not present, participate in presenting, or threaten to present criminal charges or professional disciplinary actions to obtain an advantage in a civil matter."

Louisiana adds to Rule 1.2(a): "Both lawyer and client have authority and responsibility in the objectives and means of representation. The client has ultimate authority to determine the purposes to be served by legal representation within the limits imposed by law and the lawyer's professional obligations."

Maryland adds "when appropriate" before the words "shall consult" in Rule 1.2(a).

Massachusetts: Effective January 1, 1998, Rule 1.2(a) provides that a lawyer "does not violate this rule . . . by acceding to reasonable requests of opposing counsel which do not prejudice the rights of his or her client, by being punctual in fulfilling all professional commitments, by avoiding offensive tactics, or by treating with courtesy and consideration all persons involved in the legal process.''

Michigan deletes Rule 1.2(b) and adds the following sentence to Rule 1.2(a): ''In representing a client, a lawyer may, where permissible, exercise professional judgment to waive or fail to assert a right or position of the client.'' Where the official ABA Comment to Rule 1.2, paragraph 6, refers to ''criminal or fraudulent conduct,'' the Michigan Comment refers to ''illegal or fraudulent conduct.'' Michigan places the substance of Rule 1.2(b) in the Comment to Rule 1.2.

Minnesota deletes Rule 1.2(b) entirely.

New Jersey: In Rule 1.2(d), New Jersey forbids a lawyer to assist a client ''in the preparation of a written instrument containing terms the lawyer knows are expressly prohibited by the law.''

New York: Same or substantially the same as the ABA Model Code — see Model Code Comparison above — except see New York Materials for New York's version of DR 7-102(B)(1). See also EC 2-27, EC 4-7, and DR 4-101(C)(5) of the New York Code.

Virginia: Substantially the same as the Model Code.

Related Materials

ABA Canons: Canons 16, 24, and 32 provided:

16. Restraining Clients from Improprieties

A lawyer should use his best efforts to restrain and to prevent his clients from doing those things which the lawyer himself ought not to do, particularly with reference to their conduct towards Courts, judicial officers, jurors, witnesses and suitors. If a client persists in such wrongdoing the lawyer should terminate their relation.

24. Right of Lawyer to Control the Incidents of the Trial

As to incidental matters pending the trial, not affecting the merits of the cause, or working substantial prejudice to the rights of the client, such as forcing the opposite lawyer to trial when he is under affliction or bereavement; forcing the trial on a particular day to the injury of the opposite lawyer when no harm will result from a trial at a different time; agreeing to an extension of time for signing a bill of exceptions, cross interrogatories and the like, the lawyer must be allowed to judge. In such matters no client has a right to demand that his counsel shall be illiberal, or that he do anything therein repugnant to his own sense of honor and propriety.

32. The Lawyer's Duty in Its Last Analysis

No client, corporate or individual, however powerful, nor any cause, civil or political, however important, is entitled to receive nor should any lawyer render any service or advice involving disloyalty to the law whose ministers we are, or disrespect of the judicial office, which we are bound to uphold, or corruption of any person or persons exercising a public office or private trust, or deception or betrayal of the public. When rendering any such improper service or advice, the lawyer invites and merits stern and just condemnation. Correspondingly, he advances the honor of his profession and the best interests of his client when he renders service or gives advice tending to impress upon the client and his undertaking exact compliance with the strictest principles of moral law. He must also observe and advise his client to observe the statute law, though until a statute shall have been construed and interpreted by competent adjudication, he is free and is entitled to advise as to its validity and as to what he conscientiously believes to be its just meaning and extent. But above all a lawyer will find his highest honor in a deserved reputation for fidelity to private trust and to public duty, as an honest man and as a patriotic and loyal citizen.

Aiding and abetting: In many jurisdictions, a lawyer's violation of Rule 1.2(d) would also violate criminal laws prohibiting anyone from aiding or abetting the commission of a crime.

American Academy of Matrimonial Lawyers: The "Bounds of Advocacy" drafted by the American Academy of Matrimonial Lawyers contains the following provisions and commentary:

2.13. An attorney should never encourage a client to hide or dissipate assets.

Comment to Rule 2.13

It is improper for an attorney to "counsel a client to engage, or assist a client, in conduct that the lawyer knows is criminal or fraudulent, but a lawyer may discuss the legal consequences of any proposed course of conduct with a client. . . ." Whether the client proposes opening up an out-of-state bank account or having a family member hold sums of cash for the purpose of concealment, the advice to the client must be the same: "Don't do it." Hiding assets is a fraud upon the client's spouse and likely to result in a fraud upon the court. However, advice to protect, rather than hide, assets is appropriate. The client must also be advised not to conceal data about his property, fail to furnish relevant documents, insist on placing unrealistic values on properties in, or omit assets from, sworn financial statements.

On the other hand, "[t]here is a critical distinction between presenting an analysis of legal aspects of questionable conduct and recommending the means by which a crime or fraud might be committed with impunity." It may sometimes be difficult to determine whether a client's questions concerning legal aspects of pre-divorce planning are asked to facilitate an improper purpose. Although the attorney should initially give the client the benefit of any doubt, later discovery of improper conduct mandates that the attorney cease such assistance and may require withdrawal from representation.

2.27. An attorney should refuse to assist in vindictive conduct toward a spouse or third person and should not do anything to increase the emotional level of the dispute.

Comment to Rule 2.27

Although the client has the right to determine the "objectives of representation," after consulting with the client the attorney may limit the objectives and the means by which the objectives are to be pursued. The matrimonial lawyer should make every effort to lower the emotional level of the interaction between the parties and their counsel. Some dissension and bad feelings can be avoided by a frank discussion with the client at the outset of how the attorney handles cases, including what the attorney will and will not do regarding vindictive conduct or actions likely to adversely affect the children's interests. Although not essential, a letter to the client confirming the understanding, before specific issues or requests arise, is advisable. To the extent that the client is unwilling to accept any limitations on objectives or means, the attorney should decline the representation.

If such a discussion did not occur, or the client despite a prior understanding asks the attorney to engage in conduct the attorney believes to be imprudent or repugnant, the attorney should attempt to convince the client to work toward family harmony or the interests of the children. Conduct in the interests of the children or family will almost always be in the client's long term best interests.

American Lawyer's Code of Conduct: Rules 3.3 and 3.4 provide:

3.3. A lawyer shall not advise a client about the law when the lawyer knows that the client is requesting the advice for an unlawful purpose likely to cause death or serious physical injury to another person.

3.4. A lawyer shall not knowingly encourage a client to engage in illegal conduct, except in a good faith effort to test the validity or scope of the law.

Restatement of the Law Governing Lawyers: The American Law Institute has tentatively approved the following provisions:

§30. Limitation of Client or Lawyer Duties

(1) Subject to other requirements stated in this Restatement, a client and lawyer may agree to limit a duty that a lawyer would otherwise owe to the client if:
    (a) the client is adequately informed and consents; and
    (b) the terms of the limitation are reasonable in the circumstances.
(2) A lawyer may agree to waive a client's duty to pay or other duty owed to the lawyer.

§31. Lawyer's Duty to Inform and Consult with Client

(1) A lawyer must keep a client reasonably informed about the matter and must consult with a client to a reasonable extent concerning decisions to be made by the lawyer under §§32-34.
(2) A lawyer must promptly comply with a client's reasonable requests for information.
(3) A lawyer must notify a client of decisions to be made by the client under §§32-34 and must explain a matter to the extent reasonably necessary to permit the client to make informed decisions regarding the representation.

§32. Allocating Authority to Decide Between Client and Lawyer

As between client and lawyer:

(1) A client and lawyer may agree which of them will make specified decisions, subject to the requirements stated in §§29A, 30, 33, 34, and other provisions of this Restatement. The agreement may be superseded by another valid agreement.

(2) A client may instruct a lawyer during the representation, subject to the requirements stated in §§33, 34, and other provisions of this Restatement.

(3) Subject to Subsections (1) and (2) a lawyer may take any lawful measure within the scope of representation that is reasonably calculated to advance a client's objectives as defined by the client, consulting with the client as required by §31.

(4) A client may ratify an act of a lawyer that was not previously authorized.

§33. *Authority Reserved to Client*

(1) As between client and lawyer, subject to Subsection (2) and §34, the following and comparable decisions are reserved to the client except when the client has validly authorized the lawyer to make the particular decision: whether and on what terms to settle a claim; how a criminal defendant should plead; whether a criminal defendant should waive jury trial; whether a criminal defendant should testify; and whether to appeal in a civil proceeding or criminal prosecution.

(2) A client may not validly authorize a lawyer to make the decisions described in Subsection (1) when other law (such as criminal procedure rules governing pleas, jury trial waiver, and defendant testimony) requires the client's personal participation or approval.

(3) Regardless of any contrary agreement with a lawyer, a client may revoke a lawyer's authority to make the decisions described in Subsection (1).

§34. *Authority Reserved to Lawyer*

As between client and lawyer, a lawyer retains authority that may not be overridden by an agreement with or an instruction from the client:

(1) to refuse to perform, counsel, or assist future or ongoing acts in the representation that the lawyer reasonably believes to be unlawful;

(2) to make decisions or take actions in the representation that the lawyer reasonably believes to be required by law or an order of a tribunal.

§37. *Appearance Before Tribunal*

A lawyer who enters an appearance before a tribunal on behalf of a person is presumed to represent that person as a client. The presumption may be rebutted.

§38. *Lawyer's Actual Authority*

A lawyer's act is considered to be that of a client in proceedings before a tribunal or in dealings with third persons when:

(1) the client has expressly or impliedly authorized the act;

(2) authority concerning the act is reserved to the lawyer as stated in §34; or

(3) the client ratifies the act.

§39. A Lawyer's Apparent Authority

A lawyer's act is considered to be that of a client in proceedings before a tribunal or in dealings with a third person if the tribunal or third person reasonably assumes that the lawyer is authorized to do the act on the basis of the client's (and not the lawyer's) manifestations of such authorization.

§40. Lawyer's Knowledge; Notification to Lawyer; and Statements of Lawyer

(1) Information imparted to a lawyer during and relating to the representation of a client is attributed to the client for the purpose of determining the client's rights and liabilities in matters in which the lawyer represents the client, unless those rights or liabilities require proof of the client's personal knowledge or intentions, or the lawyer's legal duties preclude disclosure of the information to the client.

(2) Unless applicable law otherwise provides, a third person may give notification to a client, in a matter in which the client is represented by a lawyer, by giving notification to the client's lawyer, unless the third person knows of circumstances reasonably indicating that the client has abrogated the lawyer's authority to receive notification.

(3) A lawyer's unprivileged statement is admissible in evidence against a client as if it were the client's statement if either:

(a) the client authorized the lawyer to make a statement concerning the subject; or

(b) the statement concerns a matter within the scope of the representation and was made by the lawyer during it.

§41. Lawyer's Act or Advice as Mitigating or Avoiding Client's Responsibility

(1) When a client's intent or mental state is in issue, a tribunal may consider otherwise admissible evidence of a lawyer's advice to the client.

(2) In deciding whether to impose a sanction on a person or to relieve a person from a criminal or civil ruling, default, or judgment, a tribunal may consider otherwise admissible evidence to prove or disprove that the lawyer who represented the person did so inadequately or contrary to the client's instructions.

§42. Lawyer's Liability to Third Person for Conduct on Behalf of Client

(1) For improper conduct while representing a client, a lawyer is subject to professional discipline as stated in [Chapter 1], to civil liability as stated in [Chapter 4], and to prosecution as provided in the criminal law.

(2) A lawyer is subject to liability to third persons on contracts the lawyer entered into on behalf of a client, unless the lawyer or third person disclaimed such liability, if:

(a) the client's existence or identity was not disclosed to the third person; or

(b) the contract is between the lawyer and a third person who provides goods or services used by lawyers and who, as the lawyer knows or reasonably should know, relies on the lawyer's credit.

(3) A lawyer is subject to liability to a third person for damages for loss proximately caused by the lawyer's acting without authority from a client under §38 if:

(a) the lawyer tortiously misrepresents to the third person that the lawyer has authority to make a contract, conveyance, or affirmation on behalf of the client and the third person reasonably relies on the misrepresentation; or

(b) the lawyer purports to make a contract, conveyance, or affirmation on behalf of the client, unless the lawyer manifests that the lawyer does not warrant that the lawyer is authorized to act or the other party knows that the lawyer is not authorized to act.

§132. Exception for Client Crime or Fraud

The attorney-client privilege does not apply to a communication occurring when a client:

(a) consults a lawyer for the purpose, later accomplished, of obtaining assistance to engage in a crime or fraud or aiding a third person to do so, or

(b) regardless of the client's purpose at the time of consultation, uses the lawyer's advice or other services to engage in or assist a crime or fraud.

§151. Advising and Assisting Client — In General

(1) A lawyer who counsels or assists a client to engage in conduct that violates the rights of a third person is subject to liability:

(a) to the third person to the extent stated in §§73 and 77-78; and

(b) to the client to the extent stated in §§72, 76A, and 77.

(2) For purposes of professional discipline, a lawyer may not counsel or assist a client to take or fail to take an action that the lawyer knows to be criminal or fraudulent or in violation of a court order with the intent of facilitating or encouraging the action, but the lawyer may counsel or assist a client to take or fail to take action for which the lawyer reasonably believes the client can assert a non-frivolous argument that the client's action will not constitute a crime or fraud or violate a court order, such as when the action constitutes a good faith effort to determine the validity, scope, meaning, or application of a law or court order.

(3) In counseling a client, a lawyer may address non-legal aspects of a proposed course of conduct, including moral, reputational, economic, social, political, and business aspects.

Rule 1.3 Diligence

A lawyer shall act with reasonable diligence and promptness in representing a client.

COMMENT

[1] A lawyer should pursue a matter on behalf of a client despite opposition, obstruction or personal inconvenience to the lawyer, and may take whatever lawful and ethical measures are required to vindicate a client's cause or endeavor. A lawyer should act with commitment and dedication to the interests of the client and with zeal in advocacy upon the client's behalf. However, a lawyer is not bound to press for every advantage that might be realized for a client. A lawyer has professional discretion in determining the means by which a matter should be pursued. See Rule 1.2. A lawyer's workload should be controlled so that each matter can be handled adequately.

[2] Perhaps no professional shortcoming is more widely resented than procrastination. A client's interests often can be adversely affected by the passage of time or the change of conditions; in extreme instances, as when a lawyer overlooks a statute of limitations, the client's legal position may be destroyed. Even when the client's interests are not affected in substance, however, unreasonable delay can cause a client needless anxiety and undermine confidence in the lawyer's trustworthiness.

[3] Unless the relationship is terminated as provided in Rule 1.16, a lawyer should carry through to conclusion all matters undertaken for a client. If a lawyer's employment is limited to a specific matter, the relationship terminates when the matter has been resolved. If a lawyer has served a client over a substantial period in a variety of matters, the client sometimes may assume that the lawyer will continue to serve on a continuing basis unless the lawyer gives notice of withdrawal. Doubt about whether a client-lawyer relationship still exists should be clarified by the lawyer, preferably in writing, so that the client will not mistakenly suppose the lawyer is looking after the client's affairs when the lawyer has ceased to do so. For example, if a lawyer has handled a judicial or administrative proceeding that produced a result adverse to the client but has not been specifically instructed concerning pursuit of an appeal, the lawyer should advise the client of the possibility of appeal before relinquishing responsibility for the matter.

Model Code Comparison

DR 6-101(A)(3) required that a lawyer not "[n]eglect a legal matter entrusted to him." EC 6-4 stated that a lawyer should "give appropriate attention to his legal work." Canon 7 stated that "a lawyer should represent a client zealously within the bounds of the law." DR 7-101(A)(1) provided that a lawyer "shall not intentionally . . . fail to seek the lawful objectives of his client through reasonably available means permitted by law and the Disciplinary Rules. . . ." DR 7-101(A)(3) provided that a lawyer "shall not intentionally . . . [p]rejudice or damage his client during the course of the relationship. . . ."

Cross-References in Rules

Rule 1.7, Comment 1: "As to whether a client-lawyer relationship exists or, having once been established, is continuing, see Comment to **Rule 1.3** and Scope."

Rule 3.2 does not refer to Rule 1.3 but does require a lawyer to make reasonable efforts to "expedite" litigation.

Legislative History

1980 Discussion Draft:

A lawyer shall attend promptly to matters undertaken for a client and give them adequate attention until completed or until the lawyer has properly withdrawn from representing the client.

1981 and 1982 Drafts were the same as adopted.

Selected State Variations

California: See Rule 3-110(B) (Failing to Act Competently).

Colorado: Rule 1.3 adds a second sentence, taken from DR 6-101 of the old Code: "A lawyer shall not neglect a legal matter entrusted to that lawyer."

District of Columbia: D.C. adds Rules 1.3(b) and (c) — see District of Columbia Rules of Professional Conduct below.

Massachusetts: Effective January 1, 1998, Rule 1.3 adds the following sentence: "The lawyer should represent a client zealously within the bounds of the law."

New Hampshire adds Rule 1.3(b), which provides:

Performance by a lawyer is prompt and diligent when:

(1) it is carried out in the manner and within the time parameters established by the agreement between the client and the lawyer; however, the lawyer may not rely upon the terms of an agreement to excuse performance which is not prompt and diligent in light of changes in circumstances, known to the lawyer, which require adjustments to the agreed upon schedule of performance.

(2) in all other matters of representation, it is carried out with no avoidable harm to the client's interest nor to the lawyer-client relationship.

New York: Same or substantially the same as the ABA Model Code — see Model Code Comparison above.

Texas omits Rule 1.3.

Virginia: DR 6-101(B) provides that a lawyer "shall attend promptly to matters undertaken for a client until completed or until the lawyer has properly and completely withdrawn from representing the client."

Related Materials

ABA Canons: Canon 21 provided:

21. Punctuality and Expedition

It is the duty of the lawyer not only to his client, but also to the Courts and to the public to be punctual in attendance, and to be concise and direct in the trial and disposition of causes.

ABA Standards for Imposing Lawyer Discipline:

4.41. Disbarment is generally appropriate when:

(a) a lawyer abandons the practice and causes serious or potentially serious injury to a client; or

(b) a lawyer knowingly fails to perform services for a client and causes serious or potentially serious injury to a client; or

(c) a lawyer engages in a pattern of neglect with respect to client matters and causes serious or potentially serious injury to a client.

4.42. Suspension is generally appropriate when:

(a) a lawyer knowingly fails to perform services for a client and causes injury or potential injury to a client; or

(b) a lawyer engages in a pattern of neglect and causes injury or potential injury to a client.

Rule 1.4 Communication

(a) A lawyer shall keep a client reasonably informed about the status of a matter and promptly comply with reasonable requests for information.

(b) A lawyer shall explain a matter to the extent reasonably necessary to permit the client to make informed decisions regarding the representation.

COMMENT

[1] The client should have sufficient information to participate intelligently in decisions concerning the objectives of the representation

and the means by which they are to be pursued, to the extent the client is willing and able to do so. For example, a lawyer negotiating on behalf of a client should provide the client with facts relevant to the matter, inform the client of communications from another party and take other reasonable steps that permit the client to make a decision regarding a serious offer from another party. A lawyer who receives from opposing counsel an offer of settlement in a civil controversy or a proffered plea bargain in a criminal case should promptly inform the client of its substance unless prior discussions with the client have left it clear that the proposal will be unacceptable. See Rule 1.2(a). Even when a client delegates authority to the lawyer, the client should be kept advised of the status of the matter.

[2] Adequacy of communication depends in part on the kind of advice or assistance involved. For example, in negotiations where there is time to explain a proposal, the lawyer should review all important provisions with the client before proceeding to an agreement. In litigation a lawyer should explain the general strategy and prospects of success and ordinarily should consult the client on tactics that might injure or coerce others. On the other hand, a lawyer ordinarily cannot be expected to describe trial or negotiation strategy in detail. The guiding principle is that the lawyer should fulfill reasonable client expectations for information consistent with the duty to act in the client's best interests, and the client's overall requirements as to the character of representation.

[3] Ordinarily, the information to be provided is that appropriate for a client who is a comprehending and responsible adult. However, fully informing the client according to this standard may be impracticable, for example, where the client is a child or suffers from mental disability. See Rule 1.14. When the client is an organization or group, it is often impossible or inappropriate to inform everyone of its members about its legal affairs; ordinarily, the lawyer should address communications to the appropriate officials of the organization. See Rule 1.13. Where many routine matters are involved, a system of limited or occasional reporting may be arranged with the client. Practical exigency may also require a lawyer to act for a client without prior consultation.

Withholding Information

[4] In some circumstances, a lawyer may be justified in delaying transmission of information when the client would be likely to react imprudently to an immediate communication. Thus, a lawyer might withhold a

psychiatric diagnosis of a client when the examining psychiatrist indicates that disclosure would harm the client. A lawyer may not withhold information to serve the lawyer's own interest or convenience. Rules or court orders governing litigation may provide that information supplied to a lawyer may not be disclosed to the client. Rule 3.4(c) directs compliance with such rules or orders.

Model Code Comparison

Rule 1.4 has no direct counterpart in the Disciplinary Rules of the Model Code. DR 6-101(A)(3) provided that a lawyer shall not "[n]eglect a legal matter entrusted to him." DR 9-102(B)(1) provided that a lawyer shall "[p]romptly notify a client of the receipt of his funds, securities, or other properties." EC 7-8 stated that a lawyer "should exert his best efforts to insure that decisions of his client are made only after the client has been informed of relevant considerations." EC 9-2 stated that a "lawyer should fully and promptly inform his client of material developments in the matters being handled for the client."

Cross-References in Rules

Rule 2.1, Comment 5: "[W]hen a lawyer knows that a client proposes a course of action that is likely to result in substantial adverse legal consequences to the client, duty to the client under **Rule 1.4** may require that the lawyer act if the client's course of action is related to the representation."

Rule 2.2, Comment 6: "In a common representation, the lawyer is still required both to keep each client adequately informed and to maintain confidentiality of information relating to the representation. See **Rules 1.4** and 1.6."

Rule 2.2, Comment 9: Paragraph (b) of Rule 2.2, requiring consultation with clients while acting as an intermediary, "is an application of the principle expressed in **Rule 1.4.**"

Legislative History

1979 Unofficial Pre-Circulation Draft (then Rule 1.3):

(a) A lawyer shall keep a client informed about a matter in which the lawyer's services are being rendered. Informing the client includes:
(1) Periodically advising the client of the status and progress of the matter;
(2) Explaining the legal and practical aspects of the matter and foreseeable effects of alternative courses of action; and . . .

(c) A lawyer may withhold information to which a client is otherwise entitled only when doing so is necessary to protect the client's interest or some superior interest.

1980 Discussion Draft prohibited a lawyer from withholding information to which a client was entitled "except when doing so is clearly necessary to protect the client's interest or to comply with the requirements of law or the rules of professional conduct."

1981 Draft provided:

(b) A lawyer shall explain the legal and practical aspects of a matter and alternative courses of action to the extent reasonably necessary to permit the client to make informed decisions regarding the representation.

1982 Draft was adopted.

Selected State Variations

California: Rule 3-500 (Communication), Rule 3-510 (Communication of Settlement Offer), and B & P Code §6068(m) (regarding communication generally).

District of Columbia: D.C. adds Rule 1.4(c) — see District of Columbia Rules of Professional Conduct below.

Florida: Florida's Statement of Client's Rights, which must be provided to every contingent fee client (see Florida Rule 1.5(D)), provides:

10. . . . Your lawyer must notify you of all offers of settlement before and after the trial. Offers during the trial must be immediately communicated and you should consult with your lawyer regarding whether to accept a settlement. However, you must make the final decision to accept or reject a settlement.

Louisiana adds to Rule 1.4(b): "The lawyer shall give the client sufficient information to participate intelligently in decisions concerning the object of the representation and the means by which they are to be pursued, to the extent the client is willing and able to do so."

Massachusetts: Effective January 1, 1998, the comment to Rule 1.4 states: "There will be circumstances in which a lawyer should advise a client concerning the advantages and disadvantages of available dispute resolution options. . . ."

Michigan adds to Rule 1.4(a): "A lawyer shall notify the client promptly of all settlement offers, mediation evaluations, and proposed plea bargains."

New Hampshire adds Rule 1.4(c), which provides: "A client is reasonably informed when information relevant to the protection of the client's interest is provided at an appropriate time and in an appropriate manner."

New York: Same or substantially the same as the ABA Model Code — see Model Code Comparison above.

Virginia: DR 6-101(D) adds that a lawyer "shall inform his client . . . of communications from another party that may significantly affect settlement or resolution of a matter."

Related Materials

ABA Canons: Canon 8 provided:

Advising upon the Merits of a Client's Cause

A lawyer should endeavor to obtain full knowledge of his client's cause before advising thereon, and he is bound to give a candid opinion of the merits and probable result of pending or contemplated litigation. The miscarriages to which justice is subject, by reason of surprises and disappointments in evidence and witnesses, and through mistakes of juries and errors of Courts, even though only occasional, admonish lawyers to beware of bold and confident assurances to clients, especially where the employment may depend upon such assurance. Whenever the controversy will admit of fair adjustment, the client should be advised to avoid or to end the litigation.

ABA Standards for Imposing Lawyer Sanctions:

4.61. Disbarment is generally appropriate when a lawyer knowingly deceives a client with the intent to benefit the lawyer or another, and causes serious injury or potentially serious injury to a client.
4.62. Suspension is generally appropriate when a lawyer knowingly deceives a client, and causes injury or potential injury to the client.

American Academy of Matrimonial Lawyers: The "Bounds of Advocacy" drafted by the American Academy of Matrimonial Lawyers contains the following provision and commentary:

2.6 An attorney should keep the client informed of developments in the representation and promptly respond to letters and telephone calls.

Comment to Rule 2.6

The duty of keeping the client reasonably informed and promptly complying with reasonable requests for information, includes the attorney or a staff member responding to telephone calls, normally by the end of the next business day. The client should be informed at the outset, however, that communications with the attorney are chargeable. In addition, the attorney should routinely: send the client a copy of all pleadings and correspondence, except in unusual circumstances; provide the client with frequent statements of costs and fees (see Standards 2.1-2.5); provide notice before incurring any major costs; provide notice of any calendar changes, scheduled court appearances, and discovery proceedings; communicate all settlement offers, no matter how trivial or facetious; advise of major changes in the law affecting the proceedings; and provide periodic status reports on progress in the case and major changes in case strategy.

Frequent communication with the client on important matters (1) empowers the client, (2) satisfies the client's need for information about the progress of the case, (3) helps to build a positive attorney-client relationship, and (4) helps the client understand the amount and nature of the work the attorney is performing, thereby reducing concern that nothing is happening and that the attorney is not earning her fees. While the attorney should understand that a pending divorce is usually the single most important matter in the life of the client, the client should understand that a successful lawyer has many clients, all of whom believe their case to be the most important.

American Lawyer's Code of Conduct: Rule 5.2 provides:

> 5.2. As soon as practicable after being retained, a lawyer shall make clear to a client, in writing, the material terms of the retainer agreement, including the scope of what the lawyer is undertaking to do for the client, the limits of that undertaking, and the fee and any other obligations the client is assuming.

Financial Institutions: Despite Rule 1.4, attorneys for banks and other financial institutions may be prohibited by federal law from disclosing certain information to their clients. In 1989, as a reaction to the savings and loan crisis, Congress passed 12 U.S.C. §3420(b), the first federal statute ever to impose an absolute ban on disclosures of certain grand jury subpoenas to "any person named" in the subpoenas. Section 3420(b) provides (with emphasis added):

> No officer, director, partner, employee, or shareholder of, or agent or *attorney* for, a financial institution shall, directly or indirectly, notify any person named in a grand jury subpoena served on such institution in connection with an investigation relating to a possible —
> (A) crime against any financial institution or supervisory agency; or
> (B) conspiracy to commit such crime,
> about the existence or contents of such subpoena, or information that has been furnished to the grand jury in response to such subpoena.

Violation of §3420(b) with intent to obstruct grand jury proceedings is punishable by up to five years in prison and/or a $250,000 fine, and violations without any obstructionist intent are punishable by up to one year in jail and/or a $100,000 fine. See Norman A. Bloch, Gagging Bankers: Grand Jury Nondisclosure Statutes and the First Amendment, 107 Banking L.J. 441 (1990).

Rule 1.5 Fees

(a) A lawyer's fee shall be reasonable. The factors to be considered in determining the reasonableness of a fee include the following:

(1) the time and labor required, the novelty and difficulty of the questions involved, and the skill requisite to perform the legal service properly;

(2) the likelihood, if apparent to the client, that the acceptance of the particular employment will preclude other employment by the lawyer;

(3) the fee customarily charged in the locality for similar legal services;

(4) the amount involved and the results obtained;

(5) the time limitations imposed by the client or by the circumstances;

(6) the nature and length of the professional relationship with the client;

(7) the experience, reputation, and ability of the lawyer or lawyers performing the services; and

(8) whether the fee is fixed or contingent.

(b) When the lawyer has not regularly represented the client, the basis or rate of the fee shall be communicated to the client, preferably in writing, before or within a reasonable time after commencing the representation.

(c) A fee may be contingent on the outcome of the matter for which the service is rendered, except in a matter in which a contingent fee is prohibited by paragraph (d) or other law. A contingent fee agreement shall be in writing and shall state the method by which the fee is to be determined, including the percentage or percentages that shall accrue to the lawyer in the event of settlement, trial or appeal, litigation and other expenses to be deducted from the recovery, and whether such expenses are to be deducted before or after the contingent fee is calculated. Upon conclusion of a contingent fee matter, the lawyer shall provide the client with a written statement stating the outcome of the matter and, if there is a recovery, showing the remittance to the client and the method of its determination.

(d) A lawyer shall not enter into an arrangement for, charge, or collect:

(1) any fee in a domestic relations matter, the payment or amount of which is contingent upon the securing of a divorce or upon the amount of alimony or support, or property settlement in lieu thereof; or

(2) a contingent fee for representing a defendant in a criminal case.

(e) A division of fee between lawyers who are not in the same firm may be made only if:

(1) the division is in proportion to the services performed by each lawyer or, by written agreement with the client, each lawyer assumes joint responsibility for the representation;

(2) the client is advised of and does not object to the participation of all the lawyers involved; and

(3) the total fee is reasonable.

COMMENT

Basis or Rate of Fee

[1] When the lawyer has regularly represented a client, they ordinarily will have evolved an understanding concerning the basis or rate of the fee. In a new client-lawyer relationship, however, an understanding as to the fee should be promptly established. It is not necessary to recite all the factors that underlie the basis of the fee, but only those that are directly involved in its computation. It is sufficient, for example, to state that the basic rate is an hourly charge or a fixed amount or an estimated amount, or to identify the factors that may be taken into account in finally fixing the fee. When developments occur during the representation that render an earlier estimate substantially inaccurate, a revised estimate should be provided to the client. A written statement concerning the fee reduces the possibility of misunderstanding. Furnishing the client with a simple memorandum or a copy of the lawyer's customary fee schedule is sufficient if the basis or rate of the fee is set forth.

Terms of Payment

[2] A lawyer may require advance payment of a fee, but is obliged to return any unearned portion. See Rule 1.16(d). A lawyer may accept property in payment for services, such as an ownership interest in an enterprise, providing this does not involve acquisition of a proprietary interest in the cause of action or subject matter of the litigation contrary to Rule 1.8(j). However, a fee paid in property instead of money may be subject to special scrutiny because it involves questions concerning both the value of the services and the lawyer's special knowledge of the value of the property.

[3] An agreement may not be made whose terms might induce the lawyer improperly to curtail services for the client or perform them in a way contrary to the client's interest. For example, a lawyer should not enter into an agreement whereby services are to be provided only up to a stated amount when it is foreseeable that more extensive services probably will be required, unless the situation is adequately explained to the client. Otherwise, the client might have to bargain for further assistance in the midst of a proceeding or transaction. However, it is proper to define the extent of services in light of the client's ability to pay. A lawyer should not exploit a fee arrangement based primarily on hourly charges by using wasteful procedures. When there is doubt whether a contingent fee is consistent with the client's best interest, the lawyer should offer the client alternative bases

for the fee and explain their implications. Applicable law may impose limitations on contingent fees, such as a ceiling on the percentage.

Division of Fee

[4] A division of fee is a single billing to a client covering the fee of two or more lawyers who are not in the same firm. A division of fee facilitates association of more than one lawyer in a matter in which neither alone could serve the client as well, and most often is used when the fee is contingent and the division is between a referring lawyer and a trial specialist. Paragraph (e) permits the lawyers to divide a fee on either the basis of the proportion of services they render or by agreement between the participating lawyers if all assume responsibility for the representation as a whole and the client is advised and does not object. It does not require disclosure to the client of the share that each lawyer is to receive. Joint responsibility for the representation entails the obligations stated in Rule 5.1 for purposes of the matter involved.

Disputes over Fees

[5] If a procedure has been established for resolution of fee disputes, such as an arbitration or mediation procedure established by the bar, the lawyer should conscientiously consider submitting to it. Law may prescribe a procedure for determining a lawyer's fee, for example, in representation of an executor or administrator, a class or a person entitled to a reasonable fee as part of the measure of damages. The lawyer entitled to such a fee and a lawyer representing another party concerned with the fee should comply with the prescribed procedure.

Model Code Comparison

DR 2-106(A) provided that a lawyer "shall not enter into an agreement for, charge, or collect an illegal or clearly excessive fee." DR 2-106(B) provided that a fee is "clearly excessive when, after a review of the facts, a lawyer of ordinary prudence would be left with a definite and firm conviction that the fee is in excess of a reasonable fee." The factors of a reasonable fee in Rule 1.5(a) are substantially identical to those listed in DR 2-106(B). EC 2-17 states that a lawyer "should not charge more than a reasonable fee. . . ."

There was no counterpart to Rule 1.5(b) in the Disciplinary Rules of the Model Code. EC 2-19 stated that it is "usually beneficial to reduce to writing the understanding of the parties regarding the fee, particularly when it is contingent.''

There was no counterpart to paragraph (c) in the Disciplinary Rules of the Model Code. EC 2-20 provided that ''[c:ontingent fee arrangements in civil cases have long been commonly accepted in the United States,'' but that ''a lawyer generally should decline to accept employment on a contingent fee basis by one who is able to pay a reasonable fixed fee. . . .''

With regard to paragraph (d), DR 2-106(C) prohibited ''a contingent fee in a criminal case.'' EC 2-20 provided that ''contingent fee arrangements in domestic relation cases are rarely justified.''

With regard to paragraph (e), DR 2-107(A) permitted division of fees only if: ''(1) The client consents to employment of the other lawyer after a full disclosure that a division of fees will be made. (2) The division is in proportion to the services performed and responsibility assumed by each. (3) The total fee does not exceed clearly reasonable compensation. . . .'' Paragraph (e) permits division with regard to the services rendered by each lawyer if they assume joint responsibility for the representation.

Cross-References in Rules

Rule 1.7, Comment 5: ''[A] lawyer's need for income should not lead the lawyer to undertake matters that cannot be handled competently and at a reasonable fee. See **Rules** 1.1 and **1.5**.''

Rule 1.8, Comment 3 states that Rule 1.8(d) (prohibiting a lawyer from acquiring media rights to a client's story until the representation is over) ''does not prohibit a lawyer from agreeing that the lawyer's fee shall consist of a share in ownership in the property, if the arrangement conforms to **Rule 1.5**'' and Rule 1.8(j).

Rule 1.8, Comment 6: Rule 1.8(j) ''states the traditional general rule that lawyers are prohibited from acquiring a proprietary interest in litigation. This general rule . . . is subject to . . . the exception for reasonable contingent fees set forth in **Rule 1.5**. . . .''

Legislative History

1979 Unofficial Pre-Circulation Draft (then Rule 1.4):

(b) A fee agreement shall . . .

(2) State with reasonable definiteness, expressly or by implication, the nature and extent of the services to be provided; and . . .

(c) A fee agreement shall be expressed or confirmed in writing before the lawyer has rendered substantial services in the matter, except:

(1) Where an agreement as to the fee is implied by the fact that the lawyer's services are of the same general kind as previously rendered to and paid for by the client;

(2) For services rendered in an emergency where a written agreement or confirmation is impracticable. . . .

1980 Discussion Draft (then Rule 1.6):

(b) The basis or rate of a lawyer's fee shall be put in writing before the lawyer has rendered substantial services in the matter, except when:

(1) An agreement as to the fee is implied by the fact that the lawyer's services are of the same general kind as previously rendered to and paid for by the client; or

(2) The services are rendered in an emergency where a writing is impracticable.

(c) The form of a fee and the terms of a fee agreement shall involve no inducement for the lawyer to perform the services in a manner inconsistent with the best interests of the client. . . .

(e) A division of fee between lawyers who are not in the same firm may be made only if:

(1) The division is in proportion to the services performed by each lawyer, or both lawyers expressly assume responsibility as if they were partners;

(2) The terms of the division are disclosed to the client. . . .

1981 Draft of Rule 1.5(b) continued to require that the "basis or rate of a lawyer's fee shall be communicated to the client in writing before the lawyer renders substantial services in a matter. . . ."

1982 Draft was substantially the same as adopted.

Selected State Variations

Alaska: Rule 1.5(b) adds: "In a case involving litigation, the lawyer shall notify the client of any costs, fees or expenses for which the client may be liable if the client is not the prevailing party." In addition, Alaska adds Rule 1.5(f), which provides that a lawyer "should be zealous in his or her efforts to avoid controversies over fees with clients and should attempt to resolve amicably any differences on the subject."

Arizona: Rule 1.5(d) Comment permits an attorney to charge a contingent fee for the enforcement of current child support or spousal maintenance orders, but the length of time that the contingency fee will apply to future payments must be spelled out in the agreement with the client and the agreement must be fair and equitable to the client.

Arkansas: Rule 1.5(d)(1) adds that in a domestic relations matter, "after a final order or decree is entered an attorney may enter into a contingent fee contract for collection of payments which are due pursuant to such decree or order."

California: See Rule 4-200 (Fees for Legal Services), B & P Code §§6147-6149 (governing contingency fee contracts and other fee arrangements), and B & P Code §§6200-6206 (establishing system and procedures for arbitrating fee disputes).

Colorado: Rule 1.5(c) adds: "A contingent fee shall meet all the requirements of Chapter 23.3 of the Colorado Rules of Civil Procedure, 'Rules Governing Contingent Fees.' " Rule 1.5(d) adds the requirements that "the client consents to the employment of an additional lawyer after a full disclosure of the division of fees to be made "and that the division is set forth in writing signed by the lawyers and the client with informed consent." Colorado also adds a section (e) prohibiting referral fees.

Connecticut: Rule 1.5(b) provides that when the lawyer has not regularly represented a client:

> the basis or rate of the fee, whether and to what extent the client will be responsible for any court costs and expenses of litigation, and the scope of the matter to be undertaken shall be communicated to the client, in writing, before or within a reasonable time after commencing the representation. This paragraph shall not apply to public defenders or in situations where the lawyer will be paid by the court or a state agency.

In addition, Connecticut's version of the fee sharing rule deletes ABA Model Rule 1.5(e)(1), and adds that the client must be advised of "the compensation sharing agreement and" of the participation of all lawyers involved.

District of Columbia: D.C. Rule 1.5(b), (d), and (e) differ significantly from the ABA Model Rule, and D.C. adds Rule 1.5(f) — see District of Columbia Rules of Professional Conduct below.

Florida has adopted an elaborate rule with these main features:

Rule 1.5(f)(4)(A)(ii) (as amended effective January 1, 1993) says that a contingent fee contract must contain the following provision (among others):

> This contract may be cancelled by written notification to the attorney at any time within three (3) business days of the date the contract was signed, and if cancelled the client shall not be obligated to pay any fees to the attorney(s) for the work performed during that time.

Florida Rule 1.5(f)(4)(B), as amended in 1995, establishes an elaborate sliding scale of maximum reasonable contingent fees. The sliding scale takes into account the stage of the litigation at which the matter is resolved (i.e., whether before or after the defendant files an answer) and the amount of money recovered (up to $1 million, $1 million to $2 million, or more than $2 million). However, maximum fees are significantly reduced "[i]f all defendants admit liability at the time of filing their answers and request a trial only on damages." (For example, if all defendants admit liability, the maximum fee allowed on a recovery up to $1 million is reduced form 40 percent to 33⅓ percent.) Unless a court approves a higher fee, any contingent fee that exceeds the standards "shall be presumed, unless rebutted, to be clearly excessive." A court may not approve a higher fee unless a "client is unable to obtain an attorney of the client's choice because of the limitations" on maximum fees. Finally, Rule 1.5(f)(4)(B) contains the following subparagraph to govern fees in structured settlements:

(iii) In cases where the client is to receive a recovery that will be paid to the client on a future structured or periodic basis, the contingent fee percentage shall only be calculated on the cost of the structured verdict or settlement or, if the cost is unknown, on the present money value of the structured verdict or settlement, whichever is less. If the damages and the fee are to be paid out over the long term future schedule, then this limitation does not apply. No attorney may separately negotiate with the defendant for that attorney's fees in a structured verdict or settlement where such separate negotiations would place the attorney in a position of conflict.

Florida Rule 1.5(f)(4)(C) provides that before a lawyer enters into a contingent fee contract, the lawyer "shall provide the client with a statement of the client's rights. . . ." The Statement of Client's Rights contains ten paragraphs and is set forth in full at the end of Florida's Rule 1.5.

With respect to Model Rule 1.5(e), Florida's statement of Client's Rights says:

5. If your lawyer intends to refer your case to another lawyer or counsel with other lawyers, your lawyer should tell you about that at the beginning. If your lawyer takes the case and later decides to refer it to another lawyer or to associate with other lawyers, you should sign a new contract which includes the new lawyers. You, the client, also have the right to consult with each lawyer working on your case and each lawyer is legally responsible to represent your interests and is legally responsible for the acts of the other lawyers involved in the case.

In addition, Florida's advertising rules (adopted in December 1990) require that advertisements describing legal fees of any kind must disclose whether the client will be liable for costs or expenses in the absence of recovery, and whether a contingent fee will be computed before or after expenses are deducted.

To prevent lawyers from advertising for cases that they have no intention of handling but intend only to refer to another lawyer in exchange for a share of the fee, Florida's advertising rules state that an advertisement "shall be presumed to be misleading if the lawyer reasonably believes that a lawyer or law firm not associated with the originally retained lawyer or law firm will be associated or act as primary counsel in representing the client. In determining whether the statement is misleading in this respect, the history of prior conduct by the lawyer in similar matters may be considered."

Florida Rule 4-7.4 prohibits "a fee for professional employment obtained in violation of" Florida's solicitation rule, and Florida Rule 1.5(a) prohibits a fee "generated by employment that was obtained through advertising or solicitation not in compliance" with Florida's advertising and solicitation rules.

Finally, in December 1990 the Florida Supreme Court gave itself the power to order any lawyer found guilty of violating the fee rules "to forfeit the fee or any part thereof," either by returning the excessive part of any fee to the client or by forfeiting all or part of an otherwise improper fee to the Florida Bar Clients' Security Fund. See Florida Rule 3-5.1(i).

Georgia's version of Rule 1.5 continues to permit fee-splitting only under the circumstances identified in the Code. DR 2-107. Georgia's Rules do not forbid contingent fees in domestic relations matters.

Idaho: Rule 1.5(d)(1) allows contingent fees in "proceedings to enforce or satisfy a judgment for property distribution or past due alimony or child support." Idaho also adds Rule 1.5(f), which provides as follows:

> (f) Upon reasonable request by the client, a lawyer shall provide, without charge, an accounting for fees and costs claimed or previously collected. Such an accounting shall include at least the following information:
>
> (1) Itemization of all hourly charges, costs, interest assessments, and past due balances.
>
> (2) For hourly rate charges, a description of the services performed and a notation of the person who performed those services. The description shall be of sufficient detail to generally apprise the client of the nature of the work. . . .

Illinois provides that "the prohibition set forth in Rule 1.5(d)(1) shall not extend to representation in matters subsequent to final judgments in such cases."

Illinois adds a new subparagraph providing:

> (e) Notwithstanding Rule 1.5(c), a contingent fee agreement regarding the collection of commercial accounts or of insurance company subrogation claims may be made in accordance with the customs and practice in the locality for such legal services.

Illinois also adds the following new subparagraphs:

> (g) A division of fees [between lawyers not in the same firm: shall be made in proportion to the services performed and responsibility assumed by each lawyer, except where the primary service performed by one lawyer is the referral of the client to another lawyer and
>
> (1) the receiving lawyer discloses that the referring lawyer has received or will receive economic benefit from the referral and the extent and basis of such economic benefit, and
>
> (2) the referring lawyer agrees to assume the same legal responsibility for the performance of the services in question as would a partner of the receiving lawyer.
>
> (h) The total fee of the lawyers shall be reasonable.
>
> (i) For purposes of Rule 1.5 "economic benefit" shall include:
>
> (1) the amount of participation in the fee received with regard to the particular matter;
>
> (2) any other form of remuneration passing to the referring lawyer from the receiving lawyer, whether or not with regard to the particular matter; and
>
> (3) an established practice of referrals to and from or from and to the receiving lawyer and the referring lawyer.
>
> (j) Notwithstanding Rule 1.5(f), a payment may be made to a lawyer formerly in the firm, pursuant to a separation or retirement agreement.

Kansas: Rule 1.5(c) adds that a court's determination that a fee is not reasonable "shall not be presumptive evidence of a violation that requires discipline of the attorney." Rule 1.5(e) adds:

Upon application by the client, all fee contracts shall be subject to review and approval by the appropriate court having jurisdiction of the matter and the court shall have the authority to determine whether the contract is reasonable. If the court finds the contract is not reasonable, it shall set and allow a reasonable fee.

Maryland adds that a fee cannot be contingent upon a client's "securing custody of a child." Maryland also prohibits fees contingent "upon the amount of an award pursuant to Section 8-201-213 of Family Law Article Annotated Code of Maryland."

Massachusetts: Effective January 1, 1998, Rule 1.5 forbids a "clearly excessive fee" instead of a requirement that a fee "shall be reasonable." However, the list of factors to consider are the same as in Rule 1.5(a). In addition, Rule 1.5(c) does not require a contingent fee to be in writing if it concerns "the collection of commercial accounts" or "insurance company subrogation claims." The rule requires greater detail in the written contingent fee agreements required in all other cases. Rule 1.5(e) permits fee division with client consent even though one lawyer does no work and has no responsibility for the other lawyer's work. The agreement need not be in writing.

Michigan retains the Code articulation in lieu of Rule 1.5(a). In Rule 1.5(d), Michigan forbids contingent fees in "a domestic relations matter" without qualification.

Michigan and *Pennsylvania* do not require a writing in Rule 1.5(e), and do not distinguish fee-sharing arrangements based on services provided from those based on assumption of responsibility.

Minnesota adds to Rule 1.5(e)(2) that the client must be "advised of the share that each lawyer is to receive."

New Jersey requires a fee agreement to be in writing if the lawyer has not regularly represented the client. In addition, New Jersey has adopted various court rules that tightly control contingent fees, especially in tort cases. Supreme Court Rule 1:21-7, for example, provides as follows:

> (c) In any matter where a client's claim for damages is based upon the alleged tortious conduct of another, including products liability claims, and the client is not a subrogee, an attorney shall not contract for, charge, or collect a contingent fee in excess of the following limits:
>> (1) 33 ⅓% on the first $250,000 recovered;
>> (2) 25% on the next $250,000 recovered;
>> (3) 20% on the next $500,000 recovered; and
>> (4) on all amounts recovered in excess of the above by application for reasonable fee in accordance with the provisions of paragraph (f) hereof; and
>> (5) where the amount recovered is for the benefit of a client who was an infant or incompetent when the contingent fee arrangement was made, the foregoing limits shall apply, except that the fee on any amount recovered by settlement without trial shall not exceed 25%.

New Jersey also controls fees in matrimonial cases. Supreme Court Rule 1:21-7A provides: "All agreements for legal services by an attorney or attorneys in connection with family actions shall be in writing signed by the attorney and client."

New York: Same or substantially the same as the ABA Model Code — see Model Code Comparison above — except that New York permits lawyers to divide fees if the division is "in proportion to the services performed by each lawyer or, by a writing given to the client, each lawyer assumes joint responsibility for the representation." See EC 2-22 and DR 2-106(C), DR 2-106(D), and DR 2-107(A)(2) of the New York Code. In addition, the New York Court of Appeals has held that it is unethical to accept "a nonrefundable fee for specific services, in advance and irrespective of whether any professional services are actually rendered." Matter of Cooperman, 83 N.Y.2d, 465, 633 N.E.2d 1069, 611 N.Y.S.2d 465 (1994). New York courts also limit attorney fees in tort litigation through court rules and equate violation of these rules to a disciplinary violation. For an example, see 22 N.Y.C.R.R. §691.20(e). Moreover, effective November 30, 1993, New York adopted special court rules governing attorney fees in divorce cases. These are reprinted in the New York materials — see "Procedure for Attorneys in Domestic Relations Matters." In addition, in domestic relations actions only, 22 N.Y.C.R.R. §§202.16(c) and (k)(3) (reprinted later in the New York materials) require lawyers to file retainer agreements with the court and to provide certain information by affidavit with any application for counsel fees.

Ohio's version of Rule 1.5(e) adopts its language but also provides for mediation or arbitration in the event of a dispute over the fees between the participating lawyers. DR 2-107(B).

Pennsylvania Rule 1.5(b) requires a written fee agreement if a lawyer has not regularly represented a client.

Rhode Island: Rule 1.5(c) provides that a contingent fee agreement "should" be in writing and "should" state the method by which the fee is to be determined. (ABA Model Rule 1.5(c) uses the word "shall" in both instances.)

Texas Rule 1.04(a) forbids "illegal" or "unconscionable" fees and lists the same considerations as in Rule 1.5. The Texas Rules do not forbid contingent fees in family law matters but the Comment says they are "rarely justified." Texas Rule 1.04(f) provides that a division "or agreement for division" of a fee between lawyers who are not in the same firm shall not be made unless the division is "(i) in proportion to the professional services performed by each lawyer; (ii) made with a forwarding lawyer; or (iii) made, by written agreement with the client, with a lawyer who assumes joint responsibility for the representation. . . ."

Utah: Rule 1.5(b) provides as follows:

> (b) When the lawyer has not regularly represented the client, and it is reasonably foreseeable that the total attorneys fees to the client will exceed $750.00, the basis or rate of the fee shall be communicated to the client, in writing, before or within a reasonable time after commencing the representation.

Virginia: DR 2-105 requires that a lawyer's fees must be reasonable "and adequately explained to the client," and that the basis or rate of the fee "shall be furnished on request of the lawyer's client." DR 2-105(D) allows a division of fees between lawyers not in the same firm only if the client "consents to the employment of additional counsel," the attorneys "expressly" assume responsibility to the client, and the "terms of the division are disclosed to the client. . . ."

Washington: Rule 1.5(d)(1) adds that a fee may not be contingent on securing an "annulment of marriage," but the rule states an exception that permits contingent fees in "postdissolution proceedings." Rule 1.5(e)(1) permits a division of fees if the division "is between the lawyer and a duly authorized lawyer referral service of either the Washington State Bar Association or of one of the county bar associations of this state."

Wyoming Rule 1.5(e)(1) provides that a division of fees between lawyers must be in proportion to the services performed by each lawyer "*and*" by written agreement with the client, each lawyer assumes joint responsibility. Wyoming also prohibits a lawyer from receiving a fee solely for making a referral to another lawyer.

Related Materials

ABA Canons: Canons 12, 13, 14, and 42 provided:

12. Fixing the Amount of the Fee

In fixing fees, lawyers should avoid charges which overestimate their advice and services, as well as those which undervalue them. A client's ability to pay cannot justify a charge in excess of the value of the service, though his poverty may require a less charge, or even none at all. The reasonable requests of brother lawyers, and of their widows and orphans without ample means, should receive special and kindly consideration.

In determining the amount of the fee, it is proper to consider: (1) the time and labor required, the novelty and difficulty of the questions involved and the skill requisite properly to conduct the cause; (2) whether the acceptance of employment in the particular case will preclude the lawyer's appearance for others in cases likely to arise out of the transaction, and in which there is a reasonable expectation that otherwise he would be employed, or will involve the loss of other employment while employed in the particular case or antagonisms with other clients; (3) the customary charges of the Bar for similar services; (4) the amount involved in the controversy and the benefits resulting to the client from the services; (5) the contingency or the certainty of the compensation; and (6) the character of the employment, whether casual or for an established and constant client. No one of these considerations in itself is controlling. They are mere guides in ascertaining the real value of the service.

In determining the customary charges of the Bar for similar services, it is proper for a lawyer to consider a schedule of minimum fees adopted by a Bar Association, but no lawyer should permit himself to be controlled thereby or to follow it as his sole guide in determining the amount of his fee.

In fixing fees it should never be forgotten that the profession is a branch of the administration of justice and not a mere money-getting trade.

13. Contingent Fees

A contract for a contingent fee, where sanctioned by law, should be reasonable under all the circumstances of the case, including the risk and uncertainty of the compensation, but should always be subject to the supervision of a court, as to its reasonableness.

14. Suing a Client for a Fee

Controversies with clients concerning compensation are to be avoided by the lawyer so far as shall be compatible with his self-respect and with his right to receive reasonable recompense for his services; and lawsuits with clients should be resorted to only to prevent injustice, imposition or fraud.

42. Expenses of Litigation

A lawyer may not properly agree with a client that the lawyer shall pay or bear the expenses of litigation; he may in good faith advance expenses as a matter of convenience, but subject to reimbursement.

ABA Model Rules for Fee Arbitration: In 1992, the ABA Commission on Evaluation of Disciplinary Enforcement ("the McKay Commission") recommended that each state establish mandatory arbitration for fee disputes. At its February 1995 Mid-Year Meeting, to assist the states in carrying out this recommendation, the ABA House of Delegates adopted Model Rules for Fee Arbitration. The ABA Model Rules for Fee Arbitration make fee arbitration mandatory if the client requests it. According to a comprehensive survey by the ABA Standing Committee on Lawyers' Responsibility for Client Protection, some form of mandatory fee arbitration at the client's option has been adopted in Alaska, California, the District of Columbia, New Jersey, North Carolina, South Carolina, and Wyoming. In addition, Minnesota has a pilot program, New York mandates fee arbitration in domestic relations matters, and at least half a dozen states are currently studying mandatory fee arbitration. Some states go further than the ABA Model Rules by making fee arbitration binding as well as mandatory. (A few states do not mandate fee arbitration, but make it binding if the lawyer and client agree to arbitrate the dispute.) No states mandate fee arbitration at the option of the lawyer. For further information, contact Charlotte (Becky) Stretch at the ABA Center for Professional Responsibility, 541 North Fairbanks Court, Chicago, IL 60611, phone 312-988-5297.

American Academy of Matrimonial Lawyers: The "Bounds of Advocacy" drafted by the American Academy of Matrimonial Lawyers contains the following provisions and commentary:

Fees

Many divorce clients have never before hired an attorney and are vulnerable because of fear and insecurity. Matrimonial lawyers and their clients may not have the long-standing relationship out of which business lawyers and their clients often evolve an understanding about fees.

It is not unusual for one party to a divorce to lack sufficient funds to pay an attorney. This lack of resources, various strictures against contingent fee contracts, the unwillingness of some courts to redress the economic imbalance between the parties with fee awards, and the tendency of overwrought clients to misunderstand the fee agreement or to blame their attorneys for undesirable results can make collection of fees extremely difficult.

These factors help to explain why the records of fee dispute committees indicate that the number of disputes arising from family law cases is several times greater than those from any other category. Thus, financial arrangements with clients should be clearly explained, agreed upon, and documented.

2.1 Fee agreements should be reduced to writing.

Comment to Rule 2.1

At the outset the matrimonial lawyer must tell the client the basis on which fees will be charged and when and how the attorney expects to be paid. Fee agreements should be presented to the client in a manner that allows the client an opportunity to reflect upon the terms, consult another attorney before signing, and obtain answers to any questions in order to fully understand the agreement prior to entering into it.

2.2 An attorney should provide periodic statements of accrued fees and costs.

Comment to Rule 2.2

This information can be part of the necessary communications concerning the case addressed in **Standard 2.6 and Comment.** The statement should be sufficiently detailed to apprise the client of the time and charges incurred. In addition, the matrimonial lawyer should comply with fee regulations in his jurisdiction which may be more detailed or restrictive in requiring information about fees and costs.

2.3 All transactions in which an attorney obtains security for fees should be properly documented.

Comment to Rule 2.3

All security agreements should be arm's-length transactions. When taking mortgages on real property from a client, the client should be independently represented. If an attorney takes personal property as security, it must be appraised, photographed and identified by a qualified appraiser in order to establish concretely its precise identity and value. The attorney must then secure it in a safe place (usually a safe deposit box) where there is no danger that it can be removed, substituted, or lost.

American Lawyer's Code of Conduct: Rule 5.4, regarding division of fees among lawyers, provides:

Lawyers who are not openly associated in the same firm shall not share a fee unless: (a) the division reflects the proportion of work performed by each attorney and the normal billing rate of each; or (b) the client has been informed pursuant to Rule 5.2 of the fact of fee-sharing and the effect on the total fee, and the client consents.

Comment to Rule 5.4

Rule 5.4, governing the division of fees by lawyers not openly associated in the same firm, is less restrictive than any other provision or proposal known to the Commission. . . .

It must be emphasized that the purpose of allowing fee splitting is to encourage lawyers to refer clients to competent specialists. The proposed [ABA Model] Rules of Professional Conduct would continue the existing practice of penalizing such referrals outside one's own firm. Such rules exalt the form of association over the substance of client consent and providing better service for the client, particularly in the context of recent increases in the number and size of multi-office firms. It prohibits some lawyers from doing something that other lawyers may do with impunity, and that many lawyers in fact do. It is more realistic to regulate a common practice than to prohibit it on a discriminatory basis, especially when the practice may actually improve the quality of service made available to clients.

ALCC Rule 5.6(d) permits contingent fee agreements even in criminal cases. The ALCC Comment to Rule 5.6(d) provides:

Rule 5.6(d) permits fees to be contingent in whole or in part on the outcome of any case. Such fees have long been recognized as proper when the client is a plaintiff in civil litigation. The principal reason is that, as a practical matter, most people would not be in a position to seek vindication of their legal rights, however meritorious, if litigating those rights could result in substantial financial loss as well as loss in time and the other burdens of litigation. . . .

There is even more reason for allowing contingent fees for the accused in criminal cases, because the accused who goes to prison, thereby losing any opportunity to earn a living, is far less able to pay a fee than is the accused who is acquitted. Also, lawyers would accept such arrangements only when the defense appeared sufficiently strong to warrant it, and the unscrupulous lawyer would be no more likely to fabricate a defense to earn a contingent fee than to earn a retainer. . . .

Costs and Expenses: Rule 1.5 governs costs and expenses as well as legal fees. In ABA Formal Ethics Opinion 93-379 (1993), the ABA discussed the application of Rule 1.5 to various billing problems, including several situations involving costs and expenses.

Private Securities Litigation Reform Act: In December of 1995, over President Clinton's veto, Congress passed the Private Securities Litigation Reform Act. Title I of the new statute, entitled ''Reduction of Abusive Litigation,'' combats unreasonable fees in such litigation by providing that total attorney fees and expenses awarded by a court ''shall not exceed a reasonable percentage of the amount of any damages and prejudgment interest actually paid to the class.'' According to the committee report, this provision is intended to replace the ''lodestar'' method of computing fees and to give courts flexibility to determine reasonable fees and expenses on a case-by-case basis.

Restatement of the Law Governing Lawyers: The American Law Institute has tentatively approved the following provisions:

§29A. Client-Lawyer Agreements

(1) An agreement between a lawyer and client concerning the client-lawyer relationship, including an agreement modifying an existing agreement, may be enforced by either party if the agreement meets other applicable requirements, except that:

(a) if the agreement or modification is made after a reasonable time after the lawyer has begun to represent the client in the matter (see §50(1)), the client may avoid it unless the lawyer shows that the agreement and the circumstances of its formation were fair and reasonable to the client; and

(b) if the agreement is made after the lawyer has finished providing services, the client may avoid it if the client was not informed of facts needed to evaluate the appropriateness of the lawyer's compensation or other benefits conferred on the lawyer by the agreement.

(2) A tribunal should construe an agreement between client and lawyer as a reasonable person in the circumstances of the client would have construed it.

§46. Reasonable and Lawful Fees

A lawyer may not charge a fee larger than is reasonable in the circumstances or that is prohibited by law.

§47. Contingent-Fee Arrangements

(1) A lawyer may agree with a client for a fee the size or payment of which is contingent on the outcome of a matter, unless the agreement violates §46 or another provision of this Restatement or the size or payment of the fee is:

(a) contingent on success in prosecuting or defending a criminal proceeding; or

(b) contingent on a specified result in a divorce proceeding or a proceeding concerning custody of a child.

(2) Unless the agreement construed in the circumstances indicates otherwise, when a lawyer has contracted for a contingent fee, the lawyer is entitled to receive the specified fee only when and to the extent the client receives payment.

§49. Partial or Complete Forfeiture of Lawyer's Compensation

A lawyer engaging in clear and serious violation of duty to a client may be required to forfeit some or all of the lawyer's compensation for the matter. In determining whether and to what extent forfeiture is appropriate, relevant considerations include the gravity and timing of the violation, its wilfulness, its effect on the value of the lawyer's work for the client, and other threatened or actual harm to the client, and the adequacy of other remedies.

§50. Client-Lawyer Fee Agreements

(1) Before or within a reasonable time after beginning to represent a client in a matter, a lawyer must communicate to the client, in writing when applicable rules so provide, the basis or rate of the fee, unless the communication is unnecessary for the client because the lawyer has previously represented that client on the same basis or at the same rate.

(2) The validity and construction of an agreement between a client and a lawyer concerning the lawyer's fees are governed by §29A.

(3) Unless an agreement construed in the circumstances indicates otherwise:

(a) a lawyer may not charge separately for the lawyer's general office and overhead expenses;

(b) payments that the law requires an opposing party or that party's lawyer to pay as attorney-fee awards or sanctions are credited to the client, not the client's lawyer, absent a contrary statute or court order; and

(c) when a lawyer requests and receives a fee payment that is not for services already rendered, that payment is to be credited against whatever fee the lawyer is entitled to collect.

§51. Lawyer's Fee in Absence of Agreement

If a client and lawyer have not made a valid agreement providing for another measure of compensation, a client owes a lawyer who has performed legal services for the client the fair value of the lawyer's services.

§53. Fee Collection Methods

In seeking compensation claimed from a client or former client, a lawyer may not employ collection methods forbidden by law, use confidential information (as defined in Chapter 5) when not permitted under §117, or harass the client.

(Restatement §117 is reprinted in the Related Materials following Model Rule 1.6.)

§54. Remedies and Burden of Persuasion

(1) A fee dispute between a lawyer and a client may be adjudicated in any appropriate proceeding, including a suit by the lawyer to recover an unpaid fee, a suit for a refund by a client, an arbitration to which both parties consent unless applicable law renders the lawyer's consent unnecessary, or in the court's discretion a proceeding ancillary to a pending suit in which the lawyer performed the services in question.

(2) In any such proceeding the lawyer has the burden of persuading the trier of fact, when relevant, of the existence and terms of any fee agreement, the making of any disclosures to the client required to render an agreement enforceable, and the extent and value of the lawyer's services.

Rule 1.6 Confidentiality of Information

(a) A lawyer shall not reveal information relating to representation of a client unless the client consents after consultation, except for disclosures that are impliedly authorized in order to carry out the representation, and except as stated in paragraph (b).

(b) A lawyer may reveal such information to the extent the lawyer reasonably believes necessary:

(1) to prevent the client from committing a criminal act that the lawyer believes is likely to result in imminent death or substantial bodily harm; or

(2) to establish a claim or defense on behalf of the lawyer in a controversy between the lawyer and the client, to establish a defense to a criminal charge or civil claim against the lawyer based upon conduct in which the client was involved, or to respond to allegations in any proceeding concerning the lawyer's representation of the client.

COMMENT

[1] The lawyer is part of a judicial system charged with upholding the law. One of the lawyer's functions is to advise clients so that they avoid any violation of the law in the proper exercise of their rights.

[2] The observance of the ethical obligation of a lawyer to hold inviolate confidential information of the client not only facilitates the full development of facts essential to proper representation of the client but also encourages people to seek early legal assistance.

[3] Almost without exception, clients come to lawyers in order to determine what their rights are and what is, in the maze of laws and regulations, deemed to be legal and correct. The common law recognizes that the client's confidences must be protected from disclosure. Based upon experience, lawyers know that almost all clients follow the advice given, and the law is upheld.

[4] A fundamental principle in the client-lawyer relationship is that the lawyer maintain confidentiality of information relating to the representation. The client is thereby encouraged to communicate fully and frankly with the lawyer even as to embarrassing or legally damaging subject matter.

[5] The principle of confidentiality is given effect in two related bodies of law, the attorney-client privilege (which includes the work product doctrine) in the law of evidence and the rule of confidentiality estab-

lished in professional ethics. The attorney-client privilege applies in judicial and other proceedings in which a lawyer may be called as a witness or otherwise required to produce evidence concerning a client. The rule of client-lawyer confidentiality applies in situations other than those where evidence is sought from the lawyer through compulsion of law. The confidentiality rule applies not merely to matters communicated in confidence by the client but also to all information relating to the representation, whatever its source. A lawyer may not disclose such information except as authorized or required by the Rules of Professional Conduct or other law. See also Scope.

[6] The requirement of maintaining confidentiality of information relating to representation applies to government lawyers who may disagree with the policy goals that their representation is designed to advance.

Authorized Disclosure

[7] A lawyer is impliedly authorized to make disclosures about a client when appropriate in carrying out the representation, except to the extent that the client's instructions or special circumstances limit that authority. In litigation, for example, a lawyer may disclose information by admitting a fact that cannot properly be disputed, or in negotiation by making a disclosure that facilitates a satisfactory conclusion.

[8] Lawyers in a firm may, in the course of the firm's practice, disclose to each other information relating to a client of the firm, unless the client has instructed that particular information be confined to specified lawyers.

Disclosure Adverse to Client

[9] The confidentiality rule is subject to limited exceptions. In becoming privy to information about a client, a lawyer may foresee that the client intends serious harm to another person. However, to the extent a lawyer is required or permitted to disclose a client's purposes, the client will be inhibited from revealing facts which would enable the lawyer to counsel against a wrongful course of action. The public is better protected if full and open communication by the client is encouraged than if it is inhibited.

[10] Several situations must be distinguished. First, the lawyer may not counsel or assist a client in conduct that is criminal or fraudulent. See Rule 1.2(d). Similarly, a lawyer has a duty under Rule 3.3(a)(4) not to use false

evidence. This duty is essentially a special instance of the duty prescribed in Rule 1.2(d) to avoid assisting a client in criminal or fraudulent conduct.

[11] Second, the lawyer may have been innocently involved in past conduct by the client that was criminal or fraudulent. In such a situation the lawyer has not violated Rule 1.2(d), because to "counsel or assist" criminal or fraudulent conduct requires knowing that the conduct is of that character.

[12] Third, the lawyer may learn that a client intends prospective conduct that is criminal and likely to result in imminent death or substantial bodily harm. As stated in paragraph (b)(1), the lawyer has professional discretion to reveal information in order to prevent such consequences. The lawyer may make a disclosure in order to prevent homicide or serious bodily injury which the lawyer reasonably believes is intended by a client. It is very difficult for a lawyer to "know" when such a heinous purpose will actually be carried out, for the client may have a change of mind.

[13] The lawyer's exercise of discretion requires consideration of such factors as the nature of the lawyer's relationship with the client and with those who might be injured by the client, the lawyer's own involvement in the transaction and factors that may extenuate the conduct in question. Where practical, the lawyer should seek to persuade the client to take suitable action. In any case, a disclosure adverse to the client's interest should be no greater than the lawyer reasonably believes necessary to the purpose. A lawyer's decision not to take preventive action permitted by paragraph (b)(1) does not violate this Rule.

Withdrawal

Editors' Note. Paragraphs 14 and 15 of the Comment to Rule 1.6 — which permit a "noisy withdrawal" — were added to the Kutak Commission's draft of the Comment after the ABA House of Delegates rejected the Kutak Commission's 1982 proposal to allow disclosure of information necessary to "rectify the consequences of a client's criminal or fraudulent act in the furtherance of which the lawyer's services had been used." The "noisy withdrawal" provision is construed in ABA Formal Ethics Opinion 92-366 (1992).

[14] If the lawyer's services will be used by the client in materially furthering a course of criminal or fraudulent conduct, the lawyer must withdraw, as stated in Rule 1.16(a)(1).

[15] After withdrawal the lawyer is required to refrain from making disclosure of the clients' confidences, except as otherwise provided in Rule 1.6. Neither this rule nor Rule 1.8(b) nor Rule 1.16(d) prevents the lawyer from giving notice of the fact of withdrawal, and the lawyer may also withdraw or disaffirm any opinion, document, affirmation, or the like.

[16] Where the client is an organization, the lawyer may be in doubt whether contemplated conduct will actually be carried out by the organization. Where necessary to guide conduct in connection with this Rule, the lawyer may make inquiry within the organization as indicated in Rule 1.13(b).

Dispute Concerning Lawyer's Conduct

[17] Where a legal claim or disciplinary charge alleges complicity of the lawyer in a client's conduct or other misconduct of the lawyer involving representation of the client, the lawyer may respond to the extent the lawyer reasonably believes necessary to establish a defense. The same is true with respect to a claim involving the conduct or representation of a former client. The lawyer's right to respond arises when an assertion of such complicity has been made. Paragraph (b)(2) does not require the lawyer to await the commencement of an action or proceeding that charges such complicity, so that the defense may be established by responding directly to a third party who has made such an assertion. The right to defend, of course, applies where a proceeding has been commenced. Where practicable and not prejudicial to the lawyer's ability to establish the defense, the lawyer should advise the client of the third party's assertion and request that the client respond appropriately. In any event, disclosure should be no greater than the lawyer reasonably believes is necessary to vindicate innocence, the disclosure should be made in a manner which limits access to the information to the tribunal or other persons having a need to know it, and appropriate protective orders or other arrangements should be sought by the lawyer to the fullest extent practicable.

[18] If the lawyer is charged with wrongdoing in which the client's conduct is implicated, the rule of confidentiality should not prevent the lawyer from defending against the charge. Such a charge can arise in a civil, criminal or professional disciplinary proceeding, and can be based on a wrong allegedly committed by the lawyer against the client, or on a wrong alleged by a third person; for example, a person claiming to have been defrauded by the lawyer and client acting together. A lawyer entitled to a fee is permitted by paragraph (b)(2) to prove the services ren-

dered in an action to collect it. This aspect of the rule expresses the principle that the beneficiary of a fiduciary relationship may not exploit it to the detriment of the fiduciary. As stated above, the lawyer must make every effort practicable to avoid unnecessary disclosure of information relating to a representation, to limit disclosure to those having the need to know it, and to obtain protective orders or make other arrangements minimizing the risk of disclosure.

Disclosures Otherwise Required or Authorized

[19] The attorney-client privilege is differently defined in various jurisdictions. If a lawyer is called as a witness to give testimony concerning a client, absent waiver by the client, Rule 1.6(a) requires the lawyer to invoke the privilege when it is applicable. The lawyer must comply with the final orders of a court or other tribunal of competent jurisdiction requiring the lawyer to give information about the client.

[20] The Rules of Professional Conduct in various circumstances permit or require a lawyer to disclose information relating to the representation. See Rules 2.2, 2.3, 3.3 and 4.1. In addition to these provisions, a lawyer may be obligated or permitted by other provisions of law to give information about a client. Whether another provision of law supersedes Rule 1.6 is a matter of interpretation beyond the scope of these Rules, but a presumption should exist against such a supersession.

Former Client

[21] The duty of confidentiality continues after the client-lawyer relationship has terminated.

Model Code Comparison

Rule 1.6 eliminates the two-pronged duty under the Model Code in favor of a single standard protecting all information about a client "relating to the representation." Under DR 4-101, the requirement applied only to information governed by the attorney-client privilege and to information "gained in" the professional relationship that "the client has requested be held inviolate or the disclosure of which would be embarrassing or would be likely to be detrimental to the client." EC 4-4 added that the duty differed from the evidentiary privilege in that it existed "without regard to the nature or source of the information or the fact that others share the knowledge." Rule 1.6 imposes confidentiality on information relating to the representation even if it is acquired before or after the relationship existed. It does not require the client to indicate information that is to be confidential, or permit the lawyer to speculate whether particular information might be embarrassing or detrimental.

Paragraph (a) permits a lawyer to disclose information where impliedly authorized to do so in order to carry out the representation. Under DR 4-101(B) and (C), a lawyer could not reveal "confidences" unless the client first consented after disclosure.

Paragraph (b) redefines the exceptions to the requirement of confidentiality. Regarding paragraph (b)(1), DR 4-101(C)(3) provided that a lawyer "may reveal . . . [t]he intention of his client to commit a crime and the information necessary to prevent the crime." This option existed regardless of the seriousness of the proposed crime.

With regard to paragraph (b)(2), DR 4-101(C)(4) provided that a lawyer may reveal "[c]onfidences or secrets necessary to establish or collect his fee or to defend himself or his employers or associates against an accusation of wrongful conduct." Paragraph (b)(2) enlarges the exception to include disclosure of information relating to claims by the lawyer other than for the lawyer's fee — for example, recovery of property from the client.

Cross-References in Rules

Scope ¶3: "Most of the duties flowing from the client-lawyer relationship attach only after the client has requested the lawyer to render legal services and the lawyer has agreed to do so. But there are some duties, such as that of confidentiality under **Rule 1.6**, that may attach when the lawyer agrees to consider whether a client-lawyer relationship shall be established."

Scope ¶7: "The fact that in exceptional situations the lawyer under the Rules has a limited discretion to disclose a client confidence does not vitiate the proposition that, as a general matter, the client has a reasonable expectation that information relating to the client will not be voluntarily disclosed and that disclosure of such information may be judicially compelled only in accordance with recognized exceptions to the attorney-client and work product privileges."

Scope ¶8: "The lawyer's exercise of discretion not to disclose information under **Rule 1.6** should not be subject to reexamination."

Rule 1.2, Comment 7: "The lawyer is not permitted to reveal the client's wrongdoing, except where permitted by **Rule 1.6**."

Rule 1.8, Comment 4: When a third party pays fees, the arrangement must "conform to the requirements of **Rule 1.6** concerning confidentiality. . . ."

Rule 1.9(b): "A lawyer shall not knowingly represent a person in the same or a substantially related matter in which a firm with which the lawyer formerly was associated had previously represented a client whose interests are materially adverse to that person and about whom the lawyer had acquired information protected by **Rules 1.6** and 1.9(c) that is material to the matter. . . ."

Rule 1.9(c): "A lawyer who has formerly represented a client in a matter or whose present or former firm has formerly represented a client . . . shall not thereafter: . . . (1) use information . . . to the disadvantage of the former client except as **Rule 1.6** or Rule 3.3 would permit or require . . . ; or (2) reveal information relating to the representation except as **Rule 1.6** or Rule 3.3 would permit or require with respect to a client."

Rule 1.9, Comment 9: "Paragraph (b) operates to disqualify the lawyer only when the lawyer involved has actual knowledge of information protected by **Rules 1.6** and 1.9(c)."

Rule 1.9, Comment 10: "Independent of the question of disqualification of a firm, a lawyer changing a professional association has a continuing duty to preserve confidentiality of information about a client formerly represented. See **Rules 1.6** and 1.9."

Rule 1.10(b)(2) restricts representation when "any lawyer remaining in the firm has information protected by **Rules 1.6** and 1.9(c) that is material to the matter."

Rule 1.10, Comment 4: When a lawyer moves from government to a private practice, or vice versa, the lawyer "is bound by the Rules generally, including **Rule 1.6**. . . ."

Rule 1.10, Comment 5: "The government is entitled to protection of its client confidences, and therefore to the protections provided in **Rule 1.6**. . . ."

Rule 1.10, Comment 7: When a lawyer who represents or formerly represented a client leaves a firm, the firm may not represent a person with interests adverse to that client where the matter is the same or substantially related and "any other lawyer currently in the firm has material information protected by **Rules 1.6** and 1.9(c)."

Rule 1.13, Comment 3: "When one of the constituents of an organizational client communicates with the organization's lawyer in that person's organizational capacity, the communication is protected by **Rule 1.6**. Thus, by way of example, if an organizational client requests its lawyer to investigate allegations of wrongdoing, interviews made in the course of that investigation between the lawyer and the client's employees or other constituents are covered by **Rule 1.6**. This does not mean, however, that constituents of an organizational client are the clients of the lawyer. The lawyer may not disclose to such constituents information relating to the representation except for disclosures explicitly or impliedly authorized by the organizational client in order to carry out the representation or as otherwise permitted by **Rule 1.6**."

Rule 1.13, Comment 6: "[T]his Rule does not limit or expand the lawyer's responsibility under **Rules 1.6**, 1.8, and 1.16, 3.3 or 4.1."

Rule 1.17, Comment 6 provides: "Negotiations between seller and prospective purchaser prior to disclosure of information relating to a specific representation of an identifiable client no more violate the confidentiality provisions of **Model Rule 1.6** than do preliminary discussions concerning the possible association of another lawyer or mergers between firms, with respect to which client consent is not required. Providing the purchaser access to client-specific information relating to the representation and to the file, however, requires client consent."

Rule 1.17, Comment 11 provides that a lawyer selling a law practice has an "obligation to protect information relating to the representation (see **Rules 1.6** and 1.9)."

Rule 2.2, Comment 6: "In a common representation, the lawyer is still required both to keep each client adequately informed and to maintain confidentiality of information relating to the representation. See **Rules** 1.4 and **1.6**."

Rule 2.3(b): "Except as disclosure is required in connection with a report of an evaluation, information relating to the evaluation is otherwise protected by **Rule 1.6**."

Rule 3.3(b): "The duties stated in paragraph (a) continue to the conclusion of the proceeding, and apply even if compliance requires disclosure of information otherwise protected by **Rule 1.6**."

Rule 4.1(b): "In the course of representing a client a lawyer shall not knowingly . . . fail to disclose a material fact to a third person when disclosure is necessary to avoid assisting a criminal or fraudulent act by a client, unless disclosure is prohibited by **Rule 1.6**."

Rule 4.1, Comment 3: "Paragraph (b) recognizes that substantive law may require a lawyer to disclose certain information to avoid being deemed to have assisted the client's crime or fraud. The requirement of disclosure created by this paragraph is, however, subject to the obligations created by **Rule 1.6**."

Rule 5.7, Comment 8: "When a lawyer is obliged to accord the recipients of such [law-related] services the protections of those Rules that apply to the client-lawyer relationship, the lawyer must . . . scrupulously adhere to the requirements of **Rule 1.6** relating to disclosure of confidential information."

Rule 8.1(b): "[T]his rule does not require disclosure of information otherwise protected by **Rule 1.6**."

Rule 8.3(c): "This rule does not require disclosure of information otherwise protected by **Rule 1.6**."

Rule 8.3, Comment 2: "A report about misconduct is not required where it would involve violation of **Rule 1.6**."

Legislative History

1979 Unofficial Pre-Circulation Draft:

(a) In giving testimony or providing evidence concerning a client's affairs, a lawyer shall not disclose matter concerning the client except as permitted under the applicable law of evidentiary privilege. In other circumstances, a lawyer shall not disclose information about a client acquired in serving the client in a professional capacity except as stated in paragraphs (b), (c) and (d).

(b) A lawyer shall disclose information about a client when directed to do so by the client and may do so when disclosure is necessary in the representation.

(c) A lawyer shall disclose information about a client

(1) to the extent necessary to prevent the client from committing an act that would seriously endanger the life or safety of a person, result in wrongful detention or incarceration of a person or wrongful destruction of substantial property, or corrupt judicial or governmental procedure;

(2) when disclosure by the lawyer is required by law or the rules of professional conduct.

(d) A lawyer may disclose information about a client

(1) to the extent necessary to prevent or rectify the consequences of a deliberately wrongful act by the client in which the lawyer's services are or were involved, except when the lawyer has been employed after the commission of such an act to represent the client concerning the act or its consequences. . . .

1980 Discussion Draft:

(b) A lawyer shall disclose information about a client to the extent it appears necessary to prevent the client from committing an act that would result in death or serious bodily harm to another person, and to the extent required by law or the rules of professional conduct.

(c) A lawyer may disclose information about a client only:

(1) For the purposes of serving the client's interest, unless it is information the client has specifically requested not to be disclosed;

(2) To the extent it appears necessary to prevent or rectify the consequences of a deliberately wrongful act by the client, except when the lawyer has been employed after the commission of such an act to represent the client concerning the act or its consequences. . . .

1981 Draft:

(b) A lawyer may reveal such information to the extent the lawyer believes necessary:

(1) to serve the client's interests, unless it is information the client has specifically requested not to be disclosed;

(2) to prevent the client from committing a criminal or fraudulent act that the lawyer believes is likely to result in death or substantial bodily harm, or substantial injury to the financial interest or property of another;

(3) to rectify the consequences of a client's criminal or fraudulent act in the commission of which the lawyer's services had been used. . . .

1982 Draft:

(b) A lawyer may reveal such information to the extent the lawyer reasonably believes necessary:

(1) to prevent the client from committing a criminal or fraudulent act that the lawyer reasonably believes is likely to result in death or substantial bodily harm, or in substantial injury to the financial interests or property of another;

(2) to rectify the consequences of a client's criminal or fraudulent act in the furtherance of which the lawyer's services had been used. . . .

1991 Proposal: At the ABA's August 1991 Annual Meeting, the Standing Committee on Ethics and Professional Responsibility proposed an amendment to Rule 1.6(b) that would have permitted a lawyer to reveal information that the lawyer reasonably believed necessary to "rectify the consequences of a client's criminal or fraudulent act in the commission of which the lawyer's services had been used." The House of Delegates defeated this proposal by a vote of 251 to 158. The rejected amendment was virtually identical to the Kutak Commission draft that was rejected by the ABA in 1982. By rejecting the 1991 proposal to amend the text of Rule 1.6, the House of Delegates also rejected the following amendments to various paragraphs of the Comment to Rule 1.6:

> To the extent a lawyer is prohibited from making disclosure, the interests of the potential victim are sacrificed in favor of preserving the client's confidences even though the client's purpose is wrongful.

> Generally speaking, information relating to the representation must be kept confidential. . . . However, where the client is or has been engaged in criminal or fraudulent conduct or the integrity of the lawyer's own conduct is involved, the principle of confidentiality may have to yield, depending on the lawyer's knowledge about and relationship to the conduct in question, and the seriousness of the conduct.

> Even if the [lawyer's] involvement was innocent . . . the fact remains that the lawyer's professional services were made the instrument of the client's crime or fraud. The lawyer, therefore, has a legitimate interest in being able to rectify the consequences of such conduct, and has the professional right, although not a professional duty, to rectify the situation. Exercising that right may require revealing information relating to the representation.

Selected State Variations

Editors' Note. American jurisdictions have adopted many variations on Rule 1.6 and its exceptions. Under the Code, a lawyer was authorized to reveal the intention of a client to commit a crime and the information necessary to prevent the crime. DR 4-101(C)(3). Rule 1.6(b)(1) limits that authority to crimes "likely to result in imminent death or substantial bodily harm." Among the questions addressed in state variations are the following:

- whether to continue the Code's authority to reveal any prospective crime;
- whether to extend the authority to conduct other than criminal conduct (such as conduct that is reckless, fraudulent, or illegal, but not criminal);
- whether to keep the authority permissive or, instead, to mandate revelation of prospective criminal or harmful conduct;
- if revelation is mandatory, the prospective conduct that will be subject to the mandatory duty to reveal;
- whether to distinguish the right or obligation to disclose depending upon whether the lawyer's information is protected by the attorney-client privilege or only protected by the jurisdiction's ethical document.

Alaska, Connecticut, Maryland, New Hampshire, New Mexico, North Dakota, Pennsylvania, and Wisconsin permit a lawyer to reveal information necessary to prevent the client from committing a criminal act "likely to result in substantial injury to the financial interest or property of another" (or words to that effect). Maryland permits the same when the act is only fraudulent.

Alaska eliminates the word "imminent" in Rule 1.6(b).

Arizona, Arkansas, Colorado, Idaho, Indiana, Kansas, Michigan, Minnesota, Mississippi, North Carolina, Washington, and *Wyoming* essentially retain the old Model Code formulation — they all permit a lawyer to reveal "the intention of a client to commit a crime" (or use words to that effect).

Arizona, Connecticut, Illinois, Nevada, North Dakota, and *Texas* mandate disclosure of information to prevent the client from committing serious violent crimes.

Arkansas places the language in paragraph 15 of the Comment in the text of the Rule as paragraph (c).

California: B & P Code §6068(e) provides that it is the duty of an attorney "[t]o maintain inviolate the confidence, and at every peril to himself or herself to preserve the secrets, of his or her client." (California's Rules of Professional Conduct do not expressly cover confidentiality.) Section 956.5 of the California Evidence Code, reprinted in our chapter on privilege and work product, suspends the privilege when the lawyer "reasonably believes" that disclosure is necessary to prevent a criminal act "likely to result in death or substantial bodily harm."

Connecticut: Rule 1.6 does not contain the word "imminent" before "death or substantial bodily harm."

Connecticut, Pennsylvania, Maryland, Michigan, New Jersey, and *Wisconsin* permit lawyers to reveal confidential information "to rectify the consequences of a client's criminal or fraudulent act in the furtherance of which the lawyer's services were used" (or words to that effect).

District of Columbia: D.C. Rule 1.6 differs significantly from the ABA Model Rule — see District of Columbia Rules of Professional Conduct below.

Florida provides that a lawyer "shall reveal" information the lawyer believes "necessary (1) to prevent a client from committing a crime or (2) to prevent death or substantial bodily harm to another." In addition, Florida Rule 1.6(c) permits a lawyer to reveal information necessary "(1) To serve the client's interest unless it is information the client specifically requires not to be disclosed . . . or (5) To comply with the Rules of Professional Conduct." Florida also adds Rule 1.6(d): "When required by a tribunal to reveal such information, a lawyer may first exhaust all appellate remedies." Finally, Florida adds Rule 1.6(e), which provides that "when disclosure is mandated or permitted, the lawyer shall disclose no more information than is required to meet the requirements or accomplish the purposes of this rule."

Georgia retains the language of DR 4-101, except that Georgia's version of DR 4-101(c)(1) deletes "but only after a full disclosure to them."

Illinois: Rule 1.6 provides:

(a) Except when required under Rule 1.6(b) or permitted under Rule 1.6(c), a lawyer shall not, during or after termination of the professional relationship with the client, use or reveal a confidence or secret of the client unless the client consents after disclosure.

(b) A lawyer shall reveal information about a client to the extent it appears necessary to prevent the client from committing an act that would result in death or serious bodily harm.

(c) A lawyer may use or reveal:

(1) confidences or secrets when permitted under these Rules or required by law or court order;

(2) the intention of a client to commit a crime in circumstances other than those enumerated in Rule 1.6(b); or

(3) confidences or secrets necessary to establish or collect the lawyer's fee or to defend the lawyer or the lawyer's employees or associates against an accusation of wrongful conduct.

Illinois also adds:

(d) The relationship of trained intervenor and a lawyer or a judge who seeks or receives assistance through the Lawyer's Assistance Program, Inc., shall be the same as that of lawyer and client for purposes of the application of Rule 8.3 and Rule 1.6.

(e) Any information received by a lawyer in a formal proceeding before a trained intervenor, or panel of intervenors, of the Lawyer's Assistance Program, Inc., shall be deemed to have been received from a client for purposes of the application of Rules 1.6 and 8.3.

Indiana: Rule 1.6 adds:

In the event of an attorney's physical or mental disability, or appointment of a Lawyers Assistance Committee as guardian or conservator of an attorney's client files, disclosure of the client names and files to the Program are deemed impliedly authorized in order to carry out the representation. . . .

Massachusetts: Effective January 1, 1998, Rule 1.6 permits a lawyer to reveal — "and to the extent required by Rule 3.3 and Rule 4. 1(b)" requires a lawyer to reveal — confidential information "to prevent the commission of a criminal or fraudulent act that the lawyer reasonably believes is likely to result in death or substantial bodily harm or in substantial injury to the financial interests or property of another, or to prevent the wrongful execution or incarceration of another." Revelation is also permitted "to the extent the lawyer reasonably believes necessary to rectify client fraud in which the lawyer's services have been used, subject to Rule 3.3(e)."

New Jersey, in addition to above, requires a lawyer to reveal confidential information "to prevent a client from committing a criminal, illegal or fraudulent act . . . likely to result in death or substantial bodily harm or substantial injury to the financial interest or property of another." New Jersey also requires a lawyer to reveal confidences to prevent a client from committing "a criminal, illegal or fraudulent act that the lawyer reasonably believes is likely to perpetrate a fraud upon a tribunal."

New York: Same or substantially the same as the ABA Model Code — see Model Code Comparison above — except see New York Materials for New York's version of DR 7-102(B)(1) and New York's versions of EC 4-7 and DR 4-101(C)(5).

Oregon: In 1995, Oregon added a new subparagraph DR 4-101(C)(5), which provides that a lawyer may reveal:

> (5) [t]he following information in discussions preliminary to the sale of a law practice under DR 2-111 with respect to each client potentially subject to the transfer: the client's identity; the identities of any adverse parties; the nature and extent of the legal services involved; and the fee and payment information. A potential purchasing lawyer shall have the same responsibilities as the selling lawyer to preserve confidences and secrets of such clients whether or not the sale of the practice closes or the client ultimately consents to representation by the purchasing lawyer.

Texas, in addition to above, Rule 1.02(d) and (e) provides:

> (d) When a lawyer has confidential information clearly establishing that a client is likely to commit a criminal or fraudulent act that is likely to result in substantial injury to the financial interests or property of another, the lawyer shall promptly make reasonable efforts under the circumstances to dissuade the client from committing the crime or fraud.
> (e) When a lawyer has confidential information clearly establishing that the lawyer's client has committed a criminal or fraudulent act in the commission of which the lawyer's services have been used, the lawyer shall make reasonable efforts under the circumstances to persuade the client to take corrective action.

Texas Rule 1.05 distinguishes between "privileged information" and "unprivileged client information." The former is information protected by the attorney-client privilege. The latter "means all information relating to a client or furnished by the client, other than privileged information, acquired by the lawyer in the course of or by reason of the representation of the client." Both categories of information comprise a third category called "confidential information." A lawyer "may reveal confidential information" in eight instances, including when "the lawyer has reason to believe it is necessary to do so in order to prevent the client from committing a criminal or fraudulent act," and to "the extent revelation reasonably appears necessary to rectify the consequences of a client's criminal or fraudulent act in the commission of which the lawyer's services had been used." Rule 1.05(c)(7) and (8).

Utah: Rule 1.6(c) states:

> (c) Representation of a client includes counseling a lawyer(s) about the need for or availability of treatment for substance abuse or psychological or emotional problems by members of the Utah State Bar serving on the Lawyers Helping Lawyers Committee.

Virginia: DR 4-101(D)(1) provides that a lawyer "shall" reveal:

> (1) The intention of his client, as stated by the client, to commit a crime and the information necessary to prevent the crime, but before revealing such information, the attorney shall, where feasible, advise his client of the possible legal consequences of his action, urge the client not to commit the crime, and advise the client that the attorney must reveal the client's criminal intention unless there-

upon abandoned, and, if the crime involves perjury by the client, that the attorney shall seek to withdraw as counsel.

Virginia DR 4-101(D)(2) retains the language of DR 7-102(B)(1) relating to a client's fraud on a tribunal, but adds that information "is clearly established when the client acknowledges to the attorney that he has perpetrated a fraud upon a tribunal."

Washington adds Rule 1.6(c): "A lawyer may reveal to the tribunal confidences or secrets which disclose any breach of fiduciary responsibility by a client who is a guardian, personal representative, receiver or other appointed fiduciary."

Related Materials

ABA Canons: Canon 37 provided:

37. Confidences of a Client

It is the duty of a lawyer to preserve his client's confidences. This duty outlasts the lawyer's employment, and extends as well to his employees; and neither of them should accept employment which involves or may involve the disclosure or use of these confidences, either for the private advantage of the lawyer or his employees or to the disadvantage of the client, without his knowledge and consent, and even though there are other available sources of such information. A lawyer should not continue employment when he discovers that this obligation prevents the performance of his full duty to his former or to his new client.

If a lawyer is accused by his client, he is not precluded from disclosing the truth in respect to this accusation. The announced intention of a client to commit a crime is not included within the confidences which he is bound to respect. He may properly make such disclosures as may be necessary to prevent the act or protect those against whom it is threatened.

ABA Standards for Imposing Lawyer Sanctions:

4.21. Disbarment is generally appropriate when a lawyer, with the intent to benefit the lawyer or another, knowingly reveals information relating to representation of a client not otherwise lawfully permitted to be disclosed, and this disclosure causes injury or potential injury to a client.

4.22. Suspension is generally appropriate when a lawyer knowingly reveals information relating to the representation of a client not otherwise lawfully permitted to be disclosed, and this disclosure causes injury or potential injury to a client.

4.23. Reprimand is generally appropriate when a lawyer negligently reveals information relating to representation of a client not otherwise lawfully permitted to be disclosed and this disclosure causes injury or potential injury to a client.

4.24. Admonition is generally appropriate when a lawyer negligently reveals information relating to representation of a client not otherwise lawfully permitted to be disclosed and this disclosure causes little or no actual or potential injury to a client.

American Academy of Matrimonial Lawyers: The "Bounds of Advocacy" drafted by the American Academy of Matrimonial Lawyers contains the following provisions and commentary:

2.10 An Attorney should not permit a client's relatives, friends, lovers, employers, or other third persons to interfere with the representation, affect the attorney's independent professional judgment, or make decisions affecting the representation, except with the client's express consent.

Comment to Rule 2.10

. . . To the extent specifically authorized by the client, the lawyer may discuss choices with third parties, provided all concerned are aware that such discussions may waive any attorney-client privilege. While it is important for persons going through a divorce to receive advice and support from those they trust, the client, with the advice of the attorney, should make the decisions with which the client must ultimately live.

Both the client and the person paying for the representation must be informed at the outset that nothing related by the client in confidence will be disclosed without the client's consent. The duty to protect confidential information also requires that the attorney raise the issue of the effect on confidentiality of the parents, friends, lovers, children or employers' being present. Usually, the presence of a third person not necessary to the rendition of legal services waives the attorney-client privilege. For this and other reasons, an attorney should discourage family members and other third persons from participating in client conferences. In addition to the potential loss of confidentiality, a more accurate account of the client's desires and best interests can usually be obtained when third persons are not present.

2.26 An attorney should disclose evidence of a substantial risk of physical or sexual abuse of a child by the attorney's client.

Comment to Rule 2.26

While engaged in efforts on the client's behalf, the matrimonial lawyer may become convinced that the client has abused one of the children. Or the client, who seems a good parent, has a live-in lover who has abused one of the children. Under traditional analysis in most jurisdictions, the attorney should refuse to assist the client. The attorney may withdraw if the client will not be adversely affected and the court grants any required permission.

It may also be appropriate to seek the appointment of a guardian ad litem or attorney for the children. The entire thrust of the family law system is intended to make the child's well-being the highest priority. The vindictiveness of a parent, the ineffective legal representation of the spouse, or the failure of the court to perceive sua sponte the need to protect the child's interests do not justify an attorney's failure to act. However, even the appointment of a guardian or lawyer for the child is insufficient if the matrimonial lawyer is aware of physical abuse or similarly extreme parental deficiency. Nor would withdrawal (even if permitted) solve the problem if the attorney is convinced that the child will suffer adverse treatment by the client.

In the most extreme cases, the attorney may reveal information reasonably believed necessary "to prevent the client from committing a criminal act that the lawyer believes is likely to result in imminent death or substantial bodily harm."

Many states permit the attorney to reveal the intention of the client to commit any crime and the information necessary to prevent it. The rules do not appear to address, however, revelation of conduct that may be severely detrimental to the well-being of the child, but not criminal.

Notwithstanding the importance of the attorney-client privilege, the obligation of the matrimonial lawyer to consider the welfare of children, coupled with the client's lack of any legitimate interest in preventing his attorney from revealing information to protect the children from likely physical abuse, requires disclosure of a substantial risk of abuse and the information necessary to prevent it. If the client insists on seeking custody or unsupervised visitation, even without the attorney's assistance, the attorney should report specific knowledge of child abuse to the authorities for the protection of the child.

American Lawyer's Code of Conduct: The terminology section states:

A *client's confidence,* protected by this Code, includes any information obtained by the client's lawyer in the course of and by reason of the lawyer-client relationship.

Rules 1.1 through 1.6 provide:

1.1. Beginning with the initial interview with a prospective client, a lawyer shall strive to establish and maintain a relationship of trust and confidence with the client. The lawyer shall impress upon the client that the lawyer cannot adequately serve the client without knowing everything that might be relevant to the client's problem, and that the client should not withhold information that the client might think is embarrassing or harmful to the client's interests. The lawyer shall explain to the client the lawyer's obligation of confidentiality.

1.2. Without the client's knowing and voluntary consent, a lawyer shall not directly or indirectly reveal a confidence of a client or former client, or use it in any way detrimental to the interests of the client, except as provided in Rules 1.3 to 1.6, and Rule 6.5. . . .

1.3. A lawyer may reveal a client's confidence to the extent required to do so by law, rule of court, or court order, but only after good faith efforts to test the validity of the law, rule, or order have been exhausted.

1.4. A lawyer may reveal a client's confidence when the lawyer knows that a judge or juror in a pending proceeding in which the lawyer is involved has been bribed or subjected to extortion. In such a case, the lawyer shall use all reasonable means to protect the client, consistent with preventing the case from going forward with a corrupted judge or juror.

1.5. A lawyer may reveal a client's confidence to the extent necessary to defend the lawyer or the lawyer's associate or employee against charges of criminal, civil, or professional misconduct asserted by the client, or against formally instituted charges of such conduct in which the client is implicated.

[1.6. A lawyer may reveal a client's confidence when and to the extent that the lawyer reasonably believes that divulgence is necessary to prevent imminent danger to human life. The lawyer shall use all reasonable means to protect the client's interests that are consistent with preventing loss of life.]

Commission's Note: Rule 1.6 was not approved by the Commission [on Professional Responsibility of the Roscoe Pound Foundation], but was supported by so many members that it is included in this Revised Draft as a Supplemental Rule.

Comment to Rules 1.1-1.6

These Rules reject the previously recognized exception permitting lawyers to violate confidentiality to collect an unpaid fee. The reason for the exception — the lawyer's financial interest — is not sufficiently weighty to justify impairing confidentiality. On the other hand, a limited exception is permitted, when a lawyer or the lawyer's associate is formally charged with criminal or unprofessional conduct. . . .

This Code rejects permitting violation of confidentiality in all cases of "future (or continuing) crimes." First, the category of "crimes" is too broad; it lumps offenses that are openly done and relatively harmless, with those that are clandestine and involve life and death. At the same time, the requirement of a crime may be too narrow; if saving a life, for example, is sufficiently important to justify an exception to confidentiality, then the exception should not turn on technicalities. . . .

Attorney-Client Privilege: Wigmore's treatise on the law of evidence defines the attorney-client privilege as follows:

(1) Where legal advice of any kind is sought (2) from a professional legal advisor in his capacity as such, (3) the communications relating to that purpose, (4) made in confidence (5) by the client, (6) are at his [the client's] instance permanently protected (7) from disclosure by himself or the legal advisor, (8) except the protection be waived.

For more detailed descriptions of the attorney-client privilege, see the chapter entitled "Attorney-Client Privilege and Work Product Provisions" later in this volume.

Federal Rules of Civil Procedure: A radically amended version of Fed. R. Civ. P. 26, which took effect on December 1, 1993, requires parties to produce lists of witnesses and documents soon after litigation commences, without any request from the other side. This "automatic discovery" provision requires parties to identify people "likely to have discoverable information relevant to disputed facts alleged with particularity in the pleadings." It also imposes a parallel duty to identify or produce relevant documents without awaiting a request. These provisions bear on Model Rule 1.6 because clients who commence litigation in federal court may be deemed to have "impliedly authorized" their lawyers to reveal the information that must be revealed under amended Rule 26(a)(1). (Note: Many federal district courts took advantage of an "opt out" provision in Rule 26(a) and did not adopt the mandatory disclosure provisions.)

Model Rules of Professional Conduct for Federal Lawyers: Rule 1.6(b) provides: "A federal lawyer shall reveal such information to the extent the Federal lawyer reasonably believes necessary to prevent the client from committing a criminal act that the Federal lawyer believes is likely to result in imminent death or substantial bodily harm, or imminent and significant impairment of national security or defense." The Comment also cautions that government lawyers have confidentiality obligations under many federal statutes and regulations, so "in addition to determining the extent to which Rule 1.6 applies to a given situation, it is always advisable for Government lawyers to review the applicable Federal law . . . and to consult with their supervisors.''

Restatement of the Law Governing Lawyers: The American Law Institute has tentatively approved the following provisions:

§26. *Formation of Client-Lawyer Relationship*

A relationship of client and lawyer arises when:

(1) a person manifests to a lawyer the person's intent that the lawyer provide legal services for the person; and either

(a) the lawyer manifests to the person consent to do so; or

(b) the lawyer fails to manifest lack of consent to do so, and the lawyer knows or reasonably should know that the person reasonably relies on the lawyer to provide the services; or

(2) a tribunal with power to do so appoints the lawyer to provide the services.

§27. *Lawyer's Duties to Prospective Client*

When a person discusses with a lawyer the possibility of their forming a client-lawyer relationship for a matter or matters, and no such relationship ensues, the lawyer must:

(1) protect the person's confidential information by:

(a) not subsequently using or disclosing confidential information learned in the consultation, except to the extent permitted with respect to confidential information of a client; and

(b) not representing a client whose interests are materially adverse to those of the prospective client in the same or a substantially related matter, but only when the lawyer (or another lawyer whose disqualification is imputed to the lawyer under the standards of §§203 & 204) has received from the prospective client confidential information that could be significantly harmful to the prospective client in the matter, unless:

(i) any personally-prohibited lawyer is screened as stated in §204(2)(b) & (c); or

(ii) both the affected client and the prospective client have given informed consent to the representation under the limitations and conditions provided in §202;

(2) protect the person's property in the lawyer's custody as stated in §§56-58; and

(3) use reasonable care to the extent the lawyer gives the person legal advice or provides other legal services for the person.

(Restatement §§56-57 are reprinted after Model Rule 1.15; §58 is reprinted after Rule 1.6; §202 is reprinted after Rule 1.7; and §§203-204 are reprinted after Rule 1.10.)

§73. Duty of Care to Certain Non-Clients

For purposes of liability under §71, a lawyer owes a duty to use care within the meaning of §74:

. . . .

(4) to a non-client when and to the extent that:

(b) circumstances known to the lawyer make it clear that appropriate action by the lawyer is necessary with respect to a matter within the scope of the representation to prevent or rectify the breach of a fiduciary duty owed by the client to the non-client, where (i) the breach is a crime or fraud or (ii) the lawyer has assisted or is assisting the breach;

(c) the non-client is not reasonably able to protect its rights; and

(d) such a duty would not significantly impair the performance of the lawyer's obligations to the client [; and

[(5) to a non-client when and to the extent that circumstances known to the lawyer make it clear that appropriate action by the lawyer is necessary with respect to a matter within the scope of the representation to prevent the client from committing a crime imminently threatening to cause death or serious bodily injury to an identifiable person who is unaware of the risk and the lawyer's act has facilitated the crime].

Editors' Note. The Reporter wrote the following footnote to explain why §73(5) appears in brackets:

By a vote of 17-14, the Council directed in 1996 that the text appearing in brackets as Subsection (5) and the accompanying Comment *i* . . . be deleted from the text tentatively approved. Nonetheless, for the information of members, the Council authorized the printing of the deleted subsection and Comment in Tentative Draft No. 8.

(Restatement §§71 and 74 and the remainder of §73 are reprinted after Model Rule 1.1.)

§111. Definition of "Confidential Client Information"

Confidential client information consists of information relating to that client, acquired by a lawyer or agent of the lawyer in the course of or as the result of representing the client, other than information that is generally known.

§112. Lawyer's Duty to Safeguard Confidential Client Information

(1) Except as provided in §§113-117A, during and after representation of a client:

(a) the lawyer may not use or disclose confidential client information as defined in §111 if there is a reasonable prospect that doing so will adversely affect a material interest of the client or if the client has instructed the lawyer not to use or disclose such information;

(b) the lawyer must take steps reasonable in the circumstances to protect confidential client information against impermissible use or disclosure by the lawyer's associates or agents that may adversely affect a material interest of the client or otherwise than as instructed by the client.

(2) Except as stated in §114, a lawyer who uses confidential information of a client for the lawyer's pecuniary gain other than in the practice of law must account to the client for any profits made.

§113. *Using or Disclosing Information to Advance Client Interests*

A lawyer may use or disclose confidential client information when the lawyer reasonably believes that doing so will advance the interests of the client in the representation.

§114. *Using or Disclosing Information with Client Consent*

A lawyer may use or disclose confidential client information when the client consents after being adequately informed concerning the use or disclosure.

§115. *Using or Disclosing Information When Required by Law*

A lawyer may use or disclose confidential client information when required by law, after the lawyer takes reasonably appropriate steps to assert that the information is privileged or otherwise protected against disclosure.

§116. *Using or Disclosing Information in Lawyer's Self-Defense*

A lawyer may use or disclose confidential client information when and to the extent that the lawyer reasonably believes it necessary in order to defend the lawyer or the lawyer's associate or agent against a charge or threatened charge by any person that the lawyer or such associate or agent acted wrongfully in the course of representing that client.

§117. *Using or Disclosing Information in Compensation Dispute*

A lawyer may use or disclose confidential client information when and to the extent that the lawyer reasonably believes necessary in order to permit the lawyer to resolve a dispute with the client concerning compensation or reimbursements that the lawyer reasonably claims to be due.

The following provision, §117A, has not been approved by the American Law Institute. At the ALI's May 1996 Annual Meeting, the membership of the ALI voted in favor of two amendments — one eliminating the requirement that the threat to human life be the result of an act by the *client*, and the other permitting a lawyer to make sufficient disclosures to rectify client frauds under certain circumstances. The membership then remanded the provision to the Reporter for revision in conformance with the amendments. As of our press deadline in September of 1997, the Reporter had not yet published a revised version of §117A.

*§117A. Using or Disclosing Information to Prevent Death, Serious
Bodily Injury, or Substantial Financial Loss*

(1) A lawyer may use or disclose confidential client information when and to the extent the lawyer reasonably believes necessary to prevent:

(a) death or serious bodily injury from occurring as the result of a crime that the client has committed or intends to commit; or

(b) substantial financial loss from occurring as the result of a crime or fraud that the client has committed or intends to commit [and in the commission of which the lawyer's services were or are being employed].

(2) In a situation described in Subsection (1), if the client has acted at the time the lawyer learns of the threat of an injury or loss to a victim, use or disclosure is permissible only if the injury or loss has not yet occurred.

(3) Before using or disclosing information pursuant to Subsection (1) or (2), if feasible, the lawyer must make a good faith effort to persuade the client either not to act or, if the client has already acted, to warn the victim.

Rule 1.7 Conflict of Interest: General Rule

(a) A lawyer shall not represent a client if the representation of that client will be directly adverse to another client, unless:

(1) the lawyer reasonably believes the representation will not adversely affect the relationship with the other client; and

(2) each client consents after consultation.

(b) A lawyer shall not represent a client if the representation of that client may be materially limited by the lawyer's responsibilities to another client or to a third person, or by the lawyer's own interests, unless:

(1) the lawyer reasonably believes the representation will not be adversely affected; and

(2) the client consents after consultation. When representation of multiple clients in a single matter is undertaken, the consultation shall include explanation of the implications of the common representation and the advantages and risks involved.

COMMENT

Loyalty to a Client

[1] Loyalty is an essential element in the lawyer's relationship to a client. An impermissible conflict of interest may exist before representation is undertaken, in which event the representation should be declined. The lawyer should adopt reasonable procedures, appropriate for the size and type of firm and practice, to determine in both litigation and non-

litigation matters the parties and issues involved and to determine whether there are actual or potential conflicts of interest.

> **Editors' Note.**   The last sentence of paragraph 1 of the Comment was added by the ABA House of Delegates in 1987.

[2] If such a conflict arises after representation has been undertaken, the lawyer should withdraw from the representation. See Rule 1.16. Where more than one client is involved and the lawyer withdraws because a conflict arises after representation, whether the lawyer may continue to represent any of the clients is determined by Rule 1.9. See also Rule 2.2(c). As to whether a client-lawyer relationship exists or, having once been established, is continuing, see Comment to Rule 1.3 and Scope.

[3] As a general proposition, loyalty to a client prohibits undertaking representation directly adverse to that client without that client's consent. Paragraph (a) expresses that general rule. Thus, a lawyer ordinarily may not act as advocate against a person the lawyer represents in some other matter, even if it is wholly unrelated. On the other hand, simultaneous representation in unrelated matters of clients whose interests are only generally adverse, such as competing economic enterprises, does not require consent of the respective clients. Paragraph (a) applies only when the representation of one client would be directly adverse to the other.

[4] Loyalty to a client is also impaired when a lawyer cannot consider, recommend or carry out an appropriate course of action for the client because of the lawyer's other responsibilities or interests. The conflict in effect forecloses alternatives that would otherwise be available to the client. Paragraph (b) addresses such situations. A possible conflict does not itself preclude the representation. The critical questions are the likelihood that a conflict will eventuate and, if it does, whether it will materially interfere with the lawyer's independent professional judgment in considering alternatives or foreclose courses of action that reasonably should be pursued on behalf of the client. Consideration should be given to whether the client wishes to accommodate the other interest involved.

Consultation and Consent

[5] A client may consent to representation notwithstanding a conflict. However, as indicated in paragraph (a)(1) with respect to represen-

tation directly adverse to a client, and paragraph (b)(1) with respect to material limitations on representation of a client, when a disinterested lawyer would conclude that the client should not agree to the representation under the circumstances, the lawyer involved cannot properly ask for such agreement or provide representation on the basis of the client's consent. When more than one client is involved, the question of conflict must be resolved as to each client. Moreover, there may be circumstances where it is impossible to make the disclosure necessary to obtain consent. For example, when the lawyer represents different clients in related matters and one of the clients refuses to consent to the disclosure necessary to permit the other client to make an informed decision, the lawyer cannot properly ask the latter to consent.

Lawyer's Interests

[6] The lawyer's own interests should not be permitted to have adverse effect on representation of a client. For example, a lawyer's need for income should not lead the lawyer to undertake matters that cannot be handled competently and at a reasonable fee. See Rules 1.1 and 1.5. If the probity of a lawyer's own conduct in a transaction is in serious question, it may be difficult or impossible for the lawyer to give a client detached advice. A lawyer may not allow related business interests to affect representation, for example, by referring clients to an enterprise in which the lawyer has an undisclosed interest.

Conflicts in Litigation

[7] Paragraph (a) prohibits representation of opposing parties in litigation. Simultaneous representation of parties whose interests in litigation may conflict, such as co-plaintiffs or co-defendants, is governed by paragraph (b). An impermissible conflict may exist by reason of substantial discrepancy in the parties' testimony, incompatibility in positions in relation to an opposing party or the fact that there are substantially different possibilities of settlement of the claims or liabilities in question. Such conflicts can arise in criminal cases as well as civil. The potential for conflict of interest in representing multiple defendants in a criminal case is so grave that ordinarily a lawyer should decline to represent more than one co-defendant. On the other hand, common representation of persons having similar interests is proper if the risk of adverse effect is minimal and the requirements of paragraph (b) are met. Compare Rule 2.2 involving intermediation between clients.

[8] Ordinarily, a lawyer may not act as advocate against a client the lawyer represents in some other matter, even if the other matter is wholly unrelated. However, there are circumstances in which a lawyer may act as advocate against a client. For example, a lawyer representing an enterprise with diverse operations may accept employment as an advocate against the enterprise in an unrelated matter if doing so will not adversely affect the lawyer's relationship with the enterprise or conduct of the suit and if both clients consent upon consultation. By the same token, government lawyers in some circumstances may represent government employees in proceedings in which a government agency is the opposing party. The propriety of concurrent representation can depend on the nature of the litigation. For example, a suit charging fraud entails conflict to a degree not involved in a suit for a declaratory judgment concerning statutory interpretation.

[9] A lawyer may represent parties having antagonistic positions on a legal question that has arisen in different cases, unless representation of either client would be adversely affected. Thus, it is ordinarily not improper to assert such positions in cases pending in different trial courts, but it may be improper to do so in cases pending at the same time in an appellate court.

Interest of Person Paying for a Lawyer's Service

[10] A lawyer may be paid from a source other than the client, if the client is informed of that fact and consents and the arrangement does not compromise the lawyer's duty of loyalty to the client. See Rule 1.8(f). For example, when an insurer and its insured have conflicting interests in a matter arising from a liability insurance agreement, and the insurer is required to provide special counsel for the insured, the arrangement should assure the special counsel's professional independence. So also, when a corporation and its directors or employees are involved in a controversy in which they have conflicting interests, the corporation may provide funds for separate legal representation of the directors or employees, if the clients consent after consultation and the arrangement ensures the lawyer's professional independence.

Other Conflict Situations

[11] Conflicts of interest in contexts other than litigation sometimes may be difficult to assess. Relevant factors in determining whether there

is potential for adverse effect include the duration and intimacy of the lawyer's relationship with the client or clients involved, the functions being performed by the lawyer, the likelihood that actual conflict will arise and the likely prejudice to the client from the conflict if it does arise. The question is often one of proximity and degree.

[12] For example, a lawyer may not represent multiple parties to a negotiation whose interests are fundamentally antagonistic to each other, but common representation is permissible where the clients are generally aligned in interest even though there is some difference of interest among them.

[13] Conflict questions may also arise in estate planning and estate administration. A lawyer may be called upon to prepare wills for several family members, such as husband and wife, and, depending upon circumstances, a conflict of interest may arise. In estate administration the identity of the client may be unclear under the law of a particular jurisdiction. Under one view, the client is the fiduciary; under another view the client is the estate or trust, including its beneficiaries. The lawyer should make clear the relationship to the parties involved.

[14] A lawyer for a corporation or other organization who is also a member of its board of directors should determine whether the responsibilities of the two roles may conflict. The lawyer may be called on to advise the corporation in matters involving actions of the directors. Consideration should be given to the frequency with which such situations may arise, the potential intensity of the conflict, the effect of the lawyer's resignation from the board and the possibility of the corporation's obtaining legal advice from another lawyer in such situations. If there is material risk that the dual role will compromise the lawyer's independence of professional judgment, the lawyer should not serve as a director.

Conflict Charged by an Opposing Party

[15] Resolving questions of conflict of interest is primarily the responsibility of the lawyer undertaking the representation. In litigation, a court may raise the question when there is reason to infer that the lawyer has neglected the responsibility. In a criminal case, inquiry by the court is generally required when a lawyer represents multiple defendants. Where the conflict is such as clearly to call in question the fair or efficient administration of justice, opposing counsel may properly raise the question. Such an objection should be viewed with caution, however, for it can be misused as a technique of harassment. See Scope.

Model Code Comparison

DR 5-101(A) provided that ''[e]xcept with the consent of his client after full disclosure, a lawyer shall not accept employment if the exercise of his professional judgment on behalf of the client will be or reasonably may be affected by his own financial, business, property, or personal interests.'' DR 5-105(A) provided that a lawyer ''shall decline proffered employment if the exercise of his independent professional judgment in behalf of a client will be or is likely to be adversely affected by the acceptance of the proffered employment, or if it would be likely to involve him in representing differing interests, except to the extent permitted under DR 5-105(C).'' DR 5-105(C) provided that ''a lawyer may represent multiple clients if it is obvious that he can adequately represent the interest of each and if each consents to the representation after full disclosure of the possible effect of such representation on the exercise of his independent professional judgment on behalf of each.'' DR 5-107(B) provided that a lawyer ''shall not permit a person who recommends, employs, or pays him to render legal services for another to direct or regulate his professional judgment in rendering such services.''

Rule 1.7 clarifies DR 5-105(A) by requiring that, when the lawyer's other interests are involved, not only must the client consent after consultation but also that, independent of such consent, the representation reasonably appears not to be adversely affected by the lawyer's other interests. This requirement appears to be the intended meaning of the provision in DR 5-105(C) that ''it is obvious that he can adequately represent'' the client, and was implicit in EC 5-2, which stated that a lawyer ''should not accept proffered employment if his personal interests or desires will, or there is a reasonable probability that they will, affect adversely the advice to be given or services to be rendered the prospective client.''

Cross-References in Rules

Rule 1.8, Comment 4: When a lawyer allows a third party to pay a client's fee, the arrangement must ''conform to the requirements of . . . **Rule 1.7** concerning conflict of interest.''

Rule 1.8, Comment 5: ''Related lawyers in the same firm are governed by **Rules 1.7,** 1.9, and 1.10.''

Rule 1.9, Comment 1: ''The principles in **Rule 1.7** determine whether the interest of the present and former client are adverse.''

Rule 1.9, Comment 14: ''With regard to an opposing party's raising a question of conflict of interest, see Comment to **Rule 1.7.''**

Rule 1.10(a): ''While lawyers are associated in a firm, none of them shall knowingly represent a client when any one of them practicing alone would be prohibited from doing so by **Rules 1.7,** 1.8(c), 1.9 or 2.2.''

Rule 1.10(c): ''A disqualification prescribed by this rule may be waived by the affected client under the conditions stated in **Rule 1.7.''**

Rule 1.10, Comment 4: A lawyer changing from government to private practice, or vice versa, "is bound by the Rules generally, including **Rules** 1.6, **1.7,** and 1.9."

Rule 1.10, Comment 7: Despite Rule 1.10(b), a law firm "may not represent a person with interests adverse to those of a present client of the firm, which would violate **Rule 1.7.**"

Rule 1.11, Comment 2: "A lawyer representing a government agency, whether employed or specially retained by the government, is subject to the Rules of Professional Conduct, including the prohibition against representing adverse interests stated in **Rule 1.7.** . . ."

Rule 1.11, Comment 8: "Paragraphs (a) and (c) do not prohibit a lawyer from jointly representing a private party and a government agency when doing so is permitted by **Rule 1.7** and is not otherwise prohibited by law."

Rule 1.13(e): "A lawyer representing an organization may also represent any of its directors, officers, employees, members, shareholders or other constituents, subject to the provisions of **Rule 1.7.** If the organization's consent to the dual representation is required by **Rule 1.7,** the consent shall be given by an appropriate official of the organization other than the individual who is to be represented, or by the shareholders."

Rule 1.13, Comment 12: If a claim involves "serious charges of wrongdoing by those in control of the organization, a conflict may arise between the lawyer's duty to the organization and the lawyer's relationship with the board. In those circumstances, **Rule 1.7** governs who should represent the directors and the organization."

Rule 1.17, Comment 5 provides that if the purchaser of a law practice "is unable to undertake all client matters because of a conflict of interest in a specific matter respecting which the purchaser is not permitted by **Rule 1.7** or another rule to represent the client, the requirement of Rule 1.17 that there be a single purchaser is nevertheless satisfied."

Rule 1.17, Comment 11 provides that a lawyer selling a law practice has an "obligation to avoid disqualifying conflicts, and to secure client consent after consultation for those conflicts which can be agreed to (see **Rule 1.7**)."

Rule 2.2: There is no formal reference to **Rule 1.7,** but note the close parallel between **Rule 1.7(b)(2)** and Rule 2.2(a)(1).

Rule 3.7(b): "A lawyer may act as advocate in a trial in which another lawyer in the lawyer's firm is likely to be called as a witness unless precluded from doing so by **Rule 1.7** or Rule 1.9."

Rule 3.7, Comment 5: "Whether the combination of roles involves an improper conflict of interest with respect to the client is determined by **Rule 1.7** or 1.9. . . . Determining whether or not such a conflict exists is primarily the responsibility of the lawyer involved. See Comment to **Rule 1.7.**"

Rule 5.2, Comment 2: "[I]f a question arises whether the interests of two clients conflict under **Rule 1.7,** the supervisor's reasonable resolution of the question should protect the subordinate professionally if the resolution is subsequently challenged."

Rule 5.7, Comment 8: "When a lawyer is obliged to accord the recipients of such [law-related] services the protections of those Rules that apply to the client-lawyer relationship, the lawyer must take special care to heed the proscriptions of the Rules addressing conflicts of interest (**Rules 1.7** through 1.11), especially **Rules 1.7(b)** and **1.8(a), (b)** and **(f)**. . . ."

Rule 6.4, Comment: In determining the nature and scope of law reform activities, "a lawyer should be mindful of obligations to clients under other Rules, particularly **Rule 1.7.**"

Rule 6.3(a): A lawyer "shall not knowingly participate in a decision or action" of a legal services organization "if participating in the decision or action would be incompatible with the lawyer's obligation to a client under **Rule 1.7.**"

Legislative History

1980 Discussion Draft (then Rule 1.8) provided as follows:

> In circumstances in which a lawyer has interests, commitments, or responsibilities that may adversely affect the representation of a client, a lawyer shall not represent the client unless:
>
> > (a) the Services contemplated in the representation can otherwise be performed in accordance with the rules of professional conduct; and
> >
> > (b) the client consents after adequate disclosure of the circumstances.

1981 Draft:

> (a) A lawyer shall not represent a client if the lawyer's ability to consider, recommend or carry out a course of action on behalf of the client will be adversely affected by the lawyer's responsibilities to another client or to a third person, or by the lawyer's own interests.
>
> (b) When a lawyer's own interests or other responsibilities might adversely affect the representation of a client, the lawyer shall not represent the client unless:
>
> > (1) the lawyer reasonably believes the other responsibilities or interests involved will not adversely affect the best interest of the client; and . . .

1982 Draft was adopted.

1987 Amendment: The ABA House of Delegates added the last sentence of Comment 1 to Rule 1.7, and placed other parts of Comment 1 into a separate paragraph, which is now Comment 2.

Selected State Variations

Alaska: Rule 1.7(a) restricts directly adverse representation only "in the same or a substantially related matter." Alaska adds Rule 1.7(c), which provides that a lawyer "shall act with reasonable diligence in determining whether a conflict of interest, as described in paragraphs (a) and (b) of this rule, or Rules 1.8, 1.9 and 1.10 exists." Alaska's Comment explains: "Substantial delay in litigation may occur as a result of a conflict of interest unless prompt efforts are made to discover any such conflicts. A lawyer should take all reasonable measures to determine whether or not a conflict of interest exists . . . ."

California: See Rule 3-310 (Avoiding the Representation of Adverse Interests). Section 2860 of the California Civil Code, adopted after the important decision in San Diego Credit Union v. Cumis, 162 Cal. App. 3d 358, 208 Cal. Rptr. 494 (1984), seeks to reconcile the multiple interests at stake when an insurance company has a duty to defend an insured whose interests might not be congruent with those of the insurer. The first paragraph of §2860 provides:

> (a) If the provisions of a policy of insurance impose a duty to defend upon an insurer and a conflict of interest arises which creates a duty on the part of the insurer to provide independent counsel to the insured, the insurer shall provide independent counsel to represent the insured unless, at the time the insured is informed that a possible conflict may arise or does exist, the insured expressly waives, in writing, the right to independent counsel. An insurance contract may contain a provision which sets forth the method of selecting that counsel consistent with this section.

The full text of §2860 is set out below in our chapter on Selected California Statutes.

Colorado: Rule 1.7 adds section (c):

> For the purposes of this Rule, a client's consent cannot be validly obtained in those instances in which a disinterested lawyer would conclude that the client should not agree to the representation under the circumstances of the particular situation.

District of Columbia: D.C. Rule 1.7 differs significantly from the ABA Model Rule — see District of Columbia Rules of Professional Conduct below.

Florida: Rule 1.7(a)(1) applies when "the representation will not adversely affect the lawyer's responsibilities to and relationship with the other client."

Georgia retains the language of DR 5-105 except that both (a) and (b) delete the phrase "or if it would be likely to involve him in representing differing interests."

Maine: Rule 3.4(a) provides:

> *Disclosure of Interest.* Before accepting any professional employment, a lawyer shall disclose to the prospective client the lawyer's relationship, if any, with the adverse party; the lawyer's interest, if any, in the subject matter of the employment; all the circumstances regarding the lawyer's relationship to the parties; and any interest or connection with the matter at hand that a lawyer knows or reasonably should know would influence the client in the selection of a lawyer.

Louisiana imports into the text of Rule 1.7 the first sentence of the Comment to ABA Model Rule 1.7: "Loyalty is an essential element in the lawyer's relationship to a client."

Massachusetts: Effective January 1, 1998, Rule 1.7 is identical to the ABA rule, but the comment is substantially different. Among other things, it addresses: the situation of the lawyer who represents one member of a corporate family while opposing another member of the family; the issue of confidentiality and privilege in multiple representation; and the responsibilities of lawyers who represent classes.

New Jersey Rule 1.7(a)(2) provides that "a public entity cannot consent to any such representation." New Jersey also adds Rule 1.7(c):

> (c) This rule shall not alter the effect of case law or ethics opinions to the effect that:
> (1) in certain cases or categories of cases involving conflicts or apparent conflicts, consent to continued representation is immaterial, and
> (2) in certain cases or situations creating an appearance of impropriety rather than an actual conflict, multiple representation is not permissible, that is, in those situations in which an ordinary knowledgeable citizen acquainted with the facts would conclude that the multiple representation poses substantial risk of disservice to either the public interest or the interest of one of the clients.

New York: Same or substantially the same as the ABA Model Code — see Model Code Comparison above.

Ohio: Effective May 1, 1996, Ohio added new subdivisions DR 5-101(A)(2)(3) that provide as follows:

> (2) Notwithstanding the consent of the client, a lawyer shall not knowingly prepare, draft, or supervise the preparation or execution of a will, codicil, or *inter vivos* trust for a client in which any of the following are named as beneficiary:
> (a) the lawyer;
> (b) the lawyer's law partner or a shareholder of the lawyer's firm;
> (c) an associate, paralegal, law clerk, or other employee in the lawyer's firm or office;
> (d) a lawyer acting "of counsel" in the lawyer's firm;
> (e) the spouses, siblings, natural or adoptive children, or natural or adoptive parents of any of those described in . . . this rule.
> (3) Division (A)(2) of this rule shall not apply if the client is related by blood or marriage to the beneficiary within the third degree of relationship as defined by the law of Ohio.

Texas: Rule 1.06 provides:

> (a) A lawyer shall not represent opposing parties to the same litigation.
> (b) In other situations and except to the extent permitted by paragraph (c), a lawyer shall not represent a person if the representation of that person:
> (1) involves a substantially related matter in which that person's interests are materially and directly adverse to the interests of another client of the lawyer or the lawyer's firm; or
> (2) reasonably appears to be or become adversely limited by the lawyer's or law firm's responsibilities to another client or to a third person or by the lawyer's or law firm's own interests.

(c) A lawyer may represent a client in the circumstances described in (b) if:

(1) the lawyer reasonably believes the representation of each client will not be materially affected; and

(2) each affected or potentially affected client consents to such representation after full disclosure of the existence, nature, implications, and possible adverse consequences of the common representation and the advantages involved, if any.

(d) A lawyer who has represented multiple parties in a matter shall not thereafter represent any of such parties in a dispute among the parties arising out of the matter, unless prior consent is obtained from all such parties to the dispute.

(e) If a lawyer has accepted representation in violation of this Rule, or if multiple representation properly accepted becomes improper under this Rule, the lawyer shall promptly withdraw from one or more representations to the extent necessary for any remaining representation not to be in violation of these Rules.

(f) If a lawyer would be prohibited by this Rule from engaging in particular conduct, no other lawyer while a member or associated with that lawyer's firm may engage in that conduct.

The Texas rule thus allows a lawyer to oppose a current client if the matter is not "substantially related" to matters currently handled on behalf of the client. However, in In re Dresser Industries, Inc., 972 F.2d 540 (5th Cir. 1992), the Fifth Circuit refused to apply Texas Rule 1.06 and disqualified a law firm suing a current client in a class action securities case. The *Dresser* court said that conflicts of interest in federal litigation are governed by "national standards," including ABA Model Rule 1.7 and the developing Restatement of the Law Governing Lawyers.

Virginia: Substantially the same as the Model Code.

Washington: Under Rules 1.7(a)(2) and 1.7(b)(2), client consent is effective only if each client "consents *in writing* after consultation and a full disclosure of the material facts (following authorization from the other client to make such a disclosure)." In addition, effective September 1, 1995, Washington added Rule 1.7(c), which provides as follows:

(c) For purposes of this rule, when a lawyer who is not a public officer or employee represents a discrete governmental agency or unit that is part of a broader governmental entity, the lawyer's client is the particular governmental agency or unit represented, and not the broader governmental entity of which the agency or unit is a part, unless:

(1) Otherwise provided in a written agreement between the lawyer and the governmental agency or unit; or

(2) The broader governmental entity gives the lawyer timely written notice to the contrary, in which case the client shall be designated by such entity. Notice under this subsection shall be given by the person designated by law as the chief legal officer of the broader governmental entity, or in the absence of such designation, by the chief executive officer of the entity.

Wisconsin requires that consent under Rule 1.7(a) and (b) be in writing after consultation.

Related Materials

ABA Canons: Canon 6 provided:

6. Adverse Influences and Conflicting Interests

It is the duty of a lawyer at the time of retainer to disclose to the client all the circumstances of his relations to the parties, and any interest in or connection with the controversy, which might influence the client in the selection of counsel.

It is unprofessional to represent conflicting interests, except by express consent of all concerned given after a full disclosure of the facts. Within the meaning of this canon, a lawyer represents conflicting interests when, in behalf of one client, it is his duty to contend for that which duty to another client requires him to oppose.

The obligation to represent the client with undivided fidelity and not to divulge his secrets or confidences forbids also the subsequent acceptance of retainers or employment from others in matters adversely affecting any interest of the client with respect to which confidence has been reposed.

ABA Standards for Imposing Lawyer Sanctions:

4.3. Failure to Avoid Conflicts of Interest

4.31. Disbarment is generally appropriate when a lawyer, without the informed consent of client(s):

(a) engages in representation of a client knowing that the lawyer's interests are adverse to the client's with the intent to benefit the lawyer or another, and causes serious or potentially serious injury to the client; or

(b) simultaneously represents clients that the lawyer knows have adverse interests with the intent to benefit the lawyer or another, and causes serious or potentially serious injury to a client; or

(c) represents a client in a matter substantially related to a matter in which the interests of a present or former client are materially adverse, and knowingly uses information relating to the representation of a client with the intent to benefit the lawyer or another, and causes serious or potentially serious injury to a client.

4.32. Suspension is generally appropriate when a lawyer knows of a conflict of interest and does not fully disclose to a client the possible effect of that conflict, and causes injury or potential injury to a client.

4.33. Reprimand is generally appropriate when a lawyer is negligent in determining whether the representation of a client may be materially affected by the lawyer's own interests, or whether the representation will adversely affect another client, and causes injury or potential injury to a client.

4.34. Admonition is generally appropriate when a lawyer engages in an isolated instance of negligence in determining whether the representation of a client may be materially affected by the lawyer's own interests, or whether the representation will adversely affect another client, and causes little or no actual or potential injury to a client.

American Academy of Matrimonial Lawyers: The "Bounds of Advocacy" drafted by the American Academy of Matrimonial Lawyers contains the following provisions and commentary:

Conflict of Interest

Conflict of interest dilutes a lawyer's loyalty to the client. A lawyer's loyalty may be diluted by a number of personal interests (financial security, prestige, and self-esteem) and interests of third persons (family, friends, business associates, employer, legal profession, and society as a whole). Under the RPC, a conflict exists if the representation of a client "may be materially limited by the lawyer's responsibilities to another client or to a third person, or by the lawyer's own interests." The key to preventing unintentional violations of the conflict of interest rules lies in anticipating the probability or possibility that a conflict situation will develop.

The influences that might dilute a matrimonial lawyer's loyalty to a client are unlimited. The interests of the children, relatives, friends, lovers, employers and the opposing party, along with a perceived obligation to the court and the interest of society, may be compelling in a given case. In family law matters, where "winning" and "losing" in the traditional sense often lose their meaning, determination of the appropriate ethical conduct can be extremely difficult.

2.10 An Attorney should not permit a client's relatives, friends, lovers, employers, or other third persons to interfere with the representation, affect the attorney's independent professional judgment, or make decisions affecting the representation, except with the client's express consent.

Comment to Rule 2.10

Third persons often try to play a part in matrimonial cases. Frequently, the client has requested that one or more of these persons be present at conferences and consulted about major decisions. The potential conflicts are exacerbated when the third person is paying expenses or the attorney's fee. Neither payment of litigation expenses nor sincere concern about the welfare of the client make those third persons clients. To the extent specifically authorized by the client, the lawyer may discuss choices with third parties, provided all concerned are aware that such discussions may waive any attorney-client privilege. While it is important for persons going through a divorce to receive advice and support from those they trust, the client, with the advice of the attorney, should make the decisions with which the client must ultimately live.

2.16 An attorney should never have a sexual relationship with a client or opposing counsel during the time of the representation.

Comment to Rule 2.16

Persons in need of a matrimonial lawyer are often in a highly vulnerable emotional state. Some degree of social contact (particularly if a social relationship existed prior to the events that occasioned the representation) may be desirable, but a more intimate relationship may endanger both the client's welfare and the lawyer's objectivity.

Attorneys are expected to maintain personal relationships with other attorneys, but must be sensitive to the threat to independent judgment and the appearance of impropriety when an intimate relationship exists with opposing counsel or others involved in the proceedings.

2.22 An attorney should not simultaneously represent both a client and a person with whom the client is sexually involved.

Comment to Rule 2.22

A matrimonial lawyer is often asked to represent a client and the client's lover. Joint representation may make it difficult to advise the client of the need to recover from the emotional trauma of divorce, the desirability of a prenuptial agreement, or the dangers of early remarriage. The testimony of either might be adverse to the other at deposition or trial. In addition, the client may desire to waive support payments because she believes she is going to marry her lover. The inherent conflicts in attempting to represent both the client and her lover render such representation improper. Even when the client's new partner is not represented by the attorney, but wishes to participate in consultations and other aspects of the representation, the attorney must be alert to the danger of the client's undermining her own best interests in an effort to accommodate her new partner.

Children

One of the most troubling issues in family law is determining a lawyer's obligations to children. The lawyer must represent the client zealously, but not at the expense of children. The parents' fiduciary obligations for the well-being of a child provide a basis for the attorney's consideration of the child's best interests consistent with traditional adversary and client loyalty principles. It is accepted doctrine that the attorney for a trustee or other fiduciary has an ethical obligation to the beneficiaries to whom the fiduciary's obligations run. To the extent that statutory or decisional law imposes a duty on the parent to act in the child's best interests, the attorney for the parent might be considered to have an obligation to the child that would, in some instances, justify subordinating the express wishes of the parent. For example, "If the lawyer represents the guardian as distinct from the ward, and is aware that the guardian is acting adversely to the ward's interest, the lawyer may have an obligation to prevent or rectify the guardian's misconduct." For this analysis to be of benefit to practitioners, however, a clearer mandate must be adopted as part of the ethical code or its official interpretations.

2.23 In representing a parent, an attorney should consider the welfare of children.

Comment to Rule 2.23

Although the substantive law in most jurisdictions concerning custody, abuse, and termination of parental rights is premised upon the "best interests of the child," the ethical codes provide little (or contradictory) guidance for an attorney whose client's expressed wishes or interests are in direct conflict with the well-being of children. This provision stresses the welfare of a client's children.

3.5 An attorney should discourage the client from interfering in the spouse's effort to obtain effective representation.

Comment to Rule 3.5

Clients who file or anticipate the filing of a divorce proceeding occasionally telephone or interview numerous attorneys as a means of denying their spouse access to effective representation. The attorney should discourage such practices and should not assist the client, for example, by responding to the client's request for a list of matrimonial lawyers if improper motives are suspected. When the client has already contacted other lawyers for the purpose of disqualifying them, the client's attorney should attempt to persuade the client to waive any conflicts so created.

Professional Cooperation and the Administration of Justice

Many jurisdictions have elaborated upon the general principles in this section by adopting codes of professional courtesy. In jurisdictions where such codes have been adopted, matrimonial lawyers should adhere to them scrupulously.

American Lawyer's Code of Conduct: Rules 2.1 and 8.8 provide:

2.1. In a matter entrusted to a lawyer by a client, the lawyer shall give undivided fidelity to the client's interests as perceived by the client, unaffected by any interest of the lawyer or of any other person, or by the lawyer's perception of the public interest.

8.8. A lawyer shall not commence having sexual relations with a client during the lawyer-client relationship.

Comment to Rule 8.8

. . . Rule 8.8 forbids a lawyer to commence having sexual relations with a client during the lawyer-client relationship. This rule . . . recognizes the dependency of a client upon a lawyer, the high degree of trust that a client is entitled to place in a lawyer, and the potential for unfair advantage in such a relationship. Other professionals, such as psychiatrists, have begun to face up to analogous problems.

Paralegal Conflicts: Courts and bar association ethics committees are devoting increasing attention to conflicts caused by paralegals and other members of a lawyer's staff. Guideline 7 of the ABA Model Guidelines for the Utilization of Legal Assistant Services (adopted in 1991) provides:

A lawyer should take reasonable measures to prevent conflicts of interest resulting from a legal assistant's other employment or interests insofar as such other employment or interests would present a conflict of interest if it were that of the lawyer.

Private Securities Litigation Reform Act: In December of 1995, over President Clinton's veto, Congress passed the Private Securities Litigation Reform Act. The new law requires courts hearing securities lawsuits to determine whether a plaintiff lawyer's ownership of securities creates a conflict of interest that disqualifies the lawyer from representing the class.

Restatement of the Law Governing Lawyers: The American Law Institute has tentatively approved the following provisions:

§201. Basic Prohibition of Conflict of Interest

Unless all affected clients and other necessary persons consent to the representation under the limitations and conditions provided in §202, a lawyer may not represent a client if the representation would involve a conflict of interest. A conflict of interest is involved if there is a substantial risk that the lawyer's representation of the client would be materially and adversely affected by the lawyer's own interests or by the lawyer's duties to another current client, a former client, or a third person.

§202. Client Consent to a Conflict of Interest

(1) A lawyer may represent a client notwithstanding a conflict of interest prohibited by §201 if each affected client or former client gives informed consent to the lawyer's representation. Informed consent requires that the client or former client have reasonably adequate information about the material risks of such representation to that client or former client.

(2) Notwithstanding the informed consent of each affected client or former client, a lawyer may not represent a client if:

(a) the representation is prohibited by law;

(b) one client will assert a claim against the other in the same litigation; or

(c) in the circumstances, it is not reasonably likely that the lawyer will be able to provide adequate representation to one or more of the clients.

§206. Lawyer's Personal Interest Affecting Representation of a Client

Unless the affected client consents to the representation under the limitations and conditions provided in §202, a lawyer may not represent a client if there is a substantial risk that the lawyer's representation of the client would be materially and adversely affected by he lawyer's financial or other personal interests.

The following provision, §209, has not been approved by American Law Institute. At its May 1996 Annual Meeting, the membership of the ALI voted to remand §209 to the Reporter for further study. The cause of the remand was a problematic example, in a single sentence in Comment d(iii) to §209, about multiple representation of unsecured creditors in a bankruptcy proceeding. The membership did not express any disagreement with the text of §209, and the Reporter does not contemplate any revision to the text.

§209. Representing Parties with Conflicting Interests in Civil Litigation

Unless all affected clients consent to the representation under the limitations and conditions provided in §202, a lawyer in civil litigation may not:

(1) represent two or more clients in a matter if there is a substantial risk that the lawyer's representation of one of the clients would be materially and adversely affected by the lawyer's duties to another client in the matter; or

(2) represent one client in asserting or defending a claim against another client currently represented by the lawyer, even if the matters are not related.

§210. *Conflicts of Interest in Criminal Litigation*

Unless all affected clients consent to the representation under the limitations and conditions provided in §202, a lawyer in a criminal matter may not represent:

(1) two or more defendants or potential defendants in the same matter; or

(2) a single defendant, if the representation would involve a conflict of interest as defined in §201.

§211. *Multiple Representation in Non-Litigated Matter*

Unless all affected clients consent to the representation under the limitations and conditions provided in §202, a lawyer may not represent two or more clients in a matter not involving litigation if there is a substantial risk that the lawyer's representation of one or more of the clients would be materially and adversely affected by the lawyer's duties to one or more of the other clients.

§216. *Lawyer with Fiduciary or Other Legal Obligation to Third Person*

Unless the affected client consents to the representation under the limitations and conditions provided in §202, a lawyer may not represent a client in any matter with respect to which the lawyer has a fiduciary or other legal obligation to another if there is a substantial risk that the lawyer's representation of the client would be materially and adversely affected by the lawyer's obligation.

With respect to "the implications of the common representation" under Rule 1.7(b), the ALI has tentatively approved the following provisions:

§125. *Privilege of Co-Clients*

(1) If two or more persons are jointly represented by the same lawyer in a matter, a communication of either co-client that otherwise qualifies as privileged under §§118-122 and relates to matters of common interest is privileged as against third persons, and any co-client may invoke the privilege, unless it has been waived by the client who made the communication.

(2) Unless the co-clients have agreed otherwise, a communication described in Subsection (1) is not privileged as between the co-clients in a subsequent adverse proceeding between them.

§126. *Common-Interest Arrangements*

(1) If two or more clients with a common interest in a litigated or non-litigated matter are represented by separate lawyers and they agree to exchange in-

formation concerning the matter, a communication of any such client that otherwise qualifies as privileged under §§118-122 that relates to the matter is privileged as against third persons. Any such client may invoke the privilege, unless it has been waived by the client who made the communication.

(2) Unless the clients have agreed otherwise, a communication described in Subsection (1) is not privileged as between clients described in Subsection (1) in a subsequent adverse proceeding between them.

(Restatement §§118-122 are reprinted below in the chapter on the attorney-client privilege.)

Rule 1.8 Conflict of Interest: Prohibited Transactions

(a) A lawyer shall not enter into a business transaction with a client or knowingly acquire an ownership, possessory, security or other pecuniary interest adverse to a client unless:

(1) the transaction and terms on which the lawyer acquires the interest are fair and reasonable to the client and are fully disclosed and transmitted in writing to the client in a manner which can be reasonably understood by the client;

(2) the client is given a reasonable opportunity to seek the advice of independent counsel in the transaction; and

(3) the client consents in writing thereto.

(b) A lawyer shall not use information relating to representation of a client to the disadvantage of the client unless the client consents after consultation, except as permitted or required by Rule 1.6 or Rule 3.3.

(c) A lawyer shall not prepare an instrument giving the lawyer or a person related to the lawyer as parent, child, sibling, or spouse any substantial gift from a client, including a testamentary gift, except where the client is related to the donee.

(d) Prior to the conclusion of representation of a client, a lawyer shall not make or negotiate an agreement giving the lawyer literary or media rights to a portrayal or account based in substantial part on information relating to the representation.

(e) A lawyer shall not provide financial assistance to a client in connection with pending or contemplated litigation, except that:

(1) a lawyer may advance court costs and expenses of litigation, the repayment of which may be contingent on the outcome of the matter; and

(2) a lawyer representing an indigent client may pay court costs and expenses of litigation on behalf of the client.

(f) A lawyer shall not accept compensation for representing a client from one other than the client unless:

(1) the client consents after consultation;

(2) there is no interference with the lawyer's independence of professional judgment or with the client-lawyer relationship; and

(3) information relating to representation of a client is protected as required by Rule 1.6.

(g) A lawyer who represents two or more clients shall not participate in making an aggregate settlement of the claims of or against the clients, or in a criminal case an aggregated agreement as to guilty or nolo contendere pleas, unless each client consents after consultation, including disclosure of the existence and nature of all the claims or pleas involved and of the participation of each person in the settlement.

(h) A lawyer shall not make an agreement prospectively limiting the lawyer's liability to a client for malpractice unless permitted by law and the client is independently represented in making the agreement, or settle a claim for such liability with an unrepresented client or former client without first advising that person in writing that independent representation is appropriate in connection therewith.

(i) A lawyer related to another lawyer as parent, child, sibling or spouse shall not represent a client in a representation directly adverse to a person who the lawyer knows is represented by the other lawyer except upon the consent by the client after consultation regarding the relationship.

(j) A lawyer shall not acquire a proprietary interest in the cause of action or subject matter of litigation the lawyer is conducting for a client, except that the lawyer may:

(1) acquire a lien granted by law to secure the lawyer's fee or expenses; and

(2) contract with a client for a reasonable contingent fee in a civil case.

COMMENT

Transactions Between Client and Lawyer

[1] As a general principle, all transactions between client and lawyer should be fair and reasonable to the client. In such transactions a review by independent counsel on behalf of the client is often advisable. Furthermore, a lawyer may not exploit information relating to the representation to the client's disadvantage. For example, a lawyer who has learned

that the client is investing in specific real estate may not, without the client's consent, seek to acquire nearby property where doing so would adversely affect the client's plan for investment. Paragraph (a) does not, however, apply to standard commercial transactions between the lawyer and the client for products or services that the client generally markets to others, for example, banking or brokerage services, medical services, products manufactured or distributed by the client, and utilities services. In such transactions, the lawyer has no advantage in dealing with the client, and the restrictions in paragraph (a) are unnecessary and impracticable.

[2] A lawyer may accept a gift from a client, if the transaction meets general standards of fairness. For example, a simple gift such as a present given at a holiday or as a token of appreciation is permitted. If effectuation of a substantial gift requires preparing a legal instrument such as a will or conveyance, however, the client should have the detached advice that another lawyer can provide. Paragraph (c) recognizes an exception where the client is a relative of the donee or the gift is not substantial.

Literary Rights

[3] An agreement by which a lawyer acquires literary or media rights concerning the conduct of the representation creates a conflict between the interests of the client and the personal interests of the lawyer. Measures suitable in the representation of the client may detract from the publication value of an account of the representation. Paragraph (d) does not prohibit a lawyer representing a client in a transaction concerning literary property from agreeing that the lawyer's fee shall consist of a share in ownership in the property, if the arrangement conforms to Rule 1.5 and paragraph (j).

Person Paying for Lawyer's Services

[4] Rule 1.8(f) requires disclosure of the fact that the lawyer's services are being paid for by a third party. Such an arrangement must also conform to the requirements of Rule 1.6 concerning confidentiality and Rule 1.7 concerning conflict of interest. Where the client is a class, consent may be obtained on behalf of the class by court-supervised procedure.

Family Relationships Between Lawyers

[5] Rule 1.8(i) applies to related lawyers who are in different firms. Related lawyers in the same firm are governed by Rules 1.7, 1.9, and 1.10. The disqualification stated in Rule 1.8(i) is personal and is not imputed to members of firms with whom the lawyers are associated.

Acquisition of Interest in Litigation

[6] Paragraph (j) states the traditional general rule that lawyers are prohibited from acquiring a proprietary interest in litigation. This general rule, which has its basis in common law champerty and maintenance, is subject to specific exceptions developed in decisional law and continued in these Rules, such as the exception for reasonable contingent fees set forth in Rule 1.5 and the exception for certain advances of the costs of litigation set forth in paragraph (e).

[7] This Rule is not intended to apply to customary qualification and limitations in legal opinions and memoranda.

Model Code Comparison

With regard to paragraph (a), DR 5-104(A) provided that a lawyer "shall not enter into a business transaction with a client if they have differing interests therein and if the client expects the lawyer to exercise his professional judgment therein for the protection of the client, unless the client has consented after full disclosure." EC 5-3 stated that a lawyer "should not seek to persuade his client to permit him to invest in an undertaking of his client nor make improper use of his professional relationship to influence his client to invest in an enterprise in which the lawyer is interested."

With regard to paragraph (b), DR 4-101(B)(3) provided that a lawyer should not use "a confidence or secret of his client for the advantage of himself, or of a third person, unless the client consents after full disclosure."

There was no counterpart to paragraph (c) in the Disciplinary Rules of the Model Code. EC 5-5 stated that a lawyer "should not suggest to his client that a gift be made to himself or for his benefit. If a lawyer accepts a gift from his client, he is peculiarly susceptible to the charge that he unduly influenced or overreached the client. If a client voluntarily offers to make a gift to his lawyer, the lawyer may accept the gift, but before doing so, he should urge that the client secure disinterested advice from an independent, competent person who is cognizant of all the circumstances. Other than in exceptional circumstances, a lawyer should insist that an instrument in which his client desires to name him beneficially be prepared by another lawyer selected by the client."

Paragraph (d) is substantially similar to DR 5-104(B), but refers to "literary or media" rights, a more generally inclusive term than "publication" rights.

Paragraph (e)(1) is similar to DR 5-103(B), but eliminates the requirement that "the client remains ultimately liable for such expenses."

Paragraph (e)(2) has no counterpart in the Model Code.

Paragraph (f) is substantially identical to DR 5-107(A)(1).

Paragraph (g) is substantially identical to DR 5-106.

The first clause of paragraph (h) is similar to DR 6-102(A). There was no counterpart in the Model Code to the second clause of paragraph (h).

Paragraph (i) has no counterpart in the Model Code.

Paragraph (j) is substantially identical to DR 5-103(A).

Cross-References in Rules

Rule 1.5, Comment 2: "A lawyer may accept property in payment for services . . . this does not involve acquisition of a proprietary interest in the cause of action or subject matter of the litigation contrary to **Rule 1.8(j).**"

Rule 1.6, Comment 15: "Neither this Rule nor **Rule 1.8(b)** . . . prevents the lawyer from giving notice of the fact of withdrawal, and the lawyer may also withdraw or disaffirm any opinion, document, affirmation, or the like."

Rule 1.7, Comment 10: "A lawyer may be paid from a source other than the client, if the client is informed of that fact and consents and the arrangement does not compromise the lawyer's duty of loyalty to the client. See **Rule 1.8(f).**"

Rule 1.10(a): "While lawyers are associated in a firm, none of them shall knowingly represent a client when any one of them practicing alone would be prohibited from doing so by **Rules** 1.7, **1.8(c),** 1.9 or 2.2."

Rule 1.13, Comment 6: Rule 1.13 "does not limit or expand the lawyer's responsibility under" **Rule 1.8.**

Rule 5.7, Comment 4: "When a client-lawyer relationship exists with a person who is referred by a lawyer to a separate law-related service entity controlled by the lawyer, individually or with others, the lawyer must comply with **Rule 1.8(a).**"

Rule 5.7, Comment 8: "When a lawyer is obliged to accord the recipients of such [law-related] services the protections of those Rules that apply to the client-lawyer relationship, the lawyer must take special care to heed the proscriptions of the Rules addressing conflicts of interest (**Rules** 1.7 through 1.11), especially **Rules 1.7(b)** and **1.8(a), (b)** and **(f)**. . . ."

Legislative History

1979 Unofficial Pre-Circulation Draft:

(e) A lawyer shall not provide financial assistance to a client in connection with pending or contemplated litigation, except that a lawyer may advance expenses, including:

Alternative (1): Court costs, expenses of investigation, medical and other experts, and obtaining and presenting evidence.

Alternative (2): Court costs, expenses of litigation, and living expenses.

1980 Discussion Draft (then called Rule 1.9):

(f) A lawyer may serve as general counsel to a corporation or other organization of which the lawyer is a director only if:

(1) There is adequate disclosure to and consent by all persons having an investment interest in the organization; or

(2) When doing so would not involve serious risk of conflict between the lawyer's responsibilities as general counsel and those as director.

1981 and 1982 Drafts were substantially the same as adopted, except that Rule 1.8(f) contained no restrictions other than the client's consent "after consultation."

Selected State Variations

Alabama adds Rule 1.8(e)(3), which provides as follows:

(3) a lawyer may advance or guarantee emergency financial assistance to the client, the repayment of which may not be contingent on the outcome of the matter, provided that no promise or assurance of financial assistance was made to the client by the lawyer, or on the lawyer's behalf, prior to the employment of the lawyer.

Alabama Rule 1.8(f) allows a lawyer to accept compensation from one other than the client without client consent if the lawyer "is appointed pursuant to an insurance contract." Alabama also adds Rule 1.8(k), which provides as follows:

(k) In no event shall a lawyer represent both parties in a divorce or domestic relations proceeding, or in matters involving custody of children, alimony or child support, whether or not contested. In an uncontested proceeding of this nature a lawyer may have contact with the non-represented party and shall be deemed to have complied with this prohibition if the non-represented party knowingly executes a document that is filed in such proceeding acknowledging:

(1) that the lawyer does not and cannot appear or serve as the lawyer for the non-represented party;

(2) that the lawyer represents only the client and will use the lawyer's best efforts to protect the client's best interests;

(3) that the non-represented party has the right to employ counsel of the party's own choosing and has been advised that it may be in the party's best interest to do so; and

(4) that having been advised of the foregoing, the non-represented party has requested the lawyer to prepare an answer and waiver under which the cause may be submitted without notice and such other pleadings and agreements as may be appropriate.

California: See Rule 3-300 (Avoiding Adverse Interests — compare to Model Rule 1.8(a)); Rule 3-310(E) (compare to Model Rule 1.8(f)); Rule 3-310(C) (compare to Model Rule 1.8(g)); Rule 3-320 (Relationship with Other Party's Lawyer — compare to Model Rule 1.8(i)); Rule 3-400 (Limiting Liability to Client — compare to Model Rule 1.8(h)); and Rule 4-210 (Payment of Personal or Business Expenses Incurred by or for a Client — compare to Model Rule 1.8(e)).

Colorado: Rule 1.8(i) adds "cohabiting relationship" to the list of relationships that require disclosure and consent prior to representation.

Connecticut: Rule 1.8(a) applies to a client "or former client," and Rule 1.8(a)(2) requires that the client "or former client is advised in writing that the client or former client should consider seeking the advice of independent counsel in the transaction and" is given a reasonable opportunity to do so. Connecticut also adds Rule 1.8(a)(4), which provides as follows:

> (4) With regard to a business transaction, the lawyer advises the client or former client in writing either (i) that the lawyer will provide legal services to the client or former client concerning the transaction, or (ii) that the lawyer is involved as a business person only and not as a lawyer representing the client or former client and that the lawyer is not one to whom the client or former client can turn for legal advice concerning the transaction.

In addition, Connecticut's version of Rule 1.8(b) deletes the phrase "except as permitted or required by Rule 1.6 or Rule 3.3."

District of Columbia: D.C. Rule 1.8(d) and (i) differ significantly from the ABA Model Rule — see District of Columbia Rules of Professional Conduct below.

Florida: On April 21, 1994, the Florida Supreme Court *rejected* a petition by 50 Florida lawyers to amend Florida's version of Rule 1.8(e). The petition was opposed by The Florida Bar. The court stated:

> [The] proposed amendment would permit a personal injury lawyer to assist a client in obtaining a third-party loan for ordinary living expense (food, clothing, shelter, and transportation). The lawyer would agree to act as trustee for the lender to ensure repayment from the proceeds of any recovery obtained. The Bar argues that the proposed amendment will result in inevitable conflicts of interest among lawyer, client, and lending institution, as well as discouraging settlements. We agree.

Georgia allows lawyers to advance litigation and related costs but the client must remain "ultimately liable" for them. Financial assistance cannot be guaranteed or advanced. DR 5-103(C).

Illinois: The Illinois version of Rule 1.8(a) provides:

> (a) Unless the client has consented after disclosure, a lawyer shall not enter into a business transaction with the client if:
> > (1) the lawyer knows or reasonably should know that the lawyer and the client have or may have conflicting interests therein; or
> > (2) the client expects the lawyer to exercise the lawyer's professional judgment therein for the protection of the client.

Illinois omits Rule 1.8(b), and modifies Rule 1.8(c) as follows:

(b) Unless all aspects of the matter giving rise to the employment have been concluded, a lawyer shall not enter into any arrangement or understanding with a client or a prospective client by which the lawyer acquires an interest in publication, media, or other literary rights with respect to the subject matter of employment or proposed employment.

Illinois modifies Rule 1.8(e) as follows:

(d) While representing a client in connection with contemplated or pending litigation, a lawyer shall not advance or guarantee financial assistance to the client, except that a lawyer may advance or guarantee the expenses of litigation, including, but not limited to, court costs, expenses of investigation, expenses of medical examination, and costs of obtaining and presenting evidence if:
   (1) the client remains ultimately liable for such expenses; or
   (2) the repayment is contingent on the outcome of the matter; or
   (3) the client is indigent.

Illinois modifies Rule 1.8(h) as follows:

(g) A lawyer shall not settle a claim against the lawyer made by an unrepresented client or former client without first advising that person in writing that independent representation is appropriate in connection therewith.

Illinois adds the following new subparagraph:

(h) A lawyer shall not enter into an agreement with a client or former client limiting or purporting to limit the right of the client or former client to file or pursue any complaint before the Attorney Registration and Disciplinary Commission.

Indiana: Effective February 1, 1996, Indiana added Rule 1.8(k), which prohibits a part-time prosecutor from "representing a private client in any matter wherein exists an issue upon which said prosecutor has statutory prosecutorial authority or responsibilities." The rule does not prohibit representation in "tort cases in which investigation and any prosecution of infractions has terminated," or in "family law matters involving no issue subject to prosecutorial authority or responsibilities."

Louisiana adds the following prior to Rule 1.8(a): "As a general principle, all transactions between client and lawyer should be fair and reasonable to the client. Furthermore, a lawyer may not exploit his representation of a client or information relating to the representation to the client's disadvantage."

Maryland also allows a gift if "the client is represented by independent counsel in connection with the gift."

Massachusetts: Effective January 1, 1998, Rule 1.8(b) forbids a lawyer to use confidential information "for the lawyer's advantage or the advantage of a third person" without consent.

Michigan: Rule 1.8(e)(1) requires nonindigent clients to remain ultimately responsible for advanced costs and expenses.

Minnesota: Rule 1.8(e)(3) allows a lawyer to guarantee a loan necessary for a client to withstand litigation delay.

Montana: On November 21, 1995, the Montana Supreme Court announced an intention to amend Rule 1.8(e) to permit lawyers to make loans to clients for living expenses, and the Court offered a proposed amendment to Rule 1.8(e) for a 150-day public comment period. The proposed amendment would have permitted a lawyer to:

> make or guarantee a loan on fair terms, the repayment of which to the lawyer may be contingent on the outcome of the matter if: (i) the loan is needed to enable the client to withstand delay in litigation that otherwise might unjustly induce the client to settle or dismiss a case because of financial hardship rather than on the merits; (ii) the loan is used only for basic living expenses; (iii) the client faces demonstrable financial hardship that relates to, and arises out of, the injuries and claims for which the lawyer is representing the client; and (iv) the lawyer does not promise, offer, or advertise the loan before being retained by the client.

Until an amended version of Rule 1.8(e) takes effect, the court allowed lawyers to petition for permission to make loans to clients on a case-by-case basis. On July 30, 1996, after considering sixteen public comments on the 1995 proposal (11 opposed, 5 in favor) and after granting five applications by attorneys to make or guarantee loans to clients for basic living expenses, the Montana Supreme Court announced the following amended version of Rule 1.8(e)(3) that permits a lawyer to guarantee a loan to a client but not to make such a loan:

> (3) a lawyer may, for the sole purpose of providing basic living expenses, guarantee a loan from a regulated financial institution whose usual business involves making loans if such loan is reasonably needed to enable the client to withstand delay in litigation that would otherwise put substantial pressure on the client to settle a case because of financial hardship rather than on the merits, provided the client remains ultimately liable for the repayment of the loan without regard to the outcome of the litigation and, further provided that neither the lawyer nor anyone on his/her behalf offers, promises or advertises such financial assistance before being retained by the client.

One of the Justices on the Montana Supreme Court, Justice Charles Erdmann, dissented on numerous grounds.

New Jersey: Rule 1.8(a)(2) adds that the client must be "advised of the desirability of seeking and is given a reasonable opportunity to seek the advice of independent counsel of the client's choice." New Jersey permits agreements prospectively limiting malpractice only when the client rejects the lawyer's advice and the lawyer continues to represent the client. The balance of Rule 1.8(h) is the same as the ABA Model Rule. New Jersey also adds a Rule 1.8(k) making the provisions of Rule 1.7(c) applicable to Rule 1.8. See Selected State Variations under Rule 1.7.

New York: Same or substantially the same as the ABA Model Code — see Model Code Comparison above. See DR 5-103(B)(2), DR 6-102(A), and DR 9-101(D) of the New York Code for the Model Rules' influence.

North Dakota adds Rule 1.8(e)(3), which permits a lawyer to "guarantee a loan reasonably needed to enable the client to withstand delay in litigation that would otherwise put substantial pressure on the client to settle a case because of financial hardship rather than on the merits, provided the client remains ultimately liable for repayment of the loan" and the lawyer did not promise financial assistance before the client retained the lawyer. North Dakota also adds Rule 1.8(i), which allows a lawyer to make an agreement prospectively limiting the lawyer's liability for malpractice in an "emergency" where (1) it is "impractical" to refer to, consult with, or associate with another lawyer, or (2) the client has "unequivocally rejected" the lawyer's advice to consult with or associate with another lawyer and the client "unequivocally" requests the lawyer's "immediate services" after the lawyer has advised the client that the lawyer "does not have the ordinary skill required to give competent representation in the matter." North Dakota Rule 1.8(g) provides that the rule restricting aggregate settlements applies "other than in class actions." In addition, North Dakota adds Rule 1.8(j), which restricts the practice of law by a part-time prosecutor or judge in certain circumstances.

Pennsylvania: Rule 1.8(a) requires the lawyer to advise the client to seek independent advice. In addition, Rule 1.8(c) applies only where the relative is "within the third degree of relationship."

Texas: Rule 1.08(c) and (d) provides:

> (c) Prior to the conclusion of all aspects of the matter giving rise to the lawyer's employment, a lawyer shall not make or negotiate an agreement with a client, prospective client, or former client giving the lawyer literary or media rights to a portrayal or account based in substantial part on information relating to the representation.

> (d) A lawyer shall not provide financial assistance to a client in connection with pending or contemplated litigation or administrative proceedings, except that:

> (1) a lawyer may advance or guarantee court costs, expenses of litigation or administrative proceedings, and reasonably necessary medical and living expenses, the repayment of which may be contingent on the outcome of the matter; and

> (2) a lawyer representing an indigent client may pay court costs and expenses of litigation on behalf of the client.

Virginia differs significantly from the Model Code.

Washington deletes Rule 1.8(e)(2).

Related Materials

ABA Canons: Canons 10, 11, and 38 provided:

10. Acquiring Interest in Litigation

The lawyer should not purchase any interest in the subject matter of the litigation which he is conducting.

11. Dealing with Trust Property

The lawyer should refrain from any action whereby for his personal benefit or gain he abuses or takes advantage of the confidence reposed in him by his client.

38. Compensation, Commissions and Rebates

A lawyer should accept no compensation, commissions, rebates or other advantages from others without the knowledge and consent of his client after full disclosure.

ABA Tort and Insurance Practice Section (TIPS): In April 1991, TIPS approved Guidelines for the Selection and Performance of Retained Counsel. The Guidelines are reprinted in the Fall 1991 issue of The Brief. The following provisions relate to Rule 1.8(f):

*c. Relationships Involving Three Parties — Attorney, Insured, and
Insurer — Must Be Balanced with Legal and Contractual
Obligations*

Counsel is charged with a high degree of care and fidelity to the client. When counsel is retained by an insurer to represent an insured, counsel's duty is owed to both clients to the extent that the interests of each party are aligned. When the interests of the insurer and the insured conflict, counsel's primary duty is to the insured.

When counsel is retained by an insurer to represent an insured and a conflict exists between insured and insurer, counsel for the insured may not provide counsel to the insurer. All potential conflicts between insurer and insured must be identified and disclosed in detail to the insured by the insurer.

If the insurer agrees to retain counsel to defend an insured (a) under a reservation of rights to deny coverage or (b) while contending that some of the allegations asserted against the insured are not covered by the insurance policy, counsel's primary duty is to the insured. In such a case, counsel should defend the action so as to avoid prejudice to, or impairment of, the rights of the insured.

Where there are matters within the policy coverage and matters potentially outside the policy coverage, the insurer should advise the insured of the excess exposure and inform the insured of the right to retain personal counsel.

American Lawyer's Code of Conduct: Rules 5.6, 8.7, and 8.8 provide:

5.6. A lawyer shall not give money or anything of substantial value to any person in order to induce that person to become or to remain a client, or to induce that person to retain or to continue the lawyer as counsel on behalf of someone else. However, a lawyer may (a) advance money to a client on any terms that are fair; (b) give money to a client as an act of charity; (c) give money to a client to enable the client to withstand delays in litigation that would otherwise induce the client to settle a case because of financial hardship, rather than on the merits of the client's claim; or (d) charge a fee that is contingent in whole or in part on the outcome of the case.

8.7. A lawyer shall not enter into a commercial transaction or other business relationship with a person who is or was recently a client, unless that person is represented by independent counsel. This Rule does not affect the specific transactions covered by Chapter V of this Code, relating to retainer agreements and financial arrangements with clients.

8.8. A lawyer shall not commence having sexual relations with a client during the lawyer-client relationship.

Restatement of the Law Governing Lawyers: The American Law Institute has tentatively approved the following provisions:

§48. Forbidden Client-Lawyer Financial Arrangements

(1) A lawyer may not acquire a proprietary interest in the cause of action or subject matter of litigation that the lawyer is conducting for a client, except that the lawyer may:

(a) acquire a lien as provided by §55 to secure the lawyer's fee or expenses; and

(b) contract with a client for a contingent fee in a civil case except when prohibited as stated in §47.

(2) A lawyer may not make or guarantee a loan to a client in connection with pending or contemplated litigation that the lawyer is conducting for the client, except that the lawyer may[:

(a)] make or guarantee a loan covering court costs and expenses of litigation, the repayment of which to the lawyer may be contingent on the outcome of the matter; and

[(b) make or guarantee a loan on fair terms, the repayment of which to the lawyer may be contingent on the outcome of the matter, if

(i) the loan is needed to enable the client to withstand delay in litigation that otherwise might unjustly induce the client to settle or dismiss a case because of financial hardship rather than on the merits; and

(ii) if the lawyer does not promise or offer the loan before being retained.]*

(3) A lawyer may not, before the lawyer ceases to represent a client, make an agreement giving the lawyer literary or media rights to a portrayal or account based in substantial part on information relating to the representation.

(Restatement §47 is reprinted above in the Related Materials following Model Rule 1.5.)

§55. Lawyer Liens

(1) Except as provided in Subsection (2) or by statute or rule, a lawyer does not acquire a lien entitling the lawyer to retain the client's property in the lawyer's possession in order to secure payment of the lawyer's fees and disbursements. A lawyer may decline to deliver to a client or former client an original or copy of any document prepared by the lawyer or at the lawyer's expense if the client or former client has not paid all fees and disbursements due for the lawyer's work in prepar-

---

*The Council [of the American Law Institute] voted in October, 1995, to delete Subsection (2)(b) and its discussion in Comment *c,* but assented to their being printed in brackets in this Proposed Final Draft. Subsection (2)(b) and its discussion in Comment *c* were tentatively approved at the Annual Meeting in 1991. [Footnote by ALI — EDS.]

ing the document and nondelivery would not unreasonably harm the client or former client.

(2) Unless otherwise provided by statute or rule, client and lawyer may agree that the lawyer shall have a security interest in property of the client recovered for the client through the lawyer's efforts, as follows:

(a) the lawyer may contract in writing with the client for a lien on the proceeds of the representation to secure payment for the lawyer's services and disbursements in that matter;

(b) the lien becomes binding on a third party when the party has notice of the lien;

(c) the lien applies only to the amount of fees and disbursements claimed reasonably and in good faith for the lawyer's services performed in the representation; and

(d) the lawyer may not unreasonably impede the speedy and inexpensive resolution of any dispute concerning those fees and disbursements or the lien.

(3) A tribunal where an action is pending may in its discretion adjudicate any fee or other dispute concerning a lien asserted by a lawyer on property of a party to the action, provide for custody of the property, release all or part of the property to the client or lawyer, and grant such other relief as justice may require.

(4) With respect to property neither in the lawyer's possession nor recovered by the client through the lawyer's efforts, the lawyer may obtain a security interest on property of a client only as provided by other law and consistent with §§29A and 207. Acquisition of such a security interest is a business or financial transaction with a client within the meaning of §207.

(Restatement §29A is reprinted following Model Rule 1.5.)

§207. Business Transaction Between Lawyer and Client

A lawyer may not participate in a business or financial transaction with a client, except a standard commercial transaction in which the lawyer does not render legal services, unless:

(1) the client has adequate information about the terms of the transaction and the risks presented by the lawyer's involvement in it;

(2) the terms and circumstances of the transaction are fair and reasonable to the client; and

(3) the client consents to the lawyer's role in the transaction under the limitations and conditions provided in §202 after being encouraged, and given a reasonable opportunity, to seek independent legal advice concerning the transaction.

§208. Client Gift to Lawyer

(1) A lawyer may not prepare any instrument effecting any gift from a client to the lawyer, including a testamentary gift, unless the lawyer is a relative or other natural object of the client's generosity and the gift is not significantly disproportionate to those given other donees similarly related to the donor.

(2) A lawyer may not accept a gift from a client, including a testamentary gift, unless:

    (a) the lawyer is a relative or other natural object of the client's generosity;

    (b) the value conferred by the client and the benefit to the lawyer are insubstantial in amount; or

    (c) the client, before making the gift, has received independent advice or has been encouraged, and given a reasonable opportunity, to seek such advice.

The following provision, §215, has not been approved by the American Law Institute. At its May 1996 Annual Meeting, the membership of the ALI voted to remand §215 to the Reporter for further study and revision.

§215. *Compensation or Direction by Third Person*

(1) A lawyer may not represent a client under circumstances in which someone other than the client will wholly or partly compensate the lawyer for the representation, unless the client consents under the limitations and conditions provided in §202, with knowledge of the circumstances and conditions of the payment.

(2) A lawyer's professional conduct on behalf of a client may be directed by someone other than the client when:

    (a) the direction is reasonable in scope and character, such as by reflecting obligations borne by the person directing the lawyer; and

    (b) the client consents to the direction under the limitations and conditions provided in §202.

(Restatement §202 is reprinted in the Related Materials following Model Rule 1.7. Proposed Restatement §76, parallels Rule 1.8(h), which is reprinted in the Related Materials following Rule 1.1.

Rule 1.9 Conflict of Interest: Former Client

> **Editors' Note.** At its February 1989 Mid-Year Meeting, the ABA House of Delegates amended Rule 1.9 and the Comment to Rule 1.9. The amendments moved the text of former Rule 1.10(b) to Rule 1.9(b), and renumbered former Rule 1.9(b) as new Rule 1.9(c). A brief explanation of the amendment is included in the Legislative History section following the rule.

(a) A lawyer who has formerly represented a client in a matter shall not thereafter represent another person in the same or a substantially related matter in which that person's interests are materially adverse to the interests of the former client unless the former client consents after consultation.

(b) A lawyer shall not knowingly represent a person in the same or a substantially related matter in which a firm with which the lawyer formerly was associated had previously represented a client,

(1) whose interests are materially adverse to that person; and

(2) about whom the lawyer had acquired information protected by Rules 1.6 and 1.9(c) that is material to the matter; unless the former client consents after consultation.

(c) A lawyer who has formerly represented a client in a matter or whose present or former firm has formerly represented a client in a matter shall not thereafter:

(1) use information relating to the representation to the disadvantage of the former client except as Rule 1.6 or Rule 3.3 would permit or require with respect to a client, or when the information has become generally known; or

(2) reveal information relating to the representation except as Rule 1.6 or Rule 3.3 would permit or require with respect to a client.

COMMENT

[1] After termination of a client-lawyer relationship, a lawyer may not represent another client except in conformity with this Rule. The principles in Rule 1.7 determine whether the interests of the present and former client are adverse. Thus, a lawyer could not properly seek to rescind on behalf of a new client a contract drafted on behalf of the former client. So also a lawyer who has prosecuted an accused person could not properly represent the accused in a subsequent civil action against the government concerning the same transaction.

[2] The scope of a "matter" for purposes of this Rule may depend on the facts of a particular situation or transaction. The lawyer's involvement in a matter can also be a question of degree. When a lawyer has been directly involved in a specific transaction, subsequent representation of other clients with materially adverse interests clearly is prohibited. On the other hand, a lawyer who recurrently handled a type of problem for a former client is not precluded from later representing another client in a wholly distinct problem of that type even though the subsequent representation involves a position adverse to the prior client. Similar considerations can apply to the reassignment of military lawyers between defense and prosecution functions within the same military jurisdiction. The underlying question is whether the lawyer was so involved in the matter that the subsequent representation can be justly regarded as a changing of sides in the matter in question.

> **Editors' Note.** Paragraphs 3 through 9 and 11 of the Comment to Rule 1.9 originally appeared as Comments 7 through 15 to Rule 1.10. In 1989, the ABA moved the substance of these comments, with minor modifications, to Rule 1.9.

Lawyers Moving Between Firms

[3] When lawyers have been associated in a firm but then end their association, the question of whether a lawyer should undertake representation is more complicated. There are several competing considerations. First, the client previously represented by the former firm must be reasonably assured that the principle of loyalty to the client is not compromised. Second, the rule should not be so broadly cast as to preclude other persons from having reasonable choice of legal counsel. Third, the rule should not unreasonably hamper lawyers from forming new associations and taking on new clients after having left a previous association. In this connection, it should be recognized that today many lawyers practice in firms, many to some degree limit their practice to one field or another, and many move from one association to another several times in their careers. If the concept of imputed disqualification were applied with unqualified rigor, the result would be radical curtailment of the opportunity of lawyers to move from one practice setting to another and of the opportunity of clients to change counsel.

[4] Reconciliation of these competing principles in the past has been attempted under two rubrics. One approach has been to seek per se rules of disqualification. For example, it has been held that a partner in a law firm is conclusively presumed to have access to all confidences concerning all clients of the firm. Under this analysis, if a lawyer has been a partner in one law firm and then becomes a partner in another law firm, there may be a presumption that all confidences known by a partner in the first firm are known to all partners in the second firm. This presumption might properly be applied in some circumstances, for example, where the client has been represented on many matters by numerous lawyers in the firm. This presumption may, however, be unrealistic in other circumstances, for example, where the client has been represented in a single matter of short duration by only one or two lawyers in a larger firm such that broad dissemination of client confidences within the firm is unlikely. Furthermore, such a rigid rule exaggerates the difference between a partner and an associate in modern law firms.

[5] The other rubric formerly used for dealing with disqualification is the appearance of impropriety proscribed in Canon 9 of the ABA Model

Code of Professional Responsibility. This rubric has a twofold problem. First, the appearance of impropriety can be taken to include any new client-lawyer relationship that might make a former client feel anxious. If that meaning were adopted, disqualification would become little more than a question of subjective judgment by the former client. Second, since "impropriety" is undefined, the term "appearance of impropriety" is question-begging. It therefore has to be recognized that the problem of disqualification cannot be properly resolved either by simple analogy to a lawyer practicing alone or by the very general concept of appearance of impropriety.

[6] A rule based on a functional analysis is more appropriate for determining the question of disqualification. Two functions are involved: preserving confidentiality and avoiding positions adverse to a client.

Confidentiality

[7] Preserving confidentiality is a question of access to information. Access to information, in turn, is essentially a question of fact in particular circumstances, aided by inferences, deductions or working presumptions that reasonably may be made about the way in which lawyers work together. A lawyer may have general access to files of all clients of a law firm and may regularly participate in discussions of their affairs; it should be inferred that such a lawyer in fact is privy to all information about all the firm's clients. In contrast, another lawyer may have access to the files of only a limited number of clients and participate in discussion of the affairs of no other clients; in the absence of information to the contrary, it should be inferred that such a lawyer in fact is privy to information about the clients actually served but not those of other clients.

[8] Application of paragraph (b) depends on a situation's particular facts. In any such inquiry, the burden of proof should rest upon the firm whose disqualification is sought.

[9] Paragraph (b) operates to disqualify the lawyer only when the lawyer involved has actual knowledge of information protected by Rules 1.6 and 1.9(c). Thus, if a lawyer while with one firm acquired no knowledge of information relating to a particular client of the firm, neither the lawyer individually nor the second firm is disqualified from representing another client in the same or a related matter even though the interests of the two clients conflict. See Rule 1.10(b) for the restrictions on a firm once a lawyer has terminated association with the firm.

118

[10] Independent of the question of disqualification of a firm, a lawyer changing professional association has a continuing duty to preserve confidentiality of information about a client formerly represented. See Rules 1.6 and 1.9.

Adverse Positions

[11] The second aspect of loyalty to client is the lawyer's obligation to decline subsequent representations involving positions adverse to a former client arising in substantially related matters. This obligation requires abstention from adverse representation by the individual lawyer involved, but does not properly entail abstention of other lawyers through imputed disqualification. Hence, this aspect of the problem is governed by Rule 1.9(a). Thus, if a lawyer left one firm for another, the new affiliation would not preclude the firms involved from continuing to represent clients with adverse interests in the same or related matters, so long as the conditions of paragraphs (b) and (c) concerning confidentiality have been met.

[12] Information acquired by the lawyer in the course of representing a client may not subsequently be revealed by the lawyer or used by the lawyer to the disadvantage of the client. However, the fact that a lawyer has once served a client does not preclude the lawyer from using generally known information about that client when later representing another client.

[13] Disqualification from subsequent representation is for the protection of clients and can be waived by them. A waiver is effective only if there is disclosure of the circumstances, including the lawyer's intended role in behalf of the new client.

[14] With regard to an opposing party's raising a question of conflict of interest, see Comment to Rule 1.7. With regard to disqualification of a firm with which a lawyer is or was formerly associated, see Rule 1.10.

Model Code Comparison

Editors' Note. The following Model Code Comparison has been revised by the editors to reflect the ABA's 1989 amendments to Rules 1.9 and 1.10.

There was no counterpart to paragraphs (a) and (c) in the Disciplinary Rules of the Model Code. The problem addressed in paragraph (a) was sometimes dealt with under the rubric of Canon 9 of the Model Code, which provided: "A lawyer should avoid even the appearance of impropriety." EC 4-6 stated that the "obligation of a lawyer to preserve the confidences and secrets of his client continues after the termination of his employment."

The provision in paragraph (a) for waiver by the former client is similar to DR 5-105(C).

The exception in the last sentence of paragraph (c) permits a lawyer to use information relating to a former client that is in the "public domain," a use that was also not prohibited by the Model Code, which protected only "confidences and secrets." Since the scope of paragraph (a) is much broader than "confidences and secrets," it is necessary to define when a lawyer may make use of information about a client after the client-lawyer relationship has terminated.

Cross-References in Rules

Terminology: " 'Firm' or 'Law firm' denotes a lawyer or lawyers in a private firm, lawyers employed in the legal department of a corporation or other organization and lawyers employed in a legal services organization. See Comment, **Rule 1.9.**"

Rule 1.7, Comment 2: "Where more than one client is involved and the lawyer withdraws because a conflict arises after representation, whether the lawyer may continue to represent any of the clients is determined by **Rule 1.9.**"

Rule 1.8, Comment 5: "Related lawyers in the same firm are governed by **Rules** 1.7, **1.9,** and 1.10."

Rule 1.10(a): "While lawyers are associated in a firm, none of them shall knowingly represent a client when any one of them practicing alone would be prohibited from doing so by **Rules** 1.7, 1.8(c), **1.9** or 2.2."

Rule 1.10(b)(2): When a lawyer leaves a firm, the firm may represent interests adverse to the departed lawyer's former clients unless "any lawyer remaining in the firm has information protected by **Rules** 1.6 and **1.9(c)** that is material to the matter."

Rule 1.10, Comment 4: A lawyer who moves from government to private practice, or vice versa, "is bound by the Rules generally, including **Rules** 1.6, 1.7, and **1.9.**"

Rule 1.10, Comment 5: "The government is entitled to protection of its client confidences, and therefore to the protections provided in **Rules** 1.6, **1.9(a) and (c),** and 1.11. However, if the more extensive disqualification in Rule **1.9(b)** were applied to former government lawyers, the potential effect on the government would be unduly burdensome. . . . The government's recruitment of lawyers would be seriously impaired if **Rule 1.9(b)** were applied to the government."

Rule 1.10, Comment 6: "When a lawyer moves from one firm to another, the situation is governed by **Rules 1.9(b)** and 1.10(b)."

Rule 1.10, Comment 7: When a lawyer who represents or formerly represented a client leaves a firm, the firm may not represent a person with interests adverse to that client where the matter is the same or substantially related and "any other lawyer currently in the firm has material information protected by **Rules** 1.6 and **1.9(c)**."

Rule 1.11, Comment 1: Rule 1.11 "is a counterpart of **Rule 1.9(b)**, which applies to lawyers moving from one firm to another."

Rule 1.11, Comment 2: "A lawyer representing a government agency . . . is subject to . . . the protections afforded former clients in **Rule 1.9**."

Rule 1.17, Comment 11 provides that a lawyer selling a law practice has an "obligation to protect information relating to the representation (see **Rules** 1.6 and **1.9**)."

Rule 2.2, Comment 10: In a common representation, each client "has the right to . . . the protection of **Rule 1.9** concerning obligations to a former client."

Rule 3.7(b): "A lawyer may act as advocate in a trial in which another lawyer in the lawyer's firm is likely to be called as a witness unless precluded from doing so by Rule 1.7 or **Rule 1.9**."

Rule 3.7, Comment 5: "Whether the combination of roles involves an improper conflict of interest with respect to the client is determined by **Rule** 1.7 or **1.9**."

Rule 5.7, Comment 8: "When a lawyer is obliged to accord the recipients of such [law-related] services the protections of those Rules that apply to the client-lawyer relationship, the lawyer must take special care to heed the proscriptions of the Rules addressing conflicts of interest (**Rules** 1.7 through **1.11**). . . ."

Legislative History

1980 Discussion Draft: Rule 1.9(c) (then Rule 1.10(a)(2)) provided that a lawyer who has represented a client in a matter shall not thereafter "make use of information acquired in service to the client in a manner disadvantageous to the client . . . unless the information has become generally known *or accessible.*"

1981 Draft was substantially the same as adopted.

1982 Draft was adopted.

1989 Amendments: At its February 1989 Mid-Year Meeting, the ABA House of Delegates moved former Rule 1.10(b) to its current position as Rule 1.9(b), amended and renumbered former Rule 1.9(b) as current Rule 1.9(c), and made some minor amendments to the balance of Rule 1.9. The Comments to Rules 1.9 and 1.10 were changed to correspond to these amendments. The Committee Report to the House of Delegates gave the following explanation for amending Rule 1.9(c):*

> The addition of explanatory language to . . . paragraph (c), is intended to eliminate another oversight in the drafting of Rule 1.9. The added language

---

*Committee Reports do not represent official policy of the ABA. They are for information only, and the opinions are those of the authors of the report.

makes clear that a lawyer's duty of confidentiality with respect to former clients applies to clients who were personally represented by the lawyer and to clients who, although not personally represented by the lawyer, were represented by the lawyer's firm. In addition, a prohibition on the "revelation" of confidential information is added to Rule 1.9. As originally drafted, Rule 1.9 prohibited only the "use" of such information to the disadvantage of the former client. . . . The Comments to Rules 1.9 and 1.10 are amended in conformity with the amendments to the black letter Rules.

Selected State Variations

California: See Rule 3-310(E) (regarding employment adverse to former clients), and B & P Code §6068(e) (regarding client confidences).

District of Columbia: D.C. Rule 1.9 differs significantly from the ABA Model Rule — see District of Columbia Rules of Professional Conduct below.

Illinois Rule 1.10(b) provides:

> (b) When a lawyer becomes associated with a firm, the firm may not represent a person in a matter that the firm knows or reasonably should know is the same or substantially related to a matter in which the newly associated lawyer, or a firm with which that lawyer was associated, had previously represented a client whose interests are materially adverse to that person unless:
>
> (1) the newly associated lawyer has no information protected by Rule 1.6 or Rule 1.9 that is material to the matter; or
>
> (2) the newly associated lawyer is screened from any participation in the matter. . . .
>
> (e) For purposes of Rule 1.10, Rule 1.11, and Rule 1.12, a lawyer in a firm will be deemed to have been screened from any participation in a matter if:
>
> (1) the lawyer has been isolated from confidences, secrets, and material knowledge concerning the matter;
>
> (2) the lawyer has been isolated from all contact with the client or any agent, officer, or employee of the client and any witness for or against the client;
>
> (3) the lawyer and the firm have been precluded from discussing the matter with each other; and
>
> (4) the firm has taken affirmative steps to accomplish the foregoing.

Massachusetts: Effective January 1, 1998, Rule 1.9(c) also forbids a lawyer to use confidential information "to the lawyer's advantage, or to the advantage of a third person" without consent.

Michigan and *Pennsylvania* also permit screening of transient lawyers who would otherwise disqualify a firm.

New Jersey adds the following language in Rule 1.10(d): "When lawyers terminate an association in a firm, none of them, nor any other lawyer with whom any of them subsequently becomes associated shall knowingly represent a client when doing so involves a material risk of violating Rule 1.6 or 1.9." Rule 1.9(a) requires "a full disclosure of the circumstances" to the former client as a condition of consent. Rule 1.9(c) applies New Jersey's Rule 1.7(c) to Rule 1.9. See Rule 1.7, Selected State Variations.

New York: Amendments to the New York version of the Code substantially adopt the provisions of Rule 1.9(a) and (c). See New York Code DR 5-105(D) and DR 5-108.

Oregon: DR 5-105(H) and (I), as amended effective January 29, 1997, permit screening but require "the personally disqualified lawyer" and his or her firm to serve affidavits at the outset and, on request, the conclusion of the matter attesting to the screen and its observance.

Texas Rule 1.09 provides:

> (a) Without prior consent, a lawyer who personally has formerly represented a client in a matter shall not thereafter represent another person in a matter adverse to the former client:
>> (1) in which such other person questions the validity of the lawyer's services or work product for the former client;
>> (2) if the representation in reasonable probability will involve a violation of Rule 1.05; or
>> (3) if it is the same or a substantially related matter.

Virginia retains the language of DR 5-105.

Related Materials

ABA Canons: Canon 37 provided:

37. Confidences of a Client

> It is the duty of a lawyer to preserve his client's confidences. This duty outlasts the lawyer's employment. . . .

ABA Standards for Imposing Lawyer Sanctions: See Standard 4.3 in the Related Materials following Model Rule 1.7.

Restatement of the Law Governing Lawyers: The American Law Institute has tentatively approved the following provision:

§213. Representation Adverse to Interest of Former Client

> Unless both the affected present and former clients consent to the representation under the limitations and conditions provided in §202, a lawyer who has represented a client in a matter may not thereafter represent another client in the same or a substantially related matter in which the interests of the former client are materially adverse. The current matter is substantially related to the earlier matter if:
>> (1) the current matter involves the work the lawyer performed for the former client; or
>> (2) there is a substantial risk that representation of the present client will involve the use of information acquired in the course of representing the former client, unless that information has become generally known.

(Restatement §202 is reprinted above in the Related Materials following Model Rule 1.7.)

Rule 1.10 Imputed Disqualification: General Rule

Editors' Note. At its February 1989 Mid-Year Meeting, the ABA House of Delegates amended Rule 1.10 and the Comment to Rule 1.10. The essence of the amendments was to move the text of former Rule 1.10(b) to Rule 1.9(b), change Rule 1.9(b) to 1.9(c), and renumber former Rules 1.10(c) and (d) as new Rules 1.10(b) and (c). A brief explanation of the amendment is included in the Legislative History section following the rule.

(a) While lawyers are associated in a firm, none of them shall knowingly represent a client when any one of them practicing alone would be prohibited from doing so by Rules 1.7, 1.8(c), 1.9 or 2.2.

(b) When a lawyer has terminated an association with a firm, the firm is not prohibited from thereafter representing a person with interests materially adverse to those of a client represented by the formerly associated lawyer, and not currently represented by the firm, unless:

(1) the matter is the same or substantially related to that in which the formerly associated lawyer represented the client; and

(2) any lawyer remaining in the firm has information protected by Rules 1.6 and 1.9(c) that is material to the matter.

(c) A disqualification prescribed by this rule may be waived by the affected client under the conditions stated in Rule 1.7.

COMMENT

Definition of "Firm"

[1] For purposes of the Rules of Professional Conduct, the term "firm" includes lawyers in a private firm, and lawyers employed in the legal department of a corporation or other organization, or in a legal services organization. Whether two or more lawyers constitute a firm within this definition can depend on the specific facts. For example, two practitioners who share office space and occasionally consult or assist each other ordinarily would not be regarded as constituting a firm. However,

if they present themselves to the public in a way suggesting that they are a firm or conduct themselves as a firm, they should be regarded as a firm for purposes of the Rules. The terms of any formal agreement between associated lawyers are relevant in determining whether they are a firm, as is the fact that they have mutual access to confidential information concerning the clients they serve. Furthermore, it is relevant in doubtful cases to consider the underlying purpose of the rule that is involved. A group of lawyers could be regarded as a firm for purposes of the rule that the same lawyer should not represent opposing parties in litigation, while it might not be so regarded for purposes of the rule that information acquired by one lawyer is attributed to another.

[2] With respect to the law department of an organization, there is ordinarily no question that the members of the department constitute a firm within the meaning of the Rules of Professional Conduct. However, there can be uncertainty as to the identity of the client. For example, it may not be clear whether the law department of a corporation represents a subsidiary or an affiliated corporation, as well as the corporation by which the members of the department are directly employed. A similar question can arise concerning an unincorporated association and its local affiliates.

[3] Similar questions can also arise with respect to lawyers in legal aid. Lawyers employed in the same unit of a legal service organization constitute a firm, but not necessarily those employed in separate units. As in the case of independent practitioners, whether the lawyers should be treated as associated with each other can depend on the particular rule that is involved, and on the specific facts of the situation.

[4] Where a lawyer has joined a private firm after having represented the government, the situation is governed by Rule 1.11(a) and (b); where a lawyer represents the government after having served private clients, the situation is governed by Rule 1.11(c)(1). The individual lawyer involved is bound by the Rules generally, including Rules 1.6, 1.7, and 1.9.

[5] Different provisions are thus made for movement of a lawyer from one private firm to another and for movement of a lawyer between a private firm and the government. The government is entitled to protection of its client confidences, and therefore to the protections provided in Rules 1.6, 1.9(a) and (c), and 1.11. However, if the more extensive disqualification in Rule 1.9(b) were applied to former government lawyers, the potential effect on the government would be unduly burdensome. The government deals with all private citizens and organizations, and thus has a much wider circle of adverse legal interests than does any private law firm. In these circumstances, the government's recruitment of lawyers would be seriously impaired if Rule 1.9(b) were applied to the

government. On balance, therefore, the government is better served in the long run by the protections stated in Rule 1.11.

Principles of Imputed Disqualification

[6] The rule of imputed disqualification stated in paragraph (a) gives effect to the principle of loyalty to the client as it applies to lawyers who practice in a law firm. Such situations can be considered from the premise that a firm of lawyers is essentially one lawyer for purposes of the rules governing loyalty to the client, or from the premise that each lawyer is vicariously bound by the obligation of loyalty owed by each lawyer with whom the lawyer is associated. Paragraph (a) operates only among the lawyers currently associated in a firm. When a lawyer moves from one firm to another, the situation is governed by Rules 1.9(b) and 1.10(b).

Editors' Note.   The following paragraph (paragraph 7) was added by the ABA House of Delegates in 1989.

[7] Rule 1.10(b) operates to permit a law firm, under certain circumstances, to represent a person with interests directly adverse to those of a client represented by a lawyer who formerly was associated with the firm. The Rule applies regardless of when the formerly associated lawyer represented the client. However, the law firm may not represent a person with interests adverse to those of a present client of the firm, which would violate Rule 1.7. Moreover, the firm may not represent the person where the matter is the same or substantially related to that in which the formerly associated lawyer represented the client and any other lawyer currently in the firm has material information protected by Rules 1.6 and 1.9(c).

Editors' Note.   At its February 1989 Mid-Year Meeting, the ABA moved the substance of the remaining paragraphs of the original Comment to Rule 1.10 (then paragraphs 7 through 15) to the Comment to Rule 1.9.

Model Code Comparison

DR 5-105(D) provided that "[i]f a lawyer is required to decline or to withdraw from employment under a Disciplinary Rule, no partner, or associate, or any other lawyer affiliated with him or his firm, may accept or continue such employment."

Cross-References in Rules

Rule 1.8, Comment 5: "Related lawyers in the same firm are governed by **Rules** 1.7, 1.9, and **1.10.**"

Rule 1.9, Comment 9: "See **Rule 1.10(b)** for the restrictions on a firm once a lawyer has terminated association with the firm."

Rule 1.9, Comment 14: "With regard to disqualification of a firm with which a lawyer is or was formerly associated, see **Rule 1.10.**"

Rule 3.7, Comment 4: "The principle of imputed disqualification in **Rule 1.10** has no application to" the problem addressed in Rule 3.7(a)(3).

Rule 3.7, Comment: "If a lawyer who is a member of a firm may not act as both advocate and witness by reason of conflict of interest, **Rule 1.10** disqualifies the firm also."

Rule 5.7, Comment 8: "When a lawyer is obliged to accord the recipients of such [law-related] services the protections of those Rules that apply to the client-lawyer relationship, the lawyer must take special care to heed the proscriptions of the Rules addressing conflicts of interest (**Rules 1.7** through **1.11**). . . ."

Legislative History

1980 Discussion Draft had no comparable provision on imputed disqualification.

1981 Draft:

(b) When lawyers terminate an association in a firm, none of them, nor any other lawyer with whom any of them subsequently become associated, shall undertake or continue representation that involves a material risk of revealing information relating to representation of a client in violation of Rule 1.6, or of making use of information to the disadvantage of a former client in violation of Rule 1.9.

1982 Draft:

(b) When lawyers terminate an association in a firm, none of them, nor any other lawyer with whom any of them subsequently becomes associated, shall knowingly represent a client when doing so involves a material risk of violating Rule 1.6 or Rule 1.9.

1989 Amendments: At its 1989 Mid-Year Meeting, the House of Delegates amended Rule 1.10 by moving former Rule 1.10(b) to its current position as Rule 1.9(b), by moving former Rule 1.10(c) to current Rule 1.10(b), by adding a phrase to new Rule 1.10(b), and by moving former Rule 1.10(d) to its current position as Rule 1.10(c). An excerpt from the Committee Report explaining the changes is reprinted in the Legislative History following Rule 1.9. The Committee's explanation regarding the amendment to former Rule 1.10(c) states:*

> Paragraph (c) (now paragraph (b)) of Rule 1.10 was never intended to permit the representation of a client whose interests are directly adverse to the interests of a present client of a firm. Such representation would violate Rule 1.7. In order to make it clear that when a lawyer leaves a law firm, this paragraph does not override the proscription in Rule 1.7, the limiting words "and not currently represented by the firm" are proposed to be added to Rule 1.10(b).

Selected State Variations

Alaska: Rule 1.10(b)(2) applies not only if any *lawyer* in the firm has information by Rule 1.6 or 1.9(c), but also if "the *firm* retains records containing such information."

California: No equivalent.

District of Columbia: D.C. Rule 1.10 differs significantly from the ABA Model Rule — see District of Columbia Rules of Professional Conduct below.

Illinois extends the prohibition of Rule 1.10(a) to any lawyer who "knows or reasonably should know" that another lawyer in the firm is disqualified. Illinois also adds a new provision, Rule 1.10(e), to define "screened." This new provision is quoted in the Selected State Variations following Rule 1.9.

Massachusetts: Effective January 1, 1998, Rule 1.10(d) provides for screening a "personally disqualified lawyer" if he or she "had neither substantial involvement nor substantial material information relating to the matter . . . and is apportioned no part of the fee therefrom." Rule 1.10(e) describes an appropriate screen, which includes a requirement of an affidavit from the lawyer and the firm describing the screening procedures. Provision is made for court reviews of the adequacy of screens.

New Jersey adds the following Rule 1.10(e):

> A disqualification prescribed by this rule may be waived by the affected client under the conditions stated in Rule 1.7 except where prohibited by law or regulation, such as the prohibition against a public entity waiving an attorney conflict of interest.

New York: For New York's imputed disqualification rule, see DR 5-105(D). In addition, on May 22, 1996, New York adopted a unique DR 5-105(E) that requires every law firm to "keep records of prior engagements" and to implement "a system by which proposed engagements are checked against current and previous engagements" so that the lawyers in the firm may comply with DR 5-105(D). Moreover: "Failure to keep records or to have a policy which complies with this subdivision, whether or not a violation of [DR 5-105(D)] occurs, shall be a violation by

---

*Committee Reports do not represent official policy of the ABA. They are for information only, and the opinions are those of the authors of the report.

the firm." Finally, if a violation of DR 5-105(E) is a "substantial factor" in a lawyer's violation of the imputed disqualification rule, then "the firm, as well as the individual lawyer, shall also be responsible for the violation of [DR 5-105(D)]."

Texas Rule 1.09 provides:

> (b) Except to the extent authorized by Rule 1.10 [concerning government lawyers], when lawyers are or have become members of or associated with a firm, none of them shall knowingly represent a client if any one of them practicing alone would be prohibited from doing so by paragraph (a).
>
> (c) When the association of a lawyer with a firm has terminated, the lawyers who were then associated with that lawyer shall not knowingly represent a client if the lawyer whose association with that firm has terminated would be prohibited from doing so by paragraph (a)(1) or if the representation in reasonable probability will involve a violation of Rule 1.05.

Virginia: Substantially the same as the Model Code.

Related Materials

Model Rules of Professional Conduct for Federal Lawyers: Rule 1.10(a) provides that "Government lawyers working in the same Federal Agency are not automatically disqualified from representing a client because any of them practicing alone would be prohibited from doing so by Rules 1.7, 1.8(c), 1.9 or 2.2." The Comment states:

> The circumstances of Government service may require representation of opposing sides by Government lawyers working in the same Federal Agency. Such representation is permissible so long as conflicts of interest are avoided and independent judgment, zealous representation, and protection of client confidences are not compromised. Thus, the principle of imputed disqualification is not automatically controlling for Government lawyers. The knowledge, action, and conflicts of interest of one Government lawyer are not to be imputed to another simply because they operate from the same office. . . .

Restatement of the Law Governing Lawyers: The American Law Institute has tentatively approved the following provisions:

§203. *Imputation of Conflicts of Interest to Affiliated Lawyers*

> Unless all affected clients consent to the representation under the limitations and conditions provided in §202 or unless imputation hereunder is removed as provided in §204, the restrictions upon a lawyer imposed by §§207-216 also restrict other affiliated lawyers who:
>
> (1) are associated with that lawyer in rendering legal services to others through a law partnership, professional corporation, sole proprietorship, or similar association;

(2) are employed with that lawyer by an organization to render legal services either to that organization or to others to advance the interests or objectives of the organizaiton; or

(3) share office facilities without reasonable adequate measures to protect confidential client information so that it will not be available to other lawyers in the shared office.

§204. Removing Imputation

(1) Imputation specified in §203 does not restrict an affiliated lawyer when the affiliation between the affiliated lawyer and the personally-prohibited lawyer that required the imputation has been terminated, and no material confidential information of the client, relevant to the matter, has been communicated by the personally-prohibited lawyer to the affiliated lawyer or that lawyer's firm.

(2) Imputation specified in §203 does not restrict an affiliated lawyer with respect to a former-client conflict under §213, when there is no reasonable apparent risk that confidential information of the former client will be used with material adverse effect on the former client because:

(a) any confidential client information communicated to the personally-prohibited lawyer is unlikely to be significant in the subsequent matter;

(b) the personally-prohibited lawyer is subject to screening measures adequate to eliminate involvement by that lawyer in the representation; and

(c) timely and adequate notice of the screening has been provided to all affected clients.

(3) Imputation specified in §203 does not restrict a lawyer affiliated with a former government lawyer with respect to a conflict under §214 if:

(a) the personally-prohibited lawyer is subject to screening measures adequate to eliminate involvement by that lawyer in the representation; and

(b) timely and adequate notice of the screening has been provided to the appropriate government agency and to affected clients.

(Restatement §§202, 209-211, and 216 are reprinted in the Related Materials following Model Rule 1.7; §§207, 208, and 215 follow Rule 1.8; §213 follows Rule 1.9; §214 follows Rule 1.11; §212 follows Rule 1.13; and "confidential client information" is defined in Restatement §111, which follows Rule 1.6.)

Rule 1.11 Successive Government and Private Employment

(a) Except as law may otherwise expressly permit, a lawyer shall not represent a private client in connection with a matter in which the lawyer participated personally and substantially as a public officer or employee, unless the appropriate government agency consents after consultation. No lawyer in a firm with which that lawyer is associated may knowingly undertake or continue representation in such a matter unless:

(1) the disqualified lawyer is screened from any participation in the matter and is apportioned no part of the fee therefrom; and

(2) written notice is promptly given to the appropriate government agency to enable it to ascertain compliance with the provisions of this rule.

(b) Except as law may otherwise expressly permit, a lawyer having information that the lawyer knows is confidential government information about a person acquired when the lawyer was a public officer or employee, may not represent a private client whose interests are adverse to that person in a matter in which the information could be used to the material disadvantage of that person. A firm with which that lawyer is associated may undertake or continue representation in the matter only if the disqualified lawyer is screened from any participation in the matter and is apportioned no part of the fee therefrom.

(c) Except as law may otherwise expressly permit, a lawyer serving as a public officer or employee shall not:

(1) participate in a matter in which the lawyer participated personally and substantially while in private practice or nongovernmental employment, unless under applicable law no one is, or by lawful delegation may be, authorized to act in the lawyer's stead in the matter; or

(2) negotiate for private employment with any person who is involved as a party or as attorney for a party in a matter in which the lawyer is participating personally and substantially, except that a lawyer serving as a law clerk to a judge, other adjudicative officer or arbitrator may negotiate for private employment as permitted by Rule 1.12(b) and subject to the conditions stated in Rule 1.12(b).

(d) As used in this rule, the term "matter" includes:

(1) any judicial or other proceeding, application, request for a ruling or other determination, contract, claim, controversy, investigation, charge, accusation, arrest or other particular matter involving a specific party or parties; and

(2) any other matter covered by the conflict of interest rules of the appropriate government agency.

(e) As used in this rule, the term "confidential government information" means information which has been obtained under governmental authority and which, at the time this rule is applied, the government is prohibited by law from disclosing to the public or has a legal privilege not to disclose, and which is not otherwise available to the public.

COMMENT

[1] This Rule prevents a lawyer from exploiting public office for the advantage of a private client. It is a counterpart of Rule 1.9(b), which applies to lawyers moving from one firm to another.

[2] A lawyer representing a government agency, whether employed or specially retained by the government, is subject to the Rules of Professional Conduct, including the prohibition against representing adverse interests stated in Rule 1.7 and the protections afforded former clients in Rule 1.9. In addition, such a lawyer is subject to Rule 1.11 and to statutes and government regulations regarding conflict of interest. Such statutes and regulations may circumscribe the extent to which the government agency may give consent under this Rule.

[3] Where the successive clients are a public agency and a private client, the risk exists that power or discretion vested in public authority might be used for the special benefit of a private client. A lawyer should not be in a position where benefit to a private client might affect performance of the lawyer's professional functions on behalf of public authority. Also, unfair advantage could accrue to the private client by reason of access to confidential government information about the client's adversary obtainable only through the lawyer's government service. However, the rules governing lawyers presently or formerly employed by a government agency should not be so restrictive as to inhibit transfer of employment to and from the government. The government has a legitimate need to attract qualified lawyers as well as to maintain high ethical standards. The provisions for screening and waiver are necessary to prevent the disqualification rule from imposing too severe a deterrent against entering public service.

[4] When the client is an agency of one government, that agency should be treated as a private client for purposes of this Rule if the lawyer thereafter represents an agency of another government, as when a lawyer represents a city and subsequently is employed by a federal agency.

[5] Paragraphs (a)(1) and (b)(1) do not prohibit a lawyer from receiving a salary or partnership share established by prior independent agreement. They prohibit directly relating the attorney's compensation to the fee in the matter in which the lawyer is disqualified.

[6] Paragraph (a)(2) does not require that a lawyer give notice to the government agency at a time when premature disclosure would injure the client; a requirement for premature disclosure might preclude engagement of the lawyer. Such notice is, however, required to be given as soon as practicable in order that the government agency or affected person will have a reasonable opportunity to ascertain that the lawyer is complying with Rule 1.11 and to take appropriate action if they believe the lawyer is not complying.

[7] Paragraph (b) operates only when the lawyer in question has knowledge of the information, which means actual knowledge; it does not operate with respect to information that merely could be imputed to the lawyer.

[8] Paragraphs (a) and (c) do not prohibit a lawyer from jointly representing a private party and a government agency when doing so is permitted by Rule 1.7 and is not otherwise prohibited by law.

[9] Paragraph (c) does not disqualify other lawyers in the agency with which the lawyer in question has become associated.

Model Code Comparison

Paragraph (a) is similar to DR 9-101(B), except that the latter used the terms "in which he had substantial responsibility while he was a public employee."

Paragraphs (b), (c), (d), and (e) have no counterparts in the Model Code.

Cross-References in Rules

Rule 1.10, Comment 4: "Where a lawyer has joined a private firm after having represented the government, the situation is governed by **Rule 1.11(a) and (b)**; where a lawyer represents the government after having served private clients, the situation is governed by **Rule 1.11(c)(1)**."

Rule 1.10, Comment 5: "The government is entitled to protection of its client confidences, and therefore to the protections provided in **Rules** 1.6, 1.9(a) and (c), and **1.11**. However, if the more extensive disqualification in Rule 1.9(b) were applied to former government lawyers, the potential effect on the government would be unduly burdensome. . . . [O]n balance, therefore, the government is better served in the long run by the protections stated in Rule **1.11**."

Rule 1.12, Comment 1: "This Rule generally parallels Rule **1.11**. . . . Compare the Comment to Rule **1.11**."

Rule 5.7, Comment 8: "When a lawyer is obliged to accord the recipients of such [law-related] services the protections of those Rules that apply to the client-lawyer relationship, the lawyer must take special care to heed the proscriptions of the Rules addressing conflicts of interest (**Rules 1.7** through **1.11**). . . ."

Legislative History

1980 Discussion Draft:

. . . (e) If a lawyer is required by this rule to decline representation on account of personal and substantial participation in a matter, except where the participation was as a judicial law clerk, no lawyer in a firm with the disqualified lawyer may accept such employment. . . .

1981 and 1982 Drafts were substantially the same as adopted.

Selected State Variations

California has no direct counterpart.

District of Columbia: D.C. Rule 1.11 differs significantly from the ABA Model Rule — see District of Columbia Rules of Professional Conduct below.

Illinois: Rule 1.11(a) covers any lawyer who knows "or reasonably should know" of the former government lawyer's prior participation. Rules 1.11(a)(1) and 1.11(b) condition the exceptions on apportioning the disqualified lawyer "no specific share" of the fee.

Iowa adds DR 8-101(b): "County attorneys and assistant county attorneys shall not engage in the defense of an accused in any criminal matter during the time they are holding this public office."

New Hampshire adds a Rule 1.11A dealing with the responsibilities of "a lawyer actively engaged in the practice of law, who is a member of [a] governmental body."

New Jersey Rules 1.11(a) and 1.11(b) provide:

> (a) Except as law may otherwise expressly permit, a lawyer shall not represent a private client in connection with a matter (i) in which the lawyer participated personally and substantially as a public officer or employee, (ii) about which the lawyer acquired knowledge of confidential information as a public officer or employee, or (iii) for which the lawyer had substantial responsibility as a public officer or employee.

> (b) An appearance of impropriety may arise from a lawyer representing a private client in connection with a matter that relates to the lawyer's former employment as public officer or employee even if the lawyer did not personally and substantially participate in it, have actual knowledge of it, or substantial responsibility for it. In such an event, the lawyer may not represent a private client, but a firm with which that lawyer is associated may undertake or continue representation if: (1) the disqualified lawyer is screened from any participation in the matter and is apportioned no part of the fee therefrom, and (2) written notice is promptly given to the appropriate government agency to enable it to ascertain compliance with the provisions of this rule.

New York: DR 9-101(B) of the New York Code substantially adopts language from Rule 1.11(a), (b), and (c), with modifications.

Pennsylvania provides in its comment that paragraphs (a)(1) and (b) "do not prohibit a lawyer from receiving a salary or distribution of firm profits established by prior independent agreement. They prohibit directly relating the attorney's compensation to the fee in the matter in which the lawyer is disqualified."

Rhode Island: Rule 1.11(a) excludes the words "personally and substantially" and provides that a lawyer "shall not represent a private client in connection with a matter in which the lawyer participated as a public officer or employee." Rhode Island also adds the following subparagraph (b) to Rule 1.11:

> Notwithstanding any other provisions of this Rule, a lawyer who has been employed by any government office or agency shall not represent a private client be-

fore the government office or agency for the period of one year following the termination of such employment.

Texas Rule 1.10(f) specifically excludes "regulation-making" and "rule-making" from the definition of "matter."

Virginia: Substantially the same as the Model Code, except that at the end of DR 9-101(B) Virginia adds, "unless the public entity by which he was employed consents after full disclosure."

Related Materials

American Lawyer's Code of Conduct: Rules 9.14 and 9.15 provide:

9.14. A lawyer shall not accept private employment relating to any matter in which the lawyer participated personally and substantially while in public service.

9.15. When a lawer is disqualified from representing a client under Rule 9.14, no partner or associate of the lawyer, and no one with an of counsel relationship to the lawyer, shall represent the client.

Comment to Rules 9.14-9.15

. . . The principal argument in favor of permitting a screening-waiver device is that the government would find it impossible to hire competent lawyers if the screening-waiver exception is rejected, because lawyers would fear becoming unemployable. But if concern over the denial of waivers would indeed result in the unemployability of former government lawyers, that problem would prevail as long as there were any significant risk that waivers would be denied in particular cases. That is, unless the waiver device were a sham, and waivers were to be granted as a matter of course whenever requested, the asserted risks of hiring former government employees would still discourage law firms from employing them, and would thus discourage lawyers from entering government service.

In fact, however, no instance has ever been given of a government employee who would be rendered unemployable by the rejection of a waiver-screening exception. Unquestionably, a particular lawyer might have to forgo employment with a particular law firm, or even with three or four firms, but that is hardly the sweeping effect that has been projected by opponents of the ethical rule.

"Confidential government information": Model Rule 1.11(e) defines "confidential government information" to include information the government is "prohibited by law from disclosing" or "has a legal privilege not to disclose," *and* (having satisfied one of those two criteria) that also is "not otherwise available to the public." As to prohibitions, various federal statutes prohibit disclosure — see, e.g., the Privacy Act, 5 U.S.C. §552a, and the Trade Secrets Act, 18 U.S.C. §1905. As to privileges, the government has successfully claimed various privileges under Federal Rule of Evidence 501, including the executive privi-

lege, the deliberate privilege, the national security privilege, and the attorney-client privilege. As to availability to the public, the Freedom of Information Act (FOIA), 5 U.S.C. §552, makes a broad range of government information available to the public on demand.

"Revolving door" provisions: Rule 1.11(d)(2) refers to "the conflict of interest rules of the appropriate government agency." All former lawyers for the federal government are covered by the "revolving door" provision in 18 U.S.C. §207, which prohibits former government lawyers from opposing the government, either directly or in matters in which the government has "a direct and substantial interest," for two years after leaving government, if the lawyer was involved in the matter while in federal government service. See 5 C.F.R. §2637 for the general implementation of 18 U.S.C. §207. In addition, several agencies of the federal government have their own "revolving door" provisions. See e.g., 45 C.F.R. §680 (National Science Foundation), 32 C.F.R. §1690 (Selective Service System), 22 C.F.R. §18 (Foreign Service). Many states have enacted parallel provisions.

Restatement of the Law Governing Lawyers: The American Law Institute has tentatively approved the following provision:

§214. *Former Government Lawyer or Officer*

(1) A lawyer may not act on behalf of a client with respect to a matter in which the lawyer participated personally and substantially while acting as a government lawyer or officer unless both the government and the client consent to the representation under the limitations and conditions provided in §202.

(2) A lawyer who acquires confidential information while acting as a government lawyer or officer may not:

(a) if the information concerns a person, represent a client whose interests are materially adverse to that person in a matter in which the information could be used to the material disadvantage of that person; or

(b) if the information concerns the governmental client or employer, represent another public or private client in circumstances described in §213(2).

(Restatement §202 is reprinted in the Related Materials following Model Rule 1.7; §213(2) is reprinted following Model Rule 1.9.)

Rule 1.12 Former Judge or Arbitrator

(a) Except as stated in paragraph (d), a lawyer shall not represent anyone in connection with a matter in which the lawyer participated personally and substantially as a judge or other adjudicative officer, arbitrator or law clerk to such a person, unless all parties to the proceeding consent after consultation.

(b) A lawyer shall not negotiate for employment with any person who is involved as a party or as attorney for a party in a matter in which the lawyer is participating personally and substantially as a judge or other adjudicative officer, or arbitrator. A lawyer serving as a law clerk to a judge, other adjudicative officer or arbitrator may negotiate for employment with a party or attorney involved in a matter in which the clerk is participating personally and substantially, but only after the lawyer has notified the judge, other adjudicative officer or arbitrator.

(c) If a lawyer is disqualified by paragraph (a), no lawyer in a firm with which that lawyer is associated may knowingly undertake or continue representation in the matter unless:

(1) the disqualified lawyer is screened from any participation in the matter and is apportioned no part of the fee therefrom; and

(2) written notice is promptly given to the appropriate tribunal to enable it to ascertain compliance with the provisions of this rule.

(d) An arbitrator selected as a partisan of a party in a multi-member arbitration panel is not prohibited from subsequently representing that party.

COMMENT

This Rule generally parallels Rule 1.11. The term "personally and substantially" signifies that a judge who was a member of a multimember court, and thereafter left judicial office to practice law, is not prohibited from representing a client in a matter pending in the court, but in which the former judge did not participate. So also the fact that a former judge exercised administrative responsibility in a court does not prevent the former judge from acting as a lawyer in a matter where the judge had previously exercised remote or incidental administrative responsibility that did not affect the merits. Compare the Comment to Rule 1.11. The term "adjudicative officer" includes such officials as judges pro tempore, referees, special masters, hearing officers and other parajudicial officers, and also lawyers who serve as part-time judges. Compliance Canons A (2), B (2) and C of the Model Code of Judicial Conduct provide that a part-time judge, judge pro tempore or retired judge recalled to active service, may not "act as a lawyer in any proceeding in which he served as a judge or in any other proceeding related thereto." Although phrased differently from this Rule, those rules correspond in meaning.

Model Code Comparison

Paragraph (a) is substantially similar to DR 9-101(A), which provided that a lawyer "shall not accept private employment in a matter upon the merits of which he has acted in a judicial capacity." Paragraph (a) differs, however, in that it is broader in scope and states more specifically the persons to whom it applies. There was no counterpart in the Model Code to paragraphs (b), (c), or (d).

With regard to arbitrators, EC 5-20 stated that "a lawyer [who] has undertaken to act as an impartial arbitrator or mediator, . . . should not thereafter represent in the dispute any of the parties involved." DR 9-101(A) did not permit a waiver of the disqualification applied to former judges by consent of the parties. However, DR 5-105(C) was similar in effect and could be construed to permit waiver.

Cross-References in Rules

None.

Legislative History

1980 Discussion Draft (then Rules 1.11(d), 1.11(e), and 1.11(f)):

(d) A lawyer who has served as a judge in an adjudicatory proceeding shall not thereafter represent anyone in connection with the subject matter of the proceeding.

(e) If a lawyer is required by this rule to decline representation on account of personal and substantial participation in a matter, except where the participation was as a judicial law clerk, no lawyer in a firm with the disqualified lawyer may accept such employment.

(f) . . . The disqualification stated in paragraph (d) may be waived by the consent of all parties to the adjudication.

1981 and 1982 Drafts: Substantially the same as adopted.

Selected State Variations

California has no direct counterpart to Rule 1.12.

District of Columbia: D.C. Rule 1.12 differs significantly from the ABA Model Rule — see District of Columbia Rules of Professional Conduct below.

Illinois: Rule 1.12(c) covers any lawyer who "knows or reasonably should know" of the former judge's or arbitrator's disqualification. Rule 1.12(c)(1) requires that the disqualified lawyer receive "no specific share" of the fee.

New Jersey deletes Rule 1.12(c).

New York: Same or substantially the same as the ABA Model Code — see Model Code Comparison above — except see New York Materials for New York's version of DR 5-105(D).

Virginia: Substantially the same as the Model Code.

Related Materials

ABA Canons: Canon 36 provided:

36. Retirement from Judicial Position of Public Employment

A lawyer should not accept employment as an advocate in any matter upon the merits of which he has previously acted in a judicial capacity.

A lawyer, having once held public office or having been in the public employ, should not after his retirement accept employment in connection with any matter which he has investigated or passed upon while in such office or employ.

Restatement of the Law Governing Lawyers: The American Law Institute has tentatively approved §204 explaining general methods of removing imputation. Section 204 is reprinted in the Related Materials following Model Rule 1.10.

Code of Conduct for Law Clerks: In a student piece entitled Ethics for Judicial Clerks, 4 Geo. L.J. 771, 786-790 (1991), the author proposes a Code of Conduct for Law Clerks. Proposed Canon 3(D) of this Code, which relates to Model Rule 1.12(b), provides:

A law clerk should inform the appointing judge of any circumstance or activity of the law clerk that might serve as a basis for disqualification of the judge, e.g., a prospective employment relation with a law firm, association of the law clerk's spouse with a law firm or litigant, etc.

Rule 1.13 Organization as Client

(a) A lawyer employed or retained by an organization represents the organization acting through its duly authorized constituents.

(b) If a lawyer for an organization knows that an officer, employee or other person associated with the organization is engaged in action, intends to act or refuses to act in a matter related to the representation that is a violation of a legal obligation to the organization, or a violation of law which reasonably might be imputed to the organization, and is likely to result in substantial injury to the organization, the lawyer shall proceed as is reasonably necessary in the best interest of the organization. In determining how to proceed, the lawyer shall give due consideration to the seriousness of the violation and its consequences, the scope and nature of the lawyer's representation, the responsibility in the organization and the apparent motivation of the person involved, the policies of the organization concerning such matters and any other relevant considerations. Any measures taken shall be designed to minimize disruption of the organization and the risk of revealing information relating to the representation to persons outside the organization. Such measures may include among others:

(1) asking reconsideration of the matter;

(2) advising that a separate legal opinion on the matter be sought for presentation to appropriate authority in the organization; and

(3) referring the matter to higher authority in the organization, including, if warranted by the seriousness of the matter, referral to the highest authority that can act in behalf of the organization as determined by applicable law.

(c) If despite the lawyer's efforts in accordance with paragraph (b), the highest authority that can act on behalf of the organization insists upon action, or a refusal to act, that is clearly a violation of law and is likely to result in substantial injury to the organization, the lawyer may resign in accordance with Rule 1.16.

(d) In dealing with an organization's directors, officers, employees, members, shareholders or other constituents, a lawyer shall explain the identity of the client when it is apparent that the organization's interests are adverse to those of the constituents with whom the lawyer is dealing.

(e) A lawyer representing an organization may also represent any of its directors, officers, employees, members, shareholders or other constituents, subject to the provisions of Rule 1.7. If the organization's consent to the dual representation is required by Rule 1.7, the consent shall be given by an appropriate official of the organization other than the individual who is to be represented, or by the shareholders.

COMMENT

The Entity as the Client

[1] An organizational client is a legal entity, but it cannot act except through its officers, directors, employees, shareholders and other constituents.

[2] Officers, directors, employees and shareholders are the constituents of the corporate organizational client. The duties defined in this Comment apply equally to unincorporated associations. "Other constituents" as used in this Comment means the positions equivalent to officers, directors, employees and shareholders held by persons acting for organizational clients that are not corporations.

[3] When one of the constituents of an organizational client communicates with the organization's lawyer in that person's organizational capacity, the communication is protected by Rule 1.6. Thus, by way of example, if an organizational client requests its lawyer to investigate allegations of wrongdoing, interviews made in the course of that investigation

between the lawyer and the client's employees or other constituents are covered by Rule 1.6. This does not mean, however, that constituents of an organizational client are the clients of the lawyer. The lawyer may not disclose to such constituents information relating to the representation except for disclosures explicitly or impliedly authorized by the organizational client in order to carry out the representation or as otherwise permitted by Rule 1.6.

[4] When constituents of the organization make decisions for it, the decisions ordinarily must be accepted by the lawyer even if their utility or prudence is doubtful. Decisions concerning policy and operations, including ones entailing serious risk, are not as such in the lawyer's province. However, different considerations arise when the lawyer knows that the organization may be substantially injured by action of constituent that is in violation of law. In such a circumstance, it may be reasonably necessary for the lawyer to ask the constituent to reconsider the matter. If that fails, or if the matter is of sufficient seriousness and importance to the organization, it may be reasonably necessary for the lawyer to take steps to have the matter reviewed by a higher authority in the organization. Clear justification should exist for seeking review over the head of the constituent normally responsible for it. The stated policy of the organization may define circumstances and prescribe channels for such review, and a lawyer should encourage the formulation of such a policy. Even in the absence of organization policy, however, the lawyer may have an obligation to refer a matter to higher authority, depending on the seriousness of the matter and whether the constituent in question has apparent motives to act at variance with the organization's interest. Review by the chief executive officer or by the board of directors may be required when the matter is of importance commensurate with their authority. At some point it may be useful or essential to obtain an independent legal opinion.

[5] In an extreme case, it may be reasonably necessary for the lawyer to refer the matter to the organization's highest authority. Ordinarily, that is the board of directors or similar governing body. However, applicable law may prescribe that under certain conditions highest authority reposes elsewhere; for example, in the independent directors of a corporation.

Relation to Other Rules

[6] The authority and responsibility provided in paragraph (b) are concurrent with the authority and responsibility provided in other Rules. In particular, this Rule does not limit or expand the lawyer's responsibil-

ity under Rules 1.6, 1.8, and 1.16, 3.3, or 4.1. If the lawyer's services are being used by an organization to further a crime or fraud by the organization, Rule 1.2(d) can be applicable.

Government Agency

[7] The duty defined in this Rule applies to governmental organizations. However, when the client is a governmental organization, a different balance may be appropriate between maintaining confidentiality and assuring that the wrongful official act is prevented or rectified, for public business is involved. In addition, duties of lawyers employed by the government or lawyers in military service may be defined by statutes and regulation. Therefore, defining precisely the identity of the client and prescribing the resulting obligations of such lawyers may be more difficult in the government context. Although in some circumstances the client may be a specific agency, it is generally the government as a whole. For example, if the action or failure to act involves the head of a bureau, either the department of which the bureau is a part or the government as a whole may be the client for purpose of this Rule. Moreover, in a matter involving the conduct of government officials, a government lawyer may have authority to question such conduct more extensively than that of a lawyer for a private organization in similar circumstances. This Rule does not limit that authority. See note on Scope.

Clarifying the Lawyer's Role

[8] There are times when the organization's interest may be or become adverse to those of one or more of its constituents. In such circumstances the lawyer should advise any constituent, whose interest he finds adverse to that of the organization of the conflict or potential conflict of interest, that the lawyer cannot represent such constituent, and that such person may wish to obtain independent representation. Care must be taken to assure that the individual understands that, when there is such adversity of interest, the lawyer for the organization cannot provide legal representation for that constituent individual, and that discussions between the lawyer for the organization and the individual may not be privileged.

[9] Whether such a warning should be given by the lawyer for the organization to any constituent individual may turn on the facts of each case.

Dual Representation

[10] Paragraph (e) recognizes that a lawyer for an organization may also represent a principal officer or major shareholder.

Derivative Actions

[11] Under generally prevailing law, the shareholders or members of a corporation may bring suit to compel the directors to perform their legal obligations in the supervision of the organization. Members of unincorporated associations have essentially the same right. Such an action may be brought nominally by the organization, but usually is, in fact, a legal controversy over management of the organization.

[12] The question can arise whether counsel for the organization may defend such an action. The proposition that the organization is the lawyer's client does not alone resolve the issue. Most derivative actions are a normal incident of an organization's affairs, to be defended by the organization's lawyer like any other suit. However, if the claim involves serious charges of wrongdoing by those in control of the organization, a conflict may arise between the lawyer's duty to the organization and the lawyer's relationship with the board. In those circumstances, Rule 1.7 governs who should represent the directors and the organization.

Model Code Comparison

There was no counterpart to this Rule in the Disciplinary Rules of the Model Code. EC 5-18 stated that a "lawyer employed or retained by a corporation or similar entity owes his allegiance to the entity and not to a stockholder, director, officer, employee, representative, or other person connected with the entity. In advising the entity, a lawyer should keep paramount its interests and his professional judgment should not be influenced by the personal desires of any person or organization. Occasionally, a lawyer for an entity is requested by a stockholder, director, officer, employee, representative, or other person connected with the entity to represent him in an individual capacity; in such case the lawyer may serve the individual only if the lawyer is convinced that differing interests are not present." EC 5-24 stated that although a lawyer "may be employed by a business corporation with non-lawyers serving as directors or officers, and they necessarily have the right to make decisions of business policy, a lawyer must decline to accept direction of his professional judgment from any layman." DR 5-107(B) provided that a lawyer "shall not permit a person who . . . employs . . .

him to render legal services for another to direct or regulate his professional judgment in rendering such legal services.''

Cross-References in Rules

Rule 1.4, Comment 3: "When the client is an organization or group, it is often impossible or inappropriate to inform every one of its members about its legal affairs; ordinarily, the lawyer should address communications to the appropriate officials of the organization. See **Rule 1.13**."

Rule 1.6, Comment 16: "The requirement of maintaining confidentiality of information relating to representation applies to government lawyers who may disagree with the policy goals that their representation is designed to advance."

Legislative History

1980 Discussion Draft:

An Organization as the Client

(a) A lawyer employed or retained by an organization represents the organization as distinct from its directors, officers, employees, members, shareholders, or other constituents.

(b) If a lawyer for an organization knows that an officer, employee, or other person associated with the organization is engaged in or intends action, or a refusal to act, that is a violation of law and is likely to result in significant harm to the organization, the lawyer shall use reasonable efforts to prevent the harm. [The rest of subparagraph (b) was substantially the same as adopted.]

(c) If, despite the lawyer's efforts in accordance with paragraph (b), the highest authority that can act on behalf of the organization insists upon action, or a refusal to act, that is clearly a violation of law and is likely to result in substantial injury to the organization, the lawyer may take further remedial action, including disclosure of client confidences to the extent necessary, if the lawyer reasonably believes such action to be in the best interest of the organization.

(d) A lawyer representing an organization may also represent any of its directors, officers, members, or shareholders subject to the provisions of Rule 1.8. A lawyer undertaking such dual representation shall disclose that fact to an appropriate official of the organization other than the person so represented.

(e) When a shareholder or member of an organization brings a derivative action, the lawyer for the organization may act as its advocate only as permitted by Rule 1.8.

(f) In dealing with an organization's officials and employees, a lawyer shall explain the identity of the client when necessary to avoid embarrassment or unfairness to them.

1981 Draft: Rule 1.13(a) was the same as 1980 Draft. In Rule 1.13(b), a lawyer discovering conduct likely to result in "material" injury (rather than "significant" injury) to the corporation was to "proceed as is reasonably necessary in the best interest of the organization." Rule 1.13(c), describing remedial action, provided:

> Such action may include revealing information relating to the representation of the organization only if the lawyer reasonably believes that:
> (1) the highest authority in the organization has acted to further the personal or financial interests of members of that authority which are in conflict with the interests of the organization; and
> (2) revealing the information is necessary in the best interest of the organization.

1982 Draft: Substantially the same as 1981 Draft.

Selected State Variations

Alaska: Rule 1.13(c), after stating that a lawyer may resign, adds "and shall act in accordance with the provisions of Rule 1.6." Rule 1.13(d) requires a lawyer not only to explain the identity of client but also "that the lawyer's first duty is to the client."

California: See Rule 3-600 (Organization as Client).

Colorado: Rule 1.13(a) adds that "the lawyer owes allegiance to the organization itself, and not its individual stockholders, directors, officers, employees, representatives or other persons connected with the entity." In addition, Rule 1.13(e) permits a lawyer to represent both the entity and its constituents "only in those instances in which the representation will not affect the lawyer's allegiance to the entity itself."

District of Columbia: D.C. Rule 1.13 differs significantly from the ABA Model Rule — see District of Columbia Rules of Professional Conduct below.

Maryland, Michigan, New Hampshire, and ***New Jersey*** permit revelation outside the corporation under the same or substantially the same circumstances described in the ABA's 1981 Draft of Rule 1.13. Michigan and New Jersey also retain the language of Rule 1.13(a) as it appeared in the Kutak Commission's 1980 draft.

Minnesota deletes "and is likely to result in substantial injury to the organization" from Rule 1.13(b). In Rule 1.13(c), Minnesota provides: "If despite the lawyer's efforts in accordance with paragraph (b), a violation of law appears likely, the lawyer may resign in accordance with Rule 1.16 and if the violation is criminal or fraudulent, may reveal it in accordance with Rules of Professional Conduct."

New York: The New York Code adopts substantial portions of Rule 1.13 in EC 5-18 and DR 5-109(A).

Texas Rule 1.12(a) says that a lawyer retained or employed by an organization "represents the entity." Texas Rule 1.12(d) relieves the lawyer of responsibilities to the entity when the lawyer properly withdraws from the representation.

Virginia omits Rule 1.13.

Washington omits Rule 1.13.

Related Materials

American Lawyer's Code of Conduct: Rule 2.5 provides:

> A lawyer representing a corporation shall, as early as possible in the lawyer-client relationship, inform the board of directors of potential conflicts that might develop among the interests of the board, corporate officers, and shareholders. The lawyer shall receive from the board instructions in advance as to how to resolve such conflicts, and shall take reasonable steps to ensure that officers with whom the lawyer deals, and the shareholders, are made aware of how the lawyer has been instructed to resolve conflicts of interest.

Model Rules of Professional Conduct for Federal Lawyers: Rule 1.13 differs significantly. It provides (with emphasis added):

> (a) Except when representing another client pursuant to paragraphs (e), (f) and (g), a *Government lawyer represents the Federal Agency that employs the Government lawyer.* Government lawyers are often formally employed by a Federal Agency but assigned to an organizational element within the Federal Agency. Unless otherwise specifically provided, the Federal Agency, not the organizational element, is ordinarily considered the client. The Federal Agency acts through its authorized officials. These officials include the heads of organizational elements within the Federal Agency. When a Government lawyer is assigned to an organizational element and designated to provide legal services and advice to the head of that organization, the client-lawyer relationship exists between the Government lawyer and the Federal Agency, as represented by the head of the organization. *The head of the organization may only invoke the attorney-client privilege or the rule of confidentiality for the benefit of the Federal Agency.* In so invoking either the attorney-client privilege or attorney-client confidentiality on behalf of the Federal Agency, the head of the organization is subject to being overruled by higher agency authority.
>
> (b) . . . [The measures a Government lawyer may take] may include, among others: . . .
>
> (3) Advising the person that the lawyer is ethically obligated to preserve the interests of the Federal agency and, as a result, must consider discussing the matter with supervisory lawyers within the Government lawyer's office or at a higher level within the Federal Agency.
>
> (c) If, despite the Government lawyer's efforts in accordance with paragraph (b), the highest authority that can act concerning the matter insists upon action, or refusal to act, that is clearly a violation of law, the Government lawyer *shall terminate representation* with respect to the matter in question. *In no event may the Government lawyer participate or assist in the illegal activity.* . . .

(e) A Government lawyer shall not form a client-lawyer relationship or represent a client other than the Federal Agency unless specifically authorized or authorized by competent authority. . . .

(g) A Government lawyer who has been duly assigned or authorized to represent an individual who is subject to disciplinary action or administrative proceedings, or to provide civil legal assistance to an individual, has, for those purposes, a lawyer-client relationship with that individual.

The Comment to these Rules states:

Except when a Government lawyer is assigned to represent the interest of another client, the Federal Agency that employs the Government lawyer is the client. This principle is critical to the application of these Rules, since the identity of the client affects significant confidentiality and conflict issues.

. . . Although arguments have been made that the Government lawyer's ultimate obligation is to serve the public interest or the "government as a whole," for practical purposes, these may be unworkable ethical guidelines, particularly with regard to client control and confidentiality.

A Federal Agency may, of course, establish different client-lawyer obligations by Executive or court order, regulation, or statute. See e.g., 5 U.S.C. 2302.

Nevertheless, the conclusion that the Government lawyer's client is the lawyer's employing agency does not answer every ethical question. There are special considerations that affect the ethical responsibilities of the Government lawyer. For example, the Government lawyer has a responsibility to question the conduct of agency officials more extensively than a lawyer for a private organization would in similar circumstances. Government lawyers, in many situations, are asked to represent diverse client interests. For example, Government lawyers in the Executive branch also represent other branches of Government in a number of different situations. Here it becomes especially clear that the Government attorney's responsibilities are affected by the attorney's more general obligations to the United States, as for example, when it is necessary to refuse to defend an unconstitutional statute or regulation or to resist the encroachment by one branch on another's sphere of power. The client-lawyer obligations of Government lawyers in other branches of Government raise still different considerations. For example, lawyers engaged by the Senate or the House of Representatives, by Congressional committees, or on the staffs of individual members of Congress may develop client-lawyer relationships with those bodies, committees or individuals. Yet these relationships must themselves be viewed in the context of the Government lawyer's broader obligations to the Congress as a whole and ultimately to the United States.

Restatement of the Law Governing Lawyers: The American Law Institute has tentatively approved the following provisions:

§123. Privilege for Organizational Client

When a client is a corporation, unincorporated association, partnership, trust, estate, sole proprietorship, or other for-profit or not-for-profit organization, the attorney-client privilege extends to a communication that:

(1) otherwise qualifies as privileged under §§118-122;

(2) is between an agent of the organization and a privileged person as defined in §120;

(3) concerns a legal matter of interest to the organization; and

(4) is disclosed only to:

(a) privileged persons as defined in §120; and

(b) other agents of the organization who reasonably need to know of the communication in order to act for the organization.

(Restatement §§118-122 are reprinted in the chapter on attorney-client privilege.)

§134A. Exception for Fiduciary-Lawyer Communication

In a proceeding in which a trustee of an express trust or similar fiduciary is charged with breach of fiduciary duties by a beneficiary, a communication otherwise wihtin §118 is nonetheless not privileged if the communication:

(a) is relevant to the claimed breach; and

(b) was between the trustee and a lawyer (or other privileged person within the meaning of §120) who was retained to advise the trustee concerning the administration of the trust.

§134B. Exception for Organizational Fiduciary

In a proceeding involving a dispute between an organizational client and shareholders, members, or other constituents of the organization toward whom the directors, officers, or similar persons managing the organization bear fiduciary responsibilities, the attorney-client privilege of the organization may be withheld from a communication otherwise within §118 if the tribunal finds that:

(a) those managing the organization are charged with breach of their obligations toward the shareholders, members, or other constituents or toward the organization itself;

(b) the communication occurred prior to the assertion of the charges and relates directly to those charges; and

(c) the need of the requesting party to discover or introduce the communication is sufficiently compelling and the threat to confidentiality sufficiently confined to justify setting the privilege aside.

§155. Representing Organization as Client

(1) When a lawyer is employed or retained to represent an organization:

(a) the lawyer represents the interests of the organization as defined by its responsible agents acting pursuant to the organization's decision-making procedures; and

(b) subject to Subsection (2), the lawyer must follow instructions in the representation, as stated in §32(2), given by persons authorized so to act on behalf of the organization.

(2) If a lawyer representing an organization knows of circumstances indicating that a constituent of the organization has engaged in action or intends to act in a way that violates a legal obligation to the organization that will likely cause

substantial injury to it, or that reasonably can be foreseen to be imputable to the organization and thus likely to result in substantial injury to it, the lawyer must proceed in what the lawyer reasonably believes to be the best interests of the organization.

(3) In the circumstances described in Subsection (2), the lawyer may, in circumstances warranting such steps, ask the constituent to reconsider the matter, recommend that a second legal opinion be sought, and seek review by appropriate supervisory authority within the organization, including referring the matter to the highest authority that can act in behalf of the organization.

§156. Representing Governmental Client

A lawyer representing a governmental client must proceed in the representation as stated in §155, except that the lawyer:

(1) possesses such rights and responsibilities as may be defined by law to make decisions on behalf of the governmental client that are within the authority of a client under §§33 and 32(2);

(2) except as otherwise provided by law, must proceed as stated in §§155(2) and 155(3) with respect to an act of a constituent of the governmental client that violates a legal obligation that will likely cause substantial public or private injury or that reasonably can be foreseen to be imputable to and thus likely result in substantial injury to the client;

(3) if a prosecutor or similar lawyer determining whether to file criminal proceedings, or take other steps in such proceedings, must do so only when based on probable cause and the lawyer's belief, formed after due investigation, that there are good factual and legal grounds to support the step taken; and

(4) must observe other applicable restrictions imposed by law on those similarly functioning for the governmental client.

(Restatement §§32(2) and 33 are reprinted in the Related Materials following Rule 1.2.)

§212. Conflicts of Interest in Representing Organization

Unless all affected clients consent to the representation under the limitations and conditions provided in §202, a lawyer may not represent both an organization and a director, officer, employee, shareholder, owner, partner, member, or other individual or organization associated with the organization if there is a substantial risk that the lawyer's representation of either would be materially and adversely affected by the lawyer's duties to the other.

(Restatement §202 is reprinted above in the Related Materials following Model Rule 1.7.)

Rule 1.14 Client Under a Disability

Editors' Note. At its 1997 Mid-Year Meeting, the ABA House of Delegates voted to amend the Comment (but not the text) of Rule 1.14. The amendment added two new paragraphs (¶¶6-7) to the Comment. The new paragraphs explain what a lawyer should do in an "emergency" that threatens the health, safety, or financial interest of a disabled person who is not yet a client. We underscore ¶¶6-7 to indicate that they are new in this edition. The full ABA Committee Report explaining the new paragraphs is reprinted in the Legislative History following Rule 1.14.

(a) When a client's ability to make adequately considered decisions in connection with the representation is impaired, whether because of minority, mental disability or for some other reason, the lawyer shall, as far as reasonably possible, maintain a normal client-lawyer relationship with the client.

(b) A lawyer may seek the appointment of a guardian or take other protective action with respect to a client, only when the lawyer reasonably believes that the client cannot adequately act in the client's own interest.

COMMENT

[1] The normal client-lawyer relationship is based on the assumption that the client, when properly advised and assisted, is capable of making decisions about important matters. When the client is a minor or suffers from a mental disorder or disability, however, maintaining the ordinary client-lawyer relationship may not be possible in all respects. In particular, an incapacitated person may have no power to make legally binding decisions. Nevertheless, a client lacking legal competence often has the ability to understand, deliberate upon, and reach conclusions about matters affecting the client's own well-being. Furthermore, to an increasing extent the law recognizes intermediate degrees of competence. For example, children as young as five or six years of age, and certainly those of ten or twelve, are regarded as having opinions that are entitled to weight in legal proceedings concerning their custody. So also, it is recognized that some persons of advanced age can be quite capable of handling routine financial matters while needing special legal protection concerning major transactions.

[2] The fact that a client suffers a disability does not diminish the lawyer's obligation to treat the client with attention and respect. If the person has no guardian or legal representative, the lawyer often must act as de facto guardian. Even if the person does have a legal representative, the lawyer should as far as possible accord the represented person the status of client, particularly in maintaining communication.

[3] If a legal representative has already been appointed for the client, the lawyer should ordinarily look to the representative for decisions on behalf of the client. If a legal representative has not been appointed, the lawyer should see to such an appointment where it would serve the client's best interests. Thus, if a disabled client has substantial property that should be sold for the client's benefit, effective completion of the transaction ordinarily requires appointment of a legal representative. In many circumstances, however, appointment of a legal representative may be expensive or traumatic for the client. Evaluation of these considerations is a matter of professional judgment on the lawyer's part.

[4] If the lawyer represents the guardian as distinct from the ward, and is aware that the guardian is acting adversely to the ward's interest, the lawyer may have an obligation to prevent or rectify the guardian's misconduct. See Rule 1.2(d).

Disclosure of the Client's Condition

[5] Rules of procedure in litigation generally provide that minors or persons suffering mental disability shall be represented by a guardian or next friend if they do not have a general guardian. However, disclosure of the client's disability can adversely affect the client's interests. For example, raising the question of disability could, in some circumstances, lead to proceedings for involuntary commitment. The lawyer's position in such cases is an unavoidably difficult one. The lawyer may seek guidance from an appropriate diagnostician.

> **Editors' Note.** Paragraphs 6 and 7 of the Comment, which follow, were added by the ABA in 1997. We underscore them to indicate that they are new.

Emergency Legal Assistance

[6] In an emergency where the health, safety, or a financial interest of a person under a disability is threatened with imminent and irreparable harm, a lawyer may take legal action on behalf of such a person even though the person is unable to establish a client-lawyer relationship or to make or express considered judgments about the matter, when the disabled person or another acting in good faith on that person's behalf has consulted the lawyer. Even in such an emergency, however, the lawyer should not act unless the lawyer reasonably believes that the person has

no other lawyer, agent or other representative available. The lawyer should take legal action on behalf of the disabled person only to the extent reasonably necessary to maintain the status quo or otherwise avoid imminent and irreparable harm. A lawyer who undertakes to represent a person in such an exigent situation has the same duties under these Rules as the lawyer would with respect to a client.

[7] A lawyer who acts on behalf of a disabled person in an emergency should keep the confidences of the disabled person as if dealing with a client, disclosing them only to the extent necessary to accomplish the intended protective action. The lawyer should disclose to any tribunal involved and to any other counsel involved the nature of his or her relationship with the disabled person. The lawyer should take steps to regularize the relationship or implement other protective solutions as soon as possible. Normally, a lawyer would not seek compensation for such emergency actions taken on behalf of a disabled person.

Model Code Comparison

There was no counterpart to this Rule in the Disciplinary Rules of the Model Code. EC 7-11 stated that the "responsibilities of a lawyer may vary according to the intelligence, experience, mental condition or age of a client. . . . Examples include the representation of an illiterate or an incompetent." EC 7-12 stated that "[a]ny mental or physical condition of a client that renders him incapable of making a considered judgment on his own behalf casts additional responsibilities upon his lawyer. Where an incompetent is acting through a guardian or other legal representative, a lawyer must look to such representative for those decisions which are normally the prerogative of the client to make. If a client under disability has no legal representative, his lawyer may be compelled in court proceedings to make decisions on behalf of the client. If the client is capable of understanding the matter in question or of contributing to the advancement of his interests, regardless of whether he is legally disqualified from performing certain acts, the lawyer should obtain from him all possible aid. If the disability of a client and the lack of a legal representative compel the lawyer to make decisions for his client, the lawyer should consider all circumstances then prevailing and act with care to safeguard and advance the interests of his client. But obviously a lawyer cannot perform any act or make any decision which the law requires his client to perform or make, either acting for himself if competent, or by a duly constituted representative if legally incompetent."

Cross-References in Rules

Rule 1.2, Comment 2: "In a case in which the client appears to be suffering mental disability, the lawyer's duty to abide by the client's decisions is to be guided by reference to **Rule 1.14.**"

Rule 1.4, Comment 3: "Ordinarily, the information to be provided is that appropriate for a client who is a comprehending and responsible adult. However, fully informing the client according to this standard may be impracticable, for example, where the client is a child or suffers from mental disability. See **Rule 1.14**."

Rule 1.16, Comment 6: "If the client is mentally incompetent, the client may lack the legal capacity to discharge the lawyer, and in any event the discharge may be seriously adverse to the client's interests. The lawyer should make special effort to help the client consider the consequences and, in an extreme case, may initiate proceedings for a conservatorship or similar protection of the client. See **Rule 1.14**."

Legislative History

1980 Discussion Draft:

... (b) A lawyer shall secure the appointment of a guardian or other legal representative, or seek a protective order with respect to a client, when doing so is necessary in the client's best interests.

1981 Draft: Rule 1.14(a) was the same as the version finally adopted. Rule 1.14(b) required a lawyer to seek appointment of a guardian or a protective order "only when the lawyer reasonably believes that the client cannot adequately communicate or exercise judgment in the client-lawyer relationship."

1982 Draft was adopted.

1995 Proposal: In May 1995, the ABA Commission on Legal Problems of the Elderly filed a proposal to amend Rule 1.14. However, the proposal was withdrawn during the ABA's August 1995 Annual Meeting so that it could be more widely circulated for public comment and so that the ABA Standing Committee on Ethics and Professional Responsibility could have an opportunity to study it. The Commission had planned to consider all comments and to present the same proposal or a similar one to the House of Delegates sometime in 1996, but that did not materialize.

The withdrawn proposal would not have touched Rule 1.14(a), but would have revised Rule 1.14(b) and added new sections 1.14(c), (d), and (e) so that those sections would have provided as follows:

(b) A lawyer may take protective action or seek the appointment of a guardian only when the lawyer reasonably believes the client cannot adequately act in the client's own interest.

(c) While it might be necessary to disclose information, the disclosure should be strictly limited to that which is necessary to accomplish the protective purpose.

(d) (1) A lawyer is an agent who acts upon the authority of a principal. In many cases, the lawyer will have a pre-existing relationship with a person or that person's family. In the absence of such a pre-existing relationship or a contractual agreement, express or implied, a lawyer generally may not act on behalf of a client.

(2) In certain circumstances, a lawyer may act as lawyer for a purported client even without express or limited agreement from the purported client, and may take those actions necessary to maintain the status quo or to avoid irreversible harm, if

i. An emergency situation exists in which the purported client's substantial health, safety, financial, or liability interests would be irreparably damaged;

ii. The purported client, in the lawyer's good faith judgment, lacks the ability to make or express considered judgments about action required to be taken because of an impairment of decision-making capacity;

iii. Time is of the essence; and

iv. The lawyer reasonably believes in good faith that no other lawyer who has an established relationship with the purported client is available or willing to act on behalf of the purported client.

(3) A "purported client" is a person who has contact with a lawyer and who would be a client but for the inability to enter into an express agreement.

(e) The lawyer should not be subject to professional discipline for invoking or failing to invoke the permissive conduct authorized by 1.14(b) if the lawyer has a reasonable basis for his or her action or inaction.

The proposal of the ABA Commission on Legal Problems of the Elderly would also have added the following language to the Comment:

Where capacity comes into question, preference should be given to staying with the situation and taking protective action over withdrawal from the case.

If the lawyer takes protective action under Model Rule 1.14(b), the lawyer's action shall be guided by:

i. The wishes and values of the client to the extent known; otherwise, according to the client's best interest;

ii. The goal of intruding into the client's decision-making autonomy to the least extent possible;

iii. The goal of maximizing client capacities; and

iv. The goal of maximizing family and social connections and community resources.

If the lawyer decides to act as *de facto* guardian, he or she, when appropriate, should seek to discontinue acting as such as soon as possible and to implement other protective solutions.

The proposal of the Commission on Legal Problems of the Elderly was accompanied by an eleven-page report, which explained that the genesis of the proposal was a conference on Ethical Issues in Representing Older Clients held at Fordham University Law School in December 1993. Much of the report quoted or cited papers from that conference, which are published in 62 Fordham L. Rev. (March 1994).

1997 Amendment: At its 1997 Mid-Year Meeting the ABA House of Delegates voted to add two new paragraphs, ¶¶6-7, to the Comment to Rule 1.14. (The amendment did not alter the text of Rule 1.14 or the existing Comment.) The new paragraphs, which were co-sponsored by the ABA Standing Committee on Ethics and Professional Responsibility and the ABA Commission on Legal Problems of the Elderly, are an outgrowth of amendments to the text of Rule 1.14 that the Commission proposed in 1995 (see 1995 entry above). They explain what a lawyer should do in an "emergency" that threatens the health, safety or financial interest of a disabled person who is not yet a client. The new paragraphs should be read in conjunction with ABA Ethics Op. 96-404 (1996), which addressed ethical issues that arise when existing clients are no longer mentally capable of handling their own affairs. The House of Delegates approved the new paragraphs exactly as proposed, by an overwhelming voice vote. (A North Carolina lawyer proposed from the floor to strike the last sentence of Comment 7 — "Normally, a lawyer would not seek compensation for such emergency actions taken on behalf of a disabled person" — but the House of Delegates rejected the amendment.) We reprint here the full text of the ABA Committee Report submitted in support of the 1997 amendment.

ABA Report Explaining 1997 Amendment to Comment*

The ABA Commission on Legal Problems of the Elderly has brought to the attention of the Standing Committee on Ethics and Professional Responsibility common situations in which a lawyer may reasonably conclude that an elderly person who has not been judged incompetent is in need of emergency legal assistance, but is, or appears to be, unable to make decisions on his or her own behalf — including a decision to retain a lawyer. Such situations fall most naturally within the spirit of Model Rule 1.14 ("Client Under a Disability"). The question is whether it is ethically permissible for a lawyer to take legal action on behalf of a disabled person who cannot, in the first instance, form a client-lawyer relationship.

The question whether and under what circumstances a lawyer may take emergency legal action on behalf of a disabled person who is not a client is not, of course, unique to the representation of the elderly. It may arise in a variety of practice settings where individuals appear to be in need of immediate legal assistance but are unable to make adequately considered decisions in connection with initiating legal representation.

Most of the duties arising under the Model Rules (the most notable exception being that of confidentiality) attach only after the formation of a client-lawyer relationship, and the Rules are silent with respect to any forms of representation that do not arise from such relationship. As noted in the Scope section of the Model Rules (at paragraph [15]), the existence of a client-lawyer relationship depends upon an express and comprehending authorization from a principal (the client) to an agent (the lawyer):

> "Furthermore, for purposes of determining the lawyer's authority and responsibility, principles of substantive law external to these Rules determine whether a client-lawyer relationship exists. Most of the duties flowing from the client-lawyer relationship attach only after the client has requested the lawyer to render legal services and the lawyer has agreed to do so. But there

*Committee Reports do not represent official policy of the ABA. They are for information only, and the opinions are those of the authors of the report.

are some duties, such as that of confidentiality under Rule 1.6, that may attach when the lawyer agrees to consider whether a client-lawyer relationship shall be established. Whether a client-lawyer relationship exists for any specific purpose can depend on the circumstances and may be a question of fact."

In light of the Model Rules' general reliance upon the concept of an established client-lawyer relationship, it is reasonable to expect that a lawyer would be uncertain about the ethical propriety of his taking legal action on behalf of an individual with whom he has not been able to establish such relationship because of the person's disability, even in an emergency. However, the Committee believes that such emergency action is permissible under the Model Rules, if properly limited. It notes as evidence of the Model Rules' acceptance of this principle the existing acknowledgment in the Comment to Model Rule 1.1 ("Competence") that some latitude to depart from the strict terms of that Rule exists in some emergency situations.

In order to allay lawyers' doubts about the propriety of taking legal action in emergency situations on behalf of disabled individuals, and to give lawyers some specific guidance respecting the limitations of such emergency responses, the Committee has developed a brief discussion of this subject for inclusion in the Comment to Model Rule 1.14. The proposed addition to the commentary makes clear that, in certain circumstances and subject to some restrictions, a lawyer is permitted to take emergency legal action on behalf of a disabled person with whom the lawyer does not have a traditional client-lawyer relationship.

Limits on and Compensation for Emergency Legal Assistance

In order to avoid undertaking a greater responsibility than is justified under any particular circumstances, a lawyer should take no greater action on behalf of the disabled person "than is reasonably necessary to maintain the status quo or otherwise avoid imminent and irreparable harm," leaving to the legal discretion of a subsequently appointed lawyer or legal representative such as a guardian any further action to advance the disabled person's interests.

Moreover, in order to render the legal position of the disabled person as normal as possible, a lawyer should take steps to regularize the client-lawyer relationship or to implement other protective actions as soon as possible. Such action will assure the disabled person the benefits of bona fide legal representation in the context of a client-lawyer relationship clearly governed by all applicable ethical and fiduciary principles.

Finally, to deter overreaching, the Comment expressly notes that a lawyer normally should disclose the nature of the emergency relationship, and not seek compensation for the emergency services.

Selected State Variations

California has no counterpart to Rule 1.14.

Colorado: Rule 1.14(b) contains the following additional language:

Not only can the mental, physical or other condition of the client impose additional responsibilities on the lawyer, the fact that a client is impaired does not relieve the lawyer of the obligation to obtain information from the client to the extent possible.

Massachusetts: Effective January 1, 1998, Rule 1.14(b) permits a lawyer who reasonably believes that a client lacks capacity as described in Rule 1.14(a) to consult "family members, adult protective agencies, or other individuals or entities that have authority to protect the client, and, if it reasonably appears necessary, the lawyer may seek the appointment of a guardian ad litem, conservator, or guardian, as the case may be."

New York: Same or substantially the same as the ABA Model Code — see Model Code Comparison above.

Texas Rule 1.02(g) provides:

> A lawyer shall take reasonable action to secure the appointment of a guardian or other legal representative for, or seek other protective orders with respect to, a client whenever the lawyer reasonably believes that the client lacks legal competence and that such action should be taken to protect the client.

Virginia omits Rule 1.14.

Related Materials

American Academy of Matrimonial Lawyers: The "Bounds of Advocacy" drafted by the American Academy of Matrimonial Lawyers contains the following provision and commentary:

> 1.2 An attorney should be sensitive to common emotional and psychological problems. When an attorney believes that such problems are interfering with effective representation or with the client's ability to function, he should suggest that the client seek the help of a mental health professional.

Comment to Rule 1.2

> Clients often come to matrimonial lawyers with "emotional baggage" that hinders their ability to make well-considered decisions about their case or interact in a constructive manner with other family members, opposing counsel, or their own attorney. Recognizing and helping the client deal with emotional problems may be essential to an effective attorney-client relationship. Competent representation may require that the attorney recommend that the client consult a mental health professional. See Standards 2.9, 2.10, 2.11 and fn. 22.

Americans with Disabilities Act: All lawyers, especially those whose clients include people with disabilities, must adhere to Title III of the Americans with Disabilities Act, which took effect in January 1992. Section 302(a) of Title III, 42 U.S.C. §12182(a), states the general rule:

> No individual shall be discriminated against on the basis of disability in the full and equal enjoyment of the goods, services, facilities, privileges, advantages, or accommodations of any place of public accommodation by any person who owns, leases (or leases to), or operates a place of public accommodation.

(The term "public accommodation" encompasses any law firm open to the public.)

Restatement of the Law Governing Lawyers: The American Law Institute has tentatively approved the following provision:

§35. Client Under Disability

(1) When a client's ability to make adequately considered decisions in connection with the representation is impaired, whether because of minority, physical illness, mental disability, or other cause, the lawyer must, as far as reasonably possible, maintain a normal client-lawyer relationship with the client and act in the best interests of the client as stated in Subsection (2).

(2) A lawyer representing a client impaired as described in Subsection (1) and for whom no guardian or other representative is available to act, must, with respect to a matter within the scope of the representation, pursue the lawyer's reasonable view of the client's objectives or interests as the client would define them if able to make adequately considered decisions on the matter, even if the client expresses no wishes or gives contrary instructions.

(3) If a client impaired as described in Subsection (1) has a guardian or other person legally entitled to act for the client, the client's lawyer must treat that person as entitled to act with respect to the client's interests in the matter, unless:

    (a) the lawyer represents the client in a matter against the interests of that person; or

    (b) that person instructs the lawyer to act in a manner that the lawyer knows will violate the person's legal duties toward the client.

(4) A lawyer representing a client impaired as described in Subsection (1) may seek the appointment of a guardian or take other protective action within the scope of the representation when doing so is practical and will advance the client's objectives or interests, determined as stated in Subsection (2).

Rule 1.15 Safekeeping Property

(a) A lawyer shall hold property of clients or third persons that is in a lawyer's possession in connection with a representation separate from the lawyer's own property. Funds shall be kept in a separate account maintained in the state where the lawyer's office is situated, or elsewhere with the consent of the client or third person. Other property shall be identified as such and appropriately safeguarded. Complete records of such account funds and other property shall be kept by the lawyer and shall be preserved for a period of [five years] after termination of the representation.

(b) Upon receiving funds or other property in which a client or third person has an interest, a lawyer shall promptly notify the client or third person. Except as stated in this rule or otherwise permitted by law or by

agreement with the client, a lawyer shall promptly deliver to the client or third person any funds or other property that the client or third person is entitled to receive and, upon request by the client or third person, shall promptly render a full accounting regarding such property.

(c) When in the course of representation a lawyer is in possession of property in which both the lawyer and another person claim interests, the property shall be kept separate by the lawyer until there is an accounting and severance of their interests. If a dispute arises concerning their respective interests, the portion in dispute shall be kept separate by the lawyer until the dispute is resolved.

COMMENT

[1] A lawyer should hold property of others with the care required of a professional fiduciary. Securities should be kept in a safe deposit box, except when some other form of safekeeping is warranted by special circumstances. All property which is the property of clients or third persons should be kept separate from the lawyer's business and personal property and, if monies, in one or more trust accounts. Separate trust accounts may be warranted when administering estate monies or acting in similar fiduciary capacities.

[2] Lawyers often receive funds from third parties from which the lawyer's fee will be paid. If there is risk that the client may divert the funds without paying the fee, the lawyer is not required to remit the portion from which the fee is to be paid. However, a lawyer may not hold funds to coerce a client into accepting the lawyer's contention. The disputed portion of the funds should be kept in trust and the lawyer should suggest means for prompt resolution of the dispute, such as arbitration. The undisputed portion of the funds shall be promptly distributed.

[3] Third parties, such as a client's creditors, may have just claims against funds or other property in a lawyer's custody. A lawyer may have a duty under applicable law to protect such third-party claims against wrongful interference by the client, and accordingly may refuse to surrender the property to the client. However, a lawyer should not unilaterally assume to arbitrate a dispute between the client and the third party.

[4] The obligations of a lawyer under this Rule are independent of those arising from activity other than rendering legal services. For example, a lawyer who serves as an escrow agent is governed by the applicable law relating to fiduciaries even though the lawyer does not render legal services in the transaction.

[5] A "client's security fund" provides a means through the collective efforts of the bar to reimburse persons who have lost money or property as a result of dishonest conduct of a lawyer. Where such a fund has been established, a lawyer should participate.

Model Code Comparison

With regard to paragraph (a), DR 9-102(A) provided that "funds of clients" are to be kept in an identifiable bank account in the state in which the lawyer's office is situated. DR 9-102(B)(2) provided that a lawyer shall "identify and label securities and properties of a client . . . and place them in . . . safekeeping. . . ." DR 9-102(B)(3) required that a lawyer "[m]aintain complete records of all funds, securities, and other properties of a client. . . ." Paragraph (a) extends these requirements to property of a third person that is in the lawyer's possession in connection with the representation.

Paragraph (b) is substantially similar to DR 9-102(B)(1), (3), and (4).

Paragraph (c) is similar to DR 9-102(A)(2), except that the requirement regarding disputes applies to property concerning which an interest is claimed by a third person as well as by a client.

Cross-References in Rules

None.

Legislative History

1980 Discussion Draft (then Rule 1.12) provided in (a) that funds "shall be kept in a *trust* account." Subparagraph (d) provided:

> (d) When a lawyer and another person both have interests in property, the property shall be treated by the lawyer as trust property until an accounting and severance of their interests. If a dispute arises concerning their respective interests, the portion in dispute shall be treated as trust property until the dispute is resolved.

1981 and 1982 Drafts were substantially the same as adopted.

Selected State Variations

Alabama: Rule 1.15(a) was amended effective July 1, 1997 to provide that "[n]o personal funds of a lawyer shall ever be deposited in such a trust account, except (1) unearned attorney fees that are being held until earned, and (2) funds sufficient to cover maintenance fees, such as service charges, on the account.'' Rule 1.15(g) requires lawyers to maintain short-term or nominal client funds in an interest-bearing account that remits the interest quarterly to the Alabama Law Foundation or the Alabama Civil Justice Foundation. Rules 1.15(i) and (j) state the many purposes of the Alabama Law Foundation and the Alabama Civil Justice Foundation.

Alaska adds Rule 1.15(d), which provides that unless a lawyer submits an election not to participate, ''a lawyer or law firm shall establish and maintain an interest bearing insured depository account into which must be deposited funds of clients which are nominal in amount or are expected to be held for a short period of time.'' The rule then sets forth detailed rules governing such accounts.

California: See Rule 4-100 (Preserving Identity of Funds and Property of a Client) and accompanying standards.

Connecticut adds Rule 1.15(d), which generally requires lawyers to deposit client funds in an interest-bearing account if the funds are less than $10,000 or are expected to be held for no more than 60 business days. The interest provides funding for ''(i) the delivery of legal services to the poor by nonprofit corporations whose principal purpose is providing legal services to the poor and (ii) law school scholarships based on financial need.'' The rule contains detailed provisions, amended effective January 28, 1997, regarding interest rates, recordkeeping, reporting, audits, and other matters. The final subparagraph, Rule 1.15(d)(7), provides:

> Nothing in this section shall prevent a lawyer or law firm from depositing a client's funds, regardless of the amount of such funds or the period for which such funds are expected to be held, in a separate interest-bearing account established on behalf of and for the benefit of the client.

Delaware adds a long list of requirements.

District of Columbia: D.C. Rule 1.15 differs significantly from the ABA Model Rule, and D.C.'s version of Rule 1.17 deals with notification of trust account overdrafts — see District of Columbia Rules of Professional Conduct below.

Florida: Effective January 1, 1994, the Florida Supreme Court approved extensive amendments to Chapter 5 of the Supreme Court Rules, which regulates lawyer trust accounts. In addition, Florida made minor amendments to Rule 4-1.15 effective April 24, 1997.

Georgia: Effective January 1, 1996, Georgia adopted a series of new Standards to regulate lawyer trust accounts. Standard 65.1 provides as follows:

> *Standard 65.1 Required Bank Accounts.* Every lawyer who . . . receives money or other property on behalf of a client or in any other fiduciary capacity shall maintain, in an approved financial institution in Georgia . . . , a trust account or accounts, separate from any business and personal accounts, into which funds received by the lawyer on behalf of a client or in any other fiduciary capacity shall be deposited.
>
> A violation of this standard may be punished by disbarment.

The other provisions adopted effective January 1, 1996 — Standards 65.2 through 65.5 — govern designation of trust and business bank accounts, criteria for approved financial institutions, the obligation to produce bank account records for an investigation, and the obligation to submit to an Audit for Cause conducted by the State Disciplinary Board.

Illinois provides:

> (d) All nominal or short-terms funds of clients paid to a lawyer or law firm, including advances for costs and expenses, shall be deposited in one or more pooled interest-bearing trust accounts established with a bank or savings and loan association, with the Lawyers Trust Fund of Illinois designated as income beneficiary. . . .

The Illinois rule then sets forth detailed guidelines for maintaining these mandatory IOLTA accounts.

Massachusetts: Effective January 1, 1998, Rule 1.15 has extensive provisions for deposit of client funds in IOLTA accounts. Rule 1.15(f) contains provisions to ensure that disciplinary authorities are notified in the event a lawyer's check is dishonored.

Michigan provides for IOLTA accounts in Rule 1.15(d).

Missouri: Rule 1.15(d) through (g) and Appendix 1 to Supreme Court Rule 4 provide for the Missouri Lawyer Trust Account Foundation, an IOLTA program.

New York: See New York version of DR 9-102.

Virginia generally keeps the language of DR 9-102, but has included an IOLTA program in DR 9-102 and has added extensive rules in DR 9-103 to govern record-keeping for client funds and property.

Related Materials

ABA Canons: Canon 11 provided:

11. Dealing with Trust Property

> Money of the client or collected for the client or other trust property coming into the possession of the lawyer should be reported and accounted for promptly, and should not under any circumstances be commingled with his own or be used by him.

ABA Financial Recordkeeping Rule: At its February 1993 Mid-Year Meeting, the ABA House of Delegates overwhelmingly approved a Model Financial Recordkeeping Rule. The rule was sponsored by the ABA Standing Committee on Lawyers' Responsibility for Client Protection and was uncontroversial. The purpose of the rule is to provide detailed guidance for compliance with Model Rule 1.15. The rule details ten separate categories of records that a lawyer must keep current and must retain for five years after termination of a representation. It also contains rules regarding deposits, withdrawals, and bookkeeping for lawyer trust accounts, and provides guidelines for dealing with trust accounts upon the dissolution of a law firm or the sale of a law practice.

ABA Random Audit Rule: At its August 1993 Annual Meeting, by the narrow vote of 110 to 105, the ABA House of Delegates approved a Model Rule for the Random Audit of Lawyer Trust Accounts. The Random Audit Rule follows through on Recommendation 16 of the "McKay Commission" (an ABA commission to study the lawyer disciplinary system, which released its widely read report in 1991). Recommendation 16, which was adopted by the ABA House of Delegates in 1992 and is official policy of the ABA, urges that the highest court of every state "should adopt a rule providing that lawyer trust accounts selected at random may be audited without having grounds to believe misconduct has occurred and also providing appropriate procedural safeguards." Like the Model Financial Recordkeeping Rule, the Random Audit Rule was sponsored by the ABA Standing Committee on Lawyers' Responsibility for Client Protection. The rule was controversial and was opposed by the ABA Section on General Practice, which is composed mainly of sole practitioners and small firms. The Random Audit Rule and the Committee Report submitted in support of the Rule provide as follows:

Random Audits of Lawyer Trust Accounts

(a) The [Supreme Court] shall approve procedures to randomly select lawyer or law firm trust accounts for audit.

(b) An audit of a lawyer or law firm trust account conducted pursuant to this rule shall be commenced by the issuance of an investigative subpoena to compel the production of records relating to a lawyer's or law firm's trust accounts. The subpoena shall contain a certification that it was issued in compliance with this rule; that the lawyer or law firm was selected at random; and that there exist no grounds to believe that professional misconduct has occurred with respect to the accounts being audited. The subpoena shall be served at least [10] business days before commencement of the audit.

(c) With respect to each audit conducted pursuant to this rule, the examiner shall:

(1) determine whether the lawyer's or law firm's records and accounts are being maintained in accordance with applicable rules of court; and

(2) employ sampling techniques to examine "selected accounts," unless discrepancies are found which indicate a need for a more detailed audit. "Selected accounts" may include money, securities and other trust assets held by the lawyer or law firm; safe deposit boxes and similar devices; deposit records; cancelled checks or their equivalent; and any other records which pertain to trust transactions affecting the lawyer's or law firm's practice of law.

(d) The examiner shall prepare a written report containing the examiner's findings, a copy of which shall be provided to the audited lawyer or law firm.

(e) In the event that the audit report asserts deficiencies in the audited lawyer's or law firm's records or procedures, the lawyer or law firm shall, within [10] business days after receipt of the report, provide evidence that the alleged deficiencies are incorrect, or that they have been corrected. If corrective action requires additional time, the lawyer or law firm shall apply for an extension of time to a date certain in which to correct the deficiencies cited in the audit report.

(f) All records produced for an audit conducted pursuant to this rule shall remain confidential, and their contents shall not be disclosed in violation of the attorney-client privilege.

(g) Records produced for an audit conducted pursuant to this rule may be disclosed to:

(1) the lawyer disciplinary agency or to a court to the extent disclosure is necessary for the purposes of the particular audit;

(2) the lawyer disciplinary agency for the purposes of a disciplinary proceeding; and

(3) any other person, including a law enforcement agency, with the permission of the Supreme Court.

(h) A lawyer or law firm shall cooperate in an audit conducted pursuant to this rule, and shall answer all questions pertaining thereto, unless the lawyer or law firm claims a privilege or right which is available to the lawyer or law firm under applicable state or federal law. A lawyer's or law firm's failure to cooperate in an audit conducted pursuant to this rule shall constitute professional misconduct.

(i) No lawyer or law firm shall be subject to an audit conducted pursuant to this rule more frequently than once every [three] years.

*Report of the Standing Committee on Lawyers' Responsibility for Client Protection**

Existing Rule 1.15 of the Model Rules of Professional Conduct requires that lawyers who hold the property of others in the practice of law must exercise the care required of professional fiduciaries, including the safeguarding of those assets in bank accounts, and the maintenance of complete records. The Model Financial Recordkeeping Rule approved by the House of Delegates on February 9, 1993 provides detailed guidance for compliance with Rule 1.15.

Random audit programs exist, or are authorized, in the jurisdictions of Delaware, Iowa, Nebraska, New Hampshire, New Jersey, New York (1st and 2nd Departments), North Carolina, and Washington.

The McKay Commission has determined that random audits are a proven deterrent to the misuse of money and property in the practice of law. The examination of trust accounts by court-paid auditors also provides practitioners with expert and practical assistance in maintaining necessary records and supporting books of account.

The proposed Model Rule of Random Audits for Lawyer Trust Accounts contains many provisions in existing state programs, and has been drafted to assist the agencies nationwide to implement Recommendation 16 in the McKay Commission report.

The Model Rule proposes a basic structure and system for a random audit program, including such procedural safeguards as adequate prior notice before the

*Committee Reports do not represent official policy of the ABA. They are for information only, and the opinions are those of the authors of the report.

commencement of an audit; written audit reports; the opportunity for an audited lawyer or law firm to respond to an examiner's report; the preservation of confidentiality for law client records; and the frequency of audits conducted by random selection.

The Model Rule contemplates that assigned agencies will tailor or augment these basic procedures to address specific conditions, needs, and concerns which exist in their jurisdictions. Such local rules will require the assignment of administrative responsibility for the jurisdiction's random audit program to the lawyer disciplinary agency, the lawyers' fund for client protection, or other appropriate entity.

ABA Standards for Imposing Lawyer Sanctions:

4.11. Disbarment is generally appropriate when a lawyer knowingly converts client property and causes injury or potential injury to a client.

4.12. Suspension is generally appropriate when a lawyer knows or should know that he is dealing improperly with client property and causes injury or potential injury to a client.

4.13. Reprimand is generally appropriate when a lawyer is negligent in dealing with client property and causes injury or potential injury to a client.

4.14. Admonition is generally appropriate when a lawyer is negligent in dealing with client property and causes little or no actual or potential injury to a client.

Client Protection Funds: In keeping with Comment 5 of Rule 1.15, many states have established client protection funds (sometimes called client security funds) for the purpose of reimbursing clients who have lost money or property as a result of dishonest conduct by lawyers. For example, chapter 7 of Florida's Supreme Court Rules authorizes establishment of a Clients' Security Fund "to provide monetary relief to persons who suffer reimbursable losses as a result of misappropriation, embezzlement, or other wrongful taking or conversion" by a Florida lawyer. In several states, these client protection funds have paid out so many claims that they have run out of money. The ABA adopted Model Rules for Lawyers' Funds for Client Protection at its 1989 Annual Meeting. These Model Rules replaced similar rules first adopted in 1981, then called Model Rules for Clients' Security Funds.

Model Rules of Professional Conduct for Federal Lawyers add a new subparagraph (d) that provides: "When property of a client or third party is admitted into evidence or otherwise included in the record of a proceeding, the Federal lawyer should take reasonable action to ensure its prompt return."

Restatement of the Law Governing Lawyers: The American Law Institute has tentatively approved the following provisions:

§56. Safeguarding and Segregating Property

(1) A lawyer holding funds or other property of a client in connection with a representation, or such funds or other property in which a client claims an interest, must take reasonable steps to safeguard the funds or property. A similar obligation may be imposed by law on funds or other property so held and owned or

claimed by a third person. In particular, the lawyer must hold such property separate from the lawyer's property, keep records of it, deposit funds in an account separate from the lawyer's own funds, identify tangible objects, and comply with related requirements imposed by regulatory authorities.

(2) Upon receiving funds or other property in a professional capacity and in which a client or a third person owns or claims an interest, a lawyer shall promptly notify the client or third person. The lawyer shall promptly render a full accounting regarding such property upon request by the client or third person.

§57. Surrendering Possession of Property

(1) Except as provided in Subsection (2), a lawyer must promptly deliver, to the client or third person so entitled, funds or other property in the lawyer's possession belonging to a client or third person.

(2) A lawyer may retain possession of funds or other property of a client or third person if:

(a) the client or third person consents;

(b) the lawyer's client is entitled to the property, the lawyer appropriately possesses the property for purposes of the representation, and the client has not asked for delivery of the property;

(c) the lawyer has a valid lien on the property (see §55);

(d) there are substantial grounds for dispute as to the person entitled to the property; or

(e) delivering the property to the client or third person would violate a court order or other legal obligation of the lawyer.

(Restatement §55 is reprinted in the Related Materials following Model Rule 1.8.)

Rule 1.16 Declining or Terminating Representation

(a) Except as stated in paragraph (c), a lawyer shall not represent a client or, where representation has commenced, shall withdraw from the representation of a client if:

(1) the representation will result in violation of the rules of professional conduct or other law; *e.g* *(1.2(d))*

(2) the lawyer's physical or mental condition materially impairs the lawyer's ability to represent the client; or

(3) the lawyer is discharged.

(b) Except as stated in paragraph (c), a lawyer may withdraw from representing a client if withdrawal can be accomplished without material adverse effect on the interests of the client, or if

(1) the client persists in a course of action involving the lawyer's services that the lawyer reasonably believes is criminal or fraudulent;

note difference

(2) the client has used the lawyer's services to perpetrate a crime or fraud;

(3) a client insists upon pursuing an objective that the lawyer considers repugnant or imprudent;

client can't pay (4) the client fails substantially to fulfill an obligation to the lawyer regarding the lawyer's services and has been given reasonable warning that the lawyer will withdraw unless the obligation is fulfilled;

(5) the representation will result in an unreasonable financial burden on the lawyer or has been rendered unreasonably difficult by the client; or *atty is on brink of not*

(6) other good cause for withdrawal exists.

(c) When ordered to do so by a tribunal, a lawyer shall continue representation notwithstanding good cause for terminating the representation.

(d) Upon termination of representation, a lawyer shall take steps to the extent reasonably practicable to protect a client's interests, such as giving reasonable notice to the client, allowing time for employment of other counsel, surrendering papers and property to which the client is entitled and refunding any advance payment of fee that has not been earned. The lawyer may retain papers relating to the client to the extent permitted by other law.

COMMENT

[1] A lawyer should not accept representation in a matter unless it can be performed competently, promptly, without improper conflict of interest and to completion.

Mandatory Withdrawal

[2] A lawyer ordinarily must decline or withdraw from representation if the client demands that the lawyer engage in conduct that is illegal or violates the Rules of Professional Conduct or other law. The lawyer is not obliged to decline or withdraw simply because the client suggests such a course of conduct; a client may make such a suggestion in the hope that a lawyer will not be constrained by a professional obligation.

[3] When a lawyer has been appointed to represent a client, withdrawal ordinarily requires approval of the appointing authority. See also Rule 6.2. Difficulty may be encountered if withdrawal is based on the client's demand that the lawyer engage in unprofessional conduct. The court

may wish an explanation for the withdrawal, while the lawyer may be bound to keep confidential the facts that would constitute such an explanation. The lawyer's statement that professional considerations require termination of the representation ordinarily should be accepted as sufficient.

Discharge

[4] A client has a right to discharge a lawyer at any time, with or without cause, subject to liability for payment for the lawyer's services. Where future dispute about the withdrawal may be anticipated, it may be advisable to prepare a written statement reciting the circumstances.

[5] Whether a client can discharge appointed counsel may depend on applicable law. A client seeking to do so should be given a full explanation of the consequences. These consequences may include a decision by the appointing authority that appointment of successor counsel is unjustified, thus requiring the client to represent himself.

[6] If the client is mentally incompetent, the client may lack the legal capacity to discharge the lawyer, and in any event the discharge may be seriously adverse to the client's interests. The lawyer should make special effort to help the client consider the consequences and, in an extreme case, may initiate proceedings for a conservatorship or similar protection of the client. See Rule 1.14.

Optional Withdrawal

[7] A lawyer may withdraw from the representation in some circumstances. The lawyer has the option to withdraw if it can be accomplished without material adverse effect on the client's interests. Withdrawal is also justified if the client persists in a course of action that the lawyer reasonably believes is criminal or fraudulent, for a lawyer is not required to be associated with such conduct even if the lawyer does not further it. Withdrawal is also permitted if the lawyer's services were misused in the past even if that would materially prejudice the client. The lawyer also may withdraw where the client insists on a repugnant or imprudent objective.

[8] A lawyer may withdraw if the client refuses to abide by the terms of an agreement relating to the representation, such as an agreement concerning fees or court costs or an agreement limiting the objectives of the representation.

Assisting the Client upon Withdrawal

[9] Even if the lawyer has been unfairly discharged by the client, a lawyer must take all reasonable steps to mitigate the consequences to the client. The lawyer may retain papers as security for a fee only to the extent permitted by law.

[10] Whether or not a lawyer for an organization may under certain unusual circumstances have a legal obligation to the organization after withdrawing or being discharged by the organization's highest authority is beyond the scope of these Rules.

Model Code Comparison

With regard to paragraph (a), DR 2-109(A) provided that a lawyer "shall not accept employment . . . if he knows or it is obvious that [the prospective client] wishes to . . . [b]ring a legal action . . . or otherwise have steps taken for him, merely for the purpose of harassing or maliciously injuring any person. . . ." Nor may a lawyer accept employment if the lawyer is aware that the prospective client wishes to "[p]resent a claim or defense . . . that is not warranted under existing law, unless it can be supported by good faith argument for an extension, modification, or reversal of existing law." DR 2-110(B) provided that a lawyer "shall withdraw from employment . . . if":

(1) He knows or it is obvious that his client is bringing the legal action . . . or is otherwise having steps taken for him, merely for the purpose of harassing or maliciously injuring any person.

(2) He knows or it is obvious that his continued employment will result in violation of a Disciplinary Rule.

(3) His mental or physical condition renders it unreasonably difficult for him to carry out the employment effectively.

(4) He is discharged by his client.

With regard to paragraph (b), DR 2-110(C) permitted withdrawal regardless of the effect on the client if:

(1) His client: (a) Insists upon presenting a claim or defense that is not warranted under existing law and cannot be supported by good faith argument for an extension, modification, or reversal of existing law; (b) Personally seeks to pursue an illegal course of conduct; (c) Insists that the lawyer pursue a course of conduct that is illegal or that is prohibited under the Disciplinary Rules; (d) By other conduct renders it unreasonably difficult for the lawyer to carry out his employment effectively; (e) Insists, in a matter not pending before a tribunal, that the lawyer engage in conduct that is contrary to the judgment and advice of the lawyer but

not prohibited under the Disciplinary Rules; (f) Deliberately disregards an agreement or obligation to the lawyer as to expenses and fees.

(2) His continued employment is likely to result in a violation of a Disciplinary Rule.

(3) His inability to work with co-counsel indicates that the best interest of the client likely will be served by withdrawal.

(4) His mental or physical condition renders it difficult for him to carry out the employment effectively.

(5) His client knowingly and freely assents to termination of his employment.

(6) He believes in good faith, in a proceeding pending before a tribunal, that the tribunal will find the existence of other good cause for withdrawal.

With regard to paragraph (c), DR 2-110(A)(1) provided: "If permission for withdrawal from employment is required by the rules of a tribunal, the lawyer shall not withdraw . . . without its permission."

The provisions of paragraph (d) are substantially identical to DR 2-110(A)(2) and (3).

Cross-References in Rules

Rule 1.3, Comment 3: "Unless the relationship is terminated as provided in **Rule 1.16**, a lawyer should carry through to conclusion all matters undertaken for a client."

Rule 1.5, Comment 2: "A lawyer may require advance payment of a fee, but is obliged to return any unearned portion. See **Rule 1.16(d)**."

Rule 1.6, Comment 14: "If the lawyer's services will be used by the client in materially furthering a course of criminal or fraudulent conduct, the lawyer must withdraw, as stated in **Rule 1.16(a)(1)**."

Rule 1.6, Comment 15: "After withdrawal the lawyer is required to refrain from making disclosure of the clients' confidences, except as otherwise provided in Rule 1.6. Neither this Rule nor Rule 1.8(b) nor **Rule 1.16(d)** prevents the lawyer from giving notice of the fact of withdrawal, and the lawyer may also withdraw or disaffirm any opinion, document, affirmation, or the like."

Rule 1.7, Comment 2: "If . . . a conflict arises after representation has been undertaken, the lawyer should withdraw from the representation. See **Rule 1.16**."

Rule 1.13(c) provides that a lawyer "may resign in accordance with **Rule 1.16**."

Rule 1.13, Comment 6: "[T]his Rule does not limit or expand the lawyer's responsibility under" **Rule 1.16**.

Rule 1.17, Comment 12 provides: "If approval of the substitution of the purchasing attorney for the selling attorney is required by the rules of any tribunal in which a matter is pending, such approval must be obtained before the matter can be included in the sale (see **Rule 1.16**)."

Rule 2.2, Comment 10: "Common representation does not diminish the rights of each client in the client-lawyer relationship. Each has the right to loyal and diligent representation, the right to discharge the lawyer as stated in **Rule 1.16**, and the protections of Rule 1.9. . . ."

Legislative History

1980 Discussion Draft: Rule 1.16(b) provided:

(b) Except as stated in paragraph (c), a lawyer may withdraw from representing a client if:
(1) Withdrawal can be effected without material prejudice to the client;
(2) The client persists in a course of conduct that is illegal or unjust; or
(3) The client fails to fulfill an obligation to the lawyer regarding the lawyer's services.

1981 and 1982 Drafts were substantially the same as adopted.

Selected State Variations

California: See Rule 3-700 (Termination of Employment).

Colorado: Rule 1.16 omits the Model Rule provision permitting withdrawal when "other good cause for withdrawal exists."

District of Columbia: A lawyer may withdraw if "obdurate or vexatious conduct on the part of the client has rendered the representation unreasonably difficult."

Georgia retains the substance of the Code provision on withdrawal.

Illinois: Rule 1.16 is substantially the same as DR 2-110.

Massachusetts: Effective January 1, 1998, Rule 1.16 permits lawyers to retain "work product" for which the client has not paid and contains a definition of work product for purposes of the rule. However, this authority is suspended "when retention would prejudice the client unfairly."

New York: Same or substantially the same as the ABA Model Code — see Model Code Comparison above.

Oregon: In 1995, to reflect a lawyer's right to sell a law practice pursuant to new DR 2-111, Oregon added a new subparagraph DR 2-110 (C) (7), which provides that a lawyer may permissively withdraw if:

(7) [t]he lawyer has sold all or part of the lawyer's practice in compliance with the requirements of DR 2-111. The selling lawyer shall comply with the requirements of DR 2-110(A) if the selling lawyer intends to withdraw from representation of the client even if the client objects to the transfer of its legal work to the purchasing lawyer.

Virginia: DR 2-107 retains the language of DR 2-109 on declining employment. DR 2-108(A)(1) mandates withdrawal if continuing the representation will result in "a course of conduct by the lawyer that is illegal or inconsistent" with the Rules. DR 2-108(B)(2) permits withdrawal if the client persists in a course of conduct that is "illegal or unjust" (as opposed to "criminal or fraudulent"), and DR 2-108(B)(3) permits withdrawal if the client fails to fulfill an obligation to the lawyer "and such failure continues after reasonable notice to the client" (in place of "reasonable warning that the lawyer will withdraw"). Virginia has no equivalent to Rule 1.16(b)(2), (3), and (6).

Related Materials

ABA Canons: Canons 7 and 44 provided:

7. *Professional Colleagues and Conflicts of Opinion*

A client's proffer of assistance of additional counsel should not be regarded as evidence of want of confidence, but the matter should be left to the determination of the client. A lawyer should decline association as colleague if it is objectionable to the original counsel, but if the lawyer first retained is relieved, another may come into the case.

When lawyers jointly associated in a cause cannot agree as to any matter vital to the interest of the client, the conflict of opinion should be frankly stated to him for his final determination. His decision should be accepted unless the nature of the difference makes it impracticable for the lawyer whose judgment has been overruled to cooperate effectively. In this event it is his duty to ask the client to relieve him.

Efforts, direct or indirect, in any way to encroach upon the professional employment of another lawyer, are unworthy of those who should be brethren at the Bar; but, nevertheless, it is the right of any lawyer, without fear or favor, to give proper advice to those seeking relief against unfaithful or neglectful counsel, generally after communication with the lawyer of whom the complaint is made.

44. *Withdrawal from Employment as Attorney or Counsel*

The right of an attorney or counsel to withdraw from employment, once assumed, arises only from good cause. Even the desire or consent of the client is not always sufficient. The lawyer should not throw up the unfinished task to the detriment of his client except for reasons of honor or self-respect. If the client insists upon an unjust or immoral course in the conduct of his case, or if he persists over the attorney's remonstrance in presenting frivolous defenses, or if he deliberately disregards an agreement or obligation as to fees or expenses, the lawyer may be warranted in withdrawing on due notice to the client, allowing him time to employ another lawyer. So also when a lawyer discovers that his client has no case and the client is determined to continue it; or even if the lawyer finds himself incapable of conducting the case effectively. Sundry other instances may arise in which withdrawal is to be justified. Upon withdrawing from a case after a retainer has been paid, the attorney should refund such part of the retainer as has not been clearly earned.

American Lawyer's Code of Conduct: Rules 5.5 and 6.2 through 6.5 provide:

5.5. A lawyer shall not impose a lien upon any part of a client's files, except upon the lawyer's own work product, and then only to the extent that the work product has not been paid for. This work-product exception shall be inapplicable when the client is in fact unable to pay, or when withholding the lawyer's work product would present a significant risk to the client of imprisonment, deportation, destruction of essential evidence, loss of custody of a child, or similar irreparable harm.

6.2. A lawyer may withdraw from representing a client at any time and for any reason if (a) withdrawal will cause no significant harm to the client's interests, (b) the client is fully informed of the consequences of withdrawal and voluntarily assents to it, or (c) withdrawal is pursuant to the terms of the retainer agreement. . . .

6.5. In any matter other than criminal litigation, a lawyer may withdraw from representing a client if the lawyer comes to know that the client has knowingly induced the lawyer to take the case or to take action on behalf of the client on the basis of material misrepresentations about the facts of the case, and if withdrawal can be accomplished without a direct violation of confidentiality.

Model Rules of Professional Conduct for Federal Lawyers: Rule 1.16(c) provides: "When properly ordered to do so by a tribunal or other competent authority, a Federal lawyer shall continue representation notwithstanding good cause for terminating the representation."

Restatement of the Law Governing Lawyers: The American Law Institute has tentatively approved the following provisions:

§29. *Client's Duties to Lawyer*

Subject to the other provisions of this Restatement, in matters covered by the representation a client must:

(1) compensate a lawyer for services and expenses as stated in Chapter 3;

(2) indemnify the lawyer for liability to which the client has exposed the lawyer without the lawyer's fault; and

(3) fulfill any valid contractual obligations to the lawyer.

§43. *Termination of Lawyer's Authority*

(1) A lawyer must comply with applicable law requiring notice to or permission of a tribunal when terminating a representation and with an order of a tribunal requiring the representation to continue.

(2) Subject to Subsection (1) and §45, a lawyer's actual authority to represent a client ends when:

(a) the client discharges the lawyer;

(b) the client dies or, in the case of a corporation or similar organization, loses its capacity to function as such;

(c) the lawyer withdraws;

(d) the lawyer dies or becomes physically or mentally incapable of providing representation, is disbarred or suspended from practicing law, or is ordered by a tribunal to cease representing a client; or

(e) the representation ends as provided by agreement or because the lawyer has completed the contemplated services.

(3) A lawyer's apparent authority to act for a client with respect to another person ends when the other person knows or should know of facts from which it can be reasonably inferred that the lawyer lacks actual authority, including knowledge of any event described in Subsection (2).

§44. Discharge by Client and Withdrawal by Lawyer

(1) Subject to Subsection (4), a client may discharge a lawyer at any time.

(2) Subject to Subsection (4), a lawyer may not represent a client or, where representation has commenced, must withdraw from the representation of a client if:

(a) the representation will result in the lawyer's violating rules of professional conduct or other law;

(b) the lawyer's physical or mental condition materially impairs the lawyer's ability to represent the client; or

(c) the client discharges the lawyer.

(3) Subject to Subsection (4), a lawyer may withdraw from representing a client if:

(a) withdrawal can be accomplished without material adverse effect on the interests of the client;

(b) the lawyer reasonably believes withdrawal is required in circumstances stated in Subsection (2);

(c) the client gives informed consent;

(d) the client persists in a course of action involving the lawyer's services that the lawyer reasonably believes is criminal, fraudulent, or in breach of the client's fiduciary duty;

(e) the lawyer reasonably believes the client has used or threatens to use the lawyer's services to perpetrate a crime or fraud;

(f) the client insists on taking action that the lawyer considers repugnant or imprudent;

(g) the client fails to fulfill a substantial financial or other obligation to the lawyer regarding the lawyer's services and the lawyer has given the client reasonable warning that the lawyer will withdraw unless the client fulfills the obligation;

(h) the representation has been rendered unreasonably difficult by the client or by the irreparable breakdown of the client-lawyer relationship; or

(i) other good cause for withdrawal exists.

(4) Notwithstanding Subsections (1), (2), and (3), a lawyer must comply with applicable law requiring notice to or permission of a tribunal when terminating a representation and with a valid order of a tribunal requiring the representation to continue.

§45. Lawyer's Duties When Representation Terminates

(1) In terminating a representation, a lawyer must take steps to the extent reasonably practicable to protect the client's interests, such as giving notice to the client of the termination, allowing time for employment of other counsel, surrendering papers and property to which the client is entitled, and refunding any advance payment of fee the lawyer has not earned.

(2) Following termination of a representation, a lawyer must:

(a) observe obligations to a former client such as those dealing with client confidences (see Chapter 5), conflicts of interest (see Chapter 8), client property and documents (see §§56-58), and fee collection (see §53);

(b) take no action on behalf of a former client without new authorization and give reasonable notice, to those who might otherwise be misled, that the lawyer lacks authority to act for the client;

(c) take reasonable steps to convey to the former client any material communication the lawyer receives relating to the matter involved in the representation; and

(d) take no unfair advantage of a former client by abusing knowledge or trust acquired by means of the representation.

§52. Fees on Termination

If a client-lawyer relationship ends before the lawyer has completed the services due for a matter and the lawyer's fee has not been forfeited under §49:

(1) a lawyer who has been discharged or withdraws may recover the lesser of the fair value of the lawyer's services as determined under §51 and the ratable proportion of the compensation provided by any otherwise enforceable agreement between lawyer and client for the services performed; except that

(2) the tribunal may allow such a lawyer to recover the ratable proportion of the compensation provided by such an agreement if:

(a) the discharge or withdrawal is not attributable to misconduct of the lawyer;

(b) the lawyer has performed severable services; and

(c) allowing contractual compensation would not burden the client's choice of counsel or the client's ability to replace counsel.

(Restatement §§49, 51, and 53 are reprinted in the Related Materials following Model Rule 1.5; §56-57 follow Rule 1.15.)

§58. Documents Relating to a Representation

(1) A lawyer must take reasonable steps to safeguard documents in the lawyer's possession relating to the representation of a client or former client.

(2) On request, a lawyer must allow a client or former client to inspect and copy any document possessed by the lawyer relating to the representation, unless substantial grounds exist to refuse.

(3) Unless a client or former client consents to nondelivery or substantial grounds exist for refusing to make delivery, a lawyer must deliver to the client or former client, at an appropriate time and in any event promptly after the representation ends, such originals and copies of other documents possessed by the lawyer relating to the representation as the client or former client reasonably needs.

(4) Notwithstanding Subsections (2) and (3), a lawyer may decline to deliver to a client or former client an original or copy of any document under circumstances permitted by §55(1).

(Section 55 is reprinted in the Related Materials following Model Rule 1.8.)

Rule 1.17 Sale of Law Practice

Editors' Note. Rule 1.17 was added by the ABA at its February 1990 Mid-Year Meeting. The reasons for adding the rule are given in the Legislative History section following the Rule.

A lawyer or a law firm may sell or purchase a law practice, including good will, if the following conditions are satisfied:

(a) The seller ceases to engage in the private practice of law [in the geographic area] [in the jurisdiction] (a jurisdiction may elect either version) in which the practice has been conducted;

(b) The practice is sold as an entirety to another lawyer or law firm;

(c) Actual written notice is given to each of the seller's clients regarding:

(1) the proposed sale;

(2) the terms of any proposed change in the fee arrangement authorized by paragraph (d);

(3) the client's right to retain other counsel or to take possession of the file; and

(4) the fact that the client's consent to the sale will be presumed if the client does not take any action or does not otherwise object within ninety (90) days of receipt of the notice.

If the client cannot be given notice, the representation of that client may be transferred to the purchaser only upon entry of an order so authorizing by a court having jurisdiction. The seller may disclose to the court *in camera* information relating to the representation only to the extent necessary to obtain an order authorizing the transfer of a file.

(d) The fees charged clients shall not be increased by reason of the sale. The purchaser may, however, refuse to undertake the representation unless the client consents to pay the purchaser fees at a rate not exceeding the fees charged by the purchaser for rendering substantially similar services prior to the initiation of the purchase negotiations.

COMMENT

[1] The practice of law is a profession, not merely a business. Clients are not commodities that can be purchased and sold at will. Pursuant to this Rule, when a lawyer or an entire firm ceases to practice and another lawyer or firm takes over the representation, the selling lawyer or firm may

obtain compensation for the reasonable value of the practice as may withdrawing partners of law firms. See Rules 5.4 and 5.6.

Termination of Practice by the Seller

[2] The requirement that all of the private practice be sold is satisfied if the seller in good faith makes the entire practice available for sale to the purchaser. The fact that a number of the seller's clients decide not to be represented by the purchaser but take their matters elsewhere, therefore, does not result in a violation. Neither does a return to private practice as a result of an unanticipated change in circumstances result in a violation. For example, a lawyer who has sold the practice to accept an appointment to judicial office does not violate the requirement that the sale be attendant to cessation of practice if the lawyer later resumes private practice upon being defeated in a contested or a retention election for the office.

[3] The requirement that the seller cease to engage in the private practice of law does not prohibit employment as a lawyer on the staff of a public agency or a legal services entity which provides legal services to the poor, or as in-house counsel to a business.

[4] The Rule permits a sale attendant upon retirement from the private practice of law within the jurisdiction. Its provisions, therefore, accommodate the lawyer who sells the practice upon the occasion of moving to another state. Some states are so large that a move from one locale therein to another is tantamount to leaving the jurisdiction in which the lawyer has engaged in the practice of law. To also accommodate lawyers so situated, states may permit the sale of the practice when the lawyer leaves the geographic area rather than the jurisdiction. The alternative desired should be indicated by selecting one of the two provided for in Rule 1.17(a).

Single Purchaser

[5] The Rule requires a single purchaser. The prohibition against piecemeal sale of a practice protects those clients whose matters are less lucrative and who might find it difficult to secure other counsel if a sale could be limited to substantial fee-generating matters. The purchaser is required to undertake all client matters in the practice, subject to client consent. If, however, the purchaser is unable to undertake all client matters because of a conflict of interest in a specific matter respecting which the purchaser is not permitted by Rule 1.7 or another rule to represent

the client, the requirement that there be a single purchaser is neverthe-less satisfied.

Client Confidences, Consent and Notice

[6] Negotiations between seller and prospective purchaser prior to disclosure of information relating to a specific representation of an iden-tifiable client no more violate the confidentiality provisions of Model Rule 1.6 than do preliminary discussions concerning the possible association of another lawyer or mergers between firms, with respect to which client consent is not required. Providing the purchaser access to client-specific information relating to the representation and to the file, however, re-quires client consent. The Rule provides that before such information can be disclosed by the seller to the purchaser the client must be given actual written notice of the contemplated sale, including the identity of the pur-chaser and any proposed change in the terms of future representation, and must be told that the decision to consent or make other arrange-ments must be made within 90 days. If nothing is heard from the client within that time, consent to the sale is presumed.

[7] A lawyer or law firm ceasing to practice cannot be required to remain in practice because some clients cannot be given actual notice of the proposed purchase. Since these clients cannot themselves consent to the purchase or direct any other disposition of their files, the Rule re-quires an order from a court having jurisdiction authorizing their trans-fer or other disposition. The Court can be expected to determine whether reasonable efforts to locate the client have been exhausted, and whether the absent client's legitimate interests will be served by authorizing the transfer of the file so that the purchaser may continue the representa-tion. Preservation of client confidences requires that the petition for a court order be considered *in camera.* (A procedure by which such an or-der can be obtained needs to be established in jurisdictions in which it presently does not exist.)

[8] All the elements of client autonomy, including the client's abso-lute right to discharge a lawyer and transfer the representation to an-other, survive the sale of the practice.

Fee Arrangements Between Client and Purchaser

[9] The sale may not be financed by increases in fees charged the clients of the practice. Existing agreements between the seller and the cli-

ent as to fees and the scope of the work must be honored by the purchaser, unless the client consents after consultation. The purchaser may, however, advise the client that the purchaser will not undertake the representation unless the client consents to pay the higher fees the purchaser usually charges. To prevent client financing of the sale, the higher fee the purchaser may charge must not exceed the fees charged by the purchaser for substantially similar service rendered prior to the initiation of the purchase negotiations.

[10] The purchaser may not intentionally fragment the practice which is the subject of the sale by charging significantly different fees in substantially similar matters. Doing so would make it possible for the purchaser to avoid the obligation to take over the entire practice by charging arbitrarily higher fees for less lucrative matters, thereby increasing the likelihood that those clients would not consent to the new representation.

Other Applicable Ethical Standards

[11] Lawyers participating in the sale of a law practice are subject to the ethical standards applicable to involving another lawyer in the representation of a client. These include, for example, the seller's obligation to exercise competence in identifying a purchaser qualified to assume the practice and the purchaser's obligation to undertake the representation competently (see Rule 1.1); the obligation to avoid disqualifying conflicts, and to secure client consent after consultation for those conflicts which can be agreed to (see Rule 1.7); and the obligation to protect information relating to the representation (see Rules 1.6 and 1.9).

[12] If approval of the substitution of the purchasing attorney for the selling attorney is required by the rules of any tribunal in which a matter is pending, such approval must be obtained before the matter can be included in the sale (see Rule 1.16).

Applicability of the Rule

[13] This Rule applies to the sale of a law practice by representatives of a deceased, disabled or disappeared lawyer. Thus, the seller may be represented by a non-lawyer representative not subject to these Rules. Since, however, no lawyer may participate in a sale of a law practice which does not conform to the requirements of this Rule, the representatives of the

seller as well as the purchasing lawyer can be expected to see to it that they are met.

[14] Admission to or retirement from a law partnership or professional association, retirement plans and similar arrangements, and a sale of tangible assets of a law practice, do not constitute a sale or purchase governed by this Rule.

[15] This Rule does not apply to the transfers of legal representation between lawyers when such transfers are unrelated to the sale of a practice.

Model Code Comparison

EC 4-6 provided that "a lawyer should not attempt to sell a law practice as a going business because, among other reasons, to do so would involve the disclosure of confidences and secrets."

Cross-References in Rules

Rule 5.4(a)(2) provides that "a lawyer who purchases the practice of a deceased, disabled, or disappeared lawyer may, pursuant to the provisions of **Rule 1.17**, pay to the estate or other representative of that lawyer the agreed-upon purchase price."

Rule 5.6, Comment 3: "This Rule does not apply to prohibit restrictions that may be included in the terms of the sale of a law practice pursuant to **Rule 1.17**."

Rule 7.2(c)(3) permits a lawyer to "pay for a law practice in accordance with **Rule 1.17**."

Rule 7.2, Comment 6: "A lawyer is allowed to pay for advertising permitted by this Rule and for the purchase of a law practice in accordance with the provisions of **Rule 1.17**, but otherwise is not permitted to pay another person for channeling professional work."

Legislative History

Rule 1.17 was adopted by the ABA House of Delegates at the ABA's February 1990 Mid-Year Meeting. It is an entirely new Rule and was not proposed in any form in Kutak Commission drafts. The proposal to add Rule 1.17 to the Model Rules was initiated by the State Bar of California, based on California Rule 2-300, and was joined by the ABA Section of General Practice and the ABA Section of

Law Practice Management. The Committee Report submitted to the House of Delegates in support of adding Rule 1.17 explained the Rule as follows:*

Impetus for Formulation of the Rule

Protection of Clients

[California] Rule of Professional Conduct 2-300 and proposed Model Rule 1.17 are consumer protection measures designed to address the disparity between the treatment of the clients of sole practitioners and the clients of law firms when the attorney handling the client matter leaves the practice, by ensuring that the client matters handled by sole practitioners are attended to when the sole practitioner leaves the practice.

If the attorney leaving the practice is or was part of a law firm, in most cases, the firm continues to handle the matter. In the majority of situations, the transition for the client is very smooth. However, if the attorney was in sole practice, the transition is not so smooth because there is no law firm standing ready to continue to handle the client matter. The clients of sole practitioners who leave the practice of law are relatively unprotected because there are no regulations in place to protect them during the transition.

Sole Practitioners in Unfair Financial Position

In addition to the issues of the client protection, sole practitioners are in an unfair financial position concerning the "good will" of their law practice. The "good will" of a business is "the expectation of continued public patronage.". . . Attorneys, like other business persons, may sell the physical assets of their law practice, such as equipment, the library or the furniture. However, case authority and ethics opinions held that the sale of "good will" of a law practice is unethical and against public policy. . . .

Treatment of "good will" in other contexts presents a mixed picture. For example, attorneys who are members of firms with two or more members may ethically enter into retirement agreements which may require lump sum payments that implicitly include sums for the attorney's share of the firm's "good will."

The estate of a deceased attorney may receive payments from the attorney who completes the unfinished client matters of the deceased attorney. However, in the absence of a rule like that which is being proposed, the payments are limited to the "proportion of the total compensation which fairly represents the services rendered by the deceased member" and thus do not permit an allowance for "good will."

Pursuant to agreements entered into between an attorney not in sole practice and the attorney's firm, partner or associate, the estate of the attorney may receive payments over a reasonable period of time after the attorney's death. Note that there is no requirement that the payments be related to any services the attorney performed. Thus, it appears that the payments to the estate can include the value of "good will."

*Committee Reports do not represent official policy of the ABA. They are for information only, and the opinions are those of the authors of the report.

In marital dissolution proceedings, the "good will" of the attorney-spouse's share in his or her law practice may be valued for the purpose of determining the community or other divisible assets.

This inconsistent treatment of "good will" resulted in a series of awkward results: the estate of a sole practitioner could not receive payment for the "good will" of the law practice, while the estate of an attorney who was a member of a law firm could; upon retirement, an attorney who was a member of a law firm could receive compensation including "good will," while the compensation received by a sole practitioner could not include "good will"; the "good will" of a sole practice may be considered an asset of the marital community for purposes of a dissolution, but could not be sold.

The Committee Report also cited two prominent cases holding that sole practitioners could not sell good will: O'Hara v. Ahlgren, Blumenfeld and Kempster, 537 N.E.2d 730 (Ill. 1989), and Geffen v. Moss, 53 Cal. App. 3d 215, 226 (1975).

Selected State Variations

California: See Rule 2-300 (Sale or Purchase of a Law Practice of a Member Living or Deceased).

District of Columbia: D.C. has not adopted any rule permitting the sale of a law practice. (D.C. has adopted a Rule 1.17, but it deals with notification of trust account overdrafts, not the sale of a law practice — see District of Columbia Rules of Professional Conduct below.)

Florida: Effective January 1, 1993, the Florida Supreme Court adopted a version of Rule 1.17 that tracks ABA Model Rule 1.17 in many respects but differs substantially in others. For example, Florida's version omits the requirement in ABA Model Rule 1.17(a) that the seller cease practicing law, and Florida adds the following new or substantially modified provisions:

(c) *Court Approval Required.* If a representation involves pending litigation, there shall be no substitution of counsel or termination of representation unless authorized by the court. . . .

(d) *Client Objections.* If a client objects to the proposed substitution of counsel, the seller shall comply with the requirements of rule 4-1.16(d) [Florida's version of ABA Model Rule 1.16(d)].

(e) *Consummation of Sale.* A sale of a law practice shall not be consummated until:

(1) with respect to clients of the seller who were served with written notice of the proposed sale, the 30-day period referred to in subdivision (b)(3) has expired or all such clients have consented to the substitution of counsel or termination of representation; and

(2) court orders have been entered authorizing substitution of counsel for all clients who could not be served with written notice of the proposed sale and whose representations involve pending litigation; provided, in the event the court fails to grant a substitution of counsel in a matter involving pending litigation, that matter shall not be included in the sale and the sale otherwise shall

be unaffected. Further, the matters not involving pending litigation of any client who cannot be served with written notice of the proposed sale shall not be included in the sale and the sale otherwise shall be unaffected.

(f) *Existing Fee Contracts Controlling.* The purchaser shall honor the fee agreements that were entered into between the seller and the seller's clients. The fees charged clients shall not be increased by reason of the sale.

Florida's Comment to subparagraph (f) provides:

> The sale may not be financed by increases in fees charged the clients of the practice. Existing agreements between the seller and the client as to fees and the scope of the work must be honored by the purchaser. This obligation of the purchaser is a factor that can be taken into account by seller and purchaser when negotiating the sale price of the practice.

Hawaii: Rule 1.17(c)(1) requires notice to the client not only of the proposed sale but also "the identity of the purchaser." Rule 1.17(d) adds a second sentence: "Existing agreements between the seller and the client as to fees and the scope of the work must be honored by the purchaser, unless the client consents in writing after consultation."

Illinois: In 1991, the Illinois State Bar Association recommended that the Supreme Court adopt Rule 1.17, but the rule was not adopted. In December of 1992, however, three new Justices were sworn in to replace retiring Justices on the seven-member Supreme Court. In July of 1993, the Supreme Court's Committee on Rules held public hearings on (among other things) a new recommendation to adopt 1.17. As of September 1996, the Court still had not taken any action on this recommendation. On March 11, 1997, the Illinois Supreme Court issued an order stating, "Petition *denied*," without explanation. Justice McMorrow dissented without opinion.

Iowa has adopted DR 2-111 to permit the sale of a law practice.

Michigan: Rule 1.17 is nearly identical to ABA Model Rule 1.17, but adds Rule 1.17(e), which permits the "sale of the good will of a law practice . . . conditioned upon the seller ceasing to engage in the private practice of law for a reasonable period of time within the geographical area in which the practice has been conducted."

Minnesota: Effective January 1, 1996, Minnesota adopted a version of Rule 1.17. It forbids the buyer from raising fees "by reason of the sale for a period of at least one year from the date of the sale." All existing fee agreements must be honored for one year from the date of the sale. All pro bono and reduced fee matters must be continued to completion. The notice to clients must include a "summary of the buying lawyer's or law firm's professional background, including education and experience and the length of time that the buyer lawyer or members of the buying law firm has been in practice." The transaction may but need not include a promise by the selling lawyer that he or she will not engage in law practice "for a reasonable period of time within a reasonable geographic area and will not advertise for or solicit clients within that area for that time."

New Jersey: Rule 1.17 permits a lawyer or firm to sell or purchase a law practice, including goodwill, if the seller is ceasing to engage in private law practice in New Jersey, the practice is sold as an entirety except for cases in which a conflict is present, and certain notices are given to the clients of the seller and by publication in the New Jersey Law Journal and the New Jersey Lawyer at least 30 days in advance of the sale.

New York: DR 2-111, added in 1996, deals with the sale of a law practice. See New York materials.

Oklahoma: In 1996, Oklahoma adopted a rule that permits the sale of a law practice, provided the buyer and seller satisfy certain conditions. The rule is based largely on ABA Model Rule 1.17, but differs in some significant ways. For example, the Oklahoma rule requires the seller to have a reasonable basis for believing that the buyer has the knowledge and skill to handle the matters being transferred or has given the seller reasonable assurance that the buyer will acquire such knowledge and skill or associate with another lawyer who possesses the requisite knowledge and skill. The Oklahoma rule also requires the seller to advice each client about any funds or property being held for the client, including advance fees.

Oregon: DR 2-111, adopted in 1995, differs in many ways from ABA Model Rule 1.17. The Oregon version provides as follows:

(A) A lawyer or a law firm may sell or purchase all or part of a law practice, including goodwill, in accordance with this rule.

(B) The selling lawyer, or the selling lawyer's legal representative, in the case of a deceased or disabled lawyer, shall provide written notice of the proposed sale to each current client whose legal work is subject to transfer by certified mail, return receipt requested, to the client's last known address. The notice shall include the following information:

(1) that a sale is proposed;

(2) the identity of the purchasing lawyer or law firm, including the office address(es), and a brief description of the size and nature of the purchasing lawyer's or law firm's practice;

(3) that the client may object to the transfer of its legal work, and may take possession of any client files and property, and may retain counsel other than the purchasing lawyer or law firm;

(4) that the client's legal work will be transferred to the purchasing lawyer or law firm, who will then take over the representation and act on the client's behalf, if the client does not object to the transfer within forty-five (45) days after the date the notice was mailed, whether or not the client consents to the transfer of its legal work.

(C) The notice may describe the purchasing lawyer or law firm's qualifications, including the selling lawyer's opinion of the purchasing lawyer or law firm's suitability and competence to assume representation of the client, but only if the selling lawyer has made a reasonable effort to arrive at an informed opinion.

(D) If certified mail is not effective to give the client notice, the selling lawyer shall take such steps as may be reasonable under the circumstances to give the client actual notice of the proposed sale and the other information required in subsection (B).

(E) A client's consent to the transfer of its legal work to the purchasing lawyer or law firm will be presumed if no objection is received within forty-five (45) days after the date the notice was mailed.

(F) If substitution of counsel is required by the rules of a tribunal in which a matter is pending, the selling lawyer shall assure that substitution of counsel is made.

(G) The fees charged clients shall not be increased by reason of the sale except upon agreement of the client.

(H) The sale of a law practice may be conditioned upon the selling lawyer ceasing to engage in the private practice of law or some particular area of practice for a reasonable period within the geographic area in which the practice has been conducted.

Oregon also amended an advertising rule (DR 2-103), its confidentiality rule (DR 4-101), and its withdrawal rule (DR 2-110) to reflect other considerations in the sale of a law practice.

West Virginia: Effective February 1, 1997, West Virginia adopted a version of Rule 1.17.

Wisconsin has adopted a rule permitting the sale of a law practice, but subdivision (d) departs significantly from ABA Model Rule 1.17(d). The Wisconsin version states:

(d) the sale may not be financed by increases in fees charged the clients of the practice. Existing agreements between the seller and the client as to fees and the scope of the work must be honored by the purchaser, unless the client consents in writing after consultation.

ARTICLE 2. COUNSELOR

Editors' Note. The *1980 Discussion Draft* contained the following Introduction to the section entitled "Attorney as Advisor":

The lawyer's professional function historically originated as attorney and advocate, that is, appearing on behalf of a party to litigation. Giving legal advice evolved from giving advice about how to proceed in litigation. Today, serving as adviser is the lawyer's predominant role.

As adviser, a lawyer informs clients about their legal rights and obligations and their practical implications. Giving advice is ordinarily an incident of other functions a lawyer performs on behalf of a client, such as advocacy or negotiation, but in many matters giving advice may be the lawyer's sole function. Legal advice may be given orally or in writing. It may be reflected in documents effectuating courses of action by the client, such as wills, articles of organization of an enterprise, by-laws, contracts, formal opinions, and draft legislation or government regulations. In giving advice, a lawyer should consider not only the literal terms of the law but also its purposes and changing course. A lawyer should also take into account equitable and ethical considerations and problems of cost and feasibility.

Rule 2.1 Advisor

In representing a client, a lawyer shall exercise independent professional judgment and render candid advice. In rendering advice, a lawyer may refer not only to law but to other considerations such as moral, economic, social and political factors, that may be relevant to the client's situation.

COMMENT

Scope of Advice

[1] A client is entitled to straightforward advice expressing the lawyer's honest assessment. Legal advice often involves unpleasant facts and alternatives that a client may be disinclined to confront. In presenting advice, a lawyer endeavors to sustain the client's morale and may put advice in as acceptable a form as honesty permits. However, a lawyer should not be deterred from giving candid advice by the prospect that the advice will be unpalatable to the client.

[2] Advice couched in narrowly legal terms may be of little value to a client, especially where practical considerations, such as cost or effects on other people, are predominant. Purely technical legal advice, therefore, can sometimes be inadequate. It is proper for a lawyer to refer to relevant moral and ethical considerations in giving advice. Although a lawyer is not a moral advisor as such, moral and ethical considerations impinge upon most legal questions and may decisively influence how the law will be applied.

[3] A client may expressly or impliedly ask the lawyer for purely technical advice. When such a request is made by a client experienced in legal matters, the lawyer may accept it at face value. When such a request is made by a client inexperienced in legal matters, however, the lawyer's responsibility as advisor may include indicating that more may be involved than strictly legal considerations.

[4] Matters that go beyond strictly legal questions may also be in the domain of another profession. Family matters can involve problems within the professional competence of psychiatry, clinical psychology or social work; business matters can involve problems within the competence of the accounting profession or of financial specialists. Where consultation with a professional in another field is itself something a competent lawyer would recommend, the lawyer should make such a recommendation. At the same time, a lawyer's advice at its best often consists of recommending a course of action in the face of conflicting recommendations of experts.

186

Offering Advice

[5] In general, a lawyer is not expected to give advice until asked by the client. However, when a lawyer knows that a client proposes a course of action that is likely to result in substantial adverse legal consequences to the client, duty to the client under Rule 1.4 may require that the lawyer act if the client's course of action is related to the representation. A lawyer ordinarily has no duty to initiate investigation of a client's affairs or to give advice that the client has indicated is unwanted, but a lawyer may initiate advice to a client when doing so appears to be in the client's interest.

Model Code Comparison

There was no direct counterpart to this Rule in the Disciplinary Rules of the Model Code. DR 5-107(B) provided that a lawyer "shall not permit a person who recommends, employs, or pays him to render legal services for another to direct or regulate his professional judgment in rendering such legal services." EC 7-8 stated that "[a]dvice of a lawyer to his client need not be confined to purely legal considerations. . . . In assisting his client to reach a proper decision, it is often desirable for a lawyer to point out those factors which may lead to a decision that is morally just as well as legally permissible. . . . In the final analysis, however, . . . the decision whether to forego legally available objectives or methods because of nonlegal factors is ultimately for the client. . . ."

Cross-References in Rules

None.

Legislative History

1980 Discussion Draft:

2.1 Independence and Candor

In advising a client a lawyer shall exercise independent and candid professional judgment, uncontrolled by the interests or wishes of a third person, or by the lawyer's own interests or wishes.

In addition, Rule 2.2 (now incorporated into Rule 2.1) provided:

Scope of Advice

In rendering advice a lawyer may refer to all relevant considerations unless in the circumstances it is evident that the client desires advice confined to strictly legal considerations.

1981 and 1982 Drafts were the same as adopted.

Selected State Variations

California has no direct counterpart to Rule 2.1.

Colorado: Rule 2.1 provides that "[i]n a matter involving or expected to involve litigation, a lawyer should advise the client of alternative forms of dispute resolution which might reasonably be pursued to attempt to resolve the legal dispute or to reach the legal objective sought." The Colorado Comment to this sentence states that depending on the circumstances, "it may be appropriate for the lawyer to discuss with the client factors such as cost, speed, effects on existing relationships, confidentiality and privacy, scope of relief, statutes of limitation, and relevant procedural rules and statutes."

Georgia: EC 7-5 provides:

A lawyer as adviser has a duty to advise the client as to various forms of dispute resolution. When a matter is likely to involve litigation, a lawyer has a duty to inform the client of forms of dispute resolution which might constitute reasonable alternatives to litigation.

Hawaii: Rule 2.1 requires lawyers to advise clients about ADR if a matter may involve litigation.

New York: Same or substantially the same as the ABA Model Code — see Model Code Comparison above.

Texas Rule 2.01 begins, "In advising or otherwise representing a client . . . ," and deletes the second sentence of ABA Model Rule 2.1.

Virginia omits Rule 2.1.

Related Materials

American Academy of Matrimonial Lawyers: The "Bounds of Advocacy" drafted by the American Academy of Matrimonial Lawyers contains the following provisions and commentary:

2.12 An attorney should advise the client of the emotional and economic impact of divorce and the possibility or advisability of reconciliation.

Comment to Rule 2.12

The duty of vigorous advocacy in no way prohibits the matrimonial lawyer from counseling the client to be cautious in embarking on divorce. The divorce process exacts a heavy economic and emotional toll. An attorney should ask if reconciliation might be possible, or at least whether the client is receptive to counseling. If the client exhibits uncertainty or ambivalence, the lawyer should assist in obtaining a counselor. In no event should an attorney urge a client to file suit, unless necessary to protect the client's interests.

It is generally assumed that a lawyer's role in family matters is to act not only as an advocate, but to some extent as a counselor or advisor. And the RPC specifically permit the lawyer to address moral, economic, social and political factors, which may be relevant to the client's situation. Further, "[w]here consultation with a professional in another field is itself something a competent lawyer would recommend, the lawyer should make such a recommendation." Although few attorneys are qualified to do personal counseling, a thorough discussion of the probable emotional and monetary repercussions of divorce is permissible.

If the client has begun counseling in hopes of reconciliation, the matrimonial lawyer should attempt to mitigate litigation-related activities that might prejudice marital harmony. It is important, however, for the attorney to be mindful that clients may make damaging admissions during joint marriage counseling. One spouse may use a "breathing spell" afforded by counseling to deplete the marital estate. The lawyer should advise the client of these risks and take precautions to protect the client in the interim.

Predivorce Planning

A client is entitled to know what laws govern divorce and the consequence of those laws on a dissolution of his marriage. A matrimonial lawyer should advise a client about the repercussions of any matrimonial litigation, including factors that are likely to be considered in economic and custody determinations. However, predivorce planning carries the potential for fraud.

2.14 An attorney should advise the client of the potential effect of the client's conduct on a custody dispute.

Comment to Rule 2.14

Predivorce conduct of the parents may significantly affect custody decisions. The client is entitled to advice where there is a custody issue. Conduct conforming to such advice often will benefit both the children and the client's spouse, independent of any custody dispute. Suggesting that the client spend more time with the child and consult from time-to-time with the child's doctor, teacher, and babysitter is appropriate. It is also proper to describe the potentially harmful legal consequences of an adulterous relationship, substance abuse, or other inappropriate behavior.

The lawyer must consider whether the custody claim will be made in good faith. If not, the lawyer must advise the client of the harmful consequences of a meritless custody claim to the client, the child, and the client's spouse. If the client still demands advice to build a spurious custody case or to use a custody claim as a bargaining chip or as a means of inflicting revenge (see Standard 2.25 and Comment), the lawyer should withdraw.

Restatement of the Law Governing Lawyers: The American Law Institute has tentatively approved §151(3), which is reprinted in the Related Materials following Rule 1.2.

Rule 2.2 Intermediary

(a) A lawyer may act as intermediary between clients if:

(1) the lawyer consults with each client concerning the implications of the common representation, including the advantages and risks involved, and the effect on the attorney-client privileges, and obtains each client's consent to the common representation;

(2) the lawyer reasonably believes that the matter can be resolved on terms compatible with the clients' best interests, that each client will be able to make adequately informed decisions in the matter and that there is little risk of material prejudice to the interests of any of the clients if the contemplated resolution is unsuccessful; and

(3) the lawyer reasonably believes that the common representation can be undertaken impartially and without improper effect on other responsibilities the lawyer has to any of the clients.

(b) While acting as intermediary, the lawyer shall consult with each client concerning the decisions to be made and the considerations relevant in making them, so that each client can make adequately informed decisions.

(c) A lawyer shall withdraw as intermediary if any of the clients so requests, or if any of the conditions stated in paragraph (a) is no longer satisfied. Upon withdrawal, the lawyer shall not continue to represent any of the clients in the matter that was the subject of the intermediation.

COMMENT

[1] A lawyer acts as intermediary under this Rule when the lawyer represents two or more parties with potentially conflicting interests. A key factor in defining the relationship is whether the parties share responsibility for the lawyer's fee, but the common representation may be inferred from other circumstances. Because confusion can arise as to the lawyer's role where each party is not separately represented, it is important that the lawyer make clear the relationship.

[2] The Rule does not apply to a lawyer acting as arbitrator or mediator between or among parties who are not clients of the lawyer, even where the lawyer has been appointed with the concurrence of the parties. In performing such a role the lawyer may be subject to applicable codes of ethics, such as the Code of Ethics for Arbitration in Commercial Disputes prepared by a joint Committee of the American Bar Association and the American Arbitration Association.

[3] A lawyer acts as intermediary in seeking to establish or adjust a relationship between clients on an amicable and mutually advantageous basis; for example, in helping to organize a business in which two or more clients are entrepreneurs, working out the financial reorganization of an enterprise in which two or more clients have an interest, arranging a property distribution in settlement of an estate or mediating a dispute between clients. The lawyer seeks to resolve potentially conflicting interests by developing the parties' mutual interests. The alternative can be that each party may have to obtain separate representation, with the possibility in some situations of incurring additional cost, complication or even litigation. Given these and other relevant factors, all the clients may prefer that the lawyer act as intermediary.

[4] In considering whether to act as intermediary between clients, a lawyer should be mindful that if the intermediation fails the result can be additional cost, embarrassment and recrimination. In some situations the risk of failure is so great that intermediation is plainly impossible. For example, a lawyer cannot undertake common representation of clients between whom contentious litigation is imminent or who contemplate contentious negotiations. More generally, if the relationship between the parties has already assumed definite antagonism, the possibility that the clients' interests can be adjusted by intermediation ordinarily is not very good.

[5] The appropriateness of intermediation can depend on its form. Forms of intermediation range from informal arbitration, where each client's case is presented by the respective client and the lawyer decides the outcome, to mediation, to common representation where the clients' interests are substantially though not entirely compatible. One form may be appropriate in circumstances where another would not. Other relevant factors are whether the lawyer subsequently will represent both parties on a continuing basis and whether the situation involves creating a relationship between the parties or terminating one.

Confidentiality and Privilege

[6] A particularly important factor in determining the appropriateness of intermediation is the effect on client-lawyer confidentiality and the attorney-client privilege. In a common representation, the lawyer is still required both to keep each client adequately informed and to maintain confidentiality of information relating to the representation. See Rules 1.4 and 1.6. Complying with both requirements while acting

as intermediary requires a delicate balance. If the balance cannot be maintained, the common representation is improper. With regard to the attorney-client privilege, the prevailing rule is that as between commonly represented clients the privilege does not attach. Hence, it must be assumed that if litigation eventuates between the clients, the privilege will not protect any such communications, and the clients should be so advised.

[7] Since the lawyer is required to be impartial between commonly represented clients, intermediation is improper when that impartiality cannot be maintained. For example, a lawyer who has represented one of the clients for a long period and in a variety of matters might have difficulty being impartial between that client and one to whom the lawyer has only recently been introduced.

Consultation

[8] In acting as intermediary between clients, the lawyer is required to consult with the clients on the implications of doing so, and proceed only upon consent based on such a consultation. The consultation should make clear that the lawyer's role is not that of partisanship normally expected in other circumstances.

[9] Paragraph (b) is an application of the principle expressed in Rule 1.4. Where the lawyer is intermediary, the clients ordinarily must assume greater responsibility for decisions than when each client is independently represented.

Withdrawal

[10] Common representation does not diminish the rights of each client in the client-lawyer relationship. Each has the right to loyal and diligent representation, the right to discharge the lawyer as stated in Rule 1.16, and the protection of Rule 1.9 concerning obligations to a former client.

Model Code Comparison

There was no direct counterpart to this Rule in the Disciplinary Rules of the Model Code. EC 5-20 stated that a "lawyer is often asked to serve as an impartial arbitrator or mediator in matters which involve present or former clients. He may serve in either capacity if he first discloses such present or former relationships.'' DR 5-105(B) provided that a lawyer ''shall not continue multiple employment if the exercise of his independent judgment in behalf of a client will be or is likely to be adversely affected by his representation of another client, or if it would be likely to involve him in representation of differing interests, except to the extent permitted under DR 5-105(C).'' DR 5-105(C) provided that ''a lawyer may represent multiple clients if it is obvious that he can adequately represent the interests of each and if each consents to the representation after full disclosure of the possible effect of such representation on the exercise of his independent professional judgment on behalf of each.''

Cross-References in Rules

Rule 1.6, Comment 20: ''The Rules of Professional Conduct in various circumstances permit or require a lawyer to disclose information relating to the representation. See **Rules 2.2**, 2.3, 3.3 and 4.1.''

Rule 1.7, Comment 2: ''Where more than one client is involved and the lawyer withdraws because a conflict arises after representation, whether the lawyer may continue to represent any of the clients is determined by Rule 1.9. See also **Rule 2.2(c)**.''

Rule 1.7, Comment 7: '' [C]ommon representation of persons having similar interests is proper if the risk of adverse effect is minimal and the requirements of paragraph (b) are met. Compare **Rule 2.2** involving intermediation between clients.''

Rule 1.10(a): ''While lawyers are associated in a firm, none of them shall knowingly represent a client when any one of them practicing alone would be prohibited from doing so by **Rules** 1.7, 1.8(c), 1.9 or **2.2**.''

Legislative History

1980 Discussion Draft (then Rules 5.1 and 5.2) began with the following Introduction:

Intermediary Between Clients

A lawyer acts as intermediary in seeking to establish or adjust a relationship between clients on an amicable and mutually advantageous basis. A lawyer acts as intermediary, for example, in drafting the documents organizing a business in which two or more clients are entrepreneurs but have differing financial or personal interests in the enterprise. A lawyer acts as intermediary in working out a plan of financial reorganization for an enterprise on behalf of two or more clients who have differing financial interests in the enterprise, or in arranging the distribution of specific property in settlement of an estate among distributees. Under some circumstances, a lawyer may act as intermediary between spouses in arranging the terms of an uncontested separation or divorce settlement. A lawyer may act as intermediary in mediating a dispute between clients.

In all such situations, the lawyer seeks to resolve potentially conflicting interests by developing the parties' mutual interests. The alternative often is that each party may have to obtain separate representation, with the possibility in some situations of incurring added burdens of cost, complication, and even litigation. In some nonlitigation situations, the stakes involved may be so modest that separate representation of the parties is financially impractical. Given these factors, all the clients may prefer that the lawyer act as intermediary. If they do, and if the lawyer's independent professional judgment indicates that acting as intermediary will further the clients' mutual interest, a lawyer may undertake that function.

This Rule does not deal with a lawyer acting as mediator or arbitrator between parties with whom the lawyer does not have a client-lawyer relationship, nor does it govern a situation where a lawyer represents a party in negotiation with a party who is unrepresented. A lawyer acts as intermediary under this Rule when the lawyer represents both parties. A key factor in defining the relationship is whether the parties share responsibility for paying the lawyer's fee, but the existence of a joint or common representation can be inferred from other circumstances. Because confusion can arise as to the lawyer's role and responsibility where each party is not separately represented, it is important that the lawyer make clear whom he represents in such situations.

Rules 5.1 and 5.2 of the 1980 Discussion Draft provided:

Conditions for Acting as an Intermediary

(a) A lawyer may act as an intermediary between clients if:
(1) the possibility of adjusting the clients' interests is strong; and
(2) each client will be able to make adequately informed decisions in the matter, and there is little likelihood that any of the clients will be significantly prejudiced if the contemplated adjustment of interests is unsuccessful; and
(3) the lawyer can act impartially and without improper effect on other services the lawyer is performing for any of the clients; and
(4) the lawyer fully explains to each client the implications of the common representation, including the advantages and risks involved, and obtains each client's consent to the common representation.

(b) Before serving as intermediary a lawyer shall explain fully to each client the decisions to be made and the considerations relevant to making them, so that each client can make adequately informed decisions.

Withdrawal as an Intermediary

A lawyer shall withdraw as intermediary if any of the clients so requests, if the conditions stated in Rule 5.1 cannot be met, or if it becomes apparent that a mutually advantageous adjustment of interests cannot be made. Upon withdrawal, the lawyer may continue to represent any of the clients only to the extent compatible with the lawyer's responsibilities to the other client or clients.

1981 Draft: Rule 2.2(c) required a lawyer to withdraw if the conditions in (a) could not be met "or if in the light of subsequent events the lawyer reasonably should know that a mutually advantageous resolution cannot be achieved."

1982 Draft: Rule 2.2(a)(1) was substantially the same as adopted except that it did not require the lawyer to explain "the effect on the attorney-client privileges." Rule 2.2(c)'s second sentence provided: "Upon withdrawal, the lawyer shall not continue to represent any of the clients unless doing so is clearly compatible with the lawyer's responsibilities to the other client or clients." The remainder of Rule 2.2 was substantially the same as adopted.

Selected State Variations

Alaska: Rule 2.2 adds paragraph (d), which prohibits a lawyer who represents a client in divorce, dissolution, custody, alimony, child support, or marital property settlement cases from acting as an intermediary in the same case.

California: See Rule 3-310(B) (generally governing concurrent conflicts — California has no direct counterpart to Rule 2.2).

Colorado: Rule 2.2(a) provides that when acting as an intermediary, the lawyer must provide "full disclosure in writing" of the implications of common representation, and that the client's consent must also be "in writing."

District of Columbia: D.C. Rule 2.2(b) differs significantly from the ABA Model Rule — see District of Columbia Rules of Professional Conduct below.

Illinois omits Rule 2.2.

Iowa: DR 5-105(a) provides: "In no event shall a lawyer represent both parties in dissolution of marriage proceedings whether or not contested or involving custody of children, alimony, child support, or property settlement."

Massachusetts has no equivalent to Rule 2.2.

New Jersey makes Rule 2.2 "subject to the provisions of Rule 1.7."

New York: Same or substantially the same as the ABA Model Code — see Model Code Comparison above.

Texas Rule 2.02 deletes paragraph (b).

Virginia omits Rule 2.2, and relies on DR 5-105 to regulate multiple representation.

Related Materials

Editors' Note.   Comment 2 to Rule 2.2 notes that the Rule "does not apply to a lawyer acting as arbitrator or mediator." However, a number of codes and standards are available to give guidance to lawyers acting as artibrators or mediators. Here are a few examples:

ABA Standards of Practice for Lawyer Mediators in Family Disputes: In 1984, the ABA House of Delegates formally adopted Standards for Lawyer Mediators in Family Disputes.

American Academy of Matrimonial Lawyers: The "Bounds of Advocacy" drafted by the American Academy of Matrimonial Lawyers contains the following provisions and commentary:

1.4 An attorney should be knowledgeable about alternative ways to resolve matrimonial disputes.

Comment to Rule 1.4

Matrimonial law is not simply a matter of winning or losing. At its best, matrimonial law should result in disputes being resolved fairly for all parties, including children. An alternative to courtroom confrontation may achieve a fair outcome. Parties are more likely to abide by their own promises than by an outcome imposed by a court. In some cases, alternative dispute resolution mechanisms may not be appropriate or workable due to the nature of the dispute or the animosity of the parties. Under certain circumstances, litigation may be the best course, but a negotiated resolution is desirable in most family law disputes.

Alternative dispute resolution mechanisms may establish a positive tone for continuing post-divorce relations by avoiding the animosity and pain of court battles. Parents who litigate their custody disputes are more likely to believe the process had a detrimental effect on relations with the divorcing spouse than parents whose custody disputes are mediated. When resolution requires complex trade-offs, the parties may be better able than the court to forge a resolution that addresses their individual values and needs. Alternatives to litigation are often less expensive; however, the client should be informed that such mechanisms may not necessarily reduce the cost because the matrimonial lawyer may need to prepare the case as thoroughly as for trial. Thus, it is essential that matrimonial lawyers have sufficient knowledge about alternative dispute resolution to enable them to understand its advantages and disadvantages. The attorney may then be able to determine when it is appropriate to recommend alternative methods to the client.

1.5 An attorney should act as a mediator or arbitrator only if competent to do so.

Comment to Rule 1.5

No one should engage in the mediation or arbitration of marital disputes without adequate education and training. There are many ways to acquire the necessary knowledge and skill, including continuing legal education, formal training programs, informal training by peers, law school training programs and experience.

A matrimonial lawyer is in the best position to understand the likely outcome of the adjudication of a legal dispute and is best able to ensure the validity of any agreement or other legal document resulting from a mediated agreement. Mediation and arbitration are skills that, like trial advocacy, require study and training.

2.15 An attorney should encourage the settlement of marital disputes through negotiation, mediation, or arbitration.

Comment to Rule 2.15

The litigation process is expensive and emotionally draining. In matrimonial matters, the highly charged atmosphere makes a speedy, cooperative resolution of disputes highly desirable. In many cases, the parties will have continuing contact with each other and need to cooperate for years to come. There is evidence that parties to a matrimonial dispute are more willing to abide by an agreement voluntarily entered into than by a court-ordered resolution following litigation. And, there is increasing evidence of the destructive effect on the children of protracted, adversarial proceedings between the spouses. It is therefore in the family's interest to seek to settle disputes cooperatively.

2.20 An attorney should not represent both husband and wife even if they do not wish to obtain independent representation.

Comment to Rule 2.20

The temptation to represent potentially conflicting interests is particularly difficult to resist in family disputes. Often the attorney is the "family lawyer" and previously represented husband, wife, family corporations, and even the children. Serving as an intermediary between husband and wife is not prohibited by the RPC. However, it is impossible for the attorney to provide impartial advice to both parties, and even a seemingly amicable separation or divorce may result in bitter litigation over financial matters or custody. A matrimonial lawyer should not attempt to represent both husband and wife even with the consent of both.

The attorney may be asked to represent family members in a nonlitigation setting. If separation or divorce is foreseeable or if one of the parents desires defense in a battered child action, the lawyer may see her role as counselor or negotiator for all concerned. This temptation should be resisted. However, this Standard does not apply in adoption proceedings or other matters where the spouses' positions are not adverse.

Association of Family Conciliation Courts Model Standards of Practice for Family and Divorce Mediation: In 1984, the Association of Family and Conciliation Courts promulgated standards "intended to assist public and private, voluntary and mandatory mediation" (Preamble). They can be found in the December 1984 Dispute Resolution Forum published by the National Institute for Dispute Resolution.

Code of Ethics for Arbitrators in Commercial Disputes: A Joint Committee of the ABA and the American Arbitration Association (AAA) has prepared a code of ethics for commercial arbitrators. It is mentioned in Comment 2 to Rule 2.2.

"Lawyer for the Situation." During the Senate hearings on the nomination of Louis Brandeis to the Supreme Court, Brandeis was criticized for alleged conflicts of interest in a complex bankruptcy where he said he was "counsel for the situation." The phrase "lawyer for the situation" has since mystified and intrigued legal scholars. A thorough recounting of the origin of the phrase is found in A. Todd, Justice on Trial: The Case of Louis D. Brandeis (1964); John Dzienkowski, Lawyers as Intermediaries: The Representation of Multiple Clients in the Modern Legal Profession, 1992 U. Ill. L. Rev. 741 (1992); and John Frank, The Legal Ethics of Louis D. Brandeis, 17 Stan. L. Rev. 683, 699-702 (1965).

Model Rules of Professional Conduct for Federal Lawyers: Federal lawyers are permitted to act as intermediaries only between two individuals. After withdrawal as an intermediary, a federal lawyer may continue to represent some of the clients in the same matter if each client consents.

Restatement of the Law Governing Lawyers: The American Law Institute has tentatively approved the following provision:

§211. Multiple Representation in Non-Litigated Matters

Unless all affected clients consent to the representation under the limitations and conditions provided in §202, a lawyer may not represent two or more clients in a matter not involving litigation if there is a substantial risk that the lawyer's representation of one or more of the clients would be materially and adversely affected by the lawyer's duties to one or more of the other clients.

(Restatement §202 is reprinted above in the Related Materials following Model Rule 1.7.)

Rule 2.3 Evaluation for Use by Third Persons

(a) A lawyer may undertake an evaluation of a matter affecting a client for the use of someone other than the client if:

(1) the lawyer reasonably believes that making the evaluation is compatible with other aspects of the lawyer's relationship with the client; and

(2) the client consents after consultation.

(b) Except as disclosure is required in connection with a report of an evaluation, information relating to the evaluation is otherwise protected by Rule 1.6.

COMMENT

Definition

[1] An evaluation may be performed at the client's direction but for the primary purpose of establishing information for the benefit of third parties; for example, an opinion concerning the title of property rendered at the behest of a vendor for the information of a prospective purchaser, or at the behest of a borrower for the information of a prospective lender. In some situations, the evaluation may be required by a government agency; for example, an opinion concerning the legality of the securities registered for sale under the securities laws. In other instances, the evaluation may be required by a third person, such as a purchaser of a business.

[2] Lawyers for the government may be called upon to give a formal opinion on the legality of contemplated government agency action. In making such an evaluation, the government lawyer acts at the behest of the government as the client but for the purpose of establishing the limits of the agency's authorized activity. Such an opinion is to be distinguished from confidential legal advice given agency officials. The critical question is whether the opinion is to be made public.

[3] A legal evaluation should be distinguished from an investigation of a person with whom the lawyer does not have a client-lawyer relationship. For example, a lawyer retained by a purchaser to analyze a vendor's title to property does not have a client-lawyer relationship with the vendor. So also, an investigation into a person's affairs by a government lawyer, or by special counsel employed by the government, is not an evaluation as that term is used in this Rule. The question is whether the lawyer is retained by the person whose affairs are being examined. When the lawyer is retained by that person, the general rules concerning loyalty to client and preservation of confidences apply, which is not the case if the lawyer is retained by someone else. For this reason, it is essential to identify the person by whom the lawyer is retained. This should be made clear not only to the person under examination, but also to others to whom the results are to be made available.

Duty to Third Person

[4] When the evaluation is intended for the information or use of a third person, a legal duty to that person may or may not arise. That legal question is beyond the scope of this Rule. However, since such an evaluation involves a departure from the normal client-lawyer relationship, careful analysis of the situation is required. The lawyer must be satisfied as a matter of professional judgment that making the evaluation is compatible with other functions undertaken in behalf of the client. For example, if the lawyer is acting as advocate in defending the client against charges of fraud, it would normally be incompatible with that responsibility for the lawyer to perform an evaluation for others concerning the same or a related transaction. Assuming no such impediment is apparent, however, the lawyer should advise the client of the implications of the evaluation, particularly the lawyer's responsibilities to third persons and the duty to disseminate the findings.

Access to and Disclosure of Information

[5] The quality of an evaluation depends on the freedom and extent of the investigation upon which it is based. Ordinarily a lawyer should have

whatever latitude of investigation seems necessary as a matter of professional judgment. Under some circumstances, however, the terms of the evaluation may be limited. For example, certain issues or sources may be categorically excluded, or the scope of search may be limited by time constraints or the noncooperation of persons having relevant information. Any such limitations which are material to the evaluation should be described in the report. If after a lawyer has commenced an evaluation, the client refuses to comply with the terms upon which it was understood the evaluation was to have been made, the lawyer's obligations are determined by law, having reference to the terms of the client's agreement and the surrounding circumstances.

Financial Auditors' Requests for Information

[6] When a question concerning the legal situation of a client arises at the instance of the client's financial auditor and the question is referred to the lawyer, the lawyer's response may be made in accordance with procedures recognized in the legal profession. Such a procedure is set forth in the American Bar Association Statement of Policy Regarding Lawyers' Responses to Auditors' Requests for Information, adopted in 1975.

Model Code Comparison

There was no counterpart to this Rule in the Model Code.

Cross-References in Rules

Rule 1.6, Comment 20: "The Rules of Professional Conduct in various circumstances permit or require a lawyer to disclose information relating to the representation. See **Rules** 2.2, **2.3**, 3.3 and 4.1."

Legislative History

1980 Discussion Draft (then Rules 6.1 through 6.3):

Confidential Evaluation (Rule 6.1)

A lawyer undertakes a confidential evaluation of a matter affecting a client when a report of the evaluation is to be given to the client alone and to be disclosed to others only at the direction of the client.

Independent Evaluation (Rule 6.2)

(a) A lawyer undertakes an independent evaluation of a matter affecting a client when a report of the evaluation is to be given to someone other than the client. A lawyer may make an independent evaluation if:

(1) Making the evaluation is compatible with other aspects of the lawyer's relationship with the client; and

(2) The terms upon which the evaluation is made are clearly described, particularly the lawyer's access to information and the persons to whom the report of the evaluation is to be made; and

(3) The client agrees that the lawyer may, within the terms upon which the evaluation is made, disclose information about the client, including matter otherwise confidential or privileged, that the lawyer determines ought to be disclosed in making a fair and accurate evaluation; and

(4) After adequate disclosure of the terms upon which the evaluation is to be made and their implications for the client, the client requests the lawyer to make the evaluation.

(b) In reporting the evaluation, the lawyer shall indicate any limitations on the scope of the inquiry that are reasonably necessary to a proper interpretation of the report.

(c) If, after a lawyer has commenced an independent evaluation, the client refuses to comply with the terms upon which it is to be made, the lawyer shall give to the person for whom the evaluation is intended the fullest report that can be made in the circumstances.

(d) Except as disclosure is required in connection with a report of the evaluation, information relating to an independent evaluation is confidential under Rule 1.7.

Financial Auditors' Requests for Information (Rule 6.3)

When a question concerning the legal situation of a client arises at the instance of the client's financial auditor and the question is referred to the lawyer, the lawyer's response shall be made in accordance with procedures recognized in the legal profession unless some other procedure is established after consent by the client upon adequate disclosure.

1981 Draft: Rule 2.3(a)(2) provided:

the terms upon which the evaluation is to be made are stated in writing, particularly the terms relating to the lawyer's access to information, the contemplated disclosure of otherwise confidential information and the persons to whom report of the evaluation is to be made . . .

Rule 2.3(b) provided: "In reporting the evaluation, the lawyer shall indicate any material limitations that were imposed on the scope of the inquiry or on the disclosure of information."

1982 Draft: Rule 2.3(a)(2) required that "the conditions of the evaluation [be] described to the client in writing, including contemplated disclosure of information otherwise protected by Rule 1.6. . . ."

Selected State Variations

California has no direct counterpart to Rule 2.3.

Florida moves subparagraph (b) to subparagraph (c) and adds the following new Rule 2.3(b):

> (b) *Limitation on Scope of Evaluation.* In reporting the evaluation, the lawyer shall indicate any material limitations that were imposed on the scope of the inquiry or on the disclosure of information.

New Jersey adds a requirement that "the conditions of the evaluation are described to the client in writing, including contemplated disclosure of information otherwise protected by Rule 1.6."

New York: No comparable provision.

Virginia omits Rule 2.3.

Related Materials

Legal Opinion Letters: A major area governed by Rule 2.3 is the "legal opinion letter" — a letter issued by a lawyer to a third party (typically a buyer or lender) assuring that the lawyer believes the transaction is legal, the seller is authorized to sell, etc. Banks, opposing parties, and others often rely upon such legal opinion letters, and a satisfactory legal opinion letter from the seller's or borrower's lawyer is often a condition of sale or a condition of making a loan. The ABA Section of Business Law has developed a Legal Opinion Accord that addresses numerous issues raised by legal opinion letters issued to third parties. The Legal Opinion Accord, which had its genesis in a 1989 conference in Silverado, California, is reprinted with extensive commentary in Third-Party Legal Opinion Report, Including the Legal Opinion Accord, of the Section of Business Law, American Bar Association, 47 Bus. Law. 167 (1991).

The Rhode Island legislature has passed a statute (R.I. Gen. Laws §19-19-10, effective January 15, 1994) prohibiting any financial institution from requiring a private borrower's lawyer to issue a legal opinion letter as a condition of making a loan. The statute — which may be the only statute of its kind in the nation — provides, in pertinent part, as follows:

§19-19-10. Attorneys' Opinions

(a) Except as provided in subsections (b)-(d), no financial institution making a loan in this state or any attorney, agent or representative for such financial institution shall directly or indirectly, as a condition of the making of a loan or advance, require any attorney representing a borrower in such loan transaction to give an opinion in relation to the validity, binding effect, or enforceability of any of the loan documents or the availability of remedies thereunder.

(b) Subsection (a) shall not apply to any transaction in which the state, or any municipality in the state . . . is the borrower.

(c) Subsection (a) shall not apply to transactions involving the public sale or underwriting of bonds, debentures, or other securities.

(d) Subsection (a) shall not prohibit, as part of a loan transaction, any requirement or condition with respect to opinions dealing with the authority and status of a borrower and matters relating to collateral.

(e) [Defines "financial institution."]

(f) No opinion obtained in violation of this section may be relied on for any purpose, and no such opinion shall give rise to or form the basis for any action against any attorney or firm rendering such opinion. Any financial institution, and any attorney, agent or representative of any financial institution knowingly violating this section shall be subject to such action as may be lawfully imposed by the regulatory authority or court which has licensing or disciplinary authority over the financial institution, attorney or other individual in question.

Restatement of the Law Governing Lawyers: The American Law Institute has tentatively approved §73 (part of the chapter on "Lawyer Civil Liability") to govern duties to non-clients who rely on or benefit from a lawyer's services in certain circumstances. Section 73 is reprinted in the Related Materials following ABA Model Rule 1.1 above. In addition, the American Law Institute has tentatively approved §152, which provides as follows:

§152. Evaluation Undertaken for Third Person

(1) In furtherance of the objectives of a client in a representation, a lawyer may provide to a non-client the results of the lawyer's investigation and analysis of facts or the lawyer's professional evaluation or opinion on the matter.

(2) When providing the information, evaluation, or opinion under Subsection (1) is reasonably likely to affect the client's interests materially and adversely, the lawyer shall first obtain the client's consent after the client is adequately informed concerning important possible effects on the client's interests.

(3) In providing the information, evaluation, or opinion under Subsection (1), the lawyer shall exercise care with respect to the non-client to the extent stated in §73(2) and not make false statements prohibited under §157.

(Restatement §73(2) is reprinted in the Related Materials following Rule 1.1; Restatement §157 is reprinted in the Related Materials following Rule 4.1.)

ARTICLE 3. ADVOCATE

Editors' Note. The *1980 Discussion Draft* contained the following Introduction to this article:

As advocate, a lawyer presents evidence and argument before a tribunal in behalf of a client. The advocate's duty in the adversary system is to present the client's case as persuasively as possible, leaving presentation of the opposing case to the other party. An advocate may not present a claim or defense lacking serious merit for the purpose of delay, although an advocate for the defendant in a criminal case may insist on proof of the offense charged. An advocate does not vouch for the justness of a client's cause but only its legal merit.

Rule 3.1 Meritorious Claims and Contentions

A lawyer shall not bring or defend a proceeding, or assert or controvert an issue therein, unless there is a basis for doing so that is not frivolous, which includes a good faith argument for an extension, modification or reversal of existing law. A lawyer for the defendant in a criminal proceeding, or the respondent in a proceeding that could result in incarceration, may nevertheless so defend the proceeding as to require that every element of the case be established.

COMMENT

[1] The advocate has a duty to use legal procedure for the fullest benefit of the client's cause, but also a duty not to abuse legal procedure. The law, both procedural and substantive, establishes the limits within which an advocate may proceed. However, the law is not always clear and never is static. Accordingly, in determining the proper scope of advocacy, account must be taken of the law's ambiguities and potential for change.

[2] The filing of an action or defense or similar action taken for a client is not frivolous merely because the facts have not first been fully substantiated or because the lawyer expects to develop vital evidence only by discovery. Such action is not frivolous even though the lawyer believes that the client's position ultimately will not prevail. The action is frivolous, however, if the client desires to have the action taken primarily for the purpose of harassing or maliciously injuring a person or if the lawyer is unable either to make a good faith argument on the merits of the action taken or to support the action taken by a good faith argument for an extension, modification or reversal of existing law.

Model Code Comparison

DR 7-102(A)(1) provided that a lawyer may not "[f]ile a suit, assert a position, conduct a defense, delay a trial, or take other action on behalf of his client when he knows or when it is obvious that such action would serve merely to harass or maliciously injure another." Rule 3.1 is to the same general effect as DR 7-102(A)(1), with three qualifications. First, the test of improper conduct is changed from "merely to harass or maliciously injure another" to the requirement that there be a basis for the litigation measure involved that is "not frivolous." This includes the concept stated in DR 7-102(A)(2) that a lawyer may advance a claim or defense unwarranted by existing law if "it can be supported by good faith argument for an extension, modification, or reversal of existing law." Second, the test in Rule 3.1 is an objective test, whereas DR 7-102(A)(1) applied only if the lawyer "knows or when it is obvious" that the litigation is frivolous. Third, Rule 3.1 has an exception that in a criminal case, or a case in which incarceration of the client may result (for example, certain juvenile proceedings), the lawyer may put the prosecution to its proof even if there is no non-frivolous basis for defense.

Cross-References in Rules

Rule 3.3, Comment 2: "An advocate is responsible for pleadings and other documents prepared for litigation, but is usually not required to have personal knowledge of matters asserted therein, for litigation documents ordinarily present assertions by the client, or by someone on the client's behalf, and not assertions by the lawyer. Compare **Rule 3.1.**"

Legislative History

1980 Discussion Draft provided:

(a) A lawyer shall not:
(1) file a complaint, motion, or pleading other than one that puts the prosecution to its proof in a criminal case, unless according to the lawyer's belief there is good ground to support it;

1982 and 1982 Drafts were substantially the same as adopted.

Selected State Variations

Alabama: Rule 3.1(a) tracks the language of DR 7-102(A)(1) — see Model Code Comparison above.
California: See Rule 3-200 (Prohibited Objectives of Employment) and B & P Code §6068(c).
District of Columbia: D.C. Rule 3.1 differs significantly from ABA Model Rule 3.1 — see District of Columbia Rules of Professional Conduct below.

New Jersey adds "the lawyer knows or reasonably believes" after "unless" in the first sentence.

New York: Same or substantially the same as the ABA Model Code — see Model Code Comparison above. See also New York Sanctioning Provisions in the New York Materials.

Texas: Rule 3.01 ends after "frivolous."

Virginia: Substantially the same as the Model Code.

Related Materials

ABA Canons: Canons 5, 15, 30, and 31 provided:

5. The Defense or Prosecution of Those Accused of Crime

It is the right of the lawyer to undertake the defense of a person accused of crime, regardless of his personal opinion as to the guilt of the accused; otherwise innocent persons, victims only of suspicious circumstances, might be denied proper defense. Having undertaken such defense, the lawyer is bound, by all fair and honorable means, to present every defense that the law of the land permits, to the end that no person may be deprived of life or liberty, but by due process of law.

15. How Far a Lawyer May Go in Supporting a Client's Cause

Nothing operates more certainly to create or to foster popular prejudice against lawyers as a class, and to deprive the profession of that full measure of public esteem and confidence which belongs to the proper discharge of its duties than does the false claim, often set up by the unscrupulous in defense of questionable transactions, that it is the duty of the lawyer to do whatever may enable him to succeed in winning his client's cause.

It is improper for a lawyer to assert in argument his personal belief in his client's innocence or in the justice of his cause.

30. Justifiable and Unjustifiable Litigations

The lawyer must decline to conduct a civil cause or to make a defense when convinced that it is intended merely to harass or to injure the opposite party or to work oppression or wrong. But otherwise it is his right, and, having accepted retainer, it becomes his duty to insist upon the judgment of the Court as to the legal merits of his client's claim. His appearance in Court should be deemed equivalent to an assertion on his honor that in his opinion his client's case is one proper for judicial determination.

31. Responsibility for Litigation

The responsibility for advising as to questionable transactions, for bringing questionable suits, for urging questionable defenses, is the lawyer's responsibility.

He cannot escape it by urging as an excuse that he is only following his client's instructions.

American Academy of Matrimonial Lawyers: The "Bounds of Advocacy" drafted by the American Academy of Matrimonial Lawyers contains the following provision and commentary:

2.25 An attorney should not contest child custody or visitation for either financial leverage or vindictiveness.

Comment to Rule 2.25

Clients in contested dissolutions sometimes ask attorneys to contest custody even though they concede that the other spouse is the better parent. It is improper for the matrimonial lawyer to assist the client in such conduct. Proper consideration of the welfare of the children requires that they not be used as pawns in the adversary process. If despite the attorney's advice the client persists, the attorney should seek to withdraw.

Federal Rules of Civil Procedure: Rule 11 was amended effective December 1, 1993; subparagraph (b) of the amended rule tracks Model Rule 3.1 closely.

Federal Rules of Appellate Procedure: Rule 38 provides that "If a court of appeals shall determine that an appeal is frivolous, it may award just damages and single or double costs to the appellee."

Private Securities Litigation Reform Act: In December of 1995, over President Clinton's veto, Congress passed the Private Securities Litigation Reform Act. Title I of the new statute, entitled "Reduction of Abusive Litigation," requires courts to make specific findings as to whether all attorneys in private securities fraud suits have complied with Rule 11 of the Federal Rules of Civil Procedure. The new law also establishes a rebuttable presumption that a losing party should pay *all* of a prevailing party's costs and attorney fees as an appropriate sanction for violating Rule 11 — but a party may rebut this presumption by showing that (1) the violation was de minimis, or (2) imposing fees and costs would be an undue burden and would be unjust. Finally, the new law gives courts express authority to require counsel for either side or both sides to post a bond to cover fees and expenses that the court may ultimately award.

Rule 3.2 Expediting Litigation

A lawyer shall make reasonable efforts to expedite litigation consistent with the interests of the client.

COMMENT

Dilatory practices bring the administration of justice into disrepute. Delay should not be indulged merely for the convenience of the advocates, or for the purpose of frustrating an opposing party's attempt to obtain rightful redress or repose. It is not a justification that similar conduct is often tolerated by the bench and bar. The question is whether a competent lawyer acting in good faith would regard the course of action as having some substantial purpose other than delay. Realizing financial or other benefit from otherwise improper delay in litigation is not a legitimate interest of the client.

Model Code Comparison

DR 7-101(A)(1) stated that a lawyer does not violate the duty to represent a client zealously "by being punctual in fulfilling all professional commitments." DR 7-102(A)(1) provided that a lawyer "shall not . . . file a suit, assert a position, conduct a defense [or] delay a trial . . . when he knows or when it is obvious that such action would serve merely to harass or maliciously injure another."

Cross-References in Rules

None.

Legislative History

1980 Discussion Draft (then Rule 3.3(a)) provided:

A lawyer shall make every effort consistent with the legitimate interests of the client to expedite litigation. Realizing financial or other benefit from otherwise improper delay in litigation is not a legitimate interest of the client. A lawyer shall not engage in any procedure or tactic having no substantial purpose other than delay or increasing the cost of litigation to another party.

1981 Draft: "A lawyer shall make reasonable effort consistent with the *legitimate* interests of the client to expedite litigation."
1982 Draft was adopted.

Selected State Variations

California: See B & P Code §6128(b). (California's Rules of Professional Conduct have no comparable provision.)
District of Columbia: D.C. Rule 3.2(a) differs significantly from the ABA Model Rule — see District of Columbia Rules of Professional Conduct below.

New Jersey adds "and shall treat with courtesy and consideration all persons involved in the legal process" at the end of Rule 3.2.

New York: Same or substantially the same as the ABA Model Code — see Model Code Comparison above.

Texas Rule 3.02 provides:

> In the course of litigation, a lawyer shall not take a position that unreasonably increases the costs or other burdens of the case or that unreasonably delays resolution of the matter.

Virginia: Substantially the same as the Model Code.

Related Materials

Alternative Dispute Resolution ("ADR"): Some lawyers believe that the obligation in Rule 3.2 to "expedite litigation" includes the obligation to inform a client about ADR methods as alternatives to litigation. For example, a Texas Bar Association Creed states: "I will advise my client regarding the availability of mediation [and] arbitration. . . ." Similarly, the Houston Bar Association has adopted guidelines stating: "When appropriate, I will counsel my client with respect to mediation, arbitration, and other alternative methods of dispute resolution." The Chicago Bar Association has circulated a draft proposal to amend Rule 3.2 to provide: "A lawyer shall make reasonable efforts to expedite *or minimize the cost of* litigation, *including the possible use of alternative dispute resolution processes,* consistent with the interests of the client." (Emphasis added.) In the context of Rule 2.1, Colorado, Georgia, and Hawaii already require lawyers to advise clients about ADR, and numerous state and federal courts have adopted mandatory ADR to move litigation along more quickly and inexpensively.

Federal Rules of Civil Procedure: Fed. R. Civ. P. 1 provides that the Federal Rules of Civil Procedure "shall be construed to secure the just, *speedy,* and inexpensive determination of every action [emphasis added]." Fed. R. Civ. P. 11 (as amended in 1993), the broadest and most frequently invoked sanctions rule, requires attorneys to sign every pleading, motion, or other paper to certify that (among other things) the paper is "not being presented for any improper purpose, such as to harass or to *cause unnecessary delay* or needless increase in the cost of litigation . . . [emphasis added]." Fed. R. Civ. P. 26(g), part of the general rule governing discovery, requires a similar certification pertaining to discovery requests, responses, and objections. Fed. R. Civ. P. 56(g), part of the rule on summary judgment, provides sanctions whenever the court finds "that any of the affidavits presented pursuant to this rule are presented in bad faith *or solely for the purpose of delay* [emphasis added]."

Federal Rules of Appellate Procedure: Rule 38, entitled "Damages for Delay," provides as follows: "If a court of appeals shall determine that an appeal is frivolous, it may award just damages and single or double costs to the appellee."

Federal Rules of Evidence: Rule 102 of the Federal Rules of Evidence provides that the Rules shall be construed to secure "elimination of unjustifiable expense and delay. . . ."

Model Rules of Professional Conduct for Federal Lawyers: Rule 3.2 provides: "A Federal lawyer shall make reasonable efforts to expedite litigation and other proceedings consistent with the interests of the client *and the lawyer's responsibilities to the tribunal to avoid unwarranted delay* [emphasis added]."

28 U.S.C. §1927: A major federal statutory provision available to penalize litigants who engage in abusive delay and other improper litigation tactics is 28 U.S.C. §1927, which provides as follows:

Counsel's Liability for Excessive Costs

Any attorney . . . who so multiplies the proceedings in any case unreasonably and vexatiously may be required by the court to satisfy personally the excess costs, expenses, and attorneys' fees reasonably incurred because of such conduct.

Rule 3.3 Candor Toward the Tribunal

(a) A lawyer shall not knowingly:

(1) make a false statement of material fact or law to a tribunal;

(2) fail to disclose a material fact to a tribunal when disclosure is necessary to avoid assisting a criminal or fraudulent act by the client;

(3) fail to disclose to the tribunal legal authority in the controlling jurisdiction known to the lawyer to be directly adverse to the position of the client and not disclosed by opposing counsel; or

(4) offer evidence that the lawyer knows to be false. If a lawyer has offered material evidence and comes to know of its falsity, the lawyer shall take reasonable remedial measures.

(b) The duties stated in paragraph (a) continue to the conclusion of the proceeding, and apply even if compliance requires disclosure of information otherwise protected by Rule 1.6.

(c) A lawyer may refuse to offer evidence that the lawyer reasonably believes is false.

(d) In an ex parte proceeding, a lawyer shall inform the tribunal of all material facts known to the lawyer which will enable the tribunal to make an informed decision, whether or not the facts are adverse.

COMMENT

[1] The advocate's task is to present the client's case with persuasive force. Performance of that duty while maintaining confidences of the cli-

ent is qualified by the advocate's duty of candor to the tribunal. However, an advocate does not vouch for the evidence submitted in a cause; the tribunal is responsible for assessing its probative value.

Representations by a Lawyer

[2] An advocate is responsible for pleadings and other documents prepared for litigation, but is usually not required to have personal knowledge of matters asserted therein, for litigation documents ordinarily present assertions by the client, or by someone on the client's behalf, and not assertions by the lawyer. Compare Rule 3.1. However, an assertion purporting to be on the lawyer's own knowledge, as in an affidavit by the lawyer or in a statement in open court, may properly be made only when the lawyer knows the assertion is true or believes it to be true on the basis of a reasonably diligent inquiry. There are circumstances where failure to make a disclosure is the equivalent of an affirmative misrepresentation. The obligation prescribed in Rule 1.2(d) not to counsel a client to commit or assist the client in committing a fraud applies in litigation. Regarding compliance with Rule 1.2(d), see the Comment to that Rule. See also the Comment to Rule 8.4(b).

Misleading Legal Argument

[3] Legal argument based on a knowingly false representation of law constitutes dishonesty toward the tribunal. A lawyer is not required to make a disinterested exposition of the law, but must recognize the existence of pertinent legal authorities. Furthermore, as stated in paragraph (a) (3), an advocate has a duty to disclose directly adverse authority in the controlling jurisdiction which has not been disclosed by the opposing party. The underlying concept is that the legal argument is a discussion seeking to determine the legal premises properly applicable to the case.

False Evidence

[4] When evidence that a lawyer knows to be false is provided by a person who is not the client, the lawyer must refuse to offer it regardless of the client's wishes.

[5] When false evidence is offered by the client, however, a conflict may arise between the lawyer's duty to keep the client's revelations confidential and the duty of candor to the court. Upon ascertaining that material evidence is false, the lawyer should seek to persuade the client that the evidence should not be offered or, if it has been offered, that its false character should immediately be disclosed. If the persuasion is ineffective, the lawyer must take reasonable remedial measures.

[6] Except in the defense of a criminal accused, the rule generally recognized is that, if necessary to rectify the situation, an advocate must disclose the existence of the client's deception to the court or to the other party. Such a disclosure can result in grave consequences to the client, including not only a sense of betrayal but also loss of the case and perhaps a prosecution for perjury. But the alternative is that the lawyer cooperate in deceiving the court, thereby subverting the truth-finding process which the adversary system is designed to implement. See Rule 1.2(d). Furthermore, unless it is clearly understood that the lawyer will act upon the duty to disclose the existence of false evidence, the client can simply reject the lawyer's advice to reveal the false evidence and insist that the lawyer keep silent. Thus the client could in effect coerce the lawyer into being a party to fraud on the court.

Perjury by a Criminal Defendant

[7] Whether an advocate for a criminally accused has the same duty of disclosure has been intensely debated. While it is agreed that the lawyer should seek to persuade the client to refrain from perjurious testimony, there has been dispute concerning the lawyer's duty when that persuasion fails. If the confrontation with the client occurs before trial, the lawyer ordinarily can withdraw. Withdrawal before trial may not be possible, however, either because trial is imminent, or because the confrontation with the client does not take place until the trial itself, or because no other counsel is available.

[8] The most difficult situation, therefore, arises in a criminal case where the accused insists on testifying when the lawyer knows that the testimony is perjurious. The lawyer's effort to rectify the situation can increase the likelihood of the client's being convicted as well as opening the possibility of a prosecution for perjury. On the other hand, if the lawyer does not exercise control over the proof, the lawyer participates, although in a merely passive way, in deception of the court.

[9] Three resolutions of this dilemma have been proposed. One is to permit the accused to testify by a narrative without guidance through

the lawyer's questioning. This compromises both contending principles; it exempts the lawyer from the duty to disclose false evidence but subjects the client to an implicit disclosure of information imparted to counsel. Another suggested resolution, of relatively recent origin, is that the advocate be entirely excused from the duty to reveal perjury if the perjury is that of the client. This is a coherent solution but makes the advocate a knowing instrument of perjury.

[10] The other resolution of the dilemma is that the lawyer must reveal the client's perjury if necessary to rectify the situation. A criminal accused has a right to the assistance of an advocate, a right to testify and a right of confidential communication with counsel. However, an accused should not have a right to assistance of counsel in committing perjury. Furthermore, an advocate has an obligation, not only in professional ethics but under the law as well, to avoid implication in the commission of perjury or other falsification of evidence. See Rule 1.2(d).

Remedial Measures

[11] If perjured testimony or false evidence has been offered, the advocate's proper course ordinarily is to remonstrate with the client confidentially. If that fails, the advocate should seek to withdraw if that will remedy the situation. If withdrawal will not remedy the situation or is impossible, the advocate should make disclosure to the court. It is for the court then to determine what should be done — making a statement about the matter to the trier of fact, ordering a mistrial or perhaps nothing. If the false testimony was that of the client, the client may controvert the lawyer's version of their communication when the lawyer discloses the situation to the court. If there is an issue whether the client has committed perjury, the lawyer cannot represent the client in resolution of the issue, and a mistrial may be unavoidable. An unscrupulous client might in this way attempt to produce a series of mistrials and thus escape prosecution. However, a second such encounter could be construed as a deliberate abuse of the right to counsel and as such a waiver of the right to further representation.

Constitutional Requirements

[12] The general rule — that an advocate must disclose the existence of perjury with respect to a material fact, even that of a client — applies to defense counsel in criminal cases, as well as in other instances.

However, the definition of the lawyer's ethical duty in such a situation may be qualified by constitutional provisions for due process and the right to counsel in criminal cases. In some jurisdictions these provisions have been construed to require that counsel present an accused as a witness if the accused wishes to testify, even if counsel knows the testimony will be false. The obligation of the advocate under these Rules is subordinate to such a constitutional requirement.

Duration of Obligation

[13] A practical time limit on the obligation to rectify the presentation of false evidence has to be established. The conclusion of the proceeding is a reasonably definite point for the termination of the obligation.

Refusing to Offer Proof Believed to Be False

[14] Generally speaking, a lawyer has authority to refuse to offer testimony or other proof that the lawyer believes is untrustworthy. Offering such proof may reflect adversely on the lawyer's ability to discriminate in the quality of evidence and thus impair the lawyer's effectiveness as an advocate. In criminal cases, however, a lawyer may, in some jurisdictions, be denied this authority by constitutional requirements governing the right to counsel.

Ex Parte Proceedings

[15] Ordinarily, an advocate has the limited responsibility of presenting one side of the matters that a tribunal should consider in reaching a decision; the conflicting position is expected to be presented by the opposing party. However, in an ex parte proceeding, such as an application for a temporary restraining order, there is no balance of presentation by opposing advocates. The object of an ex parte proceeding is nevertheless to yield a substantially just result. The judge has an affirmative responsibility to accord the absent party just consideration. The lawyer for the represented party has the correlative duty to make disclosures of material facts known to the lawyer and that the lawyer reasonably believes are necessary to an informed decision.

Model Code Comparison

Paragraph (a)(1) is substantially identical to DR 7-102(A)(5), which provided that a lawyer shall not "knowingly make a false statement of law or fact."

Paragraph (a)(2) is implicit in DR 7-102(A)(3), which provided that "a lawyer shall not . . . knowingly fail to disclose that which he is required by law to reveal."

Paragraph (a)(3) is substantially identical to DR 7-106(B)(1).

With regard to paragraph (a)(4), the first sentence of this subparagraph is similar to DR 7-102(A)(4), which provided that a lawyer shall not "knowingly use" perjured testimony or false evidence. The second sentence of paragraph (a)(4) resolves an ambiguity in the Model Code concerning the action required of a lawyer who discovers that the lawyer has offered perjured testimony or false evidence. DR 7-102(A)(4), quoted above, did not expressly deal with this situation, but the prohibition against "use" of false evidence can be construed to preclude carrying through with a case based on such evidence when that fact has become known during the trial. DR 7-102(B)(1), also noted in connection with Rule 1.6, provided that a lawyer "who receives information clearly establishing that . . . [h]is client has . . . perpetrated a fraud upon . . . a tribunal shall [if the client does not rectify the situation] . . . reveal the fraud to the . . . tribunal. . . ." Since use of perjured testimony or false evidence is usually regarded as "fraud" upon the court, DR 7-102(B)(1) apparently required disclosure by the lawyer in such circumstances. However, some states have amended DR 7-102(B)(1) in conformity with an ABA-recommended amendment to provide that the duty of disclosure does not apply when the "information is protected as a privileged communication." This qualification may be empty, for the rule of attorney-client privilege has been construed to exclude communications that further a crime, including the crime of perjury. On this interpretation of DR 7-102(B)(1), the lawyer has a duty to disclose the perjury.

Paragraph (c) confers discretion on the lawyer to refuse to offer evidence that the lawyer "reasonably believes" is false. This gives the lawyer more latitude than DR 7-102(A)(4), which prohibited the lawyer from offering evidence the lawyer "knows" is false.

There was no counterpart in the Model Code to paragraph (d).

Cross-References in Rules

Rule 1.6, Comment 10: "[A] lawyer has a duty under **Rule 3.3(a)(4)** not to use false evidence."

Rule 1.6, Comment 20: "The Rules of Professional Conduct in various circumstances permit or require a lawyer to disclose information relating to the representation. See **Rules** 2.2, 2.3, **3.3** and 4.1."

Rule 1.13, Comment 6: "[T]his Rule does not limit or expand the lawyer's responsibility under **Rules** 1.6, 1.8, and 1.16, **3.3** or 4.1."

Rule 3.8, Comment 1: "See also **Rule 3.3(d)**, governing ex parte proceedings, among which grand jury proceedings are included."

Rule 3.9: "A lawyer representing a client before a legislative or administrative tribunal in a nonadjudicative proceeding shall disclose that the appearance is in a representative capacity and shall conform to the provisions of **Rules 3.3(a)** through **(c)**, 3.4(a) through (c), and 3.5."

Legislative History

1980 Discussion Draft (then Rule 3.1) provided:

(a) A lawyer shall not: . . .

(2) make a knowing misrepresentation of fact;

(3) except as provided in paragraph (f), offer evidence that the lawyer is convinced beyond a reasonable doubt is false, or offer without suitable explanation evidence that the lawyer knows is substantially misleading; or

(4) make a representation about existing legal authority that the lawyer knows to be inaccurate or so incomplete as to be substantially misleading.

(b) Except as provided in paragraph (f), if a lawyer discovers that evidence or testimony presented by the lawyer is false, the lawyer shall disclose that fact and take suitable measures to rectify the consequences, even if doing so requires disclosure of a confidence of the client or disclosure that the client is implicated in the falsification.

(c) If a lawyer discovers that the tribunal has not been apprised of legal authority known to the lawyer that would probably have a substantial effect on the determination of a material issue, the lawyer shall advise the tribunal of that authority.

(d) Except as provided in paragraph (f), a lawyer shall disclose a fact known to the lawyer, even if the fact is adverse, when disclosure:

(1) is required by law or the Rules of Professional Conduct; or

(2) is necessary to correct a manifest misapprehension resulting from a previous representation the lawyer has made to the tribunal.

(e) Except as provided in paragraph (f), a lawyer may apprise another party of evidence favorable to that party and may refuse to offer evidence that the lawyer believes with substantial reason to be false.

(f) A lawyer for a defendant in a criminal case:

(1) is not required to apprise the prosecutor or the tribunal of evidence adverse to the accused, except as law may otherwise provide;

(2) may not disclose facts as required by paragraph (d) if doing so is prohibited by applicable law;

(3) shall offer evidence regardless of belief as to whether it is false if the client so demands and applicable law requires that the lawyer comply with such a demand.

(g) A prosecutor has the further duty of disclosure stated in Rule 3.10.

1981 Draft was substantially the same as adopted except for the following parts of subparagraph (a):

(a) A lawyer shall not knowingly:

(1) make a false statement of fact or law to a tribunal, or fail to disclose a fact in circumstances where the failure to make the disclosure is the equivalent of the lawyer's making a material misrepresentation;

(2) fail to make a disclosure of fact necessary to prevent a fraud on the tribunal. . . .

1982 Draft was adopted.

Selected State Variations

Arizona: At the end of Rule 3.3(a)(2) and (4), Arizona adds: "except as required by applicable law."

California: See Rule 5-200 (Trial Conduct), and B & P Code §6068(d) (regarding false statements to a judge) and §6128(a) (regarding intention to deceive a court).

District of Columbia: D.C. Rule 3.3 differs significantly from the ABA Model Rule — see District of Columbia Rules of Professional Conduct below.

Florida: In 1990, the Florida Supreme Court amended Rule 3.3 to provide that a lawyer shall not

> (a)(4) Permit any witness, including a criminal defendant, to offer testimony or other evidence that the lawyer knows to be false. A lawyer may not offer testimony which he knows to be false in the form of a narrative unless so ordered by the tribunal.

The next sentence of Florida's Rule 3.3(a)(4) is the same as the second sentence of ABA Model Rule 3.3(a)(4). Florida also provides in Rule 3.3(b) that the "duties stated in paragraph (a) continue beyond the conclusion of the proceeding. . . ." Effective April 21, 1994, Florida has added the following new paragraph to the Comment to its version of Rule 3.3:

> Although the offering of perjured testimony or false evidence is considered a fraud on the tribunal, these situations are distinguishable from that of a client who, upon being arrested, provides false identification to a law enforcement officer. The client's past act of lying to a law enforcement officer does not constitute a fraud on the tribunal, and thus does not trigger the disclosure obligation under this rule, because a false statement to an arresting officer is unsworn and occurs prior to the institution of a court proceeding. If the client testifies, the lawyer must attempt to have the client respond to any questions truthfully or by asserting an applicable privilege. Any false statements by the client in the course of the court proceeding will trigger the duties under this rule.

Georgia's version of Rule 3.3(a) and (b) is the Code version as originally adopted without the 1974 amendment. See Model Code Comparison above.

Hawaii: At the end of Rule 3.3(a)(4), Hawaii commands lawyers to "take remedial measures to the extent necessary to rectify the consequences." Rule 3.3(d) applies to ex parte proceedings "except grand jury proceedings and applications for search warrants," and at the end Rule 3.3(d) Hawaii adds "disclosure of which is not otherwise prohibited by law."

Illinois Rule 3.3(a) provides:

(a) In appearing in a professional capacity before a tribunal, a lawyer shall not:

(1) make a statement of material fact or law to a tribunal which the lawyer knows or reasonably should know is false; . . .

(5) participate in the creation or preservation of evidence when the lawyer knows or reasonably should know the evidence is false;

(6) counsel or assist the client in conduct the lawyer knows to be illegal or fraudulent; . . .

(8) fail to disclose the identities of the clients represented and of the persons who employed the lawyer unless such information is privileged or irrelevant;

(9) intentionally degrade a witness or other person by stating or alluding to personal facts concerning that person which are not relevant to the case; . . .

(12) fail to use reasonable efforts to restrain and to prevent clients from doing those things that the lawyer ought not to do;

(13) suppress any evidence that the lawyer or client has a legal obligation to reveal or produce;

(14) advise or cause a person to become unavailable as a witness by leaving the jurisdiction or making secret their whereabouts within the jurisdiction; or

(15) pay, offer to pay, or acquiesce in the payment of compensation to a witness contingent upon the content of the witness' testimony or the outcome of the case, but a lawyer may advance, guarantee, or acquiesce in the payment of expenses reasonably incurred in attending or testifying, and a reasonable fee for the professional services of an expert witness.

(b) The duties stated in paragraph (a) are continuing duties and apply even if compliance requires disclosure of information otherwise protected by Rule 1.6.

Illinois also adds to its Rule 1.2 the following subparagraphs, which substantially retain the language of DR 7-102(B) of the Code of Professional Responsibility as amended in 1974 (see Model Code Comparison to Rule 3.3 above):

(g) A lawyer who knows a client has, in the course of the representation, perpetrated a fraud upon a person or tribunal shall promptly call upon the client to rectify the same, and if the client refuses or is unable to do so, the lawyer shall reveal the fraud to the affected person or tribunal, except when the information is protected as a privileged communication.

(h) A lawyer who knows that a person other than the client has perpetrated a fraud upon a tribunal shall promptly reveal the fraud to the tribunal.

Iowa: DR 7-102(b)(2) requires a lawyer to disclose a client's fraud "except when barred from doing so by Iowa code section 622.10. If barred from doing so by section 622.10, the lawyer shall immediately withdraw from representation of the client unless the client fully discloses the fraud to the person or tribunal."

Maryland adds the following subparagraph (e): "notwithstanding paragraphs (a) through (d), a lawyer for an accused in a criminal case need not disclose that the accused intends to testify falsely or has testified falsely if the lawyer reasonably believes that the disclosure would jeopardize any constitutional right of the accused."

218

Massachusetts: Effective January 1, 1998, Rule 3.3(b) states that the conclusion of the proceedings includes "all appeals." Rule 3.3(e) permits a lawyer representing a criminal defendant to elicit false testimony in narrative fashion if withdrawal is not otherwise possible without prejudicing the defendant. However, "the lawyer shall not argue the probative value of the false testimony in closing argument or in any other proceedings, including appeals." A lawyer who is unable to withdraw when he or she knows that a criminal defendant will testify falsely "may not prevent the client from testifying" but must not "examine the client in such a manner as to elicit any testimony from the client the lawyer knows to be false." Comment [2A] to Rule 3.3 provides that the word "assisting" in Rule 3.3(a)(2) "is not limited to conduct that makes the lawyer liable as an aider, abettor or joint tortfeasor," but "is intended to guide the conduct of the lawyer as an officer of the court as a prophylactic measure to protect against the contamination of the judicial process. Thus, for example, a lawyer who knows that a client has committed fraud on a tribunal and has refused to rectify it must disclose the fraud to avoid assisting the client's fraudulent act." However, this obligation would not apply to a lawyer for a criminal defendant.

New Jersey adds the following subparagraph (a)(5): "fail to disclose to the tribunal a material fact with knowledge that the tribunal may tend to be misled by such failure." New Jersey adds the client's "illegal" acts to Rule 3.3(a)(2). New Jersey also requires a lawyer to reveal confidences to prevent a client from committing "a criminal, illegal or fraudulent act that the lawyer reasonably believes is likely to perpetrate a fraud upon a tribunal."

New York: Same or substantially the same as the ABA Model Code — see Model Code Comparison above — except see New York Materials for New York's versions of DR 7-102(B)(1), EC 4-7, and DR 4-101(C)(5). In addition, effective October 1, 1993, in matrimonial matters only, New York added a new §202.16(e) to its Uniform Civil Rules for the Supreme Court and the County Court. As amended effective May 1, 1996, §202.16(e) provides as follows:

> (e) *Certification by attorney.* Any paper submitted to the court by a party represented by counsel, which contains statements or allegations of fact, including the statement of net worth, shall be accompanied by a certification directed to the court, which reads as follows: "I hereby certify under penalty of perjury and as an officer of the court that I have no knowledge that the substance of any of the factual submissions contained in this document is false." This statement shall appear without qualification on any papers submitted.

> *Texas* Rule 3.03(b) and (c) provides:

> (b) If a lawyer has offered material evidence and comes to know of its falsity, the lawyer shall make a good faith effort to persuade the client to authorize the lawyer to correct or withdraw the false evidence. If such efforts are unsuccessful, the lawyer shall take reasonable remedial measures, including disclosure of the true facts.

> (c) The duties stated in paragraphs (a) and (b) continue until remedial legal measures are no longer reasonably possible.

Virginia: Substantially the same as the Model Code, except that DR 7-105 deletes the obligation to disclose adverse legal authority, and DR 7-105(C)(6) is identical to Model Rule 3.3(a)(4).

Washington's version of Rule 3.3(b) does *not* allow disclosure of information protected by Rule 1.6.

Related Materials

ABA Canons: Canons 22 and 41 provided:

22. *Candor and Fairness*

The conduct of the lawyer before the Court and with other lawyers should be characterized by candor and fairness.

It is not candid or fair for the lawyer knowingly to misquote the contents of a paper, the testimony of a witness, the language or the argument of opposing counsel, or the language of a decision or a textbook; or with knowledge of its invalidity, to cite as authority a decision that has been overruled, or a statute that has been repealed; or in argument to assert as a fact that which has not been proved, or in those jurisdictions where a side has the opening and closing arguments to mislead his opponent by concealing or withholding positions in his opening argument upon which his side then intends to rely.

It is unprofessional and dishonorable to deal other than candidly with the facts in taking the statements of witnesses, in drawing affidavits and other documents, and in the presentation of causes.

A lawyer should not offer evidence which he knows the Court should reject, in order to get the same before the jury by argument for its admissibility, nor should he address to the Judge arguments upon any point not properly calling for determination by him. Neither should he introduce into an argument, addressed to the court, remarks or statements intended to influence the jury or bystanders.

These and all kindred practices are unprofessional and unworthy of an officer of the law charged, as is the lawyer, with the duty of aiding in the administration of justice.

41. *Discovery of Imposition and Deception*

When a lawyer discovers that some fraud or deception has been practiced, which has unjustly imposed upon the court or a party, he should endeavor to rectify it; at first by advising his client, and if his client refuses to forego the advantage thus unjustly gained, he should promptly inform the injured person or his counsel, so that they may take appropriate steps.

ABA Standards for Criminal Justice: See Defense Function Standard 4-7.5. The original draft of The Defense Function contained the following version of Standard 4-7.7:

(a) If the defendant has admitted to defense counsel facts which establish guilt and counsel's independent investigation established that the admissions are true but the defendant insists on the right to trial, counsel must strongly discourage the defendant against taking the witness stand to testify perjuriously.

(b) If, in advance of trial, the defendant insists that he or she will take the stand to testify perjuriously, the lawyer may withdraw from the case, if that is feasible, seeking leave of the court if necessary, but the court should not be advised of the lawyer's reason for seeking to do so.

(c) If withdrawal from the case is not feasible or is not permitted by the court, or if the situation arises immediately preceding trial or during the trial and the defendant insists upon testifying perjuriously in his or her own behalf, it is unprofessional conduct for the lawyer to lend aid to the perjury or use the perjured testimony. Before the defendant takes the stand in these circumstances, the lawyer should make a record of the fact that the defendant is taking the stand against the advice of counsel in some appropriate manner without revealing the fact to the court. The lawyer may identify the witness as the defendant and may ask appropriate questions of the defendant when it is believed that the defendant's answers will not be perjurious. As to matters for which it is believed the defendant will offer perjurious testimony, the lawyer should seek to avoid direct examination of the defendant in the conventional manner; instead, the lawyer should ask the defendant if he or she wishes to make any additional statement concerning the case to the trier or triers of the facts. A lawyer may not later argue the defendant's known false version of facts to the jury as worthy of belief, and may not recite or rely upon the false testimony in his or her closing argument.

When Standard 4-7.7 was published, it was accompanied by the following official Editorial Note written by the ABA:

> This proposed standard was approved by the ABA Standing Committee on Association Standards for Criminal Justice but was withdrawn prior to submission of this chapter to the ABA House of Delegates. Instead, the question of what should be done in situations dealt with by the standard has been deferred until the ABA Special Commission on Evaluation of Professional Standards [the Kutak Commission] reports its final recommendations.

The final recommendation of the Kutak Commission is found in Rule 3.3 of the ABA Model Rules and in the accompanying Comments. Comment 9 to Rule 3.3 refers to the "narrative" suggested in Standard 4-7.7, but both Rule 3.3 and the accompanying Comment appear to reject the narrative proposal. ABA Formal Ethics Opinion 87-353 (1987) does so explicitly. See also Nix v. Whiteside, 475 U.S. 157 (1986). Nevertheless, some courts continue to approve the narrative method, and at least one bar's version of Rule 3.3 (D.C.) expressly permits a narrative in certain circumstances.

ABA Standards for Imposing Lawyer Sanctions:

6.11. Disbarment is generally appropriate when a lawyer, with the intent to deceive the court, makes a false statement, submits a false document, or improperly withholds material information, and causes serious or potentially serious injurt to a party, or causes a significant or potentially significant adverse effect on the legal proceeding.

6.12. Suspension is generally appropriate when a lawyer knows that false statements or documents are being submitted to the court or that material information is improperly being withheld, and takes no remedial action, and causes injury or potential injury to a party to the legal proceeding, or causes an adverse or potentially adverse effect on the legal proceeding.

6.13. Reprimand is generally appropriate when a lawyer is negligent either in determining whether statements or documents are false or in taking remedial action when material information is being withheld, and causes injury or potential injury to a party to the legal proceeding, or causes an adverse or potentially adverse effect on the legal proceeding.

6.14. Admonition is generally appropriate when a lawyer engages in an isolated instance of neglect in determining whether submitted statements or documents are false or in failing to disclose material information upon learning of its falsity, and causes little or no actual or potential injury to a party, or causes little or no adverse or potentially adverse effect on the legal proceeding.

6.31. Disbarment is generally appropriate when a lawyer:

. . . (b) makes an ex parte communication with a judge or juror with intent to affect the outcome of the proceeding, and causes serious or potentially serious injury to a party, or causes significant or potentially significant interference with the outcome of the legal proceeding. . . .

American Academy of Matrimonial Lawyers: The "Bounds of Advocacy" drafted by the American Academy of Matrimonial Lawyers contains the following provision and commentary:

3.11 An attorney should not seek an ex parte order without prior notice to opposing counsel except in exigent circumstances.

Comment to Rule 3.11

There are few things more damaging to a client's confidence in his lawyer, or to relationships between lawyers, than for a party to be served with an ex parte order about which his lawyer knows nothing. Even where there are exigent circumstances (substantial physical or financial risk to the client), or local rules permit ex parte proceedings, notice to, or the appearance of, opposing counsel usually will not prevent appropriate relief from issuing.

Federal Rules of Civil Procedure: Under the amended version of Fed. R. Civ. P. 26(e), which took effect on December 1, 1993, the duty of parties to supplement prior discovery responses is greatly expanded. The new version of Rule 26(e) covers all discovery information given to the other side, either under the "automatic discovery" provisions of amended Rule 26(a)(1) or in response to a party's specific request. (Substantial excerpts from Rule 26(e) appear below in the chapter on Federal Sanctions and Discovery Provisions.)

Model Rules of Professional Conduct for Federal Lawyers add a new Rule 3.3(a)(5), which states that a federal lawyer shall not "[d]isobey an obligation or order imposed by a tribunal, unless done openly before the tribunal in a good faith assertion that no valid obligation or order should exist." (This rule is similar to Rule 3.4(c), but the Federal Lawyers version of that rule covers only obligations to opposing parties and counsel.)

Restatement of the Law Governing Lawyers: The American Law Institute has proposed but not yet approved the following provisions:

§171. *Disclosure of Legal Authority*

In representing a client in a matter before a tribunal, a lawyer may not knowingly:

(1) make a false statement of a material proposition of law to the tribunal; or

(2) fail to disclose to the tribunal legal authority in the controlling jurisdiction known to the lawyer to be directly adverse to the position asserted by the client and not disclosed by opposing counsel.

§172. *Advocacy in Ex Parte and Other Proceedings*

In representing a client in a matter before a tribunal, a lawyer applying for ex parte relief must comply with the requirements of §170 and §§178-180 and further:

(1) must not present evidence the lawyer reasonably believes is false;

(2) must disclose all material and relevant facts known to the lawyer that will enable the tribunal to reach an informed decision; and

(3) must comply with any other applicable special requirements of candor imposed by law.

§180. *False Testimony or Evidence*

(1) A lawyer may not:

(a) knowingly counsel or assist a witness to testify falsely or otherwise to offer false evidence as to a material issue of fact;

(b) knowingly make a false statement of fact to the tribunal;

(c) offer testimony or other evidence as to a material issue of fact known by the lawyer to be false.

(2) If a lawyer has offered testimony or other evidence as to a material issue of fact and comes to know of its falsity, the lawyer must take reasonable remedial measures and may disclose confidential client information when necessary to take such a measure.

(3) A lawyer may refuse to offer testimony or other evidence that the lawyer reasonably believes is false, even if the lawyer does not know it to be false.

(Restatement §170 is reprinted in the Related Materials following Rule 3.1; §§178 and 179 are reprinted in the Related Materials following Rule 3.4.)

Rule 3.4 Fairness to Opposing Party and Counsel

A lawyer shall not:

(a) unlawfully obstruct another party's access to evidence or unlawfully alter, destroy or conceal a document or other material having poten-

tial evidentiary value. A lawyer shall not counsel or assist another person to do any such act;

(b) falsify evidence, counsel or assist a witness to testify falsely, or offer an inducement to a witness that is prohibited by law;

(c) knowingly disobey an obligation under the rules of a tribunal except for an open refusal based on an assertion that no valid obligation exists;

(d) in pretrial procedure, make a frivolous discovery request or fail to make reasonably diligent effort to comply with a legally proper discovery request by an opposing party;

(e) in trial, allude to any matter that the lawyer does not reasonably believe is relevant or that will not be supported by admissible evidence, assert personal knowledge of facts in issue except when testifying as a witness, or state a personal opinion as to the justness of a cause, the credibility of a witness, the culpability of a civil litigant or the guilt or innocence of an accused; or

(f) request a person other than a client to refrain from voluntarily giving relevant information to another party unless:

(1) the person is a relative or an employee or other agent of a client; and

(2) the lawyer reasonably believes that the person's interests will not be adversely affected by refraining from giving such information.

COMMENT

[1] The procedure of the adversary system contemplates that the evidence in a case is to be marshalled competitively by the contending parties. Fair competition in the adversary system is secured by prohibitions against destruction or concealment of evidence, improperly influencing witnesses, obstructive tactics in discovery procedure, and the like.

[2] Documents and other items of evidence are often essential to establish a claim or defense. Subject to evidentiary privileges, the right of an opposing party, including the government, to obtain evidence through discovery or subpoena is an important procedural right. The exercise of that right can be frustrated if relevant material is altered, concealed or destroyed. Applicable law in many jurisdictions makes it an offense to destroy material for purpose of impairing its availability in a pending proceeding or one whose commencement can be foreseen. Falsifying evidence is also generally a criminal offense. Paragraph (a) applies to evidentiary material generally, including computerized information.

[3] With regard to paragraph (b), it is not improper to pay a witness's expenses or to compensate an expert witness on terms permitted

by law. The common law rule in most jurisdictions is that it is improper to pay an occurrence witness any fee for testifying and that it is improper to pay an expert witness a contingent fee.

[4] Paragraph (f) permits a lawyer to advise employees of a client to refrain from giving information to another party, for the employees may identify their interests with those of the client. See also Rule 4.2.

Model Code Comparison

With regard to paragraph (a), DR 7-109(A) provided that a lawyer "shall not suppress any evidence that he or his client has a legal obligation to reveal." DR 7-109(B) provided that a lawyer "shall not advise or cause a person to secrete himself . . . for the purpose of making him unavailable as a witness. . . ." DR 7-106(C)(7) provided that a lawyer shall not "[i]ntentionally or habitually violate any established rule of procedure or of evidence."

With regard to paragraph (b), DR 7-102(A)(6) provided that a lawyer shall not participate "in the creation or preservation of evidence when he knows or it is obvious that the evidence is false." DR 7-109(C) provided that a lawyer "shall not pay, offer to pay, or acquiesce in the payment of compensation to a witness contingent upon the content of his testimony or the outcome of the case. But a lawyer may advance, guarantee or acquiesce in the payment of: (1) Expenses reasonably incurred by a witness in attending or testifying; (2) Reasonable compensation to a witness for his loss of time in attending or testifying; [or] (3) A reasonable fee for the professional services of an expert witness." EC 7-28 stated that witnesses "should always testify truthfully and should be free from any financial inducements that might tempt them to do otherwise."

Paragraph (c) is substantially similar to DR 7-106(A), which provided that "A lawyer shall not disregard . . . a standing rule of a tribunal or a ruling of a tribunal made in the course of a proceeding, but he may take appropriate steps in good faith to test the validity of such rule or ruling."

Paragraph (d) has no counterpart in the Model Code.

Paragraph (e) substantially incorporates DR 7-106(C)(1), (2), (3), and (4). DR 7-106(C)(2) proscribed asking a question "intended to degrade a witness or other person," a matter dealt with in Rule 4.4. DR 7-106(C)(5), providing that a lawyer shall not "fail to comply with known local customs of courtesy or practice," was too vague to be a rule of conduct enforceable as law.

With regard to paragraph (f), DR 7-104(A)(2) provided that a lawyer shall not "give advice to a person who is not represented . . . other than the advice to secure counsel, if the interests of such person are or have a reasonable possibility of being in conflict with the interests of his client."

Cross-References in Rules

Rule 1.4, Comment 4: "Rules or court orders governing litigation may provide that information supplied to a lawyer may not be disclosed to the client. **Rule 3.4(c)** directs compliance with such rules or orders."

Rule 3.6, Comment 3: "Special rules of confidentiality may validly govern proceedings in juvenile, domestic relations and mental disability proceedings, and perhaps other types of litigation. **Rule 3.4(c)** requires compliance with such Rules."

Rule 3.9: "A lawyer representing a client before a legislative or administrative tribunal in a nonadjudicative proceeding shall disclose that the appearance is in a representative capacity and shall conform to the provisions of **Rules** 3.3(a) through (c), **3.4(a) through (c)**, and 3.5."

Rule 4.2, Comment 4: "If an agent or employee of the organization is represented in the matter by his or her own counsel, the consent by that counsel to a communication will be sufficient for purposes of this Rule. Compare **Rule 3.4(f)**."

Legislative History

1980 Discussion Draft (then Rule 3.2):

(a) A lawyer shall be fair to other parties and their counsel, accord them their procedural rights, and fulfill obligations under the procedural law and established practices of the tribunal.

(b) A lawyer shall not:

(1) improperly obstruct another party's access to evidence, destroy, falsify or conceal evidence, or use illegal methods of obtaining evidence;

(2) disobey an obligation under procedural law, except for an open refusal based on a good faith belief that no valid obligation exists;

(3) refer in a proceeding to a matter that the lawyer has no reasonable basis to believe is relevant thereto, or does not reasonably expect will be supported by admissible evidence;

(4) make a knowing misrepresentation of fact or law to an opposing party or counsel;

(5) interview or otherwise communicate with a party who the lawyer knows is represented by other counsel concerning the subject matter of the representation, except with the consent of that party's counsel or as authorized by law.

In addition, the 1980 Discussion Draft contained the following separate Rules (then Rules 2.5 and 3.4):

2.5 Alteration or Destruction of Evidence

A lawyer shall not advise a client to alter or destroy a document or other material when the lawyer reasonably should know that the material is relevant to a pending proceeding or one that is clearly foreseeable.

3.4 Respect for the Interests of Others

    (a) In preparing and presenting a cause, a lawyer shall respect the interests of third persons, including witnesses, jurors, and persons incidentally concerned with the proceeding.

    (b) A lawyer shall not:

        (1) use means of obtaining evidence that violate a third person's legal rights; or

        (2) use a procedure having no substantial purpose other than to embarrass, delay, or burden a third person.

1981 Draft: Substantially the same as finally adopted, except subparagraph (a), which provided:

    A lawyer shall not:

    (a) unlawfully obstruct another party's access to evidence or alter, destroy or conceal a document or other material that the lawyer knows or reasonably should know is relevant to a pending proceeding or one that is reasonably foreseeable. A lawyer shall not counsel or assist another person to do any such act;

1982 Draft was adopted.

Selected State Variations

Alabama: Rule 3.4(d), equivalent to ABA Model Rule 3.4(f), adds two exceptions that allow a lawyer to ask a non-client not to give information to another party:

    (2) the person may be required by law to refrain from disclosing the information; or

    (3) the information pertains to covert law enforcement investigations in process, such as the use of undercover law enforcement agents.

California: See Rule 5-200 (Trial Conduct), Rule 5-310 (Prohibited Contact with Witnesses), and B & P Code §§6068(d), 6103, and 6128(a). In addition, California Penal Code §135, which was enacted in 1872, provides as follows:

Destroying or Concealing Documentary Evidence

    Destroying evidence. Every person who, knowing that any book, paper, record, instrument in writing, or other matter or thing, is about to be produced in evidence upon any trial, inquiry, or investigation whatever, authorized by law, willfully destroys or conceals the same, with intent thereby to prevent it from being produced, is guilty of a misdemeanor.

Connecticut forbids a lawyer to "present, participate in presenting, or threaten to present criminal charges solely to obtain an advantage in a civil matter." Rule 3.4(g).

Delaware: Rule 3.4 provides that a lawyer shall not:

falsify evidence, counsel or assist a witness to testify falsely, or pay, offer to pay or acquiesce in the payment of compensation, or participate in offering any inducement to a witness contingent upon the content of his testimony or the outcome of the case. But a lawyer may advance, guarantee or acquiesce in the payment of:
(i) expenses reasonably incurred by a witness in attending or testifying;
(ii) reasonable compensation to a witness for his loss of time in attending or testifying;
(iii) a reasonable fee for the professional services of an expert witness.

District of Columbia: D.C. Rule 3.4(a) differs significantly from the ABA Model Rule — see District of Columbia Rules of Professional Conduct below.

Florida: Rule 3.4(a) applies to evidence that a lawyer "knows or reasonably should know is relevant to a pending or a reasonably foreseeable proceeding . . . ." Rule 3.4(b) provides that a lawyer shall not "fabricate" (instead of "falsify") evidence. In addition, amplifying Comment 3 to ABA Model Rule 3.4, Florida Rule 3.4(b) provides:

[A] lawyer may pay a witness reasonable expenses incurred by the witness in attending or testifying at proceedings; a reasonable, noncontingent fee for the professional services of an expert witness; and reasonable compensation to reimburse a witness for the loss of compensation incurred by reason of preparing for, attending, or testifying at proceedings.

Florida Rule 3.4(d) eliminates the phrase "to make a reasonably diligent effort" and instead provides that a lawyer shall not "*intentionally* fail to comply with a legally proper discovery request by an opposing party."

Illinois provides, in Rule 3.3(a)(15), that a lawyer shall not "pay, offer to pay, or acquiesce in the payment of compensation to a witness contingent upon the content of the witness' testimony or the outcome of the case, but a lawyer may advance, guarantee, or acquiesce in the payment of expenses reasonably incurred in attending or testifying, and a reasonable fee for the professional services of an expert witness." In addition, Illinois omits Rules 3.4(c)-(d) and moves an amplified version of Rule 3.4(e) to Illinois Rule 3.3(a)(10).

Massachusetts: Effective January 1, 1998, Rule 3.4(h) forbids a lawyer to "present, participate in presenting, or threaten to present criminal or disciplinary charges solely to obtain an advantage in a private civil matter." Rule 3.4(i) says that a lawyer shall not "in appearing in a professional capacity before a tribunal, engage in conduct manifesting bias or prejudice based on race, sex, religion, national origin, disability, age, or sexual orientation against a party, witness, counsel, or other person. This paragraph does not preclude legitimate advocacy when [the same factors or a similar one] is an issue in the proceeding."

New Jersey Rule 3.4(d) refers to "requests" and "efforts" in the plural so that a violation will depend on showing a "pattern of behavior."

New York: Same or substantially the same as the ABA Model Code — see Model Code Comparison above.

Ohio has adopted a lengthy DR 7-111, entitled "Confidential Information," which provides, in part, as follows:

> (A)(1) A lawyer shall not disclose or cause to be disclosed, without appropriate authorization, information regarding the probable or actual decision in a case or legal proceeding pending before a court, including the vote of a justice, judge, or court in a case pending before the Supreme Court, a court of appeals, or a panel of judges of a trial court, prior to the announcement of the decision by the court or journalization of an opinion, entry, or other document reflecting that decision under either of the following circumstances:
>
> (a) The probable or actual decision is confidential because of statutory or rule provisions;
>
> (b) The probable or actual decision clearly has been designated to the justice or judge as confidential when confidentiality is warranted because of the status of the proceedings or the circumstances under which the information was received and preserving confidentiality is necessary to the proper conduct of court business.

Subparagraph (B)(1) adds that no lawyer shall "obtain or attempt to obtain" information whose disclosure would violate DR 7-111(A)(1).

Pennsylvania Rule 3.4(b) retains the substance of DR 7-109(C). Pennsylvania adds at the end of Rule 3.4(d)(2) "and such conduct is not prohibited by Rule 4.2."

Texas Rule 3.04(b) retains the substance of DR 7-109(C). Rule 3.04(a), (c), and (d) provides:

> A lawyer shall not:
>
> (a) unlawfully* obstruct another party's access to evidence; in anticipation of a dispute unlawfully alter, destroy or conceal a document or other material that a competent lawyer would believe has potential or actual evidentiary value; or counsel or assist another person to do any such act. . . .
>
> (c) except as stated in paragraph (d), in representing a client before a tribunal:
>
> (1) habitually violate an established rule of procedure or of evidence;
>
> (2) state or allude to any matter that the lawyer does not reasonably believe is relevant to such proceeding or that will not be supported by admissible evidence, or assert personal knowledge of facts in issue except when testifying as a witness;
>
> (3) state a personal opinion as to the justness of a cause, the credibility of a witness, the culpability of a civil litigant or the guilt or innocence of an accused, except that a lawyer may argue on his analysis of the evidence and other permissible considerations for any position or conclusion with respect to the matters stated herein;

---

*Texas Penal Law §37.09 makes it a felony if a person "knowing that an investigation or official proceeding is pending or in progress . . . alters, destroys, or conceals any record, document, or thing with intent to impair its verity, legibility, or availability as evidence. . . ." The section does not apply to items that are "privileged or . . . work product."

(4) ask any question intended to degrade a witness or other person except where the lawyer reasonably believes that the question will lead to relevant and admissible evidence; or

(5) engage in conduct intended to disrupt the proceedings.

(d) knowingly disobey, or advise the client to disobey, an obligation under the standing rules of or a ruling by a tribunal except for an open refusal based either on an assertion that no valid obligation exists or on the client's willingness to accept any sanctions arising from such disobedience.

Virginia: Substantially the same as the Model Code, except that Virginia's DR 7-105 (which is modeled on the ABA's DR 7-106) omits subparagraphs (c)(5) and (6).

Washington deletes subparagraph (f).

Related Materials

ABA Canons: Canons 3, 15, 25, and 39 provided:

3. Attempts to Exert Personal Influence on the Court

Marked attention and unusual hospitality on the part of a lawyer to a Judge, uncalled for by the personal relations of the parties, subject both the Judge and the lawyer to misconstructions of motive and should be avoided. A lawyer should not communicate or argue privately with the Judge as to the merits of a pending cause, and he deserves rebuke and denunciation for any device or attempt to gain from a Judge special personal consideration or favor. A self-respecting independence in the discharge of professional duty, without denial or diminution of the courtesy and respect due the Judge's station, is the only proper foundation for cordial personal and official relations between Bench and Bar.

15. How Far a Lawyer May Go in Supporting a Client's Cause

The lawyer owes "entire devotion to the interest of the client, warm zeal in the maintenance and defense of his rights and the exertion of his utmost learning and ability," to the end that nothing be taken or be withheld from him, save by the rules of law, legally applied. No fear of judicial disfavor or public unpopularity should restrain him from the full discharge of his duty. In the judicial forum the client is entitled to the benefit of any and every remedy and defense that is authorized by the law of the land, and he may expect his lawyer to assert every such remedy or defense. But it is steadfastly to be borne in mind that the great trust of the lawyer is to be performed within and not without the bounds of the law. The office of attorney does not permit, much less does it demand of him for any client, violation of law or any manner of fraud or chicane. He must obey his own conscience and not that of his client.

25. Taking Technical Advantage of Opposite Counsel; Agreements with Him

A lawyer should not ignore known customs or practice of the Bar or of a particular Court, even when the law permits, without giving timely notice to the opposing counsel. As far as possible, important agreements, affecting the rights of clients, should be reduced to writing; but it is dishonorable to avoid performance of an agreement fairly made because it is not reduced to writing, as required by rules of Court.

39. Witnesses

A lawyer may properly interview any witness or prospective witness for the opposing side in any civil or criminal action without the consent of opposing counsel or party. In doing so, however, he should scrupulously avoid any suggestion calculated to induce the witness to suppress or deviate from the truth, or in any degree to affect his free and untrammeled conduct when appearing at the trial or on the witness stand.

ABA Standards for Criminal Justice: See Prosecution Function Standards 3-5.2, 3-5.6; Defense Function Standards 4-1.2, 4-4.3, 4-4.5, 4-4.6, 4-7.1. Standard 4-4.6 is especially important because it concerns a criminal defense lawyer's obligations upon the receipt of physical evidence.
ABA Standards for Imposing Lawyer Sanctions:

6.2. Abuse of the Legal Process

6.21. Disbarment is generally appropriate when a lawyer knowingly violates a court order or rule with the intent to obtain a benefit for the lawyer or another, and causes serious injury or potentially serious injury to a party, or causes serious or potentially serious interference with a legal proceeding.
6.22. Suspension is appropriate when a lawyer knows that he is violating a court order or rule, and there is injury or potential injury to a client or a party, or interference or potential interference with a legal proceeding.

See also Standard 6.3 printed in the Related Materials following Model Rule 4.2.
American Academy of Matrimonial Lawyers: The "Bounds of Advocacy" drafted by the American Academy of Matrimonial Lawyers contains the following provision and commentary:

3.14 An attorney should promptly and completely comply with all reasonable discovery requests.

Comment to Rule 3.14

This may require convincing the client of the necessity of full compliance with such discovery requests as document production and answers to interrogatories and that concealing information is detrimental to the client's own case.

Federal Rules of Civil Procedure: Various provisions of the rules of procedure penalize the kinds of behavior condemned in Rule 3.4. With respect to Rule 3.4(c), Fed. R. Civ. P. 41(b) provides: "For failure of the plaintiff to prosecute or to comply with these rules or any order of court, a defendant may move for dismissal of an action or of any claim against the defendant," and such a dismissal ordinarily "operates as an adjudication upon the merits." Fed. R. Civ. P. 45(e) provides: "Failure by any person without adequate excuse to obey a subpoena served upon that person may be deemed a contempt of the court from which the subpoena issued." With respect to Rule 3.4(d), Fed. R. Civ. P. 26(g) provides sanctions for improper or bad faith conduct in discovery, and Fed. R. Civ. P. 37, gives courts power to compel a party to respond to discovery requests and to sanction an unjustified failure to respond to discovery.

Federal Rules of Appellate Procedure: Fed. R. App. P. 46(c) empowers a federal court of appeals, after notice and hearing, to "take any appropriate disciplinary action against any attorney who practices before it for conduct unbecoming a member of the bar or for failure to comply with these rules or any rule of the court."

Model Rules of Professional Conduct for Federal Lawyers clarify that Rule 3.4 applies to an obligation "to an opposing party and counsel." (The Rules for Federal Lawyers address obligations to a tribunal in a new Rule 3.3(a)(5), quoted after Rule 3.3.) The Comment to Rule 3.4 states:

> A federal lawyer who receives . . . an item of physical evidence implicating the client in criminal conduct shall disclose the location of or shall deliver that item to proper authorities when required by law or court order. Thus, if a Federal lawyer receives contraband, the Federal lawyer has no legal right to possess it and must always surrender it to lawful authorities. If a Federal lawyer receives stolen property, the Federal lawyer must surrender it to the owner or lawful authority to avoid violating the law. . . . When a client informs the Federal lawyer about the existence of material having potential evidentiary value adverse to the client or when the client presents, but does not relinquish possession of, such material to the Federal lawyer, the Federal lawyer should inform the client of the Federal lawyer's legal and ethical obligations regarding evidence. Frequently, the best course for the Federal lawyer is to refrain from either taking possession of such material or advising the client as to what course of action should be taken regarding it. . . . If a Federal lawyer discloses the location of or delivers an item of physical evidence to proper authorities, it should be done in the way best designed to protect the client's interest. The Federal lawyer should consider methods of return or disclosure that best protect (a) the client's identity; (b) the client's words concerning the item; (c) other confidential information; and (d) the client's privilege against self-incrimination. . . .
>
> With regard to paragraph (c), a "rule of a tribunal" includes Rule 6(e) of the Federal Rules of Criminal Procedure governing discussion of grand jury testimony.

Restatement of the Law Governing Lawyers: The American Law Institute has proposed but not yet approved §170(3) (reprinted in the Related Materials following Rule 3.1) to govern discovery requests and responses. In addition, the ALI has proposed but not yet approved the following provisions:

§165. Complying with Law and Tribunal Rulings

In representing a client in a matter before a tribunal, a lawyer must comply with applicable law, including rules of procedure and evidence and specific tribunal rulings.

§167. Prohibited Forensic Tactics

In representing a client in a matter before a tribunal, a lawyer may not, in the presence of the trier of fact:

(1) state a personal opinion about the justness of a cause, the credibility of a witness, the culpability of a civil litigant, or the guilt or innocence of an accused, but the lawyer may argue any position or conclusion adequately supported by the lawyer's analysis of the evidence; or

(2) allude to any factual matter that the lawyer does not reasonably believe is relevant or supportable by admissible evidence.

§176. Interviewing and Preparing Prospective Witness

(1) A lawyer may interview a witness for the purpose of preparing the witness to testify.

(2) A lawyer may not unlawfully obstruct another party's access to a witness.

(3) A lawyer may not unlawfully induce or assist a prospective witness to evade or ignore process obliging the witness to appear to testify.

(4) A lawyer may not request a person to refrain from voluntarily giving relevant testimony or information to another party, unless:

(a) the person is the lawyer's client in the matter; or (b) (i) the person is not the lawyer's client but is a relative or employee or other agent of the lawyer's client, and (ii) the lawyer reasonably believes compliance will not materially and adversely affect the person's interests.

§177. Compensating Witness

A lawyer may not offer or pay to a witness any consideration:

(1) in excess of the reasonable expenses of the witness incurred in providing evidence, except that an expert witness may be offered and paid a noncontingent fee;

(2) contingent on the content of the witness's testimony or the outcome of the litigation; or

(3) otherwise prohibited by law.

§178. Falsifying or Destroying Evidence

(1) A lawyer may not falsify documentary or other evidence.

(2) A lawyer may not destroy or obstruct another party's access to documentary or other evidence when doing so would violate a court order or a criminal statute dealing with obstruction of justice or a similar offense, or counsel or assist a client to do so.

§179. Physical Evidence of Client Crime

With respect to physical evidence of a client crime, a lawyer:

(1) may, when reasonably necessary for purposes of the representation, take possession of the evidence and retain it for the time reasonably necessary to examine it and subject it to tests that do not alter or destroy material characteristics of the evidence; but

(2) following possession under Subsection (1), the lawyer must:

(a) return the evidence to the site from which it was taken, when that can be accomplished without destroying or altering material characteristics of the evidence; or

(b) notify prosecuting authorities of the lawyer's possession of the evidence or turn the evidence over to them.

18 U.S.C. §201(c) and (d): These provisions, reprinted below in our chapter on Federal Conflict and Confidentiality Provisions, make it a crime to give "anything of value to any person, for or because of the testimony ... to be given by such person as a witness upon a trial. . . ." The prohibition does not apply to, among other things, payment of "the reasonable cost of travel and subsistence incurred and the reasonable value of time lost in attendance at any such trial . . . or in the case of expert witnesses, a reasonable fee for time spent in the preparation. . . ."

Rule 3.5 Impartiality and Decorum of the Tribunal

A lawyer shall not:

(a) seek to influence a judge, juror, prospective juror or other official by means prohibited by law;

(b) communicate ex parte with such a person except as permitted by law; or

(c) engage in conduct intended to disrupt a tribunal.

COMMENT

[1] Many forms of improper influence upon a tribunal are proscribed by criminal law. Others are specified in the ABA Model Code of Judicial Conduct, with which an advocate should be familiar. A lawyer is required to avoid contributing to a violation of such provisions.

[2] The advocate's function is to present evidence and argument so that the cause may be decided according to law. Refraining from abusive or obstreperous conduct is a corollary of the advocate's right to speak on behalf of litigants. A lawyer may stand firm against abuse by a judge but should avoid reciprocation; the judge's default is no justification for simi-

lar dereliction by an advocate. An advocate can present the cause, protect the record for subsequent review and preserve professional integrity by patient firmness no less effectively than by belligerence or theatrics.

Model Code Comparison

With regard to paragraphs (a) and (b), DR 7-108(A) provided that "[b]efore the trial of a case a lawyer . . . shall not communicate with . . . anyone he knows to be a member of the venire. . . ." DR 7-108(B) provided that during the trial of a case a lawyer "shall not communicate with . . . any member of the jury." DR 7-110(B) provided that a lawyer shall not "communicate . . . as to the merits of the cause with a judge or an official before whom the proceeding is pending, except . . . upon adequate notice to opposing counsel," or as "otherwise authorized by law."

With regard to paragraph (c), DR 7-106(C)(6) provided that a lawyer shall not engage in "undignified or discourteous conduct which is degrading to a tribunal."

Cross-References in Rules

Rule 3.9: "A lawyer representing a client before a legislative or administrative tribunal in a nonadjudicative proceeding shall disclose that the appearance is in a representative capacity and shall conform to the provisions of **Rules** 3.3(a) through (c), 3.4(a) through (c), and **3.5.**"

Legislative History

1980 Discussion Draft (then called Rule 3.7) provided as follows:

(a) A lawyer shall assist a tribunal in maintaining impartiality and conducting the proceedings with decorum.
(b) A lawyer shall not:
(1) seek improperly to influence a judge, juror, or other decision-maker, or, except as permitted by law, communicate ex parte with such a person;
(2) seek improperly to influence a witness;
(3) be abusive or obstreperous;
(4) refuse to comply with an obligation of procedural law or an order of the tribunal, except for an open refusal based on a good faith belief that compliance is not legally required.

1981 Draft was substantially the same as adopted, except that subparagraph (a) used the phrase "other decision-maker" instead of "other official."
1982 Draft was adopted.

Selected State Variations

Arkansas: Subparagraph (b) provides that a lawyer shall not "communicate ex parte with such a person *on the merits of the cause* except as permitted by law."

California: See Rule 5-300 (Contact with Officials).

Delaware adds the following language to subparagraph (c): "or engage in undignified or discourteous conduct which is degrading to a tribunal."

Florida, Maryland, and **Minnesota** add language to Rule 3.5 drawing on DR 7-108. (See Model Code Comparison above.)

Illinois: Rule 3.5 tracks DR 7-108 almost verbatim, but adds the following paragraph (h) prompted by the bribery and "loan" scandals uncovered in Chicago courts during Operation Greylord:

> (h) A lawyer shall not give or lend anything of value to a judge, official, or employee of a tribunal, except those gifts or loans which a judge or a member of the judge's family may receive under Rule 65(C)(4) of the Code of Judicial Conduct, and except that a lawyer may: make a gift, bequest, loan or campaign contribution to a judge that the judge is permitted to accept under the Code of Judicial Conduct, provided that no campaign contribution to a judge or candidate for judicial office may be made other than by means of a check, draft, or other instrument payable to or to the order of an entity which the lawyer reasonably believes to be a political committee supporting such judge or candidate, provided further, however, that the provision of volunteer services by a lawyer to a political committee shall not be deemed to violate this Rule.

Illinois Rule 3.5 also adds a new subparagraph (i) that tracks language from DR 7-110.

Kansas forbids a lawyer to "engage in undignified or discourteous conduct degrading to a tribunal." Rule 3.5(d).

Massachusetts: Effective January 1, 1998, Rule 3.5(d) restricts the ability of lawyers connected to a case to initiate a communication with a member of the jury after discharge without leave of the court.

Michigan's version of Rule 3.5(c) forbids a lawyer to "engage in undignified or discourteous conduct toward the tribunal."

New York: Same or substantially the same as the ABA Model Code — see Model Code Comparison above.

Texas: Rule 3.06 borrows heavily from DR 7-108, but rearranges the order somewhat, adds references to an "alternate juror," and provides in Rule 3.06(A)(2) that a lawyer shall not "seek to influence a venireman or juror concerning the merits of a pending matter by means prohibited by law or applicable rules of practice or procedure."

Virginia: Substantially the same as the Model Code, but omits the prohibition in DR 7-106(C)(6) on "undignified or discourteous conduct," and bars intentional or habitual violations of the rules of procedure or evidence "where such conduct is disruptive of the proceedings." Virginia also omits the obligation in DR 7-106(B) of the ABA Code for a lawyer to disclose the identities of clients and "the persons who employed him," and omits the prohibition in

DR 7-106(C)(7) of the ABA Code against intentionally or habitually violating a rule of procedure or evidence.

Related Materials

ABA Canons: Canons 17 and 23 provided:

17. Ill-Feeling and Personalities Between Advocates

Clients, not lawyers, are the litigants. Whatever may be the ill-feeling existing between clients, it should not be allowed to influence counsel in their conduct and demeanor toward each other or toward suitors in the case. All personalities between counsel should be scrupulously avoided. In the trial of a cause it is indecent to allude to the personal history or the personal peculiarities and idiosyncrasies of counsel on the other side. Personal colloquies between counsel which cause delay and promote unseemly wrangling should also be carefully avoided.

23. Attitude Toward Jury

All attempts to curry favor with juries by fawning, flattery or pretended solicitude for their personal comfort are unprofessional. Suggestions of counsel, looking to the comfort or convenience of jurors, and propositions to dispense with argument, should be made to the Court out of the jury's hearing. A lawyer must never converse privately with jurors about the case; and both before and during the trial he should avoid communicating with them, even as to matters foreign to the cause.

ABA Model Code of Judicial Conduct, cited in Rule 3.5, Comment 1, is reprinted in full later in this volume.

ABA Standards for Criminal Justice: See Prosecution Function Standard 3-2.8 (Relations with the Courts and Bar), Standard 3-5.2 (Courtroom Professionalism), Standard 3-5.4 (Relations with Jury), and Defense Function Standard 4-7.1 (Courtroom Professionalism) and Standard 4-7.3 (Relations with Jury). See also ABA Standards for Special Functions of the Trial Judge.

ABA Standards for Imposing Lawyer Sanctions: See Standard 6.3, which is reprinted in the Related Materials following Model Rule 4.2.

Federal Rules of Civil Procedure: Rule 65(b), governing ex parte communications in proceedings to obtain temporary restraining orders, provides, in pertinent part, as follows:

Temporary Restraining Order; Notice; Hearing; Duration. A temporary restraining order may be granted without written or oral notice to the adverse party or that party's attorney only if (1) it clearly appears from specific facts shown by affidavit or by the verified complaint that immediate and irreparable injury, loss, or damage will result to the applicant before the adverse party or that party's attorney can be heard in opposition, and (2) the applicant's attorney certifies to the court in writing the efforts, if any, which have been made to give the notice and the reasons supporting the claim that notice should not be required. . . .

Model Rules of Professional Conduct for Federal Lawyers: Rule 3.5(a) prohibits a federal lawyer from seeking to influence "a tribunal, a member of a tribunal, a prospective member of a tribunal, or other official by means prohibited by law."

Restatement of the Law Governing Lawyers: With respect to ex parte practice and improper influence, the American Law Institute has proposed but not yet approved §172, which is reprinted in the Related Materials following Rule 3.3, and §173, which provides as follows:

§173. Improperly Influencing Judicial Officer

(1) A lawyer representing a client may not knowingly communicate ex parte with a judge or an official before whom a proceeding is pending concerning the matter, except as authorized by law.

(2) A lawyer may not make a gift or loan prohibited by law to a judicial officer, attempt to influence the officer otherwise than by legally proper procedures, or state or imply an ability so to influence a judicial officer.

Rule 3.6 Trial Publicity

Editors' Note. At its August 1994 Annual Meeting, the ABA House of Delegates significantly amended Rule 3.6 for the first time since its original adoption in 1983. Work on the amendment began soon after the Supreme Court decided Gentile v. Nevada State Bar, 501 U.S. 1030 (1991), which called into question the constitutionality of some parts of Rule 3.6.

The amendment accomplishes three purposes: (1) it reformulates the types of information that a lawyer may disclose outside of court despite the general ban on extrajudicial statements likely to prejudice a court proceeding; (2) it creates a new "safe harbor" provision that allows a lawyer to protect clients against undue prejudice due to recent publicity initiated by someone else; and (3) it makes clear that all lawyers in a firm or government agency are governed by Rule 3.6. The amendment also substantially rewrites the Comment and Code Comparison. Companion amendments to Rule 3.8 were approved at the same time, also to conform to *Gentile.* Excerpts from the ABA committee report explaining the amendment to Rule 3.6 are found in the Legislative History section following this Rule.

(a) A lawyer who is participating or has participated in the investigation or litigation of a matter shall not make an extrajudicial statement that

a reasonable person would expect to be disseminated by means of public communication if the lawyer knows or reasonably should know that it will have a substantial likelihood of materially prejudicing an adjudicative proceeding in the matter.

(b) Notwithstanding paragraph (a), a lawyer may state:

(1) the claim, offense or defense involved and, except when prohibited by law, the identity of the persons involved;

(2) the information contained in a public record;

(3) that an investigation of the matter is in progress;

(4) the scheduling or result of any step in litigation;

(5) a request for assistance in obtaining evidence and information necessary thereto;

(6) a warning of danger concerning the behavior of a person involved, when there is reason to believe that there exists the likelihood of substantial harm to an individual or to the public interest; and

(7) in a criminal case, in addition to subparagraphs (1) through (6):

(i) the identity, residence, occupation and family status of the accused;

(ii) if the accused has not been apprehended, information necessary to aid in apprehension of that person;

(iii) the fact, time and place of arrest; and

(iv) the identity of investigating and arresting officers or agencies and the length of the investigation.

(c) Notwithstanding paragraph (a), a lawyer may make a statement that a reasonable lawyer would believe is required to protect a client from the substantial undue prejudicial effect of recent publicity not initiated by the lawyer or the lawyer's client. A statement made pursuant to this paragraph shall be limited to such information as is necessary to mitigate the recent adverse publicity.

(d) No lawyer associated in a firm or government agency with a lawyer subject to paragraph (a) shall make a statement prohibited by paragraph (a).

COMMENT

[1] It is difficult to strike a balance between protecting the right to a fair trial and safeguarding the right of free expression. Preserving the right to a fair trial necessarily entails some curtailment of the information that may be disseminated about a party prior to trial, particularly where trial by jury is involved. If there were no such limits, the result would be the practical nullification of the protective effect of the rules of forensic

decorum and the exclusionary rules of evidence. On the other hand, there are vital social interests served by the free dissemination of information about events having legal consequences and about legal proceedings themselves. The public has a right to know about threats to its safety and measures aimed at assuring its security. It also has a legitimate interest in the conduct of judicial proceedings, particularly in matters of general public concern. Furthermore, the subject matter of legal proceedings is often of direct significance in debate and deliberation over questions of public policy.

> **Editors' Note.** A 1994 amendment deleted all of what was formerly paragraph 2 of the Comment, renumbered the old paragraph 3 as paragraph 2, and added all of paragraphs 3 through 7 of the Comment.

[2] Special rules of confidentiality may validly govern proceedings in juvenile, domestic relations and mental disability proceedings, and perhaps other types of litigation. Rule 3.4(c) requires compliance with such rules.

[3] The Rule sets forth a basic general prohibition against a lawyer's making statements that the lawyer knows or should know will have a substantial likelihood of materially prejudicing an adjudicative proceeding. Recognizing that the public value of informed commentary is great and the likelihood of prejudice to a proceeding by the commentary of a lawyer who is not involved in the proceeding is small, the rule applies only to lawyers who are, or who have been involved in the investigation or litigation of a case, and their associates.

[4] Paragraph (b) identifies specific matters about which a lawyer's statements would not ordinarily be considered to present a substantial likelihood of material prejudice, and should not in any event be considered prohibited by the general prohibition of paragraph (a). Paragraph (b) is not intended to be an exhaustive listing of the subjects upon which a lawyer may make a statement, but statements on other matters may be subject to paragraph (a).

[5] There are, on the other hand, certain subjects which are more likely than not to have a material prejudicial effect on a proceeding, particularly when they refer to a civil matter triable to a jury, a criminal matter, or any other proceeding that could result in incarceration. These subjects relate to:

(1)   the character, credibility, reputation or criminal record of a party, suspect in a criminal investigation or witness, or the

identity of a witness, or the expected testimony of a party or witness;

(2)   in a criminal case or proceeding that could result in incarceration, the possibility of a plea of guilty to the offense or the existence or contents of any confession, admission, or statement given by a defendant or suspect or that person's refusal or failure to make a statement;

(3)   the performance or results of any examination or test or the refusal or failure of a person to submit to an examination or test, or the identity or nature of physical evidence expected to be presented;

(4)   any opinion as to the guilt or innocence of a defendant or suspect in a criminal case or proceeding that could result in incarceration;

(5)   information that the lawyer knows or reasonably should know is likely to be inadmissible as evidence in a trial and that would, if disclosed, create a substantial risk of prejudicing an impartial trial; or

(6)   the fact that a defendant has been charged with a crime, unless there is included therein a statement explaining that the charge is merely an accusation and that the defendant is presumed innocent until and unless proven guilty.

[6] Another relevant factor in determining prejudice is the nature of the proceeding involved. Criminal jury trials will be most sensitive to extra-judicial speech. Civil trials may be less sensitive. Non-jury hearings and arbitration proceedings may be even less affected. The Rule will still place limitations on prejudicial comments in these cases, but the likelihood of prejudice may be different depending on the type of proceeding.

[7] Finally, extrajudicial statements that might otherwise raise a question under this Rule may be permissible when they are made in response to statements made publicly by another party, another party's lawyer, or third persons, where a reasonable lawyer would believe a public response is required in order to avoid prejudice to the lawyer's client. When prejudicial statements have been publicly made by others, responsive statements may have the salutary effect of lessening any resulting adverse impact on the adjudicative proceeding. Such responsive statements should be limited to contain only such information as is necessary to mitigate undue prejudice created by the statements made by others.

Model Code Comparison

> **Editors' Note.** When the ABA amended Rule 3.6 in 1994, it also
> amended the Code Comparison. The Code Comparison below reflects the
> 1994 amendments. For legislative-style changes in the old Code Compari-
> son, see our 1995 edition.

Rule 3.6 is similar to DR 7-107, except as follows: First, Rule 3.6 adopts the
general criterion of "substantial likelihood of materially prejudicing an adjudicative proceeding" to describe impermissible conduct. Second, Rule 3.6 makes
clear that only lawyers who are, or have been, involved in a proceeding, or their
associates, are subject to the Rule. Third, Rule 3.6 omits the particulars in DR
7-107(b), transforming them instead into an illustrative compilation as part of
the Rule's commentary that is intended to give fair notice of the kinds of statements that are generally thought to be more likely than other kinds of statements to pose unacceptable dangers to the fair administration of justice. Whether
any statement will have a substantial likelihood of materially prejudicing an adjudicatory proceeding will depend upon the facts of each case. The particulars
of DR 7-107(c) are retained in Rule 3.6(b), except DR 7-107(C)(7), which provided that a lawyer may reveal "[a]t the time of seizure, a description of the physical evidence seized, other than a confession, admission or statement." Such
revelations may be substantially prejudicial and are frequently the subject of pretrial suppression motions whose success would be undermined by disclosure of
the suppressed evidence to the press. Finally, Rule 3.6 authorizes a lawyer to protect a client by making a limited reply to adverse publicity substantially prejudicial to the client.

Cross-References in Rules

Rule 3.8(e) provides that the prosecutor in a criminal case shall "exercise
reasonable care to prevent investigators . . . or other persons . . . from making
an extrajudicial statement that the prosecutor would be prohibited from making under **Rule 3.6**."

Rule 3.8(g) states that it "supplements **Rule 3.6** . . ." and that "Nothing in
this Comment [to Rule 3.8(g)] is intended to restrict the statements which a prosecutor may make which comply with **Rule 3.6(b) or 3.6(c).**"

Legislative History

1980 Discussion Draft (then Rule 3.8) was essentially an amalgam and reorganization of DR 7-107, except that paragraphs (F), (I), (J) of DR 7-107 were
deleted, and the following new provisions were added.

(a) To ensure a fair trial, a lawyer involved in the investigation of a criminal matter or in criminal or civil litigation shall not, except as provided in paragraph (b), make an extrajudicial statement:

(2) when the matter under investigation or in litigation is a criminal case or a civil case triable to a jury and the statement relates to:

(v) information the lawyer knows or reasonably should know would be inadmissible as evidence in a trial;

(vi) any other matter that similarly creates a serious and imminent risk of prejudicing an impartial trial.

(b) A lawyer involved in the investigation or litigation of a matter may state without elaboration;

(6) in a criminal case:

(vi) that the accused denies the charges.

(c) When evidence or information received in or relating to a proceeding is by law or order of a tribunal to be kept confidential, the lawyer shall not unlawfully disclose the evidence or information.

1981 Draft was the same as adopted, except (b)(7)(iii), which provided: "the fact, time, and place of arrest, *resistance, pursuit and use of weapons.*"

1982 Draft was adopted.

1994 Amendment: At its August 1994 Annual Meeting, by a voice vote, the ABA House of Delegates significantly amended Rule 3.6 for the first time since its original adoption in 1983. The amendment reflected three years of drafting spurred by the Supreme Court's decision in Gentile v. Nevada State Bar, 501 U.S. 1030 (1991), which cast doubt on the constitutionality of some parts of Rule 3.6. (Companion amendments to Rule 3.8 were approved at the same time, also to conform to *Gentile.*)

The amendment to Rule 3.6 has three purposes: (1) it lists various types of information that a lawyer may disclose in out-of-court statements despite the general ban on extrajudicial statements substantially likely to prejudice a court proceeding; (2) it creates a "safe harbor" that allows a lawyer to protect clients against undue prejudice resulting from recent publicity not initiated by the lawyer or client; and (3) it makes clear that all lawyers in a firm or government agency are governed by Rule 3.6. The amendment accomplished these purposes by revising paragraph (a), completely deleting the old paragraph (b), revising the old paragraph (c) and renumbering it as paragraph (b), and adding new paragraphs (c) and (d). For a legislative-style version of the Rule showing exactly what was added and deleted by the 1994 amendment, see our 1995 edition.

The 1994 amendment also substantially rewrote the Comment and Code Comparison, deleting what had been the second paragraph of the Comment and adding five completely new paragraphs. The deleted paragraph of the Comment had stated as follows:

[2] No body of rules can simultaneously satisfy all interests of fair trial and all those of free expression. The formula in this Rule is based upon the ABA Model Code of Professional Responsibility and the ABA Standards Relating to Fair Trial and Free Press, as amended in 1978.

The new paragraphs added to the Comment by the 1994 amendment are paragraphs 3 through 7. Old paragraph 3 remains in its original form, renumbered as paragraph 2.

The amendment was co-sponsored by the ABA Standing Committee on Ethics and Professional Responsibility and the ABA Criminal Justice Section. Below are substantial excerpts from the joint ABA report explaining the amendments.

Excerpts from ABA Report Explaining 1994 Amendments*

In *Gentile,* a criminal defense lawyer challenged disciplinary action taken against him by the State Bar of Nevada under its version of Rule 3.6, because of certain remarks made by him at a press conference relating to his client's anticipated defense. The lawyer challenged the state's action on grounds that his extrajudicial statements were protected by the First Amendment, and that in any event his remarks were within the Rule's "safe harbor" provision.

The Supreme Court unanimously upheld the Rule's "substantial likelihood of material prejudice" test. However, a majority of five Justices held the Rule void for vagueness as interpreted and applied by the Nevada State Bar in the circumstances of the case. Four of these Justices, in an opinion by Justice Kennedy, took the position that the lawyer's remarks at the press conference appeared to be permitted by the Rule's safe harbor provision, and that Nevada's decision nonetheless to discipline him thus raised "concerns of vagueness and selective enforcement." Justice O'Connor, writing separately, also thought that the safe harbor provision provided "insufficient guidance" to lawyers and disciplinary bodies, thus creating the possibility of discriminatory enforcement. The five members of the Court who reversed the state's disciplinary action noted that the safe harbor provision of Rule 3.6 allows a criminal lawyer to explain the "general" nature of his client's defense "without elaboration," and pointed out that the terms "general" and "elaboration" have "no settled usage or tradition of interpretation in law." As worded, they said, the provision gives a lawyer "no principle for determining when his remarks pass from the safe harbor of the general to the forbidden sea of the elaborated," and creates "a trap for the wary as well as the unwary."

The Standing Committee on Ethics and Professional Responsibility . . . proposes to revise the Rule's safe harbor provision by deleting the qualifying terms which the Supreme Court held unconstitutionally vague. . . .

The Committee considered but did not adopt a proposal from the Litigation Section that the Rule's standard be changed from "substantial likelihood" to "clear and present danger" of material prejudice. It is not clear to what extent such a change would, as a practical matter, affect the outcome in a particular case. In any event, the "substantial likelihood" test was unanimously upheld by the Supreme Court against constitutional challenge in *Gentile,* and most states have adopted it. Accordingly, we see no reason to change it.

The Committee adopted a proposal from the Criminal Justice Section to place in the text of the Rule a provision entitling a lawyer to respond where adverse

---

*Committee reports do not represent official policy of the ABA. They are for information only, and the opinions are those of the authors of the report.

publicity has been initiated by an opposing party or third persons, in order to avoid substantial undue prejudice to the lawyer's client. The Committee felt that in this situation, the danger of the second statement prejudicing the proceeding is minimized, and the rights of the client can be protected.

The Committee . . . felt that for completeness, the Rule must also extend to lawyers associated with those participating in a matter, and those who formerly participated in a matter. The need for lawyers outside a proceeding to interpret those proceedings to the public is so great, and the right of comment on government process so fundamental that the Committee felt that the lawyers affected by speech restrictions of Rule 3.6 should be clearly and narrowly defined.

The Committee also considered whether Rule 3.6 should be limited to criminal cases, or to cases involving jury trials. While a convincing argument can be made that there is less chance of prejudice from statements made in the course of a civil proceeding than in the context of a criminal matter, and in a bench trial than in a jury trial, it is the Committee's view that the nature of the proceeding and the identity of the trier of fact are relevant to but not dispositive of the issue of likelihood of prejudice. . . .

*Selected State Variations**

California: See Rule 5-120 (Trial Publicity) and B&P §6103.7 (commanding the State Bar to propose a rule governing trial publicity).

Colorado: Rule 3.6(a) uses the standard "grave danger of imminent and substantial harm to the fairness of an adjudicative matter." Colorado deletes subparagraphs (c) and (d).

District of Columbia: D.C. Rule 3.6 differs significantly from the ABA Model Rule — see District of Columbia Rules of Professional Conduct below.

Florida: Rule 3.6(a) applies to a statement that will have a substantial likelihood of materially prejudicing an adjudicative proceeding due to the statement's "creation of an imminent and substantial detrimental effect on that proceeding." Florida deletes ABA Model Rules 3.6(b), (c), and (d), and substitutes the following Rule 3.6(b):

> *Statements of Third Parties.* A lawyer shall not counsel or assist another person to make such a statement. Counsel shall exercise reasonable care to prevent investigators, employees, or other persons assisting in or associated with a case from making extrajudicial statements that are prohibited under this rule.

Illinois Rule 3.6(a) applies to statements that would "pose a serious and imminent threat to the fairness of an adjudicative proceeding." Rule 3.6(b)(1) refers to "the prior criminal record (including arrests, indictments or other charges of crime)." Illinois omits the requirement in ABA Model Rule 3.6(b)(5) that the inadmissible evidence "would if disclosed create a substan-

---

*State references are keyed to the original version of Rule 3.6. See Legislative History *supra.*

tial risk of prejudicing an impartial trial." Illinois completely omits Rule 3.6(b)(6).

Michigan places Rule 3.6(b) and (c) in its Comment to Rule 3.6.

Minnesota deletes subparagraphs (b) and (c) of Rule 3.6 in their entirety.

Montana adds the following language to (b)(4): "or a substantial likelihood of materially prejudicing the outcome of a hearing or trial."

New Jersey substitutes "reasonable lawyer" for "reasonable person" in Rule 3.6(a). Rule 3.6(b)(1) adds "other than the victim of a crime" after the words "identity of a witness."

New York: Amendments to the New York Code substantially adopt the text of Rule 3.6. See DR 7-107.

Ohio: Effective January 1, 1996, Ohio repealed its old DR 7-107 and adopted a new DR 7-107 substantively identical to the 1994 version of ABA Model Rule 3.6.

Oregon: DR 7-108(A) prohibits a lawyer from making an extrajudicial statement that a reasonable person would expect to be disseminated by means of public communication if the lawyer intends to affect the fact-finding process or the lawyer knows or reasonably should know that the statement poses "a serious and imminent threat to the fact-finding process" in an adjudicative proceeding and acts with indifference to that effect. Oregon DR 7-108(B) provides that DR 7-108(A) "does not preclude a lawyer from replying to charges of misconduct publicly made against the lawyer or from participating in the proceedings of legislative, administrative or other investigative bodies." Oregon DR 7-108(C) requires a lawyer to "exercise reasonable care to prevent the lawyer's employees from making an extrajudicial statement that the lawyer would be prohibited from making under DR 7-108 (A)."

Utah: In 1997, Utah amended Rule 3.6 to conform substantially to ABA Model Rule 3.6 as amended in 1994.

Virginia: DR 7-106(A) prohibits a lawyer "participating in or associated with the investigation or the prosecution or the defense of a criminal matter that may be tried by a jury" from making an extrajudicial statement that "constitutes a clear and present danger of interfering with the fairness of the trial by jury."

Related Materials

ABA Canons: Canon 20 provided:

20. Newspaper Discussion of Pending Litigation

Newspaper publications by a lawyer as to pending or anticipated litigation may interfere with a fair trial in the Courts and otherwise prejudice the due administration of justice. Generally they are to be condemned. If the extreme circumstances of a particular case justify a statement to the public, it is unprofessional to make it anonymously. An *ex parte* reference to the facts should not go beyond quotation from the records and papers on file in the court; but even in extreme cases it is better to avoid any *ex parte* statement.

ABA Standards of Criminal Justice: See Prosecution Function Standard 3-1.4 (Public Statements). See also Standards Relating to Fair Trial and Free Press (excerpted at pp. 544-548 of our 1997 edition), which were cited in Comment 2 to the pre-1994 version of Rule 3.6 as a basis (along with DR 7-107) for the old formulation of Rule 3.6. See especially Standard 8-1.1.

American Academy of Matrimonial Lawyers: The "Bounds of Advocacy" drafted by the American Academy of Matrimonial Lawyers contains the following provision and commentary:

2.19 An attorney should not communicate with the news media about the representation except with the client's prior consent.

Comment to Rule 2.19

Statements to the media by an attorney representing a party in a matrimonial matter are potentially improper because they tend to prejudice an adjudicative proceeding. An attorney's interest in obtaining publicity should not be allowed to obstruct settlement, cause embarrassment, diminish the opportunity for reconciliation, or harm the family. Nor should an attorney attempt to gain an advantage for the client by providing information to the media to embarrass or humiliate the opposing party or counsel.

Code of Federal Regulations: See 28 C.F.R. §50.2, reprinted later in this volume in the material on Federal Conflicts and Confidentiality Provisions.

Model Rules of Professional Conduct for Federal Lawyers: Rule 3.6(a) prohibits extrajudicial statements likely to prejudice an adjudicative proceeding "or an official review process thereof." Rule 3.6(b)(4) makes clear that Rule 3.6 applies to any proceeding that could result in incarceration "or other adverse action." The Rules for Federal Lawyers also add Rule 3.6(d), which provides: "The protection and release of information in matters pertaining to the Government shall be consistent with law."

Restatement of the Law Governing Lawyers: The American Law Institute has proposed but not yet approved the following provision:

§169. Advocate's Public Comment on Pending Litigation

(1) In representing a client in a matter before a tribunal, a lawyer may not make a statement outside the proceeding that a reasonable person would expect to be disseminated by means of public communication when the lawyer knows or reasonably should know that the statement will have a substantial likelihood of materially prejudicing a juror or influencing or intimidating a prospective witness in the proceeding. However, a lawyer may in any event make a statement that is reasonably necessary to mitigate the impact on the lawyer's client of substantial, undue, and prejudicial publicity recently initiated by one other than the lawyer or the lawyer's client.

(2) A prosecutor must, except for statements necessary to inform the public of the nature and extent of the prosecutor's action and that serve a legitimate law enforcement purpose, refrain from making extrajudicial comments that have a substantial likelihood of heightening public condemnation of the accused.

Rule 3.7 Lawyer as Witness

(a) A lawyer shall not act as advocate at a trial in which the lawyer is likely to be a necessary witness except where:
(1) the testimony relates to an uncontested issue;
(2) the testimony relates to the nature and value of legal services rendered in the case; or
(3) disqualification of the lawyer would work substantial hardship on the client.
(b) A lawyer may act as advocate in a trial in which another lawyer in the lawyer's firm is likely to be called as a witness unless precluded from doing so by Rule 1.7 or Rule 1.9.

COMMENT

[1] Combining the roles of advocate and witness can prejudice the opposing party and can involve a conflict of interest between the lawyer and client.

[2] The opposing party has proper objection where the combination of roles may prejudice that party's rights in the litigation. A witness is required to testify on the basis of personal knowledge, while an advocate is expected to explain and comment on evidence given by others. It may not be clear whether a statement by an advocate-witness should be taken as proof or as an analysis of the proof.

[3] Paragraph (a)(1) recognizes that if the testimony will be uncontested, the ambiguities in the dual role are purely theoretical. Paragraph (a)(2) recognizes that where the testimony concerns the extent and value of legal services rendered in the action in which the testimony is offered, permitting the lawyers to testify avoids the need for a second trial with new counsel to resolve that issue. Moreover, in such a situation the judge has first hand knowledge of the matter in issue; hence, there is less dependence on the adversary process to test the credibility of the testimony.

[4] Apart from these two exceptions, paragraph (a)(3) recognizes that a balancing is required between the interests of the client and those of the opposing party. Whether the opposing party is likely to suffer

prejudice depends on the nature of the case, the importance and probable tenor of the lawyer's testimony, and the probability that the lawyer's testimony will conflict with that of other witnesses. Even if there is risk of such prejudice, in determining whether the lawyer should be disqualified due regard must be given to the effect of disqualification on the lawyer's client. It is relevant that one or both parties could reasonably foresee that the lawyer would probably be a witness. The principle of imputed disqualification stated in Rule 1.10 has no application to this aspect of the problem.

[5] Whether the combination of roles involves an improper conflict of interest with respect to the client is determined by Rule 1.7 or 1.9. For example, if there is likely to be substantial conflict between the testimony of the client and that of the lawyer or a member of the lawyer's firm, the representation is improper. The problem can arise whether the lawyer is called as a witness on behalf of the client or is called by the opposing party. Determining whether or not such a conflict exists is primarily the responsibility of the lawyer involved. See Comment to Rule 1.7. If a lawyer who is a member of a firm may not act as both advocate and witness by reason of conflict of interest, Rule 1.10 disqualifies the firm also.

Model Code Comparison

DR 5-102(A) prohibited a lawyer, or the lawyer's firm, from serving as advocate if the lawyer "learns or it is obvious that he or a lawyer in his firm ought to be called as a witness on behalf of his client." DR 5-102(B) provided that a lawyer, and the lawyer's firm, may continue representation if the "lawyer learns or it is obvious that he or a lawyer in his firm may be called as a witness other than on behalf of his client . . . until it is apparent that his testimony is or may be prejudicial to his client." DR 5-101(B) permitted a lawyer to testify while representing a client: "(1) If the testimony will relate solely to an uncontested matter; (2) If the testimony will relate solely to a matter of formality and there is no reason to believe that substantial evidence will be offered in opposition to the testimony; (3) If the testimony will relate solely to the nature and value of legal services rendered in the case by the lawyer or his firm to the client; (4) As to any matter if refusal would work a substantial hardship on the client because of the distinctive value of the lawyer or his firm as counsel in the particular case."

The exception stated in paragraph (a)(1) consolidates provisions of DR 5-101(B)(1) and (2). Testimony relating to a formality, referred to in DR 5-101(B)(2), in effect defines the phrase "uncontested issue" and is redundant.

Cross-References in Rules

None.

Legislative History

1980 Discussion Draft (then Rule 3.9) prohibited a lawyer from acting as an advocate, "except on the lawyer's own behalf, in litigation in which the lawyer's own conduct is a material issue or in which the lawyer is likely to be a witness," unless the lawyer satisfied exceptions that were substantially the same as finally adopted.
1981 Draft was substantially the same as adopted.
1982 Draft was adopted.

Selected State Variations

Arkansas totally deletes subparagraph (b).
California: See Rule 5-210 (Member as Witness).
District of Columbia: D.C. Rule 3.7(b) differs significantly from the ABA Model Rule — see District of Columbia Rules of Professional Conduct below.
Florida: Rule 3.7 prohibits a lawyer from acting as advocate at a trial where the lawyer is likely to be a necessary witness "on behalf of the client" unless various exceptions apply. The exceptions are drawn from DR 5-101(B) of the ABA Model Code — see Model Code Comparison above.
Georgia's DR 5-102 provides:

> When a lawyer is a witness for his client, except as to merely formal matters, such as the attestation or custody of an instrument and the like, he should leave the trial of the case to other counsel. Except when essential to the ends of justice, a lawyer should avoid testifying in court in behalf of his client.

Illinois: Rule 3.7 distinguishes between a witness on behalf of a client and a witness not on behalf of a client. Illinois Rule 3.7(a) essentially tracks DR 5-101(B), and Illinois Rule 3.7(b) essentially tracks DR 5-102(B).
Massachusetts: Effective January 1, 1998, Rule 3.7(f) forbids a prosecutor to subpoena a lawyer to a grand jury or other criminal proceeding to present evidence about a past or present client unless "the prosecutor obtains prior judicial approval after an opportunity for an adversarial proceeding."
New Mexico deletes subparagraph (a)(3).
New York: The language of DR 5-101 and DR 5-102 is retained except that disqualification is not imputed within a firm.
Texas: Rule 3.08(a) disqualifies a lawyer whose testimony will be "necessary to establish an essential fact on behalf of the lawyer's client." Rules 3.08(b) and (c) provide:

(b) A lawyer shall not continue as an advocate in a pending adjudicatory proceeding if the lawyer believes that the lawyer will be compelled to furnish testimony that will be substantially adverse to the lawyer's client, unless the client consents after full disclosure.

(c) Without the client's informed consent, a lawyer may not act as advocate in an adjudicatory proceeding in which another lawyer in the lawyer's firm is prohibited by paragraphs (a) or (b) from serving as advocate. If the lawyer to be called as a witness could not also serve as an advocate under this Rule, that lawyer shall not take an active role before the tribunal in the presentation of the matter.

Virginia: Substantially the same as the Model Code.

Washington's version of subparagraph (a)(3) is as follows: "the trial judge finds that disqualification of the lawyer would work a substantial hardship on the client and that the likelihood of the lawyer being a necessary witness was not reasonably foreseeable before trial." Washington also adds the following new subparagraph (c): "the lawyer has been called by the opposing party and the court rules that the lawyer may continue to act as an advocate."

Related Materials

ABA Canons: Canon 19 provided:

19. *Appearance of Lawyer as Witness for His Client*

When a lawyer is a witness for his client, except as to merely formal matters, such as the attestation or custody of an instrument and the like, he should leave the trial of the case to other counsel. Except when essential to the ends of justice, a lawyer should avoid testifying in court in behalf of his client.

Model Rules of Professional Conduct for Federal Lawyers: Rule 3.7(a)(2) permits a lawyer to testify to "the nature, value, *and quality* of legal services rendered in the case."

Restatement of the Law Governing Lawyers: The American Law Institute has proposed but not yet approved the following provision:

§168. Advocate as Witness

(1) Except as provided in Subsection (2), a lawyer may not represent a client in a contested hearing or trial of a matter in which:

(a) the lawyer is expected to testify for the lawyer's client; or

(b) the lawyer does not intend to testify but (i) the lawyer's testimony would be material to establishing a claim or defense of the client, and (ii) the client has not consented as stated in §202 to the lawyer's failure to testify.

(2) A lawyer may represent a client when the lawyer will testify as stated in Subsection (1)(a) if:

(a) the lawyer's testimony relates to an issue that the lawyer reasonably believes will not be contested or to the nature and value of legal services rendered in the proceeding;

(b) deprivation of the lawyer's services as advocate would work a substantial hardship on the client; or

(c) consent has been given by (i) opposing parties who would be adversely affected by the lawyer's testimony, and (ii) if relevant, the lawyer's client, as stated in §202 with respect to any conflict of interest between lawyer and client (see §206) that the lawyer's testimony would create.

(3) A lawyer may not represent a client in a litigated matter pending before a tribunal when the lawyer or a lawyer in the lawyer's firm will give testimony materially adverse to the position of the lawyer's client or materially adverse to a former client of any such lawyer with respect to a matter substantially related to the earlier representation, unless the affected client has consented as stated in §202 with respect to any conflict of interest between lawyer and client (see §206) that the testimony would create.

(4) A tribunal should not permit a lawyer to call opposing trial counsel as a witness unless the testifying lawyer would give testimony that is not merely cumulative of evidence readily available by less intrusive means.

(Restatement §§202 and 206 are reprinted above in the Related Materials following Rule 1.7.)

Rule 3.8 Special Responsibilities of a Prosecutor

Editors' Note. At its August 1995 Annual Meeting, after a heated debate, the ABA House of Delegates amended Rule 3.8 for the third time since its adoption in 1983. The amendment completely deleted subparagraph (f)(2) from Rule 3.8. Subparagraph (f)(2) had required that if a prosecutor serves a subpoena on a lawyer in a grand jury or other criminal proceeding to obtain evidence about the lawyer's past or present clients, the prosecutor must seek "prior judicial approval after an opportunity for adversarial hearing." In a parallel change, the ABA removed the last sentence of Comment 4 to Rule 3.8, which had explained the reasons for requiring prior judicial approval. Nothing was added to Rule 3. 8 — the rest of the Rule and its Comment remain the same, except that subparagraph (f) has been renumbered to reflect the deletion of (f)(2).

For a legislative-style version of Rule 3.8 showing what was added and deleted by the 1995 amendment, see our 1996 edition. An excerpt from the ABA Committee Report explaining the amendment is reprinted in the Legislative History section after the Rule.

The prosecutor in a criminal case shall:

(a) refrain from prosecuting a charge that the prosecutor knows is not supported by probable cause;

(b) make reasonable efforts to assure that the accused has been advised of the right to, and the procedure for obtaining, counsel and has been given reasonable opportunity to obtain counsel;

(c) not seek to obtain from an unrepresented accused a waiver of important pretrial rights, such as the right to a preliminary hearing;

(d) make timely disclosure to the defense of all evidence or information known to the prosecutor that tends to negate the guilt of the accused or mitigates the offense, and, in connection with sentencing, disclose to the defense and to the tribunal all unprivileged mitigating information known to the prosecutor, except when the prosecutor is relieved of this responsibility by a protective order of the tribunal; and

(e) exercise reasonable care to prevent investigators, law enforcement personnel, employees or other persons assisting or associated with the prosecutor in a criminal case from making an extrajudicial statement that the prosecutor would be prohibited from making under Rule 3.6.

(f) not subpoena a lawyer in a grand jury or other criminal proceeding to present evidence about a past or present client unless the prosecutor reasonably believes:

(1) the information sought is not protected from disclosure by any applicable privilege;

(2) the evidence sought is essential to the successful completion of an ongoing investigation or prosecution;

(3) there is no other feasible alternative to obtain the information.

(g) except for statements that are necessary to inform the public of the nature and extent of the prosecutor's action and that serve a legitimate law enforcement purpose, refrain from making extrajudicial comments that have a substantial likelihood of heightening public condemnation of the accused.

COMMENT

[1] A prosecutor has the responsibility of a minister of justice and not simply that of an advocate. This responsibility carries with it specific obligations to see that the defendant is accorded procedural justice and that guilt is decided upon the basis of sufficient evidence. Precisely how far the prosecutor is required to go in this direction is a matter of debate and varies in different jurisdictions. Many jurisdictions have adopted the ABA Standards of Criminal Justice Relating to Prosecution Function, which in turn are the product of prolonged and careful deliberation by

lawyers experienced in both criminal prosecution and defense. See also Rule 3.3(d), governing ex parte proceedings, among which grand jury proceedings are included. Applicable law may require other measures by the prosecutor and knowing disregard of those obligations or a systematic abuse of prosecutorial discretion could constitute a violation of Rule 8.4.

[2] Paragraph (c) does not apply to an accused representing himself with the approval of the tribunal. Nor does it forbid the lawful questioning of a suspect who has knowingly waived his rights to counsel and silence.

[3] The exception in paragraph (d) recognizes that a prosecutor may seek an appropriate protective order from the tribunal if disclosure of information to the defense could result in substantial harm to an individual or to the public interest.

[4] Paragraph (f) is intended to limit the issuance of lawyer subpoenas in grand jury and other criminal proceedings to those situations in which there is a genuine need to intrude into the client-lawyer relationship.

[5] Paragraph (g) supplements Rule 3.6, which prohibits extrajudicial statements that have a substantial likelihood of prejudicing an adjudicatory proceeding. In the context of a criminal prosecution, a prosecutor's extrajudicial statement can create the additional problem of increasing public condemnation of the accused. Although the announcement of an indictment, for example, will necessarily have severe consequences for the accused, a prosecutor can, and should, avoid comments which have no legitimate law enforcement purpose and have a substantial likelihood of increasing public opprobrium of the accused. Nothing in this Comment is intended to restrict the statements which a prosecutor may make which comply with Rule 3.6(b) or 3.6(c).

Model Code Comparison

DR 7-103(A) provided that a "public prosecutor . . . shall not institute . . . criminal charges when he knows or it is obvious that the charges are not supported by probable cause." DR 7-103(B) provided that "[a] public prosecutor . . . shall make timely disclosure . . . of the existence of evidence, known to the prosecutor . . . that tends to negate the guilt of the accused, mitigate the degree of the offense, or reduce the punishment."

Paragraph (f) has no counterpart in the Model Code.

Cross-References in Rules

None.

Legislative History

1980 Discussion Draft (then Rule 3.10) provided as follows:

> The prosecutor in a criminal case shall:
> (a) refrain from prosecuting a charge that the prosecutor knows is not supported by probable cause;
> (b) advise the defendant of the right to counsel and provide assistance in obtaining counsel;
> (c) not induce an unrepresented defendant to surrender important procedural rights, such as the right to a preliminary hearing;
> (d) seek all evidence, whether or not favorable to the accused, and make timely disclosure to the defense of all evidence supporting innocence of mitigating the offense;
> (e) not discourage a person from giving relevant information to the defense;
> (f) in connection with sentencing, disclose to the defendant and to the court all unprivileged information known to the prosecution that is relevant thereto.

1980 Discussion Draft also contained a separate rule, with no counterpart in the Rules as adopted, that read as follows:

Special Responsibilities of Defense Counsel in a Criminal Case

> A lawyer for the accused in a criminal case, shall not:
> (a) agree to represent a person proposing to commit a crime, except as part of a good faith effort to determine the validity, scope, meaning, or application of the law;
> (b) act in a case in which the lawyer's partner or other professional associate is or has been the prosecutor;
> (c) accept payment of fees by one person for the defense of another except with the consent of the accused after adequate disclosure; or
> (d) charge a contingent fee.

1981 Draft: Substantially the same as adopted, except subparagraph (d), which included an obligation to "make reasonable efforts to seek all evidence, whether or not favorable to the defendant," but which did not refer to protective orders. Also, 1981 Draft did not include subparagraph (e) of the rule as adopted.

1982 Draft: Same as adopted, except that subparagraph (e) was not yet in the Rule.

1990 Amendment: At its 1990 Mid-Year Meeting, the ABA House of Delegates added subparagraph (f) to Rule 3.8 and added paragraph 4 to the Comment. The reasons for adding Rule 3.8(f) were explained in a Report and Recommendation by the ABA's Standing Committee on Ethics and Professional Responsibility that provided, in part, as follows:

Excerpt from ABA Report Explaining 1990 Amendment*

Proper operation of our adversary system of justice requires full recognition and protection of the relation of trust and confidence between a client and attorney. One, but only one, aspect of that relation is the privilege not to disclose confidential communications between the client and the attorney, the oldest privilege for confidential communications known to the common law. . . . Any rule regulating subpoenas to lawyers must, at a minimum, provide for full protection of the privilege.

A subpoena rule which does no more than recognize the attorney-client privilege, however, will ignore other important aspects of the relationship between a client and his attorney. . . . Because information protected by the attorney-client privilege is not coterminous with information which an ethical attorney is supposed to hold confidential, there is much information in the hands of an attorney which remains exposed to the subpoena power, even if that power is limited by the privilege. For example, the prevailing judicial position is that, absent special circumstances, an attorney may be compelled by subpoena to reveal information about the identity of the client and the size and source of the fee — information frequently sought by government attorneys. Similarly, an attorney in possession of documents received from a client in the course of a case may be compelled by subpoena to produce those documents, assuming that the client personally could be compelled to produce the documents were they in the client's hands.

Since a subpoena may compel production of information which, though unprivileged, is certainly confidential under Rule 1.6 and DR 4-101, the mere issuance of the subpoena undermines the client's confidence and trust. . . .

. . . Confronted by a powerful adversary and by a seemingly bewildering array of procedures, with their liberty at stake, clients rightfully expect that their lawyer will, within the constraints of the law and the profession's code of ethics, zealously argue their case at every turn. There could be few things more destructive of this expectation than the spectacle of their own attorney forced by their adversary to supply information detrimental to their interest.

1994 Amendment: At its August 1994 Annual Meeting, by a voice vote, the ABA House of Delegates amended Rule 3.8 for the second time since its original adoption in 1983. The amendment added a new subparagraph (g) that permits prosecutors to make statements "necessary to inform the public of the nature and extent of the prosecutor's action and that serve a legitimate law enforcement purpose," even if these statements may heighten "public condemnation of the accused." The amendment added a corresponding paragraph to the Comment. The amendment supplements the 1994 amendment to Rule 3.6, which generally governs extrajudicial statements by lawyers.

The amendment was co-sponsored by the ABA Standing Committee on Ethics and Professional Responsibility and the ABA Criminal Justice Section, which submitted a joint report in support of the 1994 amendment to Rule 3.6 and Rule

---

*Committee Reports do not represent official policy of the ABA. They are for information only, and the opinions are those of the authors of the report.

3.8. We reprint below the small portion of the joint ABA report explaining the amendment to Rule 3.8. (Excerpts from the remainder of the report, which provides further background and context for the amendment, are found in the Legislative History section following Rule 3.6.)

Excerpts from ABA Report Explaining 1994 Amendment*

In connection with its proposed revision of Rule 3.6, the Committee also proposes to add a new section (g) to Rule 3.8, prohibiting gratuitous comments by a prosecutor which have a substantial likelihood of increasing public opprobrium toward the accused. Not only can pretrial publicity taint the fairness of a trial, but it can also subject the accused to unfair and unnecessary condemnation before the trial takes place. Because of a prosecutor's special power and visibility, a prosecutor should use special care to avoid such publicity.

1995 Amendment: At its August 1995 Annual Meeting, the ABA House of Delegates voted 187-113 to amend Rule 3.8 by deleting subparagraph (f)(2). Subparagraph (f)(2) had required prosecutors to obtain "prior judicial approval after an opportunity for an adversarial hearing" before serving a subpoena on a lawyer in a grand jury or other criminal proceeding to seek evidence about the lawyer's past or present clients. The ABA also removed the last sentence of Comment 4 to Rule 3.8, which had explained the need for judicial approval. The amendment was jointly sponsored by the ABA's Standing Committee on Ethics and Professional Responsibility and the ABA Criminal Justice Section. We reprint below excerpts from the joint Committee Report explaining the amendment.

Excerpt from ABA Report Explaining 1995 Amendment*

Since the adoption of Model Rule 3.8(f) in 1990, it has been considered and rejected by the bars and governing courts in a number of States, and it has been judicially invalidated in the Third Circuit as exceeding a court's local rulemaking authority. See Baylson v. Disciplinary Board, 975 F.2d 102 (3d Cir. 1992), *cert. denied* 113 S. Ct. 1578 (1993) (Pennsylvania). But see Whitehouse v. U.S. District Court, 1995 U.S. App. LEXIS 9014 (1st Cir. 1995) (Rhode Island version of attorney subpoena rule, which requires prior judicial approval but does not require an adversary hearing, within the district court's rulemaking authority). This record reflects a fundamental and widespread doubt about the suitability of Rule 3.8(f) in its current form as a rule of ethics, a doubt that the Standing Committee has come to share. We have concluded, therefore, that Rule 3.8(f) should be amended. However, because we believe its defect as a provision of a professional ethics code lies not in the substantive ethical standards it sets, but in its accompanying procedural prescription, we propose to amend it solely by deleting that procedural feature.

*Committee reports do not represent official policy of the ABA. They are for information only, and the opinions are those of the authors of the report.

Subparagraph (2) of Rule 3.8(f) is an anomaly in the Model Rules. Rather than stating a substantive ethical precept, it sets out a type of implementing requirement that is properly established by rules of criminal procedure rather than established as an ethical norm. Moreover, while nominally addressed to the conduct of prosecutors, subparagraph (2) affects the operation of courts and grand juries by "requir[ing] the erection of novel court procedures and interject[ing] an additional layer of judicial supervision over the grand jury subpoena process." Baylson v. Disciplinary Board, 764 F. Supp. 328, 337 (E D. Pa. 1991). The procedural obligations it seeks to impose as a matter of professional ethics have no parallel in any other enforceable provision of the Model Rules.

We therefore recommend deletion of subparagraph (2) of Rule 3.8(f), with its requirement of prior judicial approval of a lawyer subpoena and an opportunity for an adversarial proceeding. The limiting description of the circumstances in which a prosecutor could ethically issue such a subpoena, set forth in subparagraph (1), would remain unchanged. The proposed amendment would remove the feature of the rule that courts have found objectionable, and we expect this will lead to the more widespread adoption of it substantive provisions by state bars.

Selected State Variations

Alaska deletes section (c) from its version of Rule 3.8.

California: See Rule 5-110 (Performing the Duty of Member in Government Service) and Rule 5-220 (Suppression of Evidence).

Colorado: Rule 3.8(f)(2) was amended effective February 19, 1997 to eliminate the requirement that the prosecutor obtain prior judicial approval to subpoena a lawyer.

District of Columbia: D.C. Rule 3.8 differs significantly from the ABA Model Rule — see District of Columbia Rules of Professional Conduct below.

Florida omits subparagraphs (b), (e), and (f) of Rule 3.8, and omits all of Comment 4.

Hawaii: Rule 3.8 applies to a "public prosecutor or other government lawyer." Rule 3.8(a) applies to a charge that the lawyer knows "or it is obvious" is not supported by probable cause.

Illinois has witnessed a vigorous struggle over Rule 3.8(f). In 1987, the Illinois legislature passed a law requiring judicial approval of subpoenas issued to lawyers seeking testimony against their clients, but Governor Thompson (a former U.S. Attorney) vetoed the law. Soon after the veto, the Illinois State Bar Association proposed the following rule, which the Illinois Supreme Court rejected without opinion in 1988:

> A public prosecutor or other government lawyer shall not subpoena nor cause a subpoena to be issued to an attorney without prior judicial approval after an opportunity for an adversarial proceeding in circumstances where the prosecutor seeks to compel the attorney to provide evidence obtained as a result of the attorney-client relationship concerning a person who is or was represented by the attorney.

In 1990, when Illinois adopted its new Rules of Professional Conduct, it omitted Rule 3.8(f). However, effective November 20, 1991, the Illinois Supreme Court added the language of Rule 3.8(f) by court order. (Justice Heiple dissented.) The Illinois version of Rule 3.8(f) (which is numbered 3.8(c) in Illinois) applied not only to a "public prosecutor" but also to any "other government lawyer." Immediately, the Cook County State's Attorney, the Attorney General of Illinois, and other prosecutors submitted an "emergency motion" to stay enforcement of the new rule, and on December 27, 1991, the Illinois Supreme Court issued an order staying enforcement of the rule. On October 30, 1992, just 11 months after Rule 3.8(c) took effect, the Illinois Supreme Court issued an order repealing the rule from the Illinois Rules of Professional Conduct.

Louisiana: Effective December 16, 1993, the Louisiana Supreme Court issued an order suspending all of Rule 3.8(f) as applied to federal prosecutors.

Maryland's version of subparagraph (e) extends only to an "employee or other person under the control of a prosecutor."

Massachusetts: Supreme Court Rule 3:08 (also designated PF-15) provides: "It is unprofessional conduct for a prosecutor to subpoena an attorney to a grand jury without prior judicial approval in circumstances where the prosecutor seeks to compel the attorney/witness to provide evidence concerning a person who is represented by the attorney/witness."

New Jersey deletes Rule 3.8(e) and changes Rule 3.8(c) to read "not seek to obtain from an unrepresented accused a waiver of important post-indictment pretrial rights."

New York: Same or substantially the same as the ABA Model Code — see Model Code Comparison above.

Pennsylvania: Rule 3.10 forbids a prosecutor, without judicial approval, to subpoena a lawyer before a grand jury or other tribunal investigating criminal conduct if the prosecutor seeks to compel evidence concerning a current or former client of the lawyer.

Virginia: DR 8-102 provides that a prosecutor "or other government lawyer in criminal litigation" shall not "induce an unrepresented defendant to surrender important procedural rights" or "discourage a person from giving relevant information to the defendants." DR 8-102(A)(5), a shortened version of Model Rule 3.8(f), prohibits a prosecutor from issuing a subpoena to an attorney "without prior judicial approval in circumstances where the prosecutor seeks to compel the attorney/witness to provide evidence" concerning a past or present client.

Related Materials

ABA Canons: Canon 5 provided:

5. The Defense or Prosecution of Those Accused of Crime

The primary duty of a lawyer engaged in public prosecution is not to convict, but to see that justice is done. The suppression of facts or the secreting of witnesses capable of establishing the innocence of the accused is highly reprehensible.

ABA Standards for Criminal Justice: See Prosecution Function Standard 3-3.9(a) (Discretion in the Charging Decision), Standard 3-3.11 (Disclosure of Evidence by the Prosecutor), and Standard 3-4.1 (Availability for Plea Discussions).

ABA Standards for Imposing Lawyer Sanctions: See Standard 5.2 printed in the Related Materials following Model Rule 8.4.

American Lawyer's Code of Conduct: Chapter 9 of the ALCC, entitled "Responsibilities of Government Lawyers," provides as follows:

9.1. A lawyer serving as public prosecutor shall not seek evidence to support a prosecution against a particular individual unless that individual is identified as a suspect in the course of a good faith investigation into suspected criminal conduct.

9.2. In exercising discretion to investigate or to prosecute, a lawyer serving as public prosecutor shall not show favoritism for, or invidiously discriminate against, one person among others similarly situated.

9.3. A lawyer serving as public prosecutor shall not seek or sign formal charges, or proceed to trial, unless a fair-minded juror could conclude beyond a reasonable doubt that the accused is guilty, on the basis of all of the facts that are known to the prosecutor and likely to be admissible into evidence. . . .

9.5. A lawyer serving as public prosecutor shall not use unconscionable pressures in plea bargaining, such as charging an accused in several counts for what is essentially a single offense, or charging an accused with a more serious offense than is warranted under Rule 9.3.

9.6. A lawyer serving as public prosecutor shall not condition a dismissal, nolle prosequi, or similar action on an accused's relinquishment of constitutional rights, or of rights against the government, a public official, or any other person, other than relinquishment of those rights inherent in pleading not guilty and proceeding to trial.

9.7. A lawyer serving as public prosecutor shall promptly make available to defense counsel, without request for it, any information that the prosecutor knows is likely to be useful to the defense.

9.8. A lawyer serving as public prosecutor shall not strike jurors on grounds of race, religion, national or ethnic background, or sex, except to counteract the use of such tactics initiated by the defense.

9.9. A lawyer serving as public prosecutor, who knows that a defendant is not receiving or has not received effective assistance of counsel, shall promptly advise the court, on the record when possible.

Attorney Fee Forfeitures: A topic often intertwined with subpoenas to defense attorneys is attorney fee forfeiture — seizing an attorney's fees when the government can prove that they are the fruit of federal drug crimes or RICO violations. In 1989, the Supreme Court decided two cases on fee forfeiture, Caplin & Drysdale v. United States, 491 U.S. 617 (1989), and United States v. Monsanto, 491 U.S. 600 (1989).

Department of Justice Guidelines: The United States Department of Justice maintains internal guidelines limiting the circumstances under which Justice Department lawyers may issue subpoenas to criminal defense lawyers. See D.O.J. Subpoenas Guidelines §9-2.161(B) and (F).

Due Process Clause: The constitutional basis for the disclosure obligations in Rule 3.8(d) is found in Brady v. Maryland, 373 U.S. 83, 87 (1963), which held that "the suppression by the prosecution of evidence favorable to an accused upon request violates due process where the evidence is material. . . ."

Federal Rules of Criminal Procedure: Rules 16 and 26.2 of the Federal Rules of Criminal Procedure impose disclosure obligations on both sides in criminal cases. Before trial, Rule 16(a)(1) provides that federal prosecutors must allow a criminal defendant to inspect four categories of information, including: (A) any relevant written or recorded statements made by the defendant; (B) a copy of the defendant's prior criminal record; (C) books, papers, documents, photographs, tangible objects, buildings or places that are material to the preparation of the defense, or are intended for use by the government as evidence in chief at trial, or were obtained from or belong to the defendant; and (D) results or reports of physical or mental examinations, and scientific tests or experiments, which are material to the preparation of the defense or which the government intends to use as evidence in chief at trial. However, Rule 16(a)(2) and (3) provide that the government's duty to disclose does not apply to the prosecutor's work product ("reports, memoranda, or other internal government documents made by the attorney for the government or other government agents in connection with the investigation or prosecution of the case") or to statements made by the government's witnesses or prospective witnesses "except as provided by 18 U.S.C. §3500." Conversely, Rule 16(b)(1) provides that if a defendant requests documents and tangible objects, or scientific tests and reports, and the government complies with the request, then the defendant must permit the government to inspect and copy the same categories of materials in the control of the defendant. However, Rule 16(b)(2) protects the defense attorney's work product. Rule 16(c) imposes a continuing duty to disclose on both sides, and Rule 16(d) provides for protective orders or sanctions, including an order to "prohibit the party from introducing evidence not disclosed."

At trial, Rule 26.2(a) provides that after any witness other than the defendant has testified on direct examination, the court, on motion of a party who did not call the witness, shall order whichever side called the witness to produce "any statement of the witness that is in their possession and that relates to the subject matter concerning which the witness has testified."

Guidelines for the Issuance of Search Warrants: In July 1990, the ABA's Criminal Justice Section issued Guidelines for the Issuance of Search Warrants, many of which directly or indirectly apply to prosecutors.

Model Rules of Professional Conduct for Federal Lawyers: Rule 3.8(a) mandates that a prosecutor shall "[r]efrain from prosecuting a charge that the prosecutor knows is not supported by probable cause, or if not authorized to decline the prosecution of a charge to recommend to the appropriate authority that any charge not warranted by the evidence be withdrawn." Rule 3.8(d) requires timely disclosure only to the defense, not to the tribunal. Rule 3.8(f) obligates a prosecutor to "[r]espect the attorney-client privilege of defendants and not diminish the privilege through investigative or judicial processes."

Restatement of the Law Governing Lawyers: The American Law Institute has tentatively approved §156(3) (reprinted in the Related Materials following Rule 1.13), which sets forth standards to guide prosecutors in determining whether to file criminal charges.

Witness Statements: In federal criminal trials, a prosecutor's "timely disclosure" of witness statements is governed by 18 U.S.C. §3500 (often called the Jencks Act), which provides:

> *§3500. Demands for Production of Statements and Reports of Witnesses*
>
> (b) After a witness called by the United States has testified on direct examination, the court shall, on motion of the defendant, order the United States to produce any statement (as hereinafter defined) of the witness in the possession of the United States which relates to the subject matter as to which the witness has testified. If the entire contents of any such statement relate to the subject matter of the testimony of the witness, the court shall order it to be delivered directly to the defendant for his examination and use.

Rule 3.9 Advocate in Nonadjudicative Proceedings

A lawyer representing a client before a legislative or administrative tribunal in a nonadjudicative proceeding shall disclose that the appearance is in a representative capacity and shall conform to the provisions of Rules 3.3(a) through (c), 3.4(a) through (c), and 3.5.

COMMENT

[1] In representation before bodies such as legislatures, municipal councils, and executive and administrative agencies acting in a rule-making or policy-making capacity, lawyers present facts, formulate issues and advance argument in the matters under consideration. The decision-making body, like a court, should be able to rely on the integrity of the submissions made to it. A lawyer appearing before such a body should deal with the tribunal honestly and in conformity with applicable rules of procedure.

[2] Lawyers have no exclusive right to appear before nonadjudicative bodies, as they do before a court. The requirements of this Rule therefore may subject lawyers to regulations inapplicable to advocates who are not lawyers. However, legislatures and administrative agencies have a right to expect lawyers to deal with them as they deal with courts.

[3] This Rule does not apply to representation of a client in a negotiation or other bilateral transaction with a governmental agency; representation in such a transaction is governed by Rules 4.1 through 4.4.

Model Code Comparison

EC 7-15 stated that a lawyer "appearing before an administrative agency, regardless of the nature of the proceeding it is conducting, has the continuing duty to advance the cause of his client within the bounds of the law." EC 7-16 stated that "[w]hen a lawyer appears in connection with proposed legislation, he . . . should comply with applicable laws and legislative rules." EC 8-5 stated that "[f]raudulent, deceptive, or otherwise illegal conduct by a participant in a proceeding before a . . . legislative body . . . should never be participated in . . . by lawyers." DR 7-106(B)(1) provided that "[i]n presenting a matter to a tribunal, a lawyer shall disclose . . . [u]nless privileged or irrelevant, the identity of the clients he represents and of the persons who employed him."

Cross-References in Rules

None.

Legislative History

1980 Draft (then Rule 3.12) provided as follows:

(a) A lawyer representing a client before a legislative or administrative tribunal in a nonadjudicative proceeding shall deal fairly with the body conducting the proceeding and with other persons making presentations therein and their counsel.

(b) A lawyer in such a proceeding shall:

(1) identify the client on whose behalf the lawyer appears, unless the identity of the client is privileged;

(2) conform to the provisions of Rules 3.1 and 3.4.

1981 and 1982 Drafts were the same as adopted.

Selected State Variations

Alaska replaces the phrase "legislative or administrative tribunal" with the phrase "legislative committee or administrative agency."

California has no direct counterpart.

Illinois omits Rule 3.9.

New Jersey deletes the cross-reference to Rule 3.5(b) in Rule 3.9.

New York: Same or substantially the same as the ABA Model Code — see Model Code Comparison above.

Pennsylvania does not incorporate Rule 3.4(c) in Rule 3.9.

Virginia omits Rule 3.9.

Related Materials

ABA Canons: Canon 26 provided:

26. *Professional Advocacy Other Than Before Courts*

A lawyer openly, and in his true character may render professional services before legislative or other bodies, regarding proposed legislation and in advocacy of claims before departments of government, upon the same principles of ethics which justify his appearance before the Courts; but it is unprofessional for a lawyer so engaged to conceal his attorneyship, or to employ secret personal solicitations, or to use means other than those addressed to the reason and understanding, to influence action.

ABA Standards for Criminal Justice: See Prosecution Function Standards 3-3.1, 3-3.9, 3-3.11.

Lobbying Laws: The federal government and all states have laws regulating lobbyists, including lawyers. On the federal level, the most prominent statute is the Federal Regulation of Lobbying Act (2 U.S.C. §§261-270). It applies to any person whose "principal purpose" is to "influence, directly or indirectly, the passage or defeat of any legislation by the Congress of the United States." §307(b). Lawyer-lobbyists are also regulated by a host of other federal statutes and regulations, including the Foreign Agents Registration Act, the Byrd Amendment, the HUD Reform Act of 1989, Federal Acquisition Regulations, and Office of Management and Budget Regulations. These statutes and regulations are thoroughly explained in a 1993 publication by the ABA Section of Administrative Law and Regulatory Practice entitled The Lobbying Manual.

On the state level, a recent example of a lobbying law is found in Illinois, where Governor Edgar signed a new law on August 4, 1993, providing that anyone "paid to influence executive, legislative or administrative action" must register with the Secretary of State. The lobbying laws of every state are summarized in chart form in a publication by the Council on Governmental Ethics Laws

(COGEL) entitled the Blue Book (9th ed. 1993). State and federal lobbying laws and regulations are discussed in detail in Abner Mikva & Eric Lane, The Legislative Process (Little, Brown and Co., 1995).

Restatement of the Law Governing Lawyers: The American Law Institute has proposed but not yet approved the following provision:

§164. Representing Client in Legislative and Administrative Matters

A lawyer representing a client before a legislature or administrative agency:

(1) must disclose that the appearance is in a representative capacity and not misrepresent the capacity in which the lawyer appears;

(2) must comply with applicable law and regulations governing such representations; and

(3) except as applicable law otherwise provides:

(a) in an adjudicative proceeding before a government agency or involving such an agency as a participant, has the legal rights and responsibilities of an advocate in a proceeding before a judicial tribunal; and

(b) in other types of proceedings and matters, has the legal rights and responsibilities applicable in the lawyer's dealings with a private person.

ARTICLE 4. TRANSACTIONS WITH PERSONS OTHER THAN CLIENTS

Rule 4.1 Truthfulness in Statements to Others

In the course of representing a client a lawyer shall not knowingly:

(a) make a false statement of material fact or law to a third person; or

(b) fail to disclose a material fact to a third person when disclosure is necessary to avoid assisting a criminal or fraudulent act by a client, unless disclosure is prohibited by Rule 1.6.

COMMENT

Misrepresentation

[1] A lawyer is required to be truthful when dealing with others on a client's behalf, but generally has no affirmative duty to inform an opposing party of relevant facts. A misrepresentation can occur if the lawyer incorporates or affirms a statement of another person that the lawyer knows is false. Misrepresentations can also occur by failure to act.

Statements of Fact

[2] This Rule refers to statements of fact. Whether a particular statement should be regarded as one of fact can depend on the circumstances. Under generally accepted conventions in negotiation, certain types of statements ordinarily are not taken as statements of material fact. Estimates of price or value placed on the subject of a transaction and a party's intentions as to an acceptable settlement of a claim are in this category, and so is the existence of an undisclosed principal except where nondisclosure of the principal would constitute fraud.

Fraud by Client

[3] Paragraph (b) recognizes that substantive law may require a lawyer to disclose certain information to avoid being deemed to have assisted the client's crime or fraud. The requirement of disclosure created by this paragraph is, however, subject to the obligations created by Rule 1.6.

Model Code Comparison

Paragraph (a) is substantially similar to DR 7-102(A)(5), which stated that "[i]n his representation of a client, a lawyer shall not . . . [k]nowingly make a false statement of law or fact."

With regard to paragraph (b), DR 7-102(A)(3) provided that a lawyer shall not "[c]onceal or knowingly fail to disclose that which he is required by law to reveal."

Cross-References in Rules

Rule 1.6, Comment 20: "The Rules of Professional Conduct in various circumstances permit or require a lawyer to disclose information relating to the representation. See **Rules** 2.2, 2.3, 3.3 and **4.1.**"

Rule 1.13, Comment 6: "[T]his Rule does not limit or expand the lawyer's responsibilities under **Rules** 1.6, 1.8, and 1.16, 3.3, or **4.1.**"

Rule 3.9, Comment 3: "This Rule does not apply to representation of a client in a negotiation or other bilateral transaction with a governmental agency; representation in such a transaction is governed by **Rules 4.1** through 4.4."

Legislative History

1980 Discussion Draft contained the following Introduction:

Negotiator

As negotiator a lawyer seeks agreement concerning matters of interest to a client and another party. Negotiation may concern dispute settlement, settlement of a contract, labor relations, government regulatory activity, custody and support in a family matter, and other legally significant relationships. A lawyer's function in negotiation can include presenting a bargaining position, exploring bases of common interest, reconciling differences, persuading other parties of the merits of the client's position, ironing out details, and formalizing the terms of an agreement.

A negotiator should seek the most advantageous result for the client that is consistent with the requirements of law and the lawyer's responsibilities under the Rules of Professional Conduct. As negotiator, a lawyer should consider not only the client's short-run advantage but also his or her long-run interests, such as the state of future relations between the parties. The lawyer should help the client appreciate the interests and position of the other party and should encourage concessions that will effectuate the client's larger objectives. A lawyer should not transform a bargaining situation into a demonstration of toughness or hypertechnicality or forget that the purely legal aspects of an agreement are often subordinate to its practical aspects. When the alternative to reaching agreement is likely to be litigation, the lawyer should be aware that, although litigation is wholly legitimate as a means of resolving controversy, a fairly negotiated settlement generally yields a better conclusion. A lawyer should also recognize that the lawyer's own interest in resorting to litigation may be different from a client's interest in doing so.

A lawyer's style in negotiations can have great influence on the character of the negotiations — whether they are restrained, open, and business-like, or acrimonious and permeated with distrust. Whatever their outcome, negotiations should be conducted in a civil and forthright manner. Nevertheless, it must be recognized that in negotiations a lawyer is the agent for the client and not an arbitrator or mediator. Negotiation is in part a competition for advantage between parties who have the legal competence to settle their own affairs. A lawyer as negotiator should not impose an agreement on the client, even if the lawyer believes the agreement is in the client's best interests. By the same token, a lawyer does not necessarily endorse the substance of an agreement arrived at through his or her efforts.

1980 Discussion Draft of Rule 4.1 (then called Rule 4.2) provided as follows:

Fairness to Other Participants

(a) In conducting negotiations a lawyer shall be fair in dealing with other participants.

(b) A lawyer shall not make a knowing misrepresentation of fact or law, or fail to disclose a material fact known to the lawyer, even if adverse, when disclosure is:

(1) required by law or the Rules of Professional Conduct; or

(2) necessary to correct a manifest misapprehension of fact or law resulting from a previous representation made by the lawyer or known by the lawyer to have been made by the client. . . .

1980 Discussion Draft also contained the following provision (then called Rule 4.3) that has no equivalent in the Rules as adopted:

Illegal, Fraudulent, or Unconscionable Transactions

A lawyer shall not conclude an agreement, or assist a client in concluding an agreement, that the lawyer knows or reasonably should know is illegal, contains legally prohibited terms, would work a fraud, or would be held to be unconscionable as a matter of law.

1981 Draft: Subparagraph (a) was substantially the same as adopted. Subparagraph (b) provided that a lawyer must not:

(b) knowingly fail to disclose a fact to a third person when:
(1) in the circumstances failure to make the disclosure is equivalent to making a material misrepresentation;
(2) disclosure is necessary to prevent assisting a criminal or fraudulent act, as required by Rule 1.2(d); or
(3) disclosure is necessary to comply with other law.

1982 Draft: Substantially the same as adopted, except that Rule 4.1(b) provided: "The duties stated in this Rule apply even if compliance requires disclosure of information otherwise protected by Rule 1.6."

Selected State Variations

California: See B & P Code §6128(a).

Colorado: Rule 4.1(a) applies to a false "or misleading" statement, and Colorado omits the word "material" before "fact."

Illinois: Rule 4.1(a) prohibits a lawyer from making "a statement of material fact or law to a third person which statement the lawyer knows or reasonably should know is false."

Indiana: Rule 4.1(b) provides simply that a lawyer shall not knowingly "fail to disclose that which is required by law to be revealed."

Kansas states the final clause of Rule 4.1(b) as follows: "unless disclosure is prohibited by or made discretionary under Rule 1.6."

Maryland adds a separate subparagraph providing: "The duties stated in this Rule apply even if compliance requires disclosure of information otherwise protected by Rule 1.6."

Massachusetts: Effective January 1, 1998, Comment 3 to Rule 4.1 defines "assisting" to refer "to that level of assistance that would render a third party liable for another's crime or fraud." Compare the definition of "assisting" in the comment to Massachusetts Rule 3.3.

Michigan has not adopted Rule 4.1(b). See also Michigan's version of Rule 1.6(c)(3), which is noted in the Comment to Michigan's Rule 4.1.

Mississippi deletes the wording in Rule 4.1(b), "unless disclosure is prohibited by Rule 1.6."

New Jersey: Rule 4.1 applies the duties of that Rule even if it requires revelation of information protected by Rule 1.6.

New York: Same or substantially the same as the ABA Model Code — see Model Code Comparison above — except see New York Materials for New York's versions of DR 7-102(B)(1), EC 4-7, and DR 4-101(C)(5). New York also expressly defines "fraud" (in the definitions at the beginning of the Code) as follows:

> Fraud does not include conduct, although characterized as fraudulent by statute or administrative rule, which lacks an element of scienter, deceit, intent to mislead, or knowing failure to correct misrepresentations which can be reasonably expected to induce detrimental reliance by another.

North Dakota deletes Rule 4.1(b).

Texas: Rule 4.01(b) provides in full that a lawyer shall not "fail to disclose a material fact to a third person when disclosure is necessary to avoid making the lawyer a party to a criminal act or knowingly assisting a fraudulent act perpetrated by a client."

Virginia: Substantially the same as the Model Code.

Related Materials

American Academy of Matrimonial Lawyers: The "Bounds of Advocacy" drafted by the American Academy of Matrimonial Lawyers contains the following provisions and commentary:

> 3.2 An attorney should never deceive or intentionally mislead opposing counsel.

Comment to Rule 3.2

> Attorneys are entitled to believe statements by opposing counsel. They should be able to assume that the matrimonial lawyer will correct any misimpression caused by an inaccurate or misleading prior statement by counsel or her client. Although an attorney must maintain the client's confidences, the duty of confidentiality does not require the attorney to deceive, or permit the client to deceive, opposing counsel. When the opposing party or counsel specifically requests information which the attorney is not required to provide and which the attorney has been instructed to withhold or which may be detrimental to the client's interests, the attorney should refuse to provide the information, but should not mislead opposing counsel.

> 3.3 An attorney should not induce or rely on a mistake by opposing counsel as to matters agreed upon to obtain an unfair benefit for the client.

Comment to Rule 3.3

> The need for trust between attorneys, even those representing opposing sides in a dispute, requires more than simply avoiding fraudulent and intentionally deceitful conduct. Misunderstandings should be corrected and not relied upon in the hope they will benefit the client. Thus, for example, the attorney reducing an oral agreement to writing not only should avoid misstating the understanding, but should correct inadvertent errors by opposing counsel that do not reflect prior un-

derstandings or agreements. Whether or not conduct or statements by opposing counsel that are not necessarily in her client's best interests should be corrected may not always be clear and will depend on the particular facts of a case. The crucial consideration should be whether the attorney induced the misunderstanding or is aware that opposing counsel's statements do not accurately reflect any prior agreement. It is thus unlikely that tactical, evidentiary or legal errors made by opposing counsel at trial require correction.

3.4 An attorney should not overstate his authority to settle nor represent that he has authority which he does not have.

Comment to Rule 3.4

In either case presented in the Standard, the attorney has improperly induced reliance by opposing counsel that could damage the attorney-client relationship. A matrimonial lawyer who is uncertain of his authority — or simply does not believe that opposing counsel is entitled to such information — should either truthfully disclose his uncertainty, or state that he is unwilling or unable to respond at all.

Rule 4.2 Communication with Person
Represented by Counsel

Editors' Note. At its 1995 Annual Meeting, the ABA House of Delegates voted to amend Rule 4.2. The amendment changed the word "party" to "person" in the text of the Rule and extensively revised the Comment to the Rule. For a legislative-style version of Rule 4.2 showing what was added and what was deleted by the 1995 amendment, see our 1996 edition. An excerpt from the ABA Committee Report explaining the 1995 amendment is reprinted in the Legislative History following the Rule.

In representing a client, a lawyer shall not communicate about the subject of the representation with a person the lawyer knows to be represented by another lawyer in the matter, unless the lawyer has the consent of the other lawyer or is authorized by law to do so.

COMMENT

[1] This Rule does not prohibit communication with a represented person, or an employee or agent of such a person, concerning matters outside the representation. For example, the existence of a controversy between a government agency and a private party, or between two organizations, does not prohibit a lawyer for either from communicating with

nonlawyer representatives of the other regarding a separate matter. Also, parties to a matter may communicate directly with each other and a lawyer having independent justification or legal authorization for communicating with a represented person is permitted to do so. Communications authorized by law include, for example, the right of a party to a controversy with a government agency to speak with government officials about the matter.

[2] Communications authorized by law also include constitutionally permissible investigative activities of lawyers representing governmental entities, directly or through investigative agents, prior to the commencement of criminal or civil enforcement proceedings, when there is applicable judicial precedent that either has found the activity permissible under this Rule or has found this Rule inapplicable. However, the Rule imposes ethical restrictions that go beyond those imposed by constitutional provisions.

[3] This Rule applies to communications with any person, whether or not a party to a formal adjudicative proceeding, contract or negotiation, who is represented by counsel concerning the matter to which the communication relates.

[4] In the case of an organization, this Rule prohibits communications by a lawyer for another person or entity concerning the matter in representation with persons having managerial responsibility on behalf of the organization, and with any other person whose act or omission in connection with that matter may be imputed to the organization for purposes of civil or criminal liability or whose statement may constitute an admission on the part of the organization. If an agent or employee of the organization is represented in the matter by his or her own counsel, the consent by that counsel to a communication will be sufficient for purposes of this Rule. Compare Rule 3.4(f).

[5] The prohibition on communications with a represented person only applies, however, in circumstances where the lawyer knows that the person is in fact represented in the matter to be discussed. This means that the lawyer has actual knowledge of the fact of the representation; but such actual knowledge may be inferred from the circumstances. See Terminology. Such an inference may arise in circumstances where there is substantial reason to believe that the person with whom communication is sought is represented in the matter to be discussed. Thus, a lawyer cannot evade the requirement of obtaining the consent of counsel by closing eyes to the obvious.

[6] In the event the person with whom the lawyer communicates is not known to be represented by counsel in the matter, the lawyer's communications are subject to Rule 4.3.

Model Code Comparison

This Rule is substantially identical to DR 7-104(A)(1) except for the substitution of the term "person" for "party."

Cross-References in Rules

Rule 3.4, Comment 4: "Paragraph (f) permits a lawyer to advise employees of a client to refrain from giving information to another party, for the employees may identify their interests with those of the client. See also **Rule 4.2.**"

Rule 3.9, Comment 3: "This Rule does not apply to representation of a client in a negotiation or other bilateral transaction with a governmental agency; representation in such a transaction is governed by **Rules 4.1 through 4.4.**"

Legislative History

1980 Discussion Draft (then Rule 3.2(b)(5)) provided that a lawyer shall not "interview or otherwise communicate with a party who the lawyer knows is represented by other counsel concerning the subject matter of the representation, except with the consent of that party's counsel or as authorized by law."

1981 Draft was substantially the same as adopted.

1982 Draft was adopted.

1994 Proposal (withdrawn): In May of 1994, the ABA's Standing Committee on Ethics and Professional Responsibility submitted a proposed amendment to Rule 4.2 that was intended to be considered at the ABA's August 1994 Annual Meeting. In June of 1994, however, after receiving some criticism of the proposal, the Standing Committee withdrew the proposal to circulate it for public comment.

The withdrawn 1994 proposal would have substituted the word "person" for "party" and would have added the phrase "or reasonably should know" to the text of the rule. Thus, underscoring proposed additions and striking over deletions, Rule 4.2 would have provided:

> In representing a client, a lawyer shall not communicate about the subject of the representation with a ~~party~~ person the lawyer knows or reasonably should know to be represented by another lawyer in the matter, unless the lawyer has the consent of the other lawyer or is authorized by law to do so.

A proposed addition to the Comment stated:

> Because of the interest in ensuring that persons have the assistance of counsel who represent them in a matter, a lawyer has an affirmative obligation to act as would a lawyer of reasonable prudence and competence to ascertain whether a person is represented in a matter before undertaking further communication on that matter with that person; and if the person is so represented, to communicate only as the Rule allows.

The Standing Committee's report in support of the proposed amendment explained:*

> The situation presented by the current language of the Rule permits a lawyer who believes or suspects that a person is represented in the matter by another lawyer to subvert the purpose and spirit of the Rule by avoiding learning whether that belief or suspicion is correct. The protection of represented persons the Rule is designed to foster, and the ability of those persons to receive counsel from their lawyers in dealings with counsel for other persons in the matter, would be enhanced by an amendment to Model Rule 4.2 requiring a lawyer contemplating communicating with other persons to act as a lawyer of reasonable prudence and competence would act under the circumstances and to *ascertain* whether the person with whom communication is sought is represented in the matter by another lawyer.
>
> The Standing Committee has also taken the occasion presented by this amendment to clarify the fact that the Rule protects represented persons whether or not they are, in a formal sense, actual or prospective "parties" to a proceeding or transaction. . . .

1995 Amendment: At the ABA's 1995 Annual Meeting, the House of Delegates voted to amend Rule 4.2 by changing the word "party" to "person" in Rule 4.2. (Unlike the withdrawn 1994 proposal, the 1995 proposal did not add the phrase "or reasonably should know" to the Rule.) The House of Delegates also added three new paragraphs to the Comment (paragraphs 2, 5, and 6) and revised the three existing paragraphs. The amendment was overwhelmingly approved on a voice vote, so no exact vote count was taken. For a legislative-style version of the Rule and Comment underscoring new material and striking out deleted material, see our 1996 edition.

The sole sponsor of the 1995 amendment was the ABA Standing Committee on Ethics and Professional Responsibility. The United States Department of Justice, which has its own rules on communications with represented parties and persons (reprinted in the Special Section at the end of our 1996 edition), officially opposed the amendment and spoke against it during the House of Delegates debate. The ABA Section on Criminal Justice voted against the amendment. The Standing Committee's report in support of the amendment was lengthy (about ten single-spaced pages). We reprint the most important portions of the report below (with all citations omitted).

*Excerpt from ABA Report Explaining 1995 Amendment**

[II] C.   SUBSTITUTION OF THE WORD "PERSON" for "PARTY"

In choosing whether "party" or "person" better describes the proper scope of the Rule, the Standing Committee has not sought to ascertain original intent or

---

*Committee reports do not represent official policy of the ABA. They are for information only, and the opinions are those of the authors of the report.

assess the relative precedential weight that should be assigned to the divided authority, but instead has addressed the question of what the meaning of the Rule *should* be, in light of the purposes the Rule is designed to serve.

In this light, it seems clear to the Committee that the appropriate operative term is "person," and not "party," for neither the need to protect uncounselled persons against being taken advantage of by opposing counsel nor the importance of preserving the client-attorney relationship is limited to those circumstances where the represented person is a party to an adjudicative or other formal proceeding. The interests sought to be protected by the Rule may equally well be involved when litigation is merely under consideration, even though it has not actually been instituted, and the persons who are potentially parties to the litigation have retained counsel with respect to the matter in dispute.

Concerns regarding the need to protect uncounselled persons against the wiles of opposing counsel and preserving the attorney-client relationship may also be involved where a person is a target of a criminal investigation, knows this, and has retained counsel to advise him with respect to the investigation. The same concerns may be involved where a "third-party" witness furnishes testimony in an investigation or proceeding and, even though not a formal party, has seen fit to retain counsel to advise him with respect thereto. Such concerns are equally applicable in a non-adjudicatory context, such as a commercial transaction involving a sale, a lease or some other form of contract.

    D.   PRE-INDICTMENT, NON-CUSTODIAL
          INVESTIGATIVE CONTACTS WITH
          CRIMINAL SUSPECTS

The purposes served by Rule 4.2's prohibition on communications with represented persons clearly apply with equal force in the context of pre-indictment non-custodial contacts with criminal suspects. The Standing Committee recognizes, however, that as discussed above there is case law that has sought to accommodate the needs of law enforcement by limiting the application of the anti-contact rule in this context. In the Standing Committee's view, any limitation on the Rule can be justified only if it comes within the provision for communications "authorized by law." The Committee has also concluded that, in circumstances where applicable judicial precedent has approved such investigative contacts in pre-indictment, non-custodial circumstances, and they are not prohibited by any provision of the United States Constitution or the constitution of a pertinent state, they should be considered to be authorized by law within the meaning of the Rule. The proposed new Comment [2] is intended to make this clear. That Comment also makes clear that the fact that particular communications are constitutionally permissible does not necessarily mean that they are also consistent with the Rule, for the Rule imposes ethical restrictions that go beyond those imposed by constitutional provisions.

    E.   OBJECTIONS TO THE PROPOSED CHANGE IN
          THE RULE

It has been objected [i] that the proposed change in the Rule to substitute "person" for "party" would "potentially prohibit government attorneys from ever authorizing any undercover contact with anyone who is represented by counsel''; [ii] that the change "would make it possible for anyone with means to keep an attorney on retainer in order to be insulated from undercover investigations as well as any direct questioning from law enforcement officials;'' [iii] that "[i]t could allow corporate counsel to prevent any meaningful contact with employees during the investigative phase of a criminal or civil enforcement case;'' and [iv] that it "could severely limit the ability of government attorneys and agents to communicate freely and efficiently with non-party fact witnesses.'' Letter, November 1, 1994 from Deputy Attorney General Jamie Gorelick to Margaret C. Love, Chair of the ABA Standing Committee on Ethics and Professional Responsibility.

The first of these objections is addressed immediately above. The next two objections also rest on the assumption of a much broader sweep to the Rule than is realistically to be anticipated. The Rule now applies, and as amended would continue to apply, only where the person to be contacted is known to be represented with respect to the particular matter that is the subject of the prospective communication. The fact that a particular entity or person has retained a lawyer for one matter does not mean that the representation extends to any other matter; and even a general representation for all purposes, such as might be asserted by inside counsel for a corporation, does not, for purposes of the Rule, necessarily imply a representation with respect to a matter that has not in fact been brought to the attention of such counsel. As to the fourth objection, the Standing Committee does not believe that the Rule does or will significantly limit legitimate access of lawyers, whether prosecutors or private counsel, to witnesses.

III. The Proposed Change to Clarify That an Attorney's Knowledge Regarding Representation May Be Inferred from the Circumstances

A. DESCRIPTION OF THE CHANGE

The Rule as it now stands provides that a lawyer may not communicate with an individual the lawyer "knows" is represented by counsel. . . . The proposed amendment to the Comment would draw attention to the fact that actual knowledge of the representation can be inferred from the circumstances by making clear that an attorney may not ignore circumstances that obviously indicate an individual is represented by counsel in the matter to be discussed. . . .

C. REASONS FOR THE PROPOSED CHANGE

It would not . . . be reasonable to require a lawyer in all circumstances where the lawyer wishes to speak to a third person in the course of his representation of a client first to inquire whether the person is represented by counsel: among other things, such a routine inquiry would unnecessarily complicate perfectly routine fact-finding, and might well unnecessarily obstruct such fact-finding by conveying a suggestion that there was a need for counsel in circumstances where there was none, and thus discouraging witnesses from talking. In consequence, the Rule's requirement of securing permission of counsel is reasonably limited to those circumstances where the inquiring lawyer *knows* that the person to whom he wants to speak is represented by counsel with respect to the subject of the communication.

However, a lawyer should not be able to ignore the obvious and then claim lack of certain knowledge, thus excusing a failure to secure consent of counsel whose likely involvement should have been obvious. The definition of "knows" makes clear that actual knowledge may be inferred from circumstances; and the penultimate paragraph proposed to be added to the Comment is intended to make clear that this means that a lawyer may not avoid Rule 4.2 by closing eyes to what is plainly to be seen.

The proposed final paragraph of the Comment points out that if a lawyer does not know that a person with whom he or she wishes to communicate is represented by counsel, then the lawyer must assume that he or she is dealing with an unrepresented person, and so subject to the restrictions of Rule 4.3. . . . The point is an important one, for lawyers who in good faith believe that in a particular instance they are dealing with an unrepresented person, and so need not secure prior consent of counsel before conversing with that person, must then assume that they are subject to Rule 4.3, which requires reasonable assurance that the person with whom they are communicating does not misunderstand the role the lawyer is playing in the matter.

Selected State Variations

Alaska restricts communication with a "person or party."

California: See Rule 2-100 (Communication with a Represented Party).

District of Columbia: D.C. Rule 4.2 differs significantly from the ABA Model Rule — see District of Columbia Rules of Professional Conduct below.

Florida: As amended effective January 1, 1992, Florida's version of Rule 4.2 generally tracks Model Rule 4.2 but adds:

[A]n attorney may, without such prior consent, communicate with another's client in order to meet the requirements of any statute or contract requiring notice or service of process directly on an adverse party, in which event the communication shall be strictly restricted to that required by statute or contract, and a copy shall be provided to the adverse party's attorney.

Illinois provides that a lawyer shall not communicate "or cause another to communicate" with a represented party.

Louisiana adds "A lawyer shall not effect the prohibited communication through a third person, including the lawyer's client."

Minnesota adds a second sentence to Rule 4.2 that provides:

A party who is a lawyer may communicate directly with another party unless expressly instructed to avoid communication by the lawyer for the other party, or unless the other party manifests a desire to communicate only through counsel.

New Mexico adds the following sentence to Rule 4.2: "Except for persons having a managerial responsibility on behalf of the organization, an attorney is not prohibited from communicating directly with employees of a corporation, partnership or other entity about the subject matter of the representation even though the corporation, partnership or entity itself is represented by counsel.''

New Jersey: The New Jersey Supreme Court has adopted an ''interim'' interpretation of Rule 4.2, pending further study. In re Opinion 668, 134 N.J. 294, 633 A.2d 959 (1993). Under the interim interpretation, a lawyer may not contact former and current members of an opposing corporation's control group. After indictment or filing of a civil complaint, a lawyer must give notice to the organization's lawyer before contacting other employees of the entity whose conduct might be the basis for the entity's civil or criminal liability.

New York: Same or substantially the same as the ABA Model Code — see Model Code Comparison above. However, the Association of the Bar of New York City has proposed adding the following exception, which is currently circulating among the New York bench and bar for comments and suggestions: ''. . . except that — unless such consent is explicitly withheld in writing — a lawyer in a civil matter may presume consent to cause the lawyer's client to communicate with another represented party to discuss, but not consummate, resolution of any unsettled issues.''

Oregon: DR 7-104(A)(1), as amended effective December 17, 1991, prohibits a lawyer from communicating with a represented party on the subject of the representation ''or on directly related subjects,'' but DR 7-104(A)(1)(c) makes an exception if ''a written agreement requires a written notice or demand to be sent to such other person, in which case a copy of such notice or demand shall also be sent to such other person's lawyer.'' Oregon further provides that the prohibition in DR 7-104(A)(1) ''includes a lawyer representing the lawyer's own interests.''

Texas Rule 4.02 provides:

> (a) In representing a client, a lawyer shall not communicate or cause or encourage another to communicate about the subject of the representation with a person, organization or entity of government the lawyer knows to be represented by another lawyer regarding that subject, unless the lawyer has the consent of the other lawyer or is authorized by law to do so.
>
> (b) In representing a client a lawyer shall not communicate or cause another to communicate about the subject of representation with a person or organization a lawyer knows to be employed or retained for the purpose of conferring with or advising another lawyer about the subject of the representation, unless the lawyer has the consent of the other lawyer or is authorized by law to do so.
>
> (c) For the purpose of this rule, ''organization or entity of government'' includes: (1) those persons presently having a managerial responsibility with an organization or entity of government that relates to the subject of the representation, or (2) those persons presently employed by such organization or entity and whose act or omission in connection with the subject of representation may make the organization or entity of government vicariously liable for such act or omission.
>
> (d) When a person, organization, or entity of government that is represented by a lawyer in a matter seeks advice regarding that matter from another law-

yer, the second lawyer is not prohibited by paragraph (a) from giving such advice without notifying or seeking consent of the first lawyer.

Virginia: Substantially the same as the Model Code.

Related Materials

ABA Canons: Canon 9 provided:

9. Negotiations with Opposite Party

A lawyer should not in any way communicate upon the subject of controversy with a party represented by counsel; much less should he undertake to negotiate or compromise the matter with him, but should deal only with his counsel.

ABA Standards for Criminal Justice: See Prosecution Function Standard 3-4.1(b).

ABA Standards for Imposing Lawyer Sanctions:

6.3. Improper Communications with Individuals in the Legal System

6.31. Disbarment is generally appropriate when a lawyer:

(a) intentionally tampers with a witness and causes serious or potentially serious injury to a party, or causes significant or potentially significant interference with the outcome of the legal proceeding; or . . .

(c) improperly communicates with someone in the legal system other than a witness, judge, or juror with the intent to influence or affect the outcome of the proceeding, and causes significant or potentially significant interference with the outcome of the legal proceeding.

6.32. Suspension is generally appropriate when a lawyer engages in communication with an individual in the legal system when the lawyer knows that such communication is improper, and causes injury or potential injury to a party or causes interference or potential interference with the outcome of the legal proceeding.

6.33. Reprimand is generally appropriate when a lawyer is negligent in determining whether it is proper to engage in communication with an individual in the legal system, and causes injury or potential injury to a party or interference or potential interference with the outcome of the legal proceeding.

American Lawyer's Code of Conduct: Rule 3.9 provides: "[A] lawyer may send a written offer of settlement directly to an adverse party, seven days or more after that party's attorney has received the same offer of settlement in writing."

Department of Justice "Thornburgh Memorandum" and "Reno Rules": In 1989, U.S. Attorney General Richard Thornburgh issued a memorandum stating that until an indictment Rule 4.2 did not apply to Department of Justice employees and their agents and investigators. Thornburgh argued that (1) the Supremacy

Clause prohibited state ethics rules from controlling federal employees, and (2) federal undercover investigations, including undercover contacts with suspects or unindicted grand jury targets represented by counsel, were "authorized by law" within the meaning of Rule 4.2. In 1991, however, a federal court held that the "Thornburgh Memorandum" did not have the force of law and dismissed an indictment because a prosecutor had contacted a defendant represented by counsel without being "authorized by law." United States v. Lopez, 765 F. Supp. 1433 (N.D. Cal. 1991), vacated on other grounds, 989 F.2d 1032 (9th Cir. 1993). The Bush administration sought to remedy the problem by publishing the Thornburgh Memorandum in the Federal Register on November 20, 1992, so that it would, after an appropriate period for public comment, attain the force of law. However, the proposal did not become law before the inauguration of President Clinton, and the Clinton administration withdrew the proposal on January 22, 1993, two days after taking office.

On July 26, 1993, under Attorney General Janet Reno, the Department of Justice republished the Thornburgh memorandum with only minor changes for 30 days of public comment on both the text of the proposal and on comments previously received in response to the November 1992 publication. (See 58 Fed. Reg. 39976.) Criticism was again harsh. On March 3, 1994, the Department of Justice circulated a third revised rule for public comment. (See 59 Fed. Reg. 10086.) Finally, on August 4, 1994 (effective September 6, 1994), the Department of Justice issued a "final rule" on the subject, sometimes called the "Reno rules." (See 59 Fed. Reg. 39910, codified at 28 C.F.R. Part 77.) The final rule is expressly intended "to preempt the entire field of rules concerning" contacts by government attorneys with represented parties. (We reprint the full text of the "Reno rules" in our Special Section at the end of the 1996 edition.)

The final rule distinguishes between a "represented person" and a "represented party." A "represented party" is someone who (1) has a lawyer, and (2) the representation "is ongoing and concerns the subject matter in question," and (3) the person "has been arrested or charged in a federal criminal case or is a defendant in a civil law enforcement proceeding concerning the subject matter of the representation." A "represented person" is someone who satisfies the first two criteria but not the third (i.e., the person has a lawyer concerning the subject matter but has not been criminally charged or named as a civil defendant). The final rule provides that federal prosecutors and other federal lawyers are "authorized by law," within the meaning of Rule 4.2, to communicate with represented parties or persons whenever the communication is:

- To determine if the person is represened by counsel;
- Pursuant to discovery rules or other judicial or administrative process;
- Initiated by the represented party, provided that a court finds that the party has given voluntary, knowing, and informed consent to the direct communication;
- Made at the time of arrest pursuant to a knowing and voluntary consent by the represented party after the represented party has received *Miranda* warnings;

- Made in the course of an overt or covert investigation into additional, different, or ongoing criminal activity or other unlawful conduct;
- Made on the basis of a good faith belief by the federal lawyer that the communication is necessary to protect any person from the risk of injury or death.

Moreover, as to represented persons, except as "otherwise provided" in the final rule, a federal lawyer "may communicate, or cause another to communicate, with a represented person in the process of conducting an investigation, including, but not limited to, an undercover investigation."

However, a federal lawyer may not engage in any communication with a represented party or person that would be prohibited by the Sixth Amendment right to counsel or any other Constitutional provision, or by any federal statute or procedural rule. Nor may a federal lawyer negotiate a plea agreement, settlement, or immunity agreement, or dispose of criminal charges or civil enforcement claims, or negotiate sentences or penalties, unless the communication was initiated by the represented party or person or unless the party or person's attorney consents.

Finally, even when the final rule permits communications with a represented party, the federal attorney ordinarily may not (1) inquire about lawful defense strategy or legal arguments of counsel, or (2) disparage counsel for a represented person or party or "otherwise seek to induce the person to forego representation or to disregard the advice of the person's attorney," or (3) "[o]therwise improperly seek to disrupt the relationship between the represented person or represented party and counsel." But even these three prohibitions may be overridden if a high-ranking Department of Justice official or a United States Attorney finds "substantial likelihood" of a "significant conflict of interest between a represented party or person and his or her attorney," and it is "not feasible to obtain a judicial order challenging the representation." And an undercover agent or cooperating witness may attend lawful attorney-client meetings at the request of a represented party or person, or defense counsel, or someone associated with the defense, "when reasonably necessary to protect the safety of the agent or witness or the confidentiality of an undercover operation" — but the agent or witness attending the meetings may not communicate "lawful defense strategy or trial preparation" to the federal lawyers or agents participating in the investigation or prosecution.

When the represented person or party is an organization, the rule restricts contact only with a "controlling individual" of the organization, defined as "a current high level employee who is known by the government to be participating as a decision maker in the determination of the organization's legal position in the proceeding or investigation of the subject matter."

Federal Rules of Civil Procedure: Rule 5(b) provides: "Whenever under these rules service is required or permitted to be made upon a party represented by an attorney the service shall be made upon the attorney unless service on the party is ordered by the court."

Model Rules of Professional Conduct for Federal Lawyers: Rule 4.2 provides as follows:

>   (a) In representing a client, a Federal lawyer shall not communicate about the subject of the representation with a party the lawyer knows to be represented by another lawyer in the matter, unless the Federal lawyer has the consent of the other lawyer; [or] in a criminal matter, the individual initiates the communication with the Government lawyer and voluntarily and knowingly waives the right to counsel for the purposes of that communication; or the Federal lawyer otherwise is authorized by law to do so.
>
>   (b) This Rule does not prohibit communications by a Non-Government lawyer with Federal Agency officials who have the authority to resolve a matter affecting the lawyer's client, whether or not the lawyer's communications relate to matters that are the subject of the representation, provided that the lawyer discloses the lawyer's identity; the fact that the lawyer represents a client in a matter involving the official's Federal Agency; and that the matter is being handled for the Federal Agency by a Government lawyer.

The Comment explains:

>   In a criminal case there may be times when communications between a defendant and a Federal Agency without notice to defense counsel is in the interest of the defendant. Some communications will serve to protect the defendant and to identify sham representations. For example, in certain criminal enterprises, such as organized crime or drug rings, a defendant may wish to cooperate with a Federal Agency, but the counsel may also be the counsel of others involved in the enterprise. To insure that in such instances there is no abuse, this rule would permit communications by the defendant with the Government lawyer, as long as the defendant voluntarily and knowingly waives the right to counsel.

Restatement of the Law Governing Lawyers: The American Law Institute has proposed but not yet approved the following provisions:

§158. *Represented Non-Client — General Anti-Contact Rule*

>   (1) A lawyer representing a client in a matter may not communicate about the subject of the representation with a non-client whom the lawyer knows to be represented in the matter by another lawyer, or with a representative of an organizational non-client so represented as defined in §159, unless:
>
>   (a) the communication is with a public officer or agency to the extent stated in §161;
>   (b) the lawyer is a party and represents no other client in the matter;
>   (c) the communication is authorized by law;
>   (d) the communication reasonably responds to an emergency; or
>   (e) the other lawyer consents.
>
>   (2) Subsection (1) does not prohibit the lawyer from assisting the client in otherwise proper communication by the lawyer's client with a represented non-client, unless the lawyer thereby seeks to deceive or overreach the non-client.

§159. Definition of Represented Non-Client

Within the meaning of §158, a represented non-client includes:
(1) a natural person represented by a lawyer; and
(2) a representative of an organization represented by a lawyer:
(a) who supervises, directs or regularly consults with the lawyer concerning the matter or who has power to compromise or settle the matter;
(b) whose acts or omissions may be imputed to the organization for purposes of civil or criminal liability in the matter; or
(c) whose statements, under applicable rules of evidence, would have the effect of binding the organization with respect to proof of the matter.

§161. Represented Governmental Agency or Officer

Unless otherwise provided by law and except when a represented governmental agency or officer is engaged in litigation of a specific claim that does not involve broad public policy issues, the rule stated in §158 does not apply to communications with the agency or the officer in the officer's official capacity. In specific-claim litigation, contact is permissible so long as it does not create an opportunity for substantially unfair advantage against the governmental party.

§162. Information of Non-Client Known to Be Legally Protected

A lawyer representing a client in a matter and communicating with a non-client in a situation permitted under §158 may not seek to obtain information that the lawyer reasonably should know the non-client may not reveal without violating a duty of confidentiality to another imposed by law.

Rule 4.3 Dealing with Unrepresented Person

In dealing on behalf of a client with a person who is not represented by counsel, a lawyer shall not state or imply that the lawyer is disinterested. When the lawyer knows or reasonably should know that the unrepresented person misunderstands the lawyer's role in the matter, the lawyer shall make reasonable efforts to correct the misunderstanding.

COMMENT

An unrepresented person, particularly one not experienced in dealing with legal matters, might assume that a lawyer is disinterested in loyalties or is a disinterested authority on the law even when the lawyer represents a client. During the course of a lawyer's representation of a client, the lawyer should not give advice to an unrepresented person other than the advice to obtain counsel.

Model Code Comparison

There was no direct counterpart to this Rule in the Model Code. DR 7-104(A)(2) provided that a lawyer shall not "[g]ive advice to a person who is not represented by a lawyer, other than the advice to secure counsel. . . ."

Cross-References in Rules

Rule 3.9, Comment 3: "This Rule does not apply to representation of a client in a negotiation or other bilateral transaction with a governmental agency; representation in such a transaction is governed by **Rules 4.1 through 4.4.**"

Legislative History

1980 Discussion Draft (then Rule 3.6) provided as follows:

Appearing Against an Unrepresented Party

When an opposing party is unrepresented, a lawyer shall refrain from unfairly exploiting that party's ignorance of the law or the practices of the tribunal.

1981 Draft was substantially the same as adopted.
1982 Draft was adopted.

Selected State Variations

California: No comparable provision.
Colorado adds to Rule 4.3 the following sentence taken from the old ABA Model Code: "The lawyer shall not give advice to the unrepresented person other than to secure counsel."
District of Columbia: D.C. Rule 4.3 differs significantly from the ABA Model Rule — see District of Columbia Rules of Professional Conduct below.
Louisiana: Rule 4.3 provides:

A lawyer shall assume that an unrepresented person does not understand the lawyer's role in a matter and the lawyer shall carefully explain to the unrepresented person the lawyer's role in the matter.

During the course of a lawyer's representation of a client, the lawyer should not give advice to a non-represented person other than the advice to obtain counsel.

New York: Same or substantially the same as the ABA Model Code — see Model Code Comparison above.

Pennsylvania adds the text of DR 7-104(A)(2) to Rule 4.3.

Related Materials

ABA Canons: Canon 9 provided:

9. Negotiations with Opposite Party

It is incumbent upon the lawyer most particularly to avoid everything that may tend to mislead a party not represented by counsel, and he should not undertake to advise him as to the law.

ABA Standards for Criminal Justice: Prosecution Function Standards 3-3.2(b) and 3-3.10(c).

American Academy of Matrimonial Lawyers: The "Bounds of Advocacy" drafted by the American Academy of Matrimonial Lawyers contains the following provision and commentary:

2.21 An attorney should not advise an unrepresented party.

Comment to Rule 2.21

Once it becomes apparent that an opposing party intends to proceed without a lawyer, the attorney should, at the earliest opportunity, inform the opposing party in writing as follows:

1. I am your spouse's lawyer.
2. I do not and will not represent you.
3. I will at all times look out for your spouse's interests, not yours.
4. Any statements I make to you about this case should be taken by you as negotiation or argument on behalf of your spouse and not as advice to you as to your best interest.
5. I urge you to obtain your own lawyer.

Rule 4.4 Respect for Rights of Third Persons

In representing a client, a lawyer shall not use means that have no substantial purpose other than to embarrass, delay, or burden a third person, or use methods of obtaining evidence that violate the legal rights of such a person.

COMMENT

Responsibility to a client requires a lawyer to subordinate the interests of others to those of the client, but that responsibility does not imply that a lawyer may disregard the rights of third persons. It is impractical to catalogue all such rights, but they include legal restrictions on methods of obtaining evidence from third persons.

Model Code Comparison

DR 7-106(C)(2) provided that a lawyer shall not "[a]sk any question that he has no reasonable basis to believe is relevant to the case and that is intended to degrade a witness or other person." DR 7-102(A)(1) provided that a lawyer shall not "take . . . action on behalf of his client when he knows or when it is obvious that such action would serve merely to harass or maliciously injure another." DR 7-108(D) provided that "[a]fter discharge of the jury . . . the lawyer shall not ask questions or make comments to a member of that jury that are calculated merely to harass or embarrass the juror. . . ." DR 7-108(E) provided that a lawyer "shall not conduct . . . a vexatious or harassing investigation of either a venireman or a juror."

Cross-References in Rules

Rule 3.9, Comment 3: "This Rule does not apply to representation of a client in a negotiation or other bilateral transaction with a governmental agency; representation in such a transaction is governed by **Rules** 4.1 through **4.4**."

Legislative History

1980 Discussion Draft (then Rule 3.4) provided as follows:

(a) In preparing and presenting a cause, a lawyer shall respect the interests of third persons, including witnesses, jurors, and persons incidentally concerned with the proceeding. . . .

1981 and 1982 Drafts were the same as adopted.

Selected State Variations

California: See Rule 3-200(A) (Prohibited Objectives of Employment); Rule 5-100 (Threatening Criminal, Administrative, or Disciplinary Charges); Rule

5-310(B) (Prohibited Contact with Witnesses); B & P Code §§6068(c), 6068(f), 6068(g), and 6128(b).

New York: Same or substantially the same as the ABA Model Code — see Model Code Comparison above.

Texas Rule 4.04(b) forbids lawyers to present or threaten disciplinary or criminal charges "solely to gain an advantage in a civil matter" or civil, criminal, or disciplinary charges "solely" to prevent participation by a complainant or witness in a disciplinary matter.

Virginia: Substantially the same as the Model Code.

Related Materials

ABA Canons: Canon 18 provided:

18. Treatment of Witnesses and Litigants

A lawyer should always treat adverse witnesses and suitors with fairness and due consideration, and he should never minister to the malevolence or prejudices of a client in the trial or conduct of a cause. The client cannot be made the keeper of the lawyer's conscience in professional matters. He has no right to demand that his counsel shall abuse the opposite party or indulge in offensive personalities. Improper speech is not excusable on the ground that it is what the client would say if speaking in his own behalf.

ABA Standards for Criminal Justice: See Prosecution Function Standards 3-2.9(b), 3-3.1(c), and 3-5.7(a); Defense Function Standards 4-1.2(b) and (d), 4-4.2, 4-7.1(e), and 4-7.6(a).

Restatement of the Law Governing Lawyers: The American Law Institute has tentatively approved §151 (reprinted in the Related Materials following Rule 1.2), and has proposed but not yet approved §166, which provides as follows:

§166. Dealing with Other Participants in Proceedings

In representing a client in a matter before a tribunal, a lawyer may not use means that have no substantial purpose other than to embarrass, delay, or burden a third person, or use methods of obtaining evidence that are prohibited by law.

ARTICLE 5. LAW FIRMS AND ASSOCIATIONS

Editors' Note. In the 1980 Discussion Draft, the Article entitled "Law Firms and Associations" (then beginning with Rule 7.1) had the following Introduction:

A majority of American lawyers practice in law firms or the law departments of government or private organizations. In the legal and ethical rules governing lawyers' conduct, a law firm or law department generally is treated as though it were a single practitioner. Thus, the rules prohibiting representation of opposing parties in litigation or suing one's own client apply not only to a single practitioner but also to a law firm or law department. So also, the rule that prohibits a lawyer from revealing the confidences of a client requires that all lawyers in a firm refrain from revealing confidences of a client served by any lawyer in the firm. However, a law firm or organization is in fact comprised of individual lawyers who work in association with each other. In certain circumstances, that fact is significant for purposes of professional ethics. These circumstances include the question of vicarious disqualification of lawyers in law firms and legal departments, a supervising lawyer's responsibility for ethical misconduct by a subordinate lawyer, and a subordinate lawyer's responsibility for misconduct committed at the direction of a supervisor. . . .

Rule 5.1 Responsibilities of a Partner or Supervisory Lawyer

(a) A partner in a law firm shall make reasonable efforts to ensure that the firm has in effect measures giving reasonable assurance that all lawyers in the firm conform to the rules of professional conduct.

(b) A lawyer having direct supervisory authority over another lawyer shall make reasonable efforts to ensure that the other lawyer conforms to the rules of professional conduct.

(c) A lawyer shall be responsible for another lawyer's violation of the rules of professional conduct if:

(1) the lawyer orders or, with knowledge of the specific conduct, ratifies the conduct involved; or

(2) the lawyer is a partner in the law firm in which the other lawyer practices, or has direct supervisory authority over the other lawyer, and knows of the conduct at a time when its consequences can be avoided or mitigated but fails to take reasonable remedial action.

COMMENT

[1] Paragraphs (a) and (b) refer to lawyers who have supervisory authority over the professional work of a firm or legal department of a government agency. This includes members of a partnership and the shareholders in a law firm organized as a professional corporation; lawyers having supervisory authority in the law department of an enterprise or government agency; and lawyers who have intermediate managerial responsibilities in a firm.

[2] The measures required to fulfill the responsibility prescribed in paragraphs (a) and (b) can depend on the firm's structure and the nature of its practice. In a small firm, informal supervision and occasional admonition ordinarily might be sufficient. In a large firm, or in practice situations in which intensely difficult ethical problems frequently arise, more elaborate procedures may be necessary. Some firms, for example, have a procedure whereby junior lawyers can make confidential referral of ethical problems directly to a designated senior partner or special committee. See Rule 5.2. Firms, whether large or small, may also rely on continuing legal education in professional ethics. In any event, the ethical atmosphere of a firm can influence the conduct of all its members and a lawyer having authority over the work of another may not assume that the subordinate lawyer will inevitably conform to the Rules.

[3] Paragraph (c)(1) expresses a general principle of responsibility for acts of another. See also Rule 8.4(a).

[4] Paragraph (c)(2) defines the duty of a lawyer having direct supervisory authority over performance of specific legal work by another lawyer. Whether a lawyer has such supervisory authority in particular circumstances is a question of fact. Partners of a private firm have at least indirect responsibility for all work being done by the firm, while a partner in charge of a particular matter ordinarily has direct authority over other firm lawyers engaged in the matter. Appropriate remedial action by a partner would depend on the immediacy of the partner's involvement and the seriousness of the misconduct. The supervisor is required to intervene to prevent avoidable consequences of misconduct if the supervisor knows that the misconduct occurred. Thus, if a supervising lawyer knows that a subordinate misrepresented a matter to an opposing party in negotiation, the supervisor as well as the subordinate has a duty to correct the resulting misapprehension.

[5] Professional misconduct by a lawyer under supervision could reveal a violation of paragraph (b) on the part of the supervisory lawyer even though it does not entail a violation of paragraph (c) because there was no direction, ratification or knowledge of the violation.

[6] Apart from this Rule and Rule 8.4(a), a lawyer does not have disciplinary liability for the conduct of a partner, associate or subordinate. Whether a lawyer may be liable civilly or criminally for another lawyer's conduct is a question of law beyond the scope of these Rules.

Model Code Comparison

There was no direct counterpart to this Rule in the Model Code. DR 1-103(A) provided that a lawyer "possessing unprivileged knowledge of a violation of DR 1-102 shall report such knowledge to . . . authority empowered to investigate or act upon such violation.''

Cross-References in Rules

Rule 1.5, Comment 4: For purposes of sharing fees under Rule 1.5(e): "Joint responsibility for the representation entails the obligations stated in **Rule 5.1** for purposes of the matter involved.''

Legislative History

1980 Discussion Draft of Rule 5.1 (then Rule 7.2) provided as follows:

Responsibilities of a Supervisory Lawyer

(a) A lawyer having supervisory authority over another lawyer shall make a reasonable effort to see that the conduct of the lawyer under supervision conforms to the Rules of Professional Conduct.

(b) A lawyer is chargeable with another lawyer's violation of the Rules of Professional Conduct if:

(1) the lawyer orders or ratifies the conduct involved; or

(2) the lawyer has supervisory responsibility over the other lawyer and has knowledge of the conduct at a time when its consequences can be avoided or mitigated but fails to take appropriate remedial action.

1981 Draft was substantially the same as adopted, except that Rule 5.2(a) applied to "all lawyers in the firm, *including other partners. . . .*''

1982 Draft was adopted.

Selected State Variations

California: See Rule 1-100(B) (defining "law firm" and "associate").

Georgia: EC 1-7 and EC 1-8 track Rule 5.1(a) and (b) respectively. Standard 71 is in accord.

Illinois provides that "[e]ach" partner or lawyer shall make the reasonable efforts specified in Rule 5.1(a) and (b).

New Jersey begins Rule 5.1(a) with: "Every law firm and organization authorized by the Court Rules to practice law in this jurisdiction . . .'' instead of "A partner in a law firm.'' Rule 5.1(c)(2) applies only to lawyers having "direct supervisory authority"; it deletes the phrase "is a partner in the law firm in which the other lawyer practices.''

New York: Amendment partially adopts language from Rule 5.1. See EC 1-8 and DR 1-104 of the New York Code. See DR 1-104 and EC 1-8 for partial adoption of the language of Rule 5.1. In addition, New York has adopted a rule imposing professional responsibilities on law firms as such. See DR 1-102 and DR 1-104. DR 5-105(E) imposes on law firms a duty to keep records and "have a policy implementing a system" that will assist lawyers in complying with DR 5-105(D). Failure to maintain such a system is an independent violation of the New York Code. See the New York materials.

Texas has no equivalent to Rule 5.1(a) and (b).

Virginia omits Rule 5.1.

Related Materials

Model Rules of Professional Conduct for Federal Lawyers add the following new subparagraphs to Rule 5.1:

(c) A Federal lawyer, who is a supervisory lawyer, is responsible for ensuring that the subordinate lawyer is properly trained and is competent to perform the duties to which the subordinate lawyer is assigned.

(d) A Government lawyer, who is a supervisory lawyer, should encourage subordinate lawyers to participate in pro bono publico service activities and the activities of bar associations and law reform organizations.

Partnership Law: Model Rule 5.1 roughly parallels the financial liability of general partners for the acts of others in the partnership. Section 13 of the Uniform Partnership Act, which has been adopted in nearly every state, provides:

§13 Partnership Bound by Partner's Wrongful Act

Where, by any wrongful act or omission of any partner acting in the ordinary course of the business of the partnership or with the authority of his co-partners, loss or injury is caused to any person, not being a partner in the partnership, or any penalty is incurred, the partnership is liable therefor to the same extent as the partner so acting or omitting to act.

Restatement of the Law Governing Lawyers: The American Law Institute has tentatively approved §79, reprinted in the Related Materials following Rule 1.1, to govern vicarious liability within law firms.

Rule 5.2 Responsibilities of a Subordinate Lawyer

(a) A lawyer is bound by the rules of professional conduct notwithstanding that the lawyer acted at the direction of another person.

(b) A subordinate lawyer does not violate the rules of professional conduct if that lawyer acts in accordance with a supervisory lawyer's reasonable resolution of an arguable question of professional duty.

COMMENT

[1] Although a lawyer is not relieved of responsibility for a violation by the fact that the lawyer acted at the direction of a supervisor, that fact may be relevant in determining whether a lawyer had the knowledge required to render conduct a violation of the Rules. For example, if a subordinate filed a frivolous pleading at the direction of a supervisor, the subordinate would not be guilty of a professional violation unless the subordinate knew of the document's frivolous character.

[2] When lawyers in a supervisor-subordinate relationship encounter a matter involving professional judgment as to ethical duty, the supervisor may assume responsibility for making the judgment. Otherwise a consistent course of action or position could not be taken. If the question can reasonably be answered only one way, the duty of both lawyers is clear and they are equally responsible for fulfilling it. However, if the question is reasonably arguable, someone has to decide upon the course of action. That authority ordinarily reposes in the supervisor, and a subordinate may be guided accordingly. For example, if a question arises whether the interests of two clients conflict under Rule 1.7, the supervisor's reasonable resolution of the question should protect the subordinate professionally if the resolution is subsequently challenged.

Model Code Comparison

There was no counterpart to this Rule in the Model Code.

Cross-References in Rules

Rule 5.1, Comment 2: "Some firms . . . have a procedure whereby junior lawyers can make confidential referral of ethical problems directly to a designated senior partner or special committee. See **Rule 5.2**."

Legislative History

1980 Discussion Draft (then Rule 7.3) provided as follows:

(a) A lawyer acting under the supervisory authority of another person is bound by the Rules of Professional Conduct notwithstanding the fact that the lawyer's conduct was ordered by the supervisor.

1981 Draft was substantially the same as adopted.
1982 Draft was adopted.

Selected State Variations

California: No comparable provision.
Georgia: Standard 72 is in accord with Rule 5.2(a).
New York: No comparable provision.
Virginia omits Rule 5.2.

Rule 5.3 Responsibilities Regarding Nonlawyer Assistants

With respect to a nonlawyer employed or retained by or associated with a lawyer:

(a) a partner in a law firm shall make reasonable efforts to ensure that the firm has in effect measures giving reasonable assurance that the person's conduct is compatible with the professional obligations of the lawyer;

(b) a lawyer having direct supervisory authority over the nonlawyer shall make reasonable efforts to ensure that the person's conduct is compatible with the professional obligations of the lawyer; and

(c) a lawyer shall be responsible for conduct of such a person that would be a violation of the rules of professional conduct if engaged in by a lawyer if:

(1) the lawyer orders or, with the knowledge of the specific conduct, ratifies the conduct involved; or

(2) the lawyer is a partner in the law firm in which the person is employed, or has direct supervisory authority over the person, and knows of the conduct at a time when its consequences can be avoided or mitigated but fails to take reasonable remedial action.

COMMENT

Lawyers generally employ assistants in their practice, including secretaries, investigators, law student interns, and paraprofessionals. Such assistants, whether employees or independent contractors, act for the lawyer in rendition of the lawyer's professional services. A lawyer should give such assistants appropriate instruction and supervision concerning the ethical aspects of their employment, particularly regarding the obligation not to disclose information relating to representation of the client, and should be responsible for their work product. The measures employed in supervising nonlawyers should take account of the fact that they do not have legal training and are not subject to professional discipline.

Model Code Comparison

There was no direct counterpart to this Rule in the Model Code. DR 4-101(D) provided that a lawyer "shall exercise reasonable care to prevent his employees, associates, and others whose services are utilized by him from disclosing or using confidences or secrets of a client."

Cross-References in Rules

Rule 5.5, Comment: "Paragraph (b) does not prohibit a lawyer from employing the services of paraprofessionals and delegating functions to them, so long as the lawyer supervises the delegated work and retains responsibility for their work. See **Rule 5.3.**"

Rule 5.7, Comment 7: When rendering both legal and law-related services in the same matter, "a lawyer will be responsible for assuring that both the lawyer's conduct and, to the extent required by **Rule 5.3**, that of nonlawyer employees in the distinct entity which the lawyer controls complies in all respects with the Rules of Professional Conduct."

Legislative History

1980 Discussion Draft (then Rule 7.4) provided:

Supervision of Nonlawyer Assistants

A lawyer shall use reasonable effort to ensure that nonlawyers employed or retained by the lawyer conduct themselves in a manner compatible with the professional obligations of the lawyer.

1981 Draft was substantially the same as adopted.
1982 Draft was adopted.

Selected State Variations

Alabama: Rule 7.6, entitled "Professional Cards of Nonlawyers," provides as follows:

> A lawyer shall not cause or permit a business card of a nonlawyer which contains the lawyer's or firm's name to contain a false or misleading statement or omission to the effect that the nonlawyer is a lawyer. A business card of a nonlawyer is not false and misleading which clearly identifies the nonlawyer as a "Legal Assistant," provided that the individual is employed in that capacity by a lawyer or law firm, that the lawyer or law firm supervises and is responsible for the law related tasks assigned to and performed by such individual, and that the lawyer or law firm has authorized the use of such cards.

California: No comparable provision.

Georgia: EC 1-9 tracks Rule 5.3.

Illinois: Rule 5.3(a) applies to "[t]he lawyer, and, in a law firm, each partner," and refers to the professional obligations of the lawyer "and the firm." Illinois Rule 5.3(b) applies to "each" lawyer having direct supervisory authority.

Indiana has adopted a series of "Guidelines," numbered as Guidelines 9.1 through 9.10, entitled "Use of Legal Assistants." Among other topics, the Guidelines cover "Permissible Delegation," "Prohibited Delegation," "Identification on Letterhead," and "Legal Assistant Ethics." Guideline 9.10(j) provides: "A legal assistant shall be governed by the American Bar Association Model Code of Professional Responsibility and the American Bar Association Model Rules of Professional Conduct."

New Hampshire has adopted a detailed set of rules and a lengthy commentary, accompanying Rule 5.3, to govern the use of legal assistants.

New Jersey: Rule 5.3(a) provides that "every lawyer or organization authorized by the Court Rules to practice law in this jurisdiction shall adopt and maintain reasonable efforts to ensure that the conduct of nonlawyers retained or employed by the lawyer, law firm or organization is compatible with the professional obligations of the lawyer." In addition, New Jersey has added Rule 5.3(c)(3), which provides that a lawyer is responsible for the conduct of a nonlawyer employee if "the lawyer has failed to make reasonable investigation of circumstances that would disclose past instances of conduct by the nonlawyer incompatible with the professional obligations of a lawyer, which evidence a propensity for such conduct."

New York: In addition to the Model Code Comparison above, see EC 1-8 and DR 1-104 of the New York Code for counterparts to Rule 5.3.

Virginia: DR 3-104, entitled "Non-Lawyer Personnel," contains the following unusual paragraphs:

> (C) A lawyer or law firm that employs non-lawyer personnel shall exercise a high standard of care to assure compliance by the non-lawyer personnel with the applicable provisions of the Code of Professional Responsibility. The initial and the

continuing relationship with the client must be the responsibility of the employing attorney.

(D) The delegated work of non-lawyer personnel shall be such that it will assist only the employing attorney and will be merged into the lawyer's completed product. The lawyer shall examine and be responsible for all work delegated to non-lawyer personnel.

(E) The lawyer or law firm that employs non-lawyer personnel shall not permit such non-lawyer to communicate with clients or the public, including lawyers outside his firm, without first disclosing his non-lawyer status.

Related Materials

ABA Guidelines for Approval of Paralegal Education Programs: The ABA has adopted Guidelines for the Approval of Paralegal Education Programs. These guidelines are enforced by an ABA Approval Commission that examines and approves paralegal education programs. There are currently almost 700 paralegal education programs in the United States, of which about 185 are approved by the ABA. Approved programs include programs in colleges (B.A. programs), in community colleges (A.A. programs), and in proprietary institutions (certificate or degree programs). Two universities even offer a master's degree in paraprofessionalism. The ABA works closely with the American Association for Paralegal Education (see entry below).

ABA Model Guidelines for the Utilization of Legal Assistant Services: The ABA has adopted Model Guidelines for the Utilization of Legal Assistant Services. Guidelines 1 and 6 provide as follows:

> 1. A lawyer is responsible for all of the professional actions of a legal assistant performing legal assistant services at the lawyer's direction and should take reasonable measures to ensure that the legal assistant's conduct is consistent with the lawyer's obligations under the ABA Model Rules of Professional Conduct.
>
> 6. It is the responsibility of a lawyer to take reasonable measures to ensure that all client confidences are preserved by a legal assistant.

ABA Standards for Criminal Justice: See Prosecution Function Standards 3-3.1(a) and (c); Defense Function Standard 4-4.2.

American Association for Paralegal Education: The American Association for Paralegal Education (AAfPE) is an organization for those who educate paralegals. The AAfPE represents approximately 250 paralegal training programs across America and works closely with the ABA Approval Commission to ensure that paralegal programs are providing quality education to paralegals.

Independent Paralegals: Some states allow "independent paralegals" (also called "freelance paralegals") who are retained by lawyers on an "as needed" basis but are not employees of the law firm. See, e.g., In re Opinion No. 24 of the Committee on the Unauthorized Practice of Law, 128 N.J. 114, 607 A.2d 962 (1992). Because Rule 5.3 covers non-lawyers who are "retained by or associated with" a lawyer, the rule reaches independent paralegals.

Legal Assistant Managers Association: The Legal Assistant Managers Association (LAMA) represents approximately 400 "legal assistant managers" whose job is to supervise paralegals in traditional law firm settings. LAMA strongly supports efforts to expand the role of paralegals who are employed by law firms or government agencies. For example, LAMA believes that paralegals should be permitted to appear on behalf of clients at administrative hearings and record depositions, to conduct real estate closings, and to prepare routine corporate filings, guardianship papers, and adoption papers. LAMA also supports establishing formal qualifications for paralegals and establishing a system to address complaints about unethical paralegals.

National Association of Legal Assistants: The National Association of Legal Assistants, Inc. (NALA), founded in 1975 and headquartered in Tulsa, Oklahoma, is an organization of about 17,000 legal assistants. The NALA has published Model Standards and Guidelines for Utilization of Legal Assistants Annotated. The Guidelines "represent a statement of how the legal assistant may function in the law office," and may thus help lawyers understand their supervisory responsibilities under Model Rule 5.3. The Guidelines set minimum educational standards for legal assistants and include the following provisions:

VI

Legal assistants should not:
1. Establish attorney-client relationships; set legal fees, give legal opinions or advice; or represent a client before a court; nor
2. Engage in, encourage, or contribute to any act which could constitute the unauthorized practice of law.

IX

Except as otherwise provided by statute, court rule or decision, administrative rule or regulation, or the attorney's Code of Professional Responsibility . . . a legal assistant may perform any function delegated by an attorney, including but not limited to the following:
1. Conduct client interviews and maintain general contact with the client after the establishment of the relationship, so long as the client is aware of the status and function of the legal assistant, and the client contact is under the supervision of the attorney.
2. Locate and interview witnesses, so long as the witnesses are aware of the status and function of the legal assistant.
3. Conduct investigations and statistical and documentary research for review by the attorney.
4. Conduct legal research for review by the attorney.
5. Draft legal documents for review by the attorney.
6. Draft correspondence and pleadings for review by and signature of the attorney.

7. Summarize depositions, interrogatories, and testimony for review by the attorney.

8. Attend executions of wills, real estate closings, depositions, court or administrative hearings and trials with the attorney.

9. Author and sign letters provided the legal assistant's status is clearly indicated and the correspondence does not contain independent legal opinions or legal advice.

The NALA has also adopted a very brief Code of Ethics and Professional Responsibility for legal assistants. Canon 8 of this code, which is the reciprocal of ABA Model Rule 5.3, provides: "It is the obligation of the legal assistant to avoid conduct which would cause the lawyer to be unethical or even to appear to be unethical, and loyalty to the employer is incumbent upon the legal assistant."

National Federation of Paralegal Associations: The National Federation of Paralegal Associations, Inc. (NFPA), founded in 1974 and headquartered in Kansas City, Missouri, is an organization of approximately 18,000 paralegals, almost all of whom are traditional paralegals working in corporations or private law firms. In May of 1993, the NFPA adopted a Model Code of Ethics and Professional Responsibility. The Preamble of the NFPA Code states that the purpose of the Code is "to delineate the principles for ethics and conduct to which every paralegal should aspire," and says that paralegals "should strive to expand the paralegal role in the delivery of legal services." However, the NFPA does not support the delivery of legal services directly to the public by paralegals who are not supervised by lawyers. The NFPA views paralegals as complements to lawyers, not competitors to lawyers.

Restatement of the Law Governing Lawyers: The American Law Institute has tentatively approved §79, reprinted after the Related Materials to Rule 1.1.

Student Practice Rules: Many states have student practice rules that permit law students to represent clients under certain conditions. These rules often require lawyers to provide a certain degree of supervision over law students. For example, Florida Rule 11-1.2(a), revised on April 21, 1994 provides as follows:

> An eligible law student may appear in any court or before any administrative tribunal in this state on behalf of any indigent person if the person on whose behalf the student is appearing has indicated in writing consent to that appearance and the supervising lawyer has also indicated in writing approval of that appearance. In those cases in which an indigent has a right to appointed counsel, the supervising attorney shall be personally present at all critical stages of the proceeding. In all cases, the supervising attorney shall be personally present when required by the court or administrative tribunal who shall determine the extent of the eligible law student's participation in the proceeding.

Unauthorized Practice of Law: A lawyer who fails to supervise a paralegal may be assisting the paralegal in the unauthorized practice of law, in violation of Rule 5.5.

Rule 5.4 Professional Independence of a Lawyer

(a) A lawyer or law firm shall not share legal fees with a nonlawyer, except that:

(1) an agreement by a lawyer with the lawyer's firm, partner, or associate may provide for the payment of money, over a reasonable period of time after the lawyer's death, to the lawyer's estate or to one or more specified persons;

> **Editors' Note.** The following subparagraph, (a)(2), was substantially rewritten by the ABA in 1990 to bring Rule 5.4 into line with the changes brought about by the addition of Rule 1.17 (permitting the sale of a law practice) at the ABA's February 1990 Mid-Year Meeting.

(2) a lawyer who purchases the practice of a deceased, disabled, or disappeared lawyer may, pursuant to the provisions of Rule 1.17, pay to the estate or other representative of that lawyer the agreed-upon purchase price; and

(3) a lawyer or law firm may include nonlawyer employees in a compensation or retirement plan, even though the plan is based in whole or in part on a profit-sharing arrangement.

(b) A lawyer shall not form a partnership with a nonlawyer if any of the activities of the partnership consist of the practice of law.

(c) A lawyer shall not permit a person who recommends, employs, or pays the lawyer to render legal services for another to direct or regulate the lawyer's professional judgment in rendering such legal services.

(d) A lawyer shall not practice with or in the form of a professional corporation or association authorized to practice law for a profit, if:

(1) a nonlawyer owns any interest therein, except that a fiduciary representative of the estate of a lawyer may hold the stock or interest of the lawyer for a reasonable time during administration;

(2) a nonlawyer is a corporate director or officer thereof; or

(3) a nonlawyer has the right to direct or control the professional judgment of a lawyer.

COMMENT

The provisions of this Rule express traditional limitations on sharing fees. These limitations are to protect the lawyer's professional independence of judgment. Where someone other than the client pays the lawyer's fee or salary, or recommends employment of the lawyer, that arrangement does not modify the lawyer's obligation to the client. As stated in paragraph (c), such arrangements should not interfere with the lawyer's professional judgment.

Model Code Comparison

Paragraph (a) is substantially identical to DR 3-102(A).
Paragraph (b) is substantially identical to DR 3-103(A).
Paragraph (c) is substantially identical to DR 5-107(B).
Paragraph (d) is substantially identical to DR 5-107(C).

Cross-References in Rules

Rule 1.17, Comment 1 provides that "when a lawyer or an entire firm ceases to practice and another lawyer or firm takes over the representation, the selling lawyer or firm may obtain compensation for the reasonable value of the practice as may withdrawing partners of law firms. See **Rules 5.4** and 5.6."

Legislative History

1980 Discussion Draft (then Rule 7.5) provided as follows:

Professional Independence of a Firm

A lawyer shall not practice with a firm in which an interest is owned or managerial authority is exercised by a nonlawyer, unless services can be rendered in conformity with the Rules of Professional Conduct. The terms of the relationship shall expressly provide that:
(a) there is no interference with the lawyer's independence of professional judgment or with the client-lawyer relationship; and
(b) the confidences of clients are protected as required by Rule 1.7; and
(c) the arrangement does not involve advertising or solicitation prohibited by Rules 9.2 and 9.3; and
(d) the arrangement does not result in charging a client a fee which violates Rule 1.6.

1981 Draft:

Professional Independence of a Firm

A lawyer may be employed by an organization in which a financial interest is held or managerial authority is exercised by a non-lawyer, or by a lawyer acting in a capacity other than that of representing clients, such as a business corporation, insurance company, legal services organization or government agency, but only if the terms of the relationship provide in writing that:

      (a) there is no interference with the lawyer's independence of professional judgment or with the client-lawyer relationship;

      (b) information relating to representation of a client is protected as required by Rule 1.6;

      (c) the arrangement does not involve advertising or personal contract with prospective clients prohibited by Rules 7.2 and 7.3; and

      (d) the arrangement does not result in charging a fee that violates Rule 1.5.

The *1982 Draft* was substantially the same as 1981 Draft.

Editors' Note.   The version of Rule 5.4 finally adopted in 1983 was proposed as an amendment by the General Practice Section as a substitute for the Kutak Commission's draft. Rule 5.4 was the only proposed rule from the 1982 Draft that was completely rejected and rewritten by the House of Delegates in 1983.

1990 Amendment: At its February 1990 Mid-Year Meeting, the ABA House of Delegates amended Rule 5.4(a)(2) to conform to Rule 1.17 (permitting the sale of a law practice), which was added to the Rules at the same meeting. (There was no Committee Report to explain the change, but the reason for the change is obvious.) The former version of Rule 5.4(a)(2) provided that "a lawyer who undertakes to complete unfinished legal business of a deceased lawyer may pay to the estate of the deceased lawyer that proportion of the total compensation which fairly represents the services rendered by the deceased lawyer."

Selected State Variations

California: See Rule 1-310 (Forming a Partnership with a Non-Lawyer) and Rule 1-320 (Financial Arrangements with Non-Lawyers).

District of Columbia: D.C. Rule 5.4 differs significantly from the ABA Model Rule — see District of Columbia Rules of Professional Conduct below.

Illinois does not permit the sale of a law practice, so Rule 5.4(a)(2) applies only to a lawyer "who undertakes to complete unfinished legal business of a deceased lawyer . . . ," and makes no reference to a "disabled or disappeared" lawyer. Illinois Rule 5.4(d)(2) permits a non-lawyer to serve as secretary for a professional corporation or for-profit association authorized to practice law "if such secretary performs only ministerial duties."

Maryland: Rule 8.5(b) imposes responsibility on supervisory lawyers as follows:

> (b) A lawyer not admitted by the Court of Appeals to practice in this State is subject to the disciplinary authority of this State for conduct that constitutes a violation of these Rules and that: . . .
> > (3) involves the practice of law in this State by another lawyer over whom that lawyer has the obligation of supervision or control.

Massachusetts, which retains a modified version of the Code, permits a law firm to include nonlawyer employees in a "retirement plan," but not in a "compensation . . . plan," as the Model Code allows. DR 3-102(A)(3).

Missouri: Effective January 1, 1994, Missouri's version of Rule 5.4(d) provides that a lawyer "shall not practice with or in the form of a professional corporation, *limited liability company,* or association authorized to practice law for a profit" if the conditions in the subparagraphs apply. Rule 5.4(d)(2) has been amended to prohibit such practice if a nonlawyer is "a manager of the limited liability company." The amendment was considered necessary because a number of Missouri law firms have converted to limited liability companies.

New Jersey: Rule 5.4 permits a lawyer to share legal fees with the estate of a deceased lawyer or the representative of a disabled lawyer where the first lawyer has assumed responsibility for the deceased or disabled lawyer's cases.

New York: Same or substantially the same as the ABA Model Code — see Model Code Comparison above — except see New York Materials for New York's version of DR 3-102(A)(3). The New York Code deletes DR 2-103(D)(4)(a).

North Dakota: Effective March 1, 1997, North Dakota adopted the ABA's 1990 amendments to Rule 5.4.

Ohio: Effective July 1, 1996, Ohio added a new subparagraph DR 3-102(A)(4) that allows a lawyer participating in a qualified lawyer referral service to "pay to the service a fee calculated as a percentage of legal fees earned by the lawyer in his or her capacity as a lawyer to whom the service has referred a matter." This percentage fee may be "in addition to any reasonable membership or registration fee established by the service."

Pennsylvania provides in Rule 5.4(d) that a lawyer shall not practice with or in the form of a professional corporation or other form of association organized for profit if "a nonlawyer is the beneficial owner of any interest therein [with an exception for an estate representative]; a nonlawyer is a corporate director or officer thereof or occupies the position of similar responsibility in any form of association other than a corporation; [or] . . . in the case of any form of association other than a professional corporation, the organic law governing the internal affairs of the association provides the equity owners of the association with greater liability protection than is available to the shareholders of a professional corporation." These provisions do not apply "to a lawyer employed in the legal department of a corporation or other organization."

Virginia deletes subparagraphs (b) and (c) from ABA Model Code DR 5-107.

Related Materials

ABA Canons: Canons 33, 34, and 35 provided:

33. Partnerships — Names

Partnerships between lawyers and members of other professions or non-professional persons should not be formed or permitted where any part of the partnership's employment consists of the practice of law.

34. Division of Fees

No division of fees for legal services is proper, except with another lawyer, based upon a division of service or responsibility.

35. Intermediaries

The professional services of a lawyer should not be controlled or exploited by any lay agency, personal or corporate, which intervenes between client and lawyer. A lawyer's responsibilities and qualifications are individual. He should avoid all relations which direct the performance of his duties by or in the interest of such intermediary. A lawyer's relation to his client should be personal, and the responsibility should be direct to the client. Charitable societies rendering aid to the indigents are not deemed such intermediaries.

A lawyer may accept employment from any organization, such as an association, club or trade organization, to render legal services in any matter in which the organization, as an entity, is interested, but this employment should not include the rendering of legal services to the members of such an organization in respect to their individual affairs.

ABA Model Guidelines for the Utilization of Legal Assistant Services: In 1992, the ABA House of Delegates approved Model Guidelines for the Utilization of Legal Assistant Services. Guideline 9 provides:

A lawyer may not split legal fees with a legal assistant nor pay a legal assistant for the referral of legal business. A lawyer may compensate a legal assistant based on the quantity and quality of the legal assistant's work and the value of that work to a law practice, but the legal assistant's compensation may not be contingent, by advance agreement, upon the profitability of the lawyer's practice.

American Lawyer's Code of Conduct: Rule 4.7 provides:

If a lawyer forms a partnership with a nonlawyer for the purpose of more effectively serving clients' interests, the terms of the partnership shall be consistent with the lawyer's obligations under this Code, with particular reference to Rule 2.1, requiring undivided fidelity to the client.

Limited Liability Companies: Rule 5.4(d) governs lawyers who practice with or in the form of "a professional association or association authorized to practice law for a profit" if certain enumerated circumstances apply. Some states have expressly extended coverage of Rule 5.4(d) to limited liability companies (sometimes called LLC's), which combine the benefits of partnership taxation rules with the benefits of limited liability for corporations. Many states have enacted statutes permitting LLC's. It is still not clear whether all of these states will permit law firms to practice as LLC's, because this may be a prospective limitation of the lawyer's liability to a client for legal malpractice that would violate Rule 1.8(h).

Model Rules of Professional Conduct for Federal Lawyers insert a substantially different version of Rule 5.4, which provides:

> (a) A Federal lawyer is expected to exercise professional independence of judgment during the representation of a client, consistent with these Rules.
> (b) Notwithstanding a Government lawyer's status as a Government employee, a Government lawyer detailed or assigned to represent an individual Government employee or another person as the client is expected to exercise loyalty and professional independence during the representation, consistent with these Rules and to the same extent as required by a Non-Government lawyer in private practice.
> (c) A Supervisory Government lawyer may not base an adverse evaluation or other prejudicial action against a Subordinate Government lawyer on the Subordinate Government lawyer's exercise of professional independence under (b) above.
> (d) A Government lawyer shall obey the lawful orders of superiors when representing the United States and individual clients, but a Government lawyer shall not permit a nonlawyer to direct or regulate the Government lawyer's professional judgment in rendering legal services.
> (e) A Non-Government lawyer shall not permit a nonlawyer who recommends, employs, or pays the Non-Government lawyer to render legal services for another to direct or regulate the Non-Government lawyer's professional judgment in rendering legal services.
> (f) A Non-Government lawyer shall comply with the Rules of Professional Conduct or other applicable laws of the jurisdiction in which the Non-Government lawyer is licensed or is practicing law concerning the limitations on sharing fees and the organizational form of their practice.

The Comment, which has no parallel in the ABA Model Rules, states (with headings omitted):

> A Federal lawyer subjected to outside pressures that might impair or give the appearance of impairing the effectiveness of the representation should make full disclosure of the pressures to the client. If the Federal lawyer or the client believes the effectiveness of the representation has been or will be impaired thereby, the lawyer should take proper steps to withdraw from representation of the client.

This Rule recognizes that a Government lawyer is a Government employee required by law to obey the lawful orders of superiors. Nevertheless, the practice of law requires the exercise of judgment solely for the benefit of the client and free of compromising influences and loyalties. Thus, when a Government lawyer is assigned to represent an individual client, neither the lawyer's personal interests, the interests of other clients, nor the interests of third persons should affect the loyalty to the individual client.

Rather than adopting specific rules on the sharing of fees or the organizational makeup of law practices that would apply only to Non-Government lawyers practicing before the Federal Agency, the Federal Agency defers on this matter to the rules and applicable laws of the jurisdictions in which these Non-Government lawyers are licensed.

Rule 5.5 Unauthorized Practice of Law

A lawyer shall not:

(a) practice law in a jurisdiction where doing so violates the regulation of the legal profession in that jurisdiction; or

(b) assist a person who is not a member of the bar in the performance of activity that constitutes the unauthorized practice of law.

COMMENT

The definition of the practice of law is established by law and varies from one jurisdiction to another. Whatever the definition, limiting the practice of law to members of the bar protects the public against rendition of legal services by unqualified persons. Paragraph (b) does not prohibit a lawyer from employing the services of paraprofessionals and delegating functions to them, so long as the lawyer supervises the delegated work and retains responsibility for their work. See Rule 5.3. Likewise, it does not prohibit lawyers from providing professional advice and instruction to nonlawyers whose employment requires knowledge of law; for example, claims adjusters, employees of financial or commercial institutions, social workers, accountants and persons employed in government agencies. In addition, a lawyer may counsel nonlawyers who wish to proceed pro se.

Model Code Comparison

With regard to paragraph (a), DR 3-101(B) of the Model Code provided that "[a] lawyer shall not practice law in a jurisdiction where to do so would be in violation of regulations of the profession in that jurisdiction."

With regard to paragraph (b), DR 3-101(A) of the Model Code provided that "[a] lawyer shall not aid a non-lawyer in the unauthorized practice of law."

Cross-References in Rules

Rule 8.5, Comment 1 (deleted in 1993): "If their activity in another jurisdiction is substantial and continuous, it may constitute practice of law in that jurisdiction. See **Rule 5.5.**"

Legislative History

1980 Discussion Draft (then Rule 10.4(d) and (e)) provided that it was "professional misconduct" for a lawyer to "(d) practice law in a jurisdiction in violation of the regulation of the legal profession in that jurisdiction; or (e) aid a person who is not a member of the bar in the performance of activity that constitutes the practice of law."

1981 and 1982 Drafts (then Rule 8.4(d) and (e)) were the same as adopted.

Selected State Variations

California: See Rule 1-300 (Unauthorized Practice of Law) and B & P Code §§6125-6127.

Florida: Supreme Court Rule 3-6.1 expressly permits lawyers and law firms to employ suspended, disbarred, or resigned attorneys on the same terms as other lay persons, provided the employing lawyer or firm gives notice and reports periodically to the Bar's staff counsel, and provided that "[n]o suspended, resigned, or disbarred attorney shall have direct contact with any client or receive, disburse, or otherwise handle trust funds or property." In addition, as amended effective January 1, 1993, Florida Rule 4-8.6(a) permits lawyers to practice in the form of professional service corporations organized according to Florida statutory authority "only if when such corporations are organized all shareholders are legally qualified to render legal services in this state. . . ." Rule 4-8.6(b) prohibits a professional service corporation from practicing law in Florida or rendering advice on Florida law "except through officers, directors, partners, managers, agents, or employees who are qualified to render legal services in this state." The remainder of Rule 4-8.6 imposes additional restrictions on professional service corporations.

Effective April 21, 1994, the Florida Supreme Court added an elaborate new Chapter 17, entitled "Authorized House Counsel Rule," to the Rules Regulating the Florida Bar. The purpose of the new chapter is to "authorize attorneys licensed to practice in jurisdictions other than Florida to be permitted to undertake said activities in Florida while exclusively employed by a business organization without the requirement of taking the bar examination."

Georgia: Effective October 15, 1995, to guard against the unauthorized practice of law by suspended or disbarred lawyers, Georgia adopted Standard 73, which provides:

> *Standard 73.* A lawyer shall not allow any person who has been suspended or disbarred under Part IV of these Rules and who maintains a presence in an office where the practice of law is conducted by the lawyer, to:
> > (a) represent himself or herself as a lawyer or person with similar status;
> > (b) have any contact with the clients of the lawyer either in person, by telephone, or in writing; or
> > (c) have any contact with persons who have legal dealings with the office either in person, by telephone, or in writing.
>
> A violation of this Standard may be punished by disbarment.

Maryland reinforces Rule 5.5 with the following variation on Rule 8.5 that reaches lawyers who are not admitted to practice in Maryland:

> (b) A lawyer not admitted by the Court of Appeals to practice in this State is subject to the disciplinary authority of this State for conduct that constitutes a violation of these Rules and that:
> > (1) involves the practice of law in this State by that lawyer. . . .

Missouri: Rule 5.5(c) prohibits the practice of law by a lawyer reported for failure to comply with Missouri Continuing Legal Education requirements.

Effective July 1, 1994, the Missouri Supreme Court adopted a new Rule 8.105 that authorizes limited admission to the bar for in-house counsel. Rule 8.105(a) provides as follows:

> A lawyer admitted to the practice of law in another state or territory of the United States may receive a limited license to practice law in this state when the lawyer is employed in Missouri as a lawyer exclusively for: a corporation, its subsidiaries or affiliates; an association; a business; or a governmental entity whose lawful business consists of activities other than the practice of law or the provision of legal services.

Attorneys operating under the limited license may not perform legal work for anyone other than their employer unless they are granted *pro hac vice* status. A limited license is valid for five years but is automatically terminated if the lawyer's employment terminates before that.

Also effective July 1, 1994, Missouri adopted a new version of Supreme Court Rule 9.05 to permit foreign (i.e., non-American) lawyers to work in Missouri as "foreign legal consultants." This rule addressed concerns of the state's largest law firm, which has offices in Saudi Arabia, Germany, England, and other foreign countries.

Finally, also effective July 1, 1994, Missouri adopted a new Rule 13.06 that allows a full-time law teacher at an ABA-accredited Missouri law school to supervise clinical students without being admitted to the Missouri bar if the teacher: (1) provides legal services only in connection with the law school's clinical program; (2) receives compensation only from the law school; (3) is a member in good standing of the bar of another American jurisdiction; (4) has not been denied admission to a bar or been disciplined for professional misconduct within the last five years; and (5) certifies in writing that he or she has read and is familiar with the Missouri Rules of Professional Conduct. This new rule makes it much easier for visiting professors and new clinical teachers to supervise clinical students at Missouri law schools.

New Jersey expressly permits nonprofit corporations to practice law, and permits attorneys to assist them, provided certain conditions are met. Supreme Court Rule 1:21-1(d) provides:

> (d) *Legal Services Organizations.* Nonprofit organizations incorporated in this or any other state for the purpose of providing legal services to the poor or functioning as a public interest law firm, and other federally tax exempt legal services organizations or trusts, such as those defined by 26 U.S.C.A. 120(b) and 501(c)(20), which provide legal services to a defined and limited class of clients, may practice law in their own names through staff attorneys who are members of the bar of the State of New Jersey, provided that: (1) the legal work serves the intended beneficiaries of the organizational purpose, (2) the staff attorney responsible for the matter signs all papers prepared by the organization, and (3) the relationship between staff attorney and client meets the attorney's professional responsibilities to the client and is not subject to interference, control, or direction by the organization's board or employees except for a supervising attorney who is a member of the New Jersey bar.

New York: Same or substantially the same as the ABA Model Code — see Model Code Comparison above. In addition, New York Judiciary Law §495 generally prohibits corporations from practicing law, but exempts "non-profit organizations whether incorporated or unincorporated . . . which furnish legal services as an incidental activity in furtherance of their primary purpose" and "organizations which have as their primary purpose the furnishing of legal services to indigent persons."

Virginia retains the language of DR 3-101, but adds two new paragraphs (similar to North Carolina's) prohibiting a law firm from continuing to employ disbarred or suspended lawyers who were previously associated with the firm as lawyers, or from representing the former clients of any suspended or disbarred lawyer that the firm employs.

Related Materials

ABA Canons: Canon 47 provided:

47. Aiding the Unauthorized Practice of Law

No lawyer shall permit his professional services, or his name, to be used in aid of, or to make possible, the unauthorized practice of law by any lay agency, personal or corporate.

ABA Commission on Non-Lawyer Practice: In 1992, the American Bar Association appointed a 17-member Commission on Non-Lawyer Practice to examine all aspects of work done by non-lawyers and to make recommendations in a formal report. The Commission was composed of both lawyers and non-lawyers (including representatives from two national paralegal organizations) and held hearings in nine cities around the country, taking live testimony from 337 witnesses and reviewing over 12,000 pages of additional written statements, studies, statutes, reports, and scholarly articles. The Commission issued a draft report in April 1994, and held an additional public hearing at the ABA's August 1994 Annual Meeting. The Commission had been expected to issue its final report and recommendations in late 1994 for consideration by the ABA House of Delegates sometime in 1995, but the Commission missed its deadline and the report was not included in the 1995 mailing to the ABA House of Delegates. At its August 1995 meeting, however, the Board of Governors approved funding necessary to circulate the 200-page report for public comment. But the Board of Governors did not reappoint the Commission on Non-lawyer Practice, which therefore automatically ceased to exist on August 31, 1995. Comments on the Commission's report were directed to the ABA Center for Professional Responsibility, which summarized and transmitted them to the ABA Board of Governors to decide upon further action. The report was never transmitted to the ABA House of Delegates for approval.

ABA Model Guidelines for the Utilization of Legal Assistant Services: In August of 1991, the ABA House of Delegates adopted Model Guidelines for the Utilization of Legal Assistant Services. These Model Guidelines drew upon similar guidelines already existing or proposed in 17 states. The full set of ten Guidelines, with comments, is reprinted in Therese Cannon, Ethics and Professional Responsibility for Legal Assistants 329-346 (Little, Brown and Company 1992). The most interesting guidelines relating to the unauthorized practice of law provide as follows:

> *Guideline 2:* Provided the lawyer maintains responsibility for the work product, a lawyer may delegate to a legal assistant any task normally performed by a lawyer except those tasks proscribed to one not licensed as a lawyer by statute, court rule, [etc.].
>
> *Guideline 3:* A lawyer may not delegate to a legal assistant:
> (a) Responsibility for establishing an attorney-client relationship.
> (b) Responsibility for establishing the amount of a fee to be charged for a legal service.
> (c) Responsibility for a legal opinion rendered to a client.
>
> *Guideline 4:* It is the lawyer's responsibility to take reasonable measures to ensure that clients, courts, and other lawyers are aware that a legal assistant, whose services are utilized by the lawyer in performing legal services, is not licensed to practice law.

ABA Model Rule for the Licensing of Foreign Legal Consultants: At its August 1993 Annual Meeting, the ABA House of Delegates approved a Model Rule for the Licensing of Foreign Legal Consultants. The rule was proposed by the ABA's Section of International Law and Practice and was motivated by concern that foreign countries may not allow American lawyers to practice abroad if foreign lawyers cannot practice in America. The rule, which is modeled on similar rules already in effect in New York and Washington, D.C., allows a state to license a "legal consultant" without requiring an examination if the applicant has been a member in good standing of a foreign bar for five of the past seven years. Legal consultants are not full-fledged lawyers; the rule limits the scope of their practice. However, they are subject to all disciplinary rules.

ABA Model Rules for Advisory Opinions on Unauthorized Practice of Law: In 1984, the ABA House of Delegates adopted Model Rules for Advisory Opinions on Unauthorized Practice of Law, which set forth model procedures for committees and courts to follow in issuing opinions on unauthorized practice. These rules, according to their Preamble, recognize the need "to prevent harm to the public from the unauthorized practice of law and to make public a clear and timely understanding of what is the unauthorized practice of law." The rules can be found in the ABA/BNA Lawyers' Manual on Professional Conduct.

In-House Lawyers: At least nine states (Florida, Kansas, Kentucky, Maryland, Minnesota, Missouri, Ohio, Oklahoma, and South Carolina) have statutes or court rules that permit in-house lawyers to provide legal services to their employers, subject to certain limitations, without committing the unauthorized practice of law. (California, however, rejected a special admission category for in-house lawyers in 1987.) For more information, see Carol Needham, The Multijurisdictional Practice of Law and the Corporate Lawyer: New Rules for a New Generation of Legal Practice, 36 S. Tex. L.J. 1075, 1084-1087 (1995).

Model Rules of Professional Conduct for Federal Lawyers: Rule 5.5(a) provides that "[e]xcept as authorized by law," a federal lawyer shall not practice in a jurisdiction where doing so violates the regulation of the legal profession in that jurisdiction.

National Federation of Paralegal Associations: In May of 1993, the National Federation of Paralegal Associations, Inc. (NFPA) adopted a Model Code of Ethics and Professional Responsibility. The NFPA Code defines a "paralegal" as "a person qualified through education, training, or work experience to perform substantive legal work that requires knowledge of legal concepts and is customarily, but not exclusively, performed by a lawyer."

Unauthorized Practice Laws: Most states have enacted statutes making it a crime to engage in the unauthorized practice of law. California B & P Code §6126 is typical:

§6126. Unauthorized Practice or Advertising as Misdemeanor

Any person advertising or holding himself or herself out as practicing or entitled to practice law or otherwise practicing law who is not an active member of the State Bar, is guilty of a misdemeanor.

In many states, the state bar has authority to enforce the unauthorized practice laws. In Florida, for example, the board of governors of the state bar acts "as an arm of the Supreme Court of Florida for the purpose of seeking to prohibit the unauthorized practice of law by investigating, prosecuting, and reporting'' incidents involving unlicensed practice. See Florida Supreme Court Rule 1-8.2 and Chapter 10 of those Rules (setting forth detailed procedures for investigating and prosecuting unauthorized practice cases).

Rule 5.6 Restrictions on Right to Practice

A lawyer shall not participate in offering or making:

(a) a partnership or employment agreement that restricts the rights of a lawyer to practice after termination of the relationship, except an agreement concerning benefits upon retirement; or

(b) an agreement in which a restriction on the lawyer's right to practice is part of the settlement of a controversy between private parties.

COMMENT

[1] An agreement restricting the right of partners or associates to practice after leaving a firm not only limits their professional autonomy but also limits the freedom of clients to choose a lawyer. Paragraph (a) prohibits such agreements except for restrictions incident to provisions concerning retirement benefits for service with the firm.

[2] Paragraph (b) prohibits a lawyer from agreeing not to represent other persons in connection with settling a claim on behalf of a client.

[3] This Rule does not apply to prohibit restrictions that may be included in the terms of the sale of a law practice pursuant to Rule 1.17.

Model Code Comparison

This Rule is substantially similar to DR 2-108.

Cross-References in Rules

Rule 1.17, Comment 1: "Pursuant to this Rule, when a lawyer or an entire firm ceases to practice and another lawyer or firm takes over the representation, the selling lawyer or firm may obtain compensation for the reasonable value of the practice as may withdrawing partners of law firms. See Rules 5.4 and 5.6."

Legislative History

1980 and 1981 Drafts had no equivalent to Rule 5.6.
1982 Draft was adopted.

Selected State Variations

California: See Rule 1-500 (Agreements Restricting a Member's Practice).

Georgia permits a lawyer on settling a case to agree not to "accept any other representation arising out of a transaction or event embraced in the subject matter of the controversy or suit thus settled." DR 2-108(B).

New York: Same or substantially the same as the ABA Model Code — see Model Code Comparison above.

Pennsylvania's Rule 5.6(a) forbids a lawyer to participate in offering or making "a partnership, shareholders, operating, employment or other similar type of agreement that restricts the right of a lawyer to practice after termination of the relationship, except an agreement concerning benefits upon retirement."

Virginia: DR 2-106 is substantially the same as ABA Model Code DR 2-108.

Related Materials

Arbitration Provisions: Many law partnership agreements contain terms giving greater benefits to those who do not compete with the firm after they leave. These provisions often lead to controversy because departing lawyers often argue that such terms violate Rule 5.6(a). To reduce the expense of litigating these disputes, many partnership agreements contain arbitration agreements. These arbitration provisions are encouraged by legal malpractice insurers. In Pennsylvania, for example, the well-known Bertholon-Rowland Agencies will give a 5 percent "quality of management credit" (i.e., discount) on professional liability policies that contain the following paragraph:

> Any controversy or claim arising out of or relating to the dissolution of the partnership, or relating to a partner's withdrawal from the partnership, shall be settled through mediation conducted in accordance with the then-existing rules of the Pennsylvania Bar Association Lawyer Dispute Resolution Program (the "PBA Program"). Any issues that are not resolved through such mediation shall be submitted for arbitration conducted in accordance with the then-existing rules of the PBA Program. . . .

Non-compete Provisions: Some law firm partnership agreements contain provisions that pay greater severance payments to departing lawyers who do not compete with the firm than to those who do compete. In a variation, severance payments to departing partners may be based on a sliding scale so that partners who earn more after they leave will receive less than partners who earn less (such as partners who leave to enter public service or to take a public interest job).

Many of these provisions have been held invalid under Rule 5.6(a), and many others are currently being challenged in litigation. For two dramatically different visions of the commercial aspects of law firm practice and the validity of law partnership agreements that condition post-departure payment on non-competitive practice, compare Cohen v. Lord, Day & Lord, 75 N.Y.2d 95, 550 N.E.2d 410, 551 N.Y.S.2d 157 (1989), with Howard v. Babcock, 6 Cal. 4th 409, 863 P.2d 150, 25 Cal. Rptr. 2d 80 (1994).

Rule 5.7 Responsibilities Regarding Law-Related Services

> **Editors' Note.** Rule 5.7 has a strange and complicated legislative history. The version reprinted immediately below was proposed by the Special House of Delegates Committee on Ancillary Business and was adopted by the ABA House of Delegates at its February 1994 Mid-Year Meeting. A more detailed legislative history of Rule 5.7 appears below in the Legislative History section.

(a) A lawyer shall be subject to the Rules of Professional Conduct with respect to the provision of law-related services, as defined in paragraph (b), if the law-related services are provided:

(1) by the lawyer in circumstances that are not distinct from the lawyer's provision of legal services to clients; or

(2) by a separate entity controlled by the lawyer individually or with others if the lawyer fails to take reasonable measures to assure that a person obtaining the law-related services knows that the services of the separate entity are not legal services and that the protections of the client-lawyer relationship do not exist.

(b) The term "law-related services" denotes services that might reasonably be performed in conjunction with and in substance are related to the provision of legal services, and that are not prohibited as unauthorized practice of law when provided by a nonlawyer.

COMMENT

[1] When a lawyer performs law-related services or controls an organization that does so, there exists the potential for ethical problems. Principal among these is the possibility that the person for whom the law-related services are performed fails to understand that the services may not carry with them the protections normally afforded as part of the client-lawyer relationship. The recipient of the law-related services may expect,

for example, that the protection of client confidences, prohibitions against representation of persons with conflicting interests, and obligations of a lawyer to maintain professional independence apply to the provision of law-related services when that may not be the case. Rule 5.7 applies to the provision of law-related services by a lawyer even when the lawyer does not provide any legal services to the person for whom the law-related services are performed. The Rule identifies the circumstances in which all of the Rules of Professional Conduct apply to the provision of law-related services. Even when those circumstances do not exist, however, the conduct of a lawyer involved in the provision of law-related services is subject to those Rules that apply generally to lawyer conduct, regardless of whether the conduct involves the provision of legal services. See, e.g., Rule 8.4.

[2] When law-related services are provided by a lawyer under circumstances that are not distinct from the lawyer's provision of legal services to clients, the lawyer in providing the law-related services must adhere to the requirements of the Rules of Professional Conduct as provided in Rule 5.7(a)(1).

[3] Law-related services also may be provided through an entity that is distinct from that through which the lawyer provides legal services. If the lawyer individually or with others has control of such an entity's operations, the Rule requires the lawyer to take reasonable measures to assure that each person using the services of the entity knows that the services provided by the entity are not legal services and that the Rules of Professional Conduct that relate to the client-lawyer relationship do not apply. A lawyer's control of an entity extends to the ability to direct its operation. Whether a lawyer has such control will depend upon the circumstances of the particular case.

[4] When a client-lawyer relationship exists with a person who is referred by a lawyer to a separate law-related service entity controlled by the lawyer, individually or with others, the lawyer must comply with Rule 1.8(a).

[5] In taking the reasonable measures referred to in paragraph (a)(2) to assure that a person using law-related services understands the practical effect or significance of the inapplicability of the Rules of Professional Conduct, the lawyer should communicate to the person receiving the law-related services, in a manner sufficient to assure that the person understands the significance of the fact, that the relationship of the person to the business entity will not be a client-lawyer relationship. The communication should be made before entering into an agreement for provision of or providing law-related services, and preferably should be in writing.

[6] The burden is upon the lawyer to show that the lawyer has taken reasonable measures under the circumstances to communicate the desired understanding. For instance, a sophisticated user of law-related services, such as a publicly held corporation, may require a lesser explanation than someone unaccustomed to making distinctions between legal services and law-related services, such as an individual seeking tax advice from a lawyer-accountant or investigative services in connection with a lawsuit.

[7] Regardless of the sophistication of potential recipients of law-related services, a lawyer should take special care to keep separate the provision of law-related and legal services in order to minimize the risk that the recipient will assume that the law-related services are legal services. The risk of such confusion is especially acute when the lawyer renders both types of services with respect to the same matter. Under some circumstances the legal and law-related services may be so closely entwined that they cannot be distinguished from each other, and the requirement of disclosure and consultation imposed by paragraph (a)(2) of the Rule cannot be met. In such a case a lawyer will be responsible for assuring that both the lawyer's conduct and, to the extent required by Rule 5.3, that of nonlawyer employees in the distinct entity which the lawyer controls complies in all respects with the Rules of Professional Conduct.

[8] A broad range of economic and other interests of clients may be served by lawyers' engaging in the delivery of law-related services. Examples of law-related services include providing title insurance, financial planning, accounting, trust services, real estate counseling, legislative lobbying, economic analysis, social work, psychological counseling, tax return preparation, and patent, medical or environmental consulting. When a lawyer is obliged to accord the recipients of such services the protections of those Rules that apply to the client-lawyer relationship, the lawyer must take special care to heed the proscriptions of the Rules addressing conflict of interest (Rules 1.7 through 1.11, especially Rules 1.7(b) and 1.8(a), (b) and (f)), and to scrupulously adhere to the requirements of Rule 1.6 relating to disclosure of confidential information. The promotion of the law-related services must also in all respects comply with Rules 7.1 through 7.3, dealing with advertising and solicitation. In that regard, lawyers should take special care to identify the obligations that may be imposed as a result of a jurisdiction's decisional law.

[9] When the full protections of all of the Rules of Professional Conduct do not apply to the provision of law-related services, principles of law external to the Rules, for example, the law of principal and agent, govern the legal duties owed to those receiving the services. Those other legal

principles may establish a different degree of protection for the recipient with respect to confidentiality of information, conflicts of interest and permissible business relationships with clients. See also Rule 8.4 (Misconduct).

Model Code Comparison

Rule 5.7 has no direct counterpart in the Disciplinary Rules or Ethical Considerations of the Model Code.

Cross-References in Rules

None.

Legislative History

1980, 1981, and 1982 Drafts: None of the Kutak Commission drafts had any provision equivalent to Rule 5.7.

1991 Adoption: Rule 5.7 was originally added to the Model Rules at the ABA's 1991 Annual Meeting. The rule as adopted in 1991 was proposed by the ABA's Litigation Section, which had been intensively studying ancillary businesses for several years. Before the House of Delegates voted on the Litigation Section's proposal, it rejected by voice vote an alternative version of Rule 5.7 that had been proposed by the ABA's Standing Committee on Ethics and Professional Responsibility. After rejecting the Standing Committee's proposal, the House of Delegates voted 197-186 to adopt the Litigation Section's version of Rule 5.7. The original version of Rule 5.7 provided as follows:

Provision of Ancillary Services

(a) A lawyer shall not practice law in a law firm which owns a controlling interest in, or operates, an entity which provides non-legal services which are ancillary to the practice of law, or otherwise provides such ancillary non-legal services, except as provided in paragraph (b).

(b) A lawyer may practice law in a law firm which provides non-legal services which are ancillary to the practice of law if:

(1) The ancillary services are provided solely to clients of the law firm and are incidental to, in connection with and concurrent to, the provision of legal services by the law firm to such clients;

(2) Such ancillary services are provided solely by employees of the law firm itself and not by a subsidiary or other affiliate of the law firm;

(3) The law firm makes appropriate disclosure in writing to its clients; and

(4) The law firm does not hold itself out as engaging in any non-legal activities except in conjunction with the provision of legal services, as provided in this rule.

(c) One or more lawyers who engage in the practice of law in a law firm shall neither own a controlling interest in, nor operate, an entity which provides non-legal services which are ancillary to the practice of law, nor otherwise provide such ancillary non-legal services, except that their firms may provide such services as provided in paragraph (b).

(d) Two or more lawyers who engage in the practice of law in separate law firms shall neither own a controlling interest in, nor operate, an entity which provides non-legal services which are ancillary to the practice of law, nor otherwise provide such ancillary non-legal services.

The Comment to the 1991 version of Rule 5.7 was nineteen paragraphs, making it one of the longest comments in the Model Rules. The following excerpt from the original Comment explains the origin and purpose of the 1991 version of Rule 5.7:

Excerpt from Comment to 1991 Version of Rule 5.7

[1] For many years, lawyers have provided to their clients non-legal services which are ancillary to the practice of law. Such services included title insurance, trust services and patent consulting. In most instances, these ancillary non-legal services were provided to law firm clients in connection with, and concurrent to, the provision of legal services by the lawyer or law firm. The provision of such services afforded benefits to clients, including making available a greater range of services from one source and maintaining technical expertise in various fields within a law firm. However, the provision of both legal and ancillary non-legal services raises ethical concerns, including conflicts of interest, confusion on the part of clients and possible loss (or inapplicability) of the attorney-client privilege, which may not have been addressed adequately by the other Model Rules of Professional Conduct.

[2] Eventually, law firms began to form affiliates, largely staffed by non-lawyers, to provide ancillary non-legal services to both clients and customers who were not clients for legal services. In addition to exacerbating the ethical problems of conflicts of interest, confusion and threats to confidentiality, the large-scale movement of law firms into ancillary non-legal businesses raised serious professionalism concerns, including compromising lawyers' independent judgment, the loss of the bar's right to self-regulation and the provision of legal services by entities controlled by non-lawyers.

[3] Rule 5.7 addresses both the ethical and professionalism concerns implicated by the provision of ancillary non-legal services by lawyers and law firms. It preserves the ability of lawyers to provide additional services to their clients and maintain within the law firm a broad range of technical expertise. However, Rule 5.7 restricts the ability of law firms to provide ancillary non-legal services through affiliates to non-client customers and clients alike, the rendition of which raises serious ethical and professionalism concerns.

1992 Deletion: The original version of Rule 5.7 was deleted from the ABA Model Rules at the ABA's 1992 Annual Meeting. The report urging deletion of the rule was jointly submitted by the Illinois State Bar Association, the ABA Standing Committee on Lawyers Title Guaranty Funds, and six ABA sections. The House of Delegates voted 190-183 to delete the rule. Rule 5.7 was the first rule ever to be deleted from the Model Rules.

1994 Version: The current version of Rule 5.7 was adopted by the ABA House of Delegates by a margin of 237-183 at the ABA's February 1994 Mid-Year Meeting. From August 1992 (when the original version of Rule 5.7 was deleted) until February 1994 (when the new version was adopted), the Model Rules did not contain any version of Rule 5.7. However, because the vote to adopt and then delete the original version of Rule 5.7 had been so hotly contested (a margin of less than 10 votes each time), House of Delegates Chair Phil Anderson of Arkansas appointed a Special Committee on Ancillary Business Services after the 1992 vote to "review the work that had been done by various Association entities on the subject of ancillary business activities of lawyers, and to make a recommendation to the House of Delegates for an appropriate position on that subject." The Special Committee, chaired by William G. Paul, recommended that the ABA adopt the current version of Rule 5.7. This marked the first time that a Model Rule was proposed by a Special House of Delegates Committee rather than by a Section or Standing Committee. Here are substantial excerpts from the Special Committee's Report in support of the 1994 version of Rule 5.7:

*Excerpt from Report of the Special House of Delegates Committee on
Ancillary Business in Support of the 1994 Version of Rule 5.7**

[T]he Committee made inquiries of State Bars, disciplinary agencies and entities of the ABA to ascertain what, if any, ethical or other problems have been encountered in the provision of law-related services. The Committee is satisfied that law-related services are being provided wherever lawyers practice, that law-related services are often provided by separate entities, and that there has been no reported disciplinary infraction or malpractice claim resulting from the provision of law-related services. . . . Several respondents expressed concern about potential confusion on the part of recipients of law-related services regarding the nature of their relationship with the lawyer, although no instances of actual confusion were reported to the Committee. Responses also indicated a profusion of law-related services, some traditional in the jurisdiction, and others of more recent origin. These include not only the provision of trust services, title insurance, accounting and escrow services, but also the furnishing of insurance investigation, psychological counseling, lobbying, arbitration and mediation, registered corporate agent representation, and environmental consulting services. The Committee believes that the list of law-related services is not only long, but growing longer.

The Committee concluded that law-related services should not be prohibited. Instead, the Committee proposes adoption of a rule that specifically treats law-

---

*Committee Reports do not represent official policy of the ABA. They are for information only, and the opinions are those of the authors of the report.

yers' dealings with recipients of law-related services. The proposed rule supplements existing Rules that apply to such relationships. . . .

Examples of law-related services are provided in the Comment to the proposed Rule, but these are by no means exhaustive. The Committee found that the types of law-related services are virtually unlimited, and that new types continue to be developed. Accordingly, the definition is intended to encompass a wide range of services whether or not the services are of a type currently being provided.

Controversy over law-related services arose from a concern for lawyer professionalism. The Committee believes that it is not necessary to prohibit the provision of law-related services in order to protect lawyer professionalism, but that lawyer professionalism will be fostered by permitting the delivery of law-related services under regulated conditions. . . .

Even when the recipient of law-related services is not a client of the lawyer, the law of principal and agent affords the recipient significant protections against disclosure or use of confidence, conflicts of interest, and self-dealing. The Committee notes, in this context, that it found no justification for affording recipients of law-related services through separate entities greater protection than that to which they would otherwise be entitled solely because lawyers control the separate entity.

Selected State Variations

District of Columbia has not adopted a rule equivalent to ABA Model Rule 5.7, but has adopted a version of Rule 5.4 that permits non-lawyers to become partners under certain circumstances — see District of Columbia Rules of Professional Conduct below.

Indiana adopted Rule 5.7 effective March 1, 1997.

Maine adopted a version Rule 5.7 based almost verbatim on the ABA Model Rule effective February 15, 1997 — see Maine Rule 3.2(h). The Advisory Committee Note to Rule 3.2(h) states, in part:

> In Maine the scope of "law-related services" as opposed to legal services may be quite broad, in view of the indefinite meaning of "unauthorized practice." It may be that in this jurisdiction any service other than litigation is a "law-related service." Familiar examples would include, however, the preparation of a federal income tax return, lobbying and such activities as real estate brokerage and marital counseling. . . . [T]itle insurance is the most common example of law-related services provided through a separate entity by a Maine law firm.

North Dakota adopted Rule 5.7 effective March 1, 1997.

Pennsylvania, which adopted a version of Rule 5.7 in 1996, was the first state to do so. The Pennsylvania rule, which differs significantly from ABA Model Rule 5.7, provides as follows:

RULE 5.7 Responsibilities Regarding Nonlegal Services

(a) A lawyer who provides nonlegal services to a recipient that are not distinct from legal services provided to that recipient is subject to the Rules of Professional Conduct with respect to the provision of both legal and nonlegal services.

(b) A lawyer who provides nonlegal services to a recipient that are distinct from any legal services provided to the recipient is subject to the Rules of Professional Conduct with respect to the nonlegal services if the lawyer knows or reasonably should know that the recipient might believe that the recipient is receiving the protection of a client-lawyer relationship.

(c) A lawyer who is an owner, controlling party, employee, agent, or is otherwise affiliated with an entity providing nonlegal services to a recipient is subject to the Rules of Professional Conduct with respect to the nonlegal services if the lawyer knows or reasonably should know that the recipient might believe that the recipient is receiving the protection of a client-lawyer relationship.

(d) Paragraph (b) or (c) does not apply if the lawyer makes reasonable efforts to avoid any misunderstanding by the recipient receiving nonlegal services. Those efforts must include advising the recipient that the services are not legal services and that the protection of a client-lawyer relationship does not exist with respect to the provision of nonlegal services to the recipient.

Related Materials

Professionalism Report: The ABA's Stanley Commission Report on Professionalism, 112 F.R.D. 243 (1986), called the trend toward law firm involvement in nonlegal services "disturbing" and urged the ABA to "initiate a study to see what, if any, controls or prohibitions should be imposed."

ARTICLE 6. PUBLIC SERVICE

Rule 6.1 Voluntary Pro Bono Publico Service

Editors' Note. At its February 1993 Mid-Year Meeting, the ABA House of Delegates voted by the narrow margin of 228-215 to amend Rule 6.1 substantially and to rewrite the Comment entirely. In the Legislative History section following the rule, we include a substantial excerpt from the Committee Report explaining the 1993 amendment.

A lawyer should aspire to render at least (50) hours of pro bono publico legal services per year. In fulfilling this responsibility, the lawyer should:

(a) provide a substantial majority of the (50) hours of legal services without fee or expectation of fee to:

(1) persons of limited means or

(2) charitable, religious, civic, community, governmental and educational organizations in matters which are designed primarily to address the needs of persons of limited means, and

(b) provide any additional services through:

(1) delivery of legal services at no fee or a substantially reduced fee to public service or charitable groups or organizations, individuals, groups or organizations seeking to secure or protect civil rights, civil liberties or public rights, or charitable, religious, civic, community, governmental and educational organizations in matters in furtherance of their organizational purposes, where the payment of standard legal fees would significantly deplete the organization's economic resources or would be otherwise inappropriate;

(2) delivery of legal services at a substantially reduced fee to persons of limited means; or

(3) participation in activities for improving the law, the legal system or the legal profession.

In addition, a lawyer should voluntarily contribute financial support for organizations that provide legal services to persons of limited means.

COMMENT

[1] Every lawyer, regardless of professional prominence or professional work load, has a responsibility to provide legal services to those unable to pay, and personal involvement in the problems of the disadvantaged can be one of the most rewarding experiences in the life of a lawyer. The American Bar Association urges all lawyers to provide a minimum of 50 hours of pro bono services annually. States, however, may decide to choose a higher or lower number of hours of annual service (which may be expressed as a percentage of a lawyer's professional time) depending upon local needs and local conditions. It is recognized that in some years a lawyer may render greater or fewer hours than the annual standard specified, but during the course of his or her legal career, each lawyer should render on average per year, the number of hours set forth in this Rule. Services can be performed in civil matters or in criminal or quasi-criminal matters for which there is no government obligation to provide funds for legal representation, such as post-conviction death penalty appeal cases.

[2] Paragraphs (a)(1) and (2) recognize the critical need for legal services that exists among persons of limited means by providing that a substantial majority of the legal services rendered annually to the disadvantaged be furnished without fee or expectation of fee. Legal services under these paragraphs consist of a full range of activities, including individual and class representation, the provision of legal advice, legislative lobbying, administrative rule making and the provision of free training

or mentoring to those who represent persons of limited means. The variety of these activities should facilitate participation by government attorneys, even when restrictions exist on their engaging in the outside practice of law.

[3] Persons eligible for legal services under paragraphs (a)(1) and (2) are those who qualify for participation in programs funded by the Legal Services Corporation and those whose incomes and financial resources are slightly above the guidelines utilized by such programs but, nevertheless, cannot afford counsel. Legal services can be rendered to individuals or to organizations such as homeless shelters, battered women's centers and food pantries that serve those of limited means.

[4] Because service must be provided without fee or expectation of fee, the intent of the lawyer to render free legal services is essential for the work performed to fall within the meaning of paragraphs (a)(1) and (2). Accordingly, services rendered cannot be considered pro bono if an anticipated fee is uncollected, but the award of statutory attorneys' fees in a case originally accepted as pro bono would not disqualify such services from inclusion under this section. Lawyers who do receive fees in such cases are encouraged to contribute an appropriate portion of such fees to organizations or projects that benefit persons of limited means.

[5] While it is possible for a lawyer to fulfill the annual responsibility to perform pro bono services exclusively through activities described in paragraphs (a)(1) and (2), to the extent that any hours of service remained unfulfilled, the remaining commitment can be met in a variety of ways as set forth in paragraph (b).

[6] Paragraph (b)(1) includes the provision of certain types of legal services to those whose incomes and financial resources place them above limited means. It also permits the pro bono attorney to accept a substantially reduced fee for services. Examples of the types of issues that may be addressed under this paragraph include First Amendment claims, Title VII claims and environmental protection claims. Additionally, a wide range of organizations may be represented, including social service, medical research, cultural and religious groups.

[7] Paragraph (b)(2) covers instances in which attorneys agree to and receive a modest fee for furnishing legal services to persons of limited means. Participation in judicare programs and acceptance of court appointments in which the fee is substantially below a lawyer's usual rate are encouraged under this section.

[8] Paragraph (b)(3) recognizes the value of lawyers engaging in activities that improve the law, the legal system or the legal profession. Serving on bar association committees, serving on boards of pro bono

or legal services programs, taking part in Law Day activities, acting as a continuing legal education instructor, a mediator or an arbitrator and engaging in legislative lobbying to improve the law, the legal system or the profession are a few examples of the many activities that fall within this paragraph.

[9] Because the provision of pro bono services is a professional responsibility, it is the individual ethical commitment of each lawyer. Nevertheless, there may be times when it is not feasible for a lawyer to engage in pro bono services. At such times a lawyer may discharge the pro bono responsibility by providing financial support to organizations providing free legal services to persons of limited means. Such financial support should be reasonably equivalent to the value of the hours of service that would have otherwise been provided. In addition, at times it may be more feasible to satisfy the pro bono responsibility collectively, as by a firm's aggregate pro bono activities.

[10] Because the efforts of individual lawyers are not enough to meet the need for free legal services that exists among persons of limited means, the government and the profession have instituted additional programs to provide those services. Every lawyer should financially support such programs, in addition to either providing direct pro bono services or making financial contributions when pro bono service is not feasible.

[11] The responsibility set forth in this Rule is not intended to be enforced through disciplinary process.

Model Code Comparison

There was no counterpart of this Rule in the Disciplinary Rules of the Model Code. EC 2-25 stated that the "basic responsibility for providing legal services for those unable to pay ultimately rests upon the individual lawyer. . . . Every lawyer, regardless of professional prominence or professional work load, should find time to participate in serving the disadvantaged." EC 8-9 stated that "[t]he advancement of our legal system is of vital importance in maintaining the rule of law . . . [and] lawyers should encourage, and should aid in making, needed changes and improvements." EC 8-3 stated that "[t]hose persons unable to pay for legal services should be provided needed services."

Cross-Reference in Rules

Rule 6.2, Comment 1: "All lawyers have a responsibility to assist in providing pro bono publico service. See Rule 6.1."

Legislative History

1980 Discussion Draft of Rule 6.1 (then Rule 8.1) provided as follows: "A lawyer *shall* render unpaid public interest legal services. . . . A lawyer shall make an annual report concerning such service to appropriate regulatory authority."

1981 and 1982 Drafts were the same as adopted in 1983, except that neither draft contained the final clause, "by financial support for organizations that provide legal services to persons of limited means."

1983-1993 Rule: The version of Rule 6.1 originally adopted by the ABA in 1983 (which remained in effect until its amendment in 1993) provided as follows:

> A lawyer should render public interest legal service. A lawyer may discharge this responsibility by providing professional services at no fee or a reduced fee to persons of limited means or to public service or charitable groups or organizations, by service in activities for improving the law, the legal system or the legal profession, and by financial support for organizations that provide legal services to persons of limited means.

1993 Amendment: At its 1993 Mid-Year Meeting, the ABA House of Delegates voted to amend Rule 6.1 substantially and to rewrite its Comment entirely. The amendment was controversial, and passed by the close vote of 228-215. The principal sponsor and author of the amended rule was the ABA's Standing Committee on Lawyers' Public Service Responsibility (SCLPSR). Co-sponsors of the amendment were the ABA Section of Litigation, the ABA Section of Tort and Insurance Practice (TIPS), the ABA Young Lawyers Division, the State Bar of California, and the Minnesota State Bar Association. The amendment was drafted over a period of about two years, during which the ABA held public hearings on the proposed amendment in several cities and circulated SCLPSR's draft proposals to thousands of people in the legal profession.

Because amendments to the Model Rules are usually proposed by the ABA's Standing Committee on Ethics and Professional Responsibility, SCLPSR held a number of joint meetings with that committee. However, SCLPSR and the Standing Committee on Ethics and Professional Responsibility were unable to agree on a joint proposal. The Standing Committee on Ethics and Professional Responsibility had three major problems with the amendment: (1) the Standing Committee on Ethics and Professional Responsibility opposed setting a specific target number of hours of pro bono service per year (preferring a word like "substantial" instead of a number); (2) it opposed urging lawyers to allocate most of their pro bono hours to serving the poor (out of concern that pro bono work for civil rights, the environment, and other important areas would diminish); and (3) it would have favored a "buy-out" provision allowing lawyers to substitute financial support for personal service.

We reprint below excerpts from the Committee Report issued by SCLPSR and its five co-sponsors in support of the 1993 amendment to Rule 6.1:

*Excerpts from ABA Committee Report Supporting 1993 Amendment
to Rule 6.1**

THE CURRENT CRISIS IN THE DELIVERY OF LEGAL
SERVICES TO THE POOR

[B]ecause the legal problems of the economically disadvantaged often involve areas of basic need such as minimum levels of income and entitlements, shelter, utilities and child support, their inability to obtain legal services can have dire consequences. For example, the failure of a poor person to have effective legal counsel in an eviction proceeding may well result in homelessness; the failure to have legal counsel present at a public aid hearing may result in the denial of essential food or medical benefits.

The inability of the poor to obtain needed legal services has been well documented: since 1983, when Rule 6.1 was adopted, at least one national and 13 statewide studies assessing the legal needs of the poor have been conducted. Of those studies reporting unmet legal need, there has been a consistent finding that only about 15%-20% of the legal needs of the poor are being addressed. The legal need studies also confirmed that unmet need exists in critical areas such as public benefits, utilities, shelter, medical benefits and family matters. . . .

The Committee firmly believes that the private bar alone cannot be expected to fill the gap for service that exists among the poor. Rather, the federal government, through adequate funding of the Legal Services Corporation (LSC), should bear the major responsibility for addressing the problem. Although the federal government has never provided sufficient funding for the LSC, during the past decade funding has fallen even further, causing the crisis of unmet legal needs among the poor to be exacerbated. Specifically, in FY 1981, the annual budget for LSC was $321 million, while in FY 1991, the annual budget was only $328 million. Given the fact that the consumer price index increased by well over 50% from 1980 to 1990 and that during that same time period the poverty population is estimated to have increased by 15.4%, funding for LSC is clearly inadequate.

The Association has consistently called upon the President, the Legal Services Corporation and Congress to support substantially increased funding for LSC so that sufficient resources for high quality legal services programs are available. Although the response to those requests has been inadequate, the Committee urges the Association to continue its efforts. In addition, the Association must again turn to members of the private bar and call upon them to help ease the crisis that exists in the provision of legal services to the poor. The Committee believes that one effective means of doing this is by revising Model Rule 6.1 to reflect a new emphasis on service to the disadvantaged. . . .

III. Discussion of the Proposed Revisions to Rule 6.1

In order to clarify that Rule 6.1 remains a voluntary aspirational standard, the words "aspire to" have been added to the first sentence of the Rule. The first sentence also contains one of the most notable changes proposed to Rule 6.1: the ad-

---

*Committee Reports do not represent official policy of the ABA. They are for information only, and the opinions are those of the authors of the report.

dition of language that specifies the minimum number of hours of activity on an annual basis that would be necessary to fulfill the pro bono responsibility. . . . The Committee believes that while 50 hours is a reasonable standard, each state should retain the flexibility to determine the standard that is best for it, based upon local needs and local conditions. While some states may adopt an annual standard that is lower than 50 hours, some states may decide on a higher number, as Oregon did in adopting a pro bono resolution calling upon all lawyers to render 80 hours of pro bono service annually.

To address the crisis in the delivery of legal services to the poor, the proposed revision provides that a substantial majority of the annual hours of pro bono legal services should be rendered at no cost to persons of limited means or to organizations in matters which are designed primarily to address the needs of persons of limited means. The Committee purposely chose the words "substantial majority" to make clear that a simple majority of the hours would not suffice. While the Committee recognizes the value and importance of other types of pro bono activity, it strongly believes that due to the enormity of the unmet need for legal services that exists among the disadvantaged, the provision of legal services to that group must be given priority over all other types of pro bono service. . . .

In addition to voluntarily rendering pro bono service, the revised Rule 6.1 calls upon every lawyer to voluntarily make financial contributions to organizations providing legal services to persons of limited means. In those cases in which a lawyer determines that it is not feasible to render legal services and makes a financial contribution instead, he or she is expected to make an additional contribution pursuant to the last sentence of the new Rule. The Committee firmly believes that given the severe crisis that exists in the delivery of legal services to the poor, lawyers should not only provide pro bono services directly, but also should help to financially support the very important work that is carried out by legal services programs throughout the country.

It is the Committee's intent that the ethical responsibilities set forth in Rule 6.1 apply to all lawyers and not just those currently engaged in the practice of law. Thus, any reference found to that status in the existing Comment has been eliminated in the revised one.

Although neither the Rule nor the Comment explicitly so states, it should be self evident that every lawyer is expected to provide the same quality of legal services to pro bono clients as he or she would provide to paying clients. . . . Therefore, to the extent that an attorney is unfamiliar with a given area of the law, he or she is expected to seek advice or training in that area before advising a client, either for a fee or on a pro bono basis. Many pro bono programs provide free training on a wide range of topics to assist their volunteer attorneys in attaining competency to handle the cases referred to them. The Committee strongly endorses the provision of these training events and urges pro bono attorneys to take advantage of them whenever possible.

Consistent with present Rule 6.1, the Comment to the revised Rule explicitly states that the pro bono responsibility is not intended to be enforced through the disciplinary process. Thus as drafted, revised Rule 6.1 does not mandate pro bono. Although the Committee recognizes that since 1988, mandatory pro bono proposals have been considered in many states and remain under active consideration in several of them, it nevertheless believes that it is not practical nor feasible at this time to address the issue of mandatory pro bono on a national level. Rather, the

Committee views the question of mandatory pro bono as an issue that needs to be examined by state and local bar associations. Some communities might find mandatory pro bono helpful; others may determine it to be counterproductive. . . .

Selected State Variations

Arizona: In October 1990, Arizona amended its version of Rule 6.1 so that it now contains the following key provisions:

(a) A lawyer should voluntarily render public interest legal service. A lawyer may discharge this responsibility by rendering a minimum of fifty hours of service per calendar year. . . .

(c) A law firm or other group of lawyers may satisfy their responsibility under this Rule, if they desire, collectively. For example, the designation of one or more lawyers to work on pro bono publico matters may be attributed to other lawyers within the firm or group who support the representation. . . .

(d) The efforts of individual lawyers are not enough to meet the needs of the poor. The profession and government have instituted programs to provide direct delivery of legal services to the poor. The direct support of such programs is an alternative expression of support to provide law in the public interest, and a lawyer is encouraged to provide financial support for organizations that provide legal services to persons of limited means or to the Arizona Bar Foundation for the direct delivery of legal services to the poor.

California: No comparable provision.

District of Columbia: D.C. Rule 6.1 differs significantly from the ABA Model Rule — see District of Columbia Rules of Professional Conduct below.

Florida: On June 23, 1993, in a divided opinion, the Florida Supreme Court adopted an elaborate new pro bono rule, which took effect on October 1, 1993. See 630 So. 2d 501 (Fla. 1993). The new rule provides as follows:

4-6.1 Pro Bono Public Service

(a) *Professional Responsibility.* Each member of The Florida Bar in good standing, as part of that member's professional responsibility, should (1) render pro bono legal services to the poor or (2) participate, to the extent possible, in other pro bono service activities that directly relate to the legal needs of the poor. This professional responsibility does not apply to members of the judiciary or their staffs or to government lawyers who are prohibited from performing legal services by constitutional, statutory, rule, or regulatory prohibitions. Neither does this professional responsibility apply to those members of The Bar who are retired, inactive, or suspended, or who have been placed on the inactive list for incapacity not related to discipline.

(b) *Discharge of the Professional Responsibility to Provide Pro Bono Legal Service to the Poor.* The professional responsibility to provide pro bono legal services as established under this rule is *aspirational* rather than mandatory in nature. The failure to fulfill one's professional responsibility under this rule will not subject a lawyer to discipline. The professional responsibility to provide pro bono legal service to the poor may be discharged by:

(1) annually providing at least 20 hours of pro bono legal service to the poor; or

(2) making an annual contribution of at least $350 to a legal aid organization.

(c) *Collective Discharge of the Professional Responsibility to Provide Pro Bono Legal Service to the Poor.* Each member of the bar should strive to individually satisfy the member's professional responsibility to provide pro bono legal service to the poor. Collective satisfaction of this professional responsibility is permitted by law firms only under a collective satisfaction plan that has been filed previously with the circuit pro bono committee and *only* when providing pro bono legal service to the poor:

(1) in a major case or matter involving a substantial expenditure of time and resources; or

(2) through a full-time community or public service staff; or

(3) in any other manner that has been approved by the circuit pro bono committee in the circuit in which the firm practices.

(d) *Reporting Requirement.* Each member of the bar shall annually report whether the member has satisfied the member's professional responsibility to provide pro bono legal services to the poor. Each member shall report this information through a simplified reporting form that is made a part of the member's annual dues statement. The form will contain the following categories from which each member will be allowed to choose in reporting whether the member has provided pro bono legal services to the poor:

(1) I have personally provided _____ hours of pro bono legal services;

(2) I have provided pro bono legal services collectively by: (indicate type of case and manner in which service was provided);

(3) I have contributed $_____ to: (indicate organization to which funds were provided);

(4) I have provided legal services to the poor in the following special manner: (indicate manner in which services were provided); or

(5) I have been unable to provide pro bono legal services to the poor this year; or

(6) I am deferred from the provision of pro bono legal services to the poor because I am: (indicate whether lawyer is: a member of the judiciary or judicial staff; a government lawyer prohibited by statute, rule, or regulation from providing services; retired, or inactive).

The failure to report this information shall constitute a disciplinary offense under these rules.

(e) . . .

Judge Kogan dissented because he would have preferred a mandatory pro bono requirement of at least 20 hours per year of legal services to the poor. (His views were expressed in detail in 1992 in 598 So. 2d 41, 55-60.) He also opposed the $350 "buy-out" provision, on the following grounds:

I find it ethically repugnant to suggest that an obligation inhering in each attorney personally can be discharged merely by a contribution of money. Under this provision, financially able attorneys can buy their way clear of the aspirational duty to help the poor, while less financially able attorneys who take their ethical obligations seriously will be constrained to donate services. Both should be treated equally.

Chapter 12 of the Rules Regulating the Florida Bar supplements its pro bono programs by establishing an "Emeritus Attorneys Pro Bono Participation Plan" that allows retired Florida attorneys (who are no longer licensed to practice law) to render legal services to indigents under the auspices of legal aid organizations if they are directly supervised by an active licensed attorney. Effective October 1, 1993, Florida also adopted a new Rule 6.5 to govern voluntary pro bono plans. Rule 4-6.5 provides that the "President-elect of The Florida Bar shall appoint a standing committee on legal service to the poor," and sets forth the composition and responsibilities of the standing committee. Rule 4-6.5 also requires the chief judge in each of Florida's judicial circuits to appoint a "circuit pro bono committee" that must prepare, implement, and monitor the circuit's pro bono plan, and report annually to The Florida Bar's standing committee about the plan. Finally, Rule 6.5 lists a dozen "Suggested Pro Bono Service Opportunities."

Illinois omits Rule 6.1 and explains why in its Preamble:

> It is the responsibility of those licensed as officers of the court to use their training, experience and skills to provide services in the public interest for which compensation may not be available. It is the responsibility of those who manage law firms to create an environment that is hospitable to the rendering of a reasonable amount of uncompensated service by lawyers practicing in that firm.
>
> Service in the public interest may take many forms. These include but are not limited to *pro bono* representation of persons unable to pay for legal services and assistance in the organized bar's efforts at law reform. An individual lawyer's efforts in these areas is evidence of the lawyer's good character and fitness to practice law, and the efforts of the bar as a whole are essential to the bar's maintenance of professionalism.
>
> The absence from the proposed new rules of ABA Model Rule 6.1 regarding *pro bono* and public service therefore should not be interpreted as limiting the responsibility of attorneys to render uncompensated service in the public interest. Rather, the rationale for the absence of ABA Model Rule 6.1 is that this concept is not appropriate for a disciplinary code, because an appropriate disciplinary standard regarding *pro bono* and public service is difficult, if not impossible, to articulate. That ABA Model Rule 6.1 itself uses the word "should" instead of "shall" in describing this duty reflects the uncertainty of the ABA on this issue.

Kentucky: In July 1992, Kentucky amended its Rule 6.1, entitled "Donated Legal Services," to read as follows:

> A lawyer is encouraged to voluntarily render public interest legal service. A lawyer is encouraged to accept and fulfill this responsibility to the public by rendering a minimum of fifty (50) hours of service per calendar year by providing professional services at no fee or a reduced fee to persons of limited means, and/or by financial support for organizations that provide legal services to persons of limited means. Donated legal services may be reported on the annual dues statement fur-

nished by the Kentucky Bar Association. Lawyers rendering a minimum of fifty (50) hours of donated legal service shall receive a recognition award for such service from the Kentucky Bar Association.

Minnesota: Rule 6.1 says that a lawyer "should aspire to render at least 50 hours of pro bono publico legal services per year." In addition, a lawyer "should voluntarily contribute financial support to organizations that provide legal services to persons of limited means."

Montana: Rule 6.1 says that a "lawyer should aspire to render at least (50) hours of pro bono publico legal services per year. The rule specifies that this aspiration can be fulfilled by providing no-fee services to "persons of limited means or [to] charitable, religious, civic, community, governmental and educational organizations in matters which are designed primarily to address the needs of persons of limited means." But Montana describes the "responsibility" in this rule as "a goal to which each lawyer should aspire." The rule "will not be enforced through any form of disciplinary process."

New Mexico: Effective January 1, 1997, New Mexico amended its pro bono rule, Rule 16-601, to conform almost verbatim to ABA Model Rule 6.1, except that New Mexico has modified the last sentence of ABA Model Rule 6.1 by providing that a lawyer may "alternatively, fulfill this aspiration by contributing financial support to organizations that provide legal services to persons of limited means, in the amount of three hundred fifty dollars ($350.00) per year."

New York: Same or substantially the same as the ABA Model Code — see Model Code Comparison above. See also EC 2-25 of the New York Code.

Virginia omits Rule 6.1, but adds an EC 2-29 (effective July 1, 1994 and amended on January 23, 1995) that defines pro bono services to include poverty law, civil rights law, civic or public interest law, and "[u]ncompensated activity designed to increase the availability of legal services of the types described above." EC 2-29 ends with the following statement: "Legal services should be viewed broadly as including any service which utilizes a lawyer's legal training and skills."

Related Materials

ABA Model Guidelines for the Utilization of Legal Assistant Services: In 1991, the ABA House of Delegates approved Model Guidelines for the Utilization of Legal Assistant Services. Guideline 10 provides: "A lawyer who employs a legal assistant should facilitate the legal assistant's participation in appropriate continuing education and pro bono publico activities."

ABA Standards for Programs Providing Civil Pro Bono Legal Services to Persons of Limited Means: At its February 1996 Mid-Year Meeting, the ABA House of Delegates approved Standards for Programs Providing Civil Pro Bono Legal Services to Persons of Limited Means, which were drafted by the ABA Standing

Committee on Lawyers' Public Service Responsibility ("SCLPSR"). The standards, which were adopted exactly as proposed by SCLPSR, provide guidance to newly established pro bono programs and furnish a basis for evaluating and improving existing programs. The introduction to the standards notes that organized pro bono programs have grown in number at a remarkable rate, from 80 in 1980 to more than 900 in 1995. The standards cover such things as fundraising, conflicts of interest, communication with clients, training of volunteers, and case acceptance policy. The standards were first circulated for public comment in February of 1995, and SCLPSR held three public hearings on the proposed standards. The standards replace the ABA's Standards for Providers of Civil Legal Services to the Poor, which were originally adopted in 1961 and last revised in 1986. For more information about the standards, contact Gwendolyn Rowan at the ABA Center for Professional Responsibility, 541 N. Fairbanks Court, Chicago, IL 60611, (312) 988-5756.

American Lawyer's Code of Conduct: The Comment to Chapter 8 of the ALCC states:

> This Code has no rule requiring each lawyer to do a particular amount of uncompensated public interest or *pro bono publico* work, on pain of professional discipline. That does not mean that the attorney members of the Commission are unwilling to perform such services or that the non-lawyer members do not want to share in the benefits of *pro bono* work. Rather, it is apparent to the Commission that such a rule would be inherently so vague as to be unenforceable and unenforced, and therefore hypocritical.
>
> All lawyers should do work in the public interest. But some lawyers should not be telling other lawyers how much *pro bono* work they should be doing, and for whom, and disciplining them if they do not. Nor should codes of conduct purport to impose disciplinary requirements that the codifiers know will not be enforced.

Awards for Pro Bono Work: The ABA and virtually all state and local bar associations bestow awards to recognize pro bono work. For example, in 1994 the Pro Bono Committee of the ABA's Section of Business Law created a new National Award for Public Service. The New York State Bar Association annually presents the President's Pro Bono Service Award to individual lawyers, law firms, law students, and law student groups who have distinguished themselves by rendering outstanding public service without compensation. Some pro bono awards carry cash prizes, but most include simply honor and publicity.

Federal Personnel Manual: Chapter 990 of the Federal Personnel Manual, issued in 1985, states that while federal lawyers may have an obligation to do pro bono work, "it can be argued that service as counsel to the Federal Government is pro bono publico by definition." Chapter 990 also places substantial restrictions on pro bono work by federal lawyers, such as (1) federal lawyers may not perform pro bono services on government time; (2) federal lawyers may not ask goverment clerical employees to help with pro bono matters, "even on off-duty hours on a voluntary basis." See Lisa Lerman, Public Service by Public Servants, 19 Hofstra L. Rev. 1141, 1195 (1991).

Federal Statutes: Certain federal statutes may preclude federal government lawyers from doing any pro bono work adverse to any agency or department of the United States government. For example, 18 U.S.C. §205 defines a federal lawyer's "client" as the United States government and makes it a criminal offense, punishable by up to five years in prison or a $50,000 fine, for a federal lawyer to act as an "attorney for prosecuting any claim against the United States. . . ."

Law School Pro Bono Requirements: A number of law schools now require law students to engage in a specified amount of pro bono work as a condition of graduation. Columbia Law School, for example, requires all students to perform 40 hours of public interest service between the start of the second year and graduation. Students at Columbia can register to work at any of more than 500 public interest placements, covering a wide variety of work settings. Students who do not complete the 40 hours cannot graduate. For more information on the Columbia program, contact the Columbia Law School Public Interest Program, 435 W. 116th Street, Box E-16, New York, NY 10027, (212) 854-6158.

Mandatory Pro Bono Plans: A growing number of courts and local bar associations are adopting mandatory pro bono plans.

Model Rules of Professional Conduct for Federal Lawyers add a new subparagraph (b) providing that government lawyers "should provide pro bono legal services consistent with applicable law." In addition, Rule 5.1(d) provides that a supervisory government lawyer "should encourage subordinate lawyers to participate in pro bono publico service activities and the activities of bar associations and law reform organizations." However, the Comment to Rule 6.1 explains that "18 U.S.C. §205 and §209 and other laws, including those governing off-duty employment by members of the Armed Forces, may regulate a Government lawyer's ability to provide legal services on a pro bono basis outside the scope of the Government lawyer's official duties."

Statement of Principles by Chicago Law Firms: In September of 1991, 31 major Chicago law firms formally adopted the following Statement of Principles relating to pro bono work:

> In response to the unmet legal needs of the poor and other unrepresented and disadvantaged members of our community, and in the hope that our actions will encourage similar actions by other lawyers throughout the state of Illinois, the undersigned Chicago law firms endorse and commit themselves to these principles:
>
> 1. It is the obligation of lawyers and law firms generally to use their training, experience and skills to provide services in the public interest for which compensation may not be available.
>
> 2. Those lawyers who manage law firms should take the lead in encouraging other lawyers to provide pro bono legal services and in providing an environment which is hospitable to the rendition of such services.
>
> 3. Law firms should adopt written statements of policy which encourage their partners and associates to handle legal matters on a voluntary, pro bono basis and in the public interest, with credit toward annual hourly requirements or goals.

4. Law firms should assign to one or more of their members specific responsibility for encouraging, coordination and supervising pro bono work as a regular part of the firm's practice.

5. Work done on a pro bono basis should be handled with the same care and supervision as work done for a firm's paying clients.

6. Law firms should make it a goal to contribute an average of at least 30 hours of legal services per lawyer per year to representing the poor or other persons and organizations who are unable to retain legal counsel and which serve the public interest.

7. Law firms should contribute financially to organizations, programs and agencies which provide free legal assistance. Such contributions should be commensurate with law firms' special status within the community.

Student Practice Programs: Most state and federal courts have established student practice programs that allow law students who meet certain criteria to represent indigents or government agencies, provided the students are supervised by licensed attorneys. A good example is Local Rule 46(e) of the United States Court of Appeals for the Second Circuit.

Rule 6.2 Accepting Appointments

A lawyer shall not seek to avoid appointment by a tribunal to represent a person except for good cause, such as:

(a) representing the client is likely to result in violation of the rules of professional conduct or other law;

(b) representing the client is likely to result in an unreasonable financial burden on the lawyer; or

(c) the client or the cause is so repugnant to the lawyer as to be likely to impair the client-lawyer relationship or the lawyer's ability to represent the client.

COMMENT

[1] A lawyer ordinarily is not obliged to accept a client whose character or cause the lawyer regards as repugnant. The lawyer's freedom to select clients is, however, qualified. All lawyers have a responsibility to assist in providing pro bono publico service. See Rule 6.1. An individual lawyer fulfills this responsibility by accepting a fair share of unpopular matters or indigent or unpopular clients. A lawyer may also be subject to appointment by a court to serve unpopular clients or persons unable to afford legal services.

Appointed Counsel

[2] For good cause a lawyer may seek to decline an appointment to represent a person who cannot afford to retain counsel or whose cause is unpopular. Good cause exists if the lawyer could not handle the matter competently, see Rule 1.1, or if undertaking the representation would result in an improper conflict of interest, for example, when the client or the cause is so repugnant to the lawyer as to be likely to impair the client-lawyer relationship or the lawyer's ability to represent the client. A lawyer may also seek to decline an appointment if acceptance would be unreasonably burdensome, for example, when it would impose a financial sacrifice so great as to be unjust.

[3] An appointed lawyer has the same obligations to the client as retained counsel, including the obligations of loyalty and confidentiality, and is subject to the same limitations on the client-lawyer relationship, such as the obligation to refrain from assisting the client in violation of the Rules.

Model Code Comparison

There was no counterpart to this Rule in the Disciplinary Rules of the Model Code. EC 2-29 stated that when a lawyer is "appointed by a court or requested by a bar association to undertake representation of a person unable to obtain counsel, whether for financial or other reasons, he should not seek to be excused from undertaking the representation except for compelling reasons. Compelling reasons do not include such factors as the repugnance of the subject matter of the proceeding, the identity or position of a person involved in the case, the belief of the lawyer that the defendant in a criminal proceeding is guilty, or the belief of the lawyer regarding the merits of the civil case." EC 2-30 stated that "a lawyer should decline employment if the intensity of his personal feelings, as distinguished from a community attitude, may impair his effective representation of a prospective client."

Cross-References in Rules

Rule 1.1, Comment 4: "A lawyer may accept representation where the requisite level of competence can be achieved by reasonable preparation. This applies as well to a lawyer who is appointed as counsel for an unrepresented person. See also **Rule 6.2**."

Rule 1.16, Comment 3: "When a lawyer has been appointed to represent a client, withdrawal ordinarily requires approval of the appointing authority. See also **Rule 6.2**."

Legislative History

1980 Discussion Draft and 1981 Draft were substantially the same as adopted, with only minor changes in phrasing.

1982 Draft was the same as adopted *except* that it completely omitted subparagraph (c).

Selected State Variations

California: See B & P Code §6068(h). (California's Rules of Professional Conduct have no comparable provision.)

New York: Same or substantially the same as the ABA Model Code — see Model Code Comparison above.

Texas: Rule 6.01 provides:

A lawyer shall not seek to avoid appointment by a tribunal to represent a person except for good cause, such as:

(a) representing the client is likely to result in violation of law or rules of professional conduct;

(b) representing the client is likely to result in an unreasonable financial burden on the lawyer; or

(c) the client or the cause is so repugnant to the lawyer as to be likely to impair the client-lawyer relationship or the lawyer's ability to represent the client.

Virginia omits Rule 6.2.

Related Materials

ABA Canons: Canon 4 provided:

4. When Counsel for an Indigent Prisoner

A lawyer assigned as counsel for an indigent prisoner ought not to ask to be excused for any trivial reason, and should always exert his best efforts in his behalf.

Federal Statutes: 28 U.S.C. §1915(d), which governs in forma pauperis status in civil cases, provides: "The court may request an attorney to represent any [person claiming in forma pauperis status] unable to employ counsel and may dismiss the case if the allegation of poverty is untrue. . . ." In Mallard v. United States District Court, 490 U.S. 296 (1989), the Supreme Court held that the word "request" does not give federal courts the power to compel lawyers to represent indigents in civil cases. The *Mallard* Court declined to rule on whether statutes (such as 18 U.S.C. §3005) that provide for the "assignment" or "appointment" of counsel in federal cases give courts power to compel unwilling attorneys to represent indigents.

NLADA Standards: The National Legal Aid and Defenders Association (NLADA) has proposed a set of standards to govern the appointment of counsel in criminal cases. (The American Bar Association is also considering adopting standards on this subject.)

Rule 6.3 Membership in Legal Services Organization

A lawyer may serve as a director, officer or member of a legal services organization, apart from the law firm in which the lawyer practices, notwithstanding that the organization serves persons having interests adverse to a client of the lawyer. The lawyer shall not knowingly participate in a decision or action of the organization:

(a) if participating in the decision or action would be incompatible with the lawyer's obligations to a client under Rule 1.7; or

(b) where the decision or action could have a material adverse effect on the representation of a client of the organization whose interests are adverse to a client of the lawyer.

COMMENT

[1] Lawyers should be encouraged to support and participate in legal service organizations. A lawyer who is an officer or a member of such an organization does not thereby have a client-lawyer relationship with persons served by the organization. However, there is potential conflict between the interests of such persons and the interests of the lawyer's clients. If the possibility of such conflict disqualified a lawyer from serving on the board of a legal services organization, the profession's involvement in such organizations would be severely curtailed.

[2] It may be necessary in appropriate cases to reassure a client of the organization that the representation will not be affected by conflicting loyalties of a member of a board. Established, written policies in this respect can enhance the credibility of such assurances.

Model Code Comparison

There was no counterpart to this Rule in the Model Code.

Cross-References in Rules

None.

Legislative History

1980 Discussion Draft (then Rule 8.2(c)) provided as follows:

(c) A lawyer may serve as a director, member or officer of an organization involved in reform of the law or its administration notwithstanding the fact that the reform may affect interests of a client of the lawyer if:

(1) when the interests of the client could be affected, the fact is disclosed in the course of deliberations on the matter, but the identity of the client need not be disclosed;

(2) when the client could be adversely affected, the lawyer complies with Rule 1.8 with respect to the client; and

(3) the lawyer takes no part in any decision that could result in a direct material benefit or detriment to the client.

1981 Draft was similar to the adopted version of Rule 6.3, except that it contained an additional requirement that "the organization complies with Rule 5.4 concerning the professional independence of its legal staff."

1982 Draft was adopted.

Selected State Variations

California: See Rule 1-600 (Legal Service Programs).

Illinois: Rule 6.3 applies only to a "not-for-profit" legal services organization.

New Jersey Rule 6.3 requires that the organization comply with Rule 5.4 and states the limitation in (b) to include adverse effect on the interest of "a client or class of clients of the organization or upon the independence of professional judgment of a lawyer representing such a client."

New York: See DR 5-110 of the New York Code.

North Carolina omits Rule 6.3.

Virginia omits Rule 6.3.

Rule 6.4 Law Reform Activities Affecting Client Interests

A lawyer may serve as a director, officer or member of an organization involved in reform of the law or its administration not withstanding

that the reform may affect the interests of a client of the lawyer. When the lawyer knows that the interests of a client may be materially benefitted by a decision in which the lawyer participates, the lawyer shall disclose that fact but need not identify the client.

COMMENT

Lawyers involved in organization seeking law reform generally do not have a client-lawyer relationship with the organization. Otherwise, it might follow that a lawyer could not be involved in a bar association law reform program that might indirectly affect a client. See also Rule 1.2(b). For example, a lawyer specializing in antitrust litigation might be regarded as disqualified from participating in drafting revisions of rules governing that subject. In determining the nature and scope of participation in such activities, a lawyer should be mindful of obligations to clients under other Rules, particularly Rule 1.7. A lawyer is professionally obligated to protect the integrity of the program by making an appropriate disclosure within the organization when the lawyer knows a private client might be materially benefitted.

Model Code Comparison

There was no counterpart to this Rule in the Model Code.

Cross-References in Rules

None.

Legislative History

1980 Discussion Draft (then Rule 8.2(a) and (b)) provided as follows:

Conflict of Interest in Pro Bono Publico Service

(a) A lawyer engaged in service pro bono publico shall avoid improper conflicts of interest therein.

(b) A lawyer may serve as a director, officer, or member of an organization providing legal services to persons of limited means notwithstanding that such services are provided to persons having interests adverse to a client of the lawyer if:

(1) the organization complies with Rule 7.5 [now Rule 5.4(c)] concerning the professional independence of its legal staff;

(2) when the interests of a client of the lawyer could be affected, the lawyer takes no part in any decision by the organization that could have a material adverse effect on the interest of a client of the organization or upon the independence of professional judgment of a lawyer representing such a client; and

(3) the lawyer otherwise complies with Rule 1.8 with respect to the lawyer's client.

1981 Draft:

A lawyer may serve as a director, officer or member of an organization involved in reform of the law or its administration notwithstanding the fact that the reform may affect the interests of a client of the lawyer if the lawyer takes no part in any decision that could have a direct material effect on the client.

1982 Draft was adopted.

Selected State Variations

California: No comparable provision.

District of Columbia adds the following new subparagraph to Rule 6.4:

(a) A lawyer should assist in improving the administration of justice. A lawyer may discharge this requirement by rendering services in activities for improving the law, the legal system, or the legal profession.

Florida replaces "materially benefitted" with "materially affected" in the second sentence of Rule 6.4.

Illinois: Rule 6.4 applies when the "actions" of the organization may affect a client's interests, rather than when the "reform" may affect the client's interests.

New York: Same or substantially the same as the ABA Model Code — see Model Code Comparison above. See also EC 8-4 of the New York Code.

Virginia omits Rule 6.4.

Related Materials

Model Rules of Professional Conduct for Federal Lawyers: Rule 6.4 adds a sentence providing that a federal lawyer "shall not knowingly participate in a decision or action of the organization if participating in the decision would be incompatible with the Federal lawyer's obligations to the client under Rule 1.7."

ARTICLE 7. INFORMATION ABOUT LEGAL SERVICES

Rule 7.1 Communications Concerning a Lawyer's Services

A lawyer shall not make a false or misleading communication about the lawyer or the lawyer's services. A communication is false or misleading if it:

(a) contains a material misrepresentation of fact or law, or omits a fact necessary to make the statement considered as a whole not materially misleading;

(b) is likely to create an unjustified expectation about results the lawyer can achieve, or states or implies that the lawyer can achieve results by means that violate the rules of professional conduct or other law; or

(c) compares the lawyer's services with other lawyers' services, unless the comparison can be factually substantiated.

COMMENT

This Rule governs all communications about a lawyer's services, including advertising permitted by Rule 7.2. Whatever means are used to make known a lawyer's services, statements about them should be truthful. The prohibition in paragraph (b) of statements that may create "unjustified expectations" would ordinarily preclude advertisements about results obtained on behalf of a client, such as the amount of a damage award or the lawyer's record in obtaining favorable verdicts, and advertisements containing client endorsements. Such information may create the unjustified expectation that similar results can be obtained for others without reference to the specific factual and legal circumstances.

Model Code Comparison

DR 2-101 provided that "[a] lawyer shall not . . . use . . . any form of public communication containing a false, fraudulent, misleading, deceptive, self-laudatory or unfair statement or claim." DR 2-101(B) provided that a lawyer "may publish or broadcast . . . the following information . . . in the geographic area or areas in which the lawyer resides or maintains offices or in which a significant part of the lawyer's clientele resides, provided that the information . . . complies with DR 2-101(A), and is presented in a dignified manner. . . ." DR 2-101(B) then specified 25 categories of information that may be disseminated. DR 2-101(C) provided that "[a]ny person desiring to expand the information authorized for disclosure in DR 2-101(B), or to provide for its dissemination through other forums may apply to [the agency having jurisdiction under state law]. . . . The relief granted in response to any such application shall be promulgated as an amendment to DR 2-101(B), universally applicable to all lawyers."

Cross-References in Rules

Rule 5.7, Comment 8: "The promotion of the law-related services must also in all respects comply with **Rules 7.1** through **7.3**, dealing with advertising and solicitation."

Rule 7.2(a): "Subject to the requirements of **Rule 7.1,** a lawyer may advertise services. . . ."

Rule 7.3, Comment 3: Informal public review of advertising "is itself likely to help guard against statements and claims that might constitute false and misleading communications, in violation of **Rule 7.1.**"

Rule 7.3, Comment 5: "[A]ny solicitation which contains information which is false or misleading within the meaning of **Rule 7.1** . . . is prohibited."

Rule 7.3, Comment 8: "Lawyers who participate in a legal service plan must reasonably assure that the plan sponsors are in compliance with **Rules 7.1,** 7.2, and 7.3(b)."

Rule 7.4, Comment 1: Communications claiming specialization "are subject to the 'false and misleading' standard applied in Rule 7.1 to communications concerning a lawyer's services."

Rule 7.5(a): "A lawyer shall not use a firm name, letterhead or other professional designation that violates **Rule 7.1.** A trade name may be used by a lawyer in private practice if it does not imply a connection with a government agency or with a public or charitable legal services organization and is not otherwise in violation of **Rule 7.1.**"

Legislative History

1980 Discussion Draft of Rule 7.1 (then Rule 9.1) was substantially the same as adopted, except that the first sentence prohibited a lawyer from making any "false, *fraudulent,* or misleading statement. . . ."

1981 and 1982 Drafts were the same as adopted.

Selected State Variations

Alaska: Rule 7.1 adds language prohibiting a lawyer from making a false or misleading communication regarding "any prospective client's need for legal services."

Arizona: Communications and advertisements concerning a lawyer's services must be "predominantly informational," which is defined to mean that "in both quantity and quality, the communication of factual information rationally related to the need for and selection of an attorney predominates." Rule 7.1(b).

California: See Rule 1-400 (Advertising and Solicitation) and the accompanying Standards showing presumptive violations of Rule 1-400. See also B&P Code §§6157-6159.2.

District of Columbia: D.C. Rule 7.1 differs significantly from the ABA Model Rule, and covers some material from ABA Model Rule 7.4, which D.C. omits — see District of Columbia Rules of Professional Conduct below.

Florida: Rule 7.1 provides that a lawyer shall not make "or permit to be made" a false, misleading, "deceptive or unfair" communication about the lawyer or the lawyer's services. Florida adds a new subparagraph (d) providing that a communication violates Rule 7.1 if it "[c]ontains a testimonial." The Comment explaining Rule 7.1(d) states:

> The prohibition in subdivision (d) would preclude endorsements or testimonials because they are inherently misleading to a person untrained in the law. Potential clients are likely to infer from the testimonial that the lawyer will reach similar results in future cases. Because the lawyer cannot directly make this assertion, the lawyer is not permitted to indirectly make that assertion through the use of testimonials.

As amended effective July 1, 1993, Florida also provides a mechanism for obtaining advisory opinions according to the following rule (Florida Rule 4-7.5):

> (a) *Advisory Opinion.* A lawyer may obtain an advisory opinion concerning the compliance of a contemplated advertisement or written communication with these rules . . . by submitting the material and fee . . . to the Standing Committee on Advertising at least 15 days prior to such dissemination. . . .
>
> (e) *Evaluation of Advertisements.* The committee shall evaluate all advertisements and written communications filed with it pursuant to this rule for compliance with the applicable rules. . . . If the committee does not send any communication to the lawyer within 15 days, the advertisement will be deemed approved.
>
> (f) *Substantiating Information.* If requested to do so by the committee, the filing lawyer shall submit information to substantiate representations made or implied in that lawyer's advertisement or written communication.
>
> (g) *Notice of Noncompliance; Effect of Continued Use of Advertisement.* When the committee determines that an advertisement or written communication is not in compliance with the applicable rules, the committee shall advise the lawyer that dissemination or continued dissemination . . . may result in professional discipline.

(h) *Committee Determination Not Binding; Evidence.* A finding by the committee of either compliance or noncompliance shall not be binding in a grievance proceeding, but may be offered as evidence.

In 1997, the Standing Committee on Advertising issued "Internet Guidelines" to guide lawyers who have "a presence on the Internet." The Internet Guidelines are divided into two categories: "(1) Homepage and (2) Information Beyond the Homepage." Pursuant to the filing requirement of Rule 4-7.5(b), the Guidelines generally require lawyers to submit both a hard copy of the homepage and the URL (i.e., the Internet address) to the Standing Committee on Advertising. However, information beyond the homepage "will be treated as information provided to prospective clients at their request" and need not be filed, and homepages that contain "no audio or photographs or illustrations" and only specified information are "exempt" from filing. The Guidelines end by advising that "this area will continue to be studied, and the Standing Committee on Advertising expressly reserves the right to modify its position regarding these dynamic issues as circumstances develop." A full description of the powers, duties, and composition of Florida's advertising committee is found in Chapter 15 of the Florida Supreme Court Rules.

Georgia forbids legal advertising that "makes a claim as to the quality of legal services the lawyer can provide." DR 2-101(A)(4). DR 2-101(B) requires particular language in the event the fee will be contingent. The language must include mention of the fact that such fees are not always permitted and that when they are the client will usually be responsible for other expenses. Written communications to prospective clients must contain the word "Advertisement" on the envelope and the top of each page in a typesize no smaller than the largest typesize in the body of the letter. DR 2-101(C)(2). A lawyer may not send an advertisement to a client about a specific matter if the lawyer knows or reasonably should know that the recipient has counsel on the matter. DR 2-101(C)(4)(a). Targeted mailing is not permitted in connection with personal injury or wrongful death cases. DR 2-101(C)(4)(d). DR 2-103(B) and (C) permit a lawyer to accept referrals from, and pay reasonable fees to, a "bona fide lawyer referral service operated by an organization authorized by law and qualified to do business in this state." The service must comply with certain filing and disclosure requirements. DR 2-103(D) and (E) provide:

> (D) A lawyer may assist in, cooperate with, or offer any qualified legal services plan, or assist in or cooperate with any insurer providing legal services insurance as authorized by law, to promote the use of his services, his partner or association so long as his assistance, cooperation or offer and communications of the organization are not false, fraudulent, deceptive or misleading.
>
> (E) A lawyer may assist and cooperate with a non-profit organization which provides without charge legal services to others as a form of political or associational expression in the promotion of the use of his services or those of his partner or associate provided that his assistance or the communications of the organization on his behalf are not false, fraudulent, deceptive or misleading.

Iowa has among the most restrictive rules in the country on advertising and solicitation. Iowa prohibits not only false or misleading communications but also any "self-laudatory" statement or "any statement or claim . . . which appeals to the emotions, prejudices, or likes or dislikes of a person. . . ." Iowa also continues to specify the precise categories of information a lawyer may advertise, basically along the lines of DR 2-101(B). Iowa also requires all information to be "presented in a dignified manner." With respect to legal fees, Iowa expressly prohibits use of "all subjective characterizations," including terms such as "cut-rate," "lowest," "reasonable," "moderate," "very reasonable," "give-away," "below-cost," or "special."

Missouri: Rule 7.1 adds that a communication is false or misleading if it:

(e) contains a representation of, or implication of, fact regarding the quality of legal services which is not susceptible to reasonable verification by the public;

(f) contains any statistical data or other information based on past performance which is not susceptible to reasonable verification by the public;

(g) contains any paid testimonial about, or paid endorsement of, the lawyer, without identifying the fact that payment has been made or, if the testimonial or endorsement is not made by an actual client, without identifying that fact;

(h) contains a simulated description of the lawyer, his partners or associates, his offices or facilities, or his services without identifying the fact that the description is a simulation;

(i) contains any simulated representation or visualization of the lawyer, his partners or associates, his office or facilities, without identifying the fact that the representation or visualization is a simulation.

Nevada's version of Rule 7.1 provides that a communication is false or misleading if it "[c]ontains a testimonial or endorsement." (See Nevada Supreme Court Rule 195.)

New Jersey adds a Rule 7.1(a)(4) specifying what a legal advertisement can say about fees.

New Mexico adds Rule 16-701(A)(5), which provides that a communication is false or misleading if it "states or implies that the lawyer is a specialist in any field of law other than as specifically permitted by Rule 16-704." In addition, effective March 1, 1997, New Mexico has amended its advisory opinion rule, Rule 16-707.

New York: See New York Materials for New York's version of DR 2-101.

Pennsylvania provides in Rule 7.7, entitled Lawyer Referral Service, as follows:

(a) A lawyer shall not accept referrals from a lawyer referral service if the service engaged in communication with the public or direct contact with prospective clients in a manner that would violate the Rules of Professional Conduct if the communication or contact were made by the lawyer.

(b) A "lawyer referral service" is any person, group of persons, association, organization or entity that receives a fee or charge for referring or causing the direct or indirect referral of a potential client to a lawyer drawn from a specific group or panel of lawyers.

Pennsylvania also contains other variations on Rule 7.1. Rule 7.1(b) provides that a communication is false or misleading if it:

> is likely to create an unjustified expectation about results the lawyer can achieve, such as the amount of previous damage awards, the lawyer's record in obtaining favorable verdicts, or client endorsements, or states or implies that the lawyer can achieve results by means that violate the rules of professional conduct or other law.

Rule 7.1(d) provides that a communication would be considered false or misleading if it "contains subjective claims as to the quality of legal services or a lawyer's credentials that are not capable of measurement or verification."

Texas: Texas adopted extensive amendments to its advertising rules, most of which were upheld by a federal district court in response to a challenge on constitutional grounds. See Texans Against Censorship, Inc. v. State Bar of Texas, 888 F. Supp. 1328 (E.D. Tex. 1995). The new rules were thereafter implemented by order of the Texas Supreme Court to take effect 120 days after the date of the District Court's judgment.

Wyoming: Effective December 3, 1996, Wyoming added Rule 7.1(d) to provide that advertising is false and misleading if it "contains a dramatization precluded by Rule 7.2(g), a testimonial or endorsement."

Related Materials

ABA Canons: Canons 27 and 43 provided:

27. Advertising, Direct or Indirect

It is unprofessional to solicit professional employment by circulars, advertisements, through touters or by personal communications or interviews not warranted by personal relations. Indirect advertisements for professional employment such as furnishing or inspiring newspaper comments, or procuring his photograph to be published in connection with causes in which the lawyer has been or is engaged or concerning the manner of their conduct, the magnitude of the interest involved, the importance of the lawyers's position, and all other like self-laudation, offend the traditions and lower the tone of our profession and are reprehensible; but the customary use of simple professional cards is not improper.

Publication in reputable law lists in a manner consistent with the standards of conduct imposed by these canons of brief biographical and informative data is permissible. Such data must not be misleading and may include only a statement of the lawyer's name and the names of his professsional associates; addresses, telephone numbers, cable addresses; branches of the profession practiced; date and place of birth and admission to the bar; schools attended; with dates of graduation, degrees and other educational distinctions; public or quasi-public offices; posts of honor; legal authorships; legal teaching positions; memberships and offices in bar associations and committees thereof, in legal and scientific societies and legal fraternities; foreign language ability; the fact of listings in other reputable law lists; the names and addresses of references; and, with their written consent, the names of clients regularly represented. A certificate of compliance with the Rules and Standards issued by the Standing Committee on Law Lists may be treated as evidence that such list is reputable.

It is not improper for a lawyer who is admitted to practice as a proctor in admiralty to use that designation on his letterhead or shingle or for a lawyer who has complied with the statutory requirements of admission to practice before the patent office, to so use the designation "patent attorney" or "patent lawyer" or "trademark attorney" or "trademark lawyer" or any combination of those terms.

43. Approved Law Lists

It shall be improper for a lawyer to permit his name to be published in a law list the conduct, management or contents of which are calculated or likely to deceive or injure the public or the profession, or to lower the dignity or standing of the profession.

ABA Aspirational Goals for Lawyer Advertising: In August of 1988, the ABA's House of Delegates endorsed a series of "aspirational" goals written by the ABA's Commission on Advertising. These goals are nonbinding and are not grounds for discipline. They are intended to permit lawyers to advertise "effectively yet with dignity." We reprint substantial excerpts.*

Preamble

[E]mpirical evidence suggests that undignified advertising can detract from the public's confidence in the legal profession and respect for the justice system.

Under present case law, the matter of dignity is widely believed to be so subjective as to be beyond the scope of constitutionally permitted regulation. Nevertheless, it seems entirely proper for the organized bar to suggest non-binding aspirational goals urging lawyers who wish to advertise to do so in a dignified manner. Although only aspirational, such goals must be scrupulously sensitive to fundamental constitutional rights of lawyers and the needs of the public. . . .

[I]f advertising employs false, misleading or deceptive messages or degenerates into undignified and unprofessional presentations, the public is not served, the lawyer who advertised does not benefit and the image of the judicial system may be harmed.

Accordingly, lawyer advertising should exemplify the inherent dignity and professionalism of the legal community. Dignified lawyer advertising tends to inspire public confidence in the professional competence and ability of lawyers and portrays the commitment of lawyers to serve clients' legal needs in accordance with the ethics and public service tradition of a learned profession.

Lawyer advertising is a key facet of the marketing and delivery of legal services to the public. The professional conduct rules for lawyers adopted by the states regulate some aspects of lawyer advertising, but they also leave lawyers much latitude to decide how to advertise. The following Aspirational Goals are presented in an effort to suggest how lawyers can achieve the beneficial goals of advertising while minimizing or eliminating altogether its negative implications.

The ABA does not regulate the conduct of lawyers. Absent adoption by state regulatory bodies, these Aspirational Goals have no binding effect on members of the legal profession.

Aspirational Goals

3. While "dignity" and "good taste" are terms open to subjective interpretation, lawyers should consider that advertising which reflects the ideas stated in these Aspirational Goals is likely to be dignified and suitable to the profession.

4. Since advertising must be truthful and accurate, and not false or misleading, lawyers should realize that ambiguous or confusing advertising can be misleading.

5. Particular care should be taken in describing fees and costs in advertisements. If an advertisement states a specific fee for a particular service, it should make clear whether or not all problems of that type can be handled for that specific fee. Similar care should be taken in describing the lawyer's areas of practice.

6. Lawyers should consider that the use of inappropriately dramatic music, unseemly slogans, hawkish spokespersons, premium offers, slapstick routines or outlandish settings in advertising does not instill confidence in the lawyer or the legal profession and undermines the serious purpose of legal services and the judicial system. . . .

9. Lawyers should design their advertising to attract legal matters which they are competent to handle.

10. Lawyers should be concerned with making legal services more affordable to the public. Lawyer advertising may be designed to build up client bases so that efficiencies of scale may be achieved that will translate into more affordable legal services.

ABA Commission on Advertising: The ABA has a Commission on Advertising composed of private lawyers, disciplinary counsel, a lawyer for an advertising agency, a nonlawyer, and others. The Commission was established in 1978 based on the recommendation of an ABA Task Force that studied lawyer advertising in 1977, the year *Bates* was decided. During 1994, the Commission held several open hearings around the country to explore basic issues on lawyer advertising. The Commission was especially interested in determining whether advertising was contributing to a perceived decline in the public's opinion of lawyers, and whether advertising was helping a significant number of people, especially the poor, to locate lawyers. The Commission issued its final report, findings, and recommendations in January 1995. The Commission will now focus its work on encouraging and supporting ABA entities in adopting and implementing policy recommendations that are consistent with the Commission's report. For further information on the Advertising Commission's work, contact Staff Counsel William Hornsby, 541 North Fairbanks Court, Chicago, IL 60611, phone 312-988-5761. In addition, the Commission is focusing on policy developments pertaining to the use of new technologies in client development, especially the Internet (e-mail, web sites, home pages, links, etc.).

National Federation of Paralegal Associations: In May of 1993, the National Federation of Paralegal Associations, Inc. (NFPA) adopted a Model Code of Ethics and Professional Responsibility. EC-6.1 and EC-6.2 of the NFPA Code provide:

> EC-6.1   A paralegal's title shall clearly indicate the individual's status and shall be disclosed in all business and professional communications to avoid misunderstandings and misconceptions about the paralegal's role and responsibilities.
> EC-6.2   A paralegal's title shall be included if the paralegal's name appears on business cards, letterhead, brochures, directories, and advertisements.

Rule 7.2 Advertising

> **Editors' Note.**   At its February 1989 Mid-Year Meeting, the ABA House of Delegates approved minor amendments to Rule 7.2 and far more substantial amendments to Rule 7.3 to conform to the Supreme Court's decision in Shapero v. Kentucky Bar Association, 486 U.S. 466 (1988), which held a blanket prohibition against "targeted" mail unconstitutional. At its 1990 Mid-Year Meeting, the ABA added subparagraph (c)(3) to harmonize with the addition of Rule 1.17. Excerpts from the ABA committee report explaining the 1989 amendments to Rules 7.2 and 7.3 appear in the Legislative History following Rule 7.3.

(a) **Subject to the requirements of Rules 7.1 and 7.3, a lawyer may advertise services through public media, such as a telephone directory, legal directory, newspaper or other periodical, outdoor advertising, radio or television, or through written or recorded communication.**

(b) **A copy or recording of an advertisement or written communication shall be kept for two years after its last dissemination along with a record of when and where it was used.**

(c) **A lawyer shall not give anything of value to a person for recommending the lawyer's services except that a lawyer may**

    (1) **pay the reasonable costs of advertisements or communications permitted by this Rule;**

    (2) **pay the usual charges of a not-for-profit lawyer referral service or legal service organization; and**

    (3) **pay for a law practice in accordance with Rule 1.17.**

(d) Any communication made pursuant to this rule shall include the name of at least one lawyer responsible for its content.

COMMENT

> **Editors' Note.** When the text of Rule 7.2 was amended in 1989, the Comment was not amended. However, when Rule 1.17 was added to the Model Rules in 1990, the ABA amended Comment 6 to Rule 7.2 to include a reference to Rule 1.17.

[1] To assist the public in obtaining legal services, lawyers should be allowed to make known their services not only through reputation but also through organized information campaigns in the form of advertising. Advertising involves an active quest for clients, contrary to the tradition that a lawyer should not seek clientele. However, the public's need to know about legal services can be fulfilled in part through advertising. This need is particularly acute in the case of persons of moderate means who have not made extensive use of legal services. The interest in expanding public information about legal services ought to prevail over considerations of tradition. Nevertheless, advertising by lawyers entails the risk of practices that are misleading or overreaching.

[2] This Rule permits public dissemination of information concerning a lawyer's name or firm name, address and telephone number; the kinds of services the lawyer will undertake; the basis on which the lawyer's fees are determined, including prices for specific services and payment and credit arrangements; a lawyer's foreign language ability; names of references and, with their consent, names of clients regularly represented; and other information that might invite the attention of those seeking legal assistance.

[3] Questions of effectiveness and taste in advertising are matters of speculation and subjective judgment. Some jurisdictions have had extensive prohibitions against television advertising, against advertising going beyond specified facts about a lawyer, or against "undignified" advertising. Television is now one of the most powerful media for getting information to the public, particularly persons of low and moderate income; prohibiting television advertising, therefore, would impede the flow of information about legal services to many sectors of the public. Limiting the information that may be advertised has a similar effect and assumes that the bar can accurately forecast the kind of information that the public would regard as relevant.

[4] Neither this Rule nor Rule 7.3 prohibits communications authorized by law, such as notice to members of a class in class action litigation.

Record of Advertising

[5] Paragraph (b) requires that a record of the content and use of advertising be kept in order to facilitate enforcement of this Rule. It does not require that advertising be subject to review prior to dissemination. Such a requirement would be burdensome and expensive relative to its possible benefits, and may be of doubtful constitutionality.

Paying Others to Recommend a Lawyer

[6] A lawyer is allowed to pay for advertising permitted by this Rule and for the purchase of a law practice in accordance with the provisions of Rule 1.17, but otherwise is not permitted to pay another person for channeling professional work. This restriction does not prevent an organization or person other than the lawyer from advertising or recommending the lawyer's services. Thus, a legal aid agency or prepaid legal services plan may pay to advertise legal services provided under its auspices. Likewise, a lawyer may participate in not-for-profit lawyer referral programs and pay the usual fees charged by such programs. Paragraph (c) does not prohibit paying regular compensation to an assistant, such as a secretary, to prepare communications permitted by this Rule.

Model Code Comparison

With regard to paragraph (a), DR 2-101(B) provided that a lawyer "may publish or broadcast, subject to DR 2-103, . . . in print media . . . or television or radio. . . ."

With regard to paragraph (b), DR 2-101(D) provided that if the advertisement is "communicated to the public over television or radio, . . . a recording of the actual transmission shall be retained by the lawyer."

With regard to paragraph (c), DR 2-103(B) provided that a lawyer "shall not compensate or give anything of value to a person or organization to recommend or secure his employment . . . except that he may pay the usual and reasonable fees or dues charged by any of the organizations listed in DR 2-103(D)." (DR 2-103(D) referred to legal aid and other legal services organizations.) DR 2-101(I) provided that a lawyer "shall not compensate or give anything of value to representatives of the press, radio, television, or other communication medium in anticipation of or in return for professional publicity in a news item.''

There was no counterpart to paragraph (d) in the Model Code.

Cross-References in Rules

Rule 5.7, Comment 8: ''The promotion of the law-related services must also in all respects comply with **Rules 7.1** through **7.3**, dealing with advertising and solicitations.''

Rule 7.1, Comment: ''This Rule governs all communications about a lawyer's services, including advertising permitted by **Rule 7.2**.''

Rule 7.3, Comment 2: ''This potential for abuse inherent in direct in-person or telephone solicitation of prospective clients justifies its prohibition, particularly since lawyer advertising and written and recorded communication permitted under **Rule 7.2** offer alternative means of conveying necessary information to those who may be in need of legal services.''

Rule 7.3, Comment 3: ''The contents of advertisements and communications permitted under **Rule 7.2** are permanently recorded so that they cannot be disputed and may be shared with others who know the lawyer.''

Rule 7.3, Comment 5: '' [I]f after sending a letter or other communication to a client as permitted by **Rule 7.2** the lawyer receives no response, any further effort to communicate with the prospective client may violate the provisions of Rule 7.3(b).''

Rule 7.3, Comment 6: Rule 7.3 does not prohibit lawyers from communicating with representatives of organizations or groups regarding group or prepaid legal service plans because such communications ''are functionally similar to and serve the same purpose as advertising permitted under **Rule 7.2**.''

Rule 7.3, Comment 8: ''Lawyers who participate in a legal service plan must reasonably assure that the plan sponsors are in compliance with **Rules** 7.1, **7.2**, and 7.3(b).''

Legislative History

1980 Discussion Draft (then Rule 9.2) provided as follows:

... (b) A copy or record of an advertisement in its entirety shall be kept for one year after its dissemination.

(c) A lawyer shall not give anything of value to a person for recommending the lawyer's services, except that a lawyer may pay the reasonable cost of advertising permitted by this rule.

1981 and 1982 Drafts were substantially the same as adopted, except that subparagraph (a) permitted any ''written communication not involving personal contract.''

1989 Amendments: In 1989, the ABA House of Delegates made minor amendments to Rule 7.2(a) and (c). The ABA did not amend the Comment to Rule 7.2.

1990 Amendment: At its 1990 Mid-Year Meeting, the ABA House of Delegates added subparagraph 7.2(c)(3) to reflect the addition of Rule 1.17.

Selected State Variations

Arizona: Rule 7.2(e)(1) provides that all "written communications to prospective clients for the purpose of obtaining professional employment" must "be plainly marked 'Advertisement' on the face of the envelope and at the top of each page of the written communication in type no smaller than the largest type used in the written communication." In addition, Arizona forbids a lawyer to send a written communication to a prospective client about a specific matter if the lawyer knows or reasonably should know that the recipient has a lawyer in the matter. Rule 7.2(f)(1). Finally, Rule 7.2(g) retains the language of DR 2-103(D) with some expansion.

Advertisements on the electronic media may contain the same information as permitted in print advertisements except that:

(1) Impersonations, dramatizations and recreations shall comply with all the requirements set forth in these rules, and shall be designed to further the informational purposes of legal advertisement.

(2) If a law firm advertises on television and a person appears on screen purporting to be a lawyer, such person shall in fact be a lawyer employed full-time at the advertising law firm. If a law firm advertises a particular legal service on television, and a lawyer appears on screen as the person purporting to render the service, the lawyer appearing on screen shall be the lawyer who will actually perform the service advertised unless the advertisement discloses that the service may be performed by other lawyers in the firm.

Arizona also requires advertising lawyers or firms to provide clients on request with "a factual statement detailing the background, training, and experience" of the lawyer or firm. Rule 7.2(a).

California: See Rule 1-400 (Advertising and Solicitation) and B & P Code §§6129 and 6155-6159.2.

Connecticut: Rule 7.2(e) requires lawyers who advertise a fee or fee arrangement to specify "whether and to what extent the client will be responsible for any court costs and expenses of litigation."

District of Columbia omits Rule 7.2, but see Rule 7.1(c) in District of Columbia Rules of Professional Conduct below.

Florida: An amended effective July 1, 1993, Florida's version of Rule 7.2(a) permits lawyers to advertise through "recorded messages the public may access by dialing a telephone number," and provides that Florida's Rules do not apply to any advertisement in another jurisdiction "if such advertisement complies with the rules governing lawyer advertising in that jurisdiction and is not intended for broadcast or dissemination within the State of Florida.'' Florida adds the following new language to Rule 7.2(b):

> Advertisements on the electronic media such as television and radio . . . shall be articulated by a single voice, with no background sound other than instrumental music. The voice may be that of a full-time employee of the firm whose services are advertised; it shall not be that of a celebrity whose voice is recognizable to the public. The lawyer or full-time employee of the firm whose services are being advertised may appear on screen or on radio.

Florida also adds the following new subparagraphs to Rule 7.2:

> (d) *Disclosure Statement.* Except as provided in this subdivision, all advertisements . . . shall contain the following disclosure: "The hiring of a lawyer is an important decision that should not be based solely upon advertisements. Before you decide, ask us to send you free written information about our qualifications and experience." . . . These disclosures need not appear in electronic advertisements or advertisements in the public print media that contain no illustrations and no information other than that listed in paragraph (n)(1)-(11) of this rule [which sets forth ten categories of information "presumed not to violate" Rule 7.1, including names, addresses, phone numbers, dates of bar admission, and "[a]cceptance of credit cards"].

> (e) *Dramatizations Prohibited.* There shall be no dramatization in any advertisement in any medium.

> (f) *Use of Illustrations.* Illustrations used in advertisements shall present information that can be factually substantiated and is not merely self-laudatory. . . .

> (j) *Self-Laudatory Statements.* A lawyer shall not make statements which are merely self-laudatory or statements describing or characterizing the quality of the lawyer's services [except for] information furnished to a prospective client at that person's request or . . . information supplied to existing clients. . . .

> (m) *Payment by Nonadvertising Lawyer.* No lawyer shall, directly or indirectly, pay all or a part of the cost of an advertisement by a lawyer not in the same firm unless the advertisement discloses the name and address of the nonadvertising lawyer, the relationship between the advertising lawyer and the nonadvertising lawyer, and whether the advertising lawyer may refer any case received through the advertisement to the nonadvertising lawyer. . . .

> (p) *Maintaining Copies of Advertisements.* A copy or recording of an advertisement or written or recorded communication shall be submitted to the standing committee on advertising. . . .

Florida also adds the following new Rule 4-7.3 (as amended effective January 1, 1993):

> (a) *Information Regarding Qualifications.* Each lawyer or law firm that advertises . . . shall have available in written form for delivery to any potential client:
>> (1) A factual statement detailing the background, training and experience of each lawyer or law firm. . . .
> (c) *Request for Information by Potential Client.* Whenever a potential client shall request information regarding a lawyer or law firm for the purpose of making a decision regarding employment of the lawyer or law firm:

(1) The lawyer or law firm shall promptly furnish (by mail if requested) the written information described in subdivision (a). . . .

(4) If the information furnished to the client includes a fee contract, the top of each page of the contract shall be marked "SAMPLE" in red ink . . . and the words "DO NOT SIGN" shall appear on the client signature line.

(g) *Proof of Statements or Claims.* Upon reasonable request by The Florida Bar, a lawyer shall promptly provide proof that any statement or claim made in any advertisement or written communication, as well as the information furnished to a prospective client . . . [is not directly, impliedly, or potentially false, misleading, unfair, or deceptive].

Florida has also added the following Rule 7.8 (amended effective January 1, 1993) to regulate lawyer referral services:

Rule 4-7.8 Lawyer Referral Services

(a) *When Lawyers May Accept Referrals.* A lawyer shall not accept referrals from a lawyer referral service unless the service:

(1) engages in no communication with the public and in no direct contact with prospective clients in a manner that would violate the Rules of Professional Conduct if the communication or contact were made by the lawyer;

(2) receives no fee or charge that constitutes a division or sharing of fees, unless the service is a not-for-profit service approved by The Florida Bar pursuant to chapter 8 of these rules;

(3) refers clients only to persons lawfully permitted to practice law in Florida when the services to be rendered constitute the practice of law in Florida.

(4) carries or requires each lawyer participating in the service to carry professional liability insurance in an amount not less than $100,000 per claim or occurrence;

(5) furnishes The Florida Bar, on a quarterly basis, with the names and Florida bar membership numbers of all lawyers participating in the service; and

(6) neither represents nor implies to the public that the service is endorsed or approved by The Florida Bar, unless the service is subject to chapter 8 of these rules.

(b) *Definition of Lawyer Referral Service.* A "lawyer referral service" is:

(1) any person, group of persons, association, organization, or entity that receives a fee or charge for referring or causing the direct or indirect referral of a potential client to a lawyer drawn from a specific group or panel of lawyers; or

(2) any group or pooled advertising program operated by any person, group of persons, association, organization, or entity wherein the legal services advertisements utilize a common telephone number and potential clients are then referred only to lawyers or law firms participating in the group or pooled advertising program; . . .

A pro bono referral program, in which the participating attorneys do not pay a fee or charge of any kind to receive referrals or to belong to the referral panel, and are undertaking the referred matters without expectation of remuneration, is not a lawyer referral service within the definition of this rule.

In addition, Chapter 8 of the Florida Supreme Court Rules sets forth detailed and extensive requirements for the operation of lawyer referral services by local bar associations, and no local bar association may operate a referral service without the express approval of the state bar. Chapter 9 of the Florida Supreme Court Rules provides detailed regulations governing group and prepaid legal service plans, and defines such plans as follows in Rule 9-1.2 (entitled "Definitions"):

> (a) "*Group Legal Services.*" Group legal services are plans by which legal services are rendered to individual members of a group identifiable in terms of some common interest.
> (b) "*Prepaid Legal Services Plans.*" Prepaid legal services plans are programs in which the cost of the services are prepaid by the group member or by some other person or organization in the member's behalf.

Georgia: For Georgia's version of Rule 7.2 see Selected State Variations following Rule 7.1.

Illinois prohibits giving anything of value for recommending "or having recommended" the lawyer's services.

Iowa: DR 2-101 permits written advertising in "newspapers, periodicals, trade journals, 'shoppers,' and other similar advertising media. . . ." Iowa does not expressly permit advertising through "outdoor advertising" or through "public media" in general. In addition, Iowa restricts both written and broadcast advertising to "the geographic area in which the lawyer maintains offices or in which a significant part of the lawyer's clientele resides. . . ." With respect to radio and television, Iowa permits information to be "articulated only by a single non-dramatic voice, not that of the lawyer, and with no other background sound," and on television, "no visual display shall be allowed except that allowed in print as articulated by the announcer." Moreover, Iowa adds DR 2-101(J), which provides that a lawyer shall not give anything of value "to representatives of the press, radio, television, or other communication medium in anticipation of or in return for professional publicity in a news item nor voluntarily give any information to such representatives which, if published in a news item, would be in violation of" the basic prohibition on false, deceptive, or misleading communications.

Maryland adds Rules 7.2(e) and (f), which provide as follows:

> (e) An advertisement or communication indicating that no fee will be charged in the absence of a recovery shall also disclose whether the client will be liable for any expenses.
> (f) A lawyer, including a participant in an advertising group or lawyer referral service or other program involving communications concerning the lawyer's services, shall be personally responsible for compliance with the provisions of Rules 7.1, 7.2, 7.3, 7.4 and 7.5 and shall be prepared to substantiate such compliance.

Massachusetts: See selected state variations under Rule 7.3.

Michigan's Rule 7.2(a) ends after the word "advertise" without listing the advertising media.

Missouri: Effective January 1, 1995, the Missouri Supreme Court added the following sentence to Rule 7.2(a): "All advertisements that state that legal services are available on a contingent or no-recovery-no-fee basis shall also state conspicuously that the client may be responsible for costs or expenses." Effective July 1, 1996, Missouri adopted a new Rule 10.1 to govern lawyer referral services. The rule is based largely on the ABA Model Supreme Court Rules Governing Lawyer Referral Services (see Related Materials following Rule 7.2), but adds that any person violating the new rule shall be deemed to be engaged in the unauthorized practice of law.

New Jersey: As part of its opinion in the case of Felmeister & Isaacs, 518 A.2d 188, 208 (1986), the New Jersey Supreme Court adopted the following version of Rule 7.2:

> Subject to the requirements of RPC 7.1 a lawyer may advertise services through public media, such as a telephone directory, legal directory, newspaper or other periodical, radio, or television, or through mailed written communication. All advertisements shall be predominantly informational. No drawings, animations, dramatizations, music, or lyrics shall be used in connection with televised advertising. No advertisement shall rely in any way on techniques to obtain attention that depend upon absurdity and that demonstrate a clear and intentional lack of relevance to the selection of counsel; included in this category are all advertisements that contain any extreme portrayal of counsel exhibiting characteristics clearly unrelated to legal competence.

New York: See New York Materials for New York's versions of DR 2-101 and 2-103.

Ohio: DR 2-101(A)(2) prohibits a lawyer from seeking employment if the lawyer "does not intend to actively participate in the representation" but instead intends to refer the matter to other counsel. DR 2-101(A)(3) prohibits "any testimonial of past or present clients pertaining to the lawyer's capability." DR 2-101(A)(5) prohibits "characterizations of rates or fees . . . such as 'cut-rate,' 'lowest,' 'giveaway,' 'below cost,' 'discount,' and 'special.' " Phrases such as "reasonable" and "moderate" are acceptable.

Effective July 1, 1996, Ohio significantly amended DR 2-103, drawing heavily on the ABA Model Supreme Court Rules Governing Lawyer Information and Referral Services (see Related Materials below following Rule 7.2). Some of the key provisions of the new Ohio rule are: (1) the Ohio Supreme Court will form an "oversight committee" to promulgate rules and regulations concerning lawyer referral services, and lawyers will be permitted to accept referrals only from services that report to and satisfy the requirements established by the oversight committee; (2) lawyer referral services must establish experience requirements for panel members and subject-matter panels; and (3) panel members must carry legal malpractice insurance or furnish proof of financial responsibility. The Ohio rule also permits lawyers to share a percentage of any legal fees with the referral service.

Oregon: In 1995, Oregon amended DR 2-103(A) to make clear that a lawyer may compensate or give value to another as permitted by DR 2-111, Oregon's new rule permitting the sale of a law practice. (See Selected State Variations after Rule 1.17.)

Pennsylvania omits Rule 7.2(d), but has adopted the following additional provisions in its version of Rule 7.2:

(d) No advertisement or public communication shall contain an endorsement by a celebrity or public figure.

(e) An advertisement or public communication that contains a paid endorsement shall disclose that the endorser is being paid or otherwise compensated for his or her appearance or endorsement.

(f) A non-lawyer shall not portray a lawyer or imply that he or she is a lawyer in any advertisement or public communication; nor shall an advertisement or public communication portray a fictitious entity as a law firm, use a fictitious name to refer to lawyers not associated together in a law firm, or otherwise imply that lawyers are associated together in a law firm if that is not the case.

(g) An advertisement or public communication shall not contain a portrayal of a client by a non-client; the re-enactment of any events or scenes; or, pictures or persons, which are not actual or authentic, without a disclosure that such depiction is a dramatization. . . .

(i) All advertisements and written communications shall disclose the geographic location, by city or town, of the office in which the lawyer or lawyers who will actually perform the services advertised principally practice law. If the office location is outside the city or town, the county in which the office is located must be disclosed.

(j) A lawyer shall not, directly or indirectly (whether through an advertising cooperative or otherwise), pay all or any part of the costs of an advertisement by a lawyer not in the same firm or by any for-profit entity other than the lawyer's firm, unless the advertisement discloses the name and principal office address of each lawyer or law firm involved in paying for the advertisement and, if any lawyer or law firm will receive referrals from the advertisement, the circumstances under which referrals will be made and the basis and criteria on which the referral system operates.

(k) A lawyer shall not, directly or indirectly, advertise that the lawyer or his or her law firm will only accept, or has a practice limited to, particular types of cases unless the lawyer or his or her law firm handles, as a principal part of his, her or its practice, all aspects of the cases so advertised from intake through trial. If a lawyer or law firm advertises for a particular type of case that the lawyer or law firm ordinarily does not handle from intake through trial, that fact must be disclosed. A lawyer or law firm shall not advertise as a pretext to refer cases obtained from advertising to other lawyers.

Pennsylvania has also adopted Rule 7.7 which forbids lawyers to accept referrals from a lawyer referral service "if the service engaged in communication with the public or direct contact with prospective clients in a manner that would violate the Rules of Professional Conduct if the communication or contact were made by the lawyer."

Tennessee: Under DR 2-104(C)(2)(a), as amended effective March 15, 1996, a video communication (e.g., a television ad) must display the words "THIS IS AN ADVERTISEMENT" in a prominent place and in conspicuous type size for at least five seconds at the beginning and end of the communication. An audio communication (e.g., a radio ad) must say "This is an advertisement" at the beginning and end of the communication in the same tone, clarity, and volume as used in the rest of the communication.

Texas: Rule 7.02 forbids "false or misleading communication about the qualifications or the services of any lawyer or firm." A communication will violate the rule if, among other things, it creates "an unjustified expectation about results the lawyer can achieve" or "compares the lawyer's services with other lawyers' services, unless the comparison can be substantiated by reference to verifiable, objective data."

If a lawyer advertises on the electronic media, "any person who portrays a lawyer whose services or whose firm's services are being advertised, or who narrates an advertisement as if he or she were such a lawyer, shall be one or more of the lawyers whose services are being advertised." Rule 7.04(g). If a lawyer knows or should know at the time of placing an ad that "a case or matter will likely be referred to another lawyer or firm, a statement of such facts shall be conspicuously included in such advertisement." Rule 7.04(1).

In 1997, Texas adopted guidelines for advertising on the Internet, including a requirement that "homepages" be submitted for review.

Virginia retains the language of DR 2-101(A) from the Model Code, but omits the prohibitions on "self laudatory" statements and omits all of DR 2-101(B)-(I). DR 2-101(B) requires that a paid advertisement "be identified as such unless it is apparent from the context that it is such a communication." Any electronic communication "must be prerecorded and the prerecorded communication shall be approved by the lawyer before it is broadcast." DR 2-103(D) provides that a lawyer may not compensate a person "as a reward for having made a recommendation resulting in his employment by a client," other than the usual and reasonable fees of "a lawyer referral service and any qualified legal services plan or contract of legal services insurance as authorized by law. . . ."

Related Materials

ABA Canons: Canons 28, 40, and 46 provided:

28. Stirring Up Litigation, Directly or Through Agents

It is unprofessional for a lawyer to volunteer advice to bring a lawsuit, except in rare cases where ties of blood, relationship or trust make it his duty to do so. Stirring up strife and litigation is not only unprofessional, but it is indictable at common law. It is disreputable to hunt up defects in titles or other causes of action and inform thereof in order to be employed to bring suit or collect judgment, or to breed litigation by seeking out those with claims for personal injuries or those having any other grounds of action in order to secure them as clients, or to employ agents or runners for like purposes, or to pay or reward, directly or indirectly, those who bring or influence the bringing of such cases to his office, or to remunerate policemen, court or prison officials, physicians, hospital *attachés* or others who may succeed, under the guise of giving disinterested friendly advice, in influencing the criminal, the sick and the injured, the ignorant or others, to seek his professional services. A duty to the public and to the profession devolves upon every member of the Bar having knowledge of such practices upon the part of any practitioner immediately to inform thereof, to the end that the offender may be disbarred.

40. Newspapers

A lawyer may with propriety write articles for publications in which he gives information upon the law; but he should not accept employment from such publications to advise inquirers in respect to their individual rights.

46. Notice to Local Lawyers

A lawyer available to act as an associate of other lawyers in a particular branch of the law or legal service may send to local lawyers only and publish in his local journal, a brief and dignified announcement of his availability to serve other lawyers in connection therewith. The announcement should be in a form which does not constitute a statement or representation of special experience or expertness.

ABA Model Supreme Court Rules Governing Lawyer Referral Services: At its 1993 Annual Meeting, the ABA House of Delegates voted to adopt Model Supreme Court Rules Governing Lawyer Referral Services, as well as model legislation to implement the rules. (Because many referral services are run by non-lawyers, the regulation of referral services cannot be accomplished solely through the disciplinary machinery for lawyers.) The rules and legislation are modeled on legislation governing lawyer referral services in California, Florida, and Texas. The rules provide that a referral service may be "qualified" only if (1) membership on referral panels is open to all lawyers in a given geographic area who meet reasonable experience standards and pay a reasonable membership fee to be fixed by the state bar, and (2) the referral service establishes procedures for admitting and removing lawyers from referral lists, and (3) the service establishes panels in various specific fields of law so that callers can be matched with a lawyer experienced in a particular type of law. The new rules are a step beyond the ABA's 1989 recommendation that states adopt minimum standards for lawyer referral services, and reflect increasing concern over sham referral services, often operated by lawyers who refer cases only to themselves.

Rule 7.3 Direct Contact with Prospective Clients

Editors' Note.   In Shapero v. Kentucky State Bar, 486 U.S. 466 (1988), reviewing a Kentucky rule identical to Model Rule 7.3, the Supreme Court held that Rule 7.3's blanket prohibition on mailings to people "known to need legal services of the kind provided by the lawyer in the particular matter" violated the First Amendment. At its February 1989 Mid-Year Meeting, the ABA House of Delegates substantially amended Rule 7.3's original Comment to conform to *Shapero*. A thorough report in the Legislative History section below explains the amendments and sets out deleted material from the original Comment.

On June 21, 1995, the United States Supreme Court issued another decision about targeted mail, Florida Bar v. Went for It, Inc., 115 S. Ct. 2371, 132 L. Ed. 541 (1995). By a 5-4 vote, the Court distinguished *Shapero* and upheld the constitutionality of a Florida rule that prohibited all targeted mail to accident victims and their relatives for 30 days after an accident or disaster.

(a) A lawyer shall not by in-person or live telephone contact solicit professional employment from a prospective client with whom the lawyer has no family or prior professional relationship when a significant motive for the lawyer's doing so is the lawyer's pecuniary gain.

(b) A lawyer shall not solicit professional employment from a prospective client by written or recorded communication or by in-person or telephone contact even when not otherwise prohibited by paragraph (a), if:

(1) the prospective client has made known to the lawyer a desire not to be solicited by the lawyer; or

(2) the solicitation involves coercion, duress or harassment.

(c) Every written or recorded communication from a lawyer soliciting professional employment from a prospective client known to be in need of legal services in a particular matter, and with whom the lawyer has no family or prior professional relationship, shall include the words "Advertising Material" on the outside envelope and at the beginning and ending of any recorded communication.

(d) Notwithstanding the prohibitions in paragraph (a), a lawyer may participate with a prepaid or group legal service plan operated by an organization not owned or directed by the lawyer which uses in-person or telephone contact to solicit memberships or subscriptions for the plan from persons who are not known to need legal services in a particular matter covered by the plan.

COMMENT

[1] There is a potential for abuse inherent in direct in-person or live telephone contact by a lawyer with a prospective client known to need legal services. These forms of contact between a lawyer and a prospective

client subject the lay person to the private importuning of the trained advocate in a direct interpersonal encounter. The prospective client, who may already feel overwhelmed by the circumstances giving rise to the need for legal services, may find it difficult fully to evaluate all available alternatives with reasoned judgment and appropriate self-interest in the face of the lawyer's presence and insistence upon being retained immediately. The situation is fraught with the possibility of undue influence, intimidation, and overreaching.

[2] This potential for abuse inherent in direct in-person or live telephone solicitation of prospective clients justifies its prohibition, particularly since lawyer advertising and written and recorded communication permitted under Rule 7.2 offer alternative means of conveying necessary information to those who may be in need of legal services. Advertising and written and recorded communications which may be mailed or autodialed make it possible for a prospective client to be informed about the need for legal services, and about the qualifications of available lawyers and law firms, without subjecting the prospective client to direct in-person or telephone persuasion that may overwhelm the client's judgment.

[3] The use of general advertising and written and recorded communications to transmit information from lawyer to prospective client, rather than direct in-person or live telephone contact, will help to assure that the information flows cleanly as well as freely. The contents of advertisements and communications permitted under Rule 7.2 are permanently recorded so that they cannot be disputed and may be shared with others who know the lawyer. This potential for informal review is itself likely to help guard against statements and claims that might constitute false and misleading communications, in violation of Rule 7.1. The contents of direct, in-person or live telephone conversations between a lawyer and a prospective client can be disputed and are not subject to third-party scrutiny. Consequently, they are much more likely to approach (and occasionally cross) the dividing line between accurate representations and those that are false and misleading.

[4] There is far less likelihood that a lawyer would engage in abusive practices against an individual with whom the lawyer has a prior personal or professional relationship or where the lawyer is motivated by considerations other than the lawyer's pecuniary gain. Consequently, the general prohibition in Rule 7.3(a) and the requirements of Rule 7.3(c) are not applicable in those situations.

[5] But even permitted forms of solicitation can be abused. Thus, any solicitation which contains information which is false or misleading within the meaning of Rule 7.1, which involves coercion, duress, or harassment

within the meaning of Rule 7.3(b)(2), or which involves contact with a prospective client who has made known to the lawyer a desire not to be solicited by the lawyer within the meaning of Rule 7.3(b)(1), is prohibited. Moreover, if after sending a letter or other communication to a client as permitted by Rule 7.2 the lawyer receives no response, any further effort to communicate with the prospective client may violate the provisions of Rule 7.3(b).

[6] This Rule is not intended to prohibit a lawyer from contacting representatives of organizations or groups that may be interested in establishing a group or prepaid legal plan for their members, insureds, beneficiaries or other third parties for the purpose of informing such entities of the availability of and details concerning the plan or arrangement which the lawyer or lawyer's firm is willing to offer. This form of communication is not directed to a prospective client. Rather, it is usually addressed to an individual acting in a fiduciary capacity seeking a supplier of legal services for others who may, if they choose, become prospective clients of the lawyer. Under these circumstances, the activity which the lawyer undertakes in communicating with such representatives and the type of information transmitted to the individual are functionally similar to and serve the same purpose as advertising permitted under Rule 7.2.

[7] The requirement in Rule 7.3(c) that certain communications be marked "Advertising Material" does not apply to communications sent in response to requests of potential clients or their spokespersons or sponsors. General announcements by lawyers, including changes in personnel or office location, do not constitute communications soliciting professional employment from a prospective client known to be in need of legal services within the meaning of this Rule.

[8] Paragraph (d) of this Rule would permit an attorney to participate with an organization which uses personal contact to solicit members for its group or prepaid legal services plan, provided that the personal contact is not undertaken by any lawyer who would be a provider of legal services through the plan. The organization referred to in paragraph (d) must not be owned or directed (whether as manager or otherwise) by any lawyer or law firm that participates in the plan. For example, paragraph (d) would not permit a lawyer to create an organization controlled directly or indirectly by the lawyer and use the organization for the in-person or telephone solicitation of legal employment of the lawyer through memberships in the plan or otherwise. The communication permitted by these organizations also must not be directed to a person known to need legal services in a particular matter, but is to be designed to inform potential plan members generally of another means of affordable

legal services. Lawyers who participate in a legal service plan must reasonably assure that the plan sponsors are in compliance with Rules 7.1, 7.2, and 7.3(b). See Rule 8.4(a).

Model Code Comparison

DR 2-104(A) provided with certain exceptions that "[a] lawyer who has given in-person unsolicited advice to a layperson that he should obtain counsel or take legal action shall not accept employment resulting from that advice. . . ." The exceptions include DR 2-104(A)(1), which provided that a lawyer "may accept employment by a close friend, relative, former client (if the advice is germane to the former employment), or one whom the lawyer reasonably believes to be a client." DR 2-104(A)(2) through DR 2-104(A)(5) provided other exceptions relating, respectively, to employment resulting from public educational programs, recommendation by a legal assistance organization, public speaking or writing, and representing members of a class in class action litigation.

Cross-References in Rules

Rule 5.7, Comment 8: "The promotion of the law-related services must also in all respects comply with **Rules 7.1** through **7.3**, dealing with advertising and solicitations."

Rule 7.2(a): "Subject to the requirements of **Rules** 7.1 and **7.3**, a lawyer may advertise through public media . . . or through written or recorded communication."

Rule 7.2, Comment 4: "Neither this Rule nor **Rule 7.3** prohibits communications authorized by law, such as notice to members of a class in class action litigation."

Legislative History

1980 Discussion Draft (then Rule 9.3) provided as follows:

Solicitation

(a) A lawyer shall not initiate contact with a prospective client if:

(1) the lawyer reasonably should know that the physical, emotional, or mental state of the person solicited is such that the person could not exercise reasonable judgment in employing a lawyer;

(2) the person solicited has made known a desire not to receive communications from the lawyer; or

(3) the solicitation involves coercion, duress, or harassment.

(b) subject to the requirements of paragraph (a), a lawyer may initiate contact with a prospective client in the following circumstances:

(1) if the prospective client is a close friend or relative of the lawyer;

(2) by a letter concerning a specific event or transaction if the letter is followed up only upon positive response from the addressee;

(3) under the auspices of a public or charitable legal services organization or a bona fide political, social, civic, fraternal, employee, or trade organization whose purposes include but are not limited to providing or recommending legal services.

(c) A lawyer shall not give another person anything of value to initiate contact with a prospective client on behalf of the lawyer.

1981 and 1982 Drafts both provided as follows:

Personal Contact with Prospective Clients

(a) A lawyer may initiate personal contact with a prospective client for the purpose of obtaining professional employment only in the following circumstances and subject to the requirements of paragraph (b):

(1) if the prospective client is a close friend, relative, former client or one whom the lawyer reasonably believes to be a client;

(2) under the auspices of a public or charitable legal services organization; or

(3) under the auspices of a bona fide political, social, civic, fraternal, employee or trade organization whose purposes include but are not limited to providing or recommending legal services, if the legal services are related to the principal purposes of the organization.

(b) A lawyer shall not contact, or send a written communication to, a prospective client for the purpose of obtaining professional employment if:

(1) the lawyer knows or reasonably should know that the physical, emotional or mental state of the person is such that the person could not exercise reasonable judgment in employing a lawyer;

(2) the person has made known to the lawyer a desire not to receive communications from the lawyer; or

(3) the communication involves coercion, duress or harassment.

1989 Amendments: At its February 1989 Mid-Year Meeting, the ABA House of Delegates substantially amended Rule 7.3 and its Comment. As originally promulgated, before its language was declared unconstitutional in Shapero v. Kentucky State Bar, 486 U.S. 466 (1988), Rule 7.3 provided:

A lawyer may not solicit professional employment from a prospective client with whom the lawyer has no family or prior professional relationship, by mail, in person or otherwise, when a significant motive for the lawyer's doing so is the lawyer's pecuniary gain. The term "solicit" includes contact in person, by telephone or telegraph, by letter or other writing, or by other communications directed to a specific recipient, but does not include letters addressed or advertising circulars distributed generally to persons not known to need legal services of the kind provided by the lawyer in a particular matter, but who are so situated that they might in general find such services useful.

When the ABA amended Rule 7.3 in 1989, it *completely deleted* the following two paragraphs from the original Comment to Rule 7.3:

> These dangers [of false and misleading representations] attend direct solicitation whether in-person or by mail. Direct mail solicitation cannot be effectively regulated by means less drastic than outright prohibition. One proposed safeguard is to require that the designation "Advertising" be stamped on any envelope containing a solicitation letter. This would do nothing to assure the accuracy and reliability of the contents. Another suggestion is that solicitation letters be filed with a state regulatory agency. This would be ineffective as a practical matter. State lawyer discipline agencies struggle for resources to investigate specific complaints, much less for those necessary to screen lawyers' mail solicitation material. Even if they could examine such materials, agency staff members are unlikely to know anything about the lawyer or about the prospective client's underlying problem. Without such knowledge they cannot determine whether the lawyer's representations are misleading. In any event, such review would be after the fact, potentially too late to avert the undesirable consequences of disseminating false and misleading material.
>
> General mailings not speaking to a specific matter do not pose the same danger of abuse as targeted mailings, and therefore are not prohibited by this Rule. The representations made in such mailings are necessarily general rather than tailored, less importuning than informative. They are addressed to recipients unlikely to be specially vulnerable at the time, hence who are likely to be more skeptical about unsubstantiated claims. General mailings not addressed to recipients involved in a specific legal matter or incident, therefore, more closely resemble permissible advertising rather than prohibited solicitation.

The reasons for these deletions and for other amendments to Rules 7.2 and 7.3 are explained by the ABA's Standing Committee on Ethics and Professional Responsibility in the following report that was submitted to the House of Delegates in 1989.

*ABA Committee Report Explaining 1989 Amendments to Rule 7.3**

> The Supreme Court of the United States, in Shapero v. Kentucky Bar Association, 486 U.S. 466 (1988), ruled that the First Amendment does not allow states to impose blanket bans on targeted mail solicitation by lawyers of prospective clients. Held unconstitutional was a Kentucky Supreme Court rule identical to Model Rule 7.3. The principal purpose of the amendments proposed here is to bring the Model Rules into compliance with the *Shapero* decision.
>
> The proposed amendments would make five changes in the Model Rules. The *first change,* contained in Rule 7.2(a), adds recorded communications to the types of communications covered by the advertising and solicitation Rules.

*Committee Reports do not represent official policy of the ABA. They are for information only, and the opinions are those of the authors of the report.

The *second change*, purely technical, would change the third and fourth words in Model Rule 7.3 from "may not" to "shall not." . . .

The *third change* would prohibit any solicitation even when otherwise permitted under present Model Rule 7.3 if "[t]he prospective client has made known to the lawyer a desire not to be solicited by the lawyer; or [t]he solicitation involves coercion, duress or harassment." Solicitation in-person or by telephone is permitted under present Rule 7.3, if the lawyer has a family or prior professional relationship with the prospective client or when no significant motive for the lawyer's doing so is the lawyer's pecuniary gain. The prospective client should be protected from solicitation, even under these circumstances, if the prospective client has made known a desire not to be solicited by the lawyer or if the solicitation involves coercion, duress or harassment. . . .

The *fourth change* would permit solicitation of professional employment by written and recorded communications with a prospective client known to need legal services of the kind provided by the lawyer in a particular matter (not involving in-person or telephone contact), as is required by the *Shapero* decision.

The *fifth change* requires that written or recorded communications initiated by a lawyer seeking professional employment in a particular legal matter be labelled "Advertising Material." This new requirement was suggested by the Supreme Court in *Shapero*.

The Comment to Rule 7.3 is amended to conform to the black letter Rule as amended.

Selected State Variations

Alabama: Targeted direct mail to prospective personal injury clients or their relatives is forbidden for 30 days following the injury. Rule 7.3(b)(1)(i). Direct mail solicitations of all kinds can only be sent "by regular mail," cannot resemble "a legal pleading, official government form or document (federal or state), or other legal document," and must contain the word " 'Advertisement' . . . prominently in red ink on each page of the written communication" and also on the "lower left-hand corner of the envelope in 14-point or larger type and in red ink." Further, if "the written communication is prompted by a specific occurrence [it] shall disclose how the lawyer obtained the information prompting the communication." Rule 7.3(b)(2).

Arizona: Targeted direct mail solicitation must be "clearly marked on the envelope and on the first page" as follows: "ADVERTISING MATERIAL: THIS IS A COMMERCIAL SOLICITATION." The rule continues: "Said notification shall be printed in red ink, in all capital letters, in type size at least double the largest type size used in the body of the communication." Rule 7.3(b). The communication can only be sent by regular mail not by "registered mail or other forms of restricted delivery," Rule 7.3(e), and if the communication is "prompted by a specific occurrence," it shall "disclose how the lawyer obtained the information prompting the communication." Rule 7.3(j).

California: See Rule 1-400 (Advertising and Solicitation) and B & P Code §§6152 and 6157-6158.2.

Maryland and *Missouri* have adopted versions of Rule 7.3 substantially the same as the Kutak Commission's 1981 and 1982 Drafts.

District of Columbia omits Rule 7.3. See District of Columbia Rules of Professional Conduct below.

Florida adds to its solicitation rule that a lawyer "shall not permit employees or agents of the lawyer to solicit in the lawyer's behalf." Florida also covers solicitation by "facsimile."

Florida also provides that a lawyer shall not send a communication to a prospective client or a prospective client's relative if the communication "concerns an action for personal injury or wrongful death or otherwise relates to an accident or disaster . . . unless the accident or disaster occurred more than thirty days prior to the mailing of the communication." On June 21, 1995, in a case called Florida Bar v. Went for It, Inc., 115 S. Ct. 2371, 132 L. Ed. 541 (1995), the United States Supreme Court upheld this 30-day "blackout" provision by a 5-4 vote.

Florida also imposes stringent requirements on all written communications to prospective clients. Florida Rule 4-7.4(b)(2), as amended on July 20, 1995, provides as follows:

> a. Each page of such written communications [and the envelope] shall be plainly marked "advertisement" in red ink. . . .
>
> b. A copy of each such written communication and a sample of the envelopes in which the communications are enclosed shall be filed with the Standing Committee on Advertising either prior to or concurrently with the mailing. . . .
>
> c. Written communications mailed to prospective clients shall be sent only by regular U.S. mail, not by registered mail or any other forms of restricted delivery.
>
> d. No reference shall be made in the communication about having received any kind of approval from The Florida Bar. . . .
>
> g. The first sentence of any written communication concerning a specific matter shall be: "If you have already retained a lawyer for this matter, please disregard this letter." . . .
>
> j. Any written communication prompted by a specific occurrence involving or affecting the intended recipient of the communication or a family member shall disclose how the lawyer obtained the information prompting the communication.
>
> k. A written communication seeking employment by a specific prospective client in a specific matter shall not reveal on the envelope . . . the nature of the client's legal problem.

Georgia: For Georgia's version of Rule 7.3 see Selected State Variations following Rule 7.1.

Illinois defines "solicit" as contact with a person "other than a lawyer . . ." Illinois permits solicitation "under the auspices of a public or charitable legal services organization or a *bona fide* political, social, civic, charitable, religious, fraternal, employee or trade organization whose purposes include, but are not limited to, providing or recommending legal services." Illinois prohibits solicitation when the conditions in ABA Model Rule 7.3(b)(1)-(2) exist or when "the lawyer reasonably should know that the physical or mental state of the person is such that the person could not exercise reasonable judgment in employing a lawyer.''

Kentucky has adopted an elaborate Rule 7.60 entitled "Kentucky Disaster Response Plan." Article I of Rule 7.60 explains that one purpose of the Kentucky Disaster Response Plan is to address problems that occur when lawyers and non-lawyers who are not subject to the disciplinary jurisdiction in Kentucky "engage in the provision of legal services, legal advice, and outright solicitation of persons and their families affected by a disastrous event." It is the policy of Rule 7.60 to "[m]onitor the conduct of all attorneys, both members and non-members of the Kentucky Bar Association, and thereby deter violations of the rules of ethical conduct . . . .''

Louisiana: Effective March 1, 1996, Louisiana Rule 7.2 was amended to add a new subdivision 7.2(b)(iii)(C), which provides that "if the communication . . . relates to an accident or disaster involving the person to whom the communication is addressed or a relative of that person, such communication shall not be initiated by the lawyer unless the accident or disaster occurred more than 30 days prior to the mailing of the communication.''

Massachusetts: Effective January 1, 1998, Rule 7.3 forbids in-person solicitation for profit and requires an "advertising" legend on mail solicitation.

Minnesota provides:

> A lawyer may not solicit professional employment from a prospective client with whom the lawyer has no family or prior professional relationship, by in-person or telephone contact, when a significant motive for the lawyer's doing so is the lawyer's pecuniary gain.

Missouri's version of Rule 7.3 generally follows the Kutak Commission's 1981 and 1982 drafts of Rule 7.3. However, effective January 1, 1995, the Missouri Supreme Court has added the following sentence to Rule 7.3(c):

> A written communication sent and received or a personal contact made within a reasonable period after an incident giving rise to personal injury or death is presumed to be written at a time or made at a time when the writer knows or reasonably should know that the physical, emotional, or mental state of the person makes it unlikely that the person would exercise reasonable judgment in employing a lawyer.

Also effective January 1, 1995, the Missouri Supreme Court has added the following new subparagraph (d) to Rule 7.3: "All communications or personal contacts made pursuant to this Rule 7.3 that state that legal services are available on a contingent or no-recovery-no-fee basis shall also state conspicuously that the client may be responsible for costs or expenses.''

Montana Rule 7.3(d) prohibits a lawyer from contacting a prospective client if "the lawyer reasonably should know that the person is already represented by another lawyer.''

Nevada's version of Rule 7.3., Supreme Court Rule 197, provides:

> Written communication directed to a specific prospective client who may need legal services due to a particular transaction or occurrence is prohibited in

Nevada within 45 days of the transaction or occurrence giving rise to the communication.

New Jersey: Effective May 5, 1997, to control solicitation after mass disasters, New Jersey has adopted a new Rule 7.3(b)(4), which provides that a lawyer shall not contact, or send a written communication to, a prospective client for the purpose of obtaining professional employment if:

> (4) the communication involves unsolicited direct contact with a prospective client within thirty days after a specific mass-disaster event, when such contact concerns potential compensation arising from the event.

The new rule replaced the "interim guidance" given in Matter of Anis, 126 N.J. 448, 599 A.2d 1265 (1992) (disciplining attorney for mailing solicitation letter to parents of boy killed in Pan Am Flight 103 explosion the day after the boy's remains were identified), and modified a proposed version of the mass disaster rule that had been circulated for public comment in February 1997. In response to the State Bar Association's concerns that out-of-state attorneys would continue to solicit New Jersey victims and their families after mass disasters, the Court's Clerk issued a statement saying that it "has jurisdiction over out-of-state attorneys who make such solicitations to prospective claimants in New Jersey," and the Court referred questions about out-of-state lawyers to its Committee on Attorney Advertising (CAA) for an appropriate report and recommendations.

With respect to events other than mass disasters, New Jersey Rule 7.3(b)(5) (renumbered effective May 5, 1997) provides that a targeted mail letter is generally permitted if it:

> (i) bears the word "ADVERTISEMENT" prominently displayed in capital letters at the top of the first page of text; and
> (ii) contains the following notice at the bottom of the last page of text: "Before making your choice of attorney, you should give this matter careful thought. The selection of an attorney is an important decision."; and
> (iii) contains an additional notice . . . that the recipient may, if the letter is inaccurate or misleading, report same to the Committee on Attorney Advertising, Hughes Justice Complex, CN 037, Trenton, New Jersey 08625.

Finally, New Jersey Rule 7.3(b)(1) adds that the rule applies when "the lawyer knows or reasonably should know that the physical, emotional or mental state of the person is such that the person could not exercise reasonable judgment in employing a lawyer."

New York: See New York Materials for New York's version of DR 2-103.

Ohio: Targeted direct mail solicitation must disclose "accurately and fully the manner in which the lawyer . . . became aware of and verified the identity and specific legal need of the addressee." It must also disclaim "any prior acquaintance or contact with the addressee and avoid any personalization in approach unless the facts are otherwise." The lawyer may not express "any predetermined evaluation of the merits of the addressee's case." Finally, the communication must include, in its text and on the envelope in which mailed, in red ink and in type no smaller than 10 point, the recital "ADVERTISEMENT ONLY." DR 2-101(F).

Oregon requires targeted direct mail advertisements, other than to friends, relatives, and current or prior clients, to contain the word "Advertisement" in at least "fourteen point bold type . . . on the envelope and in the text of the communication." DR 2-101(H).

Pennsylvania has not adopted Rule 7.3(c) or (d).

Rhode Island: Rule 7.3(b)(2)(A) provides that a lawyer shall not send a written solicitation to a prospective client if the written communication "concerns a specific matter and the lawyer knows or reasonably should know that the person to whom the communication is directed is represented by a lawyer in the matter."

Tennessee: Effective March 15, 1996, Tennessee amended its advertising rules. New DR 2-104(C)(1), taking advantage of the holding in Florida Bar v. Went for It, Inc., 115 S. Ct. 2371 (1995), prohibits lawyers from sending targeted communications to accident victims or their families for 30 days after an accident. If a targeted communication is prompted by a specific event, the lawyer must disclose the source of the information prompting the communication. In addition, DR 2-104(C)(2)(a) (the substance of which was moved from DR 2-101(N)) requires that every written communication to a prospective client must include the words "THIS IS AN ADVERTISEMENT" in a prominent place and conspicuous size at the beginning and end of the communication, as well as on the envelope. New DR 2-104(C)(2)(g) requires that the first sentence of any written communication concerning a specific matter must state: "If you have already hired or retained a lawyer for this matter, please disregard this letter." New DR 2-104(C)(2)(h) requires that communications mailed to a prospective client may be sent only by regular mail, not by restricted or certified mail, by express mail (such as FedEx), or by courier. However, DR 2-104(C)(2)(a)(i) permits lawyers to send written communications by "telegraph, facsimile, or computer on-line transmission." Finally, the new rule requires lawyers to file copies of all written communications with Tennessee's Board of Professional Responsibility within three days after the communication is sent.

Texas Rule 7.06 provides:

> A lawyer shall not accept or continue employment when the lawyer knows or reasonably should know that the person who seeks the lawyer's services does so as a result of conduct prohibited by these Rules.

Texas Rule 7.03(a) provides that a lawyer "shall not by in-person or telephone contact seek professional employment concerning a matter arising out of a particular occurence or event . . . when a significant motive for the lawyer's doing so is the lawyer's pecuniary gain." This rule does not apply to family members of current or former clients. The rule does not appear to prohibit in-person or telephone contact with prospective clients, where the contact is prompted by a specific event, must contain the word "Advertisement" on the first page of the communication and the envelope and must be sent by regular mail and reveal how the lawyer learned about the event. Rule 7.05.

Virginia: DR 2-103 permits telephone or in-person solicitation of strangers unless the solicitation is false, fraudulent, misleading, or deceptive, or if the solicitation

> has a substantial potential for or involves the use of coercion, duress, compulsion, intimidation, threats, unwarranted promises of benefits, overpersuasion, overreaching, or vexatious or harassing conduct, taking into account the sophistication regarding legal matters, the physical, emotional or mental state of the person to whom the communication is directed and the circumstances in which the communication is made.

However, Virginia DR 2-103(F) provides that, notwithstanding the quoted language, a lawyer "shall not initiate in-person solicitation of professional employment for compensation in a personal injury or wrongful death claim of a prospective client with whom the lawyer has no family or prior professional relationship."

Related Materials

ABA Canons: Canon 28 provided:

28. *Stirring Up Litigation, Directly or Through Agents*

> It is unprofessional for a lawyer to volunteer advice to bring a lawsuit, except in rare cases where ties of blood, relationship or trust make it his duty to do so. Stirring up strife and litigation is not only unprofessional, but it is indictable at common law. It is disreputable to hunt up defects in titles or other causes of action and inform thereof in order to be employed to bring suit or collect judgment, or to breed litigation by seeking out those with claims for personal injuries or those having any other grounds of action in order to secure them as clients, or to employ agents or runners for like purposes, or to pay or reward, directly or indirectly, those who bring or influence the bringing of such cases to his office, or to remunerate policemen, court or prison officials, physicians, hospital *attachhes* or others who may succeed, under the guise of giving disinterested friendly advice, in influencing the criminal, the sick and the injured, the ignorant or others, to seek his professional services. A duty to the public and to the profession devolves upon every member of the Bar having knowledge of such practices upon the part of any practitioner immediately to inform thereof, to the end that the offender may be disbarred.

ATLA Code of Conduct: In July 1988, following unfavorable press coverage of lawyer solicitation at various mass disaster sites, the membership of the Association of Trial Lawyers of America (ATLA), which consists largely of plaintiffs' personal injury lawyers, adopted the following Code of Conduct:

> 1. No ATLA member shall personally, or through a representative, contact any party, or an aggrieved survivor in an attempt to solicit a potential client when there has been no request for such contact from the injured party, an aggrieved survivor, or a relative of either, or the injured parties' union representative.

2. No ATLA member shall go to the scene of an event which caused injury unless requested to do so by an interested party, an aggrieved survivor, a relative of either, or by an attorney representing an injured party or survivor.

3. No ATLA member shall initiate a television appearance or initiate any comment to any news media concerning an event causing injury within 10 days of the event unless the member forgoes any financial return from the compensation of those injured or killed, provided, however, that an individual designated by a bar association to state the official position of such bar association may initiate such media contact to communicate such position.

4. No ATLA member shall personally, or through an associate attorney, file a complaint with a specific *ad damnum* amount unless required by local rules of court. If such amount is stated, it shall be based upon good faith evaluation of facts which the member can demonstrate.

5. No ATLA member shall personally, or through a representative, make representations of trial experience or past results of litigation either of which is in any way false or misleading.

6. No ATLA member shall personally, or through a representative, initiate personal contact with a potential client (who is not a client, former client, relative or close personal friend of the attorney) for the purpose of advising that individual of the possibility of an unrecognized legal claim for damages unless the member forgoes any financial interest in the compensation of the injured party.

7. No ATLA member shall file or maintain a frivolous suit, issue, or position. However, no ATLA member should refrain from urging or arguing any suit, issue or position that he believes in good faith to have merit.

8. The ATLA Board of Governors has condemned attorneys or legal clinics who advertise for clients in personal injury cases and who have no intention of handling the cases themselves, but do so for the sole purpose of brokering the case to other attorneys. Any ATLA member who enters a contract of representation on behalf of a claimant shall, at the time of retention, fully advise the client, in writing, of all relationships with other attorneys who will be involved in the presentation, the role each attorney shall play, and the proposed division of fees among them. The client shall also be promptly advised of all changes affecting the representation.

9. No ATLA member shall knowingly accept a referral from a person, whether an ATLA member or not, who obtained the representation by conduct which this code prohibits.

Victim's Bill of Rights: In January 1986, shortly after a Union Carbide gas leak killed thousands of people in Bhopal, India, the Board of Governors of ATLA adopted the following Victim's Bill of Rights:

We condemn the conduct of any attorney who, uninvited, personally, or through a representative, contacts the injured party or aggrieved survivors in an attempt to solicit a potential client.

We condemn the conduct of attorneys or representatives of insurers or companies who potentially may become defendants who, uninvited, contact the injured party or aggrieved survivors in an attempt to gain some advantage or to discourage them from contacting counsel of their choice.

We condemn the conduct of attorneys or their representatives who go, uninvited, to the scene of a disaster, set up temporary quarters and advertise for prospective clients from among the injured or the survivors of those killed in the incident.

We condemn the conduct of attorneys or legal clinics who advertise for clients in personal injury cases and who have no intention of handling the cases themselves, but do so for the sole purpose of brokering the cases to other attorneys.

We condemn false or misleading legal advertising. We condemn legal advertising that goes beyond the bounds of good taste and common decency or which creates, or attempts to create, an impression in the public's mind of an expertise or experience that does not in fact exist.

Rule 7.4 Communication of Fields of Practice and Certification

Editors' Note. At its August 1994 Annual Meeting, for the second time in three years, the ABA House of Delegates amended Rule 7.4. The amendment added a single new sentence to the rule and an identical sentence to the Comment. (The amendment made no deletions.) The new sentence makes it unnecessary for lawyers in states without certifying procedures to use a disclaimer when claiming certification by an organization accredited by the ABA Standing Committee on Specialization (which began approving certifying organizations in 1993). Excerpts from the ABA report explaining the amendment are found in the Legislative History section following this rule.

A lawyer may communicate the fact that the lawyer does or does not practice in particular fields of law. A lawyer shall not state or imply that the lawyer has been recognized or certified as a specialist in a particular field of law except as follows:

(a) a lawyer admitted to engage in patent practice before the United States Patent and Trademark Office may use the designation "Patent Attorney" or a substantially similar designation;

(b) a lawyer engaged in admiralty practice may use the designation "Admiralty," "Proctor in Admiralty" or a substantially similar designation; and

(c) [for jurisdictions where there is a regulatory authority granting certification or approving organizations that grant certification] a lawyer may communicate the fact that the lawyer has been certified as a specialist in a field of law by a named organization or authority but only if:

(1) such certification is granted by the appropriate regulatory authority or by an organization which has been approved by the appropriate regulatory authority to grant such certification; or

(2) such certification is granted by an organization that has not yet been approved by, or has been denied the approval from, the appropriate regulatory authority, and the absence or denial of approval is clearly stated in the communication, and in any advertising subject to Rule 7.2, such statement appears in the same sentence that communicates the certification.

(c) [for jurisdictions where there is no procedure either for certification or specialities or for approval of organizations granting certification] a lawyer may communicate the fact that the lawyer has been certified as a specialist in a field of law by a named organization, provided that the communication clearly states that there is no procedure in this jurisdiction for approving certifying organizations. If, however, the named organization has been accredited by the American Bar Association to certify lawyers as specialists in a particular field of law, the communication need not contain such a statement.

COMMENT

[1] This Rule permits a lawyer to indicate areas of practice in communications about the lawyer's services. If a lawyer practices only in certain fields, the lawyer is permitted to so indicate. A lawyer is generally permitted to state that the lawyer is a "specialist," practices a "specialty," or "specializes in" particular fields, but such communications are subject to the "false and misleading" standard applied in Rule 7.1 to communications concerning a lawyer's services.

[2] However, a lawyer may not communicate that the lawyer has been recognized or certified as a specialist in a particular field of law, except as provided by this Rule. Recognition of specialization in patent matters is a matter of long-established policy of the Patent and Trademark Office, as reflected in paragraph (a). Paragraph (b) recognizes that designation of admiralty practice has a long historical tradition associated with maritime commerce and the federal courts.

[3] Paragraph (c) provides for certification as a specialist in a field of law when a state authorizes an appropriate regulatory authority to grant such certification or when the state grants other organizations the right to grant certification. Certification procedures imply that an objective entity has recognized a lawyer's higher degree of specialized ability than is suggested by general licensure to practice law. Those objective entities may be expected to apply standards of competence, experience and knowledge to insure that a lawyer's recognition as a specialist is meaningful and reliable. In order to insure that consumers can obtain access to

useful information about an organization granting certification, the name of the certifying organization or agency must be included in any communication regarding the certification.

[4] Lawyers may also be certified as specialists by organizations that either have not yet been approved to grant such certification or have been disapproved. In such instances, the consumer may be misled as to the significance of the lawyer's status as a certified specialist. The Rule therefore requires that a lawyer who chooses to communicate recognition by such an organization also clearly state the absence or denial of the organization's authority to grant such certification. Since lawyer advertising through public media and written or recorded communications invites the greatest danger of misleading consumers, the absence or denial of the organization's authority to grant certification must be clearly stated in such advertising in the same sentence that communicates the certification.

[5] In jurisdictions where no appropriate regulatory authority has a procedure for approving organizations granting certification, the Rule requires that a lawyer clearly state such lack of procedure. If, however, the named organization has been accredited by the American Bar Association to certify lawyers as specialists in a particular field of law, the communication need not contain such a statement.

Model Code Comparison

DR 2-105(A) provided that a lawyer

shall not hold himself out publicly as a specialist, as practicing in certain areas of law or as limiting his practice . . . except as follows:

(1) A lawyer admitted to practice before the United States Patent and Trademark Office may use the designation "Patents," "Patent Attorney," "Patent Lawyer," or "Registered Patent Attorney" or any combination of those terms, on his letterhead and office sign.

(2) A lawyer who publicly discloses fields of law in which the lawyer . . . practices or states that his practice is limited to one or more fields of law shall do so by using designations and definitions authorized and approved by [the agency having jurisdiction of the subject under state law].

(3) A lawyer who is certified as a specialist in a particular field of law or law practice by [the authority having jurisdiction under state law over the subject of specialization by lawyers] may hold himself out as such, but only in accordance with the rules prescribed by that authority.

EC 2-14 stated that "In the absence of state controls to insure the existence of special competence, a lawyer should not be permitted to hold himself out as a specialist, . . . other than in the fields of admiralty, trademark, and patent law where a holding out as a specialist historically has been permitted."

Cross-References in Rules

None.

Legislative History

1979 Unofficial Pre-Circulation Draft (then Rule 9.3) provided, in pertinent part, as follows:

>   (a) A lawyer whose practice is limited to specified types of legal matters may communicate that fact except as otherwise provided by regulations governing specialization. A lawyer may indicate that he or she is a specialist only as permitted by paragraphs (b) and (c) and as follows: [Insert applicable provisions on designation of specialization.]

The remainder of the 1979 Draft was substantially the same as adopted.

1980 Discussion Draft was substantially the same as adopted.

1981 and 1982 Drafts were the same as adopted.

1989 Amendments: At its February 1989 Mid-Year Meeting, the ABA House of Delegates substantially amended the Comment (but not the text) to Rule 7.4. The changes were explained in the following report jointly submitted to the House of Delegates by the ABA Standing Committee on Ethics and Professional Responsibility, the ABA Standing Committee on Specialization, and the ABA Section of Taxation.

ABA Committee Report Explaining 1989 Amendment to Rule 7.4*

. . . The proposed amendment makes no change in the black-letter of Rule 7.4, but deletes from the Comment the prohibition against a lawyer stating that his or her practice is "limited to" or "concentrated in" particular fields. The proposed amendment to the Comment is consistent with Supreme Court decisions that lawyers' truthful advertising about their practices is protected by the First Amendment. Arguably, the present language in the Comment is not consistent with these decisions. . . .

B. Analysis of Rule 7.4

Rule 7.4 prohibits a lawyer from stating or implying that he or she is a "specialist," with certain limited exceptions. The Rule further provides for designation of specialty in accordance with the rules of the particular jurisdiction. Rule 7.4(c). This rule operates only to prohibit factually inaccurate or misleading information, and appears consistent with both the letter and spirit of *In re R.M.J.* and *Zauderer.*

As presently written, however, the Comment to Rule 7.4 *also* prohibits statements that the lawyer's practice is "limited to" or "concentrated in" certain fields,

---

*Committee Reports do not represent official policy of the ABA. They are for information only, and the opinions are those of the authors of the report.

under the theory that these terms also connote formal recognition of the lawyer as a "specialist." This language is called into question in light of the Court's decisions in *R.M.J.* and *Zauderer*. These cases make clear that a state may not prohibit truthful descriptions of a lawyer's practice merely because the terms raise an inference for a reader that the lawyer has some expertise in the designated fields of practice. The use of the words "limited to" or "concentrated in" in denoting areas of practice do not clearly imply *formal* recognition as a "specialist" and simply do not pose sufficient danger of misleading to warrant a proscription of their use. . . .

Therefore, the Comment to Rule 7.4 should not prohibit statements that a lawyer's practice is "limited to" or "concentrated in" a particular field.

1992 Amendments: At its 1992 Annual Meeting, the ABA House of Delegates substantially amended Rule 7.4 and its Comment to conform the rule to the holding of Peel v. Attorney Registration and Disciplinary Commission, 496 U.S. 91 (1990). The amendments are explained in the following committee report, which was jointly submitted by the ABA Standing Committee on Specialization and the ABA Standing Committee on Ethics and Professional Responsibility:

ABA Committee Report Explaining 1992 Amendment to Rule 7.4*

Background

The findings in a recent survey conducted by the ABA Young Lawyers Division . . . revealed that 64% of all lawyers in private practice spend at least 50% of their time in one substantive field of law. Further, this phenomenon is not limited to large firms. Fifty-five percent of sole practitioners responding to the survey were found to spend half or more of their time in just one field.

Lawyer specialization has proliferated largely without formal recognition by the organized bar or state and federal regulators. An ABA committee concluded in 1967 that in spite of the apparent unwillingness of the bar either to control lawyer specialization or to accept its regulation, "the fact of specialization persists and expands and the need to recognize the fact and regulate its existence and growth becomes steadily more apparent."

After several years of study, the ABA concluded in 1969 that it should not promulgate a national plan to regulate voluntary specialization. Instead, the House of Delegates resolved that the determination whether to adopt a national plan should not be made until experimental programs were conducted at the state level and their results observed.

The *Peel* Decision

In 1990 the legal specialization issue was addressed again by the Supreme Court in *Peel v. Attorney Registration and Disciplinary Commission*. . . .

The *Peel* decision invalidated the broad prohibition of ABA Model Rule 7.4 on lawyers' communications about their specialties, holding that states may not cat-

---

*Committee Reports do not represent official policy of the ABA. They are for information only, and the opinions are those of the authors of the report.

egorically ban a truthful communication by a lawyer that he or she is certified as a specialist by a bona fide private certifying organization.

The National Board of Trial Advocacy, whose certification was at issue in the *Peel* case, had certified lawyers as civil and criminal trial specialists for many years. The *Peel* decision has now spurred other private organizations to establish lawyer certification programs. The American Bankruptcy Board of Certification, a nonprofit organization sponsored by the American Bankruptcy Institute, is beginning to certify qualified lawyers as specialists, offering separate certification in business and consumer bankruptcy. The Commercial Law League of America recently announced its lawyer certification program in bankruptcy and creditors' rights law.

Other private groups such as the National Organization of Social Security Claimants Representatives and the National Academy of Elder Law Attorneys are contemplating certification plans. It is conceivable that even law schools, CLE providers and ABA Sections will become certifiers.

The proposed amendment of Model Rule 7.4 would bring the ABA Model Rules of Professional Conduct into compliance with the *Peel* decision. Although a few states have now amended their rules to comply with *Peel,* most jurisdictions will be looking to the ABA for guidance and leadership on this issue. Amending Model Rule 7.4 as we have proposed will help to insure protection of the users of legal services while authorizing legitimate, truthful advertising claims of lawyer specialists.

1994 Amendments: At its August 1994 Annual Meeting, the ABA House of Delegates amended Rule 7.4 by adding a single new sentence at the end of the existing rule and an identical sentence to the end of the Comment. (The amendment made no deletions.) The new sentence brings Rule 7.4 into line with the ABA's system for accrediting organizations that certify lawyers as specialists. (The ABA Standing Committee on Specialization began approving such organizations in 1993.) In essence, the amendment makes it unnecessary for lawyers in states without certifying procedures to use a disclaimer when claiming certification by an ABA-accredited organization. This is the first time that the American Bar Association has been mentioned by name anywhere in the ABA Model Rules of Professional Conduct.

The 1994 amendment was co-sponsored by the ABA Standing Committee on Specialization and the ABA Standing Committee on Ethics and Professional Responsibility. Below are excerpts from the joint report and recommendation submitted by the two co-sponsors in support of the amendment.

ABA Committee Report Explaining 1994 Amendment to Rule 7.4*

The purpose of this recommendation is to harmonize Model Rule 7.4 with the Association's newly enacted procedure for accrediting organizations that certify specialists in particular areas of the law. . . .

In August, 1993 the Standing Committee on Specialization reported to the House that six specialty certification programs of three separate organizations (the

---

*Committee Reports do not represent official policy of the ABA. They are for information only, and the opinions are those of the authors of the report.

National Board of Trial Advocacy, the Commercial Law League of American Academy of Commercial and Bankruptcy Law Specialists, and the American Bankruptcy Board of Certification) had met the Standards. The Standing Committee on Specialization therefore recommended that those programs be accredited, which recommendation was approved by the House.

However, under the 1992 amendments, a lawyer who is certified by one of those accredited programs, and who practices in a State that has not yet adopted a procedure for approving certifying organizations, would have to add, to any communication setting forth his or her certification, a statement to the effect that there is no procedure in that particular jurisdiction for approving certifying organizations. Many lawyers believe that such a disclaimer would dilute the positive fact of certification; therefore, those lawyers would end up refraining from publicizing their certification rather than adding the required statement, even though the certifying organization had been fully accredited by the ABA. As a consequence, the value of the ABA accreditation would be considerably diminished.

The Standing Committee on Specialization and the Standing Committee on Ethics and Professional Responsibility believe that Rule 7.4 should now be further amended to permit any accreditations authorized by the House to have their intended effect and be given recognition in those states which have not yet created a mechanism for approving organizations that grant certification. The proposed amendment, which of course would be effective only in jurisdictions that choose to adopt it, would be appropriate only in a jurisdiction that had not adopted its own procedure, either for certification of specialties of individual lawyers or for approval of organizations granting such certification. It would effectively accept the ABA's accreditation of such certifying organizations. Given the thoroughness of the procedures established by the House, there would appear to be no valid reason for suggesting to the pulic that the ABA accreditation is in some way inferior simply because a particular state has not established its own accrediting procedure. . . .

Selected State Variations

Arizona: Rule 7.4(c) permits a lawyer to state that he or she is "certified by a national entity which has standards for certification substantially the same as those established by" the Arizona Board of Legal Specialization. The Board must have recognized the entity as having equivalent standards.

Arkansas provides: "A lawyer who has been recognized as a specialist under the Arkansas Plan of Specialization approved by the Arkansas Supreme Court may communicate the fact during the period he or she is a 'Board Recognized Specialist in [insert field] of law."

California: See Standard 11 following Rule 1-400.

Colorado: Rule 7.4 permits lawyers to advertise areas of practice in which they will accept referrals, and to advertise availability as a consultant in specific areas.

Delaware: Effective January 1, 1997, the Delaware Supreme Court amended all of Article 7 of the Delaware Rules of Professional Conduct (Rules 7.1 through 7.5).

District of Columbia: D.C. omits Rule 7.4, but covers communication of fields of practice and certification in a general and limited fashion in Rule 7.1(a) — see District of Columbia Rules of Professional Conduct below.

Florida Rule 4-7.6(b) provides as follows:

> (b) *Certified Lawyers.* A lawyer who complies with the Florida certification plan as set forth in chapter 6, Rules Regulating The Florida Bar, or who is certified by an organization whose specialty certification program has been accredited by the American Bar Association may inform the public and other lawyers of the lawyer's certified areas of legal practice and may state in communications to the public that the lawyer is a "specialist in (area of certification)."

Pursuant to Supreme Court Rule 6-1.2, the Florida Bar has promulgated the following notice to the public:

> Attorneys indicating they are "board certified" have been identified by The Florida Bar as having special knowledge, skills, and proficiency in their areas of practice. "Florida Bar Designated" attorneys have met minimum experience and educational requirements under the Florida Designation Plan. "Florida Bar Members" may list their areas of practice in the Yellow Pages without meeting any specific criteria.

The rules governing Florida's designation and certification plans are detailed and elaborate, and they cover special criteria for more than 25 separate fields of law practice.

Illinois, whose old rule on specialization (DR 2-105) was struck down in Peel v. Attorney Registration and Disciplinary Commission of Illinois, 496 U.S. 91 (1990), promulgated a new rule six weeks after the *Peel* decision. The new rule requires that any lawyer advertisement using the terms "certified," "specialist," "expert," or similar terms must meet two conditions:

> (1) the reference must be truthful and verifiable and may not be misleading in violation of Rule 7.1;
> (2) the reference must state that the Supreme Court of Illinois does not recognize certifications of specialties in the practice of law and that the certificate, award or recognition is not a requirement to practice law in Illinois.

Iowa prohibits lawyers from advertising "[f]ixed fees or range of fees for specific legal services" except in the following twelve specified areas of law: (1) abstract examinations and title opinions, (2) uncontested divorces "involving no disagreement concerning custody of children, alimony, child support, or property settlement," (3) wills "leaving all property outright to one beneficiary and contingently to one beneficiary or class or beneficiaries," (4) income tax returns for wage earners, (5) uncontested personal bankruptcies, (6) changes of name, (7) simple residential deeds, (8) residential purchase and sale agreements, (9) residential leases, (10) residential mortgages and notes, (11) powers of attorney, and (12) bills of sale. In addition, Iowa prohibits a lawyer from advertising fixed fees for these services "as an indirect means of attracting clients for whom he performs other legal services not related to the specific legal services publicized."

Massachusetts: Effective January 1, 1998, Rule 7.4 permits lawyers to hold themselves out as "specialists in particular services, fields, and areas of law if the holding out does not include a deceptive statement or claim." The comment provides that lawyers who hold themselves out as specialists "shall be held to the standard of performance of specialists" in the particular area of law.

Michigan Rule 7.4 stops after the first sentence.

Minnesota provides in part:

> (a) A lawyer may communicate the fact that the lawyer does or does not practice in particular fields of law. A lawyer shall not use any false, fraudulent, misleading or deceptive statement, claim or designation in describing the lawyer's or the lawyer's firm's practice or in indicating its nature or limitations.
>
> (b) A lawyer shall not state that the lawyer is a specialist in a field of law unless the lawyer is currently certified or approved as a specialist in that field by an organization that is approved by the State Board of Legal Certification.
>
> (c) A lawyer shall not state that the lawyer is a certified specialist if the lawyer's certification has terminated, or if the statement is otherwise contrary to the terms of such certification.

Missouri amended its rule in 1991 to provide that a lawyer other than an admiralty or patent attorney shall not state or imply that the lawyer is a specialist "unless the communication contains a disclaimer that neither the Supreme Court of Missouri nor The Missouri Bar reviews or approves certifying organizations or specialist designations." Missouri's rule also requires that any communication stating that the lawyer does or does not practice in particular fields of law "shall conform to the requirements of Rule 7.1."

Montana provides:

> (c) A lawyer who is a specialist in a certain field of law by experience in the field, by specialized training or education in the field, or by certification by an authoritative professional entity in the field may communicate the fact of his or her specialty where such communication is not false or misleading under Rule 7.1. A lawyer may communicate that his or her practice is limited to or concentrated in a particular field of law, if such communication does not imply an unwarranted expertise in the field so as to be false or misleading under Rule 7.1.

New Hampshire provides:

> A lawyer who publicly discloses fields of law in which the lawyer or the law firm practices or states that his or her practice is limited to one or more fields of law shall do so by using descriptive language that is accurate, straightforward, truthful and dignified.

New Jersey provides in Rule 7.4(b) as follows:

> A lawyer may communicate that the lawyer has been certified as a specialist or certified in a field of practice only when the communication is not false or misleading, states the name of the certifying organization, and states that the certification has been granted by the Supreme Court of New Jersey or by an organization that has been approved by the American Bar Association. If the certification has been granted by an organization that has not been approved, or has been denied

approval, by the Supreme Court of New Jersey or the American Bar Association, the absence or denial of such approval shall be clearly identified in each such communication by the lawyer.

New York: See New York Materials for New York's version of DR 2-105.

Pennsylvania: Lawyers are permitted to advertise that they are certified by certain organizations approved by the Supreme Court. The Supreme Court may approve such an organization upon recommendation of the State Bar Association if the court finds that advertising by the lawyer of such certification "will provide meaningful information, which is not false, misleading or deceptive, for use of the public in selecting or retaining a lawyer." Certification must be available to all lawyers "who meet objective and consistently applied standards relevant to practice in the area of law to which the certification relates."

Texas provides that a lawyer who advertises in the public media

shall state with respect to each area advertised in which the lawyer has not been awarded a Certificate of Special Competence by the Texas Board of Legal Specialization, "Not Certified by the Texas Board of Legal Specialization," however, if an area of law so advertised has not been designated as an area in which a lawyer may be awarded a Certificate of Special Competence by the Texas Board of Legal Specialization, the lawyer may also state, "No designation has been made by the Texas board of Legal Specialization for a Certificate of Special Competence in this area." Lawyers may also advertise certification by other organizations that have been "accredited by the Texas Board of Legal Specialization as a bona fide organization that admits to membership or grants certification only on the basis of objective, exacting, publicly available standards. . . ." Rule 7.04.

Virginia generally follows the substance of DR 2-105, but expressly allows a lawyer to "state, announce or hold himself out as limiting his practice to a particular area or field of law" as long as the communication is not false, misleading, or deceptive.

Related Materials

ABA Canons: Canons 45 and 46 provided:

45. Specialists

The canons of the American Bar Association apply to all branches of the legal profession; specialists in particular branches are not to be considered as exempt from the application of these principles.

46. Notice to Local Lawyers

A lawyer available to act as an associate of other lawyers in a particular branch of the law or legal service may send to local lawyers only and publish in his local legal journal, a brief and dignified announcement of his availability to serve other lawyers in connection therewith. The announcement should be in a form which does not constitute a statement or representation of special experience or expertness.

ABA Model Plan of Specialization: In 1979, the ABA House of Delegates adopted the Model Plan of Specialization proposed by the ABA Standing Committee on Specialization. The plan is reprinted in the ABA/BNA Lawyers' Manual on Professional Conduct.

ABA Standards for Accreditation of Specialty Certification Programs for Lawyers: In 1992, when the ABA amended Rule 7.4 to allow lawyers to advertise that they were "certified" by private organizations as specialists, the ABA also asked a special committee to develop standards for accrediting private organizations that issue specialty certifications to lawyers. At the ABA's 1993 Mid-Year Meeting, the ABA House of Delegates adopted Standards for Accreditation of Specialty Certification Programs for Lawyers. The ABA Standards are strict, and the ethics rules of some states expressly allow lawyers to claim specialty certification only by an entity that has been accredited by the ABA. Under the ABA Standards, organizations must be made up primarily of lawyers and must not certify lawyers unless the lawyers meet five distinct criteria: (1) they have been involved in the specialty area for at least the past three years; (2) they devote at least 25 percent of their practice to the specialty area; (3) they have passed a written examination of "suitable length and complexity"; (4) they have been favorably recommended by five or more lawyers or judges knowledgeable in the specialty area; and (5) they have taken at least 36 hours of CLE in the specialty area during the three years before applying for certification as a specialist. The task of accrediting certifying organizations under the Standards were given to the ABA's Standing Committee on Specialization.

At its August 1993 Annual Meeting, on the recommendation of the ABA's Standing Committee on Specialization, the ABA House of Delegates voted to accredit the following specialty certification programs: (1) the Civil Trial Advocacy Program and the Criminal Trial Advocacy Program, each administered by the National Board of Trial Advocacy; (2) the Business Bankruptcy program and the Creditors' Rights program, each administered by the Commercial Law League of America Academy of Commercial and Bankruptcy Lawyer Specialists; (3) the Business Bankruptcy program and the Consumer Bankruptcy program, each administered by the American Bankruptcy Board of Certification. ABA accreditation is valid for three years. All of the specialty programs originally accredited in 1993 were reaccredited at the ABA's August 1996 Annual Meeting. The ABA was not asked to accredit or reaccredit any programs during 1997, but a few programs are up for reaccreditation in 1998, and the Standing Committee on Specialization is working with various private groups to help them develop certification programs that meet the ABA Standards. The Standing Committee also hosts an annual National Roundtable on Lawyer Specialty Certification.

Rule 7.5 Firm Names and Letterheads

(a) A lawyer shall not use a firm name, letterhead or other professional designation that violates Rule 7.1. A trade name may be used by a lawyer in private practice if it does not imply a connection with a government agency or with a public or charitable legal services organization and is not otherwise in violation of Rule 7.1.

(b) A law firm with offices in more than one jurisdiction may use the same name in each jurisdiction, but identification of the lawyers in an office of the firm shall indicate the jurisdictional limitations on those not licensed to practice in the jurisdiction where the office is located.

(c) The name of a lawyer holding a public office shall not be used in the name of a law firm, or in communications on its behalf, during any substantial period in which the lawyer is not actively and regularly practicing with the firm.

(d) Lawyers may state or imply that they practice in a partnership or other organization only when that is the fact.

COMMENT

[1] A firm may be designated by the names of all or some of its members, by the names of deceased members where there has been a continuing succession in the firm's identity or by a trade name such as the "ABC Legal Clinic." Although the United States Supreme Court has held that legislation may prohibit the use of trade names in professional practice, use of such names in law practice is acceptable so long as it is not misleading. If a private firm uses a trade name that includes a geographical name such as "Springfield Legal Clinic," an express disclaimer that it is a public legal aid agency may be required to avoid a misleading implication. It may be observed that any firm name including the name of a deceased partner is, strictly speaking, a trade name. The use of such names to designate law firms has proven a useful means of identification. However, it is misleading to use the name of a lawyer not associated with the firm or a predecessor of the firm.

[2] With regard to paragraph (d), lawyers sharing office facilities, but who are not in fact partners, may not denominate themselves as, for example, "Smith and Jones," for that title suggests partnership in the practice of law.

Model Code Comparison

With regard to paragraph (a), DR 2-102(A) provided that "[a] lawyer . . . shall not use . . . professional cards . . . letterheads, or similar professional notices or devices, [except] if they are in dignified form. . . ." DR 2-102(B) provided that "[a] lawyer in private practice shall not practice under a trade name, a name that is misleading as to the identity of the lawyer or lawyers practicing under such name, or a firm name containing names other than those of one or more of the lawyers in the firm, except that . . . a firm may use as . . . its name the name or names of one or more deceased or retired members of the firm or of a predecessor firm in a continuing line of succession."

With regard to paragraph (b), DR 2-102(D) provided that a partnership "shall not be formed or continued between or among lawyers licensed in different jurisdictions unless all enumerations of the members and associates of the firm on its letterhead and in other permissible listings make clear the jurisdictional limitations on those members and associates of the firm not licensed to practice in all listed jurisdictions; however, the same firm name may be used in each jurisdiction."

With regard to paragraph (c), DR 2-102(B) provided that "[a] lawyer who assumes a judicial, legislative, or public executive or administrative post or office shall not permit his name to remain in the name of a law firm . . . during any significant period in which he is not actively and regularly practicing law as a member of the firm. . . ."

Paragraph (d) is substantially identical to DR 2-102(C).

Cross-References in Rules

None.

Legislative History

1980 Discussion Draft (then Rule 9.5) did not include the clause in subparagraph (b) requiring lawyers to indicate their jurisdictional limitations, and did not contain subparagraph (d).

1981 Draft was generally the same as adopted, except that Rule 7.5(d) provided: "Lawyers shall not hold themselves out as practicing in a law firm unless the association is in fact a firm."

1982 Draft was adopted.

Selected State Variations

Alaska adds subparagraph (e): "The term 'of counsel' shall be used only to refer to a lawyer who has a close continuing relationship with the firm."

Arizona deletes the clause in subparagraph (a) beginning, "if it does not imply a connection. . . ."

California: See Standards 6-9 following Rule 1-400.

Colorado's Rule 7.5(d) permits the use of the name of "deceased or retired members of the firm or of a predecessor firm in a continuing line of succession," as in DR 2-102(B) of the ABA Model Code.

Florida permits a lawyer to practice under a trade name if the name is "not deceptive" and "does not imply that the firm is something other than a private law firm," and permits a lawyer to use the term "legal clinic" or "legal services" in conjunction with the lawyer's own name "if the lawyer's practice is devoted to providing routine legal services for fees that are lower than the prevailing rate in the community for those services." Florida also adds a new subparagraph to its version of Rule 7.5 (see Florida Rule 4-7.7) stating:

(c) . . . A lawyer who advertises under a trade or fictitious name shall be in violation of this rule unless the same name is the law firm name that appears on the lawyer's letterhead, business cards, office sign, and fee contracts, and appears with the lawyer's signature on pleadings and other legal documents.

Illinois amplifies Rule 7.5(c) as follows:

(a) A lawyer who assumes a judicial, legislative, or public executive or administrative post or office shall not permit the lawyer's name to remain in the name of a law firm or to be used in professional notices of the firm during any substantial period in which the lawyer is not actively and regularly practicing law as a member of the firm. . . .

Iowa: DR 2-101(G) prohibits a lawyer from using the word "clinic" in any public communication "unless the practice of the lawyer or his firm is limited to routine matters for which the costs of rendering the service can be substantially reduced because of the repetitive nature of the services performed and the use of standardized forms and office procedures."

Missouri deletes the second sentence of Rule 7.5(a), and adds two new subparagraphs providing as follows:

(b) A lawyer's firm name shall include the name of the lawyer, the name of another lawyer in the firm or the name of a deceased or retired member of the firm in a continuing line of succession.

(c) A lawyer's firm name shall not include the name of any person other than a present member of the firm or a deceased or retired member of the firm in a continuing line of succession.

New Jersey: Rule 7.5 provides:

(a) A lawyer shall not use a firm name, letterhead or other professional designation that violates RPC 7.1. Except for organizations referred to in R. 1:21-1(d), the name under which a lawyer or law firm practices shall contain only the full or last names of one or more of the lawyers in the firm or office or the names of a person or persons who have ceased to be associated with the firm through death or retirement.

(b) A law firm with offices in more than one jurisdiction may use the same name in each jurisdiction. In New Jersey, identification of all lawyers of the firm, in advertisements, on letterheads or anywhere else that the firm name is used, shall indicate the jurisdictional limitations on those not licensed to practice in New Jersey. Where the name of an attorney not licensed to practice in this State is used in a firm name, any advertisement, letterhead or other communication containing the firm name must include the name of at least one licensed New Jersey attorney who is responsible for the firm's New Jersey practice or the local office thereof.

(c) A firm name shall not contain the name of any person not actively associated with the firm as an attorney, other than that of a person or persons who have ceased to be associated with the firm through death or retirement.

(d) Lawyers may state or imply that they practice in a partnership only if the persons designated in the firm name and the principal members of the firm share in the responsibility and liability for the firm's performance of legal services.

(e) A law firm name may include additional identifying language such as "& Associates" only when such language is accurate and descriptive of the firm. Any firm name including additional identifying language such as "Legal Services" or other similar phrases shall inform all prospective clients in the retainer agreement or other writing that the law firm is not affiliated or associated with a public, quasi-public or charitable organization. However, no firm shall use the phrase "legal aid" in its name or in any additional identifying language.

(f) In any case in which an organization practices under a trade name as permitted by paragraph (a) above, the name or names of one or more of its principally responsible attorneys, licensed to practice in this State, shall be displayed on all letterheads, signs, advertisements and cards or other places where the trade name is used.

New York: Substantially the same as the ABA Model Code — see Model Code Comparison above.

Ohio DR 2-102(G) specifically provides rules for use of the term "legal clinic" in a firm name. The Rule envisions that a legal clinic will provide "standardized and multiple legal services."

Virginia combines the language of DR 2-102 and Model Rule 7.5.

Washington provides, in subparagraph (a):

A trade name may not be used by a lawyer in private practice except that the use of the words "legal clinic" may be used alone or in conjunction with a geographical designation or the name of one or more of the lawyers connected with the practice so long as the name is not otherwise in violation of Rule 7.1 and except if otherwise lawful a firm may use as, or continue to include in, its name the name or names of one or more deceased or retired members of the firm or of a predecessor firm in a continuing line of succession.

Related Materials

ABA Canons: Canon 33 provided:

33. Partnerships — Names

Partnerships among lawyers for the practice of their profession are very common and are not to be condemned. In the formation of partnerships and the use of partnership names care should be taken not to violate any law, custom, or rule of court locally applicable. Where partnerships are formed between lawyers who are not all admitted to practice in the courts of the state, care should be taken to avoid any misleading name or representation which would create a false impression as to the professional position or privileges of the member not locally admitted. In the formation of partnerships for the practice of law, no person should be admitted or held out as a practitioner or member who is not a member of the legal profession duly authorized to practice, and amenable to professional discipline. In the selection and use of a firm name, no false, misleading, assumed or trade name should be used. The continued use of the name of a deceased or former partner, when permissible by local custom, is not unethical, but care should be taken that no imposition or deception is practiced through this use. When a member of the firm, on becoming a judge, is precluded from practicing law, his name should not be continued in the firm name.

Partnership Law: Rule 7.4(d) prohibits lawyers from stating or implying that they are partners if they are not. Section 7 of the Uniform Partnership Act, entitled "Rules for Determining the Existence of a Partnership," provides: "(4) The receipt by a person of a share of the profits of a business is prima facie evidence that he is a partner in the business. . . ." The subparagraph then lists five exceptions to this general rule.

ARTICLE 8. MAINTAINING THE INTEGRITY OF THE PROFESSION

Editors' Note. In the 1980 Discussion Draft, the Article on Maintaining the Integrity of the Profession (then Rules 10.1 through 10.5) began with the following Introduction:

The legal profession is largely self-governing. Although other professions also have been granted powers of self-government, the legal profession is unique in this respect because of the close relationship between the profession and the processes of government and law enforcement. This connection is manifested in the fact that ultimate authority over the legal profession is vested largely in the courts.

Self-government of the legal profession serves important social purposes. One is reduction of the need for governmental interference in private sector activity. To the extent that the legal profession can secure conformity of its members to the obligations of their professional calling, the occasion for government regulation is obviated. Another objective of self-government is the maintenance of the legal profession's independence from government domination. An independent legal profession is an important force in preserving government under law, for abuse of legal authority is more readily challenged by a profession whose members are not dependent on government for the right to practice.

The legal profession's relative autonomy carries with it special responsibilities of self-government. From a substantive viewpoint, the profession is responsible for seeing that its regulations are conceived in the public interest and not in furtherance of parochial or self-interested concerns of the bar. From a procedural viewpoint, every law-yer is responsible for observance of the Rules of Professional Conduct; a lawyer must not only conform his or her conduct to the Rules, but also must aid in securing their observance by other lawyers. This duty involves irksome and sometimes onerous re-sponsibilities. However, neglect of these responsibilities will compromise the indepen-dence of the profession and the public interest which it serves.

Rule 8.1 Bar Admission and Disciplinary Matters

An applicant for admission to the bar, or a lawyer in connection with a bar admission application or in connection with a disciplinary matter, shall not:

(a) knowingly make a false statement of material fact; or

(b) fail to disclose a fact necessary to correct a misapprehension known by the person to have arisen in the matter, or knowingly fail to respond to a lawful demand for information from an admissions or dis-ciplinary authority, except that this Rule does not require disclosure of information otherwise protected by Rule 1.6.

COMMENT

[1] The duty imposed by this Rule extends to persons seeking ad-mission to the bar as well as to lawyers. Hence, if a person makes a mate-rial false statement in connection with an application for admission, it may be the basis for subsequent disciplinary action if the person is admitted, and in any event may be relevant in a subsequent admission application. The duty imposed by this Rule applies to a lawyer's own admission or dis-cipline as well as that of others. Thus, it is a separate professional offense for a lawyer to knowingly make a misrepresentation or omission in con-nection with a disciplinary investigation of the lawyer's own conduct. This Rule also requires affirmative clarification of any misunderstanding on the part of the admissions or disciplinary authority of which the person in-volved becomes aware.

[2] This Rule is subject to the provisions of the Fifth Amendment of the United States Constitution and corresponding provisions of state con-stitutions. A person relying on such a provision in reponse to a question, however, should do so openly and not use the right of nondisclosure as a justification for failure to comply with this Rule.

[3] A lawyer representing an applicant for admission to the bar, or representing a lawyer who is the subject of a disciplinary inquiry or

proceeding, is governed by the rules applicable to the client-lawyer relationship.

Model Code Comparison

DR 1-101(A) provided that a lawyer is "subject to discipline if he has made a materially false statement in, or if he has deliberately failed to disclose a material fact requested in connection with, his application for admission to the bar." DR 1-101(B) provided that a lawyer "shall not further the application for admission to the bar of another person known by him to be unqualified in respect to character, education, or other relevant attribute." With respect to paragraph (b), DR 1-102(A)(5) provided that a lawyer shall not engage in "conduct that is prejudicial to the administration of justice."

Cross-References in Rules

None.

Legislative History

1980 Discussion Draft of Rule 8.1 was substantially the same as adopted, except that subparagraph (a) prohibited a lawyer from making "a knowing misrepresentation of fact," and subparagraph (b) did not include the clause beginning "or knowingly fail to respond. . . ."
1981 and 1982 Drafts were substantially the same as adopted.

Selected State Variations

California: See Rule 1-200 (False Statement Regarding Admission to the State Bar).
Colorado: Rule 8.1 adds "reinstatement" to the list of proceedings to which the rule applies. Colorado also adds that 8.1(b) does not "prohibit a good faith challenge to the demand for such information."
Illinois: Rule 8.1(b) provides:

> A lawyer shall not further the application for admission to the bar of another person known by the lawyer to be unqualified in respect to character, education, or any other relevant attribute.

New York: Same or substantially the same as the ABA Model Code — see Model Code Comparison above.

Virginia retains the language of DR 1-101(A), but in place of DR 1-101(B) provides that a lawyer "is subject to discipline if he has made a materially false statement in any certification required to be filed as a condition of maintaining or renewing his license to practice law."

Related Materials

ABA Model Rules for Lawyer Disciplinary Enforcement: At its 1989 Annual Meeting, the ABA adopted a revised set of Model Rules for Lawyer Disciplinary Enforcement. These replaced the 1985 version of the Model Rules for Lawyer Disciplinary Enforcement, which had themselves replaced the 1979 Standards for Lawyer Discipline Proceedings.

Character and Fitness Standards: Nearly every state requires bar applicants to meet certain standards for "character and fitness." In New York, for example, 22 N.Y.C.R.R. §602.1(b) provides: "Every completed application shall be referred for investigation of the applicant's character and fitness to a committee on character and fitness. . . ." In Illinois, §2 of the Illinois Attorney Act provides that no person shall be entitled to receive a law license "until he shall have obtained a certificate of his good moral character from a circuit court." Neither state has adopted written standards defining good character.

Model Rules of Professional Conduct for Federal Lawyers: Rule 8.1 also applies to an "applicant for admission to a bar or employment as a lawyer with a Federal Agency, [and] a Federal lawyer seeking the right to practice before a Federal Agency. . . ."

Rule 8.2 Judicial and Legal Officials

(a) A lawyer shall not make a statement that the lawyer knows to be false or with reckless disregard as to its truth or falsity concerning the qualifications or integrity of a judge, adjudicatory officer or public legal officer, or of a candidate for election or appointment to judicial or legal office.

(b) A lawyer who is a candidate for judicial office shall comply with the applicable provisions of the code of judicial conduct.

COMMENT

[1] Assessments by lawyers are relied on in evaluating the professional or personal fitness of persons being considered for election or appointment to judicial office and to public legal offices, such as attorney general, prosecuting attorney and public defender. Expressing honest

and candid opinions on such matters contributes to improving the administration of justice. Conversely, false statements by a lawyer can unfairly undermine public confidence in the administration of justice.

[2] When a lawyer seeks judicial office, the lawyer should be bound by applicable limitations on political activity.

[3] To maintain the fair and independent administration of justice, lawyers are encouraged to continue traditional efforts to defend judges and courts unjustly criticized.

Model Code Comparison

With regard to paragraph (a), DR 8-102(A) provided that a lawyer "shall not knowingly make false statements of fact concerning the qualifications of a candidate for election or appointment to a judicial office." DR 8-102(B) provided that a lawyer "shall not knowingly make false accusations against a judge or other adjudicatory officer."

Paragraph (b) is substantially identical to DR 8-103.

Cross-References in Rules

None.

Legislative History

1980 Discussion Draft (then Rule 10.2): Subparagraph (a) provided: "A lawyer who is a candidate for judicial office shall comply with the applicable provisions of the code of judicial conduct." Subparagraph (b) was the same as adopted.
1981 and 1982 Drafts were substantially the same as adopted.

Selected State Variations

California: See B & P Code §6068(b).
District of Columbia omits Rule 8.2.
Maryland provides:

> (b) A candidate for judicial position shall not make or suffer others to make for him, promises of conduct in office which appeal to the cupidity or prejudices of the appointing or electing powers; he shall not announce in advance his conclusions of law on disputed issues to secure class support, and he shall do nothing while a candidate to create the impression that if chosen, he will administer his office with bias, partiality or improper discrimination.

New York: Same or substantially the same as the ABA Model Code — see Model Code Comparison above.

Virginia omits Rule 8.2.

Related Materials

ABA Canons: Canons 1 and 2 provided:

1. The Duty of the Lawyer to the Courts

It is the duty of the lawyer to maintain towards the Courts a respectful attitude, not for the sake of the temporary incumbent of the judicial office, but for the maintenance of its supreme importance. Judges, not being wholly free to defend themselves, are peculiarly entitled to receive the support of the Bar against unjust criticism and clamor. Whenever there is proper ground for serious complaint of a judicial officer, it is the right and duty of the lawyer to submit his grievances to the proper authorities. In such cases, but not otherwise, such charges should be encouraged and the person making them should be protected.

2. The Selection of Judges

It is the duty of the Bar to endeavor to prevent political considerations from outweighing judicial fitness in the selections of Judges. It should protest earnestly and actively against the appointment or election of those who are unsuitable for the Bench; and it should strive to have elevated thereto only those willing to forego other employments, whether of a business, political or other character, which may embarrass their free and fair consideration of questions before them for decision. The aspiration of lawyers for judicial position should be governed by an impartial estimate of their ability to add honor to the office and not by a desire for the distinction the position may bring to themselves.

ABA Code of Judicial Conduct: Rule 8.2(b) requires candidates for judicial office to "comply with the applicable provisions of the code of judicial conduct." The applicable provisions for judicial candidates are found in Canon 5 of the ABA's 1990 Code of Judicial Conduct, which is reprinted below in this volume.

Restatement of the Law Governing Lawyers: The American Law Institute has proposed but not yet approved the following provision:

§174. Lawyer Statement Concerning Judicial or Legal Officer

A lawyer may not knowingly or recklessly make publicly a false derogatory statement of fact concerning the qualifications or integrity of an incumbent of a judicial or other public legal office or a candidate for election to such an office.

Rule 8.3 Reporting Professional Misconduct

(a) A lawyer having knowledge that another lawyer has committed a violation of the rules of professional conduct that raises a substantial question as to that lawyer's honesty, trustworthiness or fitness as a lawyer in other respects, shall inform the appropriate professional authority.

(b) A lawyer having knowledge that a judge has committed a violation of applicable rules of judicial conduct that raises a substantial question as to the judge's fitness for office shall inform the appropriate authority.

(c) This rule does not require disclosure of information otherwise protected by Rule 1.6 or information gained by a lawyer or judge while serving as a member of an approved lawyers assistance program to the extent that such information would be confidential if it were communicated subject to the attorney-client privilege.

> **Editors' Note.** At its August 1991 Annual Meeting, the ABA House of Delegates amended Rule 8.3(c) to protect information gained by a lawyer workng with a lawyer assistance program. The ABA also added Comment 5 to explain the amendment. Excerpts from the Committee Report proposing the amendment are set out in the Legislative History section following this Rule.

COMMENT

[1] Self-regulation of the legal profession requires that members of the profession initiate disciplinary investigation when they know of a violation of the Rules of Professional Conduct. Lawyers have a similar obligation with respect to judicial misconduct. An apparently isolated violation may indicate a pattern of misconduct that only a disciplinary investigation can uncover. Reporting a violation is especially important where the victim is unlikely to discover the offense.

[2] A report about misconduct is not required where it would involve violation of Rule 1.6. However, a lawyer should encourage a client to consent to disclosure where prosecution would not substantially prejudice the client's interests.

[3] If a lawyer were obliged to report every violation of the Rules, the failure to report any violation would itself be a professional offense. Such a requirement existed in many jurisdictions but proved to be unenforceable. This Rule limits the reporting obligation to those offenses that a self-regulating profession must vigorously endeavor to prevent. A

measure of judgment is, therefore, required in complying with the provisions of this Rule. The term "substantial" refers to the seriousness of the possible offense and not the quantum of evidence of which the lawyer is aware. A report should be made to the bar disciplinary agency unless some other agency, such as a peer review agency, is more appropriate in the circumstances. Similar considerations apply to the reporting of judicial misconduct.

[4] The duty to report professional misconduct does not apply to a lawyer retained to represent a lawyer whose professional conduct is in question. Such a situation is governed by the rules applicable to the client-lawyer relationship.

Editors' Note. The next paragraph of the Comment was added by the ABA at its 1991 Annual Meeting.

[5] Information about a lawyer's or judge's misconduct or fitness may be received by a lawyer in the course of that lawyer's participation in an approved lawyers' or judges' assistance program. In that circumstance, providing for the confidentiality of such information encourages lawyers and judges to seek treatment through such programs. Conversely, without such confidentiality, lawyers and judges may hesitate to seek assistance from these programs, which may then result in additional harm to their professional careers and additional injury to the welfare of clients and the public. The Rule therefore exempts the lawyer from the reporting requirements of paragraphs (a) and (b) with respect to information that would be privileged if the relationship between the impaired lawyer or judge and the recipient of the information were that of a client and a lawyer. On the other hand, a lawyer who receives such information would nevertheless be required to comply with the Rule 8.3 reporting provisions to report misconduct if the impaired lawyer or judge indicates an intent to engage in illegal activity, for example, the conversion of client funds to his or her use.

Model Code Comparison

DR 1-103(A) provided that "[a] lawyer possessing unprivileged knowledge of a violation of [a Disciplinary Rule] shall report such knowledge to . . . authority empowered to investigate or act upon such violation."

Cross-References in Rules

None.

Legislative History

1980 Discussion Draft (then Rule 10.3) provided:

A lawyer having information indicating that another lawyer has committed a substantial violation of the Rules of Professional Conduct shall report the information to the appropriate disciplinary authority.

1981 Draft was substantially the same as adopted, except that it did not include any equivalent to Rule 8.3(b).

1982 Draft was adopted.

1991 Amendments: At its August 1991 Annual Meeting, the ABA House of Delegates added the clause beginning "or information gained . . ." to Rule 8.3(c). The following excerpts from the Report of the ABA Standing Committee on Ethics and Professional Responsibility explain the rationale and scope of the amendments:

ABA Committee Report Explaining 1991 Amendments to Rule 8.3*

The serious concerns that have arisen recently as a result of "lawyer impairment" have led to the creation of special programs throughout the nation to assist lawyers and judges who face alcohol or drug addiction or other serious problems which threaten to affect or have already affected the performance of their professional responsibilities. More than forty-four such programs, commonly known as "Lawyer and Judge Assistance Programs" have been established by state courts or state and local bar associations.

. . . The Committee believes that it is in the interest of the legal profession and the public that the ABA Model Rules be amended to provide for the confidentiality of information that is furnished by the impaired lawyer or judge.

Under the amendment to Model Rule 8.3, the protection of information obtained in the circumstances of a lawyer's or judge's participation in an assistance program is similar to the protection ordinarily provided by the attorney-client privilege. Where the attorney-client privilege would not apply because the information relates to the intention to commit a crime, for example where a lawyer indicates the intention to continue to convert client funds to his or her own use, such information may be disclosed to the appropriate authority, permitting the recipient of the information to comply with the obligation imposed upon him or her by paragraphs (a) or (b). In such situations concerns other than the recovery of the impaired lawyer or judge necessarily outweigh the impaired lawyer's or judge's right to confidentiality. . . . Although the Committee recognizes that disclosure of such information by one member of the profession to the det-

*Committee Reports do not represent official policy of the ABA. They are for information only, and the opinions are those of the authors of the report.

riment of a professional colleague is painful and difficult, it considers such a situation indistinguishable from other situations in which important public policy considerations require disclosure of confidential information. To extend the confidentiality protection to a lawyer's or judge's intention to commit a crime likely to result in significant harm to others, moreover, would lend support to claims that the profession is unable or unwilling to live up to its obligation to regulate itself in the public interest.

Selected State Variations

Arizona: Rule 8.3(c) provides:

> This rule does not require disclosure of information otherwise protected by [Rule 1.6] or information gained by a lawyer while serving as a member of an approved lawyers' assistance program to the extent that the information would be confidential if it were communicated subject to the attorney-client privilege and confidentiality has not otherwise been waived.

California: No comparable provision.

Connecticut: Rule 8.3(a) contains the following additional sentence: "A lawyer may not condition settlement of a civil dispute involving allegations of improprieties on the part of a lawyer on an agreement that the subject misconduct not be reported to the appropriate disciplinary authority."

Illinois: Rule 8.3(a) requires a lawyer to report knowledge "not otherwise protected as a confidence by these Rules or by law" that a lawyer has committed specified violations. Rule 8.3(c) provides that upon proper request of a tribunal or disciplinary authority, "a lawyer possessing information not otherwise protected as a confidence by these Rules or by law concerning another lawyer or a judge shall fully reveal such information." Rule 8.3(d) provides:

> A lawyer who has been disciplined as a result of a lawyer disciplinary action brought before any body other than the Illinois Attorney Registration and Disciplinary Commission shall report that fact to the Commission.

Kansas adds the following to Rule 8.3(c):

> In addition, a lawyer is not required to disclose information concerning any such violation which is discovered through participation in a Substance Abuse Committee, Service to the Bar Committee, or similar committees sponsored by a state or local bar association, or by participation in a self-help organization such as Alcoholics Anonymous, through which aid is rendered to another lawyer who may be impaired in the practice of law.

Massachusetts: Effective January 1, 1998, Rule 8.3(a) and (b) uses the phrase "should inform" instead of "shall inform." The comment states that the rule "urges but does not require lawyers to report serious violations of ethical duty by lawyers and judges."

Michigan adds the word "significant" before "violation" in Rule 8.3(a) and Rule 8.3(b). The duty under this rule is suspended if the lawyer gained the information "while serving as an employee or volunteer of the substance abuse counseling program of the State Bar of Michigan, to the extent that the information would be protected under Rule 1.6 from disclosure if it were a communication between lawyer and client." Rule 8.3(c)(2).

New York: Amendments to the New York Code substantially adopt the language of Rule 8.3(a). See EC 1-4 and DR 1-103.

Ohio: DR 1-103(C) extends a privilege if a lawyer obtains knowledge of another lawyer's wrongdoing while working for a Bar Association substance abuse committee.

Texas: Rule 8.03(a) and (b) generally track Rule 8.3(a) and (b), but the balance of the Texas rule is as follows:

> (c) A lawyer having knowledge or suspecting that another lawyer or judge whose conduct the lawyer is required to report pursuant to paragraphs (a) or (b) of this Rule is impaired by chemical dependency on alcohol or drugs or by mental illness may report that person to an approved peer assistance program rather than to an appropriate disciplinary authority. If a lawyer elects that option, the lawyer's report to the approved peer assistance program shall disclose any disciplinary violations that the reporting lawyer would otherwise have to disclose to the authorities referred to in paragraphs (a) and (b).
>
> (d) This rule does not require disclosure of knowledge or information otherwise protected as confidential information:
> > (1) by Rule 1.05 or
> > (2) by any statutory or regulatory provisions applicable to the counseling activities of the approved peer assistance program.

Virginia: DR 1-103(A) requires reporting of information "indicating that another lawyer has committed a violation of the Disciplinary Rules that raises a substantial question as to that lawyer's fitness to practice law in other respects" *unless* the information is protected by DR 4-101 (Virginia's basic rule on confidentiality). DR 1-103(B) exempts members of the Virginia Bar's Committee on Substance Abuse from any reporting duties regarding information obtained in connection with work for the Substance Abuse Committee.

Washington uses the phrase "should promptly inform" instead of "shall inform."

Related Materials

ABA Canons: Canon 29 provided:

29. Upholding the Honor of the Profession

> Lawyers should expose without fear or favor before the proper tribunals corrupt or dishonest conduct in the profession, and should accept without hesitation employment against a member of the Bar who has wronged his client. The counsel upon the trial of a cause in which perjury has been committed owe it to the pro-

fession and to the public to bring the matter to the knowledge of the prosecuting authorities. The lawyer should aid in guarding the Bar against the admission to the profession of candidates unfit or unqualified because deficient in either moral character or education. He should strive at all times to uphold the honor and to maintain the dignity of the profession and to improve not only the law but the administration of justice.

ABA Commission on Lawyer Assistance Programs: In 1988, the ABA formed a Commission on Impaired Attorneys to encourage and assist state and local bar associations in establishing programs to assist addicted lawyers and judges. Effective in August 1996, the ABA changed the name to the Commission on Lawyer Assistance Programs (CLAP). (Rule 8.3(c) expressly refers to lawyer assistance programs.) The Commission reviews lawyer assistance programs and makes recommendations for expanding and improving the programs. The Commission also circulates guidelines and policies to assist such programs. In 1990, the ABA House of Delegates approved the Commission's Model Law Firm/Legal Department Personnel Impairment Policy and Guidelines. In 1991, the House of Delegates approved the Commission's Guiding Principles for a Lawyer Assistance Program. In 1995, the House of Delegates adopted the Commission's Model Lawyer Assistance Program. The model program is designed to assist state and local bar associations in developing and maintaining effective programs to identify and assist lawyers, judges, and law sudents impaired by alcoholism, drugs, or mental health problems. The model program not only assists those who voluntarily seek help, but also provides services to lawyers referred by the disciplinary system, either as an alternative to discipline or as part of a sanction such as probation. For further information, contact the Commission's Staff Director, Donna Spilis, at the ABA Center for Professional Responsibility, 541 North Fairbanks Court, Chicago, IL 60011, telephone 312-988-5359.

Oath of Office: All states require new attorneys to take an oath upon being admitted to the bar. In Illinois, for example, §4 of the Attorney Act requires every new attorney to take the following oath:

> I do solemnly swear (or affirm, as the case may be), that I will support the constitution of the United States and the constitution of the state of Illinois, and that I will faithfully discharge the duties of the office of attorney and counselor at law to the best of my ability.

Rule 8.4 Misconduct

It is professional misconduct for a lawyer to:

(a) violate or attempt to violate the rules of professional conduct, knowingly assist or induce another to do so, or do so through the acts of another;

(b) commit a criminal act that reflects adversely on the lawyer's honesty, trustworthiness or fitness as a lawyer in other respects;

(c) engage in conduct involving dishonesty, fraud, deceit or misrepresentation;

(d) engage in conduct that is prejudicial to the administration of justice;

(e) state or imply an ability to influence improperly a government agency or official; or

(f) knowingly assist a judge or judicial officer in conduct that is a violation of applicable rules of judicial conduct or other law.

COMMENT

[1] Many kinds of illegal conduct reflect adversely on fitness to practice law, such as offenses involving fraud and the offense of willful failure to file an income tax return. However, some kinds of offense carry no such implication. Traditionally, the distinction was drawn in terms of offenses involving "moral turpitude." That concept can be construed to include offenses concerning some matters of personal morality, such as adultery and comparable offenses, that have no specific connection to fitness for the practice of law. Although a lawyer is personally answerable to the entire criminal law, a lawyer should be professionally answerable only for offenses that indicate lack of those characteristics relevant to law practice. Offenses involving violence, dishonesty, or breach of trust, or serious interference with the administration of justice are in that category. A pattern of repeated offenses, even ones of minor significance when considered separately, can indicate indifference to legal obligation.

[2] A lawyer may refuse to comply with an obligation imposed by law upon a good faith belief that no valid obligation exists. The provisions of Rule 1.2(d) concerning a good faith challenge to the validity, scope, meaning or application of the law apply to challenges of legal regulation of the practice of law.

[3] Lawyers holding public office assume legal responsibilities going beyond those of other citizens. A lawyer's abuse of public office can suggest an inability to fulfill the professional role of attorney. The same is true of abuse of positions of private trust such as trustee, executor, administrator, guardian, agent and officer, director or manager of a corporation or other organization.

Model Code Comparison

With regard to paragraphs (a) through (d), DR 1-102(A) provided that a lawyer shall not:

(1) Violate a Disciplinary Rule.

(2) Circumvent a Disciplinary Rule through actions of another.

(3) Engage in illegal conduct involving moral turpitude.

(4) Engage in conduct involving dishonesty, fraud, deceit, or misrepresentation.

(5) Engage in conduct that is prejudicial to the administration of justice.

(6) Engage in any other conduct that adversely reflects on his fitness to practice law.

Paragraph (e) is substantially similar to DR 9-101(C).

There was no direct counterpart to paragraph (f) in the Disciplinary Rules of the Model Code. EC 7-34 stated in part that "[a] lawyer . . . is never justified in making a gift or a loan to a [judicial officer] except as permitted by . . . the Code of Judicial Conduct." EC 9-1 stated that a lawyer "should promote public confidence in our [legal] system and in the legal profession."

Cross-References in Rules

Rule 3.3, Comment 2: "Regarding compliance with Rule 1.2(d), see the Comment to that Rule. See also the Comment to **Rule 8.4(b).**"

Rule 3.8, Comment 1: "Applicable law may require other measures by the prosecutor and knowing disregard of those obligations or a systematic abuse of prosecutorial discretion could constitute a violation of **Rule 8.4.**"

Rule 5.1, Comment 3: "Paragraph (c)(1) expresses a general principle of responsibility for acts of another. See also **Rule 8.4(a).**"

Rule 5.1, Comment 6: "Apart from this Rule and **Rule 8.4(a)**, a lawyer does not have disciplinary liability for the conduct of a partner, associate or subordinate."

Rule 5.7, Comment 1: "[T]he conduct of a lawyer involved in the provision of law-related services is subject to those Rules that apply generally to lawyer conduct, regardless of whether the conduct involves the provision of legal services. See, e.g., **Rule 8.4.**"

Rule 5.7, Comment 9: "When the full protections of all of the Rules of Professional Conduct do not apply to the provision of law-related services, principles of law external to the Rules, for example, the law of principal and agent, govern the legal duties owed to those receiving the services. . . . See also **Rule 8.4** (Misconduct)."

Legislative History

1980 Discussion Draft (then Rule 10.4) provided:

It is professional misconduct for a lawyer to:

(a) violate the Rules of Professional Conduct or knowingly aid another to do so;

    (b) commit a crime or other deliberately wrongful act that reflects adversely on the lawyer's honesty, trustworthiness, or fitness in other respects to practice law;

    (c) state or imply an ability to influence improperly a government agency or official;

    (d) practice law in a jurisdiction in violation of the regulation of the legal profession in that jurisdiction; or

    (e) aid a person who is not a member of the bar in the performance of activity that constitutes the practice of law.

1981 and 1982 Drafts: Subparagraph (b) of both drafts provided that it was misconduct for a lawyer to "commit a criminal *or fraudulent* act that reflects adversely . . . ," and neither draft included subparagraphs (c) and (d) of the rule as adopted. Subparagraphs (e) and (f) of both drafts were moved to Rule 5.5 of the Rules as adopted.

1994 Proposals: Two competing "anti-discrimination" proposals, each in the form of a new subparagraph (g) to Rule 8.4, were on the agenda at the ABA's February 1994 Mid-Year Meeting. However, at the last minute both proposals were withdrawn, and the competing sponsors announced their intention to work together to develop a single proposal to present at the ABA's February 1995 Mid-Year Meeting. For various reasons, the two groups did not present a joint proposal at the 1995 Mid-Year Meeting or at the ABA's 1995 Annual Meeting, and it is uncertain whether a new proposal will ever be presented to the House of Delegates.

The two proposals withdrawn in 1994 differed mainly in their scope. The narrower proposal was submitted by the ABA Standing Committee on Ethics and Professional Responsibility. It provided that it would be professional misconduct for a lawyer to:

    (g) knowingly manifest by words or conduct, in the course of representing a client, bias or prejudice based upon race, sex, religion, national origin, disability, age, sexual orientation or socio-economic status. This paragraph does not apply to a lawyer's confidential communications to a client or preclude legitimate advocacy with respect to the foregoing factors.

The Report submitted in support of the Standing Committee's 1994 proposal explained this language as follows:*

    The Committee's proposed amendment has three essential aspects.

    The first is its limitation to situations in which the lawyer is representing a client in a legal matter. The Committee considers that the lawyer's words or conduct occurring in the context of any type of legal practice should reflect respect both for the rule of law and for the sense of professionalism that distinguishes those dedicated to the practice of law. The amendment will serve this purpose.

    The second aspect is the Rule's identification of particular types of bias or prejudice that are to be prohibited. These forms of bias or prejudice have been included because they refer to factors that are generally viewed as deserving special

---

*Committee Reports do not represent official policy of the ABA. They are for information only, and the opinions are those of the authors of the report.

protection from discrimination. The proposed amendment establishes a standard of conduct broader than that mandated by statutory enactments; this standard enables the profession to set an example of fairness and impartiality that is at the core of its commitment to the public interest. In furtherance of its intention not to develop the amendment as corollary to statutory law, the Committee chose to employ the concept of "bias or prejudice" rather than the more narrowly and legally determined concept of "discrimination."

The third aspect of the rule comprises its exceptions. In order to avoid inquiry into a lawyer's confidential communications to a client, the rule excepts those communications from its ambit. The rule, as well, does not preclude legitimate advocacy by the lawyer with respect to the specified factors. An example of this would be when the national origin of a party is a factor in selecting a jury for a particular case. The Committee did not, however, intend by use of the word advocacy to limit the applicability of the exception to lawyer conduct in formal proceedings; the exception is intended to apply with equal force to the lawyer's counseling function.

A broader proposal was submitted by the ABA Young Lawyers Division. It provided that it would be professional misconduct for a lawyer to:

> (g) commit a discriminatory act prohibited by law or to harass a person on the basis of sex, race, age, creed, religion, color, national origin, disability, sexual orientation or marital status, where the act of discrimination or harassment is committed in connection with a lawyer's professional activities.

The Report submitted in support of the Young Lawyers Division's 1994 proposal explained this language as follows:

> The amendment is designed to regulate conduct in all manifestations of a lawyer's professional activities, and thereby avoid the inexplicable nuances of a rule which would allow reprehensible behavior to go unchecked merely because it is calculatedly inflicted outside the courtroom or after a case is concluded. Encompassing the all too common courtroom antics, the proposed rule will reach also to each situation where a lawyer is engaged in endeavors associated with professional activities.
>
> The proposed amendment will apply to professional activities regardless of whether the lawyer is representing a client. Implicit therein is the notion that the administration of justice must be protected from offensive conduct committed by officers of the court in all instances where a lawyer is called upon by virtue of the distinction of being a member of our profession. To do otherwise makes a mockery of the concept of fair and impartial administration of justice for all, and enhances the perception that lawyers are somehow outside or above the law. To do otherwise fuels the notion that honoring the spirit of the law is less important than knowing how to violate a law or rule in a manner where one will not be caught, or in which the offensive activity will fall between the cracks. The victim is left shaken and helpless, without recourse and questioning how our system of justice knowingly permits such shameless behavior to go unpunished.
>
> The proposal must regulate a lawyer's conduct both inside and outside the courtroom because all lawyers represent the judicial system each time they act within their professional capacity. A public perception of fairness and equality within the judicial system is essential to maintaining the integrity of the system. The proposed resolution is not unlike existing model rules that prohibit lawyers from

"engaging in conduct that is prejudicial to the administration of justice," and these rules might serve as a guide to its application.

1995 Resolution: After the Young Lawyers Division and the Standing Committee on Ethics and Professional Responsibility withdrew their competing 1994 proposals to add a new subparagraph 8.4(g), the Young Lawyers Division worked with the Standing Committee and other ABA entities in an attempt to produce a unified proposal to present to the House of Delegates. That attempt failed, partly because of concerns that a rule prohibiting bias and prejudice could infringe First Amendment rights. The Young Lawyers Division therefore decided to recommend a resolution to the House of Delegates condemning bias and prejudice by lawyers and encouraging affirmative steps to discourage bias and prejudice. The resolution passed. The full text of the resolution is reprinted in the Related Materials following this rule.

Selected State Variations

Alabama: Rule 3.10, effective January 1, 1994, provides that a lawyer "shall not present, participate in presenting, or threaten to present criminal charges solely to obtain an advantage in a civil matter," as provided in DR 7-105 of the ABA Model Code.

Alaska's version of Rule 8.4 omits paragraph (d). (See Alaska Rule 3.8.) The comment states that the phrase "prejudicial to the administration of justice" was too vague. Alaska also adds a paragraph, based on DR 7-108(D) from the Model Code, that prohibits a lawyer from harassing or embarrassing jurors or from seeking to influence the juror's actions in future jury service. (See Alaska Rule 3.10.)

Arizona: In April of 1994, the State Bar filed a petition with the Arizona Supreme Court in support of a new Rule 1.17 that would prohibit a lawyer from initiating abusive or exploitive sexual conduct with a client. On May 23, 1994, the Arizona Supreme Court denied the petition. The Court's one-sentence opinion said that the current rules already covered the issues and that the proposed rule raised more questions than it answered.

California: See B & P Code §§6101-6106.1. See also Rule 2-400, effective March 1, 1994, which provides, in part:

(B) In the management or operation of a law practice, a member shall not unlawfully discriminate or knowingly permit unlawful discrimination on the basis of race, national origin, sex, sexual orientation, religion, age or disability in:

(1) hiring, promoting, discharging or otherwise determining the conditions of employment of any person; or

(2) accepting or terminating representation of any client.

(C) No disciplinary investigation or proceeding may be initiated by the State Bar against a member under this rule unless and until a tribunal of competent jurisdiction, other than a disciplinary tribunal, shall have first adjudicated a complaint of alleged discrimination and found that unlawful conduct occurred. . . .

Colorado: Rule 1.2(f) makes it misconduct to "engage in conduct which violates accepted standards of legal ethics" or to engage in conduct that:

exhibits or is intended to appeal to or engender bias against a person on account of that person's race, gender, religion, national origin, disability, age, sexual orientation, or socioeconomic status, whether that conduct is directed to other counsel, court personnel, witnesses, parties, judges, judicial officers, or any persons involved in the legal process.

Colorado also includes a Rule 4.5 that retains the old Model Code prohibition, found in DR 7-105(A), against threatening criminal prosecution to gain an advantage in a civil proceeding.

District of Columbia: D.C. Rule 8.4(d) differs significantly from the ABA Model Rule, and D.C. adds Rule 9.1, which prohibits discrimination in employment — see District of Columbia Rules of Professional Conduct below.

Florida: Effective February 9, 1995, the Florida Supreme Court adopted a new subparagraph (h) making it professional misconduct for a lawyer to "willfully refuse, as determined by a court of competent jurisdiction, to timely pay a child support obligation." The Comment explaining the new subparagraph says that the provision was added so that lawyers will be treated like other professionals in Florida. The Comment also explains that the rule should be invoked only after all other potential remedies have been exhausted, and that the bar may not initiate a grievance proceeding until a court has made a finding of willful refusal to pay.

Effective January 1, 1994, the Florida Supreme Court adopted the following new subparagraph to its Rule 4-8.4:

> A lawyer shall not:
>
> (d) engage in conduct in connection with the practice of law that is prejudicial to the administration of justice, including to knowingly, or through callous indifference, disparage, humiliate, or discriminate against litigants, jurors, witnesses, court personnel, or other lawyers on any basis, including, but not limited to, on account of race, ethnicity, gender, religion, national origin, disability, marital status, sexual orientation, age, socioeconomic status, employment, or physical characteristic.

However, the Court *rejected* two proposals that would have addressed discriminatory employment practices. The first rejected proposal would have provided:

> If a lawyer has been adjudicated or held to have committed, in the course of the practice of law, a prohibited discriminatory practice by a final order of an agency or court of competent jurisdiction, after all appellate rights have been exhausted, such conduct shall be subject to discipline under these Rules Regulating The Florida Bar. . . .

The second rejected proposal would have provided:

> A lawyer shall not:
> (h) discriminate in employment, partnership, or compensation decisions on the basis of race, ethnicity, gender, religion, national origin, disability, marital status, sexual orientation, or age.

The Court stated: "We do not adopt either of these proposals because this Court's constitutional authority over the courts of Florida and attorney admission and discipline does not extend to the employment practices of lawyers."

In addition to adopting Model Rule 8.4, the Florida Supreme Court has promulgated Rule 3-4.7, which provides:

> Violation of the oath taken by an attorney to support the constitutions of the United States and the State of Florida is ground for disciplinary action. Membership in, alliance with, or support of any organization, group, or party advocating or dedicated to the overthrow of the government by violence or by any means in violation of the Constitution of the United States or constitution of this state shall be a violation of the oath.

On July 20, 1995, the Florida Supreme Court adopted a new Rule 4-8.4(i), which provides that a lawyer shall not "engage in sexual conduct with a client that exploits the lawyer-client relationship."

Idaho: In 1993, Idaho amended its Rule 4.4(a) to prohibit "conduct intended to appeal to or engender bias against a person on account of that person's gender, race, religion, national origin, or sexual preference. . . ."

Illinois: Effective October 15, 1993, Illinois Rule 8.4(a)(5) was amended to prohibit "adverse discriminatory treatment of litigants, jurors, witnesses, lawyers, and others, based on race, sex, religion, or national origin." Illinois Rule 8.4(a)(8) provides that a lawyer shall not "avoid in bad faith the repayment of an education loan guaranteed by the Illinois Student Assistance Commission or other governmental entity." Subparagraph (a)(8) does not prohibit a lawyer from discharging a student loan in a bankruptcy proceeding, but does provide that "the discharge shall not preclude a review of the attorney's conduct to determine if it constitutes bad faith." (A parallel Illinois statute, originally passed in 1986 and amended in 1989, provides that the state shall not issue or renew a law license for a person who has defaulted on a student loan, unless the person has established a satisfactory repayment plan and payment record.) Rule 8.4(b) provides:

> (b) A lawyer who holds public office shall not:
> (1) use that office to obtain, or attempt to obtain, a special advantage in a legislative matter for a client under circumstances where the lawyer knows or reasonably should know that such action is not in the public interest;
> (2) use that office to influence, or attempt to influence, a tribunal to act in favor of a client; or
> (3) represent any client, including a municipal corporation or other public body, in the promotion or defeat of legislative or other proposals pending before the public body of which such lawyer is a member or by which such lawyer is employed.

The Rules of the Illinois Attorney Registration and Disciplinary Commission define "misconduct" as "behavior of an attorney which violates the Illinois Code of Professional Responsibility or which tends to defeat the administration of justice or to bring the Courts or legal profession into disrepute."

Louisiana adds Rule 8.4(g), which forbids a lawyer "except upon the expressed assertion of a constitutional privilege, to fail to cooperate with the Committee on Professional Responsibility in its investigation of alleged misconduct.''

Michigan has adopted a rule numbered 6.5 and entitled "Professional Conduct," which provides:

> (a) A lawyer shall treat with courtesy and respect all persons involved in the legal process. A lawyer shall take particular care to avoid treating such a person discourteously or disrespectfully because of the person's race, gender, or other protected personal characteristic. To the extent possible, a lawyer shall require subordinate lawyers and nonlawyer assistants to provide such courteous and respectful treatment.

> (b) A lawyer serving as an adjudicative officer shall, without regard to a person's race, gender, or other protected personal characteristic, treat every person fairly, with courtesy and respect. To the extent possible, the lawyer shall require staff and others who are subject to the adjudicative officer's direction and control to provide such fair, courteous, and respectful treatment to persons who have contact with the adjudicative tribunal.

Minnesota: In 1992, to combat discrimination, Minnesota amended Rule 8.4 by providing that it is professional misconduct for a lawyer to:

> (g) harass a person on the basis of sex, race, age, creed, religion, color, national origin, disability, sexual preference or marital status in connection with a lawyer's professional activities; or

> (h) commit a discriminatory act, prohibited by federal, state, or local statute or ordinance, that reflects adversely on the lawyer's fitness as a lawyer. Whether a discriminatory act reflects adversely on a lawyer's fitness as a lawyer shall be determined after consideration of all the circumstances, including (1) the seriousness of the act, (2) whether the lawyer knew that it was prohibited by statute or ordinance, (3) whether it was part of a pattern of prohibited conduct, and (4) whether it was committed in connection with the lawyer's professional activities.

In addition, on June 20, 1994, the Minnesota Supreme Court added a new Rule 1.8(k) to govern sexual relations with clients. The rule provides as follows:

> A lawyer shall not have sexual relations with a current client unless a consensual relationship existed between them when the lawyer-client relationship commenced. For purposes of this paragraph:

> (1) "Sexual relations" means sexual intercourse or any other intentional touching of the intimate parts of a person or causing the person to touch the intimate parts of the lawyer.

> (2) If the client is an organization, any individual who oversees the representation and gives instructions to the lawyer on behalf of the organization shall be deemed to be the client. In-house attorneys while representing governmental or corporate entities are governed by Rule 1.7(b) rather than by this rule with respect to sexual relations with other employees of the entity they represent.

> (3) This paragraph does not prohibit a lawyer from engaging in sexual relations with a client of the lawyer's firm provided that the lawyer has no involvement in the performance of the legal work for the client.

(4) If a party other than the client alleges violation of this paragraph, and the complaint is not summarily dismissed, the Director [of the Office of Professional Responsibility], in determining whether to investigate the allegation and whether to charge any violation based on the allegations, shall consider the client's statement regarding whether the client would be unduly burdened by the investigation or charge.

New Mexico adds that it is professional misconduct for a lawyer to:

(e) willfully violate the Supreme Court Rules on Minimum Continuing Legal Education or the New Mexico Plan of Specialization, or the Board regulations promulgated under the authority of the Rules or the Plan.

Also, effective January 1, 1994, New Mexico has added Rule of Professional Conduct 16-300, which provides:

In the course of any judicial or quasi-judicial proceeding before a tribunal, a lawyer shall refrain from intentionally manifesting, by words or conduct, bias or prejudice based on race, gender, religion, national origin, disability, age, or sexual orientation against the judge, court personnel, parties, witnesses, counsel or others. This rule does not preclude legitimate advocacy when race, gender, religion, national origin, disability, age or sexual orientation is material to the issues in the proceeding.

The official State Bar Commentary to Rule 16-300 explains that the phrase "judicial or quasi-judicial proceeding" covers all courts, government agencies, boards, commissions, or departments, and "also encompasses arbitration or mediation proceedings, whether or not court-ordered."

New Jersey: New Jersey has adopted Rule 8.4(g), which makes it professional misconduct for a lawyer to "engage, in a professional capacity, in conduct involving discrimination (except employment discrimination unless resulting in a final agency or judicial determination) because of race, color, religion, age, sex, sexual orientation, national origin, language, marital status, socio-economic status, or handicap, where the conduct is intended or likely to cause harm." The Supreme Court's comment states that the rule

would, for example, cover activities in the court house, such as a lawyer's treatment of court support staff, as well as conduct more directly related to litigation; activities related to practice outside of the court house, whether or not related to litigation, such as treatment of other attorneys and their staff; bar association and similar activities; and activities in the lawyer's office and firm. Except to the extent that they are closely related to the foregoing, purely private activities are not intended to be covered by this rule amendment, although they may possibly constitute a violation of some other ethical rule. Nor is employment discrimination in hiring, firing, promotion, or partnership status intended to be covered unless it has resulted in either an agency or judicial determination of discriminatory conduct.

New York: Same or substantially the same as the ABA Model Code — see Model Code Comparison above — except see New York Materials for New York's version of DR 7-102(B)(1). See EC 1-7 and DR 1-102(A)(6) of the New York Code for provisions, having no counterpart in the Model Rules, prohibiting lawyers from unlawfully discriminating in the practice of law "including in hiring, promoting or otherwise determining conditions of employment on the basis of age, race, creed, color, national origin, sex, disability or marital status." In addition, effective November 30, 1993, the New York Appellate Divisions adopted a new court rule providing that it is "misconduct" for a lawyer to begin a sexual relationship with a matrimonial client during the course of the lawyer's representation of that client. N.Y.C.R.R. §1200.3(7). This rule has since been incorporated into New York's disciplinary rules as DR 1-102(A)(7).

Ohio: Effective July 1, 1994, Ohio adopted two new subparagraphs to DR 1-102:

> (A) A lawyer shall not: . . .
> (6) Engage in any other conduct that adversely reflects on the lawyer's fitness to practice law.
> (B) A lawyer shall not engage, in a professional capacity, in conduct involving discrimination prohibited by law because of race, color, religion, age, gender, sexual orientation, national origin, marital status, or disability. This prohibition does not apply to a lawyer's confidential communication to a client or preclude legitimate advocacy where race, color, religion, age, gender, sexual orientation, national origin, marital status, or disability is relevant to the proceeding where the advocacy is made.

Oregon: DR 5-110, effective December 31, 1992, provides:

> (A) A lawyer shall not have sexual relations with a current client of a lawyer unless a consensual sexual relationship existed between them before the lawyer/client relationship commenced.
> (B) A lawyer shall not have sexual relationships with a representative of a current client of the lawyer if the sexual relations would, or would likely, damage or prejudice the client in the representation.
> (C) For purposes of DR 5-110 "sexual relations" means:
> (1) Sexual intercourse; or
> (2) Any touching of the sexual or other intimate parts of a person or causing such person to touch the sexual or other intimate parts of the lawyer for the purpose of arousing or gratifying the sexual desire of either party.
> (D) For purposes of DR 5-110 "lawyer" means any lawyer who assists in the representation of the client, but does not include other firm members who provide no such assistance.

Oregon's DR 7-105(A), amended effective January 2, 1991, continues the old Code prohibition on threatening to present criminal charges to obtain an advantage in a civil matter, but continues:

> A lawyer may threaten to present such charges if, but only if, the lawyer reasonably believes the charge to be true and if the purpose of the lawyer is to compel or induce the person threatened to take reasonable action to make good the wrong which is the subject of the charge.

Rhode Island's Rule 8.4(d) prohibits conduct that is prejudicial to the administration of justice, "including but not limited to harmful or discriminatory treatment of litigants, jurors, witnesses, lawyers, and others based on race, nationality, or sex." In addition, Rhode Island adds a Rule 9.1 that establishes an ethics advisory panel to be appointed by the Supreme Court, and states: "Any lawyer who acts in accordance with an opinion given by the panel shall be conclusively presumed to have abided by the Rules of Professional Conduct."

Texas: Effective October 1, 1994, Texas Rule 5.08, entitled "Prohibited Discriminatory Activities," provides as follows:

> (a) A lawyer shall not willfully, in connection with an adjudicatory proceeding, except as provided in paragraph (b), manifest, by words or conduct, bias or prejudice based on race, color, national origin, religion, disability, age, sex, or sexual orientation towards any person involved in that proceeding in any capacity.
>
> (b) Paragraph (a) does not apply to a lawyer's decision whether to represent a particular person in connection with an adjudicatory proceeding, nor to the process of jury selection, nor to communications protected as "confidential information" under these Rules. See Rule 1.05(a), (b). It also does not preclude advocacy in connection with an adjudicatory proceeding involving any of the factors set out in paragraph (a) if that advocacy:
>
> (i) is necessary in order to address any substantive or procedural issues raised by the proceeding; and
>
> (ii) is conducted in conformity with applicable rulings and orders of a tribunal and applicable rules of practice and procedure.

Texas Rule 8.04 also forbids a lawyer to "engage in conduct that constitutes barratry as defined by the laws of this state." Rule 8.04(a) (2) forbids a lawyer to "commit a serious crime or commit any other criminal act that reflects adversely on the lawyer's honesty, trustworthiness or fitness as a lawyer in other respects." Rule 8.04(b) defines "serious crime" to include "barratry; any felony involving moral turpitude; any misdemeanor involving theft, embezzlement, or fraudulent or reckless misappropriation of money or other property; or any attempt, conspiracy, or solicitation of another to commit any of the foregoing crimes."

Utah: In 1997, Utah added a new subparagraph (g) to Rule 8.4, which provides that a lawyer shall not engage in "sexual relations with a client that exploit the lawyer-client relationship." Rule 8.4(b)(2) provides:

> Except for a spousal relationship or a sexual relationship that existed at the commencement of the lawyer-client relationship, sexual relations between a lawyer and a client shall be presumed to be exploitative. This presumption is rebuttable.

The Comment to Utah's new rule states that when the client is an organization, the "client" includes "any individual who oversees the client's interests in the representation and gives instructions to the lawyer on behalf of the organization." The Comment also states that Rule 8.4(g) "applies only to a lawyer who is directly involved in the representation of the client."

Virginia retains the language of DR 1-102(A), but adds that a lawyer shall not violate a Disciplinary Rule "or knowingly aid another to do so," and replaces the phrase "illegal conduct involving moral turpitude" with the phrase "a crime or other deliberately wrongful act." Virginia also retains the language of DR 9-101(C) (which is comparable to Model Rule 8.4(e)).

Washington: In 1993, Washington added a new subparagraph (g) to Rule 8.4, which makes it professional misconduct for a lawyer to:

> (g) Commit a discriminatory act prohibited by law on the basis of sex, race, age, creed, religion, color, national origin, disability, sexual orientation, or marital status, where the act of discrimination is committed in connection with the lawyer's professional activities.

In a related development, effective September 30, 1994, the United States District Court for the Western District of Washington adopted Local General Rule 9, which provides:

Prohibition of Bias

> Litigation, inside and outside the courtroom in the United States District Court for the Western District of Washington, must be free from prejudice and bias in any form. Fair and equal treatment must be accorded all courtroom participants, whether judges, attorneys, witnesses, litigants, jurors, or court personnel. The duty to be respectful of others includes the responsibility to avoid comment or behavior that can reasonably be interpreted as manifesting prejudice or bias toward another on the basis of categories such as gender, race, ethnicity, religion, disability, age, or sexual orientation.

However, in June 1995, without explanation, the Supreme Court of Washington rejected a proposed new Rule 1.8(h), modeled on Oregon's DR 5-110, which would have made it professional misconduct for a lawyer to:

> (1) engage in sexual relations with a current client, unless consensual sexual relations existed between them before the lawyer-client relationship commenced; and
> (2) have sexual relations with a representative of a current client if the sexual relations would, or would likely, damage or prejudice the client in the representation."

The rejected proposal added that for purposes of Rule 8.4(h), "lawyer" means "any lawyer who assists in the representation of the client, but does not include other firm members who provide no such assistance."

West Virginia adopted the following Rule 8.4(g) in 1995:

> (g) have sexual relations with a client whom the lawyer personally represents during the legal representation unless a consensual sexual relationship existed between them at the commencement of the lawyer/client relationship. For purposes of this rule, "sexual relations" means sexual intercourse or any touching of the sexual or other intimate parts of a client or causing such client to touch the sexual or other intimate parts of the lawyer for the purpose of arousing or gratifying the sexual desire of either party or as a means of abuse.

Wisconsin: On April 19, 1995, the Wisconsin Supreme Court adopted the following Rule 1.8(k):

> (1) (i) "Sexual relations" means sexual intercourse or any other intentional touching of the intimate parts of a person or causing the person to touch the intimate parts of the lawyer.

410

(ii) If the client is an organization, "client" means any individual who oversees the representation and gives instructions to the lawyer on behalf of the organization.

(2) A lawyer shall not have sexual relations with a current client unless a consensual sexual relationship existed between them when the lawyer-client relationship commenced.

(3) In-house attorneys representing governmental or corporate entities are governed by [Rule 1.7(b)] rather than by this paragraph with respect to sexual relations with other employees of the entity they represent.

Related Materials

ABA Canons: Canon 29 provided:

29. Upholding the Honor of the Profession

Lawyers should expose without fear or favor before the proper tribunals corrupt or dishonest conduct in the profession, and should accept without hesitation employment against a member of the Bar who has wronged his client. The counsel upon the trial of a cause in which perjury has been committed owe it to the profession and to the public to bring the matter to the knowledge of the prosecuting authorities. The lawyer should aid in guarding the Bar against the admission to the profession of candidates unfit or unqualified because deficient in either moral character or education. He should strive at all times to uphold the honor and to maintain the dignity of the profession and to improve not only the law but the administration of justice.

ABA Model Rules for Disciplinary Enforcement: In 1989, the ABA adopted Model Rules for Disciplinary Enforcement. These rules set forth model procedures for state disciplinary agencies to follow. At its 1993 Annual Meeting, pursuant to recommendations issued in 1992 by the ABA Commission on Evaluation of Disciplinary Enforcement (the "McKay Commission"), the House of Delegates overwhelmingly approved amendments to these rules. The rules are reprinted in full in the ABA/BNA Lawyer's Manual on Professional Conduct.

ABA Resolution Against Bias and Prejudice: At the ABA's 1995 Annual Meeting, the House of Delegates passed a resolution recommended by the ABA Young Lawyers Division to condemn bias and prejudice by lawyers in their professional activities and to encourage affirmative steps to discourage bias and prejudice among lawyers. The full resolution provides as follows:

RESOLVED, That the American Bar Association:

(a) condemns the manifestation by lawyers in the course of their professional activities, by words or conduct, of bias or prejudice against clients, opposing parties and their counsel, other litigants, witnesses, judges and court personnel, jurors and others, based upon race, sex, religion, national origin, disability, age, sexual orientation or socio-economic status, unless such words or conduct are otherwise permissible as legitimate advocacy on behalf of a client or a cause;

411

(b) opposes unlawful discrimination by lawyers in the management or operation of a law practice in hiring, promoting, discharging or otherwise determining the conditions of employment, or accepting or terminating representation of a client;

(c) condemns any conduct by lawyers that would threaten, harass, intimidate or denigrate any other person on the basis of the aforementioned categories and characteristics;

(d) discourages members from belonging to any organization that practices invidious discrimination on the basis of the aforementioned categories and characteristics;

(e) encourages affirmative steps such as continuing education, studies, and conferences to discourage the speech and conduct described above.

ABA Standards for Imposing Lawyer Sanctions:

5.1. Failure to Maintain Personal Integrity

5.11. Disbarment is generally appropriate when:

(a) a lawyer engages in serious criminal conduct a necessary element of which includes intentional interference with the administration of justice, false swearing, misrepresentation, fraud, extortion, misappropriation, or theft; or the sale, distribution or importation of controlled substances; or the intentional killing of another; or an attempt or conspiracy or solicitation of another to commit any of these offenses; or

(b) a lawyer engages in any other intentional conduct involving dishonesty, fraud, deceit, or misrepresentation that seriously adversely reflects on the lawyer's fitness to practice.

5.12. Suspension is generally appropriate when a lawyer knowingly engages in criminal conduct which does not contain the elements listed in Standard 5.11 and that seriously adversely reflects on the lawyer's fitness to practice.

5.13. Reprimand is generally appropriate when a lawyer knowingly engages in any other conduct that involves dishonesty, fraud, deceit, or misrepresentation and that adversely reflects on the lawyer's fitness to practice law.

5.14. Admonition is generally appropriate when a lawyer engages in any other conduct that reflects adversely on the lawyer's fitness to practice law.

5.2. Failure to Maintain the Public Trust

5.21. Disbarment is generally appropriate when a lawyer in an official or governmental position knowingly misuses the position with the intent to obtain a significant benefit or advantage for himself or another, or with the intent to cause serious or potentially serious injury to a party or to the integrity of the legal process.

5.22. Suspension is generally appropriate when a lawyer in an official or governmental position knowingly fails to follow proper procedures or rules and causes injury or potential injury to a party or to the integrity of the legal process.

8.0. Prior Discipline Orders

8.1. Disbarment is generally appropriate when a lawyer:

(a) intentionally or knowingly violates the terms of a prior disciplinary order and such violation causes injury or potential injury to a client, the public, the legal system, or the profession; or

(b) has been suspended for the same or similar misconduct, and intentionally or knowingly engages in further acts of misconduct that cause injury or potential injury to a client, the public, the legal system, or the profession.

8.2. Suspension is generally appropriate when a lawyer has been reprimanded for the same or similar misconduct and engages in further acts of misconduct that cause injury or potential injury to a client, the public, the legal system, or the profession.

ABA Task Force on Minorities and the Justice System: In July of 1992, an ABA Task Force on Minorities and the Justice System issued a report in which Recommendation No. 38 urged an amendment to Rule 8.4 making it misconduct for a lawyer to discriminate against minorities. Both the ABA's Standing Committee on Ethics and Professional Responsibility and the ABA Young Lawyers Division responded by drafting proposed amendments to Rule 8.4. (See Legislative History to this rule for more details.)

Federal Rules of Appellate Procedure: Fed. R. App. P. 46(b) and (c) give federal courts of appeals power to suspend or disbar or "take any appropriate disciplinary action against any attorney who practices before it for conduct unbecoming a member of the bar or for failure to comply with these rules or any rule of court."

Misconduct: Many states define "misconduct" by statute or court rule. In Washington, D.C., for example, §2(b) of the rules governing disciplinary proceedings provides: "Acts or omissions by an attorney . . . which violate the attorney's oath of office or the rules or code of professional conduct currently in effect in the District of Columbia shall constitute misconduct and shall be grounds for discipline, whether or not the act or omission occurred in the course of an attorney-client relationship. . . ."

Statutes of Limitations: Some states have adopted statutes of limitations for disciplinary matters. For example, Illinois Supreme Court Rule 751, which governs the Attorney Registration and Disciplinary Commission, contains the following provision:

> (f) *Limitations.* An attorney shall not be required to answer any charges and the Commission shall not bring a complaint against an attorney concerning alleged professional misconduct 7 or more years after the date on which the conduct was known or should reasonably have been known, unless the attorney fraudulently concealed the alleged misconduct or the alleged misconduct amounts to a criminal offense involving moral turpitude. Upon petition of the Administrator and for good cause shown, however, the Supreme Court may authorize the Commission to require an attorney to answer charges or to bring a complaint which might otherwise be barred by this paragraph.

(On May 23, 1994, the Illinois Supreme Court held public hearings on a State Bar proposal to amend this limitations provision.)

On July 20, 1995, the Florida Supreme Court adopted the following statute of limitations provision:

Rule 3-7.16 Limitation on Time to Bring Complaint

(a) *Time for Inquiries and Complaints.* Inquiries raised or complaints presented by or to The Florida Bar under these rules shall be commenced within 6 years from the time the matter giving rise to the inquiry or complaint is discovered or, with due diligence, should have been discovered.

(b) *Exception for Theft or Conviction of a Felony Criminal Offense.* There shall be no limit on the time in which to present or bring a matter alleging theft or conviction of a felony criminal offense by a member of The Florida Bar.

(c) *Tolling Based on Fraud, Concealment or Misrepresentation.* In matters covered by this rule where it can be shown that fraud, concealment, or intentional misrepresentation of fact prevented the discovery of the matter giving rise to the inquiry or complaint, the limitation of time in which to bring an inquiry or complaint within this rule shall be tolled.

Rule 8.5 Disciplinary Authority; Choice of Law

Editors' Note. At its August 1993 Annual Meeting, the ABA House of Delegates voted to amend Rule 8.5 by adding a new sentence to paragraph (a) (which had been the only paragraph) and by adding a new subparagraph (b). The new Rule 8.5(b) provides guidelines to decide which jurisdiction's disciplinary rules apply to lawyers who are admitted to practice (permanently or pro hac vice) in more than one jurisdiction, and who either engage in conduct in more than one jurisdiction or who engage in conduct in one jurisdiction having a "predominant effect" in another jurisdiction where they are also admitted to practice. Lawyers admitted in only one jurisdiction are not affected by Rule 8.5(b); they continue to be bound by the rules of their home jurisdiction, no matter where the conduct occurs, as Rule 8.5(a) provides.

The new rule basically divides conduct into two categories: (1) "conduct in connection with a proceeding in a court before which a lawyer has been admitted to practice (either generally or for purposes of that proceeding)" — as to which the disciplinary rules of the forum jurisdiction apply — and (2) "all other conduct" — as to which the disciplinary rules of the jurisdiction where the lawyer "principally practices" apply, unless the conduct has its "predominant effect" in another jurisdiction in which the lawyer is also admitted, in which case that jurisdiction's rules apply.

Rule 8.5(b) applies only if a lawyer is admitted in two (or more) jurisdictions and conduct allowed in one juridiction is prohibited in another jurisdiction. In other words, Rule 8.5(b) is a conflict-of-laws provision; it tells when a lawyer admitted in multiple jurisdictions can be disciplined for conduct that is permitted in only some of those jurisdictions. If a lawyer's conduct violates the rules in all jurisdictions where the lawyer is admitted, the lawyer can be disciplined by all jurisdictions.

The amendment was proposed by the ABA's Standing Committee on Ethics and Professional Responsibility. We reprint the amended version below. In the Legislative History section following the rule, we reprint substantial excerpts from the committee report submitted in support of the amendment.

(a) *Disciplinary Authority.* A lawyer admitted to practice in this jurisdiction is subject to the disciplinary authority of this jurisdiction, regardless of where the lawyer's conduct occurs. A lawyer may be subject to the disciplinary authority of both this jurisdiction and another jurisdiction where the lawyer is admitted for the same conduct.

(b) *Choice of Law.* In any exercise of the disciplinary authority of this jurisdiction, the rules of professional conduct to be applied shall be as follows:

(1) for conduct in connection with a proceeding in a court before which a lawyer has been admitted to practice (either generally or for purposes of that proceeding), the rules to be applied shall be the rules of the jurisdiction in which the court sits, unless the rules of the court provide otherwise; and

(2) for any other conduct,

(i) if the lawyer is licensed to practice only in this jurisdiction, the rules to be applied shall be the rules of this jurisdiction, and

(ii) if the lawyer is licensed to practice in this and another jurisdiction, the rules to be applied shall be the rules of the admitting jurisdiction in which the lawyer principally practices; provided, however, that if particular conduct clearly has its predominant effect in another jurisdiction in which the lawyer is licensed to practice, the rules of that jurisdiction shall be applied to that conduct.

COMMENT

Disciplinary Authority

[1] Paragraph (a) restates longstanding law.

Choice of Law

[2] A lawyer may be potentially subject to more than one set of rules of professional conduct which impose different obligations. The lawyer may be licensed to practice in more than one jurisdiction with differing

rules, or may be admitted to practice before a particular court with rules that differ from those of the jurisdiction or jurisdictions in which the lawyer is licensed to practice. In the past, decisions have not developed clear or consistent guidance as to which rules apply in such circumstances.

[3] Paragraph (b) seeks to resolve such potential conflicts. Its premise is that minimizing conflicts between rules, as well as uncertainty about which rules are applicable, is in the best interest of both clients and the profession (as well as the bodies having authority to regulate the profession). Accordingly, it takes the approach of (i) providing that any particular conduct of an attorney shall be subject to only one set of rules of professional conduct, and (ii) making the determination of which set of rules applies to particular conduct as straightforward as possible, consistent with vindicating appropriate regulatory interests of relevant jurisdictions.

[4] Paragraph (b) provides that as to a lawyer's conduct relating to a proceeding in a court before which the lawyer is admitted to practice (either generally or pro hac vice), the lawyer shall be subject only to the rules of professional conduct of that court. As to all other conduct, paragraph (b) provides that a lawyer licensed to practice only in this jurisdiction shall be subject to the rules of professional conduct of this jurisdiction, and that a lawyer licensed in multiple jurisdictions shall be subject only to the rules of the jurisdiction where he or she (as an individual, not his or her firm) principally practices, but with one exception: if particular conduct clearly has its predominant effect in another admitting jurisdiction, then only the rules of that jurisdiction shall apply. The intention is for the latter exception to be a narrow one. It would be appropriately applied, for example, to a situation in which a lawyer admitted in, and principally practicing in, State A, but also admitted in State B, handled an acquisition by a company whose headquarters and operations were in State B of another, similar such company. The exception would not appropriately be applied, on the other hand, if the lawyer handled an acquisition by a company whose headquarters and operations were in State A of a company whose headquarters and main operations were in State A, but which also had some operations in State B.

[5] If two admitting jurisdictions were to proceed against a lawyer for the same conduct, they should, applying this rule, identify the same governing ethics rules. They should take all appropriate steps to see that they do apply the same rule to the same conduct, and in all events should avoid proceeding against a lawyer on the basis of two inconsistent rules.

[6] The choice of law provision is not intended to apply to transnational practice. Choice of law in this context should be the subject of agreements between jurisdictions or of appropriate international law.

Model Code Comparison

There was no counterpart to this Rule in the Model Code.

Cross-References in Rules

None.

Legislative History

1980 Discussion Draft had no comparable provision.

1981 Draft was substantially the same as the 1982 draft (see next entry).

1982 Draft was adopted in 1983, and consisted of a single sentence: "A lawyer admitted to practice in this jurisdiction is subject to the disciplinary authority of this jurisdiction although engaged in practice elsewhere."

1993 Amendment: At its August 1993 Annual Meeting, the ABA House of Delegates voted to amend Rule 8.5 by rephrasing the first sentence of paragraph (a) (which had been the only sentence in the entire rule), by adding a second sentence to paragraph (a), and by adding an entirely new paragraph (b). The purpose of the new paragraph (b) is to provide guidelines for deciding which jurisdiction's disciplinary rules apply to lawyers who are licensed (generally or pro hac vice) to practice in more than one jurisdiction, or who provide legal services in jurisdictions where they are not licensed. The amendment also includes a wholesale revision of the Comment, replacing the three existing paragraphs with six completely new paragraphs, five of which explain the new choice-of-law rules contained in paragraph (b).

The amendment was proposed by the ABA's Standing Committee on Ethics and Professional Responsibility, which has traditionally been the main sponsor of amendments to the rules. We reprint here substantial excerpts from the committee report submitted in support of the amendment (with most citations omitted):

*ABA Committee Report Explaining 1993 Amendment to Rule 8.5**

The objective of this proposed change in Rule 8.5 is to bring some measure of certainty and clarity to the frequently encountered, and often difficult, decisions a lawyer must make when encountering a situation in which the lawyer is potentially subject to differing ethical requirements of more than one jurisdiction. It is generally the case that such decisions cannot await an authoritative ruling or advisory opinion from an independent source.

The most compelling circumstance of a lawyer caught between conflicting ethical obligations in all likelihood is that where a lawyer has become aware of a client's fraud committed in the course of the lawyer's representation, and the rule of one jurisdiction with authority over the lawyer would require disclosure of the fraud and that of another jurisdiction with authority would forbid it. But this is by no means the only circumstance in which the problem arises. . . .

The problem of lack of clear guidance that this proposal seeks to address is exacerbated by the fact that existing authority as to choice of law in the area of ethics rules is unclear and inconsistent. Some authorities suggest that particular conduct should be subject to only one set of rules, while others suggest that more than one set of rules can apply simultaneously to the same conduct. Widely differing approaches to how to identify the applicable rules have been taken. See, e.g., Md. Formal Op. No. 86-28, supra (rule of state in which practice occurs governs); Ala. Ethics Op. RO-81-542 (Dec. 4 & 28, 1991) (same); Mich. Informal Op. No. CI-709 (Dec. 28, 1981) (suggesting that any connection with Michigan, however small, would be sufficient to make Michigan rules applicable to lawyer admitted in both California and Michigan and practicing in California); Ariz. Op. No. 90-19 (Dec. 28, 1990) (applying the full panoply of choice-of-law factors from Restatement (Second), Conflict of Laws §6(2)); Fla. Prop. Adv. Op. No. 88-10 (1988) ("most significant relationship" test, with important factors being "the client's state of residence, the state where the cause of action arose, and the state (or states) where suit may be filed"); In re Dresser Industries, Inc., 972 F.2d 540 (5th Cir. 1992) (conduct of attorney in federal district court suit is governed by general "national standards of legal ethics," even where contrary to state rules adopted by the district court to govern attorneys practicing before it). . . .

The proposed amendment to Rule 8.5 seeks to provide clear answers to these problems in nearly all cases. In litigation, the ethical rules of the tribunal, and only those rules, would apply. In other matters, the multiply-admitted lawyer would be subject only to the rules of the jurisdiction where he or she principally practices, except when the particular conduct clearly has its predominant effect in another admitting jurisdiction. . . .

[I]t might be argued that, because of the exception for particular conduct that clearly has its predominant effect in another jurisdiction, the proposal falls short of achieving perfect clarity and certainty. This is indeed true, and there may be instances in which it is difficult to define the "particular conduct" and to decide whether it has its "predominant effect" in one jurisdiction or another. However, to provide for no exception would allow substantial conduct to occur in a second admitting jurisdiction without being subject to that jurisdiction's rules; and the exception has been crafted in a manner that is intended to minimize to the extent possible the difficulty of applying it in particular cases. . . .

Selected State Variations

Alaska: Rule 8.5 extends the state's disciplinary authority to a lawyer not admitted to practice in Alaska but who "engages in the practice of law pursuant to court rule or order."

*Committee Reports do not represent official policy of the ABA. They are for information only, and the opinions are those of the authors of the report.

California: See B & P Code §§6002.1(a)(4). California Rule 1-100(D), entitled "Geographic Scope of Rules," specifies application of California's Rules to members of the state bar and to lawyers from other jurisdictions.

Illinois: Effective February 14, 1995, Illinois became one of the first states in the nation to adopt Rule 8.5(b) verbatim.

Maryland: Rule 8.5 includes the following provision that reaches lawyers who are admitted in other states but not Maryland:

> (b) A lawyer not admitted by the Court of Appeals to practice in this State is subject to the disciplinary authority of this State for conduct that constitutes a violation of these Rules and that:
> (1) involves the practice of law in this State by that lawyer, or
> (2) involves that lawyer holding himself or herself out as practicing law in this State, or
> (3) involves the practice of law in this State by another lawyer over whom that lawyer has the obligation of supervision or control.

Massachusetts has not adopted Rule 8.5. When the Supreme Judicial Court adopted new rules in June of 1997, the Court deemed further study necessary because Rule 8.5(b) "has revealed many instances in which its application seems problematic."

Michigan: As amended effective October 6, 1995, the second sentence of Michigan Rule 8.5 provides: "A lawyer who is licensed to practice in another jurisdiction and who is admitted to practice in this jurisdiction is subject to the disciplinary authority of this jurisdiction."

Montana: Effective September 15, 1996, the Montana Supreme Court adopted the following new Rule 8.5, entitled "Jurisdiction and Certification," to insure that out-of-state lawyers who practice law in Montana "be aware of and be subject to" Montana's Rules of Professional Conduct:

> A lawyer who is not an active member in good standing of the State Bar of Montana and who seeks to practice in any court of this State pro hac vice, by motion, or before being otherwise admitted to the practice of law in this State, shall, prior to engaging in the practice of law in this State, certify in writing and under oath to this Court that, except as to Rules 6.1 through 6.4, he or she will be bound by these Rules of Professional Conduct in his or her practice of law in this State and will be subject to the disciplinary authority of this State. . . .

New York: No comparable provision.

North Dakota: A North Dakota lawyer is subject to discipline in that state "even though the conduct of the lawyer giving rise to the discipline may have occurred outside of this jurisdiction and even when that conduct may subject or has subjected the lawyer to discipline by another jurisdiction." In addition, persons not licensed in North Dakota but eligible to practice elsewhere are subject to the disciplinary authority of North Dakota if they "actually engage in this jurisdiction in the practice of law."

Rhode Island: Rule 8.5 uses the original version of ABA Model Rule 8.5, plus the following new additional sentence: "A lawyer engaged in practice in another jurisdiction who is specially admitted to appear before the courts of this jurisdiction on an ad hoc basis shall be subject to these rules.''

Virginia: DR 1-102(B) tracks Model Rule 8.5, but adds an exception if ''Disciplinary Rules of the foreign jurisdiction permit the activity.''

Related Materials

Conflicts of Interest: Despite the choice-of-law amendment to Rule 8.5, conflicts of interest in federal court may be measured by ''national standards'' rather than by the rules of the forum jurisdiction. In In re Dresser Industries, Inc., 972 F.2d 540 (5th Cir. 1992), deciding a motion to disqualify plaintiffs' counsel in a class action, the Fifth Circuit refused to apply Texas Rule 1.06 (which allows lawyers to oppose current clients as long as the matters are not ''substantially related''), and disqualified a law firm suing a current client. The *Dresser* court said that conflicts of interest in federal litigation are governed by ''national standards,'' including ABA Model Rule 1.7 and the emerging Restatement of the Law Governing Lawyers.

Federal Rules of Appellate Procedure: Fed. R. App. P. 46(b) provides:

> When it is shown to the court that any member of its bar has been suspended or disbarred from practice in any other court of record, or has been guilty of conduct unbecoming a member of the bar of the court, the member will be subject to suspension or disbarment by the court.

Limitations on Jurisdiction: A state's willingness to exercise jurisdiction over a lawyer licensed only in other states may depend on whether the alleged misconduct was directly related to the practice of law. Florida, for example, provides in Supreme Court Rule 3-4.1 that ''[j]urisdiction over an attorney of another state who is not a member of The Florida Bar shall be limited to conduct as an attorney in relation to the business for which the attorney was permitted to practice in this state. . . .''

Model Rules of Professional Conduct for Federal Lawyers: Rule 8.5 provides:

> (a) A Federal lawyer shall comply with the rules of professional conduct applicable to the Federal Agency that employs the Government lawyer or the Federal Agency before which the Federal lawyer practices.
>
> (b) If the Federal Agency has not adopted or promulgated rules of professional conduct, the Federal lawyer shall comply with the rules of professional conduct of the state bars in which the Federal lawyer is admitted to practice.

The Comment to this rule states:

> While the Federal lawyer may remain subject to the governing authority of their licensing jurisdiction, the Federal lawyer is also subject to these Rules. However, when a Government lawyer is engaged in the conduct of Federal Agency legal functions, whether servicing the Federal Agency as a client or serving an individual client in the course of official duties, these Rules are regarded as superseding any conflicting rules applicable in the jurisdictions in which the Government lawyer may be licensed.

INDEX TO THE MODEL RULES

Editors' Note. The following index was originally prepared by the American Bar Association when the Model Rules were adopted in 1983. We have revised it to reflect all amendments and additions to the Model Rules of Professional Conduct through August 1996. Our index thus reflects the deletion of Rule 3.8(f)(2) in 1995; addition of a new version of Rule 5.7 and the amendment of Rules 3.6, 3.8, and 7.4 in 1994; the amendment of Rule 6.1 and the addition of Rule 8.5(b) in 1993; the 1989 amendments that renumbered some sections of Model Rules 1.9 and 1.10; the addition of Model Rules 1.17 and 3.8(f) in 1990; the amendment to Model Rule 8.3 and the addition of Model Rule 5.7 in 1991; and the amendment of Rule 7.4 in 1992. (The original version of Rule 5.7 was deleted in 1992, but we continue to reference it in this index.)

In addition to this index, cross-reference tables relating the ABA Model Code to the Model Rules are found following each set of Disciplinary Rules and Ethical Considerations in the Model Code in this volume. Tables relating the old ABA Canons of Professional Ethics to the Model Rules and relating the emerging Restatement of the Law Governing Lawyers to the Model Rules are found in our section of Tables near the end of this volume.

Law firm,
Defined, Terminology
Nonlawyer assistants, responsibility
for, Rule 5.3
Responsibility of partner or
supervisory lawyer, Rule 5.1
Subordinate lawyer, responsibility
of, Rule 5.2
Law practice, sale of, Rule 1.17
Law reform activities,
Affecting clients' interests, Rule
6.4
Law-related services, Rule 5.7
Lawyer referral service, Rule 6.1
(Comment)
Cost of, Rule 7.2(c)
Lawyers assistance program,
confidentiality, Rule 8.3(c)
Legal education,
Duty to work to strengthen,
Preamble
Legislature,
Appearance before on behalf of
client, Rule 3.8
Letterheads,
False or misleading, Rule 7.5(a)
Jurisdictional limitations of
members, Rule 7.5(b)
Public officials, Rule 7.5(c)
Liability to client,
Agreements limiting, Rule 1.8(h)
Lien,
To secure fees and expenses, Rule
1.8(j) (1)
Literary rights,
Acquiring concerning
representation, Rule 1.8(d)
Litigation,
Expedite, duty to, Rule 3.2
Loyalty,
Duty of to client, Rule 1.7
(Comment)

M

Malpractice,
Limiting liability to client for,
Rule 1.8(h)
Meritorious claims and contentions,
Rule 3.1
Military lawyers,
Adverse interests, representation
of, Rule 1.9 (Comment)

Misconduct,
Forms of, Rule 8.4
Misleading legal argument, Rule 3.3
(Comment)
Misrepresentation,
In advertisements, Rule 7.1
To court, Rule 3.3 (Comment)
Multiple representation, see Conflict
of interest; Intermediary
Multistate law practice, Rule 8.5

N

Negotiation,
Conflicting interest,
representation of, Rule 1.7
(Comment)
Statements made during, Rule 4.1
(Comment)
Negotiator,
Lawyer as, Preamble
Nonlawyers,
Division of fees with, Rule 5.4(a)
Partnership with, Rule 5.4(b)
Non-legal services,
Provision of, Rule 5.7

O

Objectives of the representation,
Client's right to determine, Rule
1.2(a)
Lawyer's right to limit, Rule 1.2(c)
Opposing party,
Communications with represented
party, Rule 4.2
Duty of fairness to, Rule 3.4
Organization, representation of,
Board of directors, lawyer for
serving on, Rule 1.7
(Comment)
Communication with, Rule 1.4
(Comment)
Conflict of interest, Rule 1.7
(Comment)
Conflicting interests among
officers and employees, Rule
1.7 (Comment)
Constituents, representing, Rule
1.13(e)
Identity of client, Rule 1.13(a);
Rule 1.13(d)

ABA Standards for Criminal Justice*
The Prosecution Function
The Defense Function
Fair Trial and Free Press

Editors' Introduction. In 1964, ABA President Louis F. Powell, Jr. appointed a Special Committee on Standards for the Administration of Criminal Justice. The Special Committee included many distinguished figures, and was at one time chaired by Judge (later Chief Justice) Warren E. Burger. By 1973, the ABA House of Delegates had approved 17 sets of Standards, governing every phase of the criminal justice system. In 1980, all of the Standards, with commentary, were gathered together in a two-volume set, American Bar Association Standards for Criminal Justice, published by Little, Brown and Company.

In recent years, the ABA has amended many of the Standards. At the ABA's August 1990 Annual Meeting, the House of Delegates approved amendments to Chapter 5, "Providing Defense Services." At the ABA's February 1991 Mid-Year Meeting, the House of Delegates approved a complete revision of Chapter 4, "The Defense Function," and more moderate revisions to Chapter 8, "Fair Trial and Free Press." At the ABA's 1992 Mid-Year Meeting, the House of Delegates approved substantial revisions to Chapter 3, "The Prosecution Function." These changes are part of a long-term project to revise all of the chapters in the Standards. (Three other chapters were also revised recently: "Sentencing" was revised at the ABA's February 1993 Mid-Year Meeting; "Trial by Jury" was revised at the ABA's

August 1993 Annual Meeting; and "Discovery and Procedure" was revised at the ABA's August 1994 Annual Meeting. We do not reprint these chapters because they bear only tangentially on the conduct of lawyers.)

The Standards for Criminal Justice have been enormously influential. More than 40 states have revised their criminal codes on the basis of the ABA Standards and the Standards are cited dozens of times in each volume of federal court opinions. Two of the most important sets of Standards are "The Prosecution Function" and "The Defense Function." These Standards are intended to present in an organized way "guidelines that have long been adhered to by the best prosecutors and best defense advocates." We reprint here, without commentary, all of the black letter Standards for "The Prosecution Function" as amended in 1992, and "The Defense Function" as amended in 1991. In addition, we reprint selections from "Fair Trial and Free Press" as amended in 1991.

Contents

Chapter 3. The Prosecution Function

Part I. General Standards

Part II. Organization of the Prosecution Function

Part III. Investigation for Prosecution Decision

CHAPTER 3. THE PROSECUTION FUNCTION

> **Editors' Note.** Chapter 3 was originally approved by the ABA in 1971. At its 1992 Mid-Year Meeting, the ABA approved substantial revisions to "The Prosecution Function." The version that follows reflects these 1992 revisions.

Part I. General Standards

Standard 3-1.3. Conflicts of Interest

(a) A prosecutor should avoid a conflict of interest with respect to his or her official duties.

(b) A prosecutor should not represent a defendant in criminal proceedings in a jurisdiction where he or she is also employed as a prosecutor.

(c) A prosecutor should not, except as law may otherwise expressly permit, participate in a matter in which he or she participated personally and substantially while in private practice or non-governmental employment unless under applicable law no one is, or by lawful delegation may be, authorized to act in the prosecutor's stead in the matter.

(d) A prosecutor who has formerly represented a client in a matter in private practice should not thereafter use information obtained from that representation to the disadvantage of the former client unless the rules of attorney-client confidentiality do not apply or the information has become generally known.

(e) A prosecutor should not, except as law may otherwise expressly permit, negotiate for private employment with any person who is involved as an accused or as an attorney or agent for an accused in a matter in which the prosecutor is participating personally and substantially.

(f) A prosecutor should not permit his or her professional judgment or obligations to be affected by his or her own political, financial, business, property, or personal interests.

(g) A prosecutor who is related to another lawyer as parent, child, sibling or spouse should not participate in the prosecution of a person who the prosecutor knows is represented by the other lawyer. Nor should a prosecutor who has a significant personal or financial relationship

433

with another lawyer participate in the prosecution of a person who the prosecutor knows is represented by the other lawyer, unless the prosecutor's supervisor, if any, is informed and approves or unless there is no other prosecutor authorized to act in the prosecutor's stead.

(h) A prosecutor should not recommend the services of particular defense counsel to accused persons or witnesses unless requested by the accused person or witness to make such a recommendation, and should not make a referral that is likely to create a conflict of interest. Nor should a prosecutor comment upon the reputation or abilities of defense counsel to an accused person or witness who is seeking or may seek such counsel's services unless requested by such person.

Standard 3-1.4. Public Statements

(a) A prosecutor should not make or authorize the making of an extrajudicial statement that a reasonable person would expect to be disseminated by means of public communication if the prosecutor knows or reasonably should know that it will have a substantial likelihood of prejudicing a criminal proceeding.

(b) A prosecutor should exercise reasonable care to prevent investigators, law enforcement personnel, employees or other persons assisting or associated with the prosecutor from making an extrajudicial statement that the prosecutor would be prohibited from making under this standard.

Standard 3-1.5. Duty to Respond to Misconduct

(a) Where a prosecutor knows that another person associated with the prosecutor's office is engaged in action, intends to act or refuses to act in a manner that is a violation of a legal obligation to the prosecutor's office or a violation of law, the prosecutor should follow the policies of the prosecutor's office concerning such matters. If such policies are unavailing or do not exist, the prosecutor should ask the person to reconsider the action or inaction which is at issue if such a request is aptly timed to prevent such misconduct and is otherwise feasible. If such a request for reconsideration is unavailing, inapt or otherwise not feasible or if the seriousness of the matter so requires, the prosecutor should refer the matter to higher authority in the prosecutor's office, including, if warranted by the seriousness of the matter, referral to the chief prosecutor.

(b) If, despite the prosecutor's efforts in accordance with section (a), the chief prosecutor insists upon action, or a refusal to act, that is clearly a violation of law, the prosecutor may take further remedial action, including revealing the information necessary to remedy this violation to other appropriate governmental officials not in the prosecutor's office.

Part II. Organization of the Prosecution Function

Standard 3-2.8. Relations with the Courts and Bar

(a) A prosecutor should not intentionally misrepresent matters of fact or law to the court.

(b) A prosecutor's duties necessarily involve frequent and regular official contacts with the judge or judges of the prosecutor's jurisdiction. In such contacts the prosecutor should carefully strive to preserve the appearance as well as the reality of the correct relationship which professional traditions, ethical codes, and applicable law require between advocates and judges.

(c) A prosecutor should not engage in unauthorized ex parte discussions with or submission of material to a judge relating to a particular case which is or may come before the judge.

(d) A prosecutor should not fail to disclose to the tribunal legal authority in the controlling jurisdiction known to the prosecutor to be directly adverse to the prosecutor's position and not disclosed by defense counsel.

(e) A prosecutor should strive to develop good working relationships with defense counsel in order to facilitate the resolution of ethical problems. In particular, a prosecutor should assure defense counsel that if counsel finds it necessary to deliver physical items which may be relevant to a pending case or investigation to the prosecutor, the prosecutor will not offer the fact of such delivery by defense counsel as evidence before a jury for purposes of establishing defense counsel's client's culpability. However, nothing in this Standard shall prevent a prosecutor from offering evidence of the fact of such delivery in a subsequent proceeding for the purpose of proving a crime or fraud in the delivery of the evidence.

Standard 3-2.9. Prompt Disposition of Criminal Charges

(a) A prosecutor should avoid unnecessary delay in the disposition of cases. A prosecutor should not fail to act with reasonable diligence and promptness in prosecuting an accused.

(b) A prosecutor should not intentionally use procedural devices for delay for which there is no legitimate basis.

(c) The prosecution function should be so organized and supported with staff and facilities as to enable it to dispose of all criminal charges promptly. The prosecutor should be punctual in attendance in court and in the submission of all motions, briefs, and other papers. The prosecutor should emphasize to all witnesses the importance of punctuality in attendance in court.

(d) A prosecutor should not intentionally misrepresent facts or otherwise mislead the court in order to obtain a continuance.

(e) A prosecutor, without attempting to get more funding for additional staff, should not carry a workload that, by reason of its excessive size, interferes with the rendering of quality representation, endangers the interests of justice in the speedy disposition of charges, or may lead to the breach of professional obligations.

Standard 3-2.10. Supercession and Substitution of Prosecutor

(a) Procedures should be established by appropriate legislation to the end that the governor or other elected state official is empowered by law to suspend and supersede a local prosecutor upon making a public finding, after reasonable notice and hearing, that the prosecutor is incapable of fulfilling the duties of office.

(b) The governor or other elected official should be empowered by law to substitute special counsel in the place of the local prosecutor in a particular case, or category of cases, upon making a public finding that this is required for the protection of the public interest.

Standard 3-2.11. Literary or Media Agreements

A prosecutor, prior to conclusion of all aspects of a matter, should not enter into any agreement or understanding by which the prosecutor acquires an interest in literary or media rights to a portrayal or account based in substantial part on information relating to that matter.

Part III. Investigation for Prosecution Decision

Standard 3-3.1. Investigative Function of Prosecutor

(a) A prosecutor ordinarily relies on police and other investigative agencies for investigation of alleged criminal acts, but the prosecutor has an affirmative responsibility to investigate suspected illegal activity when it is not adequately dealt with by other agencies.

(b) A prosecutor should not invidiously discriminate against or in favor of any person on the basis of race, religion, sex, sexual preference, or ethnicity in exercising discretion to investigate or to prosecute. A prosecutor should not use other improper considerations in exercising such discretion.

(c) A prosecutor should not knowingly use illegal means to obtain evidence or to employ or instruct or encourage others to use such means.

(d) A prosecutor should not discourage or obstruct communication between prospective witnesses and defense counsel. A prosecutor should not advise any person or cause any person to be advised to decline to give to the defense information which such person has the right to give.

(e) A prosecutor should not secure the attendance of persons for interviews by use of any communication which has the appearance or color of a subpoena or similar judicial process unless the prosecutor is authorized by law to do so.

(f) A prosecutor should not promise not to prosecute for prospective criminal activity, except where such activity is part of an officially supervised investigative and enforcement program.

(g) Unless a prosecutor is prepared to forgo impeachment of a witness by the prosecutor's own testimony as to what the witness stated in an interview or to seek leave to withdraw from the case in order to present the impeaching testimony, a prosecutor should avoid interviewing a prospective witness except in the presence of a third person.

Standard 3-3.2. Relations with Victims and Prospective Witnesses

(a) A prosecutor should not compensate a witness, other than an expert, for giving testimony, but it is not improper to reimburse an ordinary witness for the reasonable expenses of attendance upon court, attendance for depositions pursuant to statute or court rule, or attendance for pretrial interviews. Payments to a witness may be for transportation and loss of income, provided there is no attempt to conceal the fact of reimbursement.

(b) A prosecutor should advise a witness who is to be interviewed of his or her rights against self-incrimination and the right to counsel whenever the law so requires. It is also proper for a prosecutor to so advise a witness whenever the prosecutor knows or has reason to believe that the witness may be the subject of a criminal prosecution. However, a prosecutor should not so advise a witness for the purpose of influencing the witness in favor of or against testifying.

(c) The prosecutor should readily provide victims and witnesses who request it information about the status of cases in which they are interested.

(d) The prosecutor should seek to insure that victims and witnesses who may need protections against intimidation are advised of and afforded such protections where feasible.

(e) The prosecutor should insure that victims and witnesses are given notice as soon as practicable of scheduling changes which will affect the victims' or witnesses' required attendance at judicial proceedings.

(f) The prosecutor should not require victims and witnesses to attend judicial proceedings unless their testimony is essential to the prosecution or is required by law. When their attendance is required, the prosecutor should seek to reduce to a minimum the time they must spend at the proceedings.

(g) The prosecutor should seek to insure that victims of serious crimes or their representatives are given timely notice of: (i) judicial proceedings relating to the victims' case; (ii) disposition of the case, including plea bargains, trial and sentencing; and (iii) any decision or action in the case which results in the accused's provisional or final release from custody.

(h) Where practical, the prosecutor should seek to insure that victims of serious crimes or their representatives are given an opportunity to consult with and to provide information to the prosecutor prior to the decision whether or not to prosecute, to pursue a disposition by plea, or to dismiss the charges.

Standard 3-3.3. Relations with Expert Witnesses

(a) A prosecutor who engages an expert for an opinion should respect the independence of the expert and should not seek to dictate the formation of the expert's opinion on the subject. To the extent necessary, the prosecutor should explain to the expert his or her role in the trial as an impartial expert called to aid the fact finders and the manner in which the examination of witnesses is conducted.

(b) A prosecutor should not pay an excessive fee for the purpose of influencing the expert's testimony or to fix the amount of the fee contingent upon the testimony the expert will give or the result in the case.

Standard 3-3.4. Decision to Charge

(a) The decision to institute criminal proceedings should be initially and primarily the responsibility of the prosecutor.

(b) Prosecutors should take reasonable care to ensure that investigators working at their direction or under their authority are adequately trained in the standards governing the issuance of arrest and search warrants and should inform investigators that they should seek the approval of a prosecutor in close or difficult cases.

(c) The prosecutor should establish standards and procedures for evaluating complaints to determine whether criminal proceedings should be instituted.

(d) Where the law permits a citizen to complain directly to a judicial officer or the grand jury, the citizen complainant should be required to present the complaint for prior approval to the prosecutor, and the prosecutor's action or recommendation thereon should be communicated to the judicial officer or grand jury.

Standard 3-3.5. Relations with Grand Jury

(a) Where the prosecutor is authorized to act as legal adviser to the grand jury, the prosecutor may appropriately explain the law and express an opinion on the legal significance of the evidence but should give due deference to its status as an independent legal body.

(b) The prosecutor should not make statements or arguments in an effort to influence grand jury action in a manner which would be impermissible at trial before a petit jury.

(c) The prosecutor's communications and presentations to the grand jury should be on the record.

Standard 3-3.6. Quality and Scope of Evidence Before Grand Jury

(a) A prosecutor should only make statements or arguments to the grand jury and only present evidence to the grand jury which the prosecutor believes is appropriate or authorized under law for presentation to the grand jury. In appropriate cases, the prosecutor may present witnesses to summarize admissible evidence available to the prosecutor which the prosecutor believes he or she will be able to present at trial. The prosecutor should also inform the grand jurors that they have the right to hear any available witnesses, including eyewitnesses.

(b) No prosecutor should knowingly fail to disclose to the grand jury evidence which tends to negate guilt or mitigate the offense.

(c) A prosecutor should recommend that the grand jury not indict if he or she believes the evidence presented does not warrant an indictment under governing law.

(d) If the prosecutor believes that a witness is a potential defendant, the prosecutor should not seek to compel the witness's testimony before the grand jury without informing the witness that he or she may be charged and that the witness should seek independent legal advice concerning his or her rights.

(e) The prosecutor should not compel the appearance of a witness before the grand jury whose activities are the subject of the inquiry if the witness states in advance that if called he or she will exercise the constitutional privilege not to testify, unless the prosecutor intends to judicially challenge the exercise of the privilege or to seek a grant of immunity according to the law.

(f) A prosecutor in presenting a case to a grand jury should not intentionally interfere with the independence of the grand jury, preempt a function of the grand jury, or abuse the processes of the grand jury.

(g) Unless the law of the jurisdiction so permits, a prosecutor should not use the grand jury in order to obtain tangible, documentary or testimonial evidence to assist the prosecutor in preparation for trial of a defendant who has already been charged by indictment or information.

(h) Unless the law of the jurisdiction so permits, a prosecutor should not use the grand jury for the purpose of aiding or assisting in any administrative inquiry.

Standard 3-3.7. Quality and Scope of Evidence
for Information

Where the prosecutor is empowered to charge by information, the prosecutor's decisions should be governed by the principles embodied in standards 3-3.6 and 3-3.9, where applicable.

Standard 3-3.8. Discretion as to Noncriminal
Disposition

(a) The prosecutor should consider in appropriate cases the availability of noncriminal disposition, formal or informal, in deciding whether to press criminal charges which would otherwise be supported by probable cause; especially in the case of a first offender, the nature of the offense may warrant noncriminal disposition.

(b) Prosecutors should be familiar with the resources of social agencies which can assist in the evaluation of cases for diversion from the criminal process.

Standard 3-3.9. Discretion in the Charging
Decision

(a) A prosecutor should not institute, or cause to be instituted, or permit the continued pendency of criminal charges when the prosecutor knows that the charges are not supported by probable cause. A prosecutor should not institute, cause to be instituted, or permit the continued pendency of criminal charges in the absence of sufficient admissible evidence to support a conviction.

(b) The prosecutor is not obliged to present all charges which the evidence might support. The prosecutor may in some circumstances and for good cause consistent with the public interest decline to prosecute, notwithstanding that sufficient evidence may exist which would support a conviction. Illustrative of the factors which the prosecutor may properly consider in exercising his or her discretion are:

   (i) the prosecutor's reasonable doubt that the accused is in fact guilty;

   (ii) the extent of the harm caused by the offense;

   (iii) the disproportion of the authorized punishment in relation to the particular offense or the offender;

   (iv) possible improper motives of a complainant;

    (v) reluctance of the victim to testify;

    (vi) cooperation of the accused in the apprehension or conviction of others; and

    (vii) availability and likelihood of prosecution by another jurisdiction.

    (c) A prosecutor should not be compelled by his or her supervisor to prosecute a case in which he or she has a reasonable doubt about the guilt of the accused.

    (d) In making the decision to prosecute, the prosecutor should give no weight to the personal or political advantages or disadvantages which might be involved or to a desire to enhance his or her record of convictions.

    (e) In cases which involve a serious threat to the community, the prosecutor should not be deterred from prosecution by the fact that in the jurisdiction juries have tended to acquit persons accused of the particular kind of criminal act in question.

    (f) The prosecutor should not bring or seek charges greater in number or degree than can reasonably be supported with evidence at trial or than are necessary to fairly reflect the gravity of the offense.

    (g) The prosecutor should not condition a dismissal of charges, nolle prosequi, or similar action on the accused's relinquishment of the right to seek civil redress unless the accused has agreed to the action knowingly and intelligently, freely and voluntarily, and where such waiver is approved by the court.

Standard 3-3.10. Role in First Appearance and Preliminary Hearing

    (a) A prosecutor who is present at the first appearance (however denominated) of the accused before a judicial officer should not communicate with the accused unless a waiver of counsel has been entered, except for the purpose of aiding in obtaining counsel or in arranging for the pretrial release of the accused. A prosecutor should not fail to make reasonable efforts to assure that the accused has been advised of the right to, and the procedure for obtaining, counsel and has been given reasonable opportunity to obtain counsel.

    (b) The prosecutor should cooperate in good faith in arrangements for release under the prevailing system for pretrial release.

    (c) The prosecutor should not seek to obtain from an unrepresented accused a waiver of important pretrial rights, such as the right to a preliminary hearing.

(d) The prosecutor should not seek a continuance solely for the purpose of mooting the preliminary hearing by securing an indictment.

(e) Except for good cause, the prosecutor should not seek delay in the preliminary hearing after an arrest has been made if the accused is in custody.

(f) The prosecutor should ordinarily be present at a preliminary hearing where such hearing is required by law.

Standard 3-3.11. Disclosure of Evidence by the Prosecutor

(a) A prosecutor should not intentionally fail to make timely disclosure to the defense, at the earliest feasible opportunity, of the existence of all evidence or information which tends to negate the guilt of the accused or mitigate the offense charged or which would tend to reduce the punishment of the accused.

(b) A prosecutor should not fail to make a reasonably diligent effort to comply with a legally proper discovery request.

(c) A prosecutor should not intentionally avoid pursuit of evidence because he or she believes it will damage the prosecution's case or aid the accused.

Part IV. Plea Discussions

Standard 3-4.1. Availability for Plea Discussions

(a) The prosecutor should have and make known a general policy or willingness to consult with defense counsel concerning disposition of charges by plea.

(b) A prosecutor should not engage in plea discussions directly with an accused who is represented by defense counsel, except with defense counsel's approval. Where the defendant has properly waived counsel, the prosecuting attorney may engage in plea discussions with the defendant, although, where feasible, a record of such discussions should be made and preserved.

(c) A prosecutor should not knowingly make false statements or representations as to fact or law in the course of plea discussions with defense counsel or the accused.

Standard 3-4.2. Fulfillment of Plea Discussions

(a) A prosecutor should not make any promise or commitment assuring a defendant or defense counsel that a court will impose a specific sentence or a suspension of sentence; a prosecutor may properly advise the defense what position will be taken concerning disposition.

(b) A prosecutor should not imply a greater power to influence the disposition of a case than is actually possessed.

(c) A prosecutor should not fail to comply with a plea agreement, unless a defendant fails to comply with a plea agreement or other extenuating circumstances are present.

Standard 3-4.3. Record of Reasons for Nolle Prosequi Disposition

Whenever felony criminal charges are dismissed by way of nolle prosequi (or its equivalent), the prosecutor should make a record of the reasons for the action.

Part V. The Trial

Standard 3-5.1. Calendar Control

Control over the trial calendar should be vested in the court. The prosecuting attorney should advise the court of facts relevant in determining the order of cases on the court's calendar.

Standard 3-5.2. Courtroom Professionalism

(a) As an officer of the court, the prosecutor should support the authority of the court and the dignity of the trial courtroom by strict adherence to codes of professionalism and by manifesting a professional attitude toward the judge, opposing counsel, witnesses, defendants, jurors, and others in the courtroom.

(b) When court is in session, the prosecutor should address the court, not opposing counsel, on all matters relating to the case.

(c) Prosecutor should comply promptly with all orders and directives of the court, but the prosecutor has a duty to have the record reflect adverse rulings or judicial conduct which the prosecutor considers prejudicial. The prosecutor has a right to make respectful requests for reconsideration of adverse rulings.

(d) Prosecutors should cooperate with courts and the organized bar in developing codes of professionalism for each jurisdiction.

Standard 3-5.3. Selection of Jurors

(a) The prosecutor should prepare himself or herself prior to trial to discharge effectively the prosecution function in the selection of the jury and the exercise of challenges for cause and peremptory challenges.

(b) In those cases where it appears necessary to conduct a pretrial investigation of the background of jurors, investigatory methods of the prosecutor should neither harass nor unduly embarrass potential jurors or invade their privacy and, whenever possible, should be restricted to an investigation of records and sources of information already in existence.

(c) The opportunity to question jurors personally should be used solely to obtain information for the intelligent exercise of challenges. A prosecutor should not intentionally use the voir dire to present factual matter which the prosecutor knows will not be admissible at trial or to argue the prosecution's case to the jury.

Standard 3-5.4. Relations with Jury

(a) A prosecutor should not intentionally communicate privately with persons summoned for jury duty or impaneled as jurors prior to or during trial. The prosecutor should avoid the reality or appearance of any such communications.

(b) The prosecutor should treat jurors with deference and respect, avoiding the reality or appearance of currying favor by a show of undue solicitude for their comfort or convenience.

(c) After discharge of the jury from further consideration of a case, a prosecutor should not intentionally make comments to or ask questions of a juror for the purpose of harassing or embarrassing the juror in any way which will tend to influence judgment in future jury service. If the prosecutor believes that the verdict may be subject to legal challenge, he or she may properly, if no statute or rule prohibits such course, communicate with jurors to determine whether such challenge may be available.

Standard 3-5.5. Opening Statement

The prosecutor's opening statement should be confined to a statement of the issues in the case and the evidence the prosecutor intends to offer which the prosecutor believes in good faith will be available and admissible. A prosecutor should not allude to any evidence unless there is a good faith and reasonable basis for believing that such evidence will be tendered and admitted in evidence.

Standard 3-5.6. Presentation of Evidence

(a) A prosecutor should not knowingly offer false evidence, whether by documents, tangible evidence, or the testimony of witnesses, or fail to seek withdrawal thereof upon discovery of its falsity.

(b) A prosecutor should not knowingly and for the purpose of bringing inadmissible matter to the attention of the judge or jury offer inadmissible evidence, ask legally objectionable questions, or make other impermissible comments or arguments in the presence of the judge or jury.

(c) A prosecutor should not permit any tangible evidence to be displayed in the view of the judge or jury which would tend to prejudice fair consideration by the judge or jury until such time as a good faith tender of such evidence is made.

(d) A prosecutor should not tender tangible evidence in the view of the judge or jury if it would tend to prejudice fair consideration by the judge or jury unless there is a reasonable basis for its admission in evidence. When there is any substantial doubt about the admissibility of such evidence, it should be tendered by an offer of proof and a ruling obtained.

Standard 3-5.7. Examination of Witnesses

(a) The interrogation of all witnesses should be conducted fairly, objectively, and with due regard for the dignity and legitimate privacy of the witness, and without seeking to intimidate or humiliate the witness unnecessarily.

(b) The prosecutor's belief that the witness is telling the truth does not preclude cross-examination, but may affect the method and scope of cross-examination. A prosecutor should not use the power of cross-examination to discredit or undermine a witness if the prosecutor knows the witness is testifying truthfully.

(c) A prosecutor should not call a witness in the presence of the jury who the prosecutor knows will claim a valid privilege not to testify.

(d) A prosecutor should not ask a question which implies the existence of a factual predicate for which a good faith belief is lacking.

Standard 3-5.8. Argument to the Jury

(a) In closing argument to the jury, the prosecutor may argue all reasonable inferences from evidence in the record. The prosecutor should not intentionally misstate the evidence or mislead the jury as to the inferences it may draw.

(b) The prosecutor should not express his or her personal belief or opinion as to the truth or falsity of any testimony or evidence or the guilt of the defendant.

(c) The prosecutor should not use arguments calculated to appeal to the prejudices of the jury.

(d) The prosecutor should refrain from argument which would divert the jury from its duty to decide the case on the evidence.

Standard 3-5.9. Facts Outside the Record

The prosecutor should not intentionally refer to or argue on the basis of facts outside the record whether at trial or on appeal, unless such facts are matters of common public knowledge based on ordinary human experience or matters of which the court may take judicial notice.

Standard 3-5.10. Comments by Prosecutor After Verdict

The prosecutor should not make public comments critical of a verdict, whether rendered by judge or jury.

CHAPTER 4. THE DEFENSE FUNCTION

Editors' Note. Chapter 4 was originally approved by the ABA in 1971. As noted in the Editors' Introduction to this chapter, the ABA approved substantial revisions to "The Defense Function" at its 1991 Mid-Year Meeting.

Part I. General Standards

Standard 4-1.2. The Function of Defense Counsel

(a) Counsel for the accused is an essential component of the administration of criminal justice. A court properly constituted to hear a criminal case must be viewed as a tripartite entity consisting of the judge (and jury, where appropriate), counsel for the prosecution, and counsel for the accused.

(b) The basic duty defense counsel owes to the administration of justice and as an officer of the court is to serve as the accused's counselor and advocate with courage and devotion and to render effective, quality representation.

(c) Since the death penalty differs from other criminal penalties in its finality, defense counsel in a capital case should respond to this difference by making extraordinary efforts on behalf of the accused. Defense counsel should comply with the ABA Guidelines for the Appointment and Performance of Counsel in Death Penalty Cases.

(d) Defense counsel should seek to reform and improve the administration of criminal justice. When inadequacies or injustices in the substantive or procedural law come to defense counsel's attention, he or she should stimulate efforts for remedial action.

(e) Defense counsel, in common with all members of the bar, is subject to standards of conduct stated in statutes, rules, decisions of courts, and codes, canons, or other standards of professional conduct. Defense counsel has no duty to execute any directive of the accused which does not comport with law or such standards. Defense counsel is the professional representative of the accused, not the accused's alter ego.

(f) Defense counsel should not intentionally misrepresent matters of fact or law to the court.

(g) Defense counsel should disclose to the tribunal legal authority in the controlling jurisdiction known to defense counsel to be directly adverse to the position of the accused and not disclosed by the prosecutor.

(h) It is the duty of defense counsel to know and be guided by the standards of professional conduct as defined in codes and canons of the legal profession applicable in defense counsel's jurisdiction. Once representation has been undertaken, the functions and duties of defense counsel are the same whether defense counsel is assigned, privately retained, or serving in a legal aid or defender program.

Standard 4-1.3. Delays; Punctuality; Workload

(a) Defense counsel should act with reasonable diligence and promptness in representing a client.

(b) Defense counsel should avoid unnecessary delay in the disposition of cases. Defense counsel should be punctual in attendance upon court and in the submission of all motions, briefs, and other papers. Defense counsel should emphasize to the client and all witnesses the importance of punctuality in attendance in court.

(c) Defense counsel should not intentionally misrepresent facts or otherwise mislead the court in order to obtain a continuance.

(d) Defense counsel should not intentionally use procedural devices for delay for which there is no legitimate basis.

(e) Defense counsel should not carry a workload that, by reason of its excessive size, interferes with the rendering of quality representation, endangers the client's interest in the speedy disposition of charges, or may lead to the breach of professional obligations. Defense counsel should not accept employment for the purpose of delaying trial.

Standard 4-1.4. Public Statements

Defense counsel should not make or authorize the making of an extrajudicial statement that a reasonable person would expect to be disseminated by means of public communication if defense counsel knows or reasonably should know that it will have a substantial likelihood of prejudicing a criminal proceeding.

Part III. Lawyer-Client Relationship

Standard 4-3.1. Establishment of Relationship

(a) Defense counsel should seek to establish a relationship of trust and confidence with the accused and should discuss the objectives of the representation and whether defense counsel will continue to represent the accused if there is an appeal. Defense counsel should explain the necessity of full disclosure of all facts known to the client for an effective defense, and defense counsel should explain the extent to which counsel's obligation of confidentiality makes privileged the accused's disclosures.

(b) To ensure the privacy essential for confidential communication between defense counsel and client, adequate facilities should be available for private discussions between counsel and accused in jails, prisons, courthouses, and other places where accused persons must confer with counsel.

(c) Personnel of jails, prisons, and custodial institutions should be prohibited by law or administrative regulations from examining or otherwise interfering with any communication or correspondence between client and defense counsel relating to legal action arising out of charges or incarceration.

Standard 4-3.2. Interviewing the Client

(a) As soon as practicable, defense counsel should seek to determine all relevant facts known to the accused. In so doing, defense counsel should probe for all legally relevant information without seeking to influence the direction of the client's responses.

(b) Defense counsel should not instruct the client or intimate to the client in any way that the client should not be candid in revealing facts so as to afford defense counsel free rein to take action which would be precluded by counsel's knowing of such facts.

Standard 4-3.3. Fees

(a) Defense counsel should not enter into an agreement for, charge, or collect an illegal or unreasonable fee.

(b) In determining the amount of the fee in a criminal case, it is proper to consider the time and effort required, the responsibility assumed by counsel, the novelty and difficulty of the questions involved, the skill requisite to proper representation, the likelihood that other employment will be precluded, the fee customarily charged in the locality for similar services, the gravity of the charge, the experience, reputation, and ability of defense counsel, and the capacity of the client to pay the fee.

(c) Defense counsel should not imply that his or her compensation is for anything other than professional services rendered by defense counsel or by others for defense counsel.

(d) Defense counsel should not divide a fee with a nonlawyer, except as permitted by applicable ethical codes of conduct.

(e) Defense counsel not in the same firm should not divide fees unless the division is in proportion to the services performed by each counsel or, by written agreement with the client, each counsel assumes joint responsibility for the representation, the client is advised of and does not object to the participation of all counsel involved, and the total fee is reasonable.

(f) Defense counsel should not enter into an arrangement for, charge, or collect a contingent fee for representing a defendant in a criminal case.

(g) When defense counsel has not regularly represented the client, defense counsel should communicate the basis or rate of the fee to the client, preferably in writing, before or within a reasonable time after commencing the representation.

Standard 4-3.4. Obtaining Literary or Media Rights from the Accused

Defense counsel, prior to conclusion of all aspects of the matter giving rise to his or her employment, should not enter into any agreement or understanding with a client or a prospective client by which defense counsel acquires an interest in literary or media rights to a portrayal or account based in substantial part on information relating to the employment or proposed employment.

Standard 4-3.5. Conflicts of Interest

(a) Defense counsel should not permit his or her professional judgment or obligations to be affected by his or her own political, financial, business, property, or personal interests.

(b) Defense counsel should disclose to the defendant at the earliest feasible opportunity any interest in or connection with the case or any other matter that might be relevant to the defendant's selection of counsel to represent him or her or counsel's continuing representation. Such disclosure should include communication of information reasonably sufficient to permit the client to appreciate the significance of any conflict or potential conflict of interest.

(c) Except for preliminary matters such as initial hearings or applications for bail, defense counsel who are associated in practice should not undertake to defend more than one defendant in the same criminal case if the duty to one of the defendants may conflict with the duty to another. The potential for conflict of interest in representing multiple defendants is so grave that ordinarily defense counsel should decline to act for more than one of several codefendants except in unusual situations when, after careful investigation, it is clear either that no conflict is likely to develop at trial, sentencing, or at any other time in the proceeding or that common representation will be advantageous to each of the codefendants represented and, in either case, that:

(i) the several defendants give an informed consent to such multiple representation; and

(ii) the consent of the defendants is made a matter of judicial record. In determining the presence of consent by the defendants, the trial judge should make appropriate inquiries respecting actual or potential conflicts of interest of counsel and whether the defendants fully comprehend the difficulties that defense counsel sometimes encounters in defending multiple clients.

(d) Defense counsel who has formerly represented a defendant should not thereafter use information related to the former representation to the disadvantage of the former client unless the information has become generally known or the ethical obligation of confidentiality otherwise does not apply.

(e) In accepting payment of fees by one person for the defense of another, defense counsel should be careful to determine that he or she will not be confronted with a conflict of loyalty since defense counsel's entire loyalty is due the accused. Defense counsel should not accept such compensation unless:

(i) the accused consents after disclosure;

(ii) there is no interference with defense counsel's independence of professional judgment or with the client-lawyer relationship; and

(iii) information relating to the representation of the accused is protected from disclosure as required by defense counsel's ethical obligation of confidentiality.

Defense counsel should not permit a person who recommends, employs, or pays defense counsel to render legal services for another to direct or regulate counsel's professional judgment in rendering such legal services.

(f) Defense counsel should not defend a criminal case in which counsel's partner or other professional associate is or has been the prosecutor in the same case.

(g) Defense counsel should not represent a criminal defendant in a jurisdiction in which he or she is also a prosecutor.

(h) Defense counsel who formerly participated personally and substantially in the prosecution of a defendant should not thereafter represent any person in the same or a substantially related matter. Defense counsel who was formerly a prosecutor should not use confidential information about a person acquired when defense counsel was a prosecutor in the representation of a client whose interests are adverse to that person in a matter.

(i) Defense counsel who is related to a prosecutor as parent, child, sibling or spouse should not represent a client in a criminal matter where defense counsel knows that government is represented in the matter by such prosecutor. Nor should defense counsel who has a significant personal or financial relationship with a prosecutor represent a client in a criminal matter where defense counsel knows the government is represented in the matter by such prosecutor, except upon consent by the client after consultation regarding the relationship.

(j) Defense counsel should not act as surety on a bond either for the accused represented by counsel or for any other accused in the same or a related case.

(k) Except as law may otherwise expressly permit, defense counsel should not negotiate to employ any person who is significantly involved as an attorney or employee of the government in a matter in which defense counsel is participating personally and substantially.

Standard 4-3.6. Prompt Action to Protect the Accused

Many important rights of the accused can be protected and preserved only by prompt legal action. Defense counsel should inform the accused of his or her rights at the earliest opportunity and take all necessary action to vindicate such rights. Defense counsel should consider all procedural steps which in good faith may be taken, including, for example, motions seeking pretrial release of the accused, obtaining psychiatric examination of the accused when a need appears, moving for change of venue or continuance, moving for severance from jointly charged defendants, and seeking dismissal of the charges.

Standard 4-3.7. Advice and Service on Anticipated Unlawful Conduct

(a) It is defense counsel's duty to advise a client to comply with the law, but counsel may advise concerning the meaning, scope, and validity of a law.

(b) Defense counsel should not counsel a client in or knowingly assist a client to engage in conduct which defense counsel knows to be illegal or fraudulent but defense counsel may discuss the legal consequences of any proposed course of conduct with a client.

(c) Defense counsel should not agree in advance of the commission of a crime that he or she will serve as counsel for the defendant, except as part of a bona fide effort to determine the validity, scope, meaning, or application of the law, or where the defense is incident to a general retainer for legal services to a person or enterprise engaged in legitimate activity.

(d) Defense counsel should not reveal information relating to representation of a client unless the client consents after consultation, except for disclosures that are impliedly authorized in order to carry out the representation and except that defense counsel may reveal such information to the extent he or she reasonably believes necessary to prevent the client from committing a criminal act that defense counsel believes is likely to result in imminent death or substantial bodily harm.

Standard 4-3.8. Duty to Keep Client Informed

(a) Defense counsel should keep the client informed of the developments in the case and the progress of preparing the defense and should promptly comply with reasonable requests for information.

(b) Defense counsel should explain developments in the case to the extent reasonably necessary to permit the client to make informed decisions regarding the representation.

Part IV. Investigation and Preparation

Standard 4-4.1. Duty to Investigate

(a) Defense counsel should conduct a prompt investigation of the circumstances of the case and explore all avenues leading to facts relevant to the merits of the case and the penalty in the event of conviction. The investigation should include efforts to secure information in the possession of the prosecution and law enforcement authorities. The duty to investigate exists regardless of the accused's admissions or statements to defense counsel of facts constituting guilt or the accused's stated desire to plead guilty.

(b) Defense counsel should not seek to acquire possession of physical evidence personally or through use of an investigator where defense counsel's sole purpose is to obstruct access to such evidence.

Standard 4-4.2. Illegal Investigation

Defense counsel should not knowingly use illegal means to obtain evidence or information or to employ, instruct, or encourage others to do so.

Standard 4-4.3. Relations with Prospective Witnesses

(a) Defense counsel, in representing an accused, should not use means that have no substantial purpose other than to embarrass, delay, or burden a third person, or use methods of obtaining evidence that violate the legal rights of such a person.

(b) Defense counsel should not compensate a witness, other than an expert, for giving testimony, but it is not improper to reimburse a witness for the reasonable expenses of attendance upon court, including transportation and loss of income, attendance for depositions pursuant to statute or court rule, or attendance for pretrial interviews, provided there is no attempt to conceal the fact of reimbursement.

(c) It is not necessary for defense counsel or defense counsel's investigator, in interviewing a prospective witness, to caution the witness concerning possible self-incrimination and the need for counsel.

(d) Defense counsel should not discourage or obstruct communication between prospective witnesses and the prosecutor. It is unprofessional conduct to advise any person other than a client, or cause such person to be advised, to decline to give to the prosecutor or defense counsel for codefendants information which such person has a right to give.

(e) Unless defense counsel is prepared to forgo impeachment of a witness by counsel's own testimony as to what the witness stated in an in-

455

terview or to seek leave to withdraw from the case in order to present such impeaching testimony, defense counsel should avoid interviewing a prospective witness except in the presence of a third person.

Standard 4-4.4. Relations with Expert Witnesses

(a) Defense counsel who engages an expert for an opinion should respect the independence of the expert and should not seek to dictate the formation of the expert's opinion on the subject. To the extent necessary, defense counsel should explain to the expert his or her role in the trial as an impartial witness called to aid the fact finders and the manner in which the examination of witnesses is conducted.

(b) Defense counsel should not pay an excessive fee for the purpose of influencing an expert's testimony or fix the amount of the fee contingent upon the testimony an expert will give or the result in the case.

Standard 4-4.5. Compliance with Discovery Procedure

Defense counsel should make a reasonably diligent effort to comply with a legally proper discovery request.

Standard 4-4.6. Physical Evidence

(a) Defense counsel who receives a physical item under circumstances implicating a client in criminal conduct should disclose the location of or should deliver that item to law enforcement authorities only: (1) if required by law or court order, or (2) as provided in paragraph (d).

(b) Unless required to disclose, defense counsel should return the item to the source from whom defense counsel received it, except as provided in paragraphs (c) and (d). In returning the item to the source, defense counsel should advise the source of the legal consequences pertaining to possession or destruction of the item. Defense counsel should also prepare a written record of these events for his or her file, but should not give the source a copy of such record.

(c) Defense counsel may receive the item for a reasonable period of time during which defense counsel: (1) intends to return it to the owner; (2) reasonably fears that return of the item to the source will result in destruction of the item; (3) reasonably fears that return of the item to the source will result in physical harm to anyone; (4) intends to test, examine, inspect, or use the item in any way as part of defense counsel's representation of the client; or (5) cannot return it to the source. If defense counsel tests or examines the item, he or she should thereafter return it to the source unless there is reason to believe that the evidence might be altered or destroyed or used to harm another or return is otherwise impossible. If defense counsel retains the item, he or she should retain it in his or her law office in a manner that does not impede the lawful ability of law enforcement authorities to obtain the item.

(d) If the item received is contraband, i.e. an item, possession of which is in and of itself a crime, such as narcotics, defense counsel may suggest that the client destroy it where there is no pending case or investigation relating to this evidence and where such destruction is clearly not in violation of any criminal statute. If such destruction is not permitted by law or if in defense counsel's judgment he or she cannot retain the item, whether or not it is contraband, in a way that does not pose an unreasonable risk of physical harm to anyone, defense counsel should disclose the location of or should deliver the item to law enforcement authorities.

(e) If defense counsel discloses the location of or delivers the item to law enforcement authorities under paragraphs (a) or (d), or to a third party under paragraph (c)(1), he or she should do so in the way best designed to protect the client's interests.

Part V. Control and Direction of Litigation

Standard 4-5.1. Advising the Accused

(a) After informing himself or herself fully on the facts and the law, defense counsel should advise the accused with complete candor concerning all aspects of the case, including a candid estimate of the probable outcome.

(b) Defense counsel should not intentionally understate or overstate the risks, hazards, or prospects of the case to exert undue influence on the accused's decision as to his or her plea.

(c) Defense counsel should caution the client to avoid communication about the case with witnesses, except with the approval of counsel, to avoid any contact with jurors or prospective jurors, and to avoid either the reality or the appearance of any other improper activity.

Standard 4-5.2. Control and Direction of the Case

(a) Certain decisions relating to the conduct of the case are ultimately for the accused and others are ultimately for defense counsel. The decisions which are to be made by the accused after full consultation with counsel include:

(i) what pleas to enter;

(ii) whether to accept a plea agreement;

(iii) whether to waive jury trial;

(iv) whether to testify in his or her own behalf; and

(v) whether to appeal.

(b) Strategic and tactical decisions should be made by defense counsel after consultation with the client where feasible and appropriate. Such decisions include what witnesses to call, whether and how to conduct cross-examination, what jurors to accept or strike, what trial motions should be made, and what evidence should be introduced.

(c) If a disagreement on significant matters of tactics or strategy arises between defense counsel and the client, defense counsel should make a record of the circumstances, counsel's advice and reasons, and the conclusion reached. The record should be made in a manner which protects the confidentiality of the lawyer-client relationship.

Part VI. Disposition Without Trial

Standard 4-6.1. Duty to Explore Disposition Without Trial

(a) Whenever the law, nature, and circumstances of the case permit, defense counsel should explore the possibility of an early diversion of the case from the criminal process through the use of other community agencies.

(b) Defense counsel may engage in plea discussions with the prosecutor. Under no circumstances should defense counsel recommend to a defendant acceptance of a plea unless appropriate investigation and study of the case has been completed, including an analysis of controlling law and the evidence likely to be introduced at trial.

Standard 4-6.2. Plea Discussions

(a) Defense counsel should keep the accused advised of developments arising out of plea discussions conducted with the prosecutor.

(b) Defense counsel should promptly communicate and explain to the accused all significant plea proposals made by the prosecutor.

(c) Defense counsel should not knowingly make false statements concerning the evidence in the course of plea discussions with the prosecutor.

(d) Defense counsel should not seek concessions favorable to one client by any agreement which is detrimental to the legitimate interests of a client in another case.

(e) Defense counsel representing two or more clients in the same or related cases should not participate in making an aggregated agreement as to guilty or nolo contendre pleas, unless each client consents after consultation, including disclosure of the existence and nature of all the claims or pleas involved.

Part VII. Trial

Standard 4-7.1. Courtroom Professionalism

(a) As an officer of the court, defense counsel should support the authority of the court and the dignity of the trial courtroom by strict adherence to codes of professionalism and by manifesting a professional attitude toward the judge, opposing counsel, witnesses, jurors, and others in the courtroom.

(b) Defense counsel should not engage in unauthorized ex parte discussions with or submission of material to a judge relating to a particular case which is or may come before the judge.

(c) When court is in session, defense counsel should address the court and should not address the prosecutor directly on all matters relating to the case.

(d) Defense counsel should comply promptly with all orders and directives of the court, but defense counsel has a duty to have the record reflect adverse rulings or judicial conduct which counsel considers prejudicial to his or her client's legitimate interests. Defense counsel has a right to make respectful requests for reconsiderations of adverse rulings.

(e) Defense counsel should cooperate with courts and the organized bar in developing codes of professionalism for each jurisdiction.

Standard 4-7.2. Selection of Jurors

(a) Defense counsel should prepare himself or herself prior to trial to discharge effectively his or her function in the selection of the jury,

459

Standard 4-7.2   ABA Standards for Criminal Justice

including the raising of any appropriate issues concerning the method by which the jury panel was selected and the exercise of both challenges for cause and peremptory challenges.

(b) In those cases where it appears necessary to conduct a pretrial investigation of the background of jurors, investigatory methods of defense counsel should neither harass nor unduly embarrass potential jurors or invade their privacy and, whenever possible, should be restricted to an investigation of records and sources of information already in existence.

(c) The opportunity to question jurors personally should be used solely to obtain information for the intelligent exercise of challenges. Defense counsel should not intentionally use the voir dire to present factual matter which defense counsel knows will not be admissible at trial or to argue counsel's case to the jury.

Standard 4-7.3. Relations with Jury

(a) Defense counsel should not intentionally communicate privately with persons summoned for jury duty or impaneled as jurors prior to or during the trial. Defense counsel should avoid the reality or appearance of any such communications.

(b) Defense counsel should treat jurors with deference and respect, avoiding the reality or appearance of currying favor by a show of undue solicitude for their comfort or convenience.

(c) After discharge of the jury from further consideration of a case, defense counsel should not intentionally make comments to or ask questions of a juror for the purpose of harassing or embarrassing the juror in any way which will tend to influence judgment in future jury service. If defense counsel believes that the verdict may be subject to legal challenge, he or she may properly, if no statute or rule prohibits such course, communicate with jurors to determine whether such challenge may be available.

Standard 4-7.4. Opening Statement

Defense counsel's opening statement should be confined to a statement of the issues in the case and the evidence defense counsel believes in good faith will be available and admissible. Defense counsel should not allude to any evidence unless there is a good faith and reasonable basis for believing such evidence will be tendered and admitted in evidence.

Standard 4-7.5. Presentation of Evidence

(a) Defense counsel should not knowingly offer false evidence, whether by documents, tangible evidence, or the testimony of witnesses, or fail to take reasonable remedial measures upon discovery of its falsity.

(b) Defense counsel should not knowingly and for the purpose of bringing inadmissible matter to the attention of the judge or jury offer inadmissible evidence, ask legally objectionable questions, or make other impermissible comments or arguments in the presence of the judge or jury.

(c) Defense counsel should not permit any tangible evidence to be displayed in the view of the judge or jury which would tend to prejudice fair consideration of the case by the judge or jury until such time as a good faith tender of such evidence is made.

(d) Defense counsel should not tender tangible evidence in the presence of the judge or jury if it would tend to prejudice fair consideration of the case unless there is a reasonable basis for its admission in evidence. When there is any substantial doubt about the admissibility of such evidence, it should be tendered by an offer of proof and a ruling obtained.

Standard 4-7.6. Examination of Witnesses

(a) The interrogation of all witnesses should be conducted fairly, objectively, and with due regard for the dignity and legitimate privacy of the witness, and without seeking to intimidate or humiliate the witness unnecessarily.

(b) Defense counsel's belief or knowledge that the witness is telling the truth does not preclude cross-examination.

(c) Defense counsel should not call a witness in the presence of the jury who the lawyer knows will claim a valid privilege not to testify.

(d) Defense counsel should not ask a question which implies the existence of a factual predicate for which a good faith belief is lacking.

Standard 4-7.7. Argument to the Jury

(a) In closing argument to the jury, defense counsel may argue all reasonable inferences from the evidence in the record. Defense counsel should not intentionally misstate the evidence or mislead the jury as to the inferences it may draw.

(b) Defense counsel should not express a personal belief or opinion in his or her client's innocence or personal belief or opinion in the truth or falsity of any testimony or evidence.

(c) Defense counsel should not make arguments calculated to appeal to the prejudices of the jury.

(d) Defense counsel should refrain from argument which would divert the jury from its duty to decide the case on the evidence.

Standard 4-7.8. Facts Outside the Record

Defense counsel should not intentionally refer to or argue on the basis of facts outside the record whether at trial or on appeal, unless such facts are matters of common public knowledge based on ordinary human experience or matters of which the court can take judicial notice.

ABA Code of Judicial Conduct*

Editors' Introduction. The ABA first adopted Canons of Judicial Ethics in 1924. (The original spur for judicial canons was that Kennesaw Mountain Landis, the first Commissioner of Baseball, refused to resign as a federal judge after accepting the job of Commissioner.) With occasional amendments, the Canons of Judicial Ethics served the profession well for nearly 50 years and were adopted by most states. In 1969, however, the ABA created a Special Committee on Standards of Judicial Conduct, chaired by California Supreme Court Justice Roger Traynor, "to draw up modern standards and to replace the Canons of Judicial Ethics." In August 1972, the ABA House of Delegates formally adopted the Code of Judicial Conduct to replace the Canons. The ABA made minor changes in 1982 and 1984.

The ABA Code of Judicial Conduct proved widely influential. Nearly all states (plus the District of Columbia) eventually adopted codes of judicial conduct closely modeled on the 1972 ABA Code.

In August 1990, the ABA revised the Code of Judicial Conduct. Although it is like the 1972 Code in many regards, it also contains many differences, affecting such issues as judicial membership in exclusionary clubs and judicial responsibility to prohibit race and sex discrimination and other kinds of bias in the courtroom. For a legislative history of the 1990 Code, see L. Milord, The Development of the ABA Judicial Code (1992).

At the ABA's 1997 Annual Meeting, the House of Delegates voted to amend the 1990 Judicial Code for the first time since its adoption. The amendment substantially changed the Commentary to (but not the text of) Canon 5C(2), a provision that governs the solicitation and acceptance of campaign contributions by judges and judicial candidates who are "subject to public election" (as distinct from appointed judges). The amendment to the Commentary addresses widespread concern about "the appearance of impropriety that may arise when parties whose interests may come before a judge or the lawyers who represent such parties have made contributions to the election campaigns of judicial candidates.'' We reprint the amended Commentary in legislative style, underscoring additions and striking out deletions.

According to the American Judicature Society, about 20 jurisdictions have adopted new codes of judicial conduct based on the 1990 ABA Model Code of Judicial Conduct. These are Arizona, Arkansas, California, Florida, Hawaii, Indiana, Kansas, Maine, Minnesota, Nebraska, Nevada, New Mexico, New York, North Dakota, Rhode Island, South Dakota, Utah, West Virginia, Wyoming, and the District of Columbia. In addition, the following jurisdictions have adopted various provisions of the 1990 Code: Colorado, Connecticut, Delaware, Georgia, Idaho, Illinois, Iowa, Kentucky, Louisiana, Maryland, Massachusetts, Missouri, New Jersey, Ohio, Texas, Washington, and Wisconsin. In these states, the number of provisions adopted from the 1990 Code varies widely. For example, Connecticut adopted only the ex parte communications provision of the 1990 Code, whereas Georgia has adopted the preamble, the terminology, and Canons 1 through 3 of the ABA Code. The United States Judicial Conference has adopted a new Code of Judicial Conduct that includes some provisions from the 1990 ABA Code.

At the end of Canon 3, we reprint a remarkable press release from seven United States Supreme Court Justices specifying when the participation of a lawyer-relative or the law firm of a lawyer-relative in cases before them will cause them to recuse themselves.

Contents

MODEL CODE OF JUDICIAL CONDUCT (1990)

Preamble
Terminology

Canon
1. A Judge Shall Uphold the Integrity and Independence of the Judiciary
2. A Judge Shall Avoid Impropriety and the Appearance of Impropriety in All of the Judge's Activities
3. A Judge Shall Perform the Duties of Judicial Office Impartially and Diligently
   A. Judicial Duties in General
   B. Adjudicative Responsibilities
   C. Administrative Responsibilities
   D. Disciplinary Responsibilities

MODEL CODE OF JUDICIAL CONDUCT
(1990)

PREAMBLE

Our legal system is based on the principle that an independent, fair and competent judiciary will interpret and apply the laws that govern us. The role of the judiciary is central to American concepts of justice and the rule of law. Intrinsic to all sections of this Code are the precepts that judges, individually and collectively, must respect and honor the judicial office as a public trust and strive to enhance and maintain confidence in our legal system. The judge is an arbiter of facts and law for the resolution of disputes and a highly visible symbol of government under the rule of law.

The Code of Judicial Conduct is intended to establish standards for ethical conduct of judges. It consists of broad statements called Canons, specific rules set forth in Sections under each Canon, a Terminology Section, an Application Section and Commentary. The text of the Canons and the Sections, including the Terminology and Application Sections, is authoritative. The Commentary, by explanation and example, provides guidance with respect to the purpose and meaning of the Canons and Sections. The Commentary is not intended as a statement of additional rules. When the text uses "shall" or "shall not," it is intended to impose binding obligations the violation of which can result in disciplinary action. When "should" or "should not" is used, the text is intended as hortatory and as a statement of what is or is not appropriate conduct but not as a binding rule under which a judge may be disciplined. When "may" is used, it denotes permissible discretion or, depending on the context, it refers to action that is not covered by specific proscriptions.

The Canons and Sections are rules of reason. They should be applied consistent with constitutional requirements, statutes, other court rules and decisional law and in the context of all relevant circumstances. The Code is to be construed so as not to impinge on the essential independence of judges in making judicial decisions.

The Code is designed to provide guidance to judges and candidates for judicial office and to provide a structure for regulating conduct through disciplinary agencies. It is not designed or intended as a basis for civil liability or criminal prosecution. Furthermore, the purpose of the Code would be subverted if the Code were invoked by lawyers for mere tactical advantage in a proceeding.

The text of the Canons and Sections is intended to govern conduct of judges and to be binding upon them. It is not intended, however, that every transgression will result in disciplinary action. Whether disciplinary action is appropriate, and the degree of discipline to be imposed, should be determined through a reasonable and reasoned application of the text and should depend on such factors as the seriousness of the transgression, whether there is a pattern of improper activity and the effect of the improper activity on others or on the judicial system. See ABA Standards Relating to Judicial Discipline and Disability Retirement.[1] The Code of

---

1. Judicial disciplinary procedures adopted in the jurisdictions should comport with the requirements of due process. The ABA Standards Relating to Judicial Discipline and Disability Retirement are cited as an example of how these due process requirements may be satisfied.

Judicial Conduct is not intended as an exhaustive guide for the conduct of judges. They should also be governed in their judicial and personal conduct by general ethical standards. The Code is intended, however, to state basic standards which should govern the conduct of all judges and to provide guidance to assist judges in establishing and maintaining high standards of judicial and personal conduct.

TERMINOLOGY

Terms explained below are noted with an asterisk (*) in the Sections where they appear. In addition, the Sections where terms appear are referred to after the explanation of each term below.

"Appropriate authority" denotes the authority with responsibility for initiation of disciplinary process with respect to the violation to be reported. See Sections 3D(1) and 3D(2).

"Candidate." A candidate is a person seeking selection for or retention in judicial office by election or appointment. A person becomes a candidate for judicial office as soon as he or she makes a public announcement of candidacy, declares or files as a candidate with the election or appointment authority, or authorizes solicitation or acceptance of contributions or support. The term "candidate" has the same meaning when applied to a judge seeking election or appointment to non-judicial office. See Preamble and Sections 5A, 5B, 5C and 5E.

"Continuing part-time judge." A continuing part-time judge is a judge who serves repeatedly on a part-time basis by election or under a continuing appointment, including a retired judge subject to recall who is permitted to practice law. See Application Section C.

"Court personnel" does not include the lawyers in a proceeding before a judge. See Sections 3B(7)(c) and 3B(9).

"De minimis" denotes an insignificant interest that could not raise reasonable question as to a judge's impartiality. See Sections 3E(1)(c) and 3E(1)(d).

"Economic interest" denotes ownership of a more than de minimis legal or equitable interest, or a relationship as officer, director, advisor or other active participant in the affairs of a party, except that:

(i) ownership of an interest in a mutual or common investment fund that holds securities is not an economic interest in such securities unless the judge participates in the management of the fund or a proceeding pending or impending before the judge could substantially affect the value of the interest;

(ii) service by a judge as an officer, director, advisor or other active participant in an educational, religious, charitable, fraternal or civic organization, or service by a judge's spouse, parent or child as an officer, director, advisor or other active participant in any organization does not create an economic interest in securities held by that organization;

(iii) a deposit in a financial institution, the proprietary interest of a policy holder in a mutual insurance company, of a depositor in a mutual savings association or of a member in a credit union, or a similar proprietary interest, is not an economic interest in the organization unless a proceeding pending or impending before the judge could substantially affect the value of the interest;

(iv) ownership of government securities is not an economic interest in the issuer unless a proceeding pending or impending before the judge could substantially affect the value of the securities.
See Sections 3E(1)(c) and 3E(2).

"Fiduciary" includes such relationships as executor, administrator, trustee, and guardian. See Sections 3E(2) and 4E.

"Knowingly," "knowledge," "known" or "knows" denotes actual knowledge of the fact in question. A person's knowledge may be inferred from circumstances. See Sections 3D, 3E(1), and 5A(3).

"Law" denotes court rules as well as statutes, constitutional provisions and decisional law. See Sections 2A, 3A, 3B(2), 3B(6), 4B, 4C, 4D(5), 4F, 4I, 5A(2), 5A(3), 5B(2), 5C(1), 5C(3) and 5D.

"Member of the candidate's family" denotes a spouse, child, grandchild, parent, grandparent or other relative or person with whom the candidate maintains a close familial relationship. See Section 5A(3)(a).

"Member of the judge's family" denotes a spouse, child, grandchild, parent, grandparent, or other relative or person with whom the judge maintains a close familial relationship. See Sections 4D(3), 4E and 4G.

"Member of the judge's family residing in the judge's household" denotes any relative of a judge by blood or marriage, or a person treated by a judge as a member of the judge's family, who resides in the judge's household. See Sections 3E(1) and 4D(5).

"Nonpublic information" denotes information that, by law, is not available to the public. Nonpublic information may include but is not limited to: information that is sealed by statute or court order, impounded or communicated in camera; and information offered in grand jury proceedings, presentencing reports, dependency cases or psychiatric reports. See Section 3B(11).

"Periodic part-time judge." A periodic part-time judge is a judge who serves or expects to serve repeatedly on a part-time basis but under a separate appointment for each limited period of service or for each matter. See Application Section D.

"Political organization" denotes a political party or other group, the principal purpose of which is to further the election or appointment of candidates to political office. See Sections 5A(1), 5B(2) and 5C(1).

"Pro tempore part-time judge." A pro tempore part-time judge is a judge who serves or expects to serve once or only sporadically on a part-time basis under a separate appointment for each period of service or for each case heard. See Application Section E.

"Public election." This term includes primary and general elections; it includes partisan elections, nonpartisan elections and retention elections. See Section 5C.

"Require." The rules prescribing that a judge "require" certain conduct of others are, like all of the rules in this Code, rules of reason. The use of the term "require" in that context means a judge is to exercise reasonable direction and control over the conduct of those persons subject to the judge's direction and control. See Sections 3B(3), 3B(4), 3B(5), 3B(6), 3B(9) and 3C(2).

"Third degree of relationship." The following persons are relatives within the third degree of relationship: great-grandparent, grandparent, parent, uncle, aunt, brother, sister, child, grandchild, great-grandchild, nephew or niece. See Section 3E(1)(d).

CANON 1. A JUDGE SHALL UPHOLD THE INTEGRITY AND INDEPENDENCE OF THE JUDICIARY

A. An independent and honorable judiciary is indispensable to justice in our society. A judge should participate in establishing, maintaining and enforcing high standards of conduct, and shall personally observe those standards so that the integrity and independence of the judiciary will be preserved. The provisions of this Code are to be construed and applied to further that objective.

Commentary

Deference to the judgments and rulings of courts depends upon public confidence in the integrity and independence of judges. The integrity and independence of judges depends in turn upon their acting without fear or favor. Although judges should be independent, they must comply with the law, including the provisions of this Code. Public confidence in the impartiality of the judiciary is maintained by the adherence of each judge to this responsibility. Conversely, violation of this Code diminishes public confidence in the judiciary and thereby does injury to the system of government under law.

CANON 2. A JUDGE SHALL AVOID IMPROPRIETY AND THE APPEARANCE OF IMPROPRIETY IN ALL OF THE JUDGE'S ACTIVITIES

A. A judge shall respect and comply with the law* and shall act at all times in a manner that promotes public confidence in the integrity and impartiality of the judiciary.

Commentary

Public confidence in the judiciary is eroded by irresponsible or improper conduct by judges. A judge must avoid all impropriety and appearance of impropriety. A judge must expect to be the subject of constant public scrutiny. A judge must therefore accept restrictions on the judge's conduct that might be viewed as burdensome by the ordinary citizen and should do so freely and willingly.

The prohibition against behaving with impropriety or the appearance of impropriety applies to both the professional and personal conduct of a judge. Because it is not practicable to list all prohibited acts, the proscription is necessarily cast in general terms that extend to conduct by judges that is harmful although not specifically mentioned in the Code. Actual improprieties under this standard include violations of law, court rules or other specific provisions of this Code. The test for appearance of impropriety is whether the conduct would create in reasonable minds a perception that the judge's ability to carry out judicial responsibilities with integrity, impartiality and competence is impaired.

See also Commentary under Section 2C.

*Asterisked terms are defined in the Terminology Section. — EDS.

471

B. A judge shall not allow family, social, political or other relationships to influence the judge's judicial conduct or judgment. A judge shall not lend the prestige of judicial office to advance the private interests of the judge or others; nor shall a judge convey or permit others to convey the impression that they are in a special position to influence the judge. A judge shall not testify voluntarily as a character witness.

Commentary

Maintaining the prestige of judicial office is essential to a system of government in which the judiciary functions independently of the executive and legislative branches. Respect for the judicial office facilitates the orderly conduct of legitimate judicial functions. Judges should distinguish between proper and improper use of the prestige of office in all of their activities. For example, it would be improper for a judge to allude to his or her judgeship to gain a personal advantage such as deferential treatment when stopped by a police officer for a traffic offense. Similarly, judicial letterhead must not be used for conducting a judge's personal business.

A judge must avoid lending the prestige of judicial office for the advancement of the private interests of others. For example, a judge must not use the judge's judicial position to gain advantage in a civil suit involving a member of the judge's family. In contracts for publication of a judge's writings, a judge should retain control over the advertising to avoid exploitation of the judge's office. As to the acceptance of awards, see Section 4D(5)(a) and Commentary.

Although a judge should be sensitive to possible abuse of the prestige of office, a judge may, based on the judge's personal knowledge, serve as a reference or provide a letter of recommendation. However, a judge must not initiate the communication of information to a sentencing judge or a probation or corrections officer but may provide to such persons information for the record in response to a formal request.

Judges may participate in the process of judicial selection by cooperating with appointing authorities and screening committees seeking names for consideration, and by responding to official inquiries concerning a person being considered for a judgeship. See also Canon 5 regarding use of a judge's name in political activities.

A judge must not testify voluntarily as a character witness because to do so may lend the prestige of the judicial office in support of the party for whom the judge testifies. Moreover, when a judge testifies as a witness, a lawyer who regularly appears before the judge may be placed in the awkward position of cross-examining the judge. A judge may, however, testify when properly summoned. Except in unusual circumstances where the demands of justice require, a judge should discourage a party from requiring the judge to testify as a character witness.

C. A judge shall not hold membership in any organization that practices invidious discrimination on the basis of race, sex, religion or national origin.

Commentary

Membership of a judge in an organization that practices invidious discrimination gives rise to perceptions that the judge's impartiality is impaired. Section 2C refers to the current practices of the organization. Whether an organization practices invidious discrimination is often a complex question to which judges should be sensitive. The answer cannot be determined from a mere examination of an organization's current membership rolls but rather depends on how the organization selects members and other relevant factors, such as that the organization is dedicated to the preservation of religious, ethnic or cultural values of legitimate common interest to its members, or that it is in fact and effect an intimate, purely private organization whose membership limitations could not be constitutionally prohibited. Absent such factors, an organization is generally said to discriminate invidiously if it arbitrarily excludes from membership on the basis of race, religion, sex or national origin persons who would otherwise be admitted to membership. See New York State Club Assn., Inc. v. City of New York, 108 S. Ct. 2225, 101 L. Ed. 2d 1 (1988); Board of Directors of Rotary International v. Rotary Club of Duarte, 481 U.S. 537, 107 S. Ct. 1940 (1987), 95 L. Ed. 2d 474; Roberts v. United States Jaycees, 468 U.S. 609, 104 S. Ct. 3244, 82 L. Ed. 2d 462 (1984).

Although Section 2C relates only to membership in organizations that invidiously discriminate on the basis of race, sex, religion or national origin, a judge's membership in an organization that engages in any discriminatory membership practices prohibited by the law of the jurisdiction also violates Canon 2 and Section 2A and gives the appearance of impropriety. In addition, it would be a violation of Canon 2 and Section 2A for a judge to arrange a meeting at a club that the judge knows practices invidious discrimination on the basis of race, sex, religion or national origin in its membership or other policies, or for the judge to regularly use such a club. Moreover, public manifestation by a judge of the judge's knowing approval of invidious discrimination on any basis gives the appearance of impropriety under Canon 2 and diminishes public confidence in the integrity and impartiality of the judiciary, in violation of Section 2A.

When a person who is a judge in the date this Code becomes effective [in the jurisdiction in which the person is a judge][1] learns that an organization to which the judge belongs engages in invidious discrimination that would preclude membership under Section 2C or under Canon 2 and Section 2A, the

1. The language within the brackets should be deleted when the jurisdiction adopts this provision.

judge is permitted, in lieu of resigning, to make immediate efforts to have the organization discontinue its invidiously discriminatory practices, but is required to suspend participation in any other activities of the organization. If the organization fails to discontinue its invidiously discriminatory practices as promptly as possible (and in all events within a year of the judge's first learning of the practices), the judge is required to resign immediately from the organization.

CANON 3. A JUDGE SHALL PERFORM THE DUTIES OF JUDICIAL OFFICE IMPARTIALLY AND DILIGENTLY

A. Judicial Duties in General.

The judicial duties of a judge take precedence over all the judge's other activities. The judge's judicial duties include all the duties of the judge's office prescribed by law.* In the performance of these duties, the following standards apply.

B. Adjudicative Responsibilities.

(1) A judge shall hear and decide matters assigned to the judge except those in which disqualification is required.

(2) A judge shall be faithful to the law* and maintain professional competence in it. A judge shall not be swayed by partisan interests, public clamor or fear of criticism.

(3) A judge shall require* order and decorum in proceedings before the judge.

(4) A judge shall be patient, dignified and courteous to litigants, jurors, witnesses, lawyers and others with whom the judge deals in an official capacity, and shall require* similar conduct of lawyers, and of staff, court officials and others subject to the judge's direction and control.

Commentary

The duty to hear all proceedings fairly and with patience is not inconsistent with the duty to dispose promptly of the business of the court. Judges can be efficient and businesslike while being patient and deliberate.

*Asterisked terms are defined in the Terminology Section. — EDS.

(5) A judge shall perform judicial duties without bias or prejudice. A judge shall not, in the performance of judicial duties, by words or conduct manifest bias or prejudice, including but not limited to bias or prejudice based upon race, sex, religion, national origin, disability, age, sexual orientation or socioeconomic status, and shall not permit staff, court officials and others subject to the judge's direction and control to do so.

Commentary

A judge must refrain from speech, gestures or other conduct that could reasonably be perceived as sexual harassment and must require the same standard of conduct of others subject to the judge's direction and control.

A judge must perform judicial duties impartially and fairly. A judge who manifests bias on any basis in a proceeding impairs the fairness of the proceeding and brings the judiciary into disrepute. Facial expression and body language, in addition to oral communication, can give to parties or lawyers in the proceeding, jurors, the media and others an appearance of judicial bias. A judge must be alert to avoid behavior that may be perceived as prejudicial.

(6) A judge shall require* lawyers in proceedings before the judge to refrain from manifesting, by words or conduct, bias or prejudice based upon race, sex, religion, national origin, disability, age, sexual orientation or socioeconomic status, against parties, witnesses, counsel or others. This Section 3B(6) does not preclude legitimate advocacy when race, sex, religion, national origin, disability, age, sexual orientation or socioeconomic status, or other similar factors, are issues in the proceeding.

(7) A judge shall accord to every person who has a legal interest in a proceeding, or that person's lawyer, the right to be heard according to law.* A judge shall not initiate, permit, or consider ex parte communications, or consider other communications made to the judge outside the presence of the parties concerning a pending or impending proceeding except that:

(a) Where circumstances require, ex parte communications for scheduling, administrative purposes or emergencies that do not deal with substantive matters or issues on the merits are authorized; provided:

(i) the judge reasonably believes that no party will gain a procedural or tactical advantage as a result of the ex parte communication, and

*Asterisked terms are defined in the Terminology Section. — EDS.

(ii) the judge makes provision promptly to notify all other parties of the substance of the ex parte communication and allows an opportunity to respond.

(b) A judge may obtain the advice of a disinterested expert on the law* applicable to a proceeding before the judge if the judge gives notice to the parties of the person consulted and the substance of the advice, and affords the parties reasonable opportunity to respond.

(c) A judge may consult with court personnel* whose function is to aid the judge in carrying out the judge's adjudicative responsibilities or with other judges.

(d) A judge may, with the consent of the parties, confer separately with the parties and their lawyers in an effort to mediate or settle matters pending before the judge.

(e) A judge may initiate or consider any ex parte communications when expressly authorized by law* to do so.

Commentary

The proscription against communications concerning a proceeding includes communications from lawyers, law teachers, and other persons who are not participants in the proceeding, except to the limited extent permitted.

To the extent reasonably possible, all parties or their lawyers shall be included in communications with a judge.

Whenever presence of a party or notice to a party is required by Section 3B(7), it is the party's lawyer, or if the party is unrepresented the party, who is to be present or to whom notice is to be given.

An appropriate and often desirable procedure for a court to obtain the advice of a disinterested expert on legal issues is to invite the expert to file a brief *amicus curiae.*

Certain ex parte communication is approved by Section 3B(7) to facilitate scheduling and other administrative purposes and to accommodate emergencies. In general, however, a judge must discourage ex parte communication and allow it only if all the criteria stated in Section 3B(7) are clearly met. A judge must disclose to all parties all ex parte communications described in Sections 3B(7)(a) and 3B(7)(b) regarding a proceeding pending or impending before the judge.

A judge must not independently investigate facts in a case and must consider only the evidence presented.

A judge may request a party to submit proposed findings of fact and conclusions of law, so long as the other parties are apprised of the request and are given an opportunity to respond to the proposed findings and conclusions.

*Asterisked terms are defined in the Terminology Section. — EDS.

A judge must make reasonable efforts, including the provision of appropriate supervision, to ensure that Section 3B(7) is not violated through law clerks or other personnel on the judge's staff.

If communication between the trial judge and the appellate court with respect to a proceeding is permitted, a copy of any written communication or the substance of any oral communication should be provided to all parties.

(8) A judge shall dispose of all judicial matters promptly, efficiently and fairly.

Commentary

In disposing of matters promptly, efficiently and fairly, a judge must demonstrate due regard for the rights of the parties to be heard and to have issues resolved without unnecessary cost or delay. Containing costs while preserving fundamental rights of parties also protects the interests of witnesses and the general public. A judge should monitor and supervise cases so as to reduce or eliminate dilatory practices, avoidable delays and unnecessary costs. A judge should encourage and seek to facilitate settlement, but parties should not feel coerced into surrendering the right to have their controversy resolved by the courts.

Prompt disposition of the court's business requires a judge to devote adequate time to judicial duties, to be punctual in attending court and expeditious in determining matters under submission, and to insist that court officials, litigants and their lawyers cooperate with the judge to that end.

(9) A judge shall not, while a proceeding is pending or impending in any court, make any public comment that might reasonably be expected to affect its outcome or impair its fairness or make any nonpublic comment that might substantially interfere with a fair trial or hearing. The judge shall require* similar abstention on the part of court personnel* subject to the judge's direction and control. This Section does not prohibit judges from making public statements in the course of their official duties or from explaining for public information the procedures of the court. This Section does not apply to proceedings in which the judge is a litigant in a personal capacity.

Commentary

The requirement that judges abstain from public comment regarding a pending or impending proceeding continues during any appellate process and

*Asterisked terms are defined in the Terminology Section. — EDS.

until final disposition. This Section does not prohibit a judge from commenting on proceedings in which the judge is a litigant in a personal capacity, but in cases such as a writ of mandamus where the judge is a litigant in an official capacity, the judge must not comment publicly. The conduct of lawyers relating to trial publicity is governed by [Rule 3.6 of the ABA Model Rules of Professional Conduct]. (Each jurisdiction should substitute an appropriate reference to its rule.)

(10) A judge shall not commend or criticize jurors for their verdict other than in a court order or opinion in a proceeding, but may express appreciation to jurors for their service to the judicial system and the community.

Commentary

Commending or criticizing jurors for their verdict may imply a judicial expectation in future cases and may impair a juror's ability to be fair and impartial in a subsequent case.

(11) A judge shall not disclose or use, for any purpose unrelated to judicial duties, nonpublic information* acquired in a judicial capacity.

C. Administrative Responsibilities.

(1) A judge shall diligently discharge the judge's administrative responsibilities without bias or prejudice and maintain professional competence in judicial administration, and should cooperate with other judges and court officials in the administration of court business.

(2) A judge shall require* staff, court officials and others subject to the judge's direction and control to observe the standards of fidelity and diligence that apply to the judge and to refrain from manifesting bias or prejudice in the performance of their official duties.

(3) A judge with supervisory authority for the judicial performance of other judges shall take reasonable measures to assure the prompt disposition of matters before them and the proper performance of their other judicial responsibilities.

(4) A judge shall not make unnecessary appointments. A judge shall exercise the power of appointment impartially and on the basis of merit. A judge shall avoid nepotism and favoritism. A judge shall not

---

*Asterisked terms are defined in the Terminology Section. — EDS.

approve compensation of appointees beyond the fair value of services rendered.

Commentary

Appointees of a judge include assigned counsel, officials such as referees, commissioners, special masters, receivers and guardians and personnel such as clerks, secretaries and bailiffs. Consent by the parties to an appointment or an award of compensation does not relieve the judge of the obligation prescribed by Section 3C(4).

D. Disciplinary Responsibilities.

(1) A judge who receives information indicating a substantial likelihood that another judge has committed a violation of this Code should take appropriate action. A judge having knowledge* that another judge has committed a violation of this Code that raises a substantial question as to the other judge's fitness for office shall inform the appropriate authority.*

(2) A judge who receives information indicating a substantial likelihood that a lawyer has committed a violation of the Rules of Professional Conduct [substitute correct title if the applicable rules of lawyer conduct have a different title] should take appropriate action. A judge having knowledge* that a lawyer has committed a violation of the Rules of Professional Conduct [substitute correct title if the applicable rules of lawyer conduct have a different title] that raises a substantial question as to the lawyer's honesty, trustworthiness or fitness as a lawyer in other respects shall inform the appropriate authority.*

(3) Acts of a judge, in the discharge of disciplinary responsibilities, required or permitted by Sections 3D(1) and 3D(2) are part of a judge's judicial duties and shall be absolutely privileged, and no civil action predicated thereon may be instituted against the judge.

Commentary

Appropriate action may include direct communication with the judge or lawyer who has committed the violation, other direct action if available, and reporting the violation to the appropriate authority or other agency or body.

*Asterisked terms are defined in the Terminology Section. — EDS.

E. Disqualification.

(1) A judge shall disqualify himself or herself in a proceeding in which the judge's impartiality might reasonably be questioned, including but not limited to instances where:

Commentary

Under this rule, a judge is disqualified whenever the judge's impartiality might reasonably be questioned, regardless whether any of the specific rules in Section 3E(1) apply. For example, if a judge were in the process of negotiating for employment with a law firm, the judge would be disqualified from any matters in which that law firm appeared, unless the disqualification was waived by the parties after disclosure by the judge.

A judge should disclose on the record information that the judge believes the parties or their lawyers might consider relevant to the question of disqualification, even if the judge believes there is no real basis for disqualification.

By decisional law, the rule of necessity may override the rule of disqualification. For example, a judge might be required to participate in judicial review of a judicial salary statute, or might be the only judge available in a matter requiring immediate judicial action, such as a hearing on probable cause or a temporary restraining order. In the latter case, the judge must disclose on the record the basis for possible disqualification and use reasonable efforts to transfer the matter to another judge as soon as practicable.

(a) the judge has a personal bias or prejudice concerning a party or a party's lawyer, or personal knowledge* of disputed evidentiary facts concerning the proceeding;

(b) the judge served as a lawyer in the matter in controversy, or a lawyer with whom the judge previously practiced law served during such association as a lawyer concerning the matter, or the judge has been a material witness concerning it;

Commentary

A lawyer in a government agency does not ordinarily have an association with other lawyers employed by that agency within the meaning of Section 3E(1)(b); a judge formerly employed by a government agency, however, should

---

*Asterisked terms are defined in the Terminology Section. — EDS.

disqualify himself or herself in a proceeding if the judge's impartiality might reasonably be questioned because of such association.

(c) the judge knows* that he or she, individually or as a fiduciary, or the judge's spouse, parent or child wherever residing, or any other member of the judge's family residing in the judge's household,* has an economic interest* in the subject matter in controversy or in a party to the proceeding or has any other more than de minimis* interest that could be substantially affected by the proceeding;

(d) the judge or the judge's spouse, or a person within the third degree of relationship* to either of them, or the spouse of such a person:

(i) is a party to the proceeding, or an officer, director or trustee of a party;

(ii) is acting as a lawyer in the proceeding;

(iii) is known* by the judge to have a more than de minimis* interest that could be substantially affected by the proceeding;

(iv) is to the judge's knowledge* likely to be a material witness in the proceeding.

Commentary

The fact that a lawyer in a proceeding is affiliated with a law firm with which a relative of the judge is affiliated does not of itself disqualify the judge. Under appropriate circumstances, the fact that "the judge's impartiality might reasonably be questioned" under Section 3E(1), or that the relative is known by the judge to have an interest in the law firm that could be "substantially affected by the outcome of the proceeding" under Section 3E(1)(d)(iii) may require the judge's disqualification.

(2) A judge shall keep informed about the judge's personal and fiduciary* economic interests,* and make a reasonable effort to keep informed about the personal economic interests of the judge's spouse and minor children residing in the judge's household.

F. Remittal of Disqualification.

A judge disqualified by the terms of Section 3E may disclose on the record the basis of the judge's disqualification and may ask the parties

*Asterisked terms are defined in the Terminology Section. — EDS.

and their lawyers to consider, out of the presence of the judge, whether to waive disqualification. If following disclosure of any basis for disqualification other than personal bias or prejudice concerning a party, the parties and lawyers, without participation by the judge, all agree that the judge should not be disqualified, and the judge is then willing to participate, the judge may participate in the proceeding. The agreement shall be incorporated in the record of the proceeding.

Commentary

A remittal procedure provides the parties an opportunity to proceed without delay if they wish to waive the disqualification. To assure that consideration of the question of remittal is made independently of the judge, a judge must not solicit, seek or hear comment on possible remittal or waiver of the disqualification unless the lawyers jointly propose remittal after consultation as provided in the rule. A party may act through counsel if counsel represents on the record that the party has been consulted and consents. As a practical matter, a judge may wish to have all parties and their lawyers sign the remittal agreement.

Editors' Note. In an unusual press release, seven Justices of the Supreme Court on November 1, 1993, issued the following announcement, entitled Statement of Recusal Policy. The Statement was signed by Chief Justice Rehnquist and Justices Stevens, Scalia, Thomas, O'Connor, Kennedy, and Ginsburg. Justices Blackmun and Souter did not sign.

STATEMENT OF RECUSAL POLICY

We have spouses, children or other relatives within the degree of relationship covered by 28 U.S.C. §455 who are or may become practicing attorneys. In connection with a case four Terms ago, the Chief Justice announced his policy (with which we are all in accord) regarding recusal when a covered relative is "an associate in the law firm representing one of the parties before this Court" but has "not participated in the case before the Court or at previous stages of the litigation." [The letter conclued that recusal was not required.] We think it desirable to set forth what our recusal policy will be in additional situations — specifically, when the covered lawyer HAS participated in the case at an earlier stage of the litigation, or when the covered lawyer is a *partner* in a firm appearing before us. Determining and announcing our policy in advance will make it evident that future decisions to recuse or not to recuse are unaffected by irrelevant circumstances of the particular case, and will provide needed guidance to our relatives and the firms to which they belong.

The provision of the recusal statute that deals specifically with a relative's involvement as a lawyer in the case requires recusal only when the covered relative "[i]s acting as a lawyer in the proceeding." §455(b)(5)(ii). It is well established that this provision requires personal participation in the representation, and not just membership in the representing firm, see, e.g., Potashnick v. Port City Constr. Co., 609 F.2d 1101, 1113 (CA5), *cert. denied,* 449 U.S. 820 (1980). It is also apparent, from use of the present tense, that current participation as a lawyer, and not merely past involvement in earlier stages of the litigation, is required.

A relative's partnership status, or participation in earlier stages of the litigation, is relevant, therefore, only under one of two less specific provisions of §455, which require recusal when the judge knows that the relative has "an interest that could be substantially affected by the outcome of the proceeding," §455(b)(5)(iii), or when for any reason the judge's "impartiality might reasonably be questioned," §455(a). We think that a relative's partnership in the firm appearing before us, or his or her previous work as a lawyer on a case that later comes before us, does not *automatically* trigger these provisions. If that were the intent of the law, the per se "lawyer-related recusal" requirement of §455(b)(5)(ii) would have expressed it. Per se recusal for a relative's membership in the partnership appearing here, or for a relative's work on the case below, would render the limitation of §455(b)(5)(ii) to *personal* work, and to *present* representation, meaningless.

We do not think it would serve the public interest to go beyond the requirements of the statute, and to recuse ourselves, out of an excess of caution, whenever a relative is a partner in the firm before us or acted as a lawyer at an earlier stage. Even one unnecessary recusal impairs the functioning of the Court. Given the size and number of today's national law firms, and the frequent appearance before us of many of them in a single case, recusal might become a common occurrence, and opportunities would be multiplied for "strategizing" recusals, that is, selecting law firms with an eye to producing the recusal of particular Justices. In this Court, where the absence of one Justice cannot be made up by another, needless recusal deprives litigants of the nine Justices to which they are entitled, produces the possibility of an even division on the merits of the case, and has a distorting effect upon the certiorari process, requiring the petitioner to obtain (under our current practice) four votes out of eight instead of four out of nine.

Absent some special factor, therefore, we will not recuse ourselves by reason of a relative's participation as a lawyer in earlier stages of the case. One such special factor, perhaps the most common, would be the relative's functioning as lead counsel below, so that the litigation is in effect "his" or "her" case and its outcome even at a later stage might reasonably be thought capable of substantially enhancing or damaging his or her professional reputation. We shall recuse ourselves whenever, to our knowledge, a relative has been lead counsel below.

Another special factor, of course, would be the fact that the amount of the relative's compensation could be substantially affected by the outcome here. That would require our recusal even if the relative had not worked on the case, but was merely a partner in the firm that shared the profits. It seems to us that in virtually every case before us with retained counsel there exists a genuine possibility that success or failure will affect the amount of the fee, and hence a genuine possibility that the outcome will have a substantial effect upon each partner's compensation. Since it is impractical to assure ourselves of the absence of such consequences in each individual case, we shall recuse ourselves from all cases in which appearances on behalf of parties are made by firms in which our relatives are partners, unless we have received from the firm written assurance that income from Supreme Court litigation is, on a permanent basis, excluded from our relatives' partnership shares.

CANON 4. A JUDGE SHALL SO CONDUCT THE JUDGE'S EXTRA-JUDICIAL ACTIVITIES AS TO MINIMIZE THE RISK OF CONFLICT WITH JUDICIAL OBLIGATIONS

A. Extra-Judicial Activities in General.

A judge shall conduct all of the judge's extra-judicial activities so that they do not:

(1) cast reasonable doubt on the judge's capacity to act impartially as a judge;

(2) demean the judicial office; or

(3) interfere with the proper performance of judicial duties.

Commentary

Complete separation of a judge from extra-judicial activities is neither possible nor wise; a judge should not become isolated from the community in which the judge lives.

Expressions of bias or prejudice by a judge, even outside the judge's judicial activities, may cast reasonable doubt on the judge's capacity to act impartially as a judge. Expressions which may do so include jokes or other remarks demeaning individuals on the basis of their race, sex, religion, national origin, disability, age, sexual orientation or socioeconomic status. See Section 2C and accompanying Commentary.

B. Avocational Activities.

A judge may speak, write, lecture, teach and participate in other extrajudicial activities concerning the law,* the legal system, the administration of justice and non-legal subjects, subject to the requirements of this Code.

Commentary

As a judicial officer and person specially learned in the law, a judge is in a unique position to contribute to the improvement of the law, the legal system,

*Asterisked terms are defined in the Terminology Section. — EDS.

and the administration of justice, including revision of substantive and procedural law and improvement of criminal and juvenile justice. To the extent that time permits, a judge is encouraged to do so, either independently or through a bar association, judicial conference or other organization dedicated to the improvement of the law. Judges may participate in efforts to promote the fair administration of justice, the independence of the judiciary and the integrity of the legal profession and may express opposition to the persecution of lawyers and judges in other countries because of their professional activities.

In this and other Sections of Canon 4, the phrase "subject to the requirements of this Code" is used, notably in connection with a judge's governmental, civic or charitable activities. This phrase is included to remind judges that the use of permissive language in various Sections of the Code does not relieve a judge from the other requirements of the Code that apply to the specific conduct.

C. Governmental, Civic or Charitable Activities.

(1) A judge shall not appear at a public hearing before, or otherwise consult with, an executive or legislative body or official except on matters concerning the law,* the legal system or the administration of justice or except when acting pro se in a matter involving the judge or the judge's interests.

Commentary

See Section 2B regarding the obligation to avoid improper influence.

(2) A judge shall not accept appointment to a governmental committee or commission or other governmental position that is concerned with issues of fact or policy on matters other than the improvement of the law,* the legal system or the administration of justice. A judge may, however, represent a country, state or locality on ceremonial occasions or in connection with historical, educational or cultural activities.

Commentary

Section 4C(2) prohibits a judge from accepting any governmental position except one relating to the law, legal system or administration of justice as authorized by Section 4C(3). The appropriateness of accepting extra-judicial assignments must be assessed in light of the demands on judicial resources created by

*Asterisked terms are defined in the Terminology Section. — EDS.

crowded dockets and the need to protect the courts from involvement in extra-judicial matters that may prove to be controversial. Judges should not accept governmental appointments that are likely to interfere with the effectiveness and independence of the judiciary.

Section 4C(2) does not govern a judge's service in a nongovernmental position. See Section 4C(3) permitting service by a judge with organizations devoted to the improvement of the law, the legal system or the administration of justice and with educational, religious, charitable, fraternal or civic organizations not conducted for profit. For example, service on the board of a public educational institution, unless it were a law school, would be prohibited under Section 4C(2), but service on the board of a public law school or any private educational institution would generally be permitted under Section 4C(3).

(3) A judge may serve as an officer, director, trustee or non-legal advisor of an organization or governmental agency devoted to the improvement of the law,* the legal system or the administration of justice or of an educational, religious, charitable, fraternal or civic organization not conducted for profit, subject to the following limitations and the other requirements of this Code.

Commentary

Section 4C(3) does not apply to a judge's service in a governmental position unconnected with the improvement of the law, the legal system or the administration of justice; see Section 4C(2).

See Commentary to Section 4B regarding use of the phrase "subject to the following limitations and the other requirements of this Code." As an example of the meaning of the phrase, a judge permitted by Section 4C(3) to serve on the board of a fraternal institution may be prohibited from such service by Sections 2C or 4A if the institution practices invidious discrimination or if service on the board otherwise casts reasonable doubt on the judge's capacity to act impartially as a judge.

Service by a judge on behalf of a civic or charitable organization may be governed by other provisions of Canon 4 in addition to Section 4C. For example, a judge is prohibited by Section 4G from serving as a legal advisor to a civic or charitable organization.

(a) A judge shall not serve as an officer, director, trustee or non-legal advisor if it is likely that the organization
(i) will be engaged in proceedings that would ordinarily come before the judge, or

*Asterisked terms are defined in the Terminology Section. — EDS.

(ii) will be engaged frequently in adversary proceedings in the court of which the judge is a member or in any court subject to the appellate jurisdiction of the court of which the judge is a member.

Commentary

The changing nature of some organizations and of their relationship to the law makes it necessary for a judge regularly to reexamine the activities of each organization with which the judge is affiliated to determine if it is proper for the judge to continue the affiliation. For example, in many jurisdictions charitable hospitals are now more frequently in court than in the past. Similarly, the boards of some legal aid organizations now make policy decisions that may have political significance or imply commitment to causes that may come before the courts for adjudication.

(b) A judge as an officer, director, trustee or non-legal advisor, or as a member or otherwise:

(i) may assist such an organization in planning fund-raising and may participate in the management and investment of the organization's funds, but shall not personally participate in the solicitation of funds or other fund-raising activities, except that a judge may solicit funds from other judges over whom the judge does not exercise supervisory or appellate authority;

(ii) may make recommendations to public and private fund-granting organizations on projects and programs concerning the law,* the legal system or the administration of justice;

(iii) shall not personally participate in membership solicitation if the solicitation might reasonably be perceived as coercive or, except as permitted in Section 4C(3)(b)(i), if the membership solicitation is essentially a fund-raising mechanism;

(iv) shall not use or permit the use of the prestige of judicial office for fund-raising or membership solicitation.

Commentary

A judge may solicit membership or endorse or encourage membership efforts for an organization devoted to the improvement of the law, the legal system or the administration of justice or a nonprofit educational, religious, charitable, fraternal or civic organization as long as the solicitation cannot rea-

*Asterisked terms are defined in the Terminology Section. — EDS.

sonably be perceived as coercive and is not essentially a fund-raising mechanism. Solicitation of funds for an organization and solicitation of memberships similarly involve the danger that the person solicited will feel obligated to respond favorably to the solicitor if the solicitor is in a position of influence or control. A judge must not engage in direct, individual solicitation of funds or memberships in person, in writing or by telephone except in the following cases: 1) a judge may solicit for funds or memberships other judges over whom the judge does not exercise supervisory or appellate authority, 2) a judge may solicit other persons for membership in the organizations described above if neither those persons nor persons with whom they are affiliated are likely ever to appear before the court on which the judge serves and 3) a judge who is an officer of such an organization may send a general membership solicitation mailing over the judge's signature.

Use of an organization letterhead for fund-raising or membership solicitation does not violate Section 4C(3)(b) provided the letterhead lists only the judge's name and office or other position in the organization, and, if comparable designations are listed for other persons, the judge's judicial designation. In addition, a judge must also make reasonable efforts to ensure that the judge's staff, court officials and others subject to the judge's direction and control do not solicit funds on the judge's behalf for any purpose, charitable or otherwise.

A judge must not be a speaker or guest of honor at an organization's fund-raising event, but mere attendance at such an event is permissible if otherwise consistent with this Code.

D. Financial Activities.

(1) A judge shall not engage in financial and business dealings that:
(a) may reasonably be perceived to exploit the judge's judicial position, or
(b) involve the judge in frequent transactions or continuing business relationships with those lawyers or other persons likely to come before the court on which the judge serves.

Commentary

The Time for Compliance provision of this Code (Application, Section F) postpones the time for compliance with certain provisions of this Section in some cases.

When a judge acquires in a judicial capacity information, such as material contained in filings with the court, that is not yet generally known, the judge must not use the information for private gain. See Section 2B; see also Section 3B(11).

A judge must avoid financial and business dealings that involve the judge in frequent transactions or continuing business relationships with persons likely to come either before the judge personally or before other judges in the judge's court. In addition, a judge should discourage members of the judge's family from engaging in dealings that would reasonably appear to exploit the judge's judicial position. This rule is necessary to avoid creating an appearance of exploitation of office or favoritism and to minimize the potential for disqualification. With respect to affiliation of relatives of judges with law firms appearing before the judge, see Commentary to Section 3E(1) relating to disqualification.

Participation by a judge in financial and business dealings is subject to the general prohibitions in Section 4A against activities that tend to reflect adversely on impartiality, demean the judicial office, or interfere with the proper performance of judicial duties. Such participation is also subject to the general prohibition in Canon 2 against activities involving impropriety or the appearance of impropriety and the prohibition in Section 2B against the misuse of the prestige of judicial office. In addition, a judge must maintain high standards of conduct in all of the judge's activities, as set forth in Canon 1. See Commentary for Section 4B regarding use of the phrase "subject to the requirements of this Code."

(2) A judge may, subject to the requirements of this Code, hold and manage investments of the judge and members of the judge's family,* including real estate, and engage in other remunerative activity.

Commentary

This Section provides that, subject to the requirements of this Code, a judge may hold and manage investments owned solely by the judge, investments owned solely by a member or members of the judge's family, and investments owned jointly by the judge and members of the judge's family.

(3) A judge shall not serve as an officer, director, manager, general partner, advisor or employee of any business entity except that a judge may, subject to the requirements of this Code, manage and participate in:

(a) a business closely held by the judge or members of the judge's family,* or

(b) a business entity primarily engaged in investment of the financial resources of the judge or members of the judge's family.

*Asterisked terms are defined in the Terminology Section. — EDS.

Commentary

Subject to the requirements of this Code, a judge may participate in a business that is closely held either by the judge alone, by members of the judge's family, or by the judge and members of the judge's family.

Although participation by a judge in a closely-held family business might otherwise be permitted by Section 4D(3), a judge may be prohibited from participation by other provisions of this Code when, for example, the business entity frequently appears before the judge's court or the participation requires significant time away from judicial duties. Similarly, a judge must avoid participating in a closely-held family business if the judge's participation would involve misuse of the prestige of judicial office.

(4) A judge shall manage the judge's investments and other financial interests to minimize the number of cases in which the judge is disqualified. As soon as the judge can do so without serious financial detriment, the judge shall divest himself or herself of investments and other financial interests that might require frequent disqualification.

(5) A judge shall not accept, and shall urge members of the judge's family residing in the judge's household* not to accept, a gift, bequest, favor or loan from anyone except for:

Commentary

Section 4D(5) does not apply to contributions to a judge's campaign for judicial office, a matter governed by Canon 5.

Because a gift, bequest, favor or loan to a member of the judge's family residing in the judge's household might be viewed as intended to influence the judge, a judge must inform those family members of the relevant ethical constraints upon the judge in this regard and discourage those family members from violating them. A judge cannot, however, reasonably be expected to know or control all of the financial or business activities of all family members residing in the judge's household.

(a) a gift incident to a public testimonial, books, tapes and other resource materials supplied by publishers on a complimentary basis for official use, or an invitation to the judge and the judge's spouse or guest to attend a bar-related function or an activity devoted to the improvement of the law,* the legal system or the administration of justice;

*Asterisked terms are defined in the Terminology Section. — EDS.

Commentary

Acceptance of an invitation to a law-related function is governed by Section 4D(5)(a); aceptance of an invitation paid for by an individual lawyer or group of lawyers is governed by Section 4D(5)(h).

A judge may accept a public testimonial or a gift incident thereto only if the donor organization is not an organization whose members comprise or frequently represent the same side in litigation, and the testimonial and gift are otherwise in compliance with other provisions of this Code. See Sections 4A(1) and 2B.

(b) a gift, award or benefit incident to the business, profession or other separate activity of a spouse or other family member of a judge residing in the judge's household, including gifts, awards and benefits for the use of both the spouse or other family member and the judge (as spouse or family member), provided the gift, award or benefit could not reasonably be perceived as intended to influence the judge in the performance of judicial duties;

(c) ordinary social hospitality;

(d) a gift from a relative or friend, for a special occasion, such as a wedding, anniversary or birthday, if the gift is fairly commensurate with the occasion and the relationship;

Commentary

A gift to a judge, or to a member of the judge's family living in the judge's household, that is excessive in value raises questions about the judge's impartiality and the integrity of the judicial office and might require disqualification of the judge where disqualification would not otherwise be required. See, however, Section 4D(5)(e).

(e) a gift, bequest, favor or loan from a relative or close personal friend whose appearance or interest in a case would in any event require disqualification under Section 3E;

(f) a loan from a lending institution in its regular course of business on the same terms generally available to persons who are not judges;

(g) a scholarship or fellowship awarded on the same terms and based on the same criteria applied to other applicants; or

(h) any other gift, bequest, favor or loan, only if: the donor is not a party or other person who has come or is likely to come or whose interests have come or are likely to come before the judge; and, if its value exceeds $150.00, the judge reports it in the same manner as the judge reports compensation in Section 4H.

Commentary

Section 4D(5)(h) prohibits judges from accepting gifts, favors, bequests or loans from lawyers or their firms if they have come or are likely to come before the judge; it also prohibits gifts, favors, bequests or loans from clients of lawyers or their firms when the clients' interests have come or are likely to come before the judge.

E. Fiduciary Activities.

(1) A judge shall not serve as executor, administrator or other personal representative, trustee, guardian, attorney in fact or other fiduciary,* except for the estate, trust or person of a member of the judge's family,* and then only if such service will not interfere with the proper performance of judicial duties.

(2) A judge shall not serve as a fiduciary* if it is likely that the judge as a fiduciary will be engaged in proceedings that would ordinarily come before the judge, or if the estate, trust or ward becomes involved in adversary proceedings in the court on which the judge serves or one under its appellate jurisdiction.

(3) The same restrictions on financial activities that apply to a judge personally also apply to the judge while acting in a fiduciary* capacity.

Commentary

The Time for Compliance provision of this Code (Application, Section F) postpones the time for compliance with certain provisions of this Section in some cases.

The restrictions imposed by this Canon may conflict with the judge's obligation as a fiduciary. For example, a judge should resign as trustee if detriment to the trust would result from divestiture of holdings the retention of which would place the judge in violation of Section 4D(4).

F. Service as Arbitrator or Mediator.

A judge shall not act as an arbitrator or mediator or otherwise perform judicial functions in a private capacity unless expressly authorized by law.*

*Asterisked terms are defined in the Terminology Section. — EDS.

Commentary

Section 4F does not prohibit a judge from participating in arbitration, mediation or settlement conferences performed as part of judicial duties.

G. Practice of Law.

A judge shall not practice law. Notwithstanding this prohibition, a judge may act pro se and may, without compensation, give legal advice to and draft or review documents for a member of the judge's family.*

Commentary

This prohibition refers to the practice of law in a representative capacity and not in a pro se capacity. A judge may act for himself or herself in all legal matters, including matters involving litigation and matters involving appearances before or other dealings with legislative and other governmental bodies. However, in so doing, a judge must not abuse the prestige of office to advance the interests of the judge or the judge's family. See Section 2(B).

The Code allows a judge to give legal advice to and draft legal documents for members of the judge's family, so long as the judge receives no compensation. A judge must not, however, act as an advocate or negotiator for a member of the judge's family in a legal matter.

Canon 6, new in the 1972 Code, reflected concerns about conflicts of interest and appearances of impropriety arising from compensation for off-the-bench activities. Since 1972, however, reporting requirements that are much more comprehensive with respect to what must be reported and with whom reports must be filed have been adopted by many jurisdictions. The Committee believes that although reports of compensation for extra-judicial activities should be required, reporting requirements preferably should be developed to suit the respective jurisdictions, not simply adopted as set forth in a national model code of judicial conduct. Because of the Committee's concern that deletion of this Canon might lead to the misconception that reporting compensation for extra-judicial activities is no longer important, the substance of Canon 6 is carried forward as Section 4H in this Code for adoption in those jurisdictions that do not have other reporting requirements. In jurisdictions that have separately established reporting requirements, Section 4H(2) (Public Reporting) may be deleted and the caption for Section 4H modified appropriately.

*Asterisked terms are defined in the Terminology Section. — EDS.

H. Compensation, Reimbursement and Reporting.

(1) **Compensation and Reimbursement.** A judge may receive compensation and reimbursement of expenses for the extra-judicial activities permitted by this Code, if the source of such payments does not give the appearance of influencing the judge's performance of judicial duties or otherwise give the appearance of impropriety.

(a) **Compensation** shall not exceed a reasonable amount nor shall it exceed what a person who is not a judge would receive for the same activity.

(b) **Expense reimbursement** shall be limited to the actual cost of travel, food and lodging reasonably incurred by the judge and, where appropriate to the occasion, by the judge's spouse or guest. Any payment in excess of such an amount is compensation.

(2) **Public Reports.** A judge shall report the date, place and nature of any activity for which the judge received compensation, and the name of the payor and the amount of compensation so received. Compensation or income of a spouse attributed to the judge by operation of a community property law is not extra-judicial compensation to the judge. The judge's report shall be made at least annually and shall be filed as a public document in the office of the clerk of the court on which the judge serves or other office designated by law.*

Commentary

See Section 4D(5) regarding reporting of gifts, bequests and loans.

The Code does not prohibit a judge from accepting honoraria or speaking fees provided that the compensation is reasonable and commensurate with the task performed. A judge should ensure, however, that no conflicts are created by the arrangement. A judge must not appear to trade on the judicial position for personal advantage. Nor should a judge spend significant time away from court duties to meet speaking or writing commitments for compensation. In addition, the source of the payment must not raise any question of undue influence or the judge's ability or willingness to be impartial.

I. [Disclosure of Judge's Assets]

Disclosure of a judge's income, debts, investments or other assets is required only to the extent provided in this Canon and in Sections 3E and 3F, or as otherwise required by law.*

*Asterisked terms are defined in the Terminology Section. — EDS.

Commentary

Section 3E requires a judge to disqualify himself or herself in any proceeding in which the judge has an economic interest. See "economic interest" as explained in the Terminology Section. Section 4D requires a judge to refrain from engaging in business and from financial activities that might interfere with the impartial performance of judicial duties; Section 4H requires a judge to report all compensation the judge received for activities outside judicial office. A judge has the rights of any other citizen, including the right to privacy of the judge's financial affairs, except to the extent that limitations established by law are required to safeguard the proper performance of the judge's duties.

CANON 5. A JUDGE OR JUDICIAL CANDIDATE SHALL REFRAIN FROM INAPPROPRIATE POLITICAL ACTIVITY[2]

A. All Judges and Candidates.

(1) Except as authorized in Sections 5B(2), 5C(1) and 5C(3), a judge or a candidate* for election or appointment to judicial office shall not:

2. Introductory Note to Canon 5: There is wide variation in the methods of judicial selection used, both among jurisdictions and within the jurisdictions themselves. In a given state, judges may be selected by one method initially, retained by a different method, and selected by still another method to fill interim vacancies.

According to figures compiled in 1987 by the National Center for State Courts, 32 states and the District of Columbia use a merit selection method (in which an executive such as a governor appoints a judge from a group of nominees selected by a judicial nominating commission) to select judges in the state either initially or to fill an interim vacancy. Of those 33 jurisdictions, a merit selection method is used in 18 jurisdictions to choose judges of courts of last resort, in 13 jurisdictions to choose judges of intermediate appellate courts, in 12 jurisdictions to choose judges of general jurisdiction courts and in 5 jurisdictions to choose judges of limited jurisdiction courts.

Methods of judicial selection other than merit selection include nonpartisan election (10 states use it for initial selection at all court levels, another 10 states use it for initial selection for at least one court level) and partisan election (8 states use it for initial selection at all court levels, another 7 states use it for initial selection for at least one level). In a small minority of the states, judicial selection methods include executive or legislative appointment (without nomination of a group of potential appointees by a judicial nominating commission) and court selection. In addition, the federal judicial system utilizes an executive appointment method. See State Court Organization 1987 (National Center for State Courts, 1988).

*Asterisked terms are defined in the Terminology Section. — EDS.

(a) act as a leader or hold an office in a political organization;*

(b) publicly endorse or publicly oppose another candidate for public office;

(c) make speeches on behalf of a political organization;

(d) attend political gatherings; or

(e) solicit funds for, pay an assessment to or make a contribution to a political organization or candidate, or purchase tickets for political party dinners or other functions.

Commentary

A judge or candidate for judicial office retains the right to participate in the political process as a voter.

Where false information concerning a judicial candidate is made public, a judge or another judicial candidate having knowledge of the facts is not prohibited by Section 5A(1) from making the facts public.

Section 5A(1)(a) does not prohibit a candidate for elective judicial office from retaining during candidacy a public office such as county prosecutor, which is not "an office in a political organization."

Section 5A(1)(b) does not prohibit a judge or judicial candidate from privately expressing his or her views on judicial candidates or other candidates for public office.

A candidate does not publicly endorse another candidate for public office by having that candidate's name on the same ticket.

(2) A judge shall resign from judicial office upon becoming a candidate* for a non-judicial office either in a primary or in a general election, except that the judge may continue to hold judicial office while being a candidate for election to or serving as a delegate in a state constitutional convention if the judge is otherwise permitted by law* to do so.

(3) A candidate* for a judicial office:

(a) shall maintain the dignity appropriate to judicial office and act in a manner consistent with the integrity and independence of the judiciary, and shall encourage members of the candidate's family* to adhere to the same standards of political conduct in support of the candidate as apply to the candidate;

*Asterisked terms are defined in the Terminology Section. — EDS.

Commentary

Although a judicial candidate must encourage members of his or her family to adhere to the same standards of political conduct in support of the candidate that apply to the candidate, family members are free to participate in other political activity.

(b) shall prohibit employees and officials who serve at the pleasure of the candidate,* and shall discourage other employees and officials subject to the candidate's direction and control from doing on the candidate's behalf what the candidate is prohibited from doing under the Sections of this Canon;

(c) except to the extent permitted by Section 5C(2), shall not authorize or knowingly* permit any other person to do for the candidate* what the candidate is prohibited from doing under the Sections of this Canon;

(d) shall not:

(i) make pledges or promises of conduct in office other than the faithful and impartial performance of the duties of the office;

(ii) make statements that commit or appear to commit the candidate with respect to cases, controversies or issues that are likely to come before the court; or

(iii) knowingly* misrepresent the identity, qualifications, present position or other fact concerning the candidate or an opponent;

Commentary

Section 5A(3)(d) prohibits a candidate for judicial office from making statements that appear to commit the candidate regarding cases, controversies or issues likely to come before the court. As a corollary, a candidate should emphasize in any public statement the candidate's duty to uphold the law regardless of his or her personal views. See also Section 3B(9), the general rule on public comment by judges. Section 5A(3)(d) does not prohibit a candidate from making pledges or promises respecting improvements in court administration. Nor does this Section prohibit an incumbent judge from making private statements to other judges or court personnel in the performance of judicial duties. This Section applies to any statement made in the process of securing judicial office, such as statements to commissions charged with judicial selection and tenure and legislative bodies confirming appointment. See also Rule 8.2 of the ABA Model Rules of Professional Conduct.

*Asterisked terms are defined in the Terminology Section. — EDS.

(e) may respond to personal attacks or attacks on the candidate's record as long as the response does not violate Section 5A(3)(d).

B. Candidates Seeking Appointment to Judicial or Other Governmental Office.

(1) A candidate* for appointment to judicial office or a judge seeking other governmental office shall not solicit or accept funds, personally or through a committee or otherwise, to support his or her candidacy.

(2) A candidate* for appointment to judicial office or a judge seeking other governmental office shall not engage in any political activity to secure the appointment except that:

(a) such persons may:

(i) communicate with the appointing authority, including any selection or nominating commission or other agency designated to screen candidates;

(ii) seek support or endorsement for the appointment from organizations that regularly make recommendations for reappointment or appointment to the office, and from individuals to the extent requested or required by those specified in Section 5B(2)(a); and

(iii) provide to those specified in Sections 5B(2)(a)(i) and 5B(2)(a)(ii) information as to his or her qualifications for the office;

(b) a non-judge candidate* for appointment to judicial office may, in addition, unless otherwise prohibited by law:*

(i) retain an office in a political organization,*

(ii) attend political gatherings, and

(iii) continue to pay ordinary assessments and ordinary contributions to a political organization or candidate and purchase tickets for political party dinners or other functions.

Commentary

Section 5B(2) provides a limited exception to the restrictions imposed by Sections 5A(1) and 5D. Under Section 5B(2), candidates seeking reappointment to the same judicial office or appointment to another judicial office or

---

*Asterisked terms are defined in the Terminology Section. — EDS.

other governmental office may apply for the appointment and seek appropriate support.

Although under Section 5B(2) non-judge candidates seeking appointment to judicial office are permitted during candidacy to retain office in a political organization, attend political gatherings and pay ordinary dues and assessments, they remain subject to other provisions of this Code during candidacy. See Sections 5B(1), 5B(2)(a), 5E and Application Section.

C. Judges and Candidates Subject to Public Election.

(1) A judge or a candidate* subject to public election* may, except as prohibited by law:*

    (a) at any time

        (i) purchase tickets for and attend political gatherings;

        (ii) identify himself or herself as a member of a political party; and

        (iii) contribute to a political organization;*

    (b) when a candidate for election

        (i) speak to gatherings on his or her own behalf;

        (ii) appear in newspaper, television and other media advertisements supporting his or her candidacy;

        (iii) distribute pamphlets and other promotional campaign literature supporting his or her candidacy; and

        (iv) publicly endorse or publicly oppose other candidates for the same judicial office in a public election in which the judge or judicial candidate is running.

Commentary

Section 5C(1) permits judges subject to election at any time to be involved in limited political activity. Section 5D, applicable solely to incumbent judges, would otherwise bar this activity.

(2) A candidate* shall not personally solicit or accept campaign contributions or personally solicit publicly stated support. A candidate may, however, establish committees of responsible persons to conduct campaigns for the candidate through media advertisements, brochures, mailings, candidate forums and other means not prohibited by law. Such

*Asterisked terms are defined in the Terminology Section. — EDS.

committees may solicit and accept reasonable campaign contributions, manage the expenditure of funds for the candidate's campaign and obtain public statements of support for his or her candidacy. Such com- mittees are not prohibited from soliciting and accepting reasonable campaign contributions and public support from lawyers. A candidate's committee may solicit contributions and public support for the candidate's campaign no earlier than [one year] before an election and no later than [90] days after the last election in which the candidate participates during the election year. A candidate shall not use or permit the use of campaign contributions for the private benefit of the candidate or others.

Editors' Note. At the ABA's 1997 Annual Meeting, the House of Delegates voted to amend the Commentary to Canon 5C(2). (The ABA did amend the text of Canon 5C(2).) The amendment was sponsored by the ABA's Standing Committee on Ethics and Professional Responsibility, which submitted a brief Report in support of the amendment. (Committee Reports do not represent official policy of the ABA. They are for information only, and the opinions are those of the authors of the report.)

The Committee Report noted that the ABA "strongly endorses merit selection of judges, as opposed to public election, in no small part because of the potential for conflicts of interest created by the solicitation and acceptance of significant amounts of money by committees established to manage judicial candidates' election campaigns." But the Report acknowledged that "the majority of judges are selected through the electoral process." The Report continued:

[A]lthough permissible from a legal standpoint, the fund-raising that accompanies judicial campaigns frequently gives rise to conflicts of interest that may reflect adversely upon the impartiality of the judiciary. . . .

The proposed amendment . . . suggests that election campaign contributions made by lawyers or others who appear before the judge may, by virtue of their size or source, raise questions about the judge's impartiality and be cause for disqualification.

We reprint the amended Commentary in legislative style, underscoring additions and striking out deletions.

Commentary

There is legitimate concern about a judge's impartiality when parties whose interests may come before a judge, or the lawyers who represent such parties, are known to have made contributions to the election campaigns of judicial candidates. This is among the reasons that merit selection of judges is a preferable manner in which to select the judiciary. Notwithstanding that preference, Section 5C(2) recognizes that in many jurisdictions judicial candidates must raise funds to support their candidacies for election to judicial office. It therefore ~~Section 5C(2)~~ permits a candidate, other than a candidate for appointment, to establish campaign committees to solicit and accept public support and reasonable financial contributions. ~~At the start of the campaign~~ In order to guard against the possibility that conflicts of interest will arise, the candidate must instruct his or her campaign committees at the start of the campaign to solicit or accept only contributions that are reasonable and appropriate under the circumstances. Though not prohibited, campaign contributions of which a judge has knowledge, made by lawyers or others who appear before the judge may, by virtue of their size or source, raise questions about a judge's impartiality and be cause for ~~relevant to~~ disqualification as provided under Section 3(E).

Campaign committees established under Section 5C(2) should manage campaign finances responsibly, avoiding deficits that might necessitate post-election fund-raising, to the extent possible. Such committees must at all times comply with applicable statutory provisions governing their conduct.

Section 5C(2) does not prohibit a candidate from initiating an evaluation by a judicial selection commission or bar association, or, subject to the requirements of this Code, from responding to a request for information from any organization.

(3) Except as prohibited by law,* a candidate* for judicial office in a public election* may permit the candidate's name: (a) to be listed on election materials along with the names of other candidates for elective public office, and (b) to appear in promotions of the ticket.

Commentary

Section 5C(3) provides a limited exception to the restrictions imposed by Section 5A(1).

D. Incumbent Judges.

A judge shall not engage in any political activity except (i) as authorized under any other Section of this Code, (ii) on behalf of measures to improve the law,* the legal system or the administration of justice, or (iii) as expressly authorized by law.

*Asterisked terms are defined in the Terminology Section. — EDS.

Commentary

Neither Section 5D nor any other section of the Code prohibits a judge in the exercise of administrative functions from engaging in planning and other official activities with members of the executive and legislative branches of government. With respect to a judge's activity on behalf of measures to improve the law, the legal system and the administration of justice, see Commentary to Section 4B and Section 4C(1) and its Commentary.

E. *Applicability.*

Canon 5 generally applies to all incumbent judges and judicial candidates.* A successful candidate, whether or not an incumbent, is subject to judicial discipline for his or her campaign conduct; an unsuccessful candidate who is a lawyer is subject to lawyer discipline for his or her campaign conduct. A lawyer who is a candidate for judicial office is subject to [Rule 8.2(b) of the ABA Model Rules of Professional Conduct]. (An adopting jurisdiction should substitute a reference to its applicable rule.)

APPLICATION OF THE CODE OF JUDICIAL CONDUCT

A. *[Definition of a Judge]*

Anyone, whether or not a lawyer, who is an officer of a judicial system[3] and who performs judicial functions, including an officer such as a magistrate, court commissioner, special master or referee, is a judge within the meaning of this Code. All judges shall comply with this Code except as provided below.

---

*Asterisked terms are defined in the Terminology Section. — EDS.

3. Applicability of this Code to administrative law judges should be determined by each adopting jurisdiction. Administrative law judges generally are affiliated with the executive branch of government rather than the judicial branch and each adopting jurisdiction should consider the unique characteristics of particular administrative law judge positions in adopting and adapting the Code for administrative law judges. See, e.g., Model Code of Judicial Conduct for Federal Administrative Law Judges, endorsed by the National Conference of Administrative Law Judges in February 1989.

Commentary

The four categories of judicial service in other than a full-time capacity are necessarily defined in general terms because of the widely varying forms of judicial service. For the purposes of this Section, as long as a retired judge is subject to recall the judge is considered to "perform judicial functions." The determination of which category and, accordingly, which specific Code provisions apply to an individual judicial officer, depend upon the facts of the particular judicial service.

B. Retired Judge Subject to Recall.

A retired judge subject to recall who by law is not permitted to practice law is not required to comply:
   (1) except while serving as a judge, with Section 4F; and
   (2) at any time with Section 4E.

C. Continuing Part-Time Judge.

A continuing part-time judge:*
   (1) is not required to comply
      (a) except while serving as a judge, with Section 3B(9); and
      (b) at any time with Sections 4C(2), 4D(3), 4E(1), 4F, 4G, 4H, 5A(1), 5B(2) and 5D.
   (2) shall not practice law in the court on which the judge serves or in any court subject to the appellate jurisdiction of the court on which the judge serves, and shall not act as a lawyer in a proceeding in which the judge has served as a judge or in any other proceeding related thereto.

Commentary

When a person who has been a continuing part-time judge is no longer a continuing part-time judge, including a retired judge no longer subject to recall, that person may act as a lawyer in a proceeding in which he or she has served as a judge or in any other proceeding related thereto only with the express consent of all parties pursuant to [Rule 1.12(a) of the ABA Model Rules of Professional Conduct]. (An adopting jurisdiction should substitute a reference to its applicable rule.)

*Asterisked terms are defined in the Terminology Section. — EDS.

D. *Periodic Part-Time Judge.*

A periodic part-time judge:*
(1) is not required to comply
    (a) except while serving as a judge, with Section 3B(9);
    (b) at any time, with Sections 4C(2), 4C(3)(a), 4D(1)(b), 4D(3), 4D(4), 4D(5), 4E, 4F, 4G, 4H, 5A(1), 5B(2) and 5D.
    (2) shall not practice law in the court on which the judge serves or in any court subject to the appellate jurisdiction of the court on which the judge serves, and shall not act as a lawyer in a proceeding in which the judge has served as a judge or in any other proceeding related thereto.

Commentary

When a person who has been a periodic part-time judge is no longer a periodic part-time judge (no longer accepts appointments), that person may act as a lawyer in a proceeding in which he or she has served as a judge or in any other proceeding related thereto only with the express consent of all parties pursuant to [Rule 1.12(a) of the ABA Model Rules of Professional Conduct]. (An adopting jurisdiction should substitute a reference to its applicable rule.)

E. *Pro Tempore Part-Time Judge.*

A pro tempore part-time judge:*
(1) is not required to comply
    (a) except while serving as a judge, with Sections 2A, 2B, 3B(9) and 4C(1);
    (b) at any time with Sections 2C, 4C(2), 4C(3)(a), 4C(3)(b), 4D(1)(b), 4D(3), 4D(4), 4D(5), 4E, 4F, 4G, 4H, 5A(1), 5A(2), 5B(2) and 5D.
    (2) A person who has been a pro tempore part-time judge* shall not act as a lawyer in a proceeding in which the judge has served as a judge or in any other proceeding related thereto except as otherwise permitted by [Rule 1.12(a) of the ABA Model Rules of Professional Conduct]. (An adopting jurisdiction should substitute a reference to its applicable rule.)

*Asterisked terms are defined in the Terminology Section. — EDS.

F. Time for Compliance.

A person to whom this Code becomes applicable shall comply immediately with all provisions of this Code except Sections 4D(2), 4D(3) and
4E and shall comply with these Sections as soon as reasonably possible
and shall do so in any event within the period of one year.

Commentary

If serving as a fiduciary when selected as judge, a new judge may, notwithstanding the prohibitions in Section 4E, continue to serve as fiduciary but only
for that period of time necessary to avoid serious adverse consequences to the
beneficiary of the fiduciary relationship and in no event longer than one year.
Similarly, if engaged at the time of judicial selection in a business activity, a new
judge may, notwithstanding the prohibitions in Section 4D(3), continue in that
activity for a reasonable period but in no event longer than one year.

APPENDIX. JUDICIAL ETHICS COMMITTEE

A. The [chief judge of the highest court of the jurisdiction] shall appoint a Judicial Ethics Committee consisting of [nine] members. [Five]
members shall be judges; [two] members shall be non-judge lawyers; and
[two] members shall be public members. Of the judicial members, one
member shall be appointed from each of [the highest court, the intermediate levels of courts, and the trial courts]. The remaining judicial
members shall be judges appointed from any of the above courts, but not
from the [highest court of the jurisdiction]. The [chief judge] shall designate one of the members as chairperson. Members shall serve three-
year terms; terms shall be staggered; and no individual shall serve for more
than two consecutive terms.

B. The Judicial Ethics Committee so established shall have authority
to:

(1) by the concurrence of a majority of its members, express its
opinion on proper judicial conduct with respect to the provisions of
[the code of judicial conduct adopted by the jurisdiction and any other
specified sections of law of the jurisdiction regarding the judiciary, such
as financial reporting requirements], either on its own initiative, at the
request of a judge or candidate for judicial office, or at the request of
a court or an agency charged with the administration of judicial disci-

pline in the jurisdiction, provided that an opinion may not be issued on a matter that is pending before a court or before such an agency except on request of the court or agency;

(2) make recommendations to [the highest court of the jurisdiction] for amendment of the Code of Judicial Conduct [of the jurisdiction]; and

(3) adopt rules relating to the procedures to be used in expressing opinions, including rules to assure a timely response to inquiries.

C. A judge or candidate for judicial office as defined in the Terminology Section of this Code who has requested and relied upon an opinion may not be disciplined for conduct conforming to that opinion.

D. An opinion issued pursuant to this rule shall be filed with [appropriate official of the judicial conference of the jurisdiction]. Such an opinion is confidential and not public information unless [the highest court of the jurisdiction] otherwise directs. However, the [appropriate official of the judicial conference of the jurisdiction] shall cause an edited version of each opinion to be prepared, in which the identity and geographic location of the person who has requested the opinion, the specific court involved, and the identity of other individuals, organizations or groups mentioned in the opinion are not disclosed. Opinions so edited shall be published periodically in the manner [the appropriate official of the judicial conference of the jurisdiction] deems proper.

Attorney-Client Privilege and
Work Product Provisions

Attorney-Client Privilege and Work Product Provisions

Editors' Introduction. The ethical obligation of confidentiality is closely related to the evidentiary rules governing the attorney-client privilege and the procedural rules protecting attorney work product. The materials in this chapter show how the attorney-client privilege and the work product doctrine are treated in the Federal Rules of Evidence, the Federal Rules of Civil Procedure, New York's Civil Practice Law and Rules, the California Evidence Code, and drafts of the American Law Institute's Restatement of the Law Governing Lawyers.

Contents

RESTATEMENT OF THE LAW GOVERNING LAWYERS
(PROPOSED FINAL DRAFT NO. 1):
ATTORNEY-CLIENT PRIVILEGE PROVISIONS

FEDERAL RULES OF EVIDENCE

Rule 501.　General Rule

Except as otherwise required by the Constitution of the United States or provided by Act of Congress or in rules prescribed by the Supreme Court pursuant to statutory authority, the privilege of a witness, person, government, State, or political subdivision thereof shall be governed by the principles of the common law as they may be interpreted by the courts of the United States in the light of reason and experience. However, in civil actions and proceedings, with respect to an element of a claim or defense as to which State law supplies the rule of decision, the privilege of a witness, person, government, State, or political subdivision thereof shall be determined in accordance with State law.

> **Editors' Note.** When the Supreme Court transmitted the proposed Federal Rules of Evidence to Congress in 1973, they contained thirteen separate proposed rules on privileges, including Rule 503 (defining the lawyer-client privilege) and Rules 511, 512, and 513 (governing waiver, compelled disclosure of privileged material, and comment in court about a claim of privilege). The privilege rules were extremely controversial, however, and Congress rejected all of the proposed privilege rules. (Rule 501 — the only privilege rule in the rules today — was substantially altered by Congress before its enactment.) We reprint Rule 503 here because, despite its rejection, it is an accurate general statement of the law in many jurisdictions and has been adopted nearly verbatim in the evidence codes of some states (see, e.g., Rule 503 of the Texas Rules of Criminal Evidence).

Proposed Rule 503. Lawyer-Client Privilege
(not enacted)

(a) Definitions. As used in this rule:

(1) A "client" is a person, public officer, or corporation, association, or other organization or entity, either public or private, who is rendered professional legal services by a lawyer, or who consults a lawyer with a view to obtaining professional legal services from him.

(2) A "lawyer" is a person authorized, or reasonably believed by the client to be authorized, to practice law in any state or nation.

(3) A "representative of the lawyer" is one employed to assist the lawyer in the rendition of professional legal services.

(4) A communication is "confidential" if not intended to be disclosed to third persons other than those to whom disclosure is in furtherance of the rendition of professional legal services to the client or those reasonably necessary for the transmission of the communication.

(b) General rule of privilege. A client has a privilege to refuse to disclose and to prevent any other person from disclosing confidential communications made for the purpose of facilitating the rendition of professional legal services to the client, (1) between himself or his representative and his lawyer or his lawyer's representative, or (2) between his lawyer and the lawyer's representative, or (3) by him or his lawyer to a lawyer representing another in a matter of common interest, or (4) between representatives of the client or between the client and a representative of the client, or (5) between lawyers representing the client.

(c) Who may claim the privilege? The privilege may be claimed by the client, his guardian or conservator, the personal representative of a deceased client, or the successor, trustee, or similar representative of a corporation, association, or other organization, whether or not in existence. The person who was the lawyer at the time of the communication may claim the privilege but only on behalf of the client. His authority to do so is presumed in the absence of evidence to the contrary.

(d) Exceptions. There is no privilege under this rule:

(1) *Furtherance of crime or fraud.* If the services of the lawyer were sought or obtained to enable or aid anyone to commit or plan to commit what the client knew or reasonably should have known to be a crime or fraud; or

(2) *Claimants through same deceased client.* As to a communication relevant to an issue between parties who claim through the same deceased client, regardless of whether the claims are by testate or intestate succession or by inter vivos transaction; or

(3) *Breach of duty by lawyer or client.* As to a communication relevant to an issue of breach of duty by the lawyer to his client or by the client to his lawyer; or

(4) *Document attested by lawyer.* As to a communication relevant to an issue concerning an attested document to which the lawyer is an attesting witness; or

(5) *Joint clients.* As to a communication relevant to a matter of common interest between two or more clients if the communication was made by any of them to a lawyer retained or consulted in common, when offered in an action between any of the clients.

FEDERAL RULES OF CIVIL PROCEDURE

Editors' Note. In federal courts, the work product doctrine is codified in Rules 26(b)(3)-(4) of the Federal Rules of Civil Procedure. These provisions were added to the rules by amendment in 1970 to resolve confusion and disagreement over the judicially created work product doctrine stemming from Hickman v. Taylor, 329 U.S. 495 (1947). Rule 26(b)(3) governs work product generally, including the mental opinions and impressions of lawyers, and Rule 26(b)(4) governs work product relating to experts. Effective December 1, 1993, Rule 26(b)(4) was extensively amended to the form reprinted here, but Rule 26(b)(3) was not amended at all. In addition, Rule 26(b)(5), governing claims of privilege or work product, was entirely new effective December 1, 1993; there was no comparable provision in the Federal Rules of Civil Procedure until then.

Readers should note that the Federal Rules of Criminal Procedure, in Rules 16(a)(2) and (b)(2), contain a kind of work product protection, but the criminal work product protection is subject to many exceptions, including Rule 26.2, which requires lawyers in criminal cases to turn over, upon request, any relevant statement made by a witness who has completed a direct examination at trial. We reprint all of Fed. R. Crim. P. 16 and 26.2 in our chapter on federal sanctions and discovery provisions.

Rule 26. General Provisions Governing Discovery; Duty of Disclosure

. . . **(b)(3)** *Trial Preparation: Materials.* **Subject to the provisions of subdivision (b)(4) of this rule, a party may obtain discovery of documents and tangible things otherwise discoverable under subdivision (b)(1) of this rule and prepared in anticipation of litigation or for trial by or for another party or by or for that other party's representative (including the other party's** attorney, consultant, surety, indemnitor, insurer, or agent) only upon a showing that the party seeking discovery has substantial need of the materials in the preparation of the party's case and that the party is unable without undue hardship to obtain the substantial equivalent of the materials by other means. In ordering discovery of such materials when the required showing has been made, the court shall protect against disclosure of the mental impressions, conclusions, opinions, or legal theories of an attorney or other representative of a party concerning the litigation.

A party may obtain without the required showing a statement concerning the action or its subject matter previously made by that party. Upon request, a person not a party may obtain without the required showing a statement concerning the action or its subject matter previously made by that person.

(4) *Trial Preparation: Experts.*

(A) A party may depose any person who has been identified as an expert whose opinions may be presented at trial. If a report from the expert is required under subdivision (a)(2)(B), the deposition shall not be conducted until after the report is provided.

(B) A party may, through interrogatories or by deposition, discover facts known or opinions held by an expert who has been retained or specially employed by another party in anticipation of litigation or preparation for trial and who is not expected to be called as a witness at trial, only as provided in Rule 35(b) or upon a showing of exceptional circumstances under which it is impracticable for the party seeking discovery to obtain facts or opinions on the same subject by other means.

(C) Unless manifest injustice would result, (i) the court shall require that the party seeking discovery pay the expert a reasonable fee for time spent in responding to discovery under this subdivision; and (ii) with respect to discovery obtained under subdivision (b)(4)(B) of this rule the court shall require, the party seeking discovery to pay the other party a fair portion of the fees and expenses reasonably incurred by the latter party in obtaining facts and opinions from the expert.

(5) *Claims of Privilege or Protection of Trial Preparation Materials.* When a party withholds information otherwise discoverable under these rules by claiming that it is privileged or subject to protection as trial preparation material, the party shall make the claim expressly and shall describe the nature of the documents, communications, or things not produced or disclosed in a manner that, without revealing information itself privileged or protected, will enable other parties to assess the applicability of the privilege or protection.

NEW YORK CIVIL PRACTICE LAW AND RULES

§4503. Attorney

(a) Confidential communication privileged; non-judicial proceedings. Unless the client waives the privilege, an attorney or his employee, or any person who obtains without the knowledge of the client evidence of a confidential communication made between the attorney or his employee and the client in the course of professional employment, shall not disclose, or be allowed to disclose such communication, nor shall the client be compelled to disclose such communication, in any action, disciplinary trial or hearing, or administrative action, proceeding or hearing conducted by or on behalf of any state, municipal or local governmental agency or by the legislature or any committee or body thereof. Evidence of any such communication obtained by any such person, and evidence resulting therefrom, shall not be disclosed by any state, municipal or local governmental agency or by the legislature or any committee or body thereof. The relationship of an attorney and client shall exist between a professional service corporation organized under article fifteen of the business corporation law to practice as an attorney and counselor-at-law and the clients to whom it renders legal services.

(b) Wills. In any action involving the probate, validity or construction of a will, an attorney or his employee shall be required to disclose information as to the preparation, execution or revocation of any will or other relevant instrument, but he shall not be allowed to disclose any communication privileged under subdivision (a) which would tend to disgrace the memory of the decedent.

CALIFORNIA EVIDENCE CODE

§911. General Rule as to Privileges

Except as otherwise provided by statute:
(a) No person has a privilege to refuse to be a witness.
(b) No person has a privilege to refuse to disclose any matter or to refuse to produce any writing, object, or other thing.
(c) No person has a privilege that another shall not be a witness or shall not disclose any matter or shall not produce any writing, object, or other thing.

§912. Waiver of Privilege

(a) Except as otherwise provided in this section, the right of any person to claim a privilege provided by Section 954 (lawyer-client privilege), 980 (privilege for confidential marital communications), 994 (physician-patient privilege), 1014 (psychotherapist-patient privilege), 1033 (privilege of penitent), 1034 (privilege of clergyman), or 1035.8 (sexual assault victim-counselor privilege) is waived with respect to a communication protected by such privilege if any holder of the privilege, without coercion, has disclosed a significant part of the communication or has consented to such disclosure made by anyone. Consent to disclosure is manifested by any statement or other conduct of the holder of the privilege indicating consent to the disclosure, including failure to claim the privilege in any proceeding in which the holder has the legal standing and opportunity to claim the privilege.

(b) Where two or more persons are joint holders of a privilege provided by Section 954 (lawyer-client privilege), 994 (physician-patient privilege), 1014 (psychotherapist-patient privilege), or 1035.8 (sexual assault victim-counselor privilege), a waiver of the right of a particular joint holder of the privilege to claim the privilege does not affect the right of another joint holder to claim the privilege. In the case of the privilege provided by Section 980 (privilege for confidential marital communications), a waiver of the right of one spouse to claim the privilege does not affect the right of the other spouse to claim the privilege.

(c) A disclosure that is itself privileged is not a waiver of any privilege.

(d) A disclosure in confidence of a communication that is protected by a privilege provided by Section 954 (lawyer-client privilege), 994 (physician-patient privilege), 1014 (psychotherapist-patient privilege), or 1035.8 (sexual assault victim-counselor privilege), when such disclosure is reasonably necessary for the accomplishment of the purpose for which the lawyer, physician, psychotherapist, or sexual assault counselor was consulted, is not a waiver of the privilege.

§917. Presumption That Certain Communications Are Confidential

Whenever a privilege is claimed on the ground that the matter sought to be disclosed is a communication made in confidence in the course of the lawyer-client, physician-patient, psychotherapist-patient, clergyman-penitent, or husband-wife relationship, the communication is presumed to have been made in confidence and the opponent of the claim of privilege has the burden of proof to establish that the communication was not confidential.

§950. "Lawyer"

As used in this article, "lawyer" means a person authorized, or reasonably believed by the client to be authorized, to practice law in any state or nation.

§951. "Client"

As used in this article, "client" means a person who, directly or through an authorized representative, consults a lawyer for the purpose of retaining the lawyer or securing legal service or advice from him in his professional capacity, and includes an incompetent (a) who himself so consults the lawyer or (b) whose guardian or conservator so consults the lawyer in behalf of the incompetent.

§952. "Confidential Communication Between
        Client and Lawyer"

Editors' Note. Section 952 was amended in 1994.

As used in this article, "confidential communication between client and lawyer" means information transmitted between a client and his or her lawyer in the course of that relationship and in confidence by a means which, so far as the client is aware, discloses the information to no third persons other than those who are present to further the interest of the client in the consultation or those to whom disclosure is reasonably necessary for the transmission of the information or the accomplishment of the purpose for which the lawyer is consulted, and includes a legal opinion formed and the advice given by the lawyer in the course of that relationship. A communication between a client and his or her lawyer is not deemed lacking in confidentiality solely because the communication is transmitted by facsimile, cellular telephone, or other electronic means between the client and his or her lawyer.

§953. "Holder of the privilege"

As used in this article, "holder of the privilege" means:
(a) The client when he has no guardian or conservator.
(b) A guardian or conservator of the client when the client has a guardian or conservator.
(c) The personal representative of the client if the client is dead.
(d) A successor, assign, trustee in dissolution, or any similar representative of a firm, association, organization, partnership, business trust, corporation, or public entity that is no longer in existence.

§954. Lawyer-Client Privilege

Editors' Note. Section 954 was amended in 1994 to recognize the proliferation of limited liability companies.

Subject to Section 912 and except as otherwise provided in this article, the client, whether or not a party, has a privilege to refuse to disclose, and to prevent another from disclosing, a confidential communication between client and lawyer if the privilege is claimed by:
(a) The holder of the privilege;
(b) A person who is authorized to claim the privilege by the holder of the privilege; or
(c) The person who was the lawyer at the time of the confidential communication, but such person may not claim the privilege if there is no holder of the privilege in existence or if he is otherwise instructed by a person authorized to permit disclosure.
The relationship of attorney and client shall exist between a law corporation as defined in Article 10 (commencing with Section 6160) of Chapter 4 of Division 3 of the Business and Professions Code and the persons to whom it renders professional services, as well as between such persons and members of the State Bar employed by such corporation to render services such persons. The word "persons" as used in this subdivision includes partnerships, corporations, limited liability companies, associations and other groups and entities.

§955. When Lawyer Required to Claim Privilege

The lawyer who received or made a communication subject to the privilege under this article shall claim the privilege whenever he is present when the communication is sought to be disclosed and is authorized to claim the privilege under subdivision (c) of Section 954.

§956. Exception: Crime or Fraud

There is no privilege under this article if the services of the lawyer were sought or obtained to enable or aid anyone to commit or plan to commit a crime or a fraud.

§956.5. Reasonable Belief That Disclosure of Confidential Communication Is Necessary to Prevent Criminal Act Resulting in Death or Bodily Harm; Exception to Privilege

> **Editors' Note.** Section 956.5 of the California Evidence Code was signed into law by the Governor of California on October 11, 1993. It is an entirely new provision. The language closely parallels the wording of Rule 1.6 of the ABA Model Rules of Professional Conduct, but omits the requirement in Rule 1.6 that the harm be "imminent."

There is no privilege under this article if the lawyer reasonably believes that disclosure of any confidential communication relating to representation of a client is necessary to prevent the client from committing a criminal act that the lawyer believes is likely to result in death or substantial bodily harm.

§957. Exception: Parties Claiming Through Deceased Client

There is no privilege under this article as to a communication relevant to an issue between parties all of whom claim through a deceased client, regardless of whether the claims are by testate or intestate succession or by inter vivos transaction.

§958. Exception: Breach of Duty Arising out of Lawyer-Client Relationship

There is no privilege under this article as to a communication relevant to an issue of breach, by the lawyer or by the client, of a duty arising out of the lawyer-client relationship.

§959. Exception: Lawyer as Attesting Witness

There is no privilege under this article as to a communication relevant to an issue concerning the intention or competence of a client executing an attested document of which the lawyer is an attesting witness, or concerning the execution or attestation of such a document.

§960. Exception: Intention of Deceased Client Concerning Writing Affecting Property Interest

There is no privilege under this article as to a communication relevant to an issue concerning the intention of a client, now deceased, with respect to a deed of conveyance, will, or other writing, executed by the client, purporting to affect an interest in property.

§961. Exception: Validity of Writing Affecting Property Interest

There is no privilege under this article as to a communication relevant to an issue concerning the validity of a deed of conveyance, will, or other writing, executed by a client, now deceased, purporting to affect an interest in property.

§962. Exception: Joint Clients

Where two or more clients have retained or consulted a lawyer upon a matter of common interest, none of them, nor the successor in interest of any of them, may claim a privilege under this article as to a communication made in the course of that relationship when such communication is offered in a civil proceeding between one of such clients (or his successor in interest) and another of such clients (or his successor in interest).

RESTATEMENT OF THE LAW
GOVERNING LAWYERS
(PROPOSED FINAL DRAFT NO. 1)
ATTORNEY-CLIENT PRIVILEGE PROVISIONS*

> **Editors' Note.** The attorney-client privilege provisions below were tentatively approved by the ALI in 1996. They differ significantly from equivalent provisions in earlier drafts of the Restatement. For a thorough review of the changes from earlier drafts, see the Reporter's essay at pp. xxv-lxxiii of Proposed Final Draft No. 1 (Mar. 29, 1996).

§118. The Attorney-Client Privilege

Except as otherwise provided in this Restatement, the attorney-client privilege may be invoked as provided in §135 with respect to:
    (1) a communication
    (2) made between privileged persons
    (3) in confidence
    (4) for the purpose of obtaining or providing legal assistance for the client.

§119. Attorney-Client Privilege —
"Communication"

A communication within the meaning of §118 is any expression through which a privileged person, as defined in §120, undertakes to convey information to another privileged person and any document or other record revealing such an expression.

§120. Attorney-Client Privilege —
"Privileged Persons"

Privileged persons within the meaning of §118 are the client (including a prospective client), the client's lawyer, agents of either who facili-

*Copyright © 1996 by the American Law Institute. Reprinted with the permission of the American Law Institute.

tate communications between them, and agents of the lawyer who facilitate the representation.

§121. Attorney-Client Privilege — "In Confidence"

A communication is in confidence within the meaning of §118 if, at the time and in the circumstances of the communication, the communicating person reasonably believes that no one will learn the contents of the communication except a privileged person as defined in §120 or another person with whom communications are protected under a similar evidentiary privilege.

§122. Attorney-Client Privilege — Legal Assistance as Object of Privileged Communication

A communication is made for the purpose of obtaining or providing legal assistance within the meaning of §118 if it is made to or to assist a person:

(1) who is a lawyer or who the client or prospective client reasonably believes to be a lawyer; and

(2) whom the client or prospective client consults for the purpose of obtaining legal assistance.

§123. Privilege for Organizational Client

When a client is a corporation, unincorporated association, partnership, trust, estate, sole proprietorship, or other for-profit or not-for-profit organization, the attorney-client privilege extends to a communication that:

(1) otherwise qualifies as privileged under §§118-122;

(2) is between an agent of the organization and a privileged person as defined in §120;

(3) concerns a legal matter of interest to the organization; and

(4) is disclosed only to:

(a) privileged persons as defined in §120; and

(b) other agents of the organization who reasonably need to know of the communication in order to act for the organization.

§124. Privilege for Governmental Client

Unless applicable law otherwise provides, the attorney-client privilege extends to a communication of a governmental organization as stated in §123 and of an individual officer, employee, or other agent of a governmental organization as a client with respect to his or her personal interest as stated in §§118-122.

§125. Privilege of Co-Clients

(1) If two or more persons are jointly represented by the same lawyer in a matter, a communication of either co-client that otherwise qualifies as privileged under §§118-122 and relates to matters of common interest is privileged as against third persons, and any co-client may invoke the privilege, unless it has been waived by the client who made the communication.

(2) Unless the co-clients have agreed otherwise, a communication described in Subsection (1) is not privileged as between the co-clients in a subsequent adverse proceeding between them.

§126. Common-Interest Arrangement

(1) If two or more clients with a common interest in a litigated or non-litigated matter are represented by separate lawyers and they agree to exchange information concerning the matter, a communication of any such client that otherwise qualifies as privileged under §§118-122 that relates to the matter is privileged as against third persons. Any such client may invoke the privilege, unless it has been waived by the client who made the communication.

(2) Unless the clients have agreed otherwise, a communication described in Subsection (1) is not privileged as between clients described in Subsection (1) in a subsequent adverse proceeding between them.

§127. Duration of Privilege

Unless waived (see §§128-130) or subject to exception (see §§131-134B), the attorney-client privilege may be invoked as provided in §135 at any time during or after termination of the relationship between client or prospective client and lawyer.

§128. Waiver by Agreement, Disclaimer, or
Failure to Object

The attorney-client privilege is waived if the client, the client's lawyer, or another authorized agent of the client:
   (1) agrees to waive the privilege;
   (2) disclaims protection of the privilege and
      (a) another person reasonably relies on the disclaimer to that person's detriment; or
      (b) reasons of judicial administration require that the client not be permitted to revoke the disclaimer; or
      (3) in a proceeding before a tribunal, fails to object properly to an attempt by another person to give or exact testimony or other evidence of a privileged communication.

§129. Waiver by Subsequent Disclosure

The attorney-client privilege is waived if the client, the client's lawyer, or another authorized agent of the client voluntarily discloses the communication in a non-privileged communication.

§130. Waiver by Putting Assistance or
Communication in Issue

(1) The attorney-client privilege is waived for any relevant communication if the client asserts as to a material issue in a proceeding that:
   (a) the client acted upon the advice of a lawyer or that the advice was otherwise relevant to the legal significance of the client's conduct; or
   (b) a lawyer's assistance was ineffective, negligent, or otherwise wrongful.
(2) The attorney-client privilege is waived for a recorded communication if a witness:
   (a) employs the communication to aid the witness while testifying; or
   (b) employed the communication in preparing to testify, and the tribunal finds that disclosure is required in the interests of justice.

§131. Exception for Dispute Concerning Decedent's Disposition of Property

The attorney-client privilege does not apply to a communication from or to a decedent relevant to an issue between parties who claim an interest through the same deceased client, either by testate or intestate succession or by an inter vivos transaction.

§132. Exception for Client Crime or Fraud

The attorney-client privilege does not apply to a communication occurring when a client:

(a) consults a lawyer for the purpose, later accomplished, of obtaining assistance to engage in a crime or fraud or aiding a third person to do so, or

(b) regardless of the client's purpose at the time of consultation, uses the lawyer's advice or other services to engage in or assist a crime or fraud.

§133. Exceptions for Lawyer Self-Protection

The attorney-client privilege does not apply to a communication that is relevant and reasonably necessary for a lawyer to employ in a proceeding:

(1) to resolve a dispute with a client concerning compensation or reimbursement that the lawyer reasonably claims the client owes the lawyer; or

(2) to defend the lawyer against an allegation by any person that the lawyer, an agent of the lawyer, or another person for whose conduct the lawyer is responsible acted wrongfully during the course of representing a client.

§134A. Exception for Fiduciary-Lawyer Communication

In a proceeding in which a trustee of an express trust or similar fiduciary is charged with breach of fiduciary duties by a beneficiary, a communication otherwise within §118 is nonetheless not privileged if the communication:

(a) is relevant to the claimed breach; and

(b) was between the trustee and a lawyer (or other privileged person within the meaning of §120) who was retained to advise the trustee concerning the administration of the trust.

§134B. Exception for Organizational Fiduciary

In a proceeding involving a dispute between an organizational client and shareholders, members, or other constituents of the organization toward whom the directors, officers, or similar persons managing the organization bear fiduciary responsibilities, the attorney-client privilege of the organization may be withheld from a communication otherwise within §118 if the tribunal finds that:

(a) those managing the organization are charged with breach of their obligations toward the shareholders, members, or other constituents or toward the organization itself;

(b) the communication occurred prior to the assertion of the charges and relates directly to those charges; and

(c) the need of the requesting party to discover or introduce the communication is sufficiently compelling and the threat to confidentiality sufficiently confined to justify setting the privilege aside.

§135. Invoking the Privilege and Its Exceptions

(1) When an attempt is made to introduce in evidence or obtain discovery of a communication privileged under §118:

(a) A client, a personal representative of an incompetent or deceased client, or a person succeeding to the interest of a client may invoke or waive the privilege, either personally or through counsel or another authorized agent.

(b) A lawyer, an agent of the lawyer, or an agent of a client from whom a privileged communication is sought must invoke the privilege when doing so appears reasonably appropriate, unless the client:

(i) has waived the privilege; or

(ii) has authorized the lawyer or agent to waive it.

(c) Notwithstanding failure to invoke the privilege as specified in Subsections (1)(a) and (1)(b), the tribunal has discretion to invoke the privilege.

(2) A person invoking the privilege must ordinarily object contemporaneously to an attempt to disclose the communication and, if the objection is contested, demonstrate each element of the privilege under §118.

(3) A person invoking a waiver of or exception to the privilege (§§128-134B) must assert it and, if the assertion is contested, demonstrate each element of the waiver or exception.

RESTATEMENT OF THE LAW GOVERNING LAWYERS (PROPOSED FINAL DRAFT NO. 1)

WORK PRODUCT PROVISIONS*

> **Editors' Note.** The work product provisions below differ significantly from equivalent provisions in earlier drafts of the Restatement. For a thorough review of the changes from earlier drafts, see the Reporter's essay at pp. xxv-lxxiii of Proposed Final Draft No. 1.
>
> The work product provisions have a rocky history. When they were first debated in 1992, the basic definition of work product in §136 ("Work Product Immunity") caused great controversy and the ALI membership remanded it to the Reporters for further work. In 1993, the ALI approved a revised version of §136. In 1996, the ALI again revised §136. We reprint only the 1996 version.
>
> Two other controversial work product provisions were §§141 ("Waiver of Work Product Immunity by Use in Litigation") and 141A ("Work Product as Evidence"). In 1992, both of these sections were part of a single §141 that the ALI tentatively approved. However, in light of the 1992 discussion, the reporters split the original §141 into two sections, §§141 and 141A. In 1993, these revised sections caused controversy and both sections were remanded to the reporters for further work. In 1996, the ALI approved a revised version of §141, but did not act on §141A because the reporters did not propose a new version. We reprint below the 1996 version of §141 and, for historical interest, the remanded 1992 version of §141A. (Note that former §143 is being moved to another chapter, so there is no §143 in this edition.)

§136. Work-Product Immunity

(1) Work product consists of tangible material or its intangible equivalent in unwritten or oral form, other than underlying facts, pre-

---

*Copyright © 1996 by the American Law Institute. Reprinted with the permission of the American Law Institute.

pared by a lawyer for litigation then in progress or in reasonable anticipation of future litigation.

(2) Opinion work product consists of the opinions or mental impressions of a lawyer; all other work product is ordinary work product.

(3) Except for material which by applicable law is not so protected,
work product is immune from discovery or other compelled disclosure
to the extent stated in §§137 (ordinary work product) and 138 (opinion
work product) when the immunity is invoked as described in §139.

§137. Ordinary Work Product

When work product protection is invoked as described in §139, ordinary work product (§136(2)) is immune from discovery or other compelled disclosure unless either an exception recognized in §§140-142
applies or the inquiring party:

(1) has a substantial need for the material in order to prepare for
trial; and

(2) is unable without undue hardship to obtain the substantial
equivalent of the material by other means.

§138. Opinion Work Product

When work product protection is invoked as described in §139,
opinion work product (§136(2)) is immune from discovery or other compelled disclosure unless either the immunity is waived or an exception
applies (§§140-142) or extraordinary circumstances justify disclosure.

§139. Invoking Work-Product Immunity and Its
Exceptions

(1) Work-product immunity may be invoked by or for a person on
whose behalf the work product was prepared.

(2) The person invoking work-product immunity must object and, if
the objection is contested, demonstrate each element of the immunity.

(3) Once a claim of work product has been adequately supported, a
person entitled to invoke a waiver or exception must assert it and, if
the assertion is contested, demonstrate each element of the wavier or
exception.

§140. Waiver of Work-Product Immunity by Voluntary Act

Work-product immunity is waived if the client, the client's lawyer, or another authorized agent of the client:
  (1) agrees to waive the immunity;
  (2) disclaims protection of the immunity and:
      (a) another person reasonably relies on the disclaimer to that person's detriment; or
      (b) reasons of judicial administration require that the client not be permitted to revoke the disclaimer; or
  (3) in a proceeding before a tribunal, fails to object properly to an attempt by another person to give or exact testimony or other evidence of work product; or
  (4) discloses the material to third persons in circumstances in which there is a significant likelihood that an adversary or potential adversary in anticipated litigation will obtain it.

Editors' Note. The next two sections were originally part of a single section (§141) that was tentatively approved at the ALI's 1992 Annual Meeting, but in light of the 1992 discussion §141 was edited for clarification and split into two sections. Both sections concern loss of work product protection, but §141 covers instances in which the party *claiming* work product immunity *waives* it by using the material in litigation, whereas §141A covers instances in which the party *opposing* work product immunity *overcomes* it by persuading the court that it needs the opponent's work product to obtain a fair trial. At its 1993 Annual Meeting, the ALI remanded both §141 and §141A to the Reporters for further work; both sections will be revised and resubmitted with other revisions at the end of the project. In 1996, the ALI approved a revised version of §141, but the Reporters did not forward a revised version of §141A. We reprint the 1993 version of §141A for historical interest.

§141. Waiver of Work-Product Immunity by Use in Litigation

(1) Work-product immunity is waived for any relevant material if the client asserts as to a material issue in a proceeding that:
  (a) the client acted upon the advice of a lawyer or that the advice was otherwise relevant to the legal significance of the client's conduct; or

(b) a lawyer's assistance was ineffective, negligent, or otherwise wrongful.

(2) The work-product immunity is waived for recorded material if a witness

(a) employs the material to aid the witness while testifying, or

(b) employed the material in preparing to testify, and the tribunal finds that disclosure is required in the interests of justice.

§141A. Work Product as Evidence (remanded for further consideration)

Work product that constitutes direct and substantial evidence of a material issue before a tribunal is subject to disclosure by order of the tribunal when access is required for a fair trial of the issue.

§142. Exception for Crime or Fraud

Work-product immunity does not apply to materials prepared when a client consults a lawyer for the purpose of obtaining assistance to engage in a crime or fraud or to aid a third person to do so or uses the materials for such a purpose.

[Section 143 from Tentative Draft No. 5 (dealing with turnover of workproduct) will be moved to either Chapter 1 or Chapter 4 of the Restatement.]

Federal Materials

Federal Conflict and Confidentiality Provisions

Editors' Introduction. Lawyers who work (or have worked) for the federal government are subject not only to rules of legal ethics but also to various federal statutes and regulations governing confidentiality and conflicts of interest. The statutes and regulations that follow contain detailed restrictions on the use or revelation of confidential information and on the propriety of a former government lawyer's representation of private clients in matters relating to work the lawyer did while in government service. Violation of the statutory provisions is a crime.

Contents

SELECTED PROVISIONS FROM 18 U.S.C.

§201. Bribery of Public Official and Witnesses

. . .

(c) Whoever —

(1) . . .

(2) directly or indirectly, gives, offers or promises anything of value to any person, for or because of the testimony under oath or affirmation given or to be given by such person as a witness upon a trial, hearing, or other proceeding, before any court, any committee of either House or both Houses of Congress, or any agency, commission, or officer authorized by the laws of the United States to hear evidence or take testimony, or for or because of such person's absence therefrom;

(3) directly or indirectly, demands, seeks, receives, accepts, or agrees to receive or accept anything of value personally for or because of the testimony under oath or affirmation given or to be given by such person as a witness upon any such trial, hearing, or other proceeding, or for or because of such person's absence therefrom;

shall be fined under this title or imprisoned for not more than two years, or both.

(d) Paragraphs (3) and (4) of subsection (b) and paragraphs (2) and (3) of subsection (c) shall not be construed to prohibit the payment or receipt of witness fees provided by law, or the payment, by the party upon

whose behalf a witness is called and receipt by a witness, of the reasonable cost of travel and subsistence incurred and the reasonable value of time lost in attendance at any such trial, hearing, or proceeding, or in the case of expert witnesses, a reasonable fee for time spent in the preparation of such opinion, and in appearing and testifying.

§202. Definitions

. . . (b) For the purposes of sections 205 and 207 of this title, the term "official responsibility" means the direct administrative or operating authority, whether intermediate or final, and either exercisable alone or with others, and either personally or through subordinates, to approve, disapprove, or otherwise direct Government action.

(c) Except as otherwise provided in such sections, the terms "officer" and "employee" in sections 203, 205, 207 through 209, and 218 of this title shall not include the President, the Vice President, a Member of Congress, or a Federal judge.

§207. Restrictions on Former Officers, Employees, and Elected Officials of the Executive and Legislative Branches

(a) *Restrictions on all officers and employees of the executive branch and certain other agencies. —*
(1) *Permanent restrictions on representation on particular matters.* — Any person who is an officer or employee (including any special Government employee) of the executive branch of the United States (including any independent agency of the United States), or of the District of Columbia, and who, after the termination of his or her service or employment with the United States or the District of Columbia, knowingly makes, with the intent to influence, any communication to or appearance before any officer or employee of any department, agency, court, or court-martial of the United States or the District of Columbia, on behalf of any other person (except the United States or the District of Columbia) in connection with a particular matter —
(A) in which the United States or the District of Columbia is a party or has a direct and substantial interest,
(B) in which the person participated personally and substantially as such officer or employee, and

(C) which involved a specific party or specific parties at the time of such participation,

shall be punished as provided in section 216 of this title.

(2) *Two-year restrictions concerning particular matters under official responsibility.* — Any person subject to the restrictions contained in paragraph (1) who, within 2 years after the termination of his or her service or employment with the United States or the District of Columbia, knowingly makes, with the intent to influence, any communication to or appearance before any officer or employee of any department, agency, court, or court-martial of the United States or the District of Columbia, on behalf of any other person (except the United States or the District of Columbia), in connection with a particular matter —

(A) in which the United States or the District of Columbia is a party or has a direct and substantial interest,

(B) which such person knows or reasonably should know was actually pending under his or her official responsibility as such officer or employee within a period of 1 year before the termination of his or her service or employment with the United States or the District of Columbia, and

(C) which involved a specific party or specific parties at the time it was so pending,

shall be punished as provided in section 216 of this title.

(3) *Clarification of restrictions.* — The restrictions contained in paragraphs (1) and (2) shall apply —

(A) in the case of an officer or employee of the executive branch of the United States (including any independent agency), only with respect to communications to or appearances before any officer or employee of any department, agency, court, or court-martial of the United States on behalf of any other person (except the United States), and only with respect to a matter in which the United States is a party or has a direct and substantial interest; and

(B) in the case of an officer or employee of the District of Columbia, only with respect to communications to or appearances before any officer or employee of any department, agency, or court of the District of Columbia on behalf of any other person (except the District of Columbia), and only with respect to a matter in which the District of Columbia is a party or has a direct and substantial interest.

(b) *One-year restrictions on aiding or advising.* —

(1) *In general.* — Any person who is a former officer or employee of the executive branch of the United States (including any indepen-

dent agency) and is subject to the restrictions contained in subsection (a)(1), or any person who is a former officer or employee of the legislative branch or a former Member of Congress, who personally and substantially participated in any ongoing trade or treaty negotiation on behalf of the United States within the 1-year period preceding the date on which his or her service or employment with the United States terminated, and who had access to information concerning such trade or treaty negotiation which is exempt from disclosure under section 552 of title 5, which is so designated by the appropriate department or agency, and which the person knew or should have known was so designated, shall not, on the basis of that information, knowingly represent, aid, or advise any other person (except the United States) concerning such ongoing trade or treaty negotiation for a period of 1 year after his or her service or employment with the United States terminates. Any person who violates this subsection shall be punished as provided in section 216 of this title.

(2) *Definition.* — For purposes of this paragraph —

(A) the term "trade negotiation" means negotiations which the President determines to undertake to enter into a trade agreement pursuant to section 1102 of the Omnibus Trade and Competitiveness Act of 1988, and does not include any action taken before that determination is made; and

(B) the term "treaty" means an international agreement made by the President that requires the advice and consent of the Senate.

(c) *One-year restrictions on certain senior personnel of the executive branch and independent agencies.* —

(1) *Restrictions.* — In addition to the restrictions set forth in subsections (a) and (b), any person who is an officer or employee (including any special Government employee) of the executive branch of the United States (including an independent agency), who is referred to in paragraph (2), and who, within 1 year after the termination of his or her service or employment as such officer or employee, knowingly makes, with the intent to influence, any communication to or appearance before any officer or employee of the department or agency in which such person served within 1 year before such termination, on behalf of any other person (except the United States), in connection with any matter on which such person seeks official action by any officer or employee of such department or agency, shall be punished as provided in section 216 of this title.

(2) *Persons to whom restrictions apply.* — (A) Paragraph (1) shall apply to a person (other than a person subject to the restrictions of subsection (d)) —

(i) employed at a rate of pay specified in or fixed according to subchapter II of chapter 53 of title 5,

(ii) employed in a position which is not referred to in clause (i) and for which the basic rate of pay, exclusive of any locality-based pay adjustment under section 5302 of title 5 (or any comparable adjustment pursuant to interim authority of the President), is equal to or greater than the rate of basic pay payable for level V of the Senior Executive Service,

(iii) appointed by the President to a position under section 105(a)(2)(B) of title 3 or by the Vice President to a position under section 106(a)(1)(B) of title 3, or

(iv) employed in a position which is held by an active duty commissioned officer of the uniformed services who is serving in a grade or rank for which the pay grade (as specified in section 201 of title 37) is pay grade O-7 or above.

(B) Paragraph (1) shall not apply to a special Government employee who serves less than 60 days in the 1-year period before his or her service or employment as such employee terminates.

(C) At the request of a department or agency, the Director of the Office of Government Ethics may waive the restrictions contained in paragraph (1) with respect to any position, or category of positions, referred to in clause (ii) or (iv) of subparagraph (A), in such department or agency if the Director determines that —

(i) the imposition of the restrictions with respect to such position or positions would create an undue hardship on the department or agency in obtaining qualified personnel to fill such position or positions, and

(ii) granting the waiver would not create the potential for use of undue influence or unfair advantage.

(d) *Restrictions on very senior personnel of the executive branch and independent agencies.* —

(1) *Restrictions.* — In addition to the restrictions set forth in subsections (a) and (b), any person who —

(A) serves in the position of Vice President of the United States,

(B) is employed in a position in the executive branch of the United States (including any independent agency) at a rate of pay payable for level I of the Executive Schedule or employed in a position in the Executive Office of the President at a rate of pay payable for level II of the Executive Schedule, or

(C) is appointed by the President to a position under section 105(a)(2)(A) of title 3 or by the Vice President to a position under section 106(a)(1)(A) of title 3,

and who, within 1 year after the termination of that person's service in that position, knowingly makes, with the intent to influence, any communication to or appearance before any person described in paragraph (2), on behalf of any other person (except the United States), in connection with any matter on which such person seeks official action by any officer or employee of the executive branch of the United States, shall be punished as provided in section 216 of this title.

(2) *Persons who may not be contacted.* — The persons referred to in paragraph (1) with respect to appearances or communications by a person in a position described in subparagraph (A), (B), or (C) of paragraph (1) are —

(A) any officer or employee of any department or agency in which such person served in such position within a period of 1 year before such person's service or employment with the United States Government terminated, and

(B) any person appointed to a position in the executive branch which is listed in sections 5312, 5313, 5314, 5315, or 5316 of title 5.

(e) *Restrictions on members of Congress and officers and employees of the legislative branch.* —

(1) *Members of congress and elected officers.* — (A) Any person who is a Member of Congress or an elected officer of either House of Congress and who, within 1 year after that person leaves office, knowingly makes, with the intent to influence, any communication to or appearance before any of the persons described in subparagraph (B) or (C), on behalf of any other person (except the United States) in connection with any matter on which such former Member of Congress or elected officer seeks action by a Member, officer, or employee of either House of Congress, in his or her official capacity, shall be punished as provided in section 216 of this title.

(B) The persons referred to in subparagraph (A) with respect to appearances or communications by a former Member of Congress are any Member, officer, or employee of either House of Congress, and any employee of any other legislative office of the Congress.

(C) The persons referred to in subparagraph (A) with respect to appearances or communications by a former elected officer are any Member, officer, or employee of the House of Congress in which the elected officer served.

(2) *Personal staff.* — (A) Any person who is an employee of a Senator or an employee of a Member of the House of Representatives and who, within 1 year after the termination of that employment, knowingly makes, with the intent to influence, any communication to or appearance before any of the persons described in subparagraph (B), on behalf of any other person (except the United States) in connection with any matter on which such former employee seeks action by a Member, officer, or employee of either House of Congress, in his or her official capacity, shall be punished as provided in section 216 of this title.

(B) The persons referred to in subparagraph (A) with respect to appearances or communications by a person who is a former employee are the following:

(i) the Senator or Member of the House of Representatives for whom that person was an employee; and

(ii) any employee of that Senator or Member of the House of Representatives.

(3) *Committee staff.* — Any person who is an employee of a committee of Congress and who, within 1 year after the termination of that person's employment on such committee, knowingly makes, with the intent to influence, any communication to or appearance before any person who is a Member or an employee of that committee or who was a Member of the committee in the year immediately prior to the termination of such person's employment by the committee, on behalf of any other person (except the United States) in connection with any matter on which such former employee seeks action by a Member, officer, or employee of either House of Congress, in his or her official capacity, shall be punished as provided in section 216 of this title.

(4) *Leadership staff.* — (A) Any person who is an employee on the leadership staff of the House of Representatives or an employee on the leadership staff of the Senate and who, within 1 year after the termination of that person's employment on such staff, knowingly makes, with the intent to influence, any communication to or appearance before any of the persons described in subparagraph (B), on behalf of any other person (except the United States) in connection with any matter on which such former employee seeks action by a Member, officer, or employee of either House of Congress, in his or her official capacity, shall be punished as provided in section 216 of this title.

(B) The persons referred to in subparagraph (A) with respect to appearances or communications by a former employee are the following:

(i) in the case of a former employee on the leadership staff of the House of Representatives, those persons are any Member of the leadership of the House of Representatives and any employee on the leadership staff of the House of Representatives; and

(ii) in the case of a former employee on the leadership staff of the Senate, those persons are any Member of the leadership of the Senate and any employee on the leadership staff of the Senate.

(5) *Other legislative offices.* — (A) Any person who is an employee of any other legislative office of the Congress and who, within 1 year after the termination of that person's employment in such office, knowingly makes, with the intent to influence, any communication to or appearance before any of the persons described in subparagraph (B), on behalf of any other person (except the United States) in connection with any matter on which such former employee seeks action by any officer or employee of such office, in his or her official capacity, shall be punished as provided in section 216 of this title.

(B) The persons referred to in subparagraph (A) with respect to appearances or communications by a former employee are the employees and officers of the former legislative office of the Congress of the former employee.

(6) *Limitation on restrictions.* — (A) The restrictions contained in paragraphs (2), (3), and (4) apply only to acts by a former employee who, for at least 60 days, in the aggregate, during the 1-year period before that former employee's service as such employee terminated, was paid a rate of basic pay equal to or greater than an amount which is 75 percent of the basic rate of pay payable for a Member of the House of Congress in which such employee was employed.

(B) The restrictions contained in paragraph (5) apply only to acts by a former employee who, for at least 60 days, in the aggregate, during the 1-year period before that former employee's service as such employee terminated, was employed in a position for which the rate of basic pay, exclusive of any locality-based pay adjustment under section 5302 of title 5 (or any comparable adjustment pursuant to interim authority of the President), is equal to or greater than the basic rate of pay payable for level V of the Senior Executive Service.

(7) *Definitions.* — As used in this subsection —

(A) the term "committee of Congress" includes standing committees, joint committees, and select committees;

(B) a person is an employee of a House of Congress if that person is an employee of the Senate or an employee of the House of Representatives;

(C) the term "employee of the House of Representatives" means an employee of a Member of the House of Representatives, an employee of a committee of the House of Representatives, an employee of a joint committee of the Congress whose pay is disbursed by the Clerk of the House of Representatives, and an employee on the leadership staff of the House of Representatives;

(D) the term "employee of the Senate" means an employee of a Senator, an employee of a committee of the Senate, an employee of a joint committee of the Congress whose pay is disbursed by the Secretary of the Senate, and an employee on the leadership staff of the Senate;

(E) a person is an employee of a Member of the House of Representatives if that person is an employee of a Member of the House of Representatives under the clerk hire allowance;

(F) a person is an employee of a Senator if that person is an employee in a position in the office of a Senator;

(G) the term "employee of any other legislative office of the Congress" means an officer or employee of the Architect of the Capitol, the United States Botanic Garden, the General Accounting Office, the Government Printing Office, the Library of Congress, the Office of Technology Assessment, the Congressional Budget Office, the Copyright Royalty Tribunal, the United States Capitol Police, and any other agency, entity, or office in the legislative branch not covered by paragraph (1), (2), (3), or (4) of this subsection;

(H) the term "employee on the leadership staff of the House of Representatives" means an employee of the office of a Member of the leadership of the House of Representatives described in subparagraph (L), and any elected minority employee of the House of Representatives;

(I) the term "employee on the leadership staff of the Senate" means an employee of the office of a Member of the leadership of the Senate described in subparagraph (M);

(J) the term "Member of Congress" means a Senator or a Member of the House of Representatives;

(K) the term "Member of the House of Representatives" means a Representative in, or a Delegate or Resident Commissioner to, the Congress;

(L) the term "Member of the leadership of the House of Representatives" means the Speaker, majority leader, minority leader, majority whip, minority whip, chief deputy majority whip, chief deputy minority whip, chairman of the Democratic Steering Committee, chairman and vice chairman of the Democratic Caucus, chairman, vice chairman, and secretary of the Republican Conference, chairman of the Republican Research Committee, and chairman of the Republican Policy Committee, of the House of Representatives (or any similar position created on or after the effective date set forth in section 102(a) of the Ethics Reform Act of 1989);

(M) the term "Member of the leadership of the Senate" means the Vice President, and the President pro tempore, Deputy President pro tempore, majority leader, minority leader, majority whip, minority whip, chairman and secretary of the Conference of the Majority, chairman and secretary of the Conference of the Minority, chairman and co-chairman of the Majority Policy Committee, and chairman of the Minority Policy Committee, of the Senate (or any similar position created on or after the effective date set forth in section 102(a) of the Ethics Reform Act of 1989).

(f) *Restrictions relating to foreign entities. —*

(1) *Restrictions.* — Any person who is subject to the restrictions contained in subsection (c), (d), or (e) and who knowingly, within 1 year after leaving the position, office, or employment referred to in such subsection —

(A) represents a foreign entity before any officer or employee of any department or agency of the United States with the intent to influence a decision of such officer or employee in carrying out his or her official duties, or

(B) aids or advises a foreign entity with the intent to influence a decision of any officer or employee of any department or agency of the United States, in carrying out his or her official duties,
shall be punished as provided in section 216 of this title.

(2) *Special rule for trade representative.* — With respect to a person who is the United States Trade Representative or Deputy United States Trade Representative, the restrictions described in paragraph (1) shall apply to representing, aiding, or advising foreign entities within 3 years after the termination of that person's service as the United States Trade Representative.

(3) *Definition.* — For purposes of this subsection, the term "foreign entity" means the government of a foreign country as defined in section 1(e) of the Foreign Agents Registration Act of 1938, as amended, or a foreign political party as defined in section 1(f) of that Act.

(g) *Special rules for detailees.* — For purposes of this section, a person who is detailed from one department, agency, or other entity to another department, agency, or other entity shall, during the period such person is detailed, be deemed to be an officer or employee of both departments, agencies, or such entities.

(h) *Designations of separate statutory agencies and bureaus.* —

(1) *Designations.* — For purposes of subsection (c) and except as provided in paragraph (2), whenever the Director of the Office of Government Ethics determines that an agency or bureau within a department or agency in the executive branch exercises functions which are distinct and separate from the remaining functions of the department or agency and that there exists no potential for use of undue influence or unfair advantage based on past Government service, the Director shall by rule designate such agency or bureau as a separate department or agency. On an annual basis the Director of the Office of Government Ethics shall review the designations and determinations made under this subparagraph and, in consultation with the department or agency concerned, make such additions and deletions as are necessary. Departments and agencies shall cooperate to the fullest extent with the Director of the Office of Government Ethics in the exercise of his or her responsibilities under this paragraph.

(2) *Inapplicability of designations.* — No agency or bureau within the Executive Office of the President may be designated under paragraph (1) as a separate department or agency. No designation under paragraph (1) shall apply to persons referred to in subsection (c)(2)(A)(i) or (iii).

(i) *Definitions.* — For purposes of this section —

(1) the term "officer or employee", when used to describe the person to whom a communication is made or before whom an appearance is made, with the intent to influence, shall include —

(A) in subsections (a), (c), and (d), the President and the Vice President; and

(B) in subsection (f), the President, the Vice President, and Members of Congress;

(2) the term "participated" means an action taken as an officer or employee through decision, approval, disapproval, recommendation, the rendering of advice, investigation, or other such action; and

(3) the term "particular matter" includes any investigation, application, request for a ruling or determination, rulemaking, contract, controversy, claim, charge, accusation, arrest, or judicial or other proceeding. . . .

§208. Acts Affecting a Personal Financial
Interest

(a) Except as permitted by subsection (b) hereof, whoever, being an officer or employee of the executive branch of the United States Government, or of any independent agency of the United States, a Federal Reserve bank director, officer, or employee, or an officer or employee of the District of Columbia, including a special Government employee, participates personally and substantially as a Government officer or employee, through decision, approval, disapproval, recommendation, the rendering of advice, investigation, or otherwise, in a judicial or other proceeding, application, request for a ruling or other determination, contract, claim, controversy, charge, accusation, arrest, or other particular matter in which, to his knowledge, he, his spouse, minor child, general partner, organization in which he is serving as officer, director, trustee, general partner or employee, or any person or organization with whom he is negotiating or has any arrangement concerning prospective employment, has a financial interest —

Shall be subject to the penalties set forth in section 216 of this title.

(b) Subsection (a) shall not apply —

(1) if the officer or employee first advises the Government official responsible for appointment to his or her position of the nature and circumstances of the judicial or other proceeding, application, request for a ruling or other determination, contract, claim, controversy, charge, accusation, arrest, or other particular matter and makes full disclosure of the financial interest and receives in advance a written determination made by such official that the interest is not so substantial as to be deemed likely to affect the integrity of the services which the Government may expect from such officer or employee;

(2) if, by regulation issued by the Director of the Office of Government Ethics, applicable to all or a portion of all officers and employees covered by this section, and published in the Federal Register, the financial interest has been exempted from the requirements of paragraph (a) as being too remote or too inconsequential to affect the integrity of the services of the Government officers or employees to which such regulation applies;

(3) in the case of a special Government employee serving on an advisory committee within the meaning of the Federal Advisory Committee Act (including an individual being considered for an appointment to such a position), the official responsible for the employee's appointment, after review of the financial disclosure report filed by the individual pursuant to section 107 of the Ethics in Government Act of

1978, certifies in writing that the need for the individual's services out-weighs the potential for a conflict of interest created by the financial interest involved. . . .

(d)(1) Upon request, a copy of any determination granting an exemption under subsection (b)(1) or (b)(3) shall be made available to the public by the agency granting the exemption pursuant to the proce-dures set forth in section 105 of the Ethics in Government Act of 1978. In making such determination available, the agency may withhold from dis-closure any information contained in the determination that would be ex-empt from disclosure under section 552 of title 5. For purposes of determinations under subsection (b)(3), the information describing each financial interest shall be no more extensive than that required of the in-dividual in his or her financial disclosure report under the Ethics in Gov-ernment Act of 1978.

(2) The Office of Government Ethics, after consultation with the Attorney General, shall issue uniform regulations for the issuance of waivers and exemptions under subsection (b) which shall —

(A) list and describe exemptions; and

(B) provide guidance with respect to the types of interests that are not so substantial as to be deemed likely to affect the integrity of the services the Government may expect from the employee.

§1905. Disclosure of Confidential Information
        Generally

Whoever, being an officer or employee of the United States or of any department or agency thereof, any person acting on behalf of the Of-fice of Federal Housing Enterprise Oversight, or agent of the Depart-ment of Justice as defined in the Antitrust Civil Process Act (15 U.S.C. 1311-1314), publishes, divulges, discloses, or makes known in any man-ner or to any extent not authorized by law any information coming to him in the course of his employment or official duties or by reason of any ex-amination or investigation made by, or return, report or record made to or filed with, such department or agency or officer or employee thereof, which information concerns or relates to the trade secrets, processes, op-erations, style of work, or apparatus, or to the identity, confidential sta-tistical data, amount or source of any income, profits, losses, or expenditures of any person, firm, partnership, corporation, or associa-tion; or permits any income return or copy thereof or any book contain-ing any abstract or particulars thereof to be seen or examined by any person except as provided by law; shall be fined under this title, or imprisoned not more than one year, or both; and shall be removed from office or employment.

SELECTED PROVISIONS FROM 28 U.S.C.
AND 28 C.F.R. PARTS 45 AND 50

28 U.S.C. §535. Investigation of Crimes
Involving Government Officers
and Employees; Limitations

. . . (b) Any information, allegation, or complaint received in a department or agency of the executive branch of the Government relating to violations of Title 18 involving Government officers and employees shall be expeditiously reported to the Attorney General by the head of the department or agency, unless —

(1) the responsibility to perform an investigation with respect thereto is specifically assigned otherwise by another provision of law; or

(2) as to any department or agency of the Government, the Attorney General directs otherwise with respect to a specified class of information, allegation, or complaint. . . .

> **Editors' Note.**   Under 28 U.S.C. §45.1, Department of Justice employees are subject to most of the same provisions of the Code of Federal Regulations that govern other Executive Department employees. These are set out at 5 CFR Part 2635. These are supplemented by some specific Department of Justice regulations set out at 5 CFR Part 3801. (A series of regulations numbered §45.735-4 through §45.735-12 formerly applied to Department of Justice employees — see our 1997 edition — but they were repealed effective May 2, 1997.) Executive branch employees, including Department of Justice employees, are also subject to financial disclosure regulations set out at 5 CFR Part 2634, and to regulations governing general responsibilities and conduct set out at 5 CFR Part 735.

§50.2. Release of Information by Personnel of
the Department of Justice Relating to
Criminal and Civil Proceedings

(a) General. (1) The availability to news media of information in criminal and civil cases is a matter which has become increasingly a subject of concern in the administration of justice. The purpose of this statement is to formulate specific guidelines for the release of such information by personnel of the Department of Justice.

(2) While the release of information for the purpose of influencing a trial is, of course, always improper, there are valid reasons for making available to the public information about the administration of the law. The task of striking a fair balance between the protection of individuals accused of crime or involved in civil proceedings with the Government and public understandings of the problems of controlling crime and administering government depends largely on the exercise of sound judgment by those responsible for administering the law and by representatives of the press and other media.

(3) Inasmuch as the Department of Justice has generally fulfilled its responsibilities with awareness and understanding of the competing needs in this area, this statement, to a considerable extent, reflects and formalizes the standards to which representatives of the Department have adhered in the past. Nonetheless, it will be helpful in ensuring uniformity of practice to set forth the following guidelines for all personnel of the Department of Justice.

(4) Because of the difficulty and importance of the questions they raise, it is felt that some portions of the matters covered by this statement, such as the authorization to make available Federal conviction records and a description of items seized at the time of arrest, should be the subject of continuing review and consideration by the Department on the basis of experience and suggestions from those within and outside the Department.

(b) Guidelines to criminal actions. (1) These guidelines shall apply to the release of information to news media from the time a person is the subject of a criminal investigation until any proceeding resulting from such an investigation has been terminated by trial or otherwise.

(2) At no time shall personnel of the Department of Justice furnish any statement or information for the purpose of influencing the outcome of a defendant's trial, nor shall personnel of the Department furnish any statement or information, which could reasonably be expected to be disseminated by means of public communication, if such a statement or information may reasonably be expected to influence the outcome of a pending or future trial.

(3) Personnel of the Department of Justice, subject to specific limitations imposed by law or court rule or order, may make public the following information:

(i) The defendant's name, age, residence, employment, marital status, and similar background information.

(ii) The substance or text of the charge, such as a complaint, indictment, or information.

(iii) The identity of the investigating and/or arresting agency and the length or scope of an investigation.

(iv) The circumstances immediately surrounding an arrest, resistance, pursuit, possession and use of weapons, and a description of physical items seized at the time of arrest.

Disclosures should include only incontrovertible, factual matters, and should not include subjective observations. In addition, where background information or information relating to the circumstances of an arrest or investigation would be highly prejudicial or where the release thereof would serve no law enforcement function, such information should not be made public.

(4) Personnel of the Department shall not disseminate any information concerning a defendant's prior criminal record.

(5) Because of the particular danger of prejudice resulting from statements in the period approaching and during trial, they ought strenuously to be avoided during that period. Any such statement or release shall be made only on the infrequent occasion when circumstances absolutely demand a disclosure of information and shall include only information which is clearly not prejudicial.

(6) The release of certain types of information generally tends to create dangers of prejudice without serving a significant law enforcement function. Therefore, personnel of the Department should refrain from making available the following:

(i) Observations about a defendant's character.

(ii) Statements, admissions, confessions, or alibis attributable to a defendant, or the refusal or failure of the accused to make a statement.

(iii) Reference to investigative procedures such as fingerprints, polygraph examinations, ballistic tests, or laboratory tests, or to the refusal by the defendant to submit to such tests or examinations.

(iv) Statements concerning the identity, testimony, or credibility of prospective witnesses.

(v) Statements concerning evidence or argument in the case, whether or not it is anticipated that such evidence or argument will be used at trial.

(vi) Any opinion as to the accused's guilt, or the possibility of a plea of guilty to the offense charged, or the possibility of a plea to a lesser offense.

(7) Personnel of the Department of Justice should take no action to encourage or assist news media in photographing or televising a defendant or accused person being held or transported in Federal custody. Departmental representatives should not make available photographs of a defendant unless a law enforcement function is served thereby.

(8) This statement of policy is not intended to restrict the release of information concerning a defendant who is a fugitive from justice.

(9) Since the purpose of this statement is to set forth generally applicable guidelines, there will, of course, be situations in which it will limit the release of information which would not be prejudicial under the particular circumstances. If a representative of the Department believes that in the interest of the fair administration of justice and the law enforcement process information beyond these guidelines should be released, in a particular case, he shall request the permission of the Attorney General or the Deputy Attorney General to do so.

(c) Guidelines to civil actions. Personnel of the Department of Justice associated with a civil action shall not during its investigation or litigation make or participate in making an extrajudicial statement, other than a quotation from or reference to public records, which a reasonable person would expect to be disseminated by means of public communication if there is a reasonable likelihood that such dissemination will interfere with a fair trial and which relates to:

(1) Evidence regarding the occurrence or transaction involved.

(2) The character, credibility, or criminal records of a party, witness, or prospective witness.

(3) The performance or results of any examinations or tests or the refusal or failure of a party to submit to such.

(4) An opinion as to the merits of the claims or defenses of a party, except as required by law or administrative rule.

(5) Any other matter reasonably likely to interfere with a fair trial of the action.

§50.19. Procedures to Be Followed by
Government Attorneys Prior to Filing
Recusal or Disqualification Motions

The determination to seek for any reason the disqualification or recusal of a justice, judge, or magistrate is a most significant and sensitive decision. This is particularly true for government attorneys, who should be guided by uniform procedures in obtaining the requisite authorization for such a motion. This statement is designed to establish a uniform procedure.

(a) No motion to recuse or disqualify a justice, judge, or magistrate (*see, e.g.,* 28 U.S.C. 144, 455) shall be made or supported by any Department of Justice attorney, U.S. Attorney (including Assistant U.S. Attorneys) or agency counsel conducting litigation pursuant to agreement with or authority delegated by the Attorney General, without the prior written approval of the Assistant Attorney General having ultimate supervisory power over the action in which recusal or disqualification is being considered.

(b) Prior to seeking such approval, Justice Department lawyer(s) handling the litigation shall timely seek the recommendations of the U.S. Attorney for the district in which the matter is pending, and the views of the client agencies, if any. Similarly, if agency attorneys are primarily handling any such suit, they shall seek the recommendations of the U.S. Attorney and provide them to the Department of Justice with the request for approval. In actions where the United States Attorneys are primarily handling the litigation in question, they shall seek the recommendation of the client agencies, if any, for submission to the Assistant Attorney General.

(c) In the event that the conduct and pace of the litigation does not allow sufficient time to seek the prior written approval by the Assistant Attorney General, prior oral authorization shall be sought and a written record fully reflecting that authorization shall be subsequently prepared and submitted to the Assistant Attorney General.

(d) Assistant Attorneys General may delegate the authority to approve or deny requests made pursuant to this section, but only to Deputy Assistant Attorneys General or an equivalent position.

(e) This policy statement does not create or enlarge any legal obligations upon the Department of Justice in civil or criminal litigation, and it is not intended to create any private rights enforceable by private parties in litigation with the United States.

Statutes on Disqualification and Discipline of Federal Judges

Editors' Introduction. The Code of Judicial Conduct prohibits judges from presiding over cases in which they have conflicts of interest or in which they are biased. However, the Code of Judicial Conduct does not by itself give parties the right to disqualify judges who fail to heed those prohibitions. In federal court, the right to disqualify judges derives from two federal statutes, 28 U.S.C. §§144 and 455, which we reprint below.

Federal judges appointed under Article III of the Constitution enjoy life tenure and can only be removed from office through impeachment by Congress. Provisions for discipline short of removal are contained in 28 U.S.C. §372(c), which follows the disqualification statutes below.

Contents

28 U.S.C. §144. Bias or Prejudice of Judges

Whenever a party to any proceeding in a district court makes and files a timely and sufficient affidavit that the judge before whom the matter is pending has a personal bias or prejudice either against him or in favor of any adverse party, such judge shall proceed no further therein, but another judge shall be assigned to hear such proceeding.

553

The affidavit shall state the facts and the reasons for the belief that bias or prejudice exists, and shall be filed not less than ten days before the beginning of the term at which the proceeding is to be heard, or good cause shall be shown for failure to file it within such time. A party may file only one such affidavit in any case. It shall be accompanied by a certificate of counsel of record stating that it is made in good faith.

28 U.S.C. §455. Disqualification of Justice, Judge, or Magistrate

(a) Any justice, judge, or magistrate of the United States shall disqualify himself in any proceeding in which his impartiality might reasonably be questioned.

(b) He shall also disqualify himself in the following circumstances:

(1) Where he has a personal bias or prejudice concerning a party, or personal knowledge of disputed evidentiary facts concerning the proceeding;

(2) Where in private practice he served as lawyer in the matter in controversy, or a lawyer with whom he previously practiced law served during such association as a lawyer concerning the matter, or the judge or such lawyer has been a material witness concerning it;

(3) Where he has served in governmental employment and in such capacity participated as counsel, adviser or material witness concerning the proceeding or expressed an opinion concerning the merits of the particular case in controversy;

(4) He knows that he, individually or as a fiduciary, or his spouse or minor child residing in his household, has a financial interest in the subject matter in controversy or in a party to the proceeding, or any other interest that could be substantially affected by the outcome of the proceeding;

(5) He or his spouse, or a person within the third degree of relationship to either of them, or the spouse of such a person:

(i) Is a party to the proceeding, or an officer, director, or trustee of a party;

(ii) Is acting as a lawyer in the proceeding;

(iii) Is known by the judge to have an interest that could be substantially affected by the outcome of the proceeding;

(iv) Is to the judge's knowledge likely to be a material witness in the proceeding.

(c) A judge should inform himself about his personal and fiduciary financial interests, and make a reasonable effort to inform himself about the personal financial interests of his spouse and minor children residing in his household.

(d) For the purposes of this section the following words or phrases shall have the meaning indicated:

(1) "proceeding" includes pretrial, trial, appellate review, or other stages of litigation;

(2) the degree of relationship is calculated according to the civil law system;

(3) "fiduciary" includes such relationships as executor, administrator, trustee, and guardian;

(4) "financial interest" means ownership of a legal or equitable interest, however small, or a relationship as director, adviser, or other active participant in the affairs of a party, except that:

(i) Ownership in a mutual or common investment fund that holds securities is not a "financial interest" in such securities unless the judge participates in the management of the fund;

(ii) An office in an educational, religious, charitable, fraternal, or civic organization is not a "financial interest" in securities held by the organization;

(iii) The proprietary interest of a policyholder in a mutual insurance company, of a depositor in a mutual savings association, or a similar proprietary interest, is a "financial interest" in the organization only if the outcome of the proceeding could substantially affect the value of the interest;

(iv) Ownership of governmental securities is a "financial interest" in the issuer only if the outcome of the proceeding could substantially affect the value of the securities.

(e) No justice, judge, or magistrate shall accept from the parties to the proceeding a waiver of any ground for disqualification enumerated in subsection (b). Where the ground for disqualification arises only under subsection (a), waiver may be accepted provided it is preceded by a full disclosure on the record of the basis for disqualification.

(f) Notwithstanding the preceding provisions of this section, if any justice, judge, magistrate, or bankruptcy judge to whom a matter has been assigned would be disqualified, after substantial judicial time has been devoted to the matter, because of the appearance or discovery, after the matter was assigned to him or her, that he or she individually or as a fiduciary, or his or her spouse or minor child residing in his or her household, has a financial interest in a party (other than an interest that could be substantially affected by the outcome), disqualification is not required if the justice, judge, magistrate, bankruptcy judge, spouse or minor child, as the case may be, divests himself or herself of the interest that provides the grounds for the disqualification.

Editors' Note. Subsection (f) of §455 was added by Congress in Public Law 100-702, effective November 19, 1988.

28 U.S.C. §372(c). Retirement for Disability; Substitute Judge on Failure to Retire; Judicial Discipline

. . . (c)(1) Any person alleging that a circuit, district, or bankruptcy judge, or a magistrate, has engaged in conduct prejudicial to the effective and expeditious administration of the business of the courts, or alleging that such a judge or magistrate is unable to discharge all the duties of office by reason of mental or physical disability, may file with the clerk of the court of appeals for the circuit a written complaint containing a brief statement of the facts constituting such conduct. In the interests of the effective and expeditious administration of the business of the courts and on the basis of information available to the chief judge of the circuit, the chief judge may, by written order stating reasons therefor, identify a complaint for purposes of this subsection and thereby dispense with filing of a written complaint.

(2) Upon receipt of a complaint filed under paragraph (1) of this subsection, the clerk shall promptly transmit such complaint to the chief judge of the circuit, or, if the conduct complained of is that of the chief judge, to that circuit judge in regular active service next senior in date of commission (hereafter, for purposes of this subsection only, included in the term "chief judge"). The clerk shall simultaneously transmit a copy of the complaint to the judge or magistrate whose conduct is the subject of the complaint.

(3) After expeditiously reviewing a complaint, the chief judge, by written order stating his reasons, may —

(A) dismiss the complaint, if he finds it to be (i) not in conformity with paragraph (1) of this subsection, (ii) directly related to the merits of a decision or procedural ruling, or (iii) frivolous; or

(B) conclude the proceeding if he finds that appropriate corrective action has been taken or that action on the complaint is no longer necessary because of intervening events.

The chief judge shall transmit copies of his written order to the complainant and to the judge or magistrate whose conduct is the subject of the complaint.

(4) If the chief judge does not enter an order under paragraph (3) of this subsection, such judge shall promptly —

(A) appoint himself and equal numbers of circuit and district judges of the circuit to a special committee to investigate the facts and allegations contained in the complaint;

(B) certify the complaint and any other documents pertaining thereto to each member of such committee; and

(C) provide written notice to the complainant and the judge or magistrate whose conduct is the subject of the complaint of the action taken under this paragraph.

A judge appointed to a special committee under this paragraph may continue to serve on that committee after becoming a senior judge or, in the case of the chief judge of the circuit, after his or her term as chief judge terminates under subsection (a)(3) or (c) of section 45 of this title. If a judge appointed to a committee under this paragraph dies, or retires from office under section 371(a) of this title, while serving on the committee, the chief judge of the circuit may appoint another circuit or district judge, as the case may be, to the committee.

(5) Each committee appointed under paragraph (4) of this subsection shall conduct an investigation as extensive as it considers necessary, and shall expeditiously file a comprehensive written report thereon with the judicial council of the circuit. Such report shall present both the findings of the investigation and the committee's recommendations for necessary and appropriate action by the judicial council of the circuit.

(6) Upon receipt of a report filed under paragraph (5) of this subsection, the judicial council —

(A) may conduct any additional investigation which it considers to be necessary;

(B) shall take such action as is appropriate to assure the effective and expeditious administration of the business of the courts within the circuit, including, but not limited to, any of the following actions:

(i) directing the chief judge of the district of the magistrate whose conduct is the subject of the complaint to take such action as the judicial council considers appropriate;

(ii) certifying disability of a judge appointed to hold office during good behavior whose conduct is the subject of the complaint, pursuant to the procedures and standards provided under subsection (b) of this section;

(iii) requesting that any such judge appointed to hold office during good behavior voluntarily retire, with the provision that the length of service requirements under section 371 of this title shall not apply;

(iv) ordering that, on a temporary basis for a time certain, no further cases be assigned to any judge or magistrate whose conduct is the subject of a complaint;

(v) censuring or reprimanding such judge or magistrate by means of private communication;

(vi) censuring or reprimanding such judge or magistrate by means of public announcement; or

(vii) ordering such other action as it considers appropriate under the circumstances, except that (I) in no circumstances may the council order removal from office of any judge appointed to hold office during good behavior, and (II) any removal of a magistrate shall be in accordance with section 631 of this title and any removal of a bankruptcy judge shall be in accordance with section 152 of this title;

(C) may dismiss the complaint; and

(D) shall immediately provide written notice to the complainant and to such judge or magistrate of the action taken under this paragraph.

(7)(A) In addition to the authority granted under paragraph (6) of this subsection, the judicial council may, in its discretion, refer any complaint under this subsection, together with the record of any associated proceedings and its recommendations for appropriate action, to the Judicial Conference of the United States.

(B) In any case in which the judicial council determines, on the basis of a complaint and an investigation under this subsection, or on the basis of information otherwise available to the council, that a judge appointed to hold office during good behavior may have engaged in conduct —

(i) which might constitute one or more grounds for impeachment under article II of the Constitution; or

(ii) which, in the interest of justice, is not amenable to resolution by the judicial council,

the judicial council shall promptly certify such determination, together with any complaint and a record of any associated proceedings, to the Judicial Conference of the United States.

(C) A judicial council acting under authority of this paragraph shall, unless contrary to the interests of justice, immediately submit written notice to the complainant and to the judge or magistrate whose conduct is the subject of the action taken under this paragraph.

(8)(A) Upon referral or certification of any matter under paragraph (7) of this subsection, the Judicial Conference, after consideration of the prior proceedings and such additional investigation as it considers appropriate, shall by majority vote take such action, as described in paragraph (6)(B) of this subsection, as it considers appropriate. If the Judicial Conference concurs in the determination of the council, or makes its own determination, that consideration of impeachment may be warranted, it shall so certify and transmit the determination and the record of proceedings to the House of Representatives for whatever action the House of Representatives considers to be necessary. Upon receipt of the determination and record of proceedings in the House of Representatives, the Clerk of the House of Representatives shall make available to the public the determination and any reasons for the determination.

(B) If a judge or magistrate has been convicted of a felony and has exhausted all means of obtaining direct review of the conviction, or the time for seeking further direct review of the conviction has passed and no such review has been sought, the Judicial Conference may, by majority vote and without referral or certification under paragraph (7), transmit to the House of Representatives a determination that consideration of impeachment may be warranted, together with appropriate court records, for whatever action the House of Representatives considers to be necessary.

(9)(A) In conducting any investigation under this subsection, the judicial council, or a special committee appointed under paragraph (4) of this subsection, shall have full subpoena powers as provided in section 332(d) of this title.

(B) In conducting any investigation under this subsection, the Judicial Conference, or a standing committee appointed by the Chief Justice under section 331 of this title, shall have full subpoena powers as provided in that section.

(10) A complainant, judge, or magistrate aggrieved by a final order of the chief judge under paragraph (3) of this subsection may petition the judicial council for review thereof. A complainant, judge, or magistrate aggrieved by an action of the judicial council under paragraph (6) of this subsection may petition the Judical Conference

of the United States for review thereof. The Judicial Conference, or the standing committee established under section 331 of this title, may grant a petition filed by a complainant, judge, or magistrate under this paragraph. Except as expressly provided in this paragraph, all orders and determinations, including denials of petitions for review, shall be final and conclusive and shall not be judicially reviewable on appeal or otherwise.

(11) Each judicial council and the Judicial Conference may prescribe such rules for the conduct of proceedings under this subsection, including the processing of petitions for review, as each considers to be appropriate. Such rules shall contain provisions requiring that —

(A) adequate prior notice of any investigation be given in writing to the judge or magistrate whose conduct is the subject of the complaint;

(B) the judge or magistrate whose conduct is the subject of the complaint be afforded an opportunity to appear (in person or by counsel) at proceedings conducted by the investigating panel, to present oral and documentary evidence, to compel the attendance of witnesses or the production of documents, to cross-examine witnesses, and to present argument orally or in writing; and

(C) the complainant be afforded an opportunity to appear at proceedings conducted by the investigating panel, if the panel concludes that the complainant could offer substantial information.

Any such rule shall be made or amended only after giving appropriate public notice and an opportunity for comment. Any rule promulgated under this subsection shall be a matter of public record, and any such rule promulgated by a judicial council may be modified by the Judicial Conference. No rule promulgated under this subsection may limit the period of time within which a person may file a complaint under this subsection.

(12) No judge or magistrate whose conduct is the subject of an investigation under this subsection shall serve upon a special committee appointed under paragraph (4) of this subsection, upon a judicial council, upon the Judicial Conference, or upon the standing committee established under section 331 of this title, until all related proceedings under this subsection have been finally terminated.

(13) No person shall be granted the right to intervene or to appear as amicus curiae in any proceeding before a judicial council or the Judicial Conference under this subsection.

(14) Except as provided in paragraph (8), all papers, documents, and records of proceedings related to investigations conducted under

this subsection shall be confidential and shall not be disclosed by any person in any proceeding except to the extent that —

(A) the judicial council of the circuit in its discretion releases a copy of a report of a special investigative committee under paragraph (5) to the complainant whose complaint initiated the investigation by that special committee and to the judge or magistrate whose conduct is the subject of the complaint;

(B) the judicial council of the circuit, the Judicial Conference of the United States, or the Senate or the House of Representatives by resolution, releases any such material which is believed necessary to an impeachment investigation or trial of a judge under article I of the Constitution; or

(C) such disclosure is authorized in writing by the judge or magistrate who is the subject to the complaint and by the chief judge of the circuit, the Chief Justice, or the chairman of the standing committee established under section 331 of this title.

(15) Each written order to implement any action under paragraph (6)(B) of this subsection, which is issued by a judicial council, the Judicial Conference, or the standing committee established under section 331 of this title, shall be made available to the public through the appropriate clerk's office of the court of appeals for the circuit. Unless contrary to the interests of justice, each such order issued under this paragraph shall be accompanied by written reasons therefor.

(16) Upon the request of a judge or magistrate whose conduct is the subject of a complaint under this subsection, the judicial council may, if the complaint has been finally dismissed under paragraph (6)(C), recommend that the Director of the Administrative Office of the United States Courts award reimbursement, from funds appropriated to the Federal judiciary, for those reasonable expenses, including attorneys' fees, incurred by that judge or magistrate during the investigation which would not have been incurred but for the requirements of this subsection.

(17) Except as expressly provided in this subsection, nothing in this subsection shall be construed to affect any other provision of this title, the Federal Rules of Civil Procedure, the Federal Rules of Criminal Procedure, the Federal Rules of Appellate Procedure, or the Federal Rules of Evidence.

(18) The United States Claims Court, the Court of International Trade, and the Court of Appeals for the Federal Circuit shall each prescribe rules, consistent with the foregoing provisions of this subsection, establishing procedures for the filing of complaints with respect

to the conduct of any judge of such court and for the investigation and resolution of such complaints. In investigating and taking action with respect to any such complaint, each such court shall have the powers granted to a judicial council under this subsection.

California Materials

California Rules of Professional Conduct

Editors' Note. In 1988, the California Supreme Court adopted new Rules of Professional Conduct, the first major revision of California's ethics rules since 1975. The new rules took effect in May 1989 and have been amended often. Our edition of the rules reflects amendments through our press deadline of September 1996. At the end of the rules, we include proposals pending as of our press date.

When we went to press in late September of 1997, two proposed rules were pending before the California Supreme Court. The two proposals would add a new Rule 1-700 ("Member as Candidates for Judicial Office") and a new Rule 1-710 ("Member as Temporary Judge, Referee, or Court-Appointed Arbitrator"). Both proposals incorporate California's mandatory Code of Judicial Ethics by reference, and would thus subject lawyers who are judicial candidates, temporary judges, referees, or court-appointed arbitrators to discipline by the Bar for violating the Code of Judicial Ethics. We reprint both proposed rules following the current California Rules of Professional Conduct.

For information about other proposals that are in various stages of development but have not yet reached the California Supreme Court, see the California entry in the Introduction at the front of the book, beginning on page xi. For up-to-date information on California Rules of Professional Conduct, visit the California State Bar's web site at www.calbar.org, then click first on "Bar Business," then on "Public Comment Proposals" to read proposed amendments that are being circulated for public comment, or click on "Publication 250" for a comprehensive compilation of new, amended, and repealed rules printed in legislative style.

Contents

Chapter 1. Professional Integrity in General

Chapter 2. Relationship Among Members

Chapter 3. Professional Relationship with Clients

Chapter 4. Financial Relationship with Clients

Chapter 5. Advocacy and Representation

PROPOSED AMENDMENTS PENDING AS OF PRESS DATE

CHAPTER 1. PROFESSIONAL INTEGRITY IN GENERAL

Rule 1-100. Rules of Professional Conduct, in General

(A) Purpose and Function.

The following rules are intended to regulate professional conduct of members of the State Bar through discipline. They have been adopted by the Board of Governors of the State Bar of California and approved by the Supreme Court of California pursuant to Business and Professions Code sections 6076 and 6077 to protect the public and to promote respect and confidence in the legal profession. These rules together with any standards adopted by the Board of Governors pursuant to these rules shall be binding upon all members of the State Bar.

For a willful breach of any of these rules, the Board of Governors has the power to discipline members as provided by law.

The prohibition of certain conduct in these rules is not exclusive. Members are also bound by applicable law including the State Bar Act (Bus. & Prof. Code, §6000 et seq.) and opinions of California courts. Although not binding, opinions of ethics committees in California should be consulted by members for guidance on proper professional conduct. Ethics opinions and rules and standards promulgated by other jurisdictions and bar associations may also be considered.

These rules are not intended to create new civil causes of action. Nothing in these rules shall be deemed to create, augment, diminish, or eliminate any substantive legal duty of lawyers or the non-disciplinary consequences of violating such a duty.

(B) Definitions.

(1) "Law Firm" means:

(a) two or more lawyers whose activities constitute the practice of law, and who share its profits, expenses, and liabilities; or

(b) a law corporation which employs more than one lawyer; or

(c) a division, department, office, or group within a business entity, which includes more than one lawyer who performs legal services for the business entity; or

(d) a publicly funded entity which employs more than one lawyer to perform legal services.

(2) "Member" means a member of the State Bar of California.

(3) "Lawyer" means a member of the State Bar of California or a person who is admitted in good standing of and eligible to practice

before the bar of any United States court or the highest court of the District of Columbia or any state, territory, or insular possession of the United States, or is licensed to practice law in, or is admitted in good standing and eligible to practice before the bar of the highest court of, a foreign country or any political subdivision thereof.

(4) "Associate" means an employee or fellow employee who is employed as a lawyer.

(5) "Shareholder" means a shareholder in a professional corporation pursuant to Business and Professions Code section 6160 et seq.

(C) Purpose of Discussions.

Because it is a practical impossibility to convey in black letter form all of the nuances of these disciplinary rules, the comments contained in the Discussions of the rules, while they do not add independent basis for imposing discipline, are intended to provide guidance for interpreting the rules and practicing in compliance with them.

(D) Geographic Scope of Rules.

(1) As to members: These rules shall govern the activities of members in and outside this state, except as members lawfully practicing outside this state may be specifically required by a jurisdiction in which they are practicing to follow rules of professional conduct different from these rules.

(2) As to lawyers from other jurisdictions: These rules shall also govern the activities of lawyers while engaged in the performance of lawyer functions in this state; but nothing contained in these rules shall be deemed to authorize the performance of such functions by such persons in this state except as otherwise permitted by law.

(E) These rules may be cited and referred to as "Rules of Professional Conduct of the State Bar of California."

DISCUSSION

The Rules of Professional Conduct are intended to establish the standards for members for purposes of discipline. (See Ames v. State Bar (1973) 8 Cal. 3d 910 [106 Cal. Rptr. 489].) The fact that a member has engaged in conduct that may be contrary to these rules does not automatically give rise to a civil cause of action. (See Noble v. Sears, Roebuck & Co. (1973) 33 Cal. App. 3d 654 [109 Cal. Rptr. 269]; Wilhelm v. Pray, Price, Williams & Russell (1986) 186 Cal. App. 3d 1324 [231 Cal. Rptr. 355].) These rules are not intended to supercede existing law relating to members in non-disciplinary contexts. (See, e.g., Klemm v. Superior Court (1977) 75 Cal. App. 3d 893 [142 Cal. Rptr. 509] (motion for disqualification of counsel due to a conflict of interest); Academy of California Optometrists, Inc. v. Superior Court (1975) 51 Cal. App. 3d 999 [124 Cal. Rptr. 668] (duty to return client files); Chronometrics, Inc. v. Sysgen, Inc. (1980) 110 Cal. App. 3d 597 [168 Cal. Rptr. 196] (disqualification of member appropriate remedy for improper communication with adverse party).)

Law firm, as defined by subparagraph (B)(1), is not intended to include an association of lawyers who do not share profits, expenses, and liabilities. The subparagraph is not intended to imply that a law firm may include a person who is not a member in violation of the law governing the unauthorized practice of law.

Rule 1-110. Disciplinary Authority of the State Bar

A member shall comply with conditions attached to public or private reprovals or other discipline administered by the State Bar pursuant to Business and Professions Code sections 6077 and 6078 and rule 956, California Rules of Court.

Rule 1-120. Assisting, Soliciting, or Inducing Violations

A member shall not knowingly assist in, solicit, or induce any violation of these rules or the State Bar Act.

Rule 1-200. False Statement Regarding Admission to the State Bar

(A) A member shall not knowingly make a false statement regarding a material fact or knowingly fail to disclose a material fact in connection with an application for admission to the State Bar.

(B) A member shall not further an application for admission to the State Bar of a person whom the member knows to be unqualified in respect to character, education, or other relevant attributes.

(C) This rule shall not prevent a member from serving as counsel of record for an applicant for admission to practice in proceedings related to such admission.

DISCUSSION

For purposes of rule 1-200 "admission" includes readmission.

Rule 1-300. Unauthorized Practice of Law

(A) A member shall not aid any person or entity in the unauthorized practice of law.

(B) A member shall not practice law in a jurisdiction where to do so would be in violation of regulations of the profession in that jurisdiction.

Rule 1-310. Forming a Partnership with a Non-Lawyer

A member shall not form a partnership with a person who is not a lawyer if any of the activities of that partnership consist of the practice of law.

DISCUSSION

Rule 1-310 is not intended to govern members' activities which cannot be considered to constitute the practice of law. It is intended solely to preclude a member from being involved in the practice of law with a person who is not a lawyer.

Editors' Note. On July 11, 1996, the California Supreme Court adopted a new Rule 1-311 to govern the employment of disbarred, suspended, resigned, or involuntarily inactive lawyers. The new rule, which became effective on August 1, 1996, specifies the kinds of work that such a person may and may not perform while working in a law office, and requires any lawyer who employs such a person to give the State Bar written notice of the employment and the person's current bar status.

Rule 1-311. Employment of Disbarred, Suspended, Resigned, or Involuntarily Inactive Member

(A) For purposes of this rule:

(1) "Employ" means to engage the services of another, including employees, agents, independent contractors and consultants, regardless of whether any compensation is paid;

(2) "Involuntarily inactive member" means a member who is ineligible to practice law as a result of action taken pursuant to Business and Professions Code sections 6007, 6203(c), or California Rule of Court 958(d); and

(3) "Resigned member" means a member who has resigned from the State Bar while disciplinary charges are pending.

(B) A member shall not employ, associate professionally with, or aid a person the member knows or reasonably should know is a disbarred, suspended, resigned, or involuntarily inactive member to perform the following on behalf of the member's client:

(1) Render legal consultation or advice to the client;

(2) Appear on behalf of a client in any hearing or proceeding or before any judicial officer, arbitrator, mediator, court, public agency, referee, magistrate, commissioner, or hearing officer;

(3) Appear as a representative of the client at a deposition or other discovery matter;

(4) Negotiate or transact any matter for or on behalf of the client with third parties;

(5) Receive, disburse or otherwise handle the client's funds; or

(6) Engage in activities which constitute the practice of law.

(C) A member may employ, associate professionally with, or aid a disbarred, suspended, resigned, or involuntarily inactive member to perform research, drafting or clerical activities, including but not limited to:

(1) Legal work of a preparatory nature, such as legal research, the assemblage of data and other necessary information, drafting of pleadings, briefs, and other similar documents;

(2) Direct communication with the client or third parties regarding matters such as scheduling, billing, updates, confirmation of receipt or sending of correspondence and messages; or

(3) Accompanying an active member in attending a deposition or other discovery matter for the limited purpose of providing clerical assistance to the active member who will appear as the representative of the client.

(D) Prior to or at the time of employing a person the member knows or reasonably should know is a disbarred, suspended, resigned, or involuntarily inactive member, the member shall serve upon the State Bar written notice of the employment, including a full description of such person's current bar status. The written notice shall also list the activities prohibited in paragraph (B) and state that the disbarred, suspended, resigned, or involuntarily inactive member will not perform such activities. The member shall serve similar written notice upon each client on whose specific matter such person will work, prior to or at the time of employing such person to work on the client's specific matter. The member shall obtain proof of service of the client's written notice and shall retain such proof and a true and correct copy of the client's written notice for two years following termination of the member's employment with the client.

(E) A member may, without client or State Bar notification, employ a disbarred, suspended, resigned, or involuntarily inactive member whose sole function is to perform office physical plant or equipment maintenance, courier or delivery services, catering, reception, typing or transcription, or other similar support activities.

(F) Upon termination of the disbarred, suspended, resigned, or involuntarily inactive member, the member shall promptly serve upon the State Bar written notice of the termination.

DISCUSSION

For discussion of the activities that constitute the practice of law, see Farnham v. State Bar (1976) 17 Cal.3d 605 [131 Cal. Rptr. 611]; Bluestein v. State Bar (1974) 13 Cal. 3d 162 [118 Cal. Rptr. 175]; Baron v. City of Los Angeles (1970) 2 Cal. 3d 535 [86 Cal. Rptr. 673]; Crawford v. State Bar (1960) 54 Cal. 2d 659 [7 Cal. Rptr. 746]; People v. Merchants Protective Corporation (1922) 189 Cal. 531, 535 [209 P. 363]; People v. Landlords Professional Services (1989) 215 Cal. App. 3d 1599 [264 Cal. Rptr. 548]; and People v. Sipper (1943) 61 Cal. App. 2d Supp. 844 [142 P. 2d 960].

Paragraph (D) is not intended to prevent or discourage a member from fully discussing with the client the activities that will be performed by the disbarred, suspended, resigned, or involuntarily inactive member on the client's matter. If a member's client is an organization, then the written notice required by paragraph (D) shall be served upon the highest authorized officer, employee, or constituent overseeing the particular engagement. (See rule 3-600.)

Nothing in rule 1-311 shall be deemed to limit or preclude any activity engaged in pursuant to rules 983, 983.1, 983.2, and 988 of the California Rules of Court, or any local rule of a federal district court concerning admission pro hac vice.

Rule 1-320. Financial Arrangements with Non-Lawyers

(A) Neither a member nor a law firm shall directly or indirectly share legal fees with a person who is not a lawyer, except that:

(1) An agreement between a member and a law firm, partner, or associate may provide for the payment of money after the member's death to the member's estate or to one or more specified persons over a reasonable period of time; or

(2) A member or law firm undertaking to complete unfinished legal business of a deceased member may pay to the estate of the deceased member or other person legally entitled thereto that proportion of the total compensation which fairly represents the services rendered by the deceased member;

(3) A member or law firm may include non-member employees in a compensation, profit-sharing, or retirement plan even though the plan is based in whole or in part on a profit-sharing arrangement, if such plan does not circumvent these rules or Business and Professions Code section 6000 et seq.; or

(4) A member may pay a prescribed registration, referral, or participation fee to a lawyer referral service established, sponsored, and operated in accordance with the State Bar of California's Minimum Standards for a Lawyer Referral Service in California.

(B) A member shall not compensate, give, or promise anything of value to any person or entity for the purpose of recommending or securing employment of the member or the member's law firm by a client, or as a reward for having made a recommendation resulting in employment of the member or the member's law firm by a client. A member's offering of or giving a gift or gratuity to any person or entity having made a recommendation resulting in the employment of the member or the member's law firm shall not of itself violate this rule, provided that the gift or gratuity was not offered or given in consideration of any promise, agreement, or understanding that such a gift or gratuity would be forthcoming or that referrals would be made or encouraged in the future.

(C) A member shall not compensate, give, or promise anything of value to any representative of the press, radio, television, or other communication medium in anticipation of or in return for publicity of the member, the law firm, or any other member as such in a news item, but the incidental provision of food or beverage shall not of itself violate this rule.

DISCUSSION

Rule 1-320(C) is not intended to preclude compensation to the communications media in exchange for advertising the member's or law firm's availability for professional employment.

Rule 1-400. Advertising and Solicitation

Editors' Note. Effective June 1, 1997, the California Supreme Court added a new Rule 1-400(d)(6) to govern any lawyer claiming to be a "certified specialist." The new rule replaces a similar rule repealed by the California Supreme Court effective November 30, 1992. (The repealed version did not refer to other entities accredited by the State Bar — see our 1991 edition.) Upon the adoption of Rule 1-400(d)(6), the State Bar repealed Standard 11 following Rule 1-400. (The State Bar Board of Governors may change advertising standards without Supreme Court approval.) We underscore the new rule to show that it is new, and we strike through Standard 11 to show that it has been repealed.

In a related development, also effective June 1, 1997, the State Bar Board of Governors substantially amended the Rules Governing the State Bar of California Program for Certifying Legal Specialists. These rules are lengthy and we do not reprint them, but they can be viewed on the California State Bar's web page at www.calbar.org (then click on "Legal Specialization").

(A) For purposes of this rule, "communication" means any message or offer made by or on behalf of a member concerning the availability for professional employment of a member or a law firm directed to any former, present, or prospective client, including but not limited to the following:

(1) Any use of firm name, trade name, fictitious name, or other professional designation of such member or law firm; or

(2) Any stationery, letterhead, business card, sign, brochure, or other comparable written material describing such member, law firm, or lawyers; or

(3) Any advertisement (regardless of medium) of such member or law firm directed to the general public or any substantial portion thereof; or

(4) Any unsolicited correspondence from a member or law firm directed to any person or entity.

(B) For purposes of this rule, a "solicitation" means any communication:

(1) Concerning the availability for professional employment of a member or a law firm in which a significant motive is pecuniary gain; and

(2) Which is;

(a) delivered in person or by telephone, or

(b) directed by any means to a person known to the sender to be represented by counsel in a matter which is a subject of the communication.

(C) A solicitation shall not be made by or on behalf of a member or law firm to a prospective client with whom the member or law firm has no family or prior professional relationship, unless the solicitation is protected from abridgment by the Constitution of the United States or by the Constitution of the State of California. A solicitation to a former or present client in the discharge of a member's or law firm's professional duties is not prohibited.

(D) A communication or a solicitation (as defined herein) shall not:

(1) Contain any untrue statement; or

(2) Contain any matter, or present or arrange any matter in a manner or format which is false, deceptive, or which tends to confuse, deceive, or mislead the public; or

(3) Omit to state any fact necessary to make the statements made, in the light of circumstances under which they are made, not misleading to the public; or

(4) Fail to indicate clearly, expressly, or by context, that it is a communication or solicitation, as the case may be; or

(5) Be transmitted in any manner which involves intrusion, coercion, duress, compulsion, intimidation, threats, or vexatious or harassing conduct.

(6) State that a member is a "certified specialist" unless the member holds a current certificate as a specialist issued by the Board of Legal Specialization, or any other entity accredited by the State Bar to designate specialists pursuant to standards adopted by the Board of Governors, and states the complete name of the entity which granted certification.

(E) The Board of Governors of the State Bar shall formulate and adopt standards as to communications which will be presumed to violate this rule 1-400. The standards shall only be used as presumptions affecting the burden of proof in disciplinary proceedings involving alleged violations of these rules. "Presumption affecting the burden of proof" means that presumption defined in Evidence Code sections 605 and 606. Such standards formulated and adopted by the Board, as from time to time amended, shall be effective and binding on all members.

(F) A member shall retain for two years a true and correct copy or recording of any communication made by written or electronic media. Upon written request, the member shall make any such copy or recording available to the State Bar, and, if requested, shall provide to the State Bar evidence to support any factual or objective claim contained in the communication.

Editors' Note. Effective May 11, 1994, pursuant to its authority under Rule 1-400(E), the State Bar Board of Governors amended one existing advertising standard (Standard 5) and approved five new advertising standards (Standards 12-16). Effective June 1, 1997, upon the Supreme Court's adoption of new Rule 1-400(d)(6), the State Bar repealed Standard 11, which covers the same subject matter as the new rule. (The State Bar may change the advertising standards without the approval of the California Supreme Court.)

STANDARDS

Pursuant to rule 1-400(E) the Board of Governors of the State Bar has adopted the following standards, effective May 27, 1989 as forms of "communication" defined in rule 1-400(A) which are presumed to be in violation of rule 1-400:

(1) A "communication" which contains guarantees, warranties, or predictions regarding the result of the representation.

(2) A "communication" which contains testimonials about or endorsements of a member unless such communication also contains an express disclaimer such as "this testimonial or endorsement does not constitute a guarantee, warranty, or prediction regarding the outcome of your legal matter."

(3) A "communication" which is delivered to a potential client whom the member knows or should reasonably know is in such a physical, emotional, or mental state that he or she would not be expected to exercise reasonable judgment as to the retention of counsel.

(4) A "communication" which is transmitted at the scene of an accident or at or en route to a hospital, emergency care center, or other health care facility.

(5) A "communication," except professional announcements, seeking professional employment for pecuniary gain which is transmitted by mail or equivalent means which does not bear the words "Advertisement," "Newsletter" or words of similar import in 12 point print on the first page. If such communication, including firm brochures, newsletters, recent legal developments advisories, and similar materials, is transmitted in an envelope, the envelope shall bear the word "Advertisement," "Newsletter" or words of similar import on the outside thereof.

(6) A "communication" in the form of a firm name, trade name, fictitious name, or other professional designation which states or implies a relationship between any member in private practice and a gov-

ernment agency or instrumentality or a public or non-profit legal services organization.

(7) A "communication" in the form of a firm name, trade name, fictitious name, or other professional designation which states or implies that a member has a relationship to any other lawyer or a law firm as a partner or associate, or officer or shareholder pursuant to Business and Professions Code sections 6160-6172 unless such relationship in fact exists.

(8) A "communication" which states or implies that a member or law firm is "of counsel" to another lawyer or a law firm unless the former has a relationship with the latter (other than as a partner or associate, or officer or shareholder pursuant to Business and Professions Code sections 6160-6172) which is close, personal, continuous, and regular.

(9) A "communication" in the form of a firm name, trade name, fictitious name, or other professional designation used by a member or law firm in private practice which differs materially from any other such designation used by such member or law firm at the same time in the same community.

(10) A "communication" which implies that the member or law firm is participating in a lawyer referral service which has been certified by the State Bar of California or as having satisfied the Minimum Standards for Lawyer Referral Services in California, when that is not the case.

(11) A "communication" which states or implies that a member is a "certified specialist" unless such communication also states the complete name of the entity which granted the certification as a specialist.

(12) A "communication," except professional announcements, in the form of an advertisement primarily directed to seeking professional employment primarily for pecuniary gain transmitted to the general public or any substantial portion thereof by mail or equivalent means or by means of television, radio, newspaper, magazine or other form of commercial mass media which does not state the name of the member responsible for the communication. When the communication is made on behalf of a law firm, the communication shall state the name of at least one member responsible for it.

(13) A "communication" which contains a dramatization unless such communication contains a disclaimer which states "this is a dramatization" or words of similar import.

(14) A "communication" which states or implies "no fee without recovery" unless such communication also expressly discloses whether or not the client will be liable for costs.

(15) A "communication" which states or implies that a member is able to provide legal services in a language other that English unless the member can actually provide legal services in such language or the communication also states in the language of the communication (a) the employment title of the person who speaks such language and (b) that the person is not a member of the State Bar of California, if that is the case.

(16) An unsolicited "communication" transmitted to the general public or any substantial portion thereof primarily directed to seeking professional employment primarily for pecuniary gain which sets forth a specific fee or range of fees for a particular service where, in fact, the member charges a greater fee than advertised in such communication within a period of 90 days following dissemination of such communication, unless such communication expressly specifies a shorter period of time regarding the advertised fee. Where the communication is published in the classified or "yellow pages" section of telephone, business or legal directories or in other media not published more frequently than once a year, the member shall conform to the advertised fee for a period of one year from initial publication, unless such communication expressly specifies a shorter period of time regarding the advertised fee.

Rule 1-500. Agreements Restricting a Member's Practice

(A) A member shall not be a party to or participate in offering or making an agreement, whether in connection with the settlement of a lawsuit or otherwise, if the agreement restricts the right of a member to practice law, except that this rule shall not prohibit such an agreement which:

(1) Is a part of an employment, shareholders', or partnership agreement among members provided the restrictive agreement does not survive the termination of the employment, shareholder, or partnership relationship; or

(2) Requires payments to a member upon the member's retirement from the practice of law; or

(3) Is authorized by Business & Professions Code sections 6092.5(i) or 6093.

(B) A member shall not be a party to or participate in offering or making an agreement which precludes the reporting of a violation of these rules.

DISCUSSION

Paragraph (A) makes it clear that the practice, in connection with settlement agreements, of proposing that a member refrain from representing other clients in similar litigation, is prohibited. Neither counsel may demand or suggest such provisions nor may opposing counsel accede or agree to such provisions.

Paragraph (A) permits a restrictive covenant in a law corporation, partnership, or employment agreement. The law corporation shareholder, partner, or associate may agree not to have a separate practice during the existence of the relationship; however, upon termination of the relationship (whether voluntary or involuntary), the member is free to practice law without any contractual restriction except in the case of retirement from the active practice of law.

Rule 1-600. Legal Service Programs

(A) A member shall not participate in a nongovernmental program, activity, or organization furnishing, recommending, or paying for legal services, which allows any third person or organization to interfere with the member's independence of professional judgment, or with the client-lawyer relationship, or allows unlicensed persons to practice law, or allows any third person or organization to receive directly or indirectly any part of the consideration paid to the member except as permitted by these rules, or otherwise violates the State Bar Act or these rules.

(B) The Board of Governors of the State Bar shall formulate and adopt Minimum Standards for Lawyer Referral Services, which, as from time to time amended, shall be binding on members.

DISCUSSION

The participation of a member in a lawyer referral service established, sponsored, supervised, and operated in conformity with the Minimum Standards for a Lawyer Referral Service in California is encouraged and is not, of itself, a violation of these rules.

Rule 1-600 is not intended to override any contractual agreement or relationship between insurers and insureds regarding the provision of legal services.

Rule 1-600 is not intended to apply to the activities of a public agency responsible for providing legal services to a government or to the public.

For purposes of paragraph (A), "a nongovernmental program, activity, or organization" includes, but is not limited to group, prepaid, and voluntary legal service programs, activities, or organizations.

> **Editors' Note.** Rule 1-600(b) refers to "Minimum Standards for Lawyer Referral Services." These Minimum Standards were originally adopted by the California Supreme Court in 1989 and were amended most recently effective January 1, 1997, when they were clarified and renamed "Rules and Regulations of the State Bar of California Pertaining to Lawyer Referral Services." They are too lengthy to reprint here, but can be found in California statute books following §6155 of the Business and Professions Code. For more information on lawyer referral services in California, contact the California State Bar's Office of Legal Services at 415-561-8398.

CHAPTER 2. RELATIONSHIP AMONG MEMBERS

Rule 2-100. Communication with a Represented Party

(A) While representing a client, a member shall not communicate directly or indirectly about the subject of the representation with a party the member knows to be represented by another lawyer in the matter, unless the member has the consent of the other lawyer.

(B) For purposes of this rule, a "party" includes:

(1) An officer, director, or managing agent of a corporation or association, and a partner or managing agent of a partnership; or

(2) An association member or an employee of an association, corporation, or partnership, if the subject of the communication is any act or omission of such person in connection with the matter which may be binding upon or imputed to the organization for purposes of civil or criminal liability or whose statement may constitute an admission on the part of the organization.

(C) This rule shall not prohibit:

(1) Communications with a public officer, board, committee, or body;

(2) Communications initiated by a party seeking advice or representation from an independent lawyer of the party's choice; or

(3) Communications otherwise authorized by law.

DISCUSSION

Rule 2-100 is intended to control communications between a member and persons the member knows to be represented by counsel unless a statutory scheme or case law will override the rule. There are a number of express statutory schemes which authorize communications between a member and person who would otherwise be subject to this rule. These statutes protect a variety of other rights such as the right of employees to organize and to engage in collective bargaining, employee health and safety, or equal employment opportunity. Other applicable law also includes the authority of government prosecutors and investigators to conduct criminal investigations, as limited by the relevant decisional law.

Rule 2-100 is not intended to prevent the parties themselves from communicating with respect to the subject matter of the representation, and nothing in the rule prevents a member from advising the client that such communication can be made. Moreover, the rule does not prohibit a member who is also a party to a legal matter from directly or indirectly communicating on his or her own behalf with a represented party. Such a member has independent rights as a party which should not be abrogated because of his or her professional status. To prevent any possible abuse in such situations, the counsel for the opposing party may advise that party (1) about the risks and benefits of communications with a lawyer-party, and (2) not to accept or engage in communications with the lawyer-party.

Rule 2-100 also addresses the situation in which member *A* is contacted by an opposing party who is represented and, because of dissatisfaction with that party's counsel, seeks *A*'s independent advice. Since *A* is employed by the opposition, the member cannot give independent advice.

As used in paragraph (A), "the subject of the representation," "matter," and "party" are not limited to a litigation context.

Paragraph (B) is intended to apply only to persons employed at the time of the communication.

Subparagraph (C)(2) is intended to permit a member to communicate with a party seeking to hire new counsel or to obtain a second opinion. A member contacted by such a party continues to be bound by other Rules of Professional Conduct. (See, e.g., rules 1-400 and 3-310.)

Editors' Note. During 1993, the California State Bar considered a proposed amendment to the Discussion following Rule 2-100. The proposed amendment would have clarified that Rule 2-100 does not apply to government prosecutors during the investigative phase of a criminal, disciplinary, or civil law enforcement proceeding. In August 1993, however, after considering public comments, the State Bar Board Committee on Admissions and Competence (which has oversight over rule production) determined "to take no further action on the matter."

Rule 2-200. Financial Arrangements Among Lawyers

(A) A member shall not divide a fee for legal services with a lawyer who is not a partner of, associate of, or shareholder with the member unless:

(1) The client has consented in writing thereto after a full disclosure has been made in writing that a division of fees will be made and the terms of such division; and

(2) The total fee charged by all lawyers is not increased solely by reason of the provision for division of fees and is not unconscionable as that term is defined in rule 4-200.

(B) Except as permitted in paragraph (A) of this rule or rule 2-300, a member shall not compensate, give, or promise anything of value to any lawyer for the purpose of recommending or securing employment of the member or the member's law firm by a client, or as a reward for having made a recommendation resulting in employment of the member or the member's law firm by a client. A member's offering of or giving a gift or gratuity to any lawyer who has made a recommendation resulting in the employment of the member or the member's law firm shall not of itself violate this rule, provided that the gift or gratuity was not offered in consideration of any promise, agreement, or understanding that such a gift or gratuity would be forthcoming or that referrals would be made or encouraged in the future.

Rule 2-300. Sale or Purchase of a Law Practice of a Member, Living or Deceased

All or substantially all of the law practice of a member, living or deceased, including goodwill, may be sold to another member or law firm subject to all the following conditions:

(A) Fees charged to clients shall not be increased solely by reason of such sale.

(B) If the sale contemplates the transfer of responsibility for work not yet completed or responsibility for client files or information protected by Business and Professions Code section 6068, subdivision (e), then;

(1) if the seller is deceased, or has a conservator or other person acting in a representative capacity, and no member has been appointed to act for the seller pursuant to Business and Professions Code section 6180.5, then prior to the transfer;

(a) the purchaser shall cause a written notice to be given to the client stating that the interest in the law practice is being transferred to the purchaser; that the client has the right to retain other counsel; that the client may take possession of any client papers and property, as required by rule 3-700(D); and that if no response is received to the notification within 90 days of the sending of such notice, or in the event the client's rights would be prejudiced by a failure to act during that time, the purchaser may act on behalf of the client until otherwise notified by the client. Such notice shall comply with the requirements as set forth in rule 1-400(D) and any provisions relating to attorney-client fee arrangements, and

(b) the purchaser shall obtain the written consent of the client provided that such consent shall be presumed until otherwise notified by the client if no response is received to the notification specified in subparagraph (a) within 90 days of the date of the sending of such notification to the client's last address as shown on the records of the seller, or the client's rights would be prejudiced by a failure to act during such 90-day period.

(2) in all other circumstances, not less than 90 days prior to the transfer;

(a) the seller, or the member appointed to act for the seller pursuant to Business and Professions code section 6180.5, shall cause a written notice to be given to the client stating that the interest in the law practice is being transferred to the purchaser; that the client has the right to retain other counsel; that the client may take possession of any client papers and property, as required by rule 3-700(D); and that if no response is received to the notification within 90 days of the sending of such notice, the purchaser may act on behalf of the client until otherwise notified by the client. Such notice shall comply with the requirements as set forth in rule 1-400(D) and any provisions relating to attorney-client fee arrangements, and

(b) the seller, or the member appointed to act for the seller pursuant to Business and Professions Code section 6180.5, shall obtain the written consent of the client prior to the transfer provided that such consent shall be presumed until otherwise notified by the client if no response is received to the notification specified in subparagraph (a) within 90 days of the date of the sending of such notification to the client's last address as shown on the records of the seller.

(C) If substitution is required by the rules of a tribunal in which a matter is pending, all steps necessary to substitute a member shall be taken.

(D) All activity of a purchaser or potential purchaser under this rule shall be subject to compliance with rules 3-300 and 3-310 where applicable.

(E) Confidential information shall not be disclosed to a non-member in connection with a sale under this rule.

(F) Admission to or retirement from a law partnership or law corporation, retirement plans and similar arrangements, or sale of tangible assets of a law practice shall not be deemed a sale or purchase under this rule.

DISCUSSION

Paragraph (A) is intended to prohibit the purchaser from charging the former clients of the seller a higher fee than the purchaser is charging his or her existing clients.

"All or substantially all of the law practice of a member" means, for purposes of rule 2-300, that, for example, a member may retain one or two clients who have such a longstanding personal and professional relationship with the member that transfer of those clients' files is not feasible. Conversely, rule 2-300 is not intended to authorize the sale of a law practice in a piecemeal fashion except as may be required by subparagraph (B)(1)(a) or paragraph (D).

Transfer of individual client matters, where permitted, is governed by rule 2-200. Payment of a fee to a non-lawyer broker for arranging the sale or purchase of a law practice is governed by rule 1-320.

> **Editors' Note.** Rule 2-400, which prohibits unlawful discrimination in the operation or management of a law practice, was adopted by the California Supreme Court effective March 1, 1994. It is narrower in scope than similar rules in most other states because no disciplinary investigation or proceeding may be initiated under the rule "unless and until a tribunal of competent jurisdiction, other than a disciplinary tribunal, shall have first adjudicated a complaint of alleged discrimination and found that unlawful conduct occurred."

Rule 2-400. Prohibited Discriminatory Conduct in a Law Practice

(A) For purposes of this rule:

(1) "law practice" includes sole practices, law partnerships, law corporations, corporate and governmental legal departments, and other entities which employ members to practice law;

(2) "knowingly permit" means a failure to advocate corrective action where the member knows of a discriminatory policy or practice which results in the unlawful discrimination prohibited in paragraph (B); and

(3) "unlawfully" and "unlawful" shall be determined by reference to applicable state or federal statutes or decisions making unlawful discrimination in employment and in offering goods and services to the public.

(B) In the management or operation of a law practice, a member shall not unlawfully discriminate or knowingly permit unlawful discrimination on the basis of race, national origin, sex, sexual orientation, religion, age or disability in:

(1) hiring, promoting, discharging or otherwise determining the conditions of employment of any person; or

(2) accepting or terminating representation of any client.

(C) No disciplinary investigation or proceeding may be initiated by the State Bar against a member under this rule unless and until a tribunal of competent jurisdiction, other than a disciplinary tribunal, shall have first adjudicated a complaint of alleged discrimination and found that unlawful conduct occurred. Upon such adjudication, the tribunal finding or verdict shall then be admissible evidence of the occurrence or non-occurrence of the alleged discrimination in any disciplinary proceeding initiated under this rule. In order for discipline to be imposed under this rule, however, the finding of unlawfulness must be upheld and final after appeal, the time for filing an appeal must have expired, or the appeal must have been dismissed.

DISCUSSION

In order for discriminatory conduct to be actionable under this rule, it must first be found to be unlawful by an appropriate civil administrative or judicial tribunal under applicable state or federal law. Until there is a finding of civil unlawfulness, there is no basis for disciplinary action under this rule.

A complaint of misconduct based on this rule may be filed with the State Bar following a finding of unlawfulness in the first instance even though that finding is therafter appealed.

A disciplinary investigation or proceeding for conduct coming within this rule may be initiated and maintained, however, if such conduct warrants discipline under California Business and Professions Code sections 6106 and 6068, the California Supreme Court's inherent authority to impose discipline, or other disciplinary standard.

CHAPTER 3. PROFESSIONAL RELATIONSHIP WITH CLIENTS

Editors' Note on Confidentiality. On June 3, 1993, the California Supreme Court rejected a proposed new Rule 3-100 that would have added a duty of confidentiality to California's ethics rules for the first time. California's confidentiality obligation is now solely statutory; it is found in §6068(e) of the California Business and Professions Code, which has no exceptions allowing disclosure. (Section 6068(e) is reprinted in the next chapter.) The rejected Rule 3-100 would have allowed disclosure of information necessary to prevent a client from committing a life-threatening crime. It is reprinted in full at the end of these rules.

On May 31, 1996, the State Bar circulated a new proposed draft of Rule 3-100 that would closely track Rule 1.6 of the ABA Model Rules of Professional Conduct. The draft attempts to harmonize a lawyer's absolute ethical duty of confidentiality under §6068(e) of California's Business and Professions Code with the "death or substantial bodily harm" exception to the attorney-client privilege in §956.5 of the California Evidence Code, which became law in 1993. The public comment period regarding proposed Rule 3-100 closed on September 9, 1996. The State Bar studied the comments together with representatives of the Los Angeles County Bar, which originated the proposal for a confidentiality rule. When we went to press in September of 1997, the State Bar was still deciding whether to forward the original proposal to the Supreme Court, forward a revised proposal to the Supreme Court without further public comment, circulate a revised proposal for public comment, or abandon the effort to adopt a confidentiality rule.

Rule 3-110. Failing to Act Competently

(A) A member shall not intentionally, recklessly, or repeatedly fail to perform legal services with competence.

(B) For purposes of this rule, "competence" in any legal service shall mean to apply the 1) diligence, 2) learning and skill, and 3) mental, emotional, and physical ability reasonably necessary for the performance of such service.

(C) If a member does not have sufficient learning and skill when the legal service is undertaken, the member may nonetheless perform such services competently by 1) associating with or, where appropriate, professionally consulting another lawyer reasonably believed to be competent, or 2) by acquiring sufficient learning and skill before performance is required.

DISCUSSION

The duties set forth in rule 3-110 include the duty to supervise the work of subordinate attorney and non-attorney employees or agents. (See, e.g., Waysman v. State Bar (1986) 41 Cal. 3d 452; Trousil v. State Bar (1985) 38 Cal. 3d 337, 342 [211 Cal. Rptr. 525]; Palomo v. State Bar (1984) 36 Cal. 3d 785 [205 Cal. Rptr. 834]; Crane v. State Bar (1981) 30 Cal. 3d 117, 122; Black v. State Bar (1972) 7 Cal. 3d 676, 692 [103 Cal. Rptr. 288; 499 P.2d 968]; Vaughn v. State Bar (1972) 6 Cal. 3d 847, 857-858 [100 Cal. Rptr. 713; 494 P.2d 1257]; Moore v. State Bar (1964) 62 Cal. 2d 74, 81 [41 Cal. Rptr. 161; 396 P.2d 577].)

In an emergency a lawyer may give advice or assistance in a matter in which the lawyer does not have the skill ordinarily required where referral to or consultation with another lawyer would be impractical. Even in an emergency, however, assistance should be limited to that reasonably necessary in the circumstances.

Rule 3-120. Sexual Relations with Client

Editors' Note. The following rule is a direct outgrowth of California Business and Professions Code §6106.8 (reprinted in the following chapter), enacted by the California legislature in 1989. That statute found there was "no rule that governs the propriety of sexual relationships between lawyers and clients," and commanded the Bar to submit an appropriate rule to the California Supreme Court. The Bar, slightly tardy, submitted a proposed rule to the California Supreme Court in May 1991. In August 1991, the California Supreme Court remanded the proposal for recirculation. This was done and the proposal was resubmitted to the California Supreme Court unchanged. On August 13, 1992, the California Supreme

Court adopted the rule as proposed, except that the court deleted the following proposed subparagraph E:

> (E) A member who engages in sexual relations with his or her client will be presumed to violate rule 3-120, paragraph (B)(3). This presumption shall only be used as a presumption affecting the burden of proof in disciplinary proceedings involving alleged violations of these rules. "Presumption affecting the burden of proof" means that presumption defined in Evidence Code sections 605 and 606.

Thus, violation of Rule 3-120 does not carry a presumption of incompetence in providing legal services.

California was the first state to adopt a rule of legal ethics expressly addressing sexual relationships with clients. For a parallel state statute signed into law in September 1992, see §6106.9 of the California Business and Professions Code below.

(A) For purposes of this rule, "sexual relations" means sexual intercourse or the touching of an intimate part of another person for the purpose of sexual arousal, gratification, or abuse.

(B) A member shall not:

(1) Require or demand sexual relations with a client incident to or as a condition of any professional representation; or

(2) Employ coercion, intimidation, or undue influence in entering into sexual relations with a client; or

(3) Continue representation of a client with whom the member has sexual relations if such sexual relations cause the member to perform legal services incompetently in violation of rule 3-110.

(C) Paragraph (B) shall not apply to sexual relations between members and their spouses or to ongoing consensual lawyer-client sexual relations which predate the initiation of the lawyer-client relationship.

(D) Where a lawyer in a firm has sexual relations with a client but does not participate in the representation of that client, the lawyers in the firm shall not be subject to discipline under this rule solely because of the occurrence of such sexual relations.

DISCUSSION

Rule 3-120 is intended to prohibit sexual exploitation by a lawyer in the course of a professional representation. Often, based upon the nature of the underlying representation, a client exhibits great emotional vulnerability and dependence upon the advice and guidance of counsel. Attorneys owe the utmost duty of good faith and fidelity to clients. (See, e.g., Greenbaum v. State Bar (1976) 15 Cal. 3d 893, 903 [126 Cal. Rptr. 785]; Alkow v. State Bar (1971) 3 Cal. 3d 924, 935 [92 Cal. Rptr. 278]; Cutler v. State Bar (1969) 71 Cal. 2d 241, 251 [78 Cal. Rptr. 172]; Clancy v. State Bar (1969) 71 Cal. 2d 140, 146 [77 Cal. Rptr. 657].) The relationship between an attorney and client is a fiduciary relationship of the very highest character and all dealings between an attorney and client that are beneficial to the attorney will be closely scrutinized with the utmost strictness for unfairness. (See, e.g., Giovanazzi v. State Bar (1980) 28 Cal. 3d 465, 472 [169 Cal. Rptr. 581]; Benson v. State Bar (1975) 13 Cal. 3d 581, 586 [119 Cal. Rptr. 297]; Lee v. State Bar (1970) 2 Cal. 3d 927, 939 [88 Cal. Rptr. 361]; Clancy v. State Bar (1969) 71 Cal. 2d 140, 146 [77 Cal. Rptr. 657].) Where attorneys exercise undue influence over clients or take unfair advantage of clients, discipline is appropriate. (See, e.g., Magee v. State Bar (1962) 58 Cal. 2d 423 [24 Cal. Rptr. 839]; Lantz v. State Bar (1931) 212 Cal. 213 [298 P. 497].) In all client matters, a member is advised to keep clients' interests paramount in the course of the member's representation.

For purposes of this rule, if the client is an organization, any individual overseeing the representation shall be deemed to be the client. (See rule 3-600.)

Although paragraph (C) excludes representation of certain clients from the scope of rule 3-120, such exclusion is not intended to preclude the applicability of other Rules of Professional Conduct, including rule 3-110.

Rule 3-200. Prohibited Objectives of Employment

A member shall not seek, accept, or continue employment if the member knows or should know that the objective of such employment is:

(A) To bring an action, conduct a defense, assert a position in litigation, or take an appeal, without probable cause and for the purpose of harassing or maliciously injuring any person; or

(B) To present a claim or defense in litigation that is not warranted under existing law, unless it can be supported by a good faith argument for an extension, modification, or reversal of such existing law.

Rule 3-210. Advising the Violation of Law

A member shall not advise the violation of any law, rule, or ruling of a tribunal unless the member believes in good faith that such law, rule, or ruling is invalid. A member may take appropriate steps in good faith to test the validity of any law, rule, or ruling of a tribunal.

DISCUSSION

Rule 3-210 is intended to apply not only to the prospective conduct of a client but also to the interaction between the member and client and to the specific legal service sought by the client from the member. An example of the former is the handling of physical evidence of a crime in the possession of the client and offered to the member. (See People v. Meredith (1981) 29 Cal. 3d 682 [175 Cal. Rptr. 612].) An example of the latter is a request that the member negotiate the return of stolen property in exchange for the owner's agreement not to report the theft to the police or prosecutorial authorities. (See People v. Pic'l (1982) 31 Cal. 3d 731 [183 Cal. Rptr. 685].)

Rule 3-300. Avoiding Interests Adverse to a Client

A member shall not enter into a business transaction with a client; or knowingly acquire an ownership, possessory, security, or other pecuniary interest adverse to a client, unless each of the following requirements has been satisfied:

(A) The transaction or acquisition and its terms are fair and reasonable to the client and are fully disclosed and transmitted in writing to the client in a manner which should reasonably have been understood by the client; and

(B) The client is advised in writing that the client may seek the advice of an independent lawyer of the client's choice and is given a reasonable opportunity to seek that advice; and

(C) The client thereafter consents in writing to the terms of the transaction or the terms of the acquisition.

DISCUSSION

Rule 3-300 is not intended to apply to the agreement by which the member is retained by the client, unless the agreement confers on the member an ownership, possessory, security, or other pecuniary interest adverse to the client. Such an agreement is governed, in part, by rule 4-200.

Rule 3-300 is not intended to apply where the member and client each make an investment on terms offered to the general public or a significant portion thereof. For example, rule 3-300 is not intended to apply where *A,* a member, invests in a limited partnership syndicated by a third party. *B, A*'s client, makes the same investment. Although *A* and *B* are each investing in the same business, *A* did not enter into the transaction "with" *B* for the purposes of the rule.

Rule 3-300 is intended to apply where the member wishes to obtain an interest in client's property in order to secure the amount of the member's past due or future fees.

Rule 3-310. Avoiding the Representation of Adverse Interests

(A) For purposes of this rule:

(1) "Disclosure" means informing the client or former client of the relevant circumstances and of the actual and reasonably foreseeable adverse consequences to the client or former client;

(2) "Informed written consent" means the client's or former client's written agreement to the representation following written disclosure;

(3) "Written" means any writing as defined in Evidence Code section 250.

(B) A member shall not accept or continue representation of a client without providing written disclosure to the client where:

(1) The member has a legal, business, financial, professional, or personal relationship with a party or witness in the same matter; or

(2) The member knows or reasonably should know that:

(a) the member previously had a legal, business, financial, professional, or personal relationship with a party or witness in the same matter; and

(b) the previous relationship would substantially affect the member's representation; or

(3) The member has or had a legal, business, financial, professional, or personal relationship with another person or entity the member knows or reasonably should know would be affected substantially by resolution of the matter; or

(4) The member has or had a legal, business, financial, or professional interest in the subject matter of the representation.

(C) A member shall not, without the informed written consent of each client:

(1) Accept representation of more than one client in a matter in which the interests of the clients potentially conflict; or

(2) Accept or continue representation of more than one client in a matter in which the interests of the clients actually conflict; or

(3) Represent a client in a matter and at the same time in a separate matter accept as a client a person or entity whose interest in the first matter is adverse to the client in the first matter.

(D) A member who represents two or more clients shall not enter into an aggregate settlement of the claims of or against the clients, without the informed written consent of each client.

(E) A member shall not, without the informed written consent of the client or former client, accept employment adverse to the client or former client where, by reason of the representation of the client or former client, the member has obtained confidential information material to the employment.

(F) A member shall not accept compensation for representing a client from one other than the client unless:

(1) There is no interference with the member's independence of professional judgment or with the client-lawyer relationship; and

(2) Information relating to representation of the client is protected as required by Business and Professions Code section 6068, subdivision (e); and

(3) The member obtains the client's informed written consent, provided that no disclosure or consent is required if:

(a) such nondisclosure is otherwise authorized by law; or

(b) the member is rendering legal services on behalf of any public agency which provides legal services to other public agencies or the public.

DISCUSSION

Rule 3-310 is not intended to prohibit a member from representing parties having antagonistic positions on the same legal question that has arisen in different cases, unless representation of either client would be adversely affected.

Other rules and laws may preclude making adequate disclosure under this rule. If such disclosure is precluded, informed written consent is likewise precluded. (See, e.g., Business and Professions Code section 6068, subsection (e).)

Paragraph (B) is not intended to apply to the relationship of a member to another party's lawyer. Such relationships are governed by rule 3-320.

Paragraph (B) is not intended to require either the disclosure of the new engagement to a former client or the consent of the former client to the new engagement. However, such disclosure or consent is required if paragraph (E) applies.

While paragraph (B) deals with the issues of adequate disclosure to the present client or clients of the member's present or past relationships to other parties or witnesses or present interest in the subject matter of the representation, paragraph (E) is intended to protect the confidences of another present or former client. These two paragraphs are to apply as complementary provisions.

Paragraph (B) is intended to apply only to a member's own relationships or interests, unless the member knows that a partner or associate in the same firm as the member has or had a relationship with another party or witness or has or had an interest in the subject matter of the representation.

Subparagraphs (C)(1) and (C)(2) are intended to apply to all types of legal employment, including the concurrent representation of multiple parties in litigation or in a single transaction or in some other common enterprise or legal relationship. Examples of the latter include the formation of a partnership for several partners or a corporation for several shareholders, the preparation of an ante-nuptial agreement, or joint or reciprocal wills for a husband and wife, or the resolution of an "uncontested" marital dissolution. In such situations, for the sake of convenience or economy, the parties may well prefer to employ a single counsel, but a member must disclose the potential adverse aspects of such multiple representation (e.g., Evid. Code, §962) and must obtain the informed written consent of the clients thereto pursuant to subparagraph (C)(1). Moreover, if the potential adversity should become actual, the member must obtain the further informed written consent of the clients pursuant to subparagraph (C)(2).

Subparagraph (C)(3) is intended to apply to representations of clients in both litigation and transactional matters.

There are some matters in which the conflicts are such that written consent may not suffice for non-disciplinary purposes. (See Woods v. Superior Court (1983) 149 Cal. App. 3d 931 [197 Cal. Rptr. 185]; Klemm v. Superior Court (1977) 75 Cal. App. 3d 893 [142 Cal. Rptr. 509]; Ishmael v. Millington (1966) 241 Cal. App. 2d 520 [50 Cal. Rptr. 592].)

Paragraph (D) is not intended to apply to class action settlements subject to court approval.

Paragraph (F) is not intended to abrogate existing relationships between insurers and insureds whereby the insurer has the contractual right to unilaterally select counsel for the insured, where there is no conflict of interest. (See San Diego Navy Federal Credit Union v. Cumis Insurance Society (1984) 162 Cal. App. 3d 358 [208 Cal. Rptr. 494].)

Rule 3-320. Relationship with Other Party's Lawyer

A member shall not represent a client in a matter in which another party's lawyer is a spouse, parent, child, or sibling of the member, lives with the member, is a client of the member, or has an intimate personal relationship with the member, unless the member informs the client in writing of the relationship.

DISCUSSION

Rule 3-320 is not intended to apply to circumstances in which a member fails to advise the client of a relationship with another lawyer who is merely a partner or associate in the same law firm as the adverse party's counsel, and who has no direct involvement in the matter.

Rule 3-400. Limiting Liability to Client

A member shall not:
(A) Contract with a client prospectively limiting the member's liability to the client for the member's professional malpractice; or
(B) Settle a claim or potential claim for the member's liability to the client for the member's professional malpractice unless the client is informed in writing that the client may seek the advice of an independent lawyer of the client's choice regarding the settlement and is given a reasonable opportunity to seek that advice.

DISCUSSION

Rule 3-400 is not intended to apply to customary qualifications and limitations in legal opinions and memoranda, nor is it intended to prevent a member from reasonably limiting the scope of the member's employment or representation.

Rule 3-500. Communication

A member shall keep a client reasonably informed about significant developments relating to the employment or representation and promptly comply with reasonable requests for information.

DISCUSSION

Rule 3-500 is not intended to change a member's duties to his or her clients. It is intended to make clear that, while a client must be informed of significant developments in the matter, a member will not be disciplined for failing to communicate insignificant or irrelevant information. (See Bus. & Prof. Code, §6068, subd. (m).)

Rule 3-510. Communication of Settlement Offer

(A) A member shall promptly communicate to the member's client:
    (1) All terms and conditions of any offer made to the client in a criminal matter; and
    (2) All amounts, terms, and conditions of any written offer of settlement made to the client in all other matters.
(B) As used in this rule, "client" includes a person who possesses the authority to accept an offer of settlement or plea, or, in a class action, all the named representatives of the class.

DISCUSSION

Rule 3-510 is intended to require that counsel in a criminal matter convey all offers, whether written or oral, to the client, as give and take negotiations are less common in criminal matters, and, even were they to occur, such negotiations should require the participation of the accused.

Any oral offers of settlement made to the client in a civil matter should also be communicated if they are "significant" for the purposes of rule 3-500.

Rule 3-600. Organization as Client

(A) In representing an organization, a member shall conform his or her representation to the concept that the client is the organization itself, acting through its highest authorized officer, employee, body, or constituent overseeing the particular engagement.

(B) If a member acting on behalf of an organization knows that an actual or apparent agent of the organization acts or intends or refuses to act in a manner that is or may be a violation of law reasonably imputable to the organization, or in a manner which is likely to result in substantial injury to the organization, the member shall not violate his or her duty of protecting all confidential information as provided in Business and Professions Code section 6068, subdivision (e). Subject to Business and Professions Code section 6068, subdivision (e), the member may take such actions as appear to the member to be in the best lawful interest of the organization. Such actions may include among others:

(1) Urging reconsideration of the matter while explaining its likely consequences to the organization; or

(2) Referring the matter to the next higher authority in the organization, including, if warranted by the seriousness of the matter, referral to the highest internal authority that can act on behalf of the organization.

(C) If, despite the member's actions in accordance with paragraph (B), the highest authority that can act on behalf of the organization insists upon action or a refusal to act that is a violation of law and is likely to result in substantial injury to the organization, the member's response is limited to the member's right, and, where appropriate, duty to resign in accordance with rule 3-700.

(D) In dealing with an organization's directors, officers, employees, members, shareholders, or other constituents, a member shall explain the identity of the client for whom the member acts, whenever it is or becomes apparent that the organization's interests are or may become adverse to those of the constituent(s) with whom the member is dealing. The member shall not mislead such a constituent into believing that the constituent may communicate confidential information to the member in a way that will not be used in the organization's interest if that is or becomes adverse to the constituent.

(E) A member representing an organization may also represent any of its directors, officers, employees, members, shareholders, or other constituents, subject to the provisions of rule 3-310. If the organization's consent to the dual representation is required by rule 3-310, the consent shall be given by an appropriate constituent of the organization other than the individual or constituent who is to be represented, or by the shareholder(s) or organization members.

DISCUSSION

Rule 3-600 is not intended to enmesh members in the intricacies of the entity and aggregate theories of partnership.

Rule 3-600 is not intended to prohibit members from representing both an organization and other parties connected with it, as for instance (as simply one example) in establishing employee benefit packages for closely held corporations or professional partnerships.

Rule 3-600 is not intended to create or to validate artificial distinctions between entities and their officers, employees, or members, nor is it the purpose of the rule to deny the existence or importance of such formal distinctions. In dealing with a close corporation or small association, members commonly perform professional engagements for both the organization and its major constituents. When a change in control occurs or is threatened, members are faced with complex decisions involving personal and institutional relationships and loyalties and have frequently had difficulty in perceiving their correct duty. (See People ex rel. Deukmejianv. Brown (1981) 29 Cal. 3d 150 [172 Cal. Rptr. 478]; Goldstein v. Lees (1975) 46 Cal. App. 3d 614 [120 Cal. Rptr. 253]; Woods v. Superior Court (1983) 149 Cal. App. 3d 931 [197 Cal. Rptr. 185]; In re Banks (1978) 283 Ore. 459 [584 P.2d 284]; 1 A.L.R.4th 1105.) In resolving such multiple relationships, members must rely on case law.

Rule 3-700. Termination of Employment

(A) In General.

(1) If permission for termination of employment is required by the rules of a tribunal, a member shall not withdraw from employment in a proceeding before that tribunal without its permission.

(2) A member shall not withdraw from employment until the member has taken reasonable steps to avoid reasonably foreseeable prejudice to the rights of the client, including giving due notice to the client, allowing time for employment of other counsel, complying with rule 3-700(D), and complying with applicable laws and rules.

(B) Mandatory Withdrawal.

A member representing a client before a tribunal shall withdraw from employment with the permission of the tribunal, if required by its rules, and a member representing a client in other matters shall withdraw from employment, if:

(1) The member knows or should know that the client is bringing an action, conducting a defense, asserting a position in litigation, or taking an appeal, without probable cause and for the purpose of harassing or maliciously injuring any person; or

(2) The member knows or should know that continued employment will result in violation of these rules or of the State Bar Act; or

(3) The member's mental or physical condition renders it unreasonably difficult to carry out the employment effectively.

(C) Permissive Withdrawal.

If rule 3-700(B) is not applicable, a member may not request permission to withdraw in matters pending before a tribunal, and may not withdraw in other matters, unless such request or such withdrawal is because:

(1) The client

(a) insists upon presenting a claim or defense that is not warranted under existing law and cannot be supported by good faith argument for an extension, modification, or reversal of existing law, or

(b) seeks to pursue an illegal course of conduct, or

(c) insists that the member pursue a course of conduct that is illegal or that is prohibited under these rules or the State Bar Act, or

(d) by other conduct renders it unreasonably difficult for the member to carry out the employment effectively, or

(e) insists, in a matter not pending before a tribunal, that the member engage in conduct that is contrary to the judgment and advice of the member but not prohibited under these rules or the State Bar Act, or

(f) breaches an agreement or obligation to the member as to expenses or fees.

(2) The continued employment is likely to result in a violation of these rules or of the State Bar Act; or

(3) The inability to work with co-counsel indicates that the best interests of the client likely will be served by withdrawal; or

(4) The member's mental or physical condition renders it difficult for the member to carry out the employment effectively; or

(5) The client knowingly and freely assents to termination of the employment; or

(6) The member believes in good faith, in a proceeding pending before a tribunal, that the tribunal will find the existence of other good cause for withdrawal.

(D) Papers, Property, and Fees.

A member whose employment has terminated shall:

(1) Subject to any protective order or non-disclosure agreement, promptly release to the client, at the request of the client, all the client papers and property. "Client papers and property" includes correspondence, pleadings, deposition transcripts, exhibits, physical evidence, expert's reports, and other items reasonably necessary to the client's representation, whether the client has paid for them or not; and

(2) Promptly refund any part of a fee paid in advance that has not been earned. This provision is not applicable to a true retainer fee which is paid solely for the purpose of ensuring the availability of the member for the matter.

DISCUSSION

Subparagraph (A)(2) provides that "a member shall not withdraw from employment until the member has taken reasonable steps to avoid reasonably foreseeable prejudice to the rights of the clients." What such steps would include, of course, will vary according to the circumstances. Absent special circumstances, "reasonable steps" do not include providing additional services to the client once the successor counsel has been employed and rule 3-700(D) has been satisfied.

Paragraph (D) makes clear the member's duties in the recurring situation in which new counsel seeks to obtain client files from a member discharged by the client. It codifies existing case law. (See Academy of California Optometrists v. Superior Court (1975) 51 Cal. App. 3d 999 [124 Cal. Rptr. 668]; Weiss v. Marcus (1975) 51 Cal. App. 3d 590 [124 Cal. Rptr. 297].)

Subparagraph (D)(2) requires that the member "promptly" return unearned fees paid in advance. If such fees have been placed in a trust account pursuant to rule 4-100, the member shall comply with the provisions of rule 4-100(A)(2), should the client dispute the amount to be returned. If the written fee agreement expressly provided that the fee paid in advance was nonrefundable and the engagement is not completed, the member may repay the client from the member's own funds. In any event all advances for costs and expenses must be placed in a trust account. (See Stevens v. State Bar (1990) 51 Cal. 3d 283 [272 Cal. Rptr. 167].)

Paragraph (D) is not intended to prohibit a member from making, at the member's own expense, and retaining copies of papers released to the client, nor to prohibit a claim for the recovery of the member's expense in any subsequent legal proceeding.

CHAPTER 4. FINANCIAL RELATIONSHIP WITH CLIENTS

Rule 4-100. Preserving Identity of Funds and Property of a Client

(A) All funds received or held for the benefit of clients by a member or law firm, including advances for costs and expenses, shall be deposited in one or more identifiable bank accounts labelled "Trust Account," "Client's Funds Account" or words of similar import, maintained in the State of California, or, with written consent of the client, in any other jurisdiction where there is a substantial relationship between the client or the client's business and the other jurisdiction. No funds belonging to the member or the law firm shall be deposited therein or otherwise commingled therewith except as follows:

(1) Funds reasonably sufficient to pay bank charges.

(2) In the case of funds belonging in part to a client and in part presently or potentially to the member or the law firm, the portion belonging to the member or law firm must be withdrawn at the earliest reasonable time after the member's interest in that portion becomes fixed. However, when the right of the member or law firm to receive a portion of trust funds is disputed by the client, the disputed portion shall not be withdrawn until the dispute is finally resolved.

(B) A member shall:

(1) Promptly notify a client of the receipt of the client's funds, securities, or other properties.

(2) Identify and label securities and properties of a client promptly upon receipt and place them in a safe deposit box or other place of safekeeping as soon as practicable.

(3) Maintain complete records of all funds, securities, and other properties of a client coming into the possession of the member or law firm and render appropriate accounts to the client regarding them; preserve such records for a period of no less than five years after final appropriate distribution of such funds or properties; and comply with any order for an audit of such records issued pursuant to the Rules of Procedure of the State Bar.

(4) Promptly pay or deliver, as requested by the client, any funds, securities, or other properties in the possession of the member which the client is entitled to receive.

(C) The Board of Governors of the State Bar shall have the authority to formulate and adopt standards as to what "records" shall be maintained by members and law firms in accordance with subparagraph (B)(3). The standards formulated and adopted by the Board, as from time to time amended, shall be effective and binding on all members.

TRUST ACCOUNT RECORD KEEPING STANDARDS AS ADOPTED BY THE BOARD OF GOVERNORS

Pursuant to rule 4-100(C) the Board of Governors of the State Bar has adopted the following standards, effective January 1, 1993, as to what "records" shall be maintained by members and law firms in accordance with subparagraph (B)(3).

(1) A member shall, from the date of receipt of client funds through the period ending five years from the date of appropriate disbursement of such funds, maintain:

(a) a written ledger for each client on whose behalf funds are held that sets forth

(i) the name of such client,

(ii) the date, amount and source of all funds received on behalf of such client,

(iii) the date, amount, payee and purpose of each disbursement made on behalf of such client, and

(iv) the current balance for such client;

(b) a written journal for each bank account that sets forth

(i) the name of such account,

(ii) the date, amount and client affected by each debit and credit, and

(iii) the current balance in such account;

(c) all bank statements and cancelled checks for each bank account; and

(d) each monthly reconciliation (balancing) of (a), (b), and (c).

(2) A member shall, from the date of receipt of all securities and other properties held for the benefit of client through the period ending five years from the date of appropriate disbursement of such securities and other properties, maintain a written journal that specifies:

(a) each item of security and property held;

(b) the person on whose behalf the security or property is held;

(c) the date of receipt of the security or property;

(d) the date of distribution of the security or property; and

(e) person to whom the security or property was distributed.

Rule 4-200. Fees for Legal Services

(A) A member shall not enter into an agreement for, charge, or collect an illegal or unconscionable fee.

(B) Unconscionability of a fee shall be determined on the basis of all the facts and circumstances existing at the time the agreement is entered into except where the parties contemplate that the fee will be affected by later events. Among the factors to be considered, where appropriate, in determining the conscionability of a fee are the following:

(1) The amount of the fee in proportion to the value of the services performed.

(2) The relative sophistication of the member and the client.

(3) The novelty and difficulty of the questions involved and the skill requisite to perform the legal service properly.

(4) The likelihood, if apparent to the client, that the acceptance of the particular employment will preclude other employment by the member.

(5) The amount involved and the results obtained.

(6) The time limitations imposed by the client or by the circumstances.

(7) The nature and length of the professional relationship with the client.

(8) The experience, reputation, and ability of the member or members performing the services.

(9) Whether the fee is fixed or contingent.

(10) The time and labor required.

(11) The informed consent of the client to the fee.

Rule 4-210. Payment of Personal or Business
Expenses Incurred by or for a Client

(A) A member shall not directly or indirectly pay or agree to pay, guarantee, represent, or sanction a representation that the member or member's law firm will pay the personal or business expenses of a prospective or existing client, except that this rule shall not prohibit a member:

(1) With the consent of the client, from paying or agreeing to pay such expenses to third persons from funds collected or to be collected for the client as a result of the representation; or

(2) After employment, from lending money to the client upon the client's promise in writing to repay such loan; or

(3) From advancing the costs of prosecuting or defending a claim or action or otherwise protecting or promoting the client's interests, the repayment of which may be contingent on the outcome of the matter. Such costs within the meaning of this subparagraph (3) shall be limited to all reasonable expenses of litigation or reasonable expenses in preparation for litigation or in providing any legal services to the client.

(B) Nothing in rule 4-210 shall be deemed to limit rules 3-300, 3-310, and 4-300.

Rule 4-300. Purchasing Property at a Foreclosure or a Sale Subject to Judicial Review

(A) A member shall not directly or indirectly purchase property at a probate, foreclosure, receiver's, trustee's, or judicial sale in an action or proceeding in which such member or any lawyer affiliated by reason of personal, business, or professional relationship with that member or with that member's law firm is acting as a lawyer for a party or as executor, receiver, trustee, administrator, guardian, or conservator.

(B) A member shall not represent the seller at a probate, foreclosure, receiver, trustee, or judicial sale in an action or proceeding in which the purchaser is a spouse or relative of the member or of another lawyer in the member's law firm or is an employee of the member or the member's law firm.

Rule 4-400. Gifts from Client

A member shall not induce a client to make a substantial gift, including a testamentary gift, to the member or to the member's parent, child, sibling, or spouse, except where the client is related to the member.

DISCUSSION

A member may accept a gift from a member's client, subject to general standards of fairness and absence of undue influence. The member who participates in the preparation of an instrument memorializing a gift which is otherwise permissible ought not to be subject to professional discipline. On the other hand, where impermissible influence occurred, discipline is appropriate. (See Magee v. State Bar (1962) 58 Cal. 2d 423 [24 Cal. Rptr. 839].)

Editors' Note. On February 23, 1995, the California Supreme Court rejected a proposed amendment to Rule 4-400. The amendment would have prohibited a lawyer from inducing a client to make "any" gift to the lawyer or the lawyer's relatives, not just a "substantial" gift as in the present version of Rule 4-400. The amended rule would also have prohibited a lawyer from preparing an instrument providing for "any" gift to the lawyer or the lawyer's relatives, except where the client is related to the lawyer or transferee. In its order rejecting the proposed amendment, the Court said the amendment appeared to conflict with §§21350 and 21351 of the California Probate Code.

CHAPTER 5. ADVOCACY AND REPRESENTATION

Rule 5-100. Threatening Criminal, Administrative, or Disciplinary Charges

(A) A member shall not threaten to present criminal, administrative, or disciplinary charges to obtain an advantage in a civil dispute.

(B) As used in paragraph (A) of this rule, the term "administrative charges" means the filing or lodging of a complaint with a federal, state, or local governmental entity which may order or recommend the loss or suspension of a license, or may impose or recommend the imposition of a fine, pecuniary sanction, or other sanction of a quasi-criminal nature but does not include filing charges with an administrative entity required by law as a condition precedent to maintaining a civil action.

(C) As used in paragraph (A) of this rule, the term "civil dispute" means a controversy or potential controversy over the rights and duties of two or more parties under civil law, whether or not an action has been commenced, and includes an administrative proceeding of a quasi-civil nature pending before a federal, state, or local governmental entity.

DISCUSSION

Rule 5-100 is not intended to apply to a member's threatening to initiate contempt proceedings against a party for a failure to comply with a court order.

Paragraph (B) is intended to exempt the threat of filing an administrative charge which is a prerequisite to filing a civil complaint on the same transaction or occurrence.

For purposes of paragraph (C), the definition of "civil dispute" makes clear that the rule is applicable prior to the formal filing of a civil action.

Rule 5-110. Performing the Duty of Member in Government Service

A member in government service shall not institute or cause to be instituted criminal charges when the member knows or should know that the charges are not supported by probable cause. If, after the institution of criminal charges, the member in government service having responsibility for prosecuting the charges becomes aware that those charges are not supported by probable cause, the member shall promptly so advise the court in which the criminal matter is pending.

Rule 5-120. Trial Publicity

Editors' Note. On September 14, 1995, the California Supreme Court approved a new Rule 5-120, which took effect on October 1, 1995. Up to that point, California was the only state in the country without a rule restricting extrajudicial statements by lawyers. The history of the rule is unique. The public statements by lawyers involved in the O. J. Simpson murder case, which began with Simpson's arrest in June 1994, spurred the California legislature to pass a statute commanding the State Bar to submit to the Supreme Court, no later than March 1, 1995, "a rule of professional conduct governing trial publicity and extrajudicial statements made by attorneys concerning adjudicative proceedings." Governor Wilson signed this law on September 26, 1994, the first day of jury selection in the Simpson trial. (The full text of the statute, §6103.7 of the California Business and Professions Code, is reprinted in our California statutory materials.) The State Bar dutifully drafted and submitted a proposal to the Court in February 1995 but, in an unusual move, did so "without recommendation." The proposal largely tracked ABA Model Rule 3.6 as amended in August 1994, but — unlike the ABA rule — would have applied only to jury trials and would have applied only to extrajudicial statements that posed a "clear and present danger" to trial proceedings. On March 29, 1995, the Court wrote to the State Bar suggesting that the Bar either propose a trial publicity rule that it recommended "or particularly explain the reasons why it does not recommend approval of the rule already submitted." On June 1, 1995, the State Bar President, Donald Fischbach, sent the Court a detailed five-page letter saying the State Bar opposed the proposed rule because: (1) there is no evidence that out-of-court remarks by attorneys have prejudiced anyone's right to a fair trial; (2) judges already have remedies such as gag orders to control out-of-court publicity; (3) the proposed rule would be ineffective because it would not apply to non-lawyers; (4) any trial publicity rule would be extremely difficult to enforce; (5) a trial publicity rule could "become a sword used by litigants seeking strategic advantage over one another"; and (6) the rule would "impair attorneys' duty to represent their clients zealously."

On September 14, 1995, the Supreme Court nevertheless adopted a trial publicity rule, but it tracks ABA Model Rule 3.6 rather than the State Bar proposal. The only significant differences between the ABA Rule and the new California rule are that California has dropped Rule 3.6(d), which provides that "[n]o lawyer associated in a firm or government agency with a lawyer subject to paragraph (a) shall make a statement prohibited by paragraph (a)," and the official Discussion following the California rule bears no resemblance to the Comment following Model Rule 3.6.

(A) A member who is participating or has participated in the investigation or litigation of a matter shall not make an extrajudicial statement that a reasonable person would expect to be disseminated by means of public communication if the member knows or reasonably should know that it will have a substantial likelihood of materially prejudicing an adjudicative proceeding in the matter.

(B) Notwithstanding paragraph (A), a member may state:

(1) the claim, offense or defense involved and, except when prohibited by law, the identity of the persons involved;

(2) the information contained in a public record;

(3) that an investigation of the matter is in progress;

(4) the scheduling or result of any step in litigation;

(5) a request for assistance in obtaining evidence and information necessary thereto;

(6) a warning of danger concerning the behavior of a person involved, when there is reason to believe that there exists the likelihood of substantial harm to an individual or to the public interest; and

(7) in a criminal case, in addition to subparagraphs (1) through (6):

(a) the identity, residence, occupation, and family status of the accused;

(b) if the accused has not been apprehended, information necessary to aid in apprehension of that person;

(c) the fact, time, and place of arrest; and

(d) the identity of investigating and arresting officers or agencies and the length of the investigation.

(C) Notwithstanding paragraph (A), a member may make a statement that a reasonable member would believe is required to protect a client from the substantial undue prejudicial effect of recent publicity not initiated by the member or the member's client. A statement made pursuant to this paragraph shall be limited to such information as is necessary to mitigate the recent adverse publicity.

DISCUSSION

Rule 5-120 is intended to apply equally to prosecutors and criminal defense counsel. Whether an extrajudicial statement violates rule 5-120 depends on many factors, including:

(1) whether the extrajudicial statement presents information clearly inadmissible as evidence in the matter for the purpose of proving or disproving a material fact in issue;

(2) whether the extrajudicial statement presents information the member knows is false, deceptive, or the use of which would violate Business and Professions Code section 6068(d);

(3) whether the extrajudicial statement violates a lawful "gag" order, or protective order, statute, rule of court, or special rule of confidentiality (for example, in juvenile, domestic, mental disability, and certain criminal proceedings); and

(4) the timing of the statement.

Paragraph (A) is intended to apply to statements made by or on behalf of the member. Subparagraph (B)(6) is not intended to create, augment, diminish, or eliminate any application of the lawyer-client privilege or of Business and Professions Code section 6068(e) regarding the member's duty to maintain client confidence and secrets.

Rule 5-200. Trial Conduct

In presenting a matter to a tribunal, a member:

(A) Shall employ, for the purpose of maintaining the causes confided to the member such means only as are consistent with truth;

(B) Shall not seek to mislead the judge, judicial officer, or jury by an artifice or false statement of fact or law;

(C) Shall not intentionally misquote to a tribunal the language of a book, statute, or decision;

(D) Shall not, knowing its invalidity, cite as authority a decision that has been overruled or a statute that has been repealed or declared unconstitutional; and

(E) Shall not assert personal knowledge of the facts at issue, except when testifying as a witness.

Rule 5-210. Member as Witness

A member shall not act as an advocate before a jury which will hear testimony from the member unless:

(A) The testimony relates to an uncontested matter; or

(B) The testimony relates to the nature and value of legal services rendered in the case; or

(C) The member has the informed, written consent of the client. If the member represents the People or a governmental entity, the consent shall be obtained from the head of the office or a designee of the head of the office by which the member is employed and shall be consistent with principles of recusal.

DISCUSSION

Rule 5-210 is intended to apply to situations in which the member knows or should know that he or she ought to be called as a witness in litigation in which there is a jury. This rule is not intended to encompass situations in which the member is representing the client in an adversarial proceeding and is testifying before a judge. In non-adversarial proceedings, as where the member testifies on behalf of the client in a hearing before a legislative body, rule 5-210 is not applicable.

Rule 5-210 is not intended to apply to circumstances in which a lawyer in an advocate's firm will be a witness.

Rule 5-220. Suppression of Evidence

A member shall not suppress any evidence that the member or the member's client has a legal obligation to reveal or to produce.

Rule 5-300. Contact with Officials

(A) A member shall not directly or indirectly give or lend anything of value to a judge, official, or employee of a tribunal unless the personal or family relationship between the member and the judge, official, or employee is such that gifts are customarily given and exchanged. Nothing contained in this rule shall prohibit a member from contributing to the campaign fund of a judge running for election or confirmation pursuant to applicable law pertaining to such contributions.

(B) A member shall not directly or indirectly communicate with or argue to a judge or judicial officer upon the merits of a contested matter pending before such judge or judicial officer, except:

(1) In open court; or

(2) With the consent of all other counsel in such matter; or

(3) In the presence of all other counsel in such matter; or

(4) In writing with a copy thereof furnished to such other counsel; or

(5) In ex parte matters.

(C) As used in this rule, "judge and judicial officer" shall include law clerks, research attorneys, or other court personnel who participate in the decision-making process.

Rule 5-310. Prohibited Contact with Witnesses

A member shall not:

(A) Advise or directly or indirectly cause a person to secrete himself or herself or to leave the jurisdiction of a tribunal for the purpose of making that person unavailable as a witness therein.

(B) Directly or indirectly pay, offer to pay, or acquiesce in the payment of compensation to a witness contingent upon the content of the witness's testimony or the outcome of the case. Except where prohibited by law, a member may advance, guarantee, or acquiesce in the payment of:

(1) Expenses reasonably incurred by a witness in attending or testifying.

(2) Reasonable compensation to a witness for loss of time in attending or testifying.

(3) A reasonable fee for the professional services of an expert witness.

Rule 5-320. Contact with Jurors

(A) A member connected with a case shall not communicate directly or indirectly with anyone the member knows to be a member of the venire from which the jury will be selected for trial of that case.

(B) During trial a member connected with the case shall not communicate directly or indirectly with any juror.

(C) During trial a member who is not connected with the case shall not communicate directly or indirectly concerning the case with anyone the member knows is a juror in the case.

(D) After discharge of the jury from further consideration of a case a member shall not ask questions of or make comments to a member of that jury that are intended to harass or embarrass the juror or to influence the juror's actions in future jury service.

(E) A member shall not directly or indirectly conduct an out of court investigation of a person who is either a member or the venire or a juror in a manner likely to influence the state of mind of such person in connection with present or future jury service.

(F) All restrictions imposed by this rule also apply to communications with, or investigations of, members of the family of a person who is either a member of the venire or a juror.

(G) A member shall reveal promptly to the court improper conduct by a person who is either a member of a venire or a juror, or by another toward a person who is either a member of a venire or a juror or a member of his or her family, of which the member has knowledge.

(H) This rule does not prohibit a member from communicating with persons who are members of a venire or jurors as a part of the official proceedings.

(I) For purposes of this rule, "juror" means any empaneled, discharged, or excused juror.

PROPOSED AMENDMENTS PENDING
AS OF PRESS DATE

Editors' Note. The California State Bar is extremely active and frequently proposes amendments to the Rules of Professional Conduct. However, the amendments do not take effect until they are approved by the California Supreme Court. We reprint below the only proposed new rules that were formally pending before the California Supreme Court as of our press deadline in September of 1997.

Selected California Statutes

Editors' Introduction. More than any other state, California governs the conduct of lawyers by statute. California's provision on confidentiality, for example, is found in Business and Professions Code §6068, which lists the duties of an attorney. In addition, California addresses by statute the issue of conflict of interest when an insurance company provides a lawyer for the defense of an insured. The Business and Professions Code also contains detailed provisions governing fee agreements, communication of settlement offers, legal services offices, attorney discipline, and many other matters.

We have included here the statutory materials that parallel issues usually covered in law school courses on professional responsibility. We have omitted statutes on such things as state bar administration, state bar committees, and bar dues. We have also omitted lengthy procedural rules concerning bar admission and discipline. What remains is a representative collection of the major statutes governing California lawyers.

Since our last edition went to press in September of 1996, the California legislature has not enacted any major new provisions of the State Bar Act. However, the Legislature substantially expanded §6090.5, which prohibits agreements not to file a bar complaint as part of the settlement of a civil action. The Legislature also amended several of the provisions governing fee arbitration (§§6200 through 6206), and slightly amended §§6147 and 6148, which govern attorney fees. Other amendments were generally minor. We have underscored additions and stricken through deletions in all of the amended statutes that we reprint.

For up-to-date information on California statutes, visit the California State Bar's web site at www.calbar.org. We especially recommend "Publication 250," a comprehensive compilation of new, amended, and repealed statutes printed in legislative style.

Contents

CALIFORNIA BUSINESS AND PROFESSIONS CODE

614

CALIFORNIA CIVIL CODE

CALIFORNIA BUSINESS AND
PROFESSIONS CODE

ARTICLE 1. GENERAL PROVISIONS

§6000. Short Title

This chapter of the Business and Professions Code constitutes the chapter on attorneys. It may be cited as the State Bar Act.

ARTICLE 4. ADMISSION TO THE STATE BAR

§6067. Oath

Every person on his admission shall take an oath to support the Constitution of the United States and the Constitution of the State of California, and faithfully to discharge the duties of any attorney at law to the best of his knowledge and ability. A certificate of the oath shall be indorsed upon his license.

§6068. Duties of Attorney

It is the duty of an attorney to do all of the following:

(a) To support the Constitution and laws of the United States and of this state.

(b) To maintain the respect due to the courts of justice and judicial officers.

(c) To counsel or maintain such actions, proceedings, or defenses only as appear to him or her legal or just, except the defense of a person charged with a public offense.

(d) To employ, for the purpose of maintaining the causes confided to him or her such means only as are consistent with truth, and never to seek to mislead the judge or any judicial officer by an artifice or false statement of fact or law.

(e) To maintain inviolate the confidence, and at every peril to himself or herself to preserve the secrets, of his or her client.

(f) To abstain from all offensive personality, and to advance no fact prejudicial to the honor or reputation of a party or witness, unless required by the justice of the cause with which he or she is charged.

(g) Not to encourage either the commencement or the continuance of an action or proceeding from any corrupt motive of passion or interest.

(h) Never to reject, for any consideration personal to himself or herself, the cause of the defenseless or the oppressed.

(i) To cooperate and participate in any disciplinary investigation or other regulatory or disciplinary proceeding pending against the attorney. However, this subdivision shall not be construed to deprive an attorney of any privilege guaranteed by the Fifth Amendment to the Constitution of the United States or any other constitutional or statutory privileges.

(j) To comply with the requirements of Section 6002.1.

(k) To comply with all conditions attached to any disciplinary probation, including a probation imposed with the concurrence of the attorney.

(l) To keep all agreements made in lieu of disciplinary prosecution with the agency charged with attorney discipline.

(m) To respond promptly to reasonable status inquiries of clients and to keep clients reasonably informed of significant developments in matters with regard to which the attorney has agreed to provide legal services.

(n) To provide copies to the client of certain documents under time limits and as prescribed in a rule of professional conduct which the board shall adopt.

(o) To report to the agency charged with attorney discipline, in writing, within 30 days of the time the attorney has knowledge of any of the following:

(1) The filing of three or more lawsuits in a 12-month period against the attorney for malpractice or other wrongful conduct committed in a professional capacity.

(2) The entry of judgment against the attorney in any civil action for fraud, misrepresentation, breach of fiduciary duty, or gross negligence committed in a professional capacity.

(3) The imposition of any judicial sanctions against the attorney, except for sanctions for failure to make discovery or monetary sanctions of less than one thousand dollars ($1,000).

(4) The bringing of an indictment or information charging a felony against the attorney.

(5) The conviction of the attorney, including any verdict of guilty, or plea of guilty or no contest, of any felony, or any misde-

meanor committed in the course of the practice of law, or in any manner such that a client of the attorney was the victim, or a necessary element of which, as determined by the statutory or common law definition of the misdemeanor, involves improper conduct of an attorney, including dishonesty or other moral turpitude, or an attempt or a conspiracy or solicitation of another to commit a felony or any such misdemeanor.

(6) The imposition of discipline against the attorney by any professional or occupational disciplinary agency or licensing board, whether in California or elsewhere.

(7) Reversal of judgment in a proceeding based in whole or in part upon misconduct, grossly incompetent representation, or willful misrepresentation by an attorney.

(8) As used in this subdivision, "against the attorney" includes claims and proceedings against any firm of attorneys for the practice of law in which the attorney was a partner at the time of the conduct complained of and any law corporation in which the attorney was a shareholder at the time of the conduct complained of unless the matter has to the attorney's knowledge already been reported by the law firm or corporation.

(9) The State Bar may develop a prescribed form for the making of reports required by this section, usage of which it may require by rule or regulation.

(10) This subdivision is only intended to provide that the failure to report as required herein may serve as a basis of discipline. (Amended 1985, 1986, 1988, 1990.)

ARTICLE 5. DISCIPLINARY AUTHORITY OF THE BOARD OF GOVERNORS

§6079.4. Exercise by Attorney of Constitutional or Statutory Privileges Not Deemed Failure to Cooperate

The exercise by an attorney of his or her privilege under the Fifth Amendment to the Constitution of the United States, or of any other constitutional or statutory privileges shall not be deemed a failure to cooperate within the meaning of subdivision (i) of Section 6068.
(Added 1990.)

§6086.7. Court Actions, Judgments and Sanctions Against Attorneys; Notification to State Bar

A court shall notify the State Bar of any of the following:

(a) A final order of contempt imposed against an attorney that may involve grounds warranting discipline under this chapter. The court entering the final order shall transmit to the State Bar a copy of the relevant minutes, final order, and transcript, if one exists.

(b) Whenever a modification or reversal of a judgment in a judicial proceeding is based in whole or in part on the misconduct, incompetent representation, or willful misrepresentation of an attorney.

(c) The imposition of any judicial sanctions against an attorney, except sanctions for failure to make discovery or monetary sanctions of less than one thousand dollars ($1,000).

In the event of a notification made under subdivision (a), (b), or (c), the court shall also notify the attorney involved that the matter has been referred to the State Bar.

The State Bar shall investigate any matter reported under this section as to the appropriateness of initiating disciplinary action against the attorney.

(Added 1990.)

§6086.8. Judgments for Actions Committed in a Professional Capacity; Claims or Actions for Damages; Reports to State Bar

(a) Within 20 days after a judgment by a court of this state that a member of the State Bar of California is liable for any damages resulting in a judgment against the attorney in any civil action for fraud, misrepresentation, breach of fiduciary duty, or gross negligence committed in a professional capacity, the court which rendered the judgment shall report that fact in writing to the State Bar of California.

(b) Every claim or action of damages against a member of the State Bar of California for fraud, misrepresentation, breach of fiduciary duty, or negligence committed in a professional capacity shall be reported to the State Bar of California within 30 days of receipt by the admitted insurer or licensed surplus brokers providing professional liability insurance to that member of the State Bar.

(c) An attorney who does not possess professional liability insurance shall send a complete written report to the State Bar as to any settlement, judgment, or arbitration award described in subdivision (b), in the manner specified in that subdivision.

(Added 1986, amended 1988.)

ARTICLE 5.5. MISCELLANEOUS DISCIPLINARY PROVISIONS

§6090.5. Settlements; Prohibited Agreements

> **Editors' Note.** In 1996, the California Legislature significantly amended §6090.5, rewriting virtually the entire section. We underscore the language that was added and strike through language that was deleted.

(a) It is a cause for suspension, disbarment, or other discipline for any member ~~of the State Bar to require as a condition of a settlement of a civil action for professional misconduct brought against the member that the plaintiff agree to not file a complaint with the disciplinary agency concerning that misconduct,~~ whether as a party or as an attorney for a party, to agree or seek agreement, that

(1) The professional misconduct or the terms of a settlement of a claim for professional misconduct shall not be reported to the disciplinary agency.

(2) The plaintiff shall withdraw a disciplinary complaint or shall not cooperate with the investigation or prosecution conducted by the disciplinary agency.

(3) The record of any civil action for professional misconduct shall be sealed from review by the disciplinary agency.

(b) This section applies to all settlements, whether made before or after the commencement of a civil action.

(Added 1986; amended 1996.)

§6091. Trust Funds; Investigation and Audit of Complaint Alleging Mishandling; Statement of Attorney at Client's Request

If a client files a complaint with the State Bar alleging that his or her trust fund is being mishandled, the State Bar shall investigate and may require an audit if it determines that circumstances warrant.

At the client's written request, the attorney shall furnish the client with a complete statement of the funds received and disbursed and any charges upon the trust account, within 10 calendar days after receipt of the request. Such requests may not be made more often than once each 30 days unless a client files a complaint with the State Bar and the State Bar determines that more statements are warranted.
(Added 1986.)

§6094. Privileged Communications; Immunity

(a) Communications to the disciplinary agency relating to lawyer misconduct or disability or competence, or any communication related to an investigation or proceeding and testimony given in the proceeding are privileged, and no lawsuit predicated thereon may be instituted against any person. . . .
(b) Upon application by the disciplinary agency and notice to the appropriate prosecuting authority, the superior court may grant immunity from criminal prosecution to a witness in any disciplinary agency proceeding.
(Added 1986.)

ARTICLE 6. DISCIPLINARY AUTHORITY OF THE COURTS

§6103. Disobedience of Court Order; Violation of Oath or Attorney's Duties

A wilful disobedience or violation of an order of the court requiring him to do or forbear an act connected with or in the course of his profession, which he ought in good faith to do or forbear, and any violation of the oath taken by him, or of his duties as such attorney, constitute causes for disbarment or suspension.

§6103.5. Written Offers of Settlement; Required Communication to Client; Discovery

(a) A member of the State Bar shall promptly communicate to the member's client all amounts, terms, and conditions of any written offer of settlement made by or on behalf of an opposing party. As used in this section, "client" includes any person employing the member of the State Bar who possesses the authority to accept an offer of settlement, or in a class action, who is a representative of the class.

(b) Any written offer of settlement or any required communication of a settlement offer, as described in subdivision (a), shall be discoverable by either party in any action in which the existence or communication of the offer of settlement is an issue before the trier of fact.

(Added 1986, amended 1987.)

§6103.7. [Trial Publicity and Extrajudicial Statements]

> **Editors' Note.** On September 26, 1994, Governor Wilson signed a new law commanding the State Bar to submit to the California Supreme Court, no later than March 1, 1995, "a rule of professional conduct governing trial publicity and extrajudical statements made by attorneys concerning adjudicative proceedings." The new law was prompted by publicity and extrajudicial statements surrounding the O. J. Simpson murder charges. The original bill would have codified a version of ABA Model Rule 3.6 as a California statute. Ultimately, however, the legislature decided to let the State Bar draft a rule. The California Supreme Court approved a new Rule 5-120 on September 14, 1995. For details, see our Editors' Note to Rule 5-120 in the California Rules of Professional Conduct above.

Section 1. No later than March 1, 1995, the State Bar of California shall submit to the Supreme Court for approval a rule of professional conduct governing trial publicity and extrajudicial statements made by attorneys concerning adjudicative proceedings.

Sec. 2. The Legislature finds and declares the following:

(1) Recent legal proceedings have generated extraordinary media coverage and raised serious questions regarding the potentially prejudicial and otherwise harmful effect of some media coverage. Important constitutional issues of free speech, the right to a fair trial, and related questions are implicated and require thorough review by the State Bar.

(2) In light of the fact that the American Bar Association has now reformed its rule on this subject, it is appropriate to require the State Bar to commence and complete its rulemaking process no later than March 1, 1995.

(3) During the rulemaking process, the State Bar shall, among other materials, review and consider the American Bar Association's Model Rule 3.6, as modified.

Sec. 3. It is the intent of the Legislature in enacting this act to memorialize the Supreme Court expeditiously to review and, as appropriate, approve the rule adopted by the State Bar pursuant to this section.

§6104. Unauthorized Appearance

Corruptly or wilfully and without authority appearing as attorney for a party to an action or proceeding constitutes a cause for disbarment or suspension.

§6105. Permitting Misuse of Name

Lending his name to be used as attorney by another person who is not an attorney constitutes a cause for disbarment or suspension.

§6106. Moral Turpitude, Dishonesty or Corruption Irrespective of Criminal Conviction

The commission of any act involving moral turpitude, dishonesty or corruption, whether the act is committed in the course of his relations as an attorney or otherwise, and whether the act is a felony or misdemeanor or not, constitutes a cause of disbarment or suspension.

If the act constitutes a felony or misdemeanor, conviction thereof in a criminal proceeding is not a condition precedent to disbarment or suspension from practice therefor.

§6106.1. Advocacy of Overthrow of Government

Advocating the overthrow of the Government of the United States or of this State by force, violence, or other unconstitutional means, constitutes a cause for disbarment or suspension.
(Added 1951.)

§6106.5. Insurance Claims; Fraud

It shall constitute cause for disbarment or suspension for an attorney to engage in any conduct prohibited under Section . . . 1871.4 of the Insurance Code.
(Added 1978, amended 1988, 1991.)

Editors' Note. Section 1871.4 of the California Insurance Code was enacted in 1991. Violation of the statute is punishable by a fine, imprisonment, or both. It provides, in pertinent part, as follows:

§1871.4. Unlawful Conduct; Penalties

(a) It is unlawful to do any of the following:

(1) Make or cause to be made any knowingly false or fraudulent material statement or material representation for the purpose of obtaining or denying any compensation, as defined in Section 3207 of the Labor Code.

(2) Present or cause to be presented any knowingly false or fraudulent written or oral material statement in support of, or in opposition to, any claim for compensation for the purpose of obtaining or denying any compensation. . . .

(3) Knowingly assist, abet, solicit, or conspire with any person who engages in an unlawful act under this section. . . .

§6106.8. Sexual Involvement Between Lawyers and Clients; Rule of Professional Conduct

Editors' Note. In May 1991, a few months after the deadline set forth in §6106.8(c), the California State Bar submitted a proposed rule (Rule 3-120) to the California Supreme Court to govern sexual relations with clients. On August 13, 1992, the California Supreme Court adopted the proposed rule with modifications. The rule is reprinted above in the California Rules of Professional Conduct.

(a) The Legislature hereby finds and declares that there is no rule that governs propriety of sexual relationships between lawyers and clients. The Legislature further finds and declares that it is difficult to separate sound judgment from emotion or bias which may result from sexual involvement between a lawyer and his or her client during the period that an attorney-client relationship exists, and that emotional detachment is essential to the lawyer's ability to render competent legal services. Therefore, in order to ensure that a lawyer acts in the best interest of his or her client, a rule of professional conduct governing sexual relations between attorneys and their clients shall be adopted.

(b) With the approval of the Supreme Court, the State Bar shall adopt a rule of professional conduct governing sexual relations between attorneys and their clients in cases involving, but not limited to, probate mat-

ters and domestic relations, including dissolution proceedings, child custody cases, and settlement proceedings.

(c) The State Bar shall submit the proposed rule to the Supreme Court for approval no later than January 1, 1991.

(d) Intentional violation of this rule shall constitute a cause for suspension or disbarment.

(Added 1989.)

§6106.9. Sexual Relations Between Attorney and Client; Cause for Discipline; Complaints to State Bar

(a) It shall constitute cause for the imposition of discipline of an attorney within the meaning of this chapter for an attorney to do any of the following:

(1) Expressly or impliedly condition the performance of legal services for a current or prospective client upon the client's willingness to engage in sexual relations with the attorney.

(2) Employ coercion, intimidation, or undue influence in entering into sexual relations with a client.

(3) Continue representation of a client with whom the attorney has sexual relations if the sexual relations cause the attorney to perform legal services incompetently in violation of Rule 3-110 of the Rules of Professional Conduct of the State Bar of California, or if the sexual relations would, or would be likely to, damage or prejudice the client's case.

(b) Subdivision (a) shall not apply to sexual relations between attorneys and their spouses or persons in an equivalent domestic relationship or to ongoing consensual sexual relationships that predate the initiation of the attorney-client relationship.

(c) Where an attorney in a firm has sexual relations with a client but does not participate in the representation of that client, the attorneys in the firm shall not be subject to discipline under this section solely because of the occurrence of those sexual relations.

(d) For the purposes of this section, "sexual relations" means sexual intercourse or the touching of an intimate part of another person for the purpose of sexual arousal, gratification, or abuse.

(e) Any complaint made to the State Bar alleging a violation of subdivision (a) shall be verified under oath by the person making the complaint.

SEC. 2. Commencing January 1, 1993, the State Bar shall maintain statistical data regarding the number of complaints presented and the disposition or discipline imposed pursuant to Section 6106.9 of the Business and

Professions Code. The State Bar shall submit a report to the Legislature regarding the statistical compilation on or before January 1, 1996.

The State Bar shall also develop and implement uniform standards for the implementation of Section 6106.9 of the Business and Professions Code and policies and procedures to ensure that complaints will be handled in a responsive and sensitive manner. The State Bar shall also provide appropriate training to staff on the standards, policies, and practices.

(Added 1992).

ARTICLE 7. UNLAWFUL PRACTICE OF LAW

§6126. Unauthorized Practice, Advertising or Holding Out; Penalties

(a) Any person advertising or holding himself or herself out as practicing or entitled to practice law or otherwise practicing law who is not an active member of the State Bar, is guilty of a misdemeanor.

(b) Any person who has been involuntarily enrolled as an inactive member of the State Bar, or has been suspended from membership from the State Bar, or has been disbarred, or has resigned from the State Bar with charges pending, and thereafter advertises or holds himself or herself out as practicing or otherwise entitled to practice law, is guilty of a crime punishable by imprisonment in the state prison or county jail. . . .

(Added 1939; amended 1939, 1988.)

§6128. Deceit, Collusion, Delay of Suit and Improper Receipt of Money as Misdemeanor

Every attorney is guilty of a misdemeanor who either:

(a) Is guilty of any deceit or collusion, or consents to any deceit or collusion, with intent to deceive the court or any party.

(b) Willfully delays his client's suit with a view to his own gain.

(c) Willfully receives any money or allowance for or on account of any money which he has not laid out or become answerable for.

Any violation of the provisions of this section is punishable by imprisonment in the county jail not exceeding six months, or by a fine not exceeding two thousand five hundred dollars ($2,500), or by both.

§6133. Resigned, Suspended or Disbarred Attorneys; Supervision of Activities by Firms

Any attorney or any law firm, partnership, corporation, or association employing an attorney who has resigned, or who is under actual suspension from the practice of law, or is disbarred, shall not permit that attorney to practice law or so advertise or hold himself or herself out as practicing law and shall supervise him or her in any other assigned duties. A willful violation of this section constitutes a cause for discipline.

(Added 1988.)

ARTICLE 8.5. FEE AGREEMENTS

§6146. Limitations; Periodic Payments

(a) An attorney shall not contract for or collect a contingency fee for representing any person seeking damages in connection with an action for injury or damage against a health care provider based upon such person's alleged professional negligence in excess of the following limits:

(1) Forty percent of the first fifty thousand dollars ($50,000) recovered.

(2) Thirty-three and one-third percent of the next fifty thousand dollars ($50,000) recovered.

(3) Twenty-five percent of the next five hundred thousand dollars ($500,000) recovered.

(4) Fifteen percent of any amount on which the recovery exceeds six hundred thousand dollars ($600,000).

The limitations shall apply regardless of whether the recovery is by settlement, arbitration, or judgment, or whether the person for whom the recovery is made is a responsible adult, an infant, or a person of unsound mind.

(b) If periodic payments are awarded to the plaintiff pursuant to Section 667.7 of the Code of Civil Procedure, the court shall place a total value on these payments based upon the projected life expectancy of the plaintiff and include this amount in computing the total award from which attorney's fees are calculated under this section. . . .

(Added 1975, amended 1981, 1987.)

§6147. Contingency Fee Contracts; Duplicate Copy; Contents; Effect of Noncompliance; Recovery of Workers' Compensation Benefits

> **Editors' Note.** Effective January 1, 1997, the Legislature amended subparagraph (d) of §6147 to push back the automatic repeal date from January 1, 1997 to January 1, 2000. At the same time, the Legislature enacted a different version of §6147 that will not take effect until January 1, 2000. We do not reprint the version of §6147 that will take effect on January 1, 2000 because it is identical to the current version except that the "2000" version deletes subparagraph (a)(6) and alters subparagraph (d) by noting that it "shall become operative on January 1, 2000." In the current version, we underscore the new expiration year and strike out the old expiration year to flag the amendment.

(a) An attorney who contracts to represent a client on a contingency fee basis shall, at the time the contract is entered into, provide a duplicate copy of the contract, signed by both the attorney and the client, or the client's guardian or representative, to the plaintiff, or to the client's guardian or representative. The contract shall be in writing and shall include, but is not limited to, all of the following:

(1) A statement of the contingency fee rate that the client and attorney have agreed upon.

(2) A statement as to how disbursements and costs incurred in connection with the prosecution or settlement of the claim will affect the contingency fee and the client's recovery.

(3) A statement as to what extent, if any, the client could be required to pay any compensation to the attorney for related matters that arise out of their relationship not covered by their contingency fee contract. This may include any amounts collected for the plaintiff by the attorney.

(4) Unless the claim is subject to the provisions of Section 6146, a statement that the fee is not set by law but is negotiable between attorney and client.

(5) If the claim is subject to the provisions of Section 6146, a statement that the rates set forth in that section are the maximum limits for the contingency fee agreement, and that the attorney and client may negotiate a lower rate.

(6) If the attorney does not meet any of the following criteria, a statement disclosing that fact:

(A) Maintains errors and omissions insurance coverage.

(B) Has filed with the State Bar an executed copy of a written agreement guaranteeing payment of all claims established against the attorney by his or her clients for errors or omissions arising out of the practice of law by the attorney in the amount specified in paragraph (c) of subsection (1) of Section B of Rule IV of the Law Corporation Rules of the State Bar. The State Bar may charge a filing fee not to exceed five dollars ($5).

(C) If a law corporation, has filed with the State Bar an executed copy of the written agreement required pursuant to paragraph (a), (b), or (c) of subsection (1) of Section B of Rule IV of the Law Corporation Rules of the State Bar.

(b) Failure to comply with any provision of this section renders the agreement voidable at the option of the client, and the attorney shall thereupon be entitled to collect a reasonable fee.

(c) This section shall not apply to contingency fee contracts for the recovery of workers' compensation benefits.

(d) This section shall remain in effect only until January 1, 1997 2000, and as of that date is repealed, unless a later enacted statute, which is enacted before January 1, 1997 2000, deletes or extends that date.

(Added 1982; amended 1986, 1992, 1993, 1994, 1996.)

> **Editors' Note.** Rule IV-B(1)(a)-(c) of the California State Bar's Law Corporation Rules, which is referred to in §6147(a)(6), provides, in essence, that security for claims by clients against a law corporation for errors or omissions arising out of its law practice shall consist of one of the following: (a) a legal malpractice insurance policy in the amount of $50,000 per claim times the number of lawyers in the firm, and at least $100,000 aggregate per year times the number of lawyers in the firm, but with no requirement to exceed $500,000 per claim or $5,000,000 aggregate per year; or (b) a written agreement of the firm's shareholders that they "shall jointly and severally guarantee payment by the corporation" of all malpractice claims in the amounts specified above for legal malpractice policies; or (c) a combination of written agreements by the shareholders and a legal malpractice insurance policy guaranteeing payment in the amounts specified above for legal malpractice policies.

§6147.5. Contingency Fee Contracts; Recovery of Claims Between Merchants

(a) Sections 6147 and 6148 shall not apply to contingency fee contracts for the recovery of claims between merchants as defined in Section

2104 of the Commercial Code, arising from the sale or lease of goods or services rendered, or money loaned for use, in the conduct of a business or profession if the merchant contracting for legal services employs 10 or more individuals.

(b)(1) In the instances in which no written contract for legal services exists as permitted by subdivision (a), an attorney shall not contract for or collect a contingency fee in excess of the following limits:

(A) Twenty percent of the first three hundred dollars ($300) collected.

(B) Eighteen percent of the next one thousand seven hundred dollars ($1,700) collected.

(C) Thirteen percent of sums collected in excess of two thousand dollars ($2,000).

(2) However, the following minimum charges may be charged and collected:

(A) Twenty-five dollars ($25) in collections of seventy-five dollars ($75) to one hundred twenty-five dollars ($125).

(B) Thirty-three and one-third percent of collections less than seventy-five dollars ($75).

(Added 1990.)

§6148. Contracts for Services in Cases Not Coming Within §6147; Bills Rendered by Attorney; Contents; Failure to Comply

Editors' Note. Effective January 1, 1997, the Legislature amended subparagraph (f) §6148 to push back the automatic repeal date from January 1, 1997 to January 1, 2000. At the same time, the Legislature enacted a different version of §6148 that will not take effect until January 1, 2000. We do not reprint the version of §6148 that will take effect on January 1, 2000 because it is identical to the current version except that the "2000" version deletes subparagraph (a)(4) and alters paragraph (f) by noting that it "shall become operative on January 1, 2000." In the current version, we underscore the new expiration year and strike out the old expiration year to flag the amendment.

(a) In any case not coming within Section 6147 in which it is reasonably foreseeable that total expense to a client, including attorney fees, will exceed one thousand dollars ($1,000), the contract for services in the case shall be in writing. At the time the contract is entered into, the attorney shall provide a duplicate copy of the contract signed by both the attorney and the client, or the client's guardian or representative, to the client or to the client's guardian or representative. The written contract shall contain all of the following:

(1) Any basis of compensation including, but not limited to, hourly rates, statutory fees or flat fees, and other standard rates, fees, and charges applicable to the case.

(2) The general nature of the legal services to be provided to the client.

(3) The respective responsibilities of the attorney and the client as to the performance of the contract.

(4) If the attorney does not meet any of the following criteria, a statement disclosing that fact:

(A) Maintains errors and omissions insurance coverage.

(B) Has filed with the State Bar an executed copy of a written agreement guaranteeing payment of all claims established against the attorney by his or her clients for errors or omissions arising out of the practice of law by the attorney in the amount specified in paragraph (c) of subsection (1) of Section B of Rule IV of the Law Corporation Rules of the State Bar. The State Bar may charge a filing fee not to exceed five dollars ($5).

(C) If a law corporation, has filed with the State Bar an executed copy of the written agreement required pursuant to paragraph (a), (b), or (c) of subsection (1) of Section B of Rule IV of the Law Corporation Rules of the State Bar.

(b) All bills rendered by an attorney to a client shall clearly state the basis thereof. Bills for the fee portion of the bill shall include the amount, rate, basis for calculation, or other method of determination of the attorney's fees and costs. Bills for the cost and expense portion of the bill shall clearly identify the costs and expenses incurred and the amount of the costs and expenses. Upon request by the client, the attorney shall provide a bill to the client no later than 10 days following the request. . . .

(c) Failure to comply with any provision of this section renders the agreement voidable at the option of the client, and the attorney shall, upon the agreement being voided, be entitled to collect a reasonable fee.

(d) This section shall not apply to any of the following:

(1) Services rendered in an emergency to avoid foreseeable prejudice to the rights or interests of the client or where a writing is otherwise impractical.

(2) An arrangement as to the fee implied by the fact that the attorney's services are of the same general kind as previously rendered to and paid for by the client.

(3) If the client knowingly states in writing, after full disclosure of this section, that a writing concerning fees is not required.

(4) If the client is a corporation.

(e) This section applies prospectively only to fee agreements following its operative date.

(f) This section shall remain in effect only until January 1, ~~1997~~ 2000, and as of that date is repealed, unless a later enacted statute, which is enacted before January 1, ~~1997~~ 2000, deletes or extends that date.

(Added 1986; amended 1990, 1992, 1993, 1994, 1996.)

Editors' Note. Rule IV-B(1)(a)-(c) of the California State Bar's Law Corporation Rules, referred to in §6148(a)(4), is summarized in an Editors' Note following §6147.

§6149. Written Fee Contract as Confidential Communication

A written fee contract shall be deemed to be a confidential communication within the meaning of subdivision (e) of Section 6068 and of Section 952 of the Evidence Code.

(Added 1986.)

Editors' Note. Section 6068(e) of the Business and Professions Code is reprinted above in this chapter. Section 952 of the Evidence Code is reprinted above in the chapter on the attorney-client privilege and work product.

§6149.5. Third-Party Liability Claim; Settlement by Insurer; Notice to Claimant; Effect on Action or Defense

Editors' Note. Section 6149.5 took effect on January 1, 1995. It reflects problems with attorneys who received settlement checks from insurance companies but did not inform clients.

(a) Upon the payment of one hundred dollars ($100) or more in settlement of any third-party liability claim the insurer shall provide written notice to the claimant if both of the following apply:

(1) The claimant is a natural person.

(2) The payment is delivered to the claimant's lawyer or other representative by draft, check, or otherwise.

(b) For purposes of this section, "written notice" includes providing to the claimant a copy of the cover letter sent to the claimant's attorney or other representative that accompanied the settlement payment.

(c) This section shall not create any cause of action for any person against the insurer based upon the insurer's failure to provide the notice to a claimant required by this section. This section shall not create a defense for any party to any cause of action based upon the insurer's failure to provide this notice.

(Added 1994.)

ARTICLE 9. UNLAWFUL SOLICITATION

§6151. Definitions

As used in this article:

(a) A runner or capper is any person, firm, association or corporation acting for consideration in any manner or in any capacity as an agent for an attorney at law or law firm, whether the attorney or any member of the law firm is admitted in California or any other jurisdiction, in the solicitation or procurement of business for the attorney at law or law firm as provided in this article.

(b) An agent is one who represents another in dealings with one or more third persons.

(Amended 1991.)

§6152. Prohibition of Solicitation

(a) It is unlawful for:

(1) Any person, in his individual capacity or in his capacity as a public or private employee, or for any firm, corporation, partnership or association to act as a runner or capper for any such attorneys or to solicit any business for any such attorneys in and about the state prisons, county jails, city jails, city prisons, or other places of detention of persons, city receiving hospitals, city and county receiving hospitals, county hospitals, justice courts, municipal courts, superior courts, or in any public institution or in any public place or upon any public street or highway or in and about private hospitals, sanitariums or in and about any private institution or upon private property of any character whatsoever.

(2) Any person to solicit another person to commit or join in the commission of a violation of subdivision (a).

(b) A general release from a liability claim obtained from any person during the period of the first physical confinement, whether as an inpatient or outpatient, in a clinic or health facility . . . as a result of the injury alleged to have given rise to such claim and primarily for treatment of such injury, is presumed fraudulent if such release is executed within 15 days after the commencement of such confinement or prior to release from such confinement, whichever occurs first.

(c) Nothing in this section shall be construed to prevent the recommendation of professional employment where such recommendation is not prohibited by the Rules of Professional Conduct of the State Bar of California.

(d) Nothing in this section shall be construed to mean that a public defender or assigned counsel may not make known his or her services as a criminal defense attorney to persons unable to afford legal counsel whether such persons are in custody or otherwise.

(Amended 1976, 1977.)

ARTICLE 9.5. LEGAL ADVERTISING

Editors' Note. Article 9.5 was added in 1993. These provisions must be read in conjunction with Rule 1-400 of the California Rules of Professional Conduct and the Standards adopted pursuant to Rule 1-400.

On August 30, 1994, after months of wrangling and compromise, the California legislature passed a bill that amended §§6157 and 6157.2; renumbered §§6157.5 through 6157.7 as §§6159.1 through 6159.3; and added new §§6158 through 6158.7 to govern legal advertising via electronic media. Governor Wilson signed the legislation on September 21, 1994, and it took effect on January 1, 1995.

§6157. Definitions

As used in this article, the following definitions apply:

(a) "Member" means a member in good standing of the State Bar and includes any agent of the member and any law firm or law corporation doing business in the State of California.

(b) "Lawyer" means a member of the State Bar or a person who is admitted in good standing and eligible to practice before the bar of any United States court or the highest court of the District of Columbia or any state, territory, or insular possession of the United States, or is licensed to practice law in, or is admitted in good standing and eligible to practice before the bar of the highest court of, a foreign country or any political subdivision thereof, and includes any agent of the lawyer or law firm or law corporation doing business in this state.

(c) "Advertise" or "advertisement" means any communication, disseminated by television or radio, by any print medium including, but not limited to, newspapers and billboards, or by means of a mailing directed generally to members of the public and not to a specific person, that solicits employment of legal services provided by a member, and is directed to the general public and is paid for by, or on the behalf of, an attorney.

(d) "Electronic medium" means television, radio, or computer networks.

(Added 1993; amended 1994.)

§6157.1. False, Misleading or Deceptive Statements; Prohibition

No advertisement shall contain any false, misleading, or deceptive statement or omit to state any fact necessary to make the statements made, in light of circumstances under which they are made, not false, misleading, or deceptive.

(Added 1993.)

§6157.2. Prohibited Statements Regarding Outcome; Dramatizations; Contingent Fee Basis Representations

No advertisement shall contain or refer to any of the following:

(a) Any guarantee or warranty regarding the outcome of a legal matter as a result of representation by the member.

(b) Statements or symbols stating that the member featured in the advertisement can generally obtain immediate cash or quick settlements.

(c)(1) An impersonation of the name, voice, photograph, or electronic image of any person other than the lawyer, directly or implicitly purporting to be that of a lawyer.

(2) An impersonation of the name, voice, photograph, or electronic image of any person, directly or implicitly purporting to be a

client of the member featured in the advertisement, or a dramatization of events, unless disclosure of the impersonation or dramatization is made in the advertisement.

(3) A spokesperson, including a celebrity spokesperson, unless there is disclosure of the spokesperson's title.

(d) A statement that a member offers representation on a contingent basis unless the statement also advises whether a client will be held responsible for any costs advanced by the member when no recovery is obtained on behalf of the client. If the client will not be held responsible for costs, no disclosure is required.

(Added 1993; amended 1994.)

§6157.3. Advertisements Made on Behalf of Member; Required Representations

Any advertisement made on behalf of a member, which is not paid for by the member, shall disclose any business relationship, past or present, between the member and the person paying for the advertisement.

(Added 1993.)

§6157.4. Lawyer Referral Service Advertising

Any advertisement that is created or disseminated by a lawyer referral service shall disclose whether the attorneys on the organization's referral list, panel, or system, paid any consideration, other than a proportional share of actual cost, to be included on that list, panel, or system.

(Added 1993.)

Editors' Note. In August 1994, the California legislature passed a bill renumbering former §§6157.5 through 6157.7 as new §§6159 through 6159.2. The bill made no substantive amendments to these sections. The new numbering took effect on January 1, 1995.

Sections 6158 through 6158.7, which follow, were added to the Business and Professions Code at the same time. (Note that there is no §6158.6.) Governor Wilson signed the legislation on September 21, 1994, and it took effect on January 1, 1995.

---

§6158. Electronic Media Advertising; False, Misleading or Deceptive Message; Factual Substantiation

In advertising by electronic media, to comply with Sections 6157.1 and 6157.2, the message as a whole may not be false, misleading, or deceptive, and the message as a whole must be factually substantiated. The message means the effect in combination of the spoken word, sound, background, action, symbols, visual image, or any other technique employed to create the message. Factually substantiated means capable of verification by a credible source.
(Added 1994.)

§6158.1. False, Misleading or Deceptive Messages; Rebuttable Presumption

There shall be a rebuttable presumption affecting the burden of producing evidence that the following messages are false, misleading, or deceptive within the meaning of Section 6158:

(a) A message as to the ultimate result of a specific case or cases presented out of context without adequately providing information as to the facts or law giving rise to the result.

(b) The depiction of an event through methods such as the use of displays of injuries, accident scenes, or portrayals of other injurious events which may or may not be accompanied by sound effects and which may give rise to a claim for compensation.

(c) A message referring to or implying money received by or for a client in a particular case or cases, or to potential monetary recovery for a prospective client. A reference to money or monetary recovery includes, but is not limited to, a specific dollar amount, characterization of a sum of money, monetary symbols, or the implication of wealth.
(Added 1994.)

§6158.3. Electronic Media Advertising; Required Disclosures

In addition to any disclosure required by Section 6157.2, Section 6157.3, and the Rules of Professional Conduct, the following disclosure shall appear in advertising by electronic media. Use of the following disclosure alone may not rebut any presumption created in Section 6158.1.

637

If an advertisement in the electronic media conveys a message portraying a result in a particular case or cases, the advertisement must state, in either an oral or printed communication, either of the following disclosures: The advertisement must adequately disclose the factual and legal circumstances that justify the result portrayed in the message, including the basis for liability and the nature of injury or damage sustained, or the advertisement must state that the result portrayed in the advertisement was dependent on the facts of that case, and that the results will differ if based on different facts.

(Added 1994.)

CALIFORNIA CIVIL CODE

§51.9. Sexual Harassment; Business, Service and Professional Relationships

Editors' Note. Section 51.9 of the California Civil Code, which gives clients a right to sue their lawyers for sexual harassment was signed the law on September 21, 1994, and it took effect on January 1, 1995. The law complements §12940 of the California Government Code, which prohibits a wide range of employers, including lawyers, from sexually harassing their employees.

(a) A person is liable in a cause of action for sexual harassment when the plaintiff proves all of the following elements:

(1) There is a business, service, or professional relationship between the plaintiff and defendant. Such a relationship includes any of the following:

(A) Physician, psychotherapist, or dentist-patient.

(B) Attorney, marriage, family or child counselor, licensed clinical social worker, master of social work, real estate agent, real estate appraiser, accountant, banker, trust officer, financial planner loan officer, collection service, contractor, or escrow loan officer-client.

(C) Executor, trustee, or administrator beneficiary.

(D) Landlord or property manager-tenant.

(E) Teacher-student.

(F) A relationship that is substantially similar to any of the above.

(2) The defendant has made sexual advances, solicitations, sexual requests, or demands for sexual compliance by the plaintiff that were

unwelcome and persistent or severe, continuing after a request by the plaintiff to stop.

(3) There is an inability by the plaintiff to easily terminate the relationship without tangible hardship.

(4) The plaintiff has suffered or will suffer economic loss or disadvantage or personal injury as a result of the conduct described in paragraph (2).

(b) In an action pursuant to this section, damages shall be awarded as provided by Section 52.

(c) Nothing in this section shall be construed to limit application of any other remedies provided under the law.

(d) The complaint and answer under this section shall be verified as provided for in Sections 446 and 447 of the Code of Civil Procedure.

(Added 1994.)

§2860. Conflict of Interest; Duty to Provide
         Independent Counsel; Waiver;
         Qualifications of Independent Counsel;
         Fees; Disclosure of Information

(a) If the provisions of a policy of insurance impose a duty to defend upon an insurer and a conflict of interest arises which creates a duty on the part of the insurer to provide independent counsel to the insured, the insurer shall provide independent counsel to represent the insured unless, at the time the insured is informed that a possible conflict may arise or does exist, the insured expressly waives, in writing, the right to independent counsel. An insurance contract may contain a provision which sets forth the method of selecting that counsel consistent with this section.

(b) For purposes of this section, a conflict of interest does not exist as to allegations or facts in the litigation for which the insurer denies coverage; however, when an insurer reserves its rights on a given issue and the outcome of that coverage issue can be controlled by counsel first retained by the insurer for the defense of the claim, a conflict of interest may exist. No conflict of interest shall be deemed to exist as to allegations of punitive damages or be deemed to exist solely because an insured is sued for an amount in excess of the insurance policy limits.

(c) When the insured has selected independent counsel to represent him or her, the insurer may exercise its right to require that the counsel selected by the insured possess certain minimum qualifications which may include that the selected counsel have (1) at least five years of civil litigation practice which includes substantial defense experience in the subject at issue in the litigation, and (2) errors and omissions coverage. The insurer's obligation to pay fees to the independent counsel selected by the insured is limited to the rates which are actually paid by the insurer to attorneys retained by it in the ordinary course of business in the defense of similar actions in the community where the claim arose or is being defended. This subdivision does not invalidate other different or additional policy provisions pertaining to attorney's fees or providing for methods of settlement of disputes concerning those fees. Any dispute concerning attorney's fees not resolved by these methods shall be resolved by final and binding arbitration by a single neutral arbitrator selected by the parties to the dispute.

(d) When independent counsel has been selected by the insured, it shall be the duty of that counsel and the insured to disclose to the insurer all information concerning the action except privileged materials relevant to coverage disputes, and timely to inform and consult with the insurer on all matters relating to the action. Any claim of privilege asserted is subject to in camera review in the appropriate law and motion department of the superior court. Any information disclosed by the insured or by independent counsel is not a waiver of the privilege as to any other party.

(e) The insured may waive its right to select independent counsel by signing the following statement: "I have been advised and informed of my right to select independent counsel to represent me in this lawsuit. I have considered this matter fully and freely waive my right to select independent counsel at this time. I authorize my insurer to select a defense attorney to represent me in this lawsuit."

(f) Where the insured selects independent counsel pursuant to the provisions of this section, both the counsel provided by the insurer and independent counsel selected by the insured shall be allowed to participate in all aspects of the litigation. Counsel shall cooperate fully in the exchange of information that is consistent with each counsel's ethical and legal obligation to the insured. Nothing in this section shall relieve the insured of his or her duty to cooperate with the insurer under the terms of the insurance contract.

(Added 1987; amended 1988.)

District of Columbia Materials

District of Columbia Rules of Professional Conduct

Editors' Note. The following rules were adopted by the District of Columbia Court of Appeals effective November 1, 1996. In our annotation, Selected State Variations, following each Model Rule, we identify those D.C. rules that differ significantly from the corresponding Model Rule. The D.C. Rules contain two gaps because there is no Rule 7.2, 7.3, 7.4, or 8.2.

SCOPE

The Rules of Professional Conduct are rules of reason. They should be interpreted with reference to the purposes of legal representation and of the law itself. Some of the Rules are imperatives, cast in the terms "shall" or "shall not." These define proper conduct for purposes of professional discipline. Others, generally cast in the term "may," are permissive and define areas under the Rules in which the lawyer has professional discretion. No disciplinary action should be taken when the lawyer chooses not to act or acts within the bounds of such discretion. Other Rules define the nature of relationships between the lawyer and others. The Rules are thus partly obligatory and disciplinary and partly constitutive and descriptive in that they define a lawyer's professional role. Many of the Comments use the term "should." Comments do not add obligations to the Rules but provide guidance for interpreting the Rules and practicing in compliance with them.

The Rules presuppose a larger legal context shaping the lawyer's role. That context includes court rules and statutes relating to matters of licensure, laws defining specific obligations of lawyers, and substantive and procedural law in general. Compliance with the Rules, as with all law in an open society, depends primarily upon understanding and voluntary compliance, secondarily upon reinforcement by peer and public opinion, and finally, when necessary, upon enforcement through disciplinary proceedings. The Rules do not, however, exhaust the moral and ethical considerations that should inform a lawyer, for no worthwhile human activity can be completely defined by legal rules. The Rules simply provide a framework for the ethical practice of law.

Failure to comply with an obligation or prohibition imposed by a Rule is a basis for invoking the disciplinary process. The Rules presuppose that disciplinary assessment of a lawyer's conduct will be made on the basis of the facts and circumstances as they existed at the time of the conduct in question and in recognition of the fact that a lawyer often has to act upon uncertain or incomplete evidence of the situation. Moreover, the Rules presuppose that whether or not discipline should be imposed for a violation, and the severity of a sanction, depend on all the circumstances, such as the willfulness and seriousness of the violation, extenuating factors and whether there have been previous violations.

Nothing in these Rules, the Comments associated with them, or this Scope section is intended to enlarge or restrict existing law regarding the liability of lawyers to others or the requirements that the testimony of expert witnesses or other modes of proof must be employed in determining the scope of a lawyer's duty to others. Moreover, nothing in the Rules or associated Comments or this Scope section is intended to confer rights on an adversary of a lawyer to enforce the Rules in a proceeding other than a disciplinary proceeding. A tribunal presented with claims that the conduct of a lawyer appearing before that tribunal requires, for example, disqualification of the lawyer and/or the lawyer's firm may take such action as seems appropriate in the circumstances, which may or may not involve disqualification.

In interpreting these Rules, the specific shall control the general in the sense that any rule that specifically addresses conduct shall control the disposition of matters and the outcome of such matters shall not turn upon the application of a more general rule that arguably also applies to the conduct in question. In a number of instances, there are specific rules that address specific types of conduct. The rule of interpretation expressed here is meant to make it clear that the general rule does not supplant, amend, enlarge, or extend the specific rule. So, for instance, the general terms of Rule 1.3 are not intended to govern conflicts of interest, which are particularly discussed in Rules 1.7, 1.8, and 1.9. Thus, conduct that is proper under the specific conflicts rules is not improper under the more general rule of Rule 1.3. Except where the principle of priority stated here is applicable, however, compliance with one rule does not generally excuse compliance with other rules. Accordingly, once a lawyer has analyzed the ethical considerations under a given rule, the lawyer must generally extend the analysis to ensure compliance with all other applicable rules.

The Comment accompanying each Rule explains and illustrates the meaning and purpose of the Rule. This note on Scope provides general orientation and general rules of interpretation. The Comments are intended as guides to interpretation, but the text of each Rule is controlling.

TERMINOLOGY

"Belief" or "believes" denotes that the person involved actually supposed the fact in question to be true. A person's belief may be inferred from circumstances.

"Consent" denotes a client's uncoerced assent to a proposed course of action, following consultation with the lawyer regarding the matter in question.

"Consult" or "consultation" denotes communication of information reasonably sufficient to permit the client to appreciate the significance of the matter in question.

"Firm" or "law firm" denotes a lawyer or lawyers in a private firm, lawyers employed in the legal department of a corporation or other organization, and lawyers employed in a legal services organization. See Comment, Rule 1.10.

"Fraud" or "fraudulent" denotes conduct having a purpose to deceive and not merely negligent misrepresentation or failure to apprise another of relevant information.

"Knowingly," "known," or "knows" denotes actual knowledge of the fact in question. A person's knowledge may be inferred from circumstances.

"Law clerk" denotes a person, typically a recent law school graduate, who acts, typically for a limited period, as confidential assistant to a judge or judges of a court; to an administrative law judge or a similar administrative hearing officer; or to the head of a governmental agency or to a member of a governmental commission, either of which has authority to adjudicate or to promulgate rules or regulations of general application.

"Matter" means any litigation, administrative proceeding, lobbying activity, application, claim, investigation, arrest, charge or accusation, the drafting of a contract, a negotiation, estate or family relations practice issue, or any other representation, except as expressly limited in a particular Rule.

"Partner" denotes a member of a partnership and a shareholder in a law firm organized as a professional corporation.

"Reasonable" or "reasonably" when used in relation to conduct by a lawyer denotes the conduct of a reasonably prudent and competent lawyer.

"Reasonably should know" when used in reference to a lawyer denotes that a lawyer of reasonable prudence and competence would ascertain the matter in question.

"Substantial" when used in reference to degree or extent denotes a material matter of clear and weighty importance.

"Tribunal" denotes a court, regulatory agency, commission, and any other body or individual authorized by law to render decisions of a judicial or quasi-judicial nature, based on information presented before it, regardless of the degree of formality or informality of the proceedings.

CLIENT-LAWYER RELATIONSHIP

Rule 1.1. Competence

(a) A lawyer shall provide competent representation to a client. Competent representation requires the legal knowledge, skill, thoroughness, and preparation reasonably necessary for the representation.

(b) A lawyer shall serve a client with skill and care commensurate with that generally afforded to clients by other lawyers in similar matters.

COMMENT

Legal Knowledge and Skill

[1] In determining whether a lawyer employs the requisite knowledge and skill in a particular matter, relevant factors include the relative complexity and specialized nature of the matter, the lawyer's general experience, the lawyer's training and experience in the field in question, the preparation and study the lawyer is able to give the matter, and whether it is feasible to refer the matter to, or associate or consult with, a lawyer of established competence in the field in question. In many instances, the required proficiency is that of a general practitioner. Expertise in a particular field of law may be required in some circumstances. One such circumstance would be where the lawyer, by representations made to the client, has led the client reasonably to expect a special level of expertise in the matter undertaken by the lawyer.

[2] A lawyer need not necessarily have special training or prior experience to handle legal problems of a type with which the lawyer is unfamiliar. A newly admitted lawyer can be as competent as a practitioner with long experience. Some important legal skills, such as the analysis of precedent, the evaluation of evidence and legal drafting, are required in all legal problems. Perhaps the most fundamental legal skill consists of determining what kind of legal problems a situation may involve, a skill that necessarily transcends any particular specialized knowledge. A lawyer can provide adequate representation in a wholly novel field through necessary study. Competent representation can also be provided through the association of a lawyer of established competence in the field in question.

[3] In an emergency a lawyer may give advice or assistance in a matter in which the lawyer does not have the skill ordinarily required where referral to or consultation or association with another lawyer would be impractical. Even in an emergency, however, assistance should be limited to that reasonably necessary in the circumstances, for ill-considered action under emergency conditions can jeopardize the client's interest.

[4] A lawyer may accept representation where the requisite level of competence can be achieved by reasonable preparation. This applies as well to a lawyer who is appointed as counsel for an unrepresented person. See also Rule 6.2.

Thoroughness and Preparation

[5] Competent handling of a particular matter includes inquiry into and analysis of the factual and legal elements of the problem, and use of methods and procedures meeting the standards of competent practitioners. It also includes adequate preparation, and continuing attention to the needs of the representation to assure that there is no neglect of such needs. The required attention and preparation are determined in part by what is at stake; major litigation and complex transactions ordinarily require more elaborate treatment than matters of lesser consequence.

Maintaining Competence

[6] To maintain the requisite knowledge and skill, a lawyer should engage in such continuing study and education as may be necessary to maintain competence, taking into account that the learning acquired through a lawyer's practical experience in actual representations may reduce or eliminate the need for special continuing study or education. If a system of peer review has been established, the lawyer should consider making use of it in appropriate circumstances.

Rule 1.2. Scope of Representation

(a) A lawyer shall abide by a client's decisions concerning the objectives of representation, subject to paragraphs (c), (d), and (e), and shall consult with the client as to the means by which they are to be pursued. A lawyer shall abide by a client's decision whether to accept an offer of settlement of a matter. In a criminal case, the lawyer shall abide by the client's decision, after consultation with the lawyer, as to a plea to be entered, whether to waive jury trial, and whether the client will testify.

(b) A lawyer's representation of a client, including representation by appointment, does not constitute an endorsement of the client's political, economic, social, or moral views or activities.

(c) A lawyer may limit the objectives of the representation if the client consents after consultation.

(d) A government lawyer's authority and control over decisions concerning the representation may, by statute or regulation, be expanded beyond the limits imposed by paragraphs (a) and (c).

(e) A lawyer shall not counsel a client to engage, or assist a client, in conduct that the lawyer knows is criminal or fraudulent, but a lawyer may discuss the legal consequences of any proposed course of conduct with a client and may counsel or assist a client to make a good faith effort to determine the validity, scope, meaning, or application of the law.

(f) When a lawyer knows that a client expects assistance not permitted by the rules of professional conduct or other law, the lawyer shall consult with the client regarding the relevant limitations on the lawyer's conduct.

COMMENT

Scope of Representation

[1] Both lawyer and client have authority and responsibility in the objectives and means of representation. The client has ultimate authority to determine the purposes to be served by legal representation, within the limits imposed by law and the lawyer's professional obligations. Within these limits, a client also has a right to consult with the lawyer about the means to be used in pursuing those objectives. At the same time, a lawyer is not required to pursue objectives or employ means simply because a client may wish that the lawyer do so. A clear distinction between objectives and means sometimes cannot be drawn, and in many cases the client-lawyer relationship partakes of a joint undertaking. In questions of means, the lawyer should assume responsibility for technical and legal tactical issues, but should defer to the client regarding such questions as the expense to be incurred and concern for third persons who might be adversely affected. Law defining the lawyer's scope of authority in litigation varies among jurisdictions.

[2] In a case in which the client appears to be suffering mental disability, the lawyer's duty to abide by the client's decisions is to be guided by reference to Rule 1.14.

Independence From Client's Views or Activities

[3] Legal representation should not be denied to people who are unable to afford legal services, or whose cause is controversial or the subject of popular disapproval. By the same token, representing a client does not constitute approval of the client's views or activities.

Services Limited in Objectives or Means

[4] The objectives or scope of services provided by the lawyer may be limited by agreement with the client or by terms under which the lawyer's

services are made available to the client. For example, a retainer may be for a specifically defined purpose. Representation provided through a legal aid agency may be subject to limitations on the types of cases the agency handles. When a lawyer has been retained by an insurer to represent an insured, the representation may be limited to matters related to the insurance coverage. The terms upon which representation is undertaken may exclude specific objectives or means. Such limitations may exclude objectives or means that the lawyer regards as repugnant or imprudent.

[5] An agreement concerning the scope of representation must accord with the Rules of Professional Conduct and other law. Thus, the client may not be asked to agree to representation so limited in scope as to violate Rule 1.1, or to surrender the right to terminate the lawyer's services or the right to settle litigation that the lawyer might wish to continue.

Criminal, Fraudulent, and Prohibited Transactions

[6] A lawyer is required to give an honest opinion about the actual consequences that appear likely to result from a client's conduct. The fact that a client uses advice in a course of action that is criminal or fraudulent does not, of itself, make a lawyer a party to the course of action. However, a lawyer may not knowingly assist a client in criminal or fraudulent conduct. There is a critical distinction between presenting an analysis of legal aspects of questionable conduct and recommending the means by which a crime or fraud might be committed with impunity.

[7] When the client's course of action has already begun and is continuing, the lawyer's responsibility is especially delicate. The lawyer is not permitted to reveal the client's wrongdoing, except where permitted by Rule 1.6. However, the lawyer is required to avoid furthering the purpose, for example, by suggesting how it might be concealed. A lawyer may not continue assisting a client in conduct that the lawyer originally supposes is legally proper but then discovers is criminal or fraudulent. Withdrawal from the representation, therefore, may be required.

[8] Where the client is a fiduciary, the lawyer may be charged with special obligations in dealings with a beneficiary.

[9] Paragraph (d) applies whether or not the defrauded party is a party to the transaction. Hence, a lawyer should not participate in a sham transaction; for example, a transaction to effectuate criminal or fraudulent escape of tax liability. Paragraph (d) does not preclude undertaking a criminal defense incident to a general retainer for legal services to a law-

ful enterprise. The last clause of paragraph (d) recognizes that determining the validity or interpretation of a statute or regulation may require a course of action involving disobedience of the statute or regulation or of the interpretation placed upon it by governmental authorities.

Rule 1.3. Diligence and Zeal

(a) A lawyer shall represent a client zealously and diligently within the bounds of the law.

(b) A lawyer shall not intentionally:

(1) Fail to seek the lawful objectives of a client through reasonably available means permitted by law and the disciplinary rules; or

(2) Prejudice or damage a client during the course of the professional relationship.

(c) A lawyer shall act with reasonable promptness in representing a client.

COMMENT

[1] The duty of a lawyer, both to the client and to the legal system, is to represent the client zealously within the bounds of the law, including the Rules of Professional Conduct and other enforceable professional regulations, such as agency regulations applicable to lawyers practicing before the agency. This duty requires the lawyer to pursue a matter on behalf of a client despite opposition, obstruction, or personal inconvenience to the lawyer, and to take whatever lawful and ethical measures are required to vindicate a client's cause or endeavor. A lawyer should act with commitment and dedication to the interests of the client. However, a lawyer is not bound to press for every advantage that might be realized for a client. A lawyer has professional discretion in determining the means by which a matter should be pursued. See Rule 1.2. A lawyer's work load should be controlled so that each matter can be handled adequately.

[2] This duty derives from the lawyer's membership in a profession that has the duty of assisting members of the public to secure and protect available legal rights and benefits. In our government of laws and not of individuals, each member of our society is entitled to have such member's conduct judged and regulated in accordance with the law; to seek any lawful objective through legally permissible means; and to present for adjudication any lawful claim, issue, or defense.

[3] The bounds of the law in a given case are often difficult to ascertain. The language of legislative enactments and judicial opinions may be uncertain as applied to varying factual situations. The limits and specific meaning of apparently relevant law may be made doubtful by changing or developing constitutional interpretations, ambiguous statutes, or judicial opinions, and changing public and judicial attitudes.

[4] Where the bounds of law are uncertain, the action of a lawyer may depend on whether the lawyer is serving as advocate or adviser. A lawyer may serve simultaneously as both advocate and adviser, but the two roles are essentially different. In asserting a position on behalf of a client, an advocate for the most part deals with past conduct and must take the facts as the advocate finds them. By contrast, a lawyer serving as adviser primarily assists the client in determining the course of future conduct and relationships. While serving as advocate, a lawyer should resolve in favor of the client doubts as to the bounds of the law but even when acting as an advocate, a lawyer may not institute or defend a proceeding unless the positions taken are not frivolous. See Rule 3.1. In serving a client as adviser, a lawyer, in appropriate circumstances, should give a lawyer's professional opinion as to what the ultimate decisions of the courts would likely be as to the applicable law.

[5] In the exercise of professional judgment, a lawyer should always act in a manner consistent with the best interests of the client. However, when an action in the best interests of the client seems to be unjust, a lawyer may ask the client for permission to forgo such action. If the lawyer knows that the client expects assistance that is not in accord with the Rules of Professional Conduct or other law, the lawyer must inform the client of the pertinent limitations on the lawyer's conduct. See Rule 1.2(e) and (f). Similarly, the lawyer's obligation not to prejudice the interests of the client is subject to the duty of candor toward the tribunal under Rule 3.3 and the duty to expedite litigation under Rule 3.2.

[6] The duty of a lawyer to represent the client with zeal does not militate against the concurrent obligation to treat with consideration all persons involved in the legal process and to avoid the infliction of needless harm. Thus, the lawyer's duty to pursue a client's lawful objectives zealously does not prevent the lawyer from acceding to reasonable requests of opposing counsel that do not prejudice the client's rights, being punctual in fulfilling all professional commitments, avoiding offensive tactics, or treating all persons involved in the legal process with courtesy and consideration.

[7] Perhaps no professional shortcoming is more widely resented by clients than procrastination. A client's interests often can be adversely affected by the passage of time or the change of conditions; in extreme in-

stances, as when a lawyer overlooks a statute of limitations, the client's legal position may be destroyed. Even when the client's interests are not affected in substance, however, unreasonable delay can cause a client needless anxiety and undermine confidence in the lawyer's trustworthiness. Neglect of client matters is a serious violation of the obligation of diligence.

[8] Unless the relationship is terminated as provided in Rule 1.16, a lawyer should carry through to conclusion all matters undertaken for a client. If a lawyer's employment is limited to a specific matter, the relationship terminates when the matter has been resolved. If a lawyer has served a client over a substantial period in a variety of matters, the client sometimes may assume that the lawyer will continue to serve on a continuing basis unless the lawyer gives notice of withdrawal. Doubt about whether a client-lawyer relationship still exists should be eliminated by the lawyer, preferably in writing, so that the client will not mistakenly suppose the lawyer is looking after the client's affairs when the lawyer has ceased to do so. For example, if a lawyer has handled a judicial or administrative proceeding that produced a result adverse to the client but has not been specifically instructed concerning pursuit of an appeal, the lawyer should advise the client of the possibility of appeal before relinquishing responsibility for the matter.

[9] Rule 1.3 is a rule of general applicability, and it is not meant to enlarge or restrict any specific rule. In particular, Rule 1.3 is not meant to govern conflicts of interest, which are addressed by Rules 1.7, 1.8, and 1.9.

Rule 1.4. Communication

(a) A lawyer shall keep a client reasonably informed about the status of a matter and promptly comply with reasonable requests for information.

(b) A lawyer shall explain a matter to the extent reasonably necessary to permit the client to make informed decisions regarding the representation.

(c) A lawyer who receives an offer of settlement in a civil case or a proffered plea bargain in a criminal case shall inform the client promptly of the substance of the communication.

COMMENT

[1] The client should have sufficient information to participate intelligently in decisions concerning the objectives of the representation

and the means by which they are to be pursued, to the extent the client is willing and able to do so. For example, a lawyer negotiating on behalf of a client should provide the client with facts relevant to the matter, inform the client of communications from another party, and take other reasonable steps that permit the client to make a decision regarding a serious offer from another party. A lawyer who receives from opposing counsel an offer of settlement in a civil controversy or a proffered plea bargain in a criminal case is required to inform the client promptly to inform the client of its substance. See Rule 1.2(a). Even when a client delegates authority to the lawyer, the client should be kept advised of the status of the matter.

[2] A client is entitled to whatever information the client wishes about all aspects of the subject matter of the representation unless the client expressly consents not to have certain information passed on. The lawyer must be particularly careful to ensure that decisions of the client are made only after the client has been informed of all relevant considerations. The lawyer must initiate and maintain the consultative and decision-making process if the client does not do so and must ensure that the ongoing process is thorough and complete.

[3] Adequacy of communication depends in part on the kind of advice or assistance involved. The guiding principle is that the lawyer should fulfill reasonable client expectations for information consistent with (1) the duty to act in the client's best interests, and (2) the client's overall requirements and objectives as to the character of representation.

[4] Ordinarily, the information to be provided is that appropriate for a client who is a comprehending and responsible adult. However, fully informing the client according to this standard may be impracticable, for example, where the client is a child or suffers from mental disability. See Rule 1.14. When the client is an organization or group, it is often impossible or inappropriate to inform every one of its members about its legal affairs; ordinarily, the lawyer should address communications to the appropriate officials of the organization. See Rule 1.13. Where many routine matters are involved, a system of limited or occasional reporting may be arranged with the client. Practical exigency may also require a lawyer to act for a client without prior consultation. When the lawyer is conducting a trial, it is often not possible for the lawyer to consult with the client and obtain the client's acquiescence in tactical matters arising during the course of trial. It is sufficient if the lawyer consults with the client in advance of trial on significant issues that can be anticipated as arising during the course of the trial, and consults during trial to the extent practical, given the nature of the trial process.

Withholding Information

[5] In rare circumstances, a lawyer may be justified in delaying transmission of information when the client would be likely to react imprudently to an immediate communication. Thus, a lawyer might withhold a psychiatric diagnosis of a client when the examining psychiatrist indicates that disclosure would harm the client. Similarly, a lawyer may be justified, for humanitarian reasons, in not conveying certain information, for example, where the information would merely be upsetting to a terminally ill client. A lawyer may not withhold information to serve the lawyer's own interest or convenience. Rules or court orders governing litigation (such as a protective order limiting access to certain types of discovery material to counsel only) may provide that information supplied to a lawyer may not be disclosed to the client. Rule 3.4(c) directs compliance with such rules or orders.

Rule 1.5. Fees

(a) A lawyer's fee shall be reasonable. The factors to be considered in determining the reasonableness of a fee include the following:

(1) The time and labor required, the novelty and difficulty of the questions involved, and the skill requisite to perform the legal service properly;

(2) The likelihood, if apparent to the client, that the acceptance of the particular employment will preclude other employment by the lawyer;

(3) The fee customarily charged in the locality for similar legal services;

(4) The amount involved and the results obtained;

(5) The time limitations imposed by the client or by the circumstances;

(6) The nature and length of the professional relationship with the client;

(7) The experience, reputation, and ability of the lawyer or lawyers performing the services; and

(8) Whether the fee is fixed or contingent.

(b) When the lawyer has not regularly represented the client, the basis or rate of the fee shall be communicated to the client, in writing, before or within a reasonable time after commencing the representation.

(c) A fee may be contingent on the outcome of the matter for which the service is rendered, except in a matter in which a contingent fee is prohibited by paragraph (d) or other law. A contingent fee agreement shall be in writing and shall state the method by which the fee is to be determined, including the percentage or percentages that shall accrue to the lawyer in the event of settlement, trial or appeal, litigation, and other expenses to be deducted from the recovery, and whether such expenses are to be deducted before or after the contingent fee is calculated. Upon conclusion of a contingent fee matter, the lawyer shall provide the client with a written statement stating the outcome of the matter and, if there is a recovery, showing the remittance to the client and the method of its determination.

(d) A lawyer shall not enter into an arrangement for, charge, or collect a contingent fee for representing a defendant in a criminal case.

(e) A division of a fee between lawyers who are not in the same firm may be made only if:

(1) The division is in proportion to the services performed by each lawyer or each lawyer assumes joint responsibility for the representation;

(2) The client is advised, in writing, of the identity of the lawyers who will participate in the representation, of the contemplated division of responsibility, and of the effect of the association of lawyers outside the firm on the fee to be charged;

(3) The client consents to the arrangement; and

(4) The total fee is reasonable.

(f) Any fee that is prohibited by paragraph (d) above or by law is per se unreasonable.

COMMENT

Basis or Rate of Fee

[1] When the lawyer has regularly represented a client, they ordinarily will have evolved an understanding concerning the basis or rate of the fee. In a new client-lawyer relationship, however, an understanding as to the fee should be promptly established. It is not necessary to recite all the factors that underlie the basis of the fee, but only those that are directly involved in its computation. It is sufficient, for example, to state that the basic rate is an hourly charge or a fixed amount or an estimated amount, or to identify the factors that may be taken into account in finally fixing the fee. When developments occur during the representation that render an earlier estimate substantially inaccurate, a revised estimate should be provided to the client.

[2] A written statement concerning the fee, required to be furnished in advance in most cases by paragraph (b), reduces the possibility of misunderstanding. In circumstances in which paragraph (b) requires that the basis for the lawyer's fee be in writing, an individualized writing specific to the particular client and representation is generally not required. Unless there are unique aspects of the fee arrangement, the lawyer may utilize a standardized letter, memorandum, or pamphlet explaining the lawyer's fee practices, and indicating those practices applicable to the specific representation. Such publications would, for example, explain applicable hourly billing rates, if billing on an hourly rate basis is contemplated, and indicate what charges (such as filing fees, transcript costs, duplicating costs, long-distance telephone charges) are imposed in addition to hourly rate charges.

[3] Where the services to be rendered are covered by a fixed fee schedule that adequately informs the client of the charges to be imposed, a copy of such schedule may be utilized to satisfy the requirement for a writing. Such services as routine real estate transactions, uncontested divorces, or preparation of simple wills, for example, may be suitable for description in such a fixed-fee schedule.

Terms of Payment

[4] A lawyer may require advance payment of a fee, but is obliged to return any unearned portion. See Rule 1.16(d). A lawyer may accept property in payment for services, such as an ownership interest in an enterprise. However, a fee paid in property instead of money may be subject to special scrutiny because it involves questions concerning both the value of the services and the lawyer's special knowledge of the value of the property.

[5] An agreement may not be made whose terms might induce the lawyer improperly to curtail services for the client or perform them in a way contrary to the client's interest. For example, a lawyer should not enter into an agreement whereby services are to be provided only up to a stated amount when it is foreseeable that more extensive services probably will be required, unless the situation is adequately explained to the client. Otherwise, the client might have to bargain for further assistance in the midst of a proceeding or transaction. However, it is proper to define the extent of services in light of the client's ability to pay. A lawyer should not exploit a fee arrangement based primarily on hourly charges by using wasteful procedures.

Contingent Fees

[6] Generally, contingent fees are permissible in all civil cases. However, paragraph (d) continues the prohibition, imposed under the previous Code of Professional Responsibility, against the use of a contingent fee arrangement by a lawyer representing a defendant in a criminal case. Applicable law may impose other limitations on contingent fees, such as a ceiling on the percentage. And in any case, if there is doubt whether a contingent fee is consistent with the client's best interests, the lawyer should explain any existing payment alternatives and their implications.

[7] Contingent fees in domestic relations cases, while rarely justified, are not prohibited by Rule 1.5. Contingent fees in such cases are permitted in order that lawyers may provide representation to clients who might not otherwise be able to afford to contract for the payment of fees on a noncontingent basis.

[8] Paragraph (c) requires that the contingent fee arrangement be in writing. This writing must explain the method by which the fee is to be computed. The lawyer must also provide the client with a written statement at the conclusion of a contingent fee matter, stating the outcome of the matter and explaining the computation of any remittance made to the client.

Division of Fee

[9] A division of fee is a single billing to a client covering the fee of two or more lawyers who are not in the same firm. A division of fee facilitates association of more than one lawyer in a matter in which neither alone could serve the client as well, and most often is used when the fee is contingent and the division is between a referring lawyer and a trial specialist.

[10] Paragraph (e) permits the lawyers to divide a fee either on the basis of the proportion of services they render or by agreement between the participating lawyers if all assume responsibility for the representation as a whole. Joint responsibility for the representation entails the obligations stated in Rule 5.1 for purposes of the matter involved. Permitting a division on the basis of joint responsibility, rather than on the basis of services performed, represents a change from the basis for fee divisions allowed under the prior Code of Professional Responsibility. The change is intended to encourage lawyers to affiliate other counsel, who are better

equipped by reason of experience or specialized background to serve the client's needs, rather than to retain sole responsibility for the representation in order to avoid losing the right to a fee.

[11] The concept of joint responsibility is not, however, merely a technicality or incantation. The lawyer who refers the client to another lawyer, or affiliates another lawyer in the representation, remains fully responsible to the client, and is accountable to the client for deficiencies in the discharge of the representation by the lawyer who has been brought into the representation. If a lawyer wishes to avoid such responsibility for the potential deficiencies of another lawyer, the matter must be referred to the other lawyer without retaining a right to participate in fees beyond those fees justified by services actually rendered.

[12] The concept of joint responsibility does not require the referring lawyer to perform any minimum portion of the total legal services rendered. The referring lawyer may agree that the lawyer to whom the referral is made will perform substantially all of the services to be rendered in connection with the representation, without review by the referring lawyer. Thus, the referring lawyer is not required to review pleadings or other documents, attend hearings or depositions, or otherwise participate in a significant and continuing manner. The referring lawyer does not, however, escape the implications of joint responsibility, see Comment [11], by avoiding direct participation.

[13] When fee divisions are based on assumed joint responsibility, the requirement of paragraph (a) that the fee be reasonable applies to the total fee charged for the representation by all participating lawyers.

[14] Paragraph (e) requires that the client be advised, in writing, of the fee division and states that the client must affirmatively consent to the proposed fee arrangement. The Rule does not require disclosure to the client of the share that each lawyer is to receive but does require that the client be informed of the identity of the lawyers sharing the fee, their respective responsibilities in the representation, and the effect of the association of lawyers outside the firm on the fee charged.

Disputes Over Fees

[15] If a procedure has been established for resolution of fee disputes, such as an arbitration or mediation procedure established by the Bar, the lawyer should conscientiously consider submitting to it. Law may prescribe a procedure for determining a lawyer's fee, for example, in representation of an executor or administrator, a class, or a person entitled

to a reasonable fee as part of the measure of damages. The lawyer entitled to such a fee and a lawyer representing another party concerned with the fee should comply with the prescribed procedure.

Rule 1.6. Confidentiality of Information

(a) Except when permitted under paragraph (c) or (d), a lawyer shall not knowingly:

(1) Reveal a confidence or secret of the lawyer's client;

(2) Use a confidence or secret of the lawyer's client to the disadvantage of the client;

(3) Use a confidence or secret of the lawyer's client for the advantage of the lawyer or of a third person.

(b) "Confidence" refers to information protected by the attorney-client privilege under applicable law, and "secret" refers to other information gained in the professional relationship that the client has requested be held inviolate, or the disclosure of which would be embarrassing, or would be likely to be detrimental, to the client.

(c) A lawyer may reveal client confidences and secrets, to the extent reasonably necessary:

(1) To prevent a criminal act that the lawyer reasonably believes is likely to result in death or substantial bodily harm absent disclosure of the client's secrets or confidences by the lawyer; or

(2) To prevent the bribery or intimidation of witnesses, jurors, court officials, or other persons who are involved in proceedings before a tribunal if the lawyer reasonably believes that such acts are likely to result absent disclosure of the client's confidences or secrets by the lawyer.

(d) A lawyer may use or reveal client confidences or secrets:

(1) With the consent of the client affected, but only after full disclosure to the client;

(2)(A) When permitted by these Rules or required by law or court order; and

(B) If a government lawyer, when permitted or authorized by law;

(3) To the extent reasonably necessary to establish a defense to a criminal charge, disciplinary charge, or civil claim, formally instituted against the lawyer, based upon conduct in which the client was involved, or to the extent reasonably necessary to respond to specific allegations by the client concerning the lawyer's representation of the client;

(4) When the lawyer has reasonable grounds for believing that a client has impliedly authorized disclosure of a confidence or secret in order to carry out the representation; or

(5) To the minimum extent necessary in an action instituted by the lawyer to establish or collect the lawyer's fee.

(e) A lawyer shall exercise reasonable care to prevent the lawyer's employees, associates, and others whose services are utilized by the lawyer from disclosing or using confidences or secrets of a client, except that such persons may reveal information permitted to be disclosed by paragraphs (c) or (d).

(f) The lawyer's obligation to preserve the client's confidences and secrets continues after termination of the lawyer's employment.

(g) The obligation of a lawyer under paragraph (a) also applies to confidences and secrets learned prior to becoming a lawyer in the course of providing assistance to another lawyer.

(h) A lawyer who serves as a member of the D.C. Bar Lawyer Counseling Committee, or as a trained intervenor for that Committee, shall be deemed to have a lawyer-client relationship with respect to any lawyer-counselee being counseled under programs conducted by or on behalf of the Committee. Information obtained from another lawyer being counseled under the auspices of the Committee, or in the course of and associated with such counseling, shall be treated as a confidence or secret within the terms of paragraph (b). Such information may be disclosed only to the extent permitted by this Rule.

(i) The client of the government lawyer is the agency that employs the lawyer unless expressly provided to the contrary by appropriate law, regulation, or order.

COMMENT

[1] The lawyer is part of a judicial system charged with upholding the law. One of the lawyer's functions is to advise clients so that they avoid any violation of the law in the proper exercise of their rights.

[2] The observance of the ethical obligation of a lawyer to hold inviolate confidential information of the client not only facilitates the full development of facts essential to proper representation of the client but also encourages people to seek early legal assistance.

[3] Almost without exception, clients come to lawyers in order to determine what their rights are and what is, in the maze of laws and regulations, deemed to be legal and correct. The common law recognizes that the client's confidences must be protected from disclosure. Based upon

experience, lawyers know that almost all clients follow the advice given, and the law is upheld.

[4] A fundamental principle in the client-lawyer relationship is that the lawyer holds inviolate the client's secrets and confidences. The client is thereby encouraged to communicate fully and frankly with the lawyer even as to embarrassing or legally damaging subject matter.

Relationship Between Rule 1.6 and Attorney-Client Evidentiary Privilege and Work Product Doctrine

[5] The principle of confidentiality is given effect in two related bodies of law: the attorney-client privilege and the work product doctrine in the law of evidence and the rule of confidentiality established in professional ethics. The attorney-client privilege and the work product doctrine apply in judicial and other proceedings in which a lawyer may be called as a witness or otherwise required to produce evidence concerning a client. This Rule is not intended to govern or affect judicial application of the attorney-client privilege or work product doctrine. The privilege and doctrine were developed to promote compliance with law and fairness in litigation. In reliance on the attorney-client privilege, clients are entitled to expect that communications within the scope of the privilege will be protected against compelled disclosure. The attorney-client privilege is that of the client and not of the lawyer. The fact that in exceptional situations the lawyer under this Rule has limited discretion to disclose a client confidence does not vitiate the proposition that, as a general matter, the client has a reasonable expectation that information relating to the client will not be voluntarily disclosed and that disclosure of such information may be judicially compelled only in accordance with recognized exceptions to the attorney-client privilege and work product doctrine.

[6] The rule of client-lawyer confidentiality applies in situations other than those where evidence is sought from the lawyer through compulsion of law; furthermore, it applies not merely to matters communicated in confidence by the client (i.e., confidences) but also to all information gained in the course of the professional relationship that the client has requested be held inviolate, or the disclosure of which would be embarrassing or would be likely to be detrimental to the client (i.e., secrets). This ethical precept, unlike the evidentiary privilege, exists without regard to the nature or source of the information or the fact that others

share the knowledge. It reflects not only the principles underlying the attorney-client privilege, but the lawyer's duty of loyalty to the client.

The Commencement of the Client-Lawyer Relationship

[7] Principles of substantive law external to these Rules determine whether a client-lawyer relationship exists. Although most of the duties flowing from the client-lawyer relationship attach only after the client has requested the lawyer to render legal services and the lawyer has agreed to do so, the duty of confidentiality imposed by this Rule attaches when the lawyer agrees to consider whether a client-lawyer relationship shall be established. Thus, a lawyer may be subject to a duty of confidentiality with respect to information disclosed by a client to enable the lawyer to determine whether representation of the potential client would involve a prohibited conflict of interest under Rule 1.7, 1.8, or 1.9.

Exploitation of Confidences and Secrets

[8] In addition to prohibiting the disclosure of a client's confidences and secrets, subparagraph (a)(2) provides that a lawyer may not use the client's confidences and secrets to the disadvantage of the client. For example, a lawyer who has learned that the client is investing in specific real estate may not seek to acquire nearby property where doing so would adversely affect the client's plan for investment. Similarly, information acquired by the lawyer in the course of representing a client may not be used to the disadvantage of that client even after the termination of the lawyer's representation of the client. However, the fact that a lawyer has once served a client does not preclude the lawyer from using generally known information about the former client when later representing another client. Under subparagraphs (a)(3) and (d)(1) a lawyer may use a client's confidences and secrets for the lawyer's own benefit or that of a third party only after the lawyer has made full disclosure to the client regarding the proposed use of the information and obtained the client's affirmative consent to the use in question.

Authorized Disclosure

[9] A lawyer is impliedly authorized to make disclosures about a client when appropriate in carrying out the representation, except

to the extent that the client's instructions or special circumstances limit that authority. In litigation, for example, a lawyer may disclose information by admitting a fact that cannot properly be disputed, or in negotiation by making a disclosure that facilitates a satisfactory conclusion.

[10] The obligation to protect confidences and secrets obviously does not preclude a lawyer from revealing information when the client consents after full disclosure, when necessary to perform the professional employment, when permitted by these Rules, or when required by law. Unless the client otherwise directs, a lawyer may disclose the affairs of the client to partners or associates of the lawyer's firm. It is a matter of common knowledge that the normal operation of a law office exposes confidential professional information to nonlawyer employees of the office, particularly secretaries and those having access to the files; and this obligates a lawyer to exercise care in selecting and training employees so that the sanctity of all confidences and secrets of clients may be preserved. If the obligation extends to two or more clients as to the same information, a lawyer should obtain the permission of all before revealing the information. A lawyer must always be sensitive to the rights and wishes of the client and act scrupulously in the making of decisions that may involve the disclosure of information obtained in the course of the professional relationship. Thus, in the absence of consent of the client after full disclosure, a lawyer should not associate another lawyer in the handling of a matter; nor should the lawyer, in the absence of consent, seek counsel from another lawyer if there is a reasonable possibility that the identity of the client or the client's confidences or secrets would be revealed to such lawyer. Proper concern for professional duty should cause a lawyer to shun indiscreet conversations concerning clients.

[11] Unless the client otherwise directs, it is not improper for a lawyer to give limited information from client files to an outside agency necessary for statistical, bookkeeping, accounting, data processing, banking, printing, or other legitimate purposes, provided the lawyer exercises due care in the selection of the agency and warns the agency that the information must be kept confidential.

Disclosure Adverse to Client

[12] The confidentiality rule is subject to limited exceptions. In becoming privy to information about a client, a lawyer may foresee that the client intends serious harm to another person. However, to the extent a

lawyer is required or permitted to disclose a client's purposes, the client will be inhibited from revealing facts that would enable the lawyer to counsel against a wrongful course of action. The public is better protected if full and open communication by the client is encouraged than if it is inhibited. Nevertheless, when the client's confidences or secrets are such that the lawyer knows or reasonably should know that the client or any other person is likely to kill or do substantial bodily injury to another unless the lawyer discloses client confidences or secrets, the lawyer may reveal the client's confidences and secrets if necessary to prevent harm to the third party.

[13] Several situations must be distinguished.

[14] First, the lawyer may not counsel or assist a client to engage in conduct that is criminal or fraudulent. See Rule 1.2(e). Similarly, a lawyer has a duty not to use false evidence of a non-client and may permit introduction of the false evidence of a client only in extremely limited circumstances in criminal cases when the witness is the defendant client. See Rule 3.3(a)(4) and (b). This Rule is essentially a special instance of the duty prescribed in Rule 1.2(e) to avoid assisting a client in criminal or fraudulent conduct.

[15] Second, the lawyer may have been innocently involved in past conduct by the client that was criminal or fraudulent. In such a situation the lawyer has not violated Rule 1.2(e), because to "counsel or assist" criminal or fraudulent conduct requires knowing that the conduct is of that character.

[16] Third, the lawyer may learn that a client intends prospective conduct that is criminal and likely to result in death or substantial bodily harm unless disclosure of the client's intentions is made by the lawyer. As stated in paragraph (c), the lawyer has professional discretion to reveal information in order to prevent such consequences. The lawyer may make a disclosure in order to prevent homicide or serious bodily injury which the lawyer reasonably believes is intended by a client. The "reasonably believes" standard is applied because it is very difficult for a lawyer to "know" when such a heinous purpose will actually be carried out, for the client may have a change of mind.

[17] The lawyer's exercise of discretion in determining whether to make disclosures that are reasonably likely to prevent the death or substantial bodily injury of another requires consideration of such factors as the client's tendency to commit violent acts or, conversely, to make idle threats. In any case, a disclosure adverse to the client's interest should be no greater than the lawyer reasonably believes necessary to the purpose. A lawyer's decision not to take preventive action permitted by subparagraph (c)(1) does not violate this Rule.

Withdrawal

[18] If the lawyer's services will be used by the client in materially furthering a course of criminal or fraudulent conduct, the lawyer must withdraw, as stated in Rule 1.16(a)(1). If the client persists in a course of action involving the lawyer's services that the lawyer reasonably believes is criminal or fraudulent, or if the client has used the lawyer's services to perpetrate a crime or a fraud, the lawyer may (but is not required to) withdraw, as stated in Rule 1.16(b)(1) and (2).

[19] After withdrawal under either Rule 1.16(a)(1) or Rule 1.16(b)(1) or (2), the lawyer is required to refrain from making disclosure of the client's confidences, except as otherwise provided in Rule 1.6. Giving notice of withdrawal, without elaboration, is not a disclosure of a client's confidences and is not proscribed by this Rule or by Rule 1.16(d). Furthermore, a lawyer's statement to a court that withdrawal is based upon "irreconcilable differences between the lawyer and the client," as provided under paragraph [3] of the Comment to Rule 1.16, is not elaboration. Similarly, after withdrawal under either Rule 1.16(a)(1) or Rule 1.16(b)(1) or (2), the lawyer may retract or disaffirm any opinion, document, affirmation, or the like that contains a material misrepresentation by the lawyer that the lawyer reasonably believes will be relied upon by others to their detriment.

[20] Where the client is an organization, the lawyer may be in doubt whether contemplated conduct will actually be carried out by the organization. Where necessary to guide conduct in connection with this Rule, the lawyer may make inquiry within the organization. See Comment to Rule 1.13.

Dispute Concerning Lawyer's Conduct

[21] Where a legal claim or disciplinary charge alleges complicity of the lawyer in a client's conduct or other misconduct of the lawyer involving representation of the client, the lawyer may respond to the extent the lawyer reasonably believes necessary to establish a defense. The same is true with respect to a claim involving the conduct or representation of a former client. Charges, in defense of which a lawyer may disclose client confidences and secrets, can arise in a civil, criminal, or professional disciplinary proceeding, and can be based on a wrong allegedly committed by the lawyer against the client, or on a wrong alleged by a third person; for example, a person claiming to have been defrauded by the lawyer and client acting together.

[22] The lawyer may not disclose a client's confidences or secrets to defend against informal allegations made by third parties; the Rule allows disclosure only if a third party has formally instituted a civil, criminal, or disciplinary action against the lawyer. Even if the third party has formally instituted such a proceeding, the lawyer should advise the client of the third party's action and request that the client respond appropriately, if this is practicable and would not be prejudicial to the lawyer's ability to establish a defense.

[23] If a lawyer's client, or former client, has made specific allegations against the lawyer, the lawyer may disclose that client's confidences and secrets in establishing a defense, without waiting for formal proceedings to be commenced. The requirement of subparagraph (d)(3) that there be "specific" charges of misconduct by the client precludes the lawyer from disclosing confidences or secrets in response to general criticism by a client; an example of such a general criticism would be an assertion by the client that the lawyer "did a poor job" of representing the client. But in this situation, as well as in the defense of formally instituted third-party proceedings, disclosure should be no greater than the lawyer reasonably believes is necessary to vindicate innocence, the disclosure should be made in a manner that limits access to the information to the tribunal or other persons having a need to know it, and appropriate protective orders or other arrangements should be sought by the lawyer to the fullest extent practicable.

Fee Collection Actions

[24] Subparagraph (d)(5) permits a lawyer to reveal a client's confidences or secrets if this is necessary in an action to collect fees from the client. This aspect of the Rule expresses the principle that the beneficiary of a fiduciary relationship may not exploit it to the detriment of the fiduciary. Subparagraph (d)(5) should be construed narrowly; it does not authorize broad, indiscriminate disclosure of secrets or confidences. The lawyer should evaluate the necessity for disclosure of information at each stage of the action. For example, in drafting the complaint in a fee collection suit, it would be necessary to reveal the "secrets" that the lawyer was retained by the client, that fees are due, and that the client has failed to pay those fees. Further disclosure of the client's secrets and confidences would be impermissible at the complaint stage. If possible, the lawyer should prevent even the disclosure of the client's identity through the use of John Doe pleadings.

[25] If the client's response to the lawyer's complaint raised issues implicating confidences or secrets, the lawyer would be permitted to disclose confidential or secret information pertinent to the client's claims or defenses. Even then, the Rule would require that the lawyer's response be narrowly tailored to meet the client's specific allegations, with the minimum degree of disclosure sufficient to respond effectively. In addition, the lawyer should continue, throughout the action, to make every effort to avoid unnecessary disclosure of the client's confidences and secrets and to limit the disclosure to those having the need to know it. To this end the lawyer should seek appropriate protective orders and make any other arrangements which would minimize the risk of disclosure of the confidential information in question, including the utilization of in camera proceedings.

Disclosures Otherwise Required or Authorized

[26] The attorney-client privilege is differently defined in various jurisdictions. If a lawyer is called as a witness to give testimony concerning a client, absent waiver by the client, subparagraph (d)(2) requires the lawyer to invoke the privilege when it is applicable. The lawyer may comply with the final orders of a court or other tribunal of competent jurisdiction requiring the lawyer to give information about the client. But a lawyer ordered by a court to disclose client confidences or secrets should not comply with the order until the lawyer has personally made every reasonable effort to appeal the order or has notified the client of the order and given the client the opportunity to challenge it.

[27] The Rules of Professional Conduct in various circumstances permit or require a lawyer to disclose information relating to the representation. See Rules 2.2, 2.3, 3.3, and 4.1. In addition to these provisions, a lawyer may be obligated or permitted by other provisions of law to give information about a client. Whether another provision of law supersedes Rule 1.6 is a matter of interpretation beyond the scope of these Rules, but a presumption exists against such a supersession.

Former Client

[28] The duty of confidentiality continues after the client-lawyer relationship has terminated.

Services Rendered in Assisting Another Lawyer
Before Becoming a Member of the Bar

[29] There are circumstances in which a person who ultimately becomes a lawyer provides assistance to a lawyer while serving in a non-lawyer capacity. The typical situation is that of the law clerk or summer associate in a law firm or government agency. Paragraph (g) addresses the confidentiality obligations of such a person after becoming a member of the Bar; the same confidentiality obligations are imposed as would apply if the person had been a member of the Bar at the time confidences or secrets were received. This resolution of the confidentiality obligation is consistent with the reasoning employed in D.C. Bar Legal Ethics Committee Opinion 84 (1980). For a related provision dealing with the imputation of disqualifications arising from prior participation as a law clerk, summer associate, or in a similar position, see Rule 1.10(b).

[30] Paragraph (h) adds a provision dealing specifically with the disclosure obligations of lawyers who are assisting in the counseling programs of the D.C. Bar's Lawyer Counseling Committee. Members of that committee, and lawyer-intervenors who assist the committee in counseling, may obtain information from lawyer-counselees who have sought assistance from the counseling programs offered by the committee. It is in the interests of the public to encourage lawyers who have alcohol or other substance abuse problems to seek counseling as a first step toward rehabilitation. Some lawyers who seek such assistance may have violated provisions of the Rules of Professional Conduct, or other provisions of law, including criminal statutes such as those dealing with embezzlement. In order for those who are providing counseling services to evaluate properly the lawyer-counselee's problems and enhance the prospects for rehabilitation, it is necessary for the counselors to receive completely candid information from the lawyer-counselee. Such candor is not likely if the counselor, for example, would be compelled by Rule 8.3 to report the lawyer-counselee's conduct to Bar Counsel, or if the lawyer-counselee feared that the counselor could be compelled by prosecutors or others to disclose information.

[31] These considerations make it appropriate to treat the lawyer-counselee relationship as a lawyer-client relationship, and to create an additional limited class of information treated as secrets or confidences subject to the protection of Rule 1.6. The scope of that information is set forth in paragraph (h).

[32] Rules established by the District of Columbia Court of Appeals with respect to the kinds of information protected from compelled disclosure may not be accepted by other forums or jurisdictions. Therefore,

the protections afforded to lawyer-counselees by paragraph (h) may not be available to preclude disclosure in all circumstances. Furthermore, lawyers who are members of the bar of other jurisdictions may not be entitled under the ethics rules applicable to members of the bar in such other jurisdictions, to forgo reporting violations to disciplinary authorities pursuant to the other jurisdictions' counterparts to Rule 8.3.

Government Lawyers

[33] Subparagraph (d)(2) was revised, and paragraph (i) was added, to address the unique circumstances raised by attorney-client relationships within the government.

[34] Subparagraph (d)(2)(A) applies to both private and government attorney-client relationships. Subparagraph (d)(2)(B) applies to government lawyers only. It is designed to permit disclosures that are not required by law or court order under Rule 1.6(d)(2)(A), but which the government authorizes its attorneys to make in connection with their professional services to the government. Such disclosures may be authorized or required by statute, executive order, or regulation, depending on the constitutional or statutory powers of the authorizing entity. If so authorized or required, subparagraph (d)(2)(B) governs.

[35] The term "agency" in paragraph (i) includes, inter alia, executive and independent departments and agencies, special commissions, committees of the legislature, agencies of the legislative branch such as the General Accounting Office, and the courts to the extent that they employ lawyers (e.g., staff counsel) to counsel them. The employing agency has been designated the client under this Rule to provide a commonly understood and easily determinable point for identifying the government client.

[36] Government lawyers may also be assigned to provide an individual with counsel or representation in circumstances that make clear that an obligation of confidentiality runs directly to that individual and that subparagraph (d)(2)(A), not (d)(2)(B) applies. It is, of course, acceptable in this circumstance for a government lawyer to make disclosures about the individual representation to supervisors or others within the employing governmental agency so long as such disclosures are made in the context of, and consistent with, the agency's representation program. See, e.g., 28 C.F.R. §§50.15 and 50.16. The relevant circumstances, including the agreement to represent the individual, may also indicate the extent to which the individual client to whom the government lawyer is assigned will be deemed to have granted or denied consent to disclosures

to the lawyer's employing agency. Examples of such representation include representation by a public defender, a government lawyer representing a defendant sued for damages arising out of the performance of the defendant's government employment, and a military lawyer representing a court-martial defendant.

Rule 1.7. Conflict of Interest: General Rule

(a) A lawyer shall not advance two or more adverse positions in the same matter.

(b) Except as permitted by paragraph (c) below, a lawyer shall not represent a client with respect to a matter if:

(1) That matter involves a specific party or parties, and a position to be taken by that client in that matter is adverse to a position taken or to be taken by another client in the same matter, even though that client is unrepresented or represented by a different lawyer;

(2) Such representation will be or is likely to be adversely affected by representation of another client;

(3) Representation of another client will be or is likely to be adversely affected by such representation; or

(4) The lawyer's professional judgment on behalf of the client will be or reasonably may be adversely affected by the lawyer's responsibilities to or interests in a third party or the lawyer's own financial, business, property, or personal interests.

(c) A lawyer may represent a client with respect to a matter in the circumstances described in paragraph (b) above if each potentially affected client provides consent to such representation after full disclosure of the existence and nature of the possible conflict and the possible adverse consequences of such representation.

(d) If a conflict not reasonably foreseeable at the outset of a representation arises under paragraph (b)(1) after the representation commences, and is not waived under paragraph (c), a lawyer need not withdraw from any representation unless the conflict also arises under paragraphs (b)(2), (b)(3), or (b)(4).

COMMENT

[1] Rule 1.7 is intended to provide clear notice of circumstances that may constitute a conflict of interest. Rule 1.7(a) sets out the limited circumstances in which representation of conflicting interests is absolutely

prohibited even with the consent of all involved clients. Rule 1.7(b) sets out those circumstances in which representation is barred in the absence of informed client consent. The difference between Rule 1.7(a) and Rule 1.7(b) is that in the former, the lawyer is representing multiple interests in the same matter, while in the latter the lawyer is representing a single interest, but a client of the lawyer who is represented by different counsel has an interest adverse to that advanced by the lawyer. The application of Rules 1.7(a) and 1.7(b) to specific facts must also take into consideration the principles of imputed disqualification described in Rule 1.10. Rule 1.7(c) states the procedure that must be used to obtain client consent if representation is to commence or continue in the circumstances described in Rule 1.7(b). Rule 1.7(d) governs withdrawal in cases arising under Rule 1.7(b)(1).

Representation Absolutely Prohibited — Rule 1.7(a)

[2] Institutional interests in preserving confidence in the adversary process and in the administration of justice preclude permitting a lawyer to represent adverse positions in the same matter. For that reason, paragraph (a) prohibits such conflicting representations, with or without client consent.

[3] The same lawyer (or law firm, see Rule 1.10) should not espouse adverse positions in the same matter during the course of any type of representation, whether such adverse positions are taken on behalf of clients or on behalf of the lawyer or an association of which the lawyer is a member. On the other hand, for purposes of Rule 1.7(a), an "adverse" position does not include inconsistent or alternative positions advanced by counsel on behalf of a single client. Rule 1.7(a) is intended to codify the result reached in D.C. Bar Legal Ethics Committee Opinion 204, including the conclusion that a rulemaking whose result will be applied retroactively in pending adjudications is the same matter as the adjudications, even though treated as separate proceedings by an agency. However, if the adverse positions to be taken relate to different matters, the absolute prohibition of paragraph (a) is inapplicable, even though paragraphs (b) and (c) may apply.

[4] The absolute prohibition of paragraph (a) applies only to situations in which a lawyer would be called upon to espouse adverse positions for different clients in the same matter. It is for this reason that paragraph (a) refers to adversity with respect to a "position taken or to be taken" in a matter rather than adversity with respect to the matter or

the entire representation. This approach is intended to reduce the costs of litigation in other representations where parties have common, nonadverse interests on certain issues, but have adverse (or contingently or possibly adverse) positions with respect to other issues. If, for example, a lawyer would not be required to take adverse positions in providing joint representation of two clients in the liability phase of a case, it would be permissible to undertake such a limited representation. Then, after completion of the liability phase, and upon satisfying the requirements of paragraph (c) of this Rule, and of any other applicable Rules, the lawyer could represent either one of those parties as to the damages phase of the case, even though the other, represented by separate counsel as to damages, might have an adverse position as to that phase of the case. Insofar as the absolute prohibition of paragraph (a) is concerned, a lawyer may represent two parties that may be adverse to each other as to some aspects of the case so long as the same lawyer does not represent both parties with respect to those positions. Such a representation comes within paragraph (b), rather than paragraph (a), and is therefore subject to the consent provisions of paragraph (c).

[5] The ability to represent two parties who have adverse interests as to portions of a case may be limited because the lawyer obtains confidences or secrets relating to a party while jointly representing both parties in one phase of the case. In some circumstances, such confidences or secrets might be useful, against the interests of the party to whom they relate, in a subsequent part of the case. Absent the consent of the party whose confidences or secrets are implicated, the subsequent adverse representation is governed by the substantial relationship test, which is set forth in Rule 1.9.

[6] The prohibition of paragraph (a) relates only to actual conflicts of positions, not to mere formalities. For example, a lawyer is not absolutely forbidden to provide joint or simultaneous representation if the clients' positions are only nominally but not actually adverse. Joint representation is commonly provided to incorporators of a business, to parties to a contract, in formulating estate plans for family members, and in other circumstances where the clients might be nominally adverse in some respect but have retained a lawyer to accomplish a common purpose. If no actual conflict of positions exists with respect to a matter, the absolute prohibition of paragraph (a) does not come into play. Thus, in the limited circumstances set forth in Opinion 143 of the D.C. Bar Legal Ethics Committee, this prohibition would not preclude the representation of both parties in an uncontested divorce proceeding, there being no actual conflict of positions based on the facts presented in Opinion 143.

Representation Conditionally Prohibited — Rule 1.7(b)

[7] Paragraphs (b) and (c) are based upon two principles: (1) that a client is entitled to wholehearted and zealous representation of its interests, and (2) that the client as well as the lawyer must have the opportunity to judge and be satisfied that such representation can be provided. Consistent with these principles, paragraph (b) provides a general description of the types of circumstances in which representation is improper in the absence of informed consent. The underlying premise is that disclosure and consent are required before assuming a representation if there is any reason to doubt the lawyer's ability to provide wholehearted and zealous representation of a client or if a client might reasonably consider the representation of its interest to be adversely affected by the lawyer's assumption of the other representation in question. Although the lawyer must be satisfied that the representation can be wholeheartedly and zealously undertaken, if an objective observer would have any reasonable doubt on that issue, the client has a right to disclosure of all relevant considerations and the opportunity to be the judge of its own interests.

[8] A client may, on occasion, adopt unreasonable positions with respect to having the lawyer who is representing that client also represent other parties. Such an unreasonable position may be based on an aversion to the other parties being represented by a lawyer, or on some philosophical or ideological ground having no foundation in the rules regarding representation of conflicting interests. Whatever difficulties may be presented for the lawyer in such circumstances as a matter of client relations, the unreasonable position taken by a client do not fall within the circumstances requiring notification and consent. Clients have broad discretion to terminate their representation by a lawyer and that discretion may generally be exercised on unreasonable as well as reasonable grounds.

[9] If the lawyer determines or can foresee that an issue with respect to the application of paragraph (b) exists, the only prudent course is for the lawyer to make disclosure, pursuant to paragraph (c), to each affected client and enable each to determine whether in its judgment the representation at issue is likely to affect its interests adversely.

[10] Paragraph (b) does not purport to state a uniform rule applicable to cases in which two clients may be adverse to each other in a matter in which neither is represented by the lawyer or in a situation in which two or more clients may be direct business competitors. The matter in which two clients are adverse may be so unrelated or insignificant as to

have no possible effect upon a lawyer's ability to represent both in other matters. The fact that two clients are business competitors, standing alone, is usually not a bar to simultaneous representation. Thus, in a matter involving a specific party or parties, paragraphs (b)(1) and (c) require notice and consent if the lawyer will take a position on behalf of one client adverse to another client even though the lawyer represents the latter client only on an unrelated position or in an unrelated matter. Paragraphs (b)(2), (3), (4) and (c) require disclosure and consent in any situation in which the lawyer's representation of a client may be adversely affected by representation of another client or by any of the factors specified in paragraph (b)(4).

Lawyer's Duty to Make Inquiries to Determine Potential Conflicts

[11] The scope of and parties to a "matter" are typically apparent in on-the-record adversary proceedings or other proceedings in which a written record of the identity and the position of the parties exists. In Rule 1.7(b)(1), the phrase "matter involving a specific party or parties" refers to such situations. In other situations, however, it may not be clear to a lawyer whether the representation of one client is adverse to the interests of another client. For example, a lawyer may represent a client only with respect to one or a few of the client's areas of interest. Other lawyers, or non-lawyers (such as lobbyists), or employees of the client (such as government relations personnel) may be representing that client on many issues whose scope and content are unknown to the lawyer. Clients often have many representatives acting for them, including multiple law firms, nonlawyer lobbyists, and client employees. A lawyer retained for a limited purpose may not be aware of the full range of a client's other interests or positions on issues. Except in matters involving a specific party or parties, a lawyer is not required to inquire of a client concerning the full range of that clients interests in issues, unless it is clear to the lawyer that there is a potential for adversity between the interests of clients of the lawyer. Where lawyers are associated in a firm within the meaning of Rule 1.10(a), the rule stated in the preceding sentence must be applied to all lawyers and all clients in the firm. Unless a lawyer is aware that representing one client involves seeking a result to which another client is opposed, Rule 1.7 is not violated by a representation that eventuates in the lawyer's unwittingly taking a position for one client adverse to the interests of another client. The test to be applied here is one of reasonableness and may

turn on whether the lawyer has an effective conflict checking system in place.

Situations That Frequently Arise

[12] A number of types of situations frequently arise in which disclosure and informed consent are usually required. These include joint representation of parties to criminal and civil litigation, joint representation of incorporators of a business, joint representation of a business or government agency and its employees, representation of family members seeking estate planning or the drafting of wills, joint representation of an insurer and an insured, representation in circumstances in which the personal or financial interests of the lawyer, or the lawyer's family, might be affected by the representation, and other similar situations in which experience indicates that conflicts are likely to exist or arise. For example, a lawyer might not be able to represent a client vigorously if the client's adversary is a person with whom the lawyer has longstanding personal or social ties. The client is entitled to be informed of such circumstances so that an informed decision can be made concerning the advisability of retaining the lawyer who has such ties to the adversary. The principles of disclosure and consent are equally applicable to all such circumstances, except that if the positions to be taken by two clients in a matter as to which the lawyer represents both are actually adverse, then, as provided in paragraph (a), the lawyer may not undertake or continue the representation with respect to those issues even if disclosure has been made and consent obtained.

Organization Clients

[13] As is provided in Rule 1.13, the lawyer who represents a corporation, partnership, trade association or other organization-type client is deemed to represent that specific entity, and not its shareholders, owners, partners, members or "other constituents." Thus, for purposes of interpreting this Rule, the specific entity represented by the lawyer is the "client." Ordinarily that client's affiliates (parents and subsidiaries), other stockholders and owners, partners, members, etc., are not considered to be clients of the lawyer. Generally, the lawyer for a corporation is not prohibited by legal ethics principles from representing the corporation in a matter in which the corporation's stockholders or other constituents are adverse to the corporation. See D.C. Bar Legal Ethics Committee Opin-

ion No. 216. A fortiori, and consistent with the principle reflected in Rule 1.13, the lawyer for an organization normally should not be precluded from representing an unrelated client whose interests are adverse to the interests of an affiliate (e.g., parent or subsidiary), stockholders and owners, partners, members, etc., of that organization in a matter that is separate from and not substantially related to the matter on which the lawyer represents the organization.

[14] However, there may be cases in which a lawyer is deemed to represent a constituent of an organization client. Such de facto representation has been found where a lawyer has received confidences from a constituent during the course of representing an organization client in circumstances in which the constituent reasonably believed that the lawyer was acting as the constituent's lawyer as well as the lawyer for the organization client. See generally ABA Formal Opinion 92-365. In general, representation may be implied where on the facts there is a reasonable belief by the constituent that there is individual as well as collective representation. Id. The propriety of representation adverse to an affiliate or constituent of the organization client, therefore, must first be tested by determining whether a constituent is in fact a client of the lawyer. If it is, representation adverse to the constituent requires compliance with Rule 1.7. See ABA Opinion 92-365, supra. The propriety of representation must also be tested by reference to the lawyer's obligation under Rule 1.6 to preserve confidences and secrets and to the obligations imposed by paragraphs (b)(2) through (b)(4) of this Rule. Thus, absent consent under Rule 1.7(c), such adverse representation ordinarily would be improper if:

(a) the adverse matter is the same as, or substantially related to, the matter on which the lawyer represents the organization client,

(b) during the course of representation of the organization client the lawyer has in fact acquired confidences or secrets (as defined in Rule 1.6(b)) of the organization client or an affiliate or constituent that could be used to the disadvantage of any of the organization client or its affiliate or constituents, or

(c) such representation seeks a result that is likely to have a material adverse effect on the financial condition of the organization client.

[15] In addition, the propriety of representation adverse to an affiliate or constituent of the organization client must be tested by attempting to determine whether the adverse party is in substance the "alter ego" of the organization client. The alter ego case is one in which there is likely to be a reasonable expectation by the constituents or affiliates of an organization that each has an individual as well as a collective client-lawyer relationship with the lawyer, a likelihood that a

result adverse to the constituent would also be adverse to the existing organization client, and a risk that both the new and the old representation would be so adversely affected that the conflict would not be "consentable." Although the alter ego criterion necessarily involves some imprecision, it may be usefully applied in a parent-subsidiary context, for example, by analyzing the following relevant factors: whether (i) the parent directly or indirectly owns all or substantially all of the voting stock of the subsidiary, (ii) the two companies have common directors, officers, office premises, or business activities, or (iii) a single legal department retains, supervises and pays outside lawyers for both the parent and the subsidiary. If all or most of those factors are present, for conflict of interest purposes those two entities normally would be considered alter egos of one another and the lawyer for one of them should refrain from engaging in representation adverse to the other, even on a matter where clauses (a), (b) and (c) of the preceding paragraph [14] are not applicable. Similarly, if the organization client is a corporation that is wholly owned by a single individual, in most cases for purposes of applying this Rule, that client should be deemed to be the alter ego of its sole stockholder. Therefore, the corporation's lawyer should refrain from engaging in representation adverse to the sole stockholder, even on a matter where clauses (a), (b) and (c) of the preceding paragraph [14] are not applicable.

[16] If representation otherwise appropriate under the preceding paragraphs seeks a result that is likely ultimately to have a material adverse effect on the financial condition of the organization client, such representation is prohibited by Rule 1.7(b)(3). If the likely adverse effect on the financial condition of the organization client is not material, such representation is not prohibited by Rule 1.7(b)(3). Obviously, however, a lawyer should exercise restraint and sensitivity in determining whether to undertake such representation in a case of that type, particularly if the organization client does not realistically have the option to discharge the lawyer as counsel to the organization client.

[17] The provisions of paragraphs [13] through [16] are subject to any contrary agreement or other understanding between the client and the lawyer. In particular, the client has the right by means of the original engagement letter or otherwise to restrict the lawyer from engaging in representations otherwise permissible under the foregoing guidelines. If the lawyer agrees to such restrictions in order to obtain or keep the client's business, any such agreement between client and lawyer will take precedence over these guidelines. Conversely, an organization client, in order to obtain the lawyer's services, may in the original engagement letter or otherwise give consent to the lawyer in advance to engage in rep-

resentations adverse to an affiliate, owner or other constituent of the client not otherwise permissible under the foregoing guidelines so long as the requirements of Rule 1.7(c) can be met.

[18] In any event, in all cases referred to above, the lawyer must carefully consider whether Rule 1.7(b)(2) or Rule 1.7(b)(4) requires consent from the second client whom the lawyer proposes to represent adverse to an affiliate, owner or other constituent of the first client.

Disclosure and Consent

[19] Disclosure and consent are not mere formalities. Adequate disclosure requires such disclosure of the parties and their interests and positions as to enable each potential client to make a fully informed decision as to whether to proceed with the contemplated representation. If a lawyers obligation to one or another client or to others or some other consideration precludes making such full disclosure to all affected parties, that fact alone precludes undertaking the representation at issue. Full disclosure also requires that clients be made aware of the possible extra expense, inconvenience, and other disadvantages that may arise if an actual conflict of position should later arise and the lawyer be required to terminate the representation.

[20] The Rule does not require that disclosure be in writing or in any other particular form in all cases. Nevertheless, it should be recognized that the form of disclosure sufficient for more sophisticated business clients may not be sufficient to permit less sophisticated clients to provide fully informed consent. Moreover, under District of Columbia substantive law, the lawyer bears the burden of proof to demonstrate the existence of consent. For those reasons, it would be prudent for the lawyer to provide potential joint clients with at least a written summary of the considerations disclosed and to request and receive a written consent.

[21] The term "consent" is defined in the Terminology section of these Rules. As indicated there, a client's consent must not be coerced either by the lawyer or by any other person. In particular, the lawyer should not use the client's investment in previous representation by the lawyer as leverage to obtain or maintain representation that may be contrary to the client's best interests. If a lawyer has reason to believe that undue influence has been used by anyone to obtain agreement to the representation, the lawyer should not undertake the representation.

Withdrawal

[22] It is much to be preferred that a representation that is likely to lead to a conflict be avoided before the representation begins, and a lawyer should bear this fact in mind in considering whether disclosure should be made and consent obtained at the outset. If, however, a conflict arises after a representation has been undertaken, and the conflict falls within paragraph (a), or if a conflict arises under paragraph (b) and informed and uncoerced consent is not or cannot be obtained pursuant to paragraph (c), then the lawyer should withdraw from the representation, complying with Rule 1.16. Where a conflict is not foreseeable at the outset of representation and arises only under Rule 1.7(b)(1), a lawyer should seek consent to the conflict at the time that the conflict becomes evident, but if such consent is not given by the opposing party in the matter, the lawyer need not withdraw. In determining whether a conflict is reasonably foreseeable, the test is an objective one. In determining the reasonableness of a lawyer's conduct, such factors as whether the lawyer (or lawyer's firm) has an adequate conflict-checking system in place, must be considered. Where more than one client is involved and the lawyer must withdraw because a conflict arises after representation has been undertaken, the question whether the lawyer may continue to represent any of the clients is determined by Rule 1.9.

Imputed Disqualification

[23] All of the references in Rule 1.7 and its accompanying Comment to the limitation upon a "lawyer" must be read in light of the imputed disqualification provisions of Rule 1.10, which affect lawyers practicing in a firm.

[24] In the government lawyer context, Rule 1.7(b) is not intended to apply to conflicts between agencies or components of government (federal, state, or local) where the resolution of such conflicts has been entrusted by law, order, or regulation to a specific individual or entity.

Businesses Affiliated With a Lawyer or Firm

[25] Lawyers, either alone or through firms, may have interests in enterprises that do not practice law but that, in some or all of their work, become involved with lawyers or their clients either by assisting the lawyer in providing legal services or by providing related services to the cli-

ent. Examples of such enterprises are accounting firms, consultants, real estate brokerages, and the like. The existence of such interests raises several questions under this Rule. First, a lawyer's recommendation, as part of legal advice, that the client obtain the services of an enterprise in which the lawyer has an interest implicates paragraph 1.7(b)(4). The lawyer should not make such a recommendation unless able to conclude that the lawyer's professional judgment on behalf of the client will not be adversely affected. Even then, the lawyer should not make such a recommendation without full disclosure to the client so that the client can make a fully informed choice. Such disclosure should include the nature and substance of the lawyer's or the firm's interest in the related enterprise, alternative sources for the non-legal services in question, and sufficient information so that the client understands that the related enterprise's services are not legal services and that the client's relationship to the related enterprise will not be that of client to attorney. Second, such a related enterprise may refer a potential client to the lawyer; the lawyer should take steps to assure that the related enterprise will inform the lawyer of all such referrals. The lawyer should not accept such a referral without full disclosure of the nature and substance of the lawyer's interest in the related enterprise. See also Rule 7.1(b). Third, the lawyer should be aware that the relationship of a related enterprise to its own customer may create a significant interest in the lawyer in the continuation of that relationship. The substantiality of such an interest may be enough to require the lawyer to decline a proffered client representation that would conflict with that interest; at least Rule 1.7(b)(4) and (c) may require the prospective client to be informed and to consent before the representation could be undertaken. Fourth, a lawyer's interest in a related enterprise that may also serve the lawyer's clients creates a situation in which the lawyer must take unusual care to fashion the relationship among lawyer, client, and related enterprise to assure that confidences and secrets are properly preserved pursuant to Rule 1.6 to the maximum extent possible. See Rule 5.3.

Rule 1.8. Conflict of Interest: Prohibited Transactions

(a) A lawyer shall not enter into a business transaction with a client or knowingly acquire an ownership, possessory, security or other pecuniary interest adverse to a client unless:

(1) The transaction and terms on which the lawyer acquires the interest are fair and reasonable to the client and are fully disclosed and

transmitted in writing to the client in a manner which can be reasonably understood by the client;

(2) The client is given a reasonable opportunity to seek the advice of independent counsel in the transaction; and

(3) The client consents in writing thereto.

(b) A lawyer shall not prepare an instrument giving the lawyer or a person related to the lawyer as parent, child, sibling, or spouse any substantial gift from a client, including a testamentary gift, except where the client is related to the donee.

(c) Prior to the conclusion of representation of a client, a lawyer shall not make or negotiate an agreement giving the lawyer literary or media rights to a portrayal or account based in substantial part on information relating to the representation.

(d) While representing a client in connection with contemplated or pending litigation or administrative proceedings, a lawyer shall not advance or guarantee financial assistance to the client, except that a lawyer may pay or otherwise provide:

(1) The expenses of litigation or administrative proceedings, including court costs, expenses of investigation, expenses of medical examination, costs of obtaining and presenting evidence; and

(2) Other financial assistance which is reasonably necessary to permit the client to institute or maintain the litigation or administrative proceeding.

(e) A lawyer shall not accept compensation for representing a client from one other than the client unless:

(1) The client consents after consultation;

(2) There is no interference with the lawyer's independence of professional judgment or with the client-lawyer relationship; and

(3) Information relating to representation of a client is protected as required by Rule 1.6.

(f) A lawyer who represents two or more clients shall not participate in making an aggregate settlement of the claims of or against the clients, or in a criminal case an aggregated agreement as to guilty or nolo contendere pleas, unless each client consents after consultation, including disclosure of the existence and nature of all the claims or pleas involved and of the participation of each person in the settlement.

(g) A lawyer shall not:

(1) Make an agreement prospectively limiting the lawyer's liability to a client for malpractice; or

(2) Settle a claim for such liability with an unrepresented client or former client without first advising that person in writing that independent representation is appropriate in connection therewith.

682

(h) A lawyer related to another lawyer as parent, child, sibling, or spouse shall not represent a client in a representation directly adverse to a person who the lawyer knows is represented by the other lawyer except upon consent by the client after consultation regarding the relationship.

(i) A lawyer may acquire and enforce a lien granted by law to secure the lawyer's fees or expenses, but a lawyer shall not impose a lien upon any part of a client's files, except upon the lawyer's own work product, and then only to the extent that the work product has not been paid for. This work product exception shall not apply when the client has become unable to pay, or when withholding the lawyer's work product would present a significant risk to the client of irreparable harm.

COMMENT

Transactions Between Client and Lawyer

[1] As a general principle, all transactions between client and lawyer should be fair and reasonable to the client. In such transactions a review by independent counsel on behalf of the client is often advisable. Paragraph (a) does not, however, apply to standard commercial transactions between the lawyer and the client for products or services that the client generally markets to others; for example, banking or brokerage services, medical services, products manufactured or distributed by the client, and utility services. In such transactions, the lawyer has no advantage in dealing with the client, and the restrictions in paragraph (a) are unnecessary and impracticable.

[2] A lawyer may accept a gift from a client, if the transaction meets general standards of fairness. For example, a simple gift such as a present given at a holiday or as a token of appreciation is permitted. If effectuation of a substantial gift requires preparing a legal instrument such as a will or conveyance, however, the client should be advised by the lawyer to obtain the detached advice that another lawyer can provide. Paragraph (b) recognizes an exception where the client is a relative of the donee or the gift is not substantial.

[3] This Rule does not prevent a lawyer from entering into a contingent fee arrangement with a client in a civil case, if the arrangement satisfies all the requirements of Rule 1.5(c).

Literary Rights

[4] An agreement by which a lawyer acquires literary or media rights concerning the conduct of the representation creates a conflict between

the interests of the client and the personal interests of the lawyer. Measures that might otherwise be taken in the representation of the client may detract from the publication value of an account of the representation. Paragraph (c) does not prohibit a lawyer representing a client in a transaction concerning literary property from agreeing that the lawyer's fee shall consist of a share in ownership in the property, if the arrangement conforms to Rule 1.5.

Paying Certain Litigation Costs and Client Expenses

[5] Historically, under the Code of Professional Responsibility, lawyers could only advance the costs of litigation. The client remained ultimately responsible, and was required to pay such costs even if the client lost the case. That rule was modified by this Court in 1980 in an amendment to DR 5-103(B) that eliminated the requirement that the client remain ultimately liable for costs of litigation, even if the litigation was unsuccessful. The provisions of Rule 1.8(d) embrace the result of the 1980 modification, but go further by providing that a lawyer may also pay certain expenses of a client that are not litigation expenses. Thus, under Rule 1.8(d), a lawyer may pay medical or living expenses of a client to the extent necessary to permit the client to continue the litigation. The payment of these additional expenses is limited to those strictly necessary to sustain the client during the litigation, such as medical expenses and minimum living expenses. The purpose of permitting such payments is to avoid situations in which a client is compelled by exigent financial circumstances to settle a claim on unfavorable terms in order to receive the immediate proceeds of settlement. This provision does not permit lawyers to "bid" for clients by offering financial payments beyond those minimum payments necessary to sustain the client until the litigation is completed. Regardless of the types of payments involved, assuming such payments are proper under Rule 1.8(d), client reimbursement of the lawyer is not required. However, no lawyer is required to pay litigation or other costs to a client. The Rule merely permits such payments to be made without requiring reimbursement by the client.

Person Paying for Lawyer's Services

[6] Paragraph (e) requires disclosure of the fact that the lawyer's services are being paid for by a third party. Such an arrangement must also

conform to the requirements of Rule 1.6 concerning confidentiality and Rule 1.7 concerning conflict of interest. Where the client is a class, consent may be obtained on behalf of the class by court-supervised procedure.

Family Relationships Between Lawyers

[7] Paragraph (h) applies to related lawyers who are in different firms. Related lawyers in the same firm are governed by Rules 1.7, 1.9 and 1.10. Pursuant to the provisions of Rule 1.10, the disqualification stated in paragraph (h) is personal and is not imputed to members of firms with whom the lawyers are associated. Since each of the related lawyers is subject to paragraph (h), the effect is to require the consent of all materially affected clients.

Lawyer's Liens

[8] The substantive law of the District of Columbia has long permitted lawyers to assert and enforce liens against the property of clients. See, e.g., *Redevelopment Land Agency v. Dowdey,* 618 A.2d 153, 159-60 (D.C. 1992), and cases cited therein. Whether a lawyer has a lien on money or property belonging to a client is generally a matter of substantive law as to which the ethics rules take no position. Exceptions to what the common law might otherwise permit are made with respect to contingent fees and retaining liens. See, respectively, Rule 1.5(c) and Rule 1.8(i).

[9] Rule 1.16(d) requires a lawyer to surrender papers and property to which the client is entitled when representation of the client terminates. Paragraph (i) of this Rule states a narrow exception to Rule 1.16(d): a lawyer may retain anything the law permits — including property except for files. As to files, a lawyer may retain only the lawyer's own work product, and then only if the client has not paid for the work. However, if the client has paid for the work product, the client is entitled to receive it, even if the client has not previously seen or received a copy of the work product. Furthermore, the lawyer may not retain the work product for which the client has not paid, if the client has become unable to pay or if withholding the work product might irreparably harm the client's interest.

[10] Under Rule 1.16(d), for example, a lawyer would be required to return all papers received from a client, such as birth certificates, wills,

tax returns, or "green cards." Rule 1.8(i) does not permit retention of such papers to secure payment of any fee due. Only the lawyer's own work product—results of factual investigations, legal research and analysis, and similar materials generated by the lawyer's own effort—could be retained. (The term "work product" as used in paragraph (i) is limited to materials falling within the "work product doctrine," but includes any material generated by the lawyer that would be protected under that doctrine whether or not created in connection with pending or anticipated litigation.) And a lawyer could not withhold all of the work product merely because a portion of the lawyer's fees had not been paid.

[11] There are situations in which withholding the work product would not be permissible because of irreparable harm to the client. The possibility of involuntary incarceration or criminal conviction constitutes one category of irreparable harm. The realistic possibility that a client might irretrievably lose a significant right or become subject to a significant liability because of the withholding of the work product constitutes another category of irreparable harm. On the other hand, the mere fact that the client might have to pay another lawyer to replicate the work product does not, standing alone, constitute irreparable harm. These examples are merely indicative of the meaning of the term "irreparable harm," and are not exhaustive.

Rule 1.9. Conflict of Interest: Former Client

A lawyer who has formerly represented a client in a matter shall not thereafter represent another person in the same or a substantially related matter in which that person's interests are materially adverse to the interests of the former client unless the former client consents after consultation.

COMMENT

[1] After termination of a client-lawyer relationship, a lawyer may not represent another client except in conformity with the Rule. The principles in Rule 1.7 determine whether the interests of the present and former client are adverse. Thus, a lawyer could not properly seek to rescind on behalf of a new client a contract drafted on behalf of the former client. So also a lawyer who has prosecuted an accused person could not properly represent the accused in a subsequent civil action against the government concerning the same transaction.

[2] The scope of a "matter" for purposes of this Rule may depend on the facts of a particular situation or transaction. The lawyer's involvement in a matter can also be a question of degree. When a lawyer has been directly involved in a specific transaction, subsequent representation of other clients with materially adverse interests clearly is prohibited. On the other hand, a lawyer who recurrently handled a type of problem for a former client is not precluded from later representing another client in a wholly distinct problem of that type even though the subsequent representation involves a position adverse to the prior client. Similar considerations can apply to the reassignment of military lawyers between defense and prosecution functions within the same military jurisdiction. The underlying question is whether the lawyer was so involved in the matter that the subsequent representation can be justly regarded as a changing of sides in the matter in question. Rule 1.9 is intended to incorporate federal case law defining the "substantial relationship" test. See, e.g., *T.C. Theatre Corp. v. Warner Bros. Pictures,* 113 F. Supp. 265 (S.D.N.Y. 1953), and its progeny; see also Conflicts of Interest in the Legal Profession, 94 Harv. L. Rev. 1244, 1315-1334 (1981).

[3] Disqualification from subsequent representation is for the protection of clients and can be waived by them. A waiver is effective only if there is disclosure of the circumstances, including the lawyer's intended role in behalf of the new client. The question of whether a lawyer is personally disqualified from representation in any matter on account of successive government and private employment is governed by Rule 1.11 rather than by Rule 1.9.

[4] With regard to an opposing party's raising a question of conflict of interest, see Comment to Rule 1.7. With regard to disqualification of a firm with which a lawyer is associated, see Rules 1.10 and 1.11.

Rule 1.10. Imputed Disqualification: General Rule

(a) While lawyers are associated in a firm, none of them shall knowingly represent a client when any one of them practicing alone would be prohibited from doing so by Rules 1.7, 1.8(b), 1.9, or 2.2; provided, however, that this paragraph shall not apply if an individual lawyer's disqualification results solely from the fact that the lawyer consulted with a potential client for the purpose of enabling that potential client and the firm to determine whether they desired to form a client-lawyer relationship, but no such relationship was ever formed.

(b) When a lawyer becomes associated with a firm, the firm may not knowingly represent a person in a matter which is the same as, or substantially related to, a matter with respect to which the lawyer had previously represented a client whose interests are materially adverse to that person and about whom the lawyer has in fact acquired information protected by Rule 1.6 that is material to the matter. The firm is not disqualified if the lawyer participated in a previous representation or acquired information under the circumstances covered by the proviso to paragraph (a) of this Rule or by Rule 1.6(g).

(c) When a lawyer has terminated an association with a firm, the firm is not prohibited from thereafter representing a person with interests materially adverse to those of a client represented by the formerly associated lawyer during the association unless the matter is the same or substantially related to that in which the formerly associated lawyer represented the client during such former association.

(d) A disqualification prescribed by this Rule may be waived by the affected client under the conditions stated in Rule 1.7.

(e) A lawyer who, while affiliated with a firm, is made available to assist the Office of Corporation Counsel or the District of Columbia Financial Responsibility and Management Assistance Authority in providing legal services to that agency is not considered to be associated in a firm for purposes of paragraph (a), provided, however, that no such lawyer shall represent the Office of Corporation Counsel or the District of Columbia Financial Responsibility and Management Assistance Authority with respect to a matter in which the lawyer's firm appears on behalf of an adversary.

COMMENT

Definition of "Firm"

[1] For purposes of the Rules of Professional Conduct, the term "firm" includes lawyers in a private firm, and lawyers employed in the legal department of a corporation or other organization, or in a legal services organization, but does not include a government agency or other government entity. Whether two or more lawyers constitute a firm within this definition can depend on the specific facts. For example, two practitioners who share office space and occasionally consult or assist each other ordinarily would not be regarded as constituting a firm. However, if they present themselves to the public in a way suggesting that they are a firm or conduct themselves as a firm, they should be regarded as a firm

for purposes of the Rules. The terms of any formal agreement between associated lawyers are relevant in determining whether they are a firm, as is the fact that they have mutual access to confidential information concerning the clients they serve. Furthermore, it is relevant in doubtful cases to consider the underlying purpose of the rule that is involved. A group of lawyers could be regarded as a firm for purposes of the rule that the same lawyer should not represent opposing parties in litigation, while it might not be so regarded for purposes of the rule that information acquired by one lawyer is attributed to another.

[2] With respect to the law department of an organization, there is ordinarily no question that the members of the department constitute a firm within the meaning of the Rules of Professional Conduct. However, there can be uncertainty as to the identity of the client. For example, it may not be clear whether the law department of a corporation represents a subsidiary or an affiliated corporation, as well as the corporation by which the members of the department are directly employed. A similar question can arise concerning an unincorporated association and its local affiliates.

[3] Similar questions can also arise with respect to lawyers in legal aid organizations. Lawyers employed in the same unit of a legal service organization constitute a firm, but not necessarily those employed in separate units. As in the case of independent practitioners, whether the lawyers should be treated as associated with each other can depend on the particular rule that is involved, and on the specific facts of the situation.

[4] Where a lawyer has joined a private firm after having represented the government, the situation is governed by Rule 1.11. The individual lawyer involved is bound by the Rules generally, including Rules 1.6, 1.7, and 1.9.

[5] Different provisions are thus made for movement of a lawyer from one private firm to another and for movement of a lawyer from the government to a private firm. The government is entitled to protection of its client confidences, and therefore to the protections provided in Rules 1.6 and 1.11. However, if the more extensive disqualification in Rule 1.10 were applied to former government lawyers, the potential effect on the government would be unduly burdensome. The government deals with all private citizens and organizations, and thus has a much wider circle of adverse legal interests than does any private law firm. In these circumstances, the government's recruitment of lawyers would be seriously impaired if Rule 1.10 were applied to the government. On balance, therefore, the government is better served in the long run by the protections stated in Rule 1.11.

Principles of Imputed Disqualification

[6] The rule of imputed disqualification stated in paragraph (a) gives effect to the principle of loyalty to the client as it applies to lawyers who practice in a law firm. Such situations can be considered from the premise that a firm of lawyers is essentially one lawyer for purposes of the rules governing loyalty to the client, or from the premise that each lawyer is vicariously bound by the obligation of loyalty owed by each lawyer with whom the lawyer is associated. Paragraph (a) operates only among the lawyers currently associated in a firm. When a lawyer moves from one firm to another, the situation is governed by paragraph (b) or (c).

Exception in the Case of a Prospective New Client

[7] As indicated by the proviso in paragraph (a) of this Rule, the principle of loyalty diminishes in importance if the sole reason for an individual lawyer's disqualification is the lawyer's initial consultation with a prospective new client with whom no client-lawyer relationship was ever formed, either because the lawyer detected a conflict of interest as a result of the initial consultation, or for some other reason (e.g., the prospective client decided not to retain the law firm). As provided by Rule 1.6(a), and Comment [7] thereunder, the individual lawyer involved in any such initial consultation is required to maintain in strict confidence all information obtained from the prospective client even if a client-lawyer relationship was never formed. That obligation may in turn cause the individual lawyer to be disqualified pursuant to Rule 1.7(b)(4) from representing a current or future client of the firm adverse to the prospective client because that lawyer's inability to use or disclose information obtained from the prospective client may adversely affect that lawyer's professional judgment on behalf of the current or future client of the firm whose interests are adverse to the interests of the prospective client.

[8] The individual lawyer of the firm who obtains information from a prospective client under the circumstances described in the proviso to paragraph (a) of this Rule is permitted by Rule 1.6(a) to disclose that information to other persons in the lawyer's firm only to the minimum extent necessary to enable the firm to determine whether it may ethically accept the proposed representation, and if so, whether it desires to do so. For the reasons stated in paragraph [7], any such dissemination may necessarily cause additional individual lawyers of the firm to be personally disqualified from representing a current or future client of the firm adverse

to the potential client. Nevertheless, as provided in Rule 1.10(a), the personal disqualification of individual lawyers is not imputed to the firm as a whole. Accordingly, any other lawyer in the firm who is not personally disqualified vis-a-vis the prospective client may represent a current or future client of the firm adverse to the prospective client.

[9] When a firm relies on the proviso in paragraph (a) to this Rule to avoid imputed disqualification of the firm as a whole, that firm must take affirmative steps — as soon as an actual or potential conflict is suspected — to prevent the personally disqualified lawyers from disseminating any information about the potential client that is protected by Rule 1.6, except as necessary to investigate potential conflicts of interest, to any other person in the firm, including non-lawyer staff. Conversely, the personally disqualified lawyers should not receive any confidences or secrets of the firm's clients in the conflicted matter.

Lawyers Moving Between Firms

[10] When lawyers move between firms or when lawyers have been associated in a firm but then end their association, the fiction that the law firm is the same as a single lawyer is no longer wholly realistic. There are several competing considerations. First, the client previously represented must be reasonably assured that the principle of loyalty to the client is not compromised. Second, the rule of disqualification should not be so broadly cast as to preclude other persons from having reasonable choice of legal counsel. Third, the rule of disqualification should not unreasonably hamper lawyers from forming new associations and taking on new clients after having left a previous association. In this connection, it should be recognized that today many lawyers practice in firms, that many to some degree limit their practice to one field or another, and that many move from one association to another several times in their careers. If the concept of imputed disqualification were defined with unqualified rigor, the result would be radical curtailment of the opportunity of lawyers to move from one practice setting to another and of the opportunity of clients to change counsel.

[11] Reconciliation of these competing principles in the past has been attempted under two rubrics. One approach has been to seek per se rules of disqualification. For example, it has been held that a partner in a law firm is conclusively presumed to have access to all confidences concerning all clients of the firm. Under this analysis, if a lawyer has been a partner in one law firm and then becomes a partner in another law firm, there is a presumption that all confidences known by a partner in the first

firm are known to all partners in the second firm. This presumption might properly be applied in some circumstances, especially where the client has been extensively represented, but may be unrealistic where the client was represented only for limited purposes. Furthermore, such a rigid rule exaggerates the difference between a partner and an associate in modern law firms.

[12] The other rubric formerly used for dealing with vicarious disqualification is the appearance of impropriety proscribed in Canon 9 of the Code of Professional Responsibility. Applying this rubric presents two problems. First, the appearance of impropriety can be taken to include any new client-lawyer relationship that might make a former client feel anxious. If that meaning were adopted, disqualification would become little more than a question of subjective judgment by the former client. Second, since "impropriety" is undefined, the term "appearance of impropriety" is question-begging. It therefore has to be recognized that the problem of imputed disqualification cannot be properly resolved either by simple analogy to a lawyer practicing alone or by the very general concept of appearance of impropriety.

[13] A rule based on a functional analysis is more appropriate for determining the question of vicarious disqualification. Two functions are involved: preserving confidentiality and avoiding positions adverse to a client.

Confidentiality

[14] Preserving confidentiality is a question of access to information. Access to information, in turn, is essentially a question of fact in particular circumstances, aided by inferences, deductions, or working presumptions that reasonably may be made about the way in which lawyers work together. A lawyer may have general access to files of all clients of a law firm and may regularly participate in discussions of their affairs; it should be inferred that such a lawyer in fact is privy to all information about all the firm's clients. In contrast, another lawyer may have access to the files of only a limited number of clients and participate in discussion of the affairs of no other clients; in the absence of information to the contrary, it should be inferred that such a lawyer in fact is privy to information about the clients actually served but not those of other clients.

[15] Application of paragraph (b) depends on a situation's particular facts. In any such inquiry, the burden of proof should rest upon the firm whose disqualification is sought.

[16] The provisions of paragraph (b) which refer to possession of protected information operate to disqualify the firm only when the lawyer involved has actual knowledge of information protected by Rule 1.6. Thus, if a lawyer while with one firm acquired no knowledge of information relating to a particular client of the firm, and that lawyer later joined another firm, neither the lawyer individually nor the second firm is disqualified from representing another client in the same or a substantially related matter even though the interests of the two clients conflict.

[17] Independent of the question of disqualification of a firm, a lawyer changing professional association has a continuing duty to preserve confidentiality of information about a client formerly represented. See Rule 1.6.

Adverse Positions

[18] The second aspect of loyalty to a client is the lawyer's obligation to decline subsequent representations involving positions adverse to a former client arising in substantially related matters. This obligation requires abstention from adverse representations by the individual lawyer involved, and may also entail abstention of other lawyers through imputed disqualification. Hence, this aspect of the problem is governed by the principles of Rule 1.9. Thus, under paragraph (b), if a lawyer left one firm for another, the new affiliation would preclude the lawyer's new firm from continuing to represent clients with interests materially adverse to those of the lawyer's former clients in the same or substantially related matters. In this respect paragraph (b) is at odds with — and thus must be understood to reject — the dicta expressed in the "second" hypothetical in the second paragraph of footnote 5 of *Brown v. District of Columbia Board of Zoning Adjustment,* 486 A.2d 37, 42 n.5 (D.C. 1984) (en banc), premised on *LaSalle National Bank v. County of Lake,* 703 F.2d 252, 257-59 (7th Cir. 1983).

[19] The concept of "former client" as used in paragraph (b) extends only to actual representation of the client by the newly affiliated lawyer while that lawyer was employed by the former firm. Thus, not all of the clients of the former firm during the newly affiliated lawyer's practice there are necessarily deemed former clients of the newly affiliated lawyer. Only those clients with whom the newly affiliated lawyer in fact personally had a lawyer-client relationship are former clients within the terms of paragraph (b).

[20] Conversely, when a lawyer terminates an association with a firm, paragraph (c) provides that the old firm may not thereafter represent cli-

ents whose interests are materially adverse to those of the formerly associated lawyer's client in respect to a matter that is the same or substantially related to a matter with respect to which the formerly associated lawyer represented the client during the former association. For example, if a lawyer who represented a client in a litigation while with Firm A departs the firm, taking to the lawyer's new firm the litigation, Firm A may not, despite the departure of the lawyer, who takes the matter and the client to the new firm, undertake a representation adverse to the former client in that same litigation. See Rule 1.9 and the Comment thereto for the definition of "substantially related matter."

[21] The last sentence of paragraph (b) limits the imputation rule in certain limited circumstances. Those circumstances involve situations in which any secrets or confidences obtained were received before the lawyer had become a member of the Bar, but during a time when such person was providing assistance to another lawyer. The typical situation is that of the part-time or summer law clerk, or so-called summer associate. Other types of assistance to a lawyer, such as working as a paralegal or legal assistant, could also fall within the scope of this sentence. The limitation on the imputation rule is similar to the provision dealing with judicial law clerks under Rule 1.11(b). Not applying the imputation rule reflects a policy choice that imputation in such circumstances could unduly impair the mobility of persons employed in such nonlawyer positions once they become members of the Bar. The personal disqualification of the former nonlawyer is not affected, and the lawyer who previously held the nonlegal job may not be involved in any representation with respect to which the firm would have been disqualified but for the last sentence of paragraph (b). Rule 1.6(g) provides that the former nonlawyer is subject to the requirements of Rule 1.6 (regarding protection of client confidences and secrets) just as if the person had been a member of the Bar when employed in the prior position.

Lawyers Assisting the Office of Corporation Counsel and the District of Columbia Financial Responsibility and Management Assistance Authority

[22] The Office of Corporation Counsel and the District of Columbia Financial Responsibility and Management Assistance Authority may experience periods of peak need for legal services which cannot be met by normal hiring programs, or may experience problems in dealing with a large backlog of matters requiring legal services. In such circum-

stances, the public interest is served by permitting private firms to provide the services of lawyers affiliated with such private firms on a temporary basis to assist the Office of Corporation Counsel and the District of Columbia Financial Responsibility and Management Assistance Authority. Such arrangements do not fit within the classical pattern of situations involving the general imputation rule of paragraph (a). Provided that safeguards are in place which preclude the improper disclosure of client confidences or secrets, and the improper use of one client's confidences or secrets on behalf of another client, the public interest benefits of such arrangements justify an exception to the general imputation rule, just as comment [1] excludes from the definition of "firm" lawyers employed by a government agency or other government entity. Lawyers assigned to assist the Office of Corporation Counsel or the District of Columbia Financial Responsibility and Management Assistance Authority pursuant to such temporary programs are, by virtue of paragraph (e), treated as if they were employed as government employees and as if their affiliation with the private firm did not exist during the period of temporary service with the Office of Corporation Counsel or the District of Columbia Financial Responsibility and Management Assistance Authority. See Rule 1.11(h) with respect to the procedures to be followed by lawyers participating in such temporary programs and by the firms with which such lawyers are affiliated after the participating lawyers have ended their participation in such temporary programs. (Amended Nov. 7, 1995.)

[23] The term "made available to assist the Office of the Corporation Counsel or the District of Columbia Financial Responsibility and Management Assistance Authority in providing legal services" in paragraph (e) contemplates the temporary cessation of practice with the firm during the period legal services are being made available to the Office of Corporation Counsel or the District of Columbia Financial Responsibility and Management Assistance Authority, so that during that period the lawyer's activities which involve the practice of law are devoted fully to assisting the Office of Corporation Counsel or the District of Columbia Financial Responsibility and Management Assistance Authority. (Amended Nov. 7, 1995.)

[24] Rule 1.10(e) prohibits a lawyer who is assisting the Office of Corporation Counsel or the District of Columbia Financial Responsibility and Management Assistance Authority from representing that office in any matter in which the lawyer's firm represents an adversary. Rule 1.10(e) does not, however, by its terms, prohibit lawyers assisting the Office of Corporation Counsel or the District of Columbia Financial Responsibility and Management Assistance Authority from participating in every matter in

which the Corporation Counsel or the District of Columbia Financial Responsibility and Management Assistance Authority is taking a position adverse to that of a current client of the firm with which the participating lawyer was affiliated prior to joining the program of assistance to the Office of Corporation Counsel or the District of Columbia Financial Reponsibility and Management Assistance Authority. Such an unequivocal prohibition would be overly broad, difficult to administer in practice, and inconsistent with the purpose of Rule 1.10(e). (Amended Nov. 7, 1995.)

[25] The absence of such a per se prohibition in Rule 1.10(e) does not diminish the importance of a thoughtful and restrained approach to defining those matters in which it is appropriate for a participating lawyer to be involved. An appearance of impropriety in programs of this kind can undermine the public's acceptance of the program and embarrass the Office of Corporation Counsel or the District of Columbia Financial Responsibility and Management Assistance Authority, the participating lawyer, that lawyer's law firm and clients of that firm. For example, it would not be appropriate for a participant lawyer to engage in a representation adverse to a party who is known to be a major client of the participating lawyer's firm, even though the subject matter of the representation of the Office of Corporation Counsel or the District of Columbia Financial Responsibility and Management Assistance Authority bears no substantial relationship to any representation of that party by the participating lawyer's firm. Similarly, it would be inappropriate for a participating lawyer to be involved in a representation adverse to a party that the participating lawyer has been personally involved in representing while at the firm, even if the client is not a major client of the firm. The appropriate test is that of conservative good judgment; if any reasonable doubts concerning the unrestrained vigor of the participating lawyer's representation on behalf of the Office of Corporation Counsel or the District of Columbia Financial Responsibility and Management Assistance Authority, the lawyer should advise the appropriate officials of the Office of Corporation Counsel or the District of Columbia Responsibility and Management Assistance Authority, and decline to participate. Similarly, if participation on behalf of the Office of Corporation Counsel or the District of Columbia Financial Responsibility and Management Assistance Authority might reasonably give rise to a concern on the part of a participating lawyer's firm or a client of the firm that its secrets or confidences (as defined by Rule 1.6) might be comprised, participation should be declined. It is not anticipated that situations suggesting the appropriateness of the refusal to participate will occur so frequently as to significantly impair the usefulness of the program of participation by lawyers from private firms. (Amended Nov. 7, 1995.)

696

[26] The primary responsibility for identifying situations in which representation by the participating lawyer might raise reasonable doubts as to the lawyer's zealous representation on behalf of the Office of Corporation Counsel or the District of Columbia Financial Responsibility and Management Assistance Authority must rest on the participating lawyer, who will generally be privy to nonpublic information bearing on the appropriateness of the lawyer's participation in a matter on behalf of the Office of Corporation Counsel or the District of Columbia Financial Responsibility and Management Assistance Authority. Recognizing that many representations by law firms are nonpublic matters the existence and nature of which may not be disclosed consistent with Rule 1.6, it is not anticipated that law firms from whom participating lawyers have been drawn would be asked to perform formal "conflicts checks" with respect to matters in which participating lawyers may be involved. However, consultations between participating lawyers and their law firms to identify potential areas of concern, provided that such consultations honor the requirements of Rule 1.6, are appropriate to protect the interests of all involved — the Office of Corporation Counsel, the District of Columbia Financial Responsibility and Management Assistance Authority, the participating lawyer, that lawyer's law firm and any clients whose interests are potentially implicated.

Rule 1.11. Successive Government and Private Employment

(a) A lawyer shall not accept other employment in connection with a matter which is the same as, or substantially related to, a matter in which the lawyer participated personally and substantially as a public officer or employee. Such participation includes acting on the merits of a matter in a judicial or other adjudicative capacity.

(b) If a lawyer is required to decline or to withdraw from employment under paragraph (a) on account of personal and substantial participation in a matter, no partner or associate of that lawyer, or lawyer with an of counsel relationship to that lawyer, may accept or continue such employment except as provided in paragraphs (c) and (d) below. The disqualification of such other lawyers does not apply if the sole form of participation was as a judicial law clerk.

(c) The prohibition stated in paragraph (b) shall not apply if the personally disqualified lawyer is screened from any form of participation in the matter or representation as the case may be, and from sharing in any fees resulting therefrom, and if the requirements of paragraphs (d) and (e) are satisfied.

(d) Except as provided in paragraph (e), when any of counsel, lawyer, partner, or associate of a lawyer personally disqualified under paragraph (a) accepts employment in connection with a matter giving rise to the personal disqualification, the following notifications shall be required:

(1) The personally disqualified lawyer shall submit to the public department or agency by which the lawyer was formerly employed and serve on each other party to any pertinent proceeding a signed document attesting that during the period of disqualification the personally disqualified lawyer will not participate in any manner in the matter or the representation, will not discuss the matter or the representation with any partner, associate, or of counsel lawyer, and will not share in any fees for the matter or the representation.

(2) At least one affiliated lawyer shall submit to the same department or agency and serve on the same parties a signed document attesting that all affiliated lawyers are aware of the requirement that the personally disqualified lawyer be screened from participating in or discussing the matter or the representation and describing the procedures being taken to screen the personally disqualified lawyer.

(e) If a client requests in writing that the fact and subject matter of a representation subject to paragraph (d) not be disclosed by submitting the signed statements referred to in paragraph (d), such statements shall be prepared concurrently with undertaking the representation and filed with bar counsel under seal. If at any time thereafter the fact and subject matter of the representation are disclosed to the public or become a part of the public record, the signed statements previously prepared shall be promptly submitted as required by paragraph (d).

(f) Signed documents filed pursuant to paragraph (d) shall be available to the public, except to the extent that a lawyer submitting a signed document demonstrates to the satisfaction of the public department or agency upon which such documents are served that public disclosure is inconsistent with Rule 1.6 or provisions of law.

(g) This Rule applies to any matter involving a specific party or parties.

(h) A lawyer who participates in a program of temporary service to the Office of Corporation Counsel or the District of Columbia Financial Responsibility and Management Assistance Authority of the kind described in Rule 1.10(e) shall be treated as having served as a public officer or employee for purposes of paragraph (a), and the provisions of

paragraphs (b)-(e) shall apply to the lawyer and to lawyers affiliated with the lawyer.

COMMENT

[1] This Rule deals with lawyers who leave public office and enter other employment. It applies to judges and their law clerks as well as to lawyers who act in other public capacities. It is a counterpart of Rule 1.10(b), which applies to lawyers moving from one firm to another.

[2] A lawyer representing a government agency, whether employed or specially retained by the government, is subject to the Rules of Professional Conduct, including the prohibition against representing adverse interests stated in Rule 1.7 and the protections afforded former clients in Rule 1.9. In addition, such a lawyer is subject to this Rule 1.11 and to statutes and government regulations concerning conflict of interest. In the District of Columbia, where there are so many lawyers for the federal and D.C. governments and their agencies, a number of whom are constantly leaving government and accepting other employment, particular heed must be paid to the federal conflict-of-interest statutes. See, e.g., 18 U.S.C. Chapter 11 and regulations and opinions thereunder.

[3] Rule 1.11, in paragraph (a), flatly forbids a lawyer to accept other employment in a matter in which the lawyer participated personally and substantially as a public officer or employee; participation specifically includes acting on a matter in a judicial capacity. There is no provision for waiver of the individual lawyer's disqualification. "Matter" is defined in paragraph (g) so as to encompass only matters that are particular to a specific party or parties. The making of rules of general applicability and the establishment of general policy will ordinarily not be a "matter" within the meaning of Rule 1.11. When a lawyer is forbidden by paragraph (a) to accept private employment in a matter, the partners and associates of that lawyer are likewise forbidden, by paragraph (b), to accept the employment unless the screening and disclosure procedures described in paragraphs (c) through (f) are followed.

[4] The Rule forbids lawyers to accept other employment in connection with matters that are the same as or "substantially related" to matters in which they participated personally and substantially while serving as public officers or employees. The leading case defining "substantially related" matters in the context of former government employment is *Brown v. District of Columbia Board of Zoning Adjustment,* 486 A.2d 37 (D.C. 1984) (en banc). There the D.C. Court of Appeals, en banc, held that in the "revolving door" context, a showing that a reasonable person could

699

infer that, through participation in one matter as a public officer or employee, the former government lawyer "may have had access to information legally relevant to, or otherwise useful in" a subsequent representation, is prima facie evidence that the two matters are substantially related. If this prima facie showing is made, the former government lawyer must disprove any ethical impropriety by showing that the lawyer "could not have gained access to information during the first representation that might be useful in the later representation." Id. at 49-50. In *Brown,* the Court of Appeals announced the "substantially related" test after concluding that, under former DR 9-101(B), see "Revolving Door," *445 A.2d 615 (D.C. 1982)* (en banc) (per curiam), the term "matter" was intended to embrace all matters "substantially related" to one another — a test that originated in "side-switching" litigation between private parties. See Rule 1.9, Comment [2]; *Brown,* 486 A.2d at 39-40 n.1, 41-42 & n.4. Accordingly, the words "or substantially related to" in paragraph (a) are an express statement of the judicial gloss in *Brown* interpreting "matter."

[5] Paragraph (a)'s absolute disqualification of a lawyer from matters in which the lawyer participated personally and substantially carries forward a policy of avoiding both actual impropriety and the appearance of impropriety that is expressed in the federal conflict-of-interest statutes and was expressed in the former Code of Professional Responsibility. Paragraph (c) requires the screening of a disqualified lawyer from such a matter as a condition to allowing any lawyers in the disqualified lawyer's firm to participate in it. This procedure is permitted in order to avoid imposing a serious deterrent to lawyers' entering public service. Governments have found that they benefit from having in their service both younger and more experienced lawyers who do not intend to devote their entire careers to public service. Some lawyers might not enter into short-term public service if they thought that, as a result of their active governmental practice, a firm would hesitate to hire them because of a concern that the entire firm would be disqualified from matters as a result.

[6] There is no imputed disqualification and consequently no screening requirement in the case of a judicial law clerk. But such clerks are subject to a personal obligation not to participate in matters falling within paragraph (a), since participation by a law clerk is within the term "judicial or other adjudicative capacity."

[7] Paragraph (d) imposes a further requirement that must be met before lawyers affiliated with a disqualified lawyer may participate in the representation. Except to the extent that the exception in paragraph (e) is satisfied, both the personally disqualified lawyer and at least one affiliated lawyer must submit to the agency signed documents basically stating

that the personally disqualified lawyer will be screened from participation in the matter. The personally disqualified lawyer must also state that the lawyer will not share in any fees paid for the representation in question. And the affiliated lawyer must describe the procedures to be followed to ensure that the personally disqualified lawyer is effectively screened.

[8] Paragraph (e) makes it clear that the lawyer's duty, under Rule 1.6, to maintain client confidences and secrets may preclude the submission of any notice required by paragraph (d). If the client requests in writing that the fact and subject matter of the representation not be disclosed, the lawyer must comply with that request. If the client makes such a request, the lawyer must abide by the client's wishes until such time as the fact and subject matter of the representation become public through some other means, such as a public filing. Filing a pleading or making an appearance in a proceeding before a tribunal constitutes a public filing. Once information concerning the representation is public, the notifications called for must be made promptly, and the lawyers involved may not honor a client request not to make the notifications. If a government agency has adopted rules governing practice before the agency by former government employees, members of the District of Columbia Bar are not exempted by Rule 1.11(e) from any additional or more restrictive notice requirements that the agency may impose. Thus the agency may require filing of notifications whether or not a client consents. While the lawyer cannot file a notification that the client has directed the lawyer not to file, the failure to file in accordance with agency rules may preclude the lawyer's representation of the client before the agency. Such issues are governed by the agency's rules, and Rule 1.11(e) is not intended to displace such agency requirements.

[9] Although paragraph (e) prohibits the lawyer from disclosing the fact and subject matter of the representation when the client has requested in writing that the information be kept confidential, it requires the lawyer to prepare the documents described in paragraph (d) as soon as the representation commences and to preserve the documents for possible submission to the agency and parties to any pertinent proceeding if and when the client does consent to their submission or the information becomes public.

[10] "Other employment," as used in paragraph (a) of this Rule, includes the representation of a governmental body other than an agency of the government by which the lawyer was employed as a public officer or employee, but in the case of a move from one government agency to another the prohibition provided in paragraph (a) may be waived by the government agency with which the lawyer was previously employed. As

used in paragraph (a), it would not be "other employment" for a lawyer who has left the employment of a particular government agency and taken employment with another government agency (e.g., the Department of Justice) or with a private law firm to continue or accept representation of the same government agency with which the lawyer was previously employed.

[11] Paragraph (c) does not prohibit a lawyer from receiving a salary or partnership share established by prior independent agreement. It prohibits directly relating the attorney's compensation in any way to the fee in the matter in which the lawyer is disqualified.

[12] Rule 1.10(e) provides an exception to the general imputation imposed by Rule 1.10(a) for lawyers assisting the Office of Corporation Counsel or the District of Columbia Financial Responsibility and Management Assistance Authority on a temporary basis. Rule 1.10(e) provides that lawyers providing such temporary assistance are not considered to be affiliated with their law firm during such periods of temporary assistance. However, lawyers participating in such temporary assistance programs have a potential for conflicts of interest or the abuse of information obtained while participating in such programs. It is appropriate to subject lawyers participating in temporary assistance programs to the same rules which paragraphs (a)-(g) impose on former government employees. Paragraph (h) effects this result.

[13] In addition to ethical concerns, provisions of conflict of interest statutes or regulations may impose limitations on the conduct of lawyers while they are providing assistance to the Office of Corporation Counsel or the District of Columbia Financial Responsibility and Management Assistance Authority, or after they return from such assignments. See, e.g., 18 U.S.C. §§207, 208. Compliance with the Rules of Professional Conduct does not necessarily constitute compliance with all of the obligations imposed by conflict of interest statutes or regulations.

Rule 1.12. Former Arbitrator

(a) Except as stated in paragraph (b), a lawyer shall not represent anyone in connection with a matter in which the lawyer participated personally and substantially as an arbitrator, unless all parties to the proceeding consent after disclosure.

(b) An arbitrator selected as a partisan of a party in a multimember arbitration panel is not prohibited from subsequently representing that party.

COMMENT

[1] This Rule extends the basic requirements of Rule 1.11(a) to privately employed arbitrators. Paragraph (a) is substantially similar to Rule 1.11(a), except that it allows an arbitrator to represent someone in connection with a matter with which the lawyer was substantially involved while serving as an arbitrator if the parties to the arbitration consent. Paragraph (b) makes it clear that the prohibition set forth in paragraph (a) does not apply to partisan arbitrators serving on a multimember arbitration panel.

Rule 1.13. Organization as Client

(a) A lawyer employed or retained by an organization represents the organization acting through its duly authorized constituents.

(b) In dealing with an organization's directors, officers, employees, members, shareholders, or other constituents, a lawyer shall explain the identity of the client when it is apparent that the organization's interests may be adverse to those of the constituents with whom the lawyer is dealing.

(c) A lawyer representing an organization may also represent any of its directors, officers, employees, members, shareholders, or other constituents, subject to the provisions of Rule 1.7. If the organization's consent to the dual representation is required by Rule 1.7, the consent shall be given by an appropriate official of the organization other than the individual who is to be represented, or by the shareholders.

COMMENT

The Entity as the Client

[1] An organizational client is a legal entity, but it cannot act except through its officers, directors, employees, shareholders, and other constituents.

[2] Officers, directors, employees, and shareholders are the constituents of the corporate organizational client. The duties defined in this Comment apply equally to unincorporated associations. "Other constituents" as used in this Comment means the positions equivalent to officers, directors, employees, and shareholders held by persons acting for organizational clients that are not corporations.

[3] When one of the constituents of an organizational client communicates with the organization's lawyer in that person's organizational capacity, the communication is protected by Rule 1.6. Thus, by way of example, if an organizational client requests its lawyer to investigate allegations of wrongdoing, interviews made in the course of that investigation between the lawyer and the client's employees or other constituents are covered by Rule 1.6. This does not mean, however, that constituents of an organizational client are the clients of the lawyer. The lawyer may not disclose to such constituents information relating to the representation except for disclosures explicitly or impliedly authorized by the organizational client in order to carry out the representation or as otherwise permitted by Rule 1.6.

[4] When constituents of the organization make decisions for it, the decisions ordinarily must be accepted by the lawyer even if their utility or prudence is doubtful. Decisions concerning policy and operations, including ones entailing serious risk, are not as such in the lawyer's province. However, different considerations arise when the lawyer knows that the organization may be substantially injured by tortious or illegal conduct by a constituent member of an organization that reasonably might be imputed to the organization or that might result in substantial injury to the organization. In such a circumstance, it may be reasonably necessary for the lawyer to ask the constituent to reconsider the matter. If that fails, or if the matter is of sufficient seriousness and importance to the organization, it may be reasonably necessary for the lawyer to take steps to have the matter reviewed by a higher authority in the organization. Clear justification should exist for seeking review over the head of the constituent normally responsible for it. The stated policy of the organization may define circumstances and prescribe channels for such review, and a lawyer should encourage the formulation of such a policy. Even in the absence of organization policy, however, the lawyer may have an obligation to refer a matter to a higher authority, depending on the seriousness of the matter and whether the constituent in question has apparent motives to act at variance with the organization's interest. Review by the chief executive officer or by the board of directors may be required when the matter is of importance commensurate with their authority. At some point it may be useful or essential to obtain an independent legal opinion.

[5] In an extreme case, it may be reasonably necessary for the lawyer to refer the matter to the organization's highest authority. Ordinarily, that is the board of directors or similar governing body. However, applicable law may prescribe that under certain conditions highest authority reposes elsewhere; for example, in the independent directors of a corporation.

Relation to Other Rules

[6] This Rule does not limit or expand the lawyer's responsibility under Rules 1.6, 1.8, 1.16, 3.3, and 4.1. If the lawyer's services are being used by an organization to further a crime or fraud by the organization, Rule 1.2(e) can be applicable.

Government Agency

[7] Because the government agency that employs the government lawyer is the lawyer's client, the lawyer represents the agency acting through its duly authorized constituents. Any application of Rule 1.13 to government lawyers must, however, take into account the differences between government agencies and other organizations.

Clarifying the Lawyer's Role

[8] There are times when the organization's interest may be or become adverse to those of one or more of its constituents. In such circumstances the lawyer should advise any constituent, whose interest the lawyer finds adverse to that of the organization, of the conflict or potential conflict of interest, that the lawyer cannot represent such constituent, and that such person may wish to obtain independent representation. Care must be taken to assure that the individual understands that, when there is such adversity of interest, the lawyer for the organization cannot provide legal representation for that constituent individual, and that discussions between the lawyer for the organization and the individual may not be privileged.

[9] Whether such a warning should be given by the lawyer for the organization to any constituent individual may turn on the facts of each case.

Dual Representation

[10] Paragraph (c) recognizes that a lawyer for an organization may also represent a principal officer or major shareholder.

Derivative Actions

[11] Under generally prevailing law, the shareholders or members of a corporation may bring suit to compel the directors to perform their

legal obligations in the supervision of the organization. Members of un-incorporated associations have essentially the same right. Such an action may be brought nominally by the organization, but usually is, in fact, a legal controversy over management of the organization.

[12] The question can arise whether counsel for the organization may defend such an action. The proposition that the organization is the lawyer's client does not alone resolve the issue. Most derivative actions are a normal incident of an organization's affairs, to be defended by the organization's lawyer like any other suit. However, if the claim involves serious charges of wrongdoing by those in control of the organization, a conflict may arise between the lawyer's duty to the organization and the lawyer's relationship with the board. In those circumstances, Rule 1.7 governs whether lawyers who normally serve as counsel to the corporation can properly represent both the directors and the organization.

Rule 1.14. Client Under a Disability

a) When a client's ability to make adequately considered decisions in connection with the representation is impaired, whether because of minority, mental disability, or for some other reason, the lawyer shall, as far as reasonably possible, maintain a normal client-lawyer relationship with the client.

(b) A lawyer may seek the appointment of a guardian or take other protective action with respect to a client, only when the lawyer reasonably believes that the client cannot adequately act in the client's own interest.

COMMENT

[1] The normal client-lawyer relationship is based on the assumption that the client, when properly advised and assisted, is capable of making decisions about important matters. When the client is a minor or suffers from a mental disorder or disability, however, maintaining the ordinary client-lawyer relationship may not be possible in all respects. In particular, an incapacitated person may have no power to make legally binding decisions. Nevertheless, a client lacking legal competence often has the ability to understand, deliberate upon, and reach conclusions about matters affecting the client's own well-being. Furthermore, to an

increasing extent the law recognizes intermediate degrees of competence. For example, children as young as five or six years of age, and certainly those of ten or twelve, are regarded as having opinions that are entitled to weight in legal proceedings concerning their custody. So also, it is recognized that some persons of advanced age can be quite capable of handling routine financial matters while needing special legal protection concerning major transactions.

[2] The fact that a client suffers a disability does not diminish the lawyer's obligation to treat the client with attention and respect. If the person has no guardian or legal representative, the lawyer often must act as de facto guardian. Even if the person does have a legal representative, the lawyer should as far as possible accord the represented person the status of client, particularly in maintaining communication.

[3] If a legal representative has already been appointed for the client, the lawyer should ordinarily look to the representative for decisions on behalf of the client. If a legal representative has not been appointed, the lawyer should see to such an appointment where it would serve the client's best interests. Thus, if a disabled client has substantial property that should be sold for the client's benefit, effective completion of the transaction ordinarily requires appointment of a legal representative. In many circumstances, however, appointment of a legal representative may be expensive or traumatic for the client. Evaluation of these considerations is a matter of professional judgment on the lawyer's part.

Disclosure of the Client's Condition

[4] Rules of procedure in litigation generally provide that minors or persons suffering mental disability shall be represented by a guardian or next friend if they do not have a general guardian. However, disclosure of the client's disability can adversely affect the client's interests. For example, raising the question of disability could, in some circumstances, lead to proceedings for involuntary commitment. The lawyer's position in such cases is an unavoidably difficult one. The lawyer may seek guidance from an appropriate diagnostician.

Rule 1.15. Safekeeping Property

(a) A lawyer shall hold property of clients or third persons that is in the lawyer's possession in connection with a representation separate from the lawyer's own property. Funds shall be kept in a separate account maintained in a financial institution which is authorized by federal, District of Columbia, or state law to do business in the jurisdiction where the account is maintained and which is a member of the Federal Deposit Insurance Corporation, or the Federal Savings and Loan Insurance Corporation, or successor agencies. Other property shall be identified as such and appropriately safeguarded; provided, however, that funds need not be held in an account in a financial institution if such funds (1) are permitted to be held elsewhere or in a different manner by law or court order, or (2) are held by a lawyer under an escrow or similar agreement in connection with a commercial transaction. Complete records of such account funds and other property shall be kept by the lawyer and shall be preserved for a period of five years after termination of the representation.

(b) Upon receiving funds or other property in which a client or third person has an interest, a lawyer shall promptly notify the client or third person. Except as stated in this Rule or otherwise permitted by law or by agreement with the client, a lawyer shall promptly deliver to the client or third person any funds or other property that the client or third person is entitled to receive and, upon request by the client or third person, shall promptly render a full accounting regarding such property, subject to Rule 1.6.

(c) When in the course of representation a lawyer is in possession of property in which interests are claimed by the lawyer and another person, or by two or more persons to each of whom the lawyer may have an obligation, the property shall be kept separate by the lawyer until there is an accounting and severance of interests in the property. If a dispute arises concerning the respective interests among persons claiming an interest in such property, the undisputed portion shall be distributed and the portion in dispute shall be kept separate by the lawyer until the dispute is resolved. Any funds in dispute shall be deposited in a separate account meeting the requirements of paragraph (a).

(d) Advances of legal fees and costs become the property of the lawyer upon receipt. Any unearned amount of prepaid fees must be returned to the client at the termination of the lawyer's services in accordance with Rule 1.16(d).

(e) Nothing in this Rule shall prohibit a lawyer or law firm from placing clients' funds which are nominal in amount or to be held for a short period of time in one or more interest-bearing accounts for the benefit of the charitable purposes of a court-approved "Interest on Lawyers Trust Account (IOLTA)" program.

(f) Nothing in this Rule shall prohibit a lawyer from placing a small amount of the lawyer's funds into a trust account for the sole purpose of defraying bank charges that may be made against that account.

COMMENT

[1] A lawyer should hold property of others with the care required of a professional fiduciary. Securities should be kept in a safe deposit box, except when some other form of safekeeping is warranted by special circumstances. All property that is the property of clients or third persons should be kept separate from the lawyer's business and personal property and, if monies, in one or more trust accounts maintained with financial institutions meeting the requirements of paragraph (a). Separate trust accounts may be warranted when administering estate monies or acting in similar fiduciary capacities.

[2] The District of Columbia Court of Appeals has promulgated specific rules allowing lawyers to place clients' funds that are nominal in amount, or that are to be held for a short period of time, into interest-bearing accounts for the benefit of the charitable purposes of a court-approved "Interest on Lawyers Trust Account (IOLTA)" program. On February 22, 1985, the court added to DR 9-103 a new paragraph (C) that expressly permitted IOLTA accounts meeting the requirements of Appendix B to Rule X of the court's Rules Governing the Bar of the District of Columbia. Appendix B sets forth detailed rules to be followed in establishing and administering IOLTA accounts. Paragraph (e) of this Rule is substantially identical to DR 9-103(C). The rules contained in Appendix B to Rule X are hereby incorporated and must be followed in setting up IOLTA programs pursuant to paragraph (e).

[3] Lawyers often receive funds from third parties from which the lawyer's fee will be paid. If there is risk that the client may divert the funds without paying the fee, the lawyer is not required to remit the portion from which the fee is to be paid. However, a lawyer may not hold funds to coerce a client into accepting the lawyer's contention. The disputed portion of the funds should be kept in trust and the lawyer should suggest means for prompt resolution of the dispute, such as arbitration. The undisputed portion of the funds should be promptly distributed.

[4] Third parties, such as a client's creditors, may have just claims against funds or other property in a lawyer's custody. A lawyer may have a duty under applicable law to protect such third-party claims against wrongful interference by the client, and accordingly may refuse to surrender the property to the client. However, a lawyer should not unilaterally assume to arbitrate a dispute between the client and the third party.

[5] The obligations of a lawyer under this Rule are independent of those arising from activity other than rendering legal services. For example, a lawyer who serves as an escrow agent is governed by the appli-

cable law relating to fiduciaries even though the lawyer does not render legal services in the transaction.

[6] A "clients' security fund" provides a means through the collective efforts of the Bar to reimburse persons who have lost money or property as a result of dishonest conduct of a lawyer. Where such a fund has been established, a lawyer should participate.

[7] With respect to property that constitutes evidence, such as the instruments or proceeds of crime, see Rule 3.4(a).

Rule 1.16. Declining or Terminating Representation

(a) Except as stated in paragraph (c), a lawyer shall not represent a client or, where representation has commenced, shall withdraw from the representation of a client if:

(1) The representation will result in violation of the Rules of Professional Conduct or other law;

(2) The lawyer's physical or mental condition materially impairs the lawyer's ability to represent the client; or

(3) The lawyer is discharged.

(b) Except as stated in paragraph (c), a lawyer may withdraw from representing a client if withdrawal can be accomplished without material adverse effect on the interests of the client; or if:

(1) The client persists in a course of action involving the lawyer's services that the lawyer reasonably believes is criminal or fraudulent;

(2) The client has used the lawyer's services to perpetrate a crime or fraud;

(3) The client fails substantially to fulfill an obligation to the lawyer regarding the lawyer's services and has been given reasonable warning that the lawyer will withdraw unless the obligation is fulfilled;

(4) The representation will result in an unreasonable financial burden on the lawyer or obdurate or vexatious conduct on the part of the client has rendered the representation unreasonably difficult;

(5) The lawyer believes in good faith, in a proceeding before a tribunal, that the tribunal will find the existence of other good cause for withdrawal.

(c) When ordered to do so by a tribunal, a lawyer shall continue representation notwithstanding good cause for terminating the representation.

(d) In connection with any termination of representation, a lawyer shall take timely steps to the extent reasonably practicable to protect a client's interests, such as giving reasonable notice to the client, allowing time for employment of other counsel, surrendering papers and property to which the client is entitled, and refunding any advance payment of fee that has not been earned. The lawyer may retain papers relating to the client to the extent permitted by Rule 1.8(i).

COMMENT

[1] A lawyer should not accept representation in a matter unless it can be performed competently, promptly, without improper conflict of interest, and to completion.

Mandatory Withdrawal

[2] A lawyer ordinarily must decline or withdraw from representation if the client demands that the lawyer engage in conduct that is illegal or violates the Rules of Professional Conduct or other law. The lawyer is not obliged to decline or withdraw simply because the client suggests such a course of conduct; a client may make such a suggestion in the hope that a lawyer will not be constrained by a professional obligation.

[3] When a lawyer has been appointed to represent a client, withdrawal ordinarily requires approval of the appointing authority. See also Rule 6.2. Difficulty may be encountered if withdrawal is based on the client's demand that the lawyer engage in unprofessional conduct. The court may wish an explanation for the withdrawal, while the lawyer may be bound to keep confidential the facts that would constitute such an explanation. The lawyer's statement that irreconcilable differences between the lawyer and client require termination of the representation ordinarily should be accepted as sufficient.

Discharge

[4] A client has a right to discharge a lawyer at any time, with or without cause, subject to liability for payment for the lawyer's services. Where future dispute about the withdrawal may be anticipated, it may be advisable to prepare a written statement reciting the circumstances.

[5] Whether a client can discharge appointed counsel may depend on applicable law. A client seeking to do so should be given a full explanation of the consequences. These consequences may include a decision

by the appointing authority that appointment of successor counsel is unjustified, thus requiring the client to proceed pro se.

[6] If the client is mentally incompetent, the client may lack the legal capacity to discharge the lawyer, and in any event the discharge may be seriously adverse to the client's interests. The lawyer should make a special effort to help the client consider the consequences and, in an extreme case, may initiate proceedings for a conservatorship or similar protection of the client. See Rule 1.14.

Optional Withdrawal

[7] A lawyer may withdraw from representation in some circumstances. The lawyer has the option to withdraw if the withdrawal can be accomplished without material adverse effect on the client's interests. Withdrawal is also justified if the client persists in a course of action that the lawyer reasonably believes is criminal or fraudulent, for a lawyer is not required to be associated with such conduct even if the lawyer does not further it. Withdrawal is also permitted if the lawyer's services were misused in the past even if that would materially prejudice the client.

[8] A lawyer may withdraw if the client refuses to abide by the terms of an agreement relating to the representation, such as an agreement concerning the timely payment of the lawyer's fees, court costs or other out-of-pocket expenses of the representation, or an agreement limiting the objectives of the representation.

[9] If the matter is not pending in court, a lawyer will not have "other good cause for withdrawal" unless the lawyer is acting in good faith and the circumstances are exceptional enough to outweigh the material adverse effect on the interests of the client that withdrawal will cause.

Assisting the Client Upon Withdrawal

[10] Even if the lawyer has been unfairly discharged by the client, a lawyer must take all reasonable steps to mitigate the consequences to the client. The lawyer may retain papers as security for a fee only to the extent permitted by Rule 1.8(i).

Compliance With Requirements of a Tribunal

[11] Paragraph (c) reflects the possibility that a lawyer may, by appearing before a tribunal, become subject to the tribunal's power in some

circumstances to prevent a withdrawal that would otherwise be proper. Paragraph (c) requires the lawyer who is ordered to continue a representation before a tribunal to do so. However, paragraph (c) is not intended to prevent the lawyer from challenging the tribunal's order as beyond its jurisdiction, arbitrary, or otherwise improper, while, in the interim, continuing the representation.

Return of Client's Property or Money

[12] Paragraph (d) requires a lawyer to make timely return to the client of any property or money "to which the client is entitled." Where a lawyer holds property or money of a client at the termination of a representation and there is a dispute concerning the distribution of such property or money — whether such dispute is between the lawyer and a client, the lawyer and another lawyer who is owed a fee in the matter, or between either the lawyer or the client and a third party — the lawyer must segregate the disputed portion of such property or money, hold that property or money in trust as required by Rule 1.15, and promptly distribute any undisputed amounts. See Rule 1.15 and Comment [3] thereto. Notwithstanding the foregoing, where a lawyer has a valid lien covering undisputed amounts of property or money, the lawyer may continue to hold such property or money to the extent permitted by the substantive law governing the lien asserted. See generally Rules 1.8, 1.15(b).

Rule 1.17. Trust Account Overdraft Notification

(a) Funds coming into the possession of a lawyer that are required by these Rules to be segregated from the lawyer's own funds (such segregated funds hereinafter being referred to as "trust funds") shall be deposited in one or more specially designated accounts at a financial institution. The title of each such account shall contain the words "Trust Account" or "Escrow Account," as well as the lawyer's or the lawyer's law firm's identity.

(b) The accounts required pursuant to paragraph (a) shall be maintained only in institutions that are listed as "D.C. Bar Approved Depositories" on a list maintained for this purpose by the Board on Professional Responsibility, unless (1) the account is permitted to be held elsewhere or in a different manner by law or court order, or (2) a lawyer holds trust funds under an escrow or similar agreement in connection with a commercial transaction. If a lawyer is a member of the District of Columbia

Bar and practices law outside the District of Columbia, D.C. Bar Approved Depositories shall be used for deposit of any: (1) trust funds received by the lawyer in the District of Columbia; (2) trust funds received by the lawyer from, or for the benefit of, parties or persons located in the District of Columbia; and/or (3) trust funds received by the lawyer that arise from transactions negotiated or consummated in the District of Columbia.

To be listed as an Approved Depository, a financial institution shall file an undertaking with the Board on Professional Responsibility, on a form to be provided by the Board's Office, agreeing promptly to report to the Office of Bar Counsel each instance in which an instrument that would properly be payable if sufficient funds were available has been presented against a lawyer's or law firm's specially designated account at such institution at a time when such account contained insufficient funds to pay such instrument, whether or not the instrument was honored and irrespective of any overdraft privileges that may attach to such account. In addition to undertaking to make the above-specified reports, Approved Depositories, wherever they are located, shall also undertake to respond promptly and fully to subpoenas from the Office of Bar Counsel that seek a lawyer's or law firm's specially designated account records, notwithstanding any objections that might be raised based upon the territorial limits on the effectiveness of such subpoenas or upon the jurisdiction of the District of Columbia Court of Appeals to enforce them. Such undertaking shall apply to all branches of the financial institution and shall not be cancelled by the institution except upon thirty (30) days written notice to the Office of Bar Counsel. The failure of an Approved Depository to comply with its undertaking hereunder shall be grounds for immediate removal of such institution from the list of D.C. Bar Approved Depositories.

(c) Reports to Bar Counsel by Approved Depositories pursuant to paragraph (b) above shall contain the following information:

(1) In the case of a dishonored instrument, the report shall be identical to the overdraft notice customarily forwarded to the institution's other regular account holders.

(2) In the case of an instrument that was presented against insufficient funds but was honored, the report shall identify the depository, the lawyer or law firm maintaining the account, the account number, the date of presentation for payment and the payment date of the instrument, as well as the amount of overdraft created thereby.

The report to the Office of Bar Counsel shall be made simultaneously with, and within the time period, if any, provided by law for notice of dishonor. If an instrument presented against insufficient funds was honored, the institution's report shall be mailed to Bar Counsel within five (5) business days of payment of the instrument.

(d) The establishment of a specially designated account at an Approved Depository shall be conclusively deemed to be consent by the lawyer or law firm maintaining such account to that institution's furnishing to the Office of Bar Counsel all reports and information required hereunder. No Approved Depository shall incur any liability by virtue of its compliance with the requirements of this Rule, except as might otherwise arise from bad faith, intentional misconduct, or any other acts by the Approved Depository or its employees which, unrelated to this rule, would create liability.

(e) The designation of a financial institution as an Approved Depository pursuant to this Rule shall not be deemed to be a warranty, representation, or guaranty by the District of Columbia Court of Appeals, the District of Columbia Bar, the Board on Professional Responsibility, or the Office of Bar Counsel as to the financial soundness, business practices, or other attributes of such institution. Approval of an institution under this rule means only that the institution has undertaken to meet the reporting requirements enumerated above.

(f) Nothing in this rule shall preclude a financial institution from charging a lawyer or law firm for the reasonable cost of producing the reports and records required by this rule.

(g) Definitions:

"Law Firm" — includes a partnership of lawyers, a professional or non-profit corporation of lawyers, and a combination thereof engaged in the practice of law.

"Financial Institution" — includes banks, savings and loan associations, credit unions, savings banks and any other business that accepts for deposit funds held in trust by lawyers which is authorized by Federal, District of Columbia, or state law to do business in the District of Columbia or the state in which the financial institution is situated and that maintains accounts which are insured by an agency or instrumentality of the United States.

COUNSELOR

Rule 2.1. Advisor

In representing a client, a lawyer shall exercise independent professional judgment and render candid advice. In rendering advice, a lawyer may refer not only to law but to other considerations such as moral, economic, social, and political factors, that may be relevant to the client's situation.

COMMENT

Scope of Advice

[1] A client is entitled to straightforward advice expressing the lawyer's honest assessment. Legal advice often involves unpleasant facts and alternatives that a client may be disinclined to confront. In presenting advice, a lawyer endeavors to sustain the client's morale and may put advice in as acceptable a form as honesty permits. However, a lawyer should not be deterred from giving candid advice by the prospect that the advice will be unpalatable to the client.

[2] Advice couched in narrowly legal terms may be of little value to a client, especially where practical considerations, such as cost or effects on other people, are predominant. Purely technical legal advice, therefore, can sometimes be inadequate. It is proper for a lawyer to refer to relevant moral and ethical considerations in giving advice. Although a lawyer is not a moral advisor as such, moral and ethical considerations impinge upon most legal questions and may decisively influence how the law will be applied.

[3] A client may expressly or impliedly ask the lawyer for purely technical advice. When such a request is made by a client experienced in legal matters, the lawyer may accept it at face value. When such a request is made by a client inexperienced in legal matters, however, the lawyer's responsibility as advisor may include indicating that more may be involved than strictly legal considerations.

[4] Matters that go beyond strictly legal questions may also be in the domain of another profession. Family matters can involve problems within the professional competence of psychiatry, clinical psychology, or social work; business matters can involve problems within the competence of the accounting profession or of financial specialists. Where consultation with a professional in another field is itself something a competent lawyer would recommend, the lawyer should make such a recommendation. At the same time, a lawyer's advice at its best often consists of recommending a course of action in the face of conflicting recommendations of experts.

Offering Advice

[5] In general, a lawyer is not expected to give advice until asked by the client. However, when a lawyer knows that a client proposes a course of action that is likely to result in substantial adverse legal consequences to the client, duty to the client under Rule 1.4 may require that the lawyer act if the client's course of action is related to the representation. A lawyer ordinarily has no duty to initiate investigation of a client's affairs or to give advice that the client has indicated is unwanted, but a lawyer may initiate advice to a client when doing so appears to be in the client's interest.

Rule 2.2. Intermediary

(a) A lawyer may act as intermediary between clients if:

(1) The lawyer consults with each client concerning the implications of the common representation, including the advantages and risks involved, and the effect on the attorney-client privileges, and obtains each client's consent to the common representation;

(2) The lawyer reasonably believes that the matter can be resolved on terms compatible with the clients' best interests, that each client will be able to make adequately informed decisions in the matter, and that there is little risk of material prejudice to the interests of any of the clients if the contemplated resolution is unsuccessful; and

(3) The lawyer reasonably believes that the common representation can be undertaken impartially and without improper effect on other responsibilities the lawyer has to any of the clients.

(b) A lawyer should, except in unusual circumstances that may make it infeasible, provide both clients with an explanation in writing of the risks involved in the common representation and of the circumstances that may cause separate representation later to be necessary or desirable. The consent of the clients shall also be in writing.

(c) While acting as intermediary, the lawyer shall consult with each client concerning the decisions to be made and the considerations relevant in making them, so that each client can make adequately informed decisions.

(d) A lawyer shall withdraw as intermediary if any of the clients so request, or if any of the conditions stated in paragraph (a) are no longer satisfied. Upon withdrawal, the lawyer shall not continue to represent any of the clients in the matter that was the subject of the intermediation.

COMMENT

[1] A lawyer acts as intermediary under this Rule when the lawyer represents two or more parties with potentially conflicting interests. A key factor in defining the relationship is whether the parties share responsibility for the lawyer's fee, but the common representation may be inferred from other circumstances. Because confusion can arise as to the lawyer's role where each party is not separately represented, it is important that the lawyer make clear the relationship.

[2] Because the potential for confusion is so great, paragraph (b) imposes the requirement that an explanation of the risks of the common representation be furnished in writing, except in unusual circumstances. The process of preparing the writing causes the lawyer involved to focus specifically on those risks, a process that may suggest to the lawyer that the particular situation is not suited to the use of the lawyer as an intermediary. In any event, the writing performs a valuable role in educating the client to such risks as may exist — risks that many clients may not otherwise comprehend. Mere agreement by a client to waive the requirement for a written analysis of the risks does not constitute the "unusual circumstances" that justify omitting the writing. The "unusual circumstances" requirement may be met in rare situations where an assessment of risks is not feasible at the beginning of the intermediary role. In such circumstances, the writing should be provided as soon as it becomes feasible to assess the risks with reasonable clarity. The consent required by paragraph (b) should refer to the disclosure upon which it is based.

[3] The Rule does not apply to a lawyer acting as arbitrator or mediator between or among parties who are not clients of the lawyer, even where the lawyer has been appointed with the concurrence of the parties. In performing such a role the lawyer may be subject to applicable codes of ethics, such as the Code of Ethics for Arbitration in Commercial Disputes prepared by a Joint Committee of the American Bar Association and the American Arbitration Association.

[4] A lawyer acts as intermediary in seeking to establish or adjust a relationship between clients on an amicable and mutually advantageous basis; for example, in helping to organize a business in which two or more clients are entrepreneurs, working out the financial reorganization of an enterprise in which two or more clients have an interest, arranging a property distribution in settlement of an estate, or mediating a dispute between clients. The lawyer seeks to resolve potentially conflicting interests by developing the parties' mutual interests. The alternative can be that each party may have to obtain separate representation, with the possibility in some situations of incurring additional cost, complication, or even

litigation. Given these and other relevant factors, all the clients may prefer that the lawyer act as intermediary.

[5] In considering whether to act as intermediary between clients, a lawyer should be mindful that if the intermediation fails the result can be additional cost, embarrassment, and recrimination. In some situations the risk of failure is so great that intermediation is plainly impossible. For example, a lawyer cannot undertake common representation of clients between whom contentious litigation is imminent or who contemplate contentious negotiations. More generally, if the relationship between the parties has already assumed definite antagonism, the possibility that the clients' interests can be adjusted by intermediation ordinarily is not very good.

[6] The appropriateness of intermediation can depend on its form. Forms of intermediation range from informal arbitration where each client's case is presented by the respective client and the lawyer decides the outcome, to mediation, to common representation where the clients' interests are substantially though not entirely compatible. One form may be appropriate in circumstances where another would not. Other relevant factors are whether the lawyer subsequently will represent both parties on a continuing basis and whether the situation involves creating a relationship between the parties or terminating one.

[7] Since the lawyer is required to be impartial between commonly represented clients, intermediation is improper when that impartiality cannot be maintained. For example, a lawyer who has represented one of the clients for a long period of time and in a variety of matters could have difficulty being impartial between that client and one to whom the lawyer has only recently been introduced.

Confidentiality and Privilege

[8] A particularly important factor in determining the appropriateness of intermediation is the effect on client-lawyer confidentiality and the attorney-client privilege. In a common representation, the lawyer is still required both to keep each client adequately informed and to maintain confidentiality of information relating to the representation. See Rules 1.4 and 1.6. Complying with both requirements while acting as intermediary requires a delicate balance. If the balance cannot be maintained, the common representation is improper. With regard to the attorney-client privilege, the prevailing rule is that as between commonly represented clients the privilege does not attach. Hence, it must be assumed

that if litigation eventuates between the clients, the privilege will not protect any such communications, and the clients should be so advised.

Consultation

[9] In acting as intermediary between clients, the lawyer is required to consult with the clients on the implications of doing so, and proceed only upon consent based on such a consultation. The consultation should make clear that the lawyer's role is not that of partisanship normally expected in other circumstances.

[10] Paragraph (c) is an application of the principle expressed in Rule 1.4. Where the lawyer is intermediary, the clients ordinarily must assume greater responsibility for decisions than when each client is independently represented.

Withdrawal

[11] Common representation does not diminish the rights of each client in the client-lawyer relationship. Each has the right to loyal and diligent representation, the right to discharge the lawyer as stated in Rule 1.16, and the protection of Rule 1.9 concerning obligations to a former client.

Rule 2.3. Evaluation for Use by Third Persons

(a) A lawyer may undertake an evaluation of a matter affecting a client for the use of someone other than the client if:

(1) The lawyer reasonably believes that making the evaluation is compatible with other aspects of the lawyer's relationship with the client; and

(2) The client consents after consultation.

(b) Except as disclosure is required in connection with a report of an evaluation, information relating to the evaluation is otherwise protected by Rule 1.6.

COMMENT

Definition

[1] An evaluation may be performed at the client's direction but for the primary purpose of establishing information for the benefit of third

parties; for example, an opinion concerning the title of property rendered at the behest of a vendor for the information of a prospective purchaser, or at the behest of a borrower for the information of a prospective lender. In some situations, the evaluation may be required by a government agency; for example, an opinion concerning the legality of the securities registered for sale under the securities laws. In other instances, the evaluation may be required by a third person, such as a purchaser of a business.

[2] A legal evaluation should be distinguished from an investigation of a person with whom the lawyer does not have a client-lawyer relationship. For example, a lawyer retained by a purchaser to analyze a vendor's title to property does not have a client-lawyer relationship with the vendor. So also, an investigation into a person's affairs by a government lawyer, or by special counsel employed by the government, is not an evaluation as that term is used in this Rule. The question is whether the lawyer is retained by the person whose affairs are being examined. When the lawyer is retained by that person, the general Rules concerning loyalty to client and preservation of confidences apply, which is not the case if the lawyer is retained by someone else. For this reason, it is essential to identify the person by whom the lawyer is retained. This should be made clear not only to the person under examination, but also to others to whom the results are to be made available.

Duty to Third Person

[3] When the evaluation is intended for the information or use of a third person, a legal duty to that person may or may not arise. That legal question is beyond the scope of this Rule. However, since such an evaluation involves a departure from the normal client-lawyer relationship, careful analysis of the situation is required. The lawyer must be satisfied as a matter of professional judgment that making the evaluation is compatible with other functions undertaken in behalf of the client. For example, if the lawyer is acting as advocate in defending the client against charges of fraud, it would normally be incompatible with that responsibility for the lawyer to perform an evaluation for others concerning the same or a related transaction. Assuming no such impediment is apparent, however, the lawyer should advise the client of the implications of the evaluation, particularly the lawyer's responsibilities to third persons and the duty to disseminate the findings.

Access to and Disclosure of Information

[4] The quality of an evaluation depends on the freedom and extent of the investigation upon which it is based. Ordinarily a lawyer should have whatever latitude of investigation seems necessary as a matter of professional judgment. Under some circumstances, however, the terms of the evaluation may be limited. For example, certain issues or sources may be categorically excluded, or the scope of search may be limited by time constraints or the noncooperation of persons having relevant information. Any such limitations that are material to the evaluation should be described in the report. If after a lawyer has commenced an evaluation, the client refuses to comply with the terms upon which it was understood the evaluation was to have been made, the lawyer's obligations are determined by law, having reference to the terms of the client's agreement and the surrounding circumstances.

Financial Auditors' Requests for Information

[5] When a question concerning the legal situation of a client arises at the insistence of the client's financial auditor and the question is referred to the lawyer, the lawyer's response may be made in accordance with procedures recognized in the legal profession. Such a procedure is set forth in the American Bar Association Statement of Policy Regarding Lawyers' Responses to Auditors' Requests for Information, adopted in 1975.

ADVOCATE

Rule 3.1. Meritorious Claims and Contentions

A lawyer shall not bring or defend a proceeding, or assert or controvert an issue therein, unless there is a basis for doing so that is not frivolous, which includes a good-faith argument for an extension, modification, or reversal of existing law. A lawyer for the defendant in a criminal proceeding, or for the respondent in a proceeding that could result in involuntary institutionalization, shall, if the client elects to go to trial or to a contested fact-finding hearing, nevertheless so defend the proceeding as to require that the government carry its burden of proof.

COMMENT

[1] The advocate has a duty to use legal procedure for the fullest benefit of the client's cause, but also a duty not to abuse legal procedure. The law, both procedural and substantive, establishes the limits within which an advocate may proceed. However, the law is not always clear and never is static. Accordingly, in determining the proper scope of advocacy, account must be taken of the law's ambiguities and potential for change.

[2] The filing of an action or defense or similar action taken for a client is not frivolous merely because the facts have not first been fully substantiated or because the lawyer expects to develop vital evidence only by discovery. Such action is not frivolous even though the lawyer believes that the client's position ultimately will not prevail. The action is frivolous if the lawyer is unable either to make a good-faith argument on the merits of the action taken or to support the action taken by a good-faith argument for an extension. modification, or reversal of existing law.

[3] In criminal cases or proceedings in which the respondent can be involuntarily institutionalized, such as juvenile delinquency and civil commitment cases, the lawyer is not only permitted, but is indeed required, to put the government to its proof whenever the client elects to contest adjudication.

Rule 3.2. Expediting Litigation

(a) In representing a client, a lawyer shall not delay a proceeding when the lawyer knows or when it is obvious that such action would serve solely to harass or maliciously injure another.

(b) A lawyer shall make reasonable efforts to expedite litigation consistent with the interests of the client.

COMMENT

[1] Dilatory practices bring the administration of justice into disrepute. Delay should not be indulged merely for the convenience of the advocates, or for the purpose of frustrating an opposing party's attempt to obtain rightful redress or repose. It is not a justification that similar conduct is often tolerated by the bench and bar. The question is whether a competent lawyer acting in good faith would regard the course of action as having some substantial purpose other than delay. Realizing financial

or other benefit from otherwise improper delay in litigation is not a legitimate interest of the client.

Rule 3.3. Candor Toward the Tribunal

(a) A lawyer shall not knowingly:

(1) Make a false statement of material fact or law to a tribunal;

(2) Counsel or assist a client to engage in conduct that the lawyer knows is criminal or fraudulent, but a lawyer may discuss the legal consequences of any proposed course of conduct with a client and may counsel or assist a client to make a good-faith effort to determine the validity, scope, meaning, or application of the law;

(3) Fail to disclose to the tribunal legal authority in the controlling jurisdiction not disclosed by opposing counsel and known to the lawyer to be dispositive of a question at issue and directly adverse to the position of the client; or

(4) Offer evidence that the lawyer knows to be false, except as provided in paragraph (b).

(b) When the witness who intends to give evidence that the lawyer knows to be false is the lawyer's client and is the accused in a criminal case, the lawyer shall first make a good-faith effort to dissuade the client from presenting the false evidence; if the lawyer is unable to dissuade the client, the lawyer shall seek leave of the tribunal to withdraw. If the lawyer is unable to dissuade the client or to withdraw without seriously harming the client, the lawyer may put the client on the stand to testify in a narrative fashion, but the lawyer shall not examine the client in such manner as to elicit testimony which the lawyer knows to be false, and shall not argue the probative value of the client's testimony in closing argument.

(c) The duties stated in paragraph (a) continue to the conclusion of the proceeding.

(d) A lawyer who receives information clearly establishing that a fraud has been perpetrated upon the tribunal shall promptly reveal the fraud to the tribunal unless compliance with this duty would require disclosure of information otherwise protected by Rule 1.6, in which case the lawyer shall promptly call upon the client to rectify the fraud.

COMMENT

[1] This Rule defines the duty of candor to the tribunal. In dealing with a tribunal the lawyer is also required to comply with the general re-

quirements of Rule 1.2(d) and (e). However, an advocate does not vouch for the evidence submitted in a cause; the tribunal is responsible for assessing its probative value.

Representations by a Lawyer

[2] An assertion purported to be made by the lawyer, as in an affidavit by the lawyer or in a statement in open court, may properly be made only when the lawyer knows the assertion is true or believes it to be true on the basis of a reasonably diligent inquiry. There may be circumstances where failure to make a disclosure is the equivalent of an affirmative misrepresentation. The obligation prescribed in Rule 1.2(e) not to counsel a client to commit or assist the client in committing a fraud applies in litigation but is subject to Rule 3.3(b) and (d). Regarding compliance with Rule 1.2(e), see the Comment to that Rule. See also Comment to Rule 8.4(b).

Misleading Legal Argument

[3] Legal argument based on a knowingly false representation of law constitutes dishonesty toward the tribunal. A lawyer is not required to make a disinterested exposition of the law, but must recognize the existence of pertinent legal authorities. Furthermore, as stated in subparagraph (a)(3), an advocate has a duty to disclose directly adverse authority in the controlling jurisdiction that has not been disclosed by the opposing party and that is dispositive of a question at issue. The underlying concept is that legal argument is a discussion seeking to determine the legal premises properly applicable to the case.

False Evidence

[4] When evidence that a lawyer knows to be false is provided by a person who is not the client, the lawyer must refuse to offer it regardless of the client's wishes.

[5] When false evidence is offered by the client, however, a conflict may arise between the lawyer's duty to keep the client's revelations confidential and the duty of candor to the court. Upon ascertaining that material evidence is false, the lawyer should seek to persuade the client that

the evidence should not be offered or, if it has been offered, that its false character should immediately be disclosed.

[6] Paragraph (d) provides that if a lawyer learns that a fraud has been perpetrated on the tribunal, the lawyer must reveal the fraud to the tribunal. However, if the notification of the tribunal would require disclosure of information protected by Rule 1.6, the lawyer may not inform the tribunal of the fraud; the lawyer's only duty in such an instance is to call upon the client to rectify the fraud. In other cases, the lawyer may learn of the client's intention to present false evidence before the client has had a chance to do so. In this situation, paragraphs (a)(4) and (b) forbid the lawyer to present the false evidence, except in rare instances where the witness is the accused in a criminal case, the lawyer is unsuccessful in dissuading the client from going forward, and the lawyer is unable to withdraw without causing serious harm to the client. The terms "criminal case" and "criminal defendant" as used in Rule 3.3 and its Comment include juvenile delinquency proceedings and the person who is the subject of such proceedings.

Perjury by a Criminal Defendant

[7] Paragraph (b) allows the lawyer to permit a client who is the accused in a criminal case to present false testimony in very narrowly circumscribed circumstances and in a very limited manner. Even in a criminal case the lawyer must seek to persuade the defendant-client to refrain from perjurious testimony. There has been dispute concerning the lawyer's duty when that persuasion fails. Paragraph (b) requires the lawyer to withdraw rather than offer the client's false testimony, if this can be done without seriously harming the client.

[8] Serious harm to the client sufficient to prevent the lawyer's withdrawal entails more than the usual inconveniences that necessarily result from withdrawal, such as delay in concluding the client's case or an increase in the costs of concluding the case. The term should be construed narrowly to preclude withdrawal only where the special circumstances of the case are such that the client would be significantly prejudiced, such as by express or implied divulgence of information otherwise protected by Rule 1.6. If the confrontation with the client occurs before trial, the lawyer ordinarily can withdraw. Withdrawal before trial may not be possible, however, either because trial is imminent, or because the confrontation with the client does not take place until the trial itself, or because no other counsel is available. In those rare circumstances in which withdrawal without such serious harm to the client is impossible, the lawyer may go for-

ward with examination of the client and closing argument subject to the limitations of paragraph (b).

Refusing to Offer Proof of a Nonclient Known to Be False

[9] Generally speaking, a lawyer may not offer testimony or other proof, through a nonclient, that the lawyer knows to be false. Furthermore, a lawyer may not offer evidence of a client if the evidence is known by the lawyer to be false, except to the extent permitted by paragraph (b) where the client is a defendant in a criminal case.

Rule 3.4. Fairness to Opposing Party and Counsel

A lawyer shall not:

(a) Obstruct another party's access to evidence or alter, destroy, or conceal evidence, or counsel or assist another person to do so, if the lawyer reasonably should know that the evidence is or may be the subject of discovery or subpoena in any pending or imminent proceeding. Unless prohibited by law, a lawyer may receive physical evidence of any kind from the client or from another person. If the evidence received by the lawyer belongs to anyone other than the client, the lawyer shall make a good-faith effort to preserve it and to return it to the owner, subject to Rule 1.6;

(b) Falsify evidence, counsel or assist a witness to testify falsely, or offer an inducement to a witness that is prohibited by law;

(c) Knowingly disobey an obligation under the rules of a tribunal except for an open refusal based on an assertion that no valid obligation exists;

(d) In pretrial procedure, make a frivolous discovery request or fail to make reasonably diligent effort to comply with a legally proper discovery request by an opposing party;

(e) In trial, allude to any matter that the lawyer does not reasonably believe is relevant or that will not be supported by admissible evidence, assert personal knowledge of facts in issue except when testifying as a witness, or state a personal opinion as to the justness of a cause, the credibility of a witness, the culpability of a civil litigant, or the guilt or innocence of an accused; or

(f) Request a person other than a client to refrain from voluntarily giving relevant information to another party unless:

(1) The person is a relative or an employee or other agent of a client; and

(2) The lawyer reasonably believes that the person's interests will not be adversely affected by refraining from giving such information.

COMMENT

[1] The procedure of the adversary system contemplates that the evidence in a case is to be marshaled competitively by the contending parties. Fair competition in the adversary system is secured by prohibitions against destruction or concealment of evidence, improperly influencing witnesses, obstructive tactics in discovery procedure, and the like.

[2] Documents and other items of evidence are often essential to establish a claim or defense. Subject to evidentiary privileges, the right of an opposing party, including the government, to obtain evidence through discovery or subpoena is an important procedural right. The exercise of that right can be frustrated if relevant material is altered, concealed, or destroyed. To the extent clients are involved in the effort to comply with discovery requests, the lawyer's obligations are to pursue reasonable efforts to assure that documents and other information subject to proper discovery requests are produced. Applicable law in many jurisdictions makes it an offense to destroy material for purpose of impairing its availability in a pending proceeding or a proceeding whose commencement can be foreseen. Falsifying evidence is also generally a criminal offense. Paragraph (a) applies to evidentiary material generally, including computerized information.

[3] Paragraph (a) permits, but does not require, the lawyer to accept physical evidence (including the instruments or proceeds of crime) from the client or any other person. Such receipt is, as stated in paragraph (a), subject to other provisions of law and the limitations imposed by paragraph (a) with respect to obstruction of access, alteration, destruction, or concealment, and subject also to the requirements of paragraph (a) with respect to return of property to its rightful owner, and to the obligation to comply with subpoenas and discovery requests. The term "evidence" includes any document or physical object that the lawyer reasonably should know may be the subject of discovery or subpoena in any pending or imminent litigation. See D.C. Bar Legal Ethics Committee Opinion No. 119 (March 15, 1983) (test is whether destruction of

document is directed at concrete litigation that is either pending or almost certain to be filed).

[4] A lawyer should ascertain that the lawyer's handling of documents or other physical objects does not violate any other law. Federal criminal law may forbid the destruction of documents or other physical objects in circumstances not covered by the ethical rules set forth in paragraph (a). See, e.g., 18 U.S.C. §1503 (obstruction of justice); 18 U.S.C. §1505 (obstruction of proceedings before departments, agencies, and committees); 18 U.S.C. §1510 (obstruction of criminal investigations). And it is a crime in the District of Columbia for one who knows or has reason to know that an official proceeding has begun or is likely to be instituted to alter, destroy, or conceal a document with intent to impair its integrity or availability for use in the proceeding. D.C. Code §22-723 (1981). Finally, some discovery rules having the force of law may prohibit the destruction of documents and other material even if litigation is not pending or imminent. This Rule does not set forth the scope of a lawyer's responsibilities under all applicable laws. It merely imposes on the lawyer an ethical duty to make reasonable efforts to comply fully with those laws. The provisions of paragraph (a) prohibit a lawyer from obstructing another party's access to evidence, and from altering, destroying, or concealing evidence. These prohibitions may overlap with criminal obstruction provisions and civil discovery rules, but they apply whether or not the prohibited conduct violates criminal provisions or court rules. Thus, the alteration of evidence by a lawyer, whether or not such conduct violates criminal law or court rules, constitutes a violation of paragraph (a).

[5] Because of the duty of confidentiality under Rule 1.6, the lawyer is generally forbidden to volunteer information about physical evidence received from a client without the client's consent after consultation. In some cases, the Office of Bar Counsel will accept physical evidence from a lawyer and then turn it over to the appropriate persons; in those cases this procedure is usually the best means of delivering evidence to the proper authorities without disclosing the client's confidences. However, Bar Counsel may refuse to accept evidence; thus lawyers should keep the following in mind before accepting evidence from a client, and should discuss with Bar Counsel's office the procedures that may be employed in particular circumstances.

[6] First, if the evidence received from the client is subpoenaed or otherwise requested through the discovery process while held by the lawyer, the lawyer will be obligated to deliver the evidence directly to the appropriate persons, unless there is a basis for objecting to the discovery request or moving to quash the subpoena. A lawyer should therefore ad-

vise the client of the risk that evidence may be subject to subpoena or discovery, and of the lawyer's duty to turn the evidence over in that event, before accepting it from the client.

[7] Second, if the lawyer has received physical evidence belonging to the client, for purposes of examination or testing, the lawyer may later return the property to the client pursuant to Rule 1.15, provided that the evidence has not been subpoenaed. The lawyer may not be justified in returning to a client physical evidence the possession of which by the client would be per se illegal, such as certain drugs and weapons. And if it is reasonably apparent that the evidence is not the client's property, the lawyer may not retain the evidence or return it to the client. Instead, the lawyer must, under paragraph (a), make a good-faith effort to return the evidence to its owner.

[8] With regard to paragraph (b), it is not improper to pay a witness's expenses or to compensate a witness for loss of time in preparing to testify, in attending, or in testifying. A fee for the services of a witness who will be proffered as an expert may be made contingent on the outcome of the litigation, provided, however, that the fee, while conditioned on recovery, shall not be a percentage of the recovery.

[9] Paragraph (f) permits a lawyer to advise employees of a client to refrain from giving information to another party, for the employees may identify their interests with those of the client. See also Rule 4.2.

Rule 3.5. Impartiality and Decorum of the Tribunal

A lawyer shall not:

(a) Seek to influence a judge, juror, prospective juror, or other official by means prohibited by law;

(b) Communicate ex parte with such a person except as permitted by law; or

(c) Engage in conduct intended to disrupt a tribunal.

COMMENT

[1] Many forms of improper influence upon a tribunal are proscribed by criminal law. Others are specified in the ABA Model Code of Judicial Conduct, with which an advocate should be familiar. A lawyer is required to avoid contributing to a violation of such provisions.

[2] The advocate's function is to present evidence and argument so that the cause may be decided according to law. Refraining from abusive or obstreperous conduct is a corollary of the advocate's right to speak on behalf of litigants. A lawyer may stand firm against abuse by a judge but should avoid reciprocation; the judge's default is not justification for similar dereliction by an advocate. An advocate can present the cause, protect the record for subsequent review, and preserve professional integrity by patient firmness no less effectively than by belligerence or theatrics.

Rule 3.6. Trial Publicity

A lawyer engaged in a case being tried to a judge or jury shall not make an extrajudicial statement that a reasonable person would expect to be disseminated by means of mass public communication if the lawyer knows or reasonably should know that the statement will create a serious and imminent threat to the impartiality of the judge or jury.

COMMENT

[1] It is difficult to strike a proper balance between protecting the right to a fair trial and safeguarding the right of free expression, which are both guaranteed by the Constitution. On one hand, publicity should not be allowed to influence the fair administration of justice. On the other hand, litigants have a right to present their side of a dispute to the public, and the public has an interest in receiving information about matters that are in litigation. Often a lawyer involved in the litigation is in the best position to assist in furthering these legitimate objectives. No body of rules can simultaneously satisfy all interests of fair trial and all those of free expression.

[2] The special obligations of prosecutors to limit comment on criminal matters involve considerations in addition to those implicated in this Rule, and are dealt with in Rule 3.8. Furthermore, this Rule is not intended to abrogate special court rules of confidentiality in juvenile or other cases. Lawyers are bound by Rule 3.4(c) to adhere to any such rules that have not been found invalid.

[3] Because administrative agencies should have the prerogative to determine the ethical rules for prehearing publicity, this Rule does not purport to apply to matters before administrative agencies.

Rule 3.7. Lawyer as Witness

(a) A lawyer shall not act as advocate at a trial in which the lawyer is likely to be a necessary witness except where:

　　(1) The testimony relates to an uncontested issue;

　　(2) The testimony relates to the nature and value of legal services rendered in the case; or

　　(3) Disqualification of the lawyer would work substantial hardship on the client.

(b) A lawyer may not act as advocate in a trial in which another lawyer in the lawyer's firm is likely to be called as a witness if the other lawyer would be precluded from acting as advocate in the trial by Rule 1.7 or Rule 1.9. The provisions of this paragraph (b) do not apply if the lawyer who is appearing as an advocate is employed by, and appears on behalf of, a government agency.

COMMENT

[1] Combining the roles of advocate and witness can prejudice the opposing party and can involve a conflict of interest between the lawyer and client.

[2] The opposing party has proper objection where the combination of roles may prejudice that party's rights in the litigation. A witness is required to testify on the basis of personal knowledge, while an advocate is expected to explain and comment on evidence given by others. It may not be clear whether a statement by an advocate-witness should be taken as proof or as an analysis of the proof.

[3] Subparagraph (a)(1) recognizes that if the testimony will be uncontested, the ambiguities in the dual role are purely theoretical. Subparagraph (a)(2) recognizes that where the testimony concerns the extent and value of legal services rendered in the action in which the testimony is offered, permitting the lawyers to testify avoids the need for a second trial with new counsel to resolve that issue. Moreover, in such a situation the judge has firsthand knowledge of the matter in issue; hence, there is less dependence on the adversary process to test the credibility of the testimony.

[4] Apart from these two exceptions, subparagraph (a)(3) recognizes that a balancing is required between the interests of the client and those of the opposing party. Whether the opposing party is likely to suffer prejudice depends on the nature of the case, the importance and prob-

able tenor of the lawyer's testimony, and the probability that the lawyer's testimony will conflict with that of other witnesses. Even if there is risk of such prejudice, in determining whether the lawyer should be disqualified due regard must be given to the effect of disqualification on the lawyer's client. It is relevant that one or both parties could reasonably foresee that the lawyer would probably be a witness.

[5] If the only reason for not permitting a lawyer to combine the roles of advocate and witness is possible prejudice to the opposing party, there is no reason to disqualify other lawyers in the testifying lawyer's firm from acting as advocates in that trial. In short, there is no general rule of imputed disqualification applicable to Rule 3.7. However, the combination of roles of advocate and witness may involve an improper conflict of interest between the lawyer and the client in addition to or apart from possible prejudice to the opposing party. Whether there is such a client conflict is determined by Rule 1.7 or 1.9. For example, if there is likely to be a significant conflict between the testimony of the client and that of the lawyer, the representation is improper by the standard of Rule 1.7(b) without regard to Rule 3.7(a). The problem can arise whether the lawyer is called as a witness on behalf of the client or is called by the opposing party. Determining whether such a conflict exists is, in the first instance, the responsibility of the lawyer involved. See Comment to Rule 1.7. Rule 3.7(b) states that other lawyers in the testifying lawyer's firm are disqualified only when there is such a client conflict and the testifying lawyer therefore could not represent the client under Rule 1.7 or 1.9. The principles of client consent, embodied in Rules 1.7 and 1.9, also apply to paragraph (b). Thus, the reference to Rules 1.7 and 1.9 incorporates the client consent aspects of those Rules. Paragraph (b) is designed to provide protection for the client, not rights of disqualification to the adversary. Subject to the disclosure and consultation requirements of Rules 1.7 and 1.9, the client may consent to the firm's continuing representation, despite the potential problems created by the nature of the testimony to be provided by a lawyer in the firm.

[6] Even though a lawyer's testimony does not involve a conflict with the client's interests under Rule 1.7 or 1.9 and would not be precluded under Rule 3.7, the client's interests might nevertheless be harmed by the appearance as a witness of a lawyer in the firm that represents the client. For example, the lawyer's testimony would be vulnerable to impeachment on the grounds that the lawyer-witness is testifying to support the position of the lawyer's own firm. Similarly, a lawyer whose firm colleague is testifying in the case should recognize the possibility that the lawyer might not scrutinize the testimony of the col-

league carefully enough and that this could prejudice the client's interests, whether the colleague is testifying for or against the client. In such instances, the lawyer should inform the client of any possible adverse effects on the client's interests which might result from the lawyer's relationship with the colleague-witness, so that the client may make a meaningful choice whether to retain the lawyer for the representation in question.

Rule 3.8. Special Responsibilities of a Prosecutor

The prosecutor in a criminal case shall not:

(a) In exercising discretion to investigate or to prosecute, improperly favor or invidiously discriminate against any person;

(b) File in court or maintain a charge that the prosecutor knows is not supported by probable cause;

(c) Prosecute to trial a charge that the prosecutor knows is not supported by evidence sufficient to establish a prima facie showing of guilt;

(d) Intentionally avoid pursuit of evidence or information because it may damage the prosecution's case or aid the defense;

(e) Intentionally fail to disclose to the defense, upon request and at a time when use by the defense is reasonably feasible, any evidence or information that the prosecutor knows or reasonably should know tends to negate the guilt of the accused or to mitigate the offense, or, in connection with sentencing, intentionally fail to disclose to the defense upon request any unprivileged mitigating information known to the prosecutor and not reasonably available to the defense, except when the prosecutor is relieved of this responsibility by a protective order of the tribunal;

(f) Except for statements which are necessary to inform the public of the nature and extent of the prosecutor's action and which serve a legitimate law enforcement purpose, make extrajudicial comments which serve to heighten condemnation of the accused;

(g) In presenting a case to a grand jury, intentionally interfere with the independence of the grand jury, preempt a function of the grand jury, abuse the processes of the grand jury, or fail to bring to the attention of the grand jury material facts tending substantially to negate the existence of probable cause; or

(h) Peremptorily strike jurors on grounds of race, religion, national or ethnic background, or sex.

COMMENT

[1] A prosecutor has the responsibility of a minister of justice and not simply that of an advocate. This responsibility carries with it specific obligations to see that the defendant is accorded procedural justice and that guilt is decided upon the basis of sufficient evidence. Precisely how far the prosecutor is required to go in this direction is a matter of debate and varies in different jurisdictions. Many jurisdictions have adopted the ABA Standards of Criminal Justice Relating to Prosecution Function, which in turn are the product of prolonged and careful deliberation by lawyers experienced in both criminal prosecution and defense. This Rule is intended to be a distillation of some, but not all, of the professional obligations imposed on prosecutors by applicable law. The Rule, however, is not intended either to restrict or to expand the obligations of prosecutors derived from the United States Constitution, federal or District of Columbia statutes, and court rules of procedure.

[2] Apart from the special responsibilities of a prosecutor under this Rule, prosecutors are subject to the same obligations imposed upon all lawyers by these Rules of Professional Conduct, including Rule 5.3, relating to responsibilities regarding nonlawyers who work for or in association with the lawyer's office. Indeed, because of the power and visibility of a prosecutor, the prosecutor's compliance with these Rules, and recognition of the need to refrain even from some actions technically allowed to other lawyers under the Rules, may, in certain instances, be of special importance. For example, Rule 3.6 prohibits extrajudicial statements that will have a substantial likelihood of destroying the impartiality of the judge or jury. In the context of a criminal prosecution, pretrial publicity can present the further problem of giving the public the incorrect impression that the accused is guilty before having been proven guilty through the due process of the law. It is unavoidable, of course, that the publication of an indictment may itself have severe consequences for an accused. What is avoidable, however, is extrajudicial comment by a prosecutor that serves unnecessarily to heighten public condemnation of the accused without a legitimate law enforcement purpose before the criminal process has taken its course. When that occurs, even if the ultimate trial is not prejudiced, the accused may be subjected to unfair and unnecessary condemnation before the trial takes place. Accordingly, a prosecutor should use special care to avoid publicity, such as through televised press conferences, which would unnecessarily heighten condemnation of the accused.

[3] Nothing in this Comment, however, is intended to suggest that a prosecutor may not inform the public of such matters as whether an

official investigation has ended or is continuing, or who participated in it, and the prosecutor may respond to press inquiries to clarify such things as technicalities of the indictment, the status of the matter, or the legal procedures that will follow. Also, a prosecutor should be free to respond, insofar as necessary, to any extrajudicial allegations by the defense of unprofessional or unlawful conduct on the part of the prosecutor's office.

Rule 3.9. Advocate in Nonadjudicative Proceedings

A lawyer representing a client before a legislative or administrative body in a nonadjudicative proceeding shall disclose that the appearance is in a representative capacity and shall conform to the provisions of Rules 3.3, 3.4(a) through (c), and 3.5.

COMMENT

[1] In representation before bodies such as legislatures, municipal councils, and executive and administrative agencies acting in a rule-making or policy-making capacity, lawyers present facts, formulate issues, and advance argument in the matters under consideration. The decision-making body, like a court, should be able to rely on the integrity of the submissions made to it. A lawyer appearing before such a body should deal with it honestly and in conformity with applicable rules of procedure.

[2] Lawyers have no exclusive right to appear before nonadjudicative bodies, as they do before a court. The requirements of this Rule therefore may subject lawyers to regulations inapplicable to advocates, such as nonlawyer lobbyists, who are not lawyers. However, legislatures and administrative agencies have a right to expect lawyers to deal with them as they deal with courts.

[3] This Rule does not apply to representation of a client in a negotiation or other bilateral transaction with a government agency; representation in such a transaction is governed by Rules 4.1 through 4.4.

[4] This Rule is closely related to Rules 3.3 through 3.5, which deal with conduct regarding tribunals. The term "tribunal," as defined in the Terminology section of these Rules, refers to adjudicative or quasi-adjudicative bodies.

TRANSACTIONS WITH PERSONS OTHER THAN CLIENTS

Rule 4.1. Truthfulness in Statements to Others

In the course of representing a client, a lawyer shall not knowingly:
(a) Make a false statement of material fact or law to a third person; or
(b) Fail to disclose a material fact to a third person when disclosure is necessary to avoid assisting a criminal or fraudulent act by a client, unless disclosure is prohibited by Rule 1.6.

COMMENT

Misrepresentation

[1] A lawyer is required to be truthful when dealing with others on a client's behalf, but generally has no affirmative duty to inform an opposing party of relevant facts. A misrepresentation can occur if the lawyer incorporates or affirms a statement of another person that the lawyer knows is false. Misrepresentations can also occur by failure to act. The term "third person" as used in paragraphs (a) and (b) refers to any person or entity other than the lawyer's client.

Statements of Fact

[2] This Rule refers to material statements of fact. Whether a particular statement should be regarded as material, and as one of fact, can depend on the circumstances. Under generally accepted conventions in negotiation, certain types of statements ordinarily are not taken as statements of material fact. Estimates of price or value placed on the subject of a transaction and a party's intentions as to an acceptable settlement of a claim are in this category, and so is the existence of an undisclosed principal except where nondisclosure of the principal would constitute fraud. There may be other analogous situations.

Fraud by Client

[3] Paragraph (b) recognizes that substantive law may require a lawyer to disclose certain information to avoid being deemed to have as-

sisted the client's crime or fraud. The requirement of disclosure created by this paragraph is, however, subject to the obligations created by Rule 1.6.

Rule 4.2. Communication Between Lawyer and Opposing Parties

(a) During the course of representing a client, a lawyer shall not communicate or cause another to communicate about the subject of the representation with a party known to be represented by another lawyer in the matter, unless the lawyer has the prior consent of the lawyer representing such other party or is authorized by law to do so.

(b) During the course of representing a client, a lawyer may communicate about the subject of the representation with a nonparty employee of the opposing party without obtaining the consent of that party's lawyer. However, prior to communicating with any such nonparty employee, a lawyer must disclose to such employee both the lawyer's identity and the fact that the lawyer represents a party with a claim against the employee's employer.

(c) For purposes of this Rule, the term "party" includes any person, including an employee of a party organization, who has the authority to bind a party organization as to the representation to which the communication relates.

(d) This Rule does not prohibit communication by a lawyer with government officials who have the authority to redress the grievances of the lawyer's client, whether or not those grievances or the lawyer's communications relate to matters that are the subject of the representation, provided that in the event of such communications the disclosures specified in (b) are made to the government official to whom the communication is made.

COMMENT

[1] This Rule does not prohibit communication with a party, or an employee or agent of a party, concerning matters outside the representation. For example, the existence of a controversy between two organizations does not prohibit a lawyer for either from communicating with nonlawyer representatives of the other regarding a separate matter. Also, parties to a matter may communicate directly with each other and a law-

yer having independent justification for communicating with the other party is permitted to do so.

[2] In the case of an organization, this Rule prohibits communication by a lawyer for one party concerning the matter in representation with persons having the power to bind the organization as to the particular representation to which the communication relates. If an agent or employee of the organization with authority to make binding decisions regarding the representation is represented in the matter by separate counsel, the consent by that agent's or employee's counsel to a communication will be sufficient for purposes of this Rule.

[3] The Rule does not prohibit a lawyer from communicating with employees of an organization who have the authority to bind the organization with respect to the matters underlying the representation if they do not also have authority to make binding decisions regarding the representation itself. A lawyer may therefore communicate with such persons without first notifying the organization's lawyer. See D.C. Bar Legal Ethics Committee Opinion No. 129 (1983). But before communicating with such a "nonparty employee," the lawyer must disclose to the employee the lawyer's identity and the fact that the lawyer represents a party with a claim against the employer. It is preferable that this disclosure be made in writing. The notification requirements of Rule 4.2(b) apply to contacts with government employees who do not have the authority to make binding decisions regarding the representation.

[4] This Rule also covers any person, whether or not a party to a formal proceeding, who is represented by counsel concerning the matter in question.

[5] This Rule does not apply to the situation in which a lawyer contacts employees of an organization for the purpose of obtaining information generally available to the public, or obtainable under the Freedom of Information Act, even if the information in question is related to the representation. For example, a lawyer for a plaintiff who has filed suit against an organization represented by a lawyer may telephone the organization to request a copy of a press release regarding the representation, without disclosing the lawyer's identity, obtaining the consent of the organization's lawyer, or otherwise acting as paragraphs (a) and (b) of this Rule require.

[6] Paragraph (d) recognizes that special considerations come into play when a lawyer is seeking to redress grievances involving the government. It permits communications with those in government having the authority to redress such grievances (but not with any other government personnel) without the prior consent of the lawyer representing the government in such cases. However, a lawyer making such a communication

without the prior consent of the lawyer representing the government must make the kinds of disclosures that are required by paragraph (b) in the case of communications with nonparty employees.

[7] Paragraph (d) does not permit a lawyer to bypass counsel representing the government on every issue that may arise in the course of disputes with the government. It is intended to provide lawyers access to decision makers in government with respect to genuine grievances, such as to present the view that the government's basic policy position with respect to a dispute is faulty, or that government personnel are conducting themselves improperly with respect to aspects of the dispute. It is not intended to provide direct access on routine disputes such as ordinary discovery disputes, extensions of time or other scheduling matters, or similar routine aspects of the resolution of disputes.

[8] This Rule is not intended to enlarge or restrict the law enforcement activities of the United States or the District of Columbia which are authorized and permissible under the Constitution and law of the United States or the District of Columbia. The "authorized by law" proviso to Rule 4.2(a) is intended to permit government conduct that is valid under this law. The proviso is not intended to freeze any particular substantive law, but is meant to accommodate substantive law as it may develop over time.

Rule 4.3. Dealing with Unrepresented Person

In dealing on behalf of a client with a person who is not represented by counsel, a lawyer shall not:

(a) Give advice to the unrepresented person other than the advice to secure counsel, if the interests of such person are or have a reasonable possibility of being in conflict with the interests of the lawyer's client;

(b) State or imply to unrepresented persons whose interests are not in conflict with the interests of the lawyer's client that the lawyer is disinterested. When the lawyer knows or reasonably should know that the unrepresented person misunderstands the lawyer's role in the matter, the lawyer shall make reasonable efforts to correct the misunderstanding.

COMMENT

[1] An unrepresented person, particularly one not experienced in dealing with legal matters, might assume that a lawyer will provide disin-

terested advice concerning the law even when the lawyer represents a client. In dealing personally with any unrepresented third party on behalf of the lawyer's client, a lawyer must take great care not to exploit these assumptions.

[2] The Rule distinguishes between situations involving unrepresented third parties whose interests may be adverse to those of the lawyer's client and those in which the third party's interests are not in conflict with the client's. In the former situation, the possibility of the lawyer's compromising the unrepresented person's interests is so great that the Rule prohibits the giving of any advice, apart from the advice that the unrepresented person obtain counsel. A lawyer is free to give advice to unrepresented persons whose interests are not in conflict with those of the lawyer's client, but only if it is made clear that the lawyer is acting in the interests of the client. Thus the lawyer should not represent to such persons, either expressly or implicitly, that the lawyer is disinterested. Furthermore, if it becomes apparent that the unrepresented person misunderstands the lawyer's role in the matter, the lawyer must take whatever reasonable, affirmative steps are necessary to correct the misunderstanding.

[3] This Rule is not intended to restrict in any way law enforcement efforts by government lawyers that are consistent with constitutional requirements and applicable federal law.

Rule 4.4. Respect for Rights of Third Persons

In representing a client, a lawyer shall not use means that have no substantial purpose other than to embarrass, delay, or burden a third person, or use methods of obtaining evidence that violate the legal rights of such a person.

COMMENT

[1] Responsibility to a client requires a lawyer to subordinate the interests of others to those of the client, but that responsibility does not imply that a lawyer may disregard the rights of third persons. It is impractical to catalogue all such rights, but they include legal restrictions on methods of obtaining evidence from third persons.

LAW FIRMS AND ASSOCIATIONS

Rule 5.1. Responsibilities of a Partner or Supervisory Lawyer

(a) A partner in a law firm shall make reasonable efforts to ensure that the firm has in effect measures giving reasonable assurance that all lawyers in the firm conform to the Rules of Professional Conduct.

(b) A lawyer having direct supervisory authority over another lawyer shall make reasonable efforts to ensure that the other lawyer conforms to the Rules of Professional Conduct.

(c) A lawyer shall be responsible for another lawyer's violation of the Rules of Professional Conduct if:

(1) The lawyer orders or, with knowledge of the specific conduct, ratifies the conduct involved; or

(2) The lawyer has direct supervisory authority over the other lawyer or is a partner in the law firm in which the other lawyer practices, and knows or reasonably should know of the conduct at a time when its consequences can be avoided or mitigated but fails to take reasonable remedial action.

COMMENT

[1] Paragraphs (a) and (b) refer to lawyers who have supervisory authority over the professional work of a firm or legal department of a government agency. This includes members of a partnership and the shareholders in a law firm organized as a professional corporation; lawyers having supervisory authority in the law department of an enterprise or government agency; and lawyers who have intermediate managerial responsibilities in a firm.

[2] The measures required to fulfill the responsibility prescribed in paragraphs (a) and (b) can depend on the firm's structure and the nature of its practice. In a small firm, informal supervision and occasional admonition ordinarily might be sufficient. In a large firm, or in practice situations in which intensely difficult ethical problems frequently arise, more elaborate procedures may be necessary. Some firms, for example, have a procedure whereby junior lawyers can make confidential referral of ethical problems directly to a designated senior partner or special committee. See Rule 5.2. Firms, whether large or small, may also rely on continuing legal education in professional ethics. In any event, the ethical atmosphere of a firm can influence the conduct

of all its members and a lawyer having authority over the work of another may not assume that the subordinate lawyer will inevitably conform to the Rules.

[3] Paragraph (c) sets forth general principles of imputed responsibility for the misconduct of others. Subparagraph (c)(1) makes any lawyer who orders or, with knowledge, ratifies misconduct responsible for that misconduct. See also Rule 8.4(a). Subparagraph (c)(2) extends that responsibility to any lawyer who is a partner in the firm in which the misconduct takes place, or who has direct supervisory authority over the lawyer who engages in misconduct, when the lawyer knows or should reasonably know of the conduct and could intervene to ameliorate its consequences. Whether a lawyer has such supervisory authority in particular circumstances is a question of fact. A lawyer with direct supervisory authority is a lawyer who has an actual supervisory role with respect to directing the conduct of other lawyers in a particular representation. A lawyer who is technically a "supervisor" in organizational terms, but is not involved in directing the effort of other lawyers in a particular representation, is not a supervising lawyer with respect to that representation.

[4] The existence of actual knowledge is also a question of fact; whether a lawyer should reasonably have known of misconduct by another lawyer in the same firm is an objective standard based on evaluation of all the facts, including the size and organizational structure of the firm, the lawyer's position and responsibilities within the firm, the type and frequency of contacts between the various lawyers involved, the nature of the misconduct at issue, and the nature of the supervision or other direct responsibility (if any) actually exercised. The mere fact of partnership or a position as a principal in a firm is not sufficient, without more, to satisfy this standard. Similarly, the fact that a lawyer holds a position on the management committee of a firm, or heads a department of the firm, is not sufficient, standing alone, to satisfy this standard.

[5] Appropriate remedial action would depend on the immediacy of the involvement and the seriousness of the misconduct. The supervisor is required to intervene to prevent avoidable consequences of misconduct if the supervisor knows that the misconduct occurred. Thus, if a supervising lawyer knows that a subordinate misrepresented a matter to an opposing party in a negotiation, the supervisor as well as the subordinate has a duty to correct the resulting misapprehension.

[6] Professional misconduct by a lawyer under supervision could reveal a violation of paragraph (b) on the part of the supervisory lawyer even though it does not entail a violation of paragraph (c) because there was no direction, ratification, or knowledge of the violation.

[7] Apart from this Rule and Rule 8.4(a), a lawyer does not have disciplinary liability for the conduct of a partner, associate, or subordinate. Whether a lawyer may be liable civilly or criminally for another lawyer's conduct is a question of law beyond the scope of these Rules.

Rule 5.2. Responsibilities of a Subordinate Lawyer

(a) A lawyer is bound by the Rules of Professional Conduct notwithstanding that the lawyer acted at the direction of another person.

(b) A subordinate lawyer does not violate the Rules of Professional Conduct if that lawyer acts in accordance with a supervisory lawyer's reasonable resolution of an arguable question of professional duty.

COMMENT

[1] Although a lawyer is not relieved of responsibility for a violation by the fact that the lawyer acted at the direction of a supervisor, that fact may be relevant in determining whether a lawyer had the knowledge required to render conduct a violation of the Rules. For example, if a subordinate filed a frivolous pleading at the direction of a supervisor, the subordinate would not be guilty of a professional violation unless the subordinate knew of the document's frivolous character.

[2] When lawyers in a supervisor-subordinate relationship encounter a matter involving professional judgment as to ethical duty, the supervisor may assume responsibility for making the judgment. Otherwise a consistent course of action or position could not be taken. If the question can reasonably be answered only one way, the duty of both lawyers is clear and they are equally responsible for fulfilling it. However, if the question is reasonably arguable, someone has to decide upon the course of action. That authority ordinarily reposes in the supervisor, and a subordinate may be guided accordingly. For example, if a question arises whether the interests of two clients conflict under Rule 1.7, the supervisor's reasonable resolution of the question should protect the subordinate professionally if the resolution is subsequently challenged.

Rule 5.3. Responsibilities Regarding Nonlaywer Assistants

With respect to a nonlawyer employed or retained by or associated with a lawyer:

(a) A partner in a law firm shall make reasonable efforts to ensure that the firm has in effect measures giving reasonable assurance that the person's conduct is compatible with the professional obligations of the lawyer;

(b) A lawyer having direct supervisory authority over the nonlawyer shall make reasonable efforts to ensure that the person's conduct is compatible with the professional obligations of the lawyer; and

(c) A lawyer shall be responsible for conduct of such a person that would be a violation of the Rules of Professional Conduct if engaged in by a lawyer if:

(1) The lawyer requests or, with the knowledge of the specific conduct, ratifies the conduct involved; or

(2) The lawyer has direct supervisory authority over the person, or is a partner in the law firm in which the person is employed, and knows of the conduct at a time when its consequences can be avoided or mitigated but fails to take reasonable remedial action.

COMMENT

[1] Lawyers generally employ assistants in their practice, including secretaries, investigators, law student interns, and paraprofessionals. Such assistants, whether employees or independent contractors, act for the lawyer in rendition of the lawyer's professional services. A lawyer should give such assistants appropriate instruction and supervision concerning the ethical aspects of their employment, particularly regarding the obligation not to disclose information relating to representation of the client, and should be responsible for their work product. The measures employed in supervising nonlawyers should take account of the fact that they do not have legal training and are not subject to professional discipline.

[2] Just as lawyers in private practice may direct the conduct of investigators who may be independent contractors, prosecutors and other government lawyers may effectively direct the conduct of police or other governmental investigative personnel, even though they may not have, strictly speaking, formal authority to order actions by such personnel, who report to the chief of police or the head of another enforcement agency. Such prosecutors or other government lawyers have a responsibility with respect to police or investigative personnel, whose conduct they effectively direct, equivalent to that of private lawyers with respect to investigators whom they retain. See also Comments [3], [4], and [5] to Rule 5.1, in particular, the concept of what constitutes direct supervisory authority,

and the significance of holding certain positions in a firm. Comments [3], [4], and [5] of Rule 5.1 apply as well to Rule 5.3.

Rule 5.4. Professional Independence of a Lawyer

(a) A lawyer or law firm shall not share legal fees with a nonlawyer, except that:

(1) An agreement by a lawyer with the lawyer's firm, partner, or associate may provide for the payment of money, over a reasonable period of time after the lawyer's death, to the lawyer's estate or to one or more specified persons;

(2) A lawyer who undertakes to complete unfinished legal business of a deceased lawyer may pay to the estate of the deceased lawyer that proportion of the total compensation which fairly represents the services rendered by the deceased lawyer;

(3) A lawyer or law firm may include nonlawyer employees in a compensation or retirement plan, even though the plan is based in whole or in part on a profit-sharing arrangement; and

(4) Sharing of fees is permitted in a partnership or other form of organization which meets the requirements of paragraph (b).

(b) A lawyer may practice law in a partnership or other form of organization in which a financial interest is held or managerial authority is exercised by an individual nonlawyer who performs professional services which assist the organization in providing legal services to clients, but only if:

(1) The partnership or organization has as its sole purpose providing legal services to clients;

(2) All persons having such managerial authority or holding a financial interest undertake to abide by these Rules of Professional Conduct;

(3) The lawyers who have a financial interest or managerial authority in the partnership or organization undertake to be responsible for the nonlawyer participants to the same extent as if nonlawyer participants were lawyers under Rule 5.1;

(4) The foregoing conditions are set forth in writing.

(c) A lawyer shall not permit a person who recommends, employs, or pays the lawyer to render legal services for another to direct or regulate the lawyer's professional judgment in rendering such legal services.

COMMENT

[1] The provisions of this Rule express traditional limitations on sharing fees with nonlawyers. (On sharing fees among lawyers not in the same firm, see Rule 1.5(e).) These limitations are to protect the lawyer's professional independence of judgment. Where someone other than the client pays the lawyer's fee or salary, or recommends employment of the lawyer, that arrangement does not modify the lawyer's obligation to the client. As stated in paragraph (c), such arrangements should not interfere with the lawyer's professional judgment.

[2] Traditionally, the canons of legal ethics and disciplinary rules prohibited lawyers from practicing law in a partnership that includes nonlawyers or in any other organization where a nonlawyer is a shareholder, director, or officer. Notwithstanding these strictures, the profession implicitly recognized exceptions for lawyers who work for corporate law departments, insurance companies, and legal service organizations.

[3] As the demand increased for a broad range of professional services from a single source, lawyers employed professionals from other disciplines to work for them. So long as the nonlawyers remained employees of the lawyers, these relationships did not violate the disciplinary rules. However, when lawyers and nonlawyers considered forming partnerships and professional corporations to provide a combination of legal and other services to the public, they faced serious obstacles under the former rules.

[4] This Rule rejects an absolute prohibition against lawyers and nonlawyers joining together to provide collaborative services, but continues to impose traditional ethical requirements with respect to the organization thus created. Thus, a lawyer may practice law in an organization where nonlawyers hold a financial interest or exercise managerial authority, but only if the conditions set forth in subparagraphs (b)(1), (b)(2), and (b)(3) are satisfied, and pursuant to subparagraph (b)(4), satisfaction of these conditions is set forth in a written instrument. The requirement of a writing helps ensure that these important conditions are not overlooked in establishing the organizational structure of entities in which nonlawyers enjoy an ownership or managerial role equivalent to that of a partner in a traditional law firm.

[5] Nonlawyer participants under Rule 5.4 ought not be confused with nonlawyer assistants under Rule 5.3. Nonlawyer participants are persons having managerial authority or financial interests in organizations that provide legal services. Within such organizations, lawyers with finan-

cial interests or managerial authority are held responsible for ethical misconduct by nonlawyer participants about which the lawyers know or reasonably should know. This is the same standard of liability contemplated by Rule 5.1, regarding the responsibilities of lawyers with direct supervisory authority over other lawyers.

[6] Nonlawyer assistants under Rule 5.3 do not have managerial authority or financial interests in the organization. Lawyers having direct supervisory authority over nonlawyer assistants are held responsible only for ethical misconduct by assistants about which the lawyers actually know.

[7] As the introductory portion of paragraph (b) makes clear, the purpose of liberalizing the rules regarding the possession of a financial interest or the exercise of management authority by a nonlawyer is to permit nonlawyer professionals to work with lawyers in the delivery of legal services without being relegated to the role of an employee. For example, the Rule permits economists to work in a firm with antitrust or public utility practitioners, psychologists or psychiatric social workers to work with family law practitioners to assist in counseling clients, nonlawyer lobbyists to work with lawyers who perform legislative services, certified public accountants to work in conjunction with tax lawyers or others who use accountants' services in performing legal services, and professional managers to serve as office managers, executive directors, or in similar positions. In all of these situations, the professionals may be given financial interests or managerial responsibility, so long as all of the requirements of paragraph (c) are met.

[8] Paragraph (b) does not permit an individual or entity to acquire all or any part of the ownership of a law partnership or other form of law practice organization for investment or other purposes. It thus does not permit a corporation, an investment banking firm, an investor, or any other person or entity to entitle itself to all or any portion of the income or profits of a law firm or other similar organization. Since such an investor would not be an individual performing professional services within the law firm or other organization, the requirements of paragraph (b) would not be met.

[9] The term "individual" in subparagraph (b) is not intended to preclude the participation in a law firm or other organization by an individual professional corporation in the same manner as lawyers who have incorporated as a professional corporation currently participate in partnerships that include professional corporations.

[10] Some sharing of fees is likely to occur in the kinds of organizations permitted by paragraph (b). Subparagraph (a)(4) makes it clear that such fee sharing is not prohibited.

Rule 5.5. Unauthorized Practice of Law

A lawyer shall not:

(a) Practice law in a jurisdiction where doing so violates the regulation of the legal profession in that jurisdiction; or

(b) Assist a person who is not a member of the bar in the performance of activity that constitutes the unauthorized practice of law.

COMMENT

[1] The definition of the practice of law is established by law and varies from one jurisdiction to another. Whatever the definition, limiting the practice of law to members of the bar protects the public against rendition of legal services by unqualified persons. Paragraph (b) does not prohibit a lawyer from employing the services of paraprofessionals and delegating functions to them, so long as the lawyer supervises the delegated work and retains responsibility for their work. See Rule 5.3. Likewise, it does not prohibit lawyers from providing professional advice and instruction to nonlawyers whose employment requires knowledge of law; for example, claims adjusters, employees of financial or commercial institutions, social workers, accountants and persons employed in government agencies. In addition, a lawyer may counsel nonlawyers who wish to proceed pro se.

Rule 5.6. Restrictions on Right to Practice

A lawyer shall not participate in offering or making:

(a) A partnership or employment agreement that restricts the rights of a lawyer to practice after termination of the relationship, except an agreement concerning benefits upon retirement; or

(b) An agreement in which a restriction on the lawyer's right to practice is part of the settlement of a controversy between parties.

COMMENT

[1] An agreement restricting the right of partners or associates to practice after leaving a firm not only limits their professional autonomy but also limits the freedom of clients to choose a lawyer. Paragraph (a)

prohibits such agreements except for restrictions incident to provisions concerning retirement benefits for service with the firm.

[2] Paragraph (b) prohibits a lawyer from agreeing not to represent other persons in connection with settling a claim on behalf of a client.

PUBLIC SERVICE

Rule 6.1. Pro Bono Publico Service

A lawyer should participate in serving those persons, or groups of persons, who are unable to pay all or a portion of reasonable attorneys' fees or who are otherwise unable to obtain counsel. A lawyer may discharge this responsibility by providing professional services at no fee, or at a substantially reduced fee, to persons and groups who are unable to afford or obtain counsel, or by active participation in the work of organizations that provide legal services to them. When personal representation is not feasible, a lawyer may discharge this responsibility by providing financial support for organizations that provide legal representation to those unable to obtain counsel.

COMMENT

[1] This Rule reflects the long-standing ethical principle underlying Canon 2 of the previous Code of Professional Responsibility that "A lawyer should assist the legal profession in fulfilling its duty to make legal counsel available." The Rule incorporates the legal profession's historical commitment to the principle that all persons in our society should be able to obtain necessary legal services. The Rule also recognizes that the rights and responsibilities of individuals and groups in the United States are increasingly defined in legal terms and that, as a consequence, legal assistance in coping with the web of statutes, rules, and regulations is imperative for persons of modest and limited means, as well as for the relatively well-to-do. The Rule also recognizes that a lawyer's pro bono services are sometimes needed to assert or defend public rights belonging to the public generally where no individual or group can afford to pay for the services.

[2] This Rule carries forward the ethical precepts set forth in the Code. Specifically, the Rule recognizes that the basic responsibility for providing legal services for those unable to pay ultimately rests upon the in-

dividual lawyer, and that every lawyer, regardless of professional prominence or professional work load, should find time to participate in or otherwise support the provision of legal services to the disadvantaged. [3] The Rule also acknowledges that while the provision of free legal services to those unable to pay reasonable fees continues to be an obligation of each lawyer as well as the profession generally, the efforts of individual lawyers are often not enough to meet the need. Thus, it has been necessary for the profession and government to institute additional programs to provide legal services. Accordingly, legal aid offices, lawyer referral services, and other related programs have been developed, and others will be developed by the profession and government. Every lawyer should support all proper efforts to meet this need for legal services. A lawyer also should not refuse a request from a court or bar association to undertake representation of a person unable to obtain counsel except for compelling reasons such as those listed in Rule 6.2.

[4] This Rule expresses the profession's traditional commitment to make legal counsel available, but it is not intended that the Rule be enforced through disciplinary process. Neither is it intended to place any obligation on a government lawyer that is inconsistent with laws such as 18 U.S.C. §§203 and 205 limiting the scope of permissible employment or representational activities.

[5] In determining their responsibilities under this Rule, lawyers admitted to practice in the District of Columbia should be guided by the Resolutions on Pro Bono Services passed by the Judicial Conference of the District of Columbia and the D.C. Circuit in 1980 and 1981, respectively. Those resolutions call on members of the D.C. Bar, at a minimum, each year to (1) accept one court appointment, or (2) provide 40 hours of pro bono legal service, or (3) when personal representation is not feasible, contribute the lesser of $200 or 1 percent of earned income to a legal assistance organization which services the community's economically disadvantaged, including pro bono referral and appointment offices sponsored by the Bar and the courts.

Rule 6.2. Accepting Appointments

A lawyer shall not seek to avoid appointment by a tribunal to represent a person except for good cause, such as:

(a) Representing the client is likely to result in violation of the Rules of Professional Conduct or other law;

(b) Representing the client is likely to result in a substantial and unreasonable burden on the lawyer; or

(c) The client or the cause is so repugnant to the lawyer as to be likely to impair the client-lawyer relationship or the lawyer's ability to represent the client.

COMMENT

[1] A lawyer ordinarily is not obliged to accept a client whose character or cause the lawyer regards as repugnant. The lawyer's freedom to select clients is, however, qualified. All lawyers have a responsibility to assist in providing pro bono publico service. See Rule 6.1. An individual lawyer fulfills this responsibility by accepting a fair share of unpopular matters or indigent or unpopular clients. A lawyer may also be subject to appointment by a court to serve unpopular clients or persons unable to afford legal services.

Appointed Counsel

[2] For good cause a lawyer may seek to decline an appointment to represent a person who cannot afford to retain counsel or whose cause is unpopular. Good cause exists if the lawyer could not handle the matter competently, see Rule 1.1, or if undertaking the representation would result in an improper conflict of interest; for example, when the client or the cause is so repugnant to the lawyer as to be likely to impair the client-lawyer relationship or the lawyer's ability to represent the client. A lawyer may also seek to decline an appointment if acceptance would be substantially and unreasonably burdensome, such as when it would impose a financial sacrifice so great as to be unjust.

[3] An appointed lawyer has the same obligations to the client as retained counsel, including the obligations of loyalty and confidentiality, and is subject to the same limitations on the client-lawyer relationship, such as the obligation to refrain from assisting the client in violation of the Rules.

Rule 6.3. Membership in Legal Services Organization

A lawyer may serve as a director, officer, or member of a legal services organization, apart from the law firm in which the lawyer practices, notwithstanding that the organization serves persons having interests ad-

verse to a client of the lawyer. The lawyer shall not knowingly participate in a decision or action of the organization:

(a) If participating in the decision would be incompatible with the lawyer's obligations to a client under Rule 1.7; or

(b) Where the decision could have a material adverse effect on the representation of a client of the organization whose interests are adverse to a client of the lawyer.

COMMENT

[1] Lawyers should be encouraged to support and participate in legal service organizations. A lawyer who is an officer or a member of such an organization does not thereby have a client-lawyer relationship with persons served by the organization. However, there is potential conflict between the interests of such persons and the interests of the lawyer's clients. If the possibility of such conflict disqualified a lawyer from serving on the board of a legal services organization, the profession's involvement in such organizations would be severely curtailed.

[2] It may be necessary in appropriate cases to reassure a client of the organization that the representation will not be affected by conflicting loyalties of a member of the board. Established, written policies in this respect can enhance the credibility of such assurances.

Rule 6.4. Law Reform Activities

(a) A lawyer should assist in improving the administration of justice. A lawyer may discharge this requirement by rendering services in activities for improving the law, the legal system, or the legal profession.

(b) A lawyer may serve as a director, officer, or member of an organization involved in reform of the law or its administration notwithstanding that the reform may affect the interests of a client of the lawyer. When the lawyer knows that the interests of a client may be materially benefited by a decision in which the lawyer participates, the lawyer shall disclose that fact but need not identify the client.

COMMENT

[1] Changes in human affairs and imperfections in human institutions make necessary constant efforts to maintain and improve our legal

system. This system should function in a manner that commands public respect and fosters the use of legal remedies to achieve redress of grievances. By reason of education and experience, lawyers are especially qualified to recognize deficiencies in the legal system and to initiate corrective measures therein. Thus, they should participate in proposing and supporting legislation and programs to improve the system, without regard to the general interests or desires of clients or former clients. Rules of law are deficient if they are not just, understandable, and responsive to the needs of society. If a lawyer believes that the existence or absence of a rule of law, substantive or procedural, causes or contributes to an unjust result, the lawyer should endeavor by lawful means to obtain appropriate changes in the law. This Rule expresses the policy underlying Canon 8 of the previous Code of Professional Responsibility that "A lawyer should assist in improving the legal system," but it is not intended that it be enforced through disciplinary process.

[2] Lawyers involved in organizations seeking law reform generally do not have a client-lawyer relationship with the organization. Otherwise, it might follow that a lawyer could not be involved in a bar association law reform program that might indirectly affect a client. See also Rule 1.2(b). For example, a lawyer specializing in antitrust litigation might be regarded as disqualified from participating in drafting revisions of rules governing that subject. In determining the nature and scope of participation in such activities, a lawyer should be mindful of obligations to clients under other Rules, particularly Rule 1.7. A lawyer is professionally obligated to protect the integrity of the program by making an appropriate disclosure within the organization when the lawyer knows a private client might be materially benefited.

INFORMATION ABOUT LEGAL SERVICES

Rule 7.1. Communications Concerning a Lawyer's Services

(a) A lawyer shall not make a false or misleading communication about the lawyer or the lawyer's services. A communication is false or misleading if it:

(1) Contains a material misrepresentation of fact or law, or omits a fact necessary to make the statement considered as a whole not materially misleading; or

(2) Contains an assertion about the lawyer or the lawyer's services that cannot be substantiated.

(b) A lawyer shall not seek by in-person contact, or through an intermediary, employment (or employment of a partner or associate) by a nonlawyer who has not sought the lawyer's advice regarding employment of a lawyer, if:

(1) The solicitation involves use of a statement or claim that is false or misleading, within the meaning of paragraph (a);

(2) The solicitation involves the use of undue influence;

(3) The potential client is apparently in a physical or mental condition which would make it unlikely that the potential client could exercise reasonable, considered judgment as to the selection of a lawyer;

(4) The solicitation involves use of an intermediary and the lawyer knows or could reasonably ascertain that such conduct violates the intermediary's contractual or other legal obligations; or

(5) The solicitation involves the use of an intermediary and the lawyer has not taken all reasonable steps to ensure that the potential client is informed of (a) the consideration, if any, paid or to be paid by the lawyer to the intermediary, and (b) the effect, if any, of the payment to the intermediary on the total fee to be charged.

(c) A lawyer shall not knowingly assist an organization that furnishes or pays for legal services to others to promote the use of the lawyer's services or those of the lawyer's partner or associate, or any other lawyer affiliated with the lawyer or the lawyer's firm, as a private practitioner, if the promotional activity involves the use of coercion, duress, compulsion, intimidation, threats, or vexatious or harassing conduct.

(d) No lawyer or any person acting on behalf of a lawyer shall solicit or invite or seek to solicit any person for purposes of representing that person for a fee paid by or on behalf of a client or under the Criminal Justice Act, D.C. Code Ann. §11-2601 et seq., in any present or future case in the District of Columbia Courthouse, on the sidewalks on the north, south, and west sides of the Courthouse, or within 50 feet of the building on the east side.

COMMENT

[1] This Rule governs all communications about a lawyer's services, including advertising. It is especially important that statements about a lawyer or the lawyer's services be accurate, since many members of the public lack detailed knowledge of legal matters. Certain adver-

tisements such as those that describe the amount of a damage award, the lawyer's record in obtaining favorable verdicts, or those containing client endorsements, unless suitably qualified, have a capacity to mislead by creating an unjustified expectation that similar results can be obtained for others. Advertisements comparing the lawyer's services with those of other lawyers are false or misleading if the claims made cannot be substantiated.

Advertising

[2] To assist the public in obtaining legal services, lawyers should be allowed to make known their services not only through reputation but also through organized information campaigns in the form of advertising. Advertising involves an active quest for clients, contrary to the tradition that a lawyer should not seek clientele. However, the public's need to know about legal services can be fulfilled in part through advertising. This need is particularly acute in the case of persons of moderate means who have not made extensive use of legal services. The interest in expanding public information about legal services ought to prevail over considerations of tradition.

[3] This Rule permits public dissemination of information concerning a lawyer's name or firm name, address, and telephone number; the kinds of services the lawyer will undertake; the basis on which the lawyer's fees are determined, including prices for specific services and payment and credit arrangements; a lawyer's foreign language ability; names of references and, with their consent, names of clients regularly represented; and other information that might invite the attention of those seeking legal assistance.

[4] Questions of effectiveness and taste in advertising are matters of speculation and subjective judgment. Some jurisdictions have had extensive prohibitions against television advertising, against advertising going beyond specific facts about a lawyer, or against "undignified" advertising. Television is now one of the most powerful media for getting information to the public, particularly persons of low and moderate income; prohibiting television advertising, therefore, would impede the flow of information about legal services to many sectors of the public. Limiting the information that may be advertised has a similar effect and assumes that the Bar can accurately forecast the kind of information that the public would regard as relevant.

[5] There is no significant distinction between disseminating information and soliciting clients through mass media or through individual

personal contact. In-person solicitation can, however, create additional problems because of the particular circumstances in which the solicitation takes place. This Rule prohibits in-person solicitation in circumstances or through means that are not conducive to intelligent, rational decisions.

Paying Others to Recommend a Lawyer

[6] A lawyer is allowed to pay for advertising permitted by this Rule. This Rule also permits a lawyer to pay another person for channeling professional work to the lawyer. Thus, an organization or person other than the lawyer may advertise or recommend the lawyer's services. Likewise, a lawyer may participate in lawyer referral programs and pay the usual fees charged by such programs. However, special concerns arise when a lawyer is making payments to intermediaries to recommend the lawyer's services to others. These concerns are particularly significant when the payments are not being made to a recognized or established agency or organization, such as an organized lawyer referral program. In employing intermediaries, the lawyer is bound by all of the provisions of this Rule. However, subparagraphs (b)(4) and (b)(5) contain provisions specifically relating to the use of intermediaries.

[7] Subparagraph (b)(4) forbids a lawyer to solicit clients through another person when the lawyer knows or could reasonably ascertain that such conduct violates a contractual or other legal obligation of that other person. For example, a lawyer may not solicit clients through hospital or court employees if solicitation by such employees is prohibited by their employment contracts or rules established by their employment. This prohibition applies whether or not the intermediary is being paid.

[8] Subparagraph (b)(5) imposes specific obligations on the lawyer who employs an intermediary to ensure that the potential client who is the target of the solicitation is informed of the consideration paid or to be paid by the lawyer to the intermediary, and any effect of the payment of such consideration on the total fee to be charged. The concept of payment, as incorporated in subparagraph (b)(5), includes giving anything of value to the recipient and is not limited to payments of money alone. For example, if an intermediary were provided the free use of an automobile in return for soliciting clients on behalf of the lawyer, the obligations imposed by subparagraph (b)(5) would apply and impose the specified disclosure requirements.

Solicitations in the Vicinity of the District of Columbia Courthouse

[9] Paragraph (d) is designed to prohibit unseemly solicitations of prospective clients in and around the District of Columbia Courthouse. The words ''for a fee paid by or on behalf of a client or under the Criminal Justice Act'' have been added to paragraph (d) as it was originally promulgated by the District of Columbia Court of Appeals in 1982. The purpose of the addition is to permit solicitation in the District of Columbia Courthouse for the purposes of pro bono representation. For the purposes of this Rule, pro bono representation, whether by individual lawyers or nonprofit organizations, is representation undertaken primarily for purposes other than a fee. That representation includes providing services free of charge for individuals who may be in need of legal assistance and may lack the financial means and sophistication necessary to have alternative sources of aid. Cases where fees are awarded under the Criminal Justice Act do not constitute pro bono representation for the purposes of this Rule. However, the possibility that fees may be awarded under the Equal Access to Justice Act and Civil Rights Attorneys' Fees Awards Act of 1976, as amended, or other statutory attorney fee statutes, does not prevent representation from constituting pro bono representation.

Rule 7.5. Firm Names and Letterheads

(a) A lawyer shall not use a firm name, letterhead, or other professional designation that violates Rule 7.1. A trade name may be used by a lawyer in private practice if it does not imply a connection with a government agency or with a public or charitable legal services organization and is not otherwise in violation of Rule 7.1.

(b) A law firm with offices in more than one jurisdiction may use the same name in each jurisdiction, but identification of the lawyers in an office of the firm shall indicate the jurisdictional limitations on those not licensed to practice in the jurisdiction where the office is located.

(c) The name of a lawyer holding a public office shall not be used in the name of a law firm, or in communications on its behalf, during any substantial period in which the lawyer is not actively and regularly practicing with the firm.

(d) Lawyers may state or imply that they practice in a partnership or other organization only when that is the fact.

COMMENT

[1] A firm may be designated by the names of all or some of its members, by the names of deceased members where there has been a continuing succession in the firm's identity, or by a trade name such as the ABC Legal Clinic. Although the United States Supreme Court has held that legislation may prohibit the use of trade names in professional practice, use of such names in law practice is acceptable so long as it is not misleading. If a private firm uses a trade name that includes a geographical name such as Springfield Legal Clinic, an express disclaimer that it is a public legal aid agency may be required to avoid a misleading implication. It may be observed that any firm name including the name of a deceased partner is, strictly speaking, a trade name. The use of such names to designate law firms has proven a useful means of identification. However, it is misleading to use the name of a lawyer not associated with the firm or a predecessor of the firm.

[2] With regard to paragraph (d), lawyers sharing office facilities, but who are not in fact partners, may not denominate themselves as, for example, Smith and Jones, for that title suggests partnership in the practice of law.

MAINTAINING THE INTEGRITY OF THE PROFESSION

Rule 8.1. Bar Admission and Disciplinary Matters

An applicant for admission to the Bar, or a lawyer in connection with a Bar admission application or in connection with a disciplinary matter, shall not:

(a) Knowingly make a false statement of material fact; or

(b) Fail to disclose a fact necessary to correct a misapprehension known by the lawyer or applicant to have arisen in the matter, or knowingly fail to respond reasonably to a lawful demand for information from an admissions or disciplinary authority, except that this Rule does not require disclosure of information otherwise protected by Rule 1.6.

COMMENT

[1] The duty imposed by this Rule extends to persons seeking admission to the Bar as well as to lawyers. Hence, if a person makes a ma-

terial false statement in connection with an application for admission, it may be the basis for subsequent disciplinary action if the person is admitted, and in any event may be relevant in a subsequent admission application. The duty imposed by this Rule applies to a lawyer's own admission or discipline as well as that of others. Thus, it is a separate professional offense for a lawyer knowingly to make a misrepresentation or omission in connection with a disciplinary investigation of the lawyer's own conduct. This Rule also requires affirmative clarification of any misunderstanding on the part of the admissions or disciplinary authority of which the person involved becomes aware.

[2] This Rule is subject to the provisions of the Fifth Amendment of the United States Constitution and corresponding provisions of state constitutions. A person relying on such a provision in response to a question, however, should do so openly and not use the right of nondisclosure as a justification for failure to comply with this Rule.

[3] A lawyer representing an applicant for admission to the Bar, or representing a lawyer who is the subject of a disciplinary inquiry or proceeding, is governed by the Rules applicable to the client-lawyer relationship. For example, Rule 1.6 may prohibit disclosures, which would otherwise be required, by a lawyer serving in such representative capacity.

Rule 8.3. Reporting Professional Misconduct

(a) A lawyer having knowledge that another lawyer has committed a violation of the Rules of Professional Conduct that raises a substantial question as to that lawyer's honesty, trustworthiness, or fitness as a lawyer in other respects, shall inform the appropriate professional authority.

(b) A lawyer having knowledge that a judge has committed a violation of applicable rules of judicial conduct that raises a substantial question as to the judge's fitness for office shall inform the appropriate authority.

(c) This Rule does not require disclosure of information otherwise protected by Rule 1.6.

COMMENT

[1] Self-regulation of the legal profession requires that members of the profession initiate disciplinary investigation when they know of a violation of the Rules of Professional Conduct. Lawyers have a similar obli-

gation with respect to judicial misconduct. An apparently isolated violation may indicate a pattern of misconduct that only a disciplinary investigation can uncover. Reporting a violation is especially important where the victim is unlikely to discover the offense.

[2] A report about misconduct is not required where it would involve violation of Rule 1.6. However, a lawyer should encourage a client to consent to disclosure where prosecution would not substantially prejudice the client's interests.

[3] If a lawyer were obliged to report every violation of the Rules, the failure to report any violation would itself be a professional offense. Such a requirement existed in many jurisdictions but proved to be unenforceable. This Rule limits the reporting obligation to those offenses that a self-regulating profession must vigorously endeavor to prevent. A measure of judgment is, therefore, required in complying with the provisions of this Rule. The term "substantial" refers to the seriousness of the possible offense and not the quantum of evidence of which the lawyer is aware. A report should be made to the Office of Bar Counsel. A lawyer who believes that another lawyer has a significant problem of alcohol or other substance abuse which does not require reporting to Bar Counsel under this Rule, may nonetheless wish to report the perceived situation to the Lawyer Counseling Committee, operated by the D.C. Bar, which assists lawyers having such problems.

[4] The duty to report professional misconduct does not apply to a lawyer retained to represent a lawyer whose professional conduct is in question. Such a situation is governed by the Rules applicable to the client-lawyer relationship.

[5] Rule 1.6(h) brings within the protections of Rule 1.6 certain types of information gained by lawyers participating in lawyer counseling programs of the D.C. Bar Lawyer Counseling Committee. To the extent information concerning violations of the Rules of Professional Conduct fall within the scope of Rule 1.6(h), a lawyer-counselor would not be required or permitted to inform the "appropriate professional authority" referred to in Rule 8.3. Where disclosure is permissive under Rule 1.6 (see paragraph 1.6(c) for cases of permitted disclosures), discretion to disclose to the "appropriate professional authority" would also exist pursuant to paragraph 8.3(c). See also Comment to Rule 1.6, paragraphs [29], [30], and [31].

Rule 8.4. Misconduct

It is professional misconduct for a lawyer to:

(a) Violate or attempt to violate the Rules of Professional Conduct, knowingly assist or induce another to do so, or do so through the acts of another;

(b) Commit a criminal act that reflects adversely on the lawyer's honesty, trustworthiness, or fitness as a lawyer in other respects;

(c) Engage in conduct involving dishonesty, fraud, deceit, or misrepresentation;

(d) Engage in conduct that seriously interferes with the administration of justice;

(e) State or imply an ability to influence improperly a government agency or official;

(f) Knowingly assist a judge or judicial officer in conduct that is a violation of applicable rules of judicial conduct or other law; or

(g) Seek or threaten to seek criminal charges or disciplinary charges solely to obtain an advantage in a civil matter.

COMMENT

[1] Many kinds of illegal conduct reflect adversely on fitness to practice law, such as offenses involving fraud and the offense of willful failure to file an income tax return. However, some kinds of offenses carry no such implication. Traditionally, the distinction was drawn in terms of offenses involving "moral turpitude." That concept can be construed to include offenses concerning some matters of personal morality, such as adultery and comparable offenses, that have no specific connection to fitness for the practice of law. Although a lawyer is personally answerable to the entire criminal law, a lawyer should be professionally answerable only for offenses that indicate lack of those characteristics relevant to law practice. Offenses involving violence, dishonesty, breach of trust, or serious interference with the administration of justice are in that category. A pattern of repeated offenses, even ones of minor significance when considered separately, can indicate indifference to legal obligation.

[2] Paragraph (d)'s prohibition of conduct that "seriously interferes with the administration of justice" includes conduct proscribed by the previous Code of Professional Responsibility under DR 1-102(A)(5) as "prejudicial to the administration of justice." The extensive case law on that standard, as set forth below, is hereby incorporated into this Rule.

[3] The majority of these cases involve a lawyer's failure to cooperate with Bar Counsel. A lawyer's failure to respond to Bar Counsel's inquiries or subpoenas may constitute misconduct, see *In re Cope*, 455 A.2d 1357 (D.C. 1983); *In re Haupt*, 444 A.2d 317 (D.C. 1982); *In re Lieber*, 442

A.2d 153 (D.C. 1982); *In re Whitlock*, 441 A.2d 989 (D.C. 1982); *In re Spencer*, No. M-112-82 (D.C. June 4, 1982); *In re L. Smith*, No. M-91-82 (D.C. App. Mar. 9, 1982); *In re Walsh*, No. 70 (81) (D.C. Sept. 25, 1981) en banc; *In re Schattman*, No. M-63-81 (D.C. June 2, 1981); *In re Russell*, 424 A.2d 1087 (D.C. 1980); *In re Willcher*, 404 A.2d 185 (D.C. 1979); *In re Carter*, No. D-31-79 (D.C. Oct. 28, 1979); *In re Tucker*, No. M-13-75/S-56-78 (D.C. Nov. 15, 1978); *In re Bush (Bush II)*, No. S-58-79 (D.C. Oct. 1, 1979), as may the failure to abide by agreements made with Bar Counsel; *In re Harmon*, M-79-81 (D.C. Dec. 14, 1981) (breaking promise to Bar Counsel to offer complainant refund of fee or vigorous representation constitutes conduct prejudicial to the administration of justice).

[4] A lawyer's failure to appear in court for a scheduled hearing is another common form of conduct deemed prejudicial to the administration of justice. See *In re Evans*, No. M-126-82 (D.C. Dec. 18, 1982); *In re Doud*, Bar Docket No. 442-80 (Sept. 23, 1982); *In re Bush (Bush III)*, No. S-58-79/D/39/80 (D.C. App. Apr. 30, 1980); *In re Molovinsky*, No. M-31-79 (D.C. Aug. 23, 1979). Similarly, failure to obey court orders may constitute misconduct under paragraph (d). *Whitlock*, 441 A.2d at 989-91; *In re Brown*, Bar Docket No. 222-78 (Aug. 4, 1978); *In re Bush (Bush I)*, No. DP-22-75 (D.C. July 26, 1977).

[5] While the above categories — failure to cooperate with Bar Counsel and failure to obey Court orders — encompass the major forms of misconduct proscribed by paragraph (d), that provision is to be interpreted flexibly and includes any improper behavior of an analogous nature. For example, the failure to turn over the assets of a conservatorship to the court or to the successor conservator has been held to be conduct "prejudicial to the administration of justice." *In re Burka*, 423 A.2d 181 (D.C. 1980). In *Russell, supra,* the court found that failure to keep the Bar advised of respondent's changes of address, after being warned to do so, was also misconduct under that standard. And in Schattman, supra, the court found that failure to keep the Bar advised of respondent's changes of address, after being warned to do so, was also misconduct under that standard. And in Schattman, supra, it was held that a lawyer's giving a worthless check in settlement of a claim against the lawyer by a client was improper.

Rule 8.5. Disciplinary Authority; Choice of Law

(a) **Disciplinary Authority.** A lawyer admitted to practice in this jurisdiction is subject to the disciplinary authority of this jurisdiction, regardless of where the lawyer's conduct occurs. A lawyer may be subject to the disciplinary authority of both this jurisdiction and another jurisdiction where the lawyer is admitted for the same conduct.

(b) **Choice of Law.** In any exercise of the disciplinary authority of this jurisdiction, the Rules of Professional Conduct to be applied shall be as follows:

(1) For conduct in connection with a proceeding in a court before which a lawyer has been admitted to practice (either generally or for purposes of that proceeding), the rules to be applied shall be the rules of the jurisdiction in which the court sits, unless the rules of the court provide otherwise; and

(2) for any other conduct,

(i) if the lawyer is licensed to practice only in this jurisdiction, the rules to be applied shall be the rules of this jurisdiction, and

(ii) if the lawyer is licensed to practice in this and another jurisdiction, the rules to be applied shall be the rules of the admitting jurisdiction in which the lawyer principally practices; provided, however, that if particular conduct clearly has its predominant effect in another jurisdiction in which the lawyer is licensed to practice, the rules of that jurisdiction shall be applied to that conduct.

COMMENT

Disciplinary Authority

[1] Paragraph (a) restates long-standing law.

Choice of Law

[2] A lawyer may be potentially subject to more than one set of rules of professional conduct which impose different obligations. The lawyer may be licensed to practice in more than one jurisdiction with differing rules, or may be admitted to practice before a particular court with rules that differ from those of the jurisdiction or jurisdictions in which the lawyer is licensed to practice. In the past, decisions have not developed clear or consistent guidance as to which rules apply in such circumstances.

[3] Paragraph (b) seeks to resolve such potential conflicts. Its premise is that minimizing conflicts between rules, as well as uncertainty about which rules are applicable, is in the best interest of both clients and the profession (as well as the bodies having authority to regulate the profession). Accordingly, it takes the approach of (i) providing that any par-

ticular conduct of an attorney shall be subject to only one set of rules of professional conduct, and (ii) making the determination of which set of rules applies to particular conduct as straightforward as possible, consistent with recognition of appropriate regulatory interests of relevant jurisdictions.

[4] Paragraph (b) provides that as to a lawyer's conduct relating to a proceeding in a court before which the lawyer is admitted to practice (either generally or pro hac vice), the lawyer shall be subject only to the rules of professional conduct of that court. As to all other conduct, paragraph (b) provides that a lawyer licensed to practice only in this jurisdiction shall be subject to the rules of professional conduct of this jurisdiction, and that a lawyer licensed in multiple jurisdictions shall be subject only to the rules of the jurisdiction where he or she (as an individual, not his or her firm) principally practices, but with one exception: if particular conduct clearly has its predominant effect in another admitting jurisdiction, then only the rules of that jurisdiction shall apply. The intention is for the latter exception to be a narrow one. It would be appropriately applied, for example, to a situation in which a lawyer admitted in, and principally practicing in, State A, but also admitted in State B, handled an acquisition by a company whose headquarters and operations were in State B of another, similar such company. The exception would not appropriately be applied, on the other hand, if the lawyer handled an acquisition by a company whose headquarters and operations were in State A of a company whose headquarters and main operations were in State A, but which also had some operations in State B.

[5] If two admitting jurisdictions were to proceed against a lawyer for the same conduct, they should, applying this rule, identify the same governing ethics rules. They should take all appropriate steps to see that they do apply the same rule to the same conduct, and in all events should avoid proceeding against a lawyer on the basis of two inconsistent rules.

[6] The choice of law provision is not intended to apply to transnational practice. Choice of law in this context should be the subject of agreements between jurisdictions or of appropriate international law.

NONDISCRIMINATION BY MEMBERS OF THE BAR

Rule 9.1. Discrimination in Employment

A lawyer shall not discriminate against any individual in conditions of employment because of the individual's race, color, religion, national

origin, sex, age, marital status, sexual orientation, family responsibility, or physical handicap.

COMMENT

[1] This provision is modeled after the D.C. Human Rights Act, D.C. Code §1-2512 (1981), though in some respects more limited in scope. There are also provisions of federal law that contain certain prohibitions on discrimination in employment. The rule is not intended to create ethical obligations that exceed those imposed on a lawyer by applicable law.

[2] A similar rule has been adopted by the highest court in Vermont. A similar rule is also under consideration for adoption by the courts in New York based on the recommendations of the New York State Bar Association.

[3] The investigation and adjudication of discrimination claims may involve particular expertise of the kind found within the D.C. Office of Human Rights and the federal Equal Employment Opportunity Commission. Such experience may involve, among other things, methods of analysis of statistical data regarding discrimination claims. These agencies also have, in appropriate circumstances, the power to award remedies to the victims of discrimination, such as reinstatement or back pay, which extend beyond the remedies that are available through the disciplinary process. Remedies available through the disciplinary process include such sanctions as disbarment, suspension, censure, and admonition, but do not extend to monetary awards or other remedies that could alter the employment status to take into account the impact of prior acts of discrimination.

[4] If proceedings are pending before other organizations, such as the D.C. Office of Human Rights or the Equal Employment Opportunity Commission, the processing of complaints by Bar Counsel may be deferred or abated where there is substantial similarity between the complaint filed with Bar Counsel and material allegations involved in such other proceedings. See §19(d) of Rule XI of the Rules Governing the Bar of the District of Columbia.

New York Materials

New York Code of Professional Responsibility

Editors' Introduction. New York has not adopted the Model Rules of Professional Conduct. It has instead retained a version of the Model Code of Professional Responsibility. The New York Code, which is now codified at Part 1200 of the joint rules of the Appellate Divisions, has always varied somewhat from the ABA Model Code. In the spring of 1990, the four Appellate Divisions of the New York State Supreme Court, which under §90 of the Judiciary Law have responsibility for promulgating rules of conduct for lawyers in the state, adopted amendments to the New York Code effective September 1, 1990. Many of these amendments draw upon the Model Rules. The Appellate Divisions have not adopted the Ethical Considerations of the Code as rules governing the behavior of lawyers, but the New York State Bar Association has and has modified these in response to the Model Rules.

We reprint the full text of the New York Disciplinary Rules and Ethical Considerations.

The New York Disciplinary Rules that warrant special comparison with the Model Code's equivalents are: DR 1-102 (prohibiting misconduct by lawyers *and law firms*); DR 1-102(A)(6) (discrimination in the practice of law); DR 1-104 (mandating adequate supervision by partners and supervisory lawyers); DR 2-111 (permitting the sale of a law practice); DR 4-101(C)(5) (authority to reveal confidences or secrets to the extent implicit in withdrawing a written or oral opinion or representation); DR 5-105(D) (less expansive imputed disqualification than under the Model Code); DR 5-105(E) (requiring law firms to maintain records of past engagements and to implement a system to check for conflicts); DR 5-108(A) (essentially adopting the Model Rules provision for successive representation); DR 5-109(A) (adopting a portion of Model Rule 1.13 in connection with the representation of an organizational client); DR 5-110(A) (substantially adopting the standard in Model Rule 6.3 for membership in a legal services organization with interests adverse to those of the lawyer's client); DR 7-102(B)(1) (excepting the duty to rectify a fraud if the lawyer's information "is protected as a confidence or secret"); DR 9-101(B) (dealing with former government lawyers); and DR 9-102 (dealing with preservation of client funds and property). The "definitions" section in the New York Code also contains a definition for "fraud," unlike the Model Code.

The New York State Bar Association, by resolution adopted by its House of Delegates on January 29, 1993, acknowledged that the Disciplinary Rules jointly promulgated by the Appellate Divisions are applicable to all attorneys admitted to practice in New York State, and that these same rules also appear in the Code of Professional Responsibility adopted by the New York State Bar Association; and therefore resolved that the Disciplinary Rules of its Code of Professional Responsibility shall be amended to conform to any Disciplinary Rules adopted or amended from time to time by all Appellate Divisions.

Effective November 30, 1993, the New York Court of Appeals, in conjunction with the Appellate Divisions of the New York State Supreme Court, adopted various rules applicable only to lawyers who represent clients in domestic relations matters. These rules have been codified at Part 1400 in Title 22 of the New York Codes, Rules, and Regulations (NYCRR). Part 1400 is expressly referred to in DR 2-105-a and DR 2-106(E), both of which were added to the Code in 1993 and amended in 1994 to reflect the codification of the domestic relations rules. We reprint Part 1400 in full immediately after this Code.

Since our last edition went to press in October of 1996, the Code of Professional Responsibility has not been amended in any way. However, on March 4, 1997 the New York State Bar Association forwarded to the Appellate Divisions a comprehensive set of proposed amendments to the Code. These proposals represented the culmination of more than two years of study and debate by the New York State Bar Association, especially its Special Committee to Review the Code of Professional Responsibility (commonly called the "Krane Committee," after its Chair, Steven C. Krane of New York City). There is no way of telling when the courts may act on these proposals or whether the courts will accept, modify, or reject them. For up-to-date information, call the New York State Bar Association at (518) 463-3200, or visit the New York State Bar Association's web site at www.nysba.org. For more information on New York developments related to the Code of Professional Responsibility, see our Introduction to the Regulation of Lawyers at the front of this volume.

Contents

Preamble
Preliminary Statement
Definitions

New York Code of Professional Responsibility

771

Canon 9. A Lawyer Should Avoid Even the Appearance of
Professional Impropriety

Ethical Considerations
DR 9-101.   Avoiding Even the Appearance of Impropriety
DR 9-102.   Preserving Identity of Funds and Property of Others; Fiduciary
                 Responsibility; Maintenance of Bank Accounts; Recordkeeping;
                 Examination of Records

PREAMBLE

The continued existence of a free and democratic society depends upon
recognition of the concept that justice is based upon the rule of law
grounded in respect for the dignity of the individual and the capacity of
the individual through reason for enlightened self-government. Law so
grounded makes justice possible, for only through such law does the dignity of the individual attain respect and protection. Without it, individual
rights become subject to unrestrained power, respect for law is destroyed,
and rational self-government is impossible.

Lawyers, as guardians of the law, play a vital role in the preservation
of society. The fulfillment of this role requires an understanding by lawyers of their relationship with and function in our legal system. A conse-
quent obligation of lawyers is to maintain the highest standards of ethical
conduct.

In fulfilling professional responsibilities, a lawyer necessarily assumes various roles that require the performance of many difficult tasks.
Not every situation which the lawyer may encounter can be foreseen, but
fundamental ethical principles are always present for guidance. Within
the framework of these principles, a lawyer must with courage and fore-
sight be able and ready to shape the body of the law to the ever-changing
relationships of society.

The Code of Professional Responsibility points the way to the aspiring and provides standards by which to judge the transgressor. Each lawyer's own conscience must provide the touchstone against which to test
the extent to which the lawyer's actions should rise above minimum standards. But in the last analysis it is the desire for the respect and confidence of the members of the professional and of the society which the
lawyer serves that should provide to a lawyer the incentive for the highest
possible degree of ethical conduct. So long as its practitioners are guided
by these principles, the law will continue to be a noble profession. This is
its greatness and its strength, which permit of no compromise.

PRELIMINARY STATEMENT

The Code of Professional Responsibility consists of three separate but interrelated parts: Canons, Ethical Considerations, and Disciplinary Rules. The Code is designed to be both an inspirational guide to the members of the profession and a basis for disciplinary action when the conduct of a lawyer falls below the required minimum standards stated in the Disciplinary Rules.

Obviously the Canons, Ethical Considerations, and Disciplinary Rules cannot apply to non-lawyers; however, they do define the type of ethical conduct that the public has a right to expect not only of lawyers but also of their non-professional employees and associates in all matters pertaining to professional employment. A lawyer should ultimately be responsible for the conduct of the lawyer's employees and associates in the course of the professional representation of the client.

The Canons are statements of axiomatic norms, expressing in general terms the standards of professional conduct expected of lawyers in their relationships with the public, with the legal system, and with the legal professional. They embody the general concepts from which the Ethical Considerations and the Disciplinary Rules are derived.

The Ethical Considerations are aspirational in character and represent the objectives toward which every member of the profession should strive. They constitute a body of principles upon which the lawyer can rely for guidance in many specific situations.

The Disciplinary Rules, unlike the Ethical Considerations, are mandatory in character. The Disciplinary Rules state the minimum level of conduct below which no lawyer can fall without being subject to disciplinary action. The Disciplinary Rules should be uniformly applied to all lawyers, regardless of the nature of their professional activities. The Code makes no attempt to prescribe either disciplinary procedures or penalties for violation of a Disciplinary Rule, nor does it undertake to define standards for civil liability of lawyers for professional conduct. The severity of judgment against one found guilty of violating a Disciplinary Rule should be determined by the character of the offense and the attendant circumstances. An enforcing agency, in applying the Disciplinary Rules, may find interpretive guidance in the basic principles embodied in the Canons and in the objectives reflected in the Ethical Considerations.

No codification of principles can expressly cover all situations that may arise. Accordingly, conduct that does not appear to violate the express terms of any Disciplinary Rule nevertheless may be found by an enforcing agency to be the subject of discipline on the basis of a general principle illustrated by a Disciplinary Rule or on the basis of an accepted common law principle applicable to lawyers.

DEFINITIONS

As used in the Disciplinary Rules of the Code of Professional Responsibility:

    1. "Differing interests" include every interest that will adversely affect either the judgment or the loyalty of a lawyer to a client, whether it be a conflicting, inconsistent, diverse, or other interest.

    2. "Law firm" includes, but is not limited to, a professional legal corporation, the legal department of a corporation or other organization and a legal services organization.

    3. "Person" includes a corporation, an association, a trust, a partnership, and any other organization or legal entity.

    4. "Professional legal corporation" means a corporation, or an association treated as a corporation, authorized by law to practice law for profit.

    5. "State" includes the District of Columbia, Puerto Rico, and other federal territories and possessions.

    6. "Tribunal" includes all courts and all other adjudicatory bodies. A tribunal shall be deemed "available" when it would have jurisdiction to hear a complaint, if timely brought.

    7. "Bar association" includes a bar association of specialists as referred to in DR 2-105(B).

    8. "Qualified legal assistance organization" means an office or organization of one of the four types listed in DR 2-103(D)(1) through (4), inclusive, that meets all the requirements thereof.

    9. "Fraud" does not include conduct, although characterized as fraudulent by statute or administrative rule, which lacks an element of scienter, deceit, intent to mislead, or knowing failure to correct misrepresentations which can be reasonably expected to induce detrimental reliance by another.

> **Editors' Note.** DR 4-101 defines the terms "confidence" and "secret" as follows:
>
> "Confidence" refers to information protected by the attorney-client privilege under applicable law, and "secret" refers to other information gained in the professional relationship that the client has requested be held inviolate or the disclosure of which would be embarrassing or would be likely to be detrimental to the client.

CANON 1. A LAWYER SHOULD ASSIST IN MAINTAINING THE INTEGRITY AND COMPETENCE OF THE LEGAL PROFESSION

Ethical Considerations

EC 1-1 A basic tenet of the professional responsibility of lawyers is that every person in our society should have ready access to the independent professional services of a lawyer of integrity and competence. Maintaining the integrity and improving the competence of the bar to meet the highest standards is the ethical responsibility of every lawyer.

EC 1-2 The public should be protected from those who are not qualified to be lawyers by reason of a deficiency in education or moral standards or of other relevant factors but who nevertheless seek to practice law. To assure the maintenance of high moral and educational standards of the legal profession, lawyers should affirmatively assist courts and other appropriate bodies in promulgating, enforcing, and improving requirements for admission to the bar. In like manner, the bar has a positive obligation to aid in the continued improvement of all phases of pre-admission and post-admission legal education.

EC 1-3 Before recommending an applicant for admission, a lawyer should be satisfied that the applicant is of good moral character. Although a lawyer should not become a self-appointed investigator or judge of applicants for admission, the lawyer should report to proper officials all unfavorable information the lawyer possesses relating to the character or other qualifications of an applicant.

EC 1-4 The integrity of the profession can be maintained only if conduct of lawyers in violation of the Disciplinary Rules is brought to the attention of the proper officials. A lawyer should reveal voluntarily to those officials all knowledge, other than knowledge protected as a confidence or secret, of conduct of another lawyer which the lawyer believes clearly to be a violation of the Disciplinary Rules that raises a substantial question as to the other lawyer's honesty, trustworthiness or fitness in other respects as a lawyer. A lawyer should, upon request, serve on and assist committees and boards having responsibility for the administration of the Disciplinary Rules.

EC 1-5   A lawyer should maintain high standards of professional conduct and should encourage other lawyers to do likewise. A lawyer should be temperate and dignified, and should refrain from all illegal and morally reprehensible conduct. Because of the lawyer's position in society, even minor violations of law by a lawyer may tend to lessen public confidence in the legal profession. Obedience to law exemplifies respect for law. To lawyers especially, respect for the law should be more than a platitude.

EC 1-6   An applicant for admission to the bar or a lawyer may be unqualified, temporarily or permanently, for other than moral and educational reasons, such as mental or emotional instability. Lawyers should be diligent in taking steps to see that during a period of disqualification such person is not granted a license or, if licensed, is not permitted to practice. In like manner, when the disqualification has terminated, members of the bar should assist such person in being licensed, or, if licensed, in being restored to the full right to practice.

EC 1-7   A lawyer should avoid bias and condescension toward, and treat with dignity and respect, all parties, witnesses, lawyers, court employees, and other persons involved in the legal process.

EC 1-8   A law firm should adopt measures giving reasonable assurance that all lawyers in the firm conform to the Disciplinary Rules and that the conduct of non-lawyers employed by the firm is compatible with the professional obligations of the lawyers in the firm. Such measures may include informal supervision and occasional admonition, a procedure whereby junior lawyers can make confidential referral of ethical problems directly to a designated senior lawyer or special committee, and continuing legal education in professional ethics.

DR 1-101. Maintaining Integrity and Competence of the Legal Profession

A. A lawyer is subject to discipline if the lawyer has made a materially false statement in, or has deliberately failed to disclose a material fact requested in connection with, the lawyer's application for admission to the bar.

B. A lawyer shall not further the application for admission to the bar of another person that the lawyer knows to be unqualified in respect to character, education, or other relevant attribute.

DR 1-102. Misconduct

Editors' Note. On May 22, 1996, the Appellate Divisions issued a joint order amending DR 1-102 (as well as DR 1-104 and DR 5-105). The only amendment to DR 1-102 is to add the words "or law firm" to the introductory phrase at the beginning of the rule. The effect of this small amendment, however, is to make New York the first jurisdiction in the nation to expressly prohibit professional misconduct by law firms.

A. A lawyer or law firm shall not:

1. Violate a Disciplinary Rule.

2. Circumvent a Disciplinary Rule through actions of another.

3. Engage in illegal conduct involving moral turpitude.

4. Engage in conduct involving dishonesty, fraud, deceit, or misrepresentation.

5. Engage in conduct that is prejudicial to the administration of justice.

6. Unlawfully discriminate in the practice of law, including in hiring, promoting or otherwise determining conditions of employment, on the basis of age, race, creed, color, national origin, sex, disability, or marital status.

Where there is available a tribunal of competent jurisdiction, other than a Departmental Disciplinary Committee, a complaint of professional misconduct based on unlawful discrimination shall be brought before such tribunal in the first instance. A certified copy of a determination by such a tribunal, which has become final and enforceable, and as to which the right to judicial or appellate review has been exhausted, finding that the lawyer has engaged in an unlawful discriminatory practice shall constitute prima facie evidence of professional misconduct in a disciplinary proceeding.

7. In domestic relations matters, begin a sexual relationship with a client during the course of the lawyer's representation of the client.

8. Engage in any other conduct that adversely reflects on the lawyer's fitness to practice law.

DR 1-103. Disclosure of Information to Authorities

A. A lawyer possessing knowledge, (1) not protected as a confidence or secret, of a violation, or (2) not gained in the lawyer's capacity as a member of a bona fide lawyer assistance or similar program or committee, of DR 1-102 that raises a substantial question as to another lawyer's honesty, trustworthiness or fitness in other respects as a lawyer shall report such knowledge to a tribunal or other authority empowered to investigate or act upon such violation.

B. A lawyer possessing knowledge or evidence, not protected as a confidence or secret, concerning another lawyer or a judge shall reveal fully such knowledge or evidence upon proper request of a tribunal or other authority empowered to investigate or act upon the conduct of lawyers or judges.

DR 1-104. Responsibilities of a Supervisory Lawyer

Editors' Note. On May 22, 1996, the Appellate Divisions issued a joint order significantly amending DR 1-104 (as well as DR 1-102 and DR 5-105). The amendments to DR 1-104 added completely new subdivisions (A), (B), and (C), and amended the old subdivision (A) and moved it to subdivision (D).

A. A law firm shall make reasonable efforts to ensure that all lawyers in the firm conform to the disciplinary rules.

B. A lawyer with management responsibility in the law firm or direct supervisory authority over another lawyer shall make reasonable efforts to ensure that the other lawyer conforms to the disciplinary rules.

C. A law firm shall adequately supervise, as appropriate, the work of partners, associates, and nonlawyers who work at the firm. The degree of supervision required is that which is reasonable under the circumstances, taking into account factors such as the experience of the person whose work is being supervised, the amount of work involved in a particular matter, and the likelihood that ethical problems might arise in the course of working on the matter.

D. A lawyer shall be responsible for a violation of the disciplinary rules by another lawyer or for the conduct of a nonlawyer employed or retained by or associated with the lawyer that would be a violation of the disciplinary rules if engaged in by a lawyer if:

(1) The lawyer orders, or directs the specific conduct, or, with knowledge of the specific conduct, ratifies it; or

(2) The lawyer is a partner in the law firm in which the other lawyer practices or the nonlawyer is employed, or has supervisory author-

ity over the other lawyer or the nonlawyer, and knows of such conduct, or in the exercise of reasonable management or supervisory authority should have known of the conduct so that reasonable remedial action could be or could have been taken at a time when its consequences could be or could have been avoided or mitigated.

CANON 2. A LAWYER SHOULD ASSIST THE LEGAL PROFESSION IN FULFILLING ITS DUTY TO MAKE LEGAL COUNSEL AVAILABLE

Ethical Considerations

EC 2-1   The need of members of the public for legal services is met only if they recognize their legal problems, appreciate the importance of seeking assistance, and are able to obtain the services of acceptable legal counsel. Hence, important functions of the legal profession are to educate people to recognize their problems, to facilitate the process of intelligent selection of lawyers, and to assist in making legal services fully available.

Recognition of Legal Problems

EC 2-2   The legal profession should help the public to recognize legal problems because such problems may not be self-revealing and often are not timely noticed. Therefore, lawyers should encourage and participate in educational and public relations programs concerning our legal system with particular reference to legal problems that frequently arise.

EC 2-3   Whether a lawyer acts properly in volunteering in-person advice to a non-lawyer to seek legal services depends upon the circumstances. The giving of advice that one should take legal action could well be in fulfillment of the duty of the legal profession to assist the public in recognizing legal problems.

EC 2-4   (Repealed)

EC 2-5   A lawyer who writes or speaks for the purpose of educating members of the public to recognize their legal problems should carefully refrain from giving or appearing to give a general solution applicable to all apparently similar individual problems since slight changes in fact situations may require a material variance in the applicable advice; otherwise, the public may be misled and misadvised. Talks and writings by lawyers for non-lawyers should caution them not to attempt to solve individual problems upon the basis of the information contained therein.

Selection of a Lawyer

EC 2-6   Formerly a potential client usually knew the reputations of local lawyers for competence and integrity and therefore could select a practitioner in whom he or she had confidence. This traditional selection process worked well because it was initiated by the client and the choice was an informed one.

EC 2-7   Changed conditions, however, have seriously restricted the effectiveness of the traditional selection process. Often the reputations of lawyers are not sufficiently known to enable potential users of legal services to make intelligent choices. The law has become increasingly complex and specialized. Few lawyers are willing and competent to deal with every kind of legal matter, and many people have difficulty in determining the competence of lawyers to render different types of legal services. The selection of legal counsel is particularly difficult for transients, persons moving into new areas, persons of limited education or means, and others who have little or no contact with lawyers. Lack of information about the availability of lawyers, the qualifications of particular lawyers, the areas of law in which lawyers accept representation and the cost of legal services impedes the intelligent selection of lawyers.

EC 2-8   Selection of a lawyer should be made on an informed basis. Disclosure of truthful and relevant information about lawyers and their areas of practice should assist in the making of an informed selection. Disinterested and informed advice and recommendation of third parties — relatives, friends, acquaintances, business associates, or other lawyers — may also be helpful.

Lawyer Advertising

EC 2-9   The attorney client relationship is personal and unique and should not be established as the result of pressures and deceptions.

EC 2-10   A lawyer should ensure that the information contained in any advertising which the lawyer publishes, broadcasts or causes to be published or broadcast is relevant, is disseminated in an objective and understandable fashion, and would facilitate the prospective client's ability to select a lawyer. A lawyer should strive to communicate such information without undue emphasis upon style and advertising stratagems which serve to hinder rather than to facilitate intelligent selection of counsel. In disclosing information, by advertisements or otherwise, relating to a lawyer's education, experience or professional qualifications, special care should be taken to avoid the use of any statement or claim which is false, fraudulent, misleading, deceptive or unfair, or which is violative of any statute or rule of court.

EC 2-11   The name under which a lawyer practices may be a factor in the selection process. The use of a trade name or an assumed name could mislead non-lawyers concerning the identity, responsibility, and status of those practicing thereunder. Accordingly, a lawyer in private practice should practice only under a designation containing the lawyer's own name, the name of an employing lawyer, the name of one or more of the lawyers practicing in a partnership, or, if permitted by law, in the name of a professional corporation for the practice of law, which should be clearly designated as such. For many years some law firms have used a firm name retaining one or more names of deceased or retired partners and such practice is not improper if the firm is a bona fide successor of a firm in which the deceased or retired person was a member, if the use of the name is authorized by law or by contract, and if the public is not misled thereby. However, the name of a partner who withdraws from a firm but continues to practice law should be omitted from the firm name in order to avoid misleading the public.

EC 2-12   A lawyer occupying a judicial, legislative, or public executive or administrative position who has the right to practice law concurrently may allow his or her name to remain in the name of the firm if the lawyer actively continues to practice law as a member thereof. If the lawyer does not have the right to practice law concurrently, the lawyer's name should be removed from the firm name, and the lawyer should not be identified as a past or present member of the firm; and the lawyer should not hold himself or herself out as being a practicing lawyer.

EC 2-13   In order to avoid the possibility of misleading persons with whom a lawyer deals, a lawyer should be scrupulous in the representation of professional status. A lawyer should not hold himself or herself out as being a partner or associate of a law firm if not one in fact, and thus should not hold himself or herself out as being a partner or associate if the lawyer only shares offices with another lawyer.

EC 2-14   (Repealed)

EC 2-15   The legal profession has developed lawyer referral systems designed to aid individuals who are able to pay fees but need assistance in locating lawyers competent to handle their particular problems. Use of a lawyer referral system enables an individual to avoid an uninformed selection of a lawyer because such a system makes possible the employment of competent lawyers who have indicated an interest in the subject matter involved. Lawyers should support the principle of lawyer referral systems and should encourage the evolution of other ethical plans which aid in the selection of qualified counsel.

EC 2-16   Persons unable to pay all or a portion of a reasonable fee should be able to obtain necessary legal services, and lawyers should support and participate in appropriate activities designed to achieve that objective.

Financial Ability to Employ Counsel: Persons Able to Pay Reasonable Fees

EC 2-17   The determination of a proper fee requires consideration of the interests of both client and lawyer. A lawyer should not charge more than a reasonable fee, for excessive cost of legal service would deter non-lawyers from using the legal system to protect their rights and to minimize and resolve disputes. Furthermore, an excessive charge abuses the professional relationship between lawyer and client.

EC 2-18   The determination of the reasonableness of a fee requires consideration of all relevant circumstances, including those stated in the Disciplinary Rules. The fees of a lawyer will vary according to many factors, including the time required, the lawyer's experience, ability, and reputation, the nature of the employment, the responsibility involved, and the results obtained. It is a commendable and long-standing tradition of the bar that special consideration is given in the fixing of any fee for services rendered another lawyer or a member of the lawyer's immediate family.

EC 2-19   As soon as feasible after a lawyer has been employed, it is desirable that a clear agreement be reached with the client as to the basis of the fee charges to be made. Such a course will not only prevent later misunderstanding but will also work for good relations between the lawyer and the client. It is usually beneficial to reduce to writing the understanding of the parties regarding the fee, particularly when it is contingent. A lawyer should be mindful that many persons who desire to employ a lawyer may have had little or no experience with fee charges of lawyers, and for this reason lawyers should explain fully to such persons the reasons for the particular fee arrangement proposed.

EC 2-20   Contingent fee arrangements in civil cases have long been commonly accepted in the United States in proceedings to enforce claims. The historical bases of their acceptance are that (1) they often, and in a variety of circumstances, provide the only practical means by which one having a claim against another can economically afford, finance, and obtain the services of a competent lawyer to prosecute a claim, and (2) a successful prosecution of the claim produces a fund out of which the fee can be paid. Although a lawyer generally should decline to accept employment on a contingent fee basis by one who is able to pay a reasonable fixed fee, it is not necessarily improper for a lawyer, where justified by the particular circumstances of a case, to enter into a contingent fee contract in a civil case with any client who, after being fully informed of all relevant factors, desires that arrangement. Because of the human relationships involved and the unique character of the proceedings, contingent fee arrangements in domestic relation cases are rarely justified. In administrative agency proceedings, contingent fee contracts should be governed by the same considerations as in other civil cases. Public policy properly condemns contingent fee arrangements in criminal cases, largely on the ground that legal services in criminal cases do not produce a fund out of which the fee can be paid.

EC 2-21   A lawyer should not accept compensation or anything of value incident to the lawyer's employment or services from one other than the client without the knowledge and consent of the client after full disclosure.

EC 2-22   Without the consent of the client, a lawyer should not associate in a particular matter another lawyer outside the lawyer's firm. A fee may properly be divided between lawyers properly associated if the division is in proportion to the services performed by each lawyer or, by a writing given to the client, each lawyer assumes joint responsibility for the representation and if the total fee is reasonable.

EC 2-23   A lawyer should be zealous in efforts to avoid controversies over fees with clients and should attempt to resolve amicably any differences on the subject. A lawyer should not sue a client for a fee unless necessary to prevent fraud or gross imposition by the client.

Financial Ability to Employ Counsel: Persons Unable to Pay Reasonable Fees

EC 2-24   A person whose financial ability is not sufficient to permit payment of any fee cannot obtain legal services, other than in cases where a contingent fee is appropriate, unless the services are otherwise provided. Even a person of means may be unable to pay a reasonable fee, which is large because of the complexity, novelty, or difficulty of the problem or similar factors.

EC 2-25   A lawyer has an obligation to render public interest and pro bono legal service. A lawyer may fulfill this responsibility by providing professional services at no fee or at a reduced fee to individuals of limited financial means or to public service or charitable groups or organizations, or by participation in programs and organizations specifically designed to increase the availability of legal services. In addition, lawyers or law firms are encouraged to supplement this responsibility through the financial and other support of organizations that provide legal services to persons of limited means.

Acceptance and Retention of Employment

EC 2-26   A lawyer is under no obligation to act as adviser or advocate for every person who may wish to become a client; but in furtherance of the objective of the bar to make legal services fully available, a lawyer should not lightly decline proffered employment. The fulfillment of this objective requires acceptance by a lawyer of a fair share of tendered employment which may be unattractive both to the lawyer and the bar generally.

EC 2-27   History is replete with instances of distinguished sacrificial services by lawyers who have represented unpopular clients and causes.

Regardless of personal feelings, a lawyer should not decline representation because a client or a cause is unpopular or community reaction is adverse. A lawyer's representation of a client, including representation by appointment, does not constitute an endorsement of the client's political, economic, social or moral views or activities.

EC 2-28   The personal preference of a lawyer to avoid adversary alignment against judges, other lawyers, public officials or influential members of the community does not justify rejection of tendered employment.

EC 2-29   When a lawyer is appointed by a court or requested by a bar association to undertake representation of a person unable to obtain counsel, whether for financial or other reasons, the lawyer should not seek to be excused from undertaking the representation except for compelling reasons. Compelling reasons do not include such factors as the repugnance of the subject matter of the proceeding, the identity or position of a person involved in the case, the belief of the lawyer that the defendant in a criminal proceeding is guilty, or the belief of the lawyer regarding the merits of the civil case.

EC 2-30   Employment should not be accepted by a lawyer who is unable to render competent service or who knows or it is obvious that the person seeking to employ the lawyer desires to institute or maintain an action merely for the purpose of harassing or maliciously injuring another. Likewise, a lawyer should decline employment if the intensity of personal feelings, as distinguished from a community attitude, may impair effective representation of a prospective client. If a lawyer knows that a client has previously obtained counsel, the lawyer should not accept employment in the matter unless the other counsel approves or withdraws, or the client terminates the prior employment.

EC 2-31   Full availability of legal counsel requires both that persons be able to obtain counsel and that lawyers who undertake representation complete the work involved. Trial counsel for a convicted defendant should continue to represent the client by advising whether to take an appeal and, if the appeal is prosecuted, by representing the client through the appeal unless new counsel is substituted or withdrawal is permitted by the appropriate court.

EC 2-32   A decision by a lawyer to withdraw should be made only on the basis of compelling circumstances and, in a matter pending before a tribunal, the lawyer must comply with the rules of the tribunal regarding withdrawal. A lawyer should not withdraw without considering carefully and endeavoring to minimize the possible adverse effect on the rights of the client and the possibility of prejudice to the client as a result of the withdrawal. Even when withdrawal is justifiable, a lawyer should protect the welfare of the client by giving due notice of the withdrawal, suggesting employment of other counsel, delivering to the client all papers and property to which the client is entitled, cooperating with counsel subsequently employed, and otherwise endeavoring to minimize the possibility of harm. Further, the lawyer should refund to the client any compensation not earned during the employment.

EC 2-33 As a part of the legal profession's commitment to the principle that high quality legal services should be available to all, lawyers are encouraged to cooperate with qualified legal assistance organizations providing prepaid legal services. Such participation should at all times be in accordance with the basic tenets of the profession: independence, integrity, competence and devotion to the interests of individual clients. A lawyer so participating should make certain that the relationship with a qualified legal assistance organization in no way interferes with independent, professional representation of the interests of the individual client. A lawyer should avoid situations in which officials of the organization who are not lawyers attempt to direct lawyers concerning the manner in which legal services are performed for individual members and should also avoid situations in which consideration of economy are given undue weight in determining the lawyers employed by an organization or the legal services to be performed for the member or beneficiary, rather than competence and quality of service. A lawyer interested in maintaining the historic traditions of the profession and preserving the function of a lawyer as a trusted and independent adviser to individual members of society should carefully assess such factors when accepting employment by, or otherwise participating in a particular, qualified legal assistance organization and, while so participating, should adhere to the highest professional standards of effort and competence.

Editors' Note. In January of 1996, the New York State Bar Association voted to recommend that the Appellate Divisions approve a new DR 2-111 that would permit the sale of a law practice. At the same time, the Bar approved three new Ethical Considerations, ECs 2-34, 2-35, and 2-36, contingent on judicial adoption of DR 2-111. On May 22, 1996, the Appellate Divisions adopted DR 2-111 as proposed. On the same date, the three new Ethical Considerations automatically became part of the New York Code of

Professional Responsibility as promulgated by the New York State Bar Association. (Ethical Considerations are not formally adopted by the courts, though courts may refer to them when interpreting Disciplinary Rules.)

EC 2-34 Lawyers and law firms, particularly sole practitioners, should have the ability to sell law practices, including good will, provided certain conditions, designed primarily to protect clients, are satisfied. Where a lawyer is deceased, disabled, or missing, the sale may be effected by the lawyer's personal representative. Although the sale of a law practice should ideally result in the entire practice being transferred to a single buyer, there is no single-buyer requirement.

EC 2-35 Notice to clients of the sale of the practice should be timely provided, preferably as soon as possible after an agreement has been reached by the seller and the buyer, and in any event no later than as soon as practicable after the day of closing. The sale of litigated matters does not relieve the seller of his or her obligations under DR 2-110 regarding withdrawal. To the extent that conflicts of interest preclude the buyer from undertaking the representation of any particular clients of the seller, the seller shall, to the extent reasonably practicable, assist such clients in securing successor counsel, and if the seller cannot properly withdraw from the representation under DR 2-110, the seller shall retain responsibility for the representation.

EC 2-36 Information concerning client confidences and secrets should not be disclosed to prospective buyers except to the extent permitted by DR 2-111. To the extent disclosures are made, extreme care should be taken to ensure that client confidences and secrets are protected by all lawyers who become privy to such information in the course of examining the seller's practice for possible purchase. Sellers should consider requiring prospective buyers to execute written confidentiality agreements prior to affording them access to any information concerning client matters.

DR 2-101. Publicity and Advertising

A. A lawyer on behalf of himself or herself or partners or associates, shall not use or disseminate or participate in the preparation or dissemination of any public communication containing statements or claims that are false, deceptive, misleading or cast reflection on the legal profession as a whole.

B. Advertising or other publicity by lawyers, including participation in public functions, shall not contain puffery, self-laudation, claims regarding the quality of the lawyers' legal services, or claims that cannot be measured or verified.

C. It is proper to include information, provided its dissemination does not violate the provisions of subdivisions (A) and (B) of this section, as to:

1. Education, degrees and other scholastic distinctions, dates of admission to any bar; areas of the law in which the lawyer or law firm practices, as authorized by the Code of Professional Responsibility; public offices and teaching positions held; memberships in bar associations or other professional societies or organizations, including offices and committee assignments therein; foreign language fluency;

2. Names of clients regularly represented, provided that the client has given prior written consent;

3. Bank references; credit arrangements accepted; prepaid or group legal services programs in which the attorney or firm participates; and

4. Legal fees for initial consultation, contingent fee rates in civil matters when accompanied by a statement disclosing the information required by subdivision (1) of this section; range of fees for services, provided that there be available to the public free of charge a written statement clearly describing the scope of each advertised service; hourly rates; and fixed fees for specified legal services.

D. Advertising and publicity shall be designed to educate the public to an awareness of legal needs and to provide information relevant to the selection of the most appropriate counsel. Information other than that specifically authorized in subdivision (C) of this section that is consistent with these purposes may be disseminated providing that it does not violate any other provisions of this Rule.

E. A lawyer or law firm advertising any fixed fee for specified legal services shall, at the time of fee publication, have available to the public a written statement clearly describing the scope of each advertised service, which statement shall be delivered to the client at the time of retainer for any such service. Such legal services shall include all those services which are recognized as reasonable and necessary under local custom in the area of practice in the community where the services are performed.

F. If the advertisement is broadcast, it shall be prerecorded or taped and approved for broadcast by the lawyer, and a recording or videotape of the actual transmission shall be retained by the lawyer for a period of not less than one year following such transmission. All advertisements of legal services that are mailed, or are distributed other than by radio, television, directory, newspaper, magazine or other periodical, by a lawyer or law firm with an office for the practice of law in this state, shall also be subject to the following provisions:

   1. A copy of each advertisement shall at the time of its initial mailing or distribution be filed with the Department Disciplinary Committee of the appropriate judicial department.

   2. Such advertisement shall contain no reference to the fact of filing.

   3. If such advertisement is directed to a predetermined addressee, a list, containing the names and addresses of all persons to whom the advertisement is being or will thereafter be mailed or distributed, shall be retained by the lawyer or law firm for a period of not less than one year following the last date of mailing or distribution.

   4. The advertisements filed pursuant to this subdivision shall be open to public inspection.

   5. The requirements of this subdivision shall not apply to such professional cards or other announcements the distribution of which is authorized by DR 2-102(A).

   G. If a lawyer or law firm advertises a range of fees or an hourly rate for services, the lawyer or law firm may not charge more than the fee advertised for such services. If a lawyer or law firm advertises a fixed fee for specified legal services, or performs services described in a fee schedule, the lawyer or law firm may not charge more than the fixed fee for such stated legal service as set forth in the advertisement or fee schedule, unless the client agrees in writing that the services performed or to be performed were not legal services referred to or implied in the advertisement or in the fee schedule and, further, that a different fee arrangement shall apply to the transaction.

   H. Unless otherwise specified in the advertisement, if a lawyer publishes any fee information authorized under this Disciplinary Rule in a publication which is published more frequently than once per month, the lawyer shall be bound by any representation made therein for a period of not less than 30 days after such publication. If a lawyer publishes any fee information authorized under this Rule in a publication which is published once per month or less frequently, the lawyer shall be bound by any representation made therein until the publication of the succeeding issue. If a lawyer publishes any fee information authorized under this Rule in a publication which has no fixed date for publication of a succeeding issue, the lawyer shall be bound by any representation made therein for a reasonable period of time after publication, but in no event less than 90 days.

   I. Unless otherwise specified, if a lawyer broadcasts any fee information authorized under this Rule, the lawyer shall be bound by any representation made therein for a period of not less than 30 days after such broadcast.

J. A lawyer shall not compensate or give any thing of value to representatives of the press, radio, television or other communication medium in anticipation of or in return for professional publicity in a news item.

K. All advertisements of legal services shall include the name, office address and telephone number of the attorney or law firm whose services are being offered.

L. A lawyer or law firm advertising any contingent fee rates shall, at the time of the fee publication, disclose:

1. Whether percentages are computed before or after deduction of costs, disbursements and other expenses of litigation;

2. That, in the event there is no recovery, the client shall remain liable for the expenses of litigation, including court costs and disbursements.

DR 2-102. Professional Notices, Letterheads, and Signs

A. A lawyer or law firm may use professional cards, professional announcement cards, office signs, letterheads or similar professional notices or devices, provided the same do not violate any statute or court rule, and are in accordance with DR 2-101, including the following:

1. A professional card of a lawyer identifying the lawyer by name and as a lawyer, and giving addresses, telephone numbers, the name of the law firm, and any information permitted under DR 2-105. A professional card of a law firm may also give the names of members and associates.

2. A professional announcement card stating new or changed associations or addresses, change of firm name, or similar matters pertaining to the professional offices of a lawyer or law firm. It may state biographical data, the names of members of the firm and associates and the names and dates of predecessor firms in a continuing line of succession. It shall not state the nature of the practice except as permitted under DR 2-105.

3. A sign in or near the office and in the building directory identifying the law office. The sign shall not state the nature of the practice, except as permitted under DR 2-105.

4. A letterhead identifying the lawyer by name and as a lawyer, and giving addresses, telephone numbers, the name of the law firm, associates and any information permitted under DR 2-105. A letterhead of a law firm may also give the names of members and associates, and

names and dates relating to deceased and retired members. A lawyer may be designated "Of Counsel" on a letterhead if there is a continuing relationship with a lawyer or law firm, other than as a partner or associate. A lawyer or law firm may be designated as "General Counsel" or by similar professional reference on stationery of a client if the lawyer or the firm devotes a substantial amount of professional time in the representation of that client. The letterhead of a law firm may give the names and dates of predecessor firms in a continuing line of succession.

B. A lawyer in private practice shall not practice under a trade name, a name that is misleading as to the identity of the lawyer or lawyers practicing under such name, or a firm name containing names other than those of one or more of the lawyers in the firm, except that the name of a professional corporation may contain "P.C." or such symbols permitted by law, and, if otherwise lawful, a firm may use as, or continue to include in its name the name or names of one or more deceased or retired members of the firm or of a predecessor firm in a continuing line of succession. Such terms as "legal clinic," "legal aid," "legal service office," "legal assistance office," "defender office" and the like, may be used only by qualified legal assistance organizations described in DR 2-103(D), except that the term "legal clinic" may be used by any lawyer or law firm provided the name of a participating lawyer or firm is incorporated therein. A lawyer who assumes a judicial, legislative or public executive or administrative post or office shall not permit his or her name to remain in the name of a law firm or be used in professional notices of the firm during any significant period in which the lawyer is not actively and regularly practicing law as a member of the firm and, during such period, other members of the firm shall not use the lawyer's name in the firm name or in professional notices of the firm.

C. A lawyer shall not hold himself or herself out as having a partnership with one or more other lawyers unless they are in fact partners.

D. A partnership shall not be formed or continued between or among lawyers licensed in different jurisdictions unless all enumerations of the members and associates of the firm on its letterhead and in other permissible listings make clear the jurisdictional limitations on those members and associates of the firm not licensed to practice in all listed jurisdictions; however, the same firm name may be used in each jurisdiction.

DR 2-103. Solicitation and Recommendation of Professional Employment

A. A lawyer shall not, directly or indirectly, seek professional employment for the lawyer or a partner or associate of the lawyer from a person who has not sought advice regarding employment of the lawyer in violation of any statute or existing court rule in the judicial department in which the lawyer practices.

B. A lawyer shall not compensate or give anything of value to a person or organization to recommend or obtain employment by a client, or as a reward for having made a recommendation resulting in employment by a client, except by any of the organizations listed in DR 2-103 (D).

C. A lawyer shall not request a person or organization to recommend or promote the use of the lawyer's services or those of the lawyer's partner or associate, or any other affiliated lawyer as a private practitioner, other than by advertising or publicity not proscribed by DR 2-101, except that:

1. The lawyer may request referrals from a lawyer referral service operated, sponsored or approved by a bar association and may pay its fees incident thereto.

2. The lawyer may cooperate with the legal service activities of any of the offices or organizations enumerated in DR 2-103 (D) (1) through (4) and may perform legal services for those to whom the lawyer was recommended by such an office or organization to do such work if:

a. The person to whom the recommendation is made is a member or beneficiary of such office or organization; and

b. The lawyer remains free to exercise independent professional judgment on behalf of the client.

3. The lawyer may request such a recommendation from another lawyer or an organization performing legal services.

D. A lawyer or the lawyer's partner or associate or any other affiliated lawyer may be recommended, employed or paid by, or may cooperate with one of the following offices or organizations which promote the use of the lawyer's services or those of a partner or associate or any other affiliated lawyer if there is no interference with the exercise of independent professional judgment on behalf of the client:

1. A legal aid office or public defender office

a. Operated or sponsored by a duly accredited law school;

b. Operated or sponsored by a bona fide non-profit community organization;

c. Operated or sponsored by a governmental agency; or

d. Operated, sponsored, or approved by a bar association;

2. A military legal assistance office;

3. A lawyer referral service operated, sponsored, or approved by a bar association;

4. Any bona fide organization which recommends, furnishes or pays for legal services to its members or beneficiaries provided the following conditions are satisfied:

a. Neither the lawyer, nor the lawyer's partner, nor associate, nor any other affiliated lawyer nor any non-lawyer, shall have initiated or promoted such organization for the primary purpose of providing financial or other benefit to such lawyer, partner, associate or affiliated lawyer.

b. Such organization is not operated for the purpose of procuring legal work or financial benefit for any lawyer as a private practitioner outside of the legal services program of the organization.

c. The member or beneficiary to whom the legal services are furnished, and not such organization, is recognized as the client of the lawyer in the matter.

d. Any member or beneficiary who is entitled to have legal services furnished or paid for by the organization may, if such member or beneficiary so desires, select counsel other than that furnished, selected or approved by the organization for the particular matter involved; and the legal service plan of such organization provides appropriate relief for any member or beneficiary who asserts a claim that representation by counsel furnished, selected or approved would be unethical, improper or inadequate under the circumstances of the matter involved; and the plan provides an appropriate procedure for seeking such relief.

e. The lawyer does not know or have cause to know that such organization is in violation of applicable laws, rules of court or other legal requirements that govern its legal service operations.

f. Such organization has filed with the appropriate disciplinary authority, to the extent required by such authority, at least annually a report with respect to its legal service plan, if any, showing its terms, its schedule of benefits, its subscription charges, agreements with counsel and financial results of its legal service activities or, if it has failed to do so, the lawyer does not know or have cause to know of such failure.

E. A lawyer shall not accept employment when the lawyer knows or it is obvious that the person who seeks services does so as a result of conduct prohibited under this Disciplinary Rule.

F. Advertising not proscribed under DR 2-101 shall not be deemed in violation of any provision of this Disciplinary Rule.

DR 2-104. Suggestion of Need of Legal Services

A. A lawyer who has given unsolicited advice to an individual to obtain counsel or take legal action shall not accept employment resulting from that advice, in violation of any statute or court rule.

B. A lawyer may accept employment by a close friend, relative, former client (if the advice is germane to the former employment) or one whom the lawyer reasonably believes to be a client.

C. A lawyer may accept employment which results from participation in activities designed to educate the public to recognize legal problems, to make intelligent selection of counsel or to utilize available legal services.

D. A lawyer who is recommended, furnished or paid by a qualified legal assistance organization enumerated in DR 2-103(D) (1) through (4) may represent a member or beneficiary thereof, to the extent and under the conditions prescribed therein.

E. Without affecting the right to accept employment, a lawyer may speak publicly or write for publication on legal topics so long as the lawyer does not undertake to give individual advice.

F. Subject to compliance with the provisions of DR 2-103(A), if success in asserting rights or defenses of a client in litigation in the nature of a class action is dependent upon the joinder of others, a lawyer may accept employment from those contacted for the purpose of obtaining their joinder.

DR 2-105. Identification of Practice and Specialty

A. A lawyer or law firm may publicly identify one or more areas of law in which the lawyer or the law firm practices, or may state that the practice of the lawyer or law firm is limited to one or more areas of law.

B. A lawyer who is certified as a specialist in a particular area of law or law practice by the authority having jurisdiction under the laws of this state over the subject of specialization by lawyers may hold himself or herself out as a specialist, but only in accordance with the rules prescribed by that authority.

DR 2-105-a. Client's Statements of Rights and Responsibilities in Domestic Relations Matters

Editors' Note. The New York Court of Appeals added the language of DR 2-105-a to the Code effective November 30, 1993, but did not give it a number or title. In 1994, the Appellate Divisions gave the section a number and title and added language to reflect the codification of "Procedures for Attorneys in Domestic Relations Matters" as Part 1400 of the joint rules of the Appellate Divisions. Part 1400 of the joint rules, which includes the "statement of client's rights and responsibilities" to which DR 2-105-a refers, is reprinted in full in the next section of our New York materials.

In domestic relations matters to which Part 1400 of the joint rules of the Appellate Divisions is applicable, a lawyer shall provide a prospective client with a statement of client's rights and responsibilities at the initial conference and prior to the signing of a written retainer agreement.

DR 2-106. Fee for Legal Services

A. A lawyer shall not enter into an agreement for, charge or collect an illegal or excessive fee.

B. A fee is excessive when, after a review of the facts, a lawyer of ordinary prudence would be left with a definite and firm conviction that the fee is in excess of a reasonable fee. Factors to be considered as guides in determining the reasonableness of a fee include the following:

1. The time and labor required, the novelty and difficulty of the questions involved and the skill requisite to perform the legal service properly.

2. The likelihood, if apparent or made known to the client, that the acceptance of the particular employment will preclude other employment by the lawyer.

3. The fee customarily charged in the locality for similar legal services.

4. The amount involved and the results obtained.

5. The time limitations imposed by the client or by circumstances.

6. The nature and length of the professional relationship with the client.

7. The experience, reputation and ability of the lawyer or lawyers performing the services.

8. Whether the fee is fixed or contingent.

C. A lawyer shall not enter into an arrangement for, charge or collect:

1. A contingent fee for representing a defendant in a criminal case; or

2. Any fee in a domestic relations matter, (A) The payment or amount of which is contingent upon the securing of a divorce or upon the maintenance, support, equitable distribution, or property settle-

ments; or (B) Unless a written retainer agreement is signed by the lawyer and client setting forth in plain language the nature of the relationship and the details of the fee arrangement. A lawyer shall not include in the written retainer agreement a nonrefundable fee clause; or (C) Based upon a security interest, confession of judgment or other lien, without prior notice to the client in a signed retainer agreement and approval from the Court after notice to the adversary. A lawyer shall not foreclose on a mortgage placed on the marital residence while the spouse who consents to the mortgage remains the titleholder and the residence remains the spouse's primary residence.

   3. A fee proscribed by law or rule of court.

   D. Promptly after a lawyer has been employed in a contingent fee matter, the lawyer shall provide the client with a writing stating the method by which the fee is to be determined, including the percentage or percentages that shall accrue to the lawyer in the event of settlement, trial or appeal, litigation and other expenses to be deducted from the recovery and whether such expenses are to be deducted before or after the contingent fee is calculated. Upon conclusion of a contingent fee matter, the lawyer shall provide the client with a written statement stating the outcome of the matter, and if there is a recovery, showing the remittance to the client and the method of its determination.

   E. In domestic relations matters to which Part 1400 of the joint rules of the Appellate Divisions is applicable, a lawyer shall resolve fee disputes by arbitration at the election of the client.

   Editors' Note. The New York Court of Appeals added the language of DR 2-106(E) to the Code effective November 30, 1993 and amended it slightly in 1994 to reflect the codification of "Procedures for Attorneys in Domestic Relations Matters" as Part 1400 of the joint rules of the four Appellate Divisions. We reprint Part 1400 of the joint rules in full in the next section of our New York materials.

DR 2-107. Division of Fees Among Lawyers

   A. A lawyer shall not divide a fee for legal services with another lawyer who is not a partner in or associate of the lawyer's law firm or law office, unless:

   1. The client consents to employment of the other lawyer after a full disclosure that a division of fees will be made.

   2. The division is in proportion to the services performed by each lawyer or, by a writing given to the client, each lawyer assumes joint responsibility for the representation.

3. The total fee of the lawyers does not exceed reasonable compensation for all legal services they rendered the client.

B. This Disciplinary Rule does not prohibit payment to a former partner or associate pursuant to a separation or retirement agreement.

DR 2-108. Agreements Restricting the Practice of a Lawyer

A. A lawyer shall not be a party to or participate in a partnership or employment agreement with another lawyer that restricts the right of a lawyer to practice law after the termination of a relationship created by the agreement, except as a condition to payment of retirement benefits.

B. In connection with the settlement of a controversy or suit, a lawyer shall not enter into an agreement that restricts the right of a lawyer to practice law.

DR 2-109. Acceptance of Employment

A. A lawyer shall not accept employment on behalf of a person if the lawyer knows or it is obvious that such person wishes to:

1. Bring a legal action, conduct a defense, or assert a position in litigation, or otherwise have steps taken for such person merely for the purpose of harassing or maliciously injuring any person.

2. Present a claim or defense in litigation that is not warranted under existing law, unless it can be supported by good faith argument for an extension, modification, or reversal of existing law.

DR 2-110. Withdrawal from Employment

A. In general.

1. If permission for withdrawal from employment is required by the rules of a tribunal, a lawyer shall not withdraw from employment in a proceeding before that tribunal without its permission.

2. Even when withdrawal is otherwise permitted or required under DR 2-110(A)(1), (B), or (C), a lawyer shall not withdraw from employment until the lawyer has taken steps to the extent reasonably practicable to avoid foreseeable prejudice to the rights of the client, including giving due notice to the client, allowing time for employment of other counsel, delivering to the client all papers and prop-

erty to which the client is entitled and complying with applicable laws and rules.

3. A lawyer who withdraws from employment shall refund promptly any part of a fee paid in advance that has not been earned.

B. Mandatory withdrawal. A lawyer representing a client before a tribunal, with its permission if required by its rules, shall withdraw from employment, and a lawyer representing a client in other matters shall withdraw from employment, if:

1. The lawyer knows or it is obvious that the client is bringing the legal action, conducting the defense, or asserting a position in the litigation, or is otherwise having steps taken, merely for the purpose of harassing or maliciously injuring any person.

2. The lawyer knows or it is obvious that continued employment will result in violation of a Disciplinary Rule.

3. The lawyer's mental or physical condition renders it unreasonably difficult to carry out the employment effectively.

4. The lawyer is discharged by his or her client.

C. Permissive withdrawal. Except as stated in DR 2-110(A), a lawyer may withdraw from representing a client if withdrawal can be accomplished without material adverse effect on the interests of the client, or if:

1. The client:

a. Insists upon presenting a claim or defense that is not warranted under existing law and cannot be supported by good faith argument for an extension, modification, or reversal of existing law.

b. Persists in a course of action involving the lawyer's services that the lawyer reasonably believes is criminal or fraudulent.

c. Insists that the lawyer pursue a course of conduct which is illegal or prohibited under the Disciplinary Rules.

d. By other conduct renders it unreasonably difficult for the lawyer to carry out employment effectively.

e. Insists, in a matter not pending before a tribunal, that the lawyer engage in conduct which is contrary to the judgment and advice of the lawyer but not prohibited under the Disciplinary Rules.

f. Deliberately disregards an agreement or obligation to the lawyer as to expenses or fees.

g. Has used the lawyer's services to perpetrate a crime or fraud.

2. The lawyer's continued employment is likely to result in a violation of a Disciplinary Rule.

3. The lawyer's inability to work with co-counsel indicates that the best interests of the client likely will be served by withdrawal.

4. The lawyer's mental or physical condition renders it difficult for the lawyer to carry out the employment effectively.

5. The lawyer's client knowingly and freely assents to termination of the employment.

6. The lawyer believes in good faith, in a proceeding pending before a tribunal, that the tribunal will find the existence of other good cause for withdrawal.

Editors' Note. On May 22, 1996, the Appellate Divisions issued a joint order adopting a new DR 2-111, which permits lawyers to sell a law practice provided that both the seller and the buyer abide by certain conditions before and after the sale. The new rule is based in part on Rule 1.17 of the ABA Model Rules of Professional Conduct, but differs in several important ways.

DR 2-111. Sale of Law Practice

A. A lawyer retiring from a private practice of law, a law firm one or more members of which are retiring from the private practice of law with the firm, or the personal representative of a deceased, disabled or missing lawyer, may sell a law practice, including good will, to one or more lawyers or law firms, who may purchase the practice. The seller and the buyer may agree on reasonable restrictions on the seller's private practice of law, notwithstanding any other provision of this Code. Retirement shall include the cessation of the private practice of law in the geographic area, that is, the county and city and any county or city contiguous thereto, in which the practice to be sold has been conducted.

B. Confidences and Secrets.

1. With respect to each matter subject to the contemplated sale, the seller may provide prospective buyers with any information not protected as a confidence or secret under DR 4-101.

2. Notwithstanding DR 4-101, the seller may provide the prospective buyer with information as to individual clients:

a. concerning the identity of the client, except as provided in DR 2-111(B)(6);

b. concerning the status and general nature of the matter;

c. available in public court files; and,

d. concerning the financial terms of the attorney-client relationship and the payment status of the client's account.

3. Prior to making any disclosure of confidences or secrets that may be permitted under DR 2-111(B)(2), the seller shall provide the prospective buyer with information regarding the matters involved in the proposed sale sufficient to enable the prospective buyer to determine whether any conflicts of interest exist. Where sufficient information cannot be disclosed without revealing client confidences or secrets, the seller may make the disclosures necessary for the prospective buyer to determine whether any conflict of interest exists, subject to DR 2-111(B)(6). If the prospective buyer determines that conflicts of interest exist prior to reviewing the information or determines during the course of review that a conflict of interest exists, the prospective buyer shall not review or continue to review the information unless seller shall have obtained the consent of the client in accordance with DR 4-101(C)(1).

4. Prospective buyers shall maintain the confidentiality of and shall not use any client information received in connection with the proposed sale in the same manner and to the same extent as if the prospective buyers represented the client.

5. Absent the consent of the client after full disclosure, a seller shall not provide a prospective buyer with information if doing so would cause a violation of the attorney-client privilege.

6. If the seller has reason to believe that the identity of the client or the fact of the representation itself constitutes a confidence or secret in the circumstances, the seller may not provide such information to a prospective buyer without first advising the client of the identity of the prospective buyer and obtaining the client's consent to the proposed disclosure.

C. Written notice of the sale shall be given jointly by the seller and the buyer to each of the seller's clients and shall include information regarding:

1. The client's right to retain other counsel or to take possession of the file;

2. The fact that the client's consent to the transfer of the client's file or matter to the buyer will be presumed if the client does not take any action or otherwise object within 90 days of the sending of the notice, subject to any court rule or statute requiring express approval by the client or a court;

3. The fact that agreements between the seller and the seller's clients as to fees will be honored by the buyer;

4. Proposed fee increases, if any, permitted under DR 2-111(E); and

5. The identity and background of the buyer or buyers, including principal office address, bar admissions, number of years in practice in the state, whether the buyer has even been disciplined for professional misconduct or convicted of a crime, and whether the buyer currently intends to resell the practice.

D. When the buyer's representation of a client of the seller would give rise to a waivable conflict of interest, the buyer shall not undertake such representation unless the necessary waiver or waivers have been obtained in writing.

E. The fee charged a client by the buyer shall not be increased by reason of the sale, unless permitted by a retainer agreement with the client or otherwise specifically agreed to by the client.

CANON 3. A LAWYER SHOULD ASSIST IN PREVENTING THE UNAUTHORIZED PRACTICE OF LAW

Ethical Considerations

EC 3-1 The prohibition against the practice of law by a non-lawyer is grounded in the need of the public for integrity and competence of those who undertake to render legal services. Because of the fiduciary and personal character of the lawyer-client relationship and the inherently complex nature of our legal system, the public can better be assured of the requisite responsibility and competence if the practice of law is confined to those who are subject to the requirements and regulations imposed upon members of the legal profession.

EC 3-2 The sensitive variations in the considerations that bear on legal determinations often make it difficult even for a lawyer to exercise appropriate professional judgment, and it is therefore essential that the personal nature of the relationship of client and lawyer be preserved. Competent professional judgment is the product of a trained familiarity with law and legal processes, a disciplined, analytical approach to legal problems, and a firm ethical commitment.

EC 3-3 A non-lawyer who undertakes to handle legal matters is not governed as to integrity or legal competence by the same rules that govern the conduct of a lawyer. A lawyer is not only subject to that regulation but also is committed to high standards of ethical conduct. The public interest is best served in legal matters by a regulated profession committed to such standards. The Disciplinary Rules protect the public in that they prohibit a lawyer from seeking employment by improper overtures, from acting in cases of divided loyalties, and from submitting to the control of others in the exercise of judgment. Moreover, a person who entrusts legal matters to a lawyer is protected by the attorney-client privilege and by the duty of the lawyer to hold inviolate the confidences and secrets of the client.

EC 3-4 A person who seeks legal services often is not in a position to judge whether he or she will receive proper professional attention. The entrustment of a legal matter may well involve the confidences, the reputation, the property, the freedom, or even the life of the client. Proper protection of members of the public demands that no person be permitted to act in the confidential and demanding capacity of a lawyer without being subject to the regulations of the legal profession.

EC 3-5 It is neither necessary nor desirable to attempt the formulation of a single, specific definition of what constitutes the practice of law. Functionally, the practice of law relates to the rendition of services for others that call for the professional judgment of a lawyer. The essence of the professional judgment of the lawyer is the educated ability to relate the general body and philosophy of law to a specific legal problem of a client; and thus, the public interest will be better served if only lawyers are permitted to act in matters involving professional judgment. Where this professional judgment is not involved, non-lawyers, such as court clerks, police officers, abstracters, and many governmental employees, may engage in occupations that require a special knowledge of law in certain areas. But the services of a lawyer are essential in the public interest whenever the exercise of professional legal judgment is required.

EC 3-6 A lawyer often delegates tasks to clerks, secretaries, and other lay persons. Such delegation is proper if the lawyer maintains a direct relationship with the client, supervises the delegated work, and has complete professional responsibility for the work product. This delegation enables a lawyer to render legal services more economically and efficiently.

EC 3-7 The prohibition against a non-lawyer practicing law does not prevent a non-lawyer from representing himself or herself, for then only that person is ordinarily exposed to possible injury. The purpose of the legal profession is to make educated legal representation available to the public; but anyone who does not wish to take advantage of such representation is not required to do so. Even so, the legal profession should help members of the public to recognize legal problems and to understand why it may be unwise for them to act for themselves in matters having legal consequences.

EC 3-8 Since a lawyer should not aid or encourage a non-lawyer to practice law, the lawyer should not practice law in association with a non-lawyer or otherwise share legal fees with a non-lawyer. This does not mean, however, that the pecuniary value of the interest of a deceased lawyer in a firm or practice may not be paid to the lawyer's estate or specified persons such as the lawyer's spouse or heirs. In like manner, profit-sharing retirement plans of a lawyer or law firm which include non-lawyer office employees are not improper. These limited exceptions to the rule against sharing legal fees with non-lawyers are permissible since they do not aid or encourage non-lawyers to practice law.

EC 3-9   Regulation of the practice of law is accomplished principally by the respective states. Authority to engage in the practice of law conferred in any jurisdiction is not per se a grant of the right to practice elsewhere, and it is improper for a lawyer to engage in practice where not permitted by law or by court order to do so. However, the demands of business and the mobility of our society pose distinct problems in the regulation of the practice of law by the states. In furtherance of the public interest, the legal profession should discourage regulation that unreasonably imposes territorial limitations upon the right of a lawyer to handle the legal affairs of a client or upon the opportunity of a client to obtain the services of a lawyer of the client's choice in all matters including the presentation of a contested matter in a tribunal before which the lawyer is not permanently admitted to practice.

DR 3-101. Aiding Unauthorized Practice of Law

A. A lawyer shall not aid a non-lawyer in the unauthorized practice of law.

B. A lawyer shall not practice law in a jurisdiction where to do so would be in violation of regulations of the profession in that jurisdiction.

DR 3-102. Dividing Legal Fees with a Non-Lawyer

A. A lawyer or law firm shall not share legal fees with a non-lawyer, except that:

1. An agreement by a lawyer with his or her firm, partner, or associate may provide for the payment of money, over a reasonable period of time after the lawyer's death, to the lawyer's estate or to one or more specified persons.

2. A lawyer who undertakes to complete unfinished legal business of a deceased lawyer may pay to the estate of the deceased lawyer that

proportion of the total compensation which fairly represents the services rendered by the deceased lawyer.

3. A lawyer or law firm may include non-lawyer employees in a retirement plan, even though the plan is based in whole or in part on a profit-sharing arrangement.

DR 3-103. Forming a Partnership with a Non-Lawyer

A. A lawyer shall not form a partnership with a non-lawyer if any of the activities of the partnership consist of the practice of law.

CANON 4. A LAWYER SHOULD PRESERVE THE CONFIDENCES AND SECRETS OF A CLIENT

Ethical Considerations

EC 4-1   Both the fiduciary relationship existing between lawyer and client and the proper functioning of the legal system require the preservation by the lawyer of confidences and secrets of one who has employed or sought to employ the lawyer. A client must feel free to discuss anything with his or her lawyer and a lawyer must be equally free to obtain information beyond that volunteered by the client. A lawyer should be fully informed of all the facts of the matter being handled in order for the client to obtain the full advantage of our legal system. It is for the lawyer in the exercise of independent professional judgment to separate the relevant and important from the irrelevant and unimportant. The observance of the ethical obligation of a lawyer to hold inviolate the confidences and secrets of a client not only facilitates the full development of facts essential to proper representation of the client but also encourages non-lawyers to seek early legal assistance.

EC 4-2   The obligation to protect confidences and secrets obviously does not preclude a lawyer from revealing information when the client consents after full disclosure, when necessary to perform the lawyer's professional employment, when permitted by a Disciplinary Rule, or when required by law. Unless the client otherwise directs, a lawyer may disclose the affairs of the client to partners or associates of his or her firm. It is a matter of common knowledge that the normal operation of a law office exposes confidential professional information to non-lawyer employees of the office, particularly secretaries and those having access to the files; and this obligates a lawyer to exercise care in selecting and training employees so that the sanctity of all confidences and secrets of clients may be preserved. If the obligation extends to two or more clients as to the same information, a lawyer should obtain the permission of all before revealing the information. A lawyer must always be sensitive to the rights and wishes of the client and act scrupulously in the making of decisions which may involve the disclosure of information obtained in the professional relationship. Thus, in the absence of consent of the client after full disclosure, a lawyer should not associate another lawyer in the handling of a matter; nor should the lawyer, in the absence of consent, seek counsel from another lawyer if there is a reasonable possibility that the identity of the client or the client's confidences or secrets would be revealed to such lawyer. Both social amenities and professional duty should cause a lawyer to shun indiscreet conversations concerning clients.

EC 4-3   Unless the client otherwise directs, it is not improper for a lawyer to give limited information to an outside agency necessary for statistical, bookkeeping, accounting, data processing, banking, printing, or other legitimate purposes, provided the lawyer exercises due care in the selection of the agency and warns the agency that the information must be kept confidential.

EC 4-4   The attorney-client privilege is more limited than the ethical obligation of a lawyer to guard the confidences and secrets of the client. This ethical precept, unlike the evidentiary privilege, exists without regard to the nature or source of information or the fact that others share the knowledge. A lawyer should endeavor to act in a manner which preserves the evidentiary privilege; for example, the lawyer should avoid professional discussions in the presence of persons to whom the privilege does not extend. A lawyer owes an obligation to advise the client of the attorney-client privilege and timely to assert the privilege unless it is waived by the client.

EC 4-5   A lawyer should not use information acquired in the course of the representation of a client to the disadvantage of the client and a lawyer should not use, except with the consent of the client after full disclosure, such information for the lawyer's own purposes. Likewise, a lawyer should be diligent in his or her efforts to prevent the misuse of such information by employees and associates. Care should be exercised by a lawyer to prevent the disclosure of the confidences and secrets of one client to another, and no employment should be accepted that might require such disclosure.

EC 4-6 The obligation to protect confidences and secrets of a client continues after the termination of employment. A lawyer should also provide for the protection of the confidences and secrets of the client following the termination of the practice of the lawyer, whether termination is due to death, disability, or retirement. For example, a lawyer might provide for the personal papers of the client to be returned to the client and for the papers of the lawyer to be delivered to another lawyer or to be destroyed. In determining the method of disposition, the instructions and wishes of the client should be a dominant consideration.

EC 4-7 The lawyer's exercise of discretion to disclose confidences and secrets requires consideration of a wide range of factors and should not be subject to reexamination. A lawyer is afforded the professional discretion to reveal the intention of a client to commit a crime and the information necessary to prevent the crime and cannot be subjected to discipline either for revealing or not revealing such intention or information. In exercising this discretion, however, the lawyer should consider such factors as the seriousness of the potential injury to others if the prospective crime is committed, the likelihood that it will be committed and its imminence, the apparent absence of any other feasible way in which the potential injury can be prevented, the extent to which the client may have attempted to involve the lawyer in the prospective crime, the circumstances under which the lawyer acquired the information of the client's intent, and any other possibly aggravating or extenuating circumstances. In any case, a disclosure adverse to the client's interest should be no greater than the lawyer reasonably believes necessary to the purpose.

DR 4-101. Preservation of Confidences and Secrets of a Client

A. "Confidence" refers to information protected by the attorney-client privilege under applicable law, and "secret" refers to other information gained in the professional relationship that the client has requested be held inviolate or the disclosure of which would be embarrassing or would be likely to be detrimental to the client.

B. Except when permitted under DR 4-101(C), a lawyer shall not knowingly:

1. Reveal a confidence or secret of a client.

2. Use a confidence or secret of a client to the disadvantage of the client.

3. Use a confidence or secret of a client for the advantage of the lawyer or of a third person, unless the client consents after full disclosure.

C. A lawyer may reveal:

1. Confidences or secrets with the consent of the client or clients affected, but only after a full disclosure to them.

2. Confidences or secrets when permitted under Disciplinary Rules or required by law or court order.

3. The intention of a client to commit a crime and the information necessary to prevent the crime.

4. Confidences or secrets necessary to establish or collect the lawyer's fee or to defend the lawyer or his or her employees or associates against an accusation of wrongful conduct.

5. Confidences or secrets to the extent implicit in withdrawing a written or oral opinion or representation previously given by the lawyer and believed by the lawyer still to be relied upon by a third person where the lawyer has discovered that the opinion or representation was based on materially inaccurate information or is being used to further a crime or fraud.

D. A lawyer shall exercise reasonable care to prevent his or her employees, associates, and others whose services are utilized by the lawyer from disclosing or using confidences or secrets of a client, except that a lawyer may reveal the information allowed by DR 4-101(C) through an employee.

CANON 5. A LAWYER SHOULD EXERCISE INDEPENDENT PROFESSIONAL JUDGMENT ON BEHALF OF A CLIENT

Ethical Considerations

EC 5-1   The professional judgment of a lawyer should be exercised, within the bounds of the law, solely for the benefit of the client and free of compromising influences and loyalties. Neither the lawyer's personal interests, the interests of other clients, nor the desires of third persons should be permitted to dilute the lawyer's loyalty to the client.

Interests of a Lawyer That May Affect the Lawyer's Judgment

EC 5-2   A lawyer should not accept proffered employment if the lawyer's personal interests or desires will, or there is a reasonable probability that they will, affect adversely the advice to be given or services to be rendered the prospective client. After accepting employment, a lawyer carefully should refrain from acquiring a property right or assuming a position that would tend to make his or her judgment less protective of the interests of the client.

EC 5-3   The self-interest of a lawyer resulting from ownership of property in which the client also has an interest or which may affect property of the client may interfere with the exercise of free judgment on behalf of the client. If such interference would occur with respect to a prospective client, a lawyer should decline proffered employment. After accepting employment, a lawyer should not acquire property rights that would adversely affect the lawyer's professional judgment in the representation of the client. Even if the property interests of a lawyer do not presently interfere with the exercise of independent judgment, but the likelihood of interference can be reasonably foreseen by the lawyer, the lawyer should explain the situation to the client and should decline employment or withdraw unless the client consents to the continuance of the relationship after full disclosure. A lawyer should not seek to persuade a client to permit the lawyer to invest in an undertaking of the client nor make improper use of a professional relationship to influence the client to invest in an enterprise in which the lawyer is interested.

EC 5-4   If, in the course of the representation of a client, a lawyer is permitted to receive from the client a beneficial ownership in literary or media rights relating to the subject matter of the employment, the lawyer may be tempted to subordinate the interests of the client to the lawyer's own anticipated pecuniary gain. For example, a lawyer in a criminal case who obtains from the client television, radio, motion picture, newspaper, magazine, book, or other literary or media rights with respect to the case may be influenced, consciously or unconsciously, to a course of conduct that will enhance the value of the literary or media rights to the prejudice of the client. To prevent these potentially differing interests, such arrangements should be scrupulously avoided prior to the termination of all aspects of the matter giving rise to the employment, even though the employment has previously ended.

EC 5-5   A lawyer should not suggest to the client that a gift be made to the lawyer or for the lawyer's benefit. If a lawyer accepts a gift from the client, the lawyer is peculiarly susceptible to the charge that he or she unduly influenced or overreached the client. If a client voluntarily offers to make a gift to the lawyer, the lawyer may accept the gift, but before doing so, should urge that the client secure disinterested advice from an independent, competent person who is cognizant of all the circumstances. Other than in exceptional circumstances, a lawyer should insist that an instrument in which the client desires to name the lawyer beneficially be prepared by another lawyer selected by the client.

EC 5-6   A lawyer should not consciously influence a client to name the lawyer as executor, trustee, or lawyer in an instrument. In those cases where a client wishes to name the lawyer as such, care should be taken by the lawyer to avoid even the appearance of impropriety.

EC 5-7   The possibility of an adverse effect upon the exercise of free judgment by the lawyer on behalf of the client during litigation generally makes it undesirable for the lawyer to acquire a proprietary interest in the cause of the client or otherwise to become financially interested in the outcome of the litigation. However, it is not improper for a lawyer to protect the right to collect a fee for his or her services by the assertion of legally permissible liens, even though by doing so the lawyer may acquire an interest in the outcome of litigation. Although a contingent fee arrangement gives a lawyer a financial interest in the outcome of litigation, a reasonable contingent fee is permissible in civil cases because it may be the only means by which a non-lawyer can obtain the services of a lawyer of his or her choice. But a lawyer, who is in a better position to evaluate a cause of action, should enter into a contingent fee arrangement only in those instances where the arrangement will be beneficial to the client.

EC 5-8   A financial interest in the outcome of litigation also results if monetary advances are made by the lawyer to the client. Although this assistance generally is not encouraged, there are instances when it is not improper to make loans to a client. For example, the advancing or guaranteeing of payment of the costs and expenses of litigation by a lawyer may be the only way a client can enforce a cause of action, but the ultimate liability for such costs and expenses must be that of the client except, where not prohibited by law or court rule, in the case of an indigent client represented on a pro bono basis.

EC 5-9   Occasionally a lawyer is called upon to decide in a particular case whether the lawyer will be a witness or an advocate. If a lawyer is both counsel and witness, the lawyer becomes more easily impeachable for interest and thus may be a less effective witness. Conversely, the opposing counsel may be handicapped in challenging the credibility of the lawyer when the lawyer also appears as an advocate in the case. An advocate who becomes a witness is in the unseemly and ineffective position of arguing his or her own credibility. The roles of an advocate and of a witness are inconsistent; the function of an advocate is to advance or argue the cause of another, while that of a witness is to state facts objectively.

EC 5-10   Problems incident to the lawyer-witness relationship arise at different stages; they relate either to whether a lawyer should accept employment or should withdraw from employment. Regardless of when the problem arises, the lawyer's decision is to be governed by the same basic considerations. It is not objectionable for a lawyer who is a potential witness to be an advocate if it is unlikely that he or she will be called as a witness because the testimony would be merely cumulative or if the testimony will relate only to an uncontested issue. In the exceptional situation where it will be manifestly unfair to the client for the lawyer to refuse employment or to withdraw when the lawyer will likely be a witness on a contested issue, the lawyer may serve as advocate even though he or she may be a witness. In making such decision, the lawyer should determine the personal or financial sacrifice of the client that may result from the lawyer's refusal of employment or withdrawal therefrom, the materiality of the lawyer's testimony, and the effectiveness of the lawyer's representation in view of his or her personal involvement. In weighing these factors, it should be clear that refusal or withdrawal will impose an unreasonable hardship upon the client before the lawyer accepts or continues the employment. Where the question arises, doubts should be resolved in favor of the lawyer testifying and against the lawyer's becoming or continuing as an advocate.

EC 5-11   A lawyer should not permit personal interests to influence the lawyer's advice relative to a suggestion by the client that additional counsel be employed. In like manner, the lawyer's personal interests should not deter the lawyer from suggesting that additional counsel be employed; on the contrary, the lawyer should be alert to the desirability of recommending additional counsel when, in his or her judgment, the proper representation of the client requires it. However, a lawyer should advise the client not to employ additional counsel suggested by the client if the lawyer believes that such employment would be a disservice to the client, and the lawyer should disclose the reasons for this belief.

EC 5-12   Inability of co-counsel to agree on a matter vital to the representation of their client requires that their disagreement be submitted by them jointly to their client for resolution by the client, and the decision of the client shall control the action to be taken.

EC 5-13   A lawyer should not maintain membership in or be influenced by any organization of employees that undertakes to prescribe, direct, or suggest when or how to fulfill his or her professional obligations to a person or organization that employs the lawyer. Although it is not necessarily improper for a lawyer employed by a corporation or similar entity to be a member of an organization of employees, the lawyer should be vigilant to safeguard his or her fidelity as a lawyer to the employer, free from outside influences.

Interests of Multiple Clients

EC 5-14   Maintaining the independence of professional judgment required of a lawyer precludes acceptance or continuation of employment that will adversely affect the lawyer's judgment on behalf of or dilute the lawyer's loyalty to a client. This problem arises whenever a lawyer is asked to represent two or more clients who may have differing interests, whether such interests be conflicting, inconsistent, diverse, or otherwise discordant.

EC 5-15   If a lawyer is requested to undertake or to continue representation of multiple clients having potentially differing interests, the lawyer must weigh carefully the possibility that the lawyer's judgment may be impaired or loyalty divided if the lawyer accepts or continues the employment. The lawyer should resolve all doubts against the propriety of the representation. A lawyer should never represent in litigation multiple clients with differing interests; and there are few situations in which the lawyer would be justified in representing in litigation multiple clients with potentially differing interests. If a lawyer accepted such employment and the interests did become actually differing, the lawyer would have to withdraw from employment with likelihood of resulting hardship on the clients; and for this reason it is preferable that the lawyer refuse the employment initially. On the other hand, there are many instances in which a lawyer may properly serve multiple clients having potentially differing interests in matters not involving litigation. If the interests vary only slightly, it is generally likely that the lawyer will not be subjected to an adverse influence and that the lawyer can retain his or her independent judgment on behalf of each client; and if the interests become differing, withdrawal is less likely to have a disruptive effect upon the causes of the clients.

EC 5-16   In those instances in which a lawyer is justified in representing two or more clients having differing interests, it is nevertheless essential that each client be given the opportunity to evaluate the need for representation free of any potential conflict and to obtain other counsel if the client so desires. Thus before a lawyer may represent multiple clients, the lawyer should explain fully to each client the implications of the common representation and should accept or continue employment only if the clients consent. If there are present other circumstances that might cause any of the multiple clients to question the undivided loyalty of the lawyer, the lawyer should also advise all of the clients of those circumstances.

EC 5-17   Typically recurring situations involving potentially differing interests are those in which a lawyer is asked to represent co-defendants in a criminal case, co-plaintiffs or co-defendants in a personal injury case, an insured and insurer, and beneficiaries of the estate of a decedent. Whether a lawyer can fairly and adequately protect the interests of multiple clients in these and similar situations depends upon an analysis of each case. In certain circumstances, there may exist little chance of the judgment of the lawyer being adversely affected by the slight possibility that the interests will become actually differing; in other circumstances, the chance of adverse effect upon the lawyer's judgment is not unlikely.

EC 5-18   A lawyer employed or retained by a corporation or similar entity owes allegiance to the entity and not to a stockholder, director, officer, employee, representative, or other person connected with the entity. In advising the entity, a lawyer should keep paramount its interests and the lawyer's professional judgment should not be influenced by the personal desires of any person or organization. Occasionally, the lawyer may learn that an officer, employee or other person associated with the entity is engaged in action, refuses to act, or intends to act or to refrain from acting in a matter related to the representation that is a violation of a legal obligation to the entity, or a violation of law which reasonably might be imputed to the entity, and is likely to result in substantial injury to the entity. In such event, the lawyer should proceed as is reasonably necessary in the best interest of the entity. In determining how to proceed, the lawyer should give due consideration to the seriousness of the violation and its consequences, the scope and nature of the lawyer's representation, the responsibility in the entity and the apparent motivation of the person involved, the policies of the entity concerning such matters and any other relevant considerations. Any measures taken should be designed to minimize disruption of the entity and the risk of revealing confidences and secrets of the entity. Such measures may include among others, asking reconsideration of the matter, advising that a separate legal opinion on the matter be sought for presentation to appropriate authority in the entity, and referring the matter to higher authority in the entity not involved in the wrongdoing, including, if warranted by the seriousness of the matter, referral to the highest authority that can act in behalf of the entity as determined by applicable law. Occasionally a lawyer for an entity is requested to represent a stockholder, director, officer, employee, representative, or other person connected with the entity in an individual capacity; in such case the lawyer may serve the individual only if the lawyer is convinced that differing interests are not present.

EC 5-19 A lawyer may represent several clients whose interests are not actually or potentially differing. Nevertheless, the lawyer should explain any circumstances that might cause a client to question the lawyer's undivided loyalty. Regardless of the belief of a lawyer that he or she may properly represent multiple clients, the lawyer must defer to a client who holds the contrary belief and withdraw from representation of that client.

EC 5-20 A lawyer is often asked to serve as an impartial arbitrator or mediator in matters which involve present or former clients. The lawyer may serve in either capacity after disclosing such present or former relationships. A lawyer who has undertaken to act as an impartial arbitrator or mediator should not thereafter represent in the dispute any of the parties involved.

Desires of Third Persons

EC 5-21 The obligation of a lawyer to exercise professional judgment solely on behalf of the client requires disregarding the desires of others that might impair the lawyer's free judgment. The desires of a third person will seldom adversely affect a lawyer unless that person is in a position to exert strong economic, political, or social pressures upon the lawyer. These influences are often subtle, and a lawyer must be alert to their existence. A lawyer subjected to outside pressures should make full disclosure of them to the client; and if the lawyer or the client believes that the effectiveness of the representation has been or will be impaired thereby, the lawyer should take proper steps to withdraw from representation of the client.

EC 5-22   Economic, political, or social pressures by third persons are less likely to impinge upon the independent judgment of a lawyer in a matter in which the lawyer is compensated directly by the client and the professional work is exclusively with the client. On the other hand, if a lawyer is compensated from a source other than the client, the lawyer may feel a sense of responsibility to someone other than the client.

EC 5-23   A person or organization that pays or furnishes lawyers to represent others possesses a potential power to exert strong pressures against the independent judgment of those lawyers. Some employers may be interested in furthering their own economic, political, or social goals without regard to the professional responsibility of the lawyer to an individual client. Others may be far more concerned with establishment or extension of legal principles than in the immediate protection of the rights of the lawyer's individual client. On some occasions, decisions on priority of work may be made by the employer rather than the lawyer with the result that prosecution of work already undertaken for clients is postponed to their detriment. Similarly, an employer may seek, consciously or unconsciously, to further its own economic interests through the actions of the lawyers employed by it. Since a lawyer must always be free to exercise professional judgment without regard to the interests or motives of a third person, the lawyer who is employed by one to represent another must constantly guard against erosion of professional freedom.

EC 5-24   To assist a lawyer in preserving professional independence, a number of courses are available. For example, a lawyer should not practice with or in the form of a professional legal corporation, even though the corporate form is permitted by law, if any of its directors, officers, or stockholders is a non-lawyer. Although a lawyer may be employed by a business corporation with non-lawyers serving as directors or officers, and they necessarily have the right to make decisions of business policy, a lawyer must decline to accept direction of his or her professional judgment from any non-lawyer. Various types of legal aid offices are administered by boards of directors composed of lawyers and non-lawyers. A lawyer should not accept employment from such an organization unless the board sets only broad policies and there is no interference in the relationship of the lawyer and his or her individual client. Where a lawyer is employed by an organization, a written agreement that defines the relationship between the lawyer and the organization and provides for the lawyer's independence is desirable since it may serve to prevent misunderstanding as to their respective roles. Although other innovations in the means of supplying legal counsel may develop, the responsibility of the lawyer to maintain professional independence remains constant, and the legal profession must insure that changing circumstances do not result in loss of the professional independence of the lawyer.

DR 5-101. Refusing Employment When the Interests of the Lawyer May Impair Independent Professional Judgment

A. Except with the consent of the client after full disclosure, a lawyer shall not accept employment if the exercise of professional judgment on behalf of the client will be or reasonably may be affected by the lawyer's own financial, business, property, or personal interests.

B. A lawyer shall not act, or accept employment that contemplates the lawyer's acting, as an advocate before any tribunal if the lawyer knows or it is obvious that the lawyer ought to be called as a witness on behalf of the client, except that the lawyer may act as an advocate and also testify:

1. If the testimony will relate solely to an uncontested issue.

2. If the testimony will relate solely to a matter of formality and there is no reason to believe that substantial evidence will be offered in opposition to the testimony.

3. If the testimony will relate solely to the nature and value of legal services rendered in the case by the lawyer or the lawyer's firm to the client.

4. As to any matter, if disqualification as an advocate would work a substantial hardship on the client because of the distinctive value of the lawyer as counsel in the particular case.

C. Neither a lawyer nor the lawyer's firm shall accept employment in contemplated or pending litigation if the lawyer knows or it is obvious that the lawyer or another lawyer in the lawyer's firm may be called as a witness other than on behalf of the client, and it is apparent that the testimony would or might be prejudicial to the client.

DR 5-102. Withdrawal as Counsel When the
Lawyer Becomes a Witness

A. If, after undertaking employment in contemplated or pending litigation, a lawyer learns or it is obvious that the lawyer ought to be called as a witness on behalf of the client, the lawyer shall withdraw as an advocate before the tribunal, except that the lawyer may continue as an advocate and may testify in the circumstances enumerated in DR 5-101(B)(1) through (4).

B. If, after undertaking employment in contemplated or pending litigation, a lawyer learns or it is obvious that the lawyer or a lawyer in his firm may be called as a witness other than on behalf of the client, the lawyer may continue the representation until it is apparent that the testimony is or may be prejudicial to the client at which point the lawyer and the firm must withdraw from acting as an advocate before the tribunal.

DR 5-103. Avoiding Acquisition of Interest in
Litigation

A. lawyer shall not acquire a proprietary interest in the cause of action or subject matter of litigation he or she is conducting for a client, except that the lawyer may:

1. Acquire a lien granted by law to secure the lawyer's fee or expenses.

2. Except as provided in DR 2-106(C)(2) or (3), contract with a client for a reasonable contingent fee in a civil case.

B. While representing a client in connection with contemplated or pending litigation, a lawyer shall not advance or guarantee financial assistance to the client, except that:

1. A lawyer may advance or guarantee the expenses of litigation, including court costs, expenses of investigation, expenses of medical examination, and costs of obtaining and presenting evidence, provided the client remains ultimately liable for such expenses.

2. Unless prohibited by law or rule of court, a lawyer representing an indigent client on a pro bono basis may pay court costs and reasonable expenses of litigation on behalf of the client.

DR 5-104. Limiting Business Relations with a
Client

A. A lawyer shall not enter into a business transaction with a client if they have differing interests therein and if the client expects the lawyer to exercise professional judgment therein for the protection of the client, unless the client has consented after full disclosure.

B. Prior to conclusion of all aspects of the matter giving rise to employment, a lawyer shall not enter into any arrangement or understanding with a client or a prospective client by which the lawyer acquires an interest in literary or media rights with respect to the subject matter of the employment or proposed employment.

DR 5-105. Refusing to Accept or Continue Employment if the Interests of Another Client May Impair the Independent Professional Judgment of the Lawyer

Editors' Note. On May 22, 1996, the Appellate Divisions issued a joint order amending DR 5-105 (as well as DR 1-102 and DR 1-104). The only amendment to DR 5-105 is to add a new subparagraph (E) to the rule. However, this subparagraph makes New York the first jurisdiction in the nation to hold a law firm as an entity responsible for failing to adopt or implement a system for checking and preventing conflicts of interest that would disqualify the entire firm.

A. A lawyer shall decline proffered employment if the exercise of independent professional judgment in behalf of a client will be or is likely to be adversely affected by the acceptance of the proffered employment, or if it would be likely to involve the lawyer in representing differing interests, except to the extent permitted under DR 5-105 (C).

B. A lawyer shall not continue multiple employment if the exercise of independent professional judgment in behalf of a client will be or is likely to be adversely affected by the lawyer's representation of another client, or if it would be likely to involve the lawyer in representing differing interests, except to the extent permitted under DR 5-105 (C).

C. In the situations covered by DR 5-105 (A) and (B), a lawyer may represent multiple clients if it is obvious that the lawyer can adequately represent the interest of each and if each consents to the representation after full disclosure of the possible effect of such representation on the exercise of the lawyer's independent professional judgment on behalf of each.

D. While lawyers are associated in a law firm, none of them shall knowingly accept or continue employment when any one of them practicing alone would be prohibited from doing so under DR 5-101(A), DR 5-105(A), (B) or (C), DR 5-108, or DR 9-101(B) except as otherwise provided therein.

E. A law firm shall keep records of prior engagements, which records shall be made at or near the time of such engagements and shall have a policy implementing a system by which proposed engagements are checked against current and previous engagements, so as to render effective assistance to lawyers within the firm in complying with subdivision (D) of this disciplinary rule. Failure to keep records or to have a policy which complies with this subdivision, whether or not a violation of subdivision (D) of this disciplinary rule occurs, shall be a violation by the firm. In cases where a violation of this subdivision by the firm is a substantial factor in causing a violation of subdivision (d) by a lawyer, the firm, as well as the individual lawyer, shall also be responsible for the violation of subdivision (D).

DR 5-106. Settling Similar Claims of Clients

A. A lawyer who represents two or more clients shall not make or participate in the making of an aggregate settlement of the claims of or against the clients, unless each client has consented to the settlement after being advised of the existence and nature of all the claims involved in the proposed settlement, of the total amount of the settlement, and of the participation of each person in the settlement.

DR 5-107. Avoiding Influence by Others than the Client

A. Except with the consent of the client after full disclosure a lawyer shall not:

1. Accept compensation for legal services from one other than the client.

2. Accept from one other than the client any thing of value related to his or her representation of or employment by the client.

B. A lawyer shall not permit a person who recommends, employs, or pays the lawyer to render legal service for another to direct or regulate his or her professional judgment in rendering such legal services.

C. A lawyer shall not practice with or in the form of a professional corporation or association authorized to practice law for a profit, if:

1. A non-lawyer owns any interest therein, except that a fiduciary representative of the estate of a lawyer may hold the stock or interest of the lawyer for a reasonable time during administration;

2. A non-lawyer is a corporate director or officer thereof; or

3. A non-lawyer has the right to direct or control the professional judgment of a lawyer.

DR 5-108. Conflict of Interest — Former Client

A. Except with the consent of a former client after full disclosure a lawyer who has represented the former client in a matter shall not:

1. Thereafter represent another person in the same or a substantially related matter in which that person's interests are materially adverse to the interests of the former client.

2. Use any confidences or secrets of the former client except as permitted by DR 4-101(C) or when the confidence or secret has become generally known.

DR 5-109. Conflict of Interest — Organization as Client

A. When a lawyer employed or retained by an organization is dealing with the organization's directors, officers, employees, members, shareholders or other constituents, and it appears that the organization's interests may differ from those of the constituents with whom the lawyer is dealing, the lawyer shall explain that the lawyer is the lawyer for the organization and not for any of the constituents.

DR 5-110. Membership in Legal Services Organization

A. A lawyer may serve as a director, officer or member of a not-for-profit legal services organization, apart from the law firm in which the lawyer practices, notwithstanding that the organization serves persons having interests that differ from those of a client of the lawyer or the lawyer's firm, provided that the lawyer shall not knowingly participate in a decision or action of the organization:

1. If participating in the decision or action would be incompatible with the lawyer's duty of loyalty to a client under Canon 5; or

2. Where the decision or action could have a material adverse effect on the representation of a client of the organization whose interests differ from those of a client of the lawyer or the lawyer's firm.

CANON 6. A LAWYER SHOULD REPRESENT A CLIENT COMPETENTLY

Ethical Considerations

EC 6-1 Because of the lawyer's vital role in the legal process, the lawyer should act with competence and proper care in representing clients. The lawyer should strive to become and remain proficient in his or her practice and should accept employment only in matters which he or she is or intends to become competent to handle.

EC 6-2 A lawyer is aided in attaining and maintaining competence by keeping abreast of current legal literature and developments, participating in continuing legal education programs, concentrating in particular areas of the law, and by utilizing other available means. The lawyer has the additional ethical obligation to assist in improving the legal profession, and may do so by participating in bar activities intended to advance the quality and standards of members of the profession. Of particular importance is the careful training of younger associates and the giving of sound guidance to all lawyers who consult the lawyer. In short, a lawyer should strive at all levels to aid the legal profession in advancing the highest possible standards of integrity and competence and personally to meet those standards.

EC 6-3 While the licensing of a lawyer is evidence of meeting the standards then prevailing for admission to the bar, a lawyer generally should not accept employment in any area of the law in which he or she is not qualified. However, the lawyer may accept such employment if in good faith the lawyer expects to become qualified through study and investigation, as long as such preparation would not result in unreasonable delay or expense to the client. Proper preparation and representation may require the association by the lawyer of professionals in other disciplines. A lawyer offered employment in a matter in which the lawyer is not and does not expect to become so qualified should either decline the employment or, with the consent of the client, accept the employment and associate a lawyer who is competent in the matter.

EC 6-4   Having undertaken representation, a lawyer should use proper care to safeguard the interests of the client. If a lawyer has accepted employment in a matter beyond the lawyer's competence but in which the lawyer expected to become competent, the lawyer should diligently undertake the work and study necessary to be qualified. In addition to being qualified to handle a particular matter, the lawyer's obligation to the client requires adequate preparation for and appropriate attention to the legal work, as well as promptly responding to inquiries from the client.

EC 6-5   A lawyer should have pride in his or her professional endeavors. The obligation to act competently calls for higher motivation than that arising from fear of civil liability or disciplinary penalty.

EC 6-6   A lawyer should not seek, by contract or other means, to limit prospectively the lawyer's individual liability to the client for malpractice nor shall a lawyer settle a claim for malpractice with an otherwise unrepresented client without first advising the client that independent representation is appropriate. A lawyer who handles the affairs of the client properly has no need to attempt to limit liability for professional activities and one who does not handle the affairs of the client properly should not be permitted to do so. A lawyer who is a stockholder in or is associated with a professional legal corporation may, however, limit the lawyer's liability for malpractice of associates in the corporation, but only to the extent permitted by law.

DR 6-101. Failing to Act Competently

A. A lawyer shall not:
1. Handle a legal matter which the lawyer knows or should know that he or she is not competent to handle, without associating with a lawyer who is competent to handle it.
2. Handle a legal matter without preparation adequate in the circumstances.
3. Neglect a legal matter entrusted to the lawyer.

DR 6-102. Limiting Liability to Client

A. A lawyer shall not seek, by contract or other means, to limit prospectively the lawyer's individual liability to a client for malpractice, or,

without first advising that person that independent representation is appropriate in connection therewith, to settle a claim for such liability with an unrepresented client or former client.

CANON 7. A LAWYER SHOULD REPRESENT A CLIENT ZEALOUSLY WITHIN THE BOUNDS OF THE LAW

Ethical Considerations

EC 7-1   The duty of a lawyer, both to the client and to the legal system, is to represent the client zealously within the bounds of the law, which includes Disciplinary Rules and enforceable professional regulations. The professional responsibility of a lawyer derives from membership in a profession which has the duty of assisting members of the public to secure and protect available legal rights and benefits. In our government of laws and not of individuals, each member of our society is entitled to have his or her conduct judged and regulated in accordance with the law; to seek any lawful objective through legally permissible means; and to present for adjudication any lawful claim, issue, or defense.

EC 7-2   The bounds of the law in a given case are often difficult to ascertain. The language of legislative enactments and judicial opinions may be uncertain as applied to varying factual situations. The limits and specific meaning of apparently relevant law may be made doubtful by changing or developing constitutional interpretations, inadequately expressed statutes or judicial opinions, and changing public and judicial attitudes. Certainty of law ranges from well-settled rules through areas of conflicting authority to areas without precedent.

EC 7-3   Where the bounds of law are uncertain, the action of a lawyer may depend on whether the lawyer is serving as advocate or adviser. A lawyer may serve simultaneously as both advocate and adviser, but the two roles are essentially different. In asserting a position on behalf of the client, an advocate for the most part deals with past conduct and must take the facts as they are. By contrast, a lawyer serving as adviser primarily assists the client in determining the course of future conduct and relationships. While serving as advocate, a lawyer should resolve in favor of the client doubts as to the bounds of the law. In serving a client as adviser, a lawyer in appropriate circumstances should give his or her professional opinion as to what the ultimate decisions of the courts would likely be as to the applicable law.

Duty of the Lawyer to a Client

EC 7-4   The advocate may urge any permissible construction of the law favorable to the client, without regard to the lawyer's professional opinion as to the likelihood that the construction will ultimately prevail. The lawyer's conduct is within the bounds of the law, and therefore permissible, if the position taken is supported by the law or is supportable by a good faith argument for an extension, modification, or reversal of the law. However, a lawyer is not justified in asserting a position in litigation that is frivolous.

EC 7-5   A lawyer as adviser furthers the interest of the client by giving a professional opinion as to what he or she believes would likely be the ultimate decision of the courts on the matter at hand and by informing the client of the practical effect of such decision. The lawyer may continue in the representation of the client even though the client has elected to pursue a course of conduct contrary to the advice of the lawyer so long as the lawyer does not thereby knowingly assist the client to engage in illegal conduct or to take a frivolous legal position. A lawyer should never encourage or aid the client to commit criminal acts or counsel the client on how to violate the law and avoid punishment therefor.

EC 7-6   Whether the proposed action of a lawyer is within the bounds of the law may be a perplexing question when the client is contemplating a course of conduct having legal consequences that vary according to the client's intent, motive, or desires at the time of the action. Often a lawyer is asked to assist the client in developing evidence relevant to the state of mind of the client at a particular time. The lawyer may properly assist the client in the development and preservation of evidence of existing motive, intent, or desire; obviously, the lawyer may not do anything furthering the creation or preservation of false evidence. In many cases a lawyer may not be certain as to the state of mind of the client, and in those situations the lawyer should resolve reasonable doubts in favor of the client.

EC 7-7   In certain areas of legal representation not affecting the merits of the cause or substantially prejudicing the rights of a client, a lawyer is entitled to make decisions. But otherwise the authority to make decisions is exclusively that of the client and, if made within the framework of the law, such decisions are binding on the lawyer. As typical examples in civil cases, it is for the client to decide whether to accept a settlement offer or whether to waive the right to plead an affirmative defense. A defense lawyer in a criminal case has the duty to advise the client fully on whether a particular plea to a charge appears to be desirable and as to the prospects of success on appeal, but it is for the client to decide what plea should be entered and whether an appeal should be taken.

EC 7-8   A lawyer should exert best efforts to insure that decisions of the client are made only after the client has been informed of relevant considerations. A lawyer ought to initiate this decision-making process if the client does not do so. Advice of a lawyer to the client need not be confined to purely legal considerations. A lawyer should advise the client of the possible effect of each legal alternative. A lawyer should bring to bear upon this decision-making process the fullness of his or her experience as well as the lawyer's objective viewpoint. In assisting the client to reach a proper decision, it is often desirable for a lawyer to point out those factors which may lead to a decision that is morally just as well as legally permissible. The lawyer may emphasize the possibility of harsh consequences that might result from assertion of legally permissible positions. In the final analysis, however, the lawyer should always remember that the decision whether to forego legally available objectives or methods because of non-legal factors is ultimately for the client and not for the lawyer. In the event that the client in a non-adjudicatory matter insists upon a course of conduct that is contrary to the judgment and advice of the lawyer but not prohibited by Disciplinary Rules, the lawyer may withdraw from the employment.

EC 7-9   In the exercise of the lawyer's professional judgment on those decisions which are for the lawyer's determination in the handling of a legal matter, a lawyer should always act in a manner consistent with the best interests of the client. However, when an action in the best interest of the client seems to the lawyer to be unjust, the lawyer may ask the client for permission to forego such action.

EC 7-10   The duty of a lawyer to represent the client with zeal does not militate against the concurrent obligations to treat with consideration all persons involved in the legal process and to avoid the infliction of needless harm.

EC 7-11   The responsibilities of a lawyer may vary according to the intelligence, experience, mental condition or age of a client, the obligation of a public officer, or the nature of a particular proceeding. Examples include the representation of an illiterate or an incompetent, service as a public prosecutor or other government lawyer, and appearances before administrative and legislative bodies.

EC 7-12 Any mental or physical condition that renders a client incapable of making a considered judgment on his or her own behalf casts additional responsibilities upon the lawyer. Where an incompetent is acting through a guardian or other legal representative, a lawyer must look to such representative for those decisions which are normally the prerogative of the client to make. If a client under disability has no legal representative, the lawyer may be compelled in court proceedings to make decisions on behalf of the client. If the client is capable of understanding the matter in question or of contributing to the advancement of his or her interests, regardless of whether the client is legally disqualified from performing certain acts, the lawyer should obtain from the client all possible aid. If the disability of a client and the lack of a legal representative compel the lawyer to make decisions for the client, the lawyer should consider all circumstances then prevailing and act with care to safeguard and advance the interests of the client. But obviously a lawyer cannot perform any act or make any decision which the law requires the client to perform or make, either acting alone if competent, or by a duly constituted representative if legally incompetent.

EC 7-13 The responsibility of a public prosecutor differs from that of the usual advocate; it is to seek justice, not merely to convict. This special duty exists because: (1) the prosecutor represents the sovereign and therefore should use restraint in the discretionary exercise of governmental powers, such as in the selection of cases to prosecute; (2) during trial the prosecutor is not only an advocate but also may make decisions normally made by an individual client, and those affecting the public interest should be fair to all; and (3) in our system of criminal justice the accused is to be given the benefit of all reasonable doubts. With respect to evidence and witnesses, the prosecutor has responsibilities different from those of a lawyer in private practice: the prosecutor should make timely disclosure to the defense of available evidence, known to the prosecutor, that tends to negate the guilt of the accused, mitigate the degree of the offense, or reduce the punishment. Further, a prosecutor should not intentionally avoid pursuit of evidence merely because he or she believes it will damage the prosecutor's case or aid the accused.

EC 7-14 A government lawyer who has discretionary power relative to litigation should refrain from instituting or continuing litigation that is obviously unfair. A government lawyer not having such discretionary power who believes there is lack of merit in a controversy submitted to the lawyer should so advise his or her superiors and recommend the avoidance of unfair litigation. A government lawyer in a civil action or administrative proceeding has the responsibility to seek justice and to develop a full and fair record, and should not use his or her position or the economic power of the government to harass parties or to bring about unjust settlements or results. The responsibilities of government lawyers with respect to the compulsion of testimony and other information are generally the same as those of public prosecutors.

EC 7-15   The nature and purpose of proceedings before administrative agencies vary widely. The proceedings may be legislative or quasi-judicial, or a combination of both. They may be *ex parte* in character, in which event they may originate either at the instance of the agency or upon motion of an interested party. The scope of an inquiry may be purely investigative or it may be truly adversary looking toward the adjudication of specific rights of a party or of classes of parties. The foregoing are but examples of some of the types of proceedings conducted by administrative agencies. A lawyer appearing before an administrative agency, regardless of the nature of the proceeding it is conducting, has the continuing duty to advance the cause of the client within the bounds of the law. Where the applicable rules of the agency impose specific obligations upon a lawyer, it is the lawyer's duty to comply therewith, unless the lawyer has a legitimate basis for challenging the validity thereof. In all appearances before administrative agencies, a lawyer should identify the lawyer, the client, if identity of the client is not privileged, and the representative nature of the lawyer's appearance. It is not improper, however, for a lawyer to seek from an agency information available to the public without identifying the client.

EC 7-16   The primary business of a legislative body is to enact laws rather than to adjudicate controversies, although on occasion the activities of a legislative body may take on the characteristics of an adversary proceeding, particularly in investigative and impeachment matters. The role of a lawyer supporting or opposing proposed legislation normally is quite different from the lawyer's role in representing a person under investigation or on trial by a legislative body. When a lawyer appears in connection with proposed legislation, it is to affect the lawmaking process, but when the lawyer appears on behalf of a client in investigatory or impeachment proceedings, it is to protect the rights of the client. In either event, the lawyer should identify the lawyer and the client, if identity of the client is not privileged, and should comply with applicable laws and legislative rules.

EC 7-17   The obligation of loyalty to the client applies only to a lawyer in the discharge of professional duties and implies no obligation to adopt a personal viewpoint favorable to the interests or desires of the client. While a lawyer must act always with circumspection in order that the lawyer's conduct will not adversely affect the rights of a client in a matter the lawyer is then handling, the lawyer may take positions on public issues and espouse legal reforms favored by the lawyer without regard to the individual views of any client.

EC 7-18   The legal system in its broadest sense functions best when persons in need of legal advice or assistance are represented by their own counsel. For this reason a lawyer should not communicate on the subject matter of the representation of the client with a person the lawyer knows to be represented in the matter by a lawyer, unless pursuant to law or rule of court or unless the lawyer has the consent of the lawyer for that person. If one is not represented by counsel, a lawyer representing another may have to deal directly with the unrepresented person; in such an instance, a lawyer should not undertake to give advice to the person who is not represented by a lawyer, except to advise the person to obtain a lawyer.

Duty of the Lawyer to the Adversary System of Justice

EC 7-19   Our legal system provides for the adjudication of disputes governed by the rules of substantive, evidentiary, and procedural law. An adversary presentation counters the natural human tendency to judge too swiftly in terms of the familiar that which is not yet fully known; the advocate, by zealous preparation and presentation of facts and law, enables the tribunal to come to the hearing with an open and neutral mind and to render impartial judgments. The duty of a lawyer to a client and the lawyer's duty to the legal system are the same: to represent the client zealously within the bounds of the law.

EC 7-20   In order to function properly, our adjudicative process requires an informed, impartial tribunal capable of administering justice promptly and efficiently according to procedures that command public confidence and respect. Not only must there be competent, adverse presentation of evidence and issues, but a tribunal must be aided by rules appropriate to an effective and dignified process. The procedures under which tribunals operate in our adversary system have been prescribed largely by legislative enactments, court rules and decisions, and administrative rules. Through the years certain concepts of proper professional conduct have become rules of law applicable to the adversary adjudicative process. Many of these concepts are the bases for standards of professional conduct set forth in the Disciplinary Rules.

EC 7-21   The civil adjudicative process is primarily designed for the settlement of disputes between parties, while the criminal process is designed for the protection of society as a whole. Threatening to use, or using, the criminal process to coerce adjustment of private civil claims or controversies is a subversion of that process; further, the person against whom the criminal process is so misused may be deterred from asserting legal rights and thus the usefulness of the civil process in settling private disputes is impaired. As in all cases of abuse of judicial process, the improper use of criminal process tends to diminish public confidence in our legal system.

EC 7-22   Respect for judicial rulings is essential to the proper administration of justice; however, a litigant or lawyer may, in good faith and within the framework of the law, take steps to test the correctness of a ruling of a tribunal.

EC 7-23   The complexity of law often makes it difficult for a tribunal to be fully informed unless the pertinent law is presented by the lawyers in the cause. A tribunal that is fully informed on the applicable law is better able to make a fair and accurate determination of the matter before it. The adversary system contemplates that each lawyer will present and argue the existing law in the light most favorable to the client. Where a lawyer knows of controlling legal authority directly adverse to the position of the client, the lawyer should inform the tribunal of its existence unless the adversary has done so; but, having made such disclosure, the lawyer may challenge its soundness in whole or in part.

EC 7-24   In order to bring about just and informed decisions, evidentiary and procedural rules have been established by tribunals to permit the inclusion of relevant evidence and argument and the exclusion of all other considerations. The expression by a lawyer of a personal opinion as to the justness of a cause, as to the credibility of a witness, as to the culpability of a civil litigant, or as to the guilt or innocence of an accused is not a proper subject for argument to the trier of fact. It is improper as to factual matters because admissible evidence possessed by a lawyer should be presented only as sworn testimony. It is improper as to all other matters because, were the rule otherwise, the silence of a lawyer on a given occasion could be construed unfavorably to the client. However, a lawyer may argue, based on the lawyer's analysis of the evidence, for any position or conclusion with respect to any of the foregoing matters.

EC 7-25   Rules of evidence and procedure are designed to lead to just decisions and are part of the framework of the law. Thus while a lawyer may take steps in good faith and within the framework of the law to test the validity of rules, the lawyer is not justified in consciously violating such rules and should be diligent in his or her efforts to guard against unintentional violation of them. As examples, a lawyer should subscribe to or verify only those pleadings that the lawyer believes are in compliance with applicable law and rules; a lawyer should not make any prefatory statement before a tribunal in regard to the purported facts of the case on trial unless the lawyer believes that the statement will be supported by admissible evidence; a lawyer should not ask a witness a question solely for the purpose of harassment or embarrassment; and a lawyer should not by subterfuge put before a jury matters which it cannot properly consider.

EC 7-26   The law and Disciplinary Rules prohibit the use of fraudulent, false, or perjured testimony or evidence. A lawyer who knowingly participates in introduction of such testimony or evidence is subject to discipline. A lawyer should, however, present any admissible evidence the client desires to have presented unless the lawyer knows, or from facts within the lawyer's knowledge should know, that such testimony or evidence is false, fraudulent, or perjured.

EC 7-27   Because it interferes with the proper administration of justice, a lawyer should not suppress evidence that the lawyer or the client has a legal obligation to reveal or produce. In like manner, a lawyer should not advise or cause a person to hide or to leave the jurisdiction of a tribunal for the purpose of being unavailable as a witness therein.

EC 7-28   Witnesses should always testify truthfully and should be free from any financial inducements that might tempt them to do otherwise. A lawyer should not pay or agree to pay a non-expert witness an amount in excess of reimbursement for expenses and financial loss incident to being a witness; however, a lawyer may pay or agree to pay an expert witness a reasonable fee for services as an expert. But in no event should a lawyer pay or agree to pay a contingent fee to any witness. A lawyer should exercise reasonable diligence to see that the client and lay associates conform to these standards.

EC 7-29   To safeguard the impartiality that is essential to the judicial process, members of the venire and jurors should be protected against extraneous influences. When impartiality is present, public confidence in the judicial system is enhanced. There should be no extrajudicial communication with members of the venire prior to trial or with jurors during trial or on behalf of a lawyer connected with the case. Furthermore, a lawyer who is not connected with the case should not communicate with or cause another to communicate with a member of the venire or a juror about the case. After the trial, communication by a lawyer with jurors is permitted so long as the lawyer refrains from asking questions or making comments that tend to harass or embarrass the juror or to influence actions of the juror in future cases. Were a lawyer to be prohibited from communication after trial with a juror, the lawyer could not ascertain if the verdict might be subject to legal challenge, in which event the invalidity of a verdict might go undetected. When an extrajudicial communication by a lawyer with a juror is permitted by law, it should be made considerately and with deference to the personal feelings of the juror.

EC 7-30   Vexatious or harassing investigations of members of the venire or jurors seriously impair the effectiveness of our jury system. For this reason, a lawyer or anyone on the lawyer's behalf who conducts an investigation of members of the venire or jurors should act with circumspection and restraint.

EC 7-31   Communications with or investigations of members of families of members of the venire or jurors by a lawyer or by anyone on the lawyer's behalf are subject to the restrictions imposed upon the lawyer with respect to communications with or investigations of members of the venire and jurors.

EC 7-32   Because of the duty to aid in preserving the integrity of the jury system, a lawyer who learns of improper conduct by or toward a member of the venire, a juror, or a member of the family of either should make a prompt report to the court regarding such conduct.

EC 7-33   A goal of our legal system is that each party shall have his or her case, criminal or civil, adjudicated by an impartial tribunal. The attainment of this goal may be defeated by dissemination of news or comments which tend to influence judge or jury. Such news or comments may prevent prospective jurors from being impartial at the outset of the trial and may also interfere with the obligation of jurors to base their verdict solely upon the evidence admitted in the trial. The release by a lawyer of out-of-court statements regarding an anticipated or pending trial may improperly affect the impartiality of the tribunal. For these reasons, standards for permissible and prohibited conduct of a lawyer with respect to trial publicity have been established.

EC 7-34   The impartiality of a public servant in our legal system may be impaired by the receipt of gifts or loans. A lawyer, therefore, is never justified in making a gift or a loan to a judge, a hearing officer, or an officer or employee of a tribunal except as permitted by Section C(4) of Canon 5 of the Code of Judicial Conduct, but a lawyer may make a contribution to the campaign fund of a candidate for judicial office in conformity with Section B(2) under Canon 7 of the Code of Judicial Conduct.

EC 7-35   All litigants and lawyers should have access to tribunals on an equal basis. Generally, in adversary proceedings a lawyer should not communicate with a judge relative to a matter pending before, or which is to be brought before, a tribunal over which the judge presides in circumstances which might have the effect or give the appearance of granting undue advantage to one party. For example, a lawyer should not communicate with a tribunal by a writing unless a copy thereof is promptly delivered to opposing counsel or to the adverse party if such party is not represented by a lawyer. Ordinarily an oral communication by a lawyer with a judge or hearing officer should be made only upon adequate notice to opposing counsel, or if there is none, to the opposing party. A lawyer should not condone or participate in private importunities by another with a judge or hearing officer on behalf of the lawyer or the client.

EC 7-36   Judicial hearings ought to be conducted through dignified and orderly procedures designed to protect the rights of all parties. Although a lawyer has the duty to represent the client zealously, the lawyer should not engage in any conduct that offends the dignity and decorum of proceedings. While maintaining independence, a lawyer should be respectful, courteous, and aboveboard in relations with a judge or hearing officer before whom the lawyer appears. The lawyer should avoid undue solicitude for the comfort or convenience of judge or jury and should avoid any other conduct calculated to gain special consideration.

EC 7-37   In adversary proceedings, clients are litigants and though ill feeling may exist between clients, such ill feeling should not influence a lawyer's conduct, attitude, and demeanor toward opposing lawyers. A lawyer should not make unfair or derogatory personal reference to opposing counsel. Haranguing and offensive tactics by lawyers interfere with the orderly administration of justice and have no proper place in our legal system.

EC 7-38   A lawyer should be courteous to opposing counsel and should accede to reasonable requests regarding court proceedings, settings, continuances, waiver of procedural formalities, and similar matters which do not prejudice the rights of the client. A lawyer should follow local customs of courtesy or practice, unless he or she gives timely notice to opposing counsel of the intention not to do so. A lawyer should be punctual in fulfilling all professional commitments.

EC 7-39   In the final analysis, proper functioning of the adversary system depends upon cooperation between lawyers and tribunals in utilizing procedures which will preserve the impartiality of tribunals and make their decisional processes prompt and just, without impinging upon the obligation of lawyers to represent their clients zealously within the framework of the law.

DR 7-101. Representing a Client Zealously

A. A lawyer shall not intentionally:

1. Fail to seek the lawful objectives of the client through reasonably available means permitted by law and the Disciplinary Rules, except as provided by DR 7-101(B). A lawyer does not violate this Disciplinary Rule, however, by acceding to reasonable requests of opposing counsel which do not prejudice the rights of the client, by being punctual in fulfilling all professional commitments, by avoiding offensive tactics, or by treating with courtesy and consideration all persons involved in the legal process.

2. Fail to carry out a contract of employment entered into with a client for professional services, but the lawyer may withdraw as permitted under DR 2-110, DR 5-102, and DR 5-105.

3. Prejudice or damage the client during the course of the professional relationship, except as required under DR 7-102 (B).

B. In the representation of a client, a lawyer may:

1. Where permissible, exercise professional judgment to waive or fail to assert a right or position of the client.

2. Refuse to aid or participate in conduct that the lawyer believes to be unlawful, even though there is some support for an argument that the conduct is legal.

DR 7-102. Representing a Client Within the
Bounds of the Law

A. In the representation of a client, a lawyer shall not:

1. File a suit, assert a position, conduct a defense, delay a trial, or take other action on behalf of the client when the lawyer knows or when it is obvious that such action would serve merely to harass or maliciously injure another.

2. Knowingly advance a claim or defense that is unwarranted under existing law, except that the lawyer may advance such claim or defense if it can be supported by good faith argument for an extension, modification, or reversal of existing law.

3. Conceal or knowingly fail to disclose that which the lawyer is required by law to reveal.

4. Knowingly use perjured testimony or false evidence.

5. Knowingly make a false statement of law or fact.

6. Participate in the creation or preservation of evidence when the lawyer knows or it is obvious that the evidence is false.

7. Counsel or assist the client in conduct that the lawyer knows to be illegal or fraudulent.

8. Knowingly engage in other illegal conduct or conduct contrary to a Disciplinary Rule.

B. A lawyer who receives information clearly establishing that:

1. The client has, in the course of the representation, perpetrated a fraud upon a person or tribunal shall promptly call upon the client to rectify the same, and if the client refuses or is unable to do so, the lawyer shall reveal the fraud to the affected person or tribunal, except when the information is protected as a confidence or secret.

2. A person other than the client has perpetrated a fraud upon a tribunal shall promptly reveal the fraud to the tribunal.

DR 7-103. Performing the Duty of Public
Prosecutor or Other Government
Lawyer

A. A public prosecutor or other government lawyer shall not institute or cause to be instituted criminal charges when he or she knows or it is obvious that the charges are not supported by probable cause.

B. A public prosecutor or other government lawyer in criminal litigation shall make timely disclosure to counsel for the defendant, or to a defendant who has no counsel, of the existence of evidence, known to the prosecutor or other government lawyer, that tends to negate the guilt of the accused, mitigate the degree of the offense or reduce the punishment.

DR 7-104. Communicating with One of Adverse Interest

A. During the course of the representation of a client a lawyer shall not:

1. Communicate or cause another to communicate on the subject of the representation with a party the lawyer knows to be represented by a lawyer in that matter unless the lawyer has the prior consent of the lawyer representing such other party or is authorized by law to do so.

2. Give advice to a person who is not represented by a lawyer, other than the advice to secure counsel, if the interests of such person are or have a reasonable possibility of being in conflict with the interests of the lawyer's client.

DR 7-105. Threatening Criminal Prosecution

A. A lawyer shall not present, participate in presenting, or threaten to present criminal charges solely to obtain an advantage in a civil matter.

DR 7-106. Trial Conduct

A. A lawyer shall not disregard or advise the client to disregard a standing rule of a tribunal or a ruling of a tribunal made in the course of a proceeding, but the lawyer may take appropriate steps in good faith to test the validity of such rule or ruling.

B. In presenting a matter to a tribunal, a lawyer shall disclose:

1. Controlling legal authority known to the lawyer to be directly adverse to the position of the client and which is not disclosed by opposing counsel.

2. Unless privileged or irrelevant, the identities of the clients the lawyer represents and of the persons who employed the lawyer.

C. In appearing as a lawyer before a tribunal, a lawyer shall not:

1. State or allude to any matter that he or she has no reasonable basis to believe is relevant to the case or that will not be supported by admissible evidence.

2. Ask any question that he or she has no reasonable basis to believe is relevant to the case and that is intended to degrade a witness or other person.

3. Assert personal knowledge of the facts in issue, except when testifying as a witness.

4. Assert a personal opinion as to the justness of a cause, as to the credibility of a witness, as to the culpability of a civil litigant, or as to the guilt or innocence of an accused; but the lawyer may argue, upon analysis of the evidence, for any position or conclusion with respect to the matters stated herein.

5. Fail to comply with known local customs of courtesy or practice of the bar or a particular tribunal without giving to opposing counsel timely notice of the intent not to comply.

6. Engage in undignified or discourteous conduct which is degrading to a tribunal.

7. Intentionally or habitually violate any established rule of procedure or of evidence.

DR 7-107. Trial Publicity

A. A lawyer participating in or associated with a criminal or civil matter shall not make an extrajudicial statement that a reasonable person would expect to be disseminated by means of public communication if the lawyer knows or reasonably should know that it will have a substantial likelihood of materially prejudicing an adjudicative proceeding.

B. A statement ordinarily is likely to prejudice materially an adjudicative proceeding when it refers to a civil matter triable to a jury, a criminal matter, or any other proceeding that could result in incarceration, and the statement relates to:

1. The character, credibility, reputation or criminal record of a party, suspect in a criminal investigation or witness, or the identity of a witness, or the expected testimony of a party or witness.

2. In a criminal case or proceeding that could result in incarceration, the possibility of a plea of guilty to the offense or the existence or contents of any confession, admission, or statement given by a defendant or suspect or that person's refusal or failure to make a statement.

3. The performance or results of any examination or test or the refusal or failure of a person to submit to an examination or test, or the identity or nature of physical evidence expected to be presented.

4. Any opinion as to the guilt or innocence of a defendant or suspect in a criminal case or proceeding that could result in incarceration.

5. Information the lawyer knows or reasonably should know is likely to be inadmissible as evidence in a trial and would if disclosed create a substantial risk of prejudicing an impartial trial.

6. The fact that a defendant has been charged with a crime, unless there is included therein a statement explaining that the charge is merely an accusation and that the defendant is presumed innocent until and unless proven guilty.

C. Provided that the statement complies with DR 7-107(A), a lawyer involved with the investigation or litigation of a matter may state the following without elaboration:

1. The general nature of the claim or defense.

2. The information contained in a public record.

3. That an investigation of the matter is in progress.

4. The scheduling or result of any step in litigation.

5. A request for assistance in obtaining evidence and information necessary thereto.

6. A warning of danger concerning the behavior of a person involved, when there is reason to believe that there exists the likelihood of substantial harm to an individual or to the public interest.

7. In a criminal case:

a. The identity, age, residence, occupation and family status of the accused.

b. If the accused has not been apprehended, information necessary to aid in apprehension of that person.

c. The fact, time and place of arrest, resistance, pursuit, use of weapons, and a description of physical evidence seized, other than as contained only in a confession, admission, or statement.

d. The identity of investigating and arresting officers or agencies and the length of the investigation.

DR 7-108. Communication with or Investigation
of Jurors

A. Before the trial of a case a lawyer connected therewith shall not communicate with or cause another to communicate with anyone the lawyer knows to be a member of the venire from which the jury will be selected for the trial of the case.

B. During the trial of a case:

1. A lawyer connected therewith shall not communicate with or cause another to communicate with any member of the jury.

2. A lawyer who is not connected therewith shall not communicate with or cause another to communicate with a juror concerning the case.

C. DR 7-108 (A) and (B) do not prohibit a lawyer from communicating with members of the venire or jurors in the course of official proceedings.

D. After discharge of the jury from further consideration of a case with which the lawyer was connected, the lawyer shall not ask questions of or make comments to a member of that jury that are calculated merely to harass or embarrass the juror or to influence the juror's actions in future jury service.

E. A lawyer shall not conduct or cause, by financial support or otherwise, another to conduct a vexatious or harassing investigation of either a member of the venire or a juror.

F. All restrictions imposed by DR 7-108 upon a lawyer also apply to communications with or investigations of members of a family of a member of the venire or a juror.

G. A lawyer shall reveal promptly to the court improper conduct by a member of the venire or a juror, or by another toward a member of the venire or a juror or a member of his or her family of which the lawyer has knowledge.

DR 7-109. Contact with Witnesses

A. A lawyer shall not suppress any evidence that the lawyer or the client has a legal obligation to reveal or produce.

B. A lawyer shall not advise or cause a person to hide or to leave the jurisdiction of a tribunal for the purpose of making the person unavailable as a witness therein.

C. A lawyer shall not pay, offer to pay, or acquiesce in the payment of compensation to a witness contingent upon the content of his or her testimony or the outcome of the case. But a lawyer may advance, guarantee, or acquiesce in the payment of:

1. Expenses reasonably incurred by a witness in attending or testifying.

2. Reasonable compensation to a witness for the loss of time in attending or testifying.

3. A reasonable fee for the professional services of an expert witness.

DR 7-110. Contact with Officials

A. A lawyer shall not give or lend anything of value to a judge, official, or employee of a tribunal except as permitted by Section C (4) of Canon 5 of the Code of Judicial Conduct, but a lawyer may make a contribution to the campaign fund of a candidate for judicial office in conformity with Section B (2) under Canon 7 of the Code of Judicial Conduct.

B. In an adversary proceeding, a lawyer shall not communicate, or cause another to communicate, as to the merits of the cause with a judge or an official before whom the proceeding is pending, except:

1. In the course of official proceedings in the cause.

2. In writing if the lawyer promptly delivers a copy of the writing to opposing counsel or to an adverse party who is not represented by a lawyer.

3. Orally upon adequate notice to opposing counsel or to an adverse party who is not represented by a lawyer.

4. As otherwise authorized by law, or by Section A (4) under Canon 3 of the Code of Judicial Conduct.

CANON 8.   A LAWYER SHOULD ASSIST IN IMPROVING THE LEGAL SYSTEM

Ethical Considerations

EC 8-1   Changes in human affairs and imperfections in human institutions make necessary constant efforts to maintain and improve our legal system. This system should function in a manner that commands public respect and fosters the use of legal remedies to achieve redress of grievances. By reason of education and experience, lawyers are especially qualified to recognize deficiencies in the legal system and to initiate corrective measures therein. Thus they should participate in proposing and supporting legislation and programs to improve the system, without regard to the general interests or desires of clients or former clients.

EC 8-2   Rules of law are deficient if they are not just, understandable, and responsive to the needs of society. If a lawyer believes that the existence or absence of a rule of law, substantive or procedural, causes or contributes to an unjust result, the lawyer should endeavor by lawful means to obtain appropriate changes in the law. The lawyer should encourage the simplification of laws and the repeal or amendment of laws that are outmoded. Likewise, legal procedures should be improved whenever experience indicates a change is needed.

EC 8-3   The fair administration of justice requires the availability of competent lawyers. Members of the public should be educated to recognize the existence of legal problems and the resultant need for legal services, and should be provided methods for intelligent selection of counsel. Those persons unable to pay for legal services should be provided needed services. Clients and lawyers should not be penalized by undue geographical restraints upon representation in legal matters, and the bar should address itself to improvements in licensing, reciprocity, and admission procedures consistent with the needs of modern commerce.

EC 8-4   Whenever a lawyer seeks legislative or administrative changes, the lawyer should identify the capacity in which he or she appears, whether on behalf of the lawyer, a client, or the public. A lawyer may advocate such changes on behalf of a client even though the lawyer does not agree with them. But when a lawyer purports to act on behalf of the public, the lawyer should espouse only those changes which the lawyer conscientiously believes to be in the public interest. Lawyers involved in organizations seeking law reform generally do not have a lawyer-client relationship with the organization. In determining the nature and scope of participation in reform activities, a lawyer should be mindful of obligations under Canon 5, particularly DR 5-101 through DR 5-110. A lawyer is professionally obligated to protect the integrity of the organization by making an appropriate disclosure within the organization when the lawyer knows a private client might be materially affected.

EC 8-5   Fraudulent, deceptive, or otherwise illegal conduct by a participant in a proceeding before a tribunal or legislative body is inconsistent with fair administration of justice, and it should never be participated in or condoned by lawyers. Unless constrained by the obligation to preserve the confidences and secrets of the client, a lawyer should reveal to appropriate authorities any knowledge the lawyer may have of such improper conduct.

EC 8-6:   Judges and administrative officials having adjudicatory powers ought to be persons of integrity, competence, and suitable temperament. Generally, lawyers are qualified, by personal observation or investigation, to evaluate the qualifications of persons seeking or being considered for such public offices, and for this reason they have a special responsibility to aid in the selection of only those who are qualified. It is the duty of lawyers to endeavor to prevent political considerations from outweighing judicial fitness in the selection of judges. Lawyers should protest earnestly against the appointment or election of those who are unsuited for the bench and should strive to have elected or appointed thereto only those who are willing to forego pursuits, whether of a business, political, or other nature, that may interfere with the free and fair consideration of question presented for adjudication. Adjudicatory officials, not being wholly free to defend themselves, are entitled to receive the support of the bar against unjust criticism. While a lawyer as a citizen has a right to criticize such officials publicly, the lawyer should be certain of the merit of the complaint, use appropriate language, and avoid petty criticisms, for unrestrained and intemperate statements tend to lessen public confidence in our legal system. Criticisms motivated by reasons other than a desire to improve the legal system are not justified.

EC 8-7   Since lawyers are a vital part of the legal system, they should be persons of integrity, of professional skill, and of dedication to the improvement of the system. Thus a lawyer should aid in establishing, as well as enforcing, standards of conduct adequate to protect the public by insuring that those who practice law are qualified to do so.

EC 8-8   Lawyers often serve as legislators or as holders of other public offices. This is highly desirable, as lawyers are uniquely qualified to make significant contributions to the improvement of the legal system. A lawyer who is a public officer, whether full or part-time, should not engage in activities in which the lawyer's personal or professional interests are or foreseeably may be in conflict with the lawyer's official duties.

EC 8-9   The advancement of our legal system is of vital importance in maintaining the rule of law and in facilitating orderly changes; therefore, lawyers should encourage, and should aid in making, needed changes and improvements.

DR 8-101. Action as a Public Official

A. A lawyer who holds public office shall not:
1. Use the public position to obtain, or attempt to obtain, a special advantage in legislative matters for the lawyer or for a client under circumstances where the lawyer knows or it is obvious that such action is not in the public interest.

2. Use the public position to influence, or attempt to influence, a tribunal to act in favor of the lawyer or of a client.

3. Accept any thing of value from any person when the lawyer knows or it is obvious that the offer is for the purpose of influencing the lawyer's action as a public official.

DR 8-102.　Statements Concerning Judges and Other Adjudicatory Officers

A. A lawyer shall not knowingly make false statements of fact concerning the qualifications of a candidate for election or appointment to a judicial office.

B. A lawyer shall not knowingly make false accusations against a judge or other adjudicatory officer.

DR 8-103.　Lawyer Candidate for Judicial Office

A. A lawyer who is a candidate for judicial office shall comply with the applicable provisions of Canon 7 of the Code of Judicial Conduct.

CANON 9.　A LAWYER SHOULD AVOID EVEN THE APPEARANCE OF PROFESSIONAL IMPROPRIETY

Ethical Considerations

EC 9-1　Continuation of the American concept that we are to be governed by rules of law requires that the people have faith that justice can be obtained through our legal system. A lawyer should promote public confidence in our system and in the legal profession.

EC 9-2　Public confidence in law and lawyers may be eroded by irresponsible or improper conduct of a lawyer. On occasion, ethical conduct of a lawyer may appear to non-lawyers to be unethical. In order to avoid misunderstandings and hence to maintain confidence, a lawyer should fully and promptly inform the client of material developments in the matters being handled for the client. While a lawyer should guard against otherwise proper conduct that has a tendency to diminish public confidence in the legal system or in the legal profession, the lawyer's duty to clients or to the public should never be subordinate merely because the full discharge of the lawyer's obligation may be misunderstood or may tend to subject the lawyer or the legal profession to criticism. When explicit ethical guidance does not exist a lawyer should determine prospective conduct by acting in a manner that promotes public confidence in the integrity and efficiency of the legal system and the legal profession.

EC 9-3   A lawyer who leaves judicial office or other public employment should not thereafter accept employment in connection with any matter in which the lawyer had substantial responsibility prior to leaving, since to accept employment would give the appearance of impropriety even if none exists.

EC 9-4   Because the very essence of the legal system is to provide procedures by which matters can be presented in an impartial manner so that they may be decided solely upon the merits, any statement or suggestion by a lawyer that the lawyer can or would attempt to circumvent those procedures is detrimental to the legal system and tends to undermine public confidence in it.

EC 9-5   Separation of the funds of a client from those of the lawyer not only serves to protect the client but also avoids even the appearance of impropriety, and therefore commingling of such funds should be avoided.

EC 9-6   Every lawyer owes a solemn duty to uphold the integrity and honor of the profession; to encourage respect for the law and for the courts and the judges thereof; to observe the Code of Professional Responsibility; to act as a member of a learned profession, one dedicated to public service; to cooperate with other lawyers in supporting the organized bar through devoting time, efforts, and financial support as the lawyer's professional standing and ability reasonably permit; to act so as to reflect credit on the legal profession and to inspire the confidence, respect, and trust of clients and of the public; and to strive to avoid not only professional impropriety but also the appearance of impropriety.

DR 9-101. Avoiding Even the Appearance of Impropriety

A. A lawyer shall not accept private employment in a matter upon the merits of which the lawyer has acted in a judicial capacity.

B. Except as law may otherwise expressly permit:

1. A lawyer shall not represent a private client in connection with a matter in which the lawyer participated personally and substantially as a public officer or employee, and no lawyer in a firm with which that lawyer is associated may knowingly undertake or continue representation in such a matter unless:

a. The disqualified lawyer is effectively screened from any participation, direct or indirect, including discussion, in the matter and is apportioned no part of the fee therefrom; and

b. There are no other circumstances in the particular representation that create an appearance of impropriety.

2. A lawyer having information that the lawyer knows is confidential government information about a person, acquired when the lawyer was a public officer or employee, may not represent a private client whose interests are adverse to that person in a matter in which the information could be used to the material disadvantage of that person. A firm with which that lawyer is associated may knowingly undertake or continue representation in the matter only if the disqualified lawyer is effectively screened from any participation, direct or indirect, including discussion, in the matter and is apportioned no part of the fee therefrom.

3. A lawyer serving as a public officer or employee shall not:

a. Participate in a matter in which the lawyer participated personally and substantially while in private practice or nongovernmental employment, unless under applicable law no one is, or by lawful delegation may be, authorized to act in the lawyer's stead in the matter; or

b. Negotiate for private employment with any person who is involved as a party or as attorney for a party in a matter in which the lawyer is participating personally and substantially.

C. A lawyer shall not state or imply that the lawyer is able to influence improperly or upon irrelevant grounds any tribunal, legislative body, or public official.

D. A lawyer related to another lawyer as parent, child, sibling or spouse shall not represent in any matter a client whose interests differ from those of another party to the matter who the lawyer knows is represented by the other lawyer unless the client consents to the representation after full disclosure and the lawyer concludes that the lawyer can adequately represent the interests of the client.

DR 9-102. Preserving Identity of Funds and Property of Others; Fiduciary Responsibility; Maintenance of Bank Accounts; Recordkeeping; Examination of Records

A. Prohibition Against Commingling. A lawyer in possession of any funds or other property belonging to another person, where such possession is incident to his or her practice of law, is a fiduciary, and must not commingle such property with his or her own.

B. Separate Accounts.

1. A lawyer who is in possession of funds belonging to another person incident to the lawyer's practice of law, shall maintain such funds in a banking institution within the State of New York which agrees to provide dishonored check reports in accordance with the provisions of Part 1300 of these rules (22 NYCRR Part 1300).* "Banking institution" means a state or national bank, trust company, savings bank, savings and loan association or credit union. Such funds shall be maintained, in the lawyer's own name, or in the name of a firm of lawyers of which he or she is a member, or in the name of the lawyer or firm of lawyers by whom he or she is employed, in a special account or accounts, separate from any business or personal accounts of the lawyer or lawyer's firm, and separate from any accounts which the lawyer may maintain as executor, guardian, trustee or receiver, or in any other fiduciary capacity, into which special account or accounts all funds held in escrow or otherwise entrusted to the lawyer or firm shall be deposited; provided, however, that such funds may be maintained in a banking institution located outside the State of New York if such banking institution complies with such Part 1300, and the lawyer has obtained the prior written approval of the person to whom such funds belong which specifies the name and address of the office or branch of the banking institution where such funds are to be maintained.

2. A lawyer or the lawyer's firm shall identify the special bank account or accounts required by subdivision (b)(1) of this section as an "Attorney Special Account," or "Attorney Trust Account," or "Attorney Escrow Account," and shall obtain checks and deposit slips that

---

*Part 1300 contemplates that the bank will inform the Lawyers' Fund for Client Protection "whenever a properly payable instrument is presented against an attorney special, trust, or escrow account which contains insufficient available funds, and the banking institution dishonors the instrument for that reason." After ten days, the Lawyers' Fund must forward the dishonored check report to the appropriate attorney disciplinary committee. — EDS.

bear such title. Such title may be accompanied by such other descriptive language as the lawyer may deem appropriate, provided that such additional language distinguishes such special account or accounts from other bank accounts that are maintained by the lawyer or the lawyer's firm.

3. Funds reasonably sufficient to maintain the account or to pay account charges may be deposited therein.

4. Funds belonging in part to a client or third person and in part presently or potentially to the lawyer or law firm shall be kept in such special account or accounts, but the portion belonging to the lawyer or law firm may be withdrawn when due unless the right of the lawyer or law firm to receive it is disputed by the client or third person, in which event the disputed portion shall not be withdrawn until the dispute is finally resolved.

C. Notification of Receipt of Property; Safekeeping; Rendering Accounts; Payment or Delivery of Property. A lawyer shall:

1. Promptly notify a client or third person of the receipt of funds, securities, or other properties in which the client or third person has an interest.

2. Identify and label securities and properties of a client or third person promptly upon receipt and place them in a safe deposit box or other place of safekeeping as soon as practicable.

3. Maintain complete records of all funds, securities, and other properties of a client or third person coming into the possession of the lawyer and render appropriate accounts to the client or third person regarding them.

4. Promptly pay or deliver to the client or third person as requested by the client or third person the funds, securities, or other properties in the possession of the lawyer which the client or third person is entitled to receive.

D. Required Bookkeeping Records. A lawyer shall maintain for seven years after the events which they record:

1. The records of all deposits in and withdrawals from the accounts specified in DR 9-102(B) and of any other bank account which records the operations of the lawyer's practice of law. These records shall specifically identify the date, source and description of each item deposited, as well as the date, payee and purpose of each withdrawal or disbursement.

2. A record for special accounts, showing the source of all funds deposited in such accounts, the names of all persons for whom the funds are or were held, the amount of such funds, the description and

amounts, and the names of all persons to whom such funds were disbursed.

3. Copies of all retainer and compensation agreements with clients.

4. Copies of all statements to clients or other persons showing the disbursement of funds to them or on their behalf.

5. Copies of all bills rendered to clients.

6. Copies of all records showing payments to lawyers, investigators or other persons, not in the lawyer's regular employ, for services rendered or performed.

7. Copies of all retainer and closing statements filed with the Office of Court Administration.

8. All checkbooks and checkstubs, bank statements, prenumbered cancelled checks and duplicate deposit slips with respect to the special accounts specified in DR 9-102(B) (subdivision (B) of this section) and any other bank account which records the operations of the lawyer's practice of law.

Lawyers shall make accurate entries of all financial transactions in their records of receipts and disbursements, in their special accounts, in their ledger books or similar records, and in any other books of account kept by them in the regular course of their practice, which entries shall be made at or near the time of the act, condition or event recorded.

E. Authorized Signatories. All special account withdrawals shall be made only to a named payee and not to cash. Such withdrawals shall be made by check or, with the prior written approval of the party entitled to the proceeds, by bank transfer. Only an attorney admitted to practice law in New York State shall be an authorized signatory of a special account.

Editors' Note. Effective December 13, 1994, a joint order of the four presiding justices of the Appellate Divisions amended DR 9-102(F) (Missing Clients), renumbered it as DR 9-102(F-1), and added a new section DR 9-102(F-2) (Designation of Successor Signatories). The Lawyers' Fund for Client Protection, which is referred to in the amendments, is established by §468-b of the New York Judiciary Law and is governed by Title 22, Part 7200 of the NYCRR, which we do not reprint in this volume. According to §7200.1, the purpose of the Lawyers' Fund for Client Protection is to promote public confidence in the justice system and in the integrity of the legal profession by "reimbursing losses caused by the dishonest conduct of attorneys admitted and licensed to practice law in the courts of New York State."

F-1. Missing Clients. **Whenever any sum of money is payable to a client and the lawyer is unable to locate the client, the lawyer shall apply to the court in which the action was brought if in the unified court system, or, if no action was commenced in the unified court system, to the Supreme Court in the county in which the lawyer maintains an office for the practice of law, for an order directing payment to the lawyer of any fees and disbursements that are owed by the client and the balance, if any, to the Lawyers' Fund for Client Protection for safeguarding and disbursement to persons who are entitled thereto.**

F-2. Designation of Successor Signatories.

1. Upon the death of a lawyer who was the sole signatory on an attorney trust, escrow or special account, an application may be made to the Supreme Court for an order designating a successor signatory for such trust, escrow or special account who shall be a member of the bar in good standing and admitted to the practice of law in New York State.

2. An application to designate a successor signatory shall be made to the Supreme Court in the judicial district in which the deceased lawyer maintained an office for the practice of law. The application may be made by the legal representative of the deceased lawyer's estate; a lawyer who was affiliated with the deceased lawyer in the practice of law; any person who has a beneficial interest in such trust, escrow or special account; an officer of a city or county bar association; or counsel for an attorney disciplinary committee. No lawyer may charge a legal fee for assisting with an application to designate a successor signatory pursuant to this rule.

3. The Supreme Court may designate a successor signatory and may direct the safeguarding of funds from such trust, escrow or special account, and the disbursement of such funds to persons who are entitled thereto, and may order that funds in such account be deposited with the Lawyers' Fund for Client Protection for safeguarding and disbursement to persons who are entitled thereto.

G. Dissolution of a Firm. **Upon the dissolution of any firm of lawyers, the former partners or members shall make appropriate arrangements for the maintenance by one of them or by a successor firm of the records specified in subdivision (D) of this Disciplinary Rule.**

H. Availability of Bookkeeping Records; Records Subject to Production in Disciplinary Investigations and Proceedings. **The financial records required by this Disciplinary Rule shall be located, or made available, at the principal New York State office of the lawyers subject hereto and any such records shall be produced in response to a notice or subpoena duces tecum issued in connection with a complaint before or any investigation by the appropriate grievance or departmental disciplinary committee, or** shall be produced at the direction of the appropriate Appellate Division before any person designated by it. All books and records produced pursuant to this subdivision shall be kept confidential, except for the purpose of the particular proceeding, and their contents shall not be disclosed by anyone in violation of the lawyer-client privilege.

I. Disciplinary Action. A lawyer who does not maintain and keep the accounts and records as specified and required by this Disciplinary Rule, or who does not produce any such records pursuant to this Rule, shall be deemed in violation of these Rules and shall be subject to disciplinary proceedings.

Selected Provisions of the New York State Judiciary Law

Editors' Introduction. In New York, lawyers and aspiring lawyers are heavily regulated by statute. Most of the statutes regulating lawyers are found in the New York State Judiciary Law. We reprint the most important sections of that law.

There have not been any significant amendments to these sections since our last edition, but in November of 1995 the Committee on the Profession and the Courts (commonly known as the "Craco Committee") issued a report recommending that disciplinary proceedings, which are currently closed in New York pursuant to §90 of the Judiciary Law, be open to the public as soon as the disciplinary authorities find probable cause to bring charges. In July of 1996, the Administrative Board of the New York Courts (consisting of Chief Judge Judith Kaye and the Presiding Justices of the four Appellate Divisions) endorsed this recommendation, but it cannot be implemented unless the Legislature amends §90. When we went to press in September of 1997, the Office of Court Administration had developed a proposal to amend §90 in significant ways. The most important proposed change is that charges, responses, hearings, and the referee's report and recommendation would all be public. But the proposed changes would be accompanied by four new procedural protections for lawyers: (1) before charges are brought, lawyers could appear before the grievance committee — and, with leave of court, present witnesses — to rebut the proposed charges; (2) many complaints would be subject to a four-year statute of limitations; (3) New York's current "preponderance" standard for proving disciplinary charges would be raised to the "clear and convincing" standard used in most jurisdictions; and (4) public disclosure of charges would be delayed for 40 days to allow either side time to ask the court to close the proceedings, and the courts could close proceedings for "good cause." These changes can take effect only if the Legislature enacts them. In the past, however, the Legislature has rejected past efforts to open the disciplinary process. To complicate matters, some of the disciplinary authorities in New York oppose the amendments proposed by the courts because of the restrictions that would accompany open disciplinary proceedings. For updated information, visit the New York State Bar Association's web site at www.nysba.org.

Contents

§90. Admission to and Removal from Practice by Appellate Division; Character Committees

1. a. Upon the state board of law examiners certifying that a person has passed the required examination, or that the examination has been dispensed with, the appellate division of the supreme court in the department to which such person shall have been certified by the state board of law examiners, if it shall be satisfied that such person possesses the char-

acter and general fitness requisite for an attorney and counsellor-at-law, shall admit him to practice as such attorney and counsellor-at-law in all the courts of this state, provided that he has in all respects complied with the rules of the court of appeals and the rules of the appellate divisions relating to the admission of attorneys.

b. Upon the application, pursuant to the rules of the court of appeals, of any person who has been admitted to practice law in another state or territory or the District of Columbia of the United States or in a foreign country, to be admitted to practice as an attorney and counsellor-at-law in the courts of this state without taking the regular bar examination, the appellate division of the supreme court, if it shall be satisfied that such person is currently admitted to the bar in such other jurisdiction or jurisdictions, that at least one such jurisdiction in which he is so admitted would similarly admit an attorney or counsellor-at-law admitted to practice in New York state to its bar without examination and that such person possesses the character and general fitness requisite for an attorney and counsellor-at-law, and has satisfied the requirements of section 3-503 of the general obligations law,* shall admit him to practice as such attorney and counsellor-at-law in all the courts of this state, provided, that he has in all respects complied with the rules of the court of appeals and the rules of the appellate divisions relating to the admission of attorneys. Such application, which shall conform to the requirements of section 3-503 of the general obligations law, shall be submitted to the appellate division of the supreme court in the department specified in the rules of the court of appeals.

c. The members of the committee appointed by the appellate division in each department to investigate the character and fitness of applicants for admission to the bar, shall be entitled to their necessary traveling, hotel and other expenses, incurred in the performance of their duties, payable by the state out of moneys appropriated therefor, upon certificate of the presiding justice of the appellate division by which such committee is appointed. . . .

2. The supreme court shall have power and control over attorneys and counsellors-at-law and all persons practicing or assuming to practice law, and the appellate division of the supreme court in each department is authorized to censure, suspend from practice or remove from office any attorney and counsellor-at-law admitted to practice who is guilty of

---

*General Obligations Law §3-503 addresses fulfillment of child support obligations and is described following this section.

professional misconduct, malpractice, fraud, deceit, crime or misdemeanor, or any conduct prejudicial to the administration of justice; and
the appellate division of the supreme court is hereby authorized to revoke
such admission for any misrepresentation or suppression of any information in connection with the application for admission to practice.

It shall be the duty of the appellate division to insert in each order of
suspension or removal hereafter rendered a provision which shall command the attorney and counsellor-at-law thereafter to desist and refrain
from the practice of law in any form, either as principal or as agent, clerk
or employee of another. In addition it shall forbid the performance of
any of the following acts, to wit:

a. The appearance as an attorney or counsellor-at-law before any
court, judge, justice, board, commission or other public authority.

b. The giving to another of an opinion as to the law or its application, or of any advice in relation thereto.

In case of suspension only, the order may limit the command to the
period of time within which such suspension shall continue, and if justice
so requires may further limit the scope thereof.

If an attorney and counsellor-at-law has been heretofore removed
from office, the appellate division shall upon application of any attorney
and counsellor-at-law, or of any incorporated bar association, and upon
such notice to the respondent as may be required, amend the order of
removal by adding thereto as a part thereof, provisions similar to those
required to be inserted in orders hereafter made.

If a certified copy of such order or of such amended order, be served
upon the attorney and counsellor-at-law suspended or removed from office, a violation thereof may be punished as a contempt of court.

2-a. a. The provisions of this subdivision shall apply in all cases of an
attorney licensed, registered or admitted to practice in this state who is in
arrears in payment of child support or combined child and spousal support which matter shall be referred to the appropriate appellate division
by a court pursuant to the requirements of section two hundred forty-
four-c of the domestic relations law or pursuant to section four hundred
fifty-eight-b of the family court act.

b. Upon receipt of an order from the court pursuant to one of the
foregoing provisions of law, the appropriate appellate division within
thirty days of receipt of such order, if it finds such person to be so licensed, registered or admitted, shall provide notice to such attorney
of, and initiate, a hearing which shall be held by it at least twenty days
and no more than thirty days after the sending of such notice to the attorney. The hearing shall be held solely for the purpose of determining whether there exists as of the date of the hearing proof that full

payment of all arrears of support established by the order of the court to be due from the licensed, registered or admitted attorney have been paid. Proof of such payment shall be a certifed check showing full payment of established arrears or a notice issued by the court or the support collection unit, where the order is payable to the support collection unit designated by the appropriate social services district. Such notice shall state that full payment of all arrears of support established by the order of the court to be due have been paid. The licensed attorney shall be given full opportunity to present such proof of payment at the hearing in person or by counsel. The only issue to be determined as a result of the hearing is whether the arrears have been paid. No evidence with respect to the appropriateness of the court order or ability of the respondent party in arrears to comply with such order shall be received or considered by the disciplinary committee.

c. Notwithstanding any inconsistent provision of this section or of any other provision of law to the contrary, the license to practice law in this state of an attorney admitted to practice shall be suspended by the appellate division if, at the hearing provided for by paragraph b of this subdivision, the licensed attorney fails to present proof of payments as required by such subdivision. Such suspension shall not be lifted unless the original court or the support collection unit, where the court order is payable to the support collection unit designated by the appropriate social services district, issues notice to the appellate division that full payment of all arrears of support established by the order of the original court to be due have been paid.

d. The appellate division shall inform the original court of all actions taken hereunder.

e. This subdivision two-a applies to support obligations paid pursuant to any order of child support or child and spousal support issued under provisions of article three-A or section two hundred thirty-six or two hundred forty of the domestic relations law, or article four, five, or five-A of the family court act.

f. Notwithstanding any inconsistent provision of this section or of any other provision of law to the contrary, the provisions of this subdivision two-a shall apply to the exclusion of any other requirements of this section and to the exclusion of any other requirement of law to the contrary.

3. The suspension or removal of an attorney or counsellor-at-law, by the appellate division of the supreme court, operates as a suspension or removal in every court of the state.

4. a. Any person being an attorney and counsellor-at-law who shall be convicted of a felony as defined in paragraph e of this subdivision shall

upon such conviction, cease to be an attorney and counsellor-at-law, or to be competent to practice law as such.

b. Whenever any attorney and counsellor-at-law shall be convicted of a felony as defined in paragraph e of this subdivision, there may be presented to the appellate division of the supreme court a certified or exemplified copy of the judgment of such conviction, and thereupon the name of the person so convicted shall, by order of the court, be struck from the roll of attorneys.

c. Whenever an attorney shall be convicted of a crime in a court of record of the United States or of any state, territory or district, including this state, whether by a plea of guilty or nolo contendere or from a verdict after trial or otherwise, the attorney shall file, within thirty days thereafter, with the appellate division of the supreme court, the record of such conviction.

The failure of the attorney to so file shall be deemed professional misconduct provided, however, that the appellate division may upon application of the attorney, grant an extension upon good cause shown.

d. For purposes of this subdivision, the term serious crime shall mean any criminal offense denominated a felony under the laws of any state, district or territory or of the United States which does not constitute a felony under the laws of this state, and any other crime a necessary element of which, as determined by statutory or common law definition of such crime, includes interference with the administration of justice, false swearing, misrepresentation, fraud, willful failure to file income tax returns, deceit, bribery, extortion, misappropriation, theft, or an attempt or conspiracy or solicitation of another to commit a serious crime.

e. For purposes of this subdivision, the term felony shall mean any criminal offense classified as a felony under the laws of this state or any criminal offense committed in any other state, district, or territory of the United States and classified as a felony therein which if committed within this state, would constitute a felony in this state.

f. Any attorney and counsellor-at-law convicted of a serious crime, as defined in paragraph d of this subdivision, whether by plea of guilty or nolo contendere or from a verdict after trial or otherwise, shall be suspended upon the receipt by the appellate division of the supreme court of the record of such conviction until a final order is made pursuant to paragraph g of this subdivision.

Upon good cause shown the appellate division of the supreme court may, upon application of the attorney or on its own motion, set aside such suspension when it appears consistent with the maintenance of the integrity and honor of the profession, the protection of the public and the interest of justice.

g. Upon a judgment of conviction against an attorney becoming final the appellate division of the supreme court shall order the attorney to show cause why a final order of suspension, censure or removal from office should not be made.

h. If the attorney requests a hearing, the appellate division of the supreme court shall refer the proceeding to a referee, justice or judge appointed by the appellate division for hearing, report and recommendation.

After said hearing, the appellate division may impose such discipline as it deems proper under the facts and circumstances.

5. a. If such removal or debarment was based upon conviction for a serious crime or upon a felony conviction as defined in subdivision four of this section, and such felony conviction was subsequently reversed or pardoned by the president of the United States, or governor of this or another state of the United States, the appellate division shall have power to vacate or modify such order or debarment, provided, however, that if such attorney or counsellor-at-law has been removed from practice in another jurisdiction, a pardon in said jurisdiction shall not be a basis for application for re-admission in this jurisdiction unless he shall have been readmitted in the jurisdiction where pardoned.

b. If such removal or debarment was based upon conviction for a felony as defined in subdivision four of this section, the appellate division shall have power to vacate or modify such order or debarment after a period of seven years provided that such person has not been convicted of a crime during such seven-year period.

c. An attorney and counsellor-at-law who has been convicted of a felony without the state and whose name has been struck from the roll of attorneys prior to July thirteenth, nineteen hundred seventy-nine by virtue of the provisions of subdivision four of this section may, if he alleges that such felony committed without the state would not constitute a felony if committed within the state, petition the appellate division to vacate or modify such debarment. If the appellate division finds that the felony of which the attorney and counsellor-at-law has been convicted without the state would not constitute a felony if committed within the state, it shall grant a hearing and may retroactively vacate or modify such debarment and impose such discipline as it deems just and proper under the facts and circumstances.

The attorney and counsellor-at-law shall petition for reinstatement by filing in the appellate division a copy of the order of removal together with a request for a hearing pursuant to the provisions of this paragraph. Upon such application, the order of removal shall be deemed an order of suspension for the purposes of a proceeding pursuant to this paragraph.

6. a. Where the appellate division of supreme court orders the censure, suspension from practice or removal from office of an attorney or counsellor-at-law following disciplinary proceedings at which it found, based upon a preponderance of the legally admissible evidence, that such attorney or counsellor-at-law wilfully misappropriated or misapplied money or property in the practice of law, its order may require him or her to make monetary restitution in accordance with this subdivision. Its order also may require that he or she reimburse the lawyers' fund for client protection of the state of New York for awards made to the person whose money or property was wilfully misappropriated or misapplied.

b. Monetary restitution, as authorized hereunder, shall be made to the person whose money or property was wilfully misappropriated or misapplied and shall be for the amount or value of such money or property, as found in the disciplinary proceedings. In the event that such person dies prior to completion of such restitution, any amount remaining to be paid shall be paid to the estate of the deceased.

c. Any payment made as restitution pursuant to this subdivision shall not limit, preclude or impair any liability for damages in any civil action or proceeding for an amount in excess of such payment; nor shall any order of the appellate division made hereunder deprive a criminal court of any authority pursuant to article sixty of the penal law.

d. An order issued pursuant to this subdivision may be entered as a civil judgment. Such judgment shall be enforceable as a money judgment in any court of competent jurisdiction by any person to whom payments are due thereunder, or by the lawyers' fund for client protection where it has been subrogated to the rights of such person.

e. Where an attorney or counsellor-at-law is permitted to resign from office, the appellate division may, if appropriate, issue an order as provided herein requiring him or her to make payments specified by this subdivision.

f. Notwithstanding any other provision of this subdivision, no order may be issued hereunder unless the person required to make payments under such order first is given an opportunity to be heard in opposition thereto.

7. In addition to the duties prescribed by section seven hundred of the county law, it shall be the duty of any district attorney within a department, when so designated by the justices of the appellate division of the supreme court in such department, or a majority of them, to prosecute all proceedings for the removal or suspension of attorneys and counsellors-

at-law or the said justices, or a majority of them, may appoint any attorney and counsellor-at-law to conduct a preliminary investigation and to prosecute any disciplinary proceedings and, during or upon the termination of the investigation or proceedings, may fix the compensation to be paid to such attorney and counsellor-at-law for the services rendered, which compensation shall be a charge against the county specified in his certificate and shall be paid thereon.

8. Any petitioner or respondent in a disciplinary proceeding against an attorney or counsellor-at-law under this section, including a bar association or any other corporation or association, shall have the right to appeal to the court of appeals from a final order of any appellate division in such proceeding upon questions of law involved therein, subject to the limitations prescribed by article six, section seven, of the constitution of this state. [Now Const. Art. 6, §3.]

9. No objection shall be taken to the appointment of any member of the bar to act as referee or judge in a disciplinary proceeding under this section on the ground that he is a member of a bar association or other corporation or association which is the petitioner therein.

10. Any statute or rule to the contrary notwithstanding, all papers, records and documents upon the application or examination of any person for admission as an attorney and counsellor-at-law and upon any complaint, inquiry, investigation or proceeding relating to the conduct or discipline of an attorney or attorneys, shall be sealed and be deemed private and confidential. However, upon good cause being shown, the justices of the appellate division having jurisdiction are empowered, in their discretion, by written order, to permit to be divulged all or any part of such papers, records and documents. In the discretion of the presiding or acting presiding justice of said appellate division, such order may be made either without notice to the persons or attorneys to be affected thereby or upon such notice to them as he may direct. In furtherance of the purpose of this subdivision, said justices are also empowered, in their discretion, from time to time to make such rules as they may deem necessary. Without regard to the foregoing, in the event that charges are sustained by the justices of the appellate division having jurisdiction in any complaint, investigation or proceeding relating to the conduct or discipline of any attorney, the records and documents in relation thereto shall be deemed public records.

Editors' Note. Section 3-503 of New York General Obligations Law, added in 1995, requires every applicant for a license or the renewal of a license to certify under oath that "he or she is (or is not) under an obli-

gation to pay child support and that if he or she is under such an obligation, that he or she does (or does not) meet one of the following requirements. . . ." These requirements are intended to reveal whether the
applicant is in violation of any child support obligation. If the applicant is
in violation as defined in the statute, a license may issue but must expire
within six months unless the applicant certifies under oath within that time
that the violation has been corrected. Thereafter, any licensees who are
"four months or more in arrears in child support may be subject to suspension of their business, professional and/or driver's license." "License" is
defined to include "any . . . profession."

§460. Examination and Admission of Attorneys

An applicant for admission to practice as an attorney or counsellor
in this state, must be examined and licensed to practice as prescribed in
this chapter and in the rules of the court of appeals. Race, creed, color,
national origin, alienage or sex shall constitute no cause for refusing any
person examination or admission to practice.

§460-a. Disclosure with Respect to Loans Made
or Guaranteed by the New York State
Higher Education Services Corporation

Every application for admission to practice as an attorney or counsellor in the courts in this state issued pursuant to the provisions of this
chapter shall contain a question inquiring whether the applicant has any
loans made or guaranteed by the New York state higher education services corporation currently outstanding, and if so, whether such applicant is presently in default on any such loan. The name and address of
any applicant who answers either or both of such questions in the affirmative shall be transmitted to such corporation by the appellate division
prior to the date on which such license is issued.

§466. Attorney's Oath of Office

Each person, admitted as prescribed in this chapter must, upon his
admission, take the constitutional oath of office in open court, and subscribe the same in a roll or book, to be kept in the office of the clerk of
the appellate division of the supreme court for that purpose. . . .

Editors' Note. The "constitutional oath of office" referred to in §466 is found in the New York State Constitution at Article 13, §1, which provides, in relevant part, as follows:

> Members of the legislature, and all officers, executive and judicial, except such inferior officers as shall be by law exempted, shall, before they enter on the duties of their respective offices, take and subscribe the following oath or affirmation: "I do solemnly swear (or affirm) that I will support the constitution of the United States, and the constitution of the State of New York, and that I will faithfully discharge the duties of the office of . . . ., according to the best of my ability"; and no other oath, declaration or test shall be required as a qualification for any office of public trust. . . .

§470. Attorneys Having Offices in This State May Reside in Adjoining State

A person, regularly admitted to practice as an attorney and counsellor, in the courts of record of this state, whose office for the transaction of law business is within the state, may practice as such attorney or counsellor, although he resides in an adjoining state.

§479. Soliciting Business on Behalf of an Attorney

It shall be unlawful for any person or his agent, employee or any person acting on his behalf, to solicit or procure through solicitation either directly or indirectly legal business, or to solicit or procure through solicitation a retainer, written or oral, or any agreement authorizing an attorney to perform or render legal services, or to make it a business so to solicit or procure such business, retainers or agreements.

§480. Entering Hospital to Negotiate Settlement or Obtain Release or Statement

It shall be unlawful for any person to enter a hospital for the purpose of negotiating a settlement or obtaining a general release or statement, written or oral, from any person confined in said hospital or sanitarium as a patient, with reference to any personal injuries for which said person is confined in said hospital or sanitarium within fifteen days after the injuries were sustained, unless at least five days prior to the obtaining or procuring of such general release or statement such injured party has signified in writing his willingness that such general release or statement be given. This section shall not apply to a person entering a hospital for the purpose of visiting a person therein confined, as his attorney or on behalf of his attorney.

§481. Aiding, Assisting or Abetting the
      Solicitation of Persons or the Procurement
      of a Retainer for or on Behalf of an
      Attorney

It shall be unlawful for any person in the employ of or in any capacity attached to any hospital, sanitarium, police department, prison or court, or for a person authorized to furnish bail bonds, to communicate directly or indirectly with any attorney or person acting on his behalf for the purpose of aiding, assisting or abetting such attorney in the solicitation of legal business or the procurement through solicitation of a retainer, written or oral, or any agreement authorizing the attorney to perform or render legal services.

§482. Employment by Attorney of Person to Aid,
      Assist or Abet in the Solicitation of
      Business or the Procurement Through
      Solicitation of a Retainer to Perform
      Legal Services

It shall be unlawful for an attorney to employ any person for the purpose of soliciting or aiding, assisting or abetting in the solicitation of legal business or the procurement through solicitation either directly or indirectly of a retainer, written or oral, or of any agreement authorizing the attorney to perform or render legal services.

§484. None but Attorneys to Practice in the
      State

No natural person shall ask or receive, directly or indirectly, compensation for appearing for a person other than himself as attorney in any court or before any magistrate, or for preparing deeds, mortgages, assignments, discharges, leases or any other instruments affecting real estate, wills, codicils, or any other instrument affecting the disposition of property after death, or decedents' estates, or pleadings of any kind in any action brought before any court of record in this state, or make it a business to practice for another as an attorney in any court or before any magistrate unless he has been regularly admitted to practice, as an attorney or counselor, in the courts of record in the state; but nothing in this section shall apply (1) to officers of societies for the prevention of cruelty to animals, duly appointed, when exercising the special powers conferred upon such corporations under section fourteen hundred three of the not-for-profit corporation law; or (2) to law students who have completed at least two semesters of law school or persons who have graduated from a law school, who have taken the examination for admittance to practice law in the courts of record in the state immediately available after graduation from law school, or the examination immediately available after being notified by the board of law examiners that they failed to pass said exam, and who have not been notified by the board of law examiners that they have failed to pass two such examinations, acting under the supervision of a legal aid organization, when such students and persons are acting under a program approved by the appellate division of the supreme court of the department in which the principal office of such organization is located and specifying the extent to which such students and persons may engage in activities prohibited by this statute; or (3) to persons who have graduated from a law school approved pursuant to the rules of the court of appeals for the admission of attorneys and counselors-at-law and who have taken the examination for admission to practice as an attorney and counselor-at-law immediately available after graduation from law school or the examination immediately available after being notified by the board of law examiners that they failed to pass said exam, and who have not been notified by the board of law examiners that they have failed to pass two such examinations, when such persons are acting under the supervision of the state or a subdivision thereof or of any officer or agency of the state or a subdivision thereof, pursuant to a program approved by the appellate division of the supreme court of the department within which such activities are taking place and specifying the extent to which they may engage in activities otherwise prohibited by this statute and those powers of the supervising governmental entity or officer in connection with which they may engage in such activities.

§485. Violation of Certain Preceding Sections a Misdemeanor

Any person violating the provisions of sections four hundred seventy-eight, four hundred seventy-nine, four hundred eighty, four hundred eighty-one, four hundred eighty-two, four hundred eighty-three or four hundred eighty-four, shall be guilty of a misdemeanor.

§487. Misconduct by Attorneys

An attorney or counselor who:
1. Is guilty of any deceit or collusion, or consents to any deceit or collusion, with intent to deceive the court or any party; or,
2. Wilfully delays his client's suit with a view to his own gain; or, wilfully receives any money or allowance for or on account of any money which he has not laid out, or becomes answerable for,

Is guilty of a misdemeanor, and in addition to the punishment prescribed therefor by the penal law, he forfeits to the party injured treble damages, to be recovered in a civil action.

§491. Sharing of Compensation by Attorneys Prohibited

1. It shall be unlawful for any person, partnership, corporation, or association to divide with or receive from, or to agree to divide with or receive from, any attorney-at-law or group of attorneys-at-law, whether practicing in this state or elsewhere, either before or after action brought, any portion of any fee or compensation, charged or received by such attorney-at-law or any valuable consideration or reward, as an inducement for placing, or in consideration of having placed, in the hands of such attorney-at-law, or in the hands of another person, a claim or demand of any kind for the purpose of collecting such claim, or bringing an action thereon, or of representing claimant in the pursuit of any civil remedy for the recovery thereof. But this section does not apply to an agreement between attorneys and counsellors-at-law to divide between themselves the compensation to be received.
2. Any person violating any of the provisions of this section is guilty of a misdemeanor.

§495. Corporations and Voluntary Associations Not to Practice Law

1. No corporation or voluntary association shall

(a) practice or appear as an attorney-at-law for any person in any court in this state or before any judicial body, nor

(b) make it a business to practice as an attorney-at-law, for any person, in any of said courts, nor

(c) hold itself out to the public as being entitled to practice law, or to render legal services or advice, nor

(d) furnish attorneys or counsel, nor

(e) render legal services of any kind in actions or proceedings of any nature or in any other way or manner, nor

(f) assume in any other manner to be entitled to practice law, nor

(g) assume, use or advertise the title of lawyer or attorney, attorney-at-law, or equivalent terms in any language in such manner as to convey the impression that it is entitled to practice law or to furnish legal advice, services or counsel, nor

(h) advertise that either alone or together with or by or through any person whether or not a duly and regularly admitted attorney-at-law, it has, owns, conducts or maintains a law office or an office for the practice of law, or for furnishing legal advice, services or counsel. . . .

7. This section does not apply to organizations which offer prepaid legal services; to non-profit organizations whether incorporated or unincorporated, organized and operating primarily for a purpose other than the provision of legal services and which furnish legal services as an incidental activity in furtherance of their primary purpose; or to organizations which have as their primary purpose the furnishing of legal services to indigent persons.

§496. [Prepaid Legal Services Plans; Registration Statement]

An organization described in subdivision seven of section four hundred ninety-five of this article shall file with the appellate division department in which its principal office is located a statement describing the nature and purposes of the organization, the composition of its governing body, the type of legal services being made available, and the names and addresses of any attorneys and counselors-at-law employed by the organization or with whom commitments have been made. An updating of this information shall be furnished the appropriate appellate division on or before July first of each year and the names and addresses of attorneys and counselors-at-law who rendered legal services during that year shall be included.

§498. Professional Referrals

1. There shall be no cause of action for damages arising against any association or society of attorneys and counsellors at law authorized to practice in the state of New York for referring any person or persons to a member of the profession for the purpose of obtaining legal services, provided that such referral was made without charge and as a public service by said association or society, and without malice, and in the reasonable belief that such referral was warranted, based upon the facts disclosed.

2. For the purposes of this section, "association or society of attorneys or counsellors at law" shall mean any such organization, whether incorporated or unincorporated, which offers professional referrals as an incidental service in the normal course of business, but which business does not include the providing of legal services.

§499. Lawyer Assistance Committees

1. *Confidential information privileged.* The confidential relations and communications between a member or authorized agent of a lawyer assistance committee sponsored by a state or local bar association and any person, firm or corporation communicating with such committee, its members or authorized agents shall be deemed to be privileged on the same basis as those provided by law between attorney and client. Such privilege may be waived only by the person, firm or corporation which has furnished information to the committee.

2. *Immunity from liability.* Any person, firm or corporation in good faith providing information to, or in any other way participating in the affairs of, any of the committees referred to in subdivision one of this section shall be immune from civil liability that might otherwise result by reason of such conduct. For the purpose of any proceeding, the good faith of any such person, firm or corporation shall be presumed.

Selected New York Sanctions Provisions

Editors' Introduction. This chapter reprints two of New York's main provisions for sanctioning frivolous lawsuits and frivolous conduct in litigation. The most important provision is 22 N.Y.C.R.R. Part 130, a court rule that applies to all types of litigation. The other provision is §8303-a of the Civil Practice Law and Rules (CPLR), a statute that applies only to personal injury, property damage, and wrongful death cases.

Part 130 differs in three major ways from Rule 11 of the Federal Rules of Civil Procedure, which New York's courts have expressly refused to adopt. First, Part 130 permits only monetary sanctions, whereas Rule 11 also permits a wide range of non-monetary sanctions. Second, Part 130 limits sanctions to $10,000 per "incident," whereas Rule 11 imposes no limit on sanctions for a given incident. Third, Part 130 contains a specific subsection governing sanctions for a lawyer's unjustified failure to attend a scheduled court appearance, whereas Rule 11 applies only to court papers, not to court appearances.

In April of 1997, the New York courts circulated proposed amendments to Part 130 for public comment. In September of 1997, after considering the public comments, the courts adopted significant amendments to Part 130, effective January 1, 1998. We indicate the amendments to the former version of Part 130 by underscoring additions and striking through deletions. The amendments have three main features. First, amended Part 130 requires that every paper served or filed in a civil action be signed by an attorney (or by an unrepresented party) to certify that, to the best of the signer's knowledge and belief, the filing of the paper and the contentions made in the paper are not frivolous, and the substance of the factual arguments is not false. Second, amended Part 130 rescind the current limit of $10,000 per *case* for sanctions and costs; instead, courts may now impose sanctions of up to $10,000 per *incident,* and there is no limit at all on an award of costs. Third, amended Part 130-2 would permit an award of both costs and sanctions if an attorney unjustifiably fails to attend a scheduled court appearance.

Contents

NEW YORK RULES OF COURT (22 N.Y.C.R.R.)
PART 130. COSTS AND SANCTIONS

CIVIL PRACTICE LAW AND RULES

NEW YORK RULES OF COURT (22 N.Y.C.R.R.)

Editor's Note. In September of 1997, the courts announced that significant amendments to Part 130 would take effect on January 1, 1998. Our version underscores additions and strikes through deletions from the former version of Part 130.

PART 130. COSTS AND SANCTIONS

§130-1.1. Costs; Sanctions

(a) The court, in its discretion, may award to any party or attorney in any civil action or proceeding before the court, except where prohibited by law, costs in the form of reimbursement for actual expenses reasonably incurred and reasonable attorney's fees, resulting from frivolous conduct as defined in this Part. In addition to or in lieu of awarding costs, the court, in its discretion may impose financial sanctions upon any party or attorney in a civil action or proceeding who engages in frivolous conduct as defined in this Part, which shall be payable as provided in section 130.3 of this Part. . . .

(b) The court, as appropriate, may make such award of costs or impose such financial sanctions against either an attorney or a party to the litigation or against both. Where the award or sanction is against an attorney, it may be against the attorney personally or upon a partnership, firm, corporation, government agency, prosecutor's office, legal aid society or public defender's office with which the attorney is associated and that has appeared as attorney of record. The award or sanctions may be imposed upon any attorney appearing in the action or upon a partnership, firm or corporation with which the attorney is associated.

(c) For purposes of this Part, conduct is frivolous if:

(1) it is completely without merit in law or fact and cannot be supported by a reasonable argument for an extension, modification or reversal of existing law; ~~or~~

(2) it is undertaken primarily to delay or prolong the resolution of the litigation, or to harass or maliciously injure another; or

(3) it asserts material factual statements that are false.

Frivolous conduct shall include the making of a frivolous motion for costs or sanctions under this section. In determining whether the conduct undertaken was frivolous, the court shall consider, among other issues, (1) the circumstances under which the conduct took place, including the time available for investigating the legal or factual basis of the conduct; and (2) whether or not the conduct was continued when its lack of legal or factual basis was apparent, ~~or~~ should have been apparent ~~to counsel~~, or was brought to the attention of counsel or the party.

(d) An award of costs or the imposition of sanctions may be made either upon motion in compliance with CPLR 2214 or 2215 or upon the court's own initiative, after a reasonable opportunity to be heard. The form of the hearing shall depend upon the nature of the conduct and the circumstances of the case.

§130-1.1-a Signing of Papers

(a) Signature. Every pleading, written motion, and other paper, served on another party or filed or submitted to the court shall be signed by an attorney, or by a party if the party is not represented by an attorney, with the name of the attorney or party clearly printed or typed directly below the signature. Absent good cause shown, the court shall strike any unsigned paper if the omission of the signature is not corrected promptly after being called to the attention of the attorney or party.

(b) Certification. By signing a paper, an attorney or party certifies that, to the best of that person's knowledge, information and belief, formed after an inquiry reasonable under the circumstances, the presentation of the paper or the contentions therein are not frivolous as defined in subsection (c) of section 130-1.1.

§130-1.2. Order Awarding Costs or Imposing Sanctions

The court may ~~make an~~ award ~~of~~ costs or impose sanctions or both only upon a written decision setting forth the conduct on which the award or imposition is based, the reasons why the court found the conduct to be frivolous, and the reasons why the court found the amount awarded or imposed to be appropriate. An award of costs or the imposition of sanctions or both shall be entered as a judgment of the court. In no event shall the ~~total~~ amount of ~~costs awarded and~~ sanctions imposed exceed $10,000 ~~in any action or proceeding~~ for any single occurrence of frivolous conduct.

§130-1.3. Payment of Sanctions

Payments of sanctions by an attorney shall be deposited with the Lawyers' Fund for Client Protection established pursuant to section 97-t of the State Finance Law. Payments of sanctions by a party who is not an attorney shall be deposited with the clerk of the court for transmittal to the Commissioner of Taxation and Finance. . . .

§130-2.1. Costs; Sanctions

(a) Notwithstanding and in addition to the provisions of subpart 130-1 of this Part, the court, in its discretion, may impose financial sanctions, or costs in the form of reimbursement for actual expenses reasonably incurred and reasonable attorney's fees, upon any attorney who, without good cause, fails to appear at a time and place scheduled for an action or proceeding to be heard before a designated court. This Part shall not apply to town or village courts or to proceedings in a small claims part of any court.

(b) In determining whether an attorney's failure to appear at a scheduled court appearance was without good cause and in determining the measure of sanctions or costs to be imposed, the court shall consider all of the attendant circumstances, including but not limited to: (1) the explanation, if any, offered by the attorney for his or her nonappearance; (2) the adequacy of the notice to the attorney of the time and date of the scheduled appearance; (3) whether the attorney notified the court and opposing counsel in advance that he or she would be unable to appear; (4) whether substitute counsel appeared in court at the time previously scheduled to proffer an explanation of the attorney's nonappearance and whether such substitute counsel was prepared to go forward with the case; (5) whether an affidavit or affirmation of actual engagement was filed in the manner prescribed in Part 125 of the Uniform Rules for the Trial Courts of the Unified Court System; (6) whether the attorney on prior occasions in the same action or proceeding failed to appear at a scheduled court action or proceeding; (7) whether financial sanctions have been imposed upon the attorney pursuant to this section in some other action or proceeding; and (8) the extent and nature of the harm caused by the attorney's failure to appear.

(c) The court, as appropriate, may impose any such financial sanctions or costs upon an attorney personally or upon a partnership, firm, corporation, government agency, prosecutor's office, legal aid society or public defender's office with which the attorney is associated and that has appeared as attorney of record.

(d) The imposition of sanctions may be made either upon motion or upon the court's own initiative, after a reasonable opportunity to be heard. The form of the hearing shall depend upon the nature of the attorney's failure to appear and the totality of the circumstances of the case.

§130-2.2. Order Imposing Sanctions and Costs

The court may impose sanctions or costs only upon a written memorandum decision or statement on the record setting forth the conduct on which the award or imposition is based and the reasons why the court found the attorney's failure to appear at a scheduled court appearance to be without good cause. The imposition of sanctions shall be entered as a judgment of the court. In no event shall the amount of sanctions imposed exceed $2500 for any single failure to appear at a scheduled court appearance.

§130-2.3. Payment of Sanctions

Payments of sanctions shall be deposited with the Lawyers' Fund for Client Protection established pursuant to section 97-t of the State Finance Law.

CIVIL PRACTICE LAW AND RULES

§8303-a. Costs upon Frivolous Claims and
Counterclaims in Actions to Recover
Damages for Personal Injury, Injury to
Property or Wrongful Death

(a) If in an action to recover damages for personal injury, injury to property or wrongful death, an action or claim is commenced or continued by a plaintiff or a counterclaim, defense or cross claim is commenced or continued by a defendant that is found, at any time during the proceedings or upon judgment, to be frivolous by the court, the court shall award to the successful party costs and reasonable attorney's fees not exceeding ten thousand dollars.

(b) The costs and fees awarded under subdivision (a) of this section shall be assessed either against the party bringing the action, claim, cross claim, defense or counterclaim or against the attorney for such party, or against both, as may be determined by the court, based upon the circumstances of the case. Such costs and fees shall be in addition to any other judgment awarded to the successful party.

(c) In order to find the action, claim, counterclaim, defense or cross claim to be frivolous under subdivision (a) of this section, the court must find one or more of the following:

(i) the action, claim, counterclaim, defense or cross claim was commenced, used or continued in bad faith, solely to delay or prolong the resolution of the litigation or to harass or maliciously injure another;

(ii) the action, claim, counterclaim, defense or cross claim was commenced or continued in bad faith without any reasonable basis in law or fact and could not be supported by a good faith argument for an extension, modification or reversal of existing law. If the action, claim, counterclaim, defense or cross claim was promptly discontinued when the party or the attorney learned or should have learned that the action, claim, counterclaim, defense or cross claim lacked such a reasonable basis, the court may find that the party or the attorney did not act in bad faith.

ABA Model Code
of Professional Responsibility
Cross-Referenced to the
ABA Model Rules
of Professional Conduct

Editors' Introduction. To help those who use the ABA Model Code of Professional Responsibility (or state rules numbered like the code), we reprint here a table prepared by the ABA to correlate the Model Code to the Model Rules.

Readers starting from the ABA Model Rules of Professional Conduct can find the comparable provisions of the ABA Model Code of Professional Responsibility by referring to the Code Comparison following each Model Rule. No tables are necessary for this purpose.

Contents

ABA MODEL CODE OF PROFESSIONAL RESPONSIBILITY CROSS-REFERENCED TO ABA MODEL RULES OF PROFESSIONAL CONDUCT

ABA Model Code	*ABA Model Rules of Professional Conduct*
Canon 1: Integrity of Profession	
EC 1-1	Rules 1.1, 6.1, 8.1(a)
EC 1-2	Rules 1.1, 6.1, 8.1(a)
EC 1-3	Rules 8.1(a), 8.3
EC 1-4	Rules 6.1, 8.3
EC 1-5	Rule 8.4
EC 1-6	Rules 1.16(a)(2), 8.4(a)
DR 1-101	Rule 8.1(a)
DR 1-102(A)(1)	Rule 8.4(a)
DR 1-102(A)(2)	Rules 5.1(c), 5.3(b), 8.4(a)
DR 1-102(A)(3)	Rule 8.4(b), (f)
DR 1-102(A)(4)	Rules 3.3(a)(1), (2), & (4), 3.4(a), (b), 4.1, 8.4(c), (f)
DR 1-102(A)(5)	Rules 3.1 through 3.9, Rules 8.1, 8.4(d) & (f)
DR 1-102(A)(6)	Rules 3.4(b), 8.4(b), (f)
DR 1-103(A)	Rules 5.1, 8.3
DR 1-103(B)	Rule 8.1(b)
Canon 2: Making Counsel Available	
EC 2-1	Rules 6.1, 6.2, 7.2(a), 7.4
EC 2-2	Rules 6.1, 7.2(a)
EC 2-3	Rules 4.3, 7.3
EC 2-4	Rule 7.3
EC 2-5	Rule 7.1(b)
EC 2-6	Rule 7.2(a)
EC 2-7	Rules 7.2(a), 7.4
EC 2-8	Rules 7.1, 7.2(a), (c), 7.4
EC 2-9	Rule 7.1
EC 2-10	Rule 7.1(a), (c)
EC 2-11	Rule 7.5
EC 2-12	Rule 7.5(c)
EC 2-13	Rule 7.5(a) & (d)
EC 2-14	Rule 7.4
EC 2-15	Rule 7.2(a), (c)

EC 2-16	Rules 1.5(a), 6.1, 6.2(b)
EC 2-17	Rule 1.5(a)
EC 2-18	Rule 1.5(a)
EC 2-19	Rule 1.5(b)
EC 2-20	Rule 1.5(c), (d)
EC 2-21	Rules 1.7(b), 1.8(f)
EC 2-22	Rule 1.5(e)
EC 2-23	Rule 1.5 Comment ¶5
EC 2-24	Rules 6.1, 6.2
EC 2-25	Rules 6.1, 6.2
EC 2-26	Rules 1.16(a), 6.2
EC 2-27	Rule 6.2(a), (c)
EC 2-28	Rule 6.2(a)
EC 2-29	Rules 1.16(a), 6.2
EC 2-30	Rules 1.16(a), (b)(3), 4.2, 6.2
EC 2-31	Rules 1.3, 1.16, 6.2
EC 2-32	Rule 1.16
EC 2-33	Rules 5.4, 6.3, 6.4
DR 2-101(A)	Rule 7.1
DR 2-101(B)	Rules 7.1, 7.2(a)
DR 2-101(C)	Rules 7.1, 7.2
DR 2-101(D)	Rule 7.2(b)
DR 2-101(E)	Rule 7.1(a)
DR 2-101(F)	Rule 7.1
DR 2-101(G)	Rule 7.1
DR 2-101(H)	Rules 7.1, 7.2
DR 2-101(I)	Rule 7.2(c)
DR 2-102(A)	Rules 7.2(a), 7.4, 7.5
DR 2-102(B)	Rules 7.2(a), 7.5(a), (c)
DR 2-102(C)	Rule 7.5(d)
DR 2-102(D)	Rule 7.5(a), (b)
DR 2-102(E)	Rules 7.1(a), 7.4, 7.5(a)
DR 2-103(A)	Rules 7.2(a), 7.3
DR 2-103(B)	Rules 5.4(c), 7.2(a), (c)
DR 2-103(C)	Rules 5.4(a), 7.2(c), 7.3
DR 2-103(D)	Rules 5.4, 7.2(c), 7.3
DR 2-103(E)	Rules 1.16(a), 8.4(a)
DR 2-104	Rules 1.16(a), 7.3
DR 2-105	Rule 7.4
DR 2-106(A)	Rule 1.5(a)
DR 2-106(B)	Rule 1.5(a)

ABA Model Code	*ABA Model Rules of Professional Conduct*
Canon 2: Making Counsel Available	
DR 2-106(C)	Rule 1.5(d)(2)
DR 2-107(A)	Rule 1.5(e)
DR 2-107(B)	Rule 5.4(a)(1)
DR 2-108(A)	Rule 5.6(a)
DR 2-108(B)	Rule 5.6(b)
DR 2-109(A)	Rules 1.16(a), 3.1, 3.2
DR 2-110(A)	Rule 1.16(c), (d)
DR 2-110(B)	Rules 1.16(a), 3.1, 4.4
DR 2-110(C)	Rules 1.2(e), 1.16(a), (b)
Canon 3: Unauthorized Practice	
EC 3-1	Rules 5.4, 5.5
EC 3-2	Rules 5.4, 5.5
EC 3-3	Rules 5.4, 5.5
EC 3-4	Rules 5.4, 5.5
EC 3-5	Rules 5.4, 5.5
EC 3-6	Rule 5.3
EC 3-7	Rule 5.5
EC 3-8	Rules 5.4(a), (b), (d), 5.5(b)
EC 3-9	Rules 5.5(a), 8.5
DR 3-101(A)	Rule 5.5(b)
DR 3-101(B)	Rule 5.5(a)
DR 3-102	Rule 5.4(a)
DR 3-103	Rule 5.4(b)
Canon 4: Confidences and Secrets	
EC 4-1	Rule 1.6
EC 4-2	Rules 1.6(a), (b)(1), 2.2(a)(1), 5.3(a)
EC 4-3	Rule 1.6(a)
EC 4-4	Rule 1.6(a)
EC 4-5	Rules 1.8(b), 1.9(b), 1.10(a) & (b), 5.1(a), (b) & (c), 5.3(a)
EC 4-6	Rule 1.9(b), (c)
DR 4-101(A)	Rule 1.6(a)
DR 4-101(B)	Rules 1.6(a), (b), 1.8(b), 1.9(b)
DR 4-101(C)	Rules 1.6, 1.9(b)
DR 4-101(D)	Rules 5.1(a), (b), 5.3(a), (b)

Canon 5: Independent
Judgment

EC 5-1	Rules 1.7, 1.8(c), (d), (e), (f), (g), (j)
EC 5-2	Rules 1.7, 1.8(a), (c), (d), (e), (f), (j)
EC 5-3	Rules 1.7, 1.8(a), (d), (e)
EC 5-4	Rule 1.8(d)
EC 5-5	Rule 1.8(a), (c)
EC 5-6	Rule 1.8(c)
EC 5-7	Rules 1.5(c), 1.8(e), (j), 1.15
EC 5-8	Rule 1.8(e)
EC 5-9	Rules 1.7(b), 3.7
EC 5-10	Rule 3.7
EC 5-11	Rules 1.7, 2.1
EC 5-12	Rule 1.2(a)
EC 5-13	Rule 1.7(b)
EC 5-14	Rules 1.7, 2.2(a)
EC 5-15	Rules 1.7, 2.2(a), (c)
EC 5-16	Rules 1.2(e), 1.7(b), 1.13(d), (e), 2.2(a), (b)
EC 5-17	Rule 1.7
EC 5-18	Rule 1.13
EC 5-19	Rules 1.7(b), 2.2(c)
EC 5-20	Rules 1.12, 2.2
EC 5-21	Rules 1.7, 1.16(a)(1)
EC 5-22	Rules 1.7, 1.8(f)
EC 5-23	Rules 1.7(b), 1.8(f), 5.4(c)
EC 5-24	Rules 1.13, 5.4(a), (d)
DR 5-101(A)	Rules 1.7, 1.8(j), 6.3, 6.4
DR 5-101(B)	Rules 1.7, 3.7
DR 5-102(A)	Rules 1.7, 3.7
DR 5-102(B)	Rules 1.7, 3.7
DR 5-103(A)	Rules 1.5(c), 1.8(e), (j), 1.15
DR 5-103(B)	Rule 1.8(e)
DR 5-104(A)	Rules 1.7(b), 1.8(a)
DR 5-104(B)	Rule 1.8(d)
DR 5-105(A)	Rules 1.7, 2.2
DR 5-105(B)	Rules 1.7, 1.13(e), 2.2
DR 5-105(C)	Rules 1.7, 1.9, 1.10(c), 1.13(e), 2.2
DR 5-105(D)	Rules 1.10(a), 1.12(c)
DR 5-106	Rule 1.8(g)
DR 5-107(A)	Rules 1.7, 1.8(f)

ABA Model Code	*ABA Model Rules of Professional Conduct*
Canon 5: Independent Judgment	
DR 5-107(B)	Rules 1.7, 1.8(f), 1.13(b), (c), 2.1, 5.4(c)
DR 5-107(C)	Rule 5.4(d)
Canon 6: Competence	
EC 6-1	Rule 1.1
EC 6-2	Rules 1.1, 5.1(a), (b), 6.1
EC 6-3	Rules 1.1, 1.3
EC 6-4	Rules 1.1, 1.3
EC 6-5	Rule 1.1
EC 6-6	Rule 1.8(h)
DR 6-101	Rules 1.1, 1.3, 1.4, 1.5(e)
DR 6-102	Rule 1.8(h)
Canon 7: Zeal within the Law	
EC 7-1	Rules 1.2(d), 1.3, 3.1
EC 7-2	Rule 1.2(d)
EC 7-3	Rules 1.4(b), 2.1
EC 7-4	Rule 3.1
EC 7-5	Rules 1.2(d), 1.4(a), 3.1
EC 7-6	Rule 3.4(a), (b)
EC 7-7	Rule 1.2(a)
EC 7-8	Rules 1.2(a), (c), 1.4, 2.1
EC 7-9	Rule 1.2(c)
EC 7-10	Rule 4.4
EC 7-11	Rules 1.14(a), 3.8, 3.9
EC 7-12	Rule 1.14
EC 7-13	Rule 3.8
EC 7-14	Rules 3.1, 3.8, 4.4
EC 7-15	Rule 3.9
EC 7-16	Rule 3.9
EC 7-17	Rule 1.2(b)
EC 7-18	Rules 3.8(c), 4.2, 4.3
EC 7-19	Rules 3.1 through 3.5
EC 7-20	Rules 3.1 through 3.6
EC 7-21	Rule 4.4
EC 7-22	Rules 1.2(d), 3.4(c)
EC 7-23	Rule 3.3(a)(3)

EC 7-24	Rule 3.4(e)
EC 7-25	Rules 3.1, 3.4(c), (e), 3.5, 3.6, 4.4
EC 7-26	Rule 3.3(a)(4), (c)
EC 7-27	Rules 3.3(a)(d), 3.4(a), (f)
EC 7-28	Rules 3.4(b), 5.3(a), (b)
EC 7-29	Rules 3.5(a), 4.4
EC 7-30	Rule 4.4
EC 7-31	Rules 3.5(a), (b), 4.4
EC 7-32	Rule 8.3
EC 7-33	Rule 3.6
EC 7-34	Rules 3.5(a), 8.4(f)
EC 7-35	Rule 3.5(b)
EC 7-36	Rule 3.5(c)
EC 7-37	Rules 3.5(c), 4.4
EC 7-38	Rules 1.3, 3.4(c)
EC 7-39	Rules 3.1 through 3.8
DR 7-101(A)	Rules 1.2(a), (d), 1.3, 3.2, 3.5(c), 4.4
DR 7-101(B)	Rules 1.2(a), (c), (d), 1.16(b)
DR 7-102(A)(1)	Rules 3.1, 3.2, 4.4
DR 7-102(A)(2)	Rule 3.1
DR 7-102(A)(3)	Rules 3.3(a)(2), (3), 4.1
DR 7-102(A)(4)	Rule 3.3(a)(4), (c)
DR 7-102(A)(5)	Rules 3.3(a)(1), 4.1
DR 7-102(A)(6)	Rules 1.2(b), 3.4(b)
DR 7-102(A)(7)	Rules 1.2(d), 3.3(a), 4.1
DR 7-102(A)(8)	Rules 1.2(d), 8.4(a), (b)
DR 7-102(B)	Rules 1.6(b), 3.3(a)(4), (b), 4.1(b)
DR 7-103(A)	Rule 3.8(a)
DR 7-103(B)	Rule 3.8(d)
DR 7-104	Rules 3.4(f), 4.2, 4.3
DR 7-105	None
DR 7-106(A)	Rules 1.2(d), 3.4(c), (d)
DR 7-106(B)	Rules 3.3(a)(3), 3.9
DR 7-106(C)	Rules 3.4(a), (c), (d), (e), 3.5, 4.4
DR 7-107(A)-(I)	Rule 3.6
DR 7-107(J)	Rules 5.1(a), (b), 5.3(a), (b)
DR 7-108(A)	Rule 3.5(a), (b)
DR 7-108(B)	Rules 3.5(a), (b), 5.1(c), 5.3(a), (b), 8.4(a)
DR 7-108(C)	Rule 3.5(a), (b)
DR 7-108(D)	Rules 3.5(b), 4.4
DR 7-108(E)	Rules 3.5(b), 4.4, 5.1(c), 5.3(a), (b), 8.4(a)

ABA Model Code	*ABA Model Rules of Professional Conduct*
Canon 7: Zeal within the Law	
DR 7-108(F)	Rule 4.4
DR 7-108(G)	None
DR 7-109(A)	Rules 3.3(a)(2), 3.4(a)
DR 7-109(B)	Rule 3.4(a), (f)
DR 7-109(C)	Rule 3.4(b)
DR 7-110(A)	Rules 3.5(a), 8.4(f)
DR 7-110(B)	Rule 3.5(a), (b)
Canon 8: Improving Legal System	
DR 8-1	Rules 1.2(b), 6.1
DR 8-2	Rule 6.1
DR 8-3	Rules 6.1, 6.2
DR 8-4	Rule 3.9
DR 8-5	Rules 3.3(a)(1), (2), (4), (b), 3.9
DR 8-6	Rule 8.2(a)
DR 8-7	Rules 5.5, 8.1
DR 8-8	Rule 1.11(c)
DR 8-9	Rule 6.1
DR 8-101	Rules 1.11(c), 3.5(a), 8.4(e), (f)
DR 8-102	Rule 8.2(a)
DR 8-103	Rule 8.2(b)
Canon 9: Appearance of Impropriety	
EC 9-1	Rules 3.1 through 3.8, 4.1, 8.4
EC 9-2	Rules 1.4, 3.1 through 3.8, 4.1
EC 9-3	Rules 1.11(a), 1.12(a)
EC 9-4	Rules 7.1(b), 8.4(c), (e)
EC 9-5	Rule 1.15
EC 9-6	Preamble, Rule 8.4(e)
EC 9-7	Rule 1.15
DR 9-101(A)	Rule 1.12
DR 9-101(B)	Rules 1.11(a), 1.12(a), (b)
DR 9-101(C)	Rules 1.2(e), 7.1(b), 8.4(e)
DR 9-102	Rules 1.4, 1.15

Special Section:
Office of the President
v. Office of Independent
Counsel, et al.

Is There a Government Attorney-Client Privilege?

Editors' Note: On April 9, 1997, the United States Court of Appeals for the Eighth Circuit declined, over dissent, to recognize an attorney-client privilege between a federal official and a federal lawyer when a federal prosecutor subpoenas a communication between them. In re Grand Jury Subpoena Duces Tecum, 112 F.3d 910 (8th Cir. 1997). The case, thereafter denominated Office of the President v. Office of Independent Counsel, arose after Kenneth W. Starr, Whitewater Independent Counsel, subpoenaed the notes of White House lawyers in conversations they had on two occasions with First Lady Hillary Rodham Clinton. David E. Kendall, the personal attorney for President and Mrs. Clinton, was also at these meetings. No one else was present. At one of the meetings, Mrs. Clinton discussed her activities following the death of Deputy White House Counsel Vincent Foster. The second meeting, really a series of meetings, took place on the day Mrs. Clinton testified before a federal grand jury after being called by Mr. Starr.

A federal district judge in Arkansas refused to enforce Mr. Starr's subpoena for the lawyers' notes of these meetings, but the Eighth Circuit reversed. This opinion was initially issued under seal, but released publicly on May 2, 1997 on motion of the White House and Mrs. Clinton. The White House planned to seek review in the United States Supreme Court, which does not receive papers or issue opinions under seal.

Although the case concerns the First Lady's conversations with White House counsel, the Eighth Circuit opinion does not rely on whether the First Lady is or is not a public official. Instead, the majority concludes that even assuming that there is an attorney-client privilege between government officials and government lawyers, a federal prosecutor can defeat any privilege with a federal grand jury subpoena. The Eighth Circuit's opinion applies to all federal officials in all three branches of government, without regard to the subject matter of the subpoenaed communication.

The White House filed a Petition for Certiorari in the Supreme Court. Three amicus briefs were filed in support of the Petition. The United States, acting through the Attorney General, filed one of these. A second amicus brief was filed on behalf of six prominent former government lawyers in Administrations of both parties. The third amicus brief was filed on behalf of sixteen professors of evidence and legal ethics. Hillary Clinton also filed a brief supporting the Petition. The Office of the Independent Counsel opposed the Petition. On June 23, 1997, the Supreme Court denied review without comment and the White House delivered the notes to Mr. Starr's office the same day.

Following is the amicus brief of the United States. Space does not permit us to reprint all the briefs, but we believe the following brief, read in conjunction with the majority and dissenting opinions in the Eighth Circuit opinion, cited above, suffice to define the scope of the debate.

No. 96-1783

In the Supreme Court of the United States

OCTOBER TERM, 1996

OFFICE OF THE PRESIDENT, PETITIONER

v.

OFFICE OF INDEPENDENT COUNSEL, ET AL.

*ON PETITION FOR A WRIT OF CERTIORARI
TO THE UNITED STATES COURT OF APPEALS
FOR THE EIGHTH CIRCUIT*

BRIEF AMICUS CURIAE FOR
THE UNITED STATES,
ACTING THROUGH THE ATTORNEY GENERAL,
SUPPORTING CERTIORARI

SETH P. WAXMAN
  Acting Solicitor General
FRANK W. HUNGER
  Assistant Attorney General
JOHN C. KEENEY
  *Acting Assistant Attorney
  General*
EDWIN S. KNEEDLER
MICHAEL R. DREEBEN
  Deputy Solicitors General
JAMES A. FELDMAN
  *Assistant to the Solicitor
  General
  Department of Justice
  Washington, D.C. 20530-0001
  (202) 514-2217*

QUESTIONS PRESENTED

1. Whether the Office of the President may decline to produce documents sought by a federal grand jury subpoena on the ground that the documents are protected by an attorney-client privilege.

2. Whether the Office of the President may decline to produce documents sought by a federal grand jury subpoena on the ground that they are protected by the work product doctrine because they were prepared by its attorneys in connection with grand jury proceedings and legislative proceedings.

In the Supreme Court of the United States

OCTOBER TERM, 1996

No. 96-1783

OFFICE OF THE PRESIDENT, PETITIONER

v.

OFFICE OF INDEPENDENT COUNSEL, ET AL.

*ON PETITION FOR A WRIT OF CERTIORARI
TO THE UNITED STATES COURT OF APPEALS
FOR THE EIGHTH CIRCUIT*

BRIEF AMICUS CURIAE FOR
THE UNITED STATES,
ACTING THROUGH THE ATTORNEY GENERAL,
SUPPORTING CERTIORARI

INTEREST OF THE UNITED STATES

Petitioner and respondent represent discrete interests of the United States in this specific litigation. The issues presented, however, implicate fundamental concerns of the United States that extend far beyond the particular circumstances of this case. Thus, although special counsel have been appointed by the Department of Justice to represent the Office of the President in this case, the United States has a broad and substantial interest in the ability of the President and Executive Branch agencies generally to obtain frank, fully informed, and confidential legal advice. And although the Independent Counsel has the "authority to exercise all investigative and prosecutorial functions and powers of the Department of Justice" with respect to matters within his jurisdiction, 28 U.S.C. 594(a), the Attorney General is otherwise responsible for federal criminal prosecutions. See 28 U.S.C. 597(b) (authorizing Attorney General and Solicitor General to participate as amicus curiae in independent counsel cases).

The unique nature of this case led the Attorney General to conclude at the time this dispute arose that the White House should be represented by specially appointed counsel, who would be in a position to review the attorney notes subpoenaed by the Independent Counsel and respond to the motion to compel on that basis.[1] The Attorney General reserved, however, the right to file a brief addressing legal issues of broader interest to the United States in appropriate circumstances. The opinion of the court of appeals now presents those circumstances.[2]

STATEMENT

1. a. On July 11, 1995, First Lady Hillary Rodham Clinton met with David Kendall, an attorney representing both the President and Mrs. Clinton in their personal capacities, at the White House Residence for the purpose of obtaining legal advice. Late in the meeting, two attorneys from the White House Counsel's Office, Jane Sherburne and Miriam Nemetz, joined them. Ms. Nemetz took some notes during the meeting. The subject of that part of the meeting was Mrs. Clinton's activities in the period immediately following the suicide of White House Deputy Counsel Vincent Foster in 1993. At the time of the meeting, investigations relating to what has become known as "Whitewater," including the handling of documents in the aftermath of the Foster suicide, were being conducted by the Independent Counsel, the Senate Whitewater Committee, the House Banking and Government Reform Committees, the Federal Deposit Insurance Corporation, and the Resolution Trust Corporation. The Independent Counsel had scheduled a deposition of Mrs. Clinton regarding the Foster document matter for July 22, 1995. Pet. App. 88a-89a, 94a.

b. Early in January 1996, a White House employee found in the White House Residence a copy of billing records relating to work performed by members of the Rose Law Firm, including Mrs. Clinton. Those records were responsive to a May 1994 grand jury subpoena to Mrs. Clinton. On January 19, 1996, the Independent Counsel issued a subpoena for Mrs. Clinton to testify before a Washington, D.C., grand jury regarding the discovery of the billing records. Other investigations regarding the discovery of the records were being undertaken by the Senate Whitewater Committee and other federal agencies. Mrs. Clinton testified before the grand jury on January 26, 1996. During breaks in her testimony, Mrs. Clinton met in a private room in the courthouse with Kendall, his partner

1. The Department of Justice has not reviewed the notes and is not aware of their contents.
2. The district court opinion, and all proceedings in both lower courts, were subject to a seal order, and prior to this stage we did not review them.

Nicole Seligman, White House Counsel John Quinn, and Sherburne. After the testimony was completed, Mrs. Clinton met at the White House Residence with Sherburne, Kendall, and Seligman. Sherburne took notes during those meetings. Pet. App. 66a n.3, 89a-90a, 94a.

2. On June 21, 1996, on the application of the Independent Counsel, a grand jury in the Eastern District of Arkansas issued a subpoena to "The White House c/o Jane Sherburne, Special Counsel to the President." The subpoena sought, inter alia (Resp. C.A. App. 2-3):

> All documents created during any meeting attended by any attorney from the Office of the Counsel to the President and Hillary Rodham Clinton (regardless whether any other person was present), between July 20, 1993, and the present, which relate in any way to the death of Vincent W. Foster, Jr., documents in the office of Vincent W. Foster, Jr., at the time of his death, or events between July 20 and July 27, 1993.

The White House Counsel identified nine sets of notes that were responsive to the subpoena, but refused to produce them on the ground of attorney-client privilege and the work product doctrine. The Independent Counsel then moved to compel production, but only of the Nemetz notes of the July 11, 1995, meeting, and the Sherburne notes of the January 26, 1996, meetings. Pet. App. 2a-3a.

3. On November 26, 1996, the district court denied the Independent Counsel's motion to compel production. Pet. App. 62a-83a. The court concluded that the law in this area is "uncertain," that "Mrs. Clinton, as the functional equivalent of an officer or employee of the White House, considered her communications with lawyers from the White House Counsel's Office and personal counsel, as did those lawyers, to be confidential and for the purpose of receiving legal advice," and that the attorney-client privilege should protect the conversations for that reason — regardless of whether the privilege legally applies. *Id.* at 80a. The court also held that the notes are "work product of the type that is clearly protected from disclosure to the grand jury." *Id.* at 81a.

4. a. A divided panel of the Eighth Circuit reversed. Pet. App. 1a-61a. The majority reasoned that the principal question in this case — "whether an entity of the federal government may use the attorney-client privilege to avoid complying with a subpoena by a federal grand jury," Pet. App. 5a — is governed by Rule 501 of the Federal Rules of Evidence. That Rule provides that "the privilege of a witness, person, government, State, or political subdivision thereof [is] governed by the principles of the common law as they may be interpreted by the courts of the United States in the light of reason and experience." In the majority's view, *United States* v.

Nixon, 418 U.S. 683 (1974), "is indicative of the general principle that the government's need for confidentiality may be subordinated to the needs of the government's own criminal justice processes." Pet. App. 15a. In the context of attorney-client communications, the court held, the governmental interest in confidentiality can never overcome a grand jury subpoena. See *id.* at 17a-20a.

The court rejected the argument that the governmental attorney-client privilege is supported by the same rationale — and should have the same scope — as the corporate attorney-client privilege recognized by this Court in *Upjohn Co.* v. *United States,* 449 U.S. 383 (1981). The court believed that White House lawyers require confidentiality less than their corporate counterparts because "the actions of White House personnel, whatever their capacity, cannot expose the White House as an entity to criminal liability," and the White House therefore does not have a compelling interest in ferreting out misconduct by its employees. Pet. App. 17a. In addition, the court found it "significant that executive branch employees, including attorneys, are under a statutory duty to report criminal wrongdoing by other employees to the Attorney General" pursuant to 28 U.S.C. 535(b). *Ibid.* Finally, drawing an analogy between the responsibilities of government lawyers and the responsibilities of auditors to "maintain total independence from the client at all times" and to assume "public obligations" as a "public watchdog," *id.* at 17a-18a (quoting *United States* v. *Arthur Young & Co.,* 465 U.S. 805, 817-818 (1984)), the court concluded that the "strong public interest in honest government and in exposing wrongdoing by public officials would be ill-served by recognition of a governmental attorney-client privilege applicable in criminal proceedings inquiring into the actions of public officials," *id.* at 18a.[3]

The court also rejected application of the work product doctrine, because it believed that White House Counsel was not "preparing for or anticipating some sort of adversarial proceeding involving his or her client." Pet. App. 25a-26a. It found "unpersuasive" the White House's position that its lawyers were preparing for the Independent Counsel's investigation, because the "OIC is not investigating the White House, nor could it do so." *Id.* at 26a. Nor, in the court's view, did congressional investigations trigger the work product doctrine, because they were directed not

3. The court rejected the argument that the presence of Mrs. Clinton's private attorneys "affects the calculus in this case," Pet. App. 20a, finding no "common interest" sufficient to render the private and public representations jointly privileged, *id.* at 21a-23a. And the court rejected the district court's reasoning that Mrs. Clinton's subjective belief that a privilege attached to the conversations in question was sufficient by itself to warrant refusing to enforce the subpoena. *Id.* at 23a-25a.

at the White House, but at individuals, and could result only in "political" — not legal — harm. *Id.* at 26a-27a.

b. District Judge Kopf dissented. Pet. App. 29a-61a. He believed that recognition of the attorney-client privilege in this setting falls squarely within proposed Federal Rule of Evidence 503, as well as other authoritative sources. See *id.* at 33a-38a. In his view, the fact that this is a criminal proceeding has no bearing on the application *vel non* of the attorney-client privilege, *id.* at 36a, and the public interest favors recognition of a privilege so that governmental entities may obtain legal advice about how to obey the law, *id.* at 37a-44a. Judge Kopf concluded, however, that although the ordinary prerequisites of the privilege were satisfied, see *id.* at 44a-49a, it generally can be invaded in the unique setting of a subpoena issued in connection with an independent counsel investigation on a showing of need and with appropriate procedural protections, *id.* at 51a-55a. In this case, Judge Kopf reasoned that producing the notes would unjustifiably invade Mrs. Clinton's personal attorney-client privilege, because both she and the White House Counsel reasonably expected the communications to be confidential. *Id.* at 59a-61a.

DISCUSSION

The United States is ordinarily entitled to the same attorney-client privilege that is available to private individuals and corporations. This case, however, does not arise from the ordinary situation in which the privilege is asserted by its holder against an outside entity. This case involves claims to information by prosecutorial interests of the United States represented by the Independent Counsel, on the one hand, and assertion of the attorney-client privilege for the same information by the Office of the President, on the other. The grand jury, working in conjunction with the Independent Counsel, has issued a subpoena and, through the Independent Counsel, has sought judicial enforcement of it. The primary position of the Office of the President is that the attorney-client privilege is absolute and therefore necessarily prevails against the grand jury subpoena. The position of the Independent Counsel and the court of appeals, by contrast, is that there is no attorney-client privilege in this setting and that the grand jury subpoena therefore necessarily prevails.

We see the matter from a different perspective. A purely intra-Executive Branch disagreement over the availability and use in court of information held by a federal agency would typically be resolved within the Executive Branch based on consideration of the various interests of the United States as a whole. In that setting, the Attorney General, who is charged with conducting litigation on behalf of the United States and its agencies, is in a position to reconcile all litigation and non-litigation interests and to speak for the single client (the United States) in all of its aspects — to assert or waive in litigation privileges that might otherwise be absolute as against parties outside the Executive Branch. Although in criminal cases the government's investigative and prosecutorial interests have great weight, there may be cases in which those interests are attenuated or are outweighed by the need for confidentiality.

Because this case involves a grand jury subpoena issued at the behest of an independent counsel — who is vested with responsibility for only one discrete interest of the United States and who does not operate under the direct supervision of the President or the Attorney General — there is no opportunity for the weighing of all relevant interests of the United States within the Executive Branch. That task thus necessarily falls to the district court in ruling on the Independent Counsel's motion to enforce the grand jury subpoena. In applying the law of privileges under Rule 501 in that setting, the President's interest in confidentiality supports application of the attorney-client privilege. The demands of criminal law enforcement, however, may require in a particular instance that the privilege give way. Cf. *United States* v. *Nixon,* 418 U.S. 683 (1974).

In holding that the privilege automatically gives way in response to an otherwise valid grand jury subpoena, the court of appeals' decision lays open the White House Counsel (and by extension federal agency counsel) to an ever-present potential for unrestrained intrusion into their ongoing attorney-client communications. That result would impair the ability of the President (and the heads of federal agencies) to obtain frank, fully informed, and confidential legal advice. The same is true of the court of appeals' categorical refusal to afford any protection through the work product doctrine. In light of the court of appeals' legal errors and the resulting practical consequences, review by this Court is warranted.

1. The attorney-client privilege "functions to protect communications between government attorneys and client agencies or departments * * * much as it operates to protect attorney-client communications in the private sector." Memorandum for the Attorney General re: Confidentiality of the Attorney General's Communications in Counseling the President, 6 Op. O.L.C. 481, 495 (1982) (1982 OLC Opinion).[4] The ra-

---

4. See also 6 Op. O.L.C. at 483 ("[T]he Attorney General may assert the common-law privilege for attorney-client communications, which has been codified in Rule 501 of the Federal Rules of Evidence * * *, to protect from disclosure in litigation certain confidential communications of a legal advisory nature which were prepared for the Office of the President.").

tionale for the governmental privilege is much the same as that for the corporate privilege recognized in *Upjohn Co.* v. *United States*, 449 U.S. 383 (1981). To paraphrase the Court's reasoning in *Upjohn*:

> In light of the vast and complicated array of regulatory legislation confronting [federal agencies], [agencies], like most individuals, constantly go to lawyers to find out how to obey the law, particularly since compliance with the law in this area is hardly an instinctive matter.

Id. at 392 (citations and internal quotation marks omitted). The purpose of the privilege in the governmental context, as in the private context, is "to encourage full and frank communication between attorneys and their clients and thereby promote broader public interests in the observance of law and administration of justice." *Id.* at 389.

All of the authoritative sources agree with that proposition — and none recognizes any categorical exception to the privilege in criminal proceedings. The proposed Federal Rules of Evidence, whose status as a solid indication of the scope of the "common law" of privilege under Rule 501 has frequently been recognized, see, *e.g.*, *United States* v. *Gillock*, 445 U.S. 360, 367-368 (1980), included a rule regarding the attorney-client privilege. That rule defined "client" to include "a person, *public officer*, or corporation, association, or other organization or entity, *either pulic or private.*" *Rules of Evidence for United States Courts and Magistrates*, 56 F.R.D. 183, 235 (1972) (emphasis added). Similarly, the Restatement (Third) of the Law Governing Lawyers §124, Proposed Final Draft No. 1 (approved May 28, 1996) (Restatement), states that "[t]he attorney-client privilege extends to a communication of a governmental organization," and Uniform Rule of Evidence 502(a)(1) defines "client" to include governmental bodies.[5] The attorney-client privilege of federal agencies in particular (along with the work product doctrine) has been recognized and affirmed under the Freedom of Information Act.[6]

---

5. Uniform Rule 502(d)(6) limits application of the privilege in the governmental context to situations involving a pending investigation or litigation and requires a finding by the court that disclosure will "seriously impair" the agency's pursuit of the investigation or litigation. As the court of appeals recognized (Pet. App. 8a n.5), many States that have adopted the Uniform Rules have omitted this qualification.

6. FOIA Exemption 5, 5 U.S.C. 552(b)(5), protects from disclosure materials that would normally be privileged from discovery in litigation with the agency. *NLRB* v. *Sears, Roebuck & Co.*, 421 U.S. 132, 149 (1975). In *Sears, Roebuck*, this Court found it "clear that Congress had the attorney's work-product privilege specifically in mind when it adopted Exemption 5 and that such a privilege had been recognized in the civil discovery context by the prior case law." *Id.* at 154. The lower courts have routinely held that Exemption 5 applies as well to attorney-client privileged materials. See, *e.g.*, *Mead Data Cent., Inc.*

The court of appeals' rejection of any attorney-client privilege in this setting rested on two fundamentally erroneous propositions: (1) that the White House is less in need of confidential legal advice than a corporation because the White House as an entity has no exposure to legal liability and has no compelling interest in conducting investigations to ferret out misconduct by its employees, Pet. App. 17a; and (2) that White House Counsel and other government attorneys are properly analogized to outside auditors who serve as "public watchdogs" and must "maintain total independence from the client at all times," *id.* at 17a-18a.

Contrary to the court of appeals' view, attorneys in the government, like their counterparts elsewhere, have duties of loyalty and confidentiality to their client (see ABA Standing Committee on Ethics and Professional Responsibility, Formal Opinion 97-405 (Apr. 19, 1997), slip op. 4-5; Restatement §156 cmt. d), and a governmental client plainly does have a compelling interest in investigating allegations of wrongdoing by its employees. Moreover, the need of the President and other Executive Branch officials to obtain frank, fully informed, and confidential legal advice so that they may conform their conduct to the law is at least as great as that of non-governmental clients. Thus, where a governmental attorney-client communication satisfies the ordinary prerequisites of the privilege, the communication is privileged from disclosure to outsiders to the same extent — and for the same reasons — as a corporate attorney-client communication would be.

2. a. The fact that the federal government enjoys an absolute attorney-client privilege as against outside parties does not, however, resolve this case. It is necessary to consider as well how decisions are made within the Executive Branch whether to assert or waive privileges in litigation, including in grand jury investigations. If an agency possesses information protected by the attorney-client privilege, no abrogation or waiver of that privilege would result from furnishing the information to the Attorney General, who represents the interests of the United States as a whole, including its constituent agencies. See 28 U.S.C. 511, 512, 516, 533, 547. The only question at that stage would be whether the need for the information outweighs any adverse impact on the effective provision of legal advice to the agency possessing the information that might result from the intra-Branch disclosure.[7] If information is obtained by the At-

---

v. *United States Dep't of Air Force*, 566 F.2d 242, 252-253 & n.20 (D.C. Cir. 1977); Pet. 18 n.5 (citing cases).

7. The same principles would apply within a private corporation with respect to information protected by the attorney-client privilege under *Upjohn*. No waiver of the privilege would result if counsel in one division of the corporation furnished the privileged

torney General, a further question may later arise about whether to use the information in criminal or civil litigation. Although the Attorney General's weighing of the relevant interests informing that decision would ordinarily occur in consultation with the agency involved, the agency could, if necessary, present any irreconcilable differences to the President.[8]

Where the Attorney General seeks information directly relating to the commission of a federal crime, the Justice Department's experience indicates that it would be rare for the Attorney General to strike the balance against obtaining it, given the compelling federal interest in investigation and prosecution of federal crimes.[9] The Attorney General may obtain or review the information with the understanding that there would be further consultation with the agency concerned before the material would be used in a manner that would abrogate the attorney-client (or other) privilege. After obtaining the information, there may often be situations in which the Attorney General, after again weighing the relevant considerations, would in turn choose to submit evidence protected by the governmental attorney-client privilege to a grand jury, or to introduce it into evidence at trial.[10] But there may also be situations in which the potential chilling of the effective provision of legal advice to the agency concerned would outweigh the prosecution's need to use particular information — *e.g.*, where the information bore less directly on the investigation or trial, or where the information sought reflects, not the historical matters under investigation, but rather the agency's consideration of the request for information itself. What is significant is that, in the ordinary case, the Attorney General, in consultation with other Executive Branch officials and subject to the ultimate authority of the President, would weigh all of the relevant interests of the single client, the United States.

---

information to counsel in another division, or to the general counsel of the corporation as a whole. Whether to share the information in that manner would be a matter of internal policy to be resolved by the responsible decision-makers within the corporation, taking into account the various interests of the corporation.

8. Both parties agree. See Pet. 20 n.6 ("any such intrabranch disputes would ordinarily * * * be resolved by consultation between agency heads or, if necessary, by the chief executive"); Br. in Opp. 25 (discussing "internal negotiation process within the Executive Branch").

9. That understanding is consistent with the Independent Counsel's description of the facts of this case, in which the White House has produced "numerous sets of notes taken by White House attorneys in interviews of current and former White House employees." Resp. C.A. App. 18 (Declaration of John D. Bates).

10. A similar balancing of interests takes place within the Executive Branch in deciding under the Classified Information Procedures Act, 18 U.S.C. App. III, whether classified information will be used or disclosed in a criminal prosecution.

b. When a grand jury, at the behest of an independent counsel, seeks information from an Executive Branch agency, the balancing process described above cannot fully function. Neither the President nor any other Executive Branch official is in a position to determine the extent of the independent counsel's need for the information. Those officials cannot realistically require the independent counsel to reveal the precise status of his investigation, and the very purpose of the independent counsel statute is to preclude Executive Branch officials from exercising operational control over the independent counsel's investigation. By the same token, the independent counsel, who exercises only the "investigative and prosecutorial functions and powers of the Department of Justice and the Attorney General" in a particular defined matter, 28 U.S.C. 594(a), has no institutional competence or authority to balance the prosecutorial need for the information against the potential threat to the ability of the President or other high official effectively to obtain legal advice.[11] In short, no single official is in a position to weigh all relevant considerations and speak for the United States as a whole in this situation.

Under these circumstances, a district court, in ruling on an independent counsel's motion to compel production, must resolve the dispute over the availability and use of the information. In so doing, a district court should be mindful that the governmental attorney-client privilege is absolute as against outside parties; the court should be mindful as well of the respective statutory interests and roles of the agency concerned, the Attorney General, and the independent counsel, and the constitutional office and responsibilities of the President.[12] Those considerations are fully accommodated by Rule 501 of the Federal Rules of Evidence, which states that "[e]xcept as otherwise required by the Constitution of the United States or provided by Act of Congress * * *, the privilege of a * * * government * * * shall be governed by the principles of the common law as they may be interpreted by the courts of the United States in the light of reason and experience."

We submit that against the backdrop of the governing constitutional and statutory framework, "reason and experience" suggest that the dis-

11. The independent counsel statute authorizes an independent counsel to "determin[e] whether to contest the assertion of any testimonial privilege," 28 U.S.C. 594(a)(5), but it does not authorize an independent counsel to decide whether a privilege will be asserted or waived by the United States in the first instance.

12. Our position is consistent with the Restatement, §124 cmt. b, which provides:

More particularized rules may be necessary where one agency of government claims the privilege in resisting a demand for information by another. Such rules should take account of the complex considerations of governmental structure, tradition, and regulation that are involved.

trict court should, in ruling on the motion to compel, accommodate the competing interests at stake in a manner similar to the accommodation that takes place in an ordinary, non-independent-counsel context.[13] Such an approach would not unsettle the legitimate expectations of agency officials and counsel, because it would resemble the treatment within the Executive Branch of confidential communications potentially relevant to a criminal investigation or trial. Nor would this approach hamper the investigation and prosecution of crimes, since enforcement activities outside the independent counsel setting would be governed by similar considerations.

Neither court below attempted the accommodation of interests that we believe is required, and at this stage we therefore do not address what the precise standard of review should be. A useful analogy, however, can be drawn to the resolution of assertions of executive privilege. See *Nixon* v. *Administrator of General Services*, 433 U.S. 425, 447 (1977) (*United States* v. *Nixon* held that "in the case of the general privilege of confidentiality of Presidential communications, its importance must be balanced against the inroads of the privilege upon the effective functioning of the Judicial Branch").

In this respect, the court of appeals erred in stating that the *Nixon* test would not be satisfied unless the subpoenaed party could show "that there is no reasonable possibility that the category of materials the Government seeks will produce information relevant to the general subject of the grand jury's investigation." Pet. App. 13a n.9 (quoting *United States* v. *R. Enterprises, Inc.,* 498 U.S. 292, 301 (1991)); cf. *United States* v. *North,* 910 F.2d 843, 952 (Silberman, J., concurring in part and dissenting in part), opinion withdrawn and superseded in part on other grounds on reh'g, 920 F.2d 940 (D.C. Cir. 1990), cert. denied, 500 U.S. 941 (1991). That is the standard that *any* grand jury subpoena must satisfy, even when no privilege is claimed. That standard therefore is inconsistent with this Court's direction that a district court must "treat the subpoenaed material [for which executive privilege is asserted] as presumptively privileged," *United States* v. *Nixon,* 418 U.S. at 713, and must require, as a prerequisite to disclosure, that the prosecutor demonstrate that the subpoenaed material is "essential to the justice of the [pending criminal] case," *ibid.* (quoting *United States* v. *Burr,* 25 F. Cas. 187, 192 (C.C. Va.

---

13. For example, if a government attorney learned that an official had destroyed subpoenaed documents or paid off a potential witness, see Br. in Opp. 20, the privilege should surely yield. In contrast, if a subpoena sought otherwise readily available factual material, which is embedded in a legal analysis provided by an attorney to an agency head, the privilege should ordinarily prevail.

1807) (No. 14,694) (Marshall, J.)). See also *ibid.* ("privilege must yield to the demonstrated, specific need for evidence"); *Nixon* v. *Sirica,* 487 F.2d 700, 717-719 (D.C. Cir. 1973) (en banc; per curiam) (applying need standard in grand jury setting to claim of executive privilege). As in other settings, a district court may have to receive information from the parties *ex parte* and review the materials *in camera* in order to determine whether disclosure should be ordered.[14]

c. Respondent argues (Br. in Opp. 11-16) that 28 U.S.C. 535(b) is inconsistent with the assertion of a privilege in the context of this case. Section 535(b) provides that "[a]ny information * * * received in a department or agency of the executive branch of the Government relating to violations of title 18 involving Government officers and employees" must be reported to the Attorney General, subject to certain exceptions. It was enacted to settle a dispute within the government by providing that the Department of Justice has general responsibility to investigate possible criminal wrongdoing, regardless of where in the government such wrongdoing comes to light. See H.R. Rep. No. 2622, 83d Cong., 2d Sess. 1, 2 (1954).

It is uncertain whether Section 535(b) applies of its own force to the Office of the President, compare *Franklin* v. *Massachusetts,* 505 U.S. 788, 800-801 (1992) (President not an "agency" for purposes of Administrative Procedure Act), and that Section (which applies only to violations of

---

14. Respondent argues (Br. in Opp. 24-25 & n.30) that "[t]his Court has consistently rebuffed efforts to require" the sort of accommodation approach we propose. It is true that the Court has rejected such an approach as an ordinary feature of the enforcement of grand jury subpoenas, in cases in which no privilege has been asserted. See *R. Enterprises,* 498 U.S. at 298. But such tests are routinely used in connection with certain types of privilege claims, most notably the work product doctrine. See, *e.g., Hickman* v. *Taylor,* 329 U.S. 495, 511-512 (1947) ("[A] burden rests on the one who would invade th[e] privacy [of an attorney's course of preparation] to establish adequate reasons to justify production through a subpoena or court order."); Fed. R. Civ. P. 26(b)(3) (requiring a showing that "the party seeking discovery has substantial need of the materials in the preparation of the party's case and that the party is unable without undue hardship to obtain the substantial equivalent of the materials by other means"). Other courts have applied the work product test in the context of criminal grand jury proceedings. See, *e.g., In re John Doe,* 662 F.2d 1073, 1078 (4th Cir. 1981), cert. denied, 455 U.S. 1000 (1982); *In re Grand Jury Investigation,* 599 F.2d 1224, 1228-1232 (3d Cir. 1979); *In re Grand Jury Subpoena,* 599 F.2d 504, 512-513 (2d Cir. 1979); *In re Grand Jury Proceedings,* 473 F.2d 840, 842-849 (8th Cir. 1973). See also *Roviaro* v. *United States,* 353 U.S. 53, 62 (1957) (informer privilege); *In re Certain Complaints Under Investigation,* 783 F.2d 1488, 1520 (11th Cir.) (privilege for confidential communications among judges and their staffs), cert. denied, 477 U.S. 904 (1986); *King* v. *Conde,* 121 F.R.D. 180, 190-195 (E.D.N.Y. 1988) ("governmental privilege" for confidential police materials); *Kelly* v. *City of San Jose,* 114 F.R.D. 653, 660-671 (N.D. Cal. 1987) (same); *Hartman* v. *Remington Arms Co.,* 143 F.R.D. 673, 675 (W.D. Mo. 1992) (trade secrets privilege); *Duplan Corp.* v. *Deering Milliken, Inc.,* 397 F. Supp. 1146, 1185 (D.S.C. 1974) (same).

Title 18 and only those by federal employees) does not in any event cover the full range of situations in which a federal agency may come into possession of evidence of a federal crime. We assume, however, that the President (and other Executive officials) would nevertheless recognize an equivalent duty to report to the Attorney General information received by the White House (or a federal agency) concerning federal criminal violations. Any such reporting could have no effect on the ability of the government to assert an attorney-client privilege, however, since the officer to whom the information must be reported — the Attorney General — is herself the lawyer for the Executive Branch. Indeed, it is the Attorney General who ordinarily is responsible for deciding (after weighing the relevant considerations) whether to assert or waive the government attorney-client privilege in litigation. Thus, a duty to report information concerning criminal violations to the Attorney General is entirely consistent with the approach we propose.

3. The work product doctrine also provides qualified protection in the context of this case. See *United States* v. *Nobles*, 422 U.S. 225, 239 (1975) (work product doctrine applicable in criminal cases); *Hickman* v. *Taylor*, 329 U.S. 495 (1947); *United States* v. *Davis*, 636 F.2d 1028, 1039 n.10 (5th Cir.) ("[I]t is uniformly held that the work product doctrine applies to grand jury proceedings.") (collecting cases), cert. denied, 454 U.S. 862 (1981). The court of appeals rejected that conclusion only because it believed that the materials at issue were not prepared "in anticipation of litigation." See Pet. App. 25a-26a. That view is mistaken.

Where the subpoenaed governmental entity has a legitimate interest in evaluating the assertion of applicable privileges in response to the subpoena, with the resultant potential for litigation, the attorney's work product may have been created "in anticipation of litigation" and thus be within the scope of the work product doctrine. In this case, one of Ms. Sherburne's roles at the time of the grand jury investigation was to "advise[] and assist[] the Office of the President in determining whether any privileges or other confidentiality interests should be asserted with regard to any of the information requested" and to "negotiate[] with the [Independent Counsel] * * * to accommodate interests in privileged material." Pet. App. 85a-86a.

In addition, the White House has represented that the notes at issue here were prepared, at least in part, in order to "facilitate[] advice to the Office of the President regarding responses to congressional inquiries." Pet. App. 90a; accord *id.* at 88a. The work product doctrine applies when a congressional committee is investigating matters within the Executive Branch, because the agency has a strong interest in assuring that the work of its counsel in assisting agency officials to respond to the investigation will not be subject to mandatory disclosure — either to the committee or to third parties in subsequent litigation. See Restatement §136 cmt. h (litigation "includes a proceeding such as * * * an investigative legislative hearing"). The Attorney General and the Office of Legal Counsel have consistently taken the position that work product (like attorney-client communication) is protected in this setting. See Letter from the Attorney General to the President 2 (May 23, 1996) (citing Response to Congressional Requests for Information Regarding Decisions Made Under Independent Counsel Statute, 10 Op. O.L.C. 68, 78 & n.17 (1986); 1982 OLC Opinion, 6 Op. O.L.C. at 490 n.17, 494 & n.24).[15]

4. For the foregoing reasons, the court of appeals erred in holding that neither the attorney-client privilege nor the work product doctrine provides any protection at all to the subpoenaed notes. Those holdings have sufficiently important consequences to warrant review by this Court.

The court's holding unduly diminishes the ability of the President and other high-ranking Executive Branch officials to obtain legal advice and act accordingly regarding matters that have — or that may come to have — some relevance in an independent counsel investigation (and parallel congressional inquiries). The United States has compelling interests in investigating and prosecuting crimes — inside or outside the government — and the Justice Department's performance of those tasks is aided by the duty of the President and other government officials to report evidence of criminal violations to the Attorney General. At the same time, the Constitution requires the President to adhere to and follow the law, both in his oath of office (Art. II, §1, Cl. 8), and in the requirement that "he shall take Care that the Laws be faithfully executed" (Art. II, §3). To fulfill those responsibilities, the President must have access to legal advice that is frank, fully informed, and confidential.

---

15. Respondent argues (Br. in Opp. 27) that the enforcement of the subpoena in this case was called for in any event "because the official meetings in question occurred in the presence of third parties — namely, Mrs. Clinton's personal attorneys." We disagree. There are important governmental interests in ensuring that agency counsel will be able to interview agency personnel as part of internal investigations, yet those officials may be unwilling to participate if the agency were forced to exclude their private counsel altogether in order to ensure that the investigation would be privileged. Thus, although the presence of Mrs. Clinton's private counsel does not prevent the government from waiving its privileges in the future, it did not result in an *automatic* abrogation of all protection for the information.

Respondent also maintains (Br. in Opp. 26-27) that no valid privilege can be asserted in this case because Mrs. Clinton "is not a representative of the [White House] client under *Upjohn*." The district court correctly rejected that conclusion, see Pet. App. 70a-72a, and the court of appeals did not disagree with that aspect of the district court's decision.

The court of appeals' categorical holding will have the practical effect of diminishing the ability of the President and Executive Branch agencies to obtain such advice, for it denies any protection for attorney work product and attorney-client communications that may be swept within the broad ambit of a grand jury subpoena in this or a future independent counsel investigation. Because a grand jury "can investigate merely on suspicion that the law is being violated, or even just because it wants assurance that it is not," *United States* v. *Morton Salt Co.,* 338 U.S. 632, 642-643 (1950), the court of appeals' decision threatens to have a significant chilling effect for counsel and officials in the White House and federal agencies, who would be required to operate under an ever-present potential for unrestrained examination into and disclosure of their ongoing attorney-client communications. That consequence is not necessary for effective criminal law enforcement. Such an impairment of the President's ability to obtain confidential legal advice — and to provide for the availability of legal advice for the Cabinet Officers on whom he relies in executing the laws — should not be left unreviewed.

CONCLUSION

The petition for a writ of certiorari should be granted.

Respectfully submitted.

SETH P. WAXMAN
Acting Solicitor General*
FRANK W. HUNGER
Assistant Attorney General
JOHN C. KEENEY
Acting Assistant Attorney General
EDWIN S. KNEEDLER
MICHAEL R. DREEBEN
Deputy Solicitors General
JAMES A. FELDMAN
Assistant to the Solicitor General

JUNE 1997

* Acting Solicitor General Walter Dellinger has recused himself in this case.